A PASSION FOR THE GAME

Championship golfers aren't motivated solely by the purse. They play out of a

deep passion for the game. That's why SAP is proud to sponsor this edition of

"The World of Professional Golf." For more than thirty years, we have attracted

professionals who are fiercely dedicated to excellence in technology, integrated

solutions, and the pursuit of customer goals. Not simply because it brings gratifying

success and growth. But because we truly love the game.

For more information visit our website at www.sap.com.

Presented by
SAP

THE WORLD OF
PROFESSIONAL GOLF
2002

Mark H. McCormack

An IMG PUBLISHING Book

An IMG PUBLISHING Book

Designed and produced by Davis Design

ISBN 1-878843-33-8

Printed and bound in the United States of America.

Contents

1. The Year in Retrospect

There was only one important story in 2001, a story that put golf and everything else into perspective. The terrorist attacks changed the way all of us viewed the world, and, for a time, made golf seem insignificant. Like the rest, the golf community was caught by surprise on that Tuesday morning and those who work in the professional game stopped and watched as war was waged on America.

Like everyone else, golfers went to work on September 11 without a hint of worry. The best in the game were either already in or on their way to St. Louis for the WGC American Express Championship. Other PGA Tour players were in Florida for the Tampa Bay Classic. Senior PGA Tour players were in Clemmons, North Carolina, site of the Vantage Championship, while the LPGA's best were in Portland, Oregon, preparing for the Safeway Classic.

The American Express tournament was to be the first big golf event in St. Louis since the 1992 PGA Championship. This time Bellerive Country Club was hosting a beleaguered event, which had run its course at Valderrama in Spain, before an enthusiastic Midwestern audience. Spectators got out early on Tuesday for a glimpse of Tiger Woods and others. The week seemed full of promise. By 9:00 a.m. that had changed.

Most of the players were still in the locker room when the two planes hit the World Trade Center towers. Woods was on the first nine, hitting extra shots into the par-fours and discussing possible pin placements with his caddie when the attacks occurred. He knew nothing until Mark Calcavecchia walked out of the locker room and toward the 10th tee. Woods wondered what could have caused Calcavecchia to go so pale.

Woods tried to continue his practice round, but it was no use. Joe Corless, a former FBI agent who is employed by the PGA Tour for security, kept Woods and Calcavecchia updated. "Every hole he had more bad news," Calcavecchia said. "One shocking revelation after another. We were stunned." Woods and Calcavecchia packed it in. "It's a sad, sad day for America," Woods said in the locker room. Then Woods got in his car and left the course.

Others never made it to St. Louis. Davis Love III planned to fly out of Atlanta. He made it as far as the airport before the FAA grounded all aircraft. Nick Price was flying his own plane from his home in West Palm Beach, Florida, when the call came from controllers to land immediately. Price was routed to Birmingham, Alabama. There Price rented a car and drove eight hours to Bellerive. Phil Mickelson was also in the left seat of his jet when the call to land immediately came over. Mickelson put his plane down in Austin, Texas, where he rented a car and drove back home to Phoenix. Scott Hoch was resting in the cabin of his plane when the pilot came back and said there had been a change of plans and they were landing in Nashville. It wasn't until they landed that Hoch learned what had happened. He, too, returned to his family.

LPGA player Jean Bartholomew was thinking about her family as well. Her brother had an interview at the World Trade Center on Tuesday morning, and a frantic Bartholomew spent most of the morning trying to get information on his whereabouts. By Tuesday night the Bartholomew family was intact as Jean's brother had informed them that he was unharmed. He had left the building 20 minutes before the attack.

A number of European players were stranded in St. Louis, among them Darren Clarke, Padraig Harrington and Paul McGinley, all of whom had seen their share of terrorist violence. "We're used to living with terrorism in Ireland," McGinley said. "We see it, but on a much smaller scale than this. When you read the personal stories of what happened, that's when it hits home. There was a picture of an Irish girl and her four-year-old daughter. They were on their way to San Francisco. You imagine what the last half-hour of their life was like. That's what hits home."

Most of the American players thought about their families first, then the families of those who perished. As he packed up his car and prepared for the drive home to Florida, Joe Durant said, "I think a lot of guys want to be home with their families right now to be thankful for what we have. Sometimes we get wrapped up in sports and everything else takes a back seat. It's unfortunate that things like this have to happen for us to realize what's really important in the world."

PGA Tour Commissioner Tim Finchem was in North Carolina and drove back to his Ponte Vedra Beach, Florida, office. His called the White House and learned that a national day of mourning was scheduled for Friday. Then he called his friend, former President Bush, and one of his sponsors, the chairman of American Express. It was after the last call that Finchem decided to cancel all golf for the week. The American Express offices were located very near to the World Trade Center towers. Several executives were unaccounted for. There was no way American Express should sponsor a golf tournament now, and the players should not be asked to compete during a period of national mourning.

Ty Votaw, commissioner of the LPGA Tour, came to the same conclusion, but later than Finchem. Votaw first decided to play, but to shorten the Safeway Classic to 36 holes. On Thursday morning, he cancelled the event, saying, "The thinking changed when more and more players expressed a concern over whether playing was the right thing to do."

Another issue was the Ryder Cup, scheduled to begin just 13 days after the attacks. The PGA of America, PGA European Tour and British PGA officials huddled for three and a half days before coming to what seemed like an obvious decision. American captain Curtis Strange summed it up when he said, "These players are as emotionally spent as everyone else. It is awfully tough to play golf when they're still digging bodies out of the rubble."

By Saturday morning the PGA of America agreed. "When the matches are held, they will be held at a time when the world is rightfully concentrating on a sporting event," PGA vice president M.G. Orender said.

There was a collective sigh of relief. "There was no doubt we could get over there safely," Stewart Cink said. "But why would we? This is no time to be playing an international golf tournament. What if we go to war during the middle of one of the matches?"

U.S. military forces would, indeed, go to war in October, but the second Saturday in September the PGA made the right call. "It wasn't any one thing," PGA executive director Jim Awtrey said. "When you talk about all the emotions and all the issues, combined with the effect of threats going on around the world and the possibility of military retaliation, it was an obvious decision."

Awtrey's European colleagues agreed. "There was overwhelming support," Awtrey said of his conversations with Ken Schofield and British PGA chief executive Sandy Jones. "As a matter of fact, I'll never forget trying to apologize, and they said, 'Jim, don't do it. It's going to be such a mess. Let's start working toward next year.' I just felt there was too much involved, and too many people involved, to play the Ryder Cup."

Sam Torrance, the European captain, said, "What happened last week has put the Ryder Cup and everything else into perspective. I am desperately heartbroken for all the people involved in this terrible tragedy."

The Ryder Cup was rescheduled for September of 2002 with the teams from 2001 remaining intact. "I was relieved when Curtis called," Calcavecchia said. "I was probably more excited than anybody about playing these matches, but in the past couple of days, my excitement for it really waned. I really didn't want to go."

"Whatever decision the PGA of America made I was going to support," Woods said. "I definitely think it's the right decision, especially with U.S. retaliation imminent."

"Everybody thoroughly embraced the idea of a postponement," Strange said. "Their personal feelings were all over the map, just like everybody else's, and nobody needs to know how each player felt, but this was a team decision."

The PGA Tour resumed play in the Marconi Pennsylvania Classic the week of September 17, with Arnold Palmer as the unofficial host. Palmer gave an impassioned televised introduction to the event and the tournament flags for each hole were replaced with American flags. Red, white and blue was everywhere, and the Pennsylvania tournament was an All-American comeback for professional golf.

In Europe, the beauty of Versailles was the backdrop for the Trophee Lancome. Sergio Garcia, one of the most charismatic players in the game, won in a showdown with U.S. Open champion Retief Goosen. When Garcia rolled in his final birdie putt and pumped his fist in delight, we were all reminded that we loved golf, and despite the terrible disruption of war, this was one of the most exciting seasons in the history of the professional game.

TIGER WOODS

EVENT	POSITION
Mercedes Championships	T-8
Phoenix Open	T-5
AT&T Pebble Beach National Pro-Am	T-13
Buick Invitational	4
Nissan Open	T-13
Dubai Desert Classic	T-2
Bay Hill Invitational	1
The Players Championship	1
Masters Tournament	1
Verizon Byron Nelson Classic	T-3

Deutsche Bank - SAP Open	1
Memorial Tournament	1
U.S. Open Championship	T-12
Buick Classic	T-16
Advil Western Open	T-20
British Open Championship	T-25
PGA Championship	T-29
WGC NEC Invitational	1
Bell Canadian Open	T-23
National Car Rental Classic	T-16
Tour Championship	T-13
WGC EMC World Cup	T-2
PGA Grand Slam of Golf	1
Williams World Challenge	1

Tiger Woods won his first event of the year in March at Arnold Palmer's Bay Hill Invitational, with a spectacular final-hole birdie to defeat Phil Mickelson. When and how he won wasn't as interesting as the questions that preceded the victory. Woods wasn't out of the top 15 in any tournament in the first two months of the year and he had four top-10 finishes in six events, yet some were wondering why he hadn't won. It had been all of four months. What could be wrong? No one else was being held to such a standard of expectation. But then, no other golfer was Tiger Woods.

He not only proved any critics wrong, he made them look silly. A week after winning at Bay Hill, Woods held off a challenge from Vijay Singh to win The Players Championship and capture the biggest title he had not won previously in his career. Still, Woods wasn't given the respect he had received in 2000. Winning wasn't good enough anymore. He had moved the bar so high that anything short of annihilating the field while breaking course and tournament scoring records was not enough. He was asked about the fact that no one had ever won The Players and the Masters in the same year. "We'll see," Woods said.

Two weeks later he achieved the greatest accomplishment in the history of professional golf, if not the greatest feat in all of sports. With a 20-foot birdie putt on the 18th hole at Augusta National Golf Club, Woods won his second green jacket by two strokes over David Duval. It was Woods' fourth major championship victory in a row. He became the first man in history to hold all four major professional trophies at the same time.

Palmer and Jack Nicklaus were among those who thought Woods deserved accolades for what he had done, but that you couldn't call it a Grand Slam unless all four major titles came in the same year. Since no one had ever sniffed a Grand Slam since Bobby Jones did it with different events in 1930, it was tough to come up with a name for what Woods accomplished in 2000 and 2001. Butch Harmon, Woods' swing coach during the streak, put it another way. "What this is," Harmon said, "is something no one who's ever walked this planet has ever done before."

Woods didn't get caught up in labels either. Asked if he thought what he had done constituted a Grand Slam, Woods smiled. "I can put all four of the trophies on my coffee table," he said.

Indeed he could, along with a few others. Woods won 11 times worldwide in 2000 and he picked up another eight victories worldwide in 2001, pushing his career victory total to 40 victories in just five and a half years as a professional. After the Bay Hill, Players and Masters trifecta, Woods won for the third year in a row at the Memorial Tournament in May, then won for the third year in a row in the WGC NEC Invitational. In between he won in Germany at the Deutsche Bank - SAP Open, and he closed out the year with victories at the PGA Grand Slam of Golf and at his own Williams World Challenge. His worldwide earnings were $7,771,562 and he won Player of the Year honors for the third consecutive year.

Still people said it was an "off" year for Woods. One article called it "Tiger's Lost Summer," when Woods failed to win the U.S. Open, British Open or PGA Championship. Never mind that his eight victories (including one major title) lapped the rest of the players in the game; he didn't win seven majors in a row, set tournament scoring records every time he played, and cure cancer in his spare time.

Tiger Woods is, far and away, my pick for Player of the Year. Having been around sports for over 60 years, I have no problem saying that Woods' Slam, whether or not you wish to call it Grand, was one of, if not the, greatest sporting achievement of all time.

DAVID TOMS

EVENT	POSITION
WGC Accenture Match Play	T-17
Mercedes Championships	T-8
Phoenix Open	T-9
AT&T Pebble Beach National Pro-Am	T-27
Buick Invitational	MC
Bob Hope Chrysler Classic	T-18
Genuity Championship	T-21
Bay Hill Invitational	T-56
The Players Championship	T-12
BellSouth Classic	T-17
Masters Tournament	T-31
Shell Houston Open	T-9
Compaq Classic	1
Verizon Byron Nelson Classic	T-11
MasterCard Colonial	T-8
FedEx St. Jude Classic	T-53
U.S. Open Championship	T-66
Advil Western Open	T-42
CVS/pharmacy Charity Classic	T-5
British Open Championship	MC
Buick Open	T-35
Fred Meyer Challenge	T-3
PGA Championship	1
WGC NEC Invitational	T-13
Texas Open	MC
Michelob Championship	1
National Car Rental Classic	T-6

Tour Championship	T-2
PGA Grand Slam of Golf	2
Williams World Challenge	T-11

While Tiger Woods was continuing his reign as the most recognized sports figure in the world, an unheralded 34-year-old from Shreveport, Louisiana, made a little history of his own and, with one miraculous shot and one lay-up, risked giving up his anonymity. David Toms had already won once when he arrived at Atlanta Athletic Club for the PGA Championship. But that had been way back in May, and Toms hadn't played well since that fan-friendly victory in New Orleans.

One swing on Saturday changed that. The distance was 249 yards and the club was a five wood. According to Toms, "It was the coolest shot I've ever hit. It was just the way it happened — the Saturday in a major in the last group with everyone watching. I hit a perfect shot. It's not like it bounced off a tree or rolled short of the green or anything like that. It was right on line the whole way." The ball took two hops and jumped into the hole for a one, an electrifying ace that propelled him into a two-stroke lead through 54 holes.

Phil Mickelson had taken a two-shot lead over Toms with a birdie at the 14th hole, and the momentum appeared to be in the left-hander's favor. Mickelson bogeyed the 15th to cut his lead to one. When Toms made his shot, the lead, momentum and, ultimately, the tournament swung his way.

"I had an excellent chance when I was a shot or two up to pull away," Mickelson said. "But we had that three-shot swing on 15, and that really hurt."

Toms' margin of victory over Mickelson turned out to be one stroke, a crucial par-saving putt on the 72nd hole after laying up from the rough. The shot of the tournament, and my pick for shot of the year, was the miraculous five-wood hole-in-one hit by David Toms.

Contrary to popular belief, this was not the first hole-in-one by a winner in a major championship. There were two in the early British Opens — by Young Tom Morris in 1868 and Jamie Anderson in 1878 — and there may have been others.

Toms earned double duty in that he not only hit the shot of the year; he's also my pick for the second most successful player of the 2001 season. After his PGA Championship victory, Toms won again at the Michelob Championship at Kingsmill, his third victory of what proved to be a breakout year. He moved into the top 10 in the World Ranking for the first time in his career, and won over $3.8 million for the year, a top-five-in-the-world earning performance.

RETIEF GOOSEN

EVENT	POSITION
WGC Accenture Match Play	T-17
Nashua Nedtel Cellular Masters	T-2
Alfred Dunhill Championship	T-7
Mercedes-Benz South African Open	T-21
Dimension Data Pro-Am	T-2

Dubai Desert Classic	T-17
Bay Hill Invitational	T-34
The Players Championship	MC
BellSouth Classic	WD
Masters Tournament	MC
Benson and Hedges International	T-7
Deutsche Bank - SAP Open	T-14
Volvo PGA Championship	MC
Victor Chandler British Masters	MC
Compass Group English Open	T-5
U.S. Open Championship	1
Smurfit European Open	T-6
Scottish Open at Loch Lomond	1
British Open Championship	T-13
Buick Open	MC
PGA Championship	T-37
WGC NEC Invitational	10
BMW International Open	T-23
Trophee Lancome	2
Linde German Masters	T-10
Cisco World Match Play	T-9
Dunhill Links Championship	T-9
Telefonica Open de Madrid	1
Volvo Masters	T-10
Vodacom Players Championship	T-2
WGC EMC World Cup	1
PGA Grand Slam of Golf	3
Nedbank Golf Challenge	T-8

Another newcomer to my list of outstanding players was the European Order of Merit winner, a man who almost fell into golf's infamous "blew it" category with such notables as Doug Sanders, Ed Sneed and Scott Hoch. Retief Goosen had an 18-inch putt to win the U.S. Open, the kind of putt 20-handicappers give each other every day. This one was for the biggest championship of Goosen's life, and it followed one of the gutsiest approach shots of the major season, a six iron that bounced over the hole before stopping 12 feet away on the hardest finishing hole of the year. Two putts and the championship was his. Even after he rolled the first putt past the hole, the only thing left to do was tap in the 18-incher.

Goosen missed that short one, and as he stood in disbelief on the final green, there were visions of Sanders, Sneed and Hoch. If Goosen didn't win the Monday playoff with Mark Brooks, he would forever be lumped in with those who should have won a major but didn't.

He did win, shooting even-par 70 to Brooks' 72. With the U.S. Open trophy at his side, Goosen was able to smile at his misfortunes on Sunday afternoon. It all worked out well in the end.

Goosen's season also ended well. With victories at the Scottish Open at Loch Lomond and the Telefonica Open de Madrid, Goosen became the first non-European in two decades to win the Order of Merit. Greg Norman was the last in 1980. Few are left who remember when Bobby Locke and Dale

Hayes became the only South Africans to accomplish the feat. So it was with a great deal of humility and pride that Retief Goosen accepted the trophy in Spain and the Order of Merit title it brought him.

"It's nice to win this tournament and pull off the Order of Merit title for the first time," Goosen said. "It's a great feeling, especially with so many great names on the Harry Vardon Trophy, such as Ballesteros, Faldo and Montgomerie. This is my 10th season on tour, and to be No. 1 is unbelievable. It was nice to round it off this way and it's a great feeling. It's still got to sink in a bit, but it's been a dream year. It's hard to think I am the best player in Europe this year."

Goosen went on to team with Ernie Els to win the WGC EMC World Cup in Japan, defeating the favored American squad of David Duval and Tiger Woods in a playoff, which also included the teams of Denmark and New Zealand. Goosen earned $3,478,409 in 2001 for an eighth-place spot on the World Money List and enough for him to become my pick as third best player of the year.

SERGIO GARCIA

EVENT	POSITION
Phoenix Open	T-13
AT&T Pebble Beach National Pro-Am	T-59
Greg Norman Holden International	2
Ericsson Masters	MC
Nissan Open	T-25
Bay Hill Invitational	T-4
The Players Championship	T-50
Masters Tournament	MC
WorldCom Classic	MC
Open de Espana	T-16
Verizon Byron Nelson Classic	T-8
MasterCard Colonial	1
Memorial Tournament	T-2
U.S. Open Championship	T-12
Buick Classic	1
Scottish Open at Loch Lomond	T-14
British Open Championship	T-9
The International	T-11
PGA Championship	MC
BMW International Open	T-7
Bell Canadian Open	T-5
Trophee Lancome	1
Buick Challenge	MC
Tour Championship	T-2
Casio World Open	3
WGC EMC World Cup	T-6
Nedbank Golf Challenge	1

Of course the young man in the No. 2 spot on the World Money List had a good year as well. Sergio Garcia was one major victory away from being my second choice for Player of the Year, but with four victories on three continents and almost $5.5 million in earnings, the Spaniard proved he is a force in the game and a legitimate contender to Tiger Woods.

Garcia began the year embroiled in some controversy. Leading the Greg Norman Holden International in Australia, and playing in the group with Norman, Garcia took a drop from a scoreboard under the "temporary immovable obstruction" rule. He discussed the drop with Norman, who pointed out the spot where the drop should occur.

Unfortunately, PGA European Tour rules officials disagreed, and Garcia was assessed a penalty for playing from the wrong place. To say the young man was displeased would be an understatement. Garcia was leading the tournament when the penalty was assessed, and he had some disparaging comments for the rules official. Those statements earned Garcia a fine, a reprimand and several commentaries on his behavior.

But Garcia, who is at heart a great person, regrouped and won twice in America before capturing the Trophee Lancome in France. He capped his season with a win in the Nedbank Golf Challenge in South Africa, earning $2 million, the biggest first-place check in golf. For all those reasons, and the fact that he is still just 22 years old, I think Sergio Garcia is the player to watch in the future.

DAVID DUVAL

EVENT	POSITION
Mercedes Championships	7
Phoenix Open	MC
AT&T Pebble Beach National Pro-Am	MC
Bob Hope Chrysler Classic	T-51
Genuity Championship	T-63
Masters Tournament	2
Shell Houston Open	T-26
Compaq Classic	T-18
Verizon Byron Nelson Classic	T-3
MasterCard Colonial	T-46
U.S. Open Championship	T-16
Buick Classic	T-26
Canon Greater Hartford Open	T-22
British Open Championship	1
The International	T-24
PGA Championship	T-10
Fred Meyer Challenge	T-3
WGC NEC Invitational	27
Michelob Championship	T-41
Buick Challenge	2
Tour Championship	T-7
Dunlop Phoenix	1
WGC EMC World Cup	T-2
PGA Grand Slam of Golf	4
Williams World Challenge	9

Another worthy contender made his mark by winning his first major championship. David Duval had been close so often some people may have wondered how his 0-for-26 run in the major championships had affected him. But Duval proved to be stronger than his critics thought. After enduring a nasty break-up with his chief sponsor, Titleist, and missing two critical birdie putts on the final holes that might have won him the Masters, Duval played four solid rounds at Royal Lytham & St. Annes and captured the British Open Championship. That turned out to be his only PGA Tour victory — he also won the Dunlop Phoenix in Japan — but it was enough. Duval's $3.6 million in worldwide earnings and his breakthrough win in England was good enough for me to place him in the fifth spot on my list of the top players of 2001. And with the pressure of winning his first major finally off his shoulders, I expect Duval to be a major force in the future.

PHIL MICKELSON

EVENT	POSITION
Mercedes Championships	T-28
Phoenix Open	MC
AT&T Pebble Beach National Pro-Am	T-3
Buick Invitational	1
Nissan Open	MC
Honda Classic	T-27
Bay Hill Invitational	2
The Players Championship	T-33
BellSouth Classic	T-3
Masters Tournament	3
Compaq Classic	2
Verizon Byron Nelson Classic	T-28
MasterCard Colonial	T-2
Kemper Insurance Open	T-3
FedEx St. Jude Classic	MC
U.S. Open Championship	T-7
Canon Greater Hartford Open	1
Advil Western Open	T-42
British Open Championship	T-30
The International	71
Buick Open	T-10
PGA Championship	2
WGC NEC Invitational	T-8

The same cannot be said for my sixth choice of the year. Although he won twice in America and had 10 top-three finishes, Phil Mickelson continued to be the tragic foil, failing to win when he was in contention at the Masters, U.S. Open and PGA Championship. His off-course gambling made the news. He assumed a Jimmy The Greek role in the autumn, predicting NFL games on ESPN radio. But his untapped talent made Mickelson my sixth choice for Player of the Year. He finished fourth on the World Money List with $4.4 million, but the year will be remembered for the ones that got away.

"Everyone talks about me trying to win my first major," Mickelson said.

"Well, my mindset is to win a bunch of majors, and I still can't seem to get past the first one. That's what bothers me a lot."

There were plenty of other noteworthy stories in the men's game. A 17-year-old qualified for the PGA Tour. Ty Tryon, who made a name for himself by making the cut at the Honda Classic and by leading the B.C. Open after the first round, shot a final-round 66 in the qualifying tournament and earned his player's card just months after receiving his driver's license. Could a high school junior with a penchant for hamburgers and milk shakes travel and play with the best golfers in the world? Not yet, the PGA Tour said, by imposing an 18-year-old minimum age on membership. Tryon would not be 18 until June 2002, but the precedent he set by earning his card will have repercussions for years to come.

Speaking of youth, another player who could have passed as a 17-year-old if he had tried, showed the world what Tiger Woods' competition might look like in the future. Charles Howell earned $1,546,124 in 2001, finishing the year with five top-10 performances and coming within a few thousand dollars of earning a spot in the year-end Tour Championship. The only thing the 22-year-old Howell didn't do was win a tournament, but as he put it, "I'm learning every day. Now that I'm completely exempt the only thing left to do is win."

That's the attitude many of the younger players were bringing to the game, and some of the older guys were stepping up their play as well. John Daly made the biggest jump, and for the first time in half-a-dozen years, Daly made news for his play instead of his off-course shenanigans. He won in Germany at the BMW International Open, and he jumped 450 spots in the World Ranking. He still made a couple of bone-headed errors, such as not playing enough late in the year to maintain his position in the top 50 and earn an invitation to the Masters, and making some uninformed and ill-timed comments about airline safety in the wake of September 11. But Daly was back, looking like the major champion that he once was.

Another major champion who returned to form was Ian Woosnam, who won the Cisco World Match Play and contended in the British Open. Woosnam's year will always be remembered for the most talked-about ruling since Roberto de Vicenzo's scorecard incident at the Masters. It occurred Sunday afternoon in Lytham when Woosnam, trailing by one stroke at the start of the day, hit a six-iron shot on the par-three opening hole to within inches. When he tapped in for birdie it appeared as though he had gained a share of the lead. As Woosie went to the second tee, his caddie, Miles Byrne, had some bad news.

"You're going to go ballistic," Byrne said.

"What is it?" Woosnam asked.

"We've got two drivers in the bag," Byrne said.

That was 15 clubs. And a two-shot penalty, the caddie didn't need to add.

Woosnam spat and stomped and marched around the tee, throwing his hat to the ground, then throwing it back on his head in a cockeyed manner. Then he removed the extra driver from his bag and threw it into the brush. Instead of making birdie at the first hole to draw even with the leaders, he took bogey and never recovered.

He gave Byrne a second chance, which the caddie wasted two weeks later by oversleeping and missing a tee time.

On the women's side, records were set as an old rivalry was rekindled. Just when it looked that Karrie Webb had taken the reins as the preeminent female golfer in the world, up jumped Webb's chief rival, Annika Sorenstam. The two-time U.S. Open winner had one of the most spectacular seasons in the history of the women's game. Not only did she win four times in a row (including a major title at the Nabisco Championship), Sorenstam put together an eight-victory season, worldwide earnings of $2.1 million, a single-season scoring record (69.42) and an 18-hole scoring record (59).

With a new workout regime that improved her strength and endurance and a new putting stroke that allowed her to hole many of the putts she had missed in years past, Sorenstam answered critics who claimed that she was outclassed by the longer-hitting Webb. She also put to rest rumors that she was too timid to retake the top spot. Sorenstam became the first woman in history to break 60 in a tour event, and moved to the top spot in career LPGA earnings with just over $8 million.

Webb didn't go away quietly, however. She won five times worldwide, two of those in major championships. For the second year in a row Webb won the U.S. Women's Open, and she followed it with a victory at the McDonald's LPGA Championship. At age 27, she became the youngest woman in history to complete the career Grand Slam, and she had $1.7 million in worldwide earnings.

Another player joined the mix in 2001. Se Ri Pak also won five times including one major (the Weetabix Women's British Open) and earned $1.6 million, a performance that put her second in Player of the Year points and third in worldwide earnings. Pak's scoring average was 69.69, which would have broken all previous records, except the one set in the same year by Sorenstam.

It was a frustrating year for Pak. She won more tournaments than any other season in her career, finished second in the U.S. Women's Open, and still didn't gain any post-season honors. All of which goes to show that the women's game remains competitive and healthy.

There were plenty of other stories in 2001. Ely Callaway died of cancer at age 82, leaving behind Callaway Golf, the largest golf equipment company in the history of the game. Buy.com went to dot-com purgatory when the Internet stock bubble finally burst, but the former Hogan and Nike minitour for aspiring PGA Tour pros continued to be called the Buy.com Tour despite law suits and countersuits by the company and the tour.

Bernhard Langer experienced something of a rebirth in 2001, finishing a strong third at The Players Championship and winning twice in Europe, including a victory at his own event, the Linde German Masters. Ernie Els, on the other hand, didn't win at all on the PGA Tour, making 2001 the first winless season for the big South African since 1993. Els did have a victory, however, at home in the year-end Vodacom Players Championship. David Love III returned to the winner's circle at Pebble Beach, but he lost late final-round leads three other times throughout the year.

Four women earned over $1 million worldwide — Sorenstam, Webb, Pak and Canadian Lorie Kane — two fewer than in 2000, while the LPGA announced it would seriously pare back its schedule in 2002. Another sex symbol controversy emerged, as Laura Diaz told LPGA members and anyone who would listen that capitalizing on short skirts and come-hither smiles was good for the game. Her comments sent shock waves through LPGA locker rooms, but received yawns otherwise. Outside of women's golf the fact that sex appeal sells isn't considered news.

What was breaking news in mid-summer was the $900 million the PGA Tour received for television rights through 2006. It was a deal that fell short of Tim Finchem's $1 billion goal, but it was still a record, and a sum the PGA Tour could not have commanded had the negotiations taken place after September 11.

Of course nothing was the same after the second week in September. The financial impact of the terrorist attacks remains unquantifiable. Sponsorship contracts were already in place, so very little changed in terms of 2001, but the faces and words of the players told the story. Arnold Palmer choked back tears as he spoke on television about America, while Jackie Gallagher-Smith moved her audience to tears as she led a prayer service in Portland. Players stopped and applauded 18- and 19-year-old Army recruits from Ft. Benning who came out to watch the Buick Challenge, and Justin Leonard, winner of the Texas Open, broke down in tears on the 18th green.

"I wanted to say something about all the patriotism I've seen in the last few weeks," Leonard said. "But I just got choked up. All the flags and all the support; it's just great to see."

When asked about his experience in Tampa on September 11, Ben Crenshaw said, "I was stranded like everybody else, just me in my car driving back to Austin (Texas), listening to the radio. Those were some of the happiest and most uplifting moments I've ever spent. The way this country has responded is just magnificent. It reminds us all what it means to be American."

2. Masters Tournament

Whether it was the greatest single accomplishment in the history of sports is a point that may be debated.

It was this simple. When Tiger Woods won the Masters Tournament for his fourth professional major championship title in a row, it was a feat no one who has ever played golf had accomplished — not Nicklaus, Palmer, Hogan or Snead. Nobody. The only comparison was 1930 when Bobby Jones won the Grand Slam, the Open and Amateur titles of both the United States and Great Britain, an accomplishment deemed the greatest in sports during a time when golfers wore ties and knickers and many players in any tournament didn't break 80.

In contrast, Woods demolished the U.S. Open record at Pebble Beach, rewrote the record book at the British Open at St. Andrews, set a new major championship record at the PGA Championship in Louisville (and won in one of the most dramatic playoffs in major championship history), then rolled in an 18-footer for birdie on the 72nd hole of the Masters to capture his second green jacket and his fourth major in a row — a Slam of some sort, whether or not it's considered Grand.

Two weeks earlier, Arnold Palmer had said, "No — a Grand Slam is all four majors in the same year. It's a great accomplishment if he does it, don't get me wrong, one nobody has ever done, but it's not a Grand Slam." Woods also won Arnold's Bay Hill Invitational and The Players Championship in consecutive starts before his Masters triumph. That, too, was something no one had done before.

From the beginning Woods seemed nonplused by the debate. "Obviously I'm not going to deny it's the hardest," he said. "It's harder to accomplish a Grand Slam in one year, there's no doubt about that. But I think if you can put all four trophies on your coffee table, I think you can make a pretty good case for that, too."

As impressive as the streak was the utilitarian way in which Woods dismantled the field this time around. Unlike 1997 when he broke the Masters scoring record and won by 12 shots, this one was close. Phil Mickelson was one putt away from becoming the first to shoot four consecutive rounds in the 60s at the Masters. Even if two of the short ones had fallen, Mickelson still would have lost. Woods beat him by three. "He seems to do whatever is required," Mickelson said. "I think if I had made a run, he may have followed suit."

David Duval was another casualty. He gained the lead with three holes to play only to lose it with one bogey and two missed birdies. This was from the man who finished runner-up to Mark O'Meara in 1998, made a charge in 1999 and missed another close one in 2000. Duval could do no more than shake his head at another in a list of lost opportunities at the Masters. "Been here before," Duval said. "I played very well, and I had a few opportunities coming home that I wish I could have capitalized on. I've been in this position before — a few times. I got beat by Mark O'Meara and a couple of other times I might have beaten myself. Today I didn't do that. I just came up short. It's not enjoyable sitting here under these circumstances."

Woods shot 68 on Sunday, a round that included a three-putt on the 15th hole, pars on the 16th and 17th, and an unneeded birdie at the last for a two-stroke victory over Duval and three-shot margin over Mickelson.

Not until the final putt fell did Woods show any emotion, and only briefly then. "It was a great putt (at 18)," he said. "It went in, so be it. Then I walked over to the side, and I started thinking, I don't have any more shots to play. I'm done. I just won the Masters. I started losing it a little bit." With that, he took off his cap and covered his face as he thought of what he had accomplished. He composed himself quickly to congratulate Mickelson.

"It was awfully fun to go out there and compete, and know that you have to hit the best shots and make some putts, and just hang in there," Woods said. "To see David up there and playing as solid as he did on the front nine and know that's probably going to continue on the back nine, and Phil right there in my group making birdies, I made some big putts in the middle stretch there to keep myself in the ball game."

He did just that, playing an unspectacular round, but one that accomplished the task. "That's why he's so good," said Chris DiMarco, one of the other players who played tough until the end. "He doesn't look like he's doing anything, and he still shoots 68."

DiMarco and the others didn't mean to imply that this rendition of the Masters didn't produce its fair share of drama. Before it was over, pundits were comparing it to 1975, when Nicklaus held off challenges by Johnny Miller and Tom Weiskopf, or 1986, when Nicklaus came from behind to beat Greg Norman. The names were different, but the shotmaking, tenacity and nail-biting, down-to-the-wire excitement of those events was the same.

The week was full of the usual traditions, but it also offered its share of surprises.

The first surprise was the condition of the golf course. As always the fairways were immaculate, closely mown carpet and the flowering trees and supporting flora elicited the standard oohs and ahs from the gallery. The greens, normally brick hard and lightening fast, were soft as sponges, holding long-iron shots and allowing players to take dead aim.

"I've seen firmer greens at the Bob Hope Chrysler Classic," Jesper Parnevik said after an opening 71. "I don't want to see them ridiculous, but I've never seen them like this."

The scores reflected the change. While the average score for the field on Thursday was 73.138, that included rounds of 87 by Billy Casper, 84 by Gay Brewer, and 80s, 81s and 82s from the likes of amateur Jeff Quinney and seniors Charles Coody, Arnold Palmer and Tommy Aaron. Those who had a chance of contending faired better. Thirty-two players broke par in the first round, three off the Masters record set in 1992. That was 23 more under-par scores than Thursday of 2000. There were 266 birdies and seven eagles, with a field average of 1.697 putts per green, remarkably low for a day at Augusta.

"We attacked the pins a lot more than I thought we would," defending champion Vijay Singh said. Singh shot 69 along with Jim Furyk, O'Meara and Scott Verplank. That score didn't sniff the lead.

The lead turned out to be six-under-par 66, which wasn't a course record or even a first-round record, but that it was shot by Masters rookie Chris DiMarco made the score noteworthy. Only 15 Masters rookies had ever held the first-round lead, even though two of those had come in the previous two years when Brandel Chamblee shot 69 in 1999 and Dennis Paulson shot 68 in 2000. DiMarco made it three in a row with his 65, a score only one stroke shy of the rookie opening round set by Lloyd Mangrum in 1940 and equaled by Mike Donald in 1990.

DiMarco contended the week prior to the Masters at the BellSouth Classic in Atlanta, but he lost his focus in the 36-hole Sunday finale of that event. "I really thought I was going to be in pretty rough shape when I got here," he said. Instead, a man who had never set foot on the first tee at Augusta National until Monday morning of Masters week birdied the second, fifth, sixth, seventh and ninth holes on the front nine. A lone bogey at the third hole gave DiMarco a 32 and an early share of the lead. Then DiMarco played Amen Corner in two under par, holing birdie putts at the par-three 12th and the par-five 13th. Another two-putt birdie at the 15th and DiMarco cruised in with three closing pars for 65 and a one-shot lead over Steve Stricker and Angel Cabrera.

"I was a lot less nervous than I thought I was going to be," DiMarco said. "I felt pretty comfortable. Once I hit it down the middle of the first fairway and hit a nine iron in there about five feet — I missed about a five-footer on the first hole — and it just kind of settled me down. I would have liked to have made the five-footer, but I hit a nice drive and a nice shot on the green. Relatively easy par on the first hole is a nice way to start."

DiMarco wore green and gray in the first round, but an inconspicuous color scheme couldn't hide him, not with his putting grip. "It's a normal left-hand grip like anyone else would grip the club," he said. "But my right hand is how it would be if you kind of clawed the long putter. It just takes my right side out. It helps me stay smoother on the putts and helps me stroke it a lot better. I think they call it the Psycho Grip. Since I'm such a big Florida fan, I've been trying to call it the Gator Grip."

Whatever he called it, the grip worked. DiMarco didn't three-putt a single green. "I didn't leave it on the wrong side of the hole," he said. "I didn't have that tricky five- or six-footer with a foot of break which would get away from you. I never got myself in a position where the putt could get away from me."

Three years ago he couldn't make a five- or six-footer with or without break. "He might have given up the game," DiMarco's father said. "He couldn't make a three-footer. He had the yips on second putts."

The "Gator Grip" or "Claw" changed all that, and DiMarco found himself leading the Masters. "Feels pretty good," he said. "I hope it's there Sunday afternoon. That's the main goal. Obviously you can't win the tournament today. You just put yourself in a position to not lose the tournament. I did that today. I put up a number."

Some other prominent players put up numbers as well. Mickelson broke a club on the second hole playing a shot out of a water hazard, then made five birdies in a six-hole stretch on the back nine to shoot 67 and position himself two shots behind DiMarco.

"Today was the day to score low," Mickelson said. "The golf course was playing longer than I've played it in the past, but because the greens were fairly receptive you could get at some of the pins and make some birdies. I think as the week wears on it will progressively play more difficult."

Mickelson's mishaps were self-inflicted. He pushed a drive on the second hole onto some rocks in the creek that runs adjacent to the fairway. Determined to play the shot but sure he would break a club in the process, Mickelson chose a 52-degree wedge, one of three wedges he had. Sure enough, he hit the shot across the fairway and snapped the head off the club. He then hit a six iron into the greenside bunker, blasted to five feet, and made the putt for par. Two holes later Mickelson replaced the broken club with the five iron he had taken out to make room for the third wedge. After the 67 he said he planned to keep that combination.

Another loose shot at the 11th with a wedge led to a bogey, but after that Mickelson went on a birdie run that included a tap-in two on the par-three 12th and routine birdies at the 13th, 14th and 15th holes.

"Starting out I didn't really attack many pins," Mickelson said. "I wasn't really feeling as though I had total control over where the ball was going, and where I was missing it. I didn't really do too much the first eight or nine holes. I started to feel a little bit better around the turn. I started to hit some good shots. When I bogeyed 11, that was by far the poorest swing of the day, but I still felt as though I could get at some pins. On 12, I hit a good eight iron and made a two there, which is really a bonus. After that I was able to get at some pins."

Lee Janzen and John Huston also shot 67s, but the second biggest surprise of the day behind DiMarco was 23-year-old James Driscoll, who shot 68 and became the first amateur since Mickelson in 1991 to break 70 in his first Masters round. Bruce Fleisher also accomplished the feat in 1969 when he shot 69, as did James Hallet in 1983, but none of those amateurs could match Driscoll's 68.

"I feel lucky to be four under," said Driscoll, a University of Virginia standout. "Hopefully I'll tighten up my game and shoot the same score tomorrow."

He started out like he was going for the lead. Birdies on the first, second and fourth holes moved Driscoll to the top of the leaderboard, and another birdie at the ninth kept him there for a while. The back nine was a little tougher. Bogeys at the 10th and 15th and failure to birdie the par-five 13th brought the youngster back to earth, but a great shot at the 16th turned his day around. After pushing his tee shot into the bunker at the 170-yard par-three, Driscoll blasted out onto the fringe. The ball rolled onto the green and into the hole for a two.

"I had visions of leaving it in the bunker, of it going into the water, or it going in," Driscoll said. "And it went in."

Tom Watson, who played with Driscoll, was impressed with the young man. "He was on an even keel all day," Watson said. "I saw the enjoyment on his face of playing in the Masters as a young guy. That's what you want to see."

What you didn't want to see was the kind of round Watson had. He shot 78, a round he said, "was not close to fun." Other large numbers in the first round came from Stewart Cink (75), Grant Waite (79), Nick Faldo (75), Craig Stadler (79) and Shigeki Maruyama (77).

Slipping under the radar with a bogey on the first and 10th holes and birdies at the third, seventh, ninth and 15th was Tiger Woods, who opened with 70, the same score he posted in the first round in 1997. He hit 10 of

13 fairways and 14 of 18 greens in a fairly ho-hum start.

"Any time you shoot it in the red numbers in a major championship the first day, you are going to be in the right position," he said with a smile. "This is a major championship. There are four days. Everyone knows it's awfully hard to go out there and shoot in the mid-60s every day in a major."

With one round in the books, the scoreboard looked like this:

Chris DiMarco	65	Phil Mickelson	67
Angel Cabrera	66	James Driscoll	68
Steve Stricker	66	Miguel Angel Jimenez	68
John Huston	67	Chris Perry	68
Lee Janzen	67	Kirk Triplett	68

More surprises awaited in the second round on both ends of the spectrum. Like an aging warrior still waiting to slay the dragon of his dreams, Greg Norman assumed the role of tragic foil at yet another Masters. This time he didn't roll in lengthy eagle putts only to lose balls in the azaleas later, nor did he play himself into contention only to lose it with one bad hole, one bad swing or one bad round. No one chipped in on him or shot 30 on the back nine to pass him in a trot. This one was all Norman's doing. He shot 82 on Friday, his highest score in 74 sometimes great, sometimes tragic rounds at the Masters.

"One word: Ugly," Norman said. He added, "I don't reflect on things. I move on," which is what he did after missing the cut. Moments later he was, indeed, reflecting, saying, "Of course I'd like to win a green jacket. But it's not just the jacket; it's the history. I want to be involved on the good side of it." That would have to come another day. Norman left the premises unsure of his future. Invitations for the former world No. 1 would be at the discretion of the Masters committee.

Davis Love III would likely return without much trouble, but that didn't take the sting out of missing the cut with a second-round 75. After an opening 71, Love found trouble early and often. He shot 39 on the front nine and bogeyed three of the four par-fives. He needed a birdie at the final hole to be assured of a spot in the field for the weekend, but even after watching playing partner Padraig Harrington putt from 12 feet along a similar line, Love couldn't convert a 10-footer. He shot 146 and missed the cut by one.

Joining Love in an early exit were Sergio Garcia (70-76), Dennis Paulson (73-73), Joe Durant (73-74), Nick Price (73-75), Colin Montgomerie (73-76) and the amateur sensation from round one, James Driscoll (68-78).

Driscoll turned at 38, parred the 10th and 11th, but found the water at the par-three 12th and made double bogey. He recovered briefly with a birdie at the 13th and three solid pars at the 14th, 15th and 16th. All he needed was to par out and he would make the cut by one shot. But a pushed tee shot on the 17th cost him. Driscoll clipped a tree with his approach and the ball found the bunker. From there he blasted long, chipped back and made another double bogey. "It was just disgusting," Driscoll said.

To no one's surprise except his own, Jack Nicklaus also missed the cut (73-75), and exited with some parting comments for the committee that chose to pair him with Arnold Palmer and Gary Player for the second year in a row. "I hope they don't do that again," Nicklaus said. "Arnold and Gary and I couldn't be closer friends, and we all play a lot of golf together. We're put out now as a sideshow, a ceremonial round. You can call it whatever you want, we're three guys they don't expect to compete. I played decently, but nothing happened. I just cluttered up the field."

On the other end of the leaderboard, Chris DiMarco defied the odds with another solid performance. He bogeyed the first hole, and the groans and grumbles started percolating through the crowd. As one local writer described DiMarco, "this guy's tougher than a Waffle House pork chop." He proved it with birdies on the second and third holes and solid pars throughout the rest of the front nine to go out in 35. Another birdie at the 12th followed by one at the 15th and no bogeys and, suddenly, DiMarco kept his spot atop the leaderboard with 69 for a 10-under-par 136 total.

"It was a lot like yesterday," DiMarco said. "I put myself in the positions so that when I could be aggressive, I was aggressive, and when I wasn't, I took par. I knew I didn't need to go out and shoot five or six under today, just get a couple here, a couple there and I would be all right."

When asked if he belonged in the same sentence (or on the same leaderboard) with the likes of Woods and Duval, DiMarco didn't hesitate. "I do this week," he said. "Sure, I mean, why not? Before Woods and Duval were Woods and Duval, they had to get there somehow, right? Maybe this is my week to get there."

If he were going to get there he would have to hold off some stiff competition. To the surprise of exactly no one, Woods made a move, shooting 66 to enter the weekend at eight-under 138, the same score he held going into Saturday's round in 1997 when he broke the tournament record.

"Well, I didn't start off four over par," Woods said, referring to his first-nine 40 on Thursday of 1997. "I played a little bit better yesterday. It was a lot easier 70 than it was in 1997. Going 40-30 is not exactly an ideal way to shoot 70."

Booming drives and firing at flags, Woods made his first birdie when he sank a 10-footer at the third hole. He followed with a 15-footer at the fourth and a seven iron to two feet at the sixth for a third birdie. He then hit a shot he described as a "choked-down, three-quarter bleeder, three wood" from 253 yards on the eighth hole. The ball rolled onto the green and stopped 15 feet right of the hole. Woods two-putted for his fourth birdie. The only blemish on the front nine came at the ninth, when a wedge shot flew long and he three-putted for bogey.

Solid pars on the 10th, 11th and 12th were followed by a seven-iron approach at the par-five 13th from 212 yards that flew 225 yards into the back bunker. A deft bunker shot set up a six-footer for another birdie. He reached the 15th with his second shot and two-putted for yet another birdie. He three-putted again at the 16th for his second bogey of the day, his second three-putt in nine holes. In 1997 Woods played 72 holes without three-putting a green.

"Going to 17 I just wanted to make sure I got back to at least where I was," Woods said. "If I could just get one of them back, I would be happy."

He got them both back with birdies on the 17th and 18th to shoot 33 on the back nine for 66. "I took advantage of situations I had out there," he said. "I hit good shots and I made some putts. Even though I three-putted twice, I really made my share of putts today. I think one of the reasons why is I kept a lot of the putts below the hole with my approach shots, and that's one of the keys to playing this golf course well."

Woods didn't say anything about the other players on the leaderboard, but he suggested that he liked his chances going into the final two rounds. "I think, obviously, you're going to see the guys who are really playing well probably separate themselves a little bit more than where it is now," he said. "With the tougher conditions, that's generally what happens. With the conditions a little bit more benign, the guys who are playing marginal can get away with shots and get away with misses. With the conditions getting more and more difficult, that won't be the case."

Two of those players who were not playing marginally were Mickelson and Duval, who were in the hunt with rounds of 69 and 66 respectively. Mickelson made a long putt for par on the 18th after pushing his approach, a putt he called "huge," to shoot 69 and share second place with Woods at 136.

"I don't think there's ever been a better opportunity for me to break through and win a major than this event right now," Mickelson said. "I've been playing well. The golf course sets up well for me. I feel as though I'm making, or at least know what decisions to make, and how to manage my game around Augusta National. I think this weekend provides the best opportunity for me."

Duval felt the same way. His 66 prompted Duval to say, "I'm having a great time. I was curious how things would turn out. I guess I didn't really know what to expect, but at the same time I knew my golf game was where it needed to be and I knew I was putting extremely well. So basically I just had to go out there and get out of my own way."

He did just that with seven birdies and one bogey. "You know, I came here with every intention of winning the golf tournament," he said. "And I still have that."

So the top players in the world entered the weekend with high expectations and solid platforms from which to mount their campaigns. The leaderboard at the end of the second round looked like this:

Chris DiMarco	69 - 134	David Duval	66 - 137
Phil Mickelson	69 - 136	Lee Janzen	70 - 137
Tiger Woods	66 - 136	Steve Stricker	71 - 137
Angel Cabrera	71 - 137	Toshimitsu Izawa	66 - 137

Saturday was one of those days Chris DiMarco had in mind when he said, "Tiger doesn't look like he's doing anything, and he shoots 68." Indeed, that's exactly what Woods shot on Saturday to take a one-shot lead over Mickelson into the final round.

"It was just a day when I didn't hit it close," Woods said. "I just two-putted and moved on. I didn't do anything great, anything special."

All he did was take the lead into the final round, a position from which he was unbeaten in major championship play. He did it routinely, hitting the greens, but failing to get any reasonable birdie opportunities. His only birdie on the first nine came at the seventh, when a pitch left him with his shortest putt of the day. When DiMarco followed Woods with a birdie of his own at the seventh, the leaderboard remained unchanged.

Then Woods made a long 30-footer for birdie at the 11th and things appeared to be moving in his favor. He followed that with a bogey at the 12th after missing a seven-footer. He hit a 305-yard tee shot into perfect position on the par-five 13th and an eight-iron approach from 205 yards that rolled into the swale behind the green. A deft pitch left him with a two-foot birdie, which he promptly made. Another great drive at the 14th set up a six-footer for birdie, his third on the back nine and his fourth of the day. After reaching the 15th in two, Woods two-putted for another birdie to reach 12 under and take the lead.

DiMarco struggled with a round of 72 to remain at 206, two behind Woods. Angel Cabrera spent a few fleeting moments atop the leaderboard as well. After making a four-footer for birdie at the 13th to become the first to reach 12 under, Cabrera parred the 14th, then drove the ball perfectly on the 15th. Standing in the fairway with a six iron, he thought about nothing but hitting the green and making another birdie or possibly an eagle-three. "I never even considered the front water," Cabrera said. "If I had a three wood in my hand, there's the possibility, but it was a six iron."

The ball landed on the green, then spun off the front edge and into the water. Shocked, Cabrera hit a poor pitch over the green, chipped on, and two-putted for a double-bogey seven. Another bogey at the 18th left him with a respectable but disappointing 70 for a 207 total, three behind Woods.

A similar fate could have befallen Mickelson, who had one of the more up-and-down rounds of the day. He struck the ball marvelously, but his putter let him down. On the eighth, he three-putted for bogey from eight feet to fall to eight under par. He recovered with a birdie at the ninth to move back to 10 under. Another birdie at the 13th moved Mickelson to 11 under and in position to wrestle the lead away from Woods. Then, from the fringe where he could have easily putted or chipped the ball, Mickelson attempted to hit a full-swing flop shot with his lob wedge. The ball came up 25 feet short and Mickelson three-putted for double bogey on a short par-four with no water.

He failed to birdie the 15th, but rallied after that, hitting a nine iron to 15 feet for birdie at the 17th and an eight iron to 10 feet on the 18th. When that putt for birdie went in, Mickelson was one shot behind Woods going into the final round and playing in the final group.

"I certainly have a lot of respect for Tiger as a player and as a person," Mickelson said. "With that being said, I've been able to go head-to-head with him and come out on top a few times. I do have confidence that I can prevail tomorrow. I'm looking forward to the challenge."

The challenger was confident — almost cocky — going into the final round, but he also was aware of the other players in the field with last names other than Woods. "I don't think Tiger or I will approach tomorrow as match play," Mickelson said. "If you look at the board, there are some guys behind that are incredible players, that are going to have an opportunity to get out 40 minutes in front of us, make a run, make birdies early. All of a sudden, before we tee off, we could be trailing. So I don't think the approach, by either of us, will be match play at all."

Among those other players Mickelson had in mind was Duval, who shot a 70 that included a great par at the 13th. After hitting his second shot into Rae's Creek, Duval decided to play the shot from the hazard, a decision that had cost many players at the Masters. Duval had no trouble. He hit a wedge shot from the muck and rocks across the green. A good chip left him with little more than a tap-in for his par.

Then Duval bogeyed the 14th after his tee shot hit a tree. That left him at 70 for the day and 207 for the tournament, three back of the Woods, but in a position he liked.

"I thought I played fairly well," Duval said. "I feel like I left a couple of shots out there, like the first day, but all in all, on Saturday at Augusta if you pick up a few strokes I think it is a good thing."

With that the leaders and followers entered the final round of the 2001 Masters with the leaderboard looking like this:

Tiger Woods	68 - 204	Ernie Els	68 - 207
Phil Mickelson	69 - 205	David Duval	70 - 207
Mark Calcavecchia	68 - 206	Angel Cabrera	70 - 207
Chris DiMarco	72 - 206		

There is no better front-runner in golf than Tiger Woods. With 26 PGA Tour wins, he came into the Masters having only lost twice when he led going into the final round. And he had never lost a major championship when leading after 54 holes.

But even though Woods was the favorite, the rest of the field had no intention of rolling over. Mickelson and Duval — two of the best players in the world who didn't hold major titles — wanted this one. Both saw this Masters as an opportunity to put the "best never to win" moniker behind them, and they both came out Sunday with a take-no-prisoners attitude.

The shootout that preceded the green jacket ceremony made this one special. It started with Duval's wild and woolly front nine, a stretch of holes where he shot 32 and didn't make a par for eight straight holes. He started the day with a bogey after missing the fairway on the first hole. That was followed by birdies at the second and third. Another bogey at the long par-three fourth dropped Duval back to even par on his round, but he quickly made up ground with birdies at the fifth, sixth, seventh and eighth to move to four under for the day, 13 under for the tournament and into a share of the lead.

Mickelson also made up ground. When Woods bogeyed the first hole, the left-hander shared the lead. Both players birdied the second and parred the third. The first cracks in Mickelson's game began to show at the par-three fourth when he lipped out a short putt after lagging his birdie effort. This was the third time in two rounds that Mickelson had hit a short putt too hard for the line he had chosen and the ball had ricocheted out of the hole like it had hit a tree. The bogey dropped Mickelson to one behind Woods and Duval.

Mickelson came back with a birdie at the fifth, but frittered it away with another blown three-foot putt at the sixth. Birdies at the seventh and eighth kept him one behind Woods.

Both players in the final group found themselves chasing Duval, who continued with a birdie at the 10th and solid pars at the 11th and 12th. At the 13th, the hole that cost Duval a chance at the 2000 Masters title when he hit his approach into Rae's Creek, he made another error, three-putting for par on a hole where Woods and Mickelson would certainly reach the green in two. He still had a chance, but the first problems in Duval's game appeared at the 13th.

Meanwhile Mickelson continued to make mistakes. After a par on the 10th, Mickelson pushed his tee shot on the 11th into the trees. He caught a break in that the ball bounced back into the fairway, but he left himself over 200 yards to the green. While Woods was hitting wedge into the par-four, Mickelson was faced with a four iron to a well-guarded green. He made bogey, Woods made birdie, and the margin was three.

Woods gave one back with a bogey at the 12th, but made up for it with a two-putt birdie at the 13th. Mickelson parred the difficult par-three to cut the margin to two, and kept it there with a two-putt birdie of his own at the 13th.

Up ahead, Duval was making another move with a two-putt birdie at the 15th to reach 15 under. That put him alone atop the leaderboard with three holes to play — a position he had been in before. In 1998 Duval was ahead going into the 16th and leading when he finished. He could do nothing but watch as Mark O'Meara birdied the last two holes to beat him by one shot. This year Duval held destiny in his own hands. If he could make another birdie — maybe two — coming in, the Masters would be his.

Armed with a seven iron on the 170-yard, par-three 16th, Duval hit a shot he thought was going in the hole. "I really don't have an explanation," he said. "I had 183 yards to the flag and I hit seven iron and flew it over the green. To be honest with you, I thought I might have made a one. You don't fly it 190-something yards over the green like I did. That hurts, obviously."

Duval made a four at the 16th and lost the edge he had gained at the 15th.

Woods couldn't close the door at the 15th. After reaching the green in two, he didn't hit a very good first putt and left himself with five feet for birdie. When he missed that putt and tapped in for par, both Duval and Mickelson still had chances. Mickelson got up and down from the bunker for birdie at the 15th to draw within a shot. All he had to do was made a good swing at the 16th and the pressure would be on.

"Sixteen was the killer," Mickelson said. "I finally got within a shot and I needed to step up and make a really good swing there and attack that pin."

Instead Mickelson pulled his seven iron onto the top shelf of the green, while Woods hit a shot that rolled down the hill within 20 feet. Woods two-putted and Mickelson hit a poor first putt and missed a seven-footer for par. That effectively ended Mickelson's bid, and he knew it.

"If I'm going to win with Tiger in the field, I cannot make the mistakes I've been making. I may make one or two, but I can't make as many as I've made this week," Mickelson said.

The only contender left was Duval, who had a 15-footer for birdie at the 17th that slid low, and a great chance at the 18th when he hit an approach to within six feet of the hole. He hit a slight pull and missed the putt low.

"I guess I probably pulled it a little bit," Duval said. "I had it breaking a little bit left. I don't see it, because I'm on top of it. I needed to make it, and I really felt good over that putt."

It wouldn't have mattered. Woods made pars at the 16th and 17th, then rolled in the birdie at the 18th to extend the margin of victory to two strokes.

"Certainly Tiger is the best player in the game right now," Duval said. "And I think what having him in the field will do is make my victories in these majors that much more special."

As for Woods, he appreciated the great competition his competitors provided. He knew it made accomplishing the historic feat even sweeter. "It is special," he said. "When I won in 1997 I had not been a pro a full year yet. I guess I was a little naive and didn't understand what I accomplished for at least a year or two after the event.

"This year I understand. I've been around the block. I've witnessed a lot of things since that year. I have better appreciation for winning a major championship, and to win it — to win four of them in succession, it's just — it's hard to believe. To have it happen four straight times, that's awfully nice. Some of the golfing gods are looking down on me the right way."

When asked if he considered his accomplishment a Grand Slam, Woods offered a smile and said, "I have all four trophies."

3. U.S. Open Championship

The scoreboard beside the 18th green at Southern Hills Country Club summed up this United States Open Championship better than any commentator. With little daylight left on Sunday afternoon in Tulsa, Oklahoma, the volunteers who had spent their week changing names and scores left their station with a one-word message on the board: Unbelievable.

Indeed it was. The fact there would be another 18 holes to play on Monday — the first U.S. Open playoff since 1994 — didn't diminish the shock, surprise, befuddlement and agony of Sunday's finishing events.

The bewilderment came about because of expectations. South African Retief Goosen, one of the PGA European Tour's most underrated players, who, according to conventional wisdom, was an underachiever and second-fiddle contender to his compatriot Ernie Els, appeared to have this U.S. Open within his reach. He led after the first round, and shared the top spot at the end of the second and third rounds. The question was whether one of the stars would rise to the occasion in the final round.

That didn't happen. Goosen played a spectacular fourth round, stepping onto the 18th tee at even par for the day and tied for the lead with Stewart Cink. It was the stars who folded. Phil Mickelson had another chance to win his first major title, but he shot 75, while Sergio Garcia, another favorite at the beginning of the day, shot 77. That left the seemingly unflappable Goosen and the even-keeled Cink, both of whom ground their way through the Tulsa heat to a one-hole showdown.

The green at the final hole sloped from back to front, but that was just the start of the difficulty. As Nick Price put it, "You're hitting a three iron off a downhill lie to an uphill green that can't be held with a nine iron. My caddie had the best line. He said to me, 'The green is 34 yards deep, but it has a 22-yard false front.'"

From the first day of practice, United States Golf Association executives were sweating. The green was too fast and the slope too severe. Putts were rolling off the front of the green and down the embankment some 40 or more yards. Tom Meeks, the USGA's director of rules and competitions, had visions of 1998 at the Olympic Club, where the 18th green was so severe that lip-outs rolled down the hill and four- and five-putts were common. "We had to find some way to eliminate this," Meeks said.

Water, fertilizer and fewer mowing rotations did the trick. The green held and became fair. It also rolled at least one foot slower on the Stimpmeter than the other greens on the course. A few groups ahead of the Goosen-Cink pairing, Mark Brooks was trying to cap his bid for another major championship with one of the few under-par rounds of the day. Brooks three-putted the 18th from 50 feet, saying, "I didn't pay enough attention to the speed. The 18th green definitely had a different pace. You're playing greens that are pretty darn fast all day, playing pretty big sweepers. Then you get on that green and you've got to take some of the break out of it, hit it a little firmer. It was only my second three-putt of the week."

Goosen and Cink knew the 18th green would be slower. It had been all week. Under the exhausting pressure of trying to win the U.S. Open, neither was able to adjust.

Cink played first from the fairway and missed the green. His ball nestled into the four-inch rough, a spot from which par would be a great score. Goosen followed with a six iron from the fairway. He hit what should have been the shot on which his career would be remembered. The ball never left the flag. It hit just short and ran 12 feet behind the hole, leaving Goosen with a birdie putt to win.

Cink knew he had to make a par to possibly force a playoff. When he left his chip short, misjudging the speed of the green, he made up for the mistake by rapping his 12-foot par putt harder than any putt he had hit all day, but he still thought he had made it. "You're putting on a green that's cut like fringe," Cink said. "I wish they'd left it the way it was. When you've got a green that's different than all the rest of the greens, there's something funny."

What wasn't funny was what happened next. Cink's par putt didn't break as he intended. The ball rolled 18 inches past the hole and the crowd groaned. They knew and Cink knew that he had blown his chance. Goosen would either make a birdie or two-putt for par and the championship would be over. Out of graciousness, Cink composed himself and volunteered to finish. "You take 100 guys out here and 100 of them would have done the exact same thing," he said.

He missed the 18-inch putt. "I put all my emotional energy into it," Cink said. "All day, every shot had been so meaningful. Now all of a sudden I've got this little one that doesn't mean a thing."

If only he could have known.

Moments after Cink exited with a double-bogey six, Goosen struck his 12-footer and rolled it two feet past the hole to the gasps of everyone, including those watching in the clubhouse. "I can't believe Retief," Mickelson said. "That green's slower than all the others, and he still over-judged the distance."

"Can you believe that?" Chris DiMarco shouted in the locker room. "Two putts to win the U.S. Open and he knocks it past the hole!"

That comment got Mark Brooks' attention. At four-under-par 276, Brooks assumed he would finish third or maybe tied for second, so he cleaned out his locker and changed his clothes. Now Goosen had to make a two-footer to shoot 275.

Goosen took his time but pushed the putt, missing it so badly that his third putt coming back was longer than his second.

"He didn't just do that, did he?" Brooks shouted.

Goosen had, indeed. He had just missed a two-footer to win the U.S. Open, and in so doing, joined Sam Snead (1947 U.S. Open), Bob Rosburg (1969 U.S. Open), Doug Sanders (1970 British Open), Ed Sneed (1979 Masters), Scott Hoch (1989 Masters) and Davis Love III (1996 U.S. Open) as a player who let a major title get away by missing a short putt.

The great play that had kept Goosen in the lead from the opening round, the solid ball-striking and smooth flawless swing, and the career six iron to the 72nd green were all forgotten. The only image of Goosen that would appear on television and in newspapers was the stare of disbelief he gave his ball after it skirted past the hole. The crowd wailed in collective agony at what they had just witnessed. Many wondered if Goosen could make the third putt coming back. He did, tapping in for a bogey, a one-over-par 71 and 276 total.

It was, as the scoreboard attendants aptly put it, unbelievable.

"I'm in shock," NBC announcer Roger Maltbie said afterward. "I had walked 18 holes with the guy and he looked so unflappable, so calm. I wondered why he hasn't done better in Europe. I think I know now."

Cink said, "If I knew he was going to take three to get down, yeah, I would have waited. It's not like I was hurrying to get out of his way. I'm disappointed I didn't make that putt, but I believe if I made it, I still wouldn't have tied for first. Retief would have two-putted. I honestly believe with all my heart that things happen the way they're meant to happen. This time it wasn't my turn. My turn is coming soon. What else am I going to do? I could bash in a locker, but all I'd get is a sore fist and a fine."

With that, Cink hugged his wife and kids, put on a tee shirt and khaki shorts, and left the premises in a mini-van, while Goosen and Brooks went to the media center.

"I knew I had to get down and try to make that putt or two-putt," Goosen said. "But like Mark was saying, that green is a little bit slow and putting up the hill there I just hit it too hard. I hit it right through the break. Seeing what happened to Stewart's second putt breaking so much right, I saw my putt coming back just off center right, and it went right on me. I was very surprised at that. I felt like I made a good stroke. The putt for some reason went right on me and lipped out on the right side.

"I'm not going to say I wasn't nervous. But I got down there and I hit the first putt a little too hard. The second putt I felt pretty calm over it. It just didn't go in. Probably the hardest putt was the third putt. But I just told myself to knock it in and tomorrow is another day."

The sun did, indeed, come up on Monday, and a few minutes after 10 a.m. Goosen began his journey to redemption in an 18-hole playoff with Brooks. Goosen came back from his missed putt to win — unlike Snead, Sneed, Sanders and Hoch. He shot even-par 70 to Brooks' 72 in the playoff.

But no one forgot about Sunday. How could they? It was the most bizarre fourth round anyone could remember. By Monday Goosen was the winner, Brooks was gracious in defeat, and Cink was in New York playing in a pro-am with executives from Deloitte & Touche. USGA committeemen breathed a little easier, although the criticism of the 18th would continue for days, and the Oklahoma golf faithful came out in droves to support their champion.

"Unfortunately what happened yesterday was tough," Goosen said with the U.S. Open trophy at his side. "But I told myself that day was over. I was looking forward to today."

When the USGA announced in 1994 that the 2001 U.S. Open would return to Tulsa, the first thought on everyone's mind was the weather. Oklahoma summers can be unfriendly, and June is tornado season. Even those who knew the place well, players like Tom Lehman, who won the Tour Championship when it was last played at Southern Hills, and Charles Howell, who played his college golf at nearby Oklahoma State, had reservations. "It's going to be hot," Howell said.

Even by Southwest standards, Thursday's opening round was a scorcher with humidity to boot. From the outset it wasn't a question of if there would be afternoon thunderstorms, but when they would arrive and how bad they would be. The answer turned out be 3:39 p.m., and pretty darn bad. By 3:45 p.m. the skies opened up, and a tornado watch went into effect.

If the weather wasn't a surprise, the leader when play was suspended certainly was. Three-time U.S. Open champion Hale Irwin, at age 56 years and 11 days, proved to the world that, for one day at least, age and guile can triumph over limber backs, long drives and youthful exuberance. With a three-under-par 67 that included six birdies (and one near-eagle on the 18th), the all-time winningest player on the Senior PGA Tour found himself atop the leaderboard when play was suspended.

"Let's see," Irwin said. "I'm the oldest U.S. Open winner (at age 45 at Medinah in 1990), the oldest player in the field, and now the oldest first-round leader in history. The one common denominator seems to be that I'm old."

He liked the golf course, which measured less than 7,000 yards. Hard courses had been Irwin's bread and butter for decades. "It's not a straight-forward rip it and go course," he said. "You have to know when to attack and when not to, and there aren't many holes out here to attack."

No one considered the 18th a hole anyone could attack, but Irwin did just that, ripping a two iron that almost rolled in the hole before stopping two feet away for his final birdie. "I had a tree limb in my way," he said. "My options were to hit it low and under the tree with a two iron, or sweep it high around it. That meant a four wood, and I didn't want to hit a four wood. I hit two iron in there shallow and it scooted up the hill. I hit it nearly perfect."

That was one of several near-perfect shots in his round. After bogeys on the first and second holes, Irwin came back with five birdies on the next 12. A three-putt bogey at the 15th dampened his spirits a little, and after missing the fairway at the 16th, Irwin looked like he might give another shot back. When he drained a 25-footer for par, Irwin gave the roundhouse, right-fisted uppercut reminiscent of his winning his third U.S. Open at Medinah.

"Look, age is a three-letter word," Irwin said. He claimed not to know 80 percent of the players in the field, which wasn't surprising since most of them were born after Irwin won his first U.S. Open title in 1974. "If you keep yourself young at heart, if you don't accept the words 'I can't,' then you can certainly extend your career. I know I'm capable of playing this way every day. It's just a matter of will I."

He would have to wait a while for that answer. Only 66 of 156 players finished the first round on Thursday. That put a lot of pressure on the USGA to hustle players around Friday morning. Tiger Woods was among those out on the course when play was halted, and, unlike some, Woods was happy to see the rain. At three over par through 10 holes, the defending champion needed some time to regroup. It was an erratic day for Woods, who missed the first fairway and had to scramble for par and then three-putted from 40 feet at the third hole. Just when it appeared Woods had his game together, he hit his tee shot on the ninth into the rough under a tree. Five shots later, he tapped in for a double bogey and went to the 10th tee three over par. That's when the rains came.

Unfortunately for Woods, things didn't improve on Friday. He missed half the fairways and hit only eight greens in what turned into a struggling 74.

"I put myself in some places I shouldn't put myself," Woods said. "But I kept myself in the ball game."

If Southern Hills hadn't dried out, Tom Meeks made it clear that the USGA would not play lift-clean-and-place. "If the only way we can play is to allow lift-clean-and-place, then we won't play," he said. "I'm serious. We will not sacrifice the game of golf and the foundation of golf by doing that."

Fortunately, the course drained quickly, and play resumed at 7 a.m. on Friday. Goosen went to bed on Thursday night having played only seven holes, but he was three under par. He came out early on Friday and immediately jumped to the top of the leaderboard with birdies on the eighth and ninth for a first-nine 30. Another birdie came at the 13th. Goosen had bogeys at the 16th and 17th, but he still held the lead with 66.

With the first round finishing as the second round got underway, it was tough to follow the early lead changes. But after over 30 hours, everyone in the field had completed the first 18 holes and the leaderboard looked like this:

Retief Goosen	66	Chris DiMarco	69
Hale Irwin	67	Toshimitsu Izawa	69
Mike Weir	67	Jeff Maggert	69
J.L. Lewis	68	Loren Roberts	69
Stewart Cink	69		

Friday was a grind. Some had to play as many as 35 holes in soaring temperatures and swirling winds, while others had to wait, wait, and wait some more. Stewart Cink was among those.

"It was a team effort to get in," Cink said after completing his second round. Cink and Scott Hoch rushed to the 18th tee after finishing the 17th in the hope of getting their tee shots airborne before the USGA called play due to darkness. They did with a little help from their friends. Davis Love III waved Cink up in the 18th fairway and Cink struck his tee shot seconds later. Moments later Cink returned the favor, waving up Steve Jones, Steve Flesch and Paul Lawrie.

"I knew once we finished 17 we would get in," Cink said. He and Hoch played as a twosome on Friday after Pierre Fulke withdrew with the flu. "We played fast when we were playing, but we did a lot of waiting," he said. "Scott is a fast player and he and I both had to slow down to keep our rhythm. We really took a lot of time over our shots and did anything we could do to keep from jamming up against the group ahead of us. I didn't think we were going to finish when we teed off, especially given how slow everybody was playing."

When they did finish, Cink signed for 69, his second one-under-par round of the day. Once all the scores were tallied and sense was made of the mess the rain had caused, Cink's 138 total was two off the lead. He liked his spot going into the weekend.

"I do like my chances," he said. "I like the way the USGA sets the golf course up. You feel like your back is against the wall on every shot, but you know what you have to do. I always feel like I can rise to the occasion. I like the way I'm playing right now, and I would love to win this tournament above all others. I'll be giving 110 percent effort tomorrow."

Another player who liked his chances was Brooks, who came within a stroke of equaling the record low score for a major championship when he had 64 in the afternoon. "I think you learn a little more every time you go around out here," he said. "I kind of set a goal of 62 after nine, but I really didn't hit it close enough. With those last five holes like they are, I certainly would have taken five pars and gone to the house."

He got things going early. A six-iron approach on the first hole almost went in the hole and Brooks tapped in from inside a foot. He followed that with a 12-foot putt for birdie at the second, a four-footer at the fourth and an eight iron to seven feet at the fifth. When that birdie fell, Brooks knew he was going to have a good day. The 30-footer he made for a birdie at the sixth was a bonus.

The back nine was a little less kind, but he still managed one more birdie from 14 feet at the 165-yard, par-three 11th. He saved par on the 17th after hitting his approach in the bunker and blasting out to 12 feet, and made a par at the 18th.

"It's nice to know that the golf course can be ... that you can play well on it," Brooks said, coming up short of saying Southern Hills could be "had." "It feels good to actually keep a round going."

The 64 coupled with his earlier 72 gave Brooks a share of the lead with Goosen, who had an uneventful two-birdie, two-bogey round of 70, and the surprise name on the second-round leaderboard, J.L. Lewis, who had shot two 68s.

"I don't really think it matters," Lewis said. "This golf course is very demanding and you have to play one shot at a time. If you've got a lead with two or three holes to go, then maybe that's going to matter. But right now I don't think anybody is going to benefit themselves by looking at the leaderboard and trying to figure out what they're going to do. Leads and that sort of thing probably aren't going to matter until late on Sunday."

With two rounds finally in the books, the leaderboard looked like this:

Mark Brooks	64 - 136	David Duval	69 - 139
J.L. Lewis	68 - 136	Rocco Mediate	68 - 139
Retief Goosen	70 - 136	Phil Mickelson	69 - 139
Stewart Cink	69 - 138	Matt Gogel	69 - 139

Saturday began on a peculiar note. Lee Janzen woke up in a great mood. He had birdied the 18th hole late on Friday to barely creep in under the cut at five-over-par 146, and he was ready to go on Saturday. Just as he was about to leave his hotel room, Janzen received a call. It was from Tom Meeks, and the news was not good.

An incident had occurred on Friday that would cost Janzen dearly. When the two-time U.S. Open winner returned to the ninth fairway to resume his first round after the rain delay, he noticed that the maintenance crew had swept the dew off every spot in the fairway except for one three-foot square where his ball marker was sitting. Janzen assumed that the crew didn't want to disturb his mark, so he thought nothing of taking out his towel and sopping the excess dew from the area before replacing his ball. The rest of the fairway had been swept. What would it hurt to clean the spot around his ball?

"Everything else was clean," Janzen said. "All I did was try to get the same lie. I just wiped it away."

Janzen played the remaining holes without incident. Throughout the day James Halliday, chairman of the Royal Canadian Golf Association and Janzen's official for the day, never uttered a word. According to Meeks, Halliday awoke in the middle of the night thinking he might have witnessed a violation. He put his concerns in writing and presented them to the committee on Saturday morning.

"We read it and had a decision right there on it," Meeks said. "Then I started trying to find Lee."

Janzen had removed dew, a violation of Rule 13-2. He had, through his actions, improved the position or lie of the ball as well as the area of his intended swing. The fact that he was simply swatting away a little dew to make his lie the same as everyone else's on the hole was irrelevant.

The rub came from the actions of the official. According to Ernie Els, who played with Janzen on Friday, "The way I see it, if the rules officials see a guy break a rule, tell him on the spot. Come over, show him the rule book, and tell him what the penalty is. Then the guy knows where he stands and what he has to do. We're all professionals. That's the way it should happen."

But that's not the way it happened in this case. After meeting to discuss Halliday's observations and written statement, the USGA initially decided to put out a release stating that Janzen had been disqualified for signing an incorrect scorecard. Minutes later, that was revised. Reed Mackenzie, the USGA vice president and chairman of the Rules of Golf Committee, said, "Ordinarily, when a player fails to incur a penalty and signs for a score lower than should have been recorded, the result is disqualification. But since the committeeman observed the violation and failed to notify the player of the penalty, the penalty of disqualification is waived. However, the penalty strokes must still be added to the score."

Instead of driving to the course for a little warm-up before his round, Janzen was informed that he was seven over par and had missed the cut. He accepted his fate, but he was still miffed about not knowing about his infraction sooner. Every group in the U.S. Open has a rules official, and Halliday had watched Janzen play without comment. That, Janzen thought, made the penalty tougher to swallow.

Janzen said, "The second time we came down the ninth fairway, (Mackenzie) was carrying a briefcase. I said, 'What do you have in there, the decisions book?' He said, 'Yeah, I carry it everywhere. The Rules and the Decisions." Too bad Mackenzie didn't use them.

That wasn't the only questionable ruling the USGA made on Saturday. David Duval was trying to play himself into contention after a second-round 69 that left him three strokes out of the lead. Duval could have used a break when he hit a drive on the ninth hole that landed in the middle of a crosswalk. During PGA Tour events, crosswalks are played as ground under repair. Rules officials Peter James and David Harrison denied Duval's request for relief. Duval appealed to PGA European Tour official Andy McFee, who was working the ninth hole as a roving official. McFee also denied Duval's request. "I told David it would have to be much worse than this to get relief," McFee said.

Duval chunked his pitch shot and made bogey. Adding insult to injury,

Duval received a slow play warning two holes later, even though the reason for his delay was the ruling at the ninth. He was one under par at the time of the ruling and four strokes off the lead. He ended the day at one-over 71 and five shots out of the lead.

"If thousands of people walking on an area isn't unusual damage, I don't know what is," Duval said. "It's hard to say how it affected the golf tournament. Hell, it was 75 yards. That's a flip wedge. I could have holed it."

The leaders didn't have any rules questions, but they did have a couple of new names inching toward the top. Spanish star Sergio Garcia had five birdies en route to 68 and a four-under 206 total.

"I feel like I'm playing well enough to do it," Garcia said. "I hope to go out tomorrow and play as well or better than I've been playing these days. Hopefully, if you make a couple of putts here and there you get away with it."

His two birdies on the first nine ignited the crowd, and his birdie at the 10th brought the loudest roar of the day. After leaving his second shot below the hole on the sloping green, Garcia hit his putt past the hole and watched as it rolled back and into the cup. "The ball went four or five inches past the hole and started coming back," Garcia said. "It looked like it was going to go in, then it looked like it was going to be long, and then it obviously went in the middle of the hole, but on the other side of the hole."

If Garcia was the crowd favorite, the sentimental favorite going into the final round might have been Phil Mickelson. A 68 left Mickelson at 207, one stroke behind Garcia and two off the lead.

"I don't anticipate doing anything different tomorrow," Mickelson said. "Tomorrow it's going to be very difficult to make birdies. The pins will be in the high spots and it would be very dangerous to get at some of those pins. Although I'll play the same, I would venture to say that even par will be a better score tomorrow than 68 was today."

While Garcia and Mickelson were the names everyone had waited for near the top of the leaderboard, the leaders were a couple of quiet men who could have been mistaken for actuarial agents if they had been seen on the other side of the ropes. Stewart Cink shot 67 with six birdies, a bogey and a double bogey. That his double bogey and bogey came on the first two holes only added to the quality of his score.

"I just don't ever give up," Cink said. "And I never let myself get down because of a couple of bad holes. I just don't think it's fair to myself to do that. I've worked hard enough to get here that I don't believe I'd be doing myself justice to pack it in after two holes."

The other leader, Goosen, finally broke into what could have been described as a full-fledged smile after shooting 69 and finishing with nine straight pars for a five-under 205 total.

"I think I was in more bunkers today than I've been in all year," Goosen said. "But I made a few up-and-downs, and that's why I'm still here. Hopefully tomorrow I can try and just play a little better and give myself more birdie chances."

They went home with the leaderboard looking like this:

Stewart Cink	67 - 205	Sergio Garcia	68 - 206
Retief Goosen	69 - 205	Phil Mickelson	68 - 207
Mark Brooks	70 - 206	Paul Azinger	69 - 210
Rocco Mediate	67 - 206	David Duval	71 - 210

There were some great numbers posted in the final round, but they weren't by the players anyone expected. Tom Kite, the 51-year-old special invitee who played second senior early in the week to Hale Irwin, went out early and shot a course-record-tying 64 that, in his words, "was like I was goofing around at Austin Country Club."

The score put Kite in the clubhouse at 281, the best finishing total for most of the morning, and one that ultimately finished tied for fifth with Paul Azinger.

Kite wasn't alone in going low. Vijay Singh, plagued by his putter throughout the week, also shot 64. The only problem was that Singh entered the round at 13 over par. "I just told my caddie, 'Why do I have a round like that when I can't win?'" Singh said. "The frustrating thing is I played better than what I shot. If I could have gotten anything to fall earlier in the week, maybe it would have been a different story."

It was a different story for two guys at the other end of the leaderboard when the day began. The swing that had seemed flawless earlier in the week abandoned Garcia on Sunday. A closing 77 saw him plunge from a tie for third to a tie for 12th.

"These things happen," Garcia said. "Things didn't go my way from the start. I made two mistakes and both of them cost me a lot. Still, it was a good experience and one I will learn from. I will do better next time. I will learn from this how to deal with the pressure."

Another player reflecting on what might have been after his round was Mickelson, who, like the victim of some tragic comedy, saw another major chance slip by. His final-round 75 left the left-hander six shots off the winning pace. Afterward, he looked almost punch drunk as he tried to convince himself and everyone else that it wasn't that big a deal.

"I'm just tired of beating myself up after each one," Mickelson said. "If I didn't have a shot at winning, I would be much more miserable than I am now."

He made a bogey at the ninth from the middle of the fairway, and three-putted after a questionable approach to the par-five 13th, leaving many to wonder if Mickelson's game wasn't like a shaky train running at full speed. Derailment wasn't a question of if, only when and how many casualties. He had 34 putts on Sunday, the most of any player who finished in the top 40.

"Last year I played well in the majors and didn't feel I had a shot at winning any of them," Mickelson said. "This year I've had two great shots at it. With that being the case, I don't feel like I'm far away from achieving a level of play that is extremely high. To be honest, I'm really not very upset about it."

For the most part, Cink, Brooks and Goosen weren't upset by the way they played either, with the noted exception of the final hole. Brooks had one bogey on the first nine at the par-five fifth hole, offset by two birdies on the second nine at the 11th and 13th. That got him to one under par for the day and five under for the championship. When he reached the 18th green with his second shot, he thought he had a chance to shoot 69 for the day. "I felt like five or six (under par) was the number," he said. "When I played 13 and made birdie to get to five, and I saw Goosen and Cink were both at five, that was when I knew that would probably win the golf tournament. I watched the boards. I knew what was going on."

Goosen watched as well. After his fiasco at the 18th he tried to put his round in context. "I've had my breaks today," he said. "On the second hole I hit it right and it hit a tree and stayed out of the water. I got lucky there. On the third hole I hit it in the trees and it bounced back into the fairway. I've had my breaks out there as well. Unfortunately, on the last hole I hit a perfect drive and a perfect six iron and, well, I three-putted."

Even Cink, shell-shocked by the turn of events at the last hole, didn't lament his play. "Big picture, I felt pretty comfortable coming down the stretch," he said. "I felt more comfortable on the back nine than on the front nine on Thursday. I felt really at ease and calm, and I felt confident in all my strokes and shots in the fairways and off the tees. I felt better coming into the last few holes than I did going off the first few on Thursday. That's something I'll draw off of for a long time."

Cink also learned a lot from the catastrophe at the final hole. "When you come to the last hole of a tournament, whether it's the U.S. Open or whatever, a lot of times it turns into match play," Cink said. "You can say you're playing against the course all you want to, but it turns into match play on the last hole. It's like a playoff. So I was playing not only against the hole, but I was also playing against the situation that I needed to at least tie Retief on the hole or beat him to win. After I missed the green left and chipped on, I was looking at about a 12-footer. I thought that was a pretty crucial putt because the situation dictated to me that I needed to make that, because Retief had a gimme two-putt.

"I'm not hanging my head at all. I hung in there probably better than a lot of people thought I would, maybe even better than I thought I would. I gave myself a really darn good chance at the end. I'm not going to look back and say I missed a two-footer to get myself into the playoff in the U.S. Open. I'm going to look back and say I made a great effort from 12 feet to tie."

The final leaderboard in the U.S. Open looked like this:

Retief Goosen	71 - 276	Davis Love III	70 - 282
Mark Brooks	70 - 276	Kirk Triplett	70 - 282
Stewart Cink	72 - 277	Phil Mickelson	75 - 282
Rocco Mediate	72 - 278	Tiger Woods	69 - 283
Tom Kite	64 - 281	Matt Gogel	70 - 283
Paul Azinger	71 - 281	Michael Allen	71 - 283
Vijay Singh	64 - 282	Sergio Garcia	77 - 283
Angel Cabrera	69 - 282		

Angry at himself and more determined than ever, Goosen arrived on Monday morning seeking redemption for his 72nd hole gaffe. He didn't want to be remembered for the blown putt, and the only way to put it behind him was to go out and win the trophy.

Goosen took the same number of putts through the first three holes of the playoff as he needed to finish the final hole on Sunday. But all his one-putts were for pars, as Goosen's long game appeared shaky in the early going. Brooks took the upper hand with a birdie at the fourth, but when Goosen finally found the fairway on the sixth hole, he brought things back to even with a birdie of his own.

Then Brooks' game went south. A bogey from the right rough at the seventh and another at the 10th cost him. When Goosen rolled in a 20-footer for birdie at the 10th, the margin was three shots. The same thing happened on the 11th when Brooks made bogey and Goosen made birdie. Suddenly Goosen had a five-shot margin with seven holes to play.

He maintained the margin until the 17th when the tables were reversed and Brooks made birdie to Goosen's bogey. But even another bogey by Goosen at the 18th didn't matter. He had 70 to Brooks' 72.

Afterward, Goosen was asked about other collapses, most notably, the 72nd hole triple bogey of Jean Van de Velde that cost the Frenchman the 1999 British Open.

"I know what Jean went through at Carnoustie," Goosen said. "You play so well and it all comes down to one shot at the end of the day. I think staying overnight might have helped me. I think we were all a bit shaken up over what happened on the last hole. It gave me a chance to relax and reflect on what happened. I was able to tell myself I was playing well."

Then, with a smile, he tried to put the entire Sunday incident behind him. "Today was quite a relief after yesterday," the new U.S. Open champion said. "I was able to keep my wits together."

4. British Open Championship

Some years ago, a U.S. Open champion talked about what happens when a golfer wins a major championship.

"You don't win *it*," he said. "It wins *you*."

Perhaps, but if anyone has ever taken a British Open by the throat, Tiger Woods had done it in 2000 and David Duval again in 2001. Woods, of course, won by eight strokes at St. Andrews, and Duval by three at Royal Lytham and St. Annes. While Woods may have won by the bigger margin, all the same, Duval staged one of the strongest finishes this old championship had ever seen.

Where Woods had shot 67-69–136 in his last two rounds, Duval closed 65-67–132, among the greatest of all British Open finishes. His closing 67 broke him out of a first-place tie with three others and made him the clear winner, with a 72-hole score of 274. A Swedish golfer so obscure hardly anyone knew he had entered, Niclas Fasth took second place at 277, and Ian Woosnam finished another stroke behind at 278, tied with five others — Bernhard Langer, Miguel Angel Jimenez, Darren Clarke, Ernie Els and the surprising Billy Mayfair. Although he had won the 1987 U.S. Amateur, Mayfair had never placed so high in a professional major championship.

Of the 19 men who had begun the last round either tied for first at 207 or within two strokes of it, only Duval and Ernie Els broke 70. Els had started the day tied with five others in 14th place at 209. Both Woosnam and Langer shot 71, even par, and Alex Cejka limped in with 73.

Only Fasth, Davis Love III and Kevin Sutherland matched Duval's final 67, but only Fasth had begun the last round within striking distance. Three strokes behind at the start, he gained no ground on Duval, but he passed 18 men on his way to second place.

Els, by the way, played the last 36 holes almost as well as Duval. He shot 67-69–136 and climbed from a tie for 14th after three rounds into a tie for third. Actually, Sutherland played those last 54 holes better than anyone. After a stumbling 75 start, he followed with 69-68-67–204.

Both Mikko Ilonen of Finland, a former British Amateur champion, and Bob Estes of the United States closed with 66s, but Ilonen had started six strokes behind and Estes 10 strokes back.

Woosnam might have done better, but after nearly holing his tee shot on the par-three first hole, he was handed a two-stroke penalty for carrying too many clubs.

Even without the penalty, Woosnam would have had to score better, because Duval played relentless, uncompromising golf. He had opened with a promising 69, but playing indifferent stuff through the second round, he stumbled in with 73 and began his run for the championship from a tie for 35th place.

His third-round 65 jumped him into a tie for first, and then he ran away from the field with his finishing 67. Over those last 36 holes, Duval played at a killing pace. He ran off 12 birdies, a ratio of one every three holes, and bogeyed only the 15th in the third round and the 12th in the last, two of Royal Lytham's three hardest holes.

By the 13th he had the championship in hand. After he birdied the sixth, a par-five so short that the modern golfer reaches the green with short-iron seconds, no one closed within two strokes of him, except for a brief moment after that slip on the 12th. At about the same time, Jimenez birdied the 13th and dropped to eight under par, just one stroke behind Duval. As quickly as he had closed in, Jimenez fell back. He drove into a fairway bunker on the 14th and lost the stroke he had just won, and Duval birdied the 13th.

While the championship had been a triumph for Duval, it had been a dismal disappointment for many others. Jesper Parnevik had been close in 1994, again in 1997, and once more in 1998. Two double bogeys in the third round ruined him this time.

Parnevik's close misses, though, couldn't touch Colin Montgomerie's persistent and inconsolable frustrations. For a number of years the most consistent money winner on the PGA European Tour, Montgomerie had played miserably in the British Open.

Coming to Royal Lytham, Montgomerie had played in 11 British Opens and finished within sight of the leader just once. He shot 275 at Turnberry in 1994 and tied for eighth place, seven strokes behind Nick Price. Worse, in five of the last nine, he hadn't even made the cut.

For a time Montgomerie looked as if he might break through. He opened with a blistering 65, a score no one matched, and followed with 69 — two rounds in the 60s. He's only had seven in his British Open career. Now he led halfway through, but as the tension built he dropped back to his comfort zone, and faded into a tie for 13th place.

At the end, Royal Lytham was cluttered with other disappointed and disappointing golfers. Fresh from winning both the U.S. Open a month earlier and the Scottish Open just a week before, Retief Goosen opened with a grim 74 and never recovered; always full of promise, Davis Love III never once looked like a winner; vivacious and entertaining Sergio Garcia played steady but not winning golf; Phil Mickelson, a terror in regular tour events apparently has not enough aptitude for tournaments with serious meaning; Vijay Singh, the only man since the coming of Tiger Woods to have won two major championships, played well but not well enough; Darren Clarke began the last day one stroke behind and finished four back; and Ernie Els needed a stronger finishing kick.

Perhaps none, though, ended the week more dispirited than Woods. After some unusually loose golf at Southern Hills, where he tied for 12th in the U.S. Open, Woods played worse at Royal Lytham and tied for 25th. A year earlier he had bogeyed only six holes in winning both the U.S. and British Opens. At Lytham he bogeyed nine holes, double-bogeyed one, and triple-bogeyed another in somewhat sensational style.

It was at Royal Lytham five years earlier that Woods, still an amateur, shot 66 in the second round and followed with 70s in the third and fourth, convincing himself that even though he was only 20 years old, it was time to turn to professional golf. Speaking only in terms of his golf, he was right. Since then he had run up an amazing record, and he came in as the defending champion.

Never once, though, did he look like a winner, but never once did the other players not worry that he might pull it off. It was strange: He was never in it, and yet he was always in it.

He hit more truly wild shots than anyone could remember, and adding to his misery, the putts that had so often changed course and dived into holes, teased the edges and glided past. When they didn't fall, he often looked startled and puzzled, shocked that he had missed.

Nevertheless, he battled to the end, finishing his struggle by birdieing two of the last three holes and matching Lytham's par of 71.

In 1996, his last year as an amateur, Woods shot 281 at Royal Lytham. As defending champion he shot 283, two strokes worse. His higher score, though, reflected more than an off week. Royal Lytham simply played tougher than it had five years earlier. Western England had been going through a drought in the summer of 1996. Reservoirs sat half empty and balls rolled endlessly over withered grass that barely covered the parched, hard-packed ground.

With the combination of thinnish rough, no wind, bright sunshine, warm temperatures and balls rolling indecent distances, scoring fell to unusual levels. Tom Lehman won with 271, three strokes better than Duval's winning score, and he played the first three rounds in 198, nine strokes better than Duval.

Fortunately for the integrity of the course, the weather in 2001 wasn't nearly so benign. While it wasn't bad, the ground had softened somewhat during a reasonably normal spring and summer, and the wind blew occasionally, though not powerfully.

Consequently, Royal Lytham in 2001 played more as it should play, a gratifying result because this is one of Britain's better examinations. Besides, it had a history. It was there in 1926 that Bobby Jones won the first of his three British Opens. It was there in 1963 that Bob Charles became the only left-hander to win one of the game's four premier events, and it was there in 1969 that Tony Jacklin became the first Briton to win his nation's championship since Max Faulkner back in 1951. It was there in 1996 as well that Lehman became the first American professional to win a British Open at Royal Lytham.

Royal Lytham is unique among the great courses because it opens with a par-three hole, one of three on the outward nine. Its inward nine, much the harder of the two, has one par-three, one par-five and seven testing par-fours.

As it was set up for 2001, Royal Lytham measured 6,905 yards, an insignificant 13 yards longer than in 1996. Ten of those yards were added to the first nine, which measured 3,340 yards. The second nine measured 3,565.

Royal Lytham has always been celebrated for its brutish finish, six par-four holes that together measure 2,490 yards.

This rugged run for home really begins with the 12th, the last and the hardest of the par-threes. A temperate 198 yards in length, its green sits slightly above the level of the tee, closely protected by deep bunkers. Through the four days, the 12th surrendered only 28 birdies, but it claimed 136 scores of one over par or worse. Duval bogeyed it twice and Woods took a six.

The stretch run eases with the 13th, at 342 yards the easiest of all the par-fours — it gave up 96 birdies and only 50 men scored over par. But then the serious work begins. At 445 yards, the 14th runs through borders of punishing rough, and the 15th, the hardest of them all, stretches 465 yards with a slight right-to-left bend. Over 450 rounds, the 15th yielded just 28 birdies, but took back just as many double bogeys. Overall, the players surrendered 179 scores of bogey or worse.

Taking pity, the 367-yard 16th offered some relief, but then the 17th, at 467 brutal yards, punished any error. And then comes the closing hole, just 412 yards but calling for a drive threaded through nests of bunkers set both right and left, 200 to 280 yards out. Some believe this is Royal Lytham's most exacting driving hole because, except for an exceptionally long shot, the drive must go so far and no farther. If the ball rolls into one of those deep bunkers, only exceptional shotmaking will salvage a par.

Nevertheless, in spite of all its perils and that mind-numbing finish, Royal Lytham could be beaten by the modern tournament golfer. Six years earlier, when Lytham played at its most vulnerable, 62 men either broke or equaled its par of 71 in the first round. Now, under more difficult conditions, 50 players broke or matched par. Twenty of them shot in the 60s, 13 more shot 70, and another 17 shot 71.

Leading the pack, Colin Montgomerie blistered the old course with 65, by far the best round of the day. Brad Faxon and Chris DiMarco, along with Ilonen, shot 68s. At the end of the day, the 156-man field had bunched so tightly, the next 46 men stood within two strokes of one another.

David Duval, Jose Maria Olazabal and Jesper Parnevik were among 16 men at 69; Mark O'Meara, Darren Clarke, Phil Mickelson, Vijay Singh and Sergio Garcia shot 70, and Ernie Els and Tiger Woods stood among the 18 men tied at 71.

Altogether 33 men broke par, 18 matched it, and 35 more shot within two strokes of par. Excluding Montgomerie, 85 men huddled within five strokes of one another. At different times, 52 players worked their way to two under par, and 20 of them slipped three under. Few held on.

Playing erratic golf, Mickelson fought his way to two under through the 13th even though he had parred only three holes, He birdied the second, bogeyed the next three, then scored consecutive eagle-threes on the sixth and seventh. From there on he struggled to hold what he had, gave back one of those strokes, and shot 70.

Paired with Montgomerie, Fred Couples reached three under, but he lost every one of those strokes on the 14th. Not thinking clearly when his approach buried under the lip of a greenside bunker, Couples tried to play an impossible shot rather than call the ball unplayable and drop clear. Instead, it took him four slashes, one of them left-handed, to hack it out. He made seven and fell to even par.

Even so he had done better than Jim Furyk. Two under par after the 10th, Furyk ran into all kinds of trouble on the 11th. The last of Royal Lytham's par-five holes, it gave up 18 birdies and an eagle the last day, but a combination of an unplayable ball and a shot that bounced off the revetted face of a bunker and hit him added up to a 10. From two under he soared to three over, lost three more strokes coming in, played the home nine in 43, shot 77, and had no hope of making the 36-hole cut.

Three under par after the seventh, Nick Faldo lost five strokes in four holes and shot 75.

Meantime, Goosen worked his way to two under through the 13th but bogeyed the next three, double-bogeyed the 17th, and shot 74.

Those were disappointing rounds to be sure, but they carried none of the impact of the loose play by Tiger Woods, the best player of his time. While he had played some shoddy stuff in the U.S. Open a month earlier, it seemed unlikely he would continue his sloppy golf, but the first seven holes showed he still hadn't found his game.

When he played his first stroke, at 9 o'clock Thursday morning, he looked as if he might run away with the championship. With a 10-mile-an-hour breeze at his back, Woods floated a soft seven iron to 15 feet on the opening hole and ran the putt home. After another stunning pitch to the second, half again closer to the hole, Woods appeared to be on his way to one of the great rounds.

Instead, the ball refused to fall. So sure had he been of holing it, that when the ball slid past, Woods froze, looking stunned. Worse was coming.

His pitch missed the third, but he salvaged his par four there, then played a wild drive on the fourth that put him into a unfamiliar position — his ball had burrowed into a deep pot bunker at the base of a nob covered by tall, wispy grass. A year earlier at St. Andrews, over a course pocked with more than a hundred deep, steep-faced bunkers, Woods had never hit into even one. Here he had no option but to pitch back to the fairway, then followed with a loose shot to the green's back-left corner, miles from the hole. He made his first bogey.

Next, he overshot the par-three fifth but saved par, then played two con-fidence-sapping holes.

For players of Open quality, the sixth and seventh, a pair of par-fives, aren't much of a challenge; birdies should be routine. They weren't for Woods. He pulled his drive into rough on the sixth, flew the ball into a greenside bunker, and made five. On to the seventh, where once again he drove into rough and parred a hole he should have birdied.

On and on it went. When he bogeyed the 14th, his third of the day, he had matched his total bogeys over all 72 holes of the 2000 British Open.

His had been a shabby round. He had been in five bunkers, hit only eight fairways and nine greens, and while some putts grazed the cups and slipped past, he had one-putted half the holes, six of them to save pars. Perhaps even more significantly, he hadn't birdied one of the three par-fives, each of them reachable with a decent second shot.

Nevertheless, Woods had done what all great players usually do; he had turned in a respectable score even though he had played below his usual level. Besides, while his 71 left him six strokes behind Montgomerie, Monty pointed out that Woods sat within three strokes of second place. No one ahead of him could sleep easily.

Montgomerie, though, felt no pain. It had taken awhile. It had taken years of frustration and failure, years of doubt and dejection, of anxiety and stress, of unending pressure and tension. But now, on a cool, overcast July morn-ing, Montgomerie finally began a British Open playing the caliber of golf everyone knew he could play.

Loping along in his usual long strides, Montgomerie tore through Royal Lytham's first nine in 30 strokes, came back in 35, and for all anyone knew, took a stranglehold on the championship.

This exceptional round turned him into a hero. As the birdies mounted, fans were racing after him, calling encouragement, applauding his shots, and jostling one another for a clear view. Reacting to the crowd, Monty put on a mile-wide grin that grew with every cheer.

Montgomerie had always been a puzzle. A man with enormous ability, he had never sustained a high level of scoring through 72 holes of the British Open. He had come close to winning three U.S. Opens and one PGA Championship, but someone else always played better.

Those losses hurt, but nothing matched the misery of his persistent failures in the British Open. Not only had he not won, he had played bad golf. No wonder, then, that when he led off with a barrage of birdies, the galleries flocked to him.

He began by birdieing the first from 20 feet and followed with a lovely pitch to six feet for another on the second. One stroke slipped away when he missed the fifth green, but he chipped in for an eagle-three on the sixth, then played a couple of gorgeous irons — to 10 feet on the eighth and about five feet on the ninth. Both putts fell, and Monty began the run for home five under par.

Montgomerie's gallery had grown with every hole as fans abandoned other players, and by now the fans' enthusiasm had nearly turned to frenzy, and he wallowed in their support. He had shot low rounds in important championships before, but he had never gone out in 30. Facing the punishing closing nine, he would have to hold his concentration and not let a great round slip away.

He made another birdie on the 10th, where a 30 footer fell. He was six under par after 10 holes, one stroke away from Lehman's course record of 64.

There was a struggle to save par on the easy 11th, then another par on the dangerous 12th, and a routine four on the 13th. But then Montgomerie made a three-putt bogey on the 14th, where he might have been distracted by Couples in the bunker. He was five under now, with Royal Lytham's severe finish still ahead.

Those last few holes turned into a battle. He had missed only three greens through the first 14 holes, but now he couldn't hit one. Still, his putter had turned hot, and he made his figures, holing from 20 feet on the 15th and from about 10 feet on the 16th and 17th.

Montgomerie climaxed his round by holing from 40 feet on the 18th. With the gallery's roar, the thought occurred that Colin wished the day would never end. A realist, though, he knew this might not go on very long.

"All this is is a good start," he said.

Then, thinking of the gallery, he added, "Let's hope they'll be cheering as much the rest of the week."

These were the first-round leaders:

Colin Montgomerie	65	Stuart Appleby	69
Brad Faxon	68	Pierre Fulke	69
Chris DiMarco	68	Billy Andrade	69
Mikko Ilonen	68	Alexandre Balicki	69
Justin Rose	69	Niclas Fasth	69
Miguel Angel Jimenez	69	Alex Cejka	69
Paul McGinley	69	Jesper Parnevik	69
J.P. Hayes	69	Billy Mayfair	69
David Duval	69	Greg Owen	69
Jose Maria Olazabal	69	Joe Ogilvie	69

As the first round ended, Montgomerie had looked reality squarely in the eye and cautioned, "This is the best start I've ever had in an Open, and it's nice to be in contention at last, but there is an awfully long way to go."

There was indeed, and the next day Monty gave a glimpse of just how bumpy the trip might be. Instead of another 65, he shot 70. It was another sub-par round, good enough to keep him in first place with 135, but his grin had shrunk and his brow had furrowed because overnight his game's sharp edge had worn dull. Instead of leading by three strokes, his margin was one over Swede Pierre Fulke.

The three men who had shared second place lost ground while others moved up. Brad Faxon shot 71 and fell to ninth; Chris DiMarco shot 74 and dropped to 35th place, and Mikko Ilonen did worse, falling to 45th place with 75.

Meantime, Fulke shot 67, broke away from the 16-man horde bunched in fifth place, and jumped to second at 136, and Jesper Parnevik, along with the relatively unknown Englishman Greg Owen and the equally anonymous American Joe Ogilvie, each shot 68 and shared third place at 137.

With the exception of Parnevik, Montgomerie held a good lead over the most dangerous players, but he had been looking over his shoulder at Woods. It was understandable. Woods was the most dangerous player in the game, and while he didn't challenge the course record, he did justify Montgomerie's concern by shooting 68, a score that moved him seriously close. At 139, he had climbed within four strokes of first place. On a good day, Woods could wipe away four strokes in nine holes.

Monty had been watching out for Woods all day, but his name had never shown on the leaderboards. His own round over, Montgomerie asked, without naming Woods, "What is he, three under? Four under?"

Told Woods had gone to three under, Montgomerie sighed, "Thank God he's not four under."

At this stage, though, Montgomerie had others to worry about as well. Only two strokes behind him, Parnevik had a much better British Open record, and a further two strokes behind at 139 lurked Woods, Mark O'Meara, the 1998 champion, and Darren Clarke, while Nick Price, Bernhard Langer and Ian Woosnam, three old warriors, sat another stroke behind at 140.

Price had lit up the scoreboard by going out in 31 and shooting 67, stirring 13-year-old memories of his classic battle with Seve Ballesteros over these same links in 1988. Seve administered the coup de grace with a wonderful chip to the 18th that, on video tape, still looks as if it might fall.

Hardly anyone noticed Fasth sitting quietly at 138 after a pair of 69s, and nearly everyone ignored Duval back there in 35th place.

Nor did many pay attention to Love, just five strokes behind at 140, after shooting one of the three 67s. If Love were ever to win a British Open, he would have liked best to win at Royal Lytham. It was there in 1969 that his father had played so well his name went up on the leaderboards alongside Tony Jacklin, Jack Nicklaus, Bob Charles, Peter Thomson, Roberto de Vicenzo, all of them British Open champions, and Christy O'Connor. Love died in a plane crash in 1988.

By the time Love teed off, a little after 9:30, Parnevik had been out for two hours and thrust himself into the thick of it. Parnevik began by birdieing the first hole, ran off five consecutive pars, then ripped a three-iron second onto the seventh green for a two-putt birdie. Two under for the day, he picked up another birdie at the eighth and parred the ninth. Out in 32, five under par now, he was one behind Montgomerie.

Parnevik bunkered his second shot to the par-five 11th, but pitched to six feet and birdied again. Four under for the day and six under for the 29 holes, he had caught Montgomerie.

So far Parnevik had played remarkably steady golf. He had hit every fairway through the first 13 holes, but he caught the rough on the 14th and bunkered his second — his first bogey of the round. Quickly, though, he won the stroke back with a glorious four iron to five feet on the long and hard 15th, but needing three more par holes for 67, he overshot the dangerous 17th, gambled on a daring chip shot between two bunkers that didn't work, and lost another stroke. He was in with 68, five under, one behind Montgomerie.

"The conditions were pretty good," Parnevik said later, "and I have to imagine Monty will take advantage of them."

But Monty didn't. After putting up his opening 65, Monty knew he couldn't afford to play defensively, but if he didn't intend to, he certainly gave that impression.

Montgomerie's caution was understandable. Throughout his career he had put so much pressure on himself in the big events, had come so close and yet not won, the tension must have been great.

When he was asked if he could explain Montgomerie's record in the British Open, his caddie said, in an unusually candid moment, "He doesn't like the tournament."

Like it or not, though, Montgomerie was still running ahead, more from inspired putting than precise ball-striking. Normally an exceptionally accurate driver, Montgomerie lost control of his slight fade on the third tee. His ball swerved sharply right, clattered among the trees just a few yards from the Preston-to-Blackpool railway line and, luckily, dropped clear enough to salvage a bogey five.

A scrambling birdie on the easy sixth brought him back to even par, and he missed a chance at another birdie on the seventh. In seven holes he had missed five greens he should have hit (even though he hit both par-five greens with his third shot, he could have reached both with his second), and yet he had made his figures.

A missed putt from 10 feet cost him a birdie on the eighth, and he went out in 35, even par. He came back in 35 as well, with birdies on the 11th and 13th and a bogey on the tough 15th. The birdie on the 11th must have been the work of Merlin. His three-iron second shot disappeared into the left greenside bunker, then magically popped out and glided down a gentle slope to the edge of the green. Two putts and he had his four.

Then, with a chance to shoot 69 and open a two-stroke gap, Montgomerie missed from inside 10 feet on the home hole. The mistake disappointed him, of course, but he had made it halfway through still in first place.

Just behind Montgomerie lurked Fulke, a bit of a surprise considering his recent form. He had missed the 36-hole cut in three of the six European Tour tournaments he had entered, including the Scottish Open the previous week, missed the cut in the Masters as well, and withdrew after one round of the U.S. Open. Nevertheless, he had played 36 holes at Royal Lytham with only two bogeys, both in the first round.

Holing nothing longer than a 12-footer on the 11th, he had birdied each of the par-fives and added his fourth birdie on the short 10th. Obviously, he had taken advantage of the openings Royal Lytham gave him.

For a change, so did Woods. Where he had made nothing but pars on the par-fives in the first round, like Fulke he had birdied them all in the second. Still, he wasn't the player who had won all those major tournaments. He drove the ball erratically, and the putts didn't search out the holes as they had in the past. But once again he had kept himself in position to win without playing his best.

The 36-hole cut fell at 144, two over par, and caught some great players both of the past and the present. Weakened by a case of flu, Thomas Bjorn, who had played so well in recent big events, shot 151; Mark Brooks, the playoff loser to Goosen in the U.S. Open, shot 146, and Justin Leonard, the 1997 champion, shot 145.

Forty-four years old and no longer up to playing in his old swashbuckling style, Seve Ballesteros lumbered around in 78 and 71, five strokes too many. It was sad in a way, because it was here at Royal Lytham that he had burst to the top of the game by winning the 1979 British Open, and it was here in 1988 that he played so wonderfully well, going into the last round two strokes behind, shooting 65, and winning by two.

The cut also caught Nick Faldo, the best player of his time; Tom Lehman, the last winner at Royal Lytham; John Daly, the 1995 champion; Bob Charles, who won at Royal Lytham in 1963, and Tom Watson, one of five men who had won five British Opens.

Let us not forget Gary Player, one of the most durable champions the game has known. Gary had won three British Opens over a span of 15 years, his first in 1959 at St. Andrews, his second in 1968 at Carnoustie and his last in 1974 at Royal Lytham. Player had reached 65 in 2001; he would no longer be exempt from qualifying.

These were the second-round leaders:

Colin Montgomerie	70 - 135	Raphael Jacquelin	68 - 139
Pierre Fulke	67 - 136	Rory Sabbatini	69 - 139
Jesper Parnevik	68 - 137	Des Smyth	65 - 139
Greg Owen	68 - 137	Brad Faxon	71 - 139
Joe Ogilvie	68 - 137	Mark O'Meara	69 - 139
Niclas Fasth	69 - 138	Tiger Woods	68 - 139
Alex Cejka	69 - 138	Darren Clarke	69 - 139
Eduardo Romero	68 - 138	Billy Andrade	70 - 139

Saturday was a day of shifting positions, a day when 10 men either held or shared the lead at different times, a day when the field bunched so tightly, one glorious shot jumped Greg Owen from 15th place to second.

It was a day of low scoring as well, when 23 men of the 70-man field broke par, a day when David Duval shot to the top and when Colin Montgomerie began the slide that ended another futile chase after a national championship. Montgomerie began the day in first place and ended it tied for fifth. By contrast, Duval began in a tie for 35th and ended tied for first.

It was a day when Owen holed a 240-yard three iron for a double-eagle two on the 11th, and when Jesper Parnevik four-putted the eighth.

When it ended, four men shared first place, nine tied for fifth and another six lay a further stroke behind — 19 men within two strokes of one another with 18 holes to play. A playoff seemed likely.

Among the early starters, Duval raced around Royal Lytham in 65, and reprising another decade, both Ian Woosnam and Bernhard Langer shot 67s and joined Duval and Alex Cejka at 207.

While the putts were falling for the leaders, Montgomerie's putting soured. He shot 73 and dropped one stroke out of first, tied at 208 with Parnevik, Price, Fulke, Mayfair, Ogilvie, Clarke, Jimenez and the tall Frenchman Raphael Jacquelin.

Playing under suffocating pressure, Montgomerie held his poise and good humor even as he played the costliest hole of the day, laughing while he struggled with a ridiculous situation.

With his ball lying close to the sheer wall of a tiny pot bunker on the 13th, Royal Lytham's easiest par-four, Monty pretzeled himself into a muscle-stretching stance. With room for only one leg inside the bunker, he dug his left foot into the sand and bent his right leg at an odd angle back over the bank.

Believing his pants seams were about to split, Montgomerie began giggling and climbed out. Speaking later, he laughed that splitting his pants "wouldn't have been the most embarrassing thing I've ever done."

Back in again, he took two strokes to get out and double-bogeyed. He had gone to the 13th in even par, but he never recovered and finished two over.

Meantime, Tiger Woods birdied three of the first six holes, bogeyed another, then hit a wall at the seventh. Two wild shots led to an unplayable ball penalty, and when a putt grazed the lip of the hole and refused to fall, he had taken a seven on a hole he should have birdied consistently. He shot 73, and with 212 dropped to a tie for 28th place. He was finished.

The round began on a gray though not unpleasant morning, but toward mid-afternoon the wind swept in from the Irish Sea, clouds lowered and darkened, and the temperature dropped into the 60s.

Playing in the best of the weather, Duval was off on the decisive round of the championship. Dressed in black pants, a black, long-sleeved shirt, dark blue sweater vest, black cap and his usual dark wrap-around sunglasses, and wearing a grim, tightlipped, unsmiling expression, he presented an enigmatic presence. But, then, he had a lot to overcome.

After a good 69 in the opening round, Duval had followed with 73, which may have led some to assume he was in for a spiritless finish. His first shot Saturday strengthened the feeling. It settled into an awkward position close to the lip of a greenside bunker, but here, instead of a debilitating opening bogey, Duval splashed out to six feet and holed the putt, then played a terrific six iron inside 10 feet and birdied the second.

When he missed birdieing the easy sixth, the fans seemed to accept that once again Duval wasn't up to the challenge, but quickly he changed their minds. Over the next eight holes, Duval ran off six birdies.

He began by ripping a three iron into the seventh and two-putting from 35 feet, followed with a nine iron to 12 feet and birdied the eighth, made his par three on the ninth, then holed another 12-footer on the 10th.

His putting had turned around. Balls that had skimmed past the edges in earlier rounds caught the holes, boosting his growing confidence.

He had another birdie on the 11th, got safely past the treacherous 12th, had a stunning nine iron to 18 inches on the 13th, and another pitch to eight feet on the tough 14th. Beginning the day at even par, Duval had gone to seven under par, the same as Montgomerie.

At the same time, it couldn't be said that Duval had caught up, because, as the last man off the first tee, Monty hadn't yet played a shot. Nor had anyone else close to the lead. Still, Duval stood four pars away from 64, and that could work wonders.

There would be no 64. His drive on the 15th drifted into grass so deep and tangled he took two more strokes to reach the green and bogeyed, back to six under.

Perhaps he played the best shot of the day — maybe even of the tournament — on the 17th, a wonderful par-four of 467 yards that over the four days gave up only 26 birdies. It was on this hole in 1926 that Bobby Jones played a legendary shot from a sandy lie in the left rough that carried over a dune and a patch of unkempt wasteland and sailed onto the green. The story goes that the shot so unnerved Al Watrous, who was leading and playing with Jones, that he three-putted.

Duval's shot didn't reach such heroic scope, nor would it be remembered so vividly, but it would do.

After a good drive, Duval pushed his approach into matted grass about 35 feet from the near edge of the green. From there he would have to play a delicate shot across a shallow depression to a hole not more than 15 feet from the green's edge.

Taking a lofted club, Duval played the shot perfectly. The ball popped against the upslope, jumped onto the green, and for an instant looked as if it might drop for a three. He had saved his par, and after going out in 32, had come back in 33 for 65.

When Duval finished, his six under par ranked second only to Montgomerie's seven under, but with Royal Lytham giving up low scores, any number of players probably would pass him.

A few did. After a fumbling start, Alex Cejka ran off six birdies from the fifth through the 11th and, at nine under, sprinted two strokes ahead of the field, while two others joined Montgomerie at seven under. The day had turned into a free-for-all, a struggle among nine men, including those old favorites Bernhard Langer and Ian Woosnam.

Some years had passed since those two had contended for the great prizes, but by now both had gone to the broom-handle putter and found new life. On this day they played as they had a decade or more earlier. Two under par going into the third round, Langer and Woosnam, playing together, teed off half an hour before Darren Clarke.

Starting quickly, Langer birdied the first and both par-fives, but he bogeyed the third, which played almost as tough as the 15th. Out in 33, he scored one stroke better than Woosnam, who shot a scrambling 34.

Montgomerie had started by then, but with the Open his to win or lose, he began playing shaky golf. Within two holes he had been caught not only by Fulke, playing alongside him, but by Clarke, up ahead. In truth, Monty was lucky he hadn't fallen two strokes behind, because Clarke had come within an indrawn breath of scoring eagle-threes on both par-fives. His putt on the sixth looked as if it touched the edge of the hole, and his putt on the seventh died no more than an inch or two short.

Two holes later, Montgomerie bogeyed the fourth and fell one stroke behind Fulke, who had birdied the second. Neither man would make up more ground. Montgomerie lost strokes on both the fourth and eighth, neither particularly difficult holes, went out in 37, and came back in 36. Fulke's game turned sour at the same time. He bogeyed the seventh and ninth, went out in 36, and with birdies on the 14th and 18th offset by a double bogey on the 15th, came back in 36.

Up ahead, Langer had birdied both the 10th and 11th, and Woosnam had played a glorious iron onto the 11th and holed from no more than six feet for an eagle-three. Langer was six under and Woosnam, five under. Then, when Langer birdied the 14th, he shared first place with Fulke.

Clarke had bogeyed the par-three ninth and stood six under, alongside Montgomerie, Cejka, Woosnam, Jacquelin, the 45-year-old Irishman Des Smyth and Duval. Then Nick Price slipped into the mix, going out in 33.

It was becoming more difficult by the minute to fathom who stood where.

In the end it all sorted itself out. Recovering from four-putting the eighth, Parnevik had run off four successive birdies from the ninth through the 12th, climbed into first place at seven under, then threw it away with a drive so deep in rough alongside the 17th he needed three more strokes to reach the green. He double-bogeyed, his second of the round, and with 71 settled into a tie for fifth.

Cejka, meantime, had birdied six of the seven holes from the fifth through the 11th, but he played the next seven in three over par and fell back to six under. Price came back in 35 and finished at five under, out in 32. Clarke bogeyed the 18th, came back in 37, and with 69 finished at five under. Smyth's game lost its shine on the home nine, where he shot 37, and with 70 finished at four under, tied with, among others, Retief Goosen, who sprang to life with a 67. Woosnam came back in 33, Langer in 34, and with their 67s finished at six under, tied with Duval and Cejka in first place.

At the end of the day, all those predictions that Duval's had been a good effort but he would find himself back in the pack were wrong. Of the 15 men who had begun the third round within five strokes of Montgomerie, only eight had broken par 71. Now four men shared first place, each with something to prove.

The third-round scores:

David Duval	65 - 207		Darren Clarke	69 - 208
Bernhard Langer	67 - 207		Raphael Jacquelin	69 - 208
Ian Woosnam	67 - 207		Joe Ogilvie	71 - 208
Alex Cejka	69 - 207		Pierre Fulke	72 - 208
Miguel Angel Jimenez	67 - 208		Colin Montgomerie	73 - 208
Billy Mayfair	67 - 208		Jesper Parnevik	71 - 208
Nick Price	68 - 208			

Duval had come into the British Open with a record similar to Montgomerie's in the major championships. He had risen to the top of the World Ranking for a brief time after he won the 1999 Players Championship, the most important tournament he had won, but Tiger Woods took the top spot away from him within a short time.

Twenty-nine years old in July of 2001, Duval had built a decent record in both the British and U.S. Opens over the previous few years, but he had shown no finishing kick. In first place after two rounds of the 1999 U.S. Open, Duval finished 75-75 at Pinehurst and tied for seventh. Three strokes out of first in the U.S. Open at Southern Hills in June of 2001, he closed 71-74 and tied for 16th.

Six strokes behind Tiger Woods going into the last round of the 2000 British Open, and paired with him, Duval battled to within three strokes after seven holes, but Woods tore his heart out by playing the next eight with four threes and four fours. Duval stumbled home in 43 and dropped into a tie for 11th.

He had had chances in the Masters as well, and had come very close in 1998 and earlier in 2001. Only Mark O'Meara's blinding finish denied him in 1998, and his own inept putting over the last few holes kept him from winning earlier in 2001. While terrific irons put him within birdie range on five of the last six holes, he birdied only the 15th, one of the two vulnerable par-fives on Augusta's home nine.

As the first man in at 207, Duval was the last man off the first tee, and by the time he answered the starter's call, he was already in second place. Off two hours earlier, Niclas Fasth had played the first seven holes in four under par and moved into first place at seven under.

While he was barely known, Fasth was no rookie. He had played both the European and American tours during 1998, but fared so badly he lost his playing privileges in both. He returned, concentrated solely on Europe, and won a tournament in 2000. Now, playing in his first British Open, he showed remarkable poise, especially over the last few holes when he had the championship within reach.

Fasth went out in 31, and when he birdied the 11th he had gone to eight under par. Now the field would have to catch him.

All the dangerous players were behind him, because, up ahead, Tiger Woods was having another difficult day. Starting five strokes out of first, he had picked up two strokes with 33 on the first nine, but any suspicion he might pull it out died on the 12th. There he played one of the worst holes of his career. His tee shot squirted into more deep and tangled grass right of the green, his attempted recovery darted across the green and raced 30 yards back toward the tee, his pitch back veered into the right greenside bunker, and he took three more to hole out for a triple-bogey six.

Still, Woods never gave up. He birdied both the 16th and the punishing 17th, came back in 38, shot even-par 71, and tied for 25th place. When he holed his final putt, the huge gallery cheered him as if he had won. He had indeed given all he had to give, but it just wasn't enough. The old trophy would go to someone else.

Fasth had a chance, but in the end it turned out to be no chance at all, because Duval simply wouldn't be beaten.

Who knows, though, what Woosnam might have done had he not rushed to the first tee barely in time to play his first shot, a stunning iron that hit the green and for a heart-stopping moment looked as if it might fall for a hole-in-one. He tapped it in for the birdie, then strode off bursting with confidence. When he reached the second tee he had the wind knocked out of him.

He had been testing two drivers on the practice ground, and since he had neglected to count his clubs, he hadn't realized he still had the second driver in his bag. When he stepped onto the second tee, his caddie noticed the extra club and told Ian, "You're going to go ballistic."

Wary, Woosnam asked why.

"We have 15 clubs," the caddie answered, one more than the rules allow.

Woosnam was assessed a two-stroke penalty; instead of a two on the first, he had to write down four.

No one will ever know how the penalty affected his game. A long time ago, when the great Bobby Jones was asked if the two-stroke penalty he had called on himself in the 1925 U.S. Open had cost him the championship, he said he honestly couldn't say it had, because the penalty had a mental effect. He explained that the penalty might have sparked the emotional boost to play better than he might have. In the end he tied Willie Macfarlane and lost in a playoff.

We do know, though, that after stumbling through the first four holes in three over par and dropping four strokes behind Fasth and Duval, Woosnam began playing wonderful shots. He eagled the sixth, and by the time he reached the 14th tee he had worked back to seven under, still in the hunt.

He would not catch Duval, though. After steady pars on the first two holes, Duval ran home a putt on the third that barely crept into the hole. He was seven under now, one behind Fasth, who had played through the 13th by then. Duval had scrambling pars on both the fourth and fifth, then a pulled drive into high rough on the sixth. Using brute strength, he tore the ball from the grass with his nine iron, flew it onto the green, and after a loose first putt, holed a nasty four-footer for the birdie to go eight under.

A big drive at the seventh that must have run an extra 50 yards, an eight iron that skipped past a bunker onto the green, and two putts resulted in another birdie. He was nine under.

With a routine par four on the eighth, then a timid putt that cost him a birdie on the ninth, Duval had gone out in 32.

Fasth had bogeyed the 14th by then and fallen back to seven under; Mayfair had gone out in 33 and caught Fasth; and Vijay Singh, Clarke, Langer and Jimenez all stood six under.

Duval had made some mistakes on the outward nine, but he hadn't let them ruin his round. Now he was about to take command.

He had a par on the 10th, a mis-played iron into a bunker at the 11th, but a marvelous recovery to two feet for still another birdie that dropped him to 10 under. Then he had a glitch on the 12th, where once again he was bunkered and didn't recover well enough to save par. Quickly, though, he had a pitch to 10 feet to set up still another birdie on the 13th and he was 10 under once again.

Now Duval got a lucky break on the 14th, where his pushed drive hit a spectator on the bounce, stopping the ball from bounding deeper into the rough. Once again he saved par.

By then Jimenez had bogeyed the 14th, killing his drive, and after birdieing the 16th to close to within two strokes of Duval, Clarke hit a low, running hook on the 17th that scooted into a fairway bunker and set off a series of unfortunate shots that ended with a double-bogey six. He was back to six under, four behind.

Woosnam had lost another stroke and fallen to six under as well; Langer had made no move at all, and Fasth had finished by then with 67 and 277. With four holes to play, the British Open was Duval's to win or lose.

Another drive into the rough on the 15th, and from calf-high grass 210 yards out Duval slashed a six iron onto the green. It was a remarkable shot, so stunning it startled David Pepper, the referee.

"If you'd been playing someone who hit a ball that made a sound like that," Pepper said, "you'd know you were in trouble."

Duval himself called it, "One of the best shots I've ever played."

He made his par, added two more on the 16th and 17th, then moved on to the final hole, played down that awesome avenue between the big grandstands crammed with cheering fans.

Few men have played a closing hole better. He had a monstrous drive and a glorious pitch to within 12 feet. He nearly holed the putt, but his ball died inches away. Duval had finally won his championship.

When the winning putt fell, Duval whipped off his cap and sunglasses, and waved to the crowd and smiled.

This had been a fulfilling moment, because now Duval knew not only that he could beat the best players in the game, but that he could play his best when it mattered most, and that for this one week he had been the best of them all.

5. PGA Championship

Phil Mickelson had a sinking feeling in his stomach, the kind of ache that comes from knowing something bad is about to happen and being powerless to stop it. He was standing by the 18th green in the final round of the PGA Championship. He had already tapped in for par to finish, and was propped on his putter, waiting for the dagger to plunge into his heart. He knew it was coming. He had been there before.

In 1999, Mickelson had stood on the 18th green at Pinehurst and watched as Payne Stewart rolled in a 15-footer for par to beat him by one. Stewart had barely missed the fairway at the 18th and chosen to lay up with his second shot, a play many questioned until he rolled in the winning putt at Mickelson's expense.

Two years later, Mickelson came to the 18th tee of Atlanta Athletic Club trailing David Toms by one shot in the PGA Championship. Toms barely missed the fairway with his tee shot and after a great deal of deliberation, pulled out a pitching wedge to lay up to the well-guarded green. He then hit a lob wedge to 12 feet. Mickelson rolled a 20-footer for birdie to within six inches of the hole, and tapped in for par. That left Toms standing center stage, just as Stewart had been two years earlier.

"The first thing that went through my head was '99 at Pinehurst," Mickelson said. "Payne chipped up to 15 feet and drained it to beat me by one. I had that same feeling, as though David's putt was going to go in, without a doubt."

Indeed it did. After examining his putt from various angles, Toms turned to his caddie and said, "These are the kind of putts you're supposed to make to win a major championship — especially your first one. It's supposed to be tough." Then Toms rolled the 12-footer into the hole for a 69 and a 15-under-par 265 total for a one-stroke victory.

A winner of 19 PGA Tour titles, Mickelson remained 0 for 38 in the major championships, missing opportunities to break through at the Masters, U.S. Open and PGA Championship in 2001. One shot behind at the Masters going into the final round, Mickelson three-putted the 16th to fall out of contention. Trailing by two on the final day of the U.S. Open, Mickelson missed fairways, short-sided greens and shot himself out of contention. In Atlanta he played his best golf of the year until the minute it took Toms to line up his putt at the 72nd hole. Mickelson's final-round scoring average in the majors was 72.43, a number that wouldn't put him in the top 50 on the PGA Tour.

"I think that I feel confident in the way I'm able to play these championships," Mickelson said. "I'm frustrated that I have not been able to break through or play well enough to beat every player in the field. It's certainly disappointing. Everyone talks about me trying to win my first major. Well, my mindset is to win a bunch of majors, and I still can't seem to get past the first one. That's what bothers me a lot."

It also gnawed at him that the victor at this championship wasn't Tiger Woods or David Duval or Sergio Garcia, or even Retief Goosen, but David Toms, the Louisiana native who came from behind to beat Mickelson earlier in the year at the Compaq Classic of New Orleans, and who wasn't listed on anyone's short list of best players never to win a major.

"David played in the group ahead of me at New Orleans and shot 64 and beat me," Mickelson said. "That was something that I still remember, and I would very much like to steal one from him."

But "stealing one" wouldn't be that easy. Toms was coming off his second-straight 65 on Saturday and was still riding high from the best shot of his career, a five wood on the 247-yard, par-three 15th that flew the water, landed on the green and took three hops before disappearing in the hole.

Contrary to earlier reports, this was not the first hole-in-one by a winner in a major championship. There were two in the early British Opens — by Young Tom Morris in 1868 and Jamie Anderson in 1878 — and there may have been others.

"It was the coolest shot I've ever hit," Toms said. "It was just the way it happened — the Saturday in a major in the last group with everyone watching. I hit a perfect shot."

Still, Toms understood where he stood on the "likely to win" list Saturday night. "Most people expect Phil to win, not me," he said. Conventional wisdom was that Toms would fade and Mickelson would get a major crown. This despite the fact that Toms had five career victories and had won every event he had led going into the final round.

"Don't bet on it," Rocco Mediate said. "David's got a lot of game. He does everything very well. He's won five times in a short period of time. He's a really good putter, and a good driver of the golf ball. That's a pretty solid combination. I don't see him fading. He's too good to fall apart."

Paul Azinger agreed. "He's one of the best ball-strikers in the game," Azinger said. "Week in and week out, if it's a ball-striker's golf course, he's there. If his putter gets going, he's unbelievable. If you watch him hit it, you wonder why he's not winning a lot more. He's just one of the best in the world."

No one said he was one of the smartest or most courageous. But when he came to the 72nd hole, Toms proved both those traits to be true as well. Leading by one after Mickelson three-putted the 16th, Toms hit a straight drive on the 490-yard, par-four finishing hole that rolled a few inches out of the fairway.

"I said all week that I wouldn't be afraid to lay up if I didn't have what I thought was a good shot," Toms said. He initially took out his five wood, then thought better of it. "You know I hated to do it," he said of pulling his wedge out of the bag. "The crowd was oohing and awwing and moaning like, 'You wimp.' The Chip Beck thing all over again from Augusta. But I had to put that out of my mind and just go ahead and hit two good shots and make a good putt, and I did that."

Mickelson found the fairway at the last, and his second shot left him in great shape, just 20 feet from the hole. "I felt like if I could get a one-up lead that would change the momentum," Mickelson said. "The outlook from being the leader to trailing is actually difficult to overcome sometimes and I was just never able to get ahead."

Mickelson had a chance to take the lead on the last hole. If Mickelson made birdie, Toms would have to make his 12-footer to tie. As had happened all week, when a shot had to be made, Mickelson came up short. "I was surprised that it came up short," he said. "I hit it right on line and thought I read it pretty good and hit it pretty solid. I had misjudged the speed of that green every single day, even the back right pins. I had just been pulling them up short. It just looked faster to me than what it had been playing and I consequently left the one on 18 right on line, but six inches short."

That was the story of the week. Mickelson came up short, while Toms made the gutsiest decision of the year. "That 18th green is not built for a par-four," Toms said. "It's so hard to hold it on your second shot, and I had a bad lie. I was in the first cut of rough with a sidehill, downhill lie. That translates to a low hook with no spin on it, and that's not what I needed."

What Toms needed was a par, and that's what he got. When the putt went in the hole, Toms threw up his hands in celebration while Mickelson stared at his feet and wondered if fate would ever be on his side.

"I felt as though I played well enough to win the tournament," Mickelson said, "but I did not ultimately beat all the players in the field, and David played extremely well. He played very solid, kept the ball in play and shot under par, which isn't the easiest thing to do when you are leading."

Mickelson should know. He shot 68 on Sunday — but one more than he needed for a chance to win.

Before play began, Mickelson was considered a favorite, in part because he always played well in Atlanta, and also because he said he loved the golf course. "It's nice to play a golf course where length will be a factor," Mickelson said. "To have the course playing the way it is, I think it's tremendous. I hope the tees stay back all week. I do think that the fairness of the width of the fairways at 240 to 340 yards is an asset of this golf course. I did not find the fairways bottlenecking at 300-310 yards as so many courses do. That allows all players to hit drivers, and it allows a long hitter to take advantage of his length."

The Atlanta Athletic Club course was a lot different than the course built in 1967 when the members at the old East Lake Country Club moved out of their downtown facility and took up residence in the northern suburb of Duluth. Bobby Jones, the club's most noted member, summed up the old AAC best when, in a 1971 letter to the USGA, penned just a month before his death, Jones wrote, "My home club, the Atlanta Athletic Club, has recently built a new country club consisting of two golf courses, each of 18 holes, and the four nines being so designed that they permit consecutive play. The layout also embraces a spacious clubhouse and several ponds of some beauty."

A master of the language, and a gentleman to the end, Jones believed if you couldn't say anything nice, you shouldn't say anything at all, which is what he did in pitching the Atlanta Athletic Club as the site of the 1976 U.S. Open. Those "ponds of some beauty," weren't much, especially considering Jones' basis of comparison at the time was his other club, Augusta National. And the spacious clubhouse was a low-rise, glass-fronted, post-modern cave.

The course was equally quirky. The back nine of the Highlands course, which is where all AAC's major events have been contested, was designed by Robert Trent Jones, Sr. and carried his style with flash bunkers, towering pines and sharp doglegs. The front nine, designed by Joe Finger, looked like airport runways, with big undulating greens and long, straight, treeless fairways. Redesigns by Fazio and Arnold Palmer in the 1970s and 1980s didn't help much. By the early 1990s the course looked like what it was: a hodge-podge of four different designs over 20 years.

When the club decided to make another bid for a major championship, they knew the course needed more than a facelift. So they called in re-design specialist Rees Jones, the man responsible for re-crafting such masterpieces as Congressional Country Club and Bethpage Black. As part of his efforts to give the Atlanta Athletic Club an "old course feel," as he calls it, Jones rebuilt all the greens, making them smaller and replacing the dramatic slopes with smaller, more subtle elevation changes. Several more "ponds of some beauty" were added, including a greenside hazard at the par-five 12th.

The most substantial changes Jones instituted were the new tees. In 1976 the Highlands course measured 7,015 yards and was considered a long test for a major championship. By the summer of 2001 the course played 7,213 yards with a par 70 for the championship.

"It's a lot tougher than it used to be," said Jerry Pate, who won the U.S. Open here in 1976 with a memorable five-iron shot to within a foot on the final hole. "The course is a lot longer. The 18th hole is now 490 yards, and with the wet ground and that type of length on a par-four, I'll probably go looking for a four or five wood."

The only advantage players had in the early going was the weather. Rain softened the greens, which made the course play even longer but made many of the pins more accessible. Hot air also made the balls fly farther, or at least that was Mickelson's reasoning behind the low scores in Thursday's round.

"The ball is going a long way right now with the heat," he said. "The course is not playing nearly to its length. But the reason we're seeing a great bunching of scores is because the greens are pretty receptive. When that happens guys are able to save par, get up and down better from chipping around the green, as well as hitting short irons close. When you have the golf course set up as long as it is with the rough up, you have to have the greens somewhat receptive. It's a very fair test."

Fair enough that a course record was set, not by Mickelson or Tiger Woods or any of the long hitters, but by Grant Waite, who shot 64 in the late afternoon and took a one-stroke lead.

A birdie-birdie start got Waite off on a positive note. He followed with a birdie at the par-five fifth and another at the eighth. "By that point I could really feel that things were going well and I was accomplishing my goals," he said. "It kept going in the fairway for me for the most part."

He hit a two iron from 228 yards at the par-five 12th and the ball rolled to the back of the green, where Waite two-putted for another birdie. Then he birdied the 18th after pulling his tee shot slightly and hitting a seven iron from 178 yards. "Any time you get a seven iron in your hand on 18 is a major bonus," he said. "That was a nice way to finish."

It was also a nice way to start, especially considering how low the opening-round scores were. Waite's 64 gave him a two-shot edge over nine players including Mickelson and Toms, who opened with 66s, Duval, who posted a pair of 33s, Stuart Appleby and Choi Kyung-ju.

Eleven players came in with 67s, including a few surprises like Nick Faldo, Paul Stankowski and Japan's Shingo Katayama, whose cowboy hat became the talk of the town before the weekend. Even senior special invitee Larry Nelson made an appearance on the leaderboard, shooting 32-36 for 68 which left him tied with 17 other players four strokes off the lead.

The other big surprise came from the player everyone expected to contend on such a long, tough golf course. Tiger Woods looked tired and unfocused. It was as if the nine American victories in 2000 and his four wins including the Masters in 2001 had finally take their toll. Woods shot 73 and never looked comfortable.

"I didn't hit the ball well today and I didn't make that many putts," Woods, the defending champion, said. "I made a couple here and there, but I had three three-putts. If I didn't have the three-putts, I'm right there at even par. If I play good tomorrow, I should be able to get myself back in the tournament. That's the good thing about major championships, if you go out there and play well you are going to be rewarded by moving up the leaderboard."

There was plenty of room for Woods and everyone else to navigate on the crowded first-round board. When the long day finally ended, the PGA Championship shaped up like this:

Grant Waite	64	Brad Faxon	66
Stuart Appleby	66	Fred Funk	66
Choi Kyung-ju	66	Dudley Hart	66
David Duval	66	Phil Mickelson	66
Niclas Fasth	66	David Toms	66

Grant Waite's course record didn't last long. With temperatures in the high 90s and very little wind on Friday, the course that everyone called "long" and "tough" earlier in the week was laid bare. Jim Furyk was the first to make a move, shooting a 64 that included three birdies in a row to start the back nine, and he picked up another birdie at the difficult 18th. When asked about his scores and others, Furyk continued to spout the party line.

"The golf course is very difficult and very long," Furyk said. "It's drying out nicely, so that we are getting a bit more distance on our tee shots, but I think it's just that the greens are soft. We are able to hold shots. A guy like me who has average distance with the driver, I'm hitting a lot of three and four irons, and when I get a five iron in my hands on this golf course I feel like it's a short iron. Right now I'm able to hold a three-iron shot or a four-iron within about 10 feet. That's allowing us to play well right now. That's why you're seeing scores that are good. If the greens got firmer, those scores would go up in a heartbeat."

After Furyk made those comments, a course record was set when Mark O'Meara became the 19th player in major championship history to shoot 63. He did it making only one putt outside of 20 feet. He played without making a mistake, hitting a wedge to 10 feet on the first hole and making the putt for birdie, then paring the next four holes (including the par-five fifth) before making a 10-footer for birdie at the sixth. O'Meara followed that with an 18-footer for birdie at the seventh, and he was off to the races. When he stood over his birdie putt at the 18th, he had a chance to become the first to shoot 62 in a major, but the putt broke low.

"There's no lying that the golf course does favor somebody who can get it out there," O'Meara said. "I also believe that because of the temperature and humidity the ball is definitely going. One time today I drove it by Sergio Garcia, and a couple of times I was just right behind him. Certainly I don't have the power of a David Duval or a Phil Mickelson or Tiger or Sergio, but there are a lot of facets to the game besides power. Today, it was just nice to go out there and get back into things."

Another player got back into things, but just barely. Tiger Woods stood at two over par for the championship through 14 holes on Friday when he asked a photographer what the cut was likely to be. "I found out that it was looking like the cut would be even par, so I knew I needed to make some birdies," Woods said. "I got it going. I didn't hit the ball great, but I made a few bombs on 15 and 16 and almost made another on 17."

Woods finished at 67 for the day and even-par 140, just under the wire for the weekend. "I have always believed that you've got to give it everything you have," he said. "I didn't hit the ball that great, but I hung in there. Sooner or later I knew I was going to turn things around."

Woods and everyone else in the field would need to turn on the burners over the weekend if they planned on making a run at the lead. That was because Shingo Katayama, still wearing his cowboy hat with the drawstring pulled tightly under his chin, shot 64 and entered the weekend tied for the lead with David Toms at 131, a 36-hole PGA Championship scoring record.

Katayama was about as unknown as you could be when he arrived in Atlanta, but Friday evening he was a hero with shouts of "Shingo! Shingo!" echoing through the gallery. The 28-year-old from Ibaraki, Japan, didn't disappoint his new fans. After warming up by hitting shots with a left-handed driver for balance and acknowledging that he wears a bracelet filled with "chi," a Chinese spiritual power to give him strength, he took the five woods he carried in his bag (one, three, four, seven and nine) and made seven birdies.

Katayama came into the week ranked 50th in the world, having won nine times on the Japan Tour, but he had yet to break 70 in a U.S. event. All that changed on Friday. "I would like to take a picture of the leaderboard," Katayama said. "I feel like, wow, what a place I am in now!"

He was in a place that neither he nor Toms had ever seen before, tied for the lead through 36 holes of a major championship. Toms admitted that most spectators would be watching players who had been there before. Mickelson was at 132, one shot off the lead after another round of 66. David Duval was also close, having shot 68 for a 134 total. Duval had plenty of company at that number. Ernie Els shot his second 67 for a 134 total, while Furyk's 64 got him within three of the lead. Dudley Hart, Choi Kyung-ju and Steve Lowery rounded out the group at 134.

Toms acknowledged that, even though he was leading, he was one of the lowest profile names on the board. "If I was somebody coming out to the PGA Championship to watch the last few groups, I'd probably watch Phil too," Toms said. "He's a lot of fun to watch. Makes a lot of birdies. Hits the ball forever. One of the best players in the world. The people out there watching the last few groups, they probably won't be expecting me to play all that great. They are probably like, well, I don't know what he's going to do. He's never been in a major before and so maybe the pressure is off a little bit. But I still think I can play tomorrow, and I think I can be in contention on Sunday. There's no reason why I can't."

With two rounds in the books at the Atlanta Athletic Club, the PGA Championship looked like this:

David Toms	65 - 131	Choi Kyung-ju	67 - 134
Shingo Katayama	64 - 131	Paul Azinger	67 - 135
Phil Mickelson	66 - 132	Chris DiMarco	67 - 135
Bob Estes	65 - 133	John Huston	68 - 135
Jim Furyk	64 - 134	Jonathan Kaye	65 - 135
Dudley Hart	68 - 134	Rocco Mediate	65 - 135
Steve Lowery	67 - 134	Mark O'Meara	63 - 135

The oddest thing about the third round — or "moving day" — was how little everyone moved despite some of the wackiest shotmaking of the week. In the final two groups, you had balls hitting trees and gallery members, skipping off the water, bouncing off stone walls, and one really good shot that traveled 249 yards before finding the cup for a hole-in-one. After all that, things ended pretty much the way they started. David Toms led and Phil Mickelson trailed. Shingo Katayama stayed in the hunt, along with Steve Lowery and David Duval. The only additions to the board were Davis Love III, who shot 65 after rounds of 71 and 67, and the resurrection of Stuart Appleby, who shot 68 after a second-round 70.

But Saturday was anything but dull. It started early when Tiger Woods hit his approach shot into the hole on the par-four ninth for an eagle. That came just after Chris Smith, who was playing behind Woods, flew wedge in the hole for a two at the par-four first, and just before Nick Faldo electrified the crowds with a hole-in-one at the par-three fourth.

"It was fun out there," Smith said. "Nobody is playing that good who is out there that early and yet there were roars all over the golf course. Obviously, there were a lot of good shots being hit out there, and it's a major and everyone in the gallery was excited."

None of the players who made eagles early did much else. Woods reached four under par for his round and three under for the tournament, but bogeyed the final two holes for 69. "That was a nice little dunk there at nine," Woods said. "I figured if I could shoot three or four under par on the back I could get back in it, but I couldn't do it."

Faldo finished at 71 for the day and two-over 212 for the tournament, while Smith managed to come in under par with a round of 68 for a 209 total.

There was plenty of action at the top of the leaderboard as well, but very little change in the standing. Mickelson got off to an odd start. Through five holes he had made three birdies, a double bogey and a par. The longest putt he had was 12 feet in that stretch and the double bogey came after hitting a tree and a spectator.

"The scorecard looks to be more up-and-down, but the play was very consistent," Mickelson said. "The only poor shot I felt I hit was the tee shot on number three."

On the 11th Mickelson's pitching wedge approach stopped six inches from the hole. That was five inches farther than his eight-iron approach at the 14th. With that tap-in Mickelson found himself alone atop the leaderboard with a two-stroke edge over Toms. A bogey on the par-three 15th seemed sloppy, but the lead was still one. Things finally seemed to be going Mickelson's way.

Then came Toms' shot at the 15th, a five wood that never left the flagstick and rolled in the cup. "Perfect," Toms said. "It's not like it bounced off a tree or rolled short of the green or anything like that. It was right on line the whole way."

Mickelson heard the roar from the 16th but had no idea Toms had made an ace. "It was loud, but it didn't sound like a hole-in-one roar," he said. It was, however, and suddenly Mickelson's two-shot lead was a one-shot deficit. "I had an excellent chance when I was a shot or two up to pull away. But we had that three-shot swing on 15, and that really hurt."

Toms added to his margin with a 30-footer for birdie at the 18th to shoot 65 and enter the final round at 19-under-par 196. Mickelson made eight birdies and a double bogey for 66 and a 198 total, while Lowery shot 66 to move into a tie for third at 200 with Katayama, whose legend continued to grow. On the same 15th that Mickelson bogeyed and Toms aced, Katayama hit a shot that looked short and wet all the way. The ball ricocheted off the rock wall that bordered the water hazard and Katayama was able to salvage a par. He did it again at the 18th, skipping a ball off the water and onto the fringe, where he was able to save par for a 69.

"I am proud to be Shingo Katayama," the not-so-bashful youngster said. "I love it when all the supporters call me 'Shingo, Shingo!' I enjoy playing over here, and it was my dream when I was small. Today was a great day. I had a lot of fun, and all the other players said, 'Good luck, Shingo!' so I enjoyed it."

Mickelson would have enjoyed it a little more if he had finished the day leading, but he tried to put a positive spin on his situation. "I certainly thought starting the tournament that 12-under-par 198 would be leading, but the golf course is susceptible to birdies," Mickelson said. "I know the type of player David Toms is, and he's on a mission. He not only wants to win the golf tournament, but make the Ryder Cup team. A good finish, even if he doesn't win, should secure him that. He had the game to shoot 64 earlier in the year and beat me, and I'm going to be trying to make amends. To be only two shots off the lead and in a great place to play with the leader the final day, a great opportunity to win, that's the ultimate goal."

It was Toms' goal as well, although he was a little subtler in his proclamations. "I'm in this position, so I have the game that put me here," he said. "It's just a matter of going out tomorrow and executing. I think I can win. I've played well. I played the golf course well every day that I've been here this week. I know tomorrow is going to be a different situation. I mean, I'm playing with one of the best players in the world, while he's trying to win his first major championship. But there's no reason why I couldn't win my first one too."

The leaderboard looked like this:

David Toms	65 - 196		Davis Love III	65 - 203
Phil Mickelson	66 - 198		Stuart Appleby	68 - 204
Steve Lowery	69 - 200		Paul Azinger	69 - 204
Shingo Katayama	69 - 200		Ernie Els	70 - 204
David Duval	67 - 201			

The final pairing quickly became the focus of attention. While it was not a match-play situation, when Mickelson birdied the second and both players made putts for birdie at the par-five fifth, it looked and felt like match play. When Mickelson hit the flagstick with his tee shot on the par-three seventh and made birdie, the two were even. Toms pulled ahead at the eighth, but missed a two-footer at the 10th to allow Mickelson to tie him again.

"When I missed the short putt on 10, I hate to say this, but my hands were shaking so bad," Toms said. "I was trying to breathe, and that wasn't working. I mean, I had two and a half feet there and I didn't even hit the hole. Then at 12 I missed another short putt and just didn't know if I had it in me."

Toms clawed his way back to a two-shot lead through 14 holes, but, for the second day in a row, the 15th proved pivotal. When Toms missed the green and chipped to 20 feet, Mickelson, standing pin-high on the left fringe, chipped in for birdie. Toms missed his par putt and the two were tied again.

As had happened other times in his career, Mickelson was unable to call on his swing when he needed it most. On the tee at the 16th he hit a hook that his coach, Rick Smith, thought cost him the tournament. "The club passes the body," Smith said. "He's not rotating on an even level, so to speak. He missed some fairways, and it took away his ability to control the tournament. The opportunity to make birdies was taken out of his hands."

Mickelson had to hit a four iron to the 16th, a shot that left him a 50-foot putt for birdie. "After it quieted down I had five people in the gallery telling me how slow that putt was," Mickelson said. "I tried to block it out, but it hit my subconscious. It's disappointing that I wasn't able to block that out, because I'd been focusing very well all week. I gave it a little extra and, sure enough, it ran eight feet past."

He missed the eight-footer, a three-putt Mickelson called the turning point of the event. Toms led by one stroke with two holes to play. Solid pars by both players at the 17th led to the drama at the 18th, where Toms hit a drive too straight and found the rough.

After standing in the fairway looking at his ball for the longest minute of his life, Toms' caddie, Scott Gneiser, said, "Do you think you should lay up?"

Toms said, "Yes," and Gneiser didn't flinch. "Good move," he said. "One-thirty will put you at perfect lob wedge range. The five wood wasn't going to get airborne, and if it does clear the water, it will go over the green."

Armed with a wedge and ignoring the groans from the gallery, Toms hit his lay-up perfectly, leaving himself 88 yards, a distance from which he said, "I should get up and down nine times out of 10."

He did just that, draining the most pressure-packed 12-foot putt of his career to win the PGA Championship by one stroke.

"He made a great play," Mickelson said. "That was a very intelligent play. He played right to his strength. He's a very good wedge player. He hits the ball the right yardage and it still was not an easy sand wedge, because short is water and long is the bunker, and if he goes in the bunker, there's a good chance that not only does he not win outright, he might not make a playoff either. But he hit a great shot, spun it back to 10 feet and made the putt."

As for his feelings about letting another one slip away, Mickelson said, "I know that the off-season is going to be long. I really felt like this year was a year when my game was going to break through."

6. The Players Championship

It took a fifth day to finish, but even Mother Nature couldn't stop the inevitable. Neither could great players like Vijay Singh and Bernhard Langer, nor unheralded men like Jerry Kelly, who likened his Sunday pairing with Tiger Woods to "playing golf in the middle of a freeway." The week in Ponte Vedra Beach, Florida, at The Players Championship proved that this highway song remains the same: Tiger Woods wins again. Everyone else simply makes it a good show.

The only thing that slowed the Tiger Woods convoy as it barreled down the fast lane to a 26th PGA Tour victory was wet weather on Sunday. Seven days earlier Woods had quieted the critics who claimed he was in a slump by holing a birdie on the 72nd green to beat Phil Mickelson at Arnold Palmer's Bay Hill Invitational. He was the holder of three major championship trophies and was coming into the spring having just delivered the greatest single-year performance in the history of golf. No one was going to stand between Woods and his first Players Championship title.

Just as Singh, who calls the TPC at Sawgrass his home course, made a move, pulling within one stroke of Woods after a birdie at the 13th hole in Monday's finale, the rumble behind him caused Singh to lose control. One snap-hook later Singh was taking a drop beside the lady's tee on his way to a triple-bogey seven, golf's equivalent to a three-car pileup.

Kelly pulled off onto the shoulder as well. After leading by one stroke through 36 holes and carrying a two-shot lead into the final round, Kelly shot 74 with Woods at his side. He might have finished a respectable even par and tied for third place with Langer, but a double bogey on the 72nd hole dropped him to fourth place.

"I might have proved to a few people that I can play," Kelly said. "I didn't feel like I had to prove it to myself. I really feel like I haven't achieved a whole lot. My potential is a lot greater than anything that's happened in my golf career. Today I did prove I could play under the biggest pressure we have, so I can take a positive out of it, but I leave leaning more towards bitterly disappointed than just disappointed."

"I think it's exciting to be able to play in a field this deep and to be able to come out on top," Woods said after slamming the door with a final-round 67 for a 14-under-par 274 total and a one-shot victory over Singh. "It's a big tournament, and like everybody says, it's probably the fifth major."

It was also the biggest title Woods didn't have in his growing list of victories. Already the youngest in history to complete the career Grand Slam, having won all four major titles by age 25, Woods' four-year career read like a record book of accomplishments. But this was one important trophy Woods did not own. Challenges bring out the best in him.

He almost completed the job a year before when he came from behind to pull within a shot of Hal Sutton, but Sutton responded with solid pars on the final two holes at the TPC at Sawgrass — arguably the most difficult closing stretch in championship golf — to capture the title. In 2001 it was Woods' time to stave off all comers, hitting three solid shots on two of the most intimidating holes in the world to win the title in decisive fashion.

"He's the best player in the world and he showed it," Kelly said after watching Woods dismantle the field. "I can look at what he did and see that it wasn't that much different than what I was doing. He made some putts when he got into position. When he got out of position, he made putts again."

Some thought The Players Championship would be Woods' toughest test. The TPC at Sawgrass is, by today's standards, a relatively short golf course, just under 7,000 yards. As former PGA Tour Commissioner Deane Beman said, "It was designed to be a second-shot golf course. When it first opened it didn't matter how far you hit the tee shot, the golf course rewarded precision iron play and a solid short game. Now they've introduced rough into the mix and it's a driver and putter's golf course."

Still, the first big test of the golf year always held a few surprises, and this year was no exception.

The first surprise came from off the golf course. After playing just three holes on Wednesday, David Duval walked off the course and went to see a doctor. An MRI provided some good news and some bad news. "Nothing was wrong," Duval said. "It is tendinitis." But the only sure-fire cure for tendinitis is rest. In order for Duval to be ready for the Masters, he would have to withdraw from his hometown tournament.

"I certainly am disappointed that I can't play," Duval said. "The Players Championship is very special to me and it is very frustrating not to be able to compete. However, I need to get this wrist healed, and to do so, I must take some time off. I will be consulting with doctors the rest of the week and next week about the course of therapy for the wrist and look forward to being back in action as soon as possible."

Duval was the second former champion to withdraw. Steve Elkington called it quits on Wednesday, citing a bad back.

"I think I have a few good things going for me," Duval said. "The good thing about now is I'm going to be the freshest person in the field. I'll have the clearest head of anybody at the Masters. I think it's my year."

He was still disappointed to miss an event on a course he knows as well as the TPC at Sawgrass, especially given how tough the pins were on Thursday. Heavy rains early in the week had the tour staff worried. It would have been easy for the best players in the world to set new scoring records if the superintendent wasn't careful. So he tucked the pins and let the rough grow another day without being mowed.

The results were about what everyone expected. Paul Azinger, one of the players Beman had in mind when he said the TPC at Sawgrass was designed to "reward precision iron play," set the pace with a six-under 66, his career low in The Players Championship.

"That's a nice change," Azinger said after his round. He, too, noticed the efforts to toughen up an already challenging course. "I think they were probably aware that the scores could get really low if the pins were easy," he said. "I didn't miss a green until No. 16 and I had several putts I had to be defensive on."

Defensive or not, Azinger rolled in some good putts in his round. He started with a 25-footer for birdie on the first hole, followed by a 10-foot birdie putt on the par-five second and an eight-footer for birdie on the difficult par-three third. He added another birdie at the par-five eighth and one more at the 10th, which gave him the lead. One more birdie at the 14th and Azinger could make conservative pars the rest of the way in.

"One of the things that's been getting me a little bit this year is I've played great on Tuesdays and Wednesdays and then become very frustrated with the starts to all of my tournaments," Azinger said. "I've maybe been pressing a little bit. Today I was determined that I was not going to let my start affect how I felt or change the way I did things. As it turned out, that freed me up a little bit."

Singh was one shot back with 67, and he too found the pin placements to be challenging, calling many of them "nasty." Living near the golf course, Singh thought he had an advantage. Whether sleeping in his own bed would make a difference as the week progressed, Singh believed that being near home would help, and that gave him a psychological boost. After Thursday's round he pointed out that the previous two tour winners — Jesper Parnevik, who won the Honda Classic, and Tiger Woods who won the Bay Hill Invitational — lived in the towns where they won and slept in their own beds throughout the week.

"You can go home, eat your own food, be with your family. That's very important. If you have family, you're very comfortable in your own environment, so I think that helps a lot."

Adding to Singh's comfort level was the fact that he plays and practices at Sawgrass more than any other player. "I love this golf course," he said. "I think it's challenging. You need to drive the ball well. It keeps you on your toes. It has small greens, so you can work on your irons. I was really solid tee-to-green, and when you do that, you're supposed to play a good round. I made a few putts, hit two par-fives in two. It was a round where I couldn't have played any worse."

Robert Allenby, Scott Hoch and Jonathan Kaye also shot 67s to trail by one, while Billy Mayfair and Skip Kendall finished with 68s. Kendall, playing in the final group of the day, had what could possibly have been the best finish that no one saw. Television coverage had been over for almost an hour, the crowds were long gone, and the sun had already set when Kendall rolled in an eight-footer at the 18th to cap a three consecutive birdie run, the best closing stretch of the day.

"We were joking out there that even the Internet had shut down," Kendall said. "We won't even get to see our shots at 17."

There are usually no routine birdies in the closing stretch, and Kendall's finish was anything but ordinary. After missing the fairway at the 16th, he punched out of the trees, hit an eight iron to 45 feet and made the breaking putt. At the 17th he made a 50-footer. That set up the eight-footer at the 18th, the only "routine" hole Kendall played. "I've never done that before," Kendall said. "I've birdied 16 and 17 before, and of course you feel like you're stealing there, but then to birdie 18, that was awesome. No doubt, it's certainly my best finish nobody saw."

Somewhere lost in the low scores and late-night birdies, Woods maneuvered his way around in even-par 72, a round that included more than a few lip-out putts and a double bogey on the 18th.

"Unfortunately I didn't get a whole lot out of my round today," Woods said. "That happens. The golf course is playing extremely difficult with this wind coming in all of the different directions. To be able to pick the right club, trust it and execute ... I did what I could with what I had, and was very pleased."

Friday was a shocker, and that was before Jerry Kelly leapt into the lead. A cold front moved through on Thursday night and temperatures dropped into the low 40s when play got underway. One of the first victims of the weather was Skip Kendall, whose late tee time on Thursday insured him of an early call. Seventy-eight blows later, Kendall moved from contending for the lead to calculating the cut line. He made it by two shots, but for a few quiet hours it was nip-and-tuck as to where the Kendalls would be spending their weekend.

Another player who made the cut was Tom Kite who, at 51, was the oldest man in the field. He also became the new record-holder for cuts made in The Players Championship after his 73 on Friday and one-under 143 total secured him a weekend spot for the 22nd time. "I wasn't aware of the record," he said. "That makes this even more special. It's great to come back here and play with the guys on the regular tour. And it's nice to hang in there, and hang around my friends again."

Azinger hung around as well, shooting 70 for a 136 total. "I'm going into tournaments these days with more purpose," Azinger said. "I realized that I was going through the motions a little too much — going to all these tournaments out of a sense of obligation rather than being committed. So I decided to be more patient and more prepared before I left town to go to all these tournaments."

He was both prepared and patient on Friday, as he made four birdies and two bogeys in the tough conditions. That was good enough to stay within a stroke of the lead — a lead held by the most unlikely and freshest character to emerge during the week.

Jerry Kelly's only prior claim to fame came when he lost a playoff to Loren Roberts in the 1996 Greater Milwaukee Open, the week Tiger Woods turned professional. Beyond that footnote of trivia, Kelly was considered a journeyman, ranked 118th in the world when he teed off. To shoot 66 and enter the weekend at nine-under 135 and leading by one was just short of spectacular for him.

He made one eagle, five birdies and one three-putt bogey in a round he termed "fairly safe." The only bomb he made was a 35-footer for birdie. Other than that, his round looked routine. "I played smart golf, which is kind of new to me," he said. "Patience, patience, patience. I'll keep on saying that word, because that's one thing that I've always lost in the past. This is shaping up to be my most consistent year. I really feel like I'm controlling my golf swing and controlling my emotions, and that's what it takes. I'm just happy that my fundamentals are sound enough where I feel I can go out and do whatever I want."

He was right about it being his most consistent year. In the first quarter of 2001, Kelly didn't miss a cut and posted two top-10 finishes. But he also had never led or shared the lead at the halfway point in a PGA Tour event in his career.

That was because the old Jerry Kelly suffered from "longitis," a disease that causes its victims to obsess over how far they hit the golf ball instead of how straight and how consistent they play. As a result, Kelly ranked 152nd in fairways hit coming into the week. He claimed to be a changed man. A long-time sufferer, Kelly said he came into The Players Championship as a recovering longitis patient.

"I came into the week with the swing thought of being a little shorter, and not worrying about how far I hit it," he said. "I used to come to those driving distance holes and say, 'All right, I've got to get one over 300 yards,' but now I don't really care how far I hit it. Surprisingly, I tend to be hitting it farther now that I'm shortening it up and just trying to hit it in the fairways."

Kelly missed only one fairway in his second round, an experience he had never had before at Sawgrass. "I've had some decent rounds at this golf course in the past, but my driver has always put me in some unbelievable spots," he said. "I was walking around earlier in the week saying to my caddie, 'I put it in the water here, and I put it in the water there,' and these were spots where you shouldn't be able to get it in the water. He looked at me and said, 'What did you shoot?' I actually shot about 70 or 69, but it was ugly. Now I feel really confident. I'm controlling the trajectory of my driver and that's everything. I'm able to shape a lot of different shots here with the driver, and I'm confident in my ability to do that. To get a good round under my belt and go into the weekend knowing my swing is solid, that's the most important thing."

Another player who was pleased to get a good round under his belt was Singh. Simply being on the first page of the leaderboard after two rounds in this event was encouraging. His 70 on Friday moved him to seven under par, tied for third, his best start at The Players Championship in nine years.

"I have never been in position this close to the lead here before," Singh said. "I've always been barely making the cut, so playing decent and being two off the lead is a pretty good feeling."

In his previous three trips through this championship, Singh finished tied for 54th, tied for 20th and tied for 33rd, not what you would expect from a man who calls the TPC his home course.

"It was my one thought to win this one when I started at the beginning of the year," Singh said. "I played four rounds of golf here before Bay Hill, which was important because it was windy and wet and the rough was a little longer than it is now. Getting used to all that, and putting it in the back of my mind — that it was going to be tough and hitting the fairways was important — turned out to be a good thing. Anytime you're playing in your backyard, you feel more familiar with the golf course, the bounces and where not to hit it. That's important when you're near the lead. I feel at ease on the golf course for the first time this year. I'm driving the ball well, which is important around here. Hopefully I can take it out and play even better on the weekend this week. I know I'm going to need to."

He closed his comments with a very un-Singh-like prediction. "I have some good rounds left in me on the weekend, so I'm actually looking forward to playing the next two days," he said. "I think I have a better-than-good chance of winning this thing."

Woods made no such predictions. After a 69 left him six strokes behind Kelly at the halfway mark, Woods claimed to be struggling with his game. "I didn't hit it as well as I did yesterday, that's for sure," he said. "I scored better. Made some nice putts. Just really grinded my way around the golf course. It's playing tough out there. The wind is blowing, but I know where to miss it. My lag putting just carried me around the golf course."

In the third round, Kelly kept surprising his growing fan base by hitting fairways and greens and making it look as though he had been in this position countless times in the past. The fact that he had only played in the final group on Sunday one time in his PGA Tour career, the 1996 Milwaukee Open, and the fact that no one had ever made The Players Championship their first tour win didn't bother the Wisconsin native one bit. He hit 13 of 14 fairways and 14 out of 18 greens, birdieing three of his first seven holes and posting only one bogey en route to another routine round of 70.

He also didn't seem too concerned about his Sunday pairing. "I've wanted to play with Tiger since he came out in Milwaukee," Kelly said of his final-round match-up. "He's the best player in the world. I want, more than anything, to play with the best player in the world. I want my game to match up, and I can't wait for tomorrow."

Woods showed Kelly and the rest of those watching why he was the best in the world on Saturday when he played himself back into contention with a 66 that was vintage Woods. He bogeyed the first and the last holes, but had six birdies and an eagle in between.

A routine birdie at the par-five second got things started. Another at the par-four fourth got Woods' gallery buzzing. Six straight pars dampened expectations a little, but when Woods ripped a four iron over the water and between the bunkers on the par-five 11th to set up an eagle, the rumble began anew. He followed that with a 20-footer for birdie at the 12th, and another 20-footer at the par-five 16th.

Then came the shot of the tournament. With the pin on the island par-three 17th cut on the front, Woods proceeded to hit his nine iron to the back edge of the green, as far away from the hole as possible while remaining on the putting surface. The putt was a swift, downhill double-breaker. When it went in for birdie, the gallery erupted and Woods gave one of his fist-pumps.

NBC analyst Mark Rolfing was stunned. "It was so far away and there was so much going on in terms of speed and the break and the atmosphere," Rolfing said. "It was late in the day, very noisy down there, and when it went in, it was the loudest noise I've ever heard. What was interesting was, there were three other players who saw it and everybody froze. Everything came to a surreal halt. Nobody could believe it."

Kelly, playing behind Woods and unable to see what had transpired, said, "I thought he had made a hole-in-one." Another eruption occurred behind the 18th green when the large monitor beside the grandstands replayed the putt. Colin Montgomerie had to back away from his putt on the 18th to regain his composure after witnessing the replay.

The fact that Woods followed it up with what he termed "an absolutely stupid bogey" on the 18th didn't seem to matter. He was poised in second place at nine-under 207. "It was nice to get a score out of it," Woods said. "I really didn't hit the ball good starting out, but I got it going. To shoot 66 today, under these conditions, with these pins, I'm pretty pleased with it."

Singh was also pleased. He matched Kelly's 70 and entered the final round tied with Woods at 207 while Scott Hoch continued close to the lead at 208. Bernhard Langer was four back after a 68 moved him to 209 for the week. That made Langer the low European, a title he had held more than once at The Players Championship, but one he wasn't interested in flaunting.

"Obviously I want to win the golf tournament," Langer said. "I don't know what I attribute being low European to, but that's not my goal. I try to play smart golf. I enter with a game plan and I play percentage golf. Usually my short game is pretty good, and that's it. Out here you have to stay out of the long stuff, hit fairways and greens, and hopefully roll a few in. That's all you have to do."

Kelly hoped to take that same philosophy to the first tee with him on Sunday. "I'm going to play my own game," he said, seemingly trying to convince himself as much as anyone. "If I watch Tiger's game and try to club off him, that's just plain dumb. Normally if I'm close to a guy in distance, you might want to hit the next one by him. I'm not going to be near him tomorrow in distance. So I've got to play my own game. I won't even see him. He'll be way up there somewhere. As long as I put it right on the green in front of him, who knows? Maybe I'll be making him press."

Kelly had his work cut out for him. And everyone who followed golf knew it.

Rain fell like water pouring from a boot on Sunday morning, and tour officials had to suspend play until late afternoon while they brought out squeegees and blowers to dry the golf course. The leaders only played nine holes, but they made the best of them.

Woods came out with his "A" game, making a birdie at the first hole and chipping in for eagle on the second. Kelly managed to two-putt for birdie at the second, but found himself standing on the third tee tied for the lead, his cushion gone.

"I just kind of laughed a little bit," Kelly said of Woods' start. "I said, 'This is what it's all about. This is what it's like playing with the best player in the world. He's going to make shots like that.' You know he's not going to make every one of them, though. I put myself on the green in two. I like my percentages better when I do that. But it's really fun. I love it. I can only get better watching that, knowing it can be done."

Woods rolled in another birdie putt at the ninth to move to 12 under par before play was called because of darkness, while Kelly three-putted the fourth to drop to 11 under. Singh, playing a group ahead of the leaders, birdied the fourth, fifth and seventh holes to capture temporary possession of the lead. A poor tee shot at the ninth cost Singh a bogey, and he called it quits after nine, tied with Kelly at 11 under.

"I'm quite happy with the round," Singh said before venturing home for a night's rest. "I'm looking forward to finishing tomorrow."

At 10 a.m. Monday play resumed. Singh made a move with a birdie at the 13th, but he followed it with his worst swing of the week on the 14th, a dead pull that went into the hazard so close to the tee that Singh considered re-teeing before finally taking a drop beside the lady's tee. He called it his "killer blow," and, for a moment, Singh's chances appeared dead in the water.

"It was a straight pull," he said. "It's caused by a little too quick a swing. You know, too aggressive and too anxious, I guess."

He didn't give up. After a triple-bogey seven on the 14th, Singh turned to his caddie and said, "We've got four holes left, and we need to birdie every one of them."

A birdie at the 15th barely missed, but Singh made up for it with his best shot of the tournament, a pitch with the toe of his putter from the high fringe on the 16th that rolled into the cup for an eagle. When an eight-footer for birdie at the 17th rolled into the hole, Singh found himself back within a shot of the lead.

"Playing the last three holes out here, anything can happen," Singh said. "It's all over water, and 17 has always had some drama, and 18 as well. But Tiger is not going to make any mistakes. He's too good a player for that."

Singh was right on that point. Woods reached the 16th in two and watched across the pond as Singh rolled in his birdie at the 17th. Then Woods rolled a 40-foot eagle putt that looked in all the way. When it barely slid by on the low side, Woods was as surprised as anyone.

"I don't know how my eagle putt didn't go in," he said. "It was such a pure putt. It was a triple-breaker. I know how I hit it in the right place. I just needed to get it down there. It would have been nice to top Vijay. Vijay makes birdie and loses a shot, that's how I was thinking."

The tap-in birdie gave Woods a two-shot edge with two holes to play.

On the 17th Woods hit a shot so reminiscent of his 1994 U.S. Amateur victory over Trip Kuehne that NBC announcers were calling it "déjà vu all over again." The shot, a slight push, landed on the right side of the green near the hole, and stayed out of the water by mere inches. In 1994 Woods holed his second shot for birdie to close out his match and win his first U.S. Amateur title. This year, he hit a mediocre chip and had to drain a five-footer for par to retain a two-shot edge.

That made the 18th academic after Woods found the fairway and Singh missed a 20-footer for birdie. Hardly anyone noticed the subsequent bogey Woods made at the last hole. It didn't matter. His 67 and 274 total was one better than Singh, two better than Langer, and four better than Kelly, who limped home with a double bogey at the last.

Afterward Woods responded again to the criticism that he was in a slump because he hadn't won in the first two months of 2001. "I wasn't playing that bad," he said. "It wasn't like I was missing cuts every week. I was right there with a chance to win in virtually every tournament I teed it up in, and I think that's pretty good. It's just that I had not won, and that's part of the game.

"Now I've won two tournaments in a row. I'm sure they will write about something else."

7. Cisco World Match Play

More massage, more beer. There was nothing complicated about the way Ian Woosnam approached his marathon task at the Cisco World Match Play Championship at the Wentworth Club outside London. Yet it proved mightily effectively, and the Welshman, at the age of 43, powered his way past four top-quality opponents to take the title for the third time.

First, he beat Retief Goosen, the reigning U.S. Open champion and subsequent winner of the European Order of Merit, 4 and 3. Colin Montgomerie, the seven-time former money title holder, was dispatched by the same score, while the 2000 European No. 1 Lee Westwood was brushed aside 10 and 9. In the final, Woosnam came from behind to defeat Ryder Cup player Padraig Harrington, 2 and 1.

"I'm overjoyed," Woosnam said. "To beat four great players is something I am very proud of. I was in the hardest part of the draw but played some terrific golf. I don't feel tired at all right now."

Woosnam never flagged and the more holes he played, the more the clock was turned back to his best days of a decade and more before, when he won prolifically in Europe, became the world's No. 1 golfer and won the Masters in 1991. That effortless, crisp swing was a joy to behold once more.

"My iron play was vintage Ian Woosnam," he said, "and I started driving the ball better as I got under pressure." The obvious difference with his younger days was his use of a long putter. Where he has struggled to befriend the implement on the slick and sloping greens of the American majors, on the gentle contours he knows so well on the West Course at Wentworth, he hardly missed a putt that mattered all week.

"That's how I want to play the game," Woosnam explained. "You are always after the perfect shot and I hit a lot of nearly perfect shots today. When I don't play like that, I don't want to play. It is difficult when you are chomping and hacking it about. I was really getting fed up with the game."

Back problems from the mid-1990s onwards were at the root of Woosnam's swing problems in recent seasons. Redemption has come with some hard work under the watchful eye of coach Pete Cowen. "We have worked really hard for the last two years and it is now paying off. It was great to play as well as I did this week."

Never one to stick to a fitness routine, Woosnam was allowed to play so well by the efforts of his physiotherapist, Nick Hooper.

While Woosnam relaxed with the odd libation, Hooper would administer the rub down. This was after hauling his employer's bag twice around the course himself. Hooper took over as Woosnam's caddie in the wake of Myles Byrne's non-appearance for the final round of the Scandinavian Masters. Byrne, who himself was handed the Welshman's bag only after a 12-year relationship with Phil "Wobbly" Morbey was ended earlier in the season, had been given a "second chance" after allowing a extra club into Woosnam's bag for the final round of the British Open Championship at Royal Lytham in July.

Woosnam had birdied the first hole and was determined to challenge for the claret jug when Byrne informed him they were carrying 15 clubs. Every day since, members of the gallery suggest to Woosnam's caddie that he check the number of clubs.

No one suggests the same to Woosnam himself. "You know what I would say if they did," he said. It might not be polite. But the longer Woosnam traipsed the Wentworth fairways, the more support he received. "The majority of the crowd seemed to be with me," Woosnam said of the final. "Whether it was the Open, I don't know. Maybe they just wanted an older guy to win."

Woosnam became the oldest champion and the first to win the title in three different decades after his victories in 1987 and 1990. Only Gary Player and Seve Ballesteros can claim more titles (five) and only Greg Norman and Ernie Els as many. It was his 40th professional victory but his first win anywhere for four years, his last in Europe being the 1997 Volvo PGA on the same West Course.

Woosnam only received his invitation to the 2001 Cisco World Match Play less than two weeks before the event. For the first time in the event's 38-year history, there was no American in the field. Following the terrorist attacks in America in September, both David Duval, the British Open champion, and David Toms, the PGA champion, decided to stay at home. Canadian Mike Weir's name was in the draw at the start of the week, but he also decided not to travel after the start of the U.S.-led coalition bombing in Afghanistan.

In Woosnam, Ballesteros and Nick Faldo, there were some well-known faces on standby and, after Weir withdrew, Sam Torrance, the European Ryder Cup captain, was more than happy to have his breakfast at Sunningdale interrupted on Tuesday morning to hear he too was being called up. While Westwood, the defending champion, Vijay Singh, Darren Clarke and Montgomerie all received byes into the second round, the first day still offered three former winners and the U.S. Open champion for an enthusiastic gallery.

"We have the cream of European golf — past and present — and we'll see how much has gone off," Faldo said ahead of his encounter with Harrington. Faldo was so off he suffered his worst-ever defeat in the tournament, a 9-and-8 drubbing. Faldo had never before been beaten earlier than the 33rd hole. In 2000, Faldo had taken Clarke to the 40th hole.

After bogeying the first three holes, Faldo found no way back against a player who was an approximate 12 under par for their 28 holes and who never missed a green in regulation. The 44-year-old Faldo knew he was in trouble as early as the first hole of the morning when he duffed a chip into a greenside bunker. "That was great; I couldn't believe that," Faldo said.

"Rounds like that make me wonder why I'm out there," he added. "I was really looking forward to the game and thought I might have half a chance, but to play that badly was disappointing. I don't need days like today. I am going to get my chainsaw out and go and have some fun in the garden."

Harrington had only just undergone laser eye surgery and spent most of September practicing after the cancellation of the WGC American Express Championship and the Ryder Cup. "That was a big scalp for me today," said the Irishman, who had attended a Faldo master class a decade before. "I could probably have beaten him that day by this margin because he had cut his thumb and could only play one-handed. Today I didn't make any mistakes and I didn't want to give Nick a chance of getting back into the match. I have lost too many tournaments when I thought I had them won, but in match play I've always played above my ability in stroke play."

Thomas Bjorn and Woosnam both had morning rounds of 65 and both went on to win 4 and 3 against Adam Scott and Goosen respectively. Scott, the young Australian, won the last three holes of the morning to get back to 2 down against Bjorn and holed a 40-footer at the first hole after the interval to further reduce the deficit. But the Dane surged ahead again and Scott only won two more holes, which only reduced the margin of defeat, not its inevitability.

Woosnam was 4 up by the 15th in the morning and an expected Goosen retaliation in the afternoon never materialized. "But I was pleased to hole my six-footer at the 15th to close it out," Woosnam said. "I didn't want it to go any further because, with Retief's length, he would have had the advantage over me over the closing holes."

It was the appearance of Ballesteros, the five-time former winner playing at Wentworth for the first time in seven years, that really brought out the spectators, and his supporters had plenty to enjoy before the Spaniard fell 3 and 2 to Torrance. These days when he goes in the trees, it tends to be too deep for the miraculous recoveries, but his short game and putting retain an unmistakable brilliance. Neither man had hardly made a cut all season and the Scot had lost each of his three previous first-round matches.

Torrance, at 48, four years Seve's senior, had been preoccupied with the Ryder Cup all season, but remains a more consistent player than Ballesteros and that was the only difference between them. Ballesteros was round in 68 in the morning, although Torrance birdied the 18th to draw back to only 1 down.

But after the interval, the Spaniard's birdies were replaced with bogeys. The crucial run was three dropped shots in a row from the seventh, his tree-bound drives at the eighth and ninth surrendering the initiative. Ballesteros did win the 13th and 14th to get back to 2 down, but Torrance, who was to do some television commentary on the event before his last-minute call-up, secured the win two holes later.

"This is certainly better than watching," Torrance said. "It was a great day. We both had good support, but they were definitely for Seve. He is close to playing better, but he is tough to play, no matter how he is playing. If you back him into a corner you had better duck, because you know he is going to chip stiff or hole it."

Torrance was involved in an even more remarkable victory the following day, one blessed with superb autumn sunshine. The Scot, ranked outside the top 300 in the world, proceeded to defeat Singh, the world's No. 5 player, at the last hole after twice being 3 down. Singh had a run of five successive threes on the second nine in the morning, but Torrance went one better with six in a row on the front nine after lunch as he went to the turn in 30. He three-putted the 13th to fall one behind again, but then hit a five iron to 10 feet at the short 14th to square the match.

Singh went ahead again at the next hole, but then Torrance holed from 10 feet for a birdie at the 16th, and a birdie-four at the 17th put him in front for the first time since the third hole in the morning. A fine drive and a seven wood onto the green at the 18th secured the match.

"I'm very proud of what I did today," said Torrance, the oldest semi-finalist ever. "That is as good a singles victory as I have ever had. I've got plenty of gas left in the tank and I'll be ready for tomorrow."

Torrance changed his putting stance at lunchtime, without reference to his coach and father Bob. The phone line north of the border would have been busy anyway, as Harrington, Bob Torrance's latest star pupil and Sam's semi-final opponent, was seeking advice. "It is tremendous what my dad has done for Padraig — he's now a world-class player," Sam said. "I just hope he hasn't told him all the secrets."

It was after a couple of tired swings with his driver on the 17th and 18th in the morning that Harrington got Bob to analyze him on the video between rounds. "I phoned Bob and he was able to tell me I was a bit flat-footed," Harrington explained after beating fellow Irishman Clarke 5 and 4. "That sorted out my driving but affected my pitch shots. I didn't feel comfortable at 2 up at lunch, but when I went 3 up at the 23rd I felt much better." A run of five successive threes on the first nine effectively decided the match and gave Harrington revenge for losing to Clarke in the final of the Irish Closed Championship in 1990.

Woosnam admitted to feeling tired and losing a bit of rhythm in the afternoon on the way to another impressive win, this time over Montgomerie. Woosnam's approximate 65 in the morning put him 3 up, and despite not playing quite as well later, he was again able to get off the course three holes early. "I'm enjoying myself," he said. "I was very relaxed yesterday. I didn't feel under pressure because people didn't expect me to win and it will be the same tomorrow."

In another classic match, Westwood was never in front against Bjorn until the 36th hole. "That is the only time it matters," he said. The Dane was 2 up at the interval, but there was no more than a hole in it until Westwood won the 15th to square the match. Having driven almost into the trees, Westwood put his second shot, a seven iron from 178 yards, to six feet. A birdie at the 18th, to Bjorn's par after driving into a bunker, sealed the victory.

Westwood was the only seed to receive a bye to survive the second round, and it meant that for the first time there was an Englishman, a Scotsman, an Irishman and a Welshman in the last four. Five members of the European Ryder Cup team had started the event, but the prospect of a final between the captain and vice captain was still on the cards. Woosnam, an assistant to Torrance for the postponed match, fulfilled his side of the bargain with a tremendous 10-and-9 victory over an out-of-sorts Westwood.

In a golfing sense, it had been a wretched season for Westwood following his Order of Merit victory in 2000. Off the course, however, there was the birth of his son Samuel, but the hints at an upturn in form from the previous day soon disappeared in the semis. He made only one birdie and did not win a single hole. Woosnam found himself 7 up after 13 holes and went on to equal the third best result ever. "I'll certainly settle for that," Woosnam said. "That's nine holes less than I thought I was going to have to play. Lee struggled, but I just didn't make many mistakes." But it was not to be an all-40s final because Harrington proved too strong for Torrance and ran out a 4-and-3 winner. There was little between the two men over the morning round. The fourth and the sixth holes were halved in birdies, but Torrance had holed from 18 feet for a two at the fifth to go in front.

The 11th and 12th were also halved in birdies, but Harrington's five at the 15th, his only bogey of the day, increased the Scot's lead. Harrington's response was impressive. He birdied the last three holes of the morning, with Torrance holing from four feet at the 18th to stay all square. "The way Sam had played, it was a bonus to get back to even at lunch and gave me some momentum for the afternoon," Harrington said.

Harrington was credited with an approximate 66, Torrance a 67. The Irishman resumed after a swift lunch by holing from 22 feet for a three at the first and took four of the first five holes, helped by a couple of errors from Torrance when he bunkered his approach at the third and three-putted the fifth.

At the seventh, a beautiful par-four played down into a valley and then up to a tricky elevated green, Torrance found the green with a seven iron and then holed an 18-footer for a three. At the next, he put his approach to eight feet and holed that to cut the deficit to two.

A brilliant chip out of the trees at the short 10th to a foot kept the Scot's recovery on track, but perhaps finally tiredness told and three successive bogeys from the 13th handed victory to Harrington. He missed the green at both the first two, and then drove into the trees at the 15th and could only chip back to the fairway, after which his hopes were doomed.

"Padraig played really well. It was nice to see him perform under pressure," Torrance said. "My dad will be happy that at least one of us is in the final. I wasn't feeling tired, the adrenaline keeps you going, but once I get home I will probably collapse for a couple of days."

Harrington said, "If the gallery was for Sam, they were very polite about it, because both our good shots were applauded equally. It was a big day in the Torrance household, but if Bob was sitting at home watching, he would have wanted me to score two 59s and Sam to win only by scoring a 59 and a 58. That's the way he is."

"It will be a great final," Torrance added. "I will enjoy watching it. Neither makes many mistakes. Woosie still has a class swing and loves these marathon matches. He just keeps going and grinds it out."

Torrance's assessment turned out to be fairly accurate, and ultimately, as the pair came down the back nine in the afternoon, Harrington's jaunty saunter was no match for the chest-puffed-out strut of Woosnam. But, first, the morning round was truly spectacular. Harrington holed from 35 feet for a three at the first and that set the tone. The second and fourth holes, and the seventh and eighth, were all halved in birdies. Woosnam equaled his own championship record for seven birdies in a row and set a new mark for his front nine of 28.

Harrington dropped a shot at the ninth to go 3 down, but responded with four birdies in a row to go ahead. At the short 10th, both had seven-foot putts for twos. After a measure, Woosnam was deemed away by only half a ball's width. He missed; Harrington holed. Woosnam rolled in a 20-footer on the 15th, but then Harrington birdied the last three, the Welshman pitching to 18 inches to avoid going 3 down at the interval. "That was fantastic. I don't think I have been involved in anything quite like that before," Woosnam said.

Harrington's inward 30 and his approximate 61 both equaled the existing records, while the pair's eclectic score of 56 and their combined 21 birdies were both new records. "It was unbelievable," Harrington said. "Woosie is terrific when he gets on a roll. His golf ensured that I was committed to mine. There was no point in backing off and that helped me focus and made me aggressive. Standing on the 10th tee there was no issue, I had to go for the pins all the way home."

After going 3 up after three holes in the afternoon, the 30-year-old Dubliner appeared to stop being the birdie machine he is in match play, and returned to the hesitant closer of tournaments he tends to be in stroke play. The trouble started at the seventh, when he drove into a ditch wide of the fairway and had to take a penalty drop. Normal service was briefly resumed at the eighth, where Woosnam put a six iron to nine feet and holed for a three, only to be matched by Harrington's wedge to five feet.

Harrington found more trouble at the ninth. He drove into the trees on the right and called a penalty on himself when the ball moved as he addressed it. Woosnam went over the green in two, but so did Harrington for four and had to take another penalty drop from another ditch. He was heading for an eight when he conceded that one. Woosnam evened the match by holing from 15 feet for a three at the 11th and then birdied the next two. He found the green at the par-five 12th in two and put an eight iron to 10 feet at the next, Harrington failing to get up and down at either hole.

There was one last stroke of defiance when Harrington struck a superb five wood to 15 feet at the 17th, but when he missed the putt, Woosnam holed from eight feet for the victory. "I was in control but didn't put him under pressure on the back nine," Harrington said. "Missing the greens at the 12th and 13th were bad shots. He played excellent golf, but didn't need to putt out on three key holes."

This was Harrington's seventh second place of the year, and the 16th of his career. "The run doesn't bother me in the slightest," he said. "Finishing second in a tournament can be a great performance. But at the individual event when I'm second, it does bother me. It looks like I don't like to finish the job off. I'm certainly not finishing it off. Something must change down the home stretch. Disappointed is not the word for how I feel about today. Disgusted is the word. The ball was in my court and it was totally my fault that he was not under pressure playing the back nine. I lost concentration. Why is the unanswered question. I can't always say I got unlucky or that someone else did something. It is up to me to do something. I'm reasonably patient, but I am beginning to lose my patience about this."

Woosnam won because he just did not give up. "I hung in there well and he did not quite shake me off," he said. He predicted he would be trying to shake something else off in the morning. "I know I will have a headache tomorrow, but I don't care."

8. American Tours

In what has become a familiar season-ending refrain, the biggest golf story of 2001 was Tiger Woods. He made history when he won, made news when he lost, and made headlines every time he went to play golf anywhere in the world.

The biggest question in the early part of the year was "When will he win again?" Coming off an 11-victory year in 2000 with eight wins on the U.S. PGA Tour and over $11 million in earnings, Woods was the favorite every time he teed off. Woods sometimes paid only slightly better than even money in Las Vegas and London. So, while it was silly, it shouldn't have been a surprise when fans started wondering if, in his winless winter, Woods was in a slump.

He went two whole months without winning. What other explanation was there? Forget that Woods had finished tied for eighth, tied for fifth, fourth, second and 13th twice in January and February. He hadn't obliterated the field at any event and hadn't shattered any tournament scoring records, so something must have been wrong.

Meanwhile, a few familiar names and a crop of newcomers adorned the tops of PGA Tour leaderboards. Jim Furyk won the season-opening Mercedes Championships by one shot over Rory Sabbatini, and the following week Garrett Willis beat Kevin Sutherland to win the Touchstone Energy Tucson Open. Brad Faxon reasserted himself in Honolulu at the Sony Open, while Mark Calcavecchia set a scoring record with a 256 total at the Phoenix Open.

Davis Love III shot a final-round 63 at Pebble Beach to capture the AT&T Pebble Beach National Pro-Am by one stroke over Vijay Singh. And Phil Mickelson showed us that sometimes you can't give a victory away. Mickelson won in the Buick Invitational with a double bogey on the third playoff hole to beat Frank Lickliter, who took a triple bogey.

Joe Durant surprised many by winning twice in a three-week span on two coasts. The first win came in California as Durant shot a record 324 for 90 holes at the Bob Hope Chrysler Classic, and the second came two weeks later in Miami at the Genuity Championship.

Jesper Parnevik and Robert Allenby won before Woods as well, prompting many to wonder about Tiger. He had to be in a slump. What other explanation could there be?

In three straight tournaments he made his critics look silly, stupid or both. With a birdie on the 72nd hole of the Bay Hill Invitational after a fortuitous bounce off a gallery member, Woods beat Mickelson by a stroke. That would prove to be a recurring theme throughout the remainder of the year.

Woods hit enough good shots to win. He holed birdies in the right places at the Stadium Course in Ponte Vedra Beach and won The Players Championship by one over Vijay Singh. He won his second Masters in five years, and his fourth consecutive major championship title — a Grand Slam if you gave him a mulligan and allowed for the fact that it occurred over two years. Some weren't eager to make that concession, but Woods said, "I can put all four trophies on my coffee table."

He was the first to win four consecutive professional major titles, a feat that will be remembered as one of the greatest in all of sports.

Woods would win twice more on the PGA Tour, once in Europe, and pick up two more late-year unofficial events, bringing his victory count to eight in 2001, and his yearly worldwide winnings to $7.7 million.

Mickelson, on the other hand, was the Wile E. Coyote of the PGA Tour who spent the year chasing the Road Runner, coming ever so close, only to fall off the cliff. After his victory in San Diego, Mickelson lost to Woods at Bay Hill, lost another heartbreaker at the Masters, pulled into contention at the U.S. Open only to falter on the final day, and shared the lead at the PGA Championship with three holes to play only to lose by one to David Toms.

In the course of the year Mickelson's prickly behavior — a well-masked edginess that earned him the nickname Eddie Haskel among tour regulars — was revealed to the public for the first time, and Mickelson's luster began to show a little tarnish. He was fined for gambling, a practice that had become so prevalent that Mickelson started predicting NFL games for ESPN radio. By the end of the year he was not to be seen, skipping the Tour Championship and staying at home in Arizona.

When Mickelson stumbled, Sergio Garcia stepped up as a contender. With two wins in the United States the 21-year-old proved that the early hype about his abilities wasn't overstated. By year's end Garcia was an adversary worthy of consideration when discussions reverted to the question of "Who's going to challenge Tiger?"

Garcia, Woods, Durant and Mickelson weren't the only multiple winners of the year. There were a few more surprises. Scott Hoch, wearing braces on his teeth at age 45, won twice, picking up his first wins since 1997 and earning a spot as the oldest member of the U.S. Ryder Cup team. David Toms won three times, including his PGA Championship victory, and proved that, at age 34, he was a force to be considered for the future. Bob Estes won in Memphis and Las Vegas, while Argentine Jose Coceres won at Hilton Head in April and again at Disney World in October. Both times Coceres took bed sheets from his hotel and wrote Spanish messages to his family and friends that he displayed for the television cameras after winning.

Shigeki Maruyama became the first Japanese player to win a PGA Tour event on the U.S. mainland — Isao Aoki won in Hawaii in 1983 — but it was the man Maruyama beat in Milwaukee, Charles Howell, who impressed everyone who saw him. The kid from Augusta, Georgia, proved he could play, and even though he didn't win in 2001, Howell made over $1.5 million and almost earned his way into the Tour Championship as a non-member who played solely on sponsor's exemptions. There was little question in anyone's mind that he would be a force in the future.

But they all will continue to be chasing one man. Air Canada Championship winner Joel Edwards put it best. "Tiger is our New York Yankees," Edwards said. "I mean, they can be beaten, and were in the last World Series, and he can be beaten too. But, big picture, he's the Yankees. He's our Babe Ruth. He's more than raised the bar. He's why we're earning what we're earning."

U.S. PGA Tour

Mercedes Championships—$3,500,000
Winner: Jim Furyk

Jim Furyk felt fortunate to be playing. He arrived in Hawaii unsure if he would be able to swing a club after taking two months off following a freak injury to his right wrist. Furyk hadn't played football since his early teens, but strained a ligament throwing a ball. Simply finishing the Mercedes Championships would be an accomplishment. "I would have taken 33rd place in a field of 33," he said.

Instead Furyk made a 10-foot birdie putt on the final hole for 67 and a 274 total, good enough for a one-stroke victory over Rory Sabbatini. Fighting wind and a four-shot deficit going into the final round, Furyk made a 60-foot eagle putt on the fifth hole, and finished strongly with a birdie at the 18th to take the lead.

His round also included some impressive recoveries, one at the par-five 15th when his wedge approach shot spun off the front of the green and rolled back down a slope to within 10 feet of his original position. From there Furyk hit a great chip and made the putt for par. Another recovery from a bunker at the 16th kept him in the game as third-round leader Sabbatini struggled with the wind and with his putter.

After pulling an approach shot into a greenside bunker at the 13th and failing to save par, Sabbatini lost the lead for the first time. He quickly regained a share when he made a 10-footer for birdie at the 14th, then he reached the par-five 15th green in two and two-putted for another birdie to move one ahead of Furyk.

Trouble came again on the 16th when Sabbatini rolled his par putt six feet past the hole and struggled to make bogey. His putter abandoned him again at the 18th. With a three-footer for birdie to tie the lead, Sabbatini seemed destined for a playoff. Furyk even had his driver out for the trip back to the 18th tee. Instead, Sabbatini missed the putt, shot 72 for a 275 total, and Furyk had his sixth career victory, his second in Hawaii.

"I would have liked to win this event with a little more of a heroic finish," Furyk said. "I feel for Rory. It's a pretty sick feeling."

Sabbatini was disappointed, but not disheartened by the missed putt. "There is nothing in golf that's ever a gimme," he said. "I didn't trust my line. I knew I missed it when I hit it. But I came here to give it my best, and I'm not sorry about that."

Ernie Els also gave it his best. After finishing second to Tiger Woods in this event in 2000, losing in one of the most dramatic playoffs of the season, Els had a chance at the final hole. Instead of making eagle, Els pulled his approach into the hazard and took par to shoot 69 for a 276 total and finish tied for third with Vijay Singh. "I played good enough to win this week," Els said. "I just got in my own way."

Furyk tried to avoid getting in his own or anyone else's way after coming from behind to win for the third time in his career. "Just to come here and complete the 72 holes would have made me happy," he said. "I'm pretty amazed."

Touchstone Energy Tucson Open—$3,000,000
Winner: Garrett Willis

After Garrett Willis shot 64 and 69 on the weekend to win the Touchstone Energy Tucson Open, third-round leader Mark Wiebe summed up the feelings of most when he said, "Garrett who?" Willis was less than a month out of qualifying school and playing in his first PGA Tour event after stints on the Hooters and Buy.com tours when he shocked everyone with a 15-under-par 273 total and a one-stroke victory over Kevin Sutherland.

"Just Sunday, somebody said, 'You and Garrett Willis have a lot in common," said Wiebe, who was paired with Willis in the final round. "I turned to him and said, 'Who is Garrett Willis?' I know I'm getting older, but our tour seems to be getting younger."

At 27, Willis wasn't the youngest player in the field at Tucson, but he might have been considered the least likely to come from two strokes back to become only the third player in PGA Tour history to win in his first start. "Here I am, a month out of qualifying school, and I went there not knowing where I was going to be playing this year. Now I'm a PGA Tour winner. What a country this is!"

Willis looked like an amateur qualifier throughout the week, wearing a University of Tennessee cap and carrying a logo-free golf bag. By Sunday afternoon, he had earned $540,000, moving him to third on the money list behind Steve Stricker and Jim Furyk.

Wiebe held the lead until he bogeyed the 12th, a hole Willis birdied. While Willis parred the last five holes for 69, Wiebe posted two more bogeys to shoot a final-round 74 and finish tied for fifth with Greg Kraft and Cliff Kresge at 276.

Sutherland finished strong with 68 for a 274 total, which looked like it might be good enough for a playoff after Willis missed a four-foot birdie putt at the 17th. But the leader came through at the end, two-putting from 50 feet for par.

"I just wanted to keep my head down and stroke it," Willis said. "All of a sudden my caddie is hugging me, and I'm like, 'Where am I? What's happening? Is this Oz?'" After a reality check, Willis realized where he was, and decided he liked it. "It's going to take the National Guard to get me off of this tour," he said.

Sony Open in Hawaii—$4,000,000
Winner: Brad Faxon

It seemed fitting that Brad Faxon would finish off his wire-to-wire victory in the Sony Open in Hawaii with a 30-foot eagle putt. Faxon led the tour in putting three of the previous five seasons, and was known among his colleagues as one of the best short-game players.

He showed it at the Waialae Country Club in Honolulu, chipping in from 90 feet for birdie on the second hole, and making another 30-footer at the eighth. The final eagle gave Faxon a five-under-par 65 and a 20-under-par 260 total, good enough to tie John Huston's record-setting total in 1998 and give Faxon a four-shot victory over Tom Lehman.

"Everything went as planned," Faxon said afterward. "Sometimes it went even better."

Lehman, who began the final round three behind, pulled to within one stroke after playing the first six holes in three under par, but he was even par through the remaining 12 holes for 66, which wasn't enough to catch Faxon.

"Brad had a three-shot lead and shot 65," Lehman said. "That gets the job done. He answered everything I had to give."

Faxon made so many putts that Lehman was left shaking his head. There was the six-foot par save at the first hole and the 90-foot chip-in at the second, a shot that brought a huge smile to Faxon's face. "You're only going to save par two out of 10 times from there," he said. "Making birdie is like a one-in-100 chance." He made another six-footer at the seventh for birdie and the 30-footer at the eighth, followed by another birdie from three feet at the ninth.

Ernie Els finished third at 267 after starting the final day three off the pace and tied with Lehman. He made an early charge, but stumbled at the sixth when he had to take an unplayable-lie penalty. Two holes later, Els three-putted from 10 feet for double bogey, missing a one-footer that all but ended his chances.

It was Faxon's eighth career win and his second in six months. "I have some big goals," Faxon said. "I've got to get back into the Masters. I want to play in all the majors and make the Ryder Cup team. To do that, I have to play well all year long and win a few times. Right now, though, I'm thrilled to death. I hope this is the start of a great year."

Phoenix Open—$4,000,000
Winner: Mark Calcavecchia

No one who watches golf has ever confused 41-year-old Mark Calcavecchia with Tiger Woods. But in an unseasonably cool week in Phoenix where players could see their breath and play had to be suspended once because of sleet, Calcavecchia put on a Tigeresque performance, and even stole one of Woods' more famous lines.

Before teeing off on Thursday, Calcavecchia turned to his mother and said, "I've got it." Woods had uttered those same words to his coach, Butch Harmon, back in 1999 before embarking on one of the most impressive streaks in golf history.

Rounds of 65 and 60 tied a PGA Tour record for 36 holes (held by Woods) and gave Calcavecchia a five-stroke edge over Scott Verplank. On Saturday, wearing mittens and a ski cap, Calcavecchia shot 64 and opened up a six-stroke lead on Rocco Mediate. Everyone knew he was going to win. By Sunday it was just a question of how many records Calcavecchia would break.

"I had lunch with Calcavecchia after Thursday's round," Woods said. "He was talking about how he didn't make a thing out there. He shot 65. I knew then that he might go nuts."

Calcavecchia did, indeed, go nuts, birdieing four of his last five holes to shoot a final-round 67 to finish at 256, the lowest 72-hole total in PGA Tour history. Calcavecchia entered the record books, breaking Mike Souchak's 45-year-old record by a single stroke, and tying John Huston's 1998 record for the most strokes under par at 28 under. Calcavecchia also broke the record for most birdies in a 72-hole event when he made a two-footer on the 17th for his 32nd birdie of the week.

"There was no way we were going to beat him," said Mediate, who finished second with a 264 total. "I could have shot 63, 64 and 64 the last three days and still lost the tournament. It's amazing. He was awesome. I mean, I shot 20 under and never got close. I got waxed."

Calcavecchia even had a hard time believing it. "It's semi-indescribable," he said. "I've looked at that record before, but it never crossed my mind that I could do something like that. I know I'm streaky, but I'm not that good. Looking at the board when I was out on the green and seeing a red 28, it just looked crazy."

AT&T Pebble Beach National Pro-Am—$4,000,000
Winner: Davis Love III

It had been 33 months since Davis Love III hoisted a PGA Tour trophy and received a winner's check. In that time, he had taken a barrage of criticism for his final-round falters. Love had become the media personification of the "soft" golf professional — a good player who enjoyed the luxuries of tour life, but who had lost the burning desire to win. That label wounded and insulted Love. No one wanted to win as badly as he did. In fact he admitted to being "obsessed" with winning again. He knew the only way to shed the moniker was to win a PGA Tour event in convincing fashion.

On a sunny Sunday afternoon in Monterrey, California, Love did just that, coming from seven strokes back to win the AT&T Pebble Beach National Pro-Am. A final-round nine-under-par 63 for a 16-under 272 total was good enough for a one-shot victory over Vijay Singh, but it was the way in which Love won that shattered any notion that he lacked the heart to win. The final round included one of the fastest starts in recent memory, as he played the first seven holes in eight under par.

"I think the start made it tougher on the leaders," Love said. "I knew when I was going through the hard holes, I thought if I could get another birdie these guys will be thinking they have to birdie every hole. Physically they didn't have to do it, but mentally they felt like all of a sudden they were behind."

Trailing Phil Mickelson by seven at the start of the day, Love remembered the 2000 AT&T where Tiger Woods came from seven back in the last seven holes to win by two shots.

"I had Tiger right behind me and that's where all the attention was focused early," Love said. "It took like five holes before a lot of people knew what I was doing. But I finally got their attention. There was definitely a feeling of 'take that,' of a little extra satisfaction with this one. It's nice to jump back in the spotlight after you've kind of been forgotten. And I felt like that happened to me a little bit."

A holed eagle from 104 yards on the second set things in motion for Love. He then hit his approach on the third to four feet, another shot to four feet at the fifth, and a brilliant wedge to two feet at the seventh. His only drop was a bogey at the 11th, which spurred him on to make one of the most dramatic shots of the day, a 256-yard three-wood approach to the 18th hole that landed and stopped 40 feet from the cup. Two putts later, Love was in with 63.

"There is something to be said for posting a score," Love said. "I left the 18th green thinking, 'You played a helluva round and if you had made a couple of putts coming in you would have probably won, but somebody is going to probably clip you.' That's when luck comes in a little bit."

One by one, contenders dropped off the board. Singh could have taken the lead outright, but a pulled approach to the par-three 17th that found the Pacific cost the Masters champion a chance at his first win of 2001. Mickelson also found the ocean, hitting a driver approach from the 18th fairway into the water and blowing any chance he might have had of tying or beating Love. "I had hit that shot several times already," Mickelson said. "I wanted to put the ball in the front bunker and try to make birdie from there. I simply came out of it and hit a bad shot."

An hour after finishing his round, Love finally broke into a smile as the winless streak officially ended. As for putting all the negative press and the bad thoughts behind him, Love seemed reflective and philosophic. "You always have bad thoughts," he said. "It's who conquers them the best that matters."

Buick Invitational—$3,500,000
Winner: Phil Mickelson

Despite an upset stomach early in the week that required intravenous fluids, Phil Mickelson came back to one of his favorite courses to successfully defend his Buick Invitational title in front of a friendly, hometown crowd. With a new home under construction nearby, Mickelson played Torrey Pines Golf Club like a man who grew up on the course, which is exactly what he did, playing more rounds in LaJolla, California, than anywhere else in the world.

For 74 holes, Mickelson looked confident and in control, a man destined to win. His 68, 64 and 71 in the first three rounds left him one shot behind Davis Love III, who was looking for his second win in two weeks. On Sunday Mickelson birdied the first, second, eighth and ninth holes to take the lead, then added birdies at the 11th and 13th to open up a three-shot margin. He finished with 66 for a 269 total.

But Love wasn't finished. A birdie at the 16th and a two-putt birdie at the 18th gave Love a five-under-par 67 for a 269 of his own. When Frank Lickliter made a 20-footer on the 18th for 66, he too was tied for the lead. A three-way playoff would decide the winner, but no one could have anticipated what was to come.

Love was eliminated on the second playoff hole when his tee shot at the par-three 16th plugged in the greenside bunker and he was unable to salvage par. Mickelson and Lickliter moved on to the par-four 17th. Mickelson hit first, and for the second time in two weeks he pushed a shot with his driver to the left. The previous Sunday, it had come at the 18th hole at Pebble Beach when Mickelson, trying to reach the par-five in two, pushed his second shot into the ocean and handed Love the victory. This week the same shot from the tee at the 17th put Mickelson in a terrible position in the canyon left of the fairway.

Lickliter had his opening. All he needed to do was find the fairway and play for par. But rather than take out a three wood or even a three iron, Lickliter went with the driver. "My thought was that I was going to nail this one," Lickliter said. "I had hit driver there every day. I had sand wedge or gap wedge to the green every day. That's what I was looking for. When Phil fanned his into the garbage, I just got too excited and put it right on top of his."

Both golf balls found the canyon, and both players hit provisional balls from the tee. Lickliter's ball was found first. His lie was impossible, and his only option was to head back to the tee to hit another shot. Mickelson didn't want his ball to be found. His provisional was perfect. The last thing he wanted was to trudge back to the tee and make yet another swing. But even as he was telling marshals to abandon the search, one of the volunteers discovered Mickelson's ball in the brush.

"I didn't want anybody to look for it," Mickelson said. "There was only one option if I found it, and that was to go back to the tee. I had just hit a perfect provisional drive and I didn't want to have to walk all the way back and hit another one. The marshal was just doing his job. I just wished he hadn't done it so effectively."

After a verbal tirade where Mickelson scolded the marshal, the left-hander walked back to the tee and pushed another drive. This one was destined for the canyon and would have ended up deeper in the brush than his first drive if it hadn't hit the only tree guarding the left side of the fairway. The ball ricocheted into the rough, and Mickelson was able to advance his fourth shot onto the green.

Lickliter also found the green with his fourth shot, leaving himself 12 feet for bogey. When Mickelson missed his bogey effort, Lickliter had another chance. But instead of making the putt for his only PGA Tour victory, Lickliter ran the putt five feet past the hole, then missed his double-bogey putt coming back. Mickelson won with a double bogey.

"It was certainly an awkward playoff," Mickelson said. "I'm very excited about the outcome. That's all I can say."

Bob Hope Chrysler Classic—$3,500,000
Winner: Joe Durant

Joe Durant's 65 on Wednesday didn't even sniff the lead. That was a sign of the way things would go in the windless desert during this Bob Hope Chrysler Classic, an event known for low scores and celebrity sightings. David Duval shot 59 in the final round of this event in 1999, and even Joe

Pesci regularly broke his handicap. By Thursday afternoon, once Durant made bogey at the first hole of Indian Wells and came back with 10 birdies and an eagle for 61, the record book looked to be in jeopardy. Five players shot 62 on Thursday and 36 players shot in the 60s in both the first and second rounds.

Durant kept going low, shooting 67, 66 and 65 the rest of the week, winning by four over Paul Stankowski and setting a 90-hole record of 36-under-par 324. Winner of one PGA Tour event (the 1998 Western Open), Durant wasn't expecting to set records, especially after Mark Calcavecchia's assault on par in Phoenix.

"It's a constant battle, being out here with all these guys who play so well," Durant said. "I try to keep a positive attitude, and this week was really amazing because I just didn't think I could go as low as you have to go to win here. I have no track record at this event. This is the first time I made the cut."

The cut, made after 72 holes, was 11 under par, also a record, and although he didn't get to play the final round, even Arnold Palmer got into the act by shooting 71 on Saturday to become the first man in a decade to shoot his age in a PGA Tour event.

A 63 by Stankowski on Sunday wasn't enough to make this one a battle. He never got closer than three shots behind Durant, and when it was finally over the margin was four. Calcavecchia finished third at 330 with rounds of 64, 66, 69, 65 and 66, and afterwards he shook his head in amazement at the numbers.

"My 28-under 256 in Phoenix looked pretty good until Saturday when Joe wound up at minus 29," Calcavecchia said. "Heck, I was big for almost three weeks. I don't know where it's going to end, the way things are going. I'm fat, old, out of shape and my left knee got drained last night. But I wind up 30 under here and I don't get a sniff. I'm not sure I even get lunch. How long will 36 under last? Another five years, max. Maybe five rounds."

Durant couldn't care less how long his record stands. "I don't know if I have the desire to be a top-20 player," he said. "I never had a good short game, but I'm working on it. It's getting better. So is my putting. I hope to be around for a while."

Nissan Open—$3,400,000
Winner: Robert Allenby

Australian Robert Allenby would love to win by a dozen shots, but he'll take them as they come. And so far all of Allenby's wins have come in overtime. Both his PGA Tour wins in 2000 came from playoffs, as had his four overseas victories. Allenby added a seventh playoff title on a soggy Sunday afternoon in Los Angeles when he laced a three wood through the driving rain to within five feet of the first extra hole to set up a birdie. With that shot, Allenby won the largest playoff in PGA Tour history, defeating five other players to capture the Nissan Open title, and became the ninth winner in nine events on the 2001 PGA Tour.

It wasn't supposed to be that exciting. Davis Love III started the final day with a three-stroke lead, having maneuvered his way around famed Riviera

Country Club in 10-under-par 203. With Sunday's round being played in a steady, cold downpour, Love was expected to extend his lead. According to CBS commentator Peter Kostis, "Love is hitting the ball longer than he ever has, in some cases as far as Tiger Woods." With Riviera playing longer than normal because of the raw conditions, length should have played to Love's strength.

But instead of extending his lead, Love lost it in the first three holes. From a perfect position in the first fairway, he hit a two iron over the green and over the gallery, eliminating any chance at a birdie on the benign 503-yard par-five. Then on the third hole he bladed a chip and ended up 20 feet beyond the hole. He missed that par putt. On the 236-yard fourth hole, Love missed the green with a one iron, but chipped to within two feet. Everyone was shocked when he missed a 20-inch putt to lose his lead.

Ten players shared the lead at varying stages of the final round, but Love was the one with the best chance to win. He clawed his way back to 10 under on the second nine, but played the final four holes in four over par, making double bogey from the bunker at the 15th and missing a three-foot par putt on the 16th to fall out of contention.

That opened the door for many contenders. Only moments after making bogey at the 18th to fall into a tie at eight-under 276, Allenby marched back to the tee of the long par-four for the largest playoff in history. Japan's Toshimitsu Izawa, Bob Tway, Jeff Sluman, Dennis Paulson and Brandel Chamblee, who hadn't made a cut all season until this week, joined Allenby in a scene that looked like a Monday morning shootout. Despite the size of the field, Allenby liked his chances.

"I'm pretty confident going into playoffs," he said. "It's a matter of who can get it in the hole the quickest."

Getting it in the hole was quite a task on the 18th, a hole that had only given up one birdie in the final round and played to an average of 4.544. Sluman called it, "a pretty easy par-five," but Allenby knew he needed a three.

"I was trying to hit the perfect shot," Allenby said of the three-wood approach that landed 10 feet short of the flag and rolled to within five feet. "I came up with it. To be able to pull it off in those conditions — pouring rain, five guys on your heels — that's going to be a shot that stays in my memory bank a long time."

Tway was the only other player who reached the green in two, but his birdie effort came up a foot short. Of the six players in the playoff, there were two bogeys, three pars and Allenby's birdie. Sluman was right: It played like a pretty easy par-five.

Genuity Championship—$4,500,000
Winner: Joe Durant

In Joe Durant's only Masters appearance prior to 2001 he shot 87 and 79 and finished last among those players who actually finished 36 holes. That was 1999, and the only things that kept Durant's name off the bottom of the Masters scoring list were withdrawals by Doug Ford, Gay Brewer and Billy Casper. Durant blamed a cracked rib on his performance, but to most observers it appeared as though Durant had slipped though a crack in Augusta National's invitation policy. He might have been the 1998 Western Open winner, but Joe Durant didn't look like a major championship contender.

That was then. After the Genuity Championship at the Doral Resort in Miami, the last event before Masters invitations were issued for 2001, Durant was the only PGA Tour player with two victories, and he stood atop the money list at just a few dollars shy of $1.5 million. Durant proved he could win on both coasts in all kinds of conditions in 2001, taking the Bob Hope Chrysler Classic with a record 36-under-par total, then coming from eight strokes back in his next start to play the final 36 holes of Doral's Blue Monster course in 12-under-par 132 to win the Genuity Championship by two shots. Durant's 67-65 weekend for an 18-under-par 270 total on a blustery Doral course allowed the quiet 36-year-old to pass such notables as Mike Weir, Hal Sutton, Davis Love III, Jeff Sluman and defending Masters champion Vijay Singh.

"The way I played at the Hope was validation for me," Durant said. "I usually don't expect to go that low. The conditions here were totally different, obviously. Tougher golf course, longer, but I actually think that's more of a fit for my game than when everybody's making birdies. My ball flight, I keep it down. I usually hit it pretty straight, so the tougher it is, the better I have a chance of doing."

His first two rounds weren't bad, but in warm, benign conditions a 68-70 start left Durant well behind the leaders. He made up ground on Saturday with 67 as the wind picked up, but he still trailed Weir by four strokes, Sutton by three and Love by one.

On Sunday the weather worsened and the PGA Tour moved the tee times up by four hours, sending players out in threesomes off of both sides at 7:30 to beat a storm that was moving into Miami. They didn't beat the wind, and the scores skyrocketed. Weir shot 71, his worst score of the week, for a 272 total, while Sutton limped in with 72 for an aggregate of 274. Love shot 275 after 71 on Sunday and Sluman posted 70 to tie Sutton and Singh at 274.

While the leaders were getting worse as the conditions deteriorated, Durant continued to improve. He eagled the first hole, and went to the fifth tee at four under par on the day. A two-putt birdie at the 603-yard, par-five 12th hole gave Durant the outright lead. At the 14th, his drive drifted right into a fairway bunker, but Durant made up for the error by blasting a seven iron to within 10 feet and making the putt for birdie. He capped the round with a final birdie at the 16th. Even his three-putt bogey in the rain at the 18th — his first over-par hole of the weekend — couldn't dampen Durant's enthusiasm. His 65 was seven shots better than the average score on Sunday, and two better than anyone else in the field.

"He played terrific golf and did everything right," said Sluman, who was paired with Durant and Singh. "In a wind like this, you've got to hit it solid, and Joe did."

Singh also hit it solid on Sunday, putting together a 67 to go with 66 on Saturday for the second-best weekend total of the tournament. But with a green jacket in his closet, Singh didn't have to worry about his Masters invitation getting lost in the mail. Durant did. "I really wanted to get back to the Masters," he said. "But honestly, I didn't have going back there on my radar screen this year."

Honda Classic—$3,200,000
Winner: Jesper Parnevik

You would be hard pressed to find two more diverse players on the PGA Tour than Jesper Parnevik and Mark Calcavecchia. Parnevik is known for his flashy, off-beat attire, his biting wit and his fiendish workout schedule. Calcavecchia is about as dry as they come, dressing conservatively, speaking unintelligibly and staying as far away from the fitness trailer as possible. So as the final round of the Honda Classic progressed, it seemed almost inevitable that the tournament would come down to a last-hole putting contest between the tour's oddest couple.

Parnevik won, but without any heroics. Sporting a new putter than looked more like a television antenna than a golf club, Parnevik opened with a seven-under-par 65 to share the lead with Jeff Ogilvy. A 67 on Friday gave the Swede a three-shot edge going into the weekend, and by sunset on Saturday the lead remained intact. Anything under par on Sunday and Parnevik would have won in a cakewalk.

But a cadre of contenders came gunning for the dapper leader in the final round. Two-time winner Joe Durant was the first to make a move, putting together a 66-69 weekend to post an early total of 15-under-par 273.

Ogilvy also made a last-minute run, following a lackluster 72 on Friday with rounds of 65 and 69 on the weekend. A first-nine 32 on Sunday moved Ogilvy within a shot of Parnevik, and when another birdie putt fell at the 11th, Ogilvy found himself tied for the lead. That's when his good fortune ended. Two bogeys in the closing moments left Ogilvy at 271. For a while that looked to be good enough for at least a playoff. Parnevik was struggling on Sunday, and Calcavecchia, who stood alone in second after Saturday, was having putter troubles on the final nine.

Craig Perks also made an impressive run. Opening the round with four consecutive birdies, Perks gained a temporary share of the lead. He was seven under par for his round, but a bogey at the 18th proved costly. Perks, who finished 136th on the 2000 PGA Tour money list and was forced to return to qualifying school, shot 66 and tied Ogilvy at 271.

In the closing holes it became a two-man race between Parnevik and Calcavecchia. The Swede held onto a one-shot lead, playing the first 17 holes in one under par, but allowing Calcavecchia within striking distance. It came down to the 18th, where Calcavecchia hit a four-iron shot from 205 yards onto the green. That was the 61st green Calcavecchia had hit for the week, which led the field, but the 60 feet of putting surface between his ball and the hole proved to be too much. Three putts later, Calcavecchia walked away with a bogey at the final hole, a two-under-par 70 and a tie for second place at 271.

Parnevik didn't improve matters much. Missing the last green, he chipped to within 12 feet, but missed his par effort. A tap-in bogey was all he needed. Parnevik's 270 total was good enough for his fifth PGA Tour victory. As for the television antenna putter, Parnevik could only smile. "I don't know how much longer it will last," he said. "It might be another one-week wonder."

Bay Hill Invitational—$3,500,000
Winner: Tiger Woods

It had been six months and eight golf tournaments since Tiger Woods had hoisted a winner's trophy — a dry spell that wouldn't have been noteworthy from any other golfer. But Woods' streak had been labeled a "slump," and had prompted such headlines as, "What's Wrong With Tiger?" On a windy Sunday afternoon a few miles from his Florida home, Woods answered with a 15-under-par 273 week at Arnold Palmer's home club for a one-shot, repeat victory in the Bay Hill Invitational.

"It should inspire us all to see that Tiger has finally broken out of that awful slump he was in," Lee Janzen deadpanned, prompting laughter from those who heard the comment.

"Back in the early '60s, the mid '60s and the late '60s, I had slumps," Palmer said before the start of his event. "Did it bother me? At first, yes. I felt like I was still playing pretty good golf. I'm sure Tiger feels the same way when you look at his scoring average and what he's done. I agree Tiger is in a slump, but he may win the next six tournaments he plays, too. You know golf is tough. Week in and week out you can't just hit every shot the way you want, and in this day and age when players are shooting the scores they're shooting, it doesn't take a lot of off-line shots for everyone else to catch up to you."

Woods disagreed with Palmer's "slump" reference, pointing to the fact that he entered Bay Hill 75 under par for the year. But with no wins, the 19th spot on the money list and the stinging memory of a final-hole collapse in Dubai still fresh on everyone's mind, Woods knew the only way to silence his critics was with his clubs.

Rounds of 71, 67 and 66 quieted most of the grumbling, as Woods took a one-shot lead over Sergio Garcia into the final round. Garcia got the best of Woods at the Battle at Bighorn, a made-for-television event that came on the heels of Woods' spectacular wins at the PGA Championship and the WGC NEC Invitational. This time around Woods was winless, focused, healthy and playing with something to prove.

From the early going, it looked like another erratic day for Woods. His tee shots bounded off trees and cart paths, sometimes missing the out-of-bounds stakes by mere feet. "It was ugly," Woods said. "I didn't hit the ball that solid. I didn't know where it was going but forward, and I was just trying to hit the ball between the O.B. markers."

Woods lost the lead for the first time at the 11th hole when, after using a two iron off the tee, he left himself with 222 yards to the green and missed his approach to the left. "How stupid was that?" Woods asked. A bogey dropped him one behind a charging Phil Mickelson, who was in the process of shooting 66 for a 14-under-par 274 total. Given the conditions — cool and windy, with showers coming through later in the day — Mickelson's score looked to be good enough to once again upset Woods.

Woods added to the drama when he pulled his tee shot to within two feet of the out-of-bounds stakes on the par-five 16th. He caught a break with a good lie, and proceeded to hit the green with a seven iron, leaving himself 30 feet for eagle. A two-putt birdie moved him back into a tie with Mickelson. A par at the difficult par-three 17th set up the final-hole drama. Woods pulled another drive, but this one hit a spectator in the neck, saving the ball from going perilously close to another out-of-bounds stake. After dropping from the cart path onto a hardpan lie, with water to the right of the green, Woods ripped a five iron from 190 yards to within 15 feet. With Mickelson watching from the scorer's trailer, Woods rolled in the putt for birdie, a 69 and 273 total, and the victory.

"Tiger was the only player who not only read that putt correctly, but hit it correctly," Mickelson said. "Everybody was missing it short and low. But I thought he'd make it, because he normally makes it when he needs to."

Palmer agreed. "What's gutsy was making that putt when he needed to the way he did," he said. "I asked him, 'Weren't you worried about knocking it by the hole?' He told me, 'No, I only thought about taking it over now.' But he's been playing good golf all year. The difference might have been the way the ball bounced on 18 today. He got some bad bounces earlier in the year, so he didn't win. Today he got a good one. That's all it is."

Woods approved of that assessment. "I got an 'Arnold Palmer' break," he said, explaining his fortuitous kick on the last hole. "I was able to get some wonderful breaks down the stretch. It was not a pretty round of golf, but I got the ball in the hole. It's always nice to win."

Then Woods jokingly said to reporters, "I guess the slump's over, huh?"

The Players Championship—$6,000,000
Winner: Tiger Woods

See Chapter 6.

BellSouth Classic—$3,300,000
Winner: Scott McCarron

It's sort of a cruel April Fool's joke for Jennifer McCarron. In addition to April 1 being Mrs. Scott McCarron's birthday, the bride of the 2001 BellSouth Classic champion had to watch her husband's third career PGA Tour victory on television.

"She's going to be really upset," McCarron said after shooting 72 and 73 in the 36-hole final-round marathon for an eight-under-par 280 total to win the Atlanta event by three shots over Mike Weir. "She was here all week and left. When she saw the weather forecast, she ended up taking the girls back home to California on Wednesday night. I haven't even talked to her yet. I really wish she was here right now, but I'm sure she'll get over it once I get home. It's quite a tournament, quite a day."

That description could be interpreted a lot of different ways. Rain washed out Thursday's opening round, and with the TPC at Sugerloaf course playing harder and faster than ever, the 36-hole finish proposed by officials didn't seem possible. Throw in the fact that temperatures on Sunday never climbed above 55 degrees, with winds gusting up to 30 knots, and this year's BellSouth Classic finale looked like a qualifying round for the British Open.

"Oh man," McCarron said when asked about the weather conditions during Sunday's final round. "My hands and forearms were starting to cramp up, and I was drinking so much water just to stay hydrated that I was having to go to the bathroom every two holes. The wind takes so much energy out of you — it was just a tough day."

A 67 on Saturday set up that tough day, leaving McCarron tied for the lead with Chris DiMarco at 135. Phil Mickelson stood one back after rounds of 70 and 66, and Dennis Paulson was in fourth place with rounds of 72 and 65.

The scores were much higher on Sunday. With a sunrise start and a sunset finish, the third-round scoring average was 74.53 and the field could manage no better than 74.88 in the fourth round, the highest closing round averages of the year on tour.

"I thought it was a pretty cruel April Fool's joke," Ernie Els quipped after shooting 81 and 73 on Sunday.

"Without the wind, 36 holes out here is tough," said Sugarloaf member Stewart Cink. "When you add in the wind and other elements, the course has never played this tough."

That toughness played into McCarron's hands. Hitting fairways and greens, and keeping his composure even when a bogey was inevitable, McCarron took a one-shot lead into the final round, then extended the lead, not with any charges of his own, but by watching his competitors fall by the wayside. DiMarco bogeyed four of the first six holes in the final 18 and fell away en route to 77, while Mickelson, who shot 73 in the morning 18, missed numerous short putts in the closing stretch, finishing with 75 for a 284 total and a tie for third with Paulson and Chris Smith.

McCarron hung on, making par after par, stretching his lead to six shots at one point. His 280 total was good enough for a three-shot margin over a charging Mike Weir, who managed to play the final 36 holes in 140, a score McCarron called "phenomenal."

"Go out and hit a five-footer downhill with this wind right now," McCarron said. "You'll see that one over is like shooting six or seven under the last two rounds."

Masters Tournament—$4,600,000
Winner: Tiger Woods

See Chapter 2.

WorldCom Classic—$3,500,000
Winner: Jose Coceres

It took five days and five extra holes, but the wait was worth it for Argentina's Jose Coceres. When the mist from Calabogie Sound lifted above the Harbour Town lighthouse on Monday morning, Coceres held his first PGA Tour title, having outlasted Billy Mayfair in a five-hole playoff in the WorldCom Classic that had to be carried over until Monday morning because of darkness.

Both players had lots of opportunities to win it earlier. After scores of 68, 70 and 64 and a two-under-par round in the works on Sunday, Coceres was one of the first players to get to 11 under, which is where he remained, unable to convert any closing birdie chances. His 71 for a 273 total set the bar, and no one was able to jump over it.

Mayfair had his chances. With rounds of 65, 68 and 69 he seemed in great form, especially after making a 30-footer at the 16th on Sunday to break a logjam that included Coceres, Vijay Singh, Carl Paulson, Scott Verplank and Bernhard Langer. A save from the bunker at the 18th left Mayfair tied with Coceres at 273, while the others had to settle for shares of third place.

Coceres had a chance to win on the first playoff hole, but he missed a three-footer and overtime continued. After the next hole, officials called play until Monday morning. "When you can't see, you can't see," Mayfair said.

At the par-three 17th on Monday, the fourth playoff hole, Mayfair missed another opportunity to clinch his first title in over two years. With Coceres plugged in a greenside bunker, Mayfair had a straight, uphill 15-footer for birdie that slid by the hole. Coceres then made a 12-footer for par to keep things going.

On the final hole, after pulling his approach into the marsh along the edge of the 18th green, Coceres marched into the reeds in hopes of making another recovery. Any other year the ball would have been wet, but because of a serious drought that had affected much of the Southeast, Coceres had a shot to the flag. He lobbed the ball to within five feet.

Mayfair had reached the green, but he ran his 25-footer a full six feet past the hole. After Mayfair missed his par attempt, Coceres drained the five-footer for par, punched the air, and became the first Argentine since Roberto de Vicenzo in 1968 to win a PGA Tour event.

Shell Houston Open—$3,400,000
Winner: Hal Sutton

It was the kind of day when only the grittiest survived. Winds whipped around the TPC at The Woodlands in Houston, hardening greens and blowing shots where players didn't like. It was a day for being patient, determined, smart, experienced and driven to win. It was Hal Sutton's kind of day.

"This is one I wanted more than anything," Sutton said after shooting three-under-par 69 on Sunday for a 10-under-par 278 total to pass Joe Durant by three strokes and win his first Shell Houston Open title. "I've been close here so many times, so close and yet so far. This is really good. I knew it would be tough. Today it helped to be packed with patience. There was never any let-up out there. You couldn't go to sleep or put it on cruise control. You had to think on every shot. Whoever was in control of the wind had it turned all the way up. It tests your nerves and what you have inside you."

With rounds of 70, 68 and 71, Sutton trailed Durant by two shots going into the final round, when the field averaged 73.17 in winds that gusted upwards of 25 miles an hour. The lead changed quickly in the final round as Sutton birdied his first two holes, while Durant bogeyed the second and third to fall one shot back.

Sutton could have given up on the seventh hole when a shot he thought "was one foot from the hole" splashed in the water fronting the green. He hung in and made a 20-footer for bogey to keep his round, and his lead, alive.

"I thought I hit a perfect shot with a nice eight iron," Sutton said. "Then the wind died and it dropped from the sky. But that bogey was the turning point. I could have come away with my confidence damaged, but I felt great."

Sutton followed up his gritty bogey with a birdie at the eighth and another eight iron to 15 feet to set up a fourth birdie at the 10th. The putt at the 10th opened up a two-shot lead, and nobody got close after that. A final birdie at the 17th put this one in the books. Durant finished with 74 and was tied for second at 281 with Lee Janzen, who shot 73.

Greater Greensboro Chrysler Classic—$3,500,000
Winner: Scott Hoch

In characteristic style, Scott Hoch never stopped complaining, even as he was shooting four rounds in the 60s and winning the Greater Greensboro Chrysler Classic for his first tournament victory in three years. This time it was the rough — or lack thereof — that had Hoch in a snit.

"It hurts the guy who is accurate," Hoch said of the lack of rough at Forest Oaks Country Club. "When I'm playing good, I drive it well. I get upset because a lack of rough is taking money out of my pocket. It's getting to where we have fewer and fewer courses where accuracy matters."

As he was saying this, Hoch was shooting 68, 68, 67 and a closing 69 for a 16-under-par 272 total to win by one over Scott Simpson and Brett Quigley.

"With Scott there's always got to be something to grumble about," Simpson said. "Overall he is a good guy. Sometimes he says stuff that makes you look at him funny, but there's usually an element of truth to it. I thought the rough was fine this week. I don't remember seeing Scott Hoch's name on a whole lot of U.S. Open and PGA Championship trophies. I don't know what he's complaining about."

Neither did anyone else, especially after Hoch assumed a two-shot lead through 54 holes, then came out and seized control of the tournament with birdies at the 11th, 13th and 14th holes to open a three-stroke lead. By the time he made his only bogey at the 18th, the tournament was his.

Quigley made a run, drawing even with Hoch with an eagle at the par-five 13th. Despite a pair of 67s on the weekend, the nephew of Senior PGA Tour player Dana Quigley couldn't get the putts to fall on the final five holes when it mattered. Jeff Maggert fell by the wayside as well, pulling to within one shot through 13 holes, but falling back to finish tied for fourth with Choi Kyung-ju, Gabriel Hjertstedt and Jerry Kelly at 275.

"If Tiger were a shot back I might be a little more worried," Hoch said. "But those guys are all pretty good players. They're hungry, but I'm hungry too. I'm at an age where you don't know how many more chances you'll have. I'm not ready to go quietly off into the sunset just yet."

Compaq Classic of New Orleans—$4,000,000
Winner: David Toms

In the 52 years that New Orleans had hosted a PGA Tour event, no Louisiana native had ever won. Included on that list were Hal Sutton, Fred Haas and Jay and Lionel Herbert. Not until 2001 when Shreveport native and LSU alumnus David Toms shot 63 and 64 on the weekend at English Turn and overran Phil Mickelson in the Compaq Classic did the Louisiana faithful have something to cheer about.

And cheer they did, chanting "L-S-U" and "Go Tigers" throughout the round. Toms admitted to being influenced by the partisan crowd. "I've never heard anything like it," he said.

Neither had Tom's playing partner, Ernie Els, who said, "I don't think I've ever heard so many 'Go Tigers' as I did today, and Tiger Woods wasn't even here this week." After about six holes, Els turned to Toms and said, "I take it that's the school's mascot."

Mickelson, who seemed to have righted himself after his disappointing loss to Woods at the Masters, led by six, and Toms started the final round tied for third with Els, three strokes behind second-place contender Harrison Frazar.

A course-record-tying 63 on Saturday gave Toms the confidence he needed going into the final round. That confidence coupled with the enthusiastic reception he received on every hole and a few gifts from Mickelson proved to be enough to propel Toms to victory.

"I would say that today was probably the best round of golf I've ever played," Toms said of his eight-under-par 64 final round and 22-under 266 total that broke the tournament record by three shots. It also gave Toms the second-biggest comeback of the season, eclipsed only by Davis Love's seven-shot charge at Pebble Beach.

As was the case with Love's win in Monterrey, Mickelson provided help along the way. In February the left-hander pushed a drive into the Pacific on the final hole to hand the victory to Love. In New Orleans he hooked two tee shots in the final round, one that resulted in a triple bogey on the fifth hole to drop Mickelson out of the lead. The second came after Mickelson had clawed his way back into a share of the lead. At the 15th, a reachable par-five, Mickelson hit another hook that resulted in a bogey. His 72 for a 268 total left Mickelson in second place and alone with his thoughts.

"It was a pathetic round of golf," he said. "I think when it's the final round the tendency is to just go on instinct. You can't get real mechanical. You have to let it happen as opposed to being mechanical. Just like at number 15, I tried not to think too much and just swung away, and look what happened. It was a big hook, so obviously my swing wasn't there technically."

Toms didn't have that problem. After chipping in for eagle at the 11th from a tough lie behind the green, Toms gained the lead for good. Another birdie at the 16th gave him a two-shot edge. On the 18th, Toms faced a winding 20-footer for birdie that seemed destined to go in when it left his putter. Walking after the ball as the crowd noise reached fever pitch, Toms raised his fist and let out a Tiger whoop of his own. His final-nine 30 was a record for English Turn, ending a week few in Louisiana will forget.

"It was pretty loud," Toms said. "I was screaming myself, too, so I could hear myself and them. The people were out in droves today. It was really incredible walking off that 18th green. I've never experienced anything like it."

Verizon Byron Nelson Classic—$4,500,000
Winner: Robert Damron

In this era, any event Tiger Woods plays is instantly elevated in stature. When Woods contends — as he usually does — that event becomes a spectacle destined for lead coverage. Throw in the fact that any score over 69 was considered a bad day, and the Verizon Byron Nelson Classic had all the markings of a good week.

Scott Verplank got things rolling with 62 on Thursday, a score that would have normally separated him from the field, but this week it only provided Verplank with a two-shot cushion over David Duval, Tim Herron and Chris Riley. Five players shot 65s, and Woods was one of nine who posted 66s on opening day.

Friday provided more of the same. Woods shot 68 and never sniffed the lead. Vijay Singh shot 64 and trailed by two. Even Fred Couples, all but retired from competitive golf, shot 63 in the second round. When the birdies finally stopped falling, Duval and Verplank shared the lead at 11-under-par 129, and even-par 140 missed the cut.

Justin Leonard, no fan of low-scoring golf courses, got into the act on Saturday with a course-record-tying 61 in front of his hometown crowd. "I love hard golf courses," Leonard said. "I don't think that will ever change. But, unfortunately, we don't play the most difficult golf courses under the most difficult conditions every week, so you have to be able to play under conditions where it's easy to score. I've played a lot of bad rounds on this golf course, so today is kind of nice."

Unfortunately, Leonard would have had to shoot 59 to gain the outright lead. With a Saturday 67 to go with earlier rounds of 66 and 64, Robert Damron put forth a bid for his first PGA Tour victory, tying Verplank for the lead. Leonard was one shot back, and Brian Watts, who hadn't been heard from much since his 1999 playoff loss to Mark O'Meara in the British Open, stood two back after a round of 63.

Woods shot 69 and seemed out of it. He was six shots back going into the final round. No one counted him out, especially not the leaders, who slept a little fretfully, knowing that Woods would tee off an hour or so ahead of them.

The world's No. 1 player didn't disappoint. He fired 63 at the leaders, a round the included a bogey at the 14th and a missed birdie putt at the 18th that would have given them something to shoot for. Instead, Woods settled for a tie for third with Duval and Nick Price at 266.

"I'm really pleased with the way I played this week considering that I haven't really played a whole lot this month," Woods said. The Verizon Byron Nelson Classic was Woods' first tournament since his Masters victory the first week in April. "I haven't really played at all. I've been laying low, practicing a little bit."

The rust showed, but just barely.

"Wow," Damron said as he looked up and saw Woods' name moving up the leaderboard. "I'm glad he doesn't have more holes to go. He can't birdie holes he doesn't have left."

Once Woods was in the clubhouse, Damron and Verplank knew what they had to do, which was beat each other. Both shot 32s on the second nine en route to rounds of 66 and totals of 17-under-par 263. Damron won the playoff with a 14-foot birdie putt on the fourth extra hole.

"I felt confident today, oddly enough," Damron said. "I never had any huge adrenaline rush. I never had any real butterflies. I just felt like I was going to hit the shot that I needed to hit at the time. It's a nice feeling. I don't normally feel that way."

MasterCard Colonial—$4,000,000
Winner: Sergio Garcia

To steal a quote from Yogi Berra, the MasterCard Colonial seemed like déjà vu all over again. There was Phil Mickelson, steaming toward another victory, chatting with reporters about his 66 on Saturday, and about his attitude entering the final round tied for the lead with Brett Quigley. "Confident," Mickelson said, when asked how he felt.

He was confident at the Masters, at Bay Hill, Pebble Beach, Atlanta and New Orleans, none of which Mickelson won. He was one-for-seven in 2001 when contending on Sunday, that win coming when a double bogey was good enough to beat Frank Lickliter in a playoff at the Buick Invitational.

So when Sergio Garcia, the 21-year-old Spanish phenom with all the potential in the world, starting making birdies on Sunday, history seemed destined to repeat itself. Hitting two irons off most tees to negotiate Colonial Country Club's narrow landing areas, Garcia started the final round with six straight birdies for a front-nine 29. That quickly erased the five-shot 54-hole deficit Garcia had faced when he teed off on Sunday. Then Garcia played steadily and smartly, showing a level of maturity that had been absent from some of his previous 32 U.S. starts. He made one more birdie on the second nine along with eight conservative pars for 63 and a 267 total.

Mickelson still had a chance. With Quigley shooting himself out of contention with 73 for a 272 total, the left-hander simply needed to hold on. He played the first seven holes in four under, which opened a substantial lead. Even par from the eighth to the clubhouse was all he needed.

Instead, Mickelson shot four over par on the final 11 holes. His troubles started at the eighth, when he failed to get up and down from a bunker. Then at the ninth, he power-lipped a short putt for par. From there, things only got worse. Two more bogeys and three more short misses contributed to Mickelson's second final-round collapse in his last three starts. This time his even-par 70 was only good enough for a tie for second place with Brian Gay at 269.

"It's frustrating and disappointing," Mickelson said. "The only way I know to overcome it is to try to get back in contention next week. I've had a lot of mental hurdles to overcome this year. It seems like I'm giving away my opportunities on Sundays instead of taking advantage of situations. On the front nine today I came out aggressively and played for birdies. As soon as I started playing for pars, I made some bogeys. I just seem to have a mental block on Sundays on the back nine."

This time Garcia stood by to take advantage of Mickelson's blunders. "They always say that winning the first one is the toughest," the new champion said. "Hopefully now I'll start doing some nice things."

Kemper Insurance Open—$3,500,000
Winner: Frank Lickliter

Sports columnist Thomas Boswell of *The Washington Post* dubbed the 2001 Kemper Insurance Open "The Golf Tournament from Hell." Not to dispute Mr. Boswell, but it rained like a Brazilian summer during this year's tournament. "If I ever get through this week, I'm going to buy a television without The Weather Channel because I'm so tired of looking at it," said tournament chairman Pete Cleaves.

Indeed the TPC at Avenel course looked more like American Adventures Water Park than the site of the only PGA Tour stop near Washington D.C. The sun never peeked through the clouds until after Frank Lickliter drained a par-saving 12-foot putt at the 72nd hole on Memorial Day Monday, which gave Lickliter a 68, a weeklong total of 268, and earned the Ohio native his first PGA Tour victory by one stroke over J.J. Henry.

"It wasn't the way I had hoped to finish," Lickliter said. "Toward the end it was pretty ugly. But that putt at the end felt pretty good."

By "ugly" Lickliter was referring to the bogeys he made on the 16th and 17th holes in the dawn hours of Monday after carrying a three-shot lead over Henry into the final three holes. With his lead whittled to a single shot and the pressure mounting, Lickliter was haunted by memories of another ugly finish earlier in the season. On the third playoff hole at the Buick Invitational, Lickliter had watched Phil Mickelson push his drive into a canyon, but rather than take the safe route, the then-winless 31-year-old had pulled out driver and hooked his tee shot into the same pit. Mickelson won the playoff with a double bogey.

Now, after missing only 11 greens in the last 54 holes, Lickliter pushed his approach into the rough beside the 18th green and hit a mediocre chip to set up the 12-footer for par. "I tried to remain in the moment," Lickliter said after admitting that he didn't look at the scoreboard at the 18th. "I just trusted myself."

That trust paid off. Henry, who shared the lead with Lickliter when play was finally called after three rain delays on Sunday, finished with 66, but came up one short at 269. "I played great," the 26-year-old Henry said of his best finish as a professional.

Spike McRoy followed a lackluster opening 71 with rounds of 66, 67 and 68 to finish tied for third place with Bradley Hughes and Mickelson, who finished with 65. "Finishing strong really made it worth coming out here this morning," Mickelson said. "It gives me a little momentum going into the next few weeks."

Memorial Tournament—$4,100,000
Winner: Tiger Woods

Tiger Woods continued his romp through the 2001 season, this time beating the weather, the golf course, the record book and 103 golfers while capturing his third consecutive Memorial Tournament title and winning his fifth event in six starts.

Paul Azinger, who led Woods by one stroke going into the final round, said, "Right now, he's the most dominant athlete in the history of sports. I don't know if the public appreciates it. They probably do, but if they don't, they should."

Azinger stood by as a witness to Woods' domination on Sunday. After a week plagued by weather delays, Woods went on a 45-minute tear that turned his one-stroke deficit into a four-stroke lead, hitting the kinds of shots that keep making highlight videos.

Woods played well enough to win, posting 66 to go with his previous rounds of 68, 69 and 68, and he had plenty of help from the other contenders. Azinger shot 74, after bogeying two of the par-fives. Stuart Appleby, two strokes down at sunrise, also shot 74 that included a quadruple-bogey seven on the par-three 12th.

All these disasters occurred after Woods hit the shot that defined the week, a towering 249-yard two iron on the par-five fifth hole that landed softly and stopped six feet from the hole. After watching that shot, Azinger tried an out-of-character three-wood shot from a similar distance that landed in the water and cost the leader his second bogey of the day. Woods made an eagle-three, and assumed the lead for good.

His 17-under-par 271 total won by six over Azinger and Sergio Garcia, and the margin prompted Azinger to say, "I hate that we didn't have a closer fight. I even apologized to him, because at this point, he almost looked bored. We were walking down the 17th and I said, 'I'm sorry I wasn't a better player for you today.'"

Woods said, "Thank you," and afterwards, Woods elaborated, "I've won here three different ways. The golf course does set up really well for me because I can use my driver a lot here, only because it rains every year. I'm sure it would be different if it didn't rain. You'd have to hit some iron shots and shape your ball to keep it in the fairway."

Few people remember when rain didn't dampen Jack Nicklaus' event, but the conditions seem to play into Woods' hands. "I can just bomb driver down there because it plugs," he said. He also put on a long-iron exhibition on the par-fives, playing 16 holes in 15 under par for the week, which proved to be the difference.

"I don't know about all of sports, but since I've been playing sports I've never seen anybody who dominated more," Nicklaus said. "What amazes me is that, week in and week out, he's prepared. There's never a slack. That's pretty special."

FedEx St. Jude Classic—$3,500,000

Winner: Bob Estes

When Bob Estes arrived on the first tee of the TPC at Southwind on Sunday at the FedEx St. Jude Classic, he knew two things for sure: He was going to be out-driven by 20 yards on every hole by his playing partner, and every fan in Memphis was rooting against him.

Not that Estes had done anything to offend the Tennessee faithful, it was that the other person in the final group was local resident and lovable screwup John Daly, who played himself into contention for the first time in six years on Saturday with 63.

Estes held one advantage: the lead. He led or was tied for the lead after every round, despite challenges from Daly, Bernhard Langer, Scott McCarron and even a couple of 40-somethings, Nick Price and Curtis Strange. With a course-record 61 on Thursday, Estes led by three. A second-round 66 kept him in the top spot, as did his third-round 69.

From listening to the crowd you would have never guessed Estes led on Saturday. It seemed that every spectator came for one reason: to see Big John Daly grip it and rip it. He didn't disappoint. When he hit a 216-yard six-iron shot to within eight feet on the 18th green and made the putt for 63, the golf course erupted with whistles and hog calls, cheers that would have distracted most players. But Estes made steady pars coming in to shoot 69 and lead by one.

As expected, Daly knocked his first tee shot far past Estes' golf ball. "I knew I was going to have to get used to it," Estes said. Even when Daly drew even with an eagle at the par-five fifth hole, the quiet Estes never looked rattled. He only made two bogeys in his first 54 holes, and he kept his composure on Sunday.

A birdie at the ninth, coupled with five bogeys by Daly between the seventh and 14th holes, gave Estes a four-shot lead over Strange, Langer, Scott McCarron and Tom Lehman. But Estes pulled his tee shots at the 14th and 15th holes and came away with two consecutive bogeys. That dropped him back to 17 under, only one ahead of Langer, who made five birdies in his first 16 holes to mount the most serious challenge.

The threat was short-lived, however. Langer missed birdie opportunities at the 17th and 18th, and, although Estes missed the 17th green, he made a 12-footer for par, then found the fairway with his drive at the 18th, hit a seven iron to six feet, and two-putted for an even-par 71, a 267 total and a one-shot victory over Langer, who finished with 66.

Lehman had just one bogey on the weekend and finished with a pair of 66s to tie McCarron for third place at 269, while Strange, another crowd favorite who was having his best week in recent memory, finished with two 69s for a share of fifth place at 270 with Daly and Paul Goydos.

Daly shot 73, 10 strokes worse than his Saturday score, but unlike years past, he didn't leave with a tantrum or implode with a huge number on one or two holes. "He realizes he's not going to get many more chances," said his fiancée, Shanae Chandler, herself a recovering addict. "There has been a whole change that's taken place in John's life, both on and off the course."

U.S. Open Championship—$5,000,000
Winner: Retief Goosen

See Chapter 3.

Buick Classic—$3,500,000
Winner: Sergio Garcia

Sergio Garcia picked up his second victory in four starts when he shot 16-under-par 268 at the Buick Classic in Harrison, New York. The win — with a three-shot margin over Scott Hoch — came only two weeks after Garcia was criticized for imploding in the final round of the U.S. Open. But the 77 Garcia shot in Tulsa turned out to be his only over-par round between his eighth-place finish at the Verizon Byron Nelson Classic and his win at the Buick Classic. Coupled with a second-place finish at the Memorial Tournament, the streak moved Garcia into the top five on the PGA Tour money list and the top six in the World Ranking.

In New York the young Spaniard put together one of his most consistent displays of the year. Rounds of 68 and 67 put him atop the leaderboard with Hoch. Rain washed out Saturday's round, but it didn't dampen Garcia's play. Closing rounds of 66 and 67 on the par-71 West Course at Westchester Country Club gave Garcia the victory by three strokes.

"He can do whatever he wants with the ball," Hoch said of Garcia. "I haven't seen a weakness. The thing he does best is drive the ball. He's as good a driver of the ball as I've seen since Greg Norman when it comes to distance and accuracy. Tiger Woods is not as accurate as Sergio. Sergio can hit driver on holes where Tiger hits an iron."

Garcia agreed with that assessment, although he bristled when asked on Monday if his victory was sweeter because he had beaten Woods. "Saying that is disrespectful of all the other golfers on the tour," Garcia said. "I'm hitting the ball better, putting better, and getting better breaks. Before the Byron Nelson, it was bad break after bad break. I also think I'm handling myself a lot better on the golf course. I think I'm getting closer and closer to where I want to be."

While Woods drew most of the early-week attention, he never recovered from an opening 75. By Monday afternoon he was 12 shots back. A closing 71 left Woods in a tie for 16th and looking forward to a break. When asked about his plans, he said he was "golfed out," and was looking forward to fishing. "You can't play good every week," Woods said. "I tried on every shot, but it really wasn't there. Nothing's the matter, I just don't want to play golf right now. I just need a little time off."

Leading by two when the final round began, Garcia made five opening pars and saw his lead dwindle. Hoch rolled in birdie putts at the fourth and fifth holes to temporarily gain a share of the lead, but Garcia snatched the top spot back with a birdie at the 326-yard, par-four seventh, a hole where he almost drove the green.

Both Hoch and Garcia birdied the 10th, but when Garcia hit a nine-iron approach to within a foot of the hole at the 13th and tapped in for birdie, the lead was two. Hoch was never closer. Trying to make eagle on the par-five 18th, Hoch pushed his approach into the rough, chunked his pitch shot, and settled for his eighth consecutive par on the second nine. Garcia reached the final green with a two iron and two-putted for a birdie and a three-shot edge.

"Today it could have been so low," Garcia said. "I played so well today."

He also had some words for those who continued to criticize his swing, and his swing coach, who happens to be his father, Victor. "Everybody was thinking, 'Well, you've got to change your swing,'" Garcia said. "'If you don't, you're done, you are over, you had better retire.' All of a sudden it looks like I am the best player in the world. I think everybody who said that my swing was bad and I had to change it, I think they're going to have to eat all those words. I think it's a pretty good swing."

Canon Greater Hartford Open—$3,100,000
Winner: Phil Mickelson

With only four bogeys in 72 holes and only one in his last 39 holes, Phil Mickelson went a long way toward erasing the bad memories of his blown chances in 2001 when he shot a final-round 68 to edge Billy Andrade by a single shot in the Canon Greater Hartford Open. It was Mickelson's third victory of the year, but it was the first time in 2001 he had been able to effectively close out a win after holding the 54-hole lead.

"At times this year I was letting my mind wander a little bit and just not keying on what I wanted to do down the stretch," Mickelson said. "I was confident in my physical development, but I wasn't focused mentally."

Before arriving in Hartford, Mickelson's final-round scoring average was 70.69, a full shot higher than his overall average, and the reason he was 0-4 in 2001 when holding a final-round lead. This week was a different story. After starting out with solid rounds of 67 and 68, Mickelson shot a career-best nine-under-par 61 on Saturday, equaling the 18-hole tournament record, to take a one-shot lead over David Berganio, Jr.

Berganio, playing in the final group with Mickelson, struggled with his driver in the final round and finished with a one-under 69, good enough for a 266 total and a tie for third, the best finish of his career.

"I just made a couple of mistakes," Berganio said. "I handled myself well, and I'm proud of that. I haven't fulfilled my potential coming out of college. I was one of the two best in the country my senior year. David Duval was the Jack Nicklaus Award winner and I was runner-up. Obviously he is having a great career so far, and no one has heard of me."

The $161,200 he earned in Hartford pushed Berganio's earnings over the half-million mark for the season and insured that he would keep his PGA Tour card for 2002. "The pressure is off," he said. "Now I can just go out and play. Maybe go out and win a couple."

The pressure wasn't off Mickelson, who was still handling questions about his final-round problems. "As I look on my career, it is the process that I really enjoy," Mickelson said. "When I falter or have difficulties in tournaments, that's part of the challenge. If I were to win in every one, then it wouldn't be as rewarding and fulfilling when I do win. Without those difficulties I wouldn't appreciate the times that I have been successful."

This time he was successful. While Berganio was faltering, bogeying two of his first five holes on Sunday, Mickelson birdied the third, sixth and seventh holes to get to 17 under. At the turn, his lead was three. He then made five straight pars before reaching the 296-yard, par-four 15th. Hitting a three wood off the tee in the hopes of taking advantage of a helping wind, Mickelson pushed his tee shot into the adjacent lake and made his first bogey of the weekend.

In the group ahead of Mickelson, Billy Andrade drove the 15th green and two-putted for birdie to reach 14 under, cutting Mickelson's lead to two. Andrade then sank a 20-footer for birdie at the 18th to cut the lead to one. But pars by Mickelson on the 16th and 17th, followed by a solid tee shot of 315 yards, a wedge to 20 feet and two putts for a par on the 18th silenced his critics.

"I think (those last three tee shots) were critical shots," he said. "It was very easy to get some negative thoughts and make tentative swings, but I was able to see what I wanted to do and hit the shots when I needed them."

Mickelson finished with his 68 for a 264 total and a one-shot victory over Andrade, who had his best finish since winning the Invensys Las Vegas Invitational in 2000. Berganio finished tied for third with Chris DiMarco, who also shot a final-round 68, and a charging Dudley Hart, who shot 63 on Sunday.

When it was over, Mickelson knew that this win wouldn't completely silence those who thought he should have won more. But it was a good start. "I didn't hit it any better or putt any better than I have in any other tournament," Mickelson said. "But just the way I approached each shot was from a much more positive frame of mind. I was able to see what I wanted to do and feel in my golf swing, what I needed to do to create that shot."

Advil Western Open—$3,600,000
Winner: Scott Hoch

Playing some of the best golf of his life, 45-year-old Scott Hoch could barely contain his glee as he rolled in an 18-inch par putt on the 72nd hole to win the Advil Western Open by one shot over Davis Love III. "This has got to be one of my best memories in golf," Hoch said. "This is probably the biggest tournament I've ever won, and to win two tournaments in one year, especially as old as I am, that's something special. My family being here, that's the most special of all."

In addition to defeating a cadre of younger players that included Love, Tiger Woods and Phil Mickelson, Hoch's 267 total was the lowest score in the 99-year history of the Western Open. The previous record was 268 set by Sam Snead in 1949 and equaled by Chi Chi Rodriguez in 1964.

"Gosh, I feel fortunate," Hoch said after closing with an eight-under-par 64 to set the record. "Scoring-wise, I couldn't have done much better."

Love called Hoch's round "perfect," even though he was one swing away from a perfect round of his own. Leading by one shot going into the final round, Love made three birdies in the first five holes, but the lead remained only a single shot. Hoch matched him birdie for birdie on the first nine, and by the time they reached the 10th tee it was a two-man race. Brandel Chamblee and Mike Weir were the closest players to Hoch and Love and they were both seven shots back.

Hoch finally caught Love at the par-three 12th when he rolled in a 25-foot birdie putt. Love's birdie effort from 35 feet came up inches short, and the two shared the top spot for the first time all week.

Love regained the lead at the par-four 13th when he almost holed his approach. Walking to the 14th tee, Hoch turned to Love and said, "It didn't take you long to get that shot back, did it?" Love smiled and continued to play aggressively. He ran into trouble at the long, par-four 16th when his second shot landed in the rough to the right of the green. From a tricky downhill lie, Love bladed his chip over the green and into a bunker. He got up and down for his bogey, but left the door open for Hoch, who had a 12-footer for birdie to take the lead outright. Hoch missed his birdie, but tapped in for par to regain a share of the lead with two holes to play.

Both players birdied the 17th, Love with a 17-footer and Hoch capping him with a 12-foot effort of his own. That set up the drama of the final hole. If both players made pars, they would both break the tournament scoring record. The last time anyone came close to this kind of scoring was 1993 when Nick Price shot 19-under 269 at Cog Hill to win going away. This was great scoring and great drama to boot.

It was a shame it had to end with one par and one bogey on the final hole, but when Love pushed his tee shot into the corporate hospitality tents right of the fairway, Hoch had the break he needed. "When I saw that shot I said, 'Whoo! Door's open now,'" Hoch said.

Love punched his second shot back to the fairway, then hit his third shot 12 feet beyond the hole. When his par putt slid low and left, Love dropped his head and put his hands on his knees. Hoch reached the green in two, and two-putted for the win.

"I did a lot of good things," said Love, who finished with 66 for his 268 total. "I just didn't play a perfect round like Scott did."

Hoch was also complimentary of Love, summarizing his win by saying, "Two guys just got in a groove. It was very special for me to play well against such a good player who was also playing well."

Greater Milwaukee Open—$3,100,000

Winner: Shigeki Maruyama

Shigeki Maruyama was only 13 years old in 1983 when Isao Aoki holed his approach shot for an eagle on the 72nd hole of the Hawaiian Open and became the first Japanese golfer to win a PGA Tour event. It was little wonder that when Maruyama sank a four-foot birdie putt on the first extra hole to defeat Charles Howell and win the Greater Milwaukee Open, the 31-year-old Japanese player closed his eyes, raised his arms into the air and yelled in celebration.

He had good reason to celebrate. In addition to being the first native of Japan to ever win a PGA Tour event on the U.S. mainland (although Aoki won quite a few titles on the Senior PGA Tour), Maruyama's victory earned him $558,000. He also had the privilege of beating one of the best up-and-coming players in the game. Howell birdied six of the last seven holes, including birdies on the final four holes of regulation, to shoot a closing 64 and come into the clubhouse at 18-under-par 266, tied for the lead with Maruyama.

"I didn't know if I had a chance to win," Howell said, "but I tried to make as many birdies as I could to put some pressure on him."

Howell did put pressure on the leader. Maruyama made three birdies and an eagle in his first 10 holes on Sunday before recording his only bogey at the 11th. Another birdie at the 15th moved Maruyama back to 18 under with the reachable par-five 18th still ahead. But Maruyama appeared to rush his second shot on the final hole, and the ball sailed over the green and into the grandstands. After a free drop, Maruyama chipped to 15 feet, but left his birdie putt a good two feet short. Howell was on the driving range at the time, but stopped hitting balls long enough to watch Maruyama sink the two-footer for par and a final round of 66. The two were tied at 266 and they headed back to the 18th for a playoff.

This time it was Howell who had trouble at the 18th. An errant tee shot and lackluster recovery left Howell with few options. When his third shot flew over the green, it was all but over. Maruyama hit his second shot into the back fringe and chipped to four feet. When the birdie putt found the hole, the PGA Tour had a new winner — one for whom English was still a bigger battle than the best players in the world.

"Shigeki is a great player," Howell said. "He's probably one of the nicest guys out here. He's always smiling. But now he's got a reason to smile."

Howell also had reason to smile. Although his place on the 2002 PGA Tour was almost a certainty, the $334,800 he earned for finishing second secured his place on next year's active roster. "It's nice to know you have a job," Howell said. "It's a huge relief."

J.P. Hayes shot the low round of the tournament on Sunday, carding an eight-under 63 for 269 total and a tie for third with Tim Herron. But even Hayes had nothing but praise for the winner. "I don't know what the general public thinks about Shigeki's game," Hayes said. "But all the players know that he's an excellent player. He's played quite well over here."

B.C. Open—$2,000,000
Winner: Jeff Sluman

After six failed attempts in his near-decade-long playing career, Jeff Sluman finally won a playoff at the 2001 B.C. Open. He sank an eight-foot birdie putt on the second extra hole in Endicott, New York, to beat Paul Gow. When the putt fell, Sluman dropped his head and raised his fist, relieved that the drought had finally ended.

"I've lost them in one-man, two-man, six-man playoffs, just about everything you can think of," Sluman said. "I just wanted to get off the 'schneid,' and I did. It makes me feel pretty good."

Sluman's mood swung back and forth between depression and joy in the final hour of the tournament. Coming off a disappointing final round one week before at the Milwaukee Open — a tournament Sluman led after the third round but in which he finished tied for 10th — the nine-year veteran who grew up in Rochester played himself into a share of the lead again with rounds of 67, 68 and 65. That was no consolation. In his career Sluman had held the lead going into the final round seven times, but he had only won once. Coupled with the disappointing finish at Milwaukee, Sluman wasn't sure how things would work out in Endicott.

Neither was Gow, an Australian PGA Tour rookie with only one top-20 finish on the year. Gow shot 69, 65 and 66 to hold a share of the lead going into Sunday, but he should have held the lead outright. On Friday, Gow made a mental error on the 11th green when, upset after a putt lipped the hole and failed to go in, the 30-year-old threw a penny at the ball moving it a fraction of an inch. That cost Gow a one-stroke penalty, a shot that would be sorely missed later in the week.

Sluman and Gow remained close throughout the final round, swapping birdies and bogeys for most of the day, and distancing themselves from the rest of the field. When Gow failed to get up and down from the greenside rough at the 17th, it appeared all but over. Sluman's par gave him a two-shot lead with one hole to play. An errant tee shot on the 18th by Sluman, followed by an approach that sailed over the green, and two outstanding shots by Gow, who left himself with only four feet for birdie, created more drama and anxiety than Sluman wanted. When he missed a 12-foot par putt, Sluman closed his eyes and rubbed his nose as Gow putted. The four-footer was dead center. Both men had shot 66s for totals of 266, one shy of the tournament record, but one more than either of them needed for an outright win.

Both men scrambled for pars on the first playoff hole. Then on the second playoff hole, the 18th, Sluman found the fairway and the green while Gow lost his tee shot to the right. The Aussie's ball hit a tree and careened into a concrete culvert. The culvert was a hazard, so Gow elected to chip his ball back to the fairway. From there he hit his third shot to within 13 feet, but missed the par putt. Sluman then made an eight-footer for a birdie he did not need.

"I think the way I won was very satisfying," Sluman said afterward. "I went out and played the way I thought I was capable of playing. Coming on the heels of not playing well with the lead last week, I guess you can say it's doubly satisfying."

Gow was also satisfied, despite losing. The $216,000 he received for second place surpassed his total previous earnings on tour. "I learned a lot of things," he said. "I learned I can play and compete against these guys. You know I matched one of the best players in the world all day. I'm proud of the way I held up down the stretch. Jeff just putted better than I did today. But it was great fun."

John Deere Classic—$2,800,000
Winner: David Gossett

Not long after his victory in the 1999 U.S. Amateur, David Gossett found himself responding to comparisons between himself and another successful U.S. Amateur champion, Tiger Woods. "I played with Tiger last year at the British Open," Gossett said. "I loved it. I like playing with the best."

Gossett also likes beating the best, which the 22-year-old from Germantown,

Tennessee, was accustomed to doing during most of his amateur career. But after turning professional in late 1999, Gossett's game fell on hard times. He failed to qualify for the PGA Tour in the seven sponsor's exemptions he was given, and failed again to earn his way through his play on the Buy.com Tour. In the 2000 qualifying tournament Gossett caught the attention of the media and his fellow competitors when he shot 59 in the opening round. But four scores in the 70s dropped Gossett out of the running for his player's card again, and he was relegated to another year in the minors.

All that changed on a foggy Sunday afternoon in Silvis, Illinois, when Gossett rolled in a seven-foot par putt on the 18th hole at the TPC of Deer Run and walked away as the winner of the John Deere Classic. His final-round 66 and 265 total were good enough for a one-stroke victory over Briny Baird, making Gossett the first player to win a PGA Tour event on a sponsor's exemption since the 1996 Las Vegas Invitational, when the winner was none other than Tiger Woods.

"Obviously it's great to be mentioned in the same breath with the best player in the world," Gossett said. "But I've got a long way to go."

The International—$4,000,000
Winner: Tom Pernice, Jr.

Outside the intimate traveling caravan of the PGA Tour not much was known about Tom Pernice, Jr. before his one-point victory in The International. After edging out Chris Riley in the modified-Stableford event, Pernice warmed the hearts of golf fans when he embraced his two daughters behind the 18th green at Castle Pines. Kristen Pernice, age seven, looked into her father's face and shared his smile, while Brooke, age six, could only feel dad's expression, running her hands over his damp cheeks and broad grin.

"Every time we have an eye-specialist exam, every six months, it's getting better," Pernice said of Brooke's failed eyesight. "Brooke is going to be in the first grade next year. She can read and write Braille at about a third-grade level. Her math skills are at a fourth grade level. She is unbelievably special. She's getting more light to her eyes. She's doing much better. She still can't see much, but she can see whether the lights are on or off or whether it's light out or dark out."

Pernice's face lit up when speaking of his daughter, a refreshing change from the scowl he and his fellow competitors wore throughout most of the day on Sunday. Despite the strong field in Colorado, the golf was pretty sorry. Only one player reached double digits in the points race on Sunday. Brett Quigley made 13 points in the final round, which propelled him into a tie for sixth with Brad Faxon at 30 points.

As usual, the scoring system befuddled some. Australian Paul Gow misunderstood the system and picked his ball up after missing a par putt, assuming bogey was the highest score players could take. Double bogey was the maximum score, and Gow cost himself two points. That wasn't the only error of the week. Sergio Garcia inadvertently marked and lifted his ball in the fairway on Saturday after the first two rounds were played under lift-clean-and-place rules. By the third round the course had dried, and Garcia's error cost him a one-stroke penalty.

Then there was the errant shotmaking. Pernice posted a medal score of 66 in the first round and followed it up with two rounds of 68. That equaled 33 points and Pernice entered Sunday's final round with a three-point lead. The lead evaporated quickly. Chris DiMarco began the day with 28 points, but made up ground with birdies at the fifth, sixth and seventh holes, followed by an eagle at the par-five eighth. That run gave DiMarco 39 points and a six-point lead. But the lead vanished as quickly as it was found. DiMarco made two double bogeys and one bogey in his next eight holes, falling to only four points on the day and 32 for the week. He finished tied for third.

"This is very disappointing," DiMarco said. "I've put myself in position to win a lot out here. I think this is the first win that I've really thrown away."

Others had opportunities as well. Vijay Singh, who played with Pernice on Sunday, arrived at the reachable par-five 17th needing a birdie. Instead, he made bogey. When Pernice tapped in for par, Singh knew he had thrown away his best chance at victory. A birdie instead of a bogey would have meant a three-point swing. Singh would have held a one-point lead with one hole to play. Instead, he finished tied for third with DiMarco and Ernie Els.

When all was said and done, Pernice didn't mention any of his three birdies on Sunday, but, appropriately enough, said the bogey he made at the par-three 16th hole was the turning point of the tournament. After hitting his tee shot in the greenside bunker on that hole, Pernice failed to blast out with his first shot. His second bunker shot landed within a foot of the hole, and he tapped in for bogey.

"I hit probably the worst shot I could hit there," he said. "The second (bunker) shot was miraculous. That probably won me the tournament."

Meanwhile, Riley made three birdies in his final eight holes for a 33-point total and sole possession of second place. "I didn't know how I stood," he said afterward. "I just kept playing. When they told me I finished second, it was hard to believe."

Pernice was just as excited as Riley, but being a little older, and with his family by his side, he was better able to put things into perspective. "They're the two most important things in my life," the winner said of his daughters. "We travel a lot, and don't get to see our families much. There are plenty of golf tournaments. But I only have two daughters."

One of them could see the tears that welled in her father's eyes as he said those words. The other could only touch them.

Buick Open—$3,100,000
Winner: Kenny Perry

With a major championship looming on the horizon and Ryder Cup qualifying on the line, the plots and subplots at the Buick Open were many. Kenny Perry cared about none of it. All he wanted was a victory. When Perry closed out his bogey-free round of 69 on Sunday at Warwick Hills Country Club, he had just that — the fourth victory of his career and his first since 1995.

"I didn't think I was ever going to win again, to tell you the truth," Perry said after his impressive 25-under-par 263 total beat Chris DiMarco and Jim Furyk by two shots. "It made me appreciate those three (earlier) wins even more."

Perry won with style, setting a 54-hole tournament record at 22-under 194 after rounds of 66, 64 and 64. His Friday and Saturday rounds included two nine-hole scores of 29, making Perry the first player in PGA Tour history to record two under-30 nines in one tournament. He entered Sunday with a five-shot lead over Padraig Harrington.

Before he could get his courtesy car parked on Sunday morning, the leaderboard was changing. Billy Mayfair, playing before the greens baked out, shot an early 61, which included 27 on the second nine, another PGA Tour record. Mayfair also set a record for the most consecutive holes under par, playing the eighth through the 16th with nothing but birdies and eagles. "The hole just looked as big as a tub," Mayfair said. "I just tried to stay out of my own way." Mayfair posted his 271 total before 1:00 p.m., then retired to the locker room to see how his score held up.

"That put some fear in me," Perry said of Mayfair's early blitz. Under grueling heat, scores tended to go low on Sunday, and Perry wasn't sure what it was going to take to win.

Dudley Hart pulled to within a stroke, but Perry stayed aggressive, driving the green on the par-four 14th to set up a birdie. Meanwhile, Hart bogeyed the 17th, and Perry's cushion increased to three shots. Furyk and DiMarco posted scores of 66 and 65 respectively, but neither could get closer than two shots behind the leader.

"Second place is never great," Furyk said. "It's a good spot to finish in, but it always leaves you a little empty because you got so close."

DiMarco was also disappointed. A share of second place moved him from 16th to 11th in Ryder Cup points, but, as he put it, "I'm probably going to have to earn it. I'm not going to put any more pressure on myself, but I've been playing good. I just have to keep playing good."

Perry had no Ryder Cup ambitions or dreams of contending for another PGA Championship. "I didn't even look at the Ryder Cup, I'm so far behind," he said. "I hadn't won in five years. I began to wonder, will I ever get it back? Can I do this again? Where did it go? It makes you realize how special it is to win out here. First one at The Memorial in 1991 was the sweetest because it told me I belonged out here. Second one, the New England Classic in 1994, I beat David Feherty. I saw him out there this week doing his broadcasting. He said he still hasn't forgiven me."

Furyk and DiMarco promised to hold no such grudges this time around.

PGA Championship—$5,200,000
Winner: David Toms

See Chapter 5.

WGC NEC Invitational—$5,000,000
Winner: Tiger Woods

The week before the WGC NEC Invitational, with Tiger Woods out of contention at the PGA Championship, Phil Mickelson lamented his lost opportunity for a goal he had hoped was in his grasp. "If I won the PGA, I thought I had a shot at Player of the Year," Mickelson said. "That was a goal."

A week later the door wasn't just closed on Mickelson's chances, it was nailed shut. For the sixth time in 2001, Tiger Woods hoisted a winner's trophy and cashed a first-place check, this one for a million dollars at the WGC NEC Invitational. It was Woods' third consecutive victory at the Akron, Ohio, event, and in addition to pushing his career earnings over the $25 million mark, it put a lock on the Player of the Year trophy.

A year before, Woods finished the rain-delayed WGC NEC Invitational in the dark, lofting an eight-iron approach shot to the final hole that finished six inches away from the flagstick to cap an 11-stroke rout of Justin Leonard and Phillip Price. That win came a week after Woods won his third straight major title in record fashion at the PGA Championship.

This year, Woods was supposedly struggling. He hadn't won a major since April when he picked up his second Masters title and became the first in history to hold all four major championship trophies at one time, but he had missed too many fairways and too many short putts at the 2001 PGA Championship to be a factor.

Woods bristled at suggestions of a slump, but he knew the only way to quiet his critics was with his clubs. He did just that in Akron with four rounds in the 60s, followed by a seven-hole playoff with Jim Furyk. Woods finally won the two-hour marathon when his approach to the 18th stopped two feet from the hole.

"It was a war out there," Woods said afterward. "Neither one of us was going to give an inch. When we didn't mess up — and we did make our share of mistakes out there — we recovered pretty good. We made some big putts, big saves, hole-outs, you name it. Today was a lot of fun, win or lose. It was just fun to compete like that where you were tested to the absolute utmost."

In an attempt to avoid the sunset finish of the previous year, PGA Tour officials started the final round at 7:45 a.m. due to the threat of thunderstorms in the area. That turned out to be a fortuitous move. Woods, who started Sunday's round two shots off Furyk's lead, grabbed the lead with a birdie on the 13th while Furyk was making bogey. At the 15th, the roles were reversed; Woods made bogey and Furyk regained the lead with a birdie. Woods tied it again with a birdie at the 16th. When both players made bogey from the back bunker at the 18th, they found themselves knotted at 268 and trotted back to the 18th tee for what turned out to be the longest PGA Tour playoff in over a decade.

The fireworks started early in the playoff. After finding the same bunker behind the 18th green, Furyk looked to be out of it when he left his third shot in the sand. Woods putted to five feet and appeared in command. But Furyk holed his second bunker shot for par, igniting the crowd.

"I'm thinking holing it the whole way," Furyk said. "Tiger leaves his putt short and that takes maybe a little of the aggressiveness out. I would hate to try to make it, blow it way by and give him the win. I wanted to make him make that putt."

Woods did just that, holing the five-footer to continue the playoff. He then sank a 20-footer for par on the second playoff hole to keep things moving forward. On and on they went until the fifth playoff hole when Woods hit another miraculous shot after pulling his drive into the trees. He punched back to the fairway, then took his 60-degree sand wedge, closed down the face, and played a shot he called "the two-hop skipper," to within three feet.

"If it was down-grain, I would have played a one-hopper and just flown it more toward the top of the crest," Woods said. "But I was into the grain and I couldn't afford to fly the ball there, so I tried to be a little more steep. It came out absolutely perfect."

On the sixth extra hole Woods thought he had ended it with a 50-footer. With the ball just inches from the hole, he raised his putter and stared it down only to drop the putter and fall to his knees when the ball caught the edge of the hole and didn't drop. "I don't know how that putt didn't go in," he said.

Then came the finale, another spectacular, pressure-filled approach shot from Woods that climbed out of sight before falling just behind the hole. Furyk hit his drive into the trees, failed to reach the fairway with his second shot, and came up just short of the green with his third. Even if he had holed another chip it would have been too little too late. Woods finally finished it with a routine birdie on the seventh extra hole.

"I was very lucky," Woods said. "I very easily could have missed a couple of those putts or not had shots. A lot of different scenarios could have happened where I would not have won. Win or lose I don't think either of us are going to feel real bad because of what transpired out there. We both gave absolutely everything we had."

Reno-Tahoe Open—$3,000,000
Winner: John Cook

Starting six shots off of Jerry Kelly's lead in the final round, 43-year-old John Cook thought he would be fortunate to finish in the top five at the Reno-Tahoe Open, especially after shooting 74 on Saturday.

"To stay competitive in your mid-40s is not easy," Cook said. "Especially with all the things going on in your life. Golf is maybe number five or six on my priority list."

Cook was competitive on Sunday, scorching the first nine at the Montreux Golf and Country Club with a run of birdie-eagle-birdie-birdie on the fourth through the seventh holes as part of a six-under-par 30. He closed with 34 on the second nine for an eight-under-par 64 and a 17-under-par 271 total. Still Cook trailed Kelly, who seemed destined for his first PGA Tour victory after shooting rounds of 66, 68 and 67 to take a one-stroke lead over Bryce Molder into the final round. Cook was in the locker room eating a sandwich when his fortunes changed on Sunday afternoon.

Kelly maintained a one-shot edge over Cook through 15 holes, but his tee shot on the par-three 16th found the rough. With the blade of his sand wedge opened, Kelly took a full swing from the rough, but no ball was forthcoming. The clubhead slid under the ball, moving it only a couple of feet. Still in the rough, Kelly repeated the same swing with the same result. The ball was still in the rough after Kelly's third shot. His fourth shot finally moved the ball onto the green, but well behind the hole. When Kelly's putt for double bogey lipped out, he tapped in for triple-bogey six. Just like that, Kelly had gone from leading by one to trailing by two.

"It was one of those things that makes you love and hate the game," Kelly said afterward. "I set up for the chips well, and I stroked the chips well. It wasn't like a choke kind of thing at all. I went through and I just happened to go under it. There was more grass than I thought."

Kelly missed an eight-footer for birdie at the 636-yard, par-five 17th, but he still almost forced a playoff when his second shot from 94 yards on the 18th rolled over the hole and stopped four inches away.

"I played it absolutely exactly the way I wanted to and it just missed," Kelly said of his final shot. "If that thing would have hit the flagstick, it was going in."

Instead, Kelly settled for a birdie and sole possession of second place with 71 for a 272 total.

"I feel bad for Jerry," Cook said. "It was difficult to watch. I've been there. I've done that. I've done that at the British Open with a chance to win. It happens to everybody. But I shot 64, so I didn't exactly back into it. I had made only three eagles all year, and I made three this week. Like Ken Venturi says, 'It's fun to win!'"

Air Canada Championship—$3,400,000
Winner: Joel Edwards

After more than a decade of struggle and doubt, Joel Edwards was tumbling headlong toward his 40th birthday without a victory on the PGA Tour. He had never even led after 54 holes. His best finish was a tie for second in the 1992 B.C. Open. So when Edwards posted rounds of 65, 67 and 68 at the Northview Golf and Country Club to take a four-shot lead into the final round of the Air Canada Championship, he found himself in uncharted waters.

"It's a moment in your life when all the doubt there is just washed away," Edwards said after closing with 65 to win his first tournament with a 19-under-par 265 total for a seven-stroke margin over Steve Lowery. Edwards' $612,000 first-place check doubled his earnings for the year. "It's something you think about for a long time," he said. "I started thinking about it when I was 14 and I've been playing for 25 years and I've always dreamed of this."

That dream was never really in jeopardy as Edwards ran away from the rest of the field with four straight birdies on the second nine on Sunday. He birdied the first hole to widen his lead to five, but gave two strokes back when he bogeyed the reachable par-five fourth. Fred Funk pulled to within two shots on the first nine, but Edwards quickly widened the lead again with birdies at the seventh and eighth.

"When I made that bogey it kind of calmed me down," Edwards said. "I just said to myself, 'You don't have anything to lose. Just don't look too far ahead.'"

He didn't, and when he birdied the 12th, 13th, 14th and 15th holes, the victory was secure. A bogey at the 16th didn't faze him. As they approached the 18th tee Edwards asked his caddie, "What kind of lead have we got?" The caddie laughed. "Does that mean it's more than two?" Edwards asked. "Yeah," the caddie said. "It's more than two."

Edwards hit a perfect approach over the water at the 18th to within three feet of the hole. When he rolled that birdie putt in, he covered his eyes and wept. "When you get nervous you just want to be as aggressive as possible," he said. "I felt comfortable with every club in my bag and I knew I was just playing well."

Lowery, who shot 66 for 272 total and sole possession of second place, agreed with Edwards' assessment. "For his first win to go out there and be six under today, that's great," Lowery said. "He made some good shots early and made some birdies to free himself up. The guy has been playing for so long. It's tough to come out here and not win in your whole career."

Funk's putter cooled on the second nine and he finished with 69, good enough for a tie for third with Matt Kuchar at 273, while Brent Geiberger, David Gossett and Kevin Sutherland finished tied for fifth at 274.

Bell Canadian Open—$3,800,000
Winner: Scott Verplank

Three weeks after being named as the surprise captain's pick to the U.S. Ryder Cup team, Scott Verplank answered his critics with a closing 67 and a three-shot victory at the Bell Canadian Open.

"Maybe the critics who thought I was the wrong guy can sleep better now," Verplank said with a smile. "Obviously, I'm playing okay. Not that it really matters to me, but maybe to everybody else it makes Curtis Strange look a little smarter than he was."

Strange's insight grew as the week progressed. Defending champion Tiger Woods led on Thursday after a 65, but a lost ball in the top of a pine tree on Friday cost Woods the chance at a repeat. He never recovered from his second-round 73 and finished tied for 23rd place with a 276 total. The only bright spot in Woods' week was having one of his biggest fans playing in his threesome the first two days.

"I watched every shot he took, and I'm not ashamed to admit it," Joel Edwards said. Edwards earned the pairing with Woods by virtue of his victory in the Air Canada Classic. It was a priceless experience for the 39-year-old Texan. "It was a circus," Edwards said. "But it was neat. He couldn't have been nicer. Tiger is not only filling our pockets with the trickle-down effect of his success, but he's got a good heart. I also realized I couldn't possibly deal with what Tiger does every day. I'd have to go home and sell golf balls instead."

Verplank wasn't selling golf balls or looking in the rough for very many either. He took advantage of the dry, hot conditions on Friday and Saturday to shoot rounds of 63 and 66 and take a two-shot lead over Bob Estes into Sunday.

Verplank made a 30-footer for birdie at the 15th to extend his lead to three shots, but he immediately gave that back and then some. A sloppy double bogey at the 16th allowed Estes, Joey Sindelar and John Daly all to pull within one shot. But Verplank restored order with a birdie at the par-three 17th.

The final hole provided plenty of drama, however, as Verplank pushed his driver 60 yards right of the fairway. He was so far right, in fact, that he had a great lie in the first fairway of the other course that graces the grounds of Royal Montreal Golf Club. After asking a couple of television trucks to drive out of his line, Verplank pitched back to the fairway and proceeded to hit his third shot 25 feet left of the hole. When that par putt found the hole, Verplank stared at the sky and raised both arms into the air.

"You can't call me boring anymore after that finish," he said.

You can't call him an odd pick for the Ryder Cup either. "Look, I realize there are more popular players out there, or guys with more name recognition," Verplank said. "But I didn't make the picks; Curtis did. And the feeling I get from the people I respect most, the guys in the locker room, is that I belong on the team."

Verplank finished with 266, the same score Woods shot the previous year in his victory over Grant Waite. Only this time there were plenty of others vying for the victory. Estes and Sindelar brought it home at 11-under 269 and shared second place, while Daly had the best weekend of anyone in the field, finishing with rounds of 64 and 66 for a 10-under 270 total and sole possession of fourth. David Morland, Paul Gow and Sergio Garcia finished tied for fifth at 271, with Morland making the best recovery of that group. After a Saturday 73, Morland came back with a 66 for his best finish of the year.

Marconi Pennsylvania Classic—$3,300,000
Winner: Robert Allenby

In a subdued and patriotic week where cheers were sparse and tears were plentiful, the PGA Tour resumed operations after a week off due to the terrorist attacks of September 11. Laurel Valley Golf Club in Ligonier, Pennsylvania, was the site of the Marconi Pennsylvania Classic, with Arnold Palmer acting as host and American flags adorning each of the flagsticks.

"The world has changed," said Scott Verplank, who won the Bell Canadian Open 36 hours before the World Trade Center towers collapsed. "You've got to define what normal is now, because it's different than it used to be." Still, at the urging of President Bush, the PGA Tour did what the rest of the country did: They went back to work, but with almost half-hearted effort.

After an opening round of 70, Australian Robert Allenby, who now makes his home in Orlando, said, "I was playing for the sake of playing. I wasn't concentrating." He never fully gained the level of concentration he might have had, but Allenby did return to form in the second round when he hit all 18 greens en route to 65. Saturday was more of the same. Allenby missed only two greens and shot 66, even though the third round had to be concluded on Sunday morning due to a fog embankment that rolled into Pennsylvania late Saturday afternoon.

"I don't think I could have hit it any better," Allenby said. "It was the best week tee-to-green that I've ever had."

Rocco Mediate, who grew up 20 miles from Laurel Valley and was considered a home favorite, stood alone in second place after three rounds, and was only three shots back going into the final 18.

But Allenby never faltered. Wearing a pin on his cap that displayed the American and Australian flags side by side — a gift he had received from the Australian ambassador at a dinner party in Washington — Allenby tuned out the crowds and kept his emotions in check. He matched Mediate shot for shot through the first eight holes of the final round. Then he broke away, hitting a seven iron to four feet on the ninth and making the birdie putt to move to 17 under par. He followed that up with birdies at the 10th and 11th from 30 feet and two feet respectively to extend his lead to four shots.

"He never gave us an opportunity to gain momentum," Mediate said. The local favorite did okay, shooting a final-round 68 for a share of second place with Larry Mize, who closed with 65 for 272 total. They were both three shy of Allenby's 19-under-par 269, and Allenby felt fortunate to win with his closing 68.

"If Rocco had putted well he would have lapped the field," Allenby said. "Still, I've shown I can handle pressure. To win, you've got to keep your emotions in check. I think I've shown I have that ability."

On a week when emotions were near the surface for everyone, that was more important that ever. "Golf didn't seem all that important this week," Allenby said. "And to tell you the truth, it still doesn't. But to pull off what I did, I'm proud of it."

Texas Open at LaCantera—$3,000,000
Winner: Justin Leonard

With 16 birdies in his first 36 holes and a partisan crowd clearly on his side, Justin Leonard found the Texas Open at LaCantera was his tournament to lose. The Dallas native held a four-shot lead going into the weekend, and the golf game he had worked so hard to retool over the previous two years seemed to have finally jelled.

"I wouldn't go back and change anything, because I'm going to be a better player in the long run," Leonard said of the swing changes that added length to his drives and improved the trajectory of his tee shots. "That's what I did this for. I would love to be on the Ryder Cup team. That's disappointing. But I know what I've been through this year, the work I've put in just to get to this point. To me, that's very satisfying."

Leonard wasn't as productive on the weekend as he had been in the first two rounds, but he didn't have to be. A 68 on Saturday gave him a two-shot lead over rookie Matt Kuchar, who jumped into contention with 64 on Saturday after solid scores of 67 and 68 early in the week. Kuchar and Leonard played together in the final round for the first time since the 1998 U.S. Open when Kuchar's father, Peter, caddying for his son, annoyed Leonard with some overzealous theatrics. According to Kuchar, there were no hard feelings left over from that incident.

"Justin might have been bothered by some of my dad's antics," Kuchar said. "But all that stuff afterward got blown way out of proportion. Justin and I are friends. He's one of the guys I looked up to when I was growing up."

Kuchar got the chance to look up to Leonard again. After birdieing two of the first five holes, Leonard reeled off eight straight pars to retain a three-shot advantage over a charging J.J. Henry. The match got closer at the 13th when Henry ran in a breaking 15-footer for birdie to pull within two. Leonard, playing behind Henry and watching his every move, parred the 13th, then matched Henry's birdie with one of his own at the 14th. At the 15th, Henry had a difficult 15-foot putt for birdie, which he ran past the hole. When his par putt hung on the lip and failed to drop, Henry fell three behind with three to play. Leonard got up and down for par at the 15th, but bogeyed the 16th to narrow his lead to two shots, which is where it remained.

A final-round 69 and 266 total gave Leonard a comfortable two-shot victory over Henry and Kuchar, who bogeyed two of his first four holes but recovered late in the round and finished with a 69 of his own.

Leonard became the first man since Arnold Palmer in 1960 to successfully defend his Texas Open title. Afterward he wept on the 18th green, purging many of the emotions that had built up inside him since September 11.

"I wanted to say something about the patriotism I've seen this week, and I just got choked up," he said. "All of the flags, all the patriotism you see throughout the country right now — you didn't see that a month ago. I think it's pretty special to win during this time and after what's going on and what we've all been through mentally and emotionally the last three weeks. It kind of all hit me right there on the green."

Michelob Championship at Kingsmill—$3,500,000
Winner: David Toms

The last four times David Toms had led after 54 holes, he had won. The last and most impressive of those wins had come in August when Toms carried a one-shot lead over Phil Mickelson into the final round of the PGA Championship. With a 10-foot par putt on the final hole, Toms beat Mickelson by one.

After three rounds of the Michelob Championship at Kingsmill, Toms held a two-shot lead over Esteban Toledo. "You watch him, and he doesn't hit the ball that far and you think he's nothing special," said tournament host and Ryder Cup captain Curtis Strange. "Then you tee it up with him and see what kind of heart he has, and you realize you just want no part of him as an opponent."

Toms remained uncomfortable speaking about himself in such terms, but he did add some credence to his captain's praise. "On Monday there was no way I could tell you I was going to win this golf tournament, or even contend," Toms said. "That's how far off I felt my game was. But when I get in contention, I feel like I am going to perform. I'm not scared. I feel comfortable. That's a big advantage."

Toms took advantage of that feeling on Sunday, a feeling that was only magnified in the locker room as he prepared to go out. Tying his shoes and grabbing a quick bite to eat, Toms heard the news that the United States military had begun bombing targets in Afghanistan, so he delayed his warm-up session long enough to listen to President Bush address America.

"I was already on the edge a little bit, ready to play," Toms said. "To listen to the President speak, it actually gave me a little calm. I think it got me fired up for the round."

Toms got out of the gate quickly, birdieing four of his first seven holes to leave Toledo in the dust. Neal Lancaster made something of an early move with birdies on three of his first six holes to pull to within two shots of Toms' lead, but Lancaster fell apart, playing the last 10 holes in four over par. Kirk Triplett made a run with birdies on three of his first seven holes to pull to within four, then rolled in birdies at the 14th, 15th and 17th to get within two.

When Toms made one of his few mistakes of the day at the 17th, pulling his tee shot into the trees then failing to get up and down for par, the lead dropped to a single shot. Triplett failed to birdie the 18th, finishing with 66 and 270, and Toms safely hit his approach to the center of the green and two-putted for 68 and a 15-under 269 total and his third victory of the year and his sixth in 33 months.

"No matter what he tries to tell you, he is among the elite," Triplett said of the man who beat him. "I've considered him an elite player for a long time."

Toms gave his patented "aw shucks" grin when asked about Triplett's assessment. "I might be one of the five best players in the world, but Tiger, Phil, David (Duval), and I think you can throw Ernie Els in there and maybe Vijay (Singh), they are physically more talented," Toms said. "I just think there are a handful of people that are just better than everyone else. That's just life. You can look at that in any sport."

Invensys Classic at Las Vegas—$4,500,000
Winner: Bob Estes

The Las Vegas Tourist Board would like to convince everyone that anything's possible there, and after the final round of the Invensys Classic they might have a point. Who would have thought that Bob Estes, who spent nine days in Las Vegas without wagering a dime, would take one of the biggest gambles of his career on the first nine on Sunday, then parlay that gamble into a one-shot victory over Tom Lehman and Rory Sabbatini? And who would have thought that third-round leader Scott McCarron would squander a three-stroke lead on a single hole by making a triple bogey? And how about Tom Lehman, who played his way into contention in his first competitive rounds since being bumped from the top 10 in Ryder Cup points and failing to make captain Curtis Strange's list of picks? Indeed, it seemed that anything was possible.

Estes took that thought with him to the first tee on Sunday when he set his goals high (or low, as in the score he needed to shoot). "Sixty-three was the score I had in mind," Estes said. "I was trying to visualize a 63 after my 65-66-67-68 start. I knew that 69 (the next number in the sequence) wasn't going to do it. Still, it might not have been enough. But nine under par (63) was about as good as I could do."

It wouldn't have been good enough if not for a befuddling moment early in the final round when McCarron made triple bogey from the middle of the fourth fairway. Armed with a nine iron for his second shot, McCarron's ball was blown down by a wind gust and rolled off the front of the green. He attempted to putt up the hill and onto the green, but the ball didn't make it and rolled back to his feet, twice. After finally getting the ball on the green, McCarron used the putter twice more before recording a seven on the hole.

"It's a little disappointing," he said. "It was a gust of wind, just one of those things."

That left the door open for a slue of players, including Lehman, who led after the first and second rounds of the five-round affair, but fell behind on Friday after a lackluster 72. He clawed his way back after 67 on Saturday, and after McCarron's problem on the fourth, Lehman found the top of the leaderboard again.

But Estes was still thinking about his 63, even after he drove his ball into a bush on the par-four sixth. He had already made three birdies to play himself into contention when his three wood off the tee went awry and found the desert scrub left of the fairway. After debating an unplayable lie option with his caddie, Estes took out his driver and made his only bet of the week.

"If I was going to win the golf tournament, I was going to have to try to pull off that shot somehow," he said. "I didn't know if I could make contact with the ball or not. I took a big chance playing that shot. I think I hit the ball, but I'm not positive. The bush might have propelled the ball out. That was the shot of the tournament."

The ball bounced over the cart path but stayed in the rough, leaving Estes with a nine iron that he had to hit under one tree and over another. The shot stopped 45 feet from the hole, and Estes drained the putt for par.

"It was one of the most amazing holes I've played in my life," he said. "You make a par like that, you're almost embarrassed. You've got two tour pros watching you."

The par propelled Estes to meet his goals. He birdied the ninth, 10th, 12th, 13th, 15th and 16th to take the lead. Lehman, playing behind Estes, saw the putt fall on the par-five 16th and realized what he needed to do. But instead of making birdie, Lehman's four-iron approach found the water fronting the green. After a drop, Lehman got up and down for par, but it was too little too late. Estes shot his 63 for a 329 total and walked away with his second title of the season by one stroke.

"I just didn't play good enough," Lehman said. "You have to tip your hat to someone who shoots 63."

As for Estes, he left Las Vegas without dropping any money at any of the casinos, but no one accused him of not being a gambler. "I don't think anybody can call me conservative anymore," he said with a smile. "My tournament was one shot away from being over."

National Car Rental Golf Classic—$3,400,000

Winner: Jose Coceres

It was a sign of the caliber of play at Disney World that Tiger Woods shot respectable scores of 69, 67, 67 and 69 and fared no better than a tie for 16th place. And it was a sign of the times in America that Woods had to show a photo identification before he could pass through the gates. The terrorist organizations had listed Disney as one of the possible targets, and maps of the resort were found in the apartments of some of the terrorists involved in the September 11 attacks.

"If someone wants to do something, they can," Woods said. "Golf is probably the most accessible sport there is. The gallery is right there. We pride ourselves in our accessibility, but it's one of the dangers as well."

Woods hadn't played golf in six weeks prior to his 16-under-par 272 week near his home in Orlando, but even he was surprised by how low the scores were in the tournament he has won twice. "I've never seen a leaderboard where you had to shoot 18 under just to finish in the top 10," he said.

The cut was alarmingly low at five-under-par 139, and the leader, Japan's Kaname Yokoo, was at 12 under, 132, after two days. The scores got lower from there. On Saturday, Jose Coceres, a winner earlier in the year at Hilton Head, needed 25 putts to shoot an eight-under 64 to take a three-stroke lead over Davis Love III into the final round. As he did in anticipation of his first win in April, Coceres borrowed a pillowcase from his hotel and scrawled a victory message in Spanish on it. He kept the case in his pocket throughout the final round in the hopes that it would bring him good luck.

Even though four players, including Love, pulled to within a shot on the first nine on Sunday, Coceres kept making crucial putt after putt, birdieing the ninth, 10th and 11th holes to regain a three-shot advantage. Love, who failed to capitalize on his length advantage by parring all the par-fives on Sunday, birdied the 17th to pull within two shots, but that seemed to be as close as anyone would get.

After Coceres found the fairway with his tee shot on the final hole, a thunderstorm PGA Tour officials had predicted arrived on schedule, soaking the final fairway and delaying the last approach shots by 45 minutes. When play resumed, Coceres hit his second shot safely on the front edge of the green, 20 feet away from the hole. He broke into a big smile and reached for the pillowcase in his back pocket, but his caddie stopped him. "Not yet," the caddie, Brendan McCartain, said. "You have to stay focused."

The final green was soaked, and Coceres left his first putt five feet short. Then Love made things interesting by sinking a 13-footer for birdie to shoot 66 and finish with a 266 total. If Coceres missed, they would head back to the 18th for a playoff. But Coceres made his best stroke of the week, trusting the right-edge line and punching the sky as the ball fell into the hole. He finished with 68 for the day and 265 for the week. He also joined the elite club of multiple winners in 2001.

"I left a few shots out there, and that's disappointing," Love said afterward. "But anybody who's lost a few close calls can say that, I guess. Jose did what he had to do. He was impressive."

When the final putt finally fell, Coceres reached for his pocket and showed his pillowcase to the world. It read: "Feliz Dia Para Todas las Madre Feliz Dia Ma." He dedicated the win to his mother and wished her a happy Argentine Mother's Day.

"It was very important to demonstrate that winning one tournament wasn't an accident," Coceres said. "But now that I've shown I can win two, why not three?"

Buick Challenge—$3,400,000
Winner: Chris DiMarco

After Saturday's third round at the Buick Challenge, Davis Love III, who had just shot 68, 62 and 69 and trailed by one going into the final round, was asked if the low scores on Callaway Gardens' Mountain View course surprised him.

"It doesn't seem to matter," Love said. "There are just too many good players. We thought somebody was going to shoot two or three over and win the PGA Championship this year, but somehow guys go out there and burn it up. I think we've learned not to try to predict what the score is. You have to try to birdie every hole. You can't make mistakes or somebody is going to jump up and get you, and it's not necessarily going to be somebody like David Duval or Phil Mickelson every time. There are just too many guys who can play well."

Love didn't mention Chris DiMarco by name, but that was merely an oversight, with the leaderboard at the Buick Challenge so crowded on Sunday that it took two pages to list everyone in contention.

Joel Edwards started the day in the lead after rounds of 65, 68 and 65, but by the time the final group reached the third tee, Love had caught him. By the sixth tee, Love had a two-shot lead over Bob Estes, Neal Lancaster and DiMarco, and at the turn Love was tied with DiMarco while Estes, Lancaster, Edwards and Duval lurked one shot back.

Things got more crowded from there. With four holes to play, three players were tied at 19 under par and seven were within one shot of the top spot. Jeff Maggert made an appearance on the board, pulling to within two shots of the lead then hitting a three-wood second shot to within nine feet on the par-five 15th. Maggert three-putted for par, and finished alone in sixth place at 17-under 271.

"It was crowded up there," Estes said after finishing at 19-under 269, two strokes shy of the top spot. "I tried to watch the board a little, but it was hard to keep up. I thought today that if Joel or Davis got it going, the winning score was going to be about 23 or 24 under. I thought one of those guys for sure was going to play well."

Neither played poorly, but they didn't play well enough. Love played the final 11 holes one over par to finish alone in fifth place at 18-under 270, while Edwards went backwards, shooting 74 for a 16-under total. "I think I hit two shots today the way I wanted to," Edwards said. "You can't do that out here. There are too many good players to make the kinds of mistakes I made."

No mistakes were tolerated this Sunday. After making six birdies on the final nine to shoot 63 and reach 21-under 267, Duval could only watch in amazement as DiMarco drained a 15-footer on the 18th for a final-round 65 and a 267 total of his own. Then Duval made his only mistake of the day, hitting a nine iron over the green on the first playoff hole into an impossible lie on the lip on the greenside bunker. That mistake resulted in a bogey, and DiMarco walked away with his second career win.

"I played good enough to win and I lost in a playoff, but I've done that before," Duval said. "When I made the turn I thought that if I could shoot 30 or so on the back I had a good chance."

He did have a good chance, but with so many great players still in the hunt, it just wasn't quite good enough. As Duval and DiMarco met behind the 18th green before heading back for the playoff, Duval looked at DiMarco and quipped, "Nice putt." DiMarco answered with, "What are you doing to me? You haven't won enough already?"

Afterward DiMarco clarified his remarks. "It's hard to win out here," he said. "I mean, look at David Duval. I played a great round; I had him by two shots at the beginning of the day; I shoot 65, and he goes and shoots 63. It just seems that no matter how good you play, there's somebody out there playing better. You've just got to put yourself in position to win and learn from past experience."

Tour Championship—$5,000,000
Winner: Mike Weir

In an autumn fraught with upsets and full of surprises it was no wonder that the season-ending Tour Championship would end in a four-way playoff. The only surprises were the players who weren't a part of the post-regulation play. Tiger Woods played well in the middle rounds, but two 70s on the first and final days doused his chances. Woods finished tied for 13th with a 276 total.

David Duval watched from the clubhouse as well, despite having a chance as late as the 12th tee to win his second Tour Championship at the Champions Club in Houston. An errant drive at the 12th cost Duval a bogey and he never fully recovered. A closing 71 after rounds of 69, 69 and 63 left Duval tied for seventh with Bob Estes and Jim Furyk at 272, two shots too many to make the playoff.

Second- and third-round leader Scott Verplank, who seemed on his way to his second victory of the season, lost control of his driver on Sunday. He scrambled throughout most of the day until the 17th, when a bogey dropped him to even par on the day and a shot out of the lead. That's where Verplank would finish, tied for fifth with Kenny Perry at 271.

The four players who made it into the playoff all had chances to win the event in regulation, but none could convert. Ernie Els, winless in 2001, missed a chance on the 72nd hole, as did Sergio Garcia. Both players shot three-under 68 for totals of 270. At the time that looked like it would be good enough for second place, or maybe third. They had no idea what was to come.

David Toms, capping off a career season, hoped to pull another upset like the one he had in Atlanta when he defeated Phil Mickelson at the PGA Championship, but that was not to be. Toms also missed a chance to separate himself on the final hole. He shot 67 on Sunday and joined Garcia and Els at 270.

Mike Weir could have won outright with a par on the final hole. After pulling his drive into the right rough, Weir missed the green short and left and found himself struggling for bogey and the right to round out the four-way slugfest that had Houston in a buzz.

Back at the 18th tee, Els chose a three wood, but pulled it into the trees. Garcia did the same with a driver. Toms and Weir split the fairway, but Toms could get no closer to the flag than 20 feet. Garcia maneuvered his way out of the trees and onto the back edge of the green, while Els hit his shot over a 30-foot pine to within 40 feet. When Weir finally hit, his shot headed straight for the flag, stopping just six feet beyond the hole.

Garcia putted first from off the green and fell to his knees as the ball rolled over the lip without falling in. Els followed with an equally good roll that didn't fall. When Toms failed to convert his birdie, it was all up to Weir. The Canadian took dead aim and rolled the six-footer in the middle of the cup for the win. "It was exciting," Weir said. "Everyone was having fun there with the playoff. Everyone was screaming. It was a blast."

Southern Farm Bureau Classic—$2,400,000
Winner: Cameron Beckman

After barely earning his PGA Tour card in three successive trips through qualifying school, Cameron Beckman wasn't sure how he would handle the pressure of being in contention to win. After erasing a three-shot deficit in the last five holes at the Southern Farm Bureau Classic, Beckman learned a lot about himself. He also learned he could tear up his qualifying tournament application and make plane reservations for Maui. His 19-under-par 269 total was good enough for a one-shot victory over Chad Campbell. The win gave Beckman a two-year exemption and an invitation to the winners-only Mercedes Championships in January.

"I was impressed with myself," Beckman said afterward. "I didn't know if I was capable of that. Now I know I am."

Beckman had played well all week, shooting 66, 69 and 67 in the first three rounds at Annandale Golf Club in Madison, Mississippi, to trail Campbell by three shots going into Sunday's final round. Nerves got the best of both men on the front side. Campbell, playing in only his second PGA Tour event after earning a "battlefield promotion" from the Buy.com Tour, couldn't buy a putt, while Beckman made four birdies and two bogeys on the first nine. Beckman continued to struggle with his ball-striking, but he was buoyed by two crucial par-saving putts at the 11th and 12th.

"I told my caddie as we were walking up 13, Campbell has got to start feeling it at some point," Beckman said. "If I can just start making some birdies, I've got a shot."

At the 15th, Beckman made a 30-footer for birdie, while Campbell struggled in with a bogey. That was where the momentum shifted. Both players left the 15th green tied at 18 under. With his confidence in high gear, Beckman sealed the win with a 15-foot birdie putt at the par-four 17th. Campbell, who was 30 feet away on the 17th, two-putted for par.

Despite long tee shots, both players chose to lay up in front of a water hazard on the par-five 18th. Campbell's third shot spun 25 feet below the hole, stopping on the collar of the green, while Beckman flew his wedge shot beyond the hole and spun it back to eight feet. When Campbell left his birdie effort short, Beckman calmly two-putted for par and his second consecutive round of 67, just enough to win.

No one was happier with Beckman's victory than 37-year-old Woody Austin, who was perched precariously in the 125th spot on the money list coming into this season-ending event. If Campbell had won, Austin would have been bumped from the top 125. But with Beckman's victory, Austin was able to hold on to the final fully exempt spot on the PGA Tour by $100 over Bradley Hughes.

Brandt Jobe and Dan Forsman also squeaked into the top 125 on this final week, Jobe finishing tied for 28th with a score of 280 to move from 126th on the money list to 124th, while Forsman closed with a 65-69 weekend to finish fourth at 272 and move from 137th to 114th.

Special Events

CVS/pharmacy Charity Classic—$1,100,000
Winners: Nick Price and Mark Calcavecchia

It was almost a sweet homecoming for Rhode Island native Brad Faxon. Paired with Gary Player in the 36-hole CVS/pharmacy Charity Classic, Faxon appeared poised to win at the Rhode Island Country Club in Barrington after an opening 58 gave the Faxon-Player team a share of the lead with Tim Herron and Dudley Hart.

Scores were higher in the second round, and when Faxon and Player came in with 61 for a 119 total, that looked good enough for the victory. Jay Haas and Davis Love III also shot 61 to finish at 120 along with Herron and Hart (62). Only two teams bettered their first-round scores. Peter Jacobsen and John Daly followed their opening 63 with a 62 to finish at 125, and Nick Price and Mark Calcavecchia beat their opening 60 by a stroke, shooting 59 to finish at 119. That gave them a tie for first place.

The birdie Price and Calcavecchia made on the first playoff hole was enough for the victory.

Fred Meyer Challenge—$925,000
Winners: Billy Andrade and Brad Faxon

It was a great week in the Great Northwest as two men from the Northeast put together two consistent rounds of golf to win the Fred Meyer Challenge. Billy Andrade and Brad Faxon, the only two Rhode Islanders on the PGA Tour, shot consecutive rounds of 60 for a 120 total at the Reserve Vineyards and Golf Club in Aloha, Oregon, to win the two-day, two-man event by two strokes over Fuzzy Zoeller and Jean Van de Velde.

David Duval and his father Bob shared the first-round lead with Andrade and Faxon, but 63 in the second round dropped the Duvals into a tie for third place with Stewart Cink and David Toms (61-62).

The best comeback of the week belonged to Zoeller and Van de Velde. After opening with 65, the two men shot the low round of the tournament when they partnered for a 15-under-par 57. The weakest team of the two days was the Nicklaus duo — Jack and son Gary — who shot 71 and 70.

Franklin Templeton Shootout—$2,000,000
Winners: Brad Faxon and Scott McCarron

The event moved from one side of South Florida to the other, but the defending champions didn't seem to mind. For the second year in a row Brad Faxon and Scott McCarron took advantage of the final-round scramble format to come from behind and win the Franklin Templeton Shootout.

In 2000 the duo defeated Scott Hoch and Carlos Franco in a playoff. The 2001 victims were third-round leaders John Daly and Frank Lickliter, who lost by two shots after Faxon rolled in a birdie putt at the final hole to shoot 57 for a 183 total, 33 under par.

It was a disappointment for Daly and Lickliter, who led at the end of Saturday's best-ball round and looked to be in control on Sunday. Faxon and McCarron tied for first briefly with an eagle at the first hole, but Daly rolled in a birdie to resume a one-shot lead, which they held all the way to the 15th when McCarron rolled in a birdie putt to tie.

The competition got heated on the 17th when Daly and Lickliter missed the fairway and ended up on some pine straw. Asking officials for an exact location to drop, Lickliter took exception to Faxon's presence nearby. "Just go on back over there," Lickliter snapped at Faxon.

Faxon walked away, but the friendly competition took on a greater intensity after the confrontation. "It was just the heat of the battle," Faxon said afterward in an attempt to downplay the incident. But it clearly fired up the competitors. Ten minutes later McCarron sank a double-breaking, 35-foot eagle putt to give his team the lead for the first time all day. Daly and Lickliter missed the green and failed to chip in for eagle.

Leading by a shot, McCarron found the middle of the 18th green with his second shot, a safe approach given the water that guarded the front and left side. After a booming drive, Daly and Lickliter failed to get their approach close. It proved moot anyway. Faxon rolled in the 25-footer for birdie, and the defending champs chalked up another win.

Callaway Golf Pebble Beach Invitational—$300,000
Winner: Olin Browne

It took three extra holes to do it, but Olin Browne's third birdie on the 18th hole at Pebble Beach in the span of about an hour proved to be enough for Browne to defeat Todd Barranger and win the Callaway Golf Pebble Beach Invitational.

Even though his earlier rounds of 66, 66 and 68 gave him a three-shot lead over Paul Stankowski, Browne could have used a bigger cushion. Stankowski didn't make a charge. He shot 70 and fell back to sixth place. But Barranger did make a run, coming from eight strokes back and sinking a five-foot birdie putt on the 18th to shoot 63. His 17-under-par 271 total made Barranger the leader in the clubhouse.

Browne, playing two groups behind, still had a chance to win in regulation, but bogeys at the 14th and 17th holes dropped him back to 16 under par. Then came the first birdie at the 18th, with a putt from five feet after a deft pitch from the fairway for a round of 71. That tied Browne with Barranger at 271.

The two birdied the 18th again in the playoff. The second time through they both made pars. Then, on the third playoff hole — the fourth time they had played the 18th that afternoon — Browne made another short birdie putt for the win after Barranger missed a 20-footer.

UBS Warburg Cup—$3,000,000
Winner: United States

The UBS Warburg Cup was a new rendition of an old idea, an international match-play competition similar to the Ryder Cup and Presidents Cup, but with added twists — the United States would play against the Rest of the World, including Europe, and all the participants would be over 40 years old. The Ocean Course on Kiawah Island, South Carolina, was the site, where the 1991 Ryder Cup was played. The final score was 12½ to 11½ in favor of the United States.

The World led the U.S. by a score of 7 to 5 after two days of foursomes and fourball matches.

As they have proven time and again, the U.S. golfers excelled in singles competition. It started early when Arnold Palmer defeated Gary Player 2 and 1 and Scott Hoch beat Isao Aoki by the same margin. Hale Irwin and Bernhard Langer, in a rematch of the 1991 Ryder Cup final pairing, halved their match. Also appropriate was the halve between Curtis Strange and Sam Torrance, the two current Ryder Cup captains.

The most resounding win for the U.S. came when Mark O'Meara beat Stewart Ginn 5 and 4. The U.S. lost one by a similar margin when Des Smyth beat Loren Roberts 4 and 3. John Cook kept the rally alive with a win over Jose-Maria Canizares 2 and 1.

The cup was far from won. Nick Faldo beat Tom Watson 3 and 2 and Denis Durnian won 1 up over Dana Quigley. It came down to the final three matches, where the U.S. felt they held the advantage.

In the first one, Raymond Floyd halved his match with Ian Stanley. Larry Nelson was next to finish, defeating Frank Nobilo 3 and 2. That left the cup in the hands of Mark Calcavecchia. He came through, winning over Ian Woosnam 1 up.

PGA Grand Slam of Golf—$1,000,000
Winner: Tiger Woods

If there are horses for courses, then Tiger Woods is definitely the favorite every time he plays at the Poipu Bay Golf Club in Hawaii. For the fourth year in a row, Woods won the PGA Grand Slam of Golf, which brings together the four major champions for a two-day, $1 million event.

Starting the final round one stroke behind Retief Goosen, who shot 66 the first day, Woods broke out with birdies on five of the first seven holes. A five-footer for birdie on the 573-yard, par-five sixth put Woods out front to stay.

When Goosen and David Toms bogeyed the 16th, Woods' victory was secure. Tiger shot a seven-under-par 65 and established a tournament scoring mark of 132. Toms finished second at 135. Goosen finished with 71 to take third at 137, while David Duval had shot himself out of contention with an opening 76.

Office Depot Father-Son Challenge—$919,000
Winners: Raymond and Robert Floyd

No matter which son he brings, Raymond Floyd seems to own the Office Depot Father-Son Challenge. With an 11-under-par 61 on Sunday in the scramble format, Raymond and Robert Floyd finished with a 124 total and a one-shot victory over Hale and Steve Irwin. It was Floyd's fifth win at the event in seven years, his first three coming with son Raymond, Jr. as his partner.

This time the Floyds came from behind after the Irwins opened with an impressive 59 on the Ocean Club at Paradise Island, Bahamas. "You just can't expect to make up four strokes against these teams in a scramble format," Raymond Floyd said. "We thought we would have to get to 22 under and we needed the wind to blow."

The wind did blow, but the scores didn't go as low as Floyd anticipated. When he rolled in a birdie putt at the 13th hole, the Floyds held the lead for the first time. "That's when we thought we had a chance," Raymond said. "We knew we would have to continue to make birdies, because the Irwins and Weiskopfs were playing behind us."

They did just that, birdieing the 17th to put an exclamation point on the victory. The Irwins finished with 65 to place second alone, while the Weiskopfs shot 65 to finish third, two strokes back.

Hyundai Team Matches—$1,200,000
Winners: Fred Couples and Mark Calcavecchia
        Allen Doyle and Dana Quigley
        Lorie Kane and Janice Moodie

Fred Couples mused about retiring for most of the 2001 season, but you would never have known it from his play in Dana Point, California, at the Hyundai Team Matches. Couples, paired with Mark Calcavecchia again after winning the event in 1999, made five birdies in the final 17 holes, the last coming when he rolled in a 10-footer to win 1 up over defending champions Tom Lehman and Duffy Waldorf.

"We got off to a good start," Couples said. He and Calcavecchia birdied the sixth, seventh and eighth to take a 3-up lead. "But we knew they played very well together."

Lehman and Waldorf came back, cutting their deficit to one hole when Waldorf sank a 60-foot eagle putt on the 12th and evening the match on the next hole when Lehman made a birdie. They halved the 14th, 15th and 16th before Couples closed things out with his birdie on the 17th.

On the LPGA side, Lorie Kane and Janice Moodie trounced Grace Park and Wendy Ward 5 and 4. The twosome never trailed, as Moodie sank a 20-footer for birdie on the first hole to take a 1-up lead. Another 20-footer by Moodie on the 11th for birdie all but sealed the victory. A halve on the 14th was all they needed to close out the match early.

"We jelled pretty well as a team," Moodie said. "We kind of alternated making birdies while the other made par."

The most dramatic match occurred among the seniors as Allen Doyle and Dana Quigley needed three extra holes to finally knock off Tom Watson and Andy North. That win came after Watson hit the shot of the tournament, a hole-in-one on the 170-yard, par-three 13th to bring the match back to all-square. Two holes later North pulled his team ahead with a birdie at the 15th. Doyle birdied the 16th to even the match again, and the seniors proceeded to halve the next four holes. The deadlock was finally broken when Doyle chipped in for birdie at the par-three third extra hole.

"We dodged a real bullet when Tom made that hole-in-one," Doyle said. "We thought it would give them momentum, but we hung in there, played tough and wound up on the good side."

Williams World Challenge—$4,100,000
Winner: Tiger Woods

Four strokes down with nine holes to play, Tiger Woods was struggling in the Williams World Challenge. But Woods needed only 10 putts in the final nine holes to pass Vijay Singh and win the tournament sponsored by his Tiger Woods Foundation. In the process Woods made five straight birdies, shot a course-record 64, and made an 18-footer for birdie on the final hole for a 15-under-par 273 total and a three-shot victory at Sherwood Country Club in Thousand Oaks, California.

The run actually started with a bogey at the ninth. After driving his ball so far right on the par-four that it was beyond a lateral hazard, Woods took a penalty drop from a scrub bush and proceeded to hit his third shot into the grandstands behind the green. Another drop and a poor chip left him with a 45-footer for bogey. Singh had reached the green, but was faced with 100 feet for birdie. Singh left his putt five feet short, and Woods made the uphill 45-footer for bogey. When Singh missed his par putt and both men walked away with fives, the momentum began to shift in Woods' favor.

Woods hit an approach shot at the 10th that skipped beyond the flag and rolled back to 18 inches for his first birdie. That was followed by a 12-footer for birdie at the 11th and another 12-footer at the par-three 12th to catch Singh, who had bogeyed the 11th.

The second turning point came at the par-five 13th when Woods pulled his second shot into knee-high rough. With Singh's ball sitting perfectly in the middle of the fairway, 99 yards from the hole, many were surprised when Woods flew a pitch too far. Woods followed with one of the shots for which he has become famous — a thrashing wedge that landed in the fringe and ran four feet beyond the hole.

Singh failed to get up and down for par, and Woods made his putt for birdie. Just like that a four-shot deficit had turned into a two-shot lead.

Buy.com Tour

The biggest story out of the 2001 Buy.com Tour season was the fate of the title sponsor. The Internet retailer suffered severe financial setbacks during the NASDAQ correction of 2000. The fact that the company had never shown a profit didn't help matters. The PGA Tour sued when they could no longer fund the developmental program. Then the PGA Tour entered a re-tailing arrangement with a rival Internet site, and Buy.com counter-sued. It was a mess with no end in sight.

Still, the company remained a part of the former Hogan and Nike Tour throughout the year. At the Buy.com Tour Championship in Prattville, Alabama, in October, commissioner Tim Finchem praised Buy.com executives for their commitment to the game.

Those to whom Finchem handed PGA Tour cards in Prattville couldn't have cared less. Fifteen of them, weary from a year of struggling to make it to the big leagues and teary-eyed from having finally accomplished that task, smiled and hugged each other as they rubbed the small white cards with the blue PGA Tour logo and their names embossed.

It had been a long, hard struggle, but they had finally made it. Instead of driving from Dayton to Knoxville in 2002, they would be flying from Honolulu to Palm Springs, playing in front of galleries that included more people than just their families and a few local volunteers. Getting there had been tough — the earnings to qualify were over $161,000 — but they were finally members of the PGA Tour.

Three wins earned you a "battlefield promotion" to the PGA Tour, and one player earned his way on with three weeks left in the season. Chad Campbell won in Richmond, Virginia, before capturing the Permian Basin Open and the Monterey Peninsula Classic. He finished in the top spot on the money list with $394,552, which was more than he had ever made playing golf, even though the top spot was one he had seen before. Campbell, who turned 27 just before his first win of 2001, finished No. 1 on the money list on two different tours the last four years, topping the 1998-2000 Hooters Tour list and winning the money title on the Buy.com Tour in 2001. He entered the PGA Tour with 16 professional victories.

Earlier, Heath Slocum, a Louisiana native who was motivated by the success of David Toms in 2001, won twice in three weeks and got a "battlefield promotion" five weeks after that. He finished third on the money list, and attributed his three-victory year to his improved accuracy. Slocum finished the year third in hitting greens in regulation.

No one else earned a battlefield promotion, although Pat Bates did win three events. The fact that his third victory came in the season-ending Tour Championship made the point moot. Bates got his card in Prattville by finishing second on the money list. How he got his promotion seemed irrelevant.

Richard Zokol, a former PGA Tour player who won the Greater Milwaukee Open and was known for playing golf while listening to music over headphones, was the senior member of this graduating class. At age 42, the Canadian won once at the Samsung Canadian PGA Championship, and finished 13th on the money list.

A win didn't guarantee entry this year. Paul Claxton, winner of the Louisiana Open; Chris Couch, Florida Classic champion; John Maginnes, who won the Carolina Classic; Jason Dufner, Wichita Open champion, and David Sutherland, winner of the Utah Classic, all failed to advance. Perhaps the saddest story belonged to Dayton Open winner Todd Barranger. In the 15th spot on the money list coming into the Tour Championship, Barranger needed a good week to secure his spot. Instead he started the tournament by making a quadruple-bogey eight on the first hole. Another eight on the 14th hole led to an opening 85. Barranger finished at 20-over-par 308 and 16th on the money list, just $2,273 short of his goal. "Can't do much when you're making eights all day long," Barranger said. "If it takes another year to get back on the tour, it takes another year."

Canadian Tour

The Canadian Tour showed a remarkable amount of depth and surprisingly few multiple winners in 2001. From its first event in mid-January in Panama through the Bayer Championship in September, the tour produced 13 different winners with some outstanding performances by a wealth of young and talented players. Aaron Barber from Orlando, Florida, won twice, capturing the Barefoot Classic in Myrtle Beach, South Carolina, and the Telus Edmonton Open. Barber also had one second-place finish early in the season. The only other multiple-winners were New Zealander Paul Devenport, who won in Victoria at the Shell Payless Open and later in Quebec at the Telus Open, and Kenneth Staton, who won the MTS Classic and the unofficial Niagara Classic. Other than that, the tour had a different winner every week.

It also lost one of its more promising young members in 2001. Lewis Chitengwa, a native of Zimbabwe who was sponsored by Nick Price and the only native African player on the Canadian Tour, succumbed to meningitis in the summer. He was 26 years old.

Prior to that tragic loss, the tour had been riding a wave of great play and unprecedented success. It started when Buy.com Tour member Steve Runge shot a five-under-par 67 in the Panamanian wind to pass fellow American Jonathan Byrd in the Panasonic Panama Open. Runge, who lives in Delray Beach, Florida, and whose parents are Canadian, trailed by three entering the final round, but eagled the par-five fifth hole to take the lead.

The Canadian Tour itself was in a groove as well. They moved to South Carolina and the Myrtle Beach Open. This time it was Ireland's Eamonn Brady who overcame some late jitters to win. It was an important win for Brady, who was an alternate and had to wait in the locker room for three hours before learning whether he was in the field. Three rounds later, he was at seven-under-par 206 and tied for the lead. Nerves took over a bit on Sunday, but Brady hung on with a round of even-par 71 for a 277 total.

With his first win on tour, Brady didn't have to worry about being an alternate anymore. Nor did he have to worry about traveling following his victory. The Canadian Tour spent four weeks at the Barefoot Resort in Myrtle Beach, competing on all four of the resort's courses. Brady won on the Tom Fazio-designed 18, and one week later, Aaron Barber made up for his Sunday blunder against Brady by taking the Barefoot Classic title at the Greg Norman Course with a 204 total in the rain-shortened 54-hole event. The win, Barber's first, along with the second-place finish the week before, moved Barber into the early lead on the money list.

Davis Love III designed the third course at Barefoot, where Jace Bugg shot 63 and came from six strokes back to win the South Carolina Challenge by three. Bugg's 274 total separated him from the pack, but in hindsight, it was a man who tied for third, Chitengwa, who would be remembered. With a 66 for a 278 total and a share of third place with Scott Herd and Kenneth Staton, Chitengwa posted his best finish of the season, just a few weeks before his death.

In the tour's final week in South Carolina, an eight-year Canadian Tour veteran broke a career winless drought. Scott Ford of Lake Worth, Florida, caught a break, then made a great up-and-down to shoot 71 for a total of 206 and a two-shot win over Patrick Moore of Cornelius, North Carolina, and three others.

When they finally teed off on Canadian soil three months later, in June, a local player led after three rounds and came within one stroke of winning. Victoria's Blair Piercy was one putt short of what he needed to tie New Zealand's Paul Devenport. The Kiwi shot five-under-par 67 at Gorge Vale Golf Club in Victoria for a 271 total and a one-stroke win.

An American with an interesting history won a week later in Vancouver. It was Steve Scott who got the job done, even though it took a few extra holes to complete the Telus Vancouver Open. Scott, a former University of Florida All-American who was best known for his U.S. Amateur final match against Tiger Woods in 1996, outlasted five other players at the Point Grey Country Club after shooting 67 for a 276 total.

A week later Barber won his second event of the year when he shot 65 at Edmonton Country Club for a 264 total and a two-stroke win in the Telus Edmonton Open. Casey Brown of Ft. Smith, Arkansas, also shot 65 to finish second at 266.

Slawter made it three-for-three a week later when he came within a stroke of winning the MTS Classic at Pine Ridge Golf Club in Winnipeg. That victory went to Kenneth Staton of Ormand Beach, Florida, who shot 64 for a 266 total, one better than Slawter, who also finished strong with 62.

Craig Matthew from Quebec became the first Canadian to win an event in 2001, defeating Bob Conrad in a playoff to capture the Ontario Open Heritage Classic. One week later Americans took first, second and third at the Giant Forest Products/NRCS Classic. Derek Gilchrist of Sacramento, California, won in a playoff with Rich Massey of Harrington, New Jersey, after both posted totals of 270, while Jason Bohn of Atlanta finished third.

Devenport's second win also came in a playoff, the third extra-hole affair in as many weeks. This time both Devenport and Ken Duke shot 269s at the Telus Open, and Devenport prevailed in overtime. A week later Mark Slawter and Chris Greenwood made it four playoff finishes in a row when they completed the Eagle Creek Classic knotted at 266. Slawter won on the first extra hole.

Brian Payne of Henderson, Nevada, didn't need any extra holes to take the Aliant Cup in St. John's, Newfoundland, but that was only because Jason Bohn lost his way on the weekend. Bohn had an eight-shot lead after opening with rounds of 64 and 65 at the Clovelly Golf Club. But the Atlanta resident fell apart on Saturday and Sunday, shooting 77 and 76 for a 282 total to lose by one to Payne, who shot 73 and 67 on the weekend.

Bohn made up for his blunder three weeks later by shooting the first 58 in Canadian Tour history in the final round of the Bayer Championship. His 63-58 weekend for a 260 total was good enough for a two-shot win over Jace Bugg.

South American Tour

The 2001 Tour de las Americas offered a blend of the new and the familiar as a number of well-known players from the United States and Europe as well as Central and South America made fine showings throughout the year. We also caught a glimpse of some new players who are bound for greater things in the future, but who showed their worth at the beginning and end of the year on the circuit.

Brazilian Alexandre Rocha was one such name. Rocha got the season off to a rousing start when he shot a final-round 64 at the Brisas de Chicureo Golf Club to win the Rabobank Chile Masters. His 15-under-par 265 total was two strokes better than American Dan Olsen and Paraguayan Angel Franco, brother of Carlos, and one of the rising stars of the region. Franco and Olsen came into the final round tied for the lead with Rocha one shot back. Both co-leaders shot closing 67s, not good enough as Rocha cruised to victory.

Another familiar name showed up on the leaderboard the following week at the Mexico Masters. Matt Kuchar, the former Georgia Tech All-American and U.S. Amateur champion, came within one playoff putt of winning after shooting 12-under-par 276 and tying Raul Fretes for the lead. Fretes, the third-round leader, closed poorly, shooting 74 to Kuchar's 71, but he regained the momentum in the playoff and won with a birdie on the fifth extra hole. Adam Armagost, another familiar name in America, finished third with 71 for a 277 total.

Armagost posted another third-place finish the following week when he shot 12-under-par 276 at the Isla Navidad Country Club to share third in the PGA Championship of Latin America with fellow American Dave Bishop. It was a good finish for the two Americans, but nowhere close to being good enough to win. Third-round leader Angel Romero of Colombia ran away from the field with a nine-under-par 63 for a 19-under 269 total. It gave Romero a six-shot margin of victory over Mexico's Jose Trauwitz. It also gave Romero a great deal of confidence as the tour recessed until the fall.

Meanwhile, the PGA European Tour conducted two events in Brazil and Argentina (see following pages).

Rafael Alarcon of Mexico got the autumn season off to a rousing start in November by shooting 66 and 63 on the weekend at the Lagunita Country Club to win the Movilnet Venezuela Open. Alarcon's 12-under-par 268 total was one shot better than Brazil's Alexandre Rocha, who shot 64 on Thursday and 62 on Sunday, but failed to break 70 in the middle rounds. The 62 was the lowest round of the tournament and moved Rocha into second place, one better than third-round leader Rafael Gomez of Argentina. Gomez had the most consistent week, shooting 68, 67, 66 and 69, but he failed to convert enough birdies on the final day.

Gomez continued his good play as the tour moved to Rosario Golf Club for the Litoral Open. Still he couldn't get the victory. This time it took a five-man playoff, but Paraguayan Marco Ruiz denied Gomez and three others who all shot six-under-par 278. Ruiz had 66, the lowest score of the closing day and enough to earn him a spot in the playoff with four Argentines: Gomez, Ariel Canete, Gustavo Acosta and Rodolfo Gonzalez. Ruiz won with a birdie on the first playoff hole.

A week later, a Paraguayan hero charged from behind in the final round of the Chevrolet Brazil Open to capture his first win of the season. Carlos Franco trailed American Bob Jacobson by three strokes going into the final round, but birdies on three of the first five holes quickly erased that deficit. When Jacobson found the trees on the par-five 13th and took three shots to extricate himself, Franco slammed the door with another birdie. Franco closed with a 67 for an 11-under-par 273 total and a four-shot victory.

The next week in Argentina Franco looked as if he might make it two in a row. Going to the final round of the Telefonica Masters, Franco trailed Angel Cabrera by one. Trouble came early and often for the Paraguayan, and Franco shot 74 to tie for sixth place. Edwardo Romero had the best chance of catching Cabrera, but Romero missed birdie putts on the last two holes while Cabrera shot 69 for a 272 total, 12 under par, to win by two strokes.

If losing in Argentina was a disappointment for Franco, what happened the following week in his homeland of Paraguay would have qualified as a disaster. Franco played his worst golf of the year to finish tied for 23rd place. Raul Fretes took the lead in the first round with four-under-par 67, and held on through the next three rounds to win with a 279 total.

Sao Paulo Brazil Open—£470,000
Winner: Darren Fichardt

After two days of waiting out the weather, 25-year-old South African Darren Fichardt captured his first PGA European Tour victory in stellar fashion, shooting 67 for a 54-hole tournament-record total of 195 and a five-stroke victory over Brett Rumford, Richard Johnson and Jose Coceres in the Sao Paulo Brazil Open.

Fichardt felt fortunate even to be in the field since he missed getting his PGA European Tour card last autumn, but he earned a spot in Brazil because of his recent victory in the Sunshine Tour Championship in South Africa. He made the most of it. A course-record 61 gave Fichardt a three-shot lead going into the weekend.

The weekend never happened. Violent storms postponed play for two days and shortened the event to 54 holes. When play finally resumed on Monday, Rumford was the only one ready to make a charge. He birdied two of the first four holes to cut Fichardt's lead to a single stroke, but the challenge was short-lived. With four birdies in five of the first nine holes, Fichardt moved away from the pack.

"I've never had a lead in a tournament and had to wait two nights to play," Fichardt said. "I didn't know what to expect, but once I made my first birdie at five I started to relax. Once I birdied the ninth I was very relaxed. This was a big breakthrough for me."

Open de Argentina—US$700,000
Winner: Angel Cabrera

Angel Cabrera had become known as one of the best players on the PGA European Tour never to have won a tournament. All it took to shed that label was a little home cooking and the support of his longtime friend Eduardo Romero. His final-round 67 at The Jockey Club in Buenos Aires was enough for a two-stroke victory over Carl Pettersson in the Open de Argentina.

"This is one of the most important moments of my life," Cabrera said. "I have longed for this victory for a long time. And to win in my home country … I could never do it before. Now I'm very happy."

Cabrera led after rounds of 67 and 65, but Pettersson came back with 67 to gain a share of the lead at 201 going into the final round. The lead swung back in Cabrera's favor when Pettersson bogeyed the second hole after Cabrera rolled in a birdie putt. The only other challenge came when Pettersson rolled in a long birdie effort at the 16th, but Cabrera answered with a birdie to retain the two-shot margin. Cabrera posted 67 for a 268 total, two better than Pettersson and four ahead of third-place finisher Graeme Storm.

Overcome with emotion, Cabrera thanked Romero, who sponsored Cabrera in his early years on tour. The two were paired in Buenos Aires in the 2000 WGC World Cup to give eventual winners Tiger Woods and David Duval a scare before finishing second. "Eduardo is a person who is loved and welcomed everywhere he goes," Cabrera said. "He has helped me throughout my career and supported me unconditionally. Without his help, I would not be playing the European Tour. I dedicate this win to him from my heart."

9. European Tours

A new force rose to the top of the PGA European Tour in 2001, a veteran who had been discounted as an underachiever, but who proved that his game was ripening in the 10 previous years he had spent in Europe. Retief Goosen lived in London, but was a native of Pietersburg, South Africa. He had grown up playing with (and often in the shadow of) Ernie Els. This year Goosen stepped out on his own and, in 23 European starts, became the first non-European since Greg Norman in 1980 to win the Order of Merit title.

He did it with two European victories and one major championship. Goosen's victories at the Scottish Open at Loch Lomond and the Telefonica Madrid Open, coupled with his U.S. Open victory and a second-place finish at the Trophee Lancome earned him just under €2.8 million and the Order of Merit honor as the leading money winner.

"It's a great feeling, especially with so many great names on the Harry Vardon Trophy, such as Ballesteros, Faldo and Montgomerie," Goosen said. "This is my 10th season on tour, and to be No. 1 is unbelievable. It was nice to round it off with a win, and it's a great feeling. It's still got to sink in a bit, but it's been a dream year. It's hard to think I am the best player in Europe this year."

He edged out another player who was also attempting to win his first Order of Merit title and who had a breakout year in every category except victories. Padraig Harrington led the tour in scoring average (69.23), greens in regulation (77.1 percent) and putts per green hit in regulation (1.723), but the Irishman only had one victory and it didn't come until the last week of the season.

It was a frustrating year for Harrington. He lost a playoff to Vijay Singh in February at the Carlsberg Malaysian Open. He played well enough to win the Dubai Desert Classic, but tied for second with Tiger Woods, two shots behind Thomas Bjorn. Then he shot 70 in the final round of the Algarve Open de Portugal to lose to a charging Phillip Price. By the time John Daly beat him by one stroke at the BMW International Open, Harrington had to be wondering what he had to do. His runner-up count reached seven by the last week of the season. So when Harrington rolled in a putt at the last hole to win the Volvo Masters Andalucia, even the €539,074 first-place check still left him about €800,000 short of Goosen's total. Harrington was just thrilled to chalk up a win.

"So many doubts have gone through my mind this year after all those second places," Harrington said. "So many questions. You start wondering if it will ever be your turn to win. But today it was. I knew that when the putt on 18 went in. That ball was really moving when it hit the hole."

There were a few more multiple winners on the European circuit in 2001, among them Colin Montgomerie, who returned to form midway through the year and earned a spot on the Ryder Cup team with wins at the Murphy's Irish Open and Volvo Scandinavian Masters, plus the Ericsson Masters in Australia. Also earning a berth on a team many thought he should be captaining was Bernhard Langer, who picked up two victories at age 44 at the TNT Open in The Netherlands and his own Linde German Masters.

Two Frenchmen won in 2001 and neither was named Van de Velde. Thomas Levet won a four-man playoff at the Victor Chandler British Masters and Gregory Havret sank a late birdie putt to win the Atlanet Italian Open by one shot over Bradley Dredge.

Three Argentines won as well. Ricardo Gonzalez had four rounds in the 60s at the Omega European Masters to win by three, while Angel Cabrera won the Open de Argentina, which, while played in his home country, was an official PGA European Tour event. Rounding out the group was Jorge Berendt, who shot 268 in the Cannes Open and edged out the aforementioned Jean Van de Velde by one shot.

PGA European Tour

Alfred Dunhill Championship—£500,000
Winner: Adam Scott
See African Tours chapter.

Mercedes-Benz South African Open—US$1,000,000
Winner: Mark McNulty
See African Tours chapter.

Heineken Classic—A$1,750,000
Winner: Michael Campbell
See Australasian Tour chapter.

Greg Norman Holden International—A$2,000,000
Winner: Aaron Baddeley
See Australasian Tour chapter.

Carlsberg Malaysian Open—US$910,000
Winner: Vijay Singh
See Asia/Japan Tours chapter.

Caltex Singapore Masters—US$850,000
Winner: Vijay Singh
See Asia/Japan Tours chapter.

Dubai Desert Classic—£1,000,000
Winner: Thomas Bjorn

It hasn't happened often, and until a Sunday afternoon in Dubai, it had never happened on the final hole. Even Tiger Woods can't win them all, even when he leads after 70 holes and holds a share of the top spot with one hole to play.

That was the scenario at the Emirates Golf Club when Woods played the first 71 holes of the Dubai Desert Classic in 22 under par and came to the final hole tied for the lead with Denmark's Thomas Bjorn. He had only lost three previous times after leading through 54 holes, and in a four-year professional career Woods had never lost after holding a one-shot lead through 70 holes.

Twenty minutes after the final group stepped onto the tee at the par-five 18th, Bjorn stood on the back fringe of the green needing only to four-putt to win. This change of fortune came after Woods pushed his drive into the trees, punched a second shot through the fairway and into the rough, then hit a nine-iron third shot that splashed into a pond short of the green. After a penalty shot and a drop, Woods missed the green with his fifth shot, and got down in two for a double-bogey seven.

Bjorn, assuming he would need a birdie to tie or win, hit his second shot to the back fringe. After Woods' troubles, Bjorn could four-putt and still win. Instead he three-putted, tapping in from two inches for par, finishing with 69 and a 266 total for a two-stroke victory over Woods and Padraig Harrington.

"It doesn't get any better than this," Bjorn said. "You practice for moments like this, taking on the best player in the world on Sunday. I'm proud of what I did this week. To go out with Tiger and beat him would be anyone's dream. I know I can look him in the eye and take him on. My confidence will rise from this. I know if I can beat him, I can beat anyone. This is the best performance of my life by far."

Despite the final-hole drama, it was more than a one-hole tournament. Bjorn shot 64 on Thursday to share the lead with Woods. Rounds of 66 and 67 on Friday and Saturday left the Dane one stroke behind Woods going into the final round, which would have been a great position had the leader been any other player. Only Ed Fiori in 1996 and Lee Westwood and Phil Mickelson in 2000 had ever won tournaments Woods led at the end of 54 holes. It would take a great effort for Bjorn to join that group.

Woods led outright from the third hole on Sunday, but at the 17th, after hitting his approach to 15 feet, Woods missed his birdie putt and watched as Bjorn drained a 12-footer to take a share of the lead at 22 under par. Even though Woods' collapse at the 18th made it official, Bjorn preferred to remember the putt at the 17th as the turning point.

"Coming down the stretch I could feel it was only a matter of time before I caught him," Bjorn said. "When I got that birdie on 17, I knew a good drive on 18 would put him under pressure. It's a hard shot for him because he can reach the water up the right side and no one else can. Of course, in the long term he's going to win more often than anyone else because he's in better shape, hits it longer, is the best iron player and the best putter. That all makes him the perfect golfer. In the long run you can't keep up with him. He's going to be No. 1 for a long, long time."

Qatar Masters—US$750,000
Winner: Tony Johnstone

Tony Johnstone's putting was once so bad he considered "becoming a window cleaner on very tall buildings." The 44-year-old Zimbabwean had endured three years of frustration before proclaiming that he was "not going back to another tournament until I had sorted out how to putt."

That sorting-out lesson came early in the 2001 season when sports psychologist Dr. Ken West asked Johnstone to describe the best part of his game. "My bunker play," Johnstone replied. "Then stand to your putts as if you were hitting a bunker shot," West said.

"I felt so much more comfortable," Johnstone said. "I could immediately see the line." That proved to be Johnstone's salvation as he birdied two of the final three holes at the Doha Golf Club in Qatar and made a crucial par putt on the third to shoot 70 for a 274 total, and win the Qatar Masters by two strokes over Robert Karlsson. The final putt, a 15-footer for birdie, was particularly satisfying. "I had gotten to the stage where my enjoyment of the game had been outweighed by the frustration," he said.

Karlsson, who led after every round but the last, couldn't hold on and finished with 73 and a 276 total. By the time the final group teed off, Johnstone had captured the lead with a chip-in eagle on the first hole. Karlsson regained a share of the lead when Johnstone bogeyed the fifth, but when Karlsson made a bogey at the same hole, he gave up the lead for good. Still, second place was Karlsson's best finish since 1999.

Elliot Boult of New Zealand also had his best finish, closing with 71 for a 278 total and third place. Olivier Edmond and Dean Robertson finished tied for fourth at 279 after lackluster final rounds of 73 and 75 respectively.

Madeira Island Open—£350,000
Winner: Des Smyth

With four birdies and an eagle in the final nine holes for 66 and a two-stroke victory at the Madeira Island Open, Des Smyth became the oldest winner in PGA European Tour history. At age 48, Smyth blistered the final nine to pass Italy's Massimo Florioli and England's John Bickerton. He shot 18-under-par 270 as he won his eighth PGA European Tour event.

"It just goes to show you what you can do if you keep hanging on," Smyth said. "Last year was a tough year when I finished 111th in the Order of Merit, but I came out this year playing very well. I didn't do any extra work but probably thought a little more about the game and my swing and what my ambitions were."

Among those ambitions was another victory, but Smyth didn't expect it quite so soon. He thought he might have to wait until his 50th birthday and Senior PGA Tour eligibility to cash another winner's check.

"I'm absolutely over the moon," Smyth said. "I was very nervous on the last hole because it's hard to win on the tour these days. I came out this year playing much better. I have no idea why."

After rounds of 66, 70 and 68, Smyth was three strokes behind Florioli. A three-putt at the first hole moved Smyth even further off the pace, but he made up for it with two birdies on the first nine and the eruption of under-par holes on the second nine.

Florioli fell back with 73 to finish in a four-way tie for third place at 274 with Massimo Scarpa, Stephen Dodd and defending champion Niclas Fasth. That left only Smyth and Bickerton in the hunt for the victory. When Bickerton hit his tee shot into the water at the 11th, Smyth captured the lead outright and never let go.

"I'm happy," Bickerton said after finishing with 69 and a 272 total for his third runner-up finish in a winless 10-year career. "I just let a couple of holes slip. Then I missed a couple of birdie chances coming in. Second — again."

Smyth had his own memories of near-misses at Madeira Island. "It's particularly good to win here because this course owed me one," he said. "Five years ago I four-putted the last and lost my chance. Now I've got it back. This is huge for me. It will take at least a week to sink in."

Sao Paulo Brazil Open—£470,000
Winner: Darren Fichardt

See American Tours chapter.

Open de Argentina—US$700,000
Winner: Angel Cabrera

See American Tours chapter.

Moroccan Open—£400,000
Winner: Ian Poulter

With qualification for the Ryder Cup only months away, Britain's Ian Poulter staked his claim as a contender for the European team with a 15-under-par 277 winning performance in the Moroccan Open. It was Poulter's second victory in six months.

Rounds of 71, 67 and 69 on the long Dar-es-Salam Golf Club gave Poulter a four-stroke lead over compatriot David Lynn. When Lynn made eight birdies between the fifth and 17th holes, Poulter remained cool, pouring in putts from all angles and winking at the crowd. After Lynn cut the lead to two shots, Poulter responded by draining an eagle putt on the par-five 10th, effectively sending a message that no one would catch him.

"The hard work I've put in over the last few weeks has paid off," Poulter said after finishing with 70 to win by two strokes over Lynn, who shot 67. Australian Peter Lonard mounted a charge with 67 for a 280 total and third place.

None of the challengers came close to Poulter, and none left Rabat with his determination to be playing at The Belfry in September. "I set my goals as two wins this year and possibly a place on the Ryder Cup team," Poulter said. "Now I've won one, and if I keep playing the way I am, you never know. The Ryder Cup is the sort of overall picture I want to be looking at. There's a long way to go, but it's nice to be playing well with the really big-money tournaments coming up now."

Via Digital Open de Espana—£743,000
Winner: Robert Karlsson

Miffed by what he considered a Ryder Cup snub two years ago, Sweden's Robert Karlsson was determined to take matters into his own hands and earn a spot on Europe's 2001 squad. He moved toward that goal in Valencia, Spain, when he closed out the Via Digital Open de Espana with a two-under-par 70 to win by two shots over Jean-Francois Remesy. It was Karlsson's first win since 1999, but his fourth top-10 finish of the 2001 season.

"It feels fantastic to get the payback from all the hard work I've put in," Karlsson said of his 11-under-par 277 total. "I am very happy to win again."

Karlsson finished 11th in 1999 Ryder Cup points, but was passed over by captain Mark James. The Swede hadn't forgotten, and had decided that making the team on points was the only way to secure his destiny.

He certainly impressed several Ryder Cup veterans with his performance in Valencia. Tied with Darren Clarke through 54 holes, Karlsson played the long and difficult El Saler Golf Club with three birdies and one bogey on Sunday. The bogey came at the 17th after it became evident that Karlsson would win without much challenge.

Clarke struggled, falling four behind Karlsson in the first 14 holes. At the par-five 15th, needing a birdie or better to close the gap, Clarke lost his way, finding the water and walking off the hole with a 10. He closed with 79 — his worst weekend score of the year — and dropped into a tie for 32nd place.

That allowed Remesy to slip into second place alone with 66 for a 279 total. It was the Frenchman's second 66 of the week, but 72 on Friday and 75 on Saturday dashed any chances Remesy had of winning. Miguel Angel Jimenez played well again on his home soil, posting rounds of 71, 69, 70 and 70 to finish tied for third with Soren Hanson at 280.

Algarve Open de Portugal—£634,388
Winner: Phillip Price

If Padraig Harrington had been told before teeing off in the Algarve Open de Portugal that he would be tied for the lead going into the final round and that he would hit all 18 greens in regulation on Sunday, Harrington would have chalked this one up in the victory column. All those things came true except for the winning part. After rounds of 64, 70 and 71, Harrington entered the final round tied for the lead with Sven Struver. Harrington hit every green at the Quinta do Lago Golf Club, including reaching two of the par-fives in two. But Harrington struggled to find the hole, shot 70 and ultimately lost to a charging Phillip Price. Struver and Harrington tied for second with 275 totals.

"I had 35 putts," Harrington said. "That's just too many to have any realistic chance of winning. I hit all 18 greens, and if somebody had told me I was going to play tee to green the way I did, I would have been thrilled. But I should have had a better score than 70. The par-fives hurt me badly because I did not birdie one of them. That was a big pity."

Price had the opposite experience. Trailing by four shots and looking at 14 players ahead of him on the leaderboard, Price played like a man with a dozen wins to his credit instead of being a one-time winner who hadn't tasted victory in seven years. The 34-year-old Welshman surged into the lead with five birdies in his first six holes on Sunday, followed by four more birdies in the final 10 holes. His last, a chip-in on the 407-yard 16th, put the win away. He shot eight-under-par 64 for a 273 total and the two-shot victory. With only one bogey at the 17th after the win was secure, Price played like a man destined for the Ryder Cup.

"I think I'm more relieved than anything," he said. "I've finished second so many times (eight, with the most prominent being a runner-up finish to Tiger Woods at the 2000 WGC NEC Invitational) that I was thinking over the last three holes that I really didn't want to blow this. I've found it difficult to win, so to get the job done today was very pleasing. This is going to be a big boost to my confidence."

Novotel Perrier Open de France—£818,607
Winner: Jose Maria Olazabal

The secret to Jose Maria Olazabal's success seems to be his ability to play in marathon conditions. As a Ryder Cup stalwart, the Spaniard always seemed to thrive late in the day, when exhaustion after playing 36 holes was beginning to set in. He also thrived in the finals of the Alfred Dunhill Cup, where the last day is a 36-hole affair. So it shouldn't have been a big surprise that two weeks after missing the cut in his homeland at the Via Digital Open de Espana, Olazabal would bounce back to win the Novotel Perrier Open de France in the toughest conditions the PGA European Tour had faced all season.

Torrential rains in Lyon left the Lyon Golf Club unplayable for most of the day on Friday and all day on Saturday. That forced officials to compress the final 36 holes into one day on Sunday, perfect conditions for Olazabal, who entered the final day two shots off the lead held by Marc Farry.

"I was a little tired playing two rounds," the Spaniard said. "It was especially tough with the course being so wet. That made it difficult to walk the fairways, but I never felt any lack of energy playing the last few holes. That was important."

It certainly was. Olazabal got off to a strong start in the morning session, adding a four-under-par 66 to his previous scores of 66 and 69. That was good enough for a tie atop the leaderboard with a reinvigorated Costantino Rocca, who put together his best week since 1999. Rocca's morning 64 was the low round of the week, and it left the 44-year-old Italian with a chance at his first victory in almost 24 months.

The lead see-sawed back and forth between Olazabal, Rocca and Greg Turner, who put together consistent rounds of 69, 67 and 67. Then on the 14th Olazabal rolled in a four-footer for birdie while Turner was in the process of making double bogey at the 16th, and Rocca was struggling to make bogey at the 15th. That secured the lead for Olazabal, and he never let it slip away. Another birdie at the 18th for a closing 67 and 268 total was good enough to give Olazabal a two-shot edge over Rocca, who finished with 69, Turner, who eagled the final hole to finish with his third consecutive round of 67, and Paul Eales, who shot 67 and 68 on the final day.

Georgia Tokai Classic—¥120,000,000
Winner: Toshimitsu Izawa

Toshimitsu Izawa produced his second victory in 14 days, a two-stroke triumph in the Georgia Tokai Classic that was similar to the win he earned by the same margin in the Taiheiyo Masters. Those two victories propelled him to the top of the Japan Tour money list, a position he held unchallenged for the rest of the season. Just as he had at Gotemba two weeks earlier, the 33-year-old Izawa took a lead into the final round of the Tokai Classic, then floundered a bit in the stretch before icing his third win of the year and 10th of his career.

Nobuhito Sato, one of the top performers on the 2000 circuit who had not enjoyed the same success in 2001, showed a flash of brilliance in the opening round on the West course of Miyoshi Country Club, Aichi Prefecture. He amassed 11 birdies en route to a leading eight-under-par 64 and a one-stroke advantage over Izawa, who had eight birdies and a bogey, and Mitsuhiro Tateyama, who had nine birdies and two bogeys.

Izawa took charge the rest of the way. He tacked a 68 onto the opening 65 and his 133 gave him a two-shot lead over Sato (71), Nozomi Kawahara (68) and Yoshikazu Haku (67), who got into the field through the Monday qualifier. Izawa overcame the shock of a double-bogey start Saturday, shot 70 and retained a one-stroke lead at 203, a shot ahead of unheralded Kawahara. More ominous to him was the presence of two 2000 winners, Hidemichi Tanaka and Lin Keng-chi, the latter the money leader entering the week. Both had 69s for their 205s. Izawa appeared to have things in order Sunday when he carded his fourth birdie, but his iron play faltered on the final holes. He missed all three greens but salvaged pars on each of those holes to post a 69 and 16-under-par 272 total. Although pushed back to second place on the money list, Lin matched Izawa's 69 and tied for the runner-up position with Tomohiro Kondou, who shot 68.

Japan Open—¥120,000,000
Winner: Taichi Teshima

Taichi Teshima celebrated his 33rd birthday two days early. What better gift could he have given himself than his country's national championship? Teshima, whose only victory in his nine years came in a playoff in the 1999 Okinawa Open, won the Japan Open much more easily at the Tokyo Golf Club on the outskirts of the capital city. With the scoring generally high, Teshima found that his one-under-par 70 in the final round was not only good enough for the victory but gave him the important title with a four-stroke margin.

Teshima bided his time early in the tournament, registering rounds of 68 and 72 as Nobuhito Sato wound up the first-round leader for a second straight week, then yielded the top spot to veteran Ikuo Shirahama. Sato, still winless in 2001, shot a five-under-par 66 Thursday, one in front of Mitsuhiro Tateyama and Katsuyoshi Tomori, who bogeyed two of the last four holes. Shirahama mustered a 68 Friday and went two strokes in front with his 137. A 73 dropped Sato into a second-place deadlock with the consistent Lin Keng-chi (70), Katsumasa Miyamoto (71), Tomori (72) and Tateyama (72).

Despite two back-nine bogeys, Teshima put together a 67 Saturday and slipped into a two-shot lead at 207, six under par. Tomori continued his quest for the title, holding onto second place with 70 and 209 total. Shirahama shot 73 and joined Keiichiro Fukabori at 210. Teshima had a few problems Sunday, taking four bogeys during the round, but he more than offset them with five birdies. Tsuyoshi Yoneyama eased into second place with 68 for 281, finishing a stroke ahead of Toshimitsu Izawa, the leading money winner, who shot 71, and Tomori, who lost his grip on the runner-up slot with 73 Sunday. Naomichi Ozaki, who was gunning for an unprecedented third straight Japan Open victory, was never in contention and finished in 45th place.

Bridgestone Open—¥110,000,000
Winner: Toshimitsu Izawa

No stopping Toshimitsu Izawa! Even with two of Japan's all-time greats pressing him, the Japan Tour's leading money winner rolled unruffled to his third victory in a five-tournament stretch and strengthened his hold on the coveted No. 1 position with a one-stroke victory in the Bridgestone Open. Izawa closed with a bogey-free 69 for 274, just enough to frustrate Masashi Ozaki's bid for his first win in 14 months and 113th of his storied career. Ozaki shot 68 for 275.

Tsuneyuki Nakajima, whose many successful seasons on the circuit tailed off six years earlier, continued his improved performances in 2000 with a strong start at Sodegaura Country Club in Chiba Prefecture. Nakajima, winless for six years, opened with a three-under-par 69, the leading score on a wet, chilly day that was also posted by six others — Tomohiro Kondou, Tetsuji Hiratsuka, Yoshinori Mizumaki, Toshikazu Sugihara, Anthony Gilligan of Australia and Taiwanese veteran Chen Tze-chung. Nakajima inched a stroke in front Friday with 66 for 135 total, noting that "I put myself in position to make a lot of birdies." He carded seven of them and took a single bogey. Shinichi Yokota also shot 66 to move into second place. Seven players, including Izawa (67) and Masashi Ozaki, were next at 138.

Izawa staged a stunning finish to his Saturday round. He birdied the last four holes for another 67 and was rewarded with a two-stroke lead with his 205 total. In all, he had six birdies and a bogey in establishing the two-shot margin over Ozaki, Scott Laycock and Dinesh Chand, who shot the day's best round of 66. Nakajima crippled his hopes with 73, but was still just three off the pace.

Ozaki moved within a stroke of Izawa during the final round, but he missed two short putts at the eighth and 14th holes and couldn't catch him, settling for 68 and a 275 total. Laycock, enjoying a good season in Japan, finished third with 69 and 276 total. The win, Izawa's fourth of the season, increased his career total to 11.

Philip Morris Championship—¥200,000,000
Winner: Toshimitsu Izawa

Toshimitsu Izawa, already the leading money maker on the Japan Tour, added ¥40 million to his bank account when he continued his torrid pace with a one-stroke victory in the Philip Morris Championship, one of two tournaments with the biggest purses of the season — ¥200 million. Izawa's fourth victory in six weeks ran his prize-money total over the ¥200 million mark, making him just the second player on the Japan Tour to do that. Masashi Ozaki did it twice, in 1994 and 1996.

For three days, it appeared that Nobuhito Sato might finally be ready to nail a 2001 victory after several failed bids earlier in the season, a disappointing one after his four-victory campaign in 2000. He got away running at Tojo's ABC Golf Club with a seven-under-par 65, taking a one-stroke lead over Toru Suzuki, Shoichi Yamamoto and Chen Tze-chung. Sato held onto the lead Friday, but needed an eagle at the last hole to do so. It gave him 67 for a 132 total and a one-stroke margin over South Korea's Kim Jong-duk, a two-time winner in Japan in 1999. Kim shot 65 for 133. Izawa scored his second straight 67 and settled into third place with Chen (68).

After 54 holes, the tournament was down to a two-man duel between Sato and Izawa. A string of four birdies and an eagle powered Izawa to a 66, and Sato joined him at 200 with a 68. The players next in line — Hidemasa Hoshino, Hidemichi Tanaka, Dinesh Chand and Toru Taniguchi, the defending champion — were five strokes behind the leaders at 205.

Sato's game deserted him Sunday, and Izawa struggled, too, almost opening the door to others. Sato stumbled to a 74 and Izawa, canceling his four birdies with four bogeys, managed just a par-72 round, but it was enough to nip Taniguchi and Tanaka, who was runner-up to Taniguchi at the 2000 Philip Morris. Responding to an idle question about the likelihood that he could retain the money lead for the rest of the year — four official events — Izawa quipped, "As long as Shingo doesn't go and win four tournaments." Katayama won three of the last four events to grab the 2000 money title.

Ube Kosan Open—¥140,000,000
Winner: Dean Wilson

Whatever the reason, the streaking Toshimitsu Izawa did not play in the Ube Kosan Open, the second of the four big-money tournaments that make up the rich closing stretch of the season. This was fine with Dean Wilson, who took advantage of Izawa's absence and added more luster to his outstanding season with a come-from-behind, one-stroke victory at Ube 72 Country Club on the Ebataike course. It was the third 2001 win on the circuit for the Hawaiian-born American and his fourth in Japan.

The finish turned into a duel between Wilson, the reigning Japan PGA champion, and Taichi Teshima, the current Japan Open king. Wilson prevailed when Teshima, a shot in front of him, took a double bogey at the par-three 17th hole, giving the lead to Wilson, who had made seven birdies earlier in the round and finished with 67 for 267, 21 under par. Teshima wound up with 69 and a 268 total and the disappointment of knowing that he had failed to win despite having a tour-record-tying 61 on his scorecard.

That 11-under-par round came on Friday and jumped Teshima into a third-place tie after he had shot 71 on a birdie-adorned opening day, when Naomi-chi Ozaki and Daisuke Maruyama led the field with 64s and eight others, including Wilson, shot 66. Another tour record was tied Friday as American Todd Hamilton, a seven-time winner in Japan, ran off seven straight birdies in the process of shooting 65 for 130 and the lead. Veteran Hajime Meshiai joined the scoring binge with a 63 — an eagle, eight birdies and a bogey — that put him in second place at 131, and Nozomi Kawahara fired a 62 and shared third place at 132 with Teshima, Wilson (67) and Shingo Kata-yama (67-65).

A strong second nine enabled Teshima to take the lead Saturday. He made four birdies coming in for 67 and 199 total and his one-shot edge over Wilson, who shot 68. Hamilton and Meshiai finished the day at 201, but neither man seriously challenged Sunday, Meshiai winding up behind Wilson and Teshima at 270 and Hamilton at 271.

Dunlop Phoenix—¥200,000,000
Winner: David Duval

On the international stage, the Dunlop Phoenix tournament is the most attractive event on the Japan Tour, its sizable purse and other incentives normally drawing at least a handful of prominent players from around the world to Miyazaki. Not in late 2001, though. After the September 11 tragedies, most of the leading players were avoiding air travel as much as possible, particularly overseas. The only player of particular note who flew into Japan for the Dunlop Phoenix was David Duval and he merely came a week early for the WGC EMC World Cup, in which he would be playing with Tiger Woods as the United States team in that event at the Taiheiyo Club in Gotemba City. It turned out to be a good decision for the British Open champion. He won the tournament, defeating Taichi Teshima on the first hole of a playoff after the two had deadlocked after 72 holes at 15-under-par 269. It was Duval's first victory in Japan and the second straight runner-up finish for the Japan Open champion.

The American star went wire to wire at Phoenix Country Club. He opened with 65, carding eight birdies and two bogeys, and took a one-stroke lead on Hirofumi Miyase, a two-time winner in 2000 but winless in 2001. Duval shot 67 Friday on his 30th birthday and his 132 gave him a two-stroke lead over rookie American professional David Gossett, the 1999 U.S. Amateur champion. Duval was particularly overjoyed with his position. "I had the makings of a great score and I didn't," he said, pointing to his four birdies on the first five holes, and adding, "The two holes I bogeyed are both holes I should have birdied. And I also lipped out three or four putts coming in."

Nonetheless, he widened his lead to three strokes Saturday. He shook off a late double bogey and shot 68 for a 13-under-par 200 total. Gossett fell back with 74, but another American, Jerry Kelly, replaced him in the runner-up slot. Kelly had rounds of 70, 66 and 67. Teshima and Katsunori Kuwabara were at 204. Uncharacteristically, Duval let a big lead get away from him

Sunday, forcing him to overtime to nab the title.

Six ahead with six holes to play, Duval bogeyed the 14th hole and four-putted the 17th green. By that time, Teshima was already in with his 65 and 269 total and Duval knew he needed a par at the 18th to keep his title hopes alive. He missed a downhill 12-footer for a winning birdie.

In the playoff, Teshima had tree trouble off the tee on the first extra hole, could barely advance the ball and was in a greenside bunker in three. Duval also was there, but in two, and he claimed the victory when he almost holed the sand shot.

WGC EMC World Cup—US$3,000,000
Winner: South Africa

He needed help from a friend, but Ernie Els avoided a 2001 victory white-wash when he and Retief Goosen carried the South Africa banner trium-phantly in the WGC EMC World Cup, staged before big crowds on the Taiheiyo Club's Gotemba course at the foot of Japan's famed Mt. Fuji. The two U.S. Open champions, one current and the other a double winner, emerged with the title from a four-team playoff that including the defending cham-pion United States duo of Tiger Woods and David Duval. Els had gone since the previous December without a victory. The World Cup, a variation on a half-century-old international event and the final of four events in the 2001 World Golf Championship series, idled the Japan Tour for a week.

Under the new World Cup format, the first round (and the third) was played as fourball and, on a brisk November day, three teams from cold-weather countries — Canada (Mike Weir and Ian Leggatt), Scotland (An-drew Coltart and Dean Robertson) and Sweden (Niclas Fasth and Robert Karlsson) — breezed into the lead at 62. Els-Goosen shot 64 and Woods-Duval a 66 that probably would have been at least a shot better had Duval not drawn a practice-putting penalty at the 16th hole.

A surprising development was the ascension of New Zealand to the top for the next two days. In foursomes play Friday, Michael Campbell, a PGA European Tour regular, and David Smail, a successful player on the Japan Tour this season, put together a 66 for 129 and a four-stroke lead over Scotland and the home-country gallery favorites — Toshimitsu Izawa, the year's leading money winner, and Shigeki Maruyama, the popular interna-tional golfer who won on the U.S. PGA Tour. The U.S. and South Africa teams moved closer to the lead Saturday in fourball, Woods and Duval fashioning a 63 to move into second place, but they still trailed the New Zealanders (65–194) by three. Els and Goosen also shot 63 and joined Japan, Argentina and France at 198.

Drama abounded at the final green in the fading light Sunday. First, Denmark (Thomas Bjorn and Soren Hansen) put a 264 on the board with a 65 finish, outstanding in foursomes play. Then, shortly thereafter, Els rolled in a 10-foot eagle putt after a brilliant five-iron approach by Goosen for 66 and a matching 264 total. In came the final group. New Zealand managed only a par for 70 and a 264 total, and Woods, in his remarkable fashion, holed an extremely difficult 50-foot chip-and-run for eagle, 67 and a place in the playoff.

No such luck when they played the 18th again to start the playoff. Woods drove into the trees and the U.S. and New Zealand teams departed the competition with pars as Denmark and South Africa had tap-in birdies, the latter after Goosen hit another magnificent long-iron shot — a 240-yard two-iron shot from a fairway bunker over water.

A routine par gave Els and Goosen the $1 million first prize when Bjorn drove into the trees and Hansen missed a downhill eight-foot putt on the 14th hole, the second in the playoff. Japan faded to an 11th-place tie with 72 Sunday.

Casio World Open—¥140,000,000
Winner: Kiyoshi Murota

When a tournament professional is 46 years old, he certainly has to think that his last victory may be behind him, particularly when he hadn't won in seven years. That was Kiyoshi Murota's situation when the Japan Tour resumed action with the Casio World Open, the next-to-last event of the season. Murota defied those obstacles, winning the tournament by two strokes, the fourth victory of his 19-year career, by standing off challenges in the stretch from world-class Sergio Garcia and up-and-coming Fijian Dinesh Chand, who had just partnered Vijay Singh in the World Cup at Gotemba.

Murota was the dominant player at the Ibusuki Golf Club's Kaimon course almost all week. He trailed first-round leader Brendan Jones, the 1999 Australian amateur champion, and his eight-under-par, nine-birdie 64 by a single shot, sharing the runner-up slot with another veteran, Masashi Ozaki. Then Murota went in front to stay on Friday. He mustered a six-birdie 68 for 133, but had Garcia, who also played in the World Cup; Shingo Katayama, the 2000 leading money winner; Ozaki (69) and Jones (70) on his heels at 134. Katayama shot 64, Garcia 65. Murota tied the course record with two eagles and five birdies Saturday, forging a four-stroke lead with his 63 for 196 total. Chand gained his spot in Sunday's final threesome with 64, and Garcia matched his 200 score with 68. Katayama and Jones were two back after 68s, but were never in the picture the last day.

Murota never relinquished his lead Sunday, but it was not smooth sailing. He made four birdies, but when he took his second bogey at the 17th hole, Chand and Garcia were just a shot behind him. Equal to the tense situation, the veteran drove perfectly on the 18th and striped a four iron that stopped a foot from the cup for a tap-in eagle and the victory with 68 for 264 total, an impressive 24 under par. It was Murota's first win since the 1994 Fuji-sankei Classic. Chand birdied the 18th for 66 and 266, and Garcia parred for 67 and 267.

Nippon Series JT Cup—¥90,000,000
Winner: Katsumasa Miyamoto

Final-round victory rallies had been few and far between during the long Japan Tour season, but Katsumasa Miyamoto produced a stirring one in the Nippon Series JT Cup, the concluding event of the year. Miyamoto, who had qualified for the select, 26-player field with a runaway victory in the Japan Tour Championship, came from four strokes off the lead Sunday at Tokyo Yomiuri Country Club and won by a stroke over Toshimitsu Izawa and Tsuneyuki Nakajima with his 66 for 268.

Toru Taniguchi, a two-time winner and No. 2 money winner in 2000, made a final, futile bid for a 2001 victory in the Nippon Series. He shook off two early bogeys with an eagle and seven birdies, shot 63 and began the tournament with a two-stroke lead over Nakajima, who was again to experience frustration in search of victory. Taniguchi gave way to Keiichiro Fukabori Friday. Fukabori, whose ticket into the field was his triumph in the Jyuken Sangyo Open, took over the lead with one of the day's three 64s, giving him 131 and a two-stroke margin over Takenori Hiraishi, who also had a six-under score. Taniguchi dropped into a third-place at 135 with Frankie Minoza.

Fukabori shot 67 Saturday, widening his margin to three strokes with his 198 total. Izawa and Miyamoto entered the picture that day. Izawa, going after a sixth 2001 victory to enhance his No. 1 money standing, took over second place with 65 for 201 total, and Miyamoto got into position for his hot finish with 66 for 202, joining Taniguchi (67) at that position. Izawa had five birdies and an eagle, but left the three-stroke gap when he took two late bogeys. Miyamoto won the tournament and his fourth career victory with a hot finish Sunday. He birdied two of the last four holes for 66 and 268 total, just enough to edge Nakajima, who shot his third 66 of the week for 269, and Izawa, whose birdies on the last two holes weren't enough to offset a double bogey earlier in the round.

11. Australasian Tour

Sharing events with other tours (or co-sponsoring as they call it) was nothing new for the Australians. They had been hosting events on the PGA European Tour for several years. Not since the 1998 Presidents Cup had golf fans Down Under seen the wealth of talent that came in 2001.

It started two days into the New Year when the first World Golf Championships event of the season began in Victoria. The Accenture World Match Play started at Metropolitan Golf Club on January 3, with Steve Stricker, ranked 90th in the world, emerging as the winner. He hadn't planned on going to Australia because three weeks before the event he wasn't eligible. With such notable players as Tiger Woods, Phil Mickelson, David Duval and Colin Montgomerie deciding to pass, Stricker got into the 64-player field as the 55th seed.

Stricker's win might have been the first surprise of the Australasian golf season, but it wouldn't be the last. The following week Scott Laycock won his first professional event, taking the Victorian Open by three shots and breaking a 10-year winless drought that began when Laycock turned professional at age 19. Capping off a great January, David Smail won back-to-back titles at the TelstraSaturn New Zealand Open and the Canon Challenge in Sydney.

The first week of February, Smail and everyone else on the circuit ran into a buzz saw named Michael Campbell. Campbell posted a 10-birdie 64 in the final round of the Heineken Classic to come from four shots back and defend his title with a five-stroke win over Smail in Perth. The next week, two-time Australian Open winner and world's greatest teenager Aaron Baddeley reminded the world why he was one of the young stars to watch when he defeated Sergio Garcia with a birdie on the first playoff hole to take the Greg Norman Holden International.

The Holden event was marred by a rules incident on Saturday that led to a fine and lot of discussion among the players. Garcia, who was playing with Norman, took a drop on the second hole when a billboard impeded his approach. Garcia and Norman conferred, and the Spaniard dropped his ball where Norman suggested. Unfortunately, PGA European Tour rules official John Paramour said it was the wrong spot and Garcia was assessed a two-shot penalty.

Instead of shooting 68 and holding a two-stroke lead with 18 holes to play, Garcia shot 70 and was tied with Baddeley. "Of course I'm angry," Garcia said. "It was a local rule, and luckily I am not disqualified. But if you asked 500 players, they would all tell you they would have done it the way Greg and I agreed."

The spat spilled over into the press when Garcia insinuated that some people didn't want him to win. That earned the Spaniard a fine and a reprimand from officials and some strong words from his father. At heart, Garcia couldn't be faulted for his passion, but at age 21 he still had some learning to do.

Colin Montgomerie picked up his first victory of the year at the Ericsson Masters in Melbourne. In the Australasian Tour Championship, Peter Lonard finished eagle-birdie on the final two holes at Concord Golf Club to shoot 66 for a 15-under-par 269 total and a one-shot victory.

Australian golf went on hiatus from March until November, but when it returned, two natives put an exclamation point on a poignant year. Robert Allenby defended his title at the Australian PGA Championship with a one-shot win over Geoff Ogilvy. A week later, 30-year-old Stuart Appleby shot 13-under 271 for a three-stroke victory in the Holden Australian Open. It was Appleby's first victory on his home soil since 1998. "I'm thrilled," Appleby said. "And I feel fortunate to be doing what I'm doing."

WGC Accenture Match Play—US$5,000,000
Winner: Steve Stricker

Ranked 90th in the world, Steve Stricker hadn't planned on going to Australia in early January for the WGC Accenture Match Play. Three weeks before, he wasn't eligible. With many notable players deciding to pass on the trip so close to the holidays, Stricker nudged into the 64-player field as the 55th seed. Still, his expectations weren't very high. "I just figured I would win a couple of matches and get ready for the West Coast," Stricker said.

Five days later Stricker closed out Pierre Fulke 2 and 1 on the 35th hole of the final match to win the $1 million first prize and pick up his first victory in four years. Stricker wept afterward, saying, "This means so much to me. It's just beyond my expectations."

Stricker took the lead at the 15th hole of the morning round when Fulke found the bunker. After that, the Wisconsin native never trailed. In 118 holes over six matches, Stricker was behind only for a total of nine holes. He defeated Padraig Harrington 2 and 1, Scott Verplank 3 and 2, Justin Leonard 6 and 5, Nick O'Hern on the 20th hole, and Toru Taniguchi 2 and 1 before facing Fulke in the final.

"I started feeling good about my game," Stricker said. "I was scrambling really well, and my attitude and thinking was pretty sharp."

Fulke, who upset top-seeded Ernie Els 2 and 1 in the semi-finals, had putting trouble on Sunday, missing two four-footers in the final round that could have trimmed Stricker's lead. When Fulke pulled a four iron into a bunker on the 17th and missed a 15-footer for par, it was over.

Victorian Open—A$250,000
Winner: Scott Laycock

Growing up near the Cranbourne Golf Club in Australia, Scott Laycock had always been told that persistence paid — that the longer and harder he worked, the greater the rewards he would ultimately receive. By the time he turned 29, still winless after what seemed like an eternity as a professional, the persistence argument was a little tougher to swallow. Then, two months after finishing fourth in the Australian Open, Laycock finally realized his dream, winning the Victorian Open by three shots over Richard Green.

"It's unbelievable," Laycock said. "Everyone says if you put in the hard work it eventually comes — and it did. There's no better feeling than walking down the 18th with a win or a chance of winning. To be so close so often, you have to believe it will happen, otherwise it never will."

Starting the final round one shot back of Scott Gardiner, Laycock bogeyed the par-five second hole, but came back quickly with three birdies on the first nine. Meanwhile Gardiner bogeyed the sixth and never recovered, shooting 74 on Sunday to finish eight strokes back.

Laycock and Green battled it out throughout most of the second nine. The two were tied through 15 holes, but Laycock birdied the 16th and 17th to shoot seven-under 65 for the day and 18-under-par 270 for the tournament, while Green finished with two pars and a bogey to finish the week at 273.

TelstraSaturn New Zealand Open—NZ$500,000
Winner: David Smail

It was a long time coming, but in his ninth season as a professional, New Zealander David Smail won his first title by shooting seven-under-par 273 in the TelstraSaturn New Zealand Open. That total was good enough for a two-stroke victory over defending champion Michael Campbell and three other players including Steve Alker, one of Smail's high school teammates.

Smail looked like the model of consistency throughout the week. Rounds of 66 and 68 gave him a two-shot margin heading into the weekend, and he led the rest of the way. Closing with rounds of 69 and 70, Smail was never seriously challenged. Campbell missed several good birdie opportunities in the final round before making double bogey at the 17th, while Alker got to six under through 17 holes, but bogeyed the 18th to fall into a four-way tie for second.

By the time Smail reached the 18th tee he held a five-shot lead, but a double bogey coupled with a final-hole birdie by Campbell narrowed the margin to two. "I actually thought I was only two ahead," Smail said. "But I made sure I had a look at the leaderboard as I walked down the fairway. That was a great feeling."

Canon Challenge—A$550,000
Winner: David Smail

After eight winless years as a professional, David Smail made it two in a row with an impressive victory at the Canon Challenge. One shot off the lead after rounds of 69, 64 and 69, Smail came to the 17th tee tied with David Gossett, the 1999 U.S. Amateur champion. After Smail hit an approach shot to within five feet on the 17th, Gossett three-putted for a bogey. When Smail made his birdie, he held a two-shot lead. Gossett came back with a birdie at the final hole to cut the margin to one, but Smail's closing par was enough for a five-under-par 67, a 269 total, and his second win in two weeks.

'It's unbelievable," Smail said. "It's just amazing. My first win last week seemed like a dream come true, and this was just something else. I had a lot of discussions with friends and players about how you can go along and make nice checks, and some pretty good money without actually needing to win. I was resigning myself to the fact that was what I might carry on doing for the next three years. But now, it's a dream come true."

Gossett, who failed to qualify for the PGA Tour after shooting a record 59 during the tour's qualifying tournament, shot a final-round 68 for second place at 270 while Australians Justin Cooper and Tod Power finished tied for third at 271.

Heineken Classic—A$1,750,000
Winner: Michael Campbell

The scouting report on Michael Campbell had always been that he could get hot in a hurry, and when he did there was no limit to how low he could go. Nowhere was that more evident than in Perth, Australia, where Campbell posted a 10-birdie 64 in the final round of the Heineken Classic to come from four strokes back and successfully defend his title with a 270 total for a five-shot victory over David Smail.

Third-round leader Nick O'Hern finished with an even-par round of 72 and couldn't believe his eyes when he realized that, not only had he lost by six shots to Campbell, he had to settle for third at 276. "When Michael is on his game he's as good as anyone," O'Hern said. "I don't think I've played with anyone better."

Campbell went a long way toward proving O'Hern right. After shooting 69 and 70 in the first two rounds, Campbell played a lackluster even-par first nine on Saturday before turning into a birdie machine. In the next 27 holes he posted 16 birdies, finishing with 67 on Saturday and closing with Sunday's 64. It was Campbell's sixth win in 32 starts, and his first of 2001.

After collecting the A$315,000 winner's check, Campbell set his sights on loftier goals. "My next goal is to compete against the best players in the game in the best tournaments and win a major," he said. "I think I've proved to myself after winning a few times on the PGA European Tour that it is time to go to the next level. I want to go head-to-head with Ernie Els or Tiger Woods or David Duval in majors and come out on top."

O'Hern, who never recovered from a quadruple-bogey eight on the par-four sixth hole, said of the winner, "He was on fire. You just have to take your hat off to somebody who shoots 64 on the last day."

Greg Norman Holden International—A$2,000,000
Winner: Aaron Baddeley

In a battle of young up-and-coming stars at Greg Norman's Holden Invitational, two-time Australian Open champion Aaron Baddeley came out on top, defeating Sergio Garcia with a birdie on the first playoff hole. Baddeley had already set the golf world abuzz when he won the Australian Open as an 18-year-old amateur, and successfully defended his title as a 19-year-old professional, while Garcia was labeled the wonderkid of golf before his 20th birthday.

That the two of them were neck-and-neck at the end of regulation play was a matter of good luck or terrible misfortune, depending on your perspective.

Garcia felt he should have won outright, not because of any shots he hit, but because of a ruling he received after the conclusion of play on Saturday. Paired with Norman in the third round, Garcia took a drop on the second hole when a billboard impeded his approach. Instead of taking full line-of-sight relief as the local rule required, Garcia and Norman conferred and the Spaniard dropped his ball in the wrong spot, or so said PGA European Tour rules official John Paramour, who went out to the scene after the round was completed. Garcia was assessed a two-shot penalty. Instead of shooting 68 and holding a two-stroke lead, Garcia shot 70 and was tied with Baddeley.

"Of course I'm angry," Garcia said. "It was a local rule, and luckily I am not disqualified. But if you asked 500 players they would all tell you they would have done it the way Greg and I agreed."

Garcia marched out on Sunday and shot another 68 — this one penalty-free — for a 271 total. Baddeley also shot 68, so the two returned to the 18th hole for a playoff. When Baddeley rolled in a birdie, he had captured his first PGA European Tour victory and his second win as a professional before his 20th birthday.

"This is awesome," Baddeley said. "I'm exempt in Europe until 2003."

Ericsson Masters—A$1,000,000
Winner: Colin Montgomerie

A little time off seemed to be just what the golf doctors ordered for Colin Montgomerie. After a two-month layoff, Montgomerie received a late invitation to come to Melbourne for the Ericsson Masters, an event he hadn't planned on playing after spending the holidays with his family in the Caribbean.

"I hadn't planned on coming down here, but I got a late invite, which was very kind," Montgomerie said. "I went to Houston for two days, and then came here. It's a long way down, but I'm glad I came."

With a three-under 69 on Sunday, Montgomerie finished at 278 and won by a single shot over Nathan Green and third-round leader Brett Rumford. The highlight of Green's day came at the par-three 12th, when he holed a seven iron from 176 yards. The $276,000 Green earned for the hole-in-one equaled Montgomerie's first-place prize money. But the victory was more important than the money for Montgomerie. After losing an eighth straight Order of Merit title to Lee Westwood in 2000, the 37-year-old Scot was anxious to get back on track.

For Rumford, it was a major disappointment. A course-record 64 on Saturday gave him a three-shot lead at 12-under-par 204, but Rumford bogeyed three of his first four holes on Sunday and never recovered. He remained nine under throughout the remainder of the round, but he had a chance to force a playoff on the 18th. When his birdie chip slipped past the hole, Rumford had to settle for a share of second place.

Australasian Tour Championship—A$1,500,000
Winner: Peter Lonard

With a one-shot lead on the 71st hole, 25-year-old Nathan Green felt good about his chances in the Australasian Tour Championship, especially after he reached the par-five 17th with his second shot. A two-putt for birdie and the victory should be his.

Unfortunately for Green, his playing partner had different ideas. Peter Lonard missed the 17th green with his second shot, but as he approached his ball, Lonard's caddie said, "That's the perfect place to chip it in from."

"I really needed to make eagle on 17," Lonard said, but even he had his doubts. "It was sitting pretty good on the upslope, but in my wildest dreams I didn't think I was going to hole it."

Lonard holed the chip for eagle, and when Green two-putted for birdie, the two were tied at 14 under par. When Lonard made a 10-footer for birdie at the 18th, he had captured the title with one of the best finishes in Australasian Tour Championship history. His 66 gave him a 15-under-par 269 total and a one-shot victory.

"At 33 years old I'm really getting to the stage where I've got to pull my finger out and do something or get a job," Lonard said. "It's a good start today."

Lonard's win moved him into second-place on the season-ending Australasian Order of Merit behind Aaron Baddeley, who shot seven-under 277 and finished 13th in Sydney. Michael Campbell finished third on the list after shooting 282 for the week.

Australian PGA Championship—A$1,000,000
Winner: Robert Allenby

Closing out his best season as a professional, Robert Allenby added a second straight Australian PGA Championship to his already stellar resume. And he went into the holidays with his sights set on winning a major.

"It is every golfer's ambition to win one of the four majors," Allenby said after shooting a final-round 69 for a 15-under-par 273 total at Royal Queensland to successfully defend his title by a single stroke over Geoff Ogilvy. "My goal is to win all four, not just one. If I can prepare myself right going into one of the majors, there is no reason that I can't win. I know mentally I've got it and I know I've got the game to hit any shot under pressure. Next year is a big year to get one of those. But the old story is, you can't put too much pressure on yourself. If you do, you won't get it."

That adage might have applied to Allenby in Queensland as he began the final round with a one-shot lead over Ogilvy and Craig Parry. Allenby lost that lead after a frustrating run of 12 straight pars. Then Allenby hit the shot of the tournament at the 13th. After hitting his second shot on the par-five into the greenside bunker, Allenby blasted his third shot into the hole for an eagle-three to reclaim the lead. He made a three-putt bogey at the 15th, but recovered with a birdie at the 16th to regain a one-shot lead over Ogilvy with two holes to play.

More drama was ahead at the 17th as Ogilvy hit a perfect drive on the dogleg-right, par-five hole while Allenby pushed his tee shot into the trees. With only a five iron left to the green, Ogilvy played first and hit the shot that cost him the tournament, a pull-hook that missed the green and left Ogilvy with an impossible chip.

Allenby recovered from his poor tee shot by punching back to the fairway and playing a wedge shot to 10 feet. When he made the birdie and Ogilvy failed to save par from the left side, Allenby's lead was two shots with one to play.

The tournament wasn't over yet. Ogilvy made a 20-footer for birdie at the 18th after Allenby missed the green long. With the ball sitting in a swale behind the green, Allenby made another deft chip to eight feet and rolled in the putt for the victory. Ogilvy's 69 and 274 total was enough for second place as Parry struggled in with an even-par round of 72. Parry finished at 277 and tied for third with New Zealand's Gareth Paddison.

Holden Australian Open—A$1,500,000
Winner: Stuart Appleby

Stuart Appleby didn't need to set a course record in order to win his first Holden Australian Open, but he almost did it anyway. Needing only a par at the 18th to shoot seven-under-par 64 during Sunday's final round at the Grand Golf Club on the Gold Coast, Appleby hit his worst tee shot of the day, missed the final green and left his par putt hanging on the lip of the cup.

It mattered not a whit. With a tap-in bogey for 65 and a 13-under-par 271 total, Appleby equaled the course record and won his national title by three strokes over Scott Laycock.

Tied for the lead with Laycock going into the final round, Appleby birdied four holes in a row between the ninth and 12th, but gained no ground. Laycock capped Appleby's every birdie and continued to share the lead through 14 holes. Some late bogeys cost Laycock. He shot 68 to finish second at 274.

"The way we were making that many birdies, it didn't look like anyone was going to catch us," Appleby said. "To have Scott stall at the end was very fortunate on my behalf."

12. African Tours

Southern African golfers made inroads in world golf in 2001. Retief Goosen won the U.S. Open Championship and the European Order of Merit title. In addition, Ernie Els, who won the WGC EMC World Cup for South Africa with Goosen, won a title at home in the Vodacom Players Championship. Two more Southern African veterans, Rory Sabbatini from South Africa and Mark McNulty from Zimbabwe, joined Els, Goosen and Nick Price as the only Africans in the top 100 on the World Ranking. McNulty also joined Goosen, Els and Jean Hugo (ranked 167th in the world) as top-50 finishers on the European Order of Merit.

McNulty had a good year on his home soil as well. Starting in January on the Wild Coast, the South African won the Nashua Nedtel Cellular Masters and the Mercedes-Benz South African Open in a span of three weeks. Then in February, Deane Pappas, bound for stardom in 2001 on the U.S. Buy.com Tour, captured the South African PGA Championship. It was the biggest win of the 33-year-old's career, and he was moved to tears when accepting the trophy. "It's great that my first major win should come in one of my country's premier tournaments," Pappas said.

It was Pappas' only victory in Africa, but he did all right the rest of the season, winning on the Buy.com Tour and earning his U.S. PGA Tour card for 2002.

Bradford Vaughan posted his first victory of the year at the Investec Royal Swazi Sun Open in February, and a week later, Darren Fichardt capped off the "big event" portion of the tour with a four-stroke victory over Hennie Otto in the Sunshine Tour Championship.

Vaughan wouldn't win again, but Fichardt would pick up another win late in the year at the CABS/Old Mutual Zimbabwe Open, as well as winning the San Paulo Brazil Open in March. He joined McNulty and James Kingston as multiple winners in Africa for the season. Kingston won the Randfontein Classic in late September and the Atlantic Beach Classic two weeks later.

In the last two weeks of the year, Ernie Els, frustrated by his inability to win a title in either America or Europe despite near misses on both continents, resurrected his game, first at the Nedbank Golf Challenge and again at the Vodacom Players Championship.

In the first week at Sun City, Els shot 20-under-par 268, a score that beat every player in the field except one. Sergio Garcia started the final round six strokes behind Els, but came roaring back with 63 to tie for the lead. Garcia sealed the victory and the $2 million first-place check with a chip-in from 20 feet on the first playoff hole.

A week later Els shot 15-under-par 273 on the Royal Cape Golf Club for a one-shot victory in the season-ending Vodacom Players Championship. He closed with a bang, shooting a 65 that Els called "my best round of the year."

Nashua Nedtel Cellular Masters—R1,000,000
Winner: Mark McNulty

Despite a poor final-round start, 47-year-old Mark McNulty righted a listing game and held on to win the Nashua Nedtel Cellular Masters by one stroke at Wild Coast. It was McNulty's fifth South African Masters title, one shy of the record held by Gary Player. This one didn't come easily.

Leading by three entering Sunday's round, McNulty started in abysmal fashion. An eight-iron approach from 158 yards on the first hole sailed over the green and lodged in the bushes. With nowhere to go, McNulty hacked his ball out sideways, then chipped to six feet and missed the bogey putt. After that double bogey, he hit sand wedge to the second hole and three-putted for bogey. In less than half an hour, McNulty went from nine under par to six under, and the tournament was up for grabs.

"It was a frustrating day because most of my shots were good, but nothing was happening out there," McNulty said. "It's all about emotions and I couldn't control them after the start that I had. I was very tense the whole day, which came about because of the way I started. I suppose you only need to win by one shot, but the only sad thing is that I don't like to shoot over par to win a tournament."

Three-over-par 73 was good enough for McNulty. Des Terblanche jumped into the lead early in the final round, but bogeys by Terblanche at the 11th and 14th holes allowed McNulty to edge back into the lead. Terblanche and Retief Goosen finished at 275. McNulty's 73 gave him a six-under-par 274 total, not what he wanted, but still his 49th career victory.

Alfred Dunhill Championship—£500,000
Winner: Adam Scott

From a distance 20-year-old Adam Scott bears a slight resemblance to Tiger Woods. His tall, athletic build, narrow waist and impressive swing mechanics (honed under the tutelage of Tiger's coach, Butch Harmon) made Scott the most talked-about rookie on the European circuit in 2001. He lived up to the billing, posting four rounds in the 60s at the Royal Houghton Golf Club in Johannesburg to win the Alfred Dunhill Championship by one stroke in only his eighth PGA European Tour start.

A 65 on Saturday gave Scott a one-shot lead over another young star, Justin Rose, who splashed onto the scene in 1998 when he briefly led the British Open as an 18-year-old. The two players remained close throughout the final round, with Rose making a birdie on the final hole to force Scott to make a four-foot birdie putt of his own for 69 and a 267 total. Nick Faldo, who at 42 is older than the combined ages of Scott and Rose, finished tied for third with Dean Robertson at 269.

"Adam is a world-beater with a big future," Robertson said. "He is the finished article. He oozes class. His swing is fantastic, and he has a great temperament to go with it. I think he will win majors and compete with Tiger Woods in the future."

Scott was a little more guarded in his analysis. "Hopefully this is just the start," he said. "I've got a taste of winning now and I want it even more.

I spoke to Butch Harmon, and he told me not to go out and try to win, but simply to play a round of golf."

Mercedes-Benz South African Open—US$1,000,000
Winner: Mark McNulty

For a while there was a question of whether Justin Rose would play in the Mercedes-Benz South African Open. Rose hadn't been extended an invitation because for 21 straight tournaments beginning in 1998 he had missed the cut and become a poster boy for those turning professional too soon. When Rose came within a shot of winning the Alfred Dunhill Championship, sponsors began to scramble in hopes of finding a spot for him. Their savior showed up in the form of local pro Shane Howe, who gave up his invitation in order to make room for the Englishman.

The youngster took full advantage of the opportunity, once again finishing within one shot of the winner. This time it was 47-year-old Mark McNulty, who clipped Rose by making a 20-footer for par at the final hole. The Zimbabwean finished with a final-round 71 for a 280 total to leap past third-round leader Hennie Otto and capture his 50th career title.

"This was a special win for me," McNulty said afterward. "Especially to win under such punishing conditions. It blew, it rained, the lightening flashed, it was chilly at times, and blazing hot at other times."

In the end it was McNulty's blazing hot putter that put him over the top. After Otto fell away with three early bogeys, McNulty battled for the lead with South African Roger Wessels, who entered the final round two shots back. McNulty and Wessels shared the lead through 15 holes with Rose one shot back. When Wessels bogeyed the 16th and 18th, Rose was the only player who stood a chance at forcing a playoff.

Those hopes were dashed when McNulty composed himself after a mediocre chip and nailed the 20-footer for par into the center of the hole. It was the difference between finishing with 71 for the day or 72 as Rose had done, and it was the difference between winning outright and going back to the 18th for a playoff.

Rose stood alone in second place at 281, while Wessels' two late bogeys dropped him into a tie for third with Thomas Bjorn at 282. Otto closed with 77 to tie for fifth with Mikael Lundberg at 283.

Dimension Data Pro-Am—R2,000,000
Winner: Darren Clarke

Standing in the final fairway of the Gary Player Country Club course with a three-shot lead in the Dimension Data Pro-Am, Darren Clarke was pumped up. He had elected to lay up short of the water on the par-five 18th hole, but his nine-iron shot flew further than intended, caught a downslope, and rolled into the lake.

"I wanted to finish short of that slope, but the ball ran a meter or two further than I intended," Clarke said. "When I got to the ball, I realized it was going to go into the green low, but I never expected it to come out that low."

Clarke took a drop and made what he later called "probably the best six I've ever made." He finished with 71 for a 14-under-par 274 total, two strokes better than Retief Goosen and Tjaart van der Walt.

Goosen remained close throughout the day, but a three-putt bogey at the par-four 17th put victory out of the question. He attempted to reach the 18th green in two, correctly calculating that eagle was his only chance. He found the water and settled for par. Van der Walt birdied the last hole to gain a share of second place, and Clarke fired up his ceremonial victory cigar. "It feels great," he said. "The finish was a bit touchy, but it was good enough to win."

South African PGA Championship—R1,000,000
Winner: Deane Pappas

South African Deane Pappas won the biggest tournament of his life when he posted a five-under-par 67 for a 269 total at the Woodhill County Club to capture the South African PGA Championship. No one else was close. Don Gammon, who also posted a final-round 67, finished alone in second place, three strokes behind Pappas.

Tied with Martin Maritz and Sammy Daniels at 202, Pappas got off to a quick start, birdieing the difficult par-four first hole while his two co-leaders began their rounds with bogeys. After that Pappas never gave up the lead.

"Before the round I told my caddie that our goal was to make no mistakes," Pappas said. "The only one I can think of was a three-putt at the ninth. I just kept the ball in play and hit all 18 greens. It's great that my first major win should come in one of my country's premier tournaments."

Investec Royal Swazi Sun Open—R500,000
Winner: Bradford Vaughan

With a three-shot lead going into the final round of the Investec Royal Swazi Sun Open, all Bradford Vaughan needed was a solid round to claim the title and move into third place on the South African Order of Merit. Anything under par would do.

Vaughan delivered more than expected. With six birdies and an eagle in the final round, he shot an eight-under-par 64 for a 263 total and an eight-shot victory over Mark Hilton, who finished with 69, and Trevor Immelman, who made a great run with 65.

This one belonged to Vaughan from the early moments of the final round. Four birdies and no bogeys on the first nine allowed him to separate himself from the field. "I said last night that you can't relax on this golf course," the winner said. "The best form of defense here is to attack, which may sound like a bit of a cliché, but that's exactly the way it worked out."

Sunshine Tour Championship—R2,000,000
Winner: Darren Fichardt

South African Darren Fichardt won the Sunshine Tour Championship by posting one of the most exciting final rounds in the event's history. Leading by four strokes after five holes in the final round, Fichardt was assessed a two-shot penalty when he repaired a pitch mark in the fringe. Since the pitch mark was not on the green, Fichardt was deemed to have improved his line of play, a violation of Rule 13-2.

"I was not familiar with the ruling, but it shows me that I must learn my rules better," Fichardt said.

After being assessed the penalty on the seventh tee, Fichardt bogeyed the eighth, ninth and 10th holes before righting his game to finish with 68. His 14-under-par 270 total was enough to regain his four-stroke margin over Hennie Otto, who shot 67.

"A two-shot penalty always knocks you," Fichardt said. "I had to really dig deep after that. But the spectators and my family were all cheering me on. I thought, 'Hang on, you're still in this tournament. Don't give up now.'"

Mark McNulty was also giving himself a pep talk during the final round. McNulty shot 69 to finish in a tie for 20th, but the score was good enough for him to earn a record eighth South African Order of Merit title.

"I'm delighted to have achieved this," McNulty said. "It was one of the goals I set for myself at the beginning of the year. To win three out of the six tournaments I played on tour was fantastic."

Stanbic Zambia Open—£50,000
Winner: Mark Foster

On the strength of a five-under-par 68 in the final round, England's Mark Foster was able to hold off a charge by South African Jaco Olver to win the Stanbic Zambia Open by one stroke. Foster, who saved his best round of the week for last, shot three consecutive 70s before closing with 68 on the 7,226 yard, par-73 Lusaka Golf Club for a 14-under 278 total in the event, which was co-sponsored by the European Challenge Tour.

Olver also played his best golf in the closing round. He shot nine-under-par 64 after posting scores of 71, 72 and 72 to jump into a tie for second with Englishman Stuart Little at 279. Two Scots shared fourth place as Euan Little and Roger Beames both shot 68 in the final round for 280 totals.

Cock of the North—R200,000
Winner: Sean Farrell

Thanks to a flurry of birdies in the final round and some late stumbling by the second-round leader, Sean Farrell ran away with a victory in the Cock of the North at Ndola Golf Club. Trailing by one shot going into the closing round, Farrell posted a seven-under-par 66 for a 10-under 209 total and a four-stroke margin over Graeme van der Nest.

Zimbabwean Nasho Kamungeremu held a one-shot lead at 141 when he added 69 to his opening-round 72. Mike Lamb and Andre Cruse were tied for second at 142, while Farrell and van der Nest were two off the lead.

Things turned around quickly as Farrell got off to a strong start while Kamungeremu struggled. The Zimbabwean limped in with 74 for a 215 total. That left him tied with Lamb, Cruse and the surprise player of the event, amateur Madiliso Muthiya, who followed his 72-72 start with a closing 71 for a 215 total.

FNB Botswana Open—R210,000
Winner: Marc Cayeux

It was a more exciting finish than Zimbabwe's Mark Cayeux would have liked. Leading by four strokes after two rounds on the strength of a second-round 63, Cayeux would have loved to coast in with a victory at the FNB Botswana Open. South African Hendrik Buhrmann had other plans. With a closing 63 of his own, Buhrmann posted a 199 total early and sat back to see if Cayeux could match him.

The Zimbabwean was up to the task, finishing with 68 for a 16-under-par 197 total and a two-shot victory.

Buhrmann had the low round of the final day, but he could only tie for second place, as Grant Muller shot 65 for his 199 finish. Sean Ludgater, Cayeux's closest pursuer after two rounds, followed his 68 and 65 with a closing 68 for a 201 total and a share of third place with Zambian amateur Madiliso Muthiya, who shared the first-round lead with 65.

Royal Swazi Sun Classic—R200,000
Winner: Titch Moore

In the first playoff of the season, South African Titch Moore defeated Keith Horne to take the Royal Swazi Sun Classic. The two were knotted at 16-under-par 200 at the end of regulation in a week when a half-dozen players had chances to win in the closing holes.

Horne took the first-round lead with an eight-under-par 64, but he had plenty of pursuers. Moore shot 65 and was tied for second with South African Michiel Bothma, while Leonard Loxton and Mark Murless were third with 66s.

With 68 in the second round, Horne maintained his one-shot lead at 132, although a pair of new contenders emerged. Warren Abery shot 66 to go with his earlier 67 for a 133 total, and Zimbabwean Marc Cayeux shot his second consecutive 67 to move within two strokes.

Moore shot 70 in the second round to fall three behind, but he made up ground on Sunday with a round of 65. That left him tied with Horne, who posted another 68 to finish at 200 and earn a spot in the playoff. Cayeux and Abery were one shot off the mark.

Pietersburg Industrelek Classic—R200,000
Winner: Ryan Reid

Some golfers might have given up after shooting 74. After all, the Pietersburg Industrelek Classic was only 54 holes and anyone who shot 74 in the opening round was more likely to miss the 36-hole cut than win the golf tournament. But Ryan Reid never stopped shooting at flagsticks and posted 67 and 63 to win by two strokes.

Trailing first-round leader Callie Swart by eight strokes, Reid came roaring back while the leaders faltered. Swart shot 74 in the second round and closed with 73 to tie for 20th. Reid's prospects still seemed bleak. Keith Horne shot 67 and 66 to lead by three over Naithen Moore and Bradley Davison. Reid made the cut with his second-round 67, but he still trailed by eight strokes.

That deficit was erased in the closing round when Reid shot a blistering 63, the best score of the day by four strokes and the best of the week by three, for a 12-under-par 204 total. He blew past 17 players in the final 18 holes.

Moore finished second with 70 for a 206 total.

Goldfields Powerade Classic—R200,000
Winner: Callie Swart

When it was over Callie Swart seemed more disgusted by the two bogeys he made in the final round of the Goldfields Powerade Classic than he was elated by the eagle he made on the final hole to win the title.

"I wasn't hitting the ball well at all," the winner said after posting 66 for a nine-under-par 207 total and a one-shot victory over Ryan Reid. "I missed virtually every fairway out there, not by much but just enough to put you off your game. My driver just wasn't working for me at all."

Trailing by five to Jaco Van Zyl after two rounds, Swart, who had shot 67 and 74, abandoned his driver and opted to use his three wood off most tees in the closing round. With Van Zyl falling off the leaderboard with a closing 77, Swart birdied four of the first seven holes before posting a bogey at the par-three eighth.

"Two of my three bogeys came on par-threes," he said. "I missed the green off the tee, but I knew if I could make another three birdies on the back nine I would be in with a chance."

He did just that, birdieing the 10th, 11th and 13th. What he didn't count on at the time was two more bogeys at the par-three 12th and the par-four 17th after an errant tee shot. "Ryan was in at eight-under 208," Swart said. "I knew I had to birdie the par-five 18th to at least make a playoff with him."

Swart's two three-wood shots on the final hole were perfect, the second one resulting in a five-foot putt for eagle. When Swart rolled the putt in the hole, he went from needing birdie to tie, to making eagle to win.

Bloemfontein Classic—R200,000
Winner: Andre Cruse

Andre Cruse again posted the lowest score of the day in the final round of the Bloemfontein Classic. And, again, Cruse made up four shots and leapt past a dozen contenders to win the tournament by a single stroke.

This time it was second-round leader Patrick O'Brien who fell victim to Cruse's final-round flurry. O'Brien, who shot 68s in the first two rounds, carried a one-shot lead over Jaco Van Zyl into the final 18 holes. Cruse was four shots back and well down the leaderboard when play began.

The complexion of the scoreboard changed quickly as Cruse shot 67 to go with two earlier rounds of 70. He posted a nine-under-par 207 total, then waited as his challengers fell short of the mark.

O'Brien shot 73 to tie for third with Dean van Staden at 209, while Van Zyl also shot 73 and finished in a tie for fifth at 210. Cruse's closest challenger at the end was Steve van Vuuren, who shot 71 to go with earlier rounds of 67 and 70. His 208 total left van Vuuren alone in second.

Randfontein Classic—R200,000
Winner: James Kingston

Starting the final round of the Randfontein Classic two shots behind leader Ashley Roestoff, James Kingston drew strength from the words of playing companion Andre Cruse.

"On the first hole both Crusie and I eagled and Naithen Moore (the third member of the group) had a birdie, which set the tone for a good day," Kingston said. "As we walked off the green, Crusie said, 'The winner must come from our group.' I think we fed off each other the rest of the round."

Kingston and Cruse both shot 66s to finish tied at 11-under-par 205. Sean Ludgater, who also closed with 66 after rounds of 69 and 70, joined them at 205. Moore, who started the final round one stroke ahead of the trio, shot 68 and finished a shot back at 206, while second-round leader Roestoff shot 72 for a 209 finish.

Cruse was correct: One of the members of his group would win the tournament. But it wasn't him. In the playoff, which began at the par-five 18th, Kingston made an eagle-three to win.

"Sean pulled his drive slightly (in the playoff) and wasn't in good shape to make the green in two," Kingston said. "Crusie hit a good driver, but came up just short of the green with his second. I decided that four wasn't going to be good enough to win, so I went for the green in two with a five iron from 203 meters. It was a solid shot and I hit it stiff to five feet."

Cruse came up short with his chip from 25 feet, while Ludgater hit his third shot close. When Kingston rolled in the eagle putt, he was the winner.

Bearing Man Highveld Classic—R200,000
Winner: Justin Hobday

In his 20 years as a golfer, Justin Hobday said he had never been away from the game for more than two weeks until this year. So when a stress fracture in his right hand kept Hobday sidelined for over three months, he had no idea what to expect when he returned. That made his come-from-behind playoff victory in the Bearing Man Highveld Classic one of the sweetest victories in Hobday's career.

"This is fantastic," Hobday said after rounds of 69, 69 and 65 left him tied at 203 with 23-year-old Zimbabwean Marc Cayeux, and a 12-foot par putt on the second playoff hole sealed the victory. "I've had a pretty terrible year so far with this injury. I couldn't do anything. I just had to sit at home and watch television. I had no idea what to expect coming back after such a long layoff. But I feel like things are back on track now with this win."

The final round was full of fireworks as the leader, Cayeux, struggled on the closing holes. The youngster had led since early in the first round, when he put together 64 for a four-shot lead. A 68 in the second round kept the lead at two shots over Hendrik Buhrmann and put Cayeux six ahead of Hobday.

After struggling through 16 holes of the final round in even par, Cayeux hit an approach shot to the 17th that almost went in for eagle. The tap-in birdie gave him a share of the lead at 13 under. When Cayeux parred the last hole for 71, Cayeux and Hobday were tied at 203.

Atlantic Beach Classic—R200,000
Winner: James Kingston

James Kingston fought off poor weather conditions and a field of contenders to win his second tournament in three weeks, when he closed with an even-par 72 for a 213 total at the Atlantic Beach Classic. The Rustenburg professional was the only player to finish under par on the windswept Atlantic Beach course in Cape Town.

Kingston's margin was seven shots over Justin Hobday and Wallie Coetsee, who both shot 77 in the final round for 220 totals, while Andre Cruse finished fourth after 72 left him at 222.

Kingston's total tied the 54-hole record for highest winning score on record in South Africa. The only other 213 total to win was in the 1998 Fish River Sun Pro-Am. "It was really tough out there," Kingston said. "On this course and with the wind blowing as hard as it was, I didn't expect the winning total to be anywhere near under par."

An early challenge didn't rattle Kingston. After taking a two-stroke margin into the final round, he immediately saw that lead shrink to one. Both Hobday and Keith Horne birdied the par-five opening hole. As Kingston put it, "That didn't bother me. I knew the whole course still lay ahead. I knew the tough holes were still coming, and that if I played well I would be okay."

Birdies at the eighth and ninth holes swung the tournament in Kingston's favor, and no one made any serious challenges on the final nine.

Western Cape Classic—R200,000
Winner: Lindani Ndwandwe

Lindani Ndwandwe carried a two-stroke lead into the final round of the Western Cape Classic, and he would need both of them. With a closing round of 71 for a nine-under-par 207 total, Ndwandwe held off the challenge of fellow South African Richard Kaplan to win at the Rondebosch Golf Club by a single stroke.

He trailed by three after the opening round when Brett Liddle set the pace with 63. Liddle could do little else. He finished with rounds of 77 and 74 for a 214 total. Ndwandwe followed his opening 66 with 70, and Kaplan shot 72 after opening with 66. It became a two-man race in the final round as none of the others could mount a charge. Kaplan shot 70 to finish second at 208, while Keith Horne, Clinton Whitelaw and Gerry Coetzee shared third at 211.

Vodacom Trophy—R200,000
Winner: Ulrich van den Berg

Birdies were flying in the Vodacom Trophy at Zwartkop Country Club in Pretoria and, for a while, it looked as though the last player to made a birdie might win. That wasn't exactly the case, but when Ulrich van den Berg rolled in his last putt for 64, an 18-under-par 198 total and a two-stroke victory, the only question was whether officials would lengthen the golf course and grow the rough before next year's event.

Van den Berg's victory was never secure until the final putt fell, despite rounds of 68, 66 and 64. That's because he was pressured by players such as Jaco Van Zyl, who finished second after rounds of 70, 65 and 65 left him at 200. England's Gary Birch also shot 64 in the final round. His 201 total was only good enough for a share of third with Roger Wessels and Martin Maritz.

Graceland Challenge—R200,000
Winner: Warren Abery

With a closing round of 66, Warren Abery made up five strokes in 10 holes and won the Graceland Challenge by three over second-round leader Richard Sterne. The 11-under-par 205 total earned Abery R31,400, his largest paycheck of the year.

It didn't come easy. With earlier scores of 69 and 70, Abery trailed Sterne by five. Sterne's troubles came early and often in the closing round. When the dust settled, the second-round leader had posted 74 for a total of 208. That was still one shot better than Justin Hobday, who finished with 71 for a 209 total, and two better than Wayne Bradley and Wallie Coetsee.

No one came close to Abery. His 66 in the final round was the best of the day by two shots, and equaled the best round of the tournament.

Hassan II Trophy—US$354,600
Winner: Joakim Haeggman

Sweden's Joakim Haeggman kept his composure over the closing holes to win the Hassan II Trophy at Royal Golf Dar-es-Salam in the 30th annual playing of that event in Morocco. Haeggman shot 72, one under par, in the final round for a 284 total to hold off England's Mark Roe and Spain's Santiago Luna by one stroke. He received the traditional jeweled dagger, presented by King Mohammed VI, along with prize money of $80,000.

Haeggman started the final round one stroke behind Roe and Luna, but birdied the first hole to share the lead. He had a one-stroke lead after taking 34 strokes through nine holes. Luna's chances effectively came to an end with his double bogey on the 13th, by which time Roe was three strokes behind. Haeggman dropped shots at the 14th and 16th holes, but scored pars on the last two for the victory.

Platinum Classic—R440,000
Winner: Roger Wessels

With 64 in the final round, Roger Wessels came from four shots back to finish with a 15-under-par 201 total and run away with the Platinum Classic. The margin of victory was four shots over Des Terblanche, who could do little more than watch as Wessels ripped apart the Mooinooi Golf Club in Rustenburg, bettering Terblanche's second-round 65 by one stroke.

Terblanche did manage to capture second place, following his earlier rounds of 68 and 65 with a lackluster closing score of 72 for a 205 total. Richard Sterne, still feeling the sting from his final-round collapse in the Graceland Challenge the week before, got progressively better as the week went on, shooting 73, 69 and 65 to share third place with Marc Cayeux at 207.

It was Wessels' tournament from the early moments of the final round. His closing performance was his best of the year.

CABS/Old Mutual Zimbabwe Open—R1,000,000
Winner: Darren Fichardt

With his swing failing him in the final round, Darren Fichardt had to rely on a steady putter and steely nerves to hold on and win the CABS/Old Mutual Zimbabwe Open. The Pretoria professional carried a two-shot lead after scores of 68, 68 and 69 at Chapman Golf Club, but he felt his edge slipping early. "My swing wasn't quite there the whole week," he said afterward. "I managed to work with it, but my putter and my short game got me through the week."

His putter continued working on Sunday, when he sank a 30-footer for birdie at the fourth hole to move three ahead of the field. When he failed to birdie the short par-five fifth for the second day in a row, Fichardt felt as though he had given a shot back. At the sixth, he did give a shot back, making a bogey after hitting his tee shot under a tree.

If either Richard Sterne or Andre van Staden, who started two shots off the pace, had been able to mount a charge, the outcome might have been different. But Sterne made bogey at the sixth and van Staden made double bogey, the first of what would prove to be many struggles through the day.

The only challenger turned out to be Bradford Vaughan, who started five off the pace, but rolled in an eagle putt at the fifth to cut the lead to two and move into second place alongside Michael Green and Jean Hugo.

Fichardt hit another errant tee shot at the seventh which landed behind a tree in the rough on the right, a seemingly impossible position from which to make par. Fichardt did one better, hitting the shot of the tournament from behind the tree — a seven iron that split a fork in the tree and landed six feet from the flag. The resulting birdie gave Fichardt the boost he needed.

With another birdie at the ninth, Fichardt entered the final nine holes two shots clear. He would increase that lead with a birdie at the 18th for 69, a 13-under-par 275 total and a three-shot margin over Vaughn and Mark Murless. Green and Hugo finished fourth with Nicholas Lawrence at 279, while early contenders Sterne and van Staden closed with 73s to finish in a four-way tie for seventh at 281.

PriceWaterhouseCoopers Nelson Mandela Invitational—R250,000
Winners: Martin Maritz and Simon Hobday

In an event where experience should have played a major role, it was the outstanding play of a 24-year-old rookie that ruled the day. With two days of near-flawless golf and scores that, had the PriceWaterhouseCoopers Nelson Mandela Invitational been a medal format, would have totaled 62 and 63, Martin Maritz carried his team to a five-shot victory over defending champions Retief Goosen and Allen Henning and the team of David Frost and Solly Sepeng.

Even Maritz's partner, Simon Hobday, was impressed. When Maritz, elated by the victory, said, "It's an unbelievable feeling to win, especially in my first year as a pro," the veteran Hobday responded, "Get used to it, my friend. It's not going to be the last."

The team posted best-ball scores of 61 and 62 for a total of 21-under-par 123, but at times Hobday felt like he was along for the ride. The Senior PGA Tour player didn't contribute in the second round until the final hole, when he rolled in a four-footer for birdie after victory was in the bag.

Nedbank Golf Challenge—US$4,060,000
Winner: Sergio Garcia

Never one to shy away from drama, Sergio Garcia closed out his year with one of his most dramatic wins, holing a chip shot from 20 feet to defeat Ernie Els in a playoff and win $2 million, the biggest first-place check in golf at the Nedbank Golf Challenge.

Garcia did it with the style and flair that has made him one of the most magnetic figures in the sport. After rounds of 68, 71 and 66 left him six shots behind Els, the Spaniard blazed his way around the Gary Player Country Club in nine-under-par 63 for a 20-under 268 total.

Els, a two-time champion in this event, couldn't roll in enough birdies and had to settle for 69 to tie Garcia at 268. Both were three shots clear of third-place finisher Bernhard Langer, who also shot 69 on Sunday for a 271 total. Mike Weir finished fourth at 272, and Lee Westwood rounded out the top five with a 275 performance.

In the playoff, Els seemed to have the advantage when his approach to the 18th stopped 15 feet from the hole. Garcia missed the green and was in the fringe, 25 feet away. The momentum quickly shifted when Garcia deftly chipped his ball into the left side of the hole for a birdie-three. "The kikuyu grass here made it a tough shot," Garcia said. "Even when the ball went in, I wasn't sure of winning, because Ernie still had a putt and he could have made it."

Vodacom Players Championship—R2,000,000
Winner: Ernie Els

One month after they teamed up to win the WGC EMC World Cup, Ernie Els and Retief Goosen finished first and second in the season-ending Vodacom Players Championship, with Els winning by a single stroke. His 15-under-par 273 total included a final-round 65 that Els called his "best round of the year."

Goosen shot 72 to finish tied for second with Martin Maritz, Trevor Immelman and third-round leader Alan McLean. Of those, McLean had a chance to tie Els, but his approach on the final hole found a bunker and he failed to save par.

Els made his move early, before the winds picked up and made scoring difficult. A birdie at the second hole and an eagle at the par-five fifth propelled him into the lead. He followed that with two more birdies on the sixth and seventh. "That was almost as good as I can play," Els said. "I got the start I wanted while the wind wasn't blowing too much in the morning. In golf, sometimes it happens to you, sometimes it doesn't. I kept the ball in play a lot today, tried to focus and hit the shots that I needed."

Having been on the losing end of so many close calls in 2001, the final one coming the week before when Els lost in a playoff to Sergio Garcia at the Nedbank Golf Challenge, it was very satisfying for Els to finally take home a trophy. "It's wonderful to win in South Africa again," he said.

Ernie Els Invitational—R263,000
Winner: John Bland

Senior professional John Bland won with ease in the two-round Ernie Els Invitational over Fancourt's Montagu and Outeniqua courses on the week before Christmas. Bland posted scores of 62 and 63 for a 125 total, 19 under par, and only Jean Hugo, with a 62 of his own, was able to finish reasonably close. Hugo's opening score was 67 and he had a 129 total, four stokes behind Bland. Ian Hutchings and Trevor Immelman were at 134 and Chris Davison was the only other competitor within 10 strokes, taking fifth place at 135. Host Ernie Els shot 136.

13. Senior Tours

Standing before the players on the Senior PGA Tour, Commissioner Tim Finchem didn't pull any punches. In order for golf's greatest mulligan to continue to prosper, some reconstructive surgery was needed. Sponsors deserted senior golf at an alarming rate in 2001, some citing the recession and others offering the blunt assessment that grumpy old men in golf carts no longer provided an appealing marketing partnership. The new television deal with CNBC had seemed like a great idea at the beginning of the year, but tape-delayed coverage where drama was questionable and the personality factor was at an all-time low sent viewers and advertisers scampering for other options. The present appeared bleak, and Finchem knew it.

He announced some radical changes for 2002, all centered around the original concept of the Senior Tour. In order to make old-man golf attractive, the players themselves had to be stars worth watching. As an example, Finchem pointed to the godfather of the Senior Tour, Arnold Palmer, who was still, at age 72, one of the most recognized and admired figures in professional sports.

Palmer showed some signs of brilliance throughout the year and, some-times, he showed his age. In the opening round of the Senior PGA Championship, he shot his age (71) and had the galleries cheering his every step. The following morning the crowds were so thick you would have thought Tiger Woods was marching to the first tee at Augusta National. Everyone wanted to see Palmer, to root for him and see if he could capture just a bit more of the magic from days gone by. He didn't. Palmer missed the first fairway, took a quadruple-bogey eight and finished the second round with 83. That wasn't his worst score of the year. At the 3M Championship he shot 92, the highest score of his career, but people still came and watched. He was still Arnold Palmer, and that's what they were there to see.

An edict of "be more like Arnold" wasn't an easy thing for Finchem or anyone else to tell a group of professionals, but Palmer wasn't the only example of good things that happened in 2001. Tom Watson finally added a PGA Championship to his resume, the one major that eluded him during his career on the regular tour. The fact that it was the Senior PGA Championship and Watson went head-to-head with Jim Thorpe instead of Jack Nicklaus in the final round didn't seem to matter. Watson finally got the one that got away. It was great theater, and something the seniors could package and sell.

Nicklaus made a cameo appearance in 2001 as well, playing himself into contention at the U.S. Senior Open at age 61 only to miss too many putts in the final round. Bruce Fleisher won, but Nicklaus' run was the stuff that drew the ratings.

Chi Chi Rodriguez continued to entertain, and Hale Irwin continued to impress fans around the country with his ageless play. Bruce Lietzke came on board in the summer and won twice, finishing 16th on the money list despite only playing half a season. Mike McCullough earned his first win in a PGA Tour-sanctioned event in his 612th start, providing one of the best "persistence pays" stories of the year. But that story was eclipsed later in the year when Bobby Wadkins, younger brother of Lanny, won in his first start as a senior. It was Wadkins' first PGA Tour victory in 778 tries. He also became only the eighth player (including his brother) to win in his first Senior PGA Tour start.

Doug Tewell shot 62 in a major (The Tradition), and Tom Kite had victory snatched away from him by a purple martin when the bird swooped into the path of Kite's perfectly struck six iron. The ball and bird tumbled into the water, providing one of the most memorable shots of the year.

Allen Doyle won the money title and Player of the Year honors, but no one got overly excited by the post-season awards. The biggest moment was when Doyle, a former driving range operator, donated the $1 million bonus he received for winning the Charles Schwab Cup to charity.

Not to be overlooked, outside the United States there were well-organized senior tours in Europe and Japan.

The European Seniors Tour consisted of 21 tournaments, the most prominent of which was the Senior British Open. An Australian player, Ian Stanley — one of five two-event winners on the circuit — won the Senior British title as well as leading the Order of Merit with £178,460 to £171,993 over Englishman Denis Durnian.

In addition to Stanley, the winners of two European events were Seiji Ebihara of Japan, Denis O'Sullivan of Ireland, Noel Ratcliffe of Australia and David Oakley of the United States.

The most successful European senior of all, however, was Jose Maria Canizares, who earned over $1.2 million in America and won the Toshiba Senior Classic. South Africans John Bland, Hugh Baiocchi and Gary Player were also holding their own against U.S. competition, as were Argentine Vicente Fernandez, Australians Stewart Ginn and Graham Marsh, and New Zealand's Bob Charles.

Less ambitious than the European circuit, the Japan Senior Tour consisted of 12 events. Fujio Kobayashi led with three victories including the Japan Senior Open, while Noboru Sugai and Katsunari Takahashi won twice each and Ebihara added a third title to the two he won in Europe.

U.S. Senior PGA Tour

MasterCard Championship—$1,400,000
Winner: Larry Nelson

There was a furious birdie fest in the final round of the Senior PGA Tour's season-opening event, but a familiar figure stood victorious. Larry Nelson started 2001 the way he finished 2000, winning the MasterCard Championship in Hawaii by one shot over Jim Thorpe. It was Nelson's 12th senior victory, his seventh in nine months.

"It's a good way to start the year," Nelson said. "I think I'm battle-hardened already. I think it's a continuation of how I played since August."

Nelson led after the second round and got out to a quick start on Sunday with birdies on three of the first five holes. Thorpe, who trailed by two, also made three early birdies and when he rolled in a 30-foot eagle putt on the 538-yard, par-five seventh, Thorpe found himself within a stroke of the lead. He remained a shot back after nine.

Nelson rallied with another birdie at the 12th to open a two-stroke margin, but a bogey at the 15th shrank the lead back to a single shot. He quickly rectified the situation with a birdie at the 16th. After both players parred the 17th, Thorpe had to hope for a miracle eagle at the 18th. Despite a great approach, it was not to be. Thorpe settled for another birdie at the final hole and another second-place finish to Nelson.

"I've been battling Larry for the last six months, and I just can't seem to catch him," Thorpe said. "I would shoot 66 and he would shoot 63 or 64. It's been like that. I played as good as I can play."

This time Nelson shot 66 for a 19-under-par 197 total. Thorpe finished with 65 for 198. Bruce Fleisher finished with two birdies to tie for third place with Ed Dougherty at 202, while Gary McCord and Leonard Thompson tied for fifth at 204.

Royal Caribbean Classic—$1,400,000
Winner: Larry Nelson

With his second win in a row at the Royal Caribbean Classic — his sixth in 10 starts and his eighth in nine months — Larry Nelson set the bar for senior golf. Two weeks after winning in Hawaii by one stroke over Jim Thorpe, Nelson did it again, this time winning by one point in the modified Stableford format over Isao Aoki. According to Bruce Fleisher, the man who preceded Nelson as Senior Player of the Year, "The only way to beat him is when he isn't playing."

Sometimes Nelson won by beating players at their best, and other times he won because of the mistakes of others. The latter was the case in Key Biscayne, Florida. Trailing Bob Gilder by one point, Nelson put together an eight-point final round, the 12th best of the day. It was all he needed. Gilder fell away, scoring only one point in the final round, while Bob Eastwood, Tom Jenkins, Dana Quigley and Allen Doyle all made runs with between 12 and 14 points. Eastwood had zero points and his 26-point total was good enough to tie Jenkins for third place, while Quigley finished fifth with 25 points and Doyle came in sixth with 24.

The only contender for Nelson proved to be Aoki, who had more than a few chances to win. Trailing Gilder by five points at the start of the final round, Aoki took double bogey on the first hole after he missed a short par putt then whiffed his tap-in. Aoki charged back with four birdies on the second nine to post 11 points on the day, one shy of what he needed. On the final hole, the Japanese player narrowly missed an eagle putt that would have given him the title. Instead he finished a shot behind Nelson.

"Everything being equal, the guy with the mental control is going to beat the other guy," Nelson said. "I know this streak isn't going to last forever.

I'm not going to play this way until I'm 65. But with my mental game the way it is now, and the way I'm hitting the ball, I feel like I've got a chance to do something that nobody has ever done."

ACE Group Classic—$1,400,000
Winner: Gil Morgan

After taking most of the winter off, Gil Morgan didn't expect to contend early in the 2001 season. "I really didn't expect to contend this early," he said. "I really hadn't had time to get my game in shape."

The rust didn't show in Naples, Florida, where Morgan posted a final-round 66 to win the ACE Group Classic by two strokes over Dana Quigley. After opening with rounds of 71 and 67, Morgan held a one-shot lead going into Sunday's round. It soon became a two-man race, with Morgan and Quigley swapping birdies throughout the second nine.

"Every time I made a birdie I didn't gain any ground," Quigley, who shot 69 and 70 the first two days, said of his final round pairing with Morgan. "What does that tell you? He's a tough competitor."

When Quigley birdied the 14th, Morgan made a birdie to retain the lead. When Quigley birdied the 16th, Morgan rammed in another birdie putt. The lead was one with two holes to play when Morgan hit a seven iron to the par-three 17th that stopped three feet from the hole. Quigley couldn't match that birdie, and the lead was two with one to play.

When Morgan reached the water-guarded 18th green with his second shot, it was all over. Two putts later the optometrist from Oklahoma had his 19th Senior PGA Tour victory with 66 for a 204 total as Quigley shot 67 for 206. Morgan also proved his longevity. The win gave him at least one victory in six consecutive seasons as a senior.

"I'm putting at a higher level than I did on the regular tour," Morgan said. "I putt better today than I ever did, and I'm 20 yards longer off the tee than I was on the regular tour. That coupled with the courses being a little bit shorter and the rough not so deep, it just gives me more opportunities for birdies than I used to have. I expect to do better now than I did on the regular tour. I feel like my game has matured."

Verizon Classic—$1,400,000
Winner: Bob Gilder

There were a number of Senior PGA Tour firsts on display at the TPC of Tampa during the Verizon Classic. The most noticeable change was the set-up of the golf course. After years of complaints by the stars that the senior courses were too easy, the officials finally listened. Narrow, hard fairways and tucked pins greeted the over-50 faithful who braved Tampa's toughest test.

According to Raymond Floyd, "Arnold Palmer wanted to make things harder. Jack in his first year said this tour was not about golf. Every top player has been that way, but you don't want to be critical because it's been our mulligan. But the guys who started this as an exhibition tour have basically run their course. I think those guys were protected for a lot of years. They were good for the tour, and they kept playing and the tour didn't want to embarrass them."

There was plenty of embarrassment to go around in Tampa. Not a single player posted three rounds in the 60s, a stunning turn of events. The tough conditions led to another first, or at least a first in a while. Jack Nicklaus, complete with a new hip, new corrective shoes and a new waistline that was 18 pounds lighter than the one he sported in December, shot an opening 67 to lead the tournament. The Golden Oldie backed it up on Saturday with 71 to fall two behind second-round leader Hale Irwin. Still, rumblings circulated through the galleries. Nicklaus could actually win!

"I haven't been competitive on either tour for a long time," Nicklaus said. "But it's been four years, probably five, since I've been able to do anything physically. I'm not going to blow a golf course apart anymore. But I can still play good golf."

The good golf ended on Sunday as Nicklaus putted poorly and limped in with 75 for a 213 total and a tie for 20th. "I was horrible today," Jack said. "When I was playing good golf I occasionally did this, too. I felt very composed this morning. I just need to finish off a tournament."

Senior rookie Bob Gilder had no trouble finishing off the tournament. He was another first of the week, winning the event in only his third start as a senior by shooting 67 for a 205 total and a three-stroke victory over Bruce Fleisher, Floyd, Gil Morgan and Bobby Walzel. Irwin limped in with 74 for a 210 total and a tie for ninth place.

"I've never been a big name on tour," Gilder said. "Obviously the fans like the big names, but that doesn't bother me. I just like to knock them off. These guys are my idols too. It's just nice to be able to play with them and beat them once in a while."

Mexico Senior Classic—$1,500,000
Winner: Mike McCullough

It took 29 years, 612 starts and a trip to Mexico for Mike McCullough to win his first PGA Tour-sanctioned event. When he holed a four-footer for par on the last hole of the Mexico Senior Classic for a one-shot victory, the wait seemed worth it. "I've been working hard on my game lately," a tearful McCullough said after closing with 68 for a 12-under-par 204 total. "I've been close a couple of times."

At 55, McCullough had plenty of close calls to fall back on. He finished second in the 1977 Tournament Players Championship for his best finish on the regular tour, and he posted a second place in 1998 at the Senior PGA Tour's Southwestern Bell Dominion. He had two third-place finishes in 2000 at the Cadillac NFL Classic and the IR Senior Tour Championship, but McCullough was best known as the senior tour's Iron Man, having played in over 100 consecutive events.

When McCullough hit a wedge to 12 feet on the 18th, all he needed was a two-putt for his first win. Still, it wasn't easy. McCullough ran the first putt four feet past the hole, and made the par putt coming back to edge out Jim Colbert and Bob Eastwood.

"I made key putts when I had to," McCullough said. "I wanted to make that (par) putt coming back to put the pressure squarely on Jim. It was good to make that putt. It felt great."

Putting is what kept Colbert from capturing his 20th senior title. After shooting 62 on Saturday, Colbert could only put together three birdies on Sunday in his 69. "I just missed too many short ones," he said. "I had about a half dozen that should have gone in. That was the difference."

Eastwood also finished with 69 for a 205 total and a share of second place. "I'm proud of how I played, and I'm happy for Mike," Eastwood said. "He gambled a lot and it paid off."

Toshiba Senior Classic—$1,400,000
Winner: Jose Maria Canizares

After four seasons and 43 top-10 finishes, many wondered if Jose Maria Canizares would ever win on the Senior PGA Tour. No one could have predicted that a nine-hole playoff would be the answer to Canizares' woes, but that turned out to be the prescription for success. With darkness descending on Newport Beach Country Club in California, the 54-year-old Spaniard rolled in a 20-footer for birdie on the ninth playoff hole to beat Gil Morgan and pick up his first win at the Toshiba Senior Classic.

"This is the longest playoff I've ever been in," Canizares said. "I think my longest prior to this was six holes."

The Toshiba Senior Classic was famous for protracted playoffs. In 1997 Bob Murphy took nine extra holes to eliminate Jay Sigel, and in 1999 Gary McCord required five holes to pick up his first senior victory over John Jacobs.

Canizares had to make a 10-footer for birdie on the final hole of regulation for 67 to get into the playoff after Morgan shot a closing 64 for a 202 total. The Spaniard hit the hole with two birdie putts early in the playoff when Morgan seemed in trouble, but the putts stayed out and Morgan managed to save par to keep the marathon alive. On the seventh playoff hole, Canizares stuck an approach to within four feet, but when Morgan drained a 20-footer for birdie, the Spaniard had to make the testy short one to keep things going even further.

"I had several very good long putts that touched the hole," Canizares said. "It takes a lot of concentration. I had to be strong mentally. This was a very good confrontation."

The confrontation ended at the 17th hole when Morgan missed a 40-footer for birdie, leaving Canizares with a free run at his 20-footer. "I hit a good putt and it finally went in," he said.

At the start of Sunday's round neither Canizares nor Morgan appeared to have a very good chance. Senior PGA Tour rookie Terry Mauney shot 63 on Saturday, giving him a 12-under-par 130 total and a three-shot lead over Larry Nelson. Canizares trailed Mauney by five and Morgan was eight back. Mauney found trouble, closing with 77 to tie for 10th place, while Nelson shot 72 to finish tied for seventh. That left the door open for Canizares and Morgan, who battled long after the rest of the field had cleaned out their lockers.

A few players stayed to congratulate Canizares on his victory, a win he tried to put into perspective. "It's nice to win because I am playing with some of the best players in the world," Canizares said. "In golf you have 18 holes, so you always think you have a chance to win."

Even when it takes nine extra holes at the end of a long day.

SBC Senior Classic—$1,400,000
Winner: Jim Colbert

It had been two and a half years since 60-year-old Jim Colbert needed to make a four-footer to win on the Senior PGA Tour. On a chilly Sunday afternoon in Valencia, California, Colbert found himself in contention again in the SBC Senior Classic. When he sank the four-footer on the 18th hole to save par, the Las Vegas resident had his 20th senior title.

"My teeth were chattering over the last four or five holes," Colbert said. "I'm not sure it was because it was cold. My confidence had been affected. You wonder sometimes if you are ever going to perform at the highest level again."

Colbert began questioning his ability earlier in the 2001 season when he missed a short putt in Mexico that would have earned him a spot in a playoff. "I can't ever remember missing a crucial putt from that length," Colbert said. "Not ever. That was a real shock."

The shock settled into disappointment which led to Colbert's self-doubts. "Since I won two money titles (in 1995 and 1996) I've had three operations and three years interrupted, but I really got to playing good last fall. I have high expectations for this year," he said.

Those expectations finally materialized in California when Colbert became only the 10th over-60 player to win on the Senior PGA Tour. He did it with rounds of 67, 67 and 70 for a 12-under-par 204 total, good enough to clip first-round leader Jose Maria Canizares by a shot.

Canizares, who shot 65 on Friday, couldn't hit enough greens on the weekend, even though he remained tied for the lead through 15 holes on Sunday. A five-par run on the closing six holes cost the Spaniard a chance at his second consecutive win. "I hit the ball terrible," Canizares said. "The weather was getting very cold, and I simply couldn't keep my hands warm."

Gary McCord warmed up on the weekend, posting scores of 65 and 68 after starting the week with 73. McCord, who finished tied for third at 206 with Ed Dougherty and Larry Nelson, attributed his play to a putting tip he received on Friday from Dave Stockton.

"I've been putting so bad, but Stockton helped me a bunch," McCord said. "For the last two months it's been a cornucopia of methods and grips. I've been to faith healers, to palmists, to tea readers, to graphologists; I've literally tried everything. I've run the gamut."

Stockton's advice obviously did the trick. McCord was tied for the lead with Colbert and Canizares through 14 holes in the final round, but that tie was broken when Colbert made an eight-foot birdie putt on the 15th, then thrashed a five wood 238 yards from the rough into the center of the 17th green, setting up a crucial par save.

"The challenge was could I pull the trigger and rip it," Colbert said of his shot at the 17th. "I really got excited when I got that ball on the green."

He got even more excited when the four-footer for par and the victory fell on the final hole. "It really means a lot," Colbert said. "I feel the best about this win over any other. It's hard to share. It is so fulfilling."

Siebel Classic in Silicon Valley—$1,400,000
Winner: Hale Irwin

With a course-record 65 on Coyote Creek Golf Club that was set up as tough as anyone could ever remember, Hale Irwin won the Siebel Classic in Silicon Valley in a cakewalk and became the winningest man in Senior PGA Tour history with 30 victories in five and a half seasons.

"I'm proud of reaching 30," Irwin said. "I think I've had a great career going all the way back to 1968, but when I look back I don't look at the number of wins or the money. I look at the experiences I've had, and all the people I've had them with."

Averaging more than five wins a year since turning 50 has made the experiences much more pleasant, and this was no different. Starting the final round with a one-shot lead over Allen Doyle, Irwin made an eagle at the par-five fourth hole plus five birdies to extend his lead. He lipped out a birdie putt on the 18th hole for 64 and a 206 total. "I would have liked to make that last putt for a 64," he said. "The 65 is wonderful, but you have to keep pushing. Obviously I'm delighted, to say the least. The day went better than I expected."

That could have been the understatement of the week. With hard greens, high rough, tucked pins, a wicked swirling wind and a course that stretched a few yards beyond the 7,000 mark, Coyote Creek was one of the toughest tests the seniors had faced all year.

"I love what the field staff is doing," Andy North said. As one of only 17 players to win the U.S. Open more than once, North likes courses where par is a good score. "To look up and see one or two under on the leaderboard is great. I know it's tough on a lot of the guys, but I'd like to see this every week. The scoring is still fantastic."

As one of the other players in the field with multiple U.S. Open victories, Irwin agreed. "I knew par was going to be good in 1974 when I won my first U.S. Open, and that mentality is what you have to bring to a course like this."

Doyle thought he had the mindset, but two eagles and two bogeys marked his up-and-down day. He closed with 69 to tie for second place with Tom Watson at 211. Watson came back from an opening 77 to shoot a pair of 67s on the weekend, but even though he had the second-best score on Sunday, there was no doubt in Watson's mind who was going to win.

"Nobody was going to catch Hale," Watson said. "I watched his golf swing and knew that. As for finishing second, it's a heck of a lot better than finishing 20th."

Emerald Coast Classic—$1,400,000
Winner: Mike McCullough

After a 25-year winless spell, Senior PGA Tour ironman Mike McCullough finally discovered that the Vince Lombardi axiom was true: Winning really was a habit. McCullough's first senior win came in February at the Mexico Senior Classic, after he had played in 612 official events without a victory. He had also become known as senior golf's version of Cal Ripkin, Jr., playing in 150 consecutive events since turning 50, still with no wins.

After the Mexico victory, McCullough decided he liked the view so much he did it again, this time defeating Andy North on the first hole of a playoff to capture the Emerald Coast Classic in Milton, Florida.

"This was a different kind of win," McCullough said. "When I won in Mexico the lead was never really mine until the last few holes. This time I was in a position to have the lead a good part of the final day. If you don't have good blood pressure, it can rise in that situation."

McCullough and North played mirror-image golf throughout the week, both carding rounds of 67 and 68 on Friday and Saturday, and entering the final round three shots behind leader John Schroeder (65-67) and two behind Jim Ahern (70-64).

Schroeder faded on the first nine of the final round with a couple of early bogeys. He eventually shot 72 and finished tied for fourth with Jose Maria Canizares at 204. That left the door open for Ahern, who maintained his lead through the first nine. A triple bogey on the 10th after driving the ball in a deep fairway bunker ended Ahern's chances. He finished with 70 for a 203 total, three more than he needed to get into the playoff.

Meanwhile, McCullough and North continued to match each other birdie for birdie. Both shot 65, then headed back to the 18th where McCullough won with a par after North drove his ball into a fairway bunker and missed the green.

"At times I go through stretches where I play pretty darn well," North said. "Then I hit two or three shots off the earth someplace like a 14-handicapper. I'm disappointed I didn't win, but I really feel like I'm moving in the right direction."

If North had to lose, it might as well be to someone like McCullough, who is universally liked by his peers. "Mike's having spent a lot of time with Gil Morgan has helped him realize he's a better player than he ever thought," North said. "That was Mike's deal for years — he didn't believe he was very good."

Liberty Mutual Legends of Golf—$1,800,000
Winners: Jim Colbert and Andy North

There's nothing like playing with the course architects to inspire you. At least that's what Jim Colbert and Andy North said after posting a best-ball 59 on the King and the Bear golf course while playing with co-designers Arnold Palmer and Jack Nicklaus.

"That was the most fun I've ever had playing golf," Colbert said of his team's 60-breaking performance in the opening round of the 36-hole Liberty

Mutual Legends of Golf at the World Golf Village in St. Augustine, Florida. "I hit the ball in the water four times and shot 59."

Nicklaus and Palmer were equally impressed. "It was something to see," Nicklaus said. "Andy and Jim made everybody look horrible with what they did."

Colbert and North got off to a stuttering start, parring the first four holes in Saturday's first round before reeling off nine straight birdies. They parred the 14th, then finished with four more birdies for a 13-under-par 59 total, good enough for a three-shot lead going into the second round.

"Jim is the perfect partner because he doesn't mess up," North said. "In this format, there is nothing worse than reeling off six birdies then making a bogey. You feel like you just shot yourself."

The wind picked up on Sunday, but that too worked to Colbert and North's advantage. With birdies on the par-fives and no bogeys, they shot a closing 65 for a three-shot victory over Bruce Fleisher and David Graham.

Starting six shots off the pace, Fleisher and Graham made an early charge and pulled to within one shot of the lead, but a bogey at the 10th hole dashed all hopes of catching the leaders. Even an eagle at the 18th wasn't enough. Fleisher and Graham shot 62 for a 127 total, good enough for solo second, but three shy of Colbert and North.

"Today was a really tough day with the wind," North said, "but it helped that we had managed to build a lead. It was important that we played the par-fives well, and we did that."

The Countrywide Tradition—$1,700,000
Winner: Doug Tewell

Major championships aren't supposed to be won by nine-stroke margins, and the winner isn't supposed to shoot a final round of 62. Majors aren't supposed to give up 23-under-par 265 scores. There's only one player who is supposed to dominate the game with those kinds of numbers, and Tiger Woods certainly wasn't playing in The Countrywide Tradition in Scottsdale, Arizona.

Woods still influenced the outcome as 51-year-old Doug Tewell tried to harness some of that Tiger magic during his record-setting, wire-to-wire victory.

"I never watch golf tournaments other than the Masters, and I watched Tiger and I watched his intensity," Tewell said after picking up his second major title as a senior. "In the past my intensity has been terrible, and, yes, you try to emulate what great players do. I wish I could emulate his clubhead speed. I did putt like him though. Every time I hit a putt today it felt like butter coming off the face. What a great feeling!"

With scores of 66, 67 and 70, Tewell entered on Sunday with a two-stroke lead over Larry Nelson and Mike McCullough. He widened that with a birdie on the first hole. The margin increased as McCullough, who bogeyed the first hole, made double bogey on the second and Nelson made double bogey on the third. Tewell then birdied the fourth hole to open a five-shot lead, which was as close as anyone would get the entire day.

Any lingering questions were answered on the second nine when Tewell birdied the 10th and 11th holes before rolling in a 20-foot eagle putt on the 12th. "That really won the golf tournament," Tewell said. "That three-hole stretch basically put it away."

McCullough rallied from his early travails to shoot 69 and finish in second place at 274, nine shots behind the winner, but one better than third-place finisher Hale Irwin.

"I don't shoot 14-under-par 274 too many times," McCullough said. "But Doug, he shot 62! That's the course record, and he did it in these conditions. The greens are so firm that if you dropped a ball straight down it would still roll forward. I can't say enough about what Doug did."

Tewell couldn't say enough about it either. "We talk about a zone out here," he said. "Well, the zone was there for me this week."

The winner even took a few jabs at the most notable absentee at this senior major. Tom Watson, who finished second in The Nationwide Tradition the year before, skipped this year's event to play in the WorldCom Classic on the PGA Tour. Watson missed the cut, and Tewell chastised him for being absent.

"Tom is off on Hilton Head this week because he thinks he can still beat those guys," Tewell said. "He doesn't consider this a major. I think it is. It's four rounds. We're all preparing for it like it's a major, and we need majors out here. We just have to get some of our key guys to support us. I'd like to be at Hilton Head, too. I won that tournament. But we're trying to make this a major, and I don't know why the Senior PGA Tour can't have majors. Some don't seem to think we have majors. I know Tom has had a great career and won everything in the world, and maybe this doesn't get him too fired up, but he could help us a lot. I wish he would consider it."

Las Vegas Senior Classic—$1,400,000
Winner: Bruce Fleisher

In one of the ugliest putting exhibitions of the year, Bruce Fleisher managed to jab in just enough short ones to shoot a final-round 70 and end his 2001 winless streak with a three-stroke victory in the Las Vegas Senior Classic over Jose Maria Canizares, Vicente Fernandez, Walter Hall, Hale Irwin and Doug Tewell. It ended when Fleisher three-putted the 18th hole for bogey and a 208 total.

"That's not the way you want to finish, with a three-putt," Fleisher said. "But it's a good feeling to know you can three-jack it and still win the thing. That makes things a lot easier."

Fleisher's finish was the final blow in what had been an awful putting display for the winner and all pursuers. In the final two rounds Fleisher had six putts of five feet or less that never touched the hole. Fortunately for him, second-round leader Jerry McGee was putting even worse. McGee's only birdie in the final round was a tap-in at the par-five third. After that, he played the last 15 holes in five over par, shooting 77 for the day and 213 for the week, to finish tied for eighth place, five shots behind Fleisher.

"I put a lot of pressure on myself to win," McGee said. He hasn't won a tournament since 1979, or as he put it, "Twenty-two years, six months, eight days and 42 minutes ago, or something like that." But it was not to be. "I wanted to win so bad I couldn't see straight," he said.

Hall was the second to fall away. Also searching for his first senior win, Hall pulled to within a shot of Fleisher with a birdie at the par-five 16th, only to self-destruct one hole later when he pulled his tee shot into the water on the par-three hole. A flubbed chip and missed putt later, Hall walked off the 17th green with a triple bogey, and Fleisher had a four-stroke lead with one hole to play.

"I have Walter Hall to thank," Fleisher said. "He made my job easy on 18. That last tee shot is a tough one, and I'm glad I had a little cushion there."

As for his woes on the greens, Fleisher was philosophical. "I putted like I didn't need the money," he said. "I don't know what that was all about, but I'm not complaining. A win is a win is a win."

Bruno's Memorial Classic—$1,400,000
Winner: Hale Irwin

Like grumpy old men, the over-50 players on the Senior PGA Tour didn't mince words when it came to complaining about the new tougher set-ups they faced in the first five months of 2001. Commissioner Tim Finchem listened to the players and tried to strike a balance between the U.S. Open caliber courses that marked the first half of the season, and the rough-free, pitch-and-putt birdie fests that were a weekly standard during previous seasons.

In Birmingham, Alabama, at the Bruno's Memorial Classic, the Senior PGA Tour rolled out what it hoped would be an adequate compromise. Not embarrassingly hard, but not overly easy, tour officials thought they had it just right at the Greystone Golf and Country Club. They were wrong. The course was so easy that 70-year-old Gene Littler became the first player in Senior PGA Tour history to better his age by shooting 67 in the first round, and Orville Moody three-putted the final green of the first round to miss shooting his age by one. Over half the field shot in the 60s, and Hale Irwin jokingly said, "It'll probably take three 65s to win this week."

It didn't take that, but Irwin shot it anyway, putting together three rounds of 65 for a 21-under-par 195 total and a four-stroke victory over Stewart Ginn. Irwin missed tying Raymond Floyd's 1993 Senior PGA Tour record of 22-under-par 194 by one, but that didn't seem to matter. "I'll take the check and the trophy," Irwin said. "Somebody else can have the record."

Irwin never trailed, but his victory was not a foregone conclusion either. His first-round 65 tied him for the lead with Jose Maria Canizares, but by all rights, Irwin should have finished the day trailing by at least one. At the par-five 18th, Irwin pulled his second shot into a marshy hazard. An up-and-down birdie looked improbable. Instead, Irwin chipped in for eagle.

The weekend was equally tight for the winner. Gil Morgan shot a course-record 63 on Saturday to go with an earlier 67. That forced Irwin to post another 65 just to retain a share of the lead. Ginn stood two back after rounds of 67 and 65.

"I knew I had to go out and post some low numbers early because I knew it was going to be tough to catch them," Ginn said. Unfortunately for him, those low numbers didn't materialize. A missed four-footer for birdie at the eighth after Irwin had already rolled in an eight-footer for birdie proved to be Ginn's last stand. He never got within three shots the rest of the day.

The same fate befell Morgan, who missed the eighth green and failed to get up and down, losing two shots to Irwin on one hole, and falling further behind after Irwin rolled in another birdie at the ninth.

"Hale was just a machine out there today," Ginn said. "He played a helluva round. I was glad I was able to go out and push him some. It was fun."

Irwin agreed. "I like to play with a sense of urgency," he said. "I like feeling like I don't quite have it together, but I'm trying to get it there. I played like that when I won in San Jose, and I kept that momentum going. It felt great this week."

Allen Doyle and Tom Kite both closed out with Sunday 68s to finish tied for third at 201, while Morgan struggled home with 72 for a 202 total and fifth place.

Home Depot Invitational—$1,300,000
Winner: Bruce Fleisher

With a final-round 68 in a brutal wind, Bruce Fleisher captured the Home Depot Invitational in Charlotte, North Carolina, by three strokes and became only the sixth player in Senior PGA Tour history to win the same event in three consecutive years.

"If it's in the record book, that's terrific," Fleisher said. "I think it's great."

Rounds of 68 and 67 on Friday and Saturday weren't necessarily great, but they were good enough to leave Fleisher one stroke behind Jim Colbert. Then the winds came. With swirling gusts that made it difficult to stand and sometimes caused balls to move on the greens, Fleisher understood that a conservative approach to the TPC at Piper Glen was in order. Fairways and greens were an effective strategy that paid off. With consecutive birdies at the eighth and ninth, Fleisher suddenly found himself leading by three with nine holes to play.

"I wanted to play smart and not make any stupid shots," Fleisher said. "That strategy paid off."

Colbert dropped back, shooting 73 for a 205 total. He finished tied for third with Larry Nelson and Jim Thorpe, who tied John Bland for Sunday's low round with 66s. While second place was Bland's best finish of the year, it was Fleisher who had everyone talking.

"He just went 'pop,' and just like that he had a three-shot lead," Inman said. "All of a sudden he just took off."

Fleisher's 201 total broke the tournament scoring record by two strokes. Still, Fleisher had to answer questions about his career transformation. Winless in 20 years on the PGA Tour after charging into the professional ranks as one of the top-rated amateurs in the world, Fleisher tried to put his career into perspective.

"To say I failed on the PGA Tour is so far from the truth in my mind," he said. "I just didn't reach the expectations others had for me. But I was a survivor. I just wanted to be a household name that everyone knew."

It's taken 30 years, but Bruce Fleisher has finally gotten that household name recognition.

Enterprise Rent-A-Car Match Play—$2,000,000
Winner: Leonard Thompson

With such senior stalwarts as Tom Watson, Hale Irwin, Lanny Wadkins, Tom Kite and Gil Morgan in the field, the Enterprise Rent-A-Car Match Play in Augusta, Missouri, had the potential for one of the most exciting final match-ups of the year. The final turned out to be exciting enough, but without any of the senior stalwarts. Left standing were Leonard Thompson and Vicente Fernandez, not the riveting drama the Senior PGA Tour's sponsors had hoped for, but a good story nonetheless.

Even Thompson didn't expect it. He approached Fernandez on the range early in the week and said, "I want you on Sunday. I'm going to get you," but he admitted he was only kidding. The two players had met head-to-head in the final of the 2000 Chrysler Senior Match Play Challenge in Puerto Rico, with Fernandez coming out on top, but that was without Watson, Kite and Wadkins in the field. Thompson was laughing when he mockingly called Fernandez out.

Darned if things didn't work out in Thompson's favor. "Who would have thought it," Thompson said after he defeated John Jacobs, Ted Goin and Hale Irwin to reach the final against Fernandez. "I guess it's true that anything can happen in match play."

The Argentine was equally stunned after winning his matches over Jim Thorpe, Terry Mauney and Bob Gilder to advance to the finals. "It was a great feeling," he said. "Very unexpected."

The entire event was somewhat out of the norm for the Senior PGA Tour. Instead of 54 holes of stroke play, the over-50 crowd played more than 100 holes, with Thompson playing 104 — 33 the final day — before winning the championship. In the process he played his last 42 holes without making a bogey.

That consistency ultimately won the title. After trouncing Hale Irwin 4 and 3 in the morning match, Thompson made two birdies and no bogeys on the first nine of his afternoon final with Fernandez. That put the match all-square with nine holes remaining. Fernandez birdied the 10th to go one up, but the lead was short-lived. A bogey by Fernandez made it all-square again, and one final birdie by Thompson set the advantage in his favor with three holes to play. Pars ruled the day on the final holes. Thompson simply bided his time and waited for his opponent to make a mistake.

"I try to make the guy beat me," Thompson said. "If a guy beats you, you don't feel nearly as bad about it if you lose. There's a big difference between me losing and him winning. I try not to give anything away."

Thompson never gave an inch. The mistake came from his opponent at the 18th when Fernandez hit his seven-iron approach shot into the water fronting the green. At that moment, with victory clearly in hand, Thompson sat in his golf cart, covered his face, and wept.

"I don't think people really realize how much it takes to win a golf tournament," he said. "It takes so much. You get to a level, and you have to stay there when you're winning, stay at that level the whole time. Then, when it's over, it's like turning the light off."

TD Waterhouse Championship—$1,500,000
Winner: Ed Dougherty

With a 22-under-par 194 total, which equaled the Senior PGA Tour scoring record, Ed Dougherty ran away from the field in the TD Waterhouse Championship, beating Hugh Baiocchi, Walter Morgan and Dana Quigley by eight strokes.

Dougherty birdied the first five holes in Friday's opening round on his way to a course-record 62. Dougherty's score only gave him a two-stroke cushion over Ted Goin, but that proved to be enough. On Saturday, Dougherty birdied the first five holes again on his way to 66. That increased the margin to five over Baiocchi. On Sunday he widened the gap with birdies on his first two holes and another 66, a score no one stood a chance to catch. Baiocchi shot 69 and lost three shots, while Morgan closed with 64, the low score of the day, to finish tied for second, eight shots back.

"Ed sent us a signal today," Quigley said after witnessing Dougherty's birdie eruption. "The writing was on the wall. He was on a mission out there."

Conditions helped. Soft greens and lift-clean-and-place rules made the Tiffany Greens Golf Club ideal for low scoring. None took advantage of the set-up like Dougherty. "The greens were a little soft, and you could fire right at the flags," he said. "I played one shot at a time, and I was proud of myself for handling it like that.

"I wanted to shoot one of the three lowest rounds of the day (on Sunday) and you can't do that without being aggressive. I never got out of that game plan."

Senior PGA Championship—$2,000,000
Winner: Tom Watson

Tom Watson tries not to ponder the one major championship that eluded him during his career on the PGA Tour. Like Arnold Palmer, Watson never won the PGA Championship, but Watson made amends for that gap in his record on a chilly New Jersey spring Sunday by shooting a final-round 67 to win the Senior PGA Championship by one stroke over Jim Thorpe.

"His ego doesn't need to be on the senior tour," Watson's long-time caddie, Bruce Edwards, said after Watson shot 72, 69, 66 and 67 for a 274 total to win the second senior major of the year. "He basically did everything in the game he wanted to do other than win the PGA Championship. I can understand why he's not motivated by a lot of the senior tournaments, but when you come to a tournament like this or the U.S. Senior Open, he's raring to go."

Watson putted like the man who won 34 times on the PGA Tour including two Masters, five British Opens and one U.S. Open. The stroke never looked more solid than it did on the weekend, when Watson reeled off five straight birdies, including a 45-footer on the 18th, to end Saturday's third round.

"The last hole it felt like young Tom Watson," he said. "Making a putt from that far, knowing the line, seeing the line, hitting it right on the line — I'll remember that putt for a long time."

Watson is less likely to remember the 15-footer for birdie at the eighth hole on Sunday, but that's the one that gave him the outright lead over Bob Gilder. Thorpe charged late, making a five-footer for birdie at the 14th, while Watson was missing a short par putt. That put Thorpe within one stroke, but that was as close as he could get. When a 14-footer for birdie fell at the 16th, Thorpe was tied for the lead, but Watson made an eight-footer for birdie right behind him to maintain the one-shot advantage.

Thorpe had one last chance at the 18th. After a good drive and a spinning nine-iron shot, the big man had an uphill six-footer for birdie to tie Watson and force a playoff. "I think I yanked it a little bit," Thorpe said after the putt skidded by the left side of the hole, leaving him with 68 and a 275 total. "I could probably walk up there now and make that putt half a dozen times in a row because I don't need it now. The one time I needed it, I couldn't make the stroke I needed to make."

"Watson is one of the top players, one of the drawing cards on the senior tour," Thorpe said. "If I couldn't win it, no disrespect to anyone else, but I'm glad Tom did."

Watson was glad as well, saying of his history with the PGA Championship, "This makes up for it a little bit. I had that Wanamaker Trophy in my sights a couple of times and let it get away."

BellSouth Senior Classic at Opryland—$1,600,000
Winner: Sammy Rachels

All the top names were there, and all were near the top of the leaderboard on Sunday. But like the dark humor of a Merl Haggard ballad, this Nashville duel didn't end according to the script.

With names like Hale Irwin, Bruce Fleisher, Tom Kite, Gil Morgan and Allen Doyle vying for the lead at the BellSouth Senior Classic at Opryland, a final-round 63 didn't surprise anyone. The fact that the man shooting that closing nine-under-par score was Sammy Rachels sent most Tennesseans away scratching their heads.

A native of DeFuniak, Florida, Rachels jarred a few memories when he reminded fans that his best finish in 10 years on the PGA Tour was a tie for second at the 1983 Danny Thomas Memphis Classic, Tennessee's other annual tour stop. Rachels also lured a few skeptics to his side when he claimed to be a huge Waylon Jennings and Willie Nelson fan. Nothing a little "Whiskey River" and "Cowboy Blues" can't cure in Nashville.

And nothing cures the final-round jitters like holing a 65-yard lob wedge for eagle on the first hole. That's exactly what this Senior PGA Tour rookie did on Sunday, jumping ahead of the pack with a three on the first hole after shooting 66 and 70 in the first two rounds to hold a share of the lead with Tom Wargo and Leonard Thompson. The eagle put Rachels up by two, and he extended that lead with a birdie at the fifth and another at the eighth, where he chipped in after missing the green.

Then, at the par-five 10th, with Irwin, who trailed by one at the start of the day, making a string of birdies, and Fleisher and Morgan moving up the charts as well, Rachels found the magic again, holing another wedge shot — this time from a greenside bunker — for another eagle. That extended the lead to three shots. Birdies on three of his next four holes opened up a four-shot lead, and nobody ever got closer.

Irwin finished strong with 66 on Sunday and a 203 total to take second place, while Fleisher and Kite also shot 66s to share third at 204. Morgan had the second-best score of the tournament on Sunday, shooting 64 to finish tied for fifth with Doyle at 205. But no one came close to matching Rachels' closing 63 and 199 total.

"I've learned from past mistakes," Rachels said. "I really paid attention this week, and I told myself this morning that I could shoot a low round. I didn't try to force it. This was a wonderful day for me. I was hitting it in from off the green, holing out three times today. That's probably more hole-outs than I've had all year."

NFL Golf Classic—$1,200,000
Winner: John Schroeder

No one expected John Schroeder to win the NFL Golf Classic in Clifton, New Jersey, not even Schroeder himself. "I'm probably the most surprised person in this room," the 55-year-old said after defeating Allen Doyle on the second extra hole to earn his first senior victory. "I just wanted to make birdie at 18 so I could finish second."

That was because Doyle, who started the final round two strokes behind Jim Holtgrieve and Larry Ziegler, looked poised to win this one with relative ease. After Holtgrieve and Ziegler stumbled on the early holes of the first round, Doyle got on a roll by holing a 106-yard wedge for eagle at the first. By the 13th hole, Doyle was six under par for the day and three shots ahead of Schroeder, who finished with a four-under-par 68 and a 207 total.

But Doyle let things slip away. A bogey at the 13th cut his lead to one, and another at the 17th dropped him into a tie with Schroeder. On the 18th, unaware that Schroeder had birdied the final hole, Doyle left a birdie putt of his own inches short. He finished with 68 and a 207 of his own, one better than Hugh Baiocchi and Mike Smith, but tied with Schroeder.

Both parred the first playoff hole, but at the par-three 17th, the second extra hole, Doyle found trouble for the second time in an hour, missing the green and failing to recover. When Schroeder got up and down from the fringe for a par, it was over. The former television analyst and winner of the 1973 L&M Match Play Championship had his first win in 27 years, and Doyle was left with thoughts of what might have been.

"I absolutely let this one get away," Doyle said. "I had the lead, and I was driving it in the fairway. But he's got to be thrilled to death. You've got to be happy for a guy who hasn't won before."

Schroeder was certainly happy with both the win and the $180,000 pay-check it brought. "I'm in a dogfight to maintain my status out here," he said. "I was considering doing something else if I didn't realize my goals. This will change my outlook."

Instinet Classic—$1,500,000
Winner: Gil Morgan

Sometimes a victory seems preordained, as if destiny is working in a player's favor. That was the case for Gil Morgan in Princeton, New Jersey. After leading the Instinet Classic from the opening shot on Friday, Morgan found himself in final-round battle with J.C. Snead. Then, on the sixth hole, fate intervened. A poor approach by Morgan bounced once off the cart path before striking a spectator on the leg. The ball ricocheted onto the green within 15 feet of the hole and Morgan made the putt for birdie.

"That was probably the most fortunate thing that happened to me all week," Morgan said. "Maybe in my entire career."

It was also a killing blow for Snead, who had played well enough to pull even with the leader through the fifth hole on Sunday. Snead never gave up, though. When Morgan bogeyed the 15th the two were tied again, but Morgan birdied the 17th to take a one-shot lead, and rolled in another birdie putt at the 18th for a final-round 69, a 15-under-par 201 total and a two-shot victory over Snead and Tom Jenkins.

The tournament should have belonged to Morgan from the beginning. A course-record 63 gave him a two-shot lead on Friday, and a 69 increased that lead to four. Snead had the low round of the day on Sunday, posting eight birdies and one bogey for a closing 65, but it wasn't enough. Morgan hit 39 fairways during the week, including 13 out of 14 on Sunday. Couple that with the off-the-spectator, cart-path birdie at the sixth and Morgan's win seemed a fete accompli.

"I've been hitting the ball really well lately," Morgan said. "It was also kind of neat to win with it being Father's Day and having my family here. This is a great golf course for me."

FleetBoston Classic—$1,400,000
Winner: Larry Nelson

Despite a herniated disk in his neck, Larry Nelson eased himself into the lead at the FleetBoston Classic with five birdies and a bogey in the first 16 holes on Sunday. But it wasn't until fate in the form of a bird, a purple martin, intervened that Nelson secured the victory, his first successful title defense of his 27-year career.

It happened on the 17th hole, a 167-yard par-three over water. Tom Kite, who entered the final round four shots behind Nelson and five behind second-round leader Mike Hill, had rallied to within a shot of the lead. On the 17th tee Kite hit what he thought was a perfect six-iron shot when suddenly the purple martin swooped into the ball's path. The ball struck and killed the bird. Both the bird and ball fell like stones into the pond.

Meanwhile Nelson birdied the par-five final hole for a five-under-par 67 and a three-day total of 15-under 201, good enough for a comfortable three-shot win over Bruce Fleisher (71-67-66). "You talk about the all-time bad breaks," Nelson said of Kite's misfortune. "You have a lot of bad breaks during the week, but this happened at the wrong time. You feel bad for Tom. He was playing really well."

Kite dropped behind the pond, pitched on and made a double-bogey five. He finished with 67 for a 205 total and tied for third with Hill, who closed with an even-par round of 72. "I got myself in position to win the tournament and just came up a little bit short," Kite said. "It's unfortunate when you have a chance to win the tournament. When you come that close to winning, it hurts."

Nelson played a different driver each of the three rounds, experimenting with different shafts in the hopes of finding something that wouldn't put too much pressure on his neck. The swaps didn't hurt Nelson's consistency. He shot 65, 69 and 67 on a course where he said he felt "extremely comfortable."

U.S. Senior Open—$2,400,000
Winner: Bruce Fleisher

In a year when the Senior PGA Tour went through a fair amount of tweaking of their course set-ups, the U.S. Golf Association got it just right. With pars on the final 12 holes Bruce Fleisher shot the number the USGA had in mind when it set up the Salem Country Club for the U.S. Senior Open. Fleisher posted scores of 69, 71, 72 and 68 for an even-par total of 280 to win by one stroke over Isao Aoki and Gil Morgan. It was Fleisher's first major professional victory, and he joined Arnold Palmer and Jack Nicklaus as the only men to win U.S. Amateur and U.S. Senior Open titles. Fleisher won the U.S. Amateur in 1968.

He didn't do much in the quarter-century following that, but on a hot, sunny Sunday afternoon in Peabody, Massachusetts, Fleisher made up for lost time in the biggest senior event of the season. "It's something I'm going to remember for a long time," Fleisher said. "I won on a very difficult golf course, playing with the best from the past that the game has to offer."

Among those Fleisher had in mind when he made that statement was the 61-year-old Jack Nicklaus, who contended for a title for the first time since he finished sixth in the 1998 Masters. Nicklaus put together scores of 71, 72 and 69 in the first three rounds to enter Sunday tied with Fleisher, Hale Irwin and Bob Gilder at 212, three shots off the lead held by Larry Nelson, Jim Colbert and Aoki. Morgan and Dana Quigley entered the final round two back at 211.

The race tightened ever further on Sunday. Irwin birdied the first hole and gained a share of the lead when Nelson, Aoki and Colbert posted early bogeys. It remained tight through most of the afternoon. At the turn, Nicklaus was within a shot. On the 10th green he turned to his caddie and said, "You know, I'm a little nervous. That's good. That's fun."

Six players remained within two strokes of the lead through 14 holes. The closing four holes proved to be too much for most of the contenders. Irwin bogeyed the 15th, 16th and 17th to finish with 73 and a 285 total. That was good enough for a tie for 11th place with Gilder, who closed with 73, Quigley, who shot 74, and Jay Sigel, who had tied the U.S. Senior Open record and established a course record on Saturday with a six-under-par 64, but could only manage 72 on Sunday.

Nicklaus' bid also ended on the 15th and 16h holes. After missing the green at the 223-yard 15th, Nicklaus failed to get up and down. Then Nicklaus missed a four-footer for par on the 16th and the run was over. He shot 70 for a 282 total. "That's what cost me the tournament," he said. "You can't do that coming in. All you can say is, 'At least I had a chance to win.' Maybe that means I'll try a little harder next time. At least I know I'm able to play again."

Aoki led or shared the lead through 16 holes, but missed a four-footer for par at the 17th that dropped the Japanese star out of the top spot. He shot 73 and tied Morgan for second place at 281. Colbert also stood alone at the top for a while. His 30-footer for birdie at the 15th gave him the outright lead, but a double bogey at the 18th dropped Colbert into a tie for third with Nicklaus and Allen Doyle at 282. Morgan was the last player with a chance to tie Fleisher, but after missing the 18th green to the right, he failed to save par, finished with 70 for his 281 total, and Fleisher stood alone — the only man to shoot even par.

"I knew that par would be a good score," he said. "I thought that someone would finish even and it would be a playoff, but I'm glad it didn't happen. I've got to be honest with you. I didn't want to go back out there."

Farmers Charity Classic—$1,400,000
Winner: Larry Nelson

Even though Larry Nelson, known as much for switching equipment as for winning golf tournaments, entered the final round of the Farmers Charity Classic in Grand Rapids, Michigan, with two new wedges in his bag, it was the putter that ultimately saved him. Nelson two-putted for birdie on the par-five 17th hole, then drained a tricky eight-footer at the 18th to beat Jim Ahern by a single shot and successfully defend a title for the second time in three weeks.

"The last two years I've come here hitting the ball really well," Nelson said. "It is easier to manage a golf course like this when you're hitting the ball well."

Two rounds of 67 gave Nelson a three-shot cushion going into Sunday's final round, but that evaporated quickly. Nelson missed short birdie putts on the first two holes, then made a bogey at the third while Quigley was up ahead playing the first four holes in five under par. "I hit it to five feet on the first hole and missed, hit it eight feet on the second hole and missed, and then I bogeyed the third hole," Nelson said. "I was slow getting into it, and I had a hard time reading the greens again."

He recovered well, chipping in twice with the new wedges, then rolling two critical putts on the final two holes for 68 and a 202 total to seal the victory. On the 17th, Nelson two-putted from the back of the green, tapping in for birdie after nestling his eagle putt close to the hole. "That putt is one of the hardest on this golf course," Nelson said. "There is no way you can read that much speed and that much break. The best way to make birdie is to barely miss eagle."

Moments earlier Ahern missed his best opportunity to take the lead at the 17th when he three-putted from 15 feet for par. "I underestimated how much the eagle putt broke," Ahern said. "I played a foot of break, and it was more like three feet. Then I had three and a half feet left, and it caught the lip and spun out."

Nelson's birdie moved him to 14 under for the tournament, one shot ahead with one to play. When his approach shot stopped 35 feet from the hole on the 18th, all he needed was a two-putt to win. "Putting from 35 to 40 feet is the worst part of my game," Nelson said. "For some reason I am not a very good putter from that distance."

This time he ran the first putt eight feet by the hole. The comeback putt hung on the left lip for a couple of seconds before falling in, but it did fall. Ahern was alone in second place at 203 after shooting 66, while Quigley and Walter Hall shared third with 204 totals.

Ford Senior Players Championship—$2,500,000
Winner: Allen Doyle

With a short slashing swing that even compact swinger Doug Sanders says is the shortest in golf history, former college hockey player Allen Doyle won his second major title when he beat Doug Tewell in a playoff at the Ford Senior Players Championship in Dearborn, Michigan. The winner couldn't get over what a long, strange trip his career had been.

"You can't fathom where I've come from," the 52-year-old driving range operator said after holing a par putt to win on the first extra hole. "It still blows my mind that this is my office, here at a golf course. You don't lose touch with that and don't forget that you're one of the luckiest guys in the world. Am I one up on everybody or what?"

Doyle was tied for the lead after the first round with Tom Watson, Raymond Floyd and Ed Dougherty, who all shot five-under-par 67. Hale Irwin joined the fray when he fired a second-round 65 to share the top spot at 135 with Watson.

Irwin struggled on Saturday, shooting 75 after two double bogeys on the back nine, and dropped to eighth place. Watson also struggled, but his 72 kept him tied for third with Tewell. Dougherty held the top spot with 18 holes to play, shooting 68 on Saturday to reach 205. Doyle stood one back at 206 after second- and third-round scores of 69 and 70, and found himself playing in the final group on Sunday.

When Dougherty struggled early, Doyle moved to the top of the leaderboard, but he wasn't alone. Tewell made a charge which he capped with a birdie on the 18th to shoot 66 for a 273 total to take a one-shot lead into the clubhouse. When Doyle hit an approach shot to 35 feet on the 18th, it looked like Tewell's score would be good enough for the win.

But Doyle had other ideas. "I had rolled those length putts good all week and had not made anything," he said. "I figured, 'What the hell? Why not make one now?' Those are the ones you see on TV, but they never happen to you."

They happened to Doyle this time. He drained the 35-foot birdie to shoot 67 and tie Tewell. "I kind of felt like I shut the door on Allen, but he birdied," Tewell said. "But I'm happy I'm getting my game back. I'm ticked off that I lost."

He lost on the first playoff hole, the 18th, when he pulled his tee shot into

Masters Tournament

With his victory in the Masters, Tiger Woods was the first to hold all four major titles at the same time.

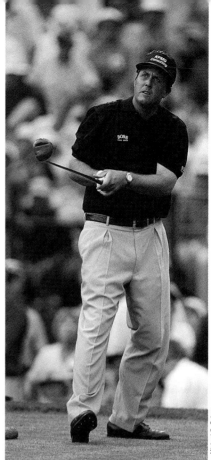

Phil Mickelson took third place.

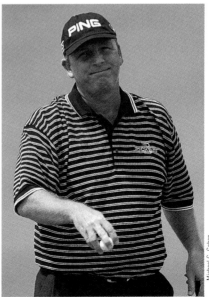

David Duval was second by two strokes.

Mark Calcavecchia shared fourth.

Toshimitsu Izawa shot 66 and 67.

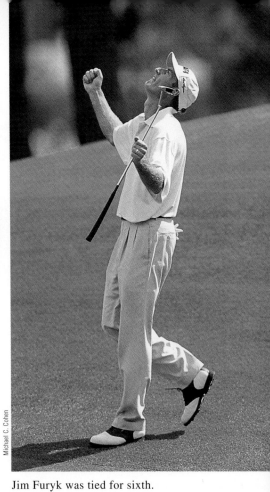

Jim Furyk was tied for sixth.

Bernhard Langer finished strongly.

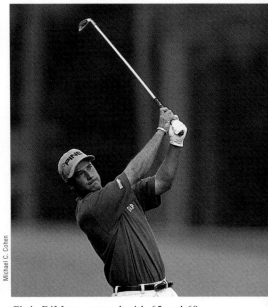

Chris DiMarco started with 65 and 69.

U.S. Open

Retief Goosen struggled to finish on Sunday, but won in a Monday playoff.

Goosen three-putted the 18th to tie.

Michael C. Cohen

Michael C. Cohen

Playoff loser Mark Brooks bogeyed the 18th on Sunday.

Stewart Cink just missed.

Michael C. Cohen

Tom Kite's 64 placed him in the top five.

Sam Greenwood

Sam Greenwood

Paul Azinger tied for fifth place.

Tiger Woods couldn't recover from a 74.

British Open

Coming from a four-man tie after 54 holes, David Duval shot 67 and won the British Open by three strokes.

Niclas Fasth rose to second place.

Colin Montgomerie led for two rounds.

Ian Woosnam was stunned at the second.

Bernhard Langer shared third place.

Tiger Woods finished nine shots behind.

Alex Cejka posted three 69s and 73.

PGA Championship

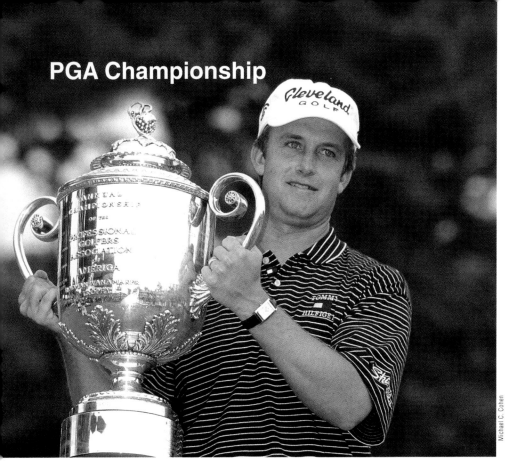

David Toms shot 66-65-65-69 and won the PGA with a conservative finish.

Phil Mickelson had a 20-foot putt for birdie but missed, and finished second by a stroke.

Michael C. Cohen

Steve Lowery finished three shots back.

Michael C. Cohen

Mark Calcavecchia tied for fourth.

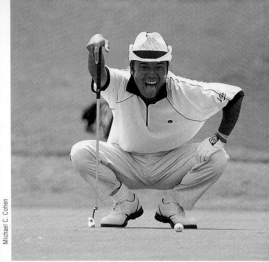

Michael C. Cohen

Shingo Katayama provided entertainment.

Michael C. Cohen

Billy Andrade shot 66 for sixth place.

Scott Halleran/Allsport

Scott Verplank earned a Ryder Cup berth.

Michael C. Cohen

He had Tiger Woods-type numbers again — five victories (eight worldwide), and first place on the World Ranking and money list.

Phil Mickelson was No. 2 for the year.

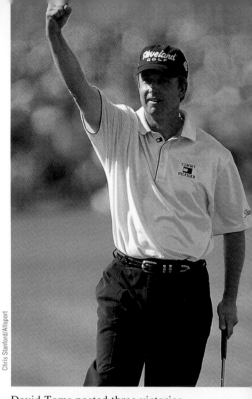

David Toms posted three victories.

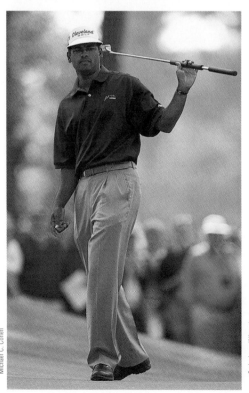

Vijay Singh won twice in Asia.

Davis Love III took the Pebble Beach title.

Sergio Garcia had two U.S. wins.

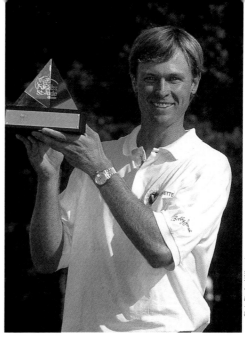

Bob Estes won in Memphis and Las Vegas.

Scott Hoch added two more titles.

David Duval was No. 8 on the U.S. money list.

Scott Verplank won in Canada.

Jim Furyk won the Mercedes title.

Chris DiMarco was 12th in the money.

Mike Weir was the Tour champion.

Joe Durant earned $2.4 million.

Ernie Els was 15th on the U.S. money list.

Robert Allenby won in Pennsylvania.

Steve Stricker won in Australia.

Jesper Parnevik took the Honda title.

Hal Sutton got a victory in Houston.

Robert Damron got his first win.

Jose Coceres was a surprise winner — twice.

Charles Howell won $1.5 million in his debut.

Ty Tryon, age 17, passed the qualifying.

Shigeki Maruyama won in Milwaukee.

The Players Championship

The Players was the second of Tiger Woods' three consecutive victories in the spring.

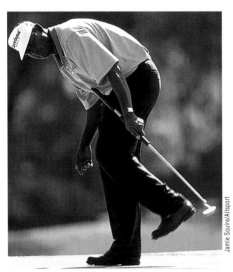

Vijay Singh took second by one.

Jerry Kelly started with 69 and 66.

a wetland area. Although Tewell was able to hack a wedge back to the fairway, his bogey wasn't good enough. Doyle hit the 18th green again and coaxed his birdie putt to within tap-in range. The par gave Doyle his first win of 2001 and his second senior major title in three years.

Irwin came back from his disappointing third round to shoot 66 and finish alone in third at 276. "If you had told me I would have three rounds of 65, 66 and 70, I would have been thrilled," Irwin said. "I just wasn't expecting the 75 that killed me."

SBC Senior Open—$1,400,000
Winner: Dana Quigley

Senior events usually last three days, but Dana Quigley didn't mind when a four-hour rain delay pushed the SBC Senior Open into a fourth day in Long Grove, Illinois. That's because Quigley had the tournament well in hand before officials decided on a Monday finish. He came back early Monday morning to play two holes with three other players. Quigley won by five strokes, and his 16-under-par 200 total established a 54-hole record for the Kemper Lakes golf course.

"I put in a full hour of practice like I was going out to play a full 18 holes," Quigley said of his warm-up routine. The effort paid off. Quigley hit his tee shot on the par-three 17th to within 20 feet and two-putted for par. He then hit his approach to five feet and sank a birdie putt at the 18th for a final-round 69.

"When I played here the first time, I thought there was no way I could shoot 70 on this course," Quigley said. "This is one of the toughest courses on the tour."

Quigley had no problems this time around. He led or shared the lead from the early going, shooting a bogey-free 65 on Friday to share the first-round lead with Gary McCord. A six-under 66 on Saturday opened up a four-shot lead for Quigley, and put him in an area with which he was unfamiliar. "The 66 the second day with that lead was uncharted territory," he said. "I never had a four-shot lead in a state Open, let alone a senior event, so I didn't know what I would do."

He would have one bogey on Sunday and three birdies to hold a four-shot edge when play was suspended. Nerves could have played a factor on Monday, and Quigley admitted he awoke at 3:23 in the morning with visions of the final two holes dancing through his brain. "I went through the scenario in my head," he said. "I knew everything that could happen."

Jay Sigel, Quigley's closest challenger, could have made things interesting if he had made a 35-footer for birdie on the 17th. "I knew Sigel was going to make that putt," Quigley said. "I told myself, 'Be prepared. Don't go into shock, three-putt and lose all of your lead.'" Sigel missed the birdie and tapped in for par. When the group arrived on the 18th tee, Quigley knew he had things well in hand.

"On the first waggle I knew I was okay," Quigley said. "It went out there perfect." He avoided the water on the par-five finishing hole, hitting wedge to five feet for the final birdie and the record.

"I've come from such a long way back to play with these guys," he said.

"I've got a tremendous passion for the game. At Crestwood Country Club (where he served as head professional from 1983 through 1996), I played every day for two dollars."

Sigel finished alone in second with a closing 70 for a 205 total, while Tom Kite had the best round of the week on Sunday, finishing with 64 for a 207 total and a share of third place with Ed Dougherty.

State Farm Senior Classic—$1,450,000
Winner: Allen Doyle

It turned out to be a duel between rivals and friends, players who stood first and second on the Senior PGA Tour money list going into the State Farm Senior Classic, who had graduated from the qualifying tournament together as the first- and second-place finishers, and who have been battling each other ever since. When the final putts fell, Allen Doyle couldn't hold back his glee at beating Bruce Fleisher, even though it took three extra holes to determine a winner.

"We've got three or four guys who carry the weight out here," Doyle said. "When you beat one of those guys it's extra special. I'm thrilled to be in that company."

Doyle earned his way by shooting a final-round 67 at the Hayfields Country Club in Hunt Valley, Maryland, for an 11-under-par 205 total. That put him into the playoff with third-round leader Fleisher, who overcame a bogey, double bogey start to shoot 69 on Sunday.

The two marched back to the 18th where they made two pars. Then on the 10th, the second playoff hole, Fleisher tried to apply some pressure by making a 15-foot birdie putt, but Doyle capped him, making his four-footer for birdie. They moved on to the par-three 17th as the skies opened up. In the midst of a driving rain, both players hit their tee shots into the front bunker. Doyle played first, blasting out to four feet. Fleisher's ball was in a precarious lie in the bunker and he couldn't get his second shot closer than 20 feet. When Fleisher missed, Doyle sank the four-footer for his second win in four weeks.

Doyle started the week slowly with an opening 73. He came back with 65 on Saturday to share third place. Then he made seven birdies and two bogeys in the final round, the final birdie coming at the 18th hole, to maintain his share of the lead with Fleisher.

Third-place finisher Jim Thorpe led by two shots through six holes on Sunday, but Thorpe's putter abandoned him. He three-putted the seventh and ninth, then missed a four-footer on the final hole that would have put him in the playoff. He shot 70 and finished alone in third place with a 206 total.

Lightpath Long Island Classic—$1,700,000
Winner: Bobby Wadkins

After 27 years and 777 professional starts in the United States, Bobby Wadkins — brother of Lanny and perennial bridesmaid — finally picked up a victory, beating Allen Doyle and Larry Nelson in the Lightpath Long Island Classic.

It was Wadkins' first win after 712 starts on the PGA Tour and 65 on the Buy.com Tour. He also became the ninth player to win a Senior PGA Tour event his first time out after reaching age 50. That list included Don January, Roberto de Vicenzo, Arnold Palmer, Rod Funseth, Gary Player, George Archer, Jack Nicklaus, Bruce Fleisher and Wadkins' brother, Lanny.

"I'm not sure my name belongs up there with those guys," Wadkins said. "But I'm happy to be there. It's kind of neat that I get to put my name by Lanny's."

Wadkins captured this one like a seasoned winner. An opening round of 65 gave him a share of the lead with Joe Inman and J.C. Snead, but 69 on Saturday dropped Wadkins to four shots back. Jay Sigel held the lead going into the final 18 holes after shooting 64 in the second round.

Sigel led by five shots after eight holes on Sunday, but things started going Wadkins' way. On the par-five third hole, he hit a short iron into the hole for a double-eagle two. He made another birdie when he drained a 20-foot putt at the 16th to gain a share of the lead. With one hole to play, he was tied with Nelson, Doyle and Sigel. But Wadkins wasn't playing for a playoff. The 18th, a 172-yard uphill par-three, was his best hope.

He struck a six iron that ran 12 feet past the hole. "All I had to do was make that putt," Wadkins said. "Obviously I wanted it to go in, but I wasn't thinking about the second putt. I only had one concern — to get that ball in the hole. You couldn't ask for a better chance to win your first one, so I had to take care of business right there."

Wadkins took care of business, draining the final birdie putt to shoot 68 for a 14-under-par 202 total. Sigel finished with a bogey for 74 and a 204 total, which dropped him into a tie for fourth with Walter Hall. Nelson had the best shot at tying Wadkins, but his uphill 25-footer came up short. "Going up that hill you don't know how hard to hit it," Nelson said. "It would have had to have been perfect. If I hit it any harder, it would have moved to the left."

Doyle also had an 18-footer to tie, but missed. Both Nelson and Doyle finished with rounds of 69 on Sunday to share second place with 203 totals.

"I was supposed to win this week, that's all there is to it," Wadkins said. "How could I have not won? Lanny and I grew up on Meadowbrook Country Club (in Richmond, Virginia) and my first tournament as a senior was at Meadow Brook (in Jericho, New York). I made a double eagle, the second I've ever made. Everything turned out like it was supposed to. I've worked hard for a year for this moment. I can't tell you how good it feels."

3M Championship—$1,750,000
Winner: Bruce Lietzke

A lot of creative descriptions have been offered for Bruce Lietzke over the years, but Lietzke himself offered probably the best analysis after winning in his second Senior PGA Tour appearance.

"I'm a freak because human nature is to want to get better, and I just want to stay the same," Lietzke said. "When most people play golf they want to be able to hit the ball 15 yards farther than they did before. Or if they can fade the ball, then they want to be able to hook the ball. If they hit the ball low, they want to be able to hit the ball high. I just want to know that when I hit a seven iron, it's going to go the same distance it did the last time. I want to have a swing that works for me every time. I don't want things to change. I don't want to get better. I want to stay the same."

Lietzke didn't hit any more range balls than normal after reaching age 50. He just went out in the 3M Championship, his second event after joining the senior circuit, and shot 72, 66 and 69 for a 207 total and a two-stroke victory over Doug Tewell. He got into contention on Saturday with a bogey-free 66, then got off to a quick start on Sunday with birdies on two of his first three holes. When he hit a lob wedge to within two feet and tapped in for birdie at the 571-yard, par-five sixth hole, Lietzke took a share of the lead.

He only needed to play even-par golf from that point on, which was what he did. Second-round co-leaders Jose Maria Canizares and Hale Irwin struggled. Both shot 74s to tie for third place with Bruce Fleisher and Gil Morgan at 210.

"I dug myself a hole at the start," Irwin said. "I got most of the way out of the hole, and then I dug myself another hole. But if I wasn't able to win, I'm glad Bruce did. His swing doesn't look any different than it did 15 or 20 years ago. And I think joining the Senior PGA Tour has got him excited and ready to show what he can do."

Lietzke found himself changing course on Sunday. "I had to adjust my thinking today," the winner said. "My thinking was to just stay within striking distance of Hale. I was flabbergasted Hale would start that way."

He found himself going from the pursuer to the pursued. Once he got to nine under par, Lietzke had two three-putt bogeys, but came back with two more birdies on the back nine. "I struggled with some of my putts today," he said. "It was a big putt at 14. I had a lot of confidence coming in. I made a few mental errors the last couple of days. I kept them to a minimum, however."

That was also the complaint the second-place finisher had. "I just didn't putt well today," Tewell said after shooting 67. "I didn't putt well on Saturday either."

Novell Utah Showdown—$1,500,000
Winner: Steven Veriato

For four years Steven Veriato qualified on Mondays for Senior PGA Tour events and wondered if he really belonged among the elite of the tour. "I never thought I would win," Veriato said, "but I always thought I could win. Sometimes you play your very best and people beat you. That's how good the competition is out here."

Conversely, sometimes you simply post three consistent rounds and watch as the field collapses around you. That's what happened to Veriato at the Novell Utah Classic in Park City. Trailing by four shots to local favorite Bruce Summerhays, Veriato went out in the afternoon and shot his third consecutive round of 68 for a 204 total, then watched as Summerhays fell apart, shooting 74 to finish tied for sixth at 206.

"It's disappointing because I was playing for the fans," Summerhays said. "I think they'll be more disappointed than me."

Summerhays was still looking for his first victory and there seemed no better place for that first win than the city where he served as a club professional for over a decade. But Summerhays felt fatigued toward the end of his final round, and when he reached the 17th tee he was exhausted. The result was a shank and an out-of-bounds tee shot followed by a lackluster finish. "Even the chip had no zip on it," he said. "That hasn't happened to me before, where I had no strength down the stretch."

With Summerhays' collapse, a number of players jumped into contention. Graham Marsh leapt into the lead when he rolled in a birdie putt at the 15th hole, but he bogeyed the 18th to shoot 68 and finish with a 205 total. That tied him with Jesse Patino, Bruce Lietzke and Tom Jenkins.

Veriato's last birdie came at the 17th hole. He hit his approach to the 18th in the front greenside bunker. "My wife told me, 'If you get up and down, you might win,'" he said. "I guess someone told her that Summerhays had hit it out of bounds on 17. I know I'm good out of the sand."

He proved it, blasting out to seven feet and making the crucial par putt. When no one behind him birdied the 18th, Veriato openly wept as he won his first Senior PGA Tour event.

"This has been a long journey in time," he said. "The last hurdle was to win. I feel like I'm one of the crew now. Jim Colbert told me the other night that it takes courage to do what I do, to keep playing even though I'd never won. This win lets you release all the stress of the doubts you carry all your life, wondering if you're good enough. Did Jim talk to me on the right week or what?"

AT&T Canada Senior Open—$1,600,000
Winner: Walter Hall

If Walter Hall had his way, he'd hang a plaque around the tree that guards the left side of the 18th green at Mississauga Golf and Country Club in Ontario. Ed Dougherty, on the other hand, would like to destroy the ancient chestnut.

"I'd blow the tree up," Dougherty said after bogeying the 18th hole three times in five tries, the last two coming on Sunday when Dougherty finished with a bogey for a final-round 65 to tie Hall at 269, and again on the first playoff hole to give Hall his first Senior PGA Tour victory at the AT&T Canada Senior Open. "You'd better get me out of Canada quick or that tree might not be there tomorrow."

Hall had the exact opposite view. "Heaven forbid they lose that tree," he said after parring the 18th to shoot a final round of 70 for a 15-under-par 269 total, then parring it again in the playoff. "I'm thinking about going out and kissing it. That's really a great spot for a tree, especially with the back left pin, for someone like me or Ed who fades the ball.

Throughout most of the final day the AT&T Canada Senior Open was Hall's tournament to lose, and Hall almost obliged. Leading by one entering the final round and with six career runner-up finishes to his credit, Hall fought the gusting winds and scrambled all day, finishing with 12 straight pars, including an up-and-down from the fairway on the 18th.

Meanwhile Dougherty was charging. Trailing by five shots going into the final round, the rangy Texan birdied four out of five holes on the front nine, then pulled within a shot of the lead with another birdie at the 12th. When his birdie putt at the 15th fell in, Dougherty tied Hall atop the leaderboard. Another 15-foot birdie putt at the 16th gave Dougherty the lead outright. Then he made the one swing that cost him the tournament, a pulled approach at the final hole that flew over the tree and into the grandstands.

"It was an absolutely horrible seven iron," Dougherty said. "I tried to hit it too hard and just pulled it. The only good thing is I didn't hit anybody."

The bogey forced a playoff, and another poor approach set up Dougherty's second bogey on the 18th in an hour's time. "It was just disappointing," he said.

Nothing was disappointing for Hall, who joined Bobby Wadkins, Bruce Lietzke and Steven Veriato as a first-time winner, the fourth in four consecutive weeks. "It's been a fantastic week," Hall said. "I was very fortunate today. I didn't play my best, but thank goodness I had my putter in the bag. It saved me time after time. I hung in there and scrambled my fanny off. Fortunately I got through it."

Kroger Senior Classic—$1,500,000
Winner: Jim Thorpe

Rain shortened the event to 36 holes, but that didn't dampen the drama of the Kroger Senior Classic in Mason, Ohio, especially after Jim Thorpe hit one of the most memorable shots of his career. Trailing Tom Jenkins by two strokes with one hole to play, Thorpe needed an eagle at the 546-yard, par-five 18th to force a playoff. He hit a perfect tee shot, then hit a 245-yard three-wood shot over a pond. The ball landed on the fringe and rolled toward the hole like a softly lobbed pitch. It looked like it might go in before stopping one foot from the hole. Thorpe tapped in for eagle to shoot his second straight 65 and tie Jenkins with a 130 total.

"It was just a perfect shot," Thorpe said. "I could probably hit a million golf balls and never do that again. It's just that sometimes we do get lucky under the gun."

Jenkins had a sinking feeling as he watched Thorpe's approach. Despite shooting a career-low round of 63 to get into the clubhouse first at 130, Jenkins knew he had left a few shots out on the course. A missed birdie putt on the 17th from 12 feet and another near miss for eagle on the 18th ultimately cost Jenkins. "I had several opportunities to close it out," he said. "It was my tournament to win. I hit a great putt at 16 and left it short going downhill. I hit another great putt at 17 that broke right instead of left. I thought 10-under 130 would win. But when you have chances and leave it open, there is always a chance of a miracle shot like the one Jim hit."

In the playoff, Thorpe once again relied on his three wood, this time hitting it onto the front edge of the 18th green and leaving himself 30 feet for eagle. Jenkins, who hit his tee shot 10 yards past Thorpe, came out of his five-wood shot and missed the green to the right. He failed to get up and down and had to settle for par.

Thorpe didn't need an eagle the second time through, but he almost made it anyway. His putt rolled inches from the hole, and he tapped in for a birdie.

"I've been close all year," Thorpe said. "Winning never comes easy. Tom Jenkins' 63 was magnificent and probably should have won the golf tournament. I've shot some very good rounds, but it seems like somebody always comes out of the pack and beats me by a shot or two. This week was just my week."

Allianz Championship—$1,750,000
Winner: Jim Thorpe

Jim Thorpe has always won tournaments in clusters. His three victories on the regular PGA Tour were closely grouped in September and October, and prior to becoming a tour regular, Thorpe won numerous mini-tour events in September, October and November. "I've won everything after September," Thorpe said after winning the Alliance Championship in Des Moines, Iowa, his second senior victory in a row, both coming in September. "It just takes me eight months to warm up," he said.

Thorpe reeled off seven birdies in 11 holes on Sunday to build an insurmountable lead. He had made a similar run on Saturday when he birdied six of the final 11 holes en route to a six-under-par 65. Coupled with the 68 he shot on Friday, Thorpe had a one-shot edge over Tom Kite and Isao Aoki going into the final 18 holes.

Thorpe stretched that lead with his birdie barrage on Sunday. After making a spectacular up-and-down for birdie from a fairway bunker on the par-five 15th, his lead was three over Bruce Lietzke. Another birdie at the 16th made the lead four. When Lietzke missed a four-footer for birdie at the 17th, the lead was five, and Thorpe was able to cruise in with a couple of bogeys on the 17th and 18th. He shot 66 and won by two strokes over Gil Morgan. His 199 total didn't break any records, but he wasn't looking for that.

"With a five-stroke lead I felt I could finish with a couple of bogeys and just try to get it over with," he said. "At this point, a win is a win, whether you win by half a dozen or by one."

Morgan jumped into second place with a flurry of birdies on the back nine to shoot 65 for a 201 total, but he missed a couple of putts late that cost him. "If I could have birdied 15 and 16, that might have changed the complexion of things," Morgan said. "But I don't know. Jim was playing well. He was making a lot of birdies."

The wet golf course and soft greens played right into Thorpe's aggressive style. "I had 19 birdies and that's not bad for 54 holes," he said. "I think what really impressed me is I birdied a lot of the tough holes. I think the reason is we had enough rain to soften the greens up so I could attack the flags on basically every shot I hit."

Then, in a reflective moment, Thorpe said, "It's good to be lucky. I feel like I've been playing good for a long time and I just haven't gotten there. I think one thing that turned my game around is I seem to be a lot more patient on the golf course right now. I don't get angry when things don't go right."

Lietzke closed with 67 for a 202 total and third place, while Kite and Aoki both closed with 69s. They tied for fourth with Bruce Summerhays at 203.

SAS Championship—$1,600,000
Winner: Bruce Lietzke

In another sign that in the wake of September 11 things will never be the same, Mike McCullough, the Ironman of the Senior PGA Tour, skipped the SAS Championship, the first event he had missed since 1996, ending his consecutive-start streak at 177 events. McCullough wasn't injured or sick. He simply wasn't ready to play golf again in the aftermath of the terrorist attacks which also resulted in the cancellation of the Vantage Championship the previous week.

Some things remained the same. Bruce Lietzke, who hadn't hit a single golf shot in almost two weeks when he teed off at the Prestonwood Country Club in Cary, North Carolina, shot rounds of 69, 66 and 66 for a 201 total to win his second senior event in only seven starts.

"I know I'm a freak," Lietzke said, repeating the claim he made after winning his senior debut. "I haven't changed my swing in 27 years. That's absolutely freakish right there. You have guys shooting 64s and they hit a bad eight iron, so they go to the practice range and hit 500 eight irons. That's human nature. I'm not like that. I'm doing things on my own terms."

On Sunday Lietzke hit all 18 greens, and he hit over 90 percent of the greens in regulation for the week. With those kinds of numbers all Lietzke had to do was putt reasonably well to win. "I had a great putting tournament," Lietzke said. "Putting is not something I can rely on every single week. I am kind of a streaky putter. I hope I can keep this streak going."

The only threat on Sunday came from Gary McCord, who managed to tie Lietzke for the lead with a birdie putt at the par-five 17th. The lead was short-lived, however. McCord's tee shot on the 18th hit a tree in the right rough and bounded into trouble.

"I hit that tree again for the third straight day," McCord said. "I kept trying to hit it over it, but it keeps hitting it and going sideways. I just kind of paid the price."

McCord recovered with an approach shot into the greenside bunker and a beautiful sand shot to two feet. When he missed the short par putt, McCord settled for 67 and a 204 total, good enough for a tie for second place with Allen Doyle, three strokes behind Lietzke.

It was McCord's best finish in over a year, but even the bogey at the 18th proved insignificant. Moments after McCord made birdie at the 17th to gain a share of the lead, Lietzke hit a great approach to the par-five and two-putted for birdie to regain the lead outright. Another birdie on the 18th gave Lietzke a comfortable three-shot cushion.

"I want to relax more on the senior tour, but I was breathing hard over the final holes," he said. "I was telling myself, 'Don't pull a Larry Nelson and do anything stupid.'"

Nelson might have taken umbrage with Lietzke's definition of "stupid," but the incident he was referring to was bizarre to say the least. Leading by four strokes after four consecutive birdies in the second round, Nelson pushed his approach on the par-four 13th under a fence. From all the hand signals he was getting from the marshals, Nelson assumed the ball was out of bounds, so he hit another ball that went into a pond in front of the green.

When he arrived at the fence, however, Nelson saw that the original ball was not out of bounds, and he played it. The only problem was that he hadn't declared his second ball a "provisional" and under the rules he was obliged to play it. With a penalty for hitting a wrong ball, plus the stroke and distance penalty, and the penalty for hitting the ball in the water hazard, Nelson walked away with a 10 on the hole and never contended again.

Gold Rush Classic—$1,300,000
Winner: Tom Kite

Runner-up Allen Doyle summed up the play at the Gold Rush Classic in El Dorado Hills, California, pretty well when he said, "Jeez, I had two weeks of birdies out here in one week and I still didn't win."

Tom Kite, leading the Senior PGA Tour in every statistical ball-striking category but still struggling with the putter, shot a final-round 67 for a tournament-record 197, tying an eight-year-old tour scoring record in relation to par with a 22-under-par total. It was just good enough. Doyle shot 63 for a 195 total, a score that would have won every other week of the 2001 season.

"That's just how it goes sometimes," Doyle said. "Normally this score was good enough to win."

Kite, who shot a course-record 62 on Saturday and carried a five-shot lead into the final round, never considered the victory a lock until the final putt fell. On Saturday night he said he wished the lead was six or seven shots. "I wish it were more," he said. "I'm not being greedy. I mean it."

He knew it would be a battle on Sunday, especially given the way he had putted throughout the year. "I've been hitting the ball as well or better than anyone on this tour and better than a lot of guys on the other tour, but I have been just worthless on the greens," Kite said.

He switched to a mid-length putter this week in an attempt to gain some sense of feel on the greens, and it appeared to work. The 62 included two eagles on the front nine, six consecutive birdies on the back nine and a total of only 24 putts. But an early stumble on Sunday cost him. Two straight leadoff bogeys opened the door for Doyle, who played ahead of Kite and tied the lead twice during the final round.

Kite's putter pulled him through in the final stretch. A birdie on the 12th gave him the lead again, and two more birdies from 10 and seven feet at the 14th and 15th extended the margin back to three shots. Late birdies by Doyle on the 16th and 17th cut the margin to one, but that was as close as he could get. Kite drained a tough six-footer for par on the 16th and cruised home with two-putt pars on the 17th and 18th, finishing the way he liked to finish — hitting fairways and greens.

"It's just a matter of trusting my putting stroke," Kite said. "Even after this week I can't say I'm totally confident, but it's a start. I was pleased I tied the record. It would have been nicer to break it. But I went 15 months without a 'W.' I'll trade the record for a win any day."

Turtle Bay Championship—$1,500,000
Winner: Hale Irwin

He wasn't the dominant force on the Senior PGA Tour in 2001 that he was in the late 1990s, but Hale Irwin had little to prove when he teed off as defending champion at the Turtle Bay Championship in Hawaii. He was already the winningest man in Senior PGA Tour history, and a two-time winner in 2001. The fact that he hadn't won since April shouldn't have bothered him, but it did.

"I've had the kind of year that's been a little frustrating," Irwin said. "I tried to convince myself that what has happened in the last five or six months had gone by me. I was frustrated at how I performed, particularly in crucial situations."

Those frustrations were washed away with the tide on Oahu's north shore as Irwin grabbed a two-shot lead through two rounds and closed out his third victory of the season and 32nd of his senior career with a final-round 68. His 11-under-par 205 total was good enough for a three-shot margin over second-place finisher John Jacobs, who finished with 69.

"It wasn't easy," Irwin said after finishing with birdies on the final two holes to secure the win. Jacobs pulled to within one shot twice during the round, the first time at the seventh when Irwin bogeyed and Jacobs rolled in a short birdie putt, and again after Jacobs birdied the 12th and 14th.

But both players conceded that the ninth hole was the turning point of the tournament. Trailing by a single shot, Jacobs pushed his tee shot into the water guarding the right side and finished with a bogey. When Irwin rolled in a 12-footer for birdie, the momentum swung in the defending champion's favor.

"The ninth hole was the difference," Jacobs said. "You can't win out here when you make mental errors, and that was a terrible mental error. I misjudged the wind. If I could have birdied, I think I could have caught Hale. I had my chances, but you've got to shoot better than 69 to beat Hale."

Irwin agreed with that assessment. "Nine was big," he said. "J.J. hit a poor tee shot, and I was able to get back the two shots I just gave to him at seven. The momentum changed at nine and then it was my tournament to lose."

The Transamerica—$1,300,000
Winner: Sammy Rachels

Even Sammy Rachels agreed that he was the most unlikely two-time rookie winner on the Senior PGA Tour this year. Playing in sneakers because of back pain, wearing a goatee because he likes it, and traveling in a motor home because of the terrorist attacks of September 11, Rachels looked more like a "roadie" for an aging rock band than a man in the midst of a breakout year on the senior circuit. But after holing a 30-foot eagle putt on the final hole to win a shootout at The Transamerica, Rachels felt like he had finally arrived.

"This win does validate me to a certain extent," he said after making the final putt for a three-under-par 69 and a 202 total, good enough for a one-shot win over Raymond Floyd and Doug Tewell. "I'm good enough to play out here, but I'm a pessimist by nature. I could win five tournaments in a row, and I'd go to the next one thinking, 'Please, don't hook it into the trees.' I'd be a good thesis for a sport psychologist."

No psychology was needed in Napa, California, as five players battled it out in the final nine holes. Rachels, who shot 63 on Saturday, entered the closing round tied for the lead with John Mahaffey and Allen Doyle. Several more players quickly joined the hunt on Sunday. The first was Floyd, who birdied the 17th hole to reach 12 under and tie Mahaffey, who stood alone in the lead at that point. Seconds later Rachels rolled in a birdie putt at the 14th to join the crowd atop the leaderboard. Tewell wasn't far behind. A few minutes later he rolled in a 12-footer for birdie at the 16th to make it a four-way tie at the top.

Hale Irwin joined the fray with an eagle at the 18th to move him to 12 under. For a few minutes he was the leader in the clubhouse with a 204 total. Floyd snatched that title a few minutes later when he rolled in a birdie putt at the 18th to shoot 64 and post a 203 total. Tewell joined him at 203 moments later when he tapped in a birdie putt on the 18th for 66 after almost holing a chip for eagle.

Mahaffey, who fell victim to an obscure rule when he accidentally dropped his ball into his ball marker on the eighth hole and incurred a one-shot penalty, clawed his way back, but missed a short birdie putt on the 16th. His chances vanished with a bogey on the 17th, but when asked about the turning point in the tournament, Mahaffey pointed to the penalty. "It's just one of those things," he said.

After marking a 12-inch bogey putt, Mahaffey lifted his ball, fumbled it, and the ball landed on the coin he'd used to mark his position. "The ball slipped out of my hand," he said. "The marker flipped over, like heads or tails. I wasn't aware of the rule, but I sure am now."

That left Rachels, who was one shot off the lead coming to the final hole, alone with a chance to win. When he reached the par-five with his second shot and stood over the 30-footer for eagle, he was simply thinking about a playoff. "My goal was to two-putt and get in a playoff," he said. "To make a long putt to win a golf tournament — that's something I've never done before. That's pretty cool."

Floyd and Tewell tied for second at 203, while Irwin, Mahaffey, Doyle and Bob Gilder shared fourth at 204. "It was a war of attrition out there today," the winner said. "It didn't feel like a birdie shootout at all."

SBC Championship—$1,400,000
Winner: Larry Nelson

Larry Nelson put an exclamation point in his season with a two-putt birdie on the final hole at the SBC Championship in San Antonio, Texas, to shoot a course-record 63 and capture the final full-field senior event of the year. His 17-under-par 199 total was good enough for a two-shot win over Gary McCord and Bob Gilder. It was Nelson's fifth victory of the year, and it rekindled his enthusiasm for the year-end Senior Tour Championship.

Nelson trailed McCord and Bob Murphy by two shots going into the final round, but he played flawlessly in the home stretch. With nine birdies and no bogeys on Sunday, Nelson leapt into the lead. But he didn't walk away with this one. Murphy didn't factor, finishing with 73 for a 207 total and tie for eighth, but McCord shot five-under 67 to keep the pressure on. Gilder also played well, making only one bogey in his closing 66.

Nelson's eighth birdie at the 17th gave him a one-shot advantage. The prudent choice on the par-five 18th would have been to lay up, make par, and be content with a one-stroke win. But Nelson wanted to go out with a bang. After a good tee shot, he hit a three wood onto the green from 230 yards. After making a good run at eagle, Nelson tapped in from 18 inches for birdie, the course record and the victory.

Senior Tour Championship—$2,500,000
Winner: Bob Gilder

Like everyone else in the field at the Senior Tour Championship in Oklahoma City, Bob Gilder struggled with the wind on Sunday. He just struggled a little less than everyone else. Gilder shot 73 for an 11-under-par 277 total and a one-shot victory over Doug Tewell at Gaillardia Country Club.

"This golf course was one of the toughest finishing golf courses I ever played on today," Gilder said after catching and passing third-round leader Bruce Lietzke and making a clutch par at the par-five 18th to avoid a play-off. "The wind just made it brutal."

The wind gusted at speeds of up to 40 miles an hour, and the scores skyrocketed as the weather worsened. Two players broke 70 on Sunday — Leonard Thompson, who played early and shot 67 for a 287 total and 14th place, and Tewell, who had the best weekend of anyone in the field, shooting 68 and 69 to fall one short of Gilder. Tewell lives in Oklahoma City, only 15 miles from the golf course, so he had an advantage. When he ran in a birdie putt at the final hole to enter the clubhouse first at 278, many thought he had a great chance of winning.

"The golf course held everybody in check," Tewell said.

Gilder held a one-shot lead with nine holes to play, but a bogey at the 10th dropped him back into a tie with Lietzke. The 11th provided a turning point. After Lietzke hit his drive into the rough, Gilder couldn't find the fairway either, hitting his tee shot into the fairway bunker. Lietzke failed to reach the green with his second shot, chipped long, then missed his par putt, while Gilder hit a recovery from the bunker to 12 feet. When he made the putt for birdie, the lead was two. That lead grew to four shots one hole later when Lietzke again missed the fairway and made another bogey. Meanwhile, Gilder hit the fairway and green, leaving himself only three feet for birdie. When he made that putt he moved to 13 under par.

Gilder gave two of those shots back in the closing holes with his final bogey coming at the 17th at the same time Tewell was birdieing the 18th. Needing a par to win, Gilder missed the fairway at the par-five finishing hole. He punched out in front of the green, chipped to eight feet and two-putted for the victory.

Senior Slam—$600,000
Winner: Allen Doyle

In an event that brought the major championship winners together for a grand finale to the senior season, the least heralded of the four players in the field turned out to be the most consistent. Allen Doyle, the driving range operator with the slap-shot swing, shot two consecutive rounds of 67 at the World Golf Village's Slammer & Squire course for a 134 total to capture the Senior Slam by two strokes over Tom Watson.

Watson, Doug Tewell and Bruce Fleisher all put up good fights. Watson was the most constant threat. After opening with a 70 to trail by three, Watson birdied the fifth, seventh and eighth holes, but still trailed by two shots at the turn.

"I knew I would need to get to double figures (under par) because of the perfect conditions and the soft greens," Watson said. He went a long way toward that goal with birdies at the 11th, 13th and 14th. But Doyle matched him with birdies of his own at the 14th and 15th.

"Tom's been sticking every iron shot and we come up to a par-three and you got to figure this guy's licking his chops," Doyle said of a man who has been enshrined in the World Golf Hall of Fame longer than Doyle has been playing professionally. "When he didn't make birdie and I did, I think the pendulum shifted back to me."

Watson made another birdie at the 16th to pull within one, but he missed a birdie putt of 20 feet on the 17th that could have earned him a share of the lead. His 40-footer for birdie on the 18th wasn't close, and when Watson missed the four-footer for par, finishing with 66, Doyle's margin expanded to two shots.

European Seniors Tour

Royal Westmoreland Barbados Open—£125,000
Winner: Priscillo Diniz

Could this have been the opening tournament of the European Seniors Tour's 2001 season? Surely not. Tommy Horton wasn't in the winner's circle. The long-time star among the European seniors had launched each of the previous four seasons with a victory. Not this time, though. In what proved to be a sign of a poor season to come, Horton finished far down in the standings at the end of the Royal Westmoreland Barbados Open.

The title instead went to Brazilian Priscillo Diniz, a lawyer turned golf pro who had become the first player from his country to win on the circuit when he took the Daily Telegraph Match Play in 2000. The 52-year-old Diniz, from Sao Paulo, one of eight golf pros in his extended family, led from the start as for the second year the tour opened in the Caribbean at the Royal

Westmoreland Golf Club at St. James, Barbados. Diniz breezed to a three-stroke victory, his 16-under-par 200 total eight strokes better than Horton's winning total in 2000.

Diniz, who missed his one chance to try to qualify for the regular tour in Europe in 1985 because of a misplaced passport, began with a blazing 64 Friday, jumping off to a two-stroke lead over David Creamer. The London native and former world-class table tennis star who plays out of Frankfurt, Germany, and Orlando, Florida, kept on Diniz's heels all the way. He trailed by two after an opening 66, then matched 67s with Diniz in Saturday's second round. Nobody else was in contention going into the final round, the nearest players five shots behind Creamer. Creamer made a run at Diniz Sunday. He led by one after a birdie at the 11th, but Diniz countered with birdies at the 14th, 15th and 18th to win going away as Creamer took two bogeys on the closing holes.

Beko Classic—US$330,000
Winner: Noel Ratcliffe

Noel Ratcliffe quickly launched his bid for a second consecutive Order of Merit title with a one-stroke victory in the Beko Classic at the Gloria Golf Resort in Turkey. Ratcliffe, four strokes off the pace after 36 holes, closed with a five-under-par 67 to snatch the title by a shot over fellow Australian Terry Gale.

Seiji Ebihara, the Japanese regular on the European tour, seized the opening-round lead with a 67, one stroke in front of Malcolm Gregson, Barry Vivian, David Creamer and Gale. Ratcliffe, who began the tournament with 69, fell four strokes behind when he shot 73 Saturday. Scotland's Mike Miller, playing in his first European Seniors event, fired a brilliant 63 that day after starting with 75 and jumped into a first-place tie with Gregson, who added 70 to his opening 68 for 138 total.

Both men struggled to 73s Sunday and dropped into a four-way tie for third place with Australians Ian Stanley and Barry Vivian at 211 as Ratcliffe and Gale sailed past them, Ratcliffe with his 67 for 209 and Gale with 70 for 210.

AIB Irish Seniors Open—£197,463
Winner: Seiji Ebihara

Seiji Ebihara, a protege of Isao Aoki who became a strong campaigner on the Japan PGA Tour in his younger days, added an international flavor to his record when he won for the first time on the European Seniors Tour in the AIB Irish Seniors Open. The victory came a week after he had a similar start in Turkey only to fall back in the two subsequent rounds. This time, his start was even better — a course-record seven-under-par 65 — and he needed that score at the end to prevail by a stroke over Simon Owen of New Zealand with his nine-under 207 total.

The 65 Friday gave Ebihara a one-shot lead over Norman Wood and two over Delroy Cambridge of Jamaica and America's John Grace. His margin vanished Saturday when Owen matched the 65 and moved three strokes ahead of Ebihara and four in front of Cambridge and Bernard Gallacher, the ex-Ryder Cupper. Owen's fortunes flip-flopped Sunday when he began the round with two bogeys. He never really recovered and shot 75, but he clung to the lead as Ebihara took a triple bogey at the fourth hole. However, Ebihara hung tough after that, birdied the 17th and won with a brilliant nine-iron approach to two feet to set up a final birdie at the last hole for 71 and the 207. Gallacher and Dennis Durnian tied for third at 209.

De Vere PGA Seniors' Championship—£200,000
Winner: Ian Stanley

Ian Stanley began his march to the 2001 Order of Merit title in the De Vere PGA Seniors' Championship, the season's first major event, outlasting Maurice Bembridge in the stretch to score a two-stroke victory at De Vere Carden Park in England. He posted a 10-under-par 278, but really didn't have victory in hand until he birdied the 71st hole to establish the final margin.

Bembridge, the Ryder Cup veteran who ended the 2000 season with three consecutive runner-up finishes and hadn't won on the senior circuit since the 1998 Swedish Seniors Open, got away fast in the opening round with a sizzling seven-under-par 65. It gave him a two-stroke lead over little-known Mike Steadman, the Somerset pro, and a three-shot edge over four others. Stanley began inconspicuously with 71, but moved into a tie for the lead Friday when he produced a 66, joining Simon Owen at 137. Bembridge faltered with 75 for 140, dropping into a fourth-place tie behind Nick Job (139).

Stanley took sole possession of first place Saturday when he followed with 68 for 205 and a three-stroke lead, which turned out to be the largest 54-hole margin of the season. Bembridge matched the 68 and slipped into second place, a shot in front of Owen, the runner-up the previous week in the Irish Seniors playing in his third tournament on the circuit. The New Zealander, who finished second to Jack Nicklaus in the 1978 Open Championship at St. Andrews, had a par 72. Interestingly, Nicklaus designed the Carden Park course.

It appeared that Stanley would roll to an easy win Sunday when Bembridge fell six strokes behind. However, the gritty Englishman fought back to within a stroke before Stanley scored the telling birdie at the 17th hole and parred the 18th for 73 and the 278.

Wales Seniors Open—£500,000
Winner: Denis Durnian

Denis Durnian got a little ahead of himself. Durnian packed his bags before heading to Royal St. David's for the second round of the Wales Seniors Open, figuring that his opening 74 had put him in danger of missing the 36-hole cut. Instead, he stood on the 18th green two days later accepting the biggest winner's check — £83,300 — in the history of the European Seniors Tour. The victory was his first, ending the frustration he had felt over the years with four second-place finishes during his career on the regular European Tour. "The most I ever won before was £32,000 when I lost to Seve Ballesteros down the road at St. Pierre," the elated Englishman recalled. "The Welsh air must agree with me."

It certainly agreed with Steve Wild on Friday. Aided by local knowledge of the course, the 54-year-old Englishman, a "country" member of St. David's for 27 of his years as a amateur, shot 67 and took a one-stroke lead over Scotland's Gordon MacDonald and Ireland's Paul Leonard. The familiarity didn't help Saturday, though. Wild stumbled to 75 as Leonard and Bernard Gallacher assumed the lead at 137, Leonard with 68-69 and Gallacher with 70-67. Gallacher, the former Ryder Cup player and captain, recovered from a three-bogey start with an eagle and three birdies in his two-under-par round. Leonard also had three bogeys, all on the second nine, but he offset them with three birdies after a one-under-par first nine.

Durnian and American Alan Tapie provided Saturday's fireworks. Durnian bounced back with 65, and Tapie, with eight birdies, set a course record with his 63 as they joined David Vaughan (71-68) at 139, a shot off the lead.

Durnian put away the title Sunday with a par 69 for 208, the only winning score of the season in over-par figures. He nosed out American Jay Horton, who also shot 69 for 209, as Gallacher faded to 74 and placed third at 211. Leonard dropped to 213 with his 76.

Microlease Jersey Seniors Masters—£110,000
Winner: Seiji Ebihara

Seiji Ebihara became the first multiple winner of the season when he captured the Microlease Jersey Seniors Masters title in mid-June, but it required three extra holes for the Japanese pro to add that one to his victory a month earlier in the AIB Irish Seniors Open. His 10-foot birdie putt the third time he played the 17th hole at breezy La Moye Golf Club ended the overtime battle with Delroy Cambridge of Jamaica and Denis Durnian, who was trying to make it two wins in a row.

The first deadlock of the week came in the first round when eight players shot 69 and led the field. Ebihara, Durnian and Cambridge were in that group, which also included Barry Vivian, Liam Higgins, Noel Ratcliffe, John Grace and Simon Owen. Then Durnian, coming off his rich victory the previous Sunday in Wales, nosed a stroke in front on a blustery Saturday with a 70 for 139, five under par. Four players finished at 140 that day — Vivian, Cambridge, Bobby Verwey of South Africa and, most notably, 66-year-old Neil Coles, the defending champion whose victory at La Moye in 2000 made him the oldest winner ever on any of the world tours. Ebihara slipped back with 73 for 142.

Ebihara managed his game better than the others in the wind Sunday and his 71 brought him into the 54-hole tie with Durnian and Cambridge at 213, the highest winning score of the season for that distance. Durnian mustered only 74 and Cambridge 73 in the rough conditions. Cambridge departed from the playoff on the first extra hole, the 17th, thanks to a wild tee shot. The surviving two each missed short par putts at the 18th, but when they returned again to the 17th, Ebihara put his approach in the center of the green and sank the winning 10-footer. Coles failed to make more history when he dropped to eighth place with 75.

Palmerston Trophy Berlin—£122,766
Winner: Denis O'Sullivan

Denis O'Sullivan was in luck when he sought a caddie for the Palmerston Trophy tournament when he arrived at Berlin's Sporting Club — Tilo Luck, to be precise. No doubt it was more than just a good caddie and the magic of his name rubbing off on him, more likely it was the tinkering the Irishman had done with his swing the previous week in Jersey that carried him to victory.

"I decided to widen my swing a bit (last week) and the end result is that I have hardly hit a bad shot since," observed O'Sullivan. "I think that's probably the best I have ever played for a whole tournament."

Seiji Ebihara, carrying a hot hand from the previous Sunday's win in the Microlease Jersey Masters, led the first day on the new Nick Faldo course at the Sporting Club with a two-under-par 70, but O'Sullivan was right on his heels at 71, along with Bernard Gallacher and Americans Jerry Bruner and Tommy Price.

O'Sullivan had only one bad hole in the windy weather Friday, a double bogey at the seventh, and continued his strong play in adverse conditions Saturday. His par 72 for 143 pushed him into the lead, a stroke ahead of Geoff Parslow of Australia and Northern Ireland's Eddie Polland. Only Jeff Van Wagenen and Delroy Cambridge broke par Saturday, both shooting 69s.

It was O'Sullivan's turn to fire a 69 Sunday. That turned a tight battle into a bit of a runaway as O'Sullivan finished at 212, four shots ahead of Ebihara, who finished with 71, and Polland, who posted his third straight 72. Of his third European Seniors Tour victory, O'Sullivan noted that "it meant an awful lot to me. Last year, when I won my first two tournaments, I did it coming from behind. This time I was there to be shot at, but I still managed to retain my composure and play golf the way I wanted to play."

Lawrence Batley Seniors—£120,000
Winner: Nick Job

Nick Job conjured up the season's lowest final round — 63 — and rolled to the year's biggest victory margin — five strokes — as he landed the title in the Lawrence Batley Seniors tournament at Huddersfield Golf Club in England. The 52-year-old Job, head pro at London's Richmond Golf Club, came from two shots off the pace to grab his second victory on the European Seniors Tour with a nine-under-par 204. The first came in 2000 in the Total-Fina Elf Seniors Open in France.

"This victory means an awful lot to me ... because of the way I played throughout the final round," Job remarked.

He had returned to a conventional putting grip and "it seems to have paid off because I putted well all week. I also played well from tee to green. You have to if you are going to shoot a 63 in tough conditions like these."

The final victory spread magnified on the last two holes. Denis Durnian, the tour's leading money winner and Job's closest pursuer, trailed Job by only a stroke after 70 holes but finished bogey, double bogey for 67 and 209 total. The remarkable Neil Coles, age 66, in contention for a second straight week, shot 70 for 210 to take third place and win the separate super seniors competition for a second straight week.

Maurice Bembridge showed the way for two days as the leader with his opening 66 (by two over John McTear) and co-leader after 36 holes with 73 for 139 with Liam Higgins (72-67) and journeyman American Jay Dolan (71-68), a long-time campaigner on the European Seniors circuit. Coles was at 140, Job at 141 and Durnian at 142. The three leaders faltered badly on Sunday, only Bembridge winding up in the top 10 after a 74. The other two took 77s.

STC Scandinavian International—£225,000
Winner: Denis O'Sullivan

Players have learned not to count Denis O'Sullivan out if he is within range of first place going into the last day. Twice in 2000, O'Sullivan came up with 67s in the final round and won the Dan Technology Tournament of Champions and the Abu Dhabi Seniors. He made an even more impressive charge to victory in the 2001 STC Scandinavian International. Trailing by four strokes going into Sunday's finale at Stockholm's Kungsangen Golf Club, O'Sullivan produced a six-under-par 65 that gave him his second win of the season by one stroke over a star-crossed Maurice Bembridge. O'Sullivan, who won the Palmerston Trophy two weeks earlier from the front, finished eight under par at 205.

Bembridge had carried a three-stroke lead into the final round as he sought to snap a string of six second-place finishes since his last (second) senior victory in Sweden in 1998, which, incidentally, came in a playoff after Bembridge three-putted the last green. This time, needing only a par at the 72nd hole at Kungsangen to nip O'Sullivan by a shot, Bembridge shanked his pitch to the last green and took a double bogey for 70 and 206 total. O'Sullivan sympathized: "I was delighted with my own game, but that was the last way I would have wanted to win. Maurice is a lovely guy and he certainly didn't deserve to lose it that way."

American Alan Tapie, a one-time winner on the circuit in 1999, held the lead at four-under-par 67 after a thunderstorm delay carried completion of the opening round to Saturday morning. O'Sullivan shot 73, then followed with 67 Saturday. At that point, he was four off the pace of Bembridge, who pieced together six birdies and 25 putts for 66 and 136 total, three strokes clear of the quartet of Tapie (72), Bobby Verwey, Ian Stanley and Eddie Polland. Scot Mike Miller and Englishman John Morgan passed all of them with 67s Sunday to claim joint third place at 209.

Senior British Open—£500,000
Winner: Ian Stanley

The Senior British Open moved closer to achieving recognition as a major championship in 2001. The tournament boasted the strongest and most prestigious international field of its 15-year history when the tee-offs began at Royal County Down. The Big Three — Arnold Palmer, Gary Player and Jack Nicklaus, the latter playing in the event for the first time — headlined a stellar field attracted to the storied course in Northern Ireland that also included three other major championship holders — Bob Charles, Tony Jacklin and Dave Stockton. In fact, Nicklaus and Charles, who won the Senior Open in 1989 and 1993 and finished second five other times, made serious runs at the title before Ian Stanley nailed down the victory.

In a finish that he compared to Retief Goosen's in the U.S. Open at Southern Hills, the 52-year-old Australian missed a short putt for the win at the 72nd hole, but annexed the championship in the subsequent playoff. It completed a European seniors double for Stanley, who had won the British PGA Seniors at De Vere in early June.

While the galleries flocked to the more famous competitors, South Africa's John Bland took command in the scoring department during the early going at Royal County Down. A second-place finisher in three of the four previous Senior Opens, Bland opened with 68 and shared first place with Denis Durnian, the European Seniors Tour's hottest player in early 2001. Nicklaus shot 70.

Durnian disappeared from view Friday as Bland took solo possession of the lead with 69 for 137 total. One stroke back was Charles, who posted his second 69, and American David Oakley (70-68). Stanley pulled within two with his 70-69 rounds, but Nicklaus slipped back with 72 for 142. When Bland lost his touch en route to 76 Saturday, Stanley edged into the lead with 70 for 209. Charles and Oakley matched 72s to remain a stroke off the pace, and Nicklaus kept his bid alive with a 70, but bogeyed the 17th and missed a birdie chance at the 18th.

Oakley fell back early on Sunday, leaving the battle to Stanley, Charles and Nicklaus. Nicklaus moved within a shot of the lead when he birdied the 10th and eagled the 12th, but a bogey at the 15th took him out of contention. He finished with 69 and tied for third with John Morgan at 281. Charles got in with 68, but it appeared to be one too many until Stanley missed a three-foot par putt at the 18th for 69 and 278 total, forcing the playoff. Replaying the 18th, the New Zealander bunkered his drive and eventually bogeyed the hole. Stanley then holed a two-footer for the prized victory.

De Vere Hotels Seniors Classic—£150,000
Winner: Noel Ratcliffe

"It was the most incredible finish I've ever had." So said Noel Ratcliffe after his victory in the De Vere Hotels Seniors Classic, an appraisal that would get no argument from any quarter. The Australian, who topped the Order of Merit in 2000, eagled two of the last three holes, one of them a par-four, to eke out a one-stroke victory over Jerry Bruner and Simon Owen, both seeking their first wins on the circuit. The remarkable stretch run gave Ratcliffe a five-under-par 67 on the De Vere Slaley Hall course and the winning 205 total. It marked the seventh time Bruner had to settle for second place during his two and a half years on the European circuit.

Owen was on course for that initial victory for two days in the second De Vere event of the season. (Ian Stanley won the Senior PGA on the Carden Park course in early June.) The New Zealander opened with a flourish, firing a 65 for a two-shot lead over Ratcliffe and three over two-time winner Seiji Ebihara. The next day, Owen posted a two-under 70 for 135 and widened his margin to two over Bruner, who shot 67. Ratcliffe (71) joined Ebihara, Denis Durnian, Graham Burroughs and Trevor Downing at 138.

The Sunday fireworks erupted after Ratcliffe went to the 16th tee trailing Bruner by three strokes. He knocked his three-wood second shot on that par-five 10 feet from the cup and holed the putt for an eagle. He parred the 17th, then put a five-wood tee shot in perfect position in the 18th fairway 100 yards from the pin — "perfect yardage for my L-wedge." Yes, it was. The ball went into the cup for the title, his second of the season to go with his win in the Beko Classic in Turkey in May. That one wasn't as spectacular, but Ratcliffe came from four strokes off the lead in the final round to win by a shot.

Bad Ragaz PGA Seniors Open—£125,000
Winner: David Huish

Defending champions had found themselves on the outside looking in until the Bad Ragaz PGA Seniors Open in Switzerland, in which David Huish successfully repeated his 2000 victory. Not without difficulty, however. Despite a closing 64, it took the year's third playoff for Huish to put away his fifth seniors title as David Good staged a brilliant finish reminiscent of the one staged by Noel Ratcliffe the previous week. Good caught Huish at 198, but succumbed on the first extra hole.

Scoring was exceptionally low all week at Bad Ragaz and the winning score was the lowest of the season. In another flashback to the Ratcliffe "miracle," American David Oakley holed a 125-yard approach on the fly at the par-four 18th for an eagle deuce and a seven-under-par 63 in the opening round, staking himself to a two-stroke lead over John Morgan, Liam Higgins and Good. Huish whipped into contention Saturday with his first of two 64s, starting and finishing the round with pairs of birdies. It moved him into a fourth-place tie at 134 with Higgins as Oakley maintained his two-stroke lead with a 67 for 130. Good and American Bob Lendzion also shot 67s, Good for 132 and Lendzion for 133.

The second 64 propelled Huish into the lead until Good, who had eagled the par-five 16th, rolled in a 16-foot birdie putt on the 18th green to overtake him and force the playoff. It was Huish's turn to make a big putt on the first extra hole, though. He ran in a 20-footer from behind the hole. "I can't begin to tell you what this means to me. It saves my season," said Huish, who had struggled with a case of shingles earlier in the season and dropped out of the top 40 on the Order of Merit.

Energis Senior Masters—£225,000
Winner: David Oakley

A chance to make amends came quickly for David Oakley. The 56-year-old American showed great resiliency at the Wentworth Club in the Energis Senior Masters. Just a week after his game failed him and he squandered a two-stroke lead in the final round at Bad Ragaz, Oakley turned his final-round fortunes around and squished to a three-stroke victory in a Sunday rainstorm. A steady 71 led to an eight-under-par 208 total and gave Oakley, not long removed from amateur golf and a furniture store job in Florida, his third win in Europe.

Oakley, who posted three sub-par rounds when he finished third on Went-worth's Edinburgh course in 2000, extended the streak to six in 2001. He opened the tournament with 68, which placed him in a first-place tie with two-time 2000 winner Noel Ratcliffe. John McTear shot 69 and five others came in with 70s. Oakley then followed with 69 and surged four strokes in front of the field. Ratcliffe faded badly with 75 as Craig Defoy, John Morgan and American Hank Woodrome moved into joint second place at 141, Morgan shooting 66, the week's low score.

Undaunted by the wet and windy weather Sunday, Oakley put together his steady 71 and was never challenged. England's Malcolm Gregson shot one of just two rounds in the 60s that day. His 69 for 211 elevated him into second place. Tommy Horton, the circuit's No. 1 player for years, shot 68 to finish seventh, just his second top-10 performance of a drab season. Defoy and Woodrome shot 71s and placed third.

Legends in Golf—£110,880
Winner: David Good

Hard to say which player was more deserving of a victory as David Good and Jerry Bruner, winless on the European Seniors Tour, went back to the 18th tee in a playoff for the Legends in Golf title in The Netherlands in late August. Australian Good had lost in a playoff to David Huish just two weeks earlier in the Bad Ragaz Open after a brilliant overtaking rally. On the other hand, Bruner was the victim of Noel Ratcliffe's preposterous finish the previous week in the De Vere Hotels Classic, relegated to second place in the event for the seventh time. Furthermore, Bruner had bogeyed the last hole with victory at hand.

Bruner's bad fortunes continued in the overtime match as Good, a quali-fier in 2000, laid a solid birdie on him — drive, eight-iron, 12-foot putt — to take his first title at Crayestein Golf Club at Dordrecht. "I can't begin to explain what this means to me," said Good, who had undergone heart sur-gery during the previous winter. "I feel sorry for Jerry, but I am sure his time will come."

The American had taken a one-stroke lead into the final day after opening with 66, the best score that day, and adding 68 Saturday for 134. Good was just one back. He shot 66 that day to go with his opening 69. Several others were in strong contention entering Sunday's finale. David Creamer (70), Jay Horton and Delroy Cambridge (both with 69-67) were two back at 136, and

T.R. Jones was at 137. Only Cambridge came close, shooting 69 for 205 total, missing the playoff by a stroke. Good shot 69 and got his unexpected chance when Bruner three-putted from 45 feet for the bogey and his 70–204.

Scottish Seniors Open—£150,000
Winner: David Oakley

David Oakley made it two victories in three weeks at the Scottish Seniors Open, but the second one nearly eluded him. Although bad weather also dogged him the Sunday he won at Wentworth in mid-August, Oakley unraveled a bit in the high winds that visited the Roxburghe Club at Kelso two Sundays later at the Scottish Seniors Open. He struggled to a 75 and dropped into a 54-hole tie with Keith MacDonald, the club pro at Goodwood in Sussex, but won at the second extra hole.

Oakley was holding a hot hand when he went to Scotland. He had not been over par in his last six rounds, including the Energis Masters win, and he continued those ways at Roxburghe. He jumped off with a 15-foot par putt on the first hole and went on to a seven-under-par 65, taking a two-stroke lead over seasoned Australian Rodger Davis, a newly minted senior who has long been one of his country's top players, both at home and internationally.

The American followed with a 70 Saturday that widened his margin to three strokes. Birdies at the ninth, 14th and 17th established that lead over Davis (71) and MacDonald (67) after a bogey-birdie switch with Davis on the first two holes. MacDonald, also a first-year player whose father was the first-round leader in the memorable 1962 Open that Arnold Palmer won at Troon, got his chance for victory Sunday. He shot a par round in the fierce conditions for 210, good enough to bring about the playoff.

Oakley found himself four over par for the round after bogeys at the 11th and 12th, but he righted things when he holed a 30-foot birdie putt at the par-five 14th — "That was absolutely vital. I felt in control after that" — and managed the deadlock with a 75. Two pars won for Oakley in the playoff when MacDonald bogeyed the second extra hole after driving in a bunker and failing to make par from 90 yards after the sand shot.

STC Bovis Lend Lease European Invitational—£225,000
Winner: Bob Shearer

It was business before pleasure for Bob Shearer, so he had no time for a celebration after his victory in the STC Bovis Lend Lease European Invitational, his first in more than two years. Shearer had three golf course design projects needing his attention in his native Australia, Indonesia and China, so he flew out of England right after his one-stroke win, "although it's a shame I can't stay on and have a few beers with my mates instead."

Shearer's victory was a bit surprising. Although one of his country's better-known players over the years, Shearer had been struggling with his putting and his driving the last two seasons and was far down the Order of Merit list before the European Invitational at Woburn Golf and Country Club in England. Armed with one of the celebrated Callaway ERCII drivers that he obtained from Bernard Gallacher at the start of the week and an improved putting stroke, he stayed within close range of the lead the first two days.

Scotland's Mike Miller and Delroy Cambridge, the Jamaican having another among many good weeks, shared the first-round lead at five-under-par 67, then Cambridge birdied his final three holes Saturday for 72 and a one-stroke lead at 139. Shearer then was two back after rounds of 70 and 71. Shearer moved in front quickly Sunday with birdies on the first three holes, then closed with two more for 67 and the winning 208 total. He won by just a stroke over Noel Ratcliffe, but his compatriot got that close when he eagled the final hole to leap into second place past Bob Charles, Jerry Bruner and Seiji Ebihara.

TEMES Seniors Open—£126,000
Winner: Russell Weir

Russell Weir, a dominant figure for years as a player in the club pro ranks in Scotland with some 100 victories and eight appearances in the PGA Cup Matches against America, carried over that talent to the European Seniors Tour, winning in just his sixth appearance in the TEMES Seniors Open in Greece. Leading all the way, the 50-year-old Scot from Cowal squeezed out a one-stroke victory over David Good, the Legends in Golf winner, who pressed him all the way.

The duel started the first day when Weir's sensational second nine gave him 66 and a two-shot lead over Good, fellow Australian Randall Vines and New Zealand's Simon Owen. Out in one-over 37, Weir blistered the incoming half with six birdies and an eagle at the par-five 15th. On Saturday, Weir shot 68 for 134 and clung to a one-stroke lead over Good and two over Owen and Peter Townsend, who shot a course-record 64 at Glyfada Golf Course. Actually, Good, who already had six top-10 finishes, had the lead after he eagled the third hole, and shared the top spot with Weir after Weir birdied the 11th. The deadlock held until Good overshot the 18th green and bogeyed.

The Scot fell behind again in the early going Sunday. He was three behind at the turn, but birdied the 10th, 11th and 13th to catch up, and retook the lead when he holed from a bunker at the 15th. Good came back with a birdie at the par-three 16th, but Weir countered with a 20-foot birdie putt at the 17th, then two-putted the last green for 68, 202 total and a one-shot victory. Good also shot 68. Three shots behind him at 206 was Delroy Cambridge, seemingly a contender every week.

Dan Technology Senior Tournament of Champions—£150,000
Winner: Delroy Cambridge

It was a bit ironic when Delroy Cambridge, who had been threatening to become a champion all season long, finally became one in early October in the Dan Technology Senior Tournament of Champions, the late-season event that took its 41-man field off the top of the Order of Merit standings, winners or not.

Nine times during the 2001 European Seniors Tour campaign, the big-hitting Jamaican had finished in the top 10. Early in the season, he had lost in a three-man playoff in Jersey. At Mere Golf and Country Club at Manchester, England, a new venue for the tournament, Cambridge found the missing ingredient — a strong finish — and became the year's fifth first-time champion. He shot 69 for 205, closing a stroke in front of Jerry Bruner, who, like Cambridge, had been challenging for the winner's circle all season.

Ian Mosey, who had not made a serious impact since turning 50 and joining the circuit in August, made his presence felt at Mere. Playing in his childhood neighborhood, Mosey, once a winner on the regular European tour, got away running Friday with an eight-birdie 64 to take a two-stroke lead over Peter Dawson and three over Bill Hardwick, Paul Leonard and Bob Lendzion. Cambridge began inconspicuously with 69, then closed in Saturday. His 67 for 136 moved him within a stroke of Mosey, who retained the lead with a par 71. Hardwick shot 69 and joined Cambridge in the No. 2 spot.

Cambridge moved fast Sunday. He birdied the first two holes to seize the lead and widened the gap to two with another birdie at the ninth. Mike Miller made a run with 10 birdies and a 65, but started too far back and took too many bogeys to catch up. Bruner eagled the par-five 18th for 68, too late, as Cambridge played the back nine in one over par, just enough to nail that elusive first victory.

Tunisian Seniors Open—£100,000
Winner: Simon Owen

A late-season pattern continued on the European Seniors Tour when, after its unplanned idle week caused by the cancellation of the Egyptian Seniors Open, the circuit traveled to North Africa for the Tunisian Seniors Open. With a two-hole playoff victory, New Zealand's Simon Owen became the third consecutive first-time winner and sixth of the season.

Owen, another player who had made several runs at titles during the season and had finished second in the AIB Irish Seniors and De Vere Hotels Classic, staged a brilliant finish to overtake American Bob Lendzion, a second-round co-leader, then defeat him with a birdie on the second extra hole.

Things did not look promising for Owen after 36 holes. He had begun the tournament at Port el Kantaoui Golf Club with 69 and was decently positioned three strokes off the lead of Denis Durnian, the No. 2 man on the Order of Merit whose game had cooled after his early-season flourishes. However, Owen managed only 73 on Saturday and slipped six strokes behind the co-leaders at 136 — Lendzion (67-69) and Jim Rhodes (68-68).

Owen came alive Sunday with a flurry of birdies. He made nine in all, six in a row starting at the eighth hole, and would have won outright but for the double bogey and bogey that gave back three strokes. He shot 66, one of only three rounds in the 60s in the final round, to finish at 208. Rhodes faded to 76, but Lendzion, whose only circuit victory came in Turkey in 1998, put up a par round to forge the deadlock. The two men matched pars on the first overtime hole before Owen bull's-eyed a wedge three feet from the cup to set up the winning birdie.

SSL International/Sodexho Match Play—£100,000
Winner: Jim Rhodes

It happened again. A new winner on the European Seniors Tour, the fourth in a row. For Englishman Jim Rhodes, victory in the SSL International/ Sodexho Match Play ended a chain of frustration that extended over 105 tournament starts and almost six full seasons. Thirty-two times during that period Rhodes finished in the top 10, four times in second place. The previous Sunday he shared the lead going into the final round and failed to convert it into a title.

Perhaps match play suited him better. He marched through the field to a final duel with Craig Defoy and scored a 2-up victory. It came down to the final two holes. Rhodes birdied the par-five 17th to go 1 up and secured the victory with a "safe" three-iron shot off the tee and a daring driver shot onto the green that gave him the 2-up win. "It certainly lifts a great weight off my mind," Rhodes said. "I'm delighted both for myself and my wife, Pauline. She's been through a lot caddieing for me and listening to all my moans and groans."

Rhodes' path to the final included victories over Peter Cowen, 4 and 3; Denis O'Sullivan, 2 and 1; Ian Stanley, the Order of Merit leader, 1 up, and, in the semi-finals, David Oakley, 3 and 2. Defoy's wins were over John Morgan, 1 up; Paul Leonard, 1 up; Jerry Bruner, 2 and 1, and Peter Dawson in a 21-hole thriller. Rhodes broke open his semi-final match against Oakley with wins at the 13th, 15th and 16th holes. Defoy trailed lefty Dawson by as much as three holes in the early going of their semi-final match, but caught up at the 14th and won at the third extra hole when Dawson failed to get up and down from just off the green.

European Seniors Tour Championship—£225,000
Winner: Jerry Bruner

Nine times during his three seasons on the European Seniors Tour, Californian Jerry Bruner endured the heartache of a second-place finish. It happened three times earlier in 2001. Finally, Bruner came from three strokes off the pace and stood in the winner's circle at the season-ending European Seniors Tour Championship at PGA Golf de Catalunya in Spain. His six-under-par 210 total gave him a one-stroke victory over Australian David Good. For the fifth time in as many tournaments, a first-time winner was crowned.

While the day brought joy to Bruner, it saw disappointment for Denis Durnian. In front by a stroke going into the final round, Durnian could have picked off the No. 1 spot on the Order of Merit and won the accompanying John Jacobs Trophy if he had held onto first place Sunday. Instead, he shot 74 and dropped into a three-way tie for third place at 213, and the 2001 title went to Ian Stanley, the second year in a row that it went to an Australian. Stanley finished a stroke further back and increased his earnings to a record £178,460.

Durnian had taken the lead Saturday, producing a 68 for 139 from six birdies and an eagle, after Mike Miller began the tournament on top with a 68 of his own. Good, another of the season's first-time winners, also shot 68 for 140. Tommy Horton, the five-time Order of Merit champion, and Jim Rhodes, the previous week's winner, checked in at 141; and Bruner, the mighty mite from Los Angeles, was in a four-way tie for fifth at 142 with Miller, David Huish and David Creamer.

Japan Senior Tour

ANA Ishigaki Senior—¥5,500,000
Winner: Fujio Kobayashi

Fujio Kobayashi, the dominant player on the 2000 Japan Senior Tour, resumed that role when the new season began, scoring a one-stroke victory in the ANA Ishigaki Senior tournament at Okinawa's Ishigaki Country Club in early February. The four-time winner during the previous season posted his ninth win with his 12-under-par 132 total.

Kobayashi came from two shots off the pace after shooting 67 in the first round and trailing Minoru Nakamura and Hisao Inoue, who led with 65s. Kobayashi's 65 established the winning margin over Hsieh Min-nan, the long-time Taiwanese star, and Wataru Horiguchi.

Castle Hill Senior Open—¥30,000,000
Winner: Noboru Sugai

Three months later, Noboru Sugai landed his first title on the Japan Senior Tour with a playoff victory in the Castle Hill Senior Open, preventing Fujio Kobayashi from making it two in a row at the start of the season. Kobayashi had come from six strokes off the pace to match Sugai's five-under-par 211 and force the overtime decision.

Seven strokes separated the two men after the first round at Castle Hill Country Club in Hoi-gun. Sugai led with 67, while Kobayashi began weakly with 74. Katsunari Takahashi held second place with 68, while Fumio Tanaka, Ichiro Teramoto, Tatsuo Fujima and Namio Takasu shared third place with 69s. Katsuji Hasegawa edged into the lead the second day with 71-68—139, a shot ahead of Sugai (73) and Takasu (71). Kobayashi followed his 74 with 71 for 145. Hasegawa slipped to 74 Sunday, opening the door for Sugai, who shot 71, and Kobayashi, who rallied with 67. Sugai won the playoff on the first extra hole.

Asahi Ryokuken Cup—¥10,000,000
Winner: Noboru Sugai

Noboru Sugai followed up his first victory on the Japan Senior Tour with another win two weeks later in the Asahi Ryokuken Cup tournament, the next stop on the circuit. He did it with the final day's best round of 67, finishing a stroke ahead of Teruo Suzumura at Ito Golf Club in Fukuoka Prefecture in early June.

Sugai came from three strokes back Sunday after starting the tournament with 72. Eiichi Itai took the first-round lead with 69, a stroke ahead of Yurio Akitomi and Katsuji Hasegawa, but tumbled far down the standings Sunday when he shot 78. Suzumura was the only other player besides Sugai to break 70 in the final round, putting a 69 with his opening 71 for 140. Akitomi was a distant third at 143.

Old Man Par Senior Open—¥5,840,000
Winner: Motomasa Aoki

Motomasa Aoki became the second first-time winner on the 2001 Japan Senior Tour when he registered a one-stroke victory in the Old Man Par Senior Open at the Southern Cross Golf Club at Shizuoka in late July.

The margin was a bit surprising, since Aoki had jumped off to a three-stroke lead Saturday with a seven-under-par 63. Kikuo Arai and Hiroshi Kaihaya were the 66 shooters. Motomasa took a 69 in the final round, just fending off Arai, Shigeru Kawamata and Fujio Kobayashi for the victory with his eight-under-par 132 on the par-72 course.

Fancl Senior Classic—¥60,000,000
Winner: Katsunari Takahashi

Katsunari Takahashi, who won both of the Japan Senior Tour's majors in his rookie 2000 season and led the money list for the year, scored his first 2001 victory with a resounding, six-stroke margin in the Fancl Senior Classic, the season's richest event with its ¥60,000,000 purse, at Susono Country Club in Shizuoka.

Takahashi trailed Kikuo Arai by a stroke after opening with a 69 and sharing the runner-up position with five other players. Two successive 66s over the weekend put the win away. The first one jumped him three strokes into the lead over Shuichi Sano (70-68) and five ahead of Arai, who shot 72 the second day. The second one established the final margin over Sano, who shot 69 Sunday. The winning total of 201 was 15 under par.

HTD Senior Classic—¥10,000,000
Winner: Fujio Kobayashi

Fujio Kobayashi joined Seiichi Kanai as the Japan Senior Tour's winningest players when he posted his 10th victory in the HTD Senior Classic at Mitsui Kanko Iris Golf Club on Hokkaido. In taking his second 2001 victory, Kobayashi recorded a 10-under-par 134 for a two-stroke win.

He had just a share of the lead Saturday despite a seven-under-par 65. That matched the start of Koichi Uehara, but they stood three strokes in front of the rest of the field, headed by Hisao Inoue and Seiji Ogawa with their 68s. Uehara paved the way for an easy victory for Kobayashi when he slumped to 75 Sunday and dropped to fifth place. Kobayashi shot 69. Inoue took second place with a second 68 for 136 total and Katsuji Hasegawa moved up to third at 137 with the day's best round of 67.

Fujita Kanko Open—¥20,000,000
Winner: Yasuzo Hagiwara

Yasuzo Hagiwara joined Noboru Sugai and Motomasa Aoki as first-time winners on the Japan Senior Tour in the Fujita Kanko Open, but it took two extra holes to accomplish the feat. Hagiwara finished the regulation 36 holes in a deadlock with Norihiko Matsumoto at 10-under-par 134, then won the playoff on the second overtime hole.

Hagiwara came from four strokes off the pace in the Sunday round at Cameria Hills Country Club, Chiba, after Matsumoto fired a sparkling 64 on opening day. He led Katsuji Hasegawa by two, Noboru Sugai, Fumio Tanaka and Koichi Uehara by three. Matsumoto managed a two-under-par 70 Sunday, but Hagiwara caught him with 66 for his 134. Uehara missed another good chance at a 2001 victory, falling one stroke short of the playoff with 67-68.

Japan PGA Senior Championship—¥30,000,000
Winner: Yasuhiro Miyamoto

Yasuhiro Miyamoto was in and out of the lead before taking charge of the Japan PGA Senior Championship and romping to a five-stroke victory in the first of the Japan Senior Tour's two "majors." Miyamoto was the only player to finish under par at the Biglayzac Country Club, a 6,834-yard course in Miyagi. He was the fourth and final first-time winner of the season.

Miyamoto tied for the first-round lead with Toyotake Nakao at 69, a stroke ahead of four players, including defending champion Katsunari Takahashi. Nakao fell back Friday and Miyamoto squeezed a stroke ahead of Takahashi (70-71) and Shuichi Sano (72-69) with his 71 for 140 total. Two behind was Hisao Inoue and he took over first place Saturday, shooting 72 for 214 as Miyamoto took a 75 and slipped a stroke behind with Masaru Amano (73-70-72). Miyamoto repeated his first-round 69 Sunday, scoring the easy victory over Amano (74), Kikuo Arai (72), Seiji Ebihara (71) and Noboru Sugai (72).

Komatsu Open—¥40,000,000
Winner: Katsunari Takahashi

Seiichi Kanai, the Japan Senior Tour's dominant player in earlier years, made his strongest bid for his first victory in three seasons in the Komatsu Open, but was turned back by a potential heir apparent in a playoff. Katsunari Takahashi, picking up his second win of the season and fourth in his first two campaigns on the tour, defeated Kanai on the third overtime hole after the two men had tied at the end of 54 holes at Katayamazu Golf Club in Ishikawa with five-under-par 211s. Going in, Kanai was tied with Fujio Kobayashi on the all-time victory list with 10 titles.

The first round belonged to unheralded Hiroaki Uenishi, who opened with 67 to take a two-stroke lead over Hisao Inoue, Koichi Uehara and Yurio Akitomi. Kanai overhauled Uenishi Saturday with his 71-69 as Uenishi shot 73. Takahashi moved into contention with 70 and 71, sharing the runner-up position with Inoue and Uehara. Takahashi, with 70, was one stroke better than Kanai on Sunday to force the season's third playoff.

Japan Senior Open Championship—¥50,000,000
Winner: Fujio Kobayashi

Fujio Kobayashi's third victory of the 2001 Japan Senior Tour season was the biggest one. It gave him the cherished Japan Senior Open Championship for the first time. In addition, as his 11th win, it made him the No. 1 career tournament winner, a distinction he had shared with Seiichi Kanai until overcoming Katsunari Takahashi, the defending champion, and Australian Terry Gale in a playoff in the national championship the last week of October at Fukuoka's Dazaifu Golf Club.

Kobayashi, Gale and Takahashi, like Kobayashi a two-time winner already during the season, reached the playoff through different routes. Kobayashi lingered just off the pace for three rounds, while Gale and Takahashi jumped into contention the third day with 67s, the best scores of the week.

Wataru Horiguchi shot a three-under-par 69 in the opening round and led by two over seven other players, including Kobayashi. Hisao Inoue took over first place Friday with 68–139, two ahead of Horiguchi (69-72) and Yasuzo Hagiwara (71-70). Kobayashi was at 143 with Shigeru Kawamata. Then, Takahashi and Gale fired their 67s, Takahashi taking over the lead at 212 after opening the week with 75 and Gale joining Kobayashi (71) at 214, a shot behind Inoue and Horiguchi.

Kobayashi and Gale matched par with their Sunday rounds to overtake Takahashi, who shot 74 for his 286 total. Kobayashi then clinched the victory with a par on the first extra hole as Takahashi and Gale bogeyed.

Takanosu Open—¥10,000,000
Winner: Tadami Ueno

Tadami Ueno broke from a first-round logjam and captured the Takanosu Open, one of two late November tournaments that closed the 2001 Japan

Senior Tour season. It was his second victory on the circuit and first in more than two years.

Ueno had shared the lead at 68 the first day at Takanosu Golf Club with Seiji Ebihara, Hisao Inoue, Takayoshi Nishikawa and Toshiki Matsui, then nailed down the victory with a par-72 round Sunday for his 139 total. Ebihara shot 73 and took second place with 140, a stroke ahead of Katsuji Hasegawa (69-72).

N. Cup Senior Open—¥15,000,000
Winner: Seiji Ebihara

Seiji Ebihara, home from a quite successful campaign on the European Seniors Tour with two victories to show for it, acquired a third 2001 title when he captured the concluding 36-hole event on the Japan Senior Tour at the end of November. Ebihara, taking his second career title in Japan, scored a two-stroke victory in the N. Cup Senior Open at Central Golf Club, his 135 two strokes better than that of runner-up Yukio Noguchi.

Ebihara and Noguchi had opened the tournament that Saturday with 68s, tied for first place with Masaji Kusakabe and Koji Nakajima. Ebihara then annexed the victory with a Sunday round of 67 for the 135 as Noguchi shot 69 and Isao Aoki, back from another season in America, posted 69 and 70 and finished third.

14. Women's Tours

Any other generation a woman shooting 59, winning eight tournaments (including four in a row and a major) and setting a scoring-average record would have been the top news story in the game. As has happened so many times in the past six years, Tiger Woods overshadowed even the most staggering accomplishments on the LPGA Tour.

What Annika Sorenstam did was, indeed, staggering. After two second-place finishes early in the year in Hawaii, Sorenstam went on a run that had many in the game hearkening back to 1978 when Nancy Lopez set a record with five consecutive victories.

It wasn't just what Sorenstam did that was so impressive, but how she did it. At the Welch's/Circle K Championship in Tucson she bracketed rounds of 68 and 67 with two rounds of 65 for a six-shot rout. One week later she become the first woman to break the 60 barrier, shooting 13-under-par 59 at the Moon Valley Country Club in Phoenix during the second round of the Standard Register Ping.

It was an accomplishment that left the golf world stunned. "I didn't think I would be leading when I got to the course," first-round leader Kris Tschetter said of arriving for her Friday afternoon tee time. "But I didn't think I'd be 11 shots behind, either."

Sorenstam followed with rounds of 69 and 68 to win by two over Se Ri Pak. One week later, Sorenstam made it three in a row when she won the Nabisco Championship by three over Karrie Webb, who had been Sorenstam's most ardent competition for the past five seasons. Suddenly people were talking about a female version of the Grand Slam as being possible. If someone could shoot 59 and win four in a row, as Sorenstam did the next week when she beat Mi Hyun Kim in a playoff at The Office Depot, then winning all four majors wasn't out of the realm of possibility.

Sorenstam won again in Atlanta at the Chick-fil-A Charity Championship, making her total victories five before mid-May. She finished third the next week in Nashville and seemed primed for a run at another U.S. Women's Open title.

Webb had other plans, such as becoming the youngest woman in history to win a career Grand Slam. She hadn't won an LPGA Tour event in the first five months of the year, and just as there were rumblings that Tiger Woods was in a slump, some mused that Webb might be burned out after her 2000 season. She admitted to being tired, but five months was plenty of time to recharge the batteries, and she had already won in 2001 in Australia and Japan. Just as she had done in 2000 with her victories at the Nabisco Championship and U.S. Women's Open, Webb ran away from the field in the U.S. Women's Open, successfully defending her USGA title in Southern Pines with an impressive eight-stroke win over Pak.

"A lot more people were worried about the state of my game than I was," Webb said after the U.S. Women's Open win. "I knew I was trying to become a better player, and I knew how close I was to having everything in the right shape at the right time. The hard work paid off. And it's just great timing to have it peak this week."

She peaked again three weeks later at the McDonald's LPGA Championship when a final-round 69 gave Webb a two-shot victory over Laura Diaz and a career Grand Slam. Suddenly, Webb was back in the limelight, and Sorenstam's streak seemed like a thing of the past. Webb won her third LPGA Tour event, and her fifth of the year worldwide, in the season-ending Tyco/ADT Championship.

Pak entered the fray with a win at the season-opening event in Orlando, followed by victories at the Longs Drugs Challenge, Jamie Farr Kroger Classic, AFLAC Champions and the fourth major of the year, the Weetabix Women's British Open, Pak earned more money than at any time in her career, over $1.6 million. Most other years, that would have been considered a Player-of-the-Year performance, but not in 2001.

Sorenstam won again at the Bank of Montreal Canadian Women's Open, the Mizuno Classic and the Cisco World Match Play in Japan, where she defeated Pak in the final for what would prove to be the decisive blow of the year. Eight wins and a scoring average of 69.42 propelled Sorenstam to the top spot in women's golf, with worldwide earnings of $2.1 million. Webb's runner-up total was $1.7 million.

With three of the greatest players in history battling head to head and all in their primes, there has never been a better time for the women's professional game. The 2001 season was one for the books, and it set the stage for what are bound to be some great rivalries in 2002 and beyond.

In the rest of the world, the Evian Ladies European Tour included two LPGA Tour co-sanctioned events, the Evian Masters and the Weetabix Women's British Open, plus two tournaments in Australia (Masters and Open), a total of 15 official events plus an unofficial season-ending tournament in Morocco. The leader of the European money list was Raquel Carriedo of Spain with £160,441 ($229,432 on the Women's World Money List). Carriedo also led the tour with three victories.

There were 33 tournaments on the Japan LPGA Tour, where the stars included Chieko Amanuma, Yuri Fudoh, Kaori Higo and Miyuki Shimabukuro. Amanuma had the most victories with five, while Fudoh posted four and Higo, three. Shimabukuro's two wins included the Japan Women's Open. The leading money winners were Fudoh with $725,593, followed by Higo with $576,631, Amanuma with $568,026 and a total of eight Japanese with Women's World Money List totals of more than $400,000 — for a very rich circuit, indeed.

There also was a five-tournament circuit in South Africa, with Annerie Wessels winning twice and Vanessa Smith taking the Open title.

U.S. LPGA Tour

YourLife Vitamins LPGA Classic—$1,000,000
Winner: Se Ri Pak

Fighting a cold all week and wondering if she would have enough energy to finish, Se Ri Pak found the perfect remedy when she fired a closing 64 at the Grand Cypress Resort in Orlando, Florida, to win the season-opening YourLife Vitamins LPGA Classic by four strokes. Pak's final-round blitz included seven birdies in her last 11 holes for 64 and a 13-under-par 203 total and a cakewalk victory over Penny Hammel and Carin Koch.

After going winless in 2000, Pak revamped her game, hiring a new coach (Tom Creavy) and a new caddie before the beginning of the season. "Last year many things happened," she said. "Everything is changing. I found a coach, found a caddie, and found a swing. I knew I was trying to get ready for this year. It looks like everything is set for 2001 — mind, swing, coach, caddie — everything."

Trailing Koch and Laura Davies by two going into the final round, Pak moved out quickly, pulling to within one shot of the lead with a 30-foot chip-in for birdie on the ninth. Another chip-in at the 14th for birdie moved Pak into sole possession of the lead. When Hammel rolled in a 20-foot birdie putt at the 15th, Pak answered with an eight-footer to maintain her lead. Another birdie at the 16th gave Pak some breathing room.

"I just kept trying to give myself opportunities," Hammel said. "I figured if something worked, great. If not, oh well. Se Ri played very good today."

That good play distracted Koch, who missed a short birdie putt at the ninth that would have moved her back into the lead. From there she never fully recovered. Despite a final-round 70, the Swede was still looking for her first LPGA victory. "I tried playing my game the best I could," she said. "But Se Ri was making all kinds of things. We saw it and heard it in front of us. It wasn't any fun at all."

From her experiences in 2000, Pak knew how Koch felt. "Last year was a bit of a struggle," she said. "I felt sometimes I had a chance to win, but a little mistake would make me drop out. But even though it was hard, somehow that gives me a lot of experience with my golf game."

Subaru Memorial of Naples—$1,000,000
Winner: Sophie Gustafson

With two LPGA and one European victory in 2000, Sophie Gustafson was arguably in the midst of the second-best streak in women's golf. But with Karrie Webb winning seven times in 12 months, including two major championships, it was tough for Gustafson to get the credit she deserved. Only a head-to-head victory over Webb could improve Gustafson's standing.

That victory came in January 2001 when Gustafson shot a tournament-record, 16-under-par 272 total for a three-stroke victory over Webb in the Subaru Memorial of Naples.

"It feels great," Gustafson said of her third LPGA victory in nine months. "Things are going well, even though I still need to improve my short game."

After a course-record 64 on Friday at The Club at the Strand, Gustafson entered Sunday's final round with a four-shot lead over Webb. At the turn the lead was five strokes. Webb attempted a charge with back-to-back birdies at the 11th and 12th, both par-fives, but Gustafson used her length to her advantage, reaching the 12th in two shots and making a birdie of her own to maintain a four-stroke edge. "Those holes really play to my advantage," she said.

A 20-foot putt for birdie at the 13th coupled with a bogey by Webb increased Gustafson's lead to six shots with six holes to play. Even a couple of bogeys coming in at the 15th and 18th didn't jeopardize the lead. Long before she tapped in for bogey at the 18th for 70, Gustafson had this one sewn up. "You can't play defensively," she said. "I knew that wouldn't work. Having a six-shot lead coming in made me feel more comfortable. It felt nice."

"I've played with Sophie when she's been in contention before," Webb said. "And I watched her play the Solheim Cup. She handles the pressure well. Her game was right on this week, and she did well. She's a long-ball hitter, and when she's on, she's long and straight. She's also a good iron player. When she got into trouble, she did well to get out of it. That's what happens when you win; you get into tough situations and get out of them. That's what you need to do. She did it, and she deserves to win."

The Office Depot—$825,000
Winner: Grace Park

For the second week in a row, Karrie Webb found herself in contention in the final round of a tournament, and for the second time she came up a little short. One week after finishing second to Sophie Gustafson at the Subaru Memorial of Naples, Webb failed to successfully defend her Office Depot title when she lost to Grace Park by a single shot at the Doral Golf Resort in Miami.

A winner in her last two visits to the Ibis Golf and Country Club in West Palm Beach, Webb trailed by one entering Sunday's final round. A birdie at the fifth hole moved Webb into at tie with Park, but the former U.S. Women's Amateur champion moved ahead again with a birdie at the eighth, hitting wedge to three feet, and another birdie at the par-five 10th, when Park's greenside bunker shot stopped eight feet from the hole and she made the putt.

Webb birdied the 14th to pull within a shot of the lead, but that was as close as she could get. Park hit her two best shots of the day at the difficult final hole, coaxing a five-iron approach to within 18 feet and two-putting for par. Her 71 and six-under-par 280 total earned Park her second career victory and a $123,750 paycheck, the largest of her short career.

"I'm glad this was the last day," Park said. "I think I aged 10 years this week."

Webb, who also finished with 71, said virtually the same thing, but for a different reason. "I played decent enough to give myself birdie opportunities, but I just couldn't make any putts," she said. "It's been the same for three weeks in a row. It's something I'll have to work on."

Takefuji Classic—$850,000
Winner: Lorie Kane

With Annika Sorenstam leading Karrie Webb by two shots going into the final 18 holes, the Takefuji Classic looked as though it would end in a showdown between the game's two most dominant female players. Lorie Kane was almost forgotten in the mix, even though she stood tied with Webb at five-under-par 139 going into the final round.

Two hours later, Sorenstam and Webb were chasing Kane. A first-nine 32 at the Kona Country Club in Hawaii gave Kane the lead as Sorenstam struggled with her putter and Webb played the first 13 holes in two over par. Kane didn't let up, posting three more birdies on the second nine for a course-record 66 and a tournament-record, 11-under-par 205 total.

Sorenstam was one over through 15 holes, but closed with three birdies at the 16th, 17th and 18th to finish with 70 and a 207 total, good for second place but two more than Kane. Webb never found a rhythm, closing with 71 for a 210 total. As for Kane, it was the Canadian's fourth win in her last 14 starts and a real confidence booster winning against the best in the game.

"I wanted to get off to a quick start this year so I would know what I did last year wasn't a thing of the past," Kane said. "I'm more confident now, and knowing I can win makes it a lot easier now. There's no panic, no rush. I felt quite peaceful all day and I had a funny feeling something good was going to happen here."

Cup Noodles Hawaiian Ladies Open—$750,000
Winner: Catriona Matthew

The constant winds that whipped through Oahu during the Cup Noodles Hawaiian Ladies Open were a hometown breeze for Scotland's Catriona Matthew. Perhaps that's why Matthew became the first player in 15 years to lead the event from start to finish. Her final-round 72 at the Kapolei Golf Course was good enough for a 210 total and a three-stroke victory over Annika Sorenstam.

"I always felt I was a good enough player to win out here," the 31-year-old Matthew said. "It probably helped being up here in contention a few times last year."

With winds gusting, Matthew played the game she learned on the links of her homeland, hitting low knock-down shots into position and remaining patient throughout all 54 holes. "The more you play in the wind, you learn how to play with the wind, not to fight it," she said. "The first two days were really difficult, especially feeling steady over putts."

Nancy Scranton gave Matthew a run in the final 18 holes, pulling even with Matthew with a birdie at the 10th. But Matthew pulled ahead quickly by holing a seven iron from the fairway for eagle at the 11th. That gave her a three-shot lead which she maintained the rest of the round.

Scranton fell back after making a disastrous double bogey at the 17th and posting 74. Her 214 total dropped her into a tie for third place with Danielle Ammaccapane and Wendy Ward, while Sorenstam sneaked into second place with a final round of 70. It was Sorenstam's second consecutive runner-up finish.

Welch's/Circle K Championship—$750,000
Winner: Annika Sorenstam

Annika Sorenstam didn't have the low round on Sunday at the Welch's/ Circle K Championship, but she didn't need it. That she shot seven-under-par 65 on Sunday was enough. Sorenstam could have played the last three or four holes with a couple of clubs and still won. Her 23-under 265 total provided a six-stroke victory and a successful title defense in Tucson, Arizona.

"This was as good as I've played in a long time," Sorenstam said. "I knew the number was 19 under here, and that's what I was shooting for."

That number would have won. Se Ri Pak, who started the final round two shots behind Sorenstam, shot 69 for a 271 total and a share of second place with Dottie Pepper, Laura Diaz and Michelle McGann. "I hit the ball pretty good today," Pak said. "Actually better than the last three days. I hit it solid, but I couldn't make any putts."

No matter how well Pak struck the ball, it would have been tough to catch Sorenstam. The Swede got out early with birdies on the first two holes to take a four-stroke lead. Another six-footer for birdie at the seventh kept Pak from gaining any ground, and a 20-footer for birdie on the ninth moved Sorenstam to 20 under par. At the turn the outcome seemed certain. Three more birdies at the 10th, 13th and 16th put the tournament out of reach.

"I look at the rankings a lot," Sorenstam said. "The money list means a lot to me, and Player of the Year means a lot. I want to be the best player out here — that's been my goal for the last 15 or 16 months."

This victory got her off to a good start.

Standard Register Ping—$1,000,000
Winner: Annika Sorenstam

Annika Sorenstam felt good about her game and her chances when she arrived in Phoenix, Arizona, for the Standard Register Ping. An opening-round 65 only bolstered those positive feelings, but nothing could have prepared Sorenstam — or the LPGA — for what followed.

Sorenstam started the second round on the 10th hole at Moon Valley, a 534-yard par-five and a reasonably easy birdie opportunity. She hit a sand wedge to nine feet and started out with a birdie. She hit a 157-yard nine-iron shot to seven feet on the par-three 11th and made that putt for birdie. When she made a 30-footer for birdie at the 12th to go three under through three holes and take the lead, the galleries started to notice.

When Sorenstam's seven-wood approach on the par-five 13th stopped 18 feet above the hole, there was a sense that this could be the start of something truly special. Two putts later, Sorenstam walked away having birdied her first four holes. The birdies kept coming. A sand wedge approach on the 14th stopped four feet from the hole and Sorenstam made another birdie. At the 15th, she made an 11-footer to go six under through six. Sorenstam remembered a saying that her coach, Pia Nilsson, used to pound home back in Sweden: Every hole on the golf course could be birdied in a round. Every hole.

The Swedes call it "54 Vision," and Sorenstam seemed to have it that morning. A seven-iron approach to 10 feet and another made putt moved Sorenstam one step closer to golf's Holy Grail, and another birdie from 18 feet at the 17th sent electric shock waves through the crowd.

Tom Sorenstam, Annika's father, called Sweden from his cell phone after every birdie, and players were trotting out to join the gallery. "I wanted to see history," Amy Benz said. So did everyone else. Players on adjacent holes would stop play and watch when Sorenstam putted, while Joanne Morley followed the action through binoculars from a nearby guesthouse. Nilsson was in the gallery, as was Sorenstam's sister, Charlotta, also an LPGA winner. Even after Sorenstam missed a 30-footer for birdie at the 18th the mood remained unchanged. She had just birdied her first eight holes and established an LPGA nine-hole record. History was, indeed, in the making.

A sand wedge approach to nine feet set up another birdie at the first hole. At the second, Sorenstam hit a seven iron from 169 yards some 22 feet beyond the hole. When that putt went in, destiny seemed to be on her side. "It was a tricky line," she said. "When that went in, I said, 'This is just my day.'"

Another sand wedge to 12 feet led to another birdie at the third, and a near chip-in for eagle at the par-five fourth kept the momentum going. "The way she was playing I thought she could have probably shot 57," said Karrie Webb. "I don't think the course played that easy because the greens were so firm, but Annika obviously got it going."

The first error, if you could call it that, occurred at the par-three fifth hole, when Sorenstam missed a nine-footer for birdie. She went on to par the sixth and seventh as well. Then on the par-five eighth she hit a seven wood to 25 feet and two-putted for birdie to be 13 under par, a figure never before reached by an LPGA player. A par at the 18th would make Sorenstam only the sixth professional, and the first female, to shoot 59.

A sand wedge approach stopped nine feet from the hole and 58 seemed not only possible, it looked probable. "I was so nervous I was shaking," said Meg Mallon, who was paired with Sorenstam. "You have to appreciate when a fellow competitor shoots close to perfection."

Sorenstam missed her birdie effort, but tapped in for par and a place in the history books.

"It takes a lot of courage to shoot 59," Webb said. "You can get way ahead of yourself. Even to make par on the last hole is big."

Even bigger was Sorenstam's eventual win two days later. Se Ri Pak threatened to steal the spotlight with 63 on Saturday that left her only three shots back. She closed that lead with quick birdies on Sunday, but fell back with two bogeys on the back nine, leaving the door open for Sorenstam, who closed with 69 and 68 for a record-setting total of 261 and a two-shot victory over Pak.

"It's been an amazing week, a grueling week," Sorenstam said. "I'm exhausted."

Nabisco Championship—$1,500,000
Winner: Annika Sorenstam

"I really don't know why this is happening to me, but I am very, very thankful. This is what golfers dream about."

Those were the first words out of Annika Sorenstam's mouth after she took the obligatory victory plunge in the pond by the 18th green after winning the Nabisco Championship, her third career major championship and her third consecutive LPGA victory. Sorenstam closed with a three-under-par 69 to pass third-round leader Rachel Teske and break away from the pack for a three-stroke win.

"I didn't shoot 59 this week," Sorenstam said, "but under the circumstances on this golf course, this really ranks up there with the 59. It's a dream come true."

The Nabisco Championship was Sorenstam's first major victory since she captured the 1995 and 1996 U.S. Women's Open titles, and she said that this one was more special than the two national titles. "When I've been home I've been putting and thinking that this putt or that putt was going to win the Nabisco Championship," she said. "These are the thoughts I've had all winter. I've walked along the 18th green here, and known that there's a spot on the Wall of Champions, and I wanted my name on it. Those are the fantasies you have."

Those fantasies came true for Sorenstam, primarily on the strength of her renewed putting and hitting 35 of 36 greens in regulation on the weekend, including 17 the final day. "She played flawless golf," said Teske, who was paired with Sorenstam in the final twosome on Sunday. "It was pretty impressive to watch."

After an exhausting stretch of golf that included wins at the Welch's/Circle K Championship and the historic 59 during her victory at the Standard Register Ping, Sorenstam took Monday and Tuesday off, foregoing practice rounds on the Dinah Shore course at Mission Hills in lieu of some rest. The strategy paid off. Scores of 72, 70 and 70 in the first three rounds left Sorenstam tied for second, one stroke behind Teske.

Hitting every fairway on the first nine, Sorenstam played the first 12 holes on Sunday in one under par, good enough to take a one-shot lead into the homestretch. But the lead was tenuous. Fighting a cold, Sorenstam had to muster the strength to hold off six strong contenders — Teske, Karrie Webb, Dottie Pepper, Pat Hurst, Akiko Fukushima and Janice Moody — lurking one stroke behind.

"I only had one round left in me," Sorenstam said. "It's been a long three weeks, and I just caught a cold. This is it. This is all I've got. I know that. I'm going to try to gather all the energy I can and hit the best shots that I can."

She did just that coming in. A birdie at the 13th increased the lead to two shots. After that, Sorenstam did what she had done best all year: She hit every fairway and every green. Although it wasn't needed, she drained a 15-footer for birdie at the final hole for a 281 total and a three-shot victory over Teske, Webb, Moodie, Pepper and Fukushima.

"Obviously Annika has stepped it up a notch," said Webb, who added her third runner-up finish of the year. "I would have liked to have won in the U.S. by now, but I've had a lot of things go my way for the last couple of years, so I can't complain. Right now, Annika is the player to beat."

That appears to be a daunting task. Even sick and tired, Sorenstam seemed unbeatable. "I feel exhausted," she said. "I need a break — probably four or five days — then I might go to the gym and just slowly get back into golf. When you're on a roll like this, you want to continue. I mean, I'm having a lot of fun."

Office Depot Hosted by Amy Alcott—$800,000
Winner: Annika Sorenstam

The Easter Bunny never visited Annika Sorenstam when she was growing up. It wasn't a Swedish thing. But Sorenstam certainly knows a gift when she sees one, and that's what she received on Easter weekend in Los Angeles. Trailing by 10 strokes, Sorenstam shot a respectable 66 in the Saturday final round of the Office Depot Hosted by Amy Alcott for a 210 total, then stood by and watched as second-round leader Pat Hurst collapsed, shooting a final-round 77 to allow Sorenstam and Mi Hyun Kim to battle out it out in a playoff for the title.

Sorenstam prevailed in the playoff with a par as Kim missed the green and failed to reach the putting surface with her first chip shot. When it was over, Sorenstam had her fourth consecutive title, tying Mickey Wright, Kathy Whitworth and Nancy Lopez as the only players in LPGA history to accomplish that. She also set a record for the largest final-round comeback by a winner, erasing Muffin Spensor-Devlin's 16-year-old record of eight strokes.

"Wow, it's unbelievable," Sorenstam said. "I don't know what I've done to deserve all this. It's got to be destiny. I asked for a miracle and it came. I've always said it's not over till it's over. Sure, I played well, but I needed some help from the leaders."

She got it. Hurst started the week with two rounds of 67 and entered the final round with a three-shot lead over Liselotte Neumann. Three straight bogeys beginning at the ninth hole started a downward trend that Hurst couldn't seem to right. Another three-putt bogey on the 16th cut Hurst's lead to one. A bogey at the 17th dropped her into a tie with Sorenstam and Kim. Then, when her tee shot at the par-three 18th plugged in a bunker, Hurst's chances were dashed. She failed to get save par and missed the playoff, finishing with 77 for a 211 total and third place.

"That was awful," Hurst said. "You can't do that and win a golf tournament."

Sorenstam could barely believe her good fortune. "If you had asked me if it would end this way, it would have been tough for me to believe," she said. As any good player knows, a win is a win, no matter how you get there. Gifts count too. Even though Sorenstam made only one bogey in her final round and had to sink a 12-footer for birdie at the final hole to have a chance at winning, she knew how fortunate she was to win this one.

"Last year I wouldn't have made that putt on 18 in regulation," she said. "This year I made it. That's the difference."

Longs Drugs Challenge—$800,000
Winner: Se Ri Pak

Any other season two victories and a second place on the LPGA Tour before May would have constituted something great, or at the very least something newsworthy. But when Se Ri Pak shot 66, 71 and 71 for a 208 total and won the rain-shortened Longs Drugs Challenge by two strokes over Laura Diaz, the first person the media wanted to talk to was 43rd-place finisher Annika Sorenstam.

"It sucks," Sorenstam said of her failed attempt to become the first woman in over two decades to win five consecutive tournaments. Still, the crowds were enormous, the media coverage tremendous and the cheers enthusiastic and sustained, even when Sorenstam was shooting 73 and 72 and, her worst round of the year, a closing 75. Her total was 220, or 12 strokes behind.

"The way Annika has played, with the attention that is coming her way, it definitely gives the LPGA a shot in the arm," said Nancy Lopez. "She's really a nice person who is giving us a push forward again, to bring people's attention to the LPGA." Once it became evident that Sorenstam wouldn't top Lopez's record on this run, the elder statesperson of the LPGA breathed a little easier. "I'll be honest with you," Lopez said, "I hope nobody breaks that record."

Of her streak, Sorenstam was as philosophical as possible under the circumstances. "It was incredible," she said. "I've enjoyed the ride. It was more than a dream come true. I would never dream of winning four in a row. But after a round like today (75 on Sunday), I'm more motivated than ever to keep working."

Pak said she only wants to beat Sorenstam at her best, and the victory in California was a good start. Pak led wire-to-wire, with the only serious challenges during the week coming from Michele Redman, who trailed by two strokes after the opening round and by one after the second. Redman had a few moments atop the leaderboard on Sunday, when she birdied the second hole after Pak had bogeyed the first, and again when Pak bogeyed the 13th, but those leads were fleeting. Pak made a 12-footer for birdie at the 16th and a seven-footer at the 17th, while Redman bogeyed two of the final three holes to fall to third place at 211, one shot behind Diaz and three behind Pak.

Diaz's charge was more sustained. Trailing by five when the final round began, the American pulled into a share of the lead by playing the first 17 holes in five under par. But a bogey on the 18th dashed her chances. When Pak birdied the 17th to expand the lead to two shots with one to play, it was over.

"I made it really difficult," Pak said afterward. "I had a lot of confidence before I teed it up, but my putter struggled the first few holes. I had a different game. I don't know why. All day I couldn't putt. I hit great shots, but I couldn't make a putt. I knew I had to hang in there and I tried to play it hole by hole. I wanted to get the trophy."

Pak also wanted to send a message that there is more than one player to watch this season. "I was not going to give up the trophy this week," Pak said. "I've lost it too many times to Annika. She plays so well, and she can play every day like that, four weeks non-stop. But it doesn't mean that she can do it every week.

"This year I think is going to be the best year ever for me. I feel really confident and comfortable and I'm really enjoying it. I trust myself mentally. I get ready on every hole, every shot, every week."

Kathy Ireland Championship Honoring Harvey Penick—$900,000
Winner: Rosie Jones

It had been six months since an American had won on the LPGA Tour. Then Rosie Jones, a California native who makes her home in Atlanta, arrived in Austin, Texas, for the Kathy Ireland Championship with some bold words for her foreign competitors. "There's so much hype about Americans not winning, it's time to put the matter to rest," Jones said. "I'm going to get it over with. I'm going to take one for the USA."

Jones followed up on her straight talk with a week of straight drives, missing only three fairways all week as she shot 66, 67 and 68 to take a one-stroke lead into the final round. In the end Jones' short game spoke the loudest, as she hit a wedge to one foot for birdie on the final hole of regulation to shoot 67 and 12-under-par 268 and force a playoff with South Korea's Mi Hyun Kim. Then Jones drained a four-footer for birdie on the first playoff hole to break the American drought.

Kim had the best weekend at the Onion Creek Golf Club, shooting 64 and 66 to gain a share of the lead after being five strokes behind at the halfway mark. Kim moved to the top of the leaderboard at the 11th hole on Sunday when she rolled in a short birdie putt, but Jones answered with a birdie of her own at the 12th to regain a one-shot advantage. Kim then had birdies at the 15th and 17th to take possession of the lead. Kim parred the 18th, then waited greenside while Jones and Colombia's Marisa Baena tried to match her 268 total.

Baena, who shared the lead with Jones on Saturday after a six-under-par 64, finished bogey-birdie for 68 and a 269 total, one stroke out of the playoff, while Jones came through with a birdie at the final hole, hitting a blind pitch shot to within a foot, followed by the playoff birdie that earned Jones her first victory since 1999.

"I'm glad it's over," she said. "The streak's been broken, finally."

Chick-fil-A Charity Championship—$1,200,000
Winner: Annika Sorenstam

With a record-setting 59 and four tournament victories under your belt, it's easy to believe that anything is possible. Annika Sorenstam proved that to be true in Atlanta when she came from four strokes behind with nine holes to play to win the Chick-fil-A Charity Championship in a playoff with defending champion Sophie Gustafson.

Scores of 70 and 67 left Sorenstam trailing by one shot going into the final round. The leaders — Gustafson, along with former Yale women's golf coach Heather Daly-Donofrio and 44-year-old Hall of Famer Beth Daniel — knew that they had better watch the group ahead of them. Sorenstam had made a habit of shooting low numbers when she needed them, especially on Sunday afternoons.

This Sunday was no exception. After making bogeys on the first two holes to drop five strokes off the lead, Sorenstam rallied with birdies at the par-five third and the short par-four seventh to decrease the deficit to four at the turn.

"I simply had to try to birdie every hole on the back nine," Sorenstam said, as if such a feat were a stroll in the park. She didn't birdie them all, but she birdied enough. Four consecutive birdies beginning at the 13th moved the Swede within a shot of the lead, held at that time by Gustafson and Dottie Pepper, who blistered the course with 64 for a 204 total. Daniel was also a shot back at 12 under par after missing a delicate putt for birdie at the 15th, but she was playing some of her best golf in years and couldn't be counted out.

Tied for the lead with one hole to play, Sorenstam hit the center of the fairway, then rolled a three wood to the back of the green. She chipped to three feet and made the putt for birdie, a final round of 67 and a 203 total, one better than Pepper, who was in the clubhouse. All Sorenstam could do at that point was wait and watch. Gustafson needed a birdie to tie and an eagle to win, while Daniel could make an eagle to tie and go into a playoff.

Daniel barely missed her 20-foot eagle putt, but tapped in for birdie and a round of 69. Her 204 total tied Pepper for third place, which was Daniel's best finish since 1999. Gustafson missed the green with her second shot, but, like Sorenstam, she chipped to three feet and rammed in the birdie for a 68 and a 203 total. The two Swedes were tied at the end of regulation.

Another trip down the 18th produced identical results. Both players made birdies, and the playoff continued on to the 10th, a tricky par-four with water guarding the left side of the fairway and fronting the green. Sorenstam found the fairway and the green. When Gustafson's approach found the water, it was all but over. Sorenstam two-putted for par and collected her fifth victory of the year.

Electrolux USA Championship—$800,000
Winner: Juli Inkster

For a while it looked like the Electrolux USA Championship was going to be a repeat of The Office Depot in April. That week, Pat Hurst had the tournament in hand, but collapsed on the final nine holes and handed Annika Sorenstam her fourth consecutive victory. This time, the Hurst-Sorenstam duel would be played out over the Legends Club of Tennessee with tournament hosts Vince Gil and Amy Grant watching every shot.

Trailing Hurst by four shots and standing three behind Sorenstam going into the final round, 40-year-old Hall of Famer Juli Inkster decided to show the youngsters on the LPGA that age and guile could still win out over youthful nerves and good putting strokes. As the rest of the players were watching the showdown between Hurst, Sorenstam and Catriona Matthew, who pulled into a tie early in the final round, Inkster rolled in three consecutive birdie putts starting at the third hole. That put her within a shot of the lead — a major accomplishment for a player who opened with a 73 that tied her for 78th place, then clawed her way up to 23rd place after 36 holes, and into a tie for sixth after the third round, having scores of 67 and 69.

"After the birdie at five I got really focused," Inkster said. It showed. A birdie at the 14th tied Inkster for the lead with Sorenstam, who seemed to struggle with her putter. When Inkster rolled in an eight-footer for birdie at the 15th, she held the lead outright. A final two-putt birdie at the par-five 18th gave Inkster 65 for a 274 total.

Hurst had another final-round disappointment, shooting 74 for a 279 total and a tie for seventh. With Inkster in the clubhouse, the only players who could challenge for the title were Sorenstam and Matthew. Sorenstam's struggles continued on the final green. Her birdie putt lipped out, leaving her with a final round of 70 and a 276 total. Matthew had an eagle putt that would have forced a playoff, but she left it below the hole. Tapping in for birdie and a final round of 69, Matthew took sole possession of second place with 275.

"It feels great," Inkster said. "Any win is good, but it's especially special to come from behind the way I did."

Champions Classic—$750,000
Winner: Wendy Doolan

An Australian won the LPGA Champions Classic in Beavercreek, Ohio, but not the Aussie you might expect. With Karrie Webb shooting 70 and 68 in the rain-shortened event to finish tied for 15th place, Sydney's Wendy Doolan won her first LPGA title, defeating Wendy Ward on the fifth playoff hole.

"You mean Karrie hasn't won this year?" Doolan said, seemingly stunned that she, not Webb, was the first Australian to break through with a 2001 win. "I'm a little numb. All I know is you can't win without putting well."

Doolan putted well all week, what little of the week there was. Dottie Pepper described the course conditions as "somewhere between a kayak race and a swamp." Conditions were so poor that LPGA officials shortened the tournament to 36 holes, which suited Doolan just fine. She managed to navigate the quagmire that was the Country Club of the North with only 56 putts and shoot 68-64–132 in the process. That was good enough for a tie with Ward, who opened the tournament with a career-low 64, but could only manage a soggy 68 on Sunday.

Beth Daniel also contended by birdieing the first four holes on Sunday to take a one-shot lead. But Doolan, who shot three-under 33 on the first nine, made birdie putts at the 14th, 15th and 16th to reach 12 under, which is where she finished. Ward caught and passed Daniel with birdies at the 12th, 15th and 16th, while the Hall of Famer finished with three straight pars to shoot 65 and finish tied for third with Maria Hjorth at 133.

Doolan and Ward trudged through the slop for five more holes, with each making pars on the first three holes and both holing birdie putts on the fourth. Then at the 18th, Ward missed a 25-footer, leaving her birdie effort hanging on the lip of the hole. Doolan took advantage, draining her eight-footer for birdie and the win.

Corning Classic—$900,000
Winner: Carin Koch

With a victory in Europe in 2000 and a heroic effort in the deciding match at the Solheim Cup, Sweden's Carin Koch knew that her winless days on the LPGA Tour were numbered. She didn't expect her maiden U.S. victory to come in Corning, New York, at the Corning Classic, an event Koch hadn't visited since a controversial disqualification five years before.

It happened in 1997 when Koch's husband Stefan was her caddie. After hitting her tee shot into a tree on the 16th hole, the ball dislodged and fell to the ground. Stefan claimed he was standing under the tree and simply watched it fall. It was later ruled that Stefan might have shaken the ball loose from the tree, and Koch was disqualified. She never returned to Corning until this year when the tight layout and firm greens proved the perfect practice ground for the U.S. Women's Open.

The trip was worth it. Rounds of 68, 67 and 69 left Koch two shots off the lead held by Scotland's Mhairi McKay going into the final round. That deficit was quickly erased as Koch played the first five holes in four under par. When a 15-foot eagle putt fell on the fifth green, the Swede found herself tied with McKay atop the leaderboard.

The two remained tied until the 11th, when McKay missed a crucial par putt to fall one back. Both players birdied the 12th, and Koch's lead remained intact.

Another challenger joined the fray late in the final round. Maria Hjorth, who had the low round of the tournament with 63 on Saturday, pulled to within two shots of the lead with birdies at the 14th and 17th, but that was as close as she would get.

McKay, the only player with a legitimate shot at catching Koch, blew her tee shot over an out-of-bounds fence right of the 17th fairway. That led to a double bogey and a final-round 70. Her 272 total tied Hjorth for second place, two behind Koch, who parred the final hole for 66.

"Winning in Europe last year helped me to know that I could do it on the last day," Koch said. "Since then I've started believing I could do it. I'm not sure I truly believed it before."

U.S. Women's Open—$2,900,000
Winner: Karrie Webb

Golf must be viewed in the long term, as many also-rans keep reminding us week in and week out. For the first eight weeks of 2001, the story was Tiger Woods' slump. By mid-June that story looked silly. The same was true of the reported "slump" Karrie Webb experienced in the first half of 2001. She had plenty of top-10 finishes, and had taken a few weeks off to rest. That didn't matter as far as the press was concerned, because women's golf had a new queen named Annika Sorenstam. Webb, the Player of the Year for the previous two seasons and winner of two major titles in 2000, was old news.

After the U.S. Women's Open, all Webb's critics looked silly.

With an eight-stroke victory over Se Ri Pak in the season's second major championship, Webb resumed her role in the spotlight of women's golf by trouncing the best players in the world on the toughest test of golf they face all year. Pine Needles, the Donald Ross-designed course in Southern Pines, North Carolina, measured 6,256 yards and played to a par of 70.

Like all USGA-modified courses, this one harbored trouble at every turn. The greens were hard and fast and the rough penal. Webb made it look easy, coming out after a rain delay and shooting a second-round 65 to open up a three-shot lead. She would extend that lead to five by the end of the third round, and while Pak was able to whittle it down to three at one point on Sunday, the outcome was never really in question.

Webb shot 70, 65, 69 and 69 for a 273 total to finish as the only player under par for the week and become only the seventh woman in history to win back-to-back U.S. Women's Opens.

"A lot more people were worried about the state of my game than I was," Webb said. "I knew I was trying to become a better player, and I knew how close I was to having everything in the right shape at the right time. The hard work paid off. And it's just great timing to have it peak this week."

Even so, the course took its toll. Grace Park, who finished tied for 39th after a closing 78, summed up the feelings of everyone when she said, "The closing holes really kicked my butt."

Even Webb had her troubles. After opening up a seven-shot lead on Saturday, Webb had to settle for bogeys at the 14th and 17th, which cut the lead to five. "You can never have too big a lead in an Open," Webb said.

She should know. Before regrouping and walking away with the 2000 U.S. Women's Open, Webb squandered a four-shot lead on the final day. She retooled her game on the final nine holes to win by five shots last year. The eight-shot margin this year was even more impressive. After having to make a 15-footer for bogey at the second hole on Sunday, Webb watched as Pak trimmed the lead with a birdie putt at the fourth. But Pak bogeyed the fifth and seventh. When Webb birdied the seventh from 15 feet, the lead was six and the outcome seemed secure. Webb added a punctuation mark to her victory with putts of 40 feet at the 17th and 20 feet at the 18th to extend the margin of victory to eight shots. Pak had scores of 69, 70, 70 and 72 for her 281 total.

Webb's 65 on Friday proved the most pivotal point of the tournament. "After shooting five under and then having the weather that we had, everyone for the most part was trying to play catch-up," Webb said. "And that was to my advantage, because this is a hard course to play that sort of golf on.

"I was definitely not ready to start the year. I may have dropped off a bit in my standards, but I don't think the standards I set the last two years are the type you're going to expect to maintain for your whole career. There have been other stories to talk about, other players to talk about, and that's just fine with me. But to walk up the 18th two years in a row with a comfortable enough lead to really enjoy the atmosphere is just a great feeling. As a little girl I never expected to be sitting here once, let alone twice."

Wegmans Rochester International—$1,000,000
Winner: Laura Davies

Even when she led by five strokes with 18 holes to play, Laura Davies wasn't convinced she had a chance at the Wegmans Rochester International in Pittsford, New York. While bemoaning that her play was so bad she had no chance to win, Davies had shot two 68s and a 69 to stand alone, five strokes clear of Maria Hjorth and Brandie Burton, who took exception to Davies' poor-mouthing.

"It's called reverse psychology," Burton said. "She's always been like that, a little negative. Maybe not as much as I've read in the paper the last couple of days, but she's played very solid."

On the most penal golf course the women face all year, Davies managed to negotiate her way with only four bogeys and one double bogey in 72 holes, and despite her own negativity, she held on with 74 for a 279 total to claim her 20th LPGA title by three shots over Hjorth and Wendy Ward.

"I'm incredibly negative right now," Davies said before trotting out to the first tee on Sunday with a commanding lead. "My problem is that I stand on the tee and look at trouble instead of looking at the middle of the fairway. I'm not expecting too much. I'm setting myself up for a big disappointment."

Instead, Davies hit fairways and greens in the final round, increasing her lead to six on the first nine. She was one under par for the day and in total control on the second nine. Even three closing bogeys to shoot 74 didn't jeopardize the victory.

"The pessimism is absolutely over," Davies said. "I'm going to the Evian Masters thinking I can win again."

Evian Ladies Masters—£1,500,000
Winner: Rachel Teske

See Ladies European Tour section.

McDonald's LPGA Championship—$1,500,000
Winner: Karrie Webb

Going to bed on Saturday night with a three-shot lead in the McDonald's LPGA Championship — the final major she needed to complete the career Grand Slam — Karrie Webb was torn by conflicting loyalties. Three days before, Webb's maternal grandfather, Mick Collinson, suffered a stroke at his home in Australia. Webb made plans to fly there on Sunday.

"I nearly didn't play today," Webb said on Sunday afternoon. "I did have a flight booked to fly back with my parents. My dad didn't sleep very well, and he talked to the rest of the family today and they all wanted me to play, because granddad would have wanted me to."

Emotions ran high as Webb played the DuPont Country Club in Wilmington, Delaware, in two-under-par 69 and became the youngest woman in history — at age 26 — to complete the career Grand Slam. Her 14-under-par 270 total was two better than Laura Diaz, who closed with 68 to finish alone in second place, and four better than Maria Hjorth and Wendy Ward. But it was never really that close, and the outcome was never in question. Midway though the final round Webb led by six shots and everyone knew it was over.

"It happens with Karrie," Helen Alfredsson said afterward. "It's sort of like the Jack Nicklaus syndrome. She is up there, and everybody starts thinking about second place."

Those thoughts crept into the players' minds early in the week as Webb played some of her best golf of the year. By Friday afternoon she had already reached double digits under par, shooting rounds of 67 and 64 to take a three-shot lead over Alfredsson and Wendy Ward. A 70 on Saturday kept the lead at three with Hjorth and Diaz as the closest pursuers.

On Sunday, Hjorth, playing in the same group as Webb, cut the lead to two with a 10-foot birdie putt on the first hole, but Webb birdied the next three holes to extend the lead to five and effectively shut the door on all challenges. Even four late birdies by Diaz to close to within three shots weren't enough to provide a serious threat. Webb bogeyed the last two holes and still won comfortably.

"She makes it look so effortless," Hall-of-Famer Juli Inkster said. "I just can't believe anybody can be as good as Karrie Webb. As far as pure golf, she's the best I've ever seen. If Karrie keeps this pace, she's going to shatter all the records."

Webb became only the fifth player in LPGA history to capture all four major titles, joining Inkster, Mickey Wright, Louise Suggs and Pat Bradley in the elite camp. But nobody did it faster than Webb (Wright was closest, completing her Slam at age 27), and nobody did it with more authority. Webb's average margin of victory in major championships was 5.7 strokes.

"To do it a year ahead of Mickey Wright at a time when the depth of talent is the best it's ever been will ultimately go down as one of the biggest achievements in women's golf," LPGA commissioner Ty Votaw said.

Despite all the accolades, Webb remained humble in victory. "It's overwhelming," she said. "It happened so quickly. This is the dream of all dreams. One day it will sink in, but right now I'm at a loss for words."

As she fought back tears, she shared her thoughts about family and the important priorities in life. "The only thing I wanted to do was win for my granddad," she said. "That's all I kept thinking about. I don't know how I did what I did today, but I don't think I was on my own."

ShopRite Classic—$1,200,000
Winner: Betsy King

When Sunday's final round of the ShopRite Classic got underway, the big question was whether 23-year-old Cristie Kerr would finally pick up her first victory? If not, would Lorie Kane earn her second title of the year? And then there was Betsy King, 45 years old and trailing by a shot going into the final round.

All that changed quickly. King, playing in the penultimate group and drawing on 25 years of experience, made a five-foot eagle putt on the par-five third hole to take the lead. She followed that up with birdies at the fifth, sixth and 11th holes. Her lone bogey of the day came at the 14th, but she recovered with good up-and-downs at the 15th and 16th, and walked off the 18th green with a four-under-par 67 for the day and a 54-hole total of 201. At the time King had no idea if this was good enough, but she knew it was the best she could do.

"I think experience and hard work helped me today," King said. "I think that if I can hit more balls than anyone else, I'm going to be a better player. If I'm making 100 three-footers on the putting green, I can make the 101st in the tournament."

That practice paid off, but so did King's patience and experience. The Donald Ross-designed Bay Course at Marriott's Seaview Resort in Atlantic City, New Jersey, is the shortest course the LPGA plays all year, but the "little gem," as it's commonly called, is full of subtleties and surprises like false fronts and mounded greens that gave players fits in the final round.

A strong bay wind also worked to King's advantage. Kerr fought the gusts all day and finished with a three-over-par 74, a round she described as "pitiful." Kane put up a better fight and had a chance to catch King. She needed an eagle-three on the par-five 18th to shoot 68 and tie for the lead, but after missing the green to the left with her second shot, Kane walked away with a par for a closing round of 70 and a 203 total, good enough for second place.

"She has a great will to win," Kane said of the winner. "And I've read quotes of hers where she said, 'Golf is a game that doesn't retire you.' She's dedicated. I was going to dinner last night, and she was still chipping on the side of the practice green."

Retirement isn't in King's vocabulary at this point, although she knows that day is coming. "When I win now, it's more of a relief than anything," the winner said after hoisting the 34th trophy of her professional career. "Each time you win, it's like, 'Is this going to be the last one?' At this point I just go year to year. I just try to think about the golf."

Jamie Farr Kroger Classic—$1,000,000
Winner: Se Ri Pak

The citizens of Sylvania, Ohio, a suburb of Toledo, haven't erected a statue of Se Ri Pak in the town square, but it's not because they don't love the South Korean star. They did name a streetcar after her, and after picking up her third Jamie Farr Kroger Classic victory in four years, Pak loves Sylvania as much as they love her.

"This town makes me feel comfortable," Pak said after her final-round 68 at the Highland Meadows Golf Club proved good enough for a two-shot victory over a hard-charging Maria Hjorth. "It is like my hometown. The people are nice to me, and that helps me play well."

A nine-under-par 62 in the second round moved Pak into the lead, a position she retained on Saturday with a two-under 69. Heather Bowie was the closest challenger entering the final round, but she stood four shots back. Hjorth was five behind after recovering from an opening 76 with rounds of 65 and 66.

Pak provided an opening on Sunday when she parred the first 11 holes before finally rolling in a 10-foot birdie putt at the 12th. By then Hjorth had erased the deficit and stood tied with Pak at 13 under.

Pak regained the lead with a six-foot birdie putt at the 13th, but she quickly gave it back with a bogey at the par-four 15th. Hjorth, playing ahead of Pak and in the midst of a six-birdie run, let a prime opportunity slip away on the short par-five 17th. The long-hitting Swede missed the fairway and was unable to reach the green from the rough. But her third shot also failed to reach the putting surface, and when she failed to get up and down, Hjorth walked off the par-five with a bogey.

"I hit one bad shot the whole day, and it cost me," Hjorth said. "I played so well. One week, hopefully, it will be my week. It just seems lately that there's always someone playing a little bit better than me. I can't be disappointed. If I finished second every week I wouldn't be disappointed."

Hjorth came back with a birdie at the par-five 18th to regain a share of the lead, but Pak seized the moment on the last two holes. Her third shot from just short of the green on the 17th rolled to within three feet, and Pak made the putt to regain the lead. On the 18th she hit a perfect drive and a perfect lay-up, then spun a wedge to within eight feet of the hole and made that birdie putt to increase the margin of victory to two shots. Her 68 and 269 total made Pak the first three-time champion in the tournament's history.

Michelob Light Classic—$800,000
Winner: Emilee Klein

With a star-studded field that included the likes of Karrie Webb, Annika Sorenstam and defending champion Lorie Kane competing in St. Louis, Emilee Klein may not have been high on anyone's list of potential winners when the Michelob Light Classic got underway. But with a renewed confidence in her putting stroke and the bread-and-butter accuracy that made Klein a world-beater in her early years on the LPGA Tour, the 27-year-old posted a five-shot, wire-to-wire victory over Sorenstam and Jill McGill.

Klein opened with an eight-under-par 64 for a three-shot lead over rookie Jennifer Hubbard, and followed that with 72 to stay two ahead of Sherri Turner and three clear of Webb. Long criticized for her lack of length, Klein had no trouble with the 6,452-yard Fox Run Golf Club, taking advantage of the narrow fairways and high rough. On Sunday Klein removed all mystery, birdieing three of her first five holes in the closing round to distance herself from the field. A final-round 69 and an 11-under-par 205 total was good enough to hold off Sorenstam, who closed with 70, and McGill, who shot a course-record 63 on Sunday after rounds of 71 and 76.

"For anyone to have had a chance, I would have had to fold and they would have had to play really well," Klein said. "I wasn't going to fold. I'm playing too good right now."

The victory was Klein's first since 1996 when she won the Ping/Welch's Championship and the Weetabix Women's British Open. "I feel like the old Emilee Klein is back," she said. "The one who knows how to win. I've won so many times, I've never been scared. I know how to do it. But it's been a long five years."

During that time Klein has changed swing coaches and caddies, and worked on her distance, but it was her improved putting that made the difference in St. Louis. "It's made all the difference in the world," she said. Klein also attributed an increase in competition to her long hiatus from the winner's circle. "The players are so much better today," she said. "Every year the players get better. If you let up at all, you can't move forward at all."

Klein became only the fourth American player to win on the LPGA in 2001, and the first under 40 years old. But those stats were meaningless as the new Michelob Light Classic winner admired her trophy. "In the long run," she said, "I feel like I'm going to win a lot more tournaments."

Sybase Big Apple Classic—$950,000

Winner: Rosie Jones

Six of the previous 11 times that Rosie Jones entered the final round as a leader, she won the golf tournament. On a sunny Sunday in New Rochelle, New York, Jones made it seven for 12, shooting a final-round 70 to defeat Laura Diaz by one stroke in the Sybase Big Apple Classic.

With a third-round 66, Jones moved to three-under-par 202 and took a three-shot lead over Nancy Scranton into Sunday's final round. Mi Hyun Kim, Nancy Redman, Betsy King and Audra Banks stood four strokes behind and Diaz was five back.

Diaz was the only contender who made a run on Sunday, birdieing two of the first three holes to cut into Jones' lead. Another birdie at the eighth hole moved Diaz one shot out of the lead. But Jones, playing two groups behind, birdied the eighth and ninth to regain a three-shot advantage with nine holes to play. Diaz cut into the lead again with a birdie at the 11th. A few minutes later, Jones bogeyed the 12th and the lead was back to one.

As Jones was tapping in for bogey at the 15th, Diaz was lining up an eagle putt on the 15th that would have given her the lead outright. She missed the eagle, but tapped in for birdie to take her first share of the lead. Jones had intentionally ignored the scoreboards throughout the round, but when she reached the 15th fairway she asked her caddie how they stood. "Tied," the caddie said. Armed with that news, Jones birdied the 15th to regain a one-shot advantage.

When Diaz hit a nine iron through the green on the 17th and failed to get up and down, Jones had her opening. She failed to take advantage, three-putting the 16th for a bogey to keep the lead at one.

On the 18th Diaz hit a nine iron from the right rough to nine feet and rolled in the birdie putt to regain a share of the lead. She pumped her fist, signed for a final-round 66 and a 273 total, and went to the range to prepare for a possible playoff.

Knowing what she had to do, Jones missed the fairway with her second shot on the 481-yard, par-five 18th. She was left with 121 yards from the thick rough. When she hit a knockdown nine iron, Jones knew it was a good shot. The ball stopped three feet from the hole, and Jones leapt in the air in celebration. She made the putt for a birdie and a final round of 70 and a 272 total. Her $142,500 winner's check made Jones the career-leading money winner in New York with over $1 million in earnings in the Empire State.

"I really love the state," Jones said. "I'm paying a lot of estimated taxes, so I'd better love it. It's not a bad problem to have."

Diaz was faced with a problem, but it, too, was a good one. The second-place finish in New Rochelle was the 26-year-old's fourth runner-up finish of the year. She remained winless in her short career. "I didn't win the tournament, but I played good golf," Diaz said. "That's all I can do."

Jones knew she had her work cut out for her. "I knew Laura was trying to get her first win, and she's kicking at the door pretty hard," Jones said. "But I have a good history at this tournament. I'm thinking better, swinging better, and I'm stronger. I never putted well today, but I'm really proud of myself for having enough faith in my game to win."

Giant Eagle Classic—$1,000,000
Winner: Dorothy Delasin

Only two times in her career has Se Ri Pak failed to win when she held the lead going into the final round. Both failures came in the Giant Eagle Classic, and both times the woman who passed Pak was young upstart Dorothy Delasin. In 2000, Delasin was a 19-year-old rookie, barely out of high school when she traveled to Ohio and solidly beat Pak and the rest of the star-studded field for her first victory. A year later, Delasin, an older and wiser 20-year-old, did it again, shooting a final-round 65 to leap past Pak and successfully defend her title.

"It's like déjà vu," Delasin said after tapping in her par putt for a 203 total. "I'm still shocked. It's hard to defend your title. I knew the second win would be even harder. I'm glad I got that off my back. I just played with my heart. I'm in shock, but it's a good shock."

Delasin birdied five of her first 10 holes, but she still trained Pak and Tammie Green, who birdied four holes on the first nine to tie the lead at 12 under par. Delasin, playing two groups ahead, was two behind when she reached the par-five 13th with her second shot. She missed the eagle putt, but tapped in for birdie to pull within one. At the 14th, Delasin hit a nine iron to seven feet and made her second birdie in a row. She made it three in a row at the 15th after hitting a knockdown five iron on the 185-yard, par-three to within five feet.

"I hadn't looked at the scoreboards all day, but at 15 I looked at my caddie and he said we were in good position," Delasin said.

Indeed she was. Pak had trouble finding the fairways, and when she three-putted for par on the 13th, she gave up the lead for good. Green had a chance to tie on the 18th, but her birdie chip ran past the hole and she had to settle for 68 and a 204 total for second place. Pak finished alone in third at 205, two behind Delasin.

"I feel great," the winner said. "I didn't know what was going to happen today. After all, I was four strokes behind. But I just played really solid. I only made one mistake — I three-putted — and I didn't let that get me."

Delasin didn't know that she was the only player to ever beat Pak when the South Korean led going into the final round. "I didn't know that," she said when told. "But I think that's cool."

Weetabix Women's British Open—£1,000,000
Winner: Se Ri Pak

See Ladies European Tour section.

Wendy's Championship for Children—$1,000,000
Winner: Wendy Ward

After three winless years and an overhaul of her golf swing and her putting stroke, Wendy Ward knew her game was back in shape. It was only a matter of time before she was back on top.

"I've been fighting hard," she said of the changes. "I needed the change for the long run, and it has taken a little time to get the confidence level there."

That confidence couldn't have been higher in New Albany, Ohio, when Ward established a 54-hole LPGA record, shooting 21-under-par 195 to win the Wendy's Championship for Children by three shots over Annika Sorenstam and Maria Dunn.

"I was hungry," Ward said. "It's not that I ever doubted that I could win again, but when you have a dry spell in there you think, 'Are you pressing too hard? Are you not pressing enough?' You start questioning yourself on a lot of things."

If there was ever an anxious moment for Ward, it came in the early stages of the final round. After missing a seven-foot birdie putt on the first hole, she failed to save par from the greenside bunker on the second, carding her only bogey of the week. Meanwhile Sorenstam was putting on the pressure with birdies at the fifth, sixth and seventh holes to cut Ward's lead in half. As the leader stepped onto the third tee, she led by two.

With doubts beginning to creep into her brain, Ward made one of her boldest decisions of the week on the par-five sixth. After driving the ball in the rough, her caddie advised her to lay up. "I saw those people chasing me, and I said, 'I've got to make a statement,'" she said.

She did just that, hitting a five wood onto the green and two-putting for a birdie to regain a three-shot lead. It was the shot of the tournament.

"That shot was something I really needed to change the momentum," Ward said. "I was waiting for the one putt or the one shot to kind of spring-board me to get the adrenaline going. I finally had to tell myself, 'When you're in contention, make the most of it, make the most of every opportunity.' That seemed to be the trick. It just happened to be my time."

A six-foot birdie putt at the ninth by Ward and another six-footer at the 11th to get to 19 under par put the tournament out of reach. Birdies at the 15th and 16th from four and six feet respectively sealed the victory. Sorenstam's hopes faded when she three-putted the 13th, missing a par putt of two feet.

"My only mistake was at 13," Sorenstam said. "You're going to make a mistake or two. If you make one, that's fine. It turned out to be a putt." But, while disappointed in her second-place finish, she couldn't be upset by her scores. "I would have taken 18-under-par 198 at the beginning of the week," she said. "I would have taken it right away."

Sorenstam closed with 66 and Maria Dunn shot 67, but neither score was enough to catch Ward, who finished with 68. "She got her game going again," Sorenstam said. "When you're trailing by five shots and the leader shoots four under, it's just very hard to catch that person."

Bank of Montreal Canadian Women's Open—$1,200,000
Winner: Annika Sorenstam

With Player of the Year honors still up for grabs, Annika Sorenstam arrived in Canada with high hopes. She'd never won in Canada despite playing well enough in 1998 and 2000 to finish second in the du Maurier Classic, and, even though the tobacco manufacturer was no longer a sponsor and the new event lacked its former major championship status, Sorenstam looked at it as one of the most important tournaments of her year.

"I was motivated early in the year to win Player of the Year," she said. "But I'll have to play well to do it. Karrie (Webb) has won the big ones, and Se Ri (Pak) is playing well. I'm right on track, but the race is still close."

The points race for Player of the Year was a lot closer than this tournament, even though Pak, Webb and nine of the top-10 players on the money list were in attendance. Sorenstam dominated, shooting a course-record 64 on Saturday to share the top spot with Kelly Robbins. Then the Swede ran away from the field on Sunday.

Birdies on the first, fifth and ninth holes while Robbins and the other leaders stumbled opened up a big lead for Sorenstam. When she made a 30-footer for birdie on the 13th and followed it up with a four-foot birdie on the par-five 15th, her lead was seven strokes.

"Annika played great," Robbins said after shooting a closing 71 to finish second at 274. She pulled to within two shots with a 30-foot birdie putt on the 18th while Sorenstam was in the process of making bogeys on the final two holes, but it was never that close, and Robbins knew it. "Once she got to 16 or 17 under, I knew I was just playing for second," she said. "But it was a good way to finish a good week."

Sorenstam finished with 69 for a 272 total. She thought her play could have been better. "I missed three putts that were less than four feet on Saturday and I could have gone three to five shots less," she said. "But I hadn't won since Atlanta (in May), so this win means a lot. At the end I probably played too conservatively. I wanted to get off to a good start. I did, and I just tried to keep it going. But I'm overwhelmed with this season. I found my game last week and I'm really happy that I was able to bring it here."

First Union Betsy King Classic—$800,000
Winner: Heather Daly-Donofrio

In a week when she thought about withdrawing due to back pain, Heather Daly-Donofrio caught every break and made every crucial putt down the stretch to pick up her first LPGA victory at the First Union Betsy King Classic. It was a week of surprises for Daly-Donofrio, who woke up Thursday morning with lower back pain so severe she considered dropping out. "Just before I was ready to play, I was afraid to pick up a club," she said.

A 65 on Thursday was the best back medicine she could find. Follow-up rounds of 71 and 68 dulled the pain even further, and suddenly Daly-Donofrio, who was coaching the woman's golf team at Yale less than 12 months before, was in the penultimate group with only two shots and two names between her and her first career victory.

She got off to a quick start in the final round with birdies on three of her first five holes to take a share of the lead with Maria Dunn. When she holed a 20-footer for birdie at the eighth, she held the lead outright. And when her long-and-left approach on the ninth ricocheted off the grandstands and landed on the green, where she made a 50-footer for par, Daly-Donofrio started thinking this might be her week.

"I felt pretty confident coming down the stretch," she said. "It was different than the first nine when I felt like I was going to be sick."

After a first-nine score of 32, Daly-Donofrio owned the lead, and the final twosome of Maria Dunn and Mhairi McKay were playing catch-up. Although her putting cooled on the second nine, Daly-Donofrio made one more birdie and two bogeys for 69. She was the leader in the clubhouse with a 72-hole total of 273.

But McKay appeared to be the player to beat. When her approach to the 17th stopped four feet away, it appeared as though the Scot would tie the lead. When she left the putt short, gasps rang out through the gallery. Then McKay blew another chance, pushing a two-foot birdie putt on the 18th hole that would have sent the tournament into a playoff.

"It's disappointing," McKay said. "I had my chance, and hopefully this will serve me well in the future. The putt on 17 went right-to-left and I didn't quite read it right. On 18, I didn't play through it like I should have."

Daly-Donofrio was as surprised as anyone when McKay missed. "I really thought Mhairi was going to make the putts at the end," she said.

When McKay missed, Daly-Donofrio had her first trophy as a professional at age 31. "I don't believe it," she said afterward. "I really didn't think this was going to happen. This whole weekend turned out to be a blessing. I didn't think I would win for a couple more years."

Dunn overcame a couple of early double bogeys with birdies on the second nine (including one at the 18th) to shoot 72 and tie McKay for second at 274. Catriona Matthew shot 275 for fifth, while Mi Hyun Kim continued her good year with 65 for a 276 total and sixth place.

State Farm Classic—$1,000,000
Winner: Kate Golden

With six victories on the season and a perfect three-for-three winning record when she led after 54 holes, nobody was ready to bet against Annika Sorenstam when she shot 67 to take a five-stroke lead into the final round of the State Farm Classic at the Rail Golf Club. But the Springfield, Illinois, event has a history of surprise endings and great drama. Four previous LPGA players made the State Farm Classic their first career victories. Texan Kate Golden hoped to become the fifth.

Six strokes back after rounds of 69, 65 and 70, and standing 103rd on the money list with earnings of just over $50,000 for the year, Golden was her one and only cheerleader when the day began. But as she put it, "My tempo was good and everything was on."

Hitting fairways and greens with pinpoint accuracy, Golden birdied the third, sixth, seventh, eighth and ninth holes to whittle away at Sorenstam's lead. On the par-three 11th, Golden made a breaking 30-footer for birdie, a putt she called "a bomb."

"When that went in, the hair stood up on the back of my neck and I said, 'Here we go again,'" Golden said.

Another birdie from 10 feet at the 12th followed by a four-footer for birdie at the 14th gave Golden a share of the lead. "My knees started shaking on the 15th tee," she said. "And they haven't stopped since."

Despite the knocking knees, Golden managed to birdie the 15th to take the outright lead, a lead that was extended to two shots when Sorenstam bogeyed the 16th. Three pars coming in gave Golden a final-round 63 and a 267 total, four shots clear of the tournament record.

Whether it would be good enough for her first victory remained to be seen. Sorenstam still had a chance to birdie the final two holes and force a playoff. She produced on the 17th, hitting a wedge approach that almost flew in the hole for eagle and rolling in the short birdie putt to pull within one. On the 18th, however, her birdie effort rolled inches right of the hole. Sorenstam closed with 70 and a 268 total, good enough for second place, one stroke shy of Golden.

"I don't think I gave it to her," Sorenstam said of Golden's win. "I think she won it. To win her first event the way she won it, she played spectacular."

Williams Championship—$1,000,000
Winner: Gloria Park

There is plenty of precedent for players calling crucial penalties on themselves, but rarely has there been a time when such a penalty came during the setting of a course record and in a circumstance where it would ultimately cost the player a victory. All that and a great deal more happened at the Williams Championship in Tulsa, the LPGA's first event in Oklahoma.

Donna Andrews, who hadn't won since the 1998 Longs Drugs Challenge, was threatening to break 60 during Saturday's second round at the 6,233-yard Tulsa Country Club course, a classic A.W. Tillinghast design. A bogey at the 16th put history out of the question. Instead, all Andrews had to do was tap in a two-footer for par on the 18th for a nine-under-par 61. Then something strange happened. As she stroked her putt, the blade of the putter struck the ball twice. Under Rule 14-4, that's a double hit, and Andrews assessed herself the obligatory one-shot penalty. Rather than 61, she carded 62, still a course record and still enough for a four-shot lead over Rachel Teske.

"I have to go by what I felt, and I felt like the putter slowed down and nicked it a second time," Andrews said. "You have to go with your gut instinct."

Andrews' instinct told her the penalty might come back to haunt her, but she had to put it out of her mind. What she couldn't have foreseen was the impressive play of Gloria Park, a second-year player from South Korea who has lived in Australia since she was 13. Trailing by five at the start of the final round, Park, who won the 1998 Australian Amateur and the 1999 Indonesian Open, got out early with four birdies on the first nine. She was tied with Andrews at the turn, but gave up the lead with a double bogey at the 10th.

"I tried to forget about that straight away," Park said. "I really didn't think about the double bogey after that. Like on 11, I tried to think about starting over."

She parred the 11th, but got the strokes back with birdies at the 12th and 13th to catch Andrews again. The leader, who struggled early, rallied with birdies on the 11th and 15th, but could fare no better than an even-par 70. That wasn't good enough. Park birdied the 16th to stay tied and rolled in a five-footer for birdie on the 17th to take the lead for good. She finished the day with 64 for a 54-hole total of 201.

"I wasn't thinking about winning," Park said. "I just wanted to try to do the best I could do. I just played a really good game today, one of my best. My target was 65, so I'm glad I made it."

Andrews had one last chance to tie at the 18th, but her 50-foot birdie putt slid below the hole.

"After a great score like a 62 it's so hard to come back and shoot under par the next day," Andrews said. "Plus, I just didn't make any putts today. I made a million miles of putts yesterday and that's the difference."

She deflected questions about the penalty, since it ultimately cost her a shot at a playoff. "To lose by one, it's hard to swallow," Andrews said. "But I don't think I'd have played as well today if I had that in the back of my mind, and if I had not done the right thing. I wouldn't have felt good about myself. That's what is really important in the game of life."

Park became the third consecutive first-time winner on the LPGA Tour, following Heather Daly-Donofrio and Kate Golden as newly crowned title-holders. She also became the third native Korean to win, joining compatriots Se Ri Pak and Grace Park.

Asahi Ryokuken International Championship—$1,200,000
Winner: Tina Fischer

The week following the September 11 attacks on America took their toll on all sports, and the LPGA Tour was no exception. Even a venue like Augusta, just across the Savannah River from one of golf's most storied sites, did little to help the newly christened Asahi Ryokuken International Championship. Most of the excitement in the area was at nearby Fort Gordon and the Savannah River nuclear weapons facility, not the Mount Vintage Plantation Golf Club.

Still, the show went on, and for the fourth tournament in a row a first-time winner was crowned. This time it was German Tina Fischer.

"I'm very happy," Fischer said after shooting 70, 66 and 70 for a 206 total in the rain-shortened event to win by one shot over Emilee Klein. "That's what everybody is trying to achieve out here, to win. I've done it in the last full field tournament of the season, so that's really wonderful."

Kris Tschetter started the final round with a two-shot lead after rounds of 68 and 66. She remained on top through seven holes until disaster struck on the eighth. After hitting her approach to 15 feet, Tschetter four-putted for a double bogey, and added two more three-putt greens that dropped her out of contention. "A four-putt and two three-putts, that pretty much sums up my day," she said.

Nancy Scranton was the first to take advantage of Tschetter's misfortune. After two rounds of 68, Scranton came out with birdies on the fourth, sixth and eighth holes to take the lead at 11 under par. Her fortunes also faded when she hit a tree with her tee shot on the 13th and took a double bogey. Scranton never recovered, finishing with 73 for a 209 total.

Tracy Hanson also made a run, jumping to a two-shot lead after a birdie at the 12th. She fell away with bogeys at the 14th and 15th. Klein's collapse came a little earlier. She bogeyed three of her first five holes. "I came out a little flat," Klein said. "I think I lost some of the momentum I had."

Hanson still had a chance at the 18th, but her 30-foot putt from the fringe came up short, and she finished with 71 and 207 to tie for second with Klein. "I was still trying to make birdies," Hanson said, "but I got a little tentative coming in."

Fischer suffered no such reservations. Needing only a par on the 18th to win, she hit a nine wood to the middle of the green and two-putted for her first career victory.

AFLAC Champions—$750,000
Winner: Se Ri Pak

With five weeks' worth of rest and relaxation behind her, Se Ri Pak reinserted herself into the Player of the Year mix in a big way at the AFLAC Champions event in Alabama. Waltzing through the magnolias of Mobile, Pak won easily, building a 10-stroke lead at one point during the final round before cruising in with a tournament record 16-under-par 272 total and a five-shot victory over Lorie Kane.

"I wasn't really sure after taking five weeks off if I was going to be the top player," Pak said. "I just kind of surprised myself."

She surprised a lot of other people too. After rounds of 72 and 67 on the difficult Magnolia Grove golf course, part of Alabama's Robert Trent Jones Golf Trail, Pak separated herself from the field by birdieing the last six holes on Saturday en route to a course-record 64. That gave her a seven-stroke lead. Through the first eight holes on Sunday, she had extended the lead to 10.

Kane cut that lead in half with four birdies in a row starting at the ninth, while Pak made her first bogey in 29 holes at the 12th. The lead went back to six shots when Kane three-putted the 14th.

The only real drama came when Pak flew her approach shot over the 15th green, chipped twice before reaching the putting surface, and two-putted for a double bogey to drop the lead back to four shots.

"I don't know why that happened," she said. "I was hitting 137 (yards) to the pin into the wind and a little uphill. I hit it and it went and I said, 'Shoot, it ran away.' I hit it 150 yards. I hit a bad shot and I took double."

She made up for the mistake on the next hole, reaching the par-five 16th in two and two-putting for birdie to extend the lead back to five shots, which is where it remained. Kane shot 69 in the final round, two shots better than Pak's 71, but the victory for the Korean star was never in question. The only unanswered query at the end of the week was whether this decisive win would be enough for Pak to challenge Annika Sorenstam for Player of the Year.

"It's getting close," Pak said. "I think I still have a chance. I feel great right now and I'm about to get pretty close to Annika. At the end of the year we'll know who's going to be on top. If it's not me, I've had a great season and I have a few years left. I'm not going to stop here, because this is not my last year. I'm much happier playing this year and the way everything is positioned."

Although she wasn't thrilled about finishing second, Kane enjoyed watching Pak make a run at the top spot. "Se Ri wants to be number one," Kane said. "I know Annika is not sitting at home twiddling her thumbs. She'll be ready to come back next week at the Samsung World Championship, but it could get interesting."

Samsung World Championship—$750,000
Winner: Dorothy Delasin

She wasn't exactly at home, but it was close enough. Dorothy Delasin grew up in Daly City, California, just across the Bay Bridge from Vallejo and the Hiddenbrooke Golf Club where the Samsung World Championship was contested. So it was no surprise that Delasin was considered the local favorite at the event, and no wonder that cheers rang out as Delasin steadily parred her way to victory in the star-studded event.

"To hear people yelling my name, it was the best feeling," Delasin said. "I wish I could have it recorded and play it again."

With three career victories before her 22nd birthday, Delasin might hear her own name a lot more in coming years. This week she showed a maturity and confidence that belied her age as she held off the world's best players to win the elite event by three shots over Karrie Webb and Se Ri Pak.

"I noticed last year that she lacked a general sense of course management," Webb said after playing in the final pairing with Delasin on Sunday. "That has definitely improved. She's got a great future. As she gets older and matures, her game will only grow with her."

She grew up a lot over the weekend near her home. Leading Pak by one going into the final round, Delasin steadily played her game, birdieing the first and last holes and carding 15 pars and one more birdie in between to finish with 69 for a 277 total. She played her last 31 holes without a bogey and went all week without three-putting a green.

In the end it was the older and more mature players who faltered. Pak missed short putts on three consecutive holes on the second nine to finish with 72 for the day and 281 for the week, three behind Delasin.

"I was thinking after the front nine that I had a pretty good chance, but the back nine was hard," Pak said. "I missed a lot of putts. It gave me a lot of stress."

Webb wasn't quite as stressed, but she wasn't in her best form either. "It's the first time in a couple of months that I've had a legitimate shot at winning," she said. "I hit the ball a lot better this week, but I still haven't been able to keep the big numbers out of my game."

Tyco/ADT Championship—$1,000,000
Winner: Karrie Webb

With conditions so windy that only two players broke par, the two women who have dominated the LPGA Tour for the past six years squared off in a final-nine duel at the Tyco/ADT Championship that had a little bit of everything. In the end Karrie Webb won the tournament, shooting a final-round score of 68 for a 279 total and a two-shot margin. Second-place finisher Annika Sorenstam also had a victory of sorts. By shooting a final-round 65, Sorenstam set a season scoring record for women's golf, finishing the year with an average of 69.42, which was .01 lower than Webb's 1999 record-setting mark.

Sorenstam also became the first woman to earn over $2 million in a single season. The $115,000 she received for second place pushed her yearly total to $2,105,868.

"I was shooting for a number, and I don't normally do that," Sorenstam said after going on a birdie blitz in the final 10 holes to set the record. "It's a great way to end the season."

Sorenstam played the final 10 holes in six under par. With wind gusts so strong that players had difficulty walking at times, she felt sure that her 281 total was good enough to at least force a playoff, especially given the strength of her finish. Down by five with four holes to play, she reached the par-five 15th with her second shot and drained a 12-foot putt for eagle. Sorenstam followed that with an eight-iron approach from 156 yards at the 17th that rolled to within four feet. When that putt fell in, Sorenstam hit seven under par for the championship, the number she was shooting for. After all the scores were tallied she learned that six-under-par 282 would have broken the record.

"Now they tell me," she joked. "After all that work!"

Webb worked pretty hard as well, leading throughout most of the week on a course near her home in South Florida. When Sorenstam's putt went in on the 17th, Webb, watching from the fairway, knew what she had to do. With water on her left and right, Webb split the fairway and found the green. She two-putted for pars on the 17th and 18th and waltzed in with her 26th career victory and her third in 2001.

"At any other regular event the score would have been 20 under," Webb said of the tough conditions. "I've had a good year, and to finish it off with a win really tops it off."

Webb's other two victories were majors — the U.S. Women's Open and the McDonald's LPGA Championship — and she became the first two-time winner of the LPGA Tour Championship. Her other win came in 1996.

Evian Ladies European Tour

Australian Ladies Masters—£200,000
Winner: Karrie Webb

Karrie Webb returned home in search of her first victory of 2001 and it was always a pretty fair bet that her journey would be successful. Webb had won the Australian Ladies Masters at the Royal Pines Resort in her native Queensland for the previous three years and the 26-year-old Australian was triumphant again.

Webb won by the little matter of eight strokes on the Gold Coast with a 17-under-par total of 271. Over her last 20 rounds at Royal Pines, she was a remarkable 87 under par. After rounds of 67 and 70, it was on the third day that Webb took the lead for good. Her 65 matched England's Diane Barnard's opening effort as the best of the week and put her five strokes ahead of the field.

In the final round Webb cruised to victory with a 69, as her compatriot Rachel Teske won the battle to finish second at nine under par. Scotland's Catriona Matthew, on the back of her first LPGA Tour win in Hawaii, was a shot further back in third place, with America's Kelly Robbins fourth.

Only Laura Davies, at the Standard Register Ping tournament from 1994 to 1997, had previously won a women's tournament four years in a row. "It was great to be in Oz again," Webb said. "It is always great to win in front of big crowds and a lot of home support. I had only two bogeys all week and it is a good kick-start to the year. Hopefully, it is a sign of things to come."

AAMI Women's Australian Open—£150,000
Winner: Sophie Gustafson

Karrie Webb was also the defending champion at her home country's other big tournament, the AAMI Women's Australian Open, but she was to be denied another success by Sweden's Sophie Gustafson. This time it was Gustafson who appeared to be cruising to victory before a dramatic finish in which the 27-year-old from Saro held on to win by only one stroke from Webb.

A 66 in the third round at Yarra Yarra put Gustafson four ahead and she birdied the first three holes in the final round to go seven clear. But with Webb not dropping a shot in a closing 68, the Swede soon came under unexpected pressure. By the turn, she was only two ahead and she had to birdie the 15th and 17th to maintain that advantage playing the 18th.

At the par-five 18th, Webb just missed her eagle putt from 35 feet, leaving Gustafson to two-putt from 12 feet for the victory. She raced her first effort four feet past the hole and had to sink the one back to prevent a playoff. Gustafson's 71 gave her a 12-under-par score of 276, while Jane Crafter took third place, six strokes behind Webb.

It was Gustafson's second win of the year after she defeated Webb in Naples, Florida, on the LPGA circuit six weeks earlier and was her fourth national crown after she won the Italian, Irish and British Opens in 2000. "I was so nervous," Gustafson said. "It is marginal whether I was in control for most of the day. Every time I go up against Karrie it is nerve-wracking and it was a tough battle again. I certainly made it harder on myself at the end, but to come out in front again makes me very happy."

Taiwan Ladies Open—£100,000
Winner: Raquel Carriedo

When she became the first Spaniard to qualify for the European Solheim Cup team in 2000, Raquel Carriedo had yet to win a tournament. In the past two years on the Ladies European Tour she had collected four runner-up finishes but finally achieved her first win at the Taiwan Ladies Open. The 29-year-old from Zaragoza led after each day in the three-round tournament, but had to make a par at the 18th to clinch the title.

Rounds of 69 and 67 at Westin Ta Shee had put Carriedo four ahead of the field, but a closing 75, for a five-under total of 211, gave her only a one-stroke victory over Sweden's Anna Berg and Germany's Elisabeth Esterl, who closed with rounds of 72 and 70 respectively.

Esterl went to the turn in 32, but playing ahead of the final twosome, missed the green at the par-three 18th and fell back to four under with a bogey. Carriedo had fallen out of the lead with a bogey at the 16th, but she immediately drew even with Berg by birdieing the 17th with an eight-foot putt. Berg, like Esterl before her, then bogeyed the last when her tee shot came up short of the green and she could only chip to 30 feet.

Carriedo found the putting surface at the back of the green and managed to two-putt for an emotional victory. "Finally, I've won," she exclaimed. "I was fighting with myself all day, but even though I'd been putting badly all day, I knew I would make it at the last."

Nedbank MasterCard South African Masters—R1,100,000
Winner: Samantha Head

See South African Ladies Tour section.

La Perla Ladies Italian Open—£120,000
Winner: Paula Marti

The consistent Raquel Carriedo was once more in contention when the Ladies European Tour began its summer season on the continent. But it was her younger compatriot Paula Marti who stole the La Perla Italian Open title at Poggio dei Medici. Marti won at the first extra hole after Carriedo, finishing runner-up for the seventh time, had the misfortune to miss a two-foot par putt when her ball hit a pitch mark and deflected wide of the hole.

However, it was still an impressive first victory for Marti, 21, who was playing in only her fifth Ladies European Tour event. The former Spanish Amateur champion from Barcelona is the daughter of a famous portrait artist. She began the final round five strokes behind Corinne Dibnah, whose 65 in the opening round had been a new course record.

While Dibnah closed with 74 to finish a stroke out of the playoff, Marti's 68 left her at nine under par following rounds of 70, 73 and 72. Marti began her round birdie-eagle-birdie and later holed from a greenside bunker for a birdie at the 11th. A fine chip set up a birdie at the 18th, which was matched by Carriedo, who had dropped a shot at the 16th, when she holed from six feet to get into a playoff after a 69.

"It's a shame for Raquel, but she has won once already and it was my turn this time," said Marti. "I was thinking if I could shoot a good round, I knew I could do it, and the start really gave me the confidence to shoot a low score. I was thinking in the playoff that if I didn't make my putt, I wanted to leave it as close as I could and put the pressure on. There is so much pressure in a playoff, you just don't know what is going to happen. I hope this will be something good for Spanish women's golf."

Ladies French Open—£175,000
Winner: Suzann Pettersen

If Paula Marti was quick off the mark, Suzann Pettersen was even quicker. The World Amateur champion in 2000, Pettersen could not play over the winter due to an ankle injury, but claimed the Ladies French Open at Arras as her first professional title in only her second tournament. Peterson, a 20-year-old from Oslo, became the first Norwegian to win on the Ladies European Tour after a birdie at the third extra hole finally saw off the challenge of another rookie, Becky Morgan from Wales.

Italy's Giulia Sergas and French rookie Karine Icher tied for third place at seven under par, a stroke out of the playoff, with Spain's Raquel Carriedo finishing alone in fifth place at five under. Icher had led after three rounds, but closed with 73 to be overtaken by Pettersen and Morgan.

A tall, powerful player, Pettersen, who had started the final round three behind, chipped in for a birdie at the 12th, added two more at the next two holes and also birdied the 372-yard 17th after driving within 50 yards of the green. A 69, after rounds of 71, 70, 70, set the clubhouse target at eight under par.

Morgan, the former Curtis Cup player who got some early season experience on the LPGA Tour, got into contention by eagling the 13th and then birdied the 17th to draw even with Pettersen. The par-five 18th was twice parred by both players in the playoff, but Morgan found the water the third time around and Pettersen took advantage to claim the last spot on offer in the following week's Evian Masters.

"I didn't get an invitation, so I thought at the start of the day I would just have to go and do it myself — my only chance to get in was to win here," Pettersen explained. "I liked it out there and I proved to myself that I wouldn't mess it up. I wasn't nervous out there at all."

Evian Masters—£1,500,000
Winner: Rachel Teske

Shaun McBride was left with mixed emotions at the end of the Evian Masters, the richest women's tournament in Europe. In his role as caddie, McBride was able to celebrate with his employer Rachel Teske when the Australian claimed a one-stroke victory over Maria Hjorth. But as Hjorth's boyfriend, he also had some consoling to do as Hjorth finished as runner-up for the third time in five weeks.

Teske, the 29-year-old from Queensland, earned £222,426 for winning an event co-sanctioned by the LPGA Tour. It was her third career win, but her first for two years. She shared the overnight lead with Hjorth and America's Beth Daniel, who went to the turn in 37 and fell out of contention.

Having missed the cut at the U.S. Women's Open two weeks earlier and been forced to withdraw the previous week with a rib injury, Teske hardly expected to post rounds of 71, 68, 66 and 68 for a 15-under-par total of 273. Much of the final day was played in heavy rain at the Evian course on the banks of Lake Geneva, but it turned into a dramatic duel.

Hjorth briefly went ahead when she holed from 15 feet for a birdie at the 10th, but Teske responded by holing a birdie putt at the 12th. Both players made fours at the par-five 15th, but the crucial hole turned out to be the 17th where Hjorth three-putted, missing a par putt from two feet.

While Teske, nee Hetherington, found the greenside bunker with her second shot to the 465-yard final hole, Hjorth hit a five iron to just 25 feet, only to leave her eagle putt agonizingly short. Teske came out of the bunker to six feet and holed the putt for victory.

"I'm ecstatic," said Teske. "I can't really believe it, it seems like quite a long time since I have won. It was a great way to finish, too. Maria had been playing well all day, and when she birdied 18, I knew I had to make birdie too, so making that putt was so important.

"I really didn't expect anything this week. I was just happy to play without pain. And Shaun was great. It was difficult, but he gives me a lot of confidence out there and I know that he gives 100 percent to his job."

Daniel finished third at 11 under par, one stroke ahead of France's Marine Monnet, who gave the home gallery plenty to shout about with a closing 66, including birdies at the last two holes. Her fourth place was the highest finish ever by a French player at the Evian Masters.

Kellogg's All-Bran Ladies British Masters—£100,000
Winner: Paula Marti

Paula Marti produced a dramatic finish to claim her second victory of the season and deny her compatriot Raquel Carriedo again. Having beaten Carriedo in a playoff at the Italian Open, Marti this time finished birdie, eagle to win the Kellogg's All-Bran Ladies British Masters at Mottram Hall.

The 21-year-old from Barcelona squeezed past the 30-year-old from Zaragoza, who had led for most of the afternoon, to win by one stroke. Marti closed with 68, after rounds of 71 and 70, for a three-round total of 10-under-par 209, while Carriedo had three successive rounds of 70.

Carriedo was four under for her first three holes as she appeared to make a determined break for her second Ladies European Tour title. Marti was four behind at the turn, but birdied the 10th and 14th and holed from eight feet for par at the 13th. Carriedo had dropped a shot at the 11th, but went two ahead again when Marti bogeyed the 16th. Carriedo might have sealed the win had her chip at the same hole not lipped out.

But then Marti struck. At the par-five 17th, she got up and down from a bunker short of the green for a birdie, and then at the 510-yard 18th she hit a drive and a five iron to nine feet and holed the putt for the eagle. Carriedo, who could only par the last, admitted, "I have to expect everything from her now."

"I am so happy," said Marti. "I never thought it was going to happen like this. I have been struggling with my putter lately, but all the ones I missed earlier in the week went in today, especially the last one.

"I knew I needed a good score today, especially when Raquel started so fast. I think I was six shots behind at one point and I knew that I could make up six shots around here, so I just stuck at it. It was so exciting when the putt went in at the last."

Dale Reid, having received her OBE for services to golf from the Queen at Holyrood Palace in Edinburgh at the start of the week, could not quite add to her 26 career titles. The 42-year-old finished in third place at eight under, a stroke ahead of Joanne Mills and Suzann Pettersen, who took a triple-bogey seven at the 14th hole after tangling with the roots of a tree.

WPGA Championship of Europe—£400,000
Winner: Helen Alfredsson

As promising as they appear to be, and as well as they have played, the Ladies European Tour is not yet all about talented youngsters. Or, as Helen Alfredsson put it, "There is life in this old bag yet."

Alfredsson, 36, held on against a fierce challenge from Norway's Suzann Pettersen to win the WPGA Championship of Europe for the second time. The Swede's four-stroke victory, her first in Europe for three years, does not yet tell the tale of the final round at Royal Porthcawl. Alfredsson, one stroke ahead after 54 holes, scored 71, following rounds of 67, 70 and 68, for a 16-under-par total of 276.

Pettersen closed with 74, but at the turn had gone three strokes clear of her more experienced opponent. An eagle at the fifth and a birdie at the sixth as Alfredsson dropped a couple of shots put the youngster from Oslo ahead, but her attempt to add to her French Open title earlier in the season went awry on the way home.

It was a brilliant run of three successive birdies from the 11th from Alfredsson that put the pressure on Pettersen. She bogeyed the 13th, where the Swede hit a six iron to four feet, to fall one behind again and dropped three more strokes over the last five holes.

"I forgot how it was to win," said Alfredsson. "Everything was perfect this week, the weather, the course, and when you really care about the game, it is great to win. I started horribly and came back, and it was so nice to make some putts when it mattered. With the wind getting up today, it took a little time to get used to it, we hadn't played in it all week, it was so calm.

"So much has been said about the youngsters this week and it was great to see them playing so well, but there is life in this old bag yet," Alfredsson added with a laugh.

Sweden's Asa Gottmo took sole possession of third place at nine under par after a final round of 68, finishing one shot clear of Becky Morgan, France's Karine Icher and fellow Swede Lisa Hed.

Weetabix Women's British Open—£1,000,000
Winner: Se Ri Pak

A brilliant final round of 66 at Sunningdale, after starting four strokes behind the leader, gave Se Ri Pak victory in the Weetabix Women's British Open. Having played well ahead of the final pairings, Pak had to wait by the 18th green to find out if anyone could match her 11-under-par total of 277.

Catriona Matthew, the 54-hole leader, finally arrived at the 18th needing to hole out with her second shot to force a playoff. As unlikely as that sounds, the Scot had done just that at the conclusion of her opening round. Three days earlier, however, she had driven into the fairway. Now, Matthew was in the rough on the right and could not even reach the green.

"The ball was not sitting well," said Matthew, who had led since making a hole-in-one at the 15th on Friday. "As soon as I saw the lie I knew a repeat of Thursday was not on."

So, as at Royal Lytham a fortnight earlier, there was no home winner of the British Open. Instead, there was a Korean one-two, with Pak, who had been unable to break 70 on the first three days, winning by two strokes over Mi Hyun Kim. Matthew dropped a shot at the 18th to tie for third with compatriot Janice Moodie, Laura Diaz and Iben Tinning.

"It is so good to win another major, and it is great for Korea that we finished first and second," Pak said. "At the start I just thought I had nothing to lose. Just go for it as hard as I can."

Pak, 23, burst on the scene in dramatic fashion by winning her first two major championships of her rookie season in 1998, the LPGA Championship and the U.S. Women's Open. She arrived at Royal Lytham for that year's British Open under an intense media glare, hated the week and the weather, and only came back this time because of the tournament's new designation as a major on the LPGA circuit.

"After 1998, I said I could never come back," Pak said. "It was so bad.

It was so windy and it was raining and the course was so foreign to me. I thought, 'I can't play this golf.' It was not fun, it was so much stress. Now this is a major, I had no choice but to come. I didn't have any idea how to play golf in this country, how to bounce the ball into the greens, but this is a really great course and I found it fun to play."

Pak won eight times in her first two years in America but missed out in 2000. "It was so busy and I did not really know what was happening," said Pak, who has now won four times this season. "Last year I realized I was pushing myself so hard, and though I did not win, it was an important season for me. Now I try to play well but also try to enjoy myself."

Diaz, an American who won the Rookie of the Year Award in Europe in 1998, showed what could be achieved by birdieing the first six holes, but then stumbled. Pak eagled the first and then parred her way to the turn. It was a homeward half of 32 that clinched her victory. Birdies at the 10th and 12th only got her into a share of the lead after Matthew fell back to nine under. But Pak suddenly broke away with birdies at the last two holes.

She got a lucky break when her drive at the 16th rebounded off a spectator's foot back onto the fairway; then on the 17th, after a drive of 280 yards, she put a wedge to three feet. At the 18th, she found the right rough, but put her seven iron to four feet and holed that as well.

Compaq Open—£325,000
Winner: Raquel Carriedo

Patience was a virtue for Spain's Raquel Carriedo as she finally added her second title of the season after a number of near-misses. Carriedo's one-under-par 72 in cold and wet conditions at Osterakers was good enough for a one-stroke victory at eight under par over France's Karine Icher.

Icher, another of the promising rookies on the Ladies European Tour, led by six strokes at the halfway stage, but back-to-back rounds of 76 were her undoing. She was still three ahead going into the final round, but was penalized a stroke at the 11th hole for slow play and then took a double bogey at the par-three 17th.

Sweden's Sophie Gustafson, after a course-record-equaling 66 in the third round, failed to mount a challenge and finished in third place, ahead of compatriot Liselotte Neumann and Germany's Elisabeth Esterl.

With Carriedo canceling out her earlier birdies with a pair of bogeys at the eighth and ninth holes, Icher was still well placed going into the second nine. But tournament director Ian Randell had put the final pairing of Icher and Gustafson on the clock from the eighth hole because they were out of position.

By the 11th, Icher and Gustafson had lost a clear hole and the French youngster received a bad time and was penalized. Understandably disconcerted, Icher proceeded to four-putt and make a triple bogey. "I spoke to Karine and Sophie after they had driven from the eighth," Randell said. "They had fallen way behind the pair in front and I informed them they were out of position. Karine then took 96 seconds to hit her second shot at the 11th, so I couldn't avoid handing out the penalty as she was 16 seconds over the time permitted."

Icher responded by birdieing the 14th, but Carriedo had not given up and she made a good par at the 15th and then a birdie from a fairway bunker at the 16th. Icher was still one ahead playing the 17th, but her seven iron tee shot came up short in the water.

"I was fighting all the way around and never gave up," said the 30-year-old from Zaragoza. "I was checking the leaderboard all the way around, which is something I don't normally do, but after finishing runner-up nine times, I thought I had better change my approach and it worked. But I feel so sorry for Karine the way she lost out, it's not the best thing to happen in the last round, but I am sure she will learn from the experience."

Icher said, "I know it's the rules. Unfair, no, because it is a rule. I know I'm not the fastest, but when there are a lot of people around and making noise and with the weather, in that situation, yes, I think it is a little unfair. But I will learn from it and now I will try and play faster."

Palmerston Ladies German Open—£100,000
Winner: Karine Icher

Just a week after losing the Compaq Open in unfortunate circumstances when she was penalized a stroke for slow play, Karine Icher achieved her first victory at the Palmerston Ladies German Open at Bad Saarow. The 22-year-old from Chateauroux became the third rookie to win during the season as she beat one of the others, Suzann Pettersen, by one stroke.

"I am so happy now," Icher said. "I tried to play a bit faster this week and it seemed to work. I was so disappointed after last week, but to win so soon after is really nice. After last week, I was trying to regulate the pressure coming down the stretch and just never gave up."

Icher scored rounds of 71, 69 and 70 for a six-under total of 210, while Pettersen closed with 72. Nicola Mount from England finished in third place a stroke further back.

Icher got back into contention by holing from 45 feet for a birdie at the ninth and then drew even with Pettersen with another birdie at the 12th. Pettersen went ahead again when she birdied the 14th, but then Icher hit a six iron to three feet at the par-three 17th to draw even again.

Pettersen found a fairway bunker at the 18th and could only play out sideways as Icher put a seven iron to 12 feet and two-putted for the victory. "Karine is a great player and played better than me today. She deserves to win at last," Pettersen said.

Waterford Crystal Ladies Irish Open—£100,000
Winner: Raquel Carriedo

Once Raquel Carriedo started winning, she could not stop. The 30-year-old Spaniard won the pro-am at the Waterford Crystal Ladies Irish Open, then the tournament itself at Faithlegg, and with it the Order of Merit. It was her third victory of the season, and under the new points system, her No. 1 position was assured.

Carriedo's form was spectacular. She opened with 68 and then added rounds of 66 and 66 for a 16-under-par total of 210. But that was only good enough to defeat Sophie Gustafson by one stroke. The Swede closed with 65, as did Laura Davies, who shared third place with Ana Belen Sanchez.

Carriedo began the final round a shot behind leader Elisabeth Esterl, who would finish fifth, but swept into the lead with a front nine of 31. Gustafson was three behind at the turn but birdied the 13th and eagled the 14th, where she needed no more than a nine iron for her second shot. Carriedo herself birdied both holes, but Gustafson drew even by birdieing the 16th and 17th. She had a 15-footer for another at the 18th, but it just stayed out.

Carriedo drove around the huge oak tree on the 18th hole to leave only a wedge shot to the green, which she hit close enough to only tap in for the victory. "It is great to win again so soon," said Carriedo, who also won the Taiwan and Compaq Opens. "And to win the Order of Merit is a big deal too. I knew it was going to be tough coming down the last couple of holes and I knew I needed to take some risks. I drove it a long way at the last, it must have been the adrenaline, and that left me with a perfect little punched wedge shot, my favorite shot."

Mexx Sport Open—£100,000
Winner: Karine Icher

To cap an extraordinary month for the French rookie Karine Icher, the 22-year-old won the Mexx Sport Open at Kennemer after taking a six-over-par 11 during her final round. Icher lost the Compaq Open after being penalized for slow play, but took her first win in Germany before adding a second victory in three weeks in Holland.

After two rounds of 70, Icher returned a 72 in the final round despite her horror score at the 12th hole and tied at four under par with Suzann Pettersen, who closed with 73. The playoff was decided at the third playing of the 18th, following halves in bogeys and pars, when Icher hit a four iron to 12 feet and made the birdie putt for the victory. Gina Scott from New Zealand, who might have been the beneficiary of Icher's collapse before she dropped strokes over the closing holes, tied for third with Valerie Van Ryckeghem, one shot out of the playoff.

Icher had taken the lead on a wet final day by heading to the turn in 33 and then birdieing the 10th to move two clear of Scott. After a good drive at the par-five 12th, the Frenchwoman hit two balls into bushes, losing both. She then laid up, hit over the green with her seventh shot and took a chip and three putts to get down.

Icher responded admirably, chipping and putting for a birdie at the long 16th hole and hitting a five iron to 10 feet for another at the short 17th. "Being mentally strong is not my best strength," Icher said, "but I learnt a lot from that today. The last time I made such a horrible score was about eight years ago. It was such a stupid mistake and I thought it was all over, but I concentrated very hard and gave myself a chance with those two birdies."

WPGA International Match Play—£400,000
Winner: Laura Davies

The addition of a match play trip was just what Laura Davies needed to inspire the 38-year-old Englishwoman to her first win in Europe for two years. Having already won in the United States earlier in the season, Davies added a transatlantic double by beating Scotland's Janice Moodie 5 and 4 in the final of the WPGA International Match Play over the PGA Centenary course at Gleneagles.

If her win in the final was comprehensive enough, her semi-final against Sophie Gustafson had a sudden and dramatic ending. The match was all-square and heading to the 19th when Gustafson's caddie, Chuck Hoersch, took a toilet break and, when offered a ride back to the first tee, jumped on without thinking.

Since no rules official had authorized the ride, his time-saving trip was against the rules and, although Davies was willing to overlook the misdemeanor, Gustafson was penalized loss of hole and effectively the match. Hoersch said, "I have just lost a great player the chance to win a great tournament. It was far too good a match for me to be the deciding factor. I am so sorry I cost Sophie the chance to win. I knew the rules, but in a bid to catch up with the group on the first tee, I made a mistake."

Gustafson went some way towards making up for her unfortunate exit against Davies by beating fellow Swede Carin Koch 4 and 3 in the playoff for third and fourth place. The final was similarly one-sided, with Davies reaching 4 up after only six holes.

"I didn't make many mistakes out there," said Davies. "Unfortunately, Janice got off to a bad start with some early bogeys, and this was a day when par was your friend. The turning point was the 13th. I made a good 15-footer there and Janice's three-putt at the 14th effectively let me have it. My confidence is back and I feel like I can take on the top guns again. As soon as this event was announced, I was looking forward to it; I love match play. It's a great idea, we need a women's match play event and I hope that it grows so that the best players in the world come over and make it develop."

Moodie, who made eight birdies in her 2-and-1 victory over Koch in the semi-finals, could not reproduce that form on the last afternoon. "I just didn't get anything going," said Moodie. "Laura played too well today and didn't allow me to get away with anything. But the whole week was great and I loved every single minute of it."

Biarritz Ladies Classic—£100,000
Winner: Rachel Kirkwood

Rachel Kirkwood, 26, from Staffordshire, England, arrived at the last official event of the season hoping to retain her Ladies European Tour card, vowing not to go back to the qualifying tournament if she did not, and even thinking about a new career in the police force. All those thoughts could be forgotten once Kirkwood had won a playoff against Marina Arruti to win the Biarritz Ladies Classic.

At the end of her third season on the tour, Kirkwood had rarely managed to finish in the top 10, but her victory gave her an exemption for another three years. Kirkwood scored rounds of 70, 65 and 67 for an eight-under-par total of 202, which Arruti tied with a closing round of 68. Kirkwood won the playoff at the first extra hole by holing from 25 feet for a birdie, with Arruti then missing from 15 feet.

Kirkwood only moved into a share of the lead when she chipped close at the 16th, and then she saved par at the next by holing from six feet. She had an eight-footer for a birdie at the 18th, but it bobbled past the hole. "It has been a shocking season and it was about time I did something," Kirkwood said. "I came here with only one thing on my mind, to get my card for next season."

Sophie Giquel, one of France's leading amateurs, took third place one stroke back after an opening 63 and a closing 67. Parisian Marine Monnet was fourth. Raquel Carriedo of Spain had already secured the Order of Merit title, while the keenly contested Bill Johnson Rookie of the Year Award went to Norway's Suzann Pettersen over Karine Icher and Paula Marti.

Princess Lalla Meriem Cup—US$50,000
Winner: Marine Monnet

Marine Monnet of France shot a final round of 73, even par, and won the Princess Lalla Meriem Cup in Morocco. She had earlier rounds of 75 and 70 for a total of 218, one under par, to edge the three players who shared second place — Johanna Head, Patricia Meunier-Lebouc and Elisabeth Esterl. Head also finished with 73 while Meunier-Lebouc shot 74 and Esterl crashed from the lead with a seven-over-par 80.

Japan LPGA Tour

Daikin Orchid Ladies—¥60,000,000
Winner: Yuri Fudoh

For the first time in Japan LPGA Tour history, the No. 1 performer of the previous season opened the new campaign with a victory in the Daikin Orchid Ladies tournament. Yuri Fudoh did this at Ryukyu Golf Club on Okinawa the first week of March and it was a sign of a season to come for the highly talented 24-year-old, who scored six of her seven career victories in 2000. She repeated as the money champion in 2001.

Fudoh staged a six-stroke rally in the final round, shot 69 and won the Daikin Orchid by three strokes with a three-under-par 213. Defending champion Orie Fujino had seemed well on the way to a repeat. She led four players — Yuko Moriguchi, Nayoko Yoshikawa, Chikayo Yamazaki and Megumi Yamanaka — by a stroke when she shot 68 in Friday's opening round, and extended her lead to three strokes when she added 70 Saturday. Seven women were at 141. Fudoh had rounds of 73 and 71 for 144. Fudoh birdied four holes on the back nine to win going away Sunday as Woo-Soon Ko suffered three consecutive bogeys coming in for 75 and dropped into a three-way tie with Kasumi Fujii and Tomoko Ueda for second place at 216.

Belluna Ladies Cup—¥60,000,000
Winner: Kasumi Fujii

The schedule resumed after a month gap with the new Belluna Ladies Cup and got a new winner as well. Kasumi Fujii, playing in her sixth season, produced back-to-back 67s and ran away with the inaugural title. She posted a seven-under-par 209 and a six-stroke victory at Misato Royale Golf Club in Saitama.

Fujii had begun the tournament with 75 as Rie Mitsuhashi opened with 70 for a two-stroke lead over Yoko Tsuchiya, Kasumi Adachi, Yoko Inoue and Jeanne Koi. Her first 67 moved Fujii into a first-place tie with Miyuki Shimabukuro as Mitsuhashi shot 74 and slipped to third place. The second 67 provided the six-stroke victory over Shimabukuro (73) and Orie Fujino (69) as Mitsuhashi finished fourth with a par round, tied with Emi Hyodoh.

Saishunkan Ladies Hinokuni Open—¥60,000,000
Winner: Kaori Higo

Kaori Higo got on the board early in the season, posting her 13th career victory in the Saishunkan Ladies Hinokuni Open. Higo shot the final round's best score of 69 to take a three-stroke victory at Kumamoto Airport Country Club, Kikuyo, where her winning score of 216 was even par, an unusually high total for tour golf.

Veteran Aki Nakano, the 2000 money runner-up, and Higo were the most prominent of the four players who shared the first-round lead at 71 Friday. Yuri Kawanami and Riko Higashio completed that quartet. Only Nakano remained on top Saturday. The 14-season veteran, seeking her 10th Japan LPGA victory, held on despite a 74 and was still tied for the lead after 36 holes, then with Rena Yamazaki, one of only three players to break par Saturday. Higashio shot 75 to finish just a stroke off the pace with Ae-Sook Kim and Shiho Ohyama, while Higo dropped two behind with 76 for 147 total, coupled at that position with Yuri Fudoh.

Higo had four birdies, including a chip-in at the 11th hole, as she rolled to victory Sunday, three in front of Kim and four ahead of Michiko Hattori. Fudoh shot 75, Nakano and Higashio 76s in their failed bids.

Nasuogawa Ladies—¥50,000,000
Winner: Michie Ohba

The early-season pattern of decisive winners continued in the Nasuogawa Ladies tournament at Nasuogawa Golf Club in Nasu as Michie Ohba clambered to a three-stroke victory with her seven-under-par 209. Victory margins of at least three strokes were posted at each of the first four events on the 2001 Japan LPGA Tour.

Yu-Chen Huang of Taiwan, who scored her only triumph of her five circuit years in 1998, led the tournament for two days. She started with a five-under-par 67, leading Miyuki Shimabukuro and Yuriko Ohtsuka by two strokes. The margin was only one after 36 holes. Huang took a 72 for 139. Ohba and Shimabukuro were at 140, Ohba firing a second 70 and Shimabukuro a 71. Ohba then notched the third victory of her career with a 69 Sunday. Shimabukuro shot 72 to snatch second place from Kasumi Adachi (70–213), as Huang faded to sixth place as she skied to 79.

Katokichi Queens—¥50,000,000
Winner: Chieko Amanuma

A new star was born at the Katokichi Queens tournament as Chieko Amanuma staged a dazzling finish and scored her first victory at Yashima Country Club at Mure, Kagawa Prefecture. It was a sign of things to come in 2001 as Amanuma went on to score four other victories and finish third on the season's money list.

The Katokichi victory came out of the blue. Amanuma was not in contention the first two days. Michie Ohba, riding the momentum of her Nasuogawa win the previous week, shot 69 in the opening round at Yashima and joined Korea's Shin Sora and Rie Murata at the top. Amanuma had a 71, then fell four shots off the pace despite a 70 as tour rookie Hiroko Yamaguchi produced a fiery 65 and jumped past 10 players into the second-round lead with 137. Yamaguchi shot a flawless, seven-birdie round, her best since qualifying for the 2001 tour the previous August after two previous unsuccessful tries. Kasumi Fujii, with 70 and 68, moved into second place, a stroke ahead of Yuri Fudoh and Mineko Nasu.

Amanuma did all of her scoring early Sunday. She rang up her five birdies on the first 11 holes en route to the 67 and 208 total. The established Junko Yasui climbed into second place with 70 and 210 and rookie nerves got to Yamaguchi, who took a 74 for 211.

Nichirei Cup World Ladies—¥60,000,000
Winner: Karrie Webb

While her main rival as the best player in women's golf was scoring her fifth victory of the season halfway around the world, Karrie Webb began the catch-up process in a visit to Japan, where she successfully defended her Nichirei Cup World Ladies title in Tokyo. Webb pulled away in the final round from Sweden's Carin Koch, the field's only other international visitor, to post a solid, six-stroke victory at Yomiuri Country Club in the season's first 72-hole event.

Kasumi Fujii, who had gotten her first victory a month earlier in the Belluna Cup, stood in Webb's way the first day. Fujii shot 67 for a two-stroke lead over Toshimi Kimura. Webb was another stroke back in third place. A solid, four-birdie 68 vaulted the Australian star two shots into the lead Friday. Fujii dropped into a three-way tie for sixth place at 141 as Koch, Chieko Amanuma, Takayo Bandoh and Aki Takamura matched 140s to tie for second.

Webb and Koch set up a two-way battle for the title Saturday. Koch, a contender but not yet a winner in America, established the challenge when she birdied three of her first five holes and shot 67 for 207, catching up to Webb, who had 69. The overseas pair left Amanuma and Takamura five strokes behind them in third place. Koch had a brief moment of glory Sunday, going two strokes ahead when Webb bogeyed the first hole and she birdied the second, but it was all Webb after that. She regained the lead with three consecutive birdies, starting at the fourth hole, and Koch's game unraveled on the back nine, allowing Webb the luxury of a double bogey coming in with her 71 and 278 total. Koch dropped into a tie for second with Fujii (71) and Amanuma (72) when she double-bogeyed the 18th hole for 77 and 284.

Vernal Ladies—¥100,000,000
Winner: Ikuyo Shiotani

Ikuyo Shiotani proved there was life in her aging golf game at the Vernal Ladies tournament. The 38-year-old Shiotani, the dominant figure on the Japan LPGA Tour in the early and mid-1990s, scored her first victory in four years in the Vernal Ladies at Fukuoka Century Golf Club, defeating Mineko Nasu on the second hole of a playoff. It was the 18th career victory for the Nagoya native, who was the leading money winner in 1992 and 1995.

Shiotani hovered just off the lead the first two days. Another veteran, Chihiro Nakajima, was in front after the first round. She shot 71, the only sub-par score of the day, leading defending champion Yuri Fudoh, Michiko Hattori and Nahoko Hirao by a stroke. Shiotani was bunched with three others at 73. She repeated the 73 Saturday, joining Fudoh, Mei-Chi Cheng, Mari Nishi and Kumiko Hiyoshi at 146, a stroke behind Nasu, who inched into the lead with scores of 73 and 72.

With three birdies and a bogey, Shiotani shot 70 Sunday to deadlock with Nasu (71) at par 216 and bring about the playoff, the first of the year on the tour. Par won for Shiotani on the second extra hole when Nasu took a double bogey. Most of the other contenders faded, Fudoh to 75. Ji-Hee Lee of South Korea, with 68, the day's best round, Fuki Kido and Cheng tied for third at 218.

Chukyo TV Bridgestone Ladies Open—¥50,000,000
Winner: Michie Ohba

Michie Ohba became the Japan LPGA Tour's first multiple winner of 2001 when she won the Chukyo TV Bridgestone Ladies Open in mid-May. The victory at Chukyo Golf Club in Aichi came a month after Ohba landed the Nasuogawa Ladies by the same three-stroke margin and was her fourth career triumph. Ohba staged a brilliant finish to win at Chukyo. Trailing two of the tour's finest players, Yuri Fudoh and Fuki Kido, by two strokes after 36 holes, Ohba fired a five-under-par 67 Sunday to nail the victory with her nine-under-par 209.

Kido shared the first-round lead with Aki Takamura, Kinue Matsubara and Hiroko Tanaka at 68, then shared the top with Fudoh after Saturday's round. Fudoh shot 68 and Kido 70 for their front-running 138s. Ohba, who had opened with 72, matched Fudoh's 68 Saturday and took over third place at 140. A blazing front nine secured the victory for Ohba. She had five of her seven birdies going out to take charge as Fudoh was on her way to 73 and Kido to 74. Veteran Korean Ok-Hee Ku equaled Ohba's final-round 67 and snatched second place at 210.

Kosaido Ladies Golf Cup—¥60,000,000
Winner: Aki Takamura

Aki Takamura, the reigning Japan LPGA champion, picked up her first 2001 title when she prevailed in a playoff in the Kosaido Ladies Golf Cup. Takamura, who has two Japan LPGA championships among her now-nine victories on the tour, caught fire late in the final round to tie Ae-Sook Kim of South Korea, then defeat her on the first extra hole.

Kumiko Hiyoshi, a 20-season veteran, made an early bid for her sixth title, opening with a three-under-par 69. Michie Ohba, coming off her Chukyo victory, Kaori Harada and the defending champion, Taiwan's Hsiu-Feng Tseng, trailed by one. Hiyoshi plummeted out of contention Saturday with 77 and first place went to another Taiwanese pro, Yu-Chen Huang, and Chihiro Nakajima, who had matching 71-69s for their 140s. Takamura, who had begun with 72, shot 70 Saturday and moved into a runner-up tie with Tseng.

Takamura wasn't doing much Sunday, running at one over par for the day, but got moving in the stretch. She birdied three of the last five holes, including a three-footer on the 18th green, for 70 and 212 total. With 68, the day's best round, Kim posted the same total, but lost her bid when Takamura sank a 12-foot birdie putt on the same green on the first playoff hole.

Resort Trust Ladies—¥50,000,000
Winner: Aki Takamura

Aki Takamura did it the easier way when she racked up her second consecutive victory at the Resort Trust Ladies tournament. Resting just off the lead, as she had been the previous week when she had to go to a playoff to win the Kosaido Ladies, the 29-year-old Takamura vanquished all of the other contenders Sunday with a five-under-par 67 that carried her to a three-stroke victory. She had a 209 total in recording her 10th career victory.

Fuki Kido, stuck at five victories since winning the PGA Championship in 1999, staked herself to a two-stroke lead over Chihiro Nakajima and Mayumi Murai with a 67 in Friday's opening round. Takamura was among the 71-shooters that day. And the next. Nakajima also shot 71 Saturday and moved up into a first-place tie with Michie Ohba, the year's only double winner.

On Sunday, Takamura birdied the first and 18th holes at Grandee Naruto

Golf Club, and three in between, for the 67 that brought the repeat triumph. Ohba fell off to 75 and dropped into a three-way tie for fourth place, while Nakajima settled for a par round and 212 total, more than enough to give her second place alone. Kaori Higo (71-72-71–214) took third.

We Love Kobe Suntory Ladies Open—¥50,000,000
Winner: Michiko Hattori

Michiko Hattori resurrected some success from her past and won her first tournament in two years, a two-stroke victory in the We Love Kobe Suntory Ladies Open. Hattori, acclaimed in Japanese golf circles since winning the 1985 U.S. Amateur championship at age 16, led through the final three rounds of the season's second 72-hole tournament and posted a nine-under-par 279. It was her 14th tour title and first since the 1999 Fujitsu Open.

Hattori had to play second fiddle only to second-year-pro Namika Omata in the first round. Omata had seven birdies and shot 67 Thursday, while Hattori, Kasumi Adachi, Kayo Yamada and Hikaru Kobayashi shared second place at 69. From there on, it was Hattori's game. The tour's leading money winner in 1998 roared to a five-stroke lead with a near-perfect 66 at Japan Memorial Golf Club, Yokawa, Friday. In the runner-up position at 140 were Junko Omote, Kayo Yamada, Hikaru Kobayashi and Omata, who shot 75 Friday.

Hattori lost control of her game Saturday and barely hung onto her lead. She took a two-over-par 74 for 209 total, absorbing two double bogeys and a pair of bogeys to go with four birdies. Yamada, winless in eight years on the tour, had second place to herself at 210 after a 70, and Omote was the only other player in sight at 212. Hattori gave up the lead early in Sunday's final round, but finished with four back-nine birdies to beat Yamada by two. Kaori Harada was a distant third at 285.

Apita Circle K Sankus Ladies—¥50,000,000
Winner: Midori Yoneyama

Three seasons, three victories. Midori Yoneyama, the 24-year-old who was the Japan LPGA Tour's Rookie of the Year in 1999, achieved that with her resounding victory in the Apita Circle K Sankus Ladies tournament in mid-June. Even without a particularly low round, Yoneyama left the rest of the field nine strokes behind when the dust settled at U Green Nakatsugawa Golf Club.

Kyoko Ono, who won the 2000 Yonex Open, was the first-round leader. With 68, she led Akane Ohshiro by one and a strong array at 70 — dual winners Aki Takamura and Michie Ohba, Kaori Harada and Yoneyama. Yoneyama rambled four strokes into the lead in Saturday's second round. She fired a five-under-par 67 for 137 total. Takamura and Harada had 71s for 141, one better than Ono after she struggled to 74.

After an early bogey Sunday, Yoneyama ran off five birdies for 68 and 205. Interestingly, Yoneyama had missed the cut in her previous six starts. She noted after securing the victory, "My golf has gone through the ceiling from as low as it could go to this." Also-ran was a fitting tag for the runners-up at 214 — Harada and Takamura with 73s, Ono with 72, Yu-Chen Huang with 70 and Mayumi Murai with 67, the day's best round.

Friskies Osaka Ladies Open—¥50,000,000
Winner: Midori Yoneyama

For the second time in a month, the Japan LPGA Tour had back-to-back winners when Midori Yoneyama hung on for a one-stroke victory in the Friskies Osaka Ladies Open a week after demolishing the field in the Apita Circle K. Aki Takamura won two in a row at the start of the month.

Dreary weather hung over Hanna Country Club, Daito, the entire week-end, but there was nothing dismal about the opening round of Mayumi Murai, the 1999 Japan Women's Open champion. The eight-time winner shot 67 and took a two-stroke lead over Yoneyama, three over three others, including Kaori Harada, again in contention. But Murai did not fare well on the drizzly Saturday, slumping to 75 and giving way at the top to Yoneyama, whose shaky 71 — five birdies, four bogeys — gave her a one-stroke lead over Harada (71) and Taiwan's Yu-Chen Huang.

Rain and fog plagued the Sunday round, forcing delays of more than two hours, but Yoneyama eventually rolled in a five-foot birdie putt on the 18th green for 71 and 211 total to subvert the late challenge of Kayo Yamada, already finished with 68 and 212. It was Yamada's second runner-up finish in three tournaments. Chihiro Nakajima, with 68, and international veteran Ayako Okamoto, with 69, tied for third at 213.

Toyo Suisan Ladies Hokkaido—¥50,000,000
Winner: Chieko Amanuma

Chieko Amanuma lived up to the promise she had been showing earlier in the 2001 season when she captured her second victory of the year in the Toyo Suisan Ladies Hokkaido. Although contending that she "really struggled in the final round," Amanuma finished a decisive four strokes ahead of veteran Toshimi Kimura at Kitahiroshima Prince Golf Club with her five-under-par 211.

High winds wreaked havoc on scoring in the opening round. Ae-Sook Kim, the South Korean who won the 1998 Daikin Orchid, was the only player to break par. Her 71 edged Amanuma and Akane Ohshiro for posses-sion of the lead by a stroke. Then, on Saturday, Amanuma established what proved to be her eventual victory margin. With 68 for 140 total, she spurted four strokes ahead of Kaori Harada, Toshimi Kimura and Ohshiro. Disaster struck Kim, who took her first of two 79s.

Kimura mounted the only challenge to Amanuma Sunday. A birdie at the 15th hole against a bogey by the leader appeared dangerous at the time, but Kimura could not make anything happen the rest of the way and had to settle for the runner-up spot. The next players, Woo-Soon Ko and Aki Takamura, were three strokes further back.

Taiheiyo Club Ladies Leben Cup—¥50,000,000
Winner: Kaori Higo

Kaori Higo became the Japan LPGA Tour's fifth double winner of the season when she picked off the Taiheiyo Club Ladies Leben Cup title and slipped into the widely contested No. 1 spot on the money list. Less than $5 million separated the top four players. Higo, who had won the Saishunkan Ladies early in the year, birdied the final hole to post a one-stroke victory in the Leben Cup event at the Taiheiyo Associates Sherwood course, the 14th career victory for the 32-year-old.

Higo had to overcome the strong early effort of Ok-Hee Ku, the long-time South Korean star, who started the tournament with a sizzling, eight-under-par 64 and a two-stroke lead over Michiko Hattori. Higo opened with 70, then made up a lot of ground Saturday with a 65. Ku shot 69 Saturday to retain her two-stroke lead, then over Higo, as Hattori took a 75.

Ku couldn't maintain her pace Sunday, dropping out of contention with a 75. Hattori bounced back with 64 and tied with Mikiyo Nishizuka (68) at 205. A playoff seemed likely until Higo rolled in her six-foot birdie putt at the 72nd hole to snatch the victory.

Golf 5 Ladies—¥50,000,000
Winner: Hsiao-Chuan Lu

Talk about getting your pro career off to a great start. Playing in just her third tournament on the Japan LPGA Tour, Taiwanese rookie Hsiao-Chuan Lu acquired her first victory, winning a playoff against Michie Ohba, who already had won twice in 2001. Lu was just the second non-Japanese winner of the season, the other being Karrie Webb in the Nichirei Cup in May.

The playoff and Lu's victory came about as a consequence of the collapse of South Korean Ae-Sook Kim, the second time in three weeks that she experienced a disastrous finish after leading early. In the Toyo Suisan, Kim followed an opening and leading 71 with a pair of 79s. In the Golf 5 event, she shot 67 in the opening round and led by one over tour rookie Yuka Arita at Mizunami Country Club, Gifu Prefecture, then added a par 72 Saturday for 139 and a three-stroke margin over Lu and Fuki Kido. Ohba shared the 143 spot with Mineko Nasu and Eika Ohtake.

Up came another 79 on Kim's card Sunday. A 73 by Lu and a 72 by Ohba forged the 215 tie and the young Taiwanese player won the title with a birdie on the second extra hole.

Vernal Open—¥80,000,000
Winner: Yuri Fudoh

The month of August "belonged" to two players and, after its four tournaments, Yuri Fudoh and Chieko Amanuma had turned the race for the No. 1 position on the money list into a two-woman duel. It began with the Vernal Open at the Privilege Golf Club at Narita, where Fudoh, the reigning champion, scored her second victory of 2001.

A second-round 66 set up Fudoh's win after Yuriko Ohtsuka had opened the tournament with the same score and led Natsuko Noro and Momoyo Kawakubo by a shot. Fudoh was two back with three others. Fudoh's 66 Saturday propelled her into a four-stroke advantage over Noro (71) and five over Hisako Ohgane.

Fudoh was not sharp Sunday, but her lackluster 73 — three birdies, two bogeys and a double bogey — was more than enough to secure the triumph. It gave her a 207 total and a three-stroke margin over Ohgane (71). Toshimi Kimura and Ikuyo Shiotani tied for third at 212. The win fattened Fudoh's victory total to nine in her six seasons.

NEC Karuizawa 72—¥60,000,000
Winner: Chieko Amanuma

It was Chieko Amanuma's turn at the NEC Karuizawa 72. Her decisive round was the third as she became the first player on the 2001 Japan LPGA Tour to put three victories into the books. Amanuma came from four shots off the pace to nail a one-stroke victory with her nine-under-par 207.

Yuri Fudoh carried a hot hand into the tournament and shared the first-round lead with little-known Megumi Higuchi at 67. Fourteen others players broke 70 on the North course of the NEC Karuizawa 72 Club. That included Amanuma at 69. Kaori Higo birdied three of the last four holes as she shot a course-record 65 Saturday and raced to the top of the leaderboard with 136, a stroke ahead of Taiwan rookie winner Hsiao-Chuan Lu. Amanuma managed just a 71 and settled into the 140 slot, four back.

Higo, a two-time winner earlier in the season, fell apart Sunday, soaring to a 79, unexpectedly leaving the door open to the others. Amanuma took the greatest advantage. She birdied two of the first four holes, then took over first place when she posted three more birdies in a four-hole stretch beginning at No. 12 following a bogey at No. 8. Amanuma finished with 67, nipping Junko Yasui by a stroke. Lu shot 73 for 210 total.

Shin Caterpillar Mitsubishi Ladies—¥60,000,000
Winner: Chieko Amanuma

Chieko Amanuma extended her hot streak in the Shin Caterpillar Mitsubishi Ladies tournament, shaking off a slow start to slip in with a one-stroke victory, her second in a row and fourth of the season. It strengthened her hold on the money list lead as well.

Amanuma shot 71 in the opening round at Daihakone Country Club at Hakone, Kanagawa Prefecture, but trailed by four strokes as Ok-Hee Ku, the South Korean standout, put up a 67, one better than the score posted by Junko Yasui, the defending champion. Amanuma made her move Saturday, producing a 69 to join Ku (73) and Masaki Maeda (71-69) in first place at 140. Seven others were within three strokes going into the final round.

Scoring was high Sunday and Amanuma's par 72 — three birdies, three bogeys — was enough to give her the one-shot win over Maeda. Ku had a 76 and dropped into a tie for fifth behind Kaori Harada and Ai-Yu Tu at 215.

Yonex Ladies Open—¥60,000,000
Winner: Yuri Fudoh

Back came Yuri Fudoh in the Yonex Ladies Open. Once again the No. 1 position on the money list changed hands as Fudoh essayed a strong finish to win her third tournament of the season and inch ahead of Chieko Amanuma, who curiously took the week off rather than go for three in a row.

Another Chieko — veteran Chieko Nishida — came up with a record performance in the opening round. A winner only once in the last eight seasons, Nishida equaled the lowest round ever at Yonex Country Club, Teradomari, with a 64 and spurted to a four-stroke lead. Nishida went from hot to cold Saturday, shooting herself out of contention with 77 as another longtime tour player, Miyuki Shimabukuro, showed the first signs of a late-season surge. She ran off six of her seven birdies in succession in shooting 65 for 136 total, but had Fudoh right at her heels. Fudoh had a 68 for 137.

As happened to Nishida, Shimabukuro faltered the next day and Fudoh finished strongly with a bogey-free 67 for 204, 12 under par. Fudoh needed that score to edge Taiwan's Hsiu-Feng Tseng, who matched the 67 for 205. Nobody else was within six strokes as Fudoh entered the 10th victory on her record.

Fujisankei Ladies Classic—¥60,000,000
Winner: Miyuki Shimabukuro

For the first time in a month, neither Yuri Fudoh nor Chieko Amanuma were factors in a tournament, and despite the presence of two of the game's top international stars at the Fujisankei Ladies Classic, Miyuki Shimabukuro was. The 17-year-old veteran mustered a huge rally in the final round at Fujizakura Country Club, Kawaguchiko, to gain her fourth career victory.

While Shimabukuro was biding her time early on, Harumi Sakagami got off to a strong start. Sakagami, idled much of the season with a thigh injury, shot 68 in her quest for her first victory since 1998 and led by a stroke over Kayo Yamada, Shin Sora, Yoko Tsuchiya, Yukiko Koyama and Ai Ogawa. Britain's great Laura Davies made her presence felt Saturday. Four off the pace starting the round, Davies carved out a seven-birdie, four-under-par 67 and rose to a one-stroke lead at 139, a shot ahead of Sakagami (72) and Tsuchiya (71).

With rounds of 73 and 71, Shimabukuro lagged five strokes behind Davies after 36 holes. With players self-destructing around her amid strong, blustery winds, Shimabukuro put together a one-under-par 70 — three birdies and a double bogey — for a one-over-par 214 and a one-stroke victory over Ji-Hee Lee of South Korea (74) and Sakagami, who suffered two double bogeys amid a 75. Davies muddled through a 78 and dropped into an eight-player deadlock for fifth place that also included America's Dottie Pepper, who never fully recovered from an opening-round 74.

Japan LPGA Championship Konica Cup—¥70,000,000
Winner: Kumiko Hiyoshi

Chalk up a big one for the veterans. Seven years after she won the Japan LPGA Championship Konica Cup, Kumiko Hiyoshi landed that prized title again in her 19th season on the Japan LPGA Tour. The 37-year-old had won just once between those major victories and only five times before the 2001 triumph at the Rope Club at Shoiya.

Although Hiyoshi led going into the final round and made it hold up, it wasn't easy. The field trailed Yoko Inoue for two days. Inoue, winless for two years, had a five-under-par 67 Thursday and led by two, then shook off a poor start Friday to post a 69 and retain a one-stroke margin, then over Hiyoshi, who shot 67. Close behind were Yuri Fudoh and Kaori Higo at 140 and, with three others, Akiko Fukushima, the U.S. tour regular, at 141.

Hiyoshi moved in front Saturday, but not by as big as margin as it could have been. With four birdies, she had built a five-stroke lead through 14 holes, but she three-putted the 15th and dropped three more strokes before the end of the round. She had to settle for 72 for 209 total and a one-stroke edge on Toshimi Kimura and Fukushima. Inoue shot 75 for 211 and Fudoh remained in contention with a 72 and 212. In Sunday's finale, Hiyoshi lost, then regained, the lead, finishing with 73 for 282. Kimura and Fukushima closed the day as they started it, one stroke behind after shooting 73s.

Munsingwear Ladies Tokai Classic—¥60,000,000
Winner: Fuki Kido

Another veteran of the Japan LPGA Tour was heard from at the Munsingwear Ladies Tokai Classic as 17-season professional Fuki Kido parlayed a course-record-tying round into a two-stroke victory in the mid-September event at Ryosen Golf Club, Inabe. It was her sixth career victory and first since she won the Japan PGA Championship in 1999.

Kido's coup de grace was her second-round 65 — an eagle, seven birdies and two bogeys — that matched the all-time low at Ryosen and brought her from three strokes off the pace into a three-stroke lead at 134, 10 under par. She replaced Michie Ohba at the top. The two-time 2001 winner had opened with 66, a shot in front of Shoko Asano and two ahead of four others including Yuri Fudoh and Miyuki Shimabukuro. Ohba shot 71 Saturday and slipped back into the runner-up slot, a stroke in front of Fudoh, Kaori Harada and Mihoko Takahashi.

A 71 provided Kido with the victory Sunday. She closed with a 205 total, two strokes ahead of Fudoh (69), Harada (69) and Kasumi Fujii (67). The runner-up money enabled Fudoh to fattened her lead in the money race as her chief rival, Chieko Amanuma, finished well down in the standings.

Miyagi TV Cup Dunlop Ladies Open—¥60,000,000
Winner: Toshimi Kimura

Toshimi Kimura, the best performing player among the non-winners of the season, shed that distinction when she seized victory in the Miyagi TV Cup Dunlop Ladies Open at Rainbow Hills Golf Club at Tomiya. For Kimura, whose achievements earlier in the year included runner-up finishes in the Japan LPGA Championship and the Toyo Suisan tournament, it was her seventh victory on the Japan LPGA Tour and first in two years, virtually insuring her a top-10 finish on the money list.

Kimura's pleasure contrasted with the disappointment of Kayo Segawa, a relative unknown who had carried the tournament lead into the final round after posting scores of 70 and 71 to stand a stroke ahead of Kimura and South Korea's Oh-Soon Lee after 36 holes. Lee, a non-winner in Japan, had been the first-round leader at 68 with Kimura at 69 and Segawa and two others at 70.

"It sure made for an interesting finish," said Kimura Sunday after she had made her fourth birdie on the final green for 71 to nip Segawa by a stroke. Her final score was 213, three under par at Rainbow Hills. Segawa had 73 for 214 total, and three players, Ok-Hee Ku, Kaori Harada and Orie Fujino, finished at 215.

Japan Women's Open—¥70,000,000
Winner: Miyuki Shimabukuro

The Japan Women's Open is automatically expected to be the toughest test of the season for the women professionals, but the 2001 examination proved to be more than that; in fact, it was a battle of survival. Miyuki Shimabukuro was that survivor, struggling in after 72 holes with the highest winning score — 302 — in the 34-year history of the championship and of any event that has been played since the formal tour was established in 1988. The usual tight fairways, heavy rough and slick greens were punctuated by heavy coastal winds that swept Hokkaido's Muroran Golf Club throughout the tournament.

It may be hard to believe, but the 41-year-old Okinawa native carried a three-stroke lead into the final round, lost five strokes to par over the final six holes, wound up with a 79 and still won the championship by four shots. Perhaps there was a premonition about it all when Shimabukuro made a hole-in-one on the sixth hole of the second round, still shot 75, but took over the lead by four strokes with 146. "I was lucky," she said. "I hope it lasts."

It certainly did. On Saturday, Shimabukuro got within a stroke of par before the winds took their toll and she finished with a 77 for 223 total on a day when more than 40 players in the reduced field shot in the 80s. Ayako Okamoto, the much-traveled international star, was the only person still within range of Shimabukuro at 226. Taiwan's Yu-Chen Huang and teenage whiz Ai Miyazato were next in line, but at 230.

Then came the astonishing finish — the stumbling final holes, the 79 and the four-stroke victory, Shimabukuro's second in five weeks and fifth of her long career. Okamoto shot 80, yet finished second, two strokes ahead of Huang, who also had an 80 during the week. Perhaps typical of the unique week, Aki Takamura, who led the championship after the first round with 70, the lowest score of the week, followed with 81-82-80.

Sankyo Ladies Open—¥60,000,000
Winner: Hiroko Yamaguchi

Hiroko Yamaguchi didn't let it happen to her twice. Earlier in her rookie season, Yamaguchi carried the tournament lead into the final round and couldn't convert it into a victory. When she put herself in front again after 36 holes of the Sankyo Ladies Open in early October, she stayed there throughout the Sunday round and etched her first title into the Japan LPGA Tour record books, winning by a stroke with her nine-under-par 207. She was the second rookie winner of the season, joining Hsiao-Chuan Lu (Golf 5), and the fourth first-time champion of 2001.

At first, it looked as though the Sankyo Open was going to be another victory stepping stone for Yuri Fudoh on her way to the seasonal championship as she opened the tournament at Akagi Country Club at Niisato, Gunma Prefecture, with a seven-under-par 65. But it wasn't her week. Instead, Yamaguchi, who shared second place behind Fudoh with Ok-Hee Ku, took over Saturday with 69 for 136 and a two-stroke lead over Taiwan's Ai-Yu Tu and three over Fudoh, Aki Takamura, Kaori Higo and Kayo Yamada. Yamaguchi's challengers Sunday were Takamura (69) and Toshimi Kimura (67), who tied for second at 208. Higo finished alone at 209.

Fujitsu Ladies—¥60,000,000
Winner: Yuri Fudoh

Talk about icing on the cake. Yuri Fudoh applied the topping at the Fujitsu Ladies tournament in mid-October. With her one-stroke victory at Fujitsu's Tokyu 700 Club in Chiba, Fudoh padded her lead in the money race to nearly ¥20 million, virtually clinching her second straight No. 1 title. It was her fourth victory of 2001 and 10th in the 2000s.

Three solid, unspectacular rounds accounted for the victory. Fudoh shot 68 in Friday's first round, sitting two strokes off the pace set by Akiko Fukushima, who was back in Japan from her annual sojourn to the U.S. LPGA Tour. Eight players had 67s, among them Michie Ohba and Orie Fujino, who reproduced them Saturday for 134s and a one-stroke lead over Fudoh (67), Fukushima (70) and Misayo Fujisawa. Fudoh returned a 68 Sunday for 203 total to squeeze out the victory over Ohba, the two-time 2001 winner, who closed with 70 for 204. Fukushima, Fujino and Mihoko Takahashi tied for third at 205.

Chako Higuchi Kibun Ladies Classic—¥60,000,000
Winner: Chieko Amanuma

Relatively silent as a contender since scoring her fourth victory of the season in August, Chieko Amanuma returned to the winner's circle at the Chako

Higuchi Kibun Ladies Classic and kept alive her chances of overtaking Yuri Fudoh in the race for the No. 1 spot on the money list. The only player with the opportunity to catch Fudoh, Amanuma cut her deficit in half with the ¥10.8 million first-place check.

Rookie Hiroko Yamaguchi, just two weeks beyond her initial victory in the Sankyo Open, had visions of another when she opened the Kibun Classic in first place with Yuri Kawanami. But Amanuma had other ideas. She came up with a three-under-par 69 at Caledonian Golf Club, Chiba, and went in front to stay at 139, a stroke ahead of Nahoko Hirao and Women's Open champion Miyuki Shimabukuro.

It wasn't totally smooth sailing for Amanuma on Sunday, though. In fact, she sank a ball in the water and took a triple-bogey six at the sixth hole, but rebounded with four birdies between the ninth and 15th holes to shoot a one-under 71 for 210 and a two-stroke victory over Shimabukuro (72) and Kaori Harada, who shot 69 after taking bogeys at the last two holes.

Cisco World Ladies Match Play—¥100,800,000
Winner: Annika Sorenstam

Both of the great players in women's golf left an imprint from their splendid 2001 seasons in Japan. Karrie Webb did it early in the season when she won the Nichirei Cup World event. Sorenstam did it twice in the autumn, first in the Cisco World Ladies Match Play, an event that brought together 16 leading players from the U.S. and Japan LPGA Tours at Sosei Country Club in Narita. Sorenstam claimed the title with a 1-up victory in a classic final match against Se Ri Pak, probably the No. 3 player in the world. Webb did not play.

The opening round paired host Japan tour's top 16 players against the 16 visitors from the American circuit, and when the action ended only Aki Takamura, Kaori Higo and Yu-Chen Huang carried the Japan Tour banner to the second round. Lorie Kane ousted Higo in the second round and Huang defeated Takamura in the quarter-finals, 1 up. The other quarter-finals winners were: Sorenstam over Mhairi McKay, 3 and 1; Kane over Emilee Klein, 4 and 3, and Pak over Rachel Teske, 3 and 2.

The attractive finale set up when Sorenstam ousted Kane, 4 and 2, and Pak eliminated Huang, 6 and 4. In the title match, the South Korean star spurted to a four-hole lead over the first six holes, only to have the brilliant Swede bounce back by winning four consecutive holes starting at the eighth, where Pak bogeyed. Sorenstam birdied the next three holes, went 1 up at the 15th, where Pak missed a three-foot par putt, and maintained that edge to the final green. The victory, Sorenstam's seventh of the season and 30th of her nine-year career, earned a check of ¥15,120,000.

Mizuno Classic—¥118,800,000
Winner: Annika Sorenstam

Annika Sorenstam completed the second half of her Japanese double with an easy, three-stroke victory in the Mizuno Classic. The early November win on the heels of her Cisco World Ladies Match Play victory brought her season to a wonderful climax. Since both events are official tournaments on both the U.S. and Japan LPGA Tours, Sorenstam's winning prize money total for the season was certain to top the $2 million mark.

With a heavy complement of women from the American circuit, including all of the players who came to Japan for the Match Play, competing with the Japanese regulars in the Mizuno Classic, Sorenstam had no easy pickings ahead when they teed it up at the Musashigaoka Golf Course in Saitama Prefecture. That makes her wire-to-wire victory performance — eighth of the year, 31st of her career — all the more impressive.

She was off and running Friday with a six-under-par 66 that placed her in a first-place tie for the lead with Colombia's Marisa Baena, a stroke in front of Akiko Fukushima, Kayo Yamada and Woo-Soon Ko, two ahead of Yuri Fudoh and France's Patricia Meunier-Lebouc. Sorenstam ripped off an eagle deuce — four wood from a fairway bunker — and three birdies for 67 on a rainy Saturday, moving two strokes in front of England's Laura Davies, who fired a seven-birdie 65 for 135 total. Fudoh, out to enhance her big money race margin, climbed into third place with 68 for 136.

Sorenstam put the title away with a conservative 70 on a windy Sunday afternoon. She carded four birdies and two bogeys over the final 18 holes for her 13-under-par total of 203. Davies shot 71 to hold onto second place at 206, two ahead of Ko and Aki Takamura as Fudoh slumped to 77 for 213 total.

Itoen Ladies—¥60,000,000
Winner: Laura Davies

The Japanese players were happy to have their tour pretty much to themselves for the Itoen Ladies tournament with the departure of virtually all of the overseas visitors who had dominated the previous two tournaments. They probably wished that Laura Davies had caught a plane, too. But, Davies' record in the Itoen Ladies was too good for her not to stick around, particularly after her runner-up finish in the preceding Mizuno Classic. Three of Davies' six previous victories in Japan had come in the Itoen — and she made it four by rolling to a three-stroke victory at the par-72 Great Island Club in Chonan.

Michie Ohba, seeking her third victory of 2001, started fast with 68 and a one-stroke lead over Davies, Hsiu-Feng Tseng and Ayako Okamoto. Ohba's game went south Saturday. A 77 took her out of contention, and Davies claimed the top spot with a four-under-par 68 for 137, two strokes ahead of South Korea's Woo-Soon Ko. Davies eagled the par-five fifth hole, reaching it in two with a five iron. She wrapped up the victory with a 70 for 207 Sunday without facing any serious challenge. Ko faded with 73 into a four-way tie for third at 212 as Junko Yasui jumped into second place with 67 for 210 total.

Daioseishi Elleair Ladies Open—¥100,000,000
Winner: Ji-Hee Lee

It was a good year for rookies on the Japan LPGA Tour. Ji-Hee Lee, a steady but little-noticed first-year player from South Korea, joined Taiwan's Hsiao-Chuan Lu and Japan's Hiroko Yamaguchi as rookie winners when she captured the Daioseishi Elleair Ladies Open in mid-November at Elleair Golf Club at Matsuyama. Lee, who missed only one cut in her 21 starts of the 2001 season, came from a stroke off the pace and won by that margin with her eight-under-par 208.

Keiko Arai, whose lone tour victory in 10 seasons came in 1995, initiated a bid for her second by taking the first-round lead in the Elleair Open with a four-under-par 68. She remained on top, but in a share of first place with another 10-year veteran, Shin Sora of South Korea, after 36 holes. Sora had rounds of 69 and 70, and Arai added a 71 for her 139. Lee was deadlocked with Yamaguchi and Ai Miyazato at 140.

From that position, Lee took the victory with a four-birdie 68 and 208 total, edging Mineko Nasu (67) by a stroke and Sora (71) by two. They finished ahead of three of the circuit's best — Kaori Higo at 211 and Yuri Fudoh and Akiko Fukushima at 212. Lee was the fifth first-time winner of the season.

Japan LPGA Tour Championship—¥60,000,000
Winner: Kaori Higo

The top 21 performers of the 2001 Japan LPGA Tour season assembled at Sadowara for the Tour Championship, the third and final major tournament on the circuit, and veteran Kaori Higo took the honors with her third victory of the season and 15th of her 13-year career. The ¥15 million prize carried her into second place on the final money list, nearly ¥20 million behind the repeating No. 1 player, Yuri Fudoh, whose third-place finish in the Tour Championship at Hibiscus Golf Club gave her a final total of ¥89,248,793. Chieko Amanuma, who began the tournament with a remote chance of overtaking Fudoh with a victory, was never a factor and finished next-to-last in the field, yielding the No. 2 money list position to Higo.

Higo played solidly all four days and was never out of first place. For two days she shared the lead with Michiko Hattori, the Suntory winner in June, as each of them posted rounds of 67 and 71. Four players — Ikuyo Shiotani, Kasumi Fujii, Aki Takamura and Mineko Nasu — were grouped at 139. Higo shed Hattori and the other close pursuers Saturday when she fired a six-under-par 66 and jumped to a four-stroke lead over Fujii and Shiotani at 210. Hattori took a 72 and dropped to fourth place at 212.

Higo slipped a bit in the early going Sunday, yielding her lead as Shiotani mounted a minor charge, but salted away the victory when she made the turn and birdied the next three holes. She wound up shooting 71 for 276, four better than Shiotani (70), who enjoyed her best season in many years, placing 12th on the money list. Fudoh punctuated her championship season with the day's best round of 65 in jumping up into third place.

South African Ladies Tour

Nedbank MasterCard Classic—R100,000
Winner: Mandy Adamson

Mandy Adamson won for the sixth time as the South African Ladies Tour opened at the Nedbank MasterCard Classic. The 28-year-old from Benoni had been second in the same event the previous year, but this time won by one stroke over Mara Larrauri of Argentina at Glendower in Johannesburg.

Larrauri led by two strokes with a round to play, but closed with 76 as Adamson rallied with 73, following rounds of 75 and 71, for an even-par total of 219. Annerie Wessels finished in third place at 221.

Telekom Ladies Classic—R125,000
Winner: Annerie Wessels

Having only just turned professional at the end of the previous year, Annerie Wessels claimed her first title at the Telekom Classic at Woodhill in Pretoria. It took four playoff holes before Wessels overcame Charlaine Coetzee-Hirst.

Caryn Louw, after 69 in the second round, was two ahead but fell away with 77 as Wessels, with rounds of 71, 74 and 70, and Coetzee-Hirst, after 71, tied at 215, one under par. Louw took third place, four strokes out of the playoff.

Vodacom Ladies Players Championship—R300,000
Winner: Annerie Wessels

Annerie Wessels won again in extra holes the following week at the Vodacom Ladies Players Championship. It took only two holes this time for Wessels to beat Mandy Adamson at Rondebosch, near Cape Town.

Adamson had made the biggest move on the final day, her 68 making up three strokes on Wessels, who had shared the lead with Vanessa Smith and Elsabe Hefer. Wessels scored rounds of 73, 69 and 71 as she tied with Adamson at six-under-par 213. Smith finished third, one stroke behind, with Hefer and America's Nicolle Flood one stroke further back.

Cape Times Women's South African Open—R100,000
Winner: Vanessa Smith

Vanessa Smith completed a remarkable hat trick of titles when she won the Cape Times Women's South African Open at Devondale in the Cape winelands of Stellenbosch. Smith, 22, had won the South African Junior title in 1999 and the South African Amateur in 2000. She turned professional at the end of 2000 after gaining a sports management degree from Damilin College.

In the 1999 Open, Smith had seen Barbara Pestana come from 13 strokes behind to take the title. This time Smith was consistency personified, moving into the lead after the second day and ultimately claiming a four-stroke victory over Charlaine Coetzee-Hirst.

Smith had rounds of 70, 70 and 71 for a five-under-par total of 211. Coetzee-Hirst lost ground on the final day by closing with 72, while Mandy Adamson, Smith's closest challenger, shot 75 to share fourth place with American Nicolle Flood. Britain's Julie Forbes took fifth place at two over par.

Nedbank MasterCard South African Masters—R1,100,000
Winner: Samantha Head

It was just as well Samantha Head had not looked at the scoreboard before approaching her six-foot putt at the final hole of the Gary Player golf course at Sun City. "I can't imagine how nervous I would have felt had I known the putt was to win," she said. Making her par, after leaving her first putt from 30 feet short, avoided a four-way playoff and gave Head the victory in the Nedbank MasterCard South African Masters.

The tournament, co-sanctioned with the Ladies European Tour, gave Head her second victory, following her 1999 Italian Open title. A closing 68, after rounds of 70 and 72, gave her a six-under score of 210. Sharing second place were Raquel Carriedo, a week after winning her first title in Taiwan, Elisabeth Esterl, for the second time in successive tournaments, and Norway's Cecilie Lundgreen.

Esterl had held a one-stroke lead going into the final round, but closed with 72, although she made a superb birdie at the last hole to get back to five under par. Carriedo had 67 but dropped a shot at the 18th by three-putting, while Lundgreen, in her second year as a professional, recorded her best-ever finish with a closing 68.

Head had gone to the turn in 33, and after dropping her first shot of the day at the 12th hole, got it back at the 14th. It was a 15-footer for birdie at the 17th that took her into the lead. "That was much harder work than my win in Italy," said Head. "I was shaking so badly at the end my putter was shaking on the backswing and coming forward. I made it my policy not to look at the scoreboards; so while I knew I was up there, I didn't know I had the outright lead."

.

APPENDIXES

Official World Golf Ranking

(As of December 31, 2001)

Ranking	Player	Country	Points Average	Total Points	No. of Events	99/00 Points Lost	2001 Points Gained
1 (1)	Tiger Woods	USA	15.67	673.64	43	-878.98	+568.11
2 (3)	Phil Mickelson	USA	9.16	430.58	47	-379.15	+411.85
3 (5)	David Duval	USA	7.98	327.14	41	-257.71	+308.89
4 (2)	Ernie Els	SAf	6.99	356.43	51	-367.64	+267.57
5 (8)	Davis Love III	USA	6.02	271.11	45	-254.19	+275.25
6 (15)	Sergio Garcia	Spn	5.86	293.22	50	-246.10	+315.46
7 (21)	David Toms	USA	5.83	332.33	57	-222.84	+320.60
8 (10)	Vijay Singh	Fiji	5.60	335.94	60	-327.19	+352.35
9 (7)	Darren Clarke	NIr	5.03	281.55	56	-260.40	+232.31
10 (36)	Retief Goosen	SAf	4.95	292.11	59	-189.14	+307.03
11 (20)	Padraig Harrington	Ire	4.93	241.51	49	-181.33	+221.19
12 (18)	Mike Weir	Can	4.92	250.71	51	-207.43	+221.94
13 (63)	Bernhard Langer	Ger	4.52	239.33	53	-125.12	+251.60
14 (6)	Colin Montgomerie	Sco	4.39	219.51	50	-300.87	+184.11
15 (17)	Jim Furyk	USA	4.28	209.95	49	-222.22	+219.35
16 (47)	Toshimitsu Izawa	Jpn	4.27	183.79	43	-121.31	+175.15
17 (48)	Scott Verplank	USA	4.23	228.54	54	-131.72	+228.55
18 (73)	Bob Estes	USA	4.08	191.57	47	-97.43	+204.91
19 (43)	Jose Coceres	Arg	4.06	166.63	41	-100.54	+156.34
20 (62)	Chris DiMarco	USA	3.90	241.89	62	-126.17	+232.94
21 (54)	Scott Hoch	USA	3.87	213.11	55	-141.79	+224.92
22 (33)	Robert Allenby	Aus	3.86	231.89	60	-166.24	+206.40
23 (11)	Tom Lehman	USA	3.82	171.72	45	-200.51	+152.83
24 (16)	Thomas Bjorn	Den	3.70	203.62	55	-209.99	+164.34
25 (31)	Paul Azinger	USA	3.58	143.06	40	-126.47	+134.66
26 (50)	Mark Calcavecchia	USA	3.56	178.23	50	-150.07	+192.17
27 (38)	Rocco Mediate	USA	3.35	143.98	43	-137.54	+145.15
28 (12)	Michael Campbell	NZl	3.33	169.73	51	-195.17	+121.51
29 (4)	Lee Westwood	Eng	3.26	166.33	51	-300.49	+48.41
30 (14)	Nick Price	Zim	3.23	148.41	46	-193.13	+117.22
31 (19)	Stewart Cink	USA	3.18	178.10	56	-198.08	+160.11
32 (13)	Jesper Parnevik	Swe	3.14	157.18	50	-208.85	+142.33
33 (85)	Kenny Perry	USA	3.14	141.22	45	-72.34	+144.15
34 (42)	Angel Cabrera	Arg	3.12	146.41	47	-125.78	+149.30
35 (66T)	Paul McGinley	Ire	3.08	160.01	52	-91.79	+156.29
36 (9)	Hal Sutton	USA	3.06	156.08	51	-239.09	+139.02
37 (40)	Shingo Katayama	Jpn	3.06	159.01	52	-105.82	+124.63
38 (148)	Niclas Fasth	Swe	2.73	117.44	43	-47.38	+126.39
39 (185)	Joe Durant	USA	2.73	141.81	52	-86.88	+187.34
40 (22)	Justin Leonard	USA	2.62	154.83	59	-179.94	+125.86
41 (64)	Steve Lowery	USA	2.62	149.19	57	-101.83	+140.42
42 (35)	Kirk Triplett	USA	2.58	139.34	54	-139.47	+118.01
43 (34)	Stuart Appleby	Aus	2.56	148.40	58	-143.20	+120.35
44 (69)	Brad Faxon	USA	2.45	134.51	55	-104.08	+152.77
45 (324)	Charles Howell	USA	2.42	99.29	41	-23.73	+107.11
46 (37)	Jose Maria Olazabal	Spn	2.40	134.12	56	-128.93	+112.23
47 (91)	Frank Lickliter	USA	2.39	140.73	59	-100.15	+153.97
48 (44)	Toru Taniguchi	Jpn	2.23	127.11	57	-104.17	+91.14
49 (145)	Adam Scott	Aus	2.21	108.09	49	-42.32	+111.72
50 (118)	Steve Stricker	USA	2.20	87.80	40	-73,38	+113.35

( ) Ranking in brackets indicates position as of December 31, 2000.

Ranking	Player	Country	Points Average	Total Points	No. of Events	99/00 Points Lost	2001 Points Gained
51 (507)	John Daly	USA	2.18	124.27	57	-28.96	+144.57
52 (95)	Billy Andrade	USA	2.18	124.15	57	-75.45	+121.09
53 (30)	Pierre Fulke	Swe	2.18	87.10	40	-95.62	+50.46
54 (206)	Scott McCarron	USA	2.18	119.69	55	-63.77	+143.48
55 (41)	Steve Flesch	USA	2.17	138.88	64	-125.50	+99.50
56 (60)	Paul Lawrie	Sco	2.13	110.95	52	-101.10	+99.33
57 (152)	Billy Mayfair	USA	2.11	120.38	57	-80.75	+145.96
58 (26)	Miguel A. Jimenez	Spn	2.08	108.24	52	-150.71	+89.34
59 (58)	Hidemichi Tanaka	Jpn	2.06	92.72	45	-84.42	+74.85
60 (52)	Phillip Price	Wal	2.04	106.17	52	-97.46	+86.32
61 (49)	Dudley Hart	USA	2.04	95.94	47	-120.93	+94.92
62 (75)	Jeff Sluman	USA	2.00	125.99	63	-119.38	+138.43
63 (56)	Shigeki Maruyama	Jpn	1.96	106.11	54	-123.25	+101.76
64 (23)	Bob May	USA	1.89	107.55	57	-144.05	+44.94
65 (116)	Kevin Sutherland	USA	1.87	104.72	56	-77.58	+118.12
66 (25)	Loren Roberts	USA	1.86	90.99	49	-132.01	+52.07
67 (164)	Taichi Teshima	Jpn	1.82	103.63	57	-54.46	+102.61
68 (24)	John Huston	USA	1.80	79.29	44	-136.62	+43.91
69 (269)	Dean Wilson	USA	1.80	75.62	42	-24.02	+79.15
70 (79)	Ian Woosnam	Wal	1.77	88.32	50	-79.40	+84.43
71 (86)	Rory Sabbatini	SAf	1.76	87.87	50	-74.36	+82.26
72 (166)	Robert Karlsson	Swe	1.72	73.76	43	-57.86	+90.69
73 (59)	Masashi Ozaki	Jpn	1.67	83.49	50	-70.21	+55.36
74 (100)	Mathias Gronberg	Swe	1.63	86.62	53	-64.72	+83.46
75 (156)	Scott Laycock	Aus	1.63	91.28	56	-33.48	+88.40
76 (103)	Peter O'Malley	Aus	1.61	86.94	54	-73.97	+88.41
77 (327)	Andrew Oldcorn	Sco	1.57	67.56	43	-31.27	+80.76
78 (105)	Ian Pouter	Eng	1.56	91.97	59	-45.73	+87.82
79 (39)	Eduardo Romero	Arg	1.55	62.05	40	-81.51	+28.74
80 (136)	Jerry Kelly	USA	1.53	98.02	64	-77.31	+110.09
81 (202)	Lin Keng-chi	Twn	1.53	84.08	55	-35.23	+80.38
82 (167)	Tom Pernice, Jr.	USA	1.50	97.74	65	-65.46	+109.73
83 (161)	Henrik Stenson	Swe	1.50	64.45	43	-36.45	+65.00
84 (65)	Andrew Coltart	Sco	1.50	85.38	57	-90.78	+69.12
85 (55)	Gary Orr	Sco	1.49	74.60	50	-90.23	+42.22
86 (256)	Brian Gay	USA	1.48	94.97	64	-45.77	+108.52
87 (32)	Duffy Waldorf	USA	1.48	74.16	50	-111.42	+30.60
88 (192)	Chris Riley	USA	1.48	88.56	60	-38.76	+84.72
89 (381T)	Warren Bennett	Eng	1.47	58.65	40	-26.02	+72,67
90 (172)	Ricardo Gonzalez	Arg	1.46	70.27	48	-39.98	+69.42
91 (122)	Keiichiro Fukabori	Jpn	1.45	77.09	53	-51.21	+60.56
92 (1043T)	Paul Casey	Eng	1.45	58.13	40	-9.50	+67.64
93 (78)	Fred Funk	USA	1.45	94.43	65	-103.62	+93.07
94 (93)	Mark McNulty	Zim	1.45	62.22	43	-61.81	+61.89
95 (144)	Robert Damron	USA	1.44	77.84	54	-65.10	+86.80
96 (171)	Katsumasa Miyamoto	Jpn	1.44	71.80	50	-34.74	+59.43
97 (29)	Chris Perry	USA	1.43	81.26	57	-168.71	+51.01
98 (61)	Dennis Paulson	USA	1.42	72.49	51	-111.23	+72.41
99 (178)	Mark Brooks	USA	1.40	78.46	56	-62.90	+90.30
100 (45)	Fred Couples	USA	1.39	55.65	40	-79.04	+36.14

( ) Ranking in brackets indicates position as of December 31, 2000.

Ranking	Player	Country	Points Average	Total Points	No. of Events	99/00 Points Lost	2001 Points Gained
101 (345)	Thomas Levet	Frn	1.38	80.21	58	-32.88	+91.93
102 (119)	Bob Tway	USA	1.36	80.50	59	-81.29	+95.07
103 (104)	Nick Faldo	Eng	1.36	58.57	43	-58.85	+53.73
104 (556)	David Gossett	USA	1.36	54.42	40	-14.49	+63.39
105 (51)	Jeff Maggert	USA	1.36	73.43	54	-98.00	+54.41
106 (89)	Lee Janzen	USA	1.36	75.91	56	-79.27	+75.40
107 (151)	John Cook	USA	1.35	71.67	53	-48.99	+69.03
108 (27)	Notah Begay	USA	1.31	52.44	40	-132.75	+7.90
109 (153)	Dean Robertson	Sco	1.31	65.52	50	-50.45	+64.65
110 (139)	Fredrik Jacobson	Swe	1.30	60.88	47	-39.18	+48.22
111 (66T)	Nobuhito Sato	Jpn	1.28	74.52	58	-69.15	+35.54
112 (28)	Carlos Franco	Par	1.27	66.03	52	-133.68	+39.14
113 (46)	Greg Norman	Aus	1.27	50.79	40	-86.99	+39.67
114 (94)	Greg Chalmers	Aus	1.27	76.02	60	-78.79	+60.95
115 (114)	Joel Edwards	USA	1.25	73.64	59	-42.52	+69.66
116 (213)	David Howell	Eng	1.24	75.63	61	-41.28	+74.52
117 (162)	Richard Green	Aus	1.24	68.12	55	-44.12	+61.39
118 (224)	Steve Webster	Eng	1.23	72.48	59	-38.50	+76.35
119 (702)	Tsuneyuki Nakajima	Jpn	1.23	50.36	41	-10.46	+57.71
120 (184)	Peter Lonard	Aus	1.21	70.40	58	-47.04	+75.93
121 (294)	Raphael Jacquelin	Frn	1.21	71.37	59	-30.20	+74.97
122 (80)	Skip Kendall	USA	1.21	77.24	64	-86.29	+65.04
123 (318)	Cameron Beckman	USA	1.20	71.00	59	-22.77	+70.23
124 (146)	Brandel Chamblee	USA	1.20	53.92	45	-48.58	+58.02
125 (254)	David Smail	NZl	1.19	61.72	52	-44.03	+75.79
126 (124)	Paul Stankowski	USA	1.19	58.15	49	-56.18	+59.60
127 (175)	Greg Owen	Eng	1.19	67.61	57	-45.30	+64.69
128 (68)	Per-Ulrik Johansson	Swe	1.17	58.42	50	-59.65	+38.56
129 (383)	Chris Smith	USA	1.16	58.25	50	-32.12	+76.06
130 (298)	Brett Quigley	USA	1.15	63.30	55	-27.76	+68.00
131 (140)	Geoff Ogilvy	Aus	1.13	61.04	54	-52.75	+63.06
132 (135)	Harrison Frazar	USA	1.12	55.03	49	-59.72	+61.54
133 (57)	Franklin Langham	USA	1.12	54.89	49	-93.93	+25.96
134 (82)	Tim Herron	USA	1.11	63.46	57	-87.01	+62.24
135 (109)	Grant Waite	NZl	1.09	62.21	57	-60.40	+48.00
136 (53)	Naomichi Ozaki	Jpn	1.09	57.81	53	-110.58	+33.08
137 (101)	Jarmo Sandelin	Swe	1.09	53.24	49	-53.51	+40.56
138 (96)	Nick O'Hern	Aus	1.07	55.73	52	-70.52	+50.51
139 (76)	Jonathan Kaye	USA	1.06	71.30	67	-90.14	+54.03
140 (391)	Darren Fichardt	SAf	1.06	42.35	40	-25.38	+56.53
141 (150)	Matt Gogel	USA	1.05	57.98	55	-37.82	+58.22
142 (475T)	J.J. Henry	USA	1.05	59.78	57	-16.22	+68.20
143 (138)	Brett Rumford	Aus	1.02	50.07	49	-42.43	+52.53
144 (107)	J.P. Hayes	USA	1.02	49.99	49	-58.59	+42.84
145 (74)	Craig Parry	Aus	1.01	56.79	56	-86.61	+51.31
146 (131)	Toru Suzuki	Jpn	1.01	55.69	55	-45.32	+35.86
147 (253)	Frankie Minoza	Phi	1.01	43.42	43	-30.99	+48.00
148 (98)	Aaron Baddeley	Aus	1.01	40.31	40	-46.25	+32.92
149 (71)	Brent Geiberger	USA	1.01	49.28	49	-90.24	+47.58
150 (179)	David Peoples	USA	1.01	58.29	58	-29.77	+55.73

( ) Ranking in brackets indicates position as of December 31, 2000.

Ranking	Player	Country	Points Average	Total Points	No. of Events	99/00 Points Lost	2001 Points Gained
151 (92)	Glen Day	USA	1.00	57.21	57	-80.94	+56.45
152 (72)	Jean Van de Velde	Frn	1.00	59.11	59	-84.94	+37.39
153 (90)	Mark O'Meara	USA	1.00	44.87	45	-60.08	+38.04
154 (125)	Brian Davis	Eng	0.99	52.72	53	-47.56	+42.70
155 (155)	Len Mattiace	USA	0.97	58.44	60	-47.87	+48.93
156 (77)	Carl Paulson	USA	0.97	62.12	64	-43.24	+40.63
157 (83)	Stephen Ames	T&T	0.97	54.27	56	-64.88	+45.02
158 (275)	Kiyoshi Murota	Jpn	0.95	52.38	55	-22.18	+46.71
159 (407)	Justin Rose	Eng	0.95	54.12	57	-25.06	+66.64
160 (379)	Thongchai Jaidee	Tha	0.95	37.97	40	-13.91	+39.77
161 (134)	Olin Browne	USA	0.95	57.85	61	-65.01	+65.44
162 (1043T)	Carl Pettersson	Swe	0.94	37.79	40	-9.30	+47.09
163 (261)	Anders Hansen	Den	0.94	50.01	53	-30.45	+51.51
164 (130)	Larry Mize	USA	0.94	41.21	44	-37.76	+34.29
165 (267)	David Lynn	Eng	0.94	50.55	54	-23.72	+53.58
166 (359)	Barry Lane	Eng	0.93	47.47	51	-14.76	+47.08
167 (205)	Jean Hugo	SAf	0.93	52.95	57	-26.05	+50.86
168 (200)	Roger Wessels	SAf	0.93	53.82	58	-36.69	+46.83
169 (120)	Paul Gow	Aus	0.90	56.59	63	-44.72	+50.59
170 (215)	Joey Sindelar	USA	0.90	48.34	54	-36.30	+49.01
171 (356)	Jeev Milkha Singh	Ind	0.89	41.13	46	-26.99	+53.44
172 (170)	Alex Cejka	Ger	0.89	40.95	46	-39.22	+37.09
173 (70)	Hirofumi Miyase	Jpn	0.88	48.59	55	-77.77	+16.80
174 (194)	Katsuyoshi Tomori	Jpn	0.87	47.14	54	-36.39	+41.47
175 (480)	Briny Baird	USA	0.86	49.21	57	-17.69	+56.56
176 (181)	Kiyoshi Maita	Jpn	0.86	35.29	41	-27.77	+20.72
177 (1043T)	Chad Campbell	USA	0.86	34.20	40	-3.60	+37.80
178 (112)	Stephen Leaney	Aus	0.85	40.93	48	-48.77	+28.42
179 (180)	Hajime Meshiai	Jpn	0.85	44.30	52	-40.22	+38.70
180 (316)	Soren Hansen	Den	0.85	48.37	57	-23.85	+49.86
181 (142)	Trevor Immelman	SAf	0.85	50.87	60	-30.78	+42.80
182 (123)	Greg Turner	NZl	0.84	37.79	45	-47.72	+37.00
183 (300)	Hiroyuki Fujita	Jpn	0.84	43.45	52	-26.40	+42.68
184 (191)	Esteban Toledo	Mex	0.83	58.08	70	-44.45	+51.10
185 (228)	Anthony Wall	Eng	0.82	43.47	53	-37.25	+45.09
186 (160)	Jay Haas	USA	0.81	38.90	48	-46.91	+40.92
187 (81)	Scott Dunlap	USA	0.81	46.87	58	-82.08	+36.02
188 (1043T)	Jamie Donaldson	Eng	0.81	32.31	40	-5.56	+37.87
189 (405)	David Berganio, Jr.	USA	0.80	41.67	52	-20.33	+51.08
190 (271)	Neal Lancaster	USA	0.80	52.85	66	-32.13	+51.31
191 (99)	Kaname Yokoo	Jpn	0.80	45.45	57	-69.04	+30.56
192 (234)	Choi Kyung-ju	Kor	0.79	46.55	59	-36.70	+53.95
193 (367)	Jorge Berendt	Arg	0.78	38.92	50	-14.78	+40.70
194 (631)	Dinesh Chand	Fiji	0.77	39.45	51	-10.33	+43.12
195 (129)	Tsuyoshi Yoneyama	Jpn	0.77	36.93	48	-52.99	+28.05
196 (147)	Steve Elkington	Aus	0.76	30.56	40	-38,37	+30.32
197 (108)	Kazuhiko Hosokawa	Jpn	0.74	40.10	54	-67.01	+28.07
198 (252)	Tony Johnstone	Zim	0.73	35.21	48	-27.86	+37.50
199 (143)	Tom Byrum	USA	0.73	38.83	53	-44.56	+32.08
200 (336T)	Des Smyth	Ire	0.73	33.43	46	-25.13	+40.77

( ) Ranking in brackets indicates position as of December 31, 2000.

Age Groups of Current Top 100 World Ranked Players

Under 25	25-28	29-30	31-32	33-34	35-36	37-38	39-42	Over 43
							Lehman	
			Mickelson				Azinger	
		Duval	Els				Calcavecchia	
		Harrington	Goosen				Mediate	
		Allenby	Weir	Toms			K.Perry	
		Bjorn	Furyk	Clarke	B.Estes		Lowery	Langer
		Fasth	Campbell	Izawa	Parnevik		Triplett	Hoch
		Leonard	Cabrera	DiMarco	McGinley	Love	Faxon	N.Price
	Woods	Appleby	Lickliter	Taniguchi	Olazabal	Singh	Huston	Sutton
	Westwood	Fulke	Lawrie	Stricker	Daly	Montgomerie	Oldcorn	Sluman
	Cink	Tanaka	Maruyama	Flesch	McCarron	Verplank	Pernice	Roberts
	Katayama	Laycock	D.Wilson	D.Hart	Mayfair	Coceres	Waldorf	Woosnam
Garcia	Sabbatini	Gay	R.Karlsson	May	P.Price	Durant	C.Perry	M.Ozaki
Howell	Poulter	Bennett	Gronberg	Teshima	O'Malley	Andrade	D.Paulson	Romero
Scott	Stenson	Damron	Coltart	Orr	Kelly	Jimenez	Brooks	Funk
Casey	Riley	Miyamoto	R.Gonzalez	Fukabori	K.C.Lin	Sutherland	Couples	McNulty

Highest-Rated Events of 2001

	Event	No. of World Ranked Players Participating					World Rating Points
		Top 5	Top 15	Top 30	Top 50	Top 100	
1	PGA Championship	5	15	30	49	95	807
2	U.S. Open Championship	5	15	30	50	74	752
3	British Open Championship	5	14	28	45	79	732
4	Masters Tournament	4	14	29	49	67	703
5	The Players Championship	5	14	26	43	78	703
6	Phoenix Open	4	10	21	31	59	535
7	Bay Hill Invitational	4	8	17	31	61	531
8	WGC NEC Invitational	5	14	24	30	38	503
9	Verizon Byron Nelson Classic	4	10	17	25	54	468
10	Volvo PGA Championship	2	6	9	14	27	247
11	MasterCard Colonial	2	8	18	27	54	429
12	Memorial Tournament	3	7	14	24	55	420
13	Advil Western Open	3	7	14	22	51	414
14	Mercedes Championships	4	8	18	23	30	391
15	The Tour Championship	4	10	17	25	29	396
16	Buick Challenge	3	7	12	26	43	395
17	WGC Accenture Match Play	1	5	13	23	61	401
18	Genuity Championship	2	8	16	20	45	360
19	AT&T Pebble Beach Pro-Am	3	9	15	21	40	353
20	NCR Classic at Walt Disney	2	6	14	21	43	364

2001 World Ranking Review

Major Movements Within Top 50

	Upward				Downward		
Name	Net Points Gained	Position 2000	2001	Name	Net Points Lost	Position 2000	2001
Retief Goosen	118	36	10	Tiger Woods	311	1	1
David Toms	98	21	7	Lee Westwood	252	4	29
Scott Verplank	97	48	17	Colin Montgomerie	117	6	14
Sergio Garcia	69	15	6	Hal Sutton	100	9	36
Jose Coceres	56	43	19	Ernie Els	100	2	4
Toshimitsu Izawa	54	47	16	Nick Price	76	14	30
David Duval	51	5	3	Michael Campbell	74	12	28
Mark Calcavecchia	42	50	26	Jesper Parnevik	67	13	32
Robert Allenby	40	33	22	Justin Leonard	54	22	40
Padraig Harrington	40	20	11	Tom Lehman	48	11	23
Phil Mickelson	33	3	2				

Major Movements Into Top 50 / Major Movements Out of Top 50

	Into Top 50				Out of Top 50		
Name	Net Points Gained	Position 2000	2001	Name	Net Points Lost	Position 2000	2001
Bernhard Langer	126	63	13	Notah Begay	125	27	108
Bob Estes	107	73	18	Chris Perry	118	29	97
Chris DiMarco	107	66	20	Bob May	99	23	64
Joe Durant	100	185	39	Carlos Franco	95	28	112
Charles Howell	83	324	45	John Huston	93	24	68
Scott Hoch	83	54	21	Duffy Waldorf	81	32	87
Niclas Fasth	79	148	38	Loren Roberts	80	25	66
Kenny Perry	72	85	33	Miguel A. Jimenez	61	26	58
Adam Scott	69	145	49	Eduardo Romero	53	39	79
Paul McGinley	65	66	35	Greg Norman	47	46	113
Frank Lickliter	54	91	46	Pierre Fulke	45	30	53
Brad Faxon	49	69	44	Fred Couples	43	45	100
Steve Stricker	40	118	50	Dudley Hart	26	49	61

Other Major Movements

	Upward				Downward		
Name	Net Points Gained	Position 2000	2001	Name	Net Points Lost	Position 2000	2001
John Daly	116	507	51	Naomichi Ozaki	76	53	136
Scott McCarron	80	206	54	Franklin Langham	68	57	133
Billy Mayfair	65	152	57	Hirofumi Miyase	61	70	173
Brian Gay	63	256	86	Gary Orr	48	55	85
Thomas Levet	59	345	101	Jean Van de Velde	48	72	151
Paul Casey	58	—	92				
Dean Wilson	55	269	69				
Scott Laycock	55	156	75				
J.J. Henry	52	475	141				
Andrew Oldcorn	49	327	77				
David Gossett	49	556	104				
Taichi Teshima	48	164	67				
Cameron Beckman	47	318	123				

World Golf Rankings 1968-2001

Year	No. 1	No. 2	No. 3	No. 4	No. 5
1968	Nicklaus	Palmer	Casper	Player	Charles
1969	Nicklaus	Player	Casper	Palmer	Charles
1970	Nicklaus	Player	Casper	Trevino	Charles
1971	Nicklaus	Trevino	Player	Palmer	Casper
1972	Nicklaus	Player	Trevino	Crampton	Palmer
1973	Nicklaus	Weiskopf	Trevino	Player	Crampton
1974	Nicklaus	Miller	Player	Weiskopf	Trevino
1975	Nicklaus	Miller	Weiskopf	Irwin	Player
1976	Nicklaus	Irwin	Miller	Player	Green
1977	Nicklaus	Watson	Green	Irwin	Crenshaw
1978	Watson	Nicklaus	Irwin	Green	Player
1979	Watson	Nicklaus	Irwin	Trevino	Player
1980	Watson	Trevino	Aoki	Crenshaw	Nicklaus
1981	Watson	Rogers	Aoki	Pate	Trevino
1982	Watson	Floyd	Ballesteros	Kite	Stadler
1983	Ballesteros	Watson	Floyd	Norman	Kite
1984	Ballesteros	Watson	Norman	Wadkins	Langer
1985	Ballesteros	Langer	Norman	Watson	Nakajima
1986	Norman	Langer	Ballesteros	Nakajima	Bean
1987	Norman	Ballesteros	Langer	Lyle	Strange
1988	Ballesteros	Norman	Lyle	Faldo	Strange
1989	Norman	Faldo	Ballesteros	Strange	Stewart
1990	Norman	Faldo	Olazabal	Woosnam	Stewart
1991	Woosnam	Faldo	Olazabal	Ballesteros	Norman
1992	Faldo	Couples	Woosnam	Olazabal	Norman
1993	Faldo	Norman	Langer	Price	Couples
1994	Price	Norman	Faldo	Langer	Olazabal
1995	Norman	Price	Langer	Els	Montgomerie
1996	Norman	Lehman	Montgomerie	Els	Couples
1997	Norman	Woods	Price	Els	Love
1998	Woods	O'Meara	Duval	Love	Els
1999	Woods	Duval	Montgomerie	Love	Els
2000	Woods	Els	Duval	Mickelson	Westwood
2001	Woods	Mickelson	Duval	Els	Love

(*The World of Professional Golf* 1968-1985; World Ranking 1986-2001)

Year	No. 6	No. 7	No. 8	No. 9	No. 10
1968	Boros	Coles	Thomson	Beard	Nagle
1969	Beard	Archer	Trevino	Barber	Sikes
1970	Devlin	Coles	Jacklin	Beard	Huggett
1971	Barber	Crampton	Charles	Devlin	Weiskopf
1972	Jacklin	Weiskopf	Oosterhuis	Heard	Devlin
1973	Miller	Oosterhuis	Wadkins	Heard	Brewer
1974	M. Ozaki	Crampton	Irwin	Green	Heard
1975	Green	Trevino	Casper	Crampton	Watson
1976	Watson	Weiskopf	Marsh	Crenshaw	Geiberger
1977	Marsh	Player	Weiskopf	Floyd	Ballesteros
1978	Crenshaw	Marsh	Ballesteros	Trevino	Aoki
1979	Aoki	Green	Crenshaw	Ballesteros	Wadkins
1980	Pate	Ballesteros	Bean	Irwin	Player
1981	Ballesteros	Graham	Crenshaw	Floyd	Lietzke
1982	Pate	Nicklaus	Rogers	Aoki	Strange
1983	Nicklaus	Nakajima	Stadler	Aoki	Wadkins
1984	Faldo	Nakajima	Stadler	Kite	Peete
1985	Wadkins	O'Meara	Strange	Pavin	Sutton
1986	Tway	Sutton	Strange	Stewart	O'Meara
1987	Woosnam	Stewart	Wadkins	McNulty	Crenshaw
1988	Crenshaw	Woosnam	Frost	Azinger	Calcavecchia
1989	Kite	Olazabal	Calcavecchia	Woosnam	Azinger
1990	Azinger	Ballesteros	Kite	McNulty	Calcavecchia
1991	Couples	Langer	Stewart	Azinger	Davis
1992	Langer	Cook	Price	Azinger	Love
1993	Azinger	Woosnam	Kite	Love	Pavin
1994	Els	Couples	Montgomerie	M. Ozaki	Pavin
1995	Pavin	Faldo	Couples	M. Ozaki	Elkington
1996	Faldo	Mickelson	M. Ozaki	Love	O'Meara
1997	Mickelson	Montgomerie	M. Ozaki	Lehman	O'Meara
1998	Price	Montgomerie	Westwood	Singh	Mickelson
1999	Westwood	Singh	Price	Mickelson	O'Meara
2000	Montgomerie	Love	Sutton	Singh	Lehman
2001	Garcia	Toms	Singh	Clarke	Goosen

World's Winners of 2001

BUY.COM TOUR

Florida Classic	Chris Couch
Monterrey Open	Deane Pappas (2)
Louisiana Open	Paul Claxton
Arkansas Classic	Brett Quigley
Charity Pro-Am at the Cliffs	Jonathan Byrd
Carolina Classic	John Maginnes
Virginia Beach Open	Trevor Dodds
Richmond Open	Chad Campbell
Steamtown Classic	Jason Hill
Samsung Canadian PGA Championship	Richard Zokol
Greater Cleveland Open	Heath Slocum
Dayton Open	Todd Barranger
Knoxville Open	Heath Slocum (2)
Hershey Open	John Rollins
Wichita Open	Jason Dufner
Siouxland Open	Pat Bates
Ozarks Open	Steve Haskins
Omaha Classic	Heath Slocum (3)
Fort Smith Classic	Jay Delsing
Permian Basin Open	Chad Campbell (2)
Utah Classic	David Sutherland
Tri-Cities Open	Guy Boros
Boise Open	Michael Long
Inland Empire Open	D.A. Points
Monterey Peninsula Classic	Chad Campbell (3)
Gila River Classic at Wild Horse Pass Resort	Ben Crane
Shreveport Open	Pat Bates (2)
Buy.com Tour Championship	Pat Bates (3)

CANADIAN TOUR

Panama Open Panasonic	Steve Runge
Myrtle Beach Open	Eamonn Brady
Barefoot Classic	Aaron Barber
South Carolina Challenge	Jace Bugg
CanAm Days Championship	Scott Ford
Shell Payless Open	Paul Devenport
Telus Vancouver Open	Steve Scott
Telus Edmonton Open	Aaron Barber (2)
MTS Classic	Kenneth Staton
Ontario Open Heritage Classic	Craig Matthew
Giant Forest Products/NRCS Classic	Derek Gilchrist
Telus Open	Paul Devenport (2)
Eagle Creek Classic	Mark Slawter
Aliant Cup	Brian Payne
Casino de Charlevoix Cup	Darren Griff/Drew Symons
Bayer Championship	Jason Bohn
Niagara Classic	Kenneth Staton (2)

SOUTH AMERICAN TOUR

Rabobank Chile Masters	Alexandre Rocha
Mexico Masters	Raul Fretes
PGA Championship of Latin America	Angel Romero
Sao Paulo Brazil Open	Darren Fichardt (2)
Open de Argentina	Angel Cabrera
Movilnet Venezuela Open	Rafael Alarcon
Litoral Open	Marco Ruiz
Chevrolet Brazil Open	Carlos Franco
Telefonica Masters Tournament	Angel Cabrera (2)
Baviera Paraguay Open	Raul Fretes (2)

PGA EUROPEAN TOUR

Dubai Desert Classic	Thomas Bjorn
Qatar Masters	Tony Johnstone
Madeira Island Open	Des Smyth
Moroccan Open	Ian Poulter
Via Digital Open de Espana	Robert Karlsson
Algarve Open de Portugal	Phillip Price
Novotel Perrier Open de France	Jose Maria Olazabal
Benson and Hedges International Open	Henrik Stenson
Deutsche Bank - SAP Open	Tiger Woods (4)
Volvo PGA Championship	Andrew Oldcorn
Victor Chandler British Masters	Thomas Levet
Compass Group English Open	Peter O'Malley
Great North Open	Andrew Coltart
Murphy's Irish Open	Colin Montgomerie (2)
Smurfit European Open	Darren Clarke (3)
Scottish Open at Loch Lomond	Retief Goosen (2)
British Open Championship	David Duval
TNT Open	Bernhard Langer
Volvo Scandinavian Masters	Colin Montgomerie (3)
Celtic Manor Resort Wales Open	Paul McGinley
North West of Ireland Open	Tobias Dier
Gleneagles Scottish PGA Championship	Paul Casey
BMW International Open	John Daly
Omega European Masters	Ricardo Gonzalez
Trophee Lancome	Sergio Garcia (3)
Linde German Masters	Bernhard Langer (2)
Cisco World Match Play	Ian Woosnam
Cannes Open	Jorge Berendt
Dunhill Links Championship	Paul Lawrie
Telefonica Open de Madrid	Retief Goosen (3)
Atlanet Italian Open	Gregory Havret
Volvo Masters Andalucia	Padraig Harrington

CHALLENGE TOUR

Tusker Kenya Open	Ashley Roestoff
Segura Viudas Challenge de Espana	Euan Little
Open Golf Montecchia - PGA Triveneta	Andrew Sherborne
Credit Suisse Private Banking Open	Greig Hutcheon
Austrian Open	Chris Gane
5th Aa Saint Omer Open	Sebastien Delagrange
NCC Open	Benn Barham
Nykredit Danish Open	Sebastien Delagrange (2)
Galeria Kaufhof Pokal Challenge	Wolfgang Huget
DEXIA-BIL Luxembourg Open	Grant Hamerton
Open des Volcans	Scott Drummond
Challenge Total Fina Elf	Kenneth Ferrie
Volvo Finnish Open	Peter Hedblom
Gunther Hamburg Classics	Peter Hanson
Charles Church Challenge Tour Championship	Mark Foster (2)
BMW Russian Open	Jamie Donaldson
Talma Finnish Challenge	Klas Eriksson
Rolex Trophy	Stuart Little
Skandia PGA Open	Christophe Pottier
Formby Hall Challenge	Sam Little
Muermans Real Estate Challenge	Dominique Nouailhac
Telia Grand Prix	Jamie Donaldson (2)
PGA of Austria Masters	Iain Pyman
San Paolo Vita & Asset Management Open	Mads Vibe-Hastrup
Hardelot Challenge de France	Marten Olander

Terme Euganee International Open Padova Chris Gane (2)
Challenge Tour Grand Final Richard Bland

ASIAN PGA DAVIDOFF TOUR

Thailand Masters	Kang Wook-soon
London Myanmar Open	Anthony Kang
Carlsberg Malaysian Open	Vijay Singh
Caltex Singapore Masters	Vijay Singh (2)
Wills Indian Open	Thongchai Jaidee
Maekyung LG Fashion Open	Choi Gwang-soo
Macau Open	Zhang Lian-wei
SK Telecom Open	Charlie Wi
Alcatel Singapore Open	Thaworn Wiratchant
Volvo Masters of Malaysia	Thaworn Wiratchant (2)
Acer Taiwan Open	Andrew Pitts
Mercuries Masters	Daniel Chopra
Kolon Cup Korean Open	*Kim Dae-sub
Shin Han Dong Hae Open	Charlie Wi (2)
Volvo China Open	Charlie Wi (3)
BMW Asian Open	Jarmo Sandelin
Omega Hong Kong Open	Jose Maria Olazabal (2)

JAPAN TOUR

Token Corporation Cup	Shingo Katayama
Dydo Drinco Shizuoka Open	Eiji Mizoguchi
Tsuruya Open	Hidemichi Tanaka
Kirin Open	Shingo Katayama (2)
Chunichi Crowns	Darren Clarke (2)
Fujisankei Classic	Frankie Minoza
Japan PGA Championship	Dean Wilson
Munsingwear Open KSB Cup	Dinesh Chand
Diamond Cup	Toshimitsu Izawa
JCB Classic Sendai	Toshiaki Odate
Tamanoi Yomiuri Open	Yoshimitsu Fukuzawa
Mizuno Open	Hidemichi Tanaka (2)
Japan Tour Championship Iiyama Cup	Katsumasa Miyamoto
Jyuken Sangyo Open Hiroshima	Keiichiro Fukabori
Aiful Cup	Lin Keng-chi
NST Niigata Open	Go Higaki
Sun Chlorella Classic	Hiroyuki Fujita
Hisamitsu-KBC Augusta	Takenori Hiraishi
Japan PGA Match Play	Dean Wilson (2)
Suntory Open	Shingo Katayama (3)
ANA Open	Lin Keng-chi (2)
Mitsui Sumitomo Visa Taiheiyo Masters	Toshimitsu Izawa (2)
Acom International	Kazuhiko Hosokawa
Georgia Tokai Classic	Toshimitsu Izawa (3)
Japan Open	Taichi Teshima
Bridgestone Open	Toshimitsu Izawa (4)
Philip Morris Championship	Toshimitsu Izawa (5)
Ube Kosan Open	Dean Wilson (3)
Dunlop Phoenix	David Duval (2)
WGC EMC World Cup	South Africa
Casio World Open	Kiyoshi Murota
Nippon Series JT Cup	Katsumasa Miyamoto (2)

AUSTRALASIAN TOUR

WGC Accenture Match Play	Steve Stricker
Victorian Open	Scott Laycock
TelstraSaturn New Zealand Open	David Smail
Canon Challenge	David Smail (2)
Heineken Classic	Michael Campbell
Greg Norman Holden International	Aaron Baddeley
Ericsson Masters	Colin Montgomerie
Australasian Tour Championship	Peter Lonard
Australian PGA Championship	Robert Allenby (3)
Holden Australian Open	Stuart Appleby

AFRICAN TOURS

Nashua Nedtel Cellular Masters	Mark McNulty
Alfred Dunhill Championship	Adam Scott
Mercedes-Benz South African Open	Mark McNulty (2)
Dimension Data Pro-Am	Darren Clarke
South Africa PGA Championship	Deane Pappas
Investec Royal Swazi Sun Open	Bradford Vaughan
Sunshine Tour Championship	Darren Fichardt
Stanbic Zambia Open	Mark Foster
Cock of the North	Sean Farrell
FNB Botswana Open	Marc Cayeux
Royal Swazi Sun Classic	Titch Moore
Pietersburg Industrelek Classic	Ryan Reid
Goldfields Powerade Classic	Callie Swart
Bloemfontein Classic	Andre Cruse
Randfontein Classic	James Kingston
Bearing Man Highveld Classic	Justin Hobday
Atlantic Beach Classic	James Kingston (2)
Western Cape Classic	Lindani Ndwandwe
Vodacom Trophy	Ulrich van den Berg
Graceland Challenge	Warren Abery
Hassan II Trophy	Joakim Haeggman
Platinum Classic	Roger Wessels
CABS/Old Mutual Zimbabwe Open	Darren Fichardt (3)
PriceWaterhouseCoopers Mandela Invitational	Simon Hobday/Martin Maritz
Nedbank Golf Challenge	Sergio Garcia (4)
Vodacom Players Championship	Ernie Els
Ernie Els Invitational	John Bland

U.S. SENIOR PGA TOUR

MasterCard Championship	Larry Nelson
Royal Caribbean Classic	Larry Nelson (2)
ACE Group Classic	Gil Morgan
Verizon Classic	Bob Gilder
Mexico Senior Classic	Mike McCullough
Toshiba Senior Classic	Jose Maria Canizares
SBC Senior Classic	Jim Colbert
Siebel Classic in Silicon Valley	Hale Irwin
Emerald Coast Classic	Mike McCullough (2)
Liberty Mutual Legends of Golf	Jim Colbert (2)/Andy North
The Countrywide Tradition	Doug Tewell
Las Vegas Senior Classic	Bruce Fleisher
Bruno's Memorial Classic	Hale Irwin (2)
Home Depot Invitational	Bruce Fleisher (2)
Enterprise Rent-A-Car Match Play	Leonard Thompson
TD Waterhouse Championship	Ed Dougherty
Senior PGA Championship	Tom Watson
BellSouth Senior Classic at Opryland	Sammy Rachels

NFL Golf Classic	John Schroeder
Instinet Classic	Gil Morgan (2)
FleetBoston Classic	Larry Nelson (3)
U.S. Senior Open	Bruce Fleisher (3)
Farmers Charity Classic	Larry Nelson (4)
Ford Senior Players Championship	Allen Doyle
SBC Senior Open	Dana Quigley
State Farm Senior Classic	Allen Doyle (2)
Lightpath Long Island Classic	Bobby Wadkins
3M Championship	Bruce Lietzke
Novell Utah Showdown	Steven Veriato
AT&T Canada Senior Open	Walter Hall
Kroger Senior Classic	Jim Thorpe
Allianz Championship	Jim Thorpe (2)
SAS Championship	Bruce Lietzke (2)
Gold Rush Classic	Tom Kite
Turtle Bay Championship	Hale Irwin (3)
The Transamerica	Sammy Rachels (2)
SBC Championship	Larry Nelson (5)
Senior Tour Championship	Bob Gilder (2)
Senior Slam	Allen Doyle (3)
Hyundai Team Matches	Allen Doyle (4)/Dana Quigley (2)

EUROPEAN SENIORS TOUR

Royal Westmoreland Barbados Open	Priscillo Diniz
Beko Classic	Noel Ratcliffe
AIB Irish Seniors Open	Seiji Ebihara
De Vere PGA Seniors' Championship	Ian Stanley
Wales Seniors Open	Denis Durnian
Microlease Jersey Seniors Masters	Seiji Ebihara (2)
Palmerston Trophy Berlin	Denis O'Sullivan
Lawrence Batley Seniors	Nick Job
STC Scandinavian International	Denis O'Sullivan (2)
Senior British Open	Ian Stanley (2)
De Vere Hotels Seniors Classic	Noel Ratcliffe (2)
Bad Ragaz PGA Seniors Open	David Huish
Energis Senior Masters	David Oakley
Legends in Golf	David Good
Scottish Seniors Open	David Oakley (2)
STC Bovis Lend Lease European Invitational	Bob Shearer
TEMES Seniors Open	Russell Weir
Dan Technology Tournament of Champions	Delroy Cambridge
Tunisian Seniors Open	Simon Owen
SSL International/Sodexho Match Play	Jim Rhodes
European Seniors Tour Championship	Jerry Bruner

JAPAN SENIOR TOUR

ANA Ishigaki Senior	Fujio Kobayashi
Castle Hill Senior Open	Noboru Sugai
Asahi Ryokuken Cup	Noboru Sugai (2)
Old Man Par Senior Open	Motomasa Aoki
Fancl Senior Classic	Katsunari Takahashi
HTD Senior Classic	Fujio Kobayashi (2)
Fujita Kanko Open	Yasuzo Hagiwara
Japan PGA Senior Championship	Yasuhiro Miyamoto
Komatsu Open	Katsunari Takahashi (2)
Japan Senior Open Championship	Fujio Kobayashi (3)
Takanosu Senior Open	Tadami Ueno
N. Cup Senior Open	Seiji Ebihara (3)

U.S. LPGA TOUR

YourLife Vitamins LPGA Classic	Se Ri Pak
Suburu Memorial of Naples	Sophie Gustafson
The Office Depot	Grace Park
Takefuji Classic	Lorie Kane
Cup Noodles Hawaiian Ladies Open	Catriona Matthew
Welch's/Circle K Championship	Annika Sorenstam
Standard Register Ping	Annika Sorenstam (2)
Nabisco Championship	Annika Sorenstam (3)
Office Depot Hosted by Amy Alcott	Annika Sorenstam (4)
Longs Drugs Challenge	Se Ri Pak (2)
Kathy Ireland Championship	Rosie Jones
Chick-fil-A Charity Championship	Annika Sorenstam (5)
Electrolux USA Championship	Juli Inkster
Champions Classic	Wendy Doolan
Corning Classic	Carin Koch
U.S. Women's Open	Karrie Webb (3)
Wegmans Rochester International	Laura Davies
McDonald's LPGA Championship	Karrie Webb (4)
ShopRite Classic	Betsy King
Jamie Farr Kroger Classic	Se Ri Pak (3)
Michelob Light Classic	Emilee Klein
Sybase Big Apple Classic	Rosie Jones (2)
Giant Eagle Classic	Dorothy Delasin
Wendy's Championship for Children	Wendy Ward
Bank of Montreal Canadian Women's Open	Annika Sorenstam (6)
First Union Betsy King Classic	Heather Daly-Donofrio
State Farm Classic	Kate Golden
Williams Championship	Gloria Park
Asahi Ryokuken International Championship	Tina Fischer
AFLAC Champions	Se Ri Pak (5)
Samsung World Championship	Dorothy Delasin (2)
Tyco/ADT Championship	Karrie Webb (5)
Hyundai Team Matches	Lorie Kane (2)/Janice Moodie

EVIAN LADIES EUROPEAN TOUR

Australian Ladies Masters	Karrie Webb
AAMI Women's Australian Open	Sophie Gustafson (2)
Taiwan Ladies Open	Raquel Carriedo
La Perla Ladies Italian Open	Paula Marti
Ladies French Open	Suzann Pettersen
Evian Masters	Rachel Teske
Kellogg's All-Bran Ladies British Masters	Paula Marti (2)
WPGA Championship of Europe	Helen Alfredsson
Weetabix Women's British Open	Se Ri Pak (4)
Compaq Open	Raquel Carriedo (2)
Palmerston Ladies German Open	Karine Icher
Waterford Crystal Ladies Irish Open	Raquel Carriedo (3)
Mexx Sport Open	Karine Icher (2)
WPGA International Match Play	Laura Davies (2)
Biarritz Ladies Classic	Rachel Kirkwood
Princess Lalla Meriem Cup	Marine Monnet

JAPAN LPGA TOUR

Daikin Orchid Ladies	Yuri Fudoh
Belluna Ladies Cup	Kasumi Fujii
Saishunkan Ladies Hinokuni Open	Kaori Higo
Nasuogawa Ladies	Michie Ohba
Katokichi Queens	Chieko Amanuma
Nichirei Cup World Ladies	Karrie Webb (2)

Vernal Ladies	Ikuyo Shiotani
Chukyo TV Bridgestone Ladies Open	Michie Ohba (2)
Kosaido Ladies Golf Cup	Aki Takamura
Resort Trust Ladies	Aki Takamura (2)
We Love Kobe Suntory Ladies Open	Michiko Hattori
Apita Circle K Sankus Ladies	Midori Yoneyama
Friskies Osaka Ladies Open	Midori Yoneyama (2)
Toyo Suisan Ladies Hokkaido	Chieko Amanuma (2)
Taiheiyo Club Ladies Leben Cup	Kaori Higo (2)
Golf 5 Ladies	Hsiao-Chuan Lu
Vemal Open	Yuri Fudoh (2)
NEC Karuizawa 72	Chieko Amanuma (3)
Shin Caterpillar Mitsubishi Ladies	Chieko Amanuma (4)
Yonex Ladies Open	Yuri Fudoh (3)
Fujisankei Ladies Classic	Miyuki Shimabukuro
Japan LPGA Championship Konica Cup	Kumiko Hiyoshi
Munsingwear Ladies Tokai Classic	Fuki Kido
Miyagi TV Cup Dunlop Ladies Open	Toshimi Kimura
Japan Women's Open	Miyuki Shimabukuro (2)
Sankyo Ladies Open	Hiroko Yamaguchi
Fujitsu Ladies	Yuri Fudoh (4)
Chako Higuchi Kibun Ladies Classic	Chieko Amanuma (5)
Cisco World Ladies Match Play	Annika Sorenstam (7)
Mizuno Classic	Annika Sorenstam (8)
Itoen Ladies	Laura Davies (3)
Daiohseishi Elleair Ladies Open	Ji-Hee Lee
Japan LPGA Tour Championship	Kaori Higo (3)

SOUTH AFRICAN WOMEN'S TOUR

Nedbank MasterCard Classic	Mandy Adamson
Telekom Ladies Classic	Annerie Wessels
Vodacom Ladies Players Championship	Annerie Wessels (2)
Cape Times Women's South African Open	Vanessa Smith
Nedbank MasterCard South African Masters	Samantha Head

Multiple Winners of 2001

PLAYER	WINS	PLAYER	WINS
Annika Sorenstam	8	Mark Foster	2
Tiger Woods	8	Raul Fretes	2
Chieko Amanuma	5	Chris Gane	2
Toshimitsu Izawa	5	Bob Gilder	2
Larry Nelson	5	Sophie Gustafson	2
Se Ri Pak	5	Scott Hoch	2
Karrie Webb	5	Karine Icher	2
Allen Doyle	4	Rosie Jones	2
Yuri Fudoh	4	Lorie Kane	2
Sergio Garcia	4	James Kingston	2
Robert Allenby	3	Bernhard Langer	2
Pat Bates	3	Bruce Lietzke	2
Mark Calcavecchia	3	Lin Keng-chi	2
Chad Campbell	3	Paula Marti	2
Raquel Carriedo	3	Scott McCarron	2
Darren Clarke	3	Mike McCullough	2
Laura Davies	3	Mark McNulty	2
Seiji Ebihara	3	Phil Mickelson	2
Brad Faxon	3	Katsumasa Miyamoto	2
Darren Fichardt	3	Gil Morgan	2
Bruce Fleisher	3	David Oakley	2
Retief Goosen	3	Michie Ohba	2
Kaori Higo	3	Jose Maria Olazabal	2
Hale Irwin	3	Denis O'Sullivan	2
Shingo Katayama	3	Deane Pappas	2
Fujio Kobayashi	3	Dana Quigley	2
Colin Montgomerie	3	Sammy Rachels	2
Heath Slocum	3	Noel Ratcliffe	2
David Toms	3	Miyuki Shimabukuro	2
Charlie Wi	3	Vijay Singh	2
Dean Wilson	3	David Smail	2
Aaron Barber	2	Ian Stanley	2
Angel Cabrera	2	Kenneth Staton	2
Jose Coceres	2	Noboru Sugai	2
Jim Colbert	2	Katsunari Takahashi	2
Sebastien Delagrange	2	Aki Takamura	2
Dorothy Delasin	2	Hidemichi Tanaka	2
Paul Devenport	2	Jim Thorpe	2
Jamie Donaldson	2	Annerie Wessels	2
Joe Durant	2	Thaworn Wiratchant	2
David Duval	2	Midori Yoneyama	2
Bob Estes	2		

World Money List

This list of the 400 leading money winners in the world of professional golf in 2001 was compiled from the results of men's (excluding seniors) tournaments carried in the Appendixes of this edition. This list includes tournaments with a minimum of 36 holes and four contestants and does not include such competitions as skins games, pro-ams and shootouts.

In the 36 years during which World Money Lists have been compiled, the earnings of the player in the 200th position have risen from a total of $3,326 in 1966 to $397,714 in 2001. The top 200 players in 1966 earned a total of $4,680,287. In 2001, the comparable total was $227,808,919.

The world money list of the International Federation of PGA Tours was used for the official money list events of the U.S. PGA Tour, PGA European Tour, PGA Tour of Japan, Davidoff Asian PGA Tour, Southern African PGA and Vodacom Tours and PGA Tour of Australia. The conversion rates used for 2001 for other events and other tours were: British pound = US$1.43; Japanese yen = US$0.00813; South African rand = US$0.12; Australian dollar = US$0.52; Canadian dollar = US$0.65.

POS.	PLAYER, COUNTRY	TOTAL MONEY
1	Tiger Woods, USA	$7,771,562
2	Sergio Garcia, Spain	5,490,441
3	Vijay Singh, Fiji	4,478,038
4	Phil Mickelson, USA	4,440,383
5	David Toms, USA	4,296,845
6	Ernie Els, South Africa	3,841,114
7	David Duval, USA	3,635,284
8	Retief Goosen, South Africa	3,478,409
9	Scott Hoch, USA	3,392,198
10	Davis Love III, USA	3,361,963
11	Bernhard Langer, Germany	3,233,980
12	Mike Weir, Canada	3,050,436
13	Scott Verplank, USA	2,913,401
14	Jim Furyk, USA	2,823,234
15	Bob Estes, USA	2,795,477
16	Chris DiMarco, USA	2,595,201
17	Padraig Harrington, Ireland	2,511,365
18	Joe Durant, USA	2,494,184
19	Mark Calcavecchia, USA	2,476,576
20	Darren Clarke, N. Ireland	2,425,771
21	Robert Allenby, Australia	2,410,975
22	Brad Faxon, USA	2,346,412
23	Scott McCarron, USA	2,102,006
24	Frank Lickliter, USA	2,081,911
25	Tom Lehman, USA	2,046,375
26	Toshimitsu Izawa, Japan	2,046,213
27	Jeff Sluman, USA	1,955,702
28	Colin Montgomerie, Scotland	1,912,941
29	Thomas Bjorn, Denmark	1,908,489
30	Jesper Parnevik, Sweden	1,890,992
31	Stewart Cink, USA	1,872,028

POS.	PLAYER, COUNTRY	TOTAL MONEY
32	Kenny Perry, USA	1,786,066
33	Justin Leonard, USA	1,783,842
34	Billy Mayfair, USA	1,753,252
35	Steve Lowery, USA	1,738,820
36	Hal Sutton, USA	1,723,946
37	Steve Stricker, USA	1,676,229
38	John Daly, USA	1,670,188
39	Jose Coceres, Argentina	1,640,308
40	Nick Price, Zimbabwe	1,562,506
41	Charles Howell, USA	1,546,124
42	Jerry Kelly, USA	1,533,494
43	Kevin Sutherland, USA	1,530,323
44	Paul Azinger, USA	1,509,130
45	Shigeki Maruyama, Japan	1,502,969
46	Rocco Mediate, USA	1,474,435
47	Billy Andrade, USA	1,441,797
48	Kirk Triplett, USA	1,400,202
49	Paul McGinley, Ireland	1,337,824
50	Tom Pernice, Jr., USA	1,318,762
51	Brian Gay, USA	1,299,361
52	Michael Campbell, New Zealand	1,268,842
53	John Cook, USA	1,267,528
54	Fred Funk, USA	1,237,004
55	Steve Flesch, USA	1,227,552
56	Paul Lawrie, Scotland	1,225,659
57	Chris Riley, USA	1,202,282
58	Ian Woosnam, Wales	1,198,344
59	Joel Edwards, USA	1,193,528
60	Stuart Appleby, Australia	1,191,699
61	Angel Cabrera, Argentina	1,143,243
62	Brett Quigley, USA	1,125,875
63	Bob Tway, USA	1,121,858
64	Shingo Katayama, Japan	1,120,667
65	Toru Taniguchi, Japan	1,103,873
66	J.J. Henry, USA	1,094,247
67	Dudley Hart, USA	1,093,210
68	Niclas Fasth, Sweden	1,090,702
69	Jose Maria Olazabal, Spain	1,085,179
70	Cameron Beckman, USA	1,071,343
71	Robert Damron, USA	1,059,187
72	Adam Scott, Australia	1,040,816
73	Rory Sabbatini, South Africa	1,038,590
74	Tim Herron, USA	1,002,941
75	Lee Janzen, USA	988,128
76	Dean Wilson, USA	980,421
77	David Gossett, USA	943,491
78	Olin Browne, USA	941,886
79	Chris Smith, USA	935,360
80	Taichi Teshima, Japan	925,030
81	Mark Brooks, USA	899,444
82	Miguel Angel Jimenez, Spain	890,801
83	Mark O'Meara, USA	845,870
84	Lee Westwood, England	831,193
85	Lin Keng-chi, Taiwan	816,617

POS.	PLAYER, COUNTRY	TOTAL MONEY
86	Briny Baird, USA	812,001
87	Dennis Paulson, USA	811,105
88	Choi Kyung-ju, Korea	800,326
89	Harrison Frazar, USA	795,331
90	Robert Karlsson, Sweden	794,122
91	Hidemichi Tanaka, Japan	790,619
92	David Howell, England	784,579
93	Skip Kendall, USA	783,701
94	Jeff Maggert, USA	776,107
95	Peter O'Malley, Australia	762,074
96	Thomas Levet, France	753,542
97	Paul Stankowski, USA	751,603
98	Mathias Gronberg, Sweden	751,326
99	Paul Casey, England	745,277
100	Loren Roberts, USA	734,072
101	Matt Gogel, USA	733,408
102	Greg Chalmers, Australia	730,586
103	Glen Day, USA	715,780
104	David Peoples, USA	712,657
105	Katsumasa Miyamoto, Japan	711,243
106	Brent Geiberger, USA	711,194
107	David Smail, New Zealand	707,921
108	Ian Poulter, England	703,450
109	Fred Couples, USA	702,484
110	Pierre Fulke, Sweden	699,886
111	Phillip Price, Wales	698,214
112	Geoff Ogilvy, Australia	686,791
113	David Berganio, Jr., USA	685,082
114	Garrett Willis, USA	684,038
115	Esteban Toledo, Mexico	683,751
116	Jonathan Kaye, USA	683,210
117	Jay Haas, USA	677,641
118	Neal Lancaster, USA	657,580
119	Chad Campbell, USA	656,040
120	Joey Sindelar, USA	654,864
121	Nick Faldo, England	645,858
122	Ricardo Gonzalez, Argentina	643,964
123	Soren Hansen, Denmark	634,684
124	Paul Gow, Australia	632,903
125	Matt Kuchar, USA	625,040
126	J.P. Hayes, USA	622,964
127	Andrew Oldcorn, Scotland	620,984
128	Raphael Jacquelin, France	618,654
129	Scott Laycock, Australia	611,705
130	Craig Parry, Australia	601,404
131	Andrew Coltart, Scotland	596,824
132	Steve Webster, England	596,202
133	Len Mattiace, USA	592,781
134	Jerry Smith, USA	592,030
135	Peter Lonard, Australia	588,146
136	Edward Fryatt, England	586,668
137	Carlos Franco, Paraguay	585,688
138	Brandel Chamblee, USA	582,086
139	Warren Bennett, England	580,369

POS.	PLAYER, COUNTRY	TOTAL MONEY
140	Stephen Ames, Trinidad & Tobago	578,901
141	Mike Sposa, USA	576,312
142	Per-Ulrik Johansson, Sweden	570,306
143	Chris Perry, USA	568,391
144	Justin Rose, England	564,973
145	Tsuneyuki Nakajima, Japan	563,720
146	John Huston, USA	562,752
147	Frank Nobilo, New Zealand	562,650
148	Steve Elkington, Australia	560,200
149	Greg Owen, England	559,420
150	Grant Waite, New Zealand	539,587
151	Jean Hugo, South Africa	537,552
152	Bob May, USA	537,486
153	Dean Robertson, Scotland	534,143
154	Masashi Ozaki, Japan	530,941
155	Keiichiro Fukabori, Japan	529,694
156	Brian Watts, USA	528,469
157	Hiroyuki Fujita, Japan	523,316
158	Scott Simpson, USA	515,405
159	J.L. Lewis, USA	515,368
160	Corey Pavin, USA	513,401
161	Carl Paulson, USA	508,208
162	David Frost, South Africa	504,376
163	Greg Kraft, USA	503,605
164	Dinesh Chand, Fiji	502,105
165	Kiyoshi Murota, Japan	498,178
166	Kaname Yokoo, Japan	492,284
167	Barry Lane, England	488,003
168	Duffy Waldorf, USA	479,431
169	Fredrik Jacobson, Sweden	476,606
170	Frankie Minoza, Philippines	476,180
171	Jay Williamson, USA	476,031
172	Hajime Meshiai, Japan	463,279
173	Rich Beem, USA	461,917
174	Craig Stadler, USA	461,877
175	Nick O'Hern, Australia	458,987
176	Craig Perks, New Zealand	457,127
177	Dan Forsman, USA	456,194
178	Larry Mize, USA	440,179
179	David Lynn, England	437,659
180	Jay Don Blake, USA	436,576
181	Anders Hansen, Denmark	436,429
182	Glen Hnatiuk, Canada	434,524
183	Scott Dunlap, USA	422,002
184	Jarmo Sandelin, Sweden	420,632
185	Mark McNulty, Zimbabwe	418,451
186	Ian Leggatt, Canada	418,406
187	Jean Van de Velde, France	416,503
188	Naomichi Ozaki, Japan	416,417
189	Craig Barlow, USA	414,139
190	Michael Muehr, USA	411,270
191	Jeev Milkha Singh, India	408,788
192	Brandt Jobe, USA	407,065
193	Woody Austin, USA	406,352

POS.	PLAYER, COUNTRY	TOTAL MONEY
194	Bradley Hughes, Australia	406,258
195	Gary Orr, Scotland	404,076
196	Brian Davis, England	402,986
197	Spike McRoy, USA	401,654
198	Carl Pettersson, Sweden	401,639
199	Brett Rumford, Australia	399,372
200	Rodney Pampling, Australia	397,714
201	Nobuhito Sato, Japan	397,612
202	Brad Elder, USA	396,967
203	Greg Norman, Australia	396,191
204	Tom Byrum, USA	391,925
205	Thongchai Jaidee, Thailand	388,326
206	Henrik Stenson, Sweden	388,207
207	Katsuyoshi Tomori, Japan	386,835
208	Pete Jordan, USA	386,088
209	Heath Slocum, USA	385,340
210	Richard Green, Australia	379,224
211	John Bickerton, England	376,443
212	Paul Goydos, USA	375,557
213	Daren Lee, England	374,726
214	Soren Kjeldsen, Denmark	373,309
215	Anthony Wall, England	366,170
216	Russ Cochran, USA	362,556
217	Charlie Wi, Korea	358,724
218	Shinichi Yokota, Japan	358,126
219	Bob Burns, USA	353,046
220	Pat Bates, USA	352,261
221	Takenori Hiraishi, Japan	351,706
222	Shaun Micheel, USA	351,095
223	Alex Cejka, Germany	350,778
224	Kazuhiko Hosokawa, Japan	349,511
225	Jim Carter, USA	347,866
226	Lee Porter, USA	346,462
227	Joe Ogilvie, USA	343,189
228	Roger Wessels, South Africa	342,581
229	John Riegger, USA	342,221
230	Gary Evans, England	341,509
231	Tsukasa Watanabe, Japan	337,906
232	Toru Suzuki, Japan	336,426
233	Mark Mouland, Wales	334,761
234	Franklin Langham, USA	332,538
235	Gregory Havret, France	324,810
236	Des Smyth, Ireland	323,766
237	Brent Schwarzrock, USA	322,336
238	Greg Turner New Zealand	320,663
239	Ian Garbutt, England	320,253
240	Jim McGovern, USA	316,802
241	Henrik Bjornstadt, Norway	311,672
242	Aaron Baddeley, Australia	309,576
243	Mark Wiebe, USA	308,792
244	Ted Tryba, USA	308,049
245	Deane Pappas, South Africa	305,694
246	Tommy Tolles, USA	304,644
247	Mathew Goggin, Australia	304,061

POS.	PLAYER, COUNTRY	TOTAL MONEY
248	Eduardo Herrera, Colombia	303,846
249	Joakim Haeggman, Sweden	300,307
250	Tripp Isenhour, USA	299,452
251	Tony Johnstone, Zimbabwe	299,037
252	Curtis Strange, USA	298,632
253	Eiji Mizoguchi, Japan	297,660
254	Gabriel Hjertstedt, Sweden	296,273
255	Kenichi Kuboya, Japan	292,450
256	Raymond Russell, Scotland	290,162
257	Mikael Lundberg, Sweden	289,844
258	Tomohiro Kondou, Japan	289,314
259	Stephen Gallacher, Scotland	284,015
260	Blaine McCallister, USA	280,589
261	David Morland, Canada	279,877
262	Eduardo Romero, Argentina	279,173
263	Sven Struver, Germany	278,443
264	Steve Pate, USA	271,967
265	Ronnie Black, USA	271,686
266	Shigemasa Higaki, Japan	270,249
267	Hideki Kase, Japan	266,926
268	Tetsuji Hiratsuka, Japan	265,912
269	Steve Jones, USA	264,456
270	Olle Karlsson, Sweden	262,312
271	Jamie Donaldson, Wales	260,822
272	Sam Torrance, Scotland	258,530
273	Roger Chapman, England	255,547
274	Tim Petrovic, USA	255,263
275	Jarrod Moseley, Australia	254,179
276	Markus Brier, Austria	251,963
277	Danny Ellis, USA	250,817
278	Jonathan Byrd, USA	250,144
279	Robin Freeman, USA	248,543
280	Bradley Dredge, Wales	247,340
281	Emanuele Canonica, Italy	245,043
282	Gary Nicklaus, USA	244,893
283	Katsumune Imai, Japan	243,655
284	John Rollins, USA	242,841
285	Zaw Moe, Myanmar	242,008
286	Fulton Allem, South Africa	241,680
287	Jorge Berendt, Argentina	239,830
288	Tommy Armour III, USA	238,091
289	Michael Clark, USA	236,991
290	Darren Fichardt, South Africa	236,973
291	John Senden, Australia	234,308
292	Jonathan Lomas, England	233,463
293	Willie Wood, USA	232,675
294	Tsuyoshi Yoneyama, Japan	232,650
295	Trevor Immelman, South Africa	232,514
296	Yeh Chang-ting, Taiwan	227,800
297	Anders Forsbrand, Sweden	225,628
298	Kiyoshi Maita, Japan	225,354
299	Gary Emerson, England	223,479
300	Stephen Leaney, Australia	222,579
301	Jean-Francois Remesy, France	220,819

POS.	PLAYER, COUNTRY	TOTAL MONEY
302	Cliff Kresge, USA	220,649
303	Jeff Hart, USA	219,386
304	Costantino Rocca, Italy	218,331
305	Simon Dyson, England	217,961
306	Nobuo Serizawa, Japan	215,851
307	Jimmy Green, USA	213,942
308	Tom Scherrer, USA	213,443
309	Toshiaki Odate, Japan	212,062
310	Bryce Molder, USA	211,105
311	Stephen Dodd, Wales	210,410
312	Brenden Pappas, South Africa	210,174
313	Ben Bates, USA	209,866
314	Diego Borrego, Spain	209,075
315	Peter Jacobsen, USA	209,047
316	David Carter, England	208,444
317	Ignacio Garrido, Spain	208,064
318	Dicky Pride, USA	207,127
319	Satoshi Higashi, Japan	206,760
320	Peter Baker, England	206,571
321	Kevin Johnson, USA	205,242
322	Todd Hamilton, USA	204,015
323	Phil Tataurangi, New Zealand	203,902
324	Stephen Scahill, New Zealand	203,576
325	Shigeru Nonaka, Japan	203,244
326	Jeff Gove, USA	201,687
327	Mark Pilkington, Wales	201,358
328	Richard Zokol, Canada	199,995
329	Todd Barranger, USA	199,292
330	Prayad Marksaeng, Thailand	198,130
331	Brian Henninger, USA	196,814
332	Robert Gamez, USA	196,045
333	Tjaart van der Walt, South Africa	195,689
334	Jim Benepe, USA	195,075
335	Nathan Green, Australia	194,195
336	Patrik Sjoland, Sweden	192,650
337	Trevor Dodds, Namibia	192,373
338	Chris Tidland, USA	191,738
339	Yoshimitsu Fukuzawa, Japan	191,691
340	Hirofumi Miyase, Japan	190,488
341	Brendan Jones, New Zealand	188,602
342	Ben Ferguson, Australia	187,970
343	Christopher Hanell, Sweden	187,214
344	Richard Johnson, Sweden	186,987
345	Scott Gardiner, New Zealand	186,661
346	Marc Farry, France	186,012
347	Johan Rystrom, Sweden	185,395
348	Michael Long, New Zealand	184,901
349	Go Higaki, Japan	182,500
350	Mark Roe, England	182,151
351	Katsunori Kuwabara, Japan	182,039
352	Maarten Lafeber, Holland	181,526
353	Peter Hanson, Sweden	181,399
354	Paul Eales, England	180,664
355	Jason Gore, USA	180,451

POS.	PLAYER, COUNTRY	TOTAL MONEY
356	Bill Glasson, USA	180,441
357	Bo Van Pelt, USA	175,947
358	Henrik Nystrom, Sweden	175,412
359	Andrew Magee, USA	175,108
360	Jeff Brehaut, USA	175,046
361	Marco Dawson, USA	172,738
362	Matt Peterson, USA	169,947
363	Brian Wilson, USA	169,440
364	Jason Hill, USA	166,899
365	Kazuhiro Kinjo, Japan	165,832
366	Desvond Botes, South Africa	165,051
367	Masayuki Kawamura, Japan	164,359
368	Anthony Gilligan, Australia	163,656
369	James Kingston, South Africa	163,590
370	Brad Fabel, USA	162,706
371	Rolf Muntz, Holland	162,253
372	Paul Claxton, USA	161,260
373	Andrew McLardy, South Africa	160,362
374	Malcolm Mackenzie, England	160,080
375	Brian Claar, USA	160,065
376	Andrew Pitts, USA	158,564
377	Omar Uresti, USA	158,419
378	Steve Haskins, USA	157,615
379	Ryuji Imada, Japan	157,544
380	Steve Allan, Australia	156,686
381	Christian Cevaer, France	156,121
382	Donnie Hammond, USA	155,977
383	Mark Hensby, Australia	155,629
384	Arjun Atwal, India	154,857
385	Jason Dufner, USA	151,784
386	Michael Allen, USA	151,598
387	Tom Carter, USA	149,576
388	Elliot Boult, New Zealand	148,470
389	Mitsutaka Kusakabe, Japan	148,146
390	Ben Crane, USA	147,474
391	Santiago Luna, Spain	146,781
392	Sonny Skinner, USA	145,706
393	Kelly Gibson, USA	145,551
394	Chris Couch, USA	145,536
395	Nozomi Kawahara, Japan	145,282
396	Kosaku Makisaka, Japan	144,987
397	Carlos Rodiles, Spain	144,005
398	Eric Meeks, USA	143,751
399	Christian Pena, USA	143,542
400	Keoke Cotner, Mexico	143,317

World Money List Leaders

YEAR	PLAYER, COUNTRY	TOTAL MONEY
1966	Jack Nicklaus, USA	$168,088
1967	Jack Nicklaus, USA	276,166
1968	Billy Casper, USA	222,436
1969	Frank Beard, USA	186,993
1970	Jack Nicklaus, USA	222,583
1971	Jack Nicklaus, USA	285,897
1972	Jack Nicklaus, USA	341,792
1973	Tom Weiskopf, USA	349,645
1974	Johnny Miller, USA	400,255
1975	Jack Nicklaus, USA	332,610
1976	Jack Nicklaus, USA	316,086
1977	Tom Watson, USA	358,034
1978	Tom Watson, USA	384,388
1979	Tom Watson, USA	506,912
1980	Tom Watson, USA	651,921
1981	Johnny Miller, USA	704,204
1982	Raymond Floyd, USA	738,699
1983	Seve Ballesteros, Spain	686,088
1984	Seve Ballesteros, Spain	688,047
1985	Bernhard Langer, Germany	860,262
1986	Greg Norman, Australia	1,146,584
1987	Ian Woosnam, Wales	1,793,268
1988	Seve Ballesteros, Spain	1,261,275
1989	David Frost, South Africa	1,650,230
1990	Jose Maria Olazabal, Spain	1,633,640
1991	Bernhard Langer, Germany	2,186,700
1992	Nick Faldo, England	2,748,248
1993	Nick Faldo, England	2,825,280
1994	Ernie Els, South Africa	2,862,854
1995	Corey Pavin, USA	2,746,340
1996	Colin Montgomerie, Scotland	3,071,442
1997	Colin Montgomerie, Scotland	3,366,900
1998	Tiger Woods, USA	2,927,946
1999	Tiger Woods, USA	7,681,625
2000	Tiger Woods, USA	11,034,530
2001	Tiger Woods, USA	7,771,562

Career World Money List

Here is a list of the 50 leading money winners for their careers through the 2001 season. It includes players active on both the regular and senior tours of the world. The World Money List from this and the 35 previous editions of the annual and a table prepared for a companion book, *The Wonderful World of Professional Golf* (Atheneum, 1973) form the basis for this compilation. Additional figures were taken from official records of major golf associations, although shortcomings in records-keeping outside the United States in the 1950s and 1960s and a few exclusions from U.S. records during those years prevent these figures from being completely accurate, although the careers of virtually all of these top 50 players began after that time. Conversion of foreign currency figures to U.S. dollars is based on average values during the particular years involved.

POS.	PLAYER, COUNTRY	TOTAL MONEY
1	Tiger Woods, USA	$32,690,554
2	Ernie Els, South Africa	26,589,295
3	Davis Love III, USA	24,212,138
4	Nick Price, Zimbabwe	23,612,139
5	Colin Montgomerie, Scotland	23,558,412
6	Hale Irwin, USA	23,245,925
7	Greg Norman, Australia	22,937,310
8	Bernhard Langer, Germany	22,267,009
9	Vijay Singh, Fiji	22,110,263
10	Fred Couples, USA	21,042,703
11	Masashi Ozaki, Japan	20,548,992
12	Phil Mickelson, USA	19,673,917
13	Scott Hoch, USA	18,673,183
14	David Duval, USA	18,545,825
15	Raymond Floyd, USA	18,159,917
16	Nick Faldo, England	17,878,403
17	Mark Calcavecchia, USA	17,476,817
18	Tom Lehman, USA	17,102,009
19	Tom Kite, USA	16,775,104
20	Gil Morgan, USA	16,608,483
21	Mark O'Meara, USA	16,606,118
22	Lee Trevino, USA	16,373,448
23	Ian Woosnam, Wales	15,902,805
24	Isao Aoki, Japan	15,586,432
25	Jose Maria Olazabal, Spain	15,144,981
26	David Frost, South Africa	15,015,251
27	Tom Watson, USA	14,675,821
28	Hal Sutton, USA	14,639,497
29	Payne Stewart, USA	14,617,674
30	Larry Nelson, USA	14,306,778
31	Jim Colbert, USA	14,188,911
32	Paul Azinger, USA	13,723,744
33	Naomichi Ozaki, Japan	13,205,508
34	Corey Pavin, USA	13,049,735
35	Jim Furyk, USA	12,973,778
36	Lee Westwood, England	12,539,301
37	Brad Faxon, USA	12,421,043

POS.	PLAYER, COUNTRY	TOTAL MONEY
38	Jeff Sluman, USA	12,362,574
39	Bob Charles, New Zealand	12,320,509
40	Justin Leonard, USA	12,262,835
41	Graham Marsh, Australia	12,243,097
42	Steve Elkington, Australia	12,129,539
43	Jesper Parnevik, Sweden	12,073,986
44	Bob Murphy, USA	12,019,255
45	Dave Stockton, USA	11,962,876
46	Seve Ballesteros, Spain	11,913,366
47	Darren Clarke, N. Ireland	11,885,274
48	George Archer, USA	11,774,821
49	John Cook, USA	11,671,487
50	Craig Stadler, USA	11,607,477

These 50 players have won $824,904,319 in their careers.

Senior World Money List

This list includes official earnings from the world money list of the International Federation of PGA Tours, U.S. Senior PGA Tour, European Seniors Tour and Japan Senior Tour, along with other winnings in established unofficial events when reliable figures could be obtained.

POS.	PLAYER, COUNTRY	TOTAL MONEY
1	Allen Doyle, USA	$2,953,582
2	Bruce Fleisher, USA	2,643,563
3	Hale Irwin, USA	2,415,586
4	Larry Nelson, USA	2,314,936
5	Gil Morgan, USA	1,924,704
6	Jim Thorpe, USA	1,850,048
7	Doug Tewell, USA	1,846,339
8	Dana Quigley, USA	1,826,681
9	Bob Gilder, USA	1,704,713
10	Tom Kite, USA	1,675,054
11	Tom Watson, USA	1,391,497
12	Jim Colbert, USA	1,368,638
13	Walter Hall, USA	1,339,059
14	Mike McCullough, USA	1,335,040
15	Ed Dougherty, USA	1,330,818
16	Jose Maria Canizares, Spain	1,291,094
17	Tom Jenkins, USA	1,156,576
18	Bruce Lietzke, USA	1,128,413
19	Raymond Floyd, USA	978,690
20	Leonard Thompson, USA	968,881
21	Sammy Rachels, USA	932,031
22	Bruce Summerhays, USA	916,617
23	Vicente Fernandez, Argentina	872,226

POS.	PLAYER, COUNTRY	TOTAL MONEY
24	Gary McCord, USA	871,132
25	Jim Ahern, USA	831,480
26	Stewart Ginn, Australia	799,254
27	Isao Aoki, Japan	797,184
28	John Bland, South Africa	772,835
29	J.C. Snead, USA	768,421
30	John Jacobs, USA	743,421
31	Bob Charles, New Zealand	732,662
32	John Schroeder, USA	716,197
33	Terry Mauney, USA	695,474
34	Hugh Baiocchi, South Africa	693,131
35	Mike Hill, USA	691,612
36	Graham Marsh, Australia	668,093
37	Andy North, USA	612,890
38	Dave Stockton, USA	588,891
39	Bobby Wadkins, USA	583,869
40	George Archer, USA	545,596
41	Walter Morgan, USA	535,312
42	Steven Veriato, USA	527,703
43	Jim Dent, USA	519,631
44	Jim Albus, USA	517,794
45	Jay Sigel, USA	516,027
46	Gary Player, South Africa	505,467
47	Bobby Walzel, USA	487,452
48	Bob Eastwood, USA	482,993
49	John Mahaffey, USA	482,400
50	Rocky Thompson, USA	481,594
51	Dave Eichelberger, USA	481,076
52	Joe Inman, USA	468,056
53	Howard Twitty, USA	431,932
54	Mike Smith, USA	426,313
55	Hubert Green, USA	424,441
56	Lee Trevino, USA	397,834
57	Ted Goin, USA	394,516
58	Jim Holtgrieve, USA	376,498
59	Terry Dill, USA	370,308
60	Ian Stanley, Australia	357,407
61	Jack Nicklaus, USA	352,014
62	Denis Durnian, England	344,597
63	Tom Wargo, USA	331,631
64	Fred Gibson, USA	325,538
65	Gibby Gilbert, USA	321,861
66	Dale Douglass, USA	310,464
67	Jesse Patino, USA	306,573
68	Don Pooley, USA	303,271
69	Katsunari Takahashi, Japan	280,744
70	Al Geiberger, USA	278,007
71	Seiji Ebihara, Japan	273,131
72	Arnold Palmer, USA	271,697
73	DeWitt Weaver, USA	268,640
74	Tom McGinnis, USA	267,390
75	Bob Murphy, USA	263,844
76	Dick Mast, USA	261,547
77	Bill Brask, USA	248,329

POS.	PLAYER, COUNTRY	TOTAL MONEY
78	Jimmy Powell, USA	244,453
79	David Lundstrom, USA	229,920
80	Jerry Bruner, USA	224,128
81	David Graham, Australia	223,487
82	Jerry McGee, USA	222,377
83	Don Bies, USA	220,864
84	Lanny Wadkins, USA	207,833
85	Larry Ziegler, USA	203,694
86	Mark Hayes, USA	196,847
87	Noel Ratcliffe, Australia	193,366
88	David Good, Australia	189,665
89	Simon Owen, New Zealand	180,025
90	Jay Overton, USA	173,800
91	David Oakley, USA	169,988
92	Frank Conner, Austria	161,068
93	Roy Vucinich, USA	158,509
94	Delroy Cambridge, Jamaica	157,279
95	Fujio Kobayashi, Japan	152,424
96	John Morgan, England	151,866
97	Tom Shaw, USA	150,574
98	Charles Coody, USA	149,832
99	Bernard Gallacher, Scotland	147,333
100	Denis O'Sullivan, Ireland	146,711

Women's World Money List

This list includes official earnings on the U.S. LPGA Tour, Evian Ladies European Tour and Japan LPGA Tour, along with other winnings in established unofficial events when reliable figures could be obtained.

POS.	PLAYER, COUNTRY	TOTAL MONEY
1	Annika Sorenstam, Sweden	$2,105,868
2	Karrie Webb, Australia	1,719,847
3	Se Ri Pak, Korea	1,623,009
4	Lorie Kane, Canada	1,047,489
5	Maria Hjorth, Sweden	907,680
6	Dottie Pepper, USA	810,921
7	Janice Moodie, Scotland	795,563
8	Sophie Gustafson, Sweden	794,267
9	Rosie Jones, USA	785,010
10	Laura Diaz, USA	784,356
11	Laura Davies, England	780,945
12	Catriona Matthew, Scotland	768,930
13	Mi Hyun Kim, Korea	762,363
14	Rachel Teske, Australia	742,102
15	Wendy Ward, USA	736,906
16	Yuri Fudoh, Japan	725,593
17	Emilee Klein, USA	649,380

POS.	PLAYER, COUNTRY	TOTAL MONEY
18	Dorothy Delasin, USA	620,442
19	Kaori Higo, Japan	576,631
20	Chieko Amanuma, Japan	568,026
21	Michele Redman, USA	552,317
22	Carin Koch, Sweden	533,724
23	Kelly Robbins, USA	530,754
24	Kasumi Fujii, Japan	513,527
25	Grace Park, Korea	496,670
26	Meg Mallon, USA	488,235
27	Juli Inkster, USA	482,883
28	Nancy Scranton, USA	465,673
29	Toshimi Kimura, Japan	462,778
30	Aki Takamura, Japan	452,792
31	Miyuki Shimabukuro, Japan	447,637
32	Mhairi McKay, Scotland	439,024
33	Kaori Harada, Japan	422,837
34	Michie Ohba, Japan	417,436
35	Beth Daniel, USA	410,540
36	Ji-Hee Lee, Korea	405,721
37	Wendy Doolan, Australia	405,135
38	Akiko Fukushima, Japan	393,013
39	Woo-Soon Ko, Korea	375,883
40	Ikuyo Shiotani, Japan	375,504
41	Cristie Kerr, USA	373,947
42	Pat Hurst, USA	367,303
43	Betsy King, USA	358,756
44	Jill McGill, USA	340,991
45	Moira Dunn, USA	335,307
46	Yu-Chen Huang, Taiwan	329,038
47	Helen Alfredsson, Sweden	319,398
48	Marisa Baena, Colombia	318,819
49	Fuki Kido, Japan	309,947
50	Kelli Kuehne, USA	300,729
51	Mineko Nasu, Japan	293,399
52	Kris Tschetter, USA	290,191
53	Gloria Park, Korea	289,468
54	Michiko Hattori, Japan	282,489
55	Midori Yoneyama, Japan	274,200
56	Brandie Burton, USA	265,853
57	Donna Andrews, USA	263,754
58	Vicki Goetze-Ackerman, USA	261,446
59	Yu Ping Lin, Taiwan	253,771
60	Sherri Turner, USA	253,724
61	Kumiko Hiyoshi, Japan	252,713
62	Danielle Ammaccapane, USA	251,992
63	Tina Fischer, Germany	251,218
64	Tracy Hanson, USA	249,978
65	Hiroko Yamaguchi, Japan	245,444
66	Ok-Hee Ku, Korea	245,095
67	Leta Lindley, USA	243,597
68	Heather Daly-Donofrio, USA	242,176
69	Junko Yasui, Japan	241,303
70	Becky Iverson, USA	233,602
71	Raquel Carriedo, Spain	229,432

POS.	PLAYER, COUNTRY	TOTAL MONEY
72	Heather Bowie, USA	226,291
73	Kate Golden, USA	223,879
74	Jackie Gallagher-Smith, USA	216,940
75	Ae-Sook Kim, Korea	214,740
76	Michelle McGann, USA	214,289
77	Hisako Ohgane, Japan	214,117
78	Orie Fujino, Japan	210,753
79	Suzann Pettersen, Norway	208,132
80	Tammie Green, USA	203,734
81	Kayo Yamada, Japan	203,458
82	Hsui-Feng Tseng, Taiwan	199,161
83	Kathryn Marshall, Scotland	191,160
84	Amy Fruhwirth, USA	188,984
85	Karen Weiss, USA	186,228
86	Marine Monnet, France	184,307
87	Chihiro Nakajima, Japan	183,062
88	Liselotte Neumann, Sweden	182,120
89	Ayako Okamoto, Japan	180,055
90	Shin Sora, Korea	179,778
91	Sherri Steinhauer, USA	175,431
92	Dina Ammaccapane, USA	173,306
93	Barb Mucha, USA	172,526
94	Becky Morgan, Wales	169,594
95	A.J. Eathorne, Canada	157,833
96	Hsiao-Chuan Lu, Taiwan	148,696
97	Audra Burks, USA	147,012
98	Karine Icher, France	146,598
99	Marnie McGuire, New Zealand	145,237
100	Leslie Spalding, USA	144,918
101	Mayumi Murai, Japan	140,264
102	Hiromi Kobayashi, Japan	139,726
103	Alicia Dibos, Peru	139,251
104	Penny Hammel, USA	139,034
105	Patricia Meunier Lebouc, France	136,678
106	Jenny Lidback, Peru	136,115
107	Jane Crafter, Australia	133,503
108	Charlotte Sorenstam, Sweden	132,917
109	Hee-Won Han, Korea	131,669
110	Michelle Estill, USA	130,541
111	Dawn Coe-Jones, Canada	130,366
112	Kristi Albers, USA	128,912
113	Jean Bartholomew, USA	126,209
114	Fumiko Muraguchi, Japan	121,571
115	Silvia Cavalleri, Italy	121,559
116	Shani Waugh, Australia	120,436
117	Alison Nicholas, England	119,034
118	Akane Ohshiro, Japan	118,732
119	Tina Barrett, USA	116,241
120	Paula Marti, Spain	115,567
121	Elisabeth Esterl, Germany	114,957
122	Kyoko Ono, Japan	114,744
123	Cindy Figg-Currier, USA	114,635
124	Nahoko Hirao, Japan	113,434
125	Iben Tinning, Denmark	112,830

American Tours

Mercedes Championships

Plantation Course, Kapalua, Maui, Hawaii
Par 36-37–73; 7,263 yards

January 11-14
purse, $3,500,000

	SCORES				TOTAL	MONEY
Jim Furyk	69	69	69	67	274	$630,000
Rory Sabbatini	69	69	65	72	275	380,000
Ernie Els	68	66	73	69	276	203,000
Vijay Singh	71	67	67	71	276	203,000
John Huston	74	67	69	67	277	140,000
Rocco Mediate	70	69	70	69	278	126,000
David Duval	73	71	65	70	279	118,000
Michael Clark	69	70	72	69	280	99,000
Justin Leonard	67	73	69	71	280	99,000
David Toms	70	71	67	72	280	99,000
Tiger Woods	70	73	68	69	280	99,000
Billy Andrade	69	70	69	73	281	78,000
Stewart Cink	69	71	69	72	281	78,000
Dennis Paulson	70	72	67	72	281	78,000
Mike Weir	70	70	68	73	281	78,000
Kirk Triplett	71	73	68	70	282	70,000
Paul Azinger	70	70	68	75	283	66,000
Chris DiMarco	71	73	69	70	283	66,000
Carlos Franco	70	76	68	70	284	60,000
Dudley Hart	70	77	69	68	284	60,000
Loren Roberts	74	69	71	70	284	60,000
Duffy Waldorf	70	70	71	73	284	60,000
Brad Faxon	71	70	71	73	285	54,500
Jesper Parnevik	76	66	72	71	285	54,500
Hal Sutton	70	74	73	69	286	53,000
Tom Lehman	74	73	71	71	289	51,500
Tom Scherrer	74	71	72	72	289	51,500
Robert Allenby	72	74	73	71	290	49,500
Phil Mickelson	72	73	72	73	290	49,500
Scott Verplank	74	73	71	73	291	48,000
Jim Carter	80	72	72	72	296	47,000
Notah Begay	75	76	71	75	297	46,000
Steve Lowery	80	73	71	75	299	45,000

Touchstone Energy Tucson Open

Omni Tucson National Resort: Par 36-36–72; 7,019 yards
Gallery Golf Club: Par 36-36–72; 7,360 yards
Tucson, Arizona

January 11-14
purse, $3,000,000

	SCORES				TOTAL	MONEY
Garrett Willis	71	69	64	69	273	$540,000
Kevin Sutherland	67	72	67	68	274	324,000
Geoff Ogilvy	67	72	68	68	275	174,000
Bob Tway	73	69	67	66	275	174,000
Choi Kyung-ju	70	70	70	66	276	105,375

	SCORES			TOTAL	MONEY
Greg Kraft	74	65	69	68	276	105,375
Cliff Kresge	72	67	71	66	276	105,375
Mark Wiebe	69	67	66	74	276	105,375
Rich Beem	70	69	71	67	277	72,000
Steve Flesch	72	69	66	70	277	72,000
Harrison Frazar	68	73	66	70	277	72,000
Mark Hensby	69	68	69	71	277	72,000
Bernhard Langer	68	69	70	70	277	72,000
Jeff Maggert	70	68	70	69	277	72,000
Mark Calcavecchia	71	71	67	69	278	48,000
Hunter Haas	71	68	68	71	278	48,000
Glen Hnatiuk	71	69	66	72	278	48,000
Brandt Jobe	72	69	66	71	278	48,000
Jerry Kelly	70	69	70	69	278	48,000
Bob Burns	70	70	70	69	279	32,500
Russ Cochran	71	69	68	71	279	32,500
Fred Funk	70	73	67	69	279	32,500
Craig Kanada	70	70	72	67	279	32,500
Chris Riley	69	70	68	72	279	32,500
Mike Sposa	71	70	69	69	279	32,500
Jay Don Blake	70	72	68	70	280	21,750
Tim Clark	67	73	71	69	280	21,750
Fred Couples	71	69	68	72	280	21,750
Robert Gamez	69	70	72	69	280	21,750
Paul Goydos	70	71	69	70	280	21,750
Len Mattiace	70	71	68	71	280	21,750
Olin Browne	68	74	69	70	281	15,566.67
Ben Ferguson	74	70	66	71	281	15,566.67
Tim Herron	67	76	66	72	281	15,566.67
Jonathan Kaye	72	68	71	70	281	15,566.67
Scott McCarron	71	69	71	70	281	15,566.67
David Peoples	71	70	72	68	281	15,566.67
Mike Reid	73	67	68	73	281	15,566.66
Willie Wood	67	75	69	70	281	15,566.66
Kaname Yokoo	68	70	72	71	281	15,566.66
Neal Lancaster	68	76	68	70	282	11,400
Jim McGovern	74	67	70	71	282	11,400
Chris Perry	70	74	68	70	282	11,400
Tommy Tolles	71	70	71	70	282	11,400
Andrew Magee	70	66	70	77	283	9,300
Larry Mize	73	70	70	70	283	9,300
Grant Waite	71	71	71	70	283	9,300
Stephen Ames	69	71	73	71	284	7,387.50
John Daly	70	72	71	71	284	7,387.50
Glen Day	67	76	73	68	284	7,387.50
Jeff Gallagher	70	73	72	69	284	7,387.50
Carl Paulson	70	68	74	72	284	7,387.50
Lee Porter	69	65	76	74	284	7,387.50
Chris Tidland	71	70	72	71	284	7,387.50
Mark Wurtz	74	70	69	71	284	7,387.50
Craig Barlow	71	70	72	72	285	6,720
Jim Gallagher, Jr.	72	72	73	68	285	6,720
Jason Gore	71	72	72	70	285	6,720
Jeff Hart	70	73	69	73	285	6,720
Brent Schwarzrock	72	71	66	76	285	6,720
Steve Allan	76	67	73	70	286	6,390
Ronnie Black	70	69	75	72	286	6,390
Steve Jones	70	66	72	78	286	6,390
Sean Murphy	70	71	70	75	286	6,390

		SCORES			TOTAL	MONEY
Tom Pernice, Jr.	74	70	73	69	286	6,390
Kenny Perry	73	71	70	72	286	6,390
John Cook	71	71	74	71	287	6,120
Donnie Hammond	70	73	71	73	287	6,120
Tom Purtzer	73	70	74	70	287	6,120
Ted Tryba	72	71	71	74	288	6,000
Jeff Brehaut	71	70	73	75	289	5,850
Matt Gogel	72	72	73	72	289	5,850
John Riegger	73	71	73	72	289	5,850
Mike Springer	71	72	72	74	289	5,850
Brad Elder	72	71	76	71	290	5,670
Steve Elkington	70	74	70	76	290	5,670
Dave Stockton, Jr.	73	71	76	71	291	5,580
Yoshinori Mizumaki	70	74	73	75	292	5,520
Robert Damron	71	73	74	75	293	5,460
Rick Fehr	70	74	76	74	294	5,400
Barry Cheesman	73	71	79	72	295	5,340
Emanuele Canonica	69	72	77	78	296	5,280
Cameron Beckman	72	70	73		WD	

Sony Open in Hawaii

Waialae Country Club, Honolulu, Hawaii
Par 35-35–70; 7,060 yards

January 18-21
purse, $4,000,000

		SCORES			TOTAL	MONEY
Brad Faxon	64	64	67	65	260	$720,000
Tom Lehman	66	67	65	66	264	432,000
Ernie Els	68	65	65	69	267	272,000
Billy Andrade	69	69	66	65	269	192,000
Briny Baird	68	70	68	65	271	135,600
Greg Chalmers	69	69	66	67	271	135,600
Fred Funk	66	69	69	67	271	135,600
Naomichi Ozaki	66	70	68	67	271	135,600
Loren Roberts	67	67	69	68	271	135,600
Tom Byrum	68	70	67	67	272	96,000
Brian Gay	71	65	70	66	272	96,000
Davis Love III	70	68	65	69	272	96,000
Jeff Sluman	66	73	66	67	272	96,000
Stephen Ames	68	68	68	69	273	68,000
Jim Furyk	66	67	69	71	273	68,000
John Huston	68	66	69	70	273	68,000
Spike McRoy	66	69	71	67	273	68,000
Shaun Micheel	67	68	69	69	273	68,000
Michael Clark	72	66	69	67	274	52,000
Carlos Franco	66	67	69	72	274	52,000
Duffy Waldorf	73	66	70	65	274	52,000
Bradley Hughes	67	66	71	71	275	36,057.15
Vijay Singh	68	70	67	70	275	36,057.15
Chris DiMarco	67	69	67	72	275	36,057.14
Scott Dunlap	68	68	68	71	275	36,057.14
Steve Lowery	68	70	69	68	275	36,057.14
Shigeki Maruyama	69	66	70	70	275	36,057.14
Craig Parry	69	69	66	71	275	36,057.14
Robert Allenby	70	67	68	71	276	24,350
Jim Carter	70	69	68	69	276	24,350
Choi Kyung-ju	68	70	69	69	276	24,350

	SCORES				TOTAL	MONEY
Joe Durant	68	69	68	71	276	24,350
Jerry Kelly	69	65	73	69	276	24,350
Franklin Langham	66	69	69	72	276	24,350
Jerry Smith	71	66	67	72	276	24,350
Kaname Yokoo	70	66	72	68	276	24,350
Stuart Appleby	72	67	69	69	277	17,600
David Berganio, Jr.	71	66	67	73	277	17,600
Bill Glasson	67	68	68	74	277	17,600
J.L. Lewis	66	69	70	72	277	17,600
Jeff Maggert	69	70	69	69	277	17,600
David Peoples	67	70	73	67	277	17,600
Olin Browne	67	68	71	72	278	13,600
Cliff Kresge	68	68	70	72	278	13,600
Rory Sabbatini	71	68	66	73	278	13,600
Esteban Toledo	71	66	73	68	278	13,600
Steve Allan	70	69	69	71	279	10,760
Dudley Hart	69	70	70	70	279	10,760
Larry Mize	64	71	71	73	279	10,760
Ted Tryba	68	70	75	66	279	10,760
Bob Burns	68	70	69	73	280	9,413.34
Richie Coughlan	65	71	70	74	280	9,413.34
Craig Barlow	69	67	75	69	280	9,413.33
Pete Jordan	68	71	72	69	280	9,413.33
Corey Pavin	73	66	71	70	280	9,413.33
Chris Perry	67	72	68	73	280	9,413.33
John Cook	71	68	70	72	281	9,000
John Riegger	68	70	75	68	281	9,000
Paul Goydos	68	71	71	72	282	8,760
Kelly Grunewald	71	68	74	69	282	8,760
Chris Smith	70	69	68	75	282	8,760
Garrett Willis	68	70	68	76	282	8,760
John Daly	64	72	76	71	283	8,480
Frank Lickliter	71	66	74	72	283	8,480
Sean Murphy	66	71	70	76	283	8,480
J.J. Henry	67	71	72	74	284	8,280
Peter Jacobsen	69	64	75	76	284	8,280
Jeremy Anderson	72	67	75	71	285	8,080
Michael Muehr	68	70	75	72	285	8,080
Gary Nicklaus	66	71	70	78	285	8,080

Phoenix Open

TPC of Scottsdale, Scottsdale, Arizona
Par 35-36–71; 7,083 yards

January 25-28
purse, $4,000,000

	SCORES				TOTAL	MONEY
Mark Calcavecchia	65	60	64	67	256	$720,000
Rocco Mediate	68	63	64	69	264	432,000
Steve Lowery	69	67	64	68	268	272,000
Scott Verplank	64	66	70	70	270	192,000
Chris DiMarco	68	67	65	71	271	152,000
Tiger Woods	65	73	68	65	271	152,000
Tom Lehman	64	70	69	69	272	129,000
Steve Stricker	71	62	72	67	272	129,000
Stewart Cink	65	66	71	71	273	104,000
John Daly	67	70	70	66	273	104,000
Fred Funk	68	69	70	66	273	104,000

	SCORES				TOTAL	MONEY
David Toms	69	69	68	67	273	104,000
Edward Fryatt	66	69	72	67	274	72,800
Sergio Garcia	67	71	70	66	274	72,800
Billy Mayfair	68	71	70	65	274	72,800
Chris Perry	65	70	72	67	274	72,800
Nick Price	70	70	69	65	274	72,800
Frank Lickliter	70	66	70	69	275	60,000
Harrison Frazar	67	71	72	66	276	52,000
Paul Goydos	70	68	72	66	276	52,000
Shigeki Maruyama	69	65	72	70	276	52,000
Stephen Ames	69	68	71	69	277	44,800
Bob Burns	69	65	72	72	278	31,400
Fred Couples	67	70	72	69	278	31,400
Steve Flesch	67	71	71	69	278	31,400
Mathew Goggin	67	68	74	69	278	31,400
Mark Hensby	70	69	70	69	278	31,400
Tim Herron	69	70	71	68	278	31,400
Jonathan Kaye	71	69	71	67	278	31,400
Frank Nobilo	65	69	72	72	278	31,400
Steve Pate	65	71	76	66	278	31,400
Mike Weir	66	74	69	69	278	31,400
Steve Jones	70	70	71	68	279	22,600
Davis Love III	68	66	77	68	279	22,600
Scott McCarron	67	65	73	74	279	22,600
Tommy Armour III	68	67	72	73	280	17,625
Brad Elder	64	75	71	70	280	17,625
Brian Gay	67	68	74	71	280	17,625
Matt Gogel	69	71	71	69	280	17,625
Brandt Jobe	72	67	71	70	280	17,625
Bob May	66	71	72	71	280	17,625
Vijay Singh	71	69	69	71	280	17,625
Hal Sutton	72	66	75	67	280	17,625
Jay Don Blake	70	67	76	68	281	12,432
Joe Durant	70	68	73	70	281	12,432
Glen Hnatiuk	71	67	69	74	281	12,432
Andrew Magee	66	71	72	72	281	12,432
Len Mattiace	71	69	73	68	281	12,432
Stuart Appleby	72	66	72	72	282	9,773.34
Nolan Henke	69	70	72	71	282	9,773.34
Joel Edwards	70	70	71	71	282	9,773.33
Dan Forsman	70	65	71	76	282	9,773.33
Skip Kendall	71	68	71	72	282	9,773.33
David Peoples	67	68	76	71	282	9,773.33
Steve Allan	72	66	71	74	283	9,040
Paul Azinger	72	68	70	73	283	9,040
Brian Henninger	67	73	73	70	283	9,040
Bradley Hughes	69	69	71	74	283	9,040
Paul Stankowski	69	67	72	75	283	9,040
Greg Chalmers	68	71	75	70	284	8,640
Michael Clark	68	71	73	72	284	8,640
Miguel Angel Jimenez	68	70	73	73	284	8,640
Jose Maria Olazabal	68	72	73	71	284	8,640
Kenny Perry	68	68	75	73	284	8,640
Scott Dunlap	69	70	72	74	285	8,360
Blaine McCallister	66	72	76	71	285	8,360
Jim Carter	67	72	70	77	286	8,240
Franklin Langham	69	69	74	76	288	8,160
Olin Browne	68	69	79	73	289	8,080
Brent Geiberger	68	72	77	73	290	7,960
J.P. Hayes	70	69	74	77	290	7,960

AT&T Pebble Beach National Pro-Am

Pebble Beach GL: Par 36-36–72; 6,799 yards
Poppy Hills: Par 36-36–72; 6,833 yards
Spyglass Hill GC: Par 36-36–72; 6,855 yards
Pebble Beach, California

February 1-4
purse, $4,000,000

		SCORES			TOTAL	MONEY
Davis Love III	71	69	69	63	272	$720,000
Vijay Singh	66	68	70	69	273	432,000
Olin Browne	68	69	65	73	275	232,000
Phil Mickelson	70	66	66	73	275	232,000
Ronnie Black	67	68	70	71	276	160,000
Craig Barlow	67	71	67	72	277	139,000
Glen Day	68	75	69	65	277	139,000
Jerry Kelly	69	68	68	73	278	112,000
Franklin Langham	70	70	70	68	278	112,000
Frank Nobilo	70	70	67	71	278	112,000
Mike Weir	70	70	65	73	278	112,000
Scott McCarron	68	73	65	73	279	92,000
Brad Faxon	71	67	69	73	280	68,571.43
Tim Herron	67	70	74	69	280	68,571.43
Mike Springer	72	70	71	67	280	68,571.43
Kirk Triplett	71	69	70	70	280	68,571.43
Grant Waite	70	73	71	66	280	68,571.43
Tiger Woods	66	73	69	72	280	68,571.43
Kenny Perry	70	70	69	71	280	68,571.42
David Berganio, Jr.	64	73	71	73	281	48,266.67
Kevin Sutherland	72	69	70	70	281	48,266.67
Willie Wood	67	69	73	72	281	48,266.66
Steve Flesch	71	72	66	73	282	36,800
Jonathan Kaye	69	73	68	72	282	36,800
Jose Maria Olazabal	71	76	67	68	282	36,800
Garrett Willis	71	74	69	68	282	36,800
Choi Kyung-ju	68	72	72	71	283	26,066.67
Edward Fryatt	66	72	74	71	283	26,066.67
Matt Gogel	69	62	81	71	283	26,066.67
Joe Ogilvie	72	73	68	70	283	26,066.67
John Riegger	73	68	70	72	283	26,066.67
Esteban Toledo	72	70	72	69	283	26,066.67
Jerry Smith	71	70	69	73	283	26,066.66
Jeff Hart	73	69	71	70	283	26,066.66
David Toms	70	69	70	74	283	26,066.66
Jay Don Blake	70·	67	72	75	284	18,028.58
Scott Dunlap	71	71	69	73	284	18,028.57
Brad Elder	66	69	75	74	284	18,028.57
Kevin Johnson	67	72	72	73	284	18,028.57
Tom Pernice, Jr.	70	69	72	73	284	18,028.57
Hal Sutton	70	71	73	70	284	18,028.57
Richard Johnson	67	71	72	74	284	18,028.57
Mark Johnson	65	74	73	73	285	13,600
Corey Pavin	71	69	71	74	285	13,600
Kevin Wentworth	72	71	71	71	285	13,600
Fuzzy Zoeller	73	68	73	71	285	13,600
Paul Azinger	72	70	71	73	286	10,413.34
Peter Jacobsen	71	74	68	73	286	10,413.34
Dan Forsman	71	70	73	72	286	10,413.33
Mike Heinen	70	73	71	72	286	10,413.33
Joey Sindelar	73	68	71	74	286	10,413.33
Chris Smith	71	71	71	73	286	10,413.33

	SCORES				TOTAL	MONEY
Richie Coughlan	74	71	68	74	287	9,360
Gary Hallberg	71	73	70	73	287	9,360
Woody Austin	74	70	70	74	288	9,080
Tom Scherrer	68	67	73	80	288	9,080
Craig Stadler	68	71	73	76	288	9,080
Tripp Isenhour	71	70	73	74	288	9,080
Michael Clark	73	71	70	75	289	8,760
Sergio Garcia	68	70	75	76	289	8,760
Frank Lickliter	69	66	78	76	289	8,760
Mark O'Meara	73	70	70	76	289	8,760
Chris DiMarco	70	73	70	77	290	8,360
Scott Gump	71	68	75	76	290	8,360
Donnie Hammond	70	69	75	76	290	8,360
Pete Jordan	69	72	71	78	290	8,360
Jim McGovern	70	69	71	80	290	8,360
Paul Stankowski	70	72	71	77	290	8,360
Cameron Beckman	72	72	67	80	291	8,000
Jeff Maggert	72	71	70	78	291	8,000
Steve Elkington	70	71	73	77	291	8,000
Jesper Parnevik	72	70	71	80	293	7,840

Buick Invitational

Torrey Pines Golf Course, LaJolla, California
South Course: Par 36-36–72; 7,055 yards
North Course: Par 36-36–72; 6,874 yards

February 8-11
purse, $3,500,000

	SCORES				TOTAL	MONEY
Phil Mickelson	68	64	71	66	269	$630,000
Frank Lickliter	68	67	68	66	269	308,000
Davis Love III	65	67	70	67	269	308,000
(Mickelson defeated Love on second and Lickliter on third playoff hole.)						
Tiger Woods	70	67	67	67	271	168,000
Brent Geiberger	64	69	70	69	272	133,000
Mike Weir	68	67	68	69	272	133,000
Jay Williamson	68	69	71	65	273	109,083.34
Jay Don Blake	68	68	68	69	273	109,083.33
Greg Kraft	69	68	66	70	273	109,083.33
Cameron Beckman	70	68	68	68	274	87,500
Harrison Frazar	68	68	70	68	274	87,500
Chris Smith	66	70	71	67	274	87,500
Brandt Jobe	69	70	67	69	275	60,000
Tom Lehman	68	68	69	70	275	60,000
Shigeki Maruyama	69	69	69	68	275	60,000
Jose Maria Olazabal	68	68	70	69	275	60,000
Mike Sposa	70	68	69	68	275	60,000
Kevin Sutherland	70	68	69	68	275	60,000
Jean Van de Velde	70	67	69	69	275	60,000
J.L. Lewis	71	66	69	70	276	39,340
Dennis Paulson	69	66	69	72	276	39,340
Chris Riley	67	71	70	68	276	39,340
Brent Schwarzrock	67	71	70	68	276	39,340
Bob Tway	68	69	70	69	276	39,340
Bernhard Langer	71	69	67	70	277	29,400
Frank Nobilo	67	70	69	71	277	29,400
Ronnie Black	71	68	69	70	278	22,808.34
Steve Jones	68	71	71	68	278	22,808.34

	SCORES				TOTAL	MONEY
Corey Pavin	68	72	68	70	278	22,808.34
Fred Funk	68	69	69	72	278	22,808.33
J.J. Henry	73	66	69	70	278	22,808.33
Bob May	71	68	67	72	278	22,808.33
Billy Mayfair	73	66	68	71	278	22,808.33
David Morland	67	69	68	74	278	22,808.33
Chris Tidland	67	68	71	72	278	22,808.33
Joe Durant	69	70	71	69	279	16,485
Robin Freeman	69	70	73	67	279	16,485
Jason Gore	72	69	70	68	279	16,485
Tom Pernice, Jr.	73	65	71	70	279	16,485
Jeff Sluman	71	70	69	69	279	16,485
Rich Beem	70	71	72	67	280	12,250
Bob Estes	70	71	68	71	280	12,250
Michael Muehr	67	73	70	70	280	12,250
Naomichi Ozaki	68	70	72	70	280	12,250
Chris Perry	67	72	70	71	280	12,250
Lee Porter	72	68	68	72	280	12,250
Hal Sutton	72	67	72	69	280	12,250
Choi Kyung-ju	69	65	74	73	281	8,796.67
John Daly	71	69	70	71	281	8,796.67
Blaine McCallister	71	68	71	71	281	8,796.67
Toru Taniguchi	72	65	72	72	281	8,796.67
Doug Barron	70	66	69	76	281	8,796.66
Fred Couples	70	71	72	68	281	8,796.66
Bob Burns	70	69	72	71	282	8,015
Hunter Haas	70	69	72	71	282	8,015
Glen Hnatiuk	69	71	73	69	282	8,015
Steve Lowery	73	67	73	69	282	8,015
Stephen Ames	70	69	73	71	283	7,490
David Berganio, Jr.	70	69	73	71	283	7,490
Jeff Brehaut	72	69	74	68	283	7,490
Brad Faxon	67	69	72	75	283	7,490
Edward Fryatt	70	71	69	73	283	7,490
Paul Goydos	72	69	71	71	283	7,490
Tripp Isenhour	71	68	73	71	283	7,490
Craig Kanada	68	73	72	70	283	7,490
Skip Kendall	68	71	72	72	283	7,490
Spike McRoy	68	70	73	72	283	7,490
Ted Tryba	69	72	70	72	283	7,490
Jeff Gallagher	71	70	72	71	284	7,000
Mark O'Meara	68	73	73	70	284	7,000
Paul Stankowski	68	67	71	78	284	7,000
Craig Barlow	69	70	75	71	285	6,790
Mark Hensby	71	70	74	70	285	6,790
Esteban Toledo	69	70	68	78	285	6,790
Jerry Kelly	71	70	68	77	286	6,580
Tommy Tolles	67	73	73	73	286	6,580
Kirk Triplett	71	65	76	74	286	6,580
Jeremy Anderson	70	70	70	77	287	6,370
Kent Jones	73	68	74	72	287	6,370
Rocky Walcher	70	70	74	73	287	6,370
Robert Damron	70	71	75	72	288	6,230
Mathew Goggin	71	70	76	73	290	6,125
Fuzzy Zoeller	71	69	75	75	290	6,125
Sean Murphy	72	68	78	73	291	6,020
David Stephens	69	72	76	80	297	5,950

Bob Hope Chrysler Classic

PGA West, Palmer Course: Par 36-36–72; 6,950 yards
Bermuda Dunes CC: Par 36-36–72; 6,927 yards
La Quinta CC: Par 36-36–72; 7,060 yards
Indian Wells CC: Par 36-36–72; 6,478 yards
La Quinta, California

February 14-18
purse, $3,500,000

	SCORES					TOTAL	MONEY
Joe Durant	65	61	67	66	65	324	$630,000
Paul Stankowski	67	64	65	69	63	328	378,000
Mark Calcavecchia	64	66	69	65	66	330	238,000
Brad Faxon	66	67	70	65	65	333	144,666.67
Scott Verplank	66	68	70	62	67	333	144,666.67
Bob Tway	68	62	68	68	67	333	144,666.66
Frank Lickliter	70	66	64	68	66	334	112,875
Tom Pernice, Jr.	64	68	66	70	66	334	112,875
Billy Mayfair	71	62	67	69	66	335	98,000
Kevin Sutherland	64	67	66	67	71	335	98,000
Brad Elder	67	68	67	66	69	337	69,500
Robert Gamez	73	72	64	67	61	337	69,500
Miguel Angel Jimenez	68	62	68	68	71	337	69,500
Kevin Johnson	66	73	67	65	66	337	69,500
J.L. Lewis	69	67	71	63	67	337	69,500
Jeff Maggert	64	70	71	65	67	337	69,500
Jeff Sluman	67	69	66	66	69	337	69,500
Brent Geiberger	65	70	68	68	67	338	47,250
Scott McCarron	70	68	63	69	68	338	47,250
Chris Perry	68	68	72	64	66	338	47,250
David Toms	67	68	66	69	68	338	47,250
Harrison Frazar	63	71	69	67	69	339	35,000
Jim Furyk	68	68	67	69	67	339	35,000
Jason Gore	65	73	70	66	65	339	35,000
Blaine McCallister	69	66	67	66	71	339	35,000
Steve Allan	66	70	67	67	70	340	26,425
John Cook	72	67	69	69	63	340	26,425
Jerry Kelly	67	67	68	71	67	340	26,425
Spike McRoy	68	68	72	62	70	340	26,425
Stuart Appleby	67	68	69	68	69	341	20,343.75
Jay Don Blake	66	75	66	68	66	341	20,343.75
Robert Damron	68	70	67	66	70	341	20,343.75
Glen Day	64	67	72	71	67	341	20,343.75
Fred Funk	69	68	71	68	65	341	20,343.75
Mathew Goggin	68	67	71	68	67	341	20,343.75
Jay Haas	69	70	65	72	65	341	20,343.75
Joey Sindelar	70	73	64	68	66	341	20,343.75
Chris Smith	65	64	69	69	75	342	16,100
Steve Stricker	70	67	66	69	70	342	16,100
Robin Freeman	71	67	72	66	67	343	13,300
Lee Janzen	70	68	70	68	67	343	13,300
Justin Leonard	69	69	67	69	69	343	13,300
Loren Roberts	72	70	70	65	66	343	13,300
Hal Sutton	70	74	66	65	68	343	13,300
Mark Wiebe	71	68	69	68	67	343	13,300
Greg Chalmers	69	66	71	65	73	344	9,702
David Gossett	66	69	68	69	72	344	9,702
Donnie Hammond	71	65	67	70	71	344	9,702
Skip Kendall	66	71	73	67	67	344	9,702
Garrett Willis	65	72	67	71	69	344	9,702
Stephen Ames	64	71	69	73	68	345	8,288

	SCORES					TOTAL	MONEY
David Duval	65	68	70	68	74	345	8,288
Neal Lancaster	67	69	70	68	71	345	8,288
David Morland	69	73	66	68	69	345	8,288
Brian Wilson	70	68	68	70	69	345	8,288
Fred Couples	72	66	72	67	69	346	7,805
Bob Estes	66	69	68	70	73	346	7,805
Brandt Jobe	71	69	65	72	69	346	7,805
Jose Maria Olazabal	71	69	70	67	69	346	7,805
Kirk Triplett	72	64	65	73	72	346	7,805
Ted Tryba	66	72	73	66	69	346	7,805
Robert Allenby	65	69	72	68	73	347	7,420
Billy Andrade	69	73	66	67	72	347	7,420
Paul Azinger	72	70	67	67	71	347	7,420
Cameron Beckman	64	76	67	70	70	347	7,420
Andrew McLardy	66	69	71	70	71	347	7,420
Russ Cochran	71	66	71	66	74	348	7,140
Joe Ogilvie	69	71	67	70	71	348	7,140
Fuzzy Zoeller	68	69	67	70	74	348	7,140
Mark Brooks	69	71	70	67	72	349	6,930
Olin Browne	69	67	71	70	72	349	6,930
Shaun Micheel	74	65	71	67	72	349	6,930
Rich Beem	72	72	65	67	74	350	6,790
Rory Sabbatini	71	68	66	71	76	352	6,720
Jonathan Kaye	73	69	66	68	80	356	6,650

Nissan Open

Riviera Country Club, Pacific Palisades, California
Par 35-36–71; 7,035 yards

February 22-25
purse, $3,400,000

	SCORES				TOTAL	MONEY
Robert Allenby	73	64	69	70	276	$612,000
Brandel Chamblee	68	68	73	67	276	204,000
Toshimitsu Izawa	73	68	69	66	276	204,000
Dennis Paulson	70	68	68	70	276	204,000
Jeff Sluman	68	69	70	69	276	204,000
Bob Tway	67	71	70	68	276	204,000
(Allenby won on first playoff hole.)						
Emanuele Canonica	68	70	71	68	277	113,900
David Berganio, Jr.	71	67	70	70	278	91,800
Jerry Kelly	72	69	70	67	278	91,800
Neal Lancaster	69	68	71	70	278	91,800
Davis Love III	68	67	68	75	278	91,800
Chris Perry	68	68	72	70	278	91,800
Greg Chalmers	67	70	71	71	279	58,285.72
Jeff Maggert	71	70	68	70	279	58,285.72
Jesper Parnevik	70	68	71	70	279	58,285.72
Craig Barlow	68	68	70	73	279	58,285.71
Scott Dunlap	71	69	68	71	279	58,285.71
Michael Muehr	74	63	70	72	279	58,285.71
Tiger Woods	71	68	69	71	279	58,285.71
Rich Beem	70	72	68	70	280	38,216
Stewart Cink	69	69	70	72	280	38,216
Edward Fryatt	67	73	72	68	280	38,216
Corey Pavin	71	68	67	74	280	38,216
Nick Price	68	70	69	73	280	38,216
Jeff Brehaut	72	70	70	69	281	24,862.50

	SCORES				TOTAL	MONEY
Robin Freeman	72	69	70	70	281	24,862.50
Sergio Garcia	66	72	71	72	281	24,862.50
Paul Gow	69	70	71	71	281	24,862.50
Miguel Angel Jimenez	69	66	73	73	281	24,862.50
Rocco Mediate	67	70	74	70	281	24,862.50
Frank Nobilo	72	69	70	70	281	24,862.50
Brent Schwarzrock	66	75	69	71	281	24,862.50
Tommy Armour III	70	71	70	71	282	16,490
Cameron Beckman	72	68	71	71	282	16,490
Choi Kyung-ju	69	71	72	70	282	16,490
Bradley Hughes	67	71	73	71	282	16,490
Kevin Johnson	69	69	75	69	282	16,490
J.L. Lewis	73	69	67	73	282	16,490
Billy Mayfair	68	69	72	73	282	16,490
Tom Scherrer	66	71	72	73	282	16,490
Esteban Toledo	70	72	69	71	282	16,490
Scott Verplank	72	70	71	69	282	16,490
Mark Brooks	70	71	72	70	283	10,353
Andrew Magee	70	70	71	72	283	10,353
Len Mattiace	70	68	74	71	283	10,353
Scott McCarron	68	68	76	71	283	10,353
Chris Riley	68	70	76	69	283	10,353
Paul Stankowski	70	71	72	70	283	10,353
Ted Tryba	72	70	71	70	283	10,353
Brian Wilson	71	71	71	70	283	10,353
Steve Elkington	69	71	71	73	284	8,001.34
Jason Gore	69	71	73	71	284	8,001.34
Brent Geiberger	69	71	68	76	284	8,001.33
J.P. Hayes	69	72	72	71	284	8,001.33
Scott Simpson	75	66	72	71	284	8,001.33
Kevin Sutherland	71	71	71	71	284	8,001.33
Jay Don Blake	71	68	74	72	285	7,514
Olin Browne	73	68	71	73	285	7,514
John Daly	69	73	70	73	285	7,514
Ben Ferguson	71	69	73	72	285	7,514
Shigeki Maruyama	67	69	75	74	285	7,514
Duffy Waldorf	71	70	73	71	285	7,514
Jay Haas	70	71	72	73	286	7,208
Peter Jacobsen	71	71	71	73	286	7,208
Steve Lowery	71	69	73	73	286	7,208
Dan Forsman	72	70	70	75	287	7,038
Rory Sabbatini	72	69	75	71	287	7,038
Doug Barron	71	67	75	75	288	6,766
John Cook	71	70	71	76	288	6,766
Hunter Haas	70	72	68	78	288	6,766
Tripp Isenhour	72	70	73	73	288	6,766
Justin Leonard	71	70	72	75	288	6,766
Tom Pernice, Jr.	69	70	77	72	288	6,766
Steve Pate	71	69	74	75	289	6,494
Dicky Pride	71	70	72	76	289	6,494
Naomichi Ozaki	67	74	75	74	290	6,392
Sean Murphy	72	68	74	79	293	6,324
*Gary Birch, Jr.	70	72	75	76	293	
Doug Dunakey	71	70	73	80	294	6,256

Genuity Championship

Doral Golf Resort & Spa, Blue Course, Miami, Florida
Par 36-36–72; 7,125 yards

March 1-4

purse, $4,500,000

	SCORES				TOTAL	MONEY
Joe Durant	68	70	67	65	270	$810,000
Mike Weir	62	70	69	71	272	486,000
Vijay Singh	70	71	66	67	274	234,000
Jeff Sluman	69	66	69	70	274	234,000
Hal Sutton	66	66	70	72	274	234,000
Davis Love III	65	70	69	71	275	162,000
Nick Price	71	68	71	67	277	150,750
Billy Andrade	67	67	74	70	278	126,000
Bob Estes	68	69	71	70	278	126,000
Lee Porter	69	69	69	71	278	126,000
Chris Smith	69	66	76	67	278	126,000
Craig Barlow	67	70	70	72	279	88,200
Greg Chalmers	67	66	75	71	279	88,200
Stewart Cink	64	66	75	74	279	88,200
Esteban Toledo	70	69	68	72	279	88,200
Scott Verplank	67	71	69	72	279	88,200
Ben Bates	67	69	72	72	280	65,250
Jim Furyk	69	72	66	73	280	65,250
Billy Mayfair	68	69	71	72	280	65,250
Jesper Parnevik	68	70	71	71	280	65,250
Glen Day	64	71	74	72	281	48,600
Lee Janzen	67	67	77	70	281	48,600
Geoff Ogilvy	72	67	69	73	281	48,600
David Toms	73	68	71	69	281	48,600
Brandel Chamblee	73	65	72	72	282	32,200
Choi Kyung-ju	65	72	73	72	282	32,200
Robert Damron	69	72	71	70	282	32,200
Ernie Els	66	71	72	73	282	32,200
Jerry Kelly	69	69	71	73	282	32,200
Skip Kendall	68	73	69	72	282	32,200
J.L. Lewis	69	69	71	73	282	32,200
Chris Perry	71	68	70	73	282	32,200
Grant Waite	70	65	73	74	282	32,200
Stuart Appleby	67	72	74	70	283	22,725
Cameron Beckman	69	71	71	72	283	22,725
Brad Elder	69	72	73	69	283	22,725
Brian Gay	71	70	69	73	283	22,725
Greg Kraft	67	72	69	75	283	22,725
Steve Stricker	69	72	70	72	283	22,725
Steve Allan	69	72	72	71	284	15,363
Steve Elkington	68	70	73	73	284	15,363
Matt Gogel	71	70	71	72	284	15,363
Paul Gow	67	73	71	73	284	15,363
Glen Hnatiuk	72	69	68	75	284	15,363
Pete Jordan	69	71	70	74	284	15,363
Craig Kanada	67	71	70	76	284	15,363
Bernhard Langer	68	70	73	73	284	15,363
Steve Lowery	68	73	69	74	284	15,363
Hidemichi Tanaka	71	69	72	72	284	15,363
Robert Allenby	66	67	75	77	285	10,631.25
Ronnie Black	70	70	74	71	285	10,631.25
Joel Edwards	68	69	75	73	285	10,631.25
Fred Funk	72	68	68	77	285	10,631.25
John Huston	69	72	70	74	285	10,631.25

	SCORES				TOTAL	MONEY
Neal Lancaster	73	64	75	73	285	10,631.25
Frank Nobilo	72	68	78	67	285	10,631.25
Joe Ogilvie	67	72	76	70	285	10,631.25
Steve Flesch	65	72	78	71	286	9,900
Harrison Frazar	65	71	81	69	286	9,900
Justin Leonard	71	70	73	72	286	9,900
Mike Sposa	68	73	72	73	286	9,900
Bob Tway	69	70	71	76	286	9,900
Briny Baird	71	70	75	71	287	9,270
Jim Carter	68	68	75	76	287	9,270
David Duval	69	69	77	72	287	9,270
Edward Fryatt	70	68	79	70	287	9,270
Mathew Goggin	68	71	74	74	287	9,270
Shigeki Maruyama	70	66	74	77	287	9,270
David Morland	69	71	75	72	287	9,270
Kenny Perry	68	72	74	73	287	9,270
Larry Rinker	68	70	75	74	287	9,270
Russ Cochran	69	71	72	76	288	8,640
Doug Dunakey	74	67	78	69	288	8,640
Nick Faldo	72	69	75	72	288	8,640
Shaun Micheel	68	69	75	76	288	8,640
John Riegger	69	71	71	77	288	8,640
Chris Riley	70	69	75	75	289	8,325
Kaname Yokoo	66	75	76	72	289	8,325
Andy Bean	66	74	77	77	294	8,190

Honda Classic

TPC at Heron Bay, Coral Springs, Florida
Par 36-36–72; 7,268 yards

March 8-11
purse, $3,200,000

	SCORES				TOTAL	MONEY
Jesper Parnevik	65	67	66	72	270	$576,000
Craig Perks	67	70	68	66	271	238,933.34
Mark Calcavecchia	67	68	66	70	271	238,933.33
Geoff Ogilvy	65	72	65	69	271	238,933.33
Joe Durant	67	71	66	69	273	121,600
Joel Edwards	69	67	68	69	273	121,600
Stuart Appleby	68	70	67	69	274	96,400
Steve Flesch	69	70	67	68	274	96,400
Jim Furyk	70	72	67	65	274	96,400
Kaname Yokoo	71	69	69	65	274	96,400
Fulton Allem	66	71	68	70	275	63,542.86
Skip Kendall	68	70	67	70	275	63,542.86
Scott McCarron	69	71	68	67	275	63,542.86
Adam Scott	70	68	67	70	275	63,542.86
Tommy Tolles	71	69	67	68	275	63,542.86
John Daly	71	65	67	72	275	63,542.85
Chris Smith	67	68	69	71	275	63,542.85
Chris DiMarco	69	73	68	66	276	36,266.67
Glen Hnatiuk	70	70	67	69	276	36,266.67
John Huston	68	67	71	70	276	36,266.67
Joey Sindelar	70	71	69	66	276	36,266.67
Mike Sposa	70	71	69	66	276	36,266.67
Garrett Willis	70	69	69	68	276	36,266.67
Briny Baird	69	68	67	72	276	36,266.66
Brad Faxon	69	67	69	71	276	36,266.66

	SCORES				TOTAL	MONEY
Hal Sutton	69	68	67	72	276	36,266.66
Ben Ferguson	65	75	70	67	277	19,573.34
Gene Fieger	68	73	69	67	277	19,573.34
Tom Lehman	68	72	70	67	277	19,573.34
Esteban Toledo	69	73	68	67	277	19,573.34
Brian Gay	70	67	68	72	277	19,573.33
Pete Jordan	69	70	67	71	277	19,573.33
Bernhard Langer	66	73	68	70	277	19,573.33
Spike McRoy	67	69	69	72	277	19,573.33
Phil Mickelson	69	70	67	71	277	19,573.33
Joe Ogilvie	67	72	69	69	277	19,573.33
Kenny Perry	69	71	69	68	277	19,573.33
Paul Stankowski	68	69	71	69	277	19,573.33
Dan Forsman	67	70	65	76	278	12,480
Carlos Franco	69	68	68	73	278	12,480
Jeff Hart	68	72	68	70	278	12,480
Lee Janzen	70	69	64	75	278	12,480
Neal Lancaster	69	68	70	71	278	12,480
Shaun Micheel	70	68	66	74	278	12,480
Mark O'Meara	72	69	69	68	278	12,480
*Ty Tryon	67	73	70	68	278	
Mark Brooks	67	75	70	67	279	8,224
Jim Carter	70	71	65	73	279	8,224
John Cook	69	70	69	71	279	8,224
Marco Dawson	72	68	70	69	279	8,224
Doug Dunakey	70	71	65	73	279	8,224
Harrison Frazar	72	70	69	68	279	8,224
Jim Gallagher, Jr.	66	72	70	71	279	8,224
Dudley Hart	70	71	69	69	279	8,224
J.P. Hayes	66	71	72	70	279	8,224
Mark Wiebe	73	69	70	67	279	8,224
Craig Barlow	69	69	68	74	280	7,200
Per-Ulrik Johansson	71	71	69	69	280	7,200
Jonathan Kaye	69	71	68	72	280	7,200
Craig Parry	73	69	71	67	280	7,200
Cameron Beckman	72	69	68	72	281	6,880
Bill Glasson	69	71	69	72	281	6,880
Paul Gow	70	71	72	68	281	6,880
Gabriel Hjertstedt	67	72	73	69	281	6,880
Kevin Johnson	67	70	71	73	281	6,880
David Morland	70	70	67	74	281	6,880
Stephen Ames	70	70	73	69	282	6,560
Tim Herron	69	71	72	70	282	6,560
Tripp Isenhour	67	74	70	71	282	6,560
Jay Williamson	71	71	69	71	282	6,560
Mathew Goggin	73	68	67	75	283	6,368
Cliff Kresge	71	70	72	70	283	6,368
David Berganio, Jr.	72	69	71	72	284	6,208
Jeff Brehaut	71	71	70	72	284	6,208
Robin Freeman	72	68	71	73	284	6,208
Richie Coughlan	71	71	72	71	285	5,984
Jimmy Green	69	73	72	71	285	5,984
Hunter Haas	66	71	71	77	285	5,984
Scott Simpson	66	76	71	72	285	5,984

Bay Hill Invitational

Bay Hill Club & Lodge, Orlando, Florida
Par 36-36–72; 7,208 yards

March 15-18
purse, $3,500,000

	SCORES				TOTAL	MONEY
Tiger Woods	71	67	66	69	273	$630,000
Phil Mickelson	66	72	70	66	274	378,000
Grant Waite	66	71	72	69	278	238,000
Sergio Garcia	71	66	68	74	279	137,812.50
Steve Lowery	68	70	70	71	279	137,812.50
Greg Norman	69	71	68	71	279	137,812.50
Vijay Singh	71	70	66	72	279	137,812.50
Paul Goydos	68	68	73	71	280	91,000
Scott Hoch	68	72	69	71	280	91,000
Lee Janzen	67	72	69	72	280	91,000
Dennis Paulson	66	75	69	70	280	91,000
Chris Perry	71	66	69	74	280	91,000
Jeff Sluman	67	74	68	71	280	91,000
Harrison Frazar	70	70	68	73	281	66,500
Paul Azinger	71	70	71	70	282	61,250
Fred Funk	70	72	71	69	282	61,250
Robert Damron	72	66	73	72	283	47,366.67
Bob Estes	69	74	69	71	283	47,366.67
Gary Nicklaus	71	70	71	71	283	47,366.67
Lee Westwood	71	72	68	72	283	47,366.67
Brandt Jobe	70	73	66	74	283	47,366.66
Scott McCarron	67	70	71	75	283	47,366.66
Fulton Allem	70	67	73	74	284	28,787.50
Olin Browne	70	75	68	71	284	28,787.50
Dan Forsman	72	71	69	72	284	28,787.50
Skip Kendall	70	75	67	72	284	28,787.50
Frank Lickliter	70	71	70	73	284	28,787.50
Rocco Mediate	77	67	67	73	284	28,787.50
Frank Nobilo	72	69	70	73	284	28,787.50
Steve Pate	66	73	71	74	284	28,787.50
David Berganio, Jr.	70	71	70	74	285	21,700
Mark Calcavecchia	66	72	75	72	285	21,700
Kevin Sutherland	73	69	69	74	285	21,700
Robert Allenby	72	72	74	68	286	17,675
Greg Chalmers	71	70	73	72	286	17,675
Nick Faldo	72	72	68	74	286	17,675
Retief Goosen	72	72	71	71	286	17,675
Tripp Isenhour	69	72	75	70	286	17,675
Bernhard Langer	72	70	70	74	286	17,675
Tim Herron	68	72	73	74	287	14,350
Naomichi Ozaki	74	71	69	73	287	14,350
Carl Paulson	72	70	70	75	287	14,350
Jay Don Blake	72	72	73	71	288	11,900
Brandel Chamblee	73	70	69	76	288	11,900
Tom Lehman	71	71	68	78	288	11,900
Kenny Perry	73	72	69	74	288	11,900
Brad Faxon	75	70	75	69	289	9,415
Peter Jacobsen	73	72	71	73	289	9,415
Loren Roberts	72	71	71	75	289	9,415
Jean Van de Velde	69	76	72	72	289	9,415
Choi Kyung-ju	71	72	70	77	290	8,288
Brad Elder	69	73	77	71	290	8,288
David Frost	68	70	75	77	290	8,288
Colin Montgomerie	75	69	75	71	290	8,288

	SCORES				TOTAL	MONEY
Geoff Ogilvy	69	72	70	79	290	8,288
Notah Begay	73	72	71	75	291	7,805
Joe Durant	70	75	73	73	291	7,805
Brian Gay	72	72	70	77	291	7,805
J.L. Lewis	74	70	76	71	291	7,805
Corey Pavin	71	73	70	77	291	7,805
David Toms	71	74	73	73	291	7,805
Ernie Els	73	70	74	75	292	7,525
Len Mattiace	70	75	71	76	292	7,525
Stephen Ames	74	70	72	77	293	7,385
Kirk Triplett	69	74	75	75	293	7,385
Craig Barlow	68	76	75	75	294	7,245
Steve Stricker	74	70	77	73	294	7,245
Fred Couples	73	70	73	79	295	7,070
Craig Parry	71	73	72	79	295	7,070
Adam Scott	71	74	75	75	295	7,070
Jay Haas	72	72	76	76	296	6,825
Gary Koch	73	71	72	80	296	6,825
Tom Pernice, Jr.	70	74	77	75	296	6,825
Paul Stankowski	72	72	77	75	296	6,825

The Players Championship

TPC at Sawgrass, Stadium Course,
Ponte Vedra Beach, Florida
Par 36-36–72; 7,093 yards

March 22-25
purse, $6,000,000

	SCORES				TOTAL	MONEY
Tiger Woods	72	69	66	67	274	$1,080,000
Vijay Singh	67	70	70	68	275	648,000
Bernhard Langer	73	68	68	67	276	408,000
Jerry Kelly	69	66	70	73	278	288,000
Billy Mayfair	68	72	70	71	281	228,000
Hal Sutton	72	71	68	70	281	228,000
Paul Azinger	66	70	74	72	282	187,000
Scott Hoch	67	70	71	74	282	187,000
Frank Lickliter	72	72	70	68	282	187,000
Joe Durant	73	73	67	70	283	156,000
Nick Price	70	74	71	68	283	156,000
Tom Lehman	71	71	72	70	284	126,000
Jose Maria Olazabal	71	76	68	69	284	126,000
David Toms	70	77	66	71	284	126,000
Michael Campbell	72	71	69	73	285	102,000
Scott Dunlap	70	73	73	69	285	102,000
Franklin Langham	73	71	71	70	285	102,000
Lee Janzen	77	67	69	73	286	84,000
Jonathan Kaye	67	72	76	71	286	84,000
Kenny Perry	71	66	74	75	286	84,000
Robert Allenby	68	75	71	73	287	62,400
Jim Furyk	72	75	72	68	287	62,400
J.P. Hayes	72	69	76	70	287	62,400
Tim Herron	73	74	71	69	287	62,400
Corey Pavin	73	72	69	73	287	62,400
Angel Cabrera	72	70	74	72	288	44,400
Darren Clarke	75	70	72	71	288	44,400
Brad Faxon	72	74	73	69	288	44,400
Skip Kendall	68	78	69	73	288	44,400

	SCORES				TOTAL	MONEY
Naomichi Ozaki	77	68	72	71	288	44,400
Dennis Paulson	74	70	73	72	289	38,100
Kirk Triplett	72	71	76	70	289	38,100
Stuart Appleby	74	73	75	68	290	31,029
Fred Funk	70	71	77	72	290	31,029
Padraig Harrington	70	75	73	72	290	31,029
Phil Mickelson	73	68	72	77	290	31,029
Craig Parry	71	73	76	70	290	31,029
Jeff Sluman	72	71	75	72	290	31,029
Mark Wiebe	73	73	69	75	290	31,029
Steve Flesch	70	73	76	72	291	24,000
Brian Gay	73	74	72	72	291	24,000
Colin Montgomerie	71	71	75	74	291	24,000
Bob Tway	72	73	74	72	291	24,000
Billy Andrade	72	73	74	73	292	18,140
Tom Kite	70	73	75	74	292	18,140
Scott McCarron	71	75	77	69	292	18,140
Paul Stankowski	72	74	73	73	292	18,140
Scott Verplank	69	75	72	76	292	18,140
Mike Weir	77	69	72	74	292	18,140
Jay Don Blake	74	73	73	73	293	14,472
Jim Carter	69	73	75	76	293	14,472
Nick Faldo	73	73	75	72	293	14,472
Sergio Garcia	73	74	74	72	293	14,472
Steve Jones	72	71	72	78	293	14,472
Tom Byrum	73	71	75	75	294	13,680
John Cook	71	72	75	76	294	13,680
Chris DiMarco	74	73	74	73	294	13,680
Greg Chalmers	71	73	72	79	295	13,080
Fred Couples	71	75	70	79	295	13,080
Glen Hnatiuk	74	70	71	80	295	13,080
Steve Pate	72	72	76	75	295	13,080
Chris Riley	71	75	73	76	295	13,080
Kevin Sutherland	71	74	73	77	295	13,080
Jay Williamson	78	69	77	71	295	13,080
Mark Brooks	71	74	76	76	297	12,480
Greg Kraft	73	71	72	81	297	12,480
Rocco Mediate	73	73	75	76	297	12,480
Paul Goydos	73	74	76	75	298	12,180
Carl Paulson	74	73	76	75	298	12,180
Brent Geiberger	72	75	82	70	299	11,880
Mathew Goggin	72	75	72	80	299	11,880
Ian Woosnam	73	73	81	72	299	11,880
Brad Elder	69	72	81	78	300	11,520
Robin Freeman	73	72	79	76	300	11,520
J.L. Lewis	73	72	78	77	300	11,520
Joel Edwards	72	74	77		DQ	

BellSouth Classic

TPC at Sugarloaf, Duluth, Georgia
Par 36-36—72; 7,259 yards

March 29-April 1
purse, $3,300,000

	SCORES				TOTAL	MONEY
Scott McCarron	68	67	72	73	280	$594,000
Mike Weir	76	67	73	67	283	356,400
Phil Mickelson	70	66	73	75	284	171,600

	SCORES				TOTAL	MONEY
Dennis Paulson	72	65	72	75	284	171,600
Chris Smith	73	70	72	69	284	171,600
Stewart Cink	70	71	71	73	285	103,290
Chris DiMarco	68	67	73	77	285	103,290
Mathew Goggin	69	73	69	74	285	103,290
Charles Howell	70	68	74	73	285	103,290
Joey Sindelar	73	70	72	70	285	103,290
Scott Dunlap	74	65	75	72	286	67,650
Brandt Jobe	68	74	73	71	286	67,650
Jerry Kelly	69	69	72	76	286	67,650
Skip Kendall	74	67	73	72	286	67,650
Davis Love III	70	71	71	74	286	67,650
Shaun Micheel	72	71	70	73	286	67,650
Harrison Frazar	73	68	73	73	287	51,150
David Toms	69	69	74	75	287	51,150
Choi Kyung-ju	72	70	69	77	288	44,550
Steve Flesch	68	75	71	74	288	44,550
Jeff Brehaut	70	68	78	73	289	35,640
Bob Burns	73	70	73	73	289	35,640
Billy Mayfair	70	70	74	75	289	35,640
Jesper Parnevik	72	71	75	71	289	35,640
Gary Nicklaus	73	69	76	72	290	27,720
Mike Sposa	69	70	77	74	290	27,720
Doug Barron	74	67	73	77	291	22,440
John Daly	69	71	76	75	291	22,440
Shigeki Maruyama	69	73	75	74	291	22,440
Greg Norman	73	67	76	75	291	22,440
Jose Maria Olazabal	73	70	71	77	291	22,440
Craig Parry	71	70	74	76	291	22,440
Scott Simpson	73	69	73	76	291	22,440
Marco Dawson	67	72	79	74	292	16,665
Kelly Grunewald	71	71	75	75	292	16,665
Mark Hensby	69	72	73	78	292	16,665
Andrew McLardy	71	70	78	73	292	16,665
Tom Pernice, Jr.	73	70	75	74	292	16,665
Kaname Yokoo	68	69	77	78	292	16,665
Bradley Hughes	73	70	75	75	293	13,530
Frank Lickliter	70	68	72	83	293	13,530
Bob Tway	72	70	74	77	293	13,530
Blaine McCallister	70	71	78	75	294	12,210
Ernie Els	74	67	81	73	295	11,550
Robin Freeman	72	70	74	80	296	10,890
Michael Clark	71	72	80	74	297	9,614
Pierre Fulke	72	70	78	77	297	9,614
Ted Tryba	70	69	79	79	297	9,614
Robert Damron	71	69	79	79	298	8,448
Andrew Magee	73	69	76	80	298	8,448
Kevin Johnson	73	70	75	81	299	8,118
Tommy Armour III	72	67	84	78	301	7,920

Masters Tournament

Augusta National Golf Club, Augusta, Georgia
Par 36-36–72; 6,985 yards

April 5-8
purse, $4,600,000

	SCORES			TOTAL	MONEY
Tiger Woods	70	66	68	272	$1,008,000
David Duval	71	66	70	67	274	604,800
Phil Mickelson	67	69	69	70	275	380,800
Mark Calcavecchia	72	66	68	72	278	246,400
Toshimitsu Izawa	71	66	74	67	278	246,400
Ernie Els	71	68	68	72	279	181,300
Jim Furyk	69	71	70	69	279	181,300
Bernhard Langer	73	69	68	69	279	181,300
Kirk Triplett	68	70	70	71	279	181,300
Angel Cabrera	66	71	70	73	280	128,800
Chris DiMarco	65	69	72	74	280	128,800
Brad Faxon	73	68	68	71	280	128,800
Miguel Angel Jimenez	68	72	71	69	280	128,800
Steve Stricker	66	71	72	71	280	128,800
Paul Azinger	70	71	71	69	281	95,200
Rocco Mediate	72	70	66	73	281	95,200
Jose Maria Olazabal	70	68	71	72	281	95,200
Tom Lehman	75	68	71	68	282	81,200
Vijay Singh	69	71	73	69	282	81,200
John Huston	67	75	72	69	283	65,240
Jeff Maggert	72	70	70	71	283	65,240
Mark O'Meara	69	74	72	68	283	65,240
Jesper Parnevik	71	71	72	69	283	65,240
Darren Clarke	72	67	72	73	284	53,760
Tom Scherrer	71	71	70	73	285	49,280
Fred Couples	74	71	73	68	286	44,800
Padraig Harrington	75	69	72	71	287	40,600
Steve Jones	74	70	72	71	287	40,600
Justin Leonard	73	71	72	71	287	40,600
Mike Weir	74	69	72	72	287	40,600
Stuart Appleby	72	70	70	76	288	33,208
Mark Brooks	70	71	77	70	288	33,208
Lee Janzen	67	70	72	79	288	33,208
David Toms	72	72	71	73	288	33,208
Duffy Waldorf	72	70	71	75	288	33,208
Hal Sutton	74	69	71	75	289	28,840
Scott Hoch	74	70	72	74	290	26,320
Chris Perry	68	74	74	74	290	26,320
Loren Roberts	71	74	73	72	290	26,320
Shingo Katayama	75	70	73	74	292	22,960
Franklin Langham	72	73	75	72	292	22,960
Steve Lowery	72	72	78	70	292	22,960
Dudley Hart	74	70	78	71	293	19,600
Jonathan Kaye	74	71	74	74	293	19,600
Bob May	71	74	73	75	293	19,600
Carlos Franco	71	71	77	75	294	17,360
Robert Allenby	71	74	75	75	295	16,240

Out of Final 36 Holes

			TOTAL	
Thomas Bjorn	70	76	146	
Davis Love III	71	75	146	
Dennis Paulson	73	73	146	
Notah Begay	73	73	146	

	SCORES		TOTAL
Sergio Garcia	70	76	146
Jose Coceres	77	69	146
James Driscoll	68	78	146
Joe Durant	73	74	147
Sandy Lyle	74	73	147
Shigeki Maruyama	77	70	147
Scott Verplank	69	78	147
Larry Mize	74	74	148
Jack Nicklaus	73	75	148
Nick Price	73	75	148
Eduardo Romero	75	73	148
Tom Watson	78	70	148
Ian Woosnam	71	77	148
Greg Chalmers	76	72	148
Rory Sabbatini	73	75	148
Stewart Cink	75	74	149
Colin Montgomerie	73	76	149
Fuzzy Zoeller	77	72	149
Gary Player	73	76	149
Retief Goosen	75	74	149
Paul Lawrie	73	76	149
Grant Waite	79	71	150
Steve Flesch	74	76	150
*Aaron Baddeley	75	75	150
Nick Faldo	75	76	151
Raymond Floyd	76	75	151
*Mikko Ilonen	72	79	151
Seve Ballesteros	76	76	152
Craig Stadler	79	73	152
Charles Coody	80	72	152
Pierre Fulke	73	79	152
Michael Campbell	78	75	153
Greg Norman	71	82	153
D.J. Trahan	78	75	153
Jeff Quinney	80	76	156
Greg Puga	76	80	156
Arnold Palmer	82	76	158
Ben Crenshaw	81	78	159
Tommy Aaron	81	82	163
Billy Casper	87	80	167
Gay Brewer, Jr.	84		WD

(Professionals who did not complete 72 holes received $5,000.)

WorldCom Classic

Harbour Town Golf Links, Hilton Head Island, South Carolina
Par 36-36–72; 6,916 yards
(Playoff extended to Monday due to darkness.)

April 12-16
purse, $3,500,000

	SCORES				TOTAL	MONEY
Jose Coceres	68	70	64	71	273	$630,000
Billy Mayfair	65	68	69	71	273	378,000
(Coceres defeated Mayfair on fifth playoff hole.)						
Bernhard Langer	69	69	67	69	274	168,000
Carl Paulson	71	63	71	69	274	168,000
Vijay Singh	65	68	67	74	274	168,000

	SCORES				TOTAL	MONEY
Scott Verplank	68	67	69	70	274	168,000
Steve Flesch	71	69	72	63	275	109,083.34
Mark Brooks	66	69	71	69	275	109,083.33
Davis Love III	68	67	71	69	275	109,083.33
Billy Andrade	66	67	73	70	276	91,000
Stewart Cink	69	71	70	66	276	91,000
Paul Azinger	69	71	68	69	277	60,666.67
Thomas Bjorn	69	70	71	67	277	60,666.67
Michael Campbell	72	65	69	71	277	60,666.67
Brad Elder	66	69	72	70	277	60,666.67
David Frost	69	69	72	67	277	60,666.67
Rocco Mediate	66	71	74	66	277	60,666.67
Dudley Hart	66	71	69	71	277	60,666.66
Len Mattiace	68	68	68	73	277	60,666.66
Dennis Paulson	71	68	67	71	277	60,666.66
Fulton Allem	73	67	71	67	278	33,850
Stephen Ames	71	69	69	69	278	33,850
Joe Durant	69	68	72	69	278	33,850
Lee Janzen	69	71	67	71	278	33,850
Bob May	69	71	70	68	278	33,850
Corey Pavin	69	70	69	70	278	33,850
Mike Sposa	67	67	70	74	278	33,850
John Cook	69	66	73	71	279	21,350
Glen Day	70	68	67	74	279	21,350
Joel Edwards	74	65	72	68	279	21,350
Glen Hnatiuk	67	72	75	65	279	21,350
Scott Hoch	67	69	71	72	279	21,350
Tom Lehman	66	66	72	75	279	21,350
Jesper Parnevik	68	69	72	70	279	21,350
Chris Smith	71	66	72	70	279	21,350
Ted Tryba	69	70	70	70	279	21,350
D.A. Weibring	69	73	68	69	279	21,350
Mark Calcavecchia	66	71	71	72	280	15,400
Fred Funk	68	72	72	68	280	15,400
Greg Norman	69	71	71	69	280	15,400
Mark Wiebe	71	71	70	68	280	15,400
Greg Chalmers	66	71	69	75	281	11,570
Doug Dunakey	65	71	76	69	281	11,570
Bob Estes	70	69	67	75	281	11,570
Brian Gay	67	71	72	71	281	11,570
Skip Kendall	72	66	71	72	281	11,570
Steve Lowery	71	68	73	69	281	11,570
Bob Tway	69	68	73	71	281	11,570
John Daly	73	66	67	76	282	8,960
Nick Price	70	72	69	71	282	8,960
Nick Faldo	70	71	70	72	283	8,347.50
Carlos Franco	67	72	76	68	283	8,347.50
Chris Riley	68	68	75	72	283	8,347.50
Tom Scherrer	69	70	70	74	283	8,347.50
Tommy Armour III	66	74	73	71	284	7,945
Cameron Beckman	70	69	74	71	284	7,945
Neal Lancaster	67	75	70	72	284	7,945
Garrett Willis	70	68	72	74	284	7,945
Todd Barranger	68	73	69	75	285	7,700
Padraig Harrington	70	71	72	72	285	7,700
Shaun Micheel	72	69	72	72	285	7,700
Craig Barlow	73	69	73	71	286	7,455
Brandel Chamblee	70	71	72	73	286	7,455
Jay Haas	71	71	72	72	286	7,455

	SCORES				TOTAL	MONEY
Loren Roberts	67	73	72	74	286	7,455
Bob Burns	68	74	75	70	287	7,140
Michael Clark	73	68	72	74	287	7,140
Brad Faxon	69	72	77	69	287	7,140
Franklin Langham	69	70	76	72	287	7,140
Jeff Sluman	67	71	73	76	287	7,140
Jay Don Blake	74	68	73	73	288	6,895
Chris Perry	72	70	73	73	288	6,895
Robert Damron	71	71	72	75	289	6,790
Jimmy Green	71	71	72	76	290	6,720
Robert Allenby	71	69	74	78	292	6,650

Shell Houston Open

TPC at The Woodlands, The Woodlands, Texas
Par 36-36–72; 7,018 yards

April 19-22
purse, $3,400,000

	SCORES				TOTAL	MONEY
Hal Sutton	70	68	71	69	278	$612,000
Joe Durant	67	69	71	74	281	299,200
Lee Janzen	67	68	73	73	281	299,200
John Cook	69	72	72	69	282	149,600
Justin Leonard	71	70	72	69	282	149,600
Len Mattiace	72	69	73	69	283	113,900
Billy Mayfair	70	72	71	70	283	113,900
Vijay Singh	73	70	69	71	283	113,900
Chris DiMarco	69	70	71	74	284	88,400
Ben Ferguson	72	71	68	73	284	88,400
Kevin Sutherland	69	69	72	74	284	88,400
David Toms	73	68	73	70	284	88,400
Stewart Cink	73	70	71	71	285	65,733.34
Joel Edwards	70	69	73	73	285	65,733.33
Brian Gay	74	70	68	73	285	65,733.33
Phil Blackmar	70	72	71	73	286	49,300
Marco Dawson	71	69	73	73	286	49,300
David Frost	72	72	71	71	286	49,300
Paul Gow	73	72	68	73	286	49,300
Scott Hoch	72	72	67	75	286	49,300
Chris Riley	71	71	72	72	286	49,300
Fred Couples	68	76	72	71	287	34,000
Nick Faldo	75	70	70	72	287	34,000
Carlos Franco	72	71	68	76	287	34,000
Shigeki Maruyama	73	72	72	70	287	34,000
Jeremy Anderson	72	72	72	72	288	23,138.89
Jim Carter	72	69	77	70	288	23,138.89
John Daly	71	69	73	75	288	23,138.89
David Duval	72	70	72	74	288	23,138.89
Brian Henninger	74	69	74	71	288	23,138.89
Brandt Jobe	69	73	74	72	288	23,138.89
Frank Lickliter	75	68	71	74	288	23,138.89
Chris Smith	71	72	70	75	288	23,138.89
Tom Pernice, Jr.	70	67	74	77	288	23,138.88
Briny Baird	74	71	72	72	289	16,405
David Morland	72	69	72	76	289	16,405
Carl Paulson	68	73	76	72	289	16,405
Scott Simpson	72	71	74	72	289	16,405
Mike Sposa	75	70	68	76	289	16,405

	SCORES				TOTAL	MONEY
Esteban Toledo	71	73	69	76	289	16,405
Greg Chalmers	71	72	74	73	290	12,580
Brad Elder	75	68	71	76	290	12,580
Robert Gamez	71	70	75	74	290	12,580
Bradley Hughes	71	72	74	73	290	12,580
Tim Thelen	75	70	70	75	290	12,580
Stephen Ames	72	71	75	73	291	8,959
Tom Byrum	74	71	69	77	291	8,959
Fred Funk	72	70	76	73	291	8,959
J.J. Henry	71	74	71	75	291	8,959
Joe Ogilvie	72	69	76	74	291	8,959
Jerry Smith	71	72	73	75	291	8,959
Brian Wilson	73	72	71	75	291	8,959
Kaname Yokoo	69	76	75	71	291	8,959
Jeff Brehaut	73	72	74	73	292	7,718
Jimmy Green	70	71	76	75	292	7,718
Craig Kanada	69	76	74	73	292	7,718
Andrew Magee	70	71	73	78	292	7,718
Shaun Micheel	72	71	68	81	292	7,718
Garrett Willis	74	70	76	72	292	7,718
Doug Barron	75	67	75	76	293	7,446
Matt Gogel	70	69	79	75	293	7,446
Robert Allenby	69	74	70	81	294	7,208
Choi Kyung-ju	73	71	74	76	294	7,208
Greg Kraft	73	72	69	80	294	7,208
Lee Porter	73	72	72	77	294	7,208
Adam Scott	68	73	77	76	294	7,208
Tommy Armour III	73	72	76	74	295	6,936
Paul Stankowski	73	69	80	73	295	6,936
Robert Thompson	75	70	75	75	295	6,936
Cliff Kresge	70	72	79	75	296	6,766
Steve Pate	72	73	81	70	296	6,766
J.P. Hayes	72	70	74	81	297	6,664
Jeff Gallagher	71	71	74	83	299	6,596

Greater Greensboro Chrysler Classic

Forest Oaks Country Club, Greensboro, North Carolina   April 26-29
Par 36-36–72; 7,062 yards   purse, $3,500,000

	SCORES				TOTAL	MONEY
Scott Hoch	68	68	67	69	272	$630,000
Brett Quigley	68	71	67	67	273	308,000
Scott Simpson	66	69	70	68	273	308,000
David Berganio, Jr.	70	66	68	71	275	131,950
Choi Kyung-ju	72	66	70	67	275	131,950
Gabriel Hjertstedt	70	69	67	69	275	131,950
Jerry Kelly	67	70	67	71	275	131,950
Jeff Maggert	69	67	70	69	275	131,950
Olin Browne	71	67	69	69	276	94,500
Jim Furyk	69	72	66	69	276	94,500
Kaname Yokoo	71	69	65	71	276	94,500
Rich Beem	71	65	70	71	277	68,600
Mike Sposa	68	66	70	73	277	68,600
Kevin Sutherland	69	72	65	71	277	68,600
Phil Tataurangi	69	72	66	70	277	68,600
Brian Watts	70	68	69	70	277	68,600

	SCORES				TOTAL	MONEY
Matt Kuchar	72	68	70	68	278	54,250
Esteban Toledo	70	69	69	70	278	54,250
Briny Baird	75	67	66	71	279	42,420
Donnie Hammond	71	68	69	71	279	42,420
Scott McCarron	69	68	72	70	279	42,420
David Peoples	70	72	70	67	279	42,420
Joey Sindelar	68	70	70	71	279	42,420
Stephen Ames	68	70	72	70	280	29,050
Dudley Hart	67	70	70	73	280	29,050
Kenny Perry	69	69	70	72	280	29,050
Hal Sutton	70	71	68	71	280	29,050
Omar Uresti	71	65	73	71	280	29,050
Stuart Appleby	71	70	68	72	281	21,775
Jim Carter	71	68	73	69	281	21,775
Marco Dawson	71	70	72	68	281	21,775
Edward Fryatt	74	68	66	73	281	21,775
Jeffrey Lankford	67	73	69	72	281	21,775
Frank Nobilo	69	71	69	72	281	21,775
Steve Stricker	70	70	72	69	281	21,775
Mark Calcavecchia	73	69	69	71	282	14,365.91
Trevor Dodds	70	69	69	74	282	14,365.91
Scott Dunlap	68	73	69	72	282	14,365.91
Steve Gangluff	71	70	72	69	282	14,365.91
Jonathan Kaye	68	69	73	72	282	14,365.91
Neal Lancaster	69	72	71	70	282	14,365.91
Ian Leggatt	68	74	68	72	282	14,365.91
Lee Porter	71	69	70	72	282	14,365.91
Brent Schwarzrock	71	68	70	73	282	14,365.91
Scott Verplank	73	67	71	71	282	14,365.91
Cliff Kresge	71	69	68	74	282	14,365.90
Russ Cochran	69	71	72	71	283	8,990
Robert Damron	67	71	70	75	283	8,990
Glen Day	70	71	68	74	283	8,990
Kelly Grunewald	69	73	70	71	283	8,990
Tripp Isenhour	74	65	68	76	283	8,990
Craig Kanada	71	67	72	73	283	8,990
Jim McGovern	73	69	72	69	283	8,990
Joel Edwards	70	69	73	72	284	7,910
Steve Elkington	71	69	73	71	284	7,910
Fred Funk	70	70	70	74	284	7,910
Jimmy Green	72	69	70	73	284	7,910
Pete Jordan	72	70	70	72	284	7,910
Greg Kraft	68	72	72	72	284	7,910
Andrew Magee	71	70	69	74	284	7,910
Aaron Baddeley	67	74	66	78	285	7,490
Jeff Brehaut	69	71	74	71	285	7,490
Robin Freeman	69	69	73	74	285	7,490
Mathew Goggin	70	72	68	75	285	7,490
Shaun Micheel	67	74	74	70	285	7,490
Hunter Haas	72	70	73	71	286	7,175
Kevin Johnson	71	71	73	71	286	7,175
John Riegger	73	67	74	72	286	7,175
Willie Wood	70	70	73	73	286	7,175
Spike McRoy	67	71	74	75	287	6,930
David Morland	70	70	70	77	287	6,930
Michael Muehr	70	68	78	71	287	6,930
Mike Heinen	70	70	77	71	288	6,720
Mike Springer	73	69	72	74	288	6,720
Jay Williamson	73	69	74	72	288	6,720

	SCORES				TOTAL	MONEY
Mike Hulbert	75	67	71	76	289	6,580
Steve Allan	72	68	72	78	290	6,475
Ted Tryba	71	70	73	76	290	6,475
Garrett Willis	70	68	71	82	291	6,370

Compaq Classic of New Orleans

English Turn Golf & Country Club,
New Orleans, Louisiana
Par 36-36–72; 7,116 yards

May 3-6
purse, $4,000,000

	SCORES				TOTAL	MONEY
David Toms	66	73	63	64	266	$720,000
Phil Mickelson	66	66	64	72	268	432,000
Ernie Els	67	69	65	68	269	272,000
Harrison Frazar	68	65	66	71	270	192,000
Brian Gay	66	66	70	69	271	152,000
Chris Smith	73	66	66	66	271	152,000
Charles Howell	69	71	63	69	272	134,000
Stephen Ames	69	70	65	69	273	116,000
Frank Lickliter	67	71	67	68	273	116,000
Steve Lowery	71	67	66	69	273	116,000
David Peoples	68	69	71	66	274	79,428.58
Greg Chalmers	70	71	66	67	274	79,428.57
Joe Durant	67	71	68	68	274	79,428.57
Dudley Hart	71	70	65	68	274	79,428.57
Scott Hoch	69	72	63	70	274	79,428.57
Bob May	67	73	66	68	274	79,428.57
Jeff Sluman	69	72	66	67	274	79,428.57
David Duval	69	68	69	69	275	52,160
Joel Edwards	69	69	70	67	275	52,160
Brad Fabel	67	70	67	71	275	52,160
Jerry Kelly	68	67	71	69	275	52,160
Tom Pernice, Jr.	66	74	68	67	275	52,160
Shigeki Maruyama	67	71	70	68	276	38,400
Nick Price	69	69	69	69	276	38,400
Bob Tway	69	71	68	68	276	38,400
Danny Ellis	73	66	70	68	277	29,000
Jeff Hart	70	69	69	69	277	29,000
Neal Lancaster	70	71	65	71	277	29,000
J.L. Lewis	69	69	74	65	277	29,000
Steve Stricker	69	72	65	71	277	29,000
Chris Tidland	66	69	71	71	277	29,000
Scott Dunlap	69	72	67	70	278	24,200
Brian Watts	64	72	71	71	278	24,200
John Cook	70	71	67	71	279	18,933.34
Bill Glasson	68	73	70	68	279	18,933.34
Kirk Triplett	68	71	69	71	279	18,933.34
Woody Austin	68	72	65	74	279	18,933.33
Keith Clearwater	65	70	72	72	279	18,933.33
Russ Cochran	68	74	66	71	279	18,933.33
Carlos Franco	69	68	70	72	279	18,933.33
Paul Gow	70	70	66	73	279	18,933.33
Gabriel Hjertstedt	70	70	66	73	279	18,933.33
Brian Henninger	68	70	67	75	280	12,480
Blaine McCallister	69	69	68	74	280	12,480
Kenny Perry	64	77	69	70	280	12,480

	SCORES			TOTAL	MONEY
Scott Simpson	68	71	67	74	280	12,480
Hal Sutton	67	73	68	72	280	12,480
Scott Verplank	67	73	69	71	280	12,480
Brian Wilson	65	70	74	71	280	12,480
Cameron Beckman	72	70	70	69	281	9,840
Jim Carter	65	71	75	70	281	9,840
Robin Freeman	71	68	71	71	281	9,840
Pete Jordan	71	70	70	71	282	9,306.67
Paul Stankowski	61	77	72	72	282	9,306.67
Jonathan Kaye	69	73	64	76	282	9,306.66
Fulton Allem	69	72	70	72	283	8,960
Brent Geiberger	68	73	70	72	283	8,960
Craig Kanada	71	70	72	70	283	8,960
Greg Norman	70	72	71	70	283	8,960
Dicky Pride	71	69	69	74	283	8,960
Michael Clark	70	71	68	75	284	8,560
Marco Dawson	71	71	68	74	284	8,560
Tommy Tolles	67	75	69	73	284	8,560
Ted Tryba	67	72	71	74	284	8,560
Mike Weir	68	74	74	68	284	8,560
John Riegger	69	73	71	72	285	8,240
Grant Waite	71	69	70	75	285	8,240
Kaname Yokoo	70	72	67	76	285	8,240
Bradley Hughes	70	70	69	77	286	8,080
Andrew Magee	68	73	73	73	287	7,960
Andrew McLardy	70	71	72	74	287	7,960
Mathew Goggin	69	73	75	74	291	7,840

Verizon Byron Nelson Classic

TPC at Four Seasons Resort Las Colinas:
Par 35-35–70; 6,924 yards
Cottonwood Valley Golf Club:
Par 35-35–70; 6,846 yards
Irving, Texas

May 10-13
purse, $4,500,000

	SCORES			TOTAL	MONEY
Robert Damron	66	64	67	66	263	$810,000
Scott Verplank	62	67	68	66	263	486,000
(Damron defeated Verplank on fourth playoff hole.)					
David Duval	64	65	70	67	266	234,000
Nick Price	69	65	65	67	266	234,000
Tiger Woods	66	68	69	63	266	234,000
Justin Leonard	68	69	61	69	267	156,375
Brian Watts	68	68	63	68	267	156,375
Sergio Garcia	71	68	64	65	268	130,500
David Peoples	66	69	67	66	268	130,500
Kenny Perry	68	65	67	68	268	130,500
Rich Beem	69	66	68	66	269	78,954.55
Glen Day	66	68	69	66	269	78,954.55
Brad Faxon	70	65	67	67	269	78,954.55
David Frost	72	66	65	66	269	78,954.55
Dudley Hart	67	66	69	67	269	78,954.55
Tim Herron	64	70	67	68	269	78,954.55
Fred Couples	71	63	66	69	269	78,954.54
Vijay Singh	67	64	67	71	269	78,954.54
Esteban Toledo	66	71	63	69	269	78,954.54

	SCORES				TOTAL	MONEY
David Toms	68	71	62	68	269	78,954.54
Mike Weir	66	68	65	70	269	78,954.54
Tommy Armour III	66	67	70	67	270	46,800
Olin Browne	69	67	64	70	270	46,800
Ted Tryba	68	67	73	62	270	46,800
Len Mattiace	69	70	64	68	271	36,750
Chris Riley	64	69	71	67	271	36,750
Paul Stankowski	71	67	68	65	271	36,750
Russ Cochran	65	70	70	67	272	28,050
Scott Dunlap	66	73	67	66	272	28,050
Brent Geiberger	68	68	68	68	272	28,050
J.L. Lewis	68	67	70	67	272	28,050
Frank Lickliter	68	66	66	72	272	28,050
Phil Mickelson	72	66	68	66	272	28,050
Loren Roberts	70	65	69	68	272	28,050
Hal Sutton	68	70	66	68	272	28,050
Kirk Triplett	70	67	67	68	272	28,050
Mark Brooks	69	67	67	70	273	19,800
Chris DiMarco	71	67	67	68	273	19,800
Jim Furyk	72	66	66	69	273	19,800
Scott McCarron	68	69	66	70	273	19,800
Scott Simpson	69	70	67	67	273	19,800
Grant Waite	69	66	67	71	273	19,800
Robert Allenby	70	68	66	70	274	13,702.50
Stuart Appleby	67	68	70	69	274	13,702.50
Jim Carter	68	67	67	72	274	13,702.50
John Cook	69	70	67	68	274	13,702.50
Steve Flesch	69	68	70	67	274	13,702.50
Brian Gay	68	68	69	69	274	13,702.50
Andrew Magee	69	68	68	69	274	13,702.50
Shigeki Maruyama	69	70	66	69	274	13,702.50
Tom Byrum	68	71	69	67	275	10,317.28
Jose Coceres	71	68	70	66	275	10,317.28
Harrison Frazar	68	67	72	68	275	10,317.28
Perry Arthur	70	68	65	72	275	10,317.27
Craig Barlow	66	71	69	69	275	10,317.27
Dan Forsman	69	70	67	69	275	10,317.27
Gabriel Hjertstedt	66	69	69	71	275	10,317.27
Bob May	65	69	68	73	275	10,317.27
Rocco Mediate	67	69	67	72	275	10,317.27
Steve Pate	70	68	66	71	275	10,317.27
D.A. Weibring	70	68	69	68	275	10,317.27
Steve Lowery	67	70	68	71	276	9,630
Jesper Parnevik	70	64	68	74	276	9,630
Chris Smith	71	68	65	72	276	9,630
Kevin Johnson	69	70	69	69	277	9,360
Michael Muehr	67	67	72	71	277	9,360
Rory Sabbatini	70	67	71	69	277	9,360
Greg Chalmers	67	70	70	71	278	9,000
Fred Funk	68	71	70	69	278	9,000
Bradley Hughes	75	64	66	73	278	9,000
Joe Ogilvie	69	66	72	71	278	9,000
Brent Schwarzrock	67	70	72	69	278	9,000
Briny Baird	71	68	70	70	279	8,595
Cameron Beckman	70	65	68	76	279	8,595
Brandel Chamblee	66	71	72	70	279	8,595
Billy Mayfair	65	70	74	70	279	8,595
Edward Fryatt	67	65	73	75	280	8,325
Jerry Smith	69	70	66	75	280	8,325

	SCORES				TOTAL	MONEY
Jason Gore	65	69	72	76	282	8,100
Glen Hnatiuk	70	64	72	76	282	8,100
Larry Mize	67	70	75	70	282	8,100
Jay Williamson	69	70	75	69	283	7,920
Emanuele Canonica	71	65	72	76	284	7,830

MasterCard Colonial

Colonial Country Club, Ft. Worth, Texas
Par 35-35–70; 7,080 yards

May 17-20
purse, $4,000,000

	SCORES				TOTAL	MONEY
Sergio Garcia	69	69	66	63	267	$720,000
Brian Gay	66	69	69	65	269	352,000
Phil Mickelson	65	68	66	70	269	352,000
Glen Day	68	72	64	66	270	192,000
Justin Leonard	69	67	70	66	272	146,000
Shigeki Maruyama	72	65	65	70	272	146,000
Brett Quigley	69	64	66	73	272	146,000
Rocco Mediate	72	62	69	70	273	116,000
Corey Pavin	68	64	73	68	273	116,000
David Toms	67	70	66	70	273	116,000
Per-Ulrik Johansson	69	68	68	69	274	88,000
Jesper Parnevik	70	69	67	68	274	88,000
Vijay Singh	69	68	69	68	274	88,000
Mike Sposa	71	66	67	70	274	88,000
Robert Allenby	72	68	65	70	275	64,000
Greg Chalmers	71	69	67	68	275	64,000
Tom Lehman	67	68	68	72	275	64,000
Jeff Sluman	71	64	69	71	275	64,000
Kirk Triplett	68	67	70	70	275	64,000
Fred Funk	70	68	67	71	276	50,000
Billy Mayfair	71	68	69	68	276	50,000
Jim Carter	73	67	68	69	277	40,000
Jim Furyk	65	71	69	72	277	40,000
Blaine McCallister	71	64	71	71	277	40,000
Scott McCarron	68	67	72	70	277	40,000
Fulton Allem	68	73	67	70	278	27,800
Stephen Ames	68	71	66	73	278	27,800
Rich Beem	70	68	71	69	278	27,800
Stewart Cink	71	70	67	70	278	27,800
Brad Elder	70	71	67	70	278	27,800
Bob Estes	68	73	64	73	278	27,800
Brent Geiberger	68	69	72	69	278	27,800
Kenny Perry	72	67	70	69	278	27,800
Jose Coceres	70	67	70	72	279	20,200
John Cook	71	71	70	67	279	20,200
Jonathan Kaye	71	65	70	73	279	20,200
Tom Kite	68	71	69	71	279	20,200
Joe Ogilvie	75	66	68	70	279	20,200
Geoff Ogilvy	70	70	68	71	279	20,200
Brandel Chamblee	71	66	73	70	280	15,200
Chris DiMarco	71	71	66	72	280	15,200
J.L. Lewis	71	67	69	73	280	15,200
Frank Nobilo	70	68	72	70	280	15,200
Joey Sindelar	74	67	72	67	280	15,200
Hal Sutton	73	69	66	72	280	15,200

	SCORES				TOTAL	MONEY
David Duval	69	68	73	71	281	10,880
Steve Flesch	69	69	69	74	281	10,880
Brandt Jobe	71	70	68	72	281	10,880
Skip Kendall	69	68	73	71	281	10,880
Greg Kraft	69	69	71	72	281	10,880
Bob Tway	75	67	66	73	281	10,880
David Frost	73	69	70	70	282	9,520
Bob May	70	72	69	71	282	9,520
Craig Barlow	72	70	69	72	283	9,160
Scott Dunlap	69	71	68	75	283	9,160
Harrison Frazar	73	65	69	76	283	9,160
Len Mattiace	74	68	70	71	283	9,160
Robert Damron	70	71	73	70	284	8,840
J.P. Hayes	73	67	68	76	284	8,840
Bruce Lietzke	71	71	69	73	284	8,840
Mike Weir	70	71	68	75	284	8,840
Briny Baird	72	68	71	74	285	8,520
Mark Brooks	67	72	72	74	285	8,520
Steve Pate	70	70	69	76	285	8,520
Brian Wilson	70	70	74	71	285	8,520
Keith Clearwater	72	70	68	76	286	8,320
D.A. Weibring	69	71	72	75	287	8,240
Ronnie Black	69	70	74	75	288	8,160
Tim Herron	70	71	75	74	290	8,080
Tom Purtzer	70	69	73	79	291	8,000
Dave Stockton, Jr.	70	71	77	76	294	7,920

Kemper Insurance Open

TPC at Avenel, Potomac, Maryland   May 24-28
Par 36-36–72; 7,005 yards   purse, $3,500,000
(Tournament extended to Monday — rain.)

	SCORES				TOTAL	MONEY
Frank Lickliter	69	65	66	68	268	$630,000
J.J. Henry	65	71	67	66	269	378,000
Bradley Hughes	70	63	72	67	272	182,000
Spike McRoy	71	66	67	68	272	182,000
Phil Mickelson	68	67	72	65	272	182,000
Tim Herron	69	68	68	69	274	117,250
Scott Hoch	68	70	66	70	274	117,250
Per-Ulrik Johansson	68	69	66	71	274	117,250
Chris DiMarco	65	70	68	72	275	94,500
Dan Forsman	68	67	67	73	275	94,500
Brent Schwarzrock	68	67	71	69	275	94,500
Robert Allenby	69	67	67	73	276	77,000
Chris Riley	67	69	69	71	276	77,000
Cameron Beckman	69	69	69	70	277	63,000
Charles Howell	71	65	71	70	277	63,000
Brian Watts	72	67	69	69	277	63,000
Fred Funk	71	69	71	67	278	49,000
Jay Haas	69	67	71	71	278	49,000
Frank Nobilo	66	72	71	69	278	49,000
Craig Parry	70	70	71	67	278	49,000
Phil Tataurangi	68	68	71	71	278	49,000
Bill Glasson	73	68	72	66	279	29,944.45
Lee Janzen	71	68	69	71	279	29,944.45

		SCORES			TOTAL	MONEY
Greg Kraft	71	70	69	69	279	29,944.45
Esteban Toledo	70	71	73	65	279	29,944.45
Bob Estes	66	69	73	71	279	29,944.44
Matt Gogel	71	70	69	69	279	29,944.44
Mike Heinen	72	69	67	71	279	29,944.44
Kazuhiko Hosokawa	70	65	73	71	279	29,944.44
Lee Porter	66	68	71	74	279	29,944.44
Stuart Appleby	65	71	70	74	280	20,300
Brandel Chamblee	72	69	70	69	280	20,300
Kevin Johnson	68	68	71	73	280	20,300
Skip Kendall	69	68	71	72	280	20,300
Ian Leggatt	71	69	71	69	280	20,300
Steve Lowery	68	68	71	73	280	20,300
Briny Baird	69	68	72	72	281	15,050
Jeff Brehaut	73	68	68	72	281	15,050
Donnie Hammond	71	66	73	71	281	15,050
Jeff Julian	69	66	76	70	281	15,050
Mark O'Meara	67	73	72	69	281	15,050
Brett Quigley	69	68	77	67	281	15,050
Willie Wood	67	70	74	70	281	15,050
Mark Brooks	69	72	70	71	282	11,550
Gary Nicklaus	69	70	72	71	282	11,550
Tom Pernice, Jr.	70	68	70	74	282	11,550
Mark Hensby	71	68	73	71	283	9,111.67
Larry Mize	72	69	73	69	283	9,111.67
Carl Paulson	71	68	73	71	283	9,111.67
Loren Roberts	70	70	70	73	283	9,111.67
Michael Bradley	70	71	71	71	283	9,111.66
Pete Jordan	71	70	69	73	283	9,111.66
Woody Austin	68	73	70	73	284	8,012.50
Bob Burns	69	72	69	74	284	8,012.50
Jim Carter	71	68	72	73	284	8,012.50
Justin Leonard	68	68	78	70	284	8,012.50
Chris Tidland	68	73	70	74	285	7,875
Tommy Tolles	68	69	69	79	285	7,875
Ben Crenshaw	70	70	74	72	286	7,770
Brad Elder	71	66	72	78	287	7,665
Steve Flesch	68	73	72	74	287	7,665
Ben Bates	69	71	74	75	289	7,560
Steve Allan	70	71	77	75	293	7,490

Memorial Tournament

Muirfield Village Golf Club, Dublin, Ohio
Par 36-36–72; 7,193 yards

May 31-June 3
purse, $4,100,000

		SCORES			TOTAL	MONEY
Tiger Woods	68	69	68	66	271	$738,000
Paul Azinger	68	67	69	74	278	360,800
Sergio Garcia	68	69	70	71	278	360,800
Stewart Cink	72	69	67	71	279	196,800
Vijay Singh	70	66	73	71	280	155,800
Toru Taniguchi	68	74	69	69	280	155,800
Kenny Perry	72	69	71	69	281	127,783.34
Robert Allenby	69	69	70	73	281	127,783.33
Stuart Appleby	67	71	69	74	281	127,783.33
Scott Hoch	70	69	69	74	282	110,700

		SCORES			TOTAL	MONEY
Steve Flesch	72	67	71	73	283	90,200
Fred Funk	71	68	71	73	283	90,200
Lee Janzen	74	71	71	67	283	90,200
Kevin Sutherland	69	72	71	71	283	90,200
Fred Couples	72	75	72	65	284	65,600
Charles Howell	73	68	70	73	284	65,600
Peter Lonard	75	69	71	69	284	65,600
Gary Nicklaus	72	72	70	70	284	65,600
Jeff Sluman	67	73	73	71	284	65,600
Greg Chalmers	72	68	71	74	285	47,765
John Cook	72	68	72	73	285	47,765
John Daly	73	68	75	69	285	47,765
Jay Haas	68	76	72	69	285	47,765
Mark Brooks	72	72	72	70	286	33,210
Jim Furyk	69	69	74	74	286	33,210
Skip Kendall	73	70	72	71	286	33,210
Len Mattiace	72	67	73	74	286	33,210
Naomichi Ozaki	69	69	74	74	286	33,210
Scott Verplank	66	72	72	76	286	33,210
Brad Faxon	70	71	75	71	287	24,365.72
Jonathan Kaye	71	71	74	71	287	24,365.72
Jesper Parnevik	68	75	73	71	287	24,365.72
Chris DiMarco	74	70	74	69	287	24,365.71
Justin Leonard	71	73	74	69	287	24,365.71
Grant Waite	68	71	72	76	287	24,365.71
Mike Weir	72	69	71	75	287	24,365.71
Shigeki Maruyama	70	75	70	73	288	19,270
Steve Stricker	74	70	72	72	288	19,270
Bob Tway	72	72	68	76	288	19,270
Mark Calcavecchia	69	73	74	73	289	16,810
Dennis Paulson	68	74	70	77	289	16,810
Mike Sposa	68	78	72	71	289	16,810
David Frost	71	72	75	72	290	14,350
Billy Mayfair	68	74	76	72	290	14,350
Garrett Willis	72	70	73	75	290	14,350
Aaron Baddeley	71	73	73	74	291	11,944.67
Rich Beem	71	70	76	74	291	11,944.67
David Peoples	74	72	74	71	291	11,944.66
J.P. Hayes	71	76	74	71	292	10,229.50
Franklin Langham	74	73	73	72	292	10,229.50
Andrew Magee	74	70	74	74	292	10,229.50
Paul Stankowski	72	71	74	75	292	10,229.50
Hal Sutton	71	71	75	76	293	9,539.34
Bob May	75	71	76	71	293	9,539.33
Carl Paulson	71	73	76	73	293	9,539.33
Robert Damron	74	71	70	79	294	9,225
Shingo Katayama	71	76	76	71	294	9,225
Frank Nobilo	73	72	77	72	294	9,225
Chris Smith	66	71	81	76	294	9,225
Brian Gay	71	74	78	72	295	8,938
Cliff Kresge	71	75	74	75	295	8,938
Rory Sabbatini	73	69	77	76	295	8,938
Billy Andrade	72	71	74	79	296	8,692
Ernie Els	69	75	75	77	296	8,692
Duffy Waldorf	68	75	80	73	296	8,692
Steve Lowery	72	70	78	77	297	8,528
Carlos Franco	69	74	77	78	298	8,446
Harrison Frazar	76	71	75	78	300	8,364
Curtis Strange	71	75	77	78	301	8,282
Esteban Toledo	76	70	82	74	302	8,200

FedEx St. Jude Classic

TPC at Southwind, Germantown, Tennessee
Par 36-35–71; 7,006 yards

June 7-10
purse, $3,500,000

	SCORES				TOTAL	MONEY
Bob Estes	61	66	69	71	267	$630,000
Bernhard Langer	69	65	68	66	268	378,000
Tom Lehman	69	68	66	66	269	203,000
Scott McCarron	66	65	66	72	269	203,000
John Daly	69	65	63	73	270	127,750
Paul Goydos	66	67	69	68	270	127,750
Curtis Strange	65	67	69	69	270	127,750
Jesper Parnevik	67	64	71	69	271	105,000
Nick Price	68	67	69	67	271	105,000
Nick Faldo	66	70	67	69	272	91,000
Scott Hoch	68	68	67	69	272	91,000
Ben Bates	70	69	70	64	273	64,500
Bob Burns	71	67	67	68	273	64,500
Chris DiMarco	66	69	69	69	273	64,500
Jay Haas	69	68	70	66	273	64,500
Len Mattiace	69	69	67	68	273	64,500
Billy Mayfair	69	67	68	69	273	64,500
Craig Parry	67	66	72	68	273	64,500
Choi Kyung-ju	67	66	72	69	274	45,500
Jose Coceres	68	69	67	70	274	45,500
Mathew Goggin	69	69	65	71	274	45,500
Brandt Jobe	68	68	72	67	275	32,491.67
Pete Jordan	71	66	70	68	275	32,491.67
Brent Schwarzrock	64	67	75	69	275	32,491.67
Ted Tryba	67	69	69	70	275	32,491.67
Joel Edwards	67	67	71	70	275	32,491.66
Glen Hnatiuk	69	70	64	72	275	32,491.66
David Gossett	67	70	70	69	276	25,375
Bob May	69	68	69	70	276	25,375
Russ Cochran	69	66	71	71	277	20,800
Bill Glasson	68	71	68	70	277	20,800
Per-Ulrik Johansson	70	65	73	69	277	20,800
Steve Jones	71	67	72	67	277	20,800
J.L. Lewis	68	70	70	69	277	20,800
Scott Simpson	71	66	72	68	277	20,800
Mike Sposa	70	68	70	69	277	20,800
Stewart Cink	70	69	71	68	278	15,750
Jimmy Green	71	66	71	70	278	15,750
Shaun Micheel	68	66	72	72	278	15,750
John Riegger	65	70	73	70	278	15,750
Chris Tidland	71	68	68	71	278	15,750
Brandel Chamblee	68	70	74	67	279	11,570
Richie Coughlan	64	72	71	72	279	11,570
Robert Damron	68	67	73	71	279	11,570
Kelly Grunewald	67	69	77	66	279	11,570
Cliff Kresge	66	72	73	68	279	11,570
Frank Nobilo	70	67	69	73	279	11,570
Jeff Sluman	68	69	69	73	279	11,570
Notah Begay	68	70	71	71	280	8,732.50
Tom Byrum	64	70	72	74	280	8,732.50
Angel Cabrera	71	67	73	69	280	8,732.50
J.P. Hayes	66	70	71	73	280	8,732.50
Barry Cheesman	67	70	72	72	281	8,064
Andrew McLardy	68	71	74	68	281	8,064

		SCORES			TOTAL	MONEY
Jerry Smith	69	69	72	71	281	8,064
David Toms	70	68	73	70	281	8,064
Jean Van de Velde	69	70	69	73	281	8,064
Brad Elder	66	69	75	72	282	7,700
Hunter Haas	68	71	68	75	282	7,700
Kent Jones	71	66	75	70	282	7,700
Sean Murphy	66	69	74	73	282	7,700
Tommy Tolles	65	74	68	75	282	7,700
Bobby Cochran	67	69	74	73	283	7,455
Jason Gore	69	69	76	69	283	7,455
Bart Bryant	70	68	68	78	284	7,315
David Morland	71	66	74	73	284	7,315
Joe Ogilvie	69	70	71	75	285	7,210
Jeff Hart	70	68	75	73	286	7,105
Spike McRoy	71	66	73	76	286	7,105
Rob Bradley	70	69	73	75	287	7,000

U.S. Open Championship

Southern Hills Country Club, Tulsa, Oklahoma　　　　　　　June 14-18
Par 35-35-70; 6,973 yards　　　　　　　　　　　　purse, $5,000,000

		SCORES			TOTAL	MONEY
Retief Goosen	66	70	69	71	276	$900,000
Mark Brooks	72	64	70	70	276	530,000
(Goosen defeated Brooks in 18-hole playoff, 70-72.)						
Stewart Cink	69	69	67	72	277	325,310
Rocco Mediate	71	68	67	72	278	226,777
Tom Kite	73	72	72	64	281	172,912
Paul Azinger	74	67	69	71	281	172,912
Vijay Singh	74	70	74	64	282	125,172
Angel Cabrera	70	71	72	69	282	125,172
Davis Love III	72	69	71	70	282	125,172
Kirk Triplett	72	69	71	70	282	125,172
Phil Mickelson	70	69	68	75	282	125,172
Tiger Woods	74	71	69	69	283	91,734
Matt Gogel	70	69	74	70	283	91,734
Michael Allen	77	68	67	71	283	91,734
Sergio Garcia	70	68	68	77	283	91,734
Scott Hoch	73	73	69	69	284	75,337
Chris DiMarco	69	73	70	72	284	75,337
David Duval	70	69	71	74	284	75,337
Chris Perry	72	71	73	69	285	63,426
Corey Pavin	70	75	68	72	285	63,426
Mike Weir	67	76	68	74	285	63,426
Scott Verplank	71	71	73	71	286	54,813
Thomas Bjorn	72	69	73	72	286	54,813
Mark Calcavecchia	70	74	73	70	287	42,523
Steve Lowery	71	73	72	71	287	42,523
Hal Sutton	70	75	71	71	287	42,523
Olin Browne	71	74	71	71	287	42,523
Joe Durant	71	74	70	72	287	42,523
Tom Lehman	76	68	69	74	287	42,523
Jesper Parnevik	73	73	74	68	288	30,055
Steve Jones	73	73	72	70	288	30,055
Bob Estes	70	72	75	71	288	30,055
Dean Wilson	71	74	72	71	288	30,055

	SCORES				TOTAL	MONEY
Darren Clarke	74	71	71	72	288	30,055
Gabriel Hjertstedt	72	74	70	72	288	30,055
Padraig Harrington	73	70	71	74	288	30,055
*Bryce Molder	75	71	68	74	288	
J.L. Lewis	68	68	77	75	288	30,055
Bob May	72	72	69	75	288	30,055
Shaun Micheel	73	70	75	71	289	23,933
Tim Herron	71	74	73	71	289	23,933
Bernhard Langer	71	73	71	74	289	23,933
Briny Baird	71	72	70	76	289	23,933
Kevin Sutherland	73	72	73	72	290	18,780
Tom Byrum	74	72	72	72	290	18,780
Toshimitsu Izawa	69	74	74	73	290	18,780
Fred Funk	78	68	71	73	290	18,780
Jeff Maggert	69	73	72	76	290	18,780
Brandel Chamblee	72	71	71	76	290	18,780
Duffy Waldorf	75	68	69	78	290	18,780
Eduardo Romero	74	72	72	73	291	15,035
Mark Wiebe	73	72	74	73	292	13,164
Jimmy Walker	79	66	74	73	292	13,164
Colin Montgomerie	71	70	77	74	292	13,164
Jose Coceres	70	73	75	74	292	13,164
Bob Tway	75	71	72	74	292	13,164
Scott Dunlap	74	70	73	75	292	13,164
Hale Irwin	67	75	74	76	292	13,164
Brandt Jobe	77	68	71	76	292	13,164
Frank Lickliter	75	71	70	76	292	13,164
Loren Roberts	69	76	69	78	292	13,164
Tim Petrovic	74	71	75	73	293	11,443
Dudley Hart	71	73	74	75	293	11,443
Richard Zokol	72	71	74	76	293	11,443
Jim Furyk	70	70	71	82	293	11,443
Dan Forsman	75	71	77	71	294	10,368
Ernie Els	71	74	77	72	294	10,368
Harrison Frazar	73	73	76	72	294	10,368
David Toms	71	71	77	75	294	10,368
David Peoples	73	73	72	76	294	10,368
Peter Lonard	76	69	70	79	294	10,368
Franklin Langham	75	71	75	74	295	9,508
Nick Faldo	76	70	74	75	295	9,508
Anthony Kang	74	72	77	73	296	8,863
Gary Orr	74	72	74	76	296	8,863
Thongchai Jaidee	73	73	72	78	296	8,863
Mathias Gronberg	74	69	74	79	296	8,863
Jim McGovern	71	73	77	76	297	8,325
Stephen Gangluff	74	72	78	77	301	8,105

Out of Final 36 Holes

Rich Beem	74	73		147
Chad Campbell	76	71		147
Robert Damron	73	74		147
Brad Faxon	73	74		147
Mike Hulbert	75	72		147
Lee Janzen	77	70		147
Pete Jordan	77	70		147
Gary Koch	75	72		147
Tom Pernice, Jr.	74	73		147
Brett Quigley	71	76		147

	SCORES		TOTAL
Choi Kyung-ju	78	70	148
Robert Gamez	74	74	148
Skip Kendall	74	74	148
Mark O'Meara	74	74	148
Dennis Paulson	75	73	148
Nick Price	74	74	148
Steve Stricker	73	75	148
Robert Allenby	74	75	149
Billy Andrade	75	74	149
Charles Howell	75	74	149
Jose Maria Olazabal	77	72	149
Carl Paulson	73	76	149
Toru Taniguchi	78	71	149
Ronnie Black	76	74	150
Kyle Blackman	74	76	150
Fred Couples	76	74	150
Steve Flesch	81	69	150
Chris Gonzales	75	75	150
Tripp Isenhour	73	77	150
Miguel Angel Jimenez	77	73	150
Paul Lawrie	73	77	150
Joey Maxon	74	76	150
Jay Don Blake	75	76	151
Todd Fischer	76	75	151
Paul Goydos	76	75	151
Donnie Hammond	76	75	151
John Huston	75	76	151
Joel Kribel	74	77	151
Justin Leonard	78	73	151
Mike Sposa	78	73	151
Esteban Toledo	74	77	151
Lee Westwood	75	76	151
Jess Daley	80	72	152
John Douma	77	75	152
Jason Dufner	74	78	152
Jeff Freeman	77	75	152
Shingo Katayama	77	75	152
Brad Klapprott	75	77	152
Gary Nicklaus	78	74	152
Charles Raulerson, Jr.	77	75	152
Chris Smith	74	78	152
Glen Day	77	76	153
*John Harris	76	77	153
Brian Henninger	75	78	153
Kevin Johnson	77	76	153
Michael Campbell	77	77	154
Stuart Appleby	80	75	155
Ben Bates	75	80	155
Carlos Franco	76	79	155
Jeff Hart	80	75	155
Scott Johnson	82	73	155
John Maginnes	79	76	155
Dicky Pride	77	78	155
*Jeff Quinney	82	73	155
Chris Anderson	77	79	156
Notah Begay	78	78	156
Clark Dennis	79	77	156
Wes Heffernan	77	79	156
Willie Wood	75	81	156

	SCORES			TOTAL	
Marty Schiene	78	79		157	
Jeff Barlow	78	81		159	
Chris Wall	81	79		160	
George Frake	84	77		161	
Phillip Price				WD	
Jarmo Sandelin	72			WD	
Jay Williamson	75			DQ	
Pierre Fulke	76			WD	

(Professionals who did not complete 72 holes received $5,000.)

Buick Classic

Westchester Country Club, Harrison, New York   June 21-24
Par 36-35–71; 6,722 yards   purse, $3,500,000

	SCORES				TOTAL	MONEY
Sergio Garcia	68	67	66	67	268	$630,000
Scott Hoch	67	68	68	68	271	378,000
Billy Andrade	70	69	68	66	273	182,000
Stewart Cink	65	72	69	67	273	182,000
J.P. Hayes	68	69	67	69	273	182,000
Brad Faxon	69	72	66	67	274	121,625
Vijay Singh	67	70	70	67	274	121,625
Robert Allenby	69	68	74	64	275	105,000
Russ Cochran	71	68	67	69	275	105,000
Jay Williamson	70	72	65	69	276	94,500
Olin Browne	71	71	69	67	278	84,000
Kevin Sutherland	70	70	69	69	278	84,000
Steve Elkington	70	68	72	69	279	67,666.67
Craig Parry	71	69	67	72	279	67,666.67
Gabriel Hjertstedt	68	70	68	73	279	67,666.66
Paul Azinger	71	70	68	71	280	56,000
Chris Smith	72	70	69	69	280	56,000
Tiger Woods	75	66	68	71	280	56,000
Steve Allan	69	71	72	69	281	39,500
Jim Furyk	71	72	67	71	281	39,500
Per-Ulrik Johansson	69	69	72	71	281	39,500
Skip Kendall	72	70	69	70	281	39,500
J.L. Lewis	72	71	69	69	281	39,500
Chris Perry	70	73	69	69	281	39,500
Mark Wiebe	68	68	73	72	281	39,500
Stuart Appleby	73	68	70	71	282	25,375
David Duval	71	73	68	70	282	25,375
Harrison Frazar	71	67	72	72	282	25,375
Paul Gow	71	68	72	71	282	25,375
Jay Haas	68	73	72	69	282	25,375
Frank Nobilo	73	69	69	71	282	25,375
Cameron Beckman	72	69	72	70	283	19,810
John Cook	69	73	69	72	283	19,810
Fred Couples	72	68	70	73	283	19,810
David Frost	70	71	72	70	283	19,810
Ian Leggatt	70	69	71	73	283	19,810
Tommy Armour III	74	69	71	70	284	14,000
Tom Byrum	69	69	75	71	284	14,000
Danny Ellis	72	72	68	72	284	14,000
Nick Faldo	73	68	70	73	284	14,000

	SCORES				TOTAL	MONEY
Brian Gay	71	71	71	71	284	14,000
Brent Geiberger	70	69	73	72	284	14,000
Matt Gogel	70	71	71	72	284	14,000
Glen Hnatiuk	71	68	71	74	284	14,000
Kevin Johnson	69	70	74	71	284	14,000
Jonathan Kaye	70	74	71	69	284	14,000
Rich Beem	74	67	71	73	285	9,613.34
Edward Fryatt	70	71	74	70	285	9,613.33
Loren Roberts	72	72	71	70	285	9,613.33
Jim McGovern	70	72	74	70	286	8,715
Tom Pernice, Jr.	71	69	71	75	286	8,715
Brandel Chamblee	73	69	74	71	287	8,207.50
Dennis Paulson	71	73	74	69	287	8,207.50
Corey Pavin	69	72	71	75	287	8,207.50
Dicky Pride	71	72	71	73	287	8,207.50
Jim Carter	73	67	72	76	288	7,770
Steve Flesch	71	73	70	74	288	7,770
Jason Gore	73	69	68	78	288	7,770
Jeff Hart	69	71	73	75	288	7,770
Jerry Kelly	72	72	73	71	288	7,770
Justin Leonard	69	75	72	72	288	7,770
Jerry Smith	77	66	74	71	288	7,770
Bob Estes	72	69	73	75	289	7,455
Brian Watts	69	73	70	77	289	7,455
David Berganio, Jr.	69	73	71	77	290	7,245
Brad Elder	73	67	78	72	290	7,245
Kent Jones	76	67	74	73	290	7,245
David Morland	71	73	70	76	290	7,245
Michael Campbell	72	72	75	72	291	6,895
Tripp Isenhour	72	66	79	74	291	6,895
Gary Nicklaus	73	71	74	73	291	6,895
Brett Quigley	70	73	72	76	291	6,895
Chris Riley	73	71	74	73	291	6,895
Rocky Walcher	74	70	74	73	291	6,895
Larry Mize	72	72	72	76	292	6,650
Mike Reid	76	68	74	75	293	6,580
Jeff Julian	73	71	75	76	295	6,475
Brent Schwarzrock	71	73	78	73	295	6,475
Keith Clearwater	73	70	78	75	296	6,370

Canon Greater Hartford Open

TPC at River Highlands, Cromwell, Connecticut
Par 35-35–70; 6,820 yards

June 28-July 1
purse, $3,100,000

	SCORES				TOTAL	MONEY
Phil Mickelson	67	68	61	68	264	$558,000
Billy Andrade	68	65	66	66	265	334,800
David Berganio, Jr.	67	66	64	69	266	161,200
Chris DiMarco	65	67	66	68	266	161,200
Dudley Hart	70	63	70	63	266	161,200
Tom Pernice, Jr.	68	68	66	65	267	111,600
Olin Browne	68	71	67	63	269	83,921.43
Tripp Isenhour	69	70	67	63	269	83,921.43
Frank Lickliter	65	69	68	67	269	83,921.43
Shigeki Maruyama	63	69	73	64	269	83,921.43
Kenny Perry	68	68	70	63	269	83,921.43

	SCORES				TOTAL	MONEY
Kirk Triplett	68	71	65	65	269	83,921.43
Jerry Kelly	67	65	69	68	269	83,921.42
Paul Azinger	70	64	69	67	270	55,800
Tim Herron	66	68	67	69	270	55,800
Hal Sutton	67	67	69	67	270	55,800
Mark Brooks	66	69	68	68	271	43,400
Joe Ogilvie	68	64	70	69	271	43,400
Scott Simpson	65	67	70	69	271	43,400
Kevin Sutherland	68	67	68	68	271	43,400
Scott Verplank	72	67	71	61	271	43,400
Jay Don Blake	64	68	72	68	272	27,944.29
John Daly	67	70	70	65	272	27,944.29
Edward Fryatt	65	67	72	68	272	27,944.29
Billy Mayfair	70	70	68	64	272	27,944.29
David Duval	67	66	70	69	272	27,944.28
Frank Nobilo	67	66	70	69	272	27,944.28
Geoff Ogilvy	67	68	69	68	272	27,944.28
Briny Baird	67	69	70	67	273	19,286.43
Mark Calcavecchia	68	68	71	66	273	19,286.43
David Frost	69	68	69	67	273	19,286.43
Charles Howell	66	72	70	65	273	19,286.43
Jonathan Kaye	62	71	72	68	273	19,286.43
Jay Williamson	66	72	70	65	273	19,286.43
Paul Gow	67	69	68	69	273	19,286.42
Jeremy Anderson	70	67	71	66	274	13,659.38
Jim Carter	68	68	71	67	274	13,659.38
Brian Gay	68	72	68	66	274	13,659.38
Steve Pate	68	67	71	68	274	13,659.38
Doug Dunakey	67	65	71	71	274	13,659.37
Jay Haas	71	68	68	67	274	13,659.37
Jeff Sluman	67	69	69	69	274	13,659.37
Duffy Waldorf	71	69	65	69	274	13,659.37
Len Mattiace	67	69	72	67	275	10,850
Cameron Beckman	70	70	69	67	276	9,076.80
Joel Edwards	73	67	66	70	276	9,076.80
Jimmy Green	66	73	70	67	276	9,076.80
Andrew McLardy	66	71	72	67	276	9,076.80
Chris Smith	70	66	72	68	276	9,076.80
Kevin Johnson	68	71	67	71	277	7,477.20
J.L. Lewis	70	70	69	68	277	7,477.20
Larry Mize	65	72	71	69	277	7,477.20
Carl Paulson	68	69	71	69	277	7,477.20
Esteban Toledo	66	74	71	66	277	7,477.20
Michael Clark	69	69	69	71	278	6,975
Nick Faldo	66	73	72	67	278	6,975
Andrew Magee	67	71	71	69	278	6,975
Corey Pavin	69	71	71	67	278	6,975
David Peoples	71	68	69	70	278	6,975
Chris Tidland	70	70	69	69	278	6,975
Keith Clearwater	71	67	73	68	279	6,603
Jim Furyk	72	67	71	69	279	6,603
Jeff Hart	74	66	69	70	279	6,603
Glen Hnatiuk	73	67	71	68	279	6,603
Bradley Hughes	69	71	69	70	279	6,603
Sean Murphy	67	73	74	65	279	6,603
Woody Austin	69	71	70	70	280	6,231
Bart Bryant	70	69	74	67	280	6,231
Steve Elkington	68	72	69	71	280	6,231
Pete Jordan	69	66	73	72	280	6,231

	SCORES				TOTAL	MONEY
Ian Leggatt	67	73	71	69	280	6,231
Paul Stankowski	67	72	70	71	280	6,231
Greg Kraft	68	72	74	67	281	5,983
Chris Riley	65	70	78	68	281	5,983
Emanuele Canonica	71	68	71	72	282	5,859
Robin Freeman	73	67	74	68	282	5,859
Kelly Grunewald	69	70	75	69	283	5,735
Dicky Pride	68	71	74	70	283	5,735
Spike McRoy	68	71	76	69	284	5,642
John Huston	71	68	71	75	285	5,549
Neal Lancaster	69	69	74	73	285	5,549
Brent Geiberger	70	69	78	69	286	5,425
Franklin Langham	70	67	78	71	286	5,425
Kent Jones	71	65	77	74	287	5,332
Mathew Goggin	67	72	72	77	288	5,270

Advil Western Open

Cog Hill Golf & Country Club, Dubsdread Course,   July 5-8
Lemont, Illinois   purse, $3,600,000
Par 36-36–72; 7,073 yards

	SCORES				TOTAL	MONEY
Scott Hoch	69	68	66	64	267	$648,000
Davis Love III	66	67	69	66	268	388,800
Brandel Chamblee	69	67	70	69	275	208,800
Mike Weir	71	70	67	67	275	208,800
Jerry Kelly	67	73	69	67	276	136,800
Rory Sabbatini	71	68	70	67	276	136,800
Steve Flesch	71	70	67	69	277	112,200
Dudley Hart	70	70	69	68	277	112,200
Kevin Sutherland	70	70	69	68	277	112,200
Matt Gogel	69	74	66	69	278	82,800
Frank Lickliter	70	71	70	67	278	82,800
Vijay Singh	69	70	70	69	278	82,800
Steve Stricker	72	70	68	68	278	82,800
Mark Wiebe	65	74	67	72	278	82,800
Bob Estes	70	68	71	70	279	57,600
Brian Gay	74	68	67	70	279	57,600
Billy Mayfair	72	70	67	70	279	57,600
Carl Paulson	68	71	72	68	279	57,600
Scott Verplank	69	69	70	71	279	57,600
Stephen Ames	72	69	68	71	280	33,381.82
Brad Faxon	68	70	72	70	280	33,381.82
David Frost	72	71	70	67	280	33,381.82
Justin Leonard	69	72	70	69	280	33,381.82
Frank Nobilo	68	69	72	71	280	33,381.82
Joe Ogilvie	71	67	73	69	280	33,381.82
Kenny Perry	68	74	70	68	280	33,381.82
Chris Smith	71	68	71	70	280	33,381.82
Tiger Woods	73	68	68	71	280	33,381.82
Cameron Beckman	71	72	66	71	280	33,381.81
Bob Tway	68	74	67	71	280	33,381.81
John Cook	69	72	72	68	281	20,880
Jonathan Kaye	69	71	75	66	281	20,880
Tom Lehman	74	68	70	69	281	20,880
Bob May	72	70	74	65	281	20,880

	SCORES				TOTAL	MONEY
Scott McCarron	69	73	72	67	281	20,880
Hal Sutton	70	71	70	70	281	20,880
Briny Baird	70	71	70	71	282	16,200
Robert Damron	70	72	68	72	282	16,200
Joey Gullion	72	69	71	70	282	16,200
Charles Howell	72	69	73	68	282	16,200
Joey Sindelar	72	69	70	71	282	16,200
Bob Burns	71	68	72	72	283	11,583
Greg Chalmers	69	74	72	68	283	11,583
Brandt Jobe	70	70	72	71	283	11,583
Ian Leggatt	69	73	70	71	283	11,583
Shaun Micheel	70	72	67	74	283	11,583
Phil Mickelson	66	74	67	76	283	11,583
Larry Mize	70	73	69	71	283	11,583
David Toms	67	73	73	70	283	11,583
Glen Hnatiuk	71	69	73	71	284	8,964
Nick Price	72	71	68	73	284	8,964
J.J. Henry	74	69	71	71	285	8,395.20
Tim Herron	70	73	72	70	285	8,395.20
Skip Kendall	71	72	72	70	285	8,395.20
Loren Roberts	70	69	73	73	285	8,395.20
Mark Wilson	71	67	73	74	285	8,395.20
Russ Cochran	72	69	73	72	286	8,064
Brent Geiberger	69	73	70	74	286	8,064
J.L. Lewis	69	71	74	72	286	8,064
Rich Beem	70	73	75	69	287	7,848
Choi Kyung-ju	71	71	76	69	287	7,848
Robin Freeman	74	69	69	75	287	7,848
Jim Carter	71	72	74	71	288	7,596
Kevin Johnson	70	73	76	69	288	7,596
Jeff Maggert	70	71	70	77	288	7,596
Chris Perry	74	68	74	72	288	7,596
Ted Tryba	71	72	74	72	289	7,416
Craig Kanada	74	69	73	74	290	7,308
Gary Nicklaus	71	72	74	73	290	7,308
Shigeki Maruyama	72	71	76	75	294	7,164
Jean Van de Velde	73	70	76	75	294	7,164

Greater Milwaukee Open

Brown Deer Park Golf Course, Milwaukee, Wisconsin   July 12-15
Par 36-35–71; 6,759 yards   purse, $3,100,000

	SCORES				TOTAL	MONEY
Shigeki Maruyama	68	65	67	66	266	$558,000
Charles Howell	66	69	67	64	266	334,800
(Maruyama defeated Howell on first playoff hole.)						
J.P. Hayes	69	66	71	63	269	179,800
Tim Herron	69	69	64	67	269	179,800
Choi Kyung-ju	70	68	66	66	270	105,090
Harrison Frazar	70	68	62	70	270	105,090
Brent Geiberger	65	68	70	67	270	105,090
Blaine McCallister	69	65	70	66	270	105,090
Kenny Perry	66	63	71	70	270	105,090
Jay Haas	64	71	69	67	271	71,300
Scott Hoch	67	68	68	68	271	71,300
Steve Lowery	72	69	66	64	271	71,300

	SCORES				TOTAL	MONEY
Jeff Sluman	67	68	64	72	271	71,300
Bob Tway	69	72	66	64	271	71,300
Skip Kendall	73	67	65	67	272	52,700
David Peoples	71	68	66	67	272	52,700
Steve Stricker	68	66	69	69	272	52,700
Tommy Armour III	73	66	67	67	273	37,731.43
Brian Claar	68	68	71	66	273	37,731.43
Glen Day	72	69	66	66	273	37,731.43
Jonathan Kaye	70	71	65	67	273	37,731.43
Michael Muehr	69	70	67	67	273	37,731.43
Brett Quigley	72	67	67	67	273	37,731.43
Tom Byrum	70	67	66	70	273	37,731.42
Richie Coughlan	69	70	67	68	274	25,316.67
Carlos Franco	71	66	68	69	274	25,316.67
Craig Spence	68	65	70	71	274	25,316.66
Briny Baird	67	67	73	68	275	19,743.13
Brad Elder	68	67	70	70	275	19,743.13
Paul Goydos	72	68	68	67	275	19,743.13
Frank Lickliter	73	66	70	66	275	19,743.13
Jay Don Blake	67	69	67	72	275	19,743.12
Marco Dawson	65	69	68	73	275	19,743.12
Bradley Hughes	68	70	67	70	275	19,743.12
D.A. Weibring	65	75	70	65	275	19,743.12
John Riegger	71	66	69	70	276	12,724.10
Woody Austin	71	70	70	65	276	12,724.09
Craig Barlow	72	69	69	66	276	12,724.09
Jimmy Green	67	73	69	67	276	12,724.09
Cliff Kresge	72	65	67	72	276	12,724.09
Neal Lancaster	71	70	68	67	276	12,724.09
Jim McGovern	70	70	68	68	276	12,724.09
Corey Pavin	70	68	70	68	276	12,724.09
Loren Roberts	74	67	67	68	276	12,724.09
Scott Simpson	71	70	64	71	276	12,724.09
Chris Smith	66	66	72	72	276	12,724.09
Jerry Kelly	68	71	67	71	277	7,784.45
Larry Mize	68	72	68	69	277	7,784.45
Joe Ogilvie	75	65	67	70	277	7,784.45
Lee Porter	70	69	67	71	277	7,784.45
Cameron Beckman	72	68	71	66	277	7,784.44
Robert Damron	72	69	67	69	277	7,784.44
Dan Forsman	71	70	68	68	277	7,784.44
Tom Purtzer	71	70	67	69	277	7,784.44
Jerry Smith	69	70	65	73	277	7,784.44
Bob Burns	68	69	69	72	278	6,944
Doug Dunakey	75	66	70	67	278	6,944
Scott Gump	70	69	69	70	278	6,944
Pete Jordan	70	71	70	67	278	6,944
Steve Pate	66	71	68	73	278	6,944
Joel Edwards	70	69	71	69	279	6,541
Brad Fabel	69	69	67	74	279	6,541
Donnie Hammond	69	70	68	72	279	6,541
J.J. Henry	72	69	70	68	279	6,541
Peter Jacobsen	69	72	66	72	279	6,541
Chris Perry	68	70	66	75	279	6,541
Craig Stadler	69	66	73	71	279	6,541
Fuzzy Zoeller	69	71	68	71	279	6,541
Rich Beem	70	68	72	70	280	6,107
Craig Bowden	68	70	69	73	280	6,107
Michael Bradley	69	72	70	69	280	6,107

	SCORES				TOTAL	MONEY
Sean Murphy	70	71	71	68	280	6,107
Esteban Toledo	68	66	71	75	280	6,107
Brian Watts	66	70	73	71	280	6,107
Brandt Jobe	67	70	69	75	281	5,766
Franklin Langham	69	71	71	70	281	5,766
Craig Perks	70	69	69	73	281	5,766
Mike Reid	69	71	74	67	281	5,766
Mike Standly	70	70	73	68	281	5,766
Spike McRoy	68	73	69	72	282	5,549
Dave Stockton, Jr.	68	72	68	74	282	5,549
Gary Nicklaus	70	71	72	70	283	5,425
Ted Tryba	72	69	72	70	283	5,425
Mark Wilson	71	67	70	76	284	5,332
Dicky Pride	71	70	73	71	285	5,270
Tripp Isenhour	69	70	73	74	286	5,177
Kevin Johnson	73	68	76	69	286	5,177
Jeff Hart	69	71	75	72	287	5,084

B.C. Open

En-Joie Golf Club, Endicott, New York
Par 37-35–72; 6,994 yards

July 19-22
purse, $2,000,000

	SCORES				TOTAL	MONEY
Jeff Sluman	67	68	65	66	266	$360,000
Paul Gow	69	65	66	66	266	216,000
(Sluman defeated Gow on second playoff hole.)						
Jonathan Kaye	67	65	70	67	269	136,000
Jay Haas	68	68	66	68	270	96,000
Steve Pate	69	69	67	66	271	80,000
Stephen Ames	70	70	69	63	272	69,500
Jim McGovern	67	66	68	71	272	69,500
Brett Quigley	67	62	72	72	273	60,000
Brian Watts	66	72	67	68	273	60,000
Trevor Dodds	74	67	69	64	274	52,000
Brad Fabel	66	71	69	68	274	52,000
Ronnie Black	67	69	69	70	275	39,200
Edward Fryatt	65	68	73	69	275	39,200
Charles Howell	70	71	68	66	275	39,200
Tim Thelen	73	66	68	68	275	39,200
Ted Tryba	68	68	69	70	275	39,200
Michael Bradley	71	68	68	69	276	27,066.67
Brad Elder	72	65	69	70	276	27,066.67
Jerry Smith	69	66	71	70	276	27,066.67
D.A. Weibring	67	69	72	68	276	27,066.67
Dan Forsman	70	68	68	70	276	27,066.66
John Riegger	71	64	69	72	276	27,066.66
Ben Bates	70	69	68	70	277	18,400
Cliff Kresge	70	69	70	68	277	18,400
Esteban Toledo	69	69	70	69	277	18,400
Omar Uresti	70	69	69	69	277	18,400
Brad Bryant	68	71	69	70	278	12,760
Barry Cheesman	70	70	69	69	278	12,760
Keith Clearwater	69	71	67	71	278	12,760
Joel Edwards	73	66	68	71	278	12,760
Ed Fiori	69	67	74	68	278	12,760
Mark Hensby	66	66	70	76	278	12,760

	SCORES				TOTAL	MONEY
Bradley Hughes	70	69	68	71	278	12,760
Ian Leggatt	73	66	69	70	278	12,760
Craig Parry	69	68	69	72	278	12,760
Chris Riley	70	71	69	68	278	12,760
Jeremy Anderson	71	69	69	70	279	8,400
Jonathan Byrd	69	70	70	70	279	8,400
Mark Carnevale	67	73	65	74	279	8,400
Doug Dunakey	67	70	70	72	279	8,400
Michael Muehr	68	70	72	69	279	8,400
Gene Sauers	68	73	67	71	279	8,400
Dave Stockton, Jr.	71	65	71	72	279	8,400
Brian Wilson	72	68	70	69	279	8,400
*Ty Tryon	65	72	72	70	279	
Ben Curtis	68	73	68	71	280	6,020
J.J. Henry	71	66	73	70	280	6,020
Sam Randolph	68	72	70	70	280	6,020
Willie Wood	71	69	71	69	280	6,020
Jay Delsing	70	69	71	71	281	4,886.67
Pete Jordan	71	70	71	69	281	4,886.67
Blaine McCallister	71	68	72	70	281	4,886.67
Bobby Wadkins	71	70	71	69	281	4,886.67
Mike Sposa	67	67	72	75	281	4,886.66
Chris Tidland	67	73	70	71	281	4,886.66
Scott Gump	71	68	74	69	282	4,520
Nolan Henke	71	69	70	72	282	4,520
Glen Hnatiuk	73	66	71	72	282	4,520
Mike Hulbert	67	73	71	71	282	4,520
Dicky Pride	73	68	68	73	282	4,520
Steve Allan	74	67	71	71	283	4,300
Andy Bean	68	69	73	73	283	4,300
Danny Ellis	71	70	69	73	283	4,300
Donnie Hammond	69	70	68	76	283	4,300
Kent Jones	72	66	73	72	283	4,300
Bob Lohr	69	69	73	72	283	4,300
Woody Austin	69	70	70	75	284	4,120
Jeff Hart	66	73	72	73	284	4,120
Sean Murphy	68	68	72	76	284	4,120
Bart Bryant	69	69	74	73	285	4,000
Morris Hatalsky	75	64	72	74	285	4,000
Dick Mast	70	71	68	76	285	4,000
Doug Barron	69	68	73	76	286	3,880
Wayne Levi	69	69	73	75	286	3,880
John Morse	72	69	72	73	286	3,880
Dave Barr	69	71	72	75	287	3,760
Robin Freeman	67	72	72	76	287	3,760
Mike Heinen	68	68	72	79	287	3,760
Tim Conley	68	70	74	76	288	3,680
Jason Gore	69	72	74	74	289	3,640
Marco Dawson	70	71	75	74	290	3,540
Jeff Julian	71	69	72	78	290	3,540
Greg Twiggs	71	66	76	77	290	3,540
Stan Utley	73	68	74	75	290	3,540
Ernie Gonzalez	68	73	76	83	300	3,440

John Deere Classic

TPC at Deere Run, Silvis, Illinois
Par 35-36–71; 7,183 yards

July 26-29
purse, $2,800,000

	SCORES				TOTAL	MONEY
David Gossett	67	64	68	66	265	$504,000
Briny Baird	69	65	66	66	266	302,400
Pete Jordan	69	68	65	65	267	190,400
Jeff Sluman	70	65	68	65	268	134,400
Matt Gogel	68	66	67	68	269	106,400
Ian Leggatt	67	68	68	66	269	106,400
Paul Stankowski	67	67	66	70	270	93,800
Woody Austin	69	66	69	67	271	84,000
Brian Claar	66	69	66	70	271	84,000
Barry Cheesman	71	67	66	68	272	67,200
Paul Gow	65	69	69	69	272	67,200
Bradley Hughes	69	65	66	72	272	67,200
Jerry Smith	65	69	67	71	272	67,200
John Riegger	67	69	72	65	273	53,200
Olin Browne	68	71	65	70	274	38,136
Edward Fryatt	66	67	69	72	274	38,136
Bill Glasson	72	69	67	66	274	38,136
Kent Jones	68	64	73	69	274	38,136
Steve Jones	70	67	66	71	274	38,136
Neal Lancaster	69	71	67	67	274	38,136
Steve Lowery	66	70	67	71	274	38,136
Scott McCarron	70	69	67	68	274	38,136
Andrew McLardy	64	71	70	69	274	38,136
Kirk Triplett	73	68	66	67	274	38,136
Bart Bryant	68	70	69	68	275	22,330
Brad Elder	68	69	69	69	275	22,330
Donnie Hammond	68	70	69	68	275	22,330
Charles Howell	70	69	66	70	275	22,330
Matt Kuchar	69	66	73	68	276	17,803.34
Tommy Tolles	67	72	69	68	276	17,803.34
Steve Allan	65	76	68	67	276	17,803.33
David Berganio, Jr.	70	67	67	72	276	17,803.33
Fred Funk	70	70	69	67	276	17,803.33
Bob May	67	67	70	72	276	17,803.33
Spike McRoy	70	69	69	69	277	12,078.19
Craig Perks	69	70	69	69	277	12,078.19
Doug Barron	69	70	68	70	277	12,078.18
Cameron Beckman	70	70	71	66	277	12,078.18
Glen Day	67	68	70	72	277	12,078.18
Brad Fabel	69	71	70	67	277	12,078.18
Scott Gump	69	72	70	66	277	12,078.18
Len Mattiace	70	71	68	68	277	12,078.18
David Morland	66	68	73	70	277	12,078.18
Craig Parry	68	69	71	69	277	12,078.18
Lee Porter	70	68	69	70	277	12,078.18
Michael Christensen	67	70	70	71	278	7,616
Kevin Johnson	71	70	71	66	278	7,616
Dicky Pride	70	70	69	69	278	7,616
Brett Quigley	67	72	70	69	278	7,616
Jay Williamson	71	66	70	71	278	7,616
Willie Wood	69	69	72	68	278	7,616
Dan Forsman	70	71	66	72	279	6,496
Jimmy Green	69	69	71	70	279	6,496
Jim McGovern	69	70	68	72	279	6,496

	SCORES				TOTAL	MONEY
Michael Muehr	74	67	69	69	279	6,496
Brent Schwarzrock	70	71	69	69	279	6,496
D.A. Weibring	69	71	70	69	279	6,496
Jeremy Anderson	69	72	68	71	280	6,216
Shaun Micheel	70	69	67	74	280	6,216
Esteban Toledo	69	70	72	69	280	6,216
Ronnie Black	72	69	70	70	281	5,936
Jim Carter	70	70	73	68	281	5,936
Gary Hallberg	67	71	73	70	281	5,936
Brian Henninger	71	67	71	72	281	5,936
John Huston	72	68	68	73	281	5,936
J.L. Lewis	64	72	69	76	281	5,936
Gary Nicklaus	73	66	69	73	281	5,936
Michael Bradley	70	68	71	73	282	5,600
Jason Gore	68	70	75	69	282	5,600
Jeff Hart	69	71	71	71	282	5,600
Joey Sindelar	70	71	70	71	282	5,600
Chris Zambri	73	67	68	74	282	5,600
Harrison Frazar	73	68	71	71	283	5,432
Mark Carnevale	69	72	70	73	284	5,292
Tim Herron	69	72	70	73	284	5,292
Craig Kanada	71	69	67	77	284	5,292
Brian Watts	69	67	73	75	284	5,292
Joe Ogilvie	71	70	75	69	285	5,124
Fuzzy Zoeller	70	71	73	71	285	5,124
Dave Stockton, Jr.	67	74	74	71	286	5,040
Guy Boros	68	73	75	71	287	4,956
Nolan Henke	71	70	73	73	287	4,956
Ben Bates	70	71	71	76	288	4,872
Jeff Julian	71	70	75	76	292	4,816

The International

Castle Pines Golf Club, Castle Rock, Colorado
Par 36-36–72; 7,559 yards

August 2-5
purse, $4,000,000

	POINTS				TOTAL	MONEY
Tom Pernice, Jr.	12	12	9	1	34	$720,000
Chris Riley	16	5	8	4	33	432,000
Ernie Els	9	7	10	6	32	208,000
Chris DiMarco	7	13	8	4	32	208,000
Vijay Singh	9	9	12	2	32	208,000
Brett Quigley	9	6	2	13	30	139,000
Brad Faxon	8	10	4	8	30	139,000
Woody Austin	11	8	8	1	28	124,000
Mark O'Meara	12	3	4	8	27	112,000
Edward Fryatt	9	11	2	5	27	112,000
Charles Howell	11	8	8	-1	26	92,000
Sergio Garcia	7	12	7	0	26	92,000
Kenny Perry	0	10	11	5	26	92,000
Tim Herron	9	11	2	3	25	76,000
Jose Maria Olazabal	12	5	0	7	24	68,000
Bob May	3	8	6	7	24	68,000
Kirk Triplett	10	7	3	4	24	68,000
Jay Don Blake	7	1	10	5	23	58,000
Steve Flesch	6	8	6	3	23	58,000
Scott McCarron	13	3	0	6	22	46,600

	POINTS				TOTAL	MONEY
Steve Jones	6	2	10	4	22	46,600
Duffy Waldorf	13	0	5	4	22	46,600
Justin Leonard	7	12	3	0	22	46,600
Harrison Frazar	11	2	3	5	21	36,800
David Duval	11	5	2	3	21	36,800
Stewart Cink	8	14	-4	2	20	31,400
Rory Sabbatini	14	0	5	1	20	31,400
Cameron Beckman	5	2	9	3	19	28,400
Jean Van de Velde	8	2	10	-1	19	28,400
Stuart Appleby	2	12	9	-4	19	28,400
Ted Tryba	3	12	4	-1	18	26,000
Brent Geiberger	12	8	-3	0	17	24,800
Stephen Ames	3	7	7	-1	16	23,600
Spike McRoy	4	5	7	-1	15	21,600
Bill Glasson	6	7	3	-1	15	21,600
Lee Janzen	17	-1	4	-5	15	21,600
Paul Gow	7	8	1	-5	11	19,600

Out of Final 18 Holes

	POINTS			TOTAL	MONEY
Billy Andrade	5	8	2	15	17,600
John Huston	7	7	1	15	17,600
Bob Tway	7	3	5	15	17,600
Briny Baird	1	7	7	15	17,600
John Cook	9	4	1	14	14,800
Chris Tidland	1	10	3	14	14,800
Jeff Brehaut	0	9	5	14	14,800
Paul Stankowski	3	9	1	13	12,440
David Berganio, Jr.	9	3	1	13	12,440
Mike Sposa	5	3	5	13	12,440
Choi Kyung-ju	10	7	-4	13	12,440
Jay Haas	1	7	5	13	12,440
Jerry Kelly	4	3	6	13	12,440
Russ Cochran	7	4	1	12	9,720
Jim McGovern	2	8	2	12	9,720
Joey Sindelar	9	4	-2	11	9,260
Greg Norman	5	5	1	11	9,260
Craig Stadler	6	3	2	11	9,260
David Peoples	8	0	3	11	9,260
Angel Cabrera	5	6	-1	10	9,000
Glen Day	1	6	3	10	9,000
Lee Porter	3	8	-2	9	8,800
Tommy Tolles	11	0	-2	9	8,800
Jonathan Kaye	5	5	-1	9	8,800
Tripp Isenhour	8	4	-4	8	8,560
Mathew Goggin	11	4	-7	8	8,560
Craig Parry	1	6	1	8	8,560
Shaun Micheel	11	-1	-3	7	8,360
Glen Hnatiuk	-1	11	-3	7	8,360
Olin Browne	7	4	-5	6	8,120
Bob Burns	8	1	-3	6	8,120
Dan Forsman	6	2	-2	6	8,120
Chris Smith	8	-1	-1	6	8,120
Phil Mickelson	11	5	-11	5	7,920
Andrew Magee	5	6	-9	2	7,800
Steve Elkington	1	6	-5	2	7,800

Buick Open

Warwick Hills Golf & Country Club,
Grand Blanc, Michigan
Par 36-36–72; 7,105 yards

August 9-12
purse, $3,100,000

	SCORES				TOTAL	MONEY
Kenny Perry	66	64	64	69	263	$558,000
Chris DiMarco	68	67	65	65	265	272,800
Jim Furyk	64	69	66	66	265	272,800
Dudley Hart	68	70	65	64	267	136,400
Tom Pernice, Jr.	68	67	66	66	267	136,400
Brian Gay	70	67	66	65	268	107,725
Padraig Harrington	67	67	65	69	268	107,725
Ian Leggatt	66	68	69	66	269	93,000
Jeff Maggert	69	66	68	66	269	93,000
Justin Leonard	69	68	63	70	270	74,400
Frank Lickliter	68	70	69	63	270	74,400
Phil Mickelson	65	70	71	64	270	74,400
Bob Tway	68	65	67	70	270	74,400
Stephen Ames	69	66	68	68	271	51,150
Tom Byrum	73	63	67	68	271	51,150
Skip Kendall	69	70	66	66	271	51,150
Billy Mayfair	69	70	71	61	271	51,150
Craig Perks	66	68	68	69	271	51,150
Scott Verplank	68	67	68	68	271	51,150
Brian Wilson	67	70	64	71	272	40,300
Woody Austin	67	68	68	70	273	31,000
Russ Cochran	68	71	68	66	273	31,000
Fred Funk	73	63	72	65	273	31,000
Brian Henninger	64	71	70	68	273	31,000
Loren Roberts	69	69	67	68	273	31,000
Jeff Sluman	68	69	68	68	273	31,000
John Cook	66	68	70	70	274	23,405
Jay Williamson	70	65	69	70	274	23,405
Craig Barlow	70	69	71	65	275	19,710.84
Brandt Jobe	72	68	69	66	275	19,710.84
Ben Bates	69	66	69	71	275	19,710.83
Stewart Cink	73	67	67	68	275	19,710.83
Donnie Hammond	67	69	70	69	275	19,710.83
Jean Van de Velde	66	71	70	68	275	19,710.83
Jim Carter	68	70	68	70	276	14,318.13
Katsumune Imai	69	70	71	66	276	14,318.13
Jonathan Kaye	67	67	71	71	276	14,318.13
David Toms	68	69	70	69	276	14,318.13
Stuart Appleby	68	71	64	73	276	14,318.12
Jay Don Blake	67	68	70	71	276	14,318.12
Steve Flesch	66	70	67	73	276	14,318.12
Larry Mize	67	71	67	71	276	14,318.12
Olin Browne	69	71	70	67	277	9,940.67
Bob Burns	71	69	69	68	277	9,940.67
Barry Cheesman	72	65	75	65	277	9,940.67
Rocco Mediate	70	68	71	68	277	9,940.67
Greg Chalmers	67	72	68	70	277	9,940.66
Neal Lancaster	68	72	68	69	277	9,940.66
Paul Azinger	70	70	70	68	278	7,455.50
Michael Clark	71	69	69	69	278	7,455.50
Joel Edwards	67	69	69	73	278	7,455.50
David Frost	68	70	71	69	278	7,455.50
Jay Haas	70	69	69	70	278	7,455.50

	SCORES				TOTAL	MONEY
David Peoples	66	69	69	74	278	7,455.50
Brett Quigley	68	65	72	73	278	7,455.50
Heath Slocum	73	66	70	69	278	7,455.50
Briny Baird	66	72	69	72	279	6,882
Glen Day	69	70	70	70	279	6,882
Brad Elder	69	70	74	66	279	6,882
Paul Gow	68	71	71	69	279	6,882
Spike McRoy	69	71	71	68	279	6,882
J.P. Hayes	70	70	68	72	280	6,603
Tripp Isenhour	70	69	73	68	280	6,603
Mark O'Meara	67	72	72	69	280	6,603
Dicky Pride	69	66	74	71	280	6,603
Jerry Smith	70	69	69	73	281	6,448
David Berganio, Jr.	68	71	73	70	282	6,355
Jeff Brehaut	68	71	71	72	282	6,355
Joe Ogilvie	72	67	72	72	283	6,231
Craig Spence	71	69	78	65	283	6,231
Carlos Franco	73	67	71	73	284	6,138

PGA Championship

Atlanta Athletic Club, Duluth, Georgia
Par 35-35–70; 7,213 yards

August 16-19
purse, $5,200,000

	SCORES				TOTAL	MONEY
David Toms	66	65	65	69	265	$936,000
Phil Mickelson	66	66	66	68	266	562,000
Steve Lowery	67	67	66	68	268	354,000
Mark Calcavecchia	71	68	66	65	270	222,500
Shingo Katayama	67	64	69	70	270	222,500
Billy Andrade	68	70	68	66	272	175,000
Jim Furyk	70	64	71	69	274	152,333
Scott Hoch	68	70	69	67	274	152,333
Scott Verplank	69	68	70	67	274	152,333
David Duval	66	68	67	74	275	122,000
Justin Leonard	70	69	67	69	275	122,000
Kirk Triplett	68	70	71	66	275	122,000
Ernie Els	67	67	70	72	276	94,666
Steve Flesch	73	67	70	66	276	94,666
Jesper Parnevik	70	68	70	68	276	94,666
Robert Allenby	69	67	73	68	277	70,666
Stuart Appleby	66	70	68	73	277	70,666
Jose Coceres	69	68	73	67	277	70,666
Chris DiMarco	68	67	71	71	277	70,666
Dudley Hart	66	68	73	70	277	70,666
Mike Weir	69	72	66	70	277	70,666
Paul Azinger	68	67	69	74	278	44,285
Briny Baird	70	69	72	67	278	44,285
Brian Gay	70	68	69	71	278	44,285
Charles Howell	71	67	69	71	278	44,285
Shigeki Maruyama	68	72	71	67	278	44,285
Paul McGinley	68	72	71	67	278	44,285
Mark O'Meara	72	63	70	73	278	44,285
Choi Kyung-ju	66	68	72	73	279	29,437
Niclas Fasth	66	69	72	72	279	29,437
Carlos Franco	67	72	71	69	279	29,437
Greg Norman	70	68	71	70	279	29,437

	SCORES				TOTAL	MONEY
Jose Maria Olazabal	70	70	68	71	279	29,437
Nick Price	71	67	71	70	279	29,437
Chris Smith	69	71	68	71	279	29,437
Bob Tway	69	69	71	70	279	29,437
Tiger Woods	73	67	69	70	279	29,437
Angel Cabrera	69	69	70	72	280	21,000
Andrew Coltart	67	72	71	70	280	21,000
Fred Couples	70	69	70	71	280	21,000
Retief Goosen	69	70	66	75	280	21,000
Davis Love III	71	67	65	77	280	21,000
Greg Chalmers	68	70	69	74	281	14,250
Bob Estes	68	65	75	73	281	14,250
Jerry Kelly	69	67	72	73	281	14,250
Andrew Oldcorn	73	67	74	67	281	14,250
Kenny Perry	68	70	71	72	281	14,250
Rick Schuller	68	70	72	71	281	14,250
Hal Sutton	67	71	73	70	281	14,250
Lee Westwood	71	68	68	74	281	14,250
Scott Dunlap	69	72	70	71	282	11,343
Joe Durant	68	71	72	71	282	11,343
Nick Faldo	67	74	71	70	282	11,343
Frank Lickliter	71	69	71	71	282	11,343
Tom Pernice, Jr.	69	69	74	70	282	11,343
Chris Riley	68	71	73	70	282	11,343
Vijay Singh	73	68	70	71	282	11,343
Ian Woosnam	71	70	73	68	282	11,343
Stewart Cink	68	72	71	72	283	10,650
Brad Faxon	66	70	74	73	283	10,650
Phillip Price	68	69	76	70	283	10,650
Grant Waite	64	74	73	72	283	10,650
Thomas Bjorn	67	71	73	73	284	10,300
Jonathan Kaye	67	68	78	71	284	10,300
Skip Kendall	72	67	73	72	284	10,300
Rocco Mediate	70	65	73	76	284	10,300
Robert Damron	68	73	71	73	285	9,950
Steve Stricker	75	65	75	70	285	9,950
Tom Watson	69	70	76	70	285	9,950
Fred Funk	66	74	71	75	286	9,725
Scott McCarron	69	67	73	77	286	9,725
John Huston	67	68	75	77	287	9,650
Bob May	71	70	76	74	291	9,600
Paul Stankowski	67	71	76	79	293	9,550
Steve Pate	71	69	71	83	294	9,500
Colin Montgomerie	71	69	74		DQ	2,000

Out of Final 36 Holes

				TOTAL	
Olin Browne	70	72		142	
Jeff Maggert	70	72		142	
Garrett Willis	70	72		142	
Mark Brooks	71	71		142	
Stephen Keppler	72	70		142	
Larry Nelson	68	74		142	
Bernhard Langer	69	73		142	
Darren Clarke	73	69		142	
Gary Orr	73	70		143	
Jerry Pate	73	70		143	
Brett Quigley	71	72		143	
Paul Lawrie	69	74		143	

	SCORES		TOTAL
Loren Roberts	74	69	143
Sergio Garcia	68	75	143
David Gossett	72	71	143
Glen Day	74	69	143
Kevin Sutherland	73	70	143
Adam Scott	71	72	143
Tom Kite	72	71	143
Tom Lehman	72	72	144
Lee Janzen	70	74	144
Bruce Zabriski	69	76	145
Don Berry	73	72	145
Tim Thelen	74	71	145
Eduardo Romero	73	72	145
Nick O'Hern	73	72	145
Len Mattiace	74	71	145
Billy Mayfair	73	72	145
Carl Paulson	72	73	145
Ian Poulter	73	73	146
Tim Herron	72	74	146
Dennis Paulson	73	73	146
Notah Begay	78	68	146
Harrison Frazar	73	73	146
Franklin Langham	70	76	146
Steve Schneiter	72	74	146
Robert Karlsson	74	73	147
John Mazza	70	77	147
Duffy Waldorf	75	72	147
John Aber	74	73	147
Tim Fleming	75	72	147
Miguel Angel Jimenez	74	74	148
Chris Perry	74	74	148
Mark Brown	75	73	148
Jeff Sluman	72	76	148
Michael Clark	70	78	148
John Daly	72	77	149
Mathias Gronberg	75	74	149
Pierre Fulke	71	78	149
Padraig Harrington	75	74	149
Craig Stevens	73	76	149
Wayne DeFrancesco	76	74	150
Darrell Kestner	73	77	150
Bob Sowards	78	72	150
Toru Taniguchi	72	78	150
Jim Woodward	77	73	150
Michael Campbell	72	79	151
Jeffrey Lankford	77	74	151
Curtis Strange	74	77	151
Naomichi Ozaki	78	73	151
Ken Schall	74	77	151
Mark McNulty	71	80	151
Larry Emery	74	78	152
Hidemichi Tanaka	80	73	153
Steve Brady	77	76	153
James Blair	80	74	154
Rory Sabbatini	78	76	154
Mark Mielke	80	77	157
Dean Prowse	78	79	157
Mike Northern	78	79	157
Bill Loeffler	78	81	159

	SCORES		TOTAL
Robert Wilkin	86	75	161
Lanny Wadkins	86	85	171
Steve Elkington	77		WD

(Professionals who did not complete 72 holes received $2,000.)

WGC NEC Invitational

Firestone Country Club, South Course, Akron, Ohio
Par 35-35–70; 7,139 yards

August 23-26
purse, $5,000,000

	SCORES				TOTAL	MONEY
Tiger Woods	66	67	66	69	268	$1,000,000
Jim Furyk	65	66	66	71	268	500,000
(Woods defeated Furyk on seventh playoff hole.)						
Darren Clarke	66	68	68	69	271	375,000
Colin Montgomerie	66	71	66	70	273	300,000
Stuart Appleby	70	64	70	70	274	201,666.67
Davis Love III	68	68	70	68	274	201,666.67
Paul Azinger	67	70	65	72	274	201,666.66
Ernie Els	67	70	66	72	275	147,500
Phil Mickelson	67	66	70	72	275	147,500
Retief Goosen	72	69	64	71	276	131,000
Bernhard Langer	69	67	68	73	277	118,500
Hal Sutton	69	71	67	70	277	118,500
Stewart Cink	69	67	70	72	278	100,500
Ian Poulter	67	72	69	70	278	100,500
Vijay Singh	68	68	69	73	278	100,500
David Toms	68	70	70	70	278	100,500
Pierre Fulke	73	71	65	70	279	83,000
Padraig Harrington	68	66	73	72	279	83,000
Scott Verplank	69	71	70	69	279	83,000
Carlos Franco	68	71	68	73	280	73,000
Niclas Fasth	74	67	68	72	281	66,000
Scott Hoch	71	70	69	71	281	66,000
Robert Allenby	68	67	75	72	282	58,000
Steve Elkington	73	68	73	68	282	58,000
Mike Weir	69	70	71	73	283	53,000
Paul McGinley	68	73	71	72	284	51,000
David Duval	69	69	72	75	285	49,000
Phillip Price	70	71	74	71	286	47,000
Nick Price	71	70	71	76	288	44,000
Loren Roberts	72	70	67	79	288	44,000
Notah Begay	77	71	72	69	289	38,000
Thomas Bjorn	66	79	73	71	289	38,000
Michael Campbell	71	71	75	72	289	38,000
Shigeki Maruyama	68	75	73	73	289	38,000
Greg Norman	65	71	74	80	290	33,000
Mark Calcavecchia	72	69	72	79	292	30,000
Miguel Angel Jimenez	70	72	74	76	292	30,000
Lee Westwood	70	78			WD	
Kirk Triplett	70	70			DQ	

Reno-Tahoe Open

Montreux Golf & Country Club, Reno, Nevada
Par 36-36–72; 7,552 yards

August 23-26
purse, $3,000,000

	SCORES				TOTAL	MONEY
John Cook	69	64	74	64	271	$540,000
Jerry Kelly	66	68	67	71	272	324,000
Bryce Molder	70	65	67	71	273	204,000
Charles Howell	68	66	69	71	274	144,000
Justin Leonard	71	69	69	66	275	114,000
Duffy Waldorf	71	67	69	68	275	114,000
Dan Forsman	71	68	68	69	276	93,500
J.P. Hayes	68	68	71	69	276	93,500
Tim Herron	66	70	71	69	276	93,500
Steve Flesch	67	74	67	69	277	78,000
Brian Gay	69	69	69	70	277	78,000
Edward Fryatt	65	73	71	69	278	66,000
Bob Tway	68	69	72	69	278	66,000
Mark Brooks	73	67	73	66	279	54,000
Corey Pavin	69	72	71	67	279	54,000
Chris Riley	70	71	68	70	279	54,000
John Daly	71	71	69	69	280	46,500
John Riegger	69	70	69	72	280	46,500
David Berganio, Jr.	66	68	74	73	281	36,360
Joel Edwards	67	70	75	69	281	36,360
Neal Lancaster	71	68	72	70	281	36,360
Mark O'Meara	66	72	73	70	281	36,360
Brian Watts	64	71	71	75	281	36,360
Cameron Beckman	71	67	71	73	282	24,300
Brad Elder	72	69	72	69	282	24,300
Brent Geiberger	71	67	70	74	282	24,300
Gabriel Hjertstedt	71	67	72	72	282	24,300
Scott McCarron	70	70	73	69	282	24,300
Jean Van de Velde	71	70	72	69	282	24,300
Bart Bryant	71	67	73	72	283	18,225
Hunter Haas	76	66	68	73	283	18,225
Tripp Isenhour	70	72	72	69	283	18,225
Kent Jones	72	70	71	70	283	18,225
Ian Leggatt	72	70	75	66	283	18,225
Craig Perks	71	70	74	68	283	18,225
Jim Carter	68	67	72	77	284	13,218.75
Robin Freeman	67	72	75	70	284	13,218.75
Jeff Hart	71	71	72	70	284	13,218.75
Jonathan Kaye	71	66	71	76	284	13,218.75
Greg Kraft	71	71	73	69	284	13,218.75
Michael Muehr	72	70	75	67	284	13,218.75
Craig Stadler	71	68	71	74	284	13,218.75
Chris Tidland	70	68	73	73	284	13,218.75
Ben Bates	68	69	73	75	285	9,070
Greg Chalmers	72	70	72	71	285	9,070
Lee Janzen	70	65	75	75	285	9,070
Billy Mayfair	70	69	74	72	285	9,070
Andrew McLardy	72	70	71	72	285	9,070
Jeff Sluman	68	73	69	75	285	9,070
Ronnie Black	68	73	74	71	286	7,236
Lee Porter	73	65	75	73	286	7,236
Brett Quigley	72	65	74	75	286	7,236
Mike Sposa	69	71	73	73	286	7,236
Esteban Toledo	73	68	76	69	286	7,236

	SCORES				TOTAL	MONEY
Donnie Hammond	72	69	75	71	287	6,840
J.L. Lewis	71	70	72	74	287	6,840
Carl Paulson	70	72	68	77	287	6,840
Danny Ellis	69	71	75	73	288	6,660
Brian Henninger	68	74	78	68	288	6,660
Glen Hnatiuk	70	72	75	71	288	6,660
Steve Allan	67	69	79	74	289	6,510
Woody Austin	71	66	75	77	289	6,510
Craig Kanada	70	71	76	73	290	6,390
Brian Wilson	69	72	73	76	290	6,390
Rich Beem	74	68	77	72	291	6,240
Joe Ogilvie	73	69	71	78	291	6,240
Dicky Pride	71	70	77	73	291	6,240
Ben Ferguson	70	72	79	71	292	6,120
Brent Schwarzrock	69	72	77	75	293	6,060
Tommy Armour III	72	68	79	80	299	6,000

Air Canada Championship

Northview Golf & Country Club, Surrey,
British Columbia, Canada
Par 36-35–71; 7,009 yards

August 30-September 2
purse, $3,400,000

	SCORES				TOTAL	MONEY
Joel Edwards	65	67	68	65	265	$612,000
Steve Lowery	73	65	68	66	272	367,200
Fred Funk	70	67	67	69	273	197,200
Matt Kuchar	68	66	72	67	273	197,200
Brent Geiberger	66	70	70	68	274	124,100
David Gossett	67	68	69	70	274	124,100
Kevin Sutherland	70	69	68	67	274	124,100
Bob Estes	69	69	69	68	275	82,025
Edward Fryatt	72	67	66	70	275	82,025
J.J. Henry	67	72	66	70	275	82,025
Brett Quigley	68	70	67	70	275	82,025
Chris Riley	66	71	71	67	275	82,025
Brent Schwarzrock	68	68	69	70	275	82,025
Jerry Smith	71	70	67	67	275	82,025
Grant Waite	70	68	65	72	275	82,025
Dennis Paulson	70	69	70	67	276	54,400
John Riegger	70	71	68	67	276	54,400
Joey Sindelar	71	67	69	69	276	54,400
Ben Ferguson	67	71	67	72	277	45,900
Jesper Parnevik	67	71	72	67	277	45,900
Craig Barlow	67	71	69	71	278	31,917.50
Danny Ellis	69	69	70	70	278	31,917.50
Tripp Isenhour	71	69	67	71	278	31,917.50
Shigeki Maruyama	68	68	73	69	278	31,917.50
Scott McCarron	67	72	70	69	278	31,917.50
David Peoples	70	70	70	68	278	31,917.50
Esteban Toledo	69	69	70	70	278	31,917.50
Brian Wilson	72	68	70	68	278	31,917.50
Tommy Armour III	67	69	71	72	279	20,697.50
Tony Carolan	72	68	69	70	279	20,697.50
David Frost	69	72	70	68	279	20,697.50
J.P. Hayes	69	71	71	68	279	20,697.50
Tim Herron	71	68	74	66	279	20,697.50

	SCORES				TOTAL	MONEY
Bob May	70	70	69	70	279	20,697.50
Rory Sabbatini	67	70	71	71	279	20,697.50
Chris Tidland	67	70	71	71	279	20,697.50
Jim Carter	72	68	69	71	280	14,960
Peter Jacobsen	69	71	72	68	280	14,960
Neal Lancaster	68	72	70	70	280	14,960
David Morland	68	71	70	71	280	14,960
Tom Pernice, Jr.	68	69	72	71	280	14,960
Jean Van de Velde	72	69	72	67	280	14,960
Woody Austin	71	68	70	72	281	10,132
Jay Don Blake	70	71	68	72	281	10,132
Guy Boros	70	68	72	71	281	10,132
Brian Henninger	70	69	73	69	281	10,132
Charles Howell	68	73	68	72	281	10,132
Gary Nicklaus	71	70	68	72	281	10,132
Lee Porter	69	68	73	71	281	10,132
Brian Watts	72	67	71	71	281	10,132
Kaname Yokoo	69	69	70	73	281	10,132
Choi Kyung-ju	73	68	72	69	282	7,973
Paul Goydos	70	70	70	72	282	7,973
Pete Jordan	68	71	72	71	282	7,973
Craig Stadler	69	70	71	72	282	7,973
Dan Forsman	69	71	75	68	283	7,684
Brandt Jobe	67	70	70	76	283	7,684
Heath Slocum	67	71	75	70	283	7,684
Jeff Brehaut	70	71	77	66	284	7,480
Greg Kraft	65	71	74	74	284	7,480
Steve Pate	70	68	73	73	284	7,480
Michael Combs	68	69	77	71	285	7,208
James Driscoll	70	68	75	72	285	7,208
Todd Fanning	68	70	73	74	285	7,208
Per-Ulrik Johansson	68	66	76	75	285	7,208
John Restino	69	72	70	74	285	7,208
Bart Bryant	70	70	75	71	286	6,902
Mark Hensby	68	73	74	71	286	6,902
Steve Jones	68	72	74	72	286	6,902
Ted Tryba	70	71	72	73	286	6,902
Brandel Chamblee	68	71	73	76	288	6,698
Dave Stockton, Jr.	70	71	77	70	288	6,698
Carlos Franco	68	73	73	75	289	6,596

Bell Canadian Open

Royal Montreal Golf Club, Ile Bizard, Quebec, Canada
Par 35-35–70; 6,859 yards

September 6-9
purse, $3,800,000

	SCORES				TOTAL	MONEY
Scott Verplank	70	63	66	67	266	$684,000
Bob Estes	69	65	67	68	269	334,400
Joey Sindelar	66	69	69	65	269	334,400
John Daly	66	74	64	66	270	182,400
Sergio Garcia	69	68	65	69	271	138,700
Paul Gow	67	67	66	71	271	138,700
David Morland	69	63	73	66	271	138,700
Robert Allenby	70	68	69	65	272	98,800
David Berganio, Jr.	69	68	69	66	272	98,800
Choi Kyung-ju	67	68	69	68	272	98,800

		SCORES			TOTAL	MONEY
Matt Gogel	65	67	71	69	272	98,800
Dudley Hart	69	68	71	64	272	98,800
Michael Muehr	65	70	68	69	272	98,800
Fulton Allem	70	71	67	66	274	66,500
Brad Faxon	70	67	69	68	274	66,500
J.J. Henry	72	68	66	68	274	66,500
Dicky Pride	67	64	69	74	274	66,500
Luke Donald	71	69	68	67	275	49,552
Brian Gay	70	71	65	69	275	49,552
Ian Leggatt	70	71	65	69	275	49,552
Mike Sposa	70	69	71	65	275	49,552
Steve Stricker	67	68	69	71	275	49,552
Nick Price	69	69	70	68	276	32,028.58
Stuart Appleby	72	67	66	71	276	32,028.57
Fred Funk	69	68	70	69	276	32,028.57
Jay Haas	73	68	67	68	276	32,028.57
Per-Ulrik Johansson	68	72	67	69	276	32,028.57
Bob Tway	69	72	66	69	276	32,028.57
Tiger Woods	65	73	69	69	276	32,028.57
Olin Browne	70	68	71	68	277	24,130
Robin Freeman	71	66	73	67	277	24,130
Mark O'Meara	66	68	72	71	277	24,130
Jeff Sluman	73	68	64	72	277	24,130
Steve Elkington	68	69	72	69	278	17,986.67
Robert Gamez	70	70	70	68	278	17,986.67
Jimmy Green	68	70	76	64	278	17,986.67
Jeff Julian	68	68	73	69	278	17,986.67
Steve Pate	69	69	70	70	278	17,986.67
Mike Weir	68	69	69	72	278	17,986.67
Glen Hnatiuk	69	70	67	72	278	17,986.66
Len Mattiace	68	71	67	72	278	17,986.66
Shaun Micheel	70	67	66	75	278	17,986.66
Ronnie Black	68	70	71	70	279	11,324
Mark Carnevale	68	71	70	70	279	11,324
Jose Coceres	73	64	69	73	279	11,324
David Gossett	71	68	68	72	279	11,324
Donnie Hammond	69	71	73	66	279	11,324
Jim McGovern	65	73	68	73	279	11,324
Spike McRoy	69	69	67	74	279	11,324
Jesper Parnevik	71	67	74	67	279	11,324
Willie Wood	71	67	72	69	279	11,324
Joel Edwards	74	66	70	70	280	8,968
Sam Randolph	69	68	65	78	280	8,968
Kaname Yokoo	68	70	69	73	280	8,968
Steve Alker	68	73	71	69	281	8,550
Jeff Brehaut	70	70	73	68	281	8,550
Neal Lancaster	72	69	71	69	281	8,550
Justin Leonard	71	70	70	70	281	8,550
Andrew McLardy	69	71	67	74	281	8,550
Jerry Smith	70	71	67	73	281	8,550
Jim Carter	70	71	72	69	282	8,208
Cliff Kresge	73	67	71	71	282	8,208
Chris Tidland	70	70	68	74	282	8,208
Mike Hulbert	73	67	70	73	283	8,018
Craig Perks	72	65	71	75	283	8,018
*Gareth Paddison	70	67	72	74	283	
Ben Bates	72	68	70	74	284	7,828
Steve Jones	68	67	72	77	284	7,828
Scott Simpson	71	70	71	72	284	7,828

	SCORES				TOTAL	MONEY
Heath Slocum	70	67	76	72	285	7,676
J.L. Lewis	69	72	72	73	286	7,562
Brian Watts	72	68	75	71	286	7,562
Richie Coughlan	72	68	70	78	288	7,448
Geoff Ogilvy	72	67	72	78	289	7,372
Derek Gillespie	67	74	70	79	290	7,296
Kevin Wentworth	69	71	76	77	293	7,220

Marconi Pennsylvania Classic

Laurel Valley Golf Club, Ligonier, Pennsylvania
Par 36-36–72; 7,244 yards

September 20-23
purse, $3,300,000

	SCORES				TOTAL	MONEY
Robert Allenby	70	65	66	68	269	$594,000
Rocco Mediate	69	68	67	68	272	290,400
Larry Mize	73	67	67	65	272	290,400
Kevin Sutherland	76	65	64	68	273	158,400
Nick Price	66	71	68	69	274	132,000
Steve Elkington	70	68	69	70	277	110,550
Matt Gogel	70	73	66	68	277	110,550
Jay Williamson	74	68	67	68	277	110,550
Glen Hnatiuk	70	73	66	69	278	95,700
Cameron Beckman	70	71	65	73	279	89,100
Jim Furyk	72	72	68	68	280	65,528.58
Chris DiMarco	69	70	69	72	280	65,528.57
Robert Gamez	70	73	73	64	280	65,528.57
Jay Haas	74	66	66	74	280	65,528.57
Jeff Hart	70	71	68	71	280	65,528.57
Charles Howell	68	74	66	72	280	65,528.57
Paul Stankowski	70	72	70	68	280	65,528.57
Olin Browne	69	71	72	69	281	44,550
Fred Funk	69	68	70	74	281	44,550
Joe Ogilvie	75	69	72	65	281	44,550
Jerry Smith	71	69	72	69	281	44,550
Stuart Appleby	76	64	73	69	282	30,635
Marco Dawson	69	74	67	72	282	30,635
Steve Flesch	69	67	74	72	282	30,635
Brian Gay	71	70	72	69	282	30,635
John Huston	71	71	71	69	282	30,635
John Riegger	72	72	70	68	282	30,635
Jeff Brehaut	72	72	69	70	283	22,440
Tim Herron	72	68	70	73	283	22,440
Greg Kraft	72	68	72	71	283	22,440
Jeff Sluman	72	67	71	73	283	22,440
Willie Wood	70	70	71	72	283	22,440
Billy Andrade	70	73	70	71	284	17,820
Tom Byrum	69	73	70	72	284	17,820
John Cook	72	70	71	71	284	17,820
Per-Ulrik Johansson	67	73	71	73	284	17,820
Shigeki Maruyama	72	69	72	71	284	17,820
Jonathan Kaye	70	72	71	72	285	14,850
Andrew McLardy	74	68	70	73	285	14,850
Duffy Waldorf	75	69	69	72	285	14,850
Michael Clark	69	73	71	73	286	12,210
Chris Smith	72	69	71	74	286	12,210
Ted Tryba	74	70	66	76	286	12,210

	SCORES				TOTAL	MONEY
Bob Tway	70	73	71	72	286	12,210
Brian Watts	70	72	71	73	286	12,210
Briny Baird	69	71	73	74	287	8,976
J.L. Lewis	71	70	75	71	287	8,976
Steve Lowery	71	68	76	72	287	8,976
Len Mattiace	71	71	72	73	287	8,976
Corey Pavin	72	72	73	70	287	8,976
Tommy Tolles	74	70	73	70	287	8,976
Brian Claar	73	69	76	70	288	7,788
Edward Fryatt	71	71	73	73	288	7,788
Lee Janzen	72	72	72	72	288	7,788
Kelly Grunewald	73	69	73	74	289	7,524
Kevin Johnson	71	72	72	74	289	7,524
Lee Porter	71	70	75	73	289	7,524
Paul Azinger	70	74	72	74	290	7,326
Jerry Kelly	71	68	73	78	290	7,326
David Peoples	75	69	73	73	290	7,326
Andrew Magee	72	72	71	76	291	7,095
Carl Paulson	70	74	75	72	291	7,095
Mike Reid	70	72	76	73	291	7,095
Scott Verplank	74	70	72	75	291	7,095
Mark Calcavecchia	69	73	78	72	292	6,864
David Frost	70	69	70	83	292	6,864
Heath Slocum	71	71	72	78	292	6,864
John Daly	70	71	82	70	293	6,732
Dan Forsman	71	71	73	79	294	6,666
John Restino	72	71	78	75	296	6,600
Ryan Dillon	71	72	81	77	301	6,534

Texas Open at LaCantera

LaCantera Golf Club, San Antonio, Texas
Par 35-35–70; 6,905 yards

September 27-30
purse, $3,000,000

	SCORES				TOTAL	MONEY
Justin Leonard	65	64	68	69	266	$540,000
J.J. Henry	70	64	68	66	268	264,000
Matt Kuchar	67	68	64	69	268	264,000
Bob Estes	67	68	69	67	271	132,000
Tommy Tolles	68	69	66	68	271	132,000
Steve Elkington	67	70	68	67	272	104,250
Kaname Yokoo	67	69	68	68	272	104,250
Bob Burns	66	72	67	68	273	87,000
David Frost	70	65	70	68	273	87,000
J.L. Lewis	71	68	69	65	273	87,000
Jaxon Brigman	67	71	67	69	274	61,500
Brent Geiberger	67	69	68	70	274	61,500
Jesper Parnevik	67	66	71	70	274	61,500
Carl Paulson	66	66	68	74	274	61,500
Jerry Smith	68	69	69	68	274	61,500
Jay Williamson	65	68	71	70	274	61,500
Jay Haas	68	67	71	69	275	39,257.15
Larry Mize	67	71	71	66	275	39,257.15
Joel Edwards	67	71	68	69	275	39,257.14
Carlos Franco	68	70	65	72	275	39,257.14
Tripp Isenhour	68	65	72	70	275	39,257.14
Bob May	68	66	71	70	275	39,257.14

	SCORES				TOTAL	MONEY
Tom Scherrer	69	66	67	73	275	39,257.14
Tom Byrum	68	71	68	69	276	24,300
Brian Gay	68	71	70	67	276	24,300
David Gossett	67	72	69	68	276	24,300
Glen Hnatiuk	68	70	69	69	276	24,300
Scott Simpson	71	68	71	66	276	24,300
Paul Stankowski	69	70	66	71	276	24,300
Brandel Chamblee	66	70	73	68	277	16,363.64
Danny Ellis	70	66	71	70	277	16,363.64
Pete Jordan	70	69	70	68	277	16,363.64
Andrew Magee	69	69	69	70	277	16,363.64
Frank Nobilo	67	73	66	71	277	16,363.64
Craig Perks	67	69	70	71	277	16,363.64
Hal Sutton	69	69	69	70	277	16,363.64
Choi Kyung-ju	68	69	68	72	277	16,363.63
Charles Howell	70	68	67	72	277	16,363.63
Jonathan Kaye	69	71	70	67	277	16,363.63
Esteban Toledo	69	71	69	68	277	16,363.63
Brandt Jobe	69	70	71	68	278	11,400
Michael Muehr	71	67	71	69	278	11,400
Jeff Quinney	69	68	72	69	278	11,400
Chris Riley	71	67	69	71	278	11,400
Paul Casey	71	69	68	71	279	8,580
Doug Dunakey	69	69	68	73	279	8,580
Paul Goydos	70	66	70	73	279	8,580
Jeff Maggert	71	69	72	67	279	8,580
Scott McCarron	66	70	71	72	279	8,580
Lee Porter	69	70	70	70	279	8,580
Jay Don Blake	69	69	71	71	280	7,020
Marco Dawson	64	68	70	78	280	7,020
Per-Ulrik Johansson	70	68	70	72	280	7,020
Jim McGovern	68	68	72	72	280	7,020
Gary Nicklaus	71	69	70	70	280	7,020
Joe Ogilvie	73	65	70	72	280	7,020
Dave Stockton, Jr.	70	68	72	70	280	7,020
Steve Allan	71	68	71	71	281	6,630
John Riegger	69	71	70	71	281	6,630
Heath Slocum	69	68	68	76	281	6,630
D.A. Weibring	71	68	68	74	281	6,630
Tim Herron	69	68	69	76	282	6,450
Len Mattiace	67	70	67	78	282	6,450
Barry Cheesman	69	70	72	72	283	6,330
Greg Kraft	72	66	72	73	283	6,330
Rich Beem	70	67	73	74	284	6,180
Robert Gamez	69	71	70	74	284	6,180
Lucas Glover	70	70	74	70	284	6,180
David Ogrin	69	67	73	77	286	6,030
Duffy Waldorf	70	69	74	73	286	6,030
Mark Brooks	69	71	73	74	287	5,820
Luke Donald	67	70	76	74	287	5,820
Robin Freeman	67	73	73	74	287	5,820
Dennis Paulson	69	70	76	72	287	5,820
Phil Tataurangi	70	70	70	77	287	5,820
Tommy Armour III	68	72	74	75	289	5,610
Richie Coughlan	72	68	75	74	289	5,610

Michelob Championship at Kingsmill

Kingsmill Golf Club, Williamsburg, Virginia   October 4-7
Par 36-35–71; 6,853 yards   purse, $3,500,000

	SCORES				TOTAL	MONEY
David Toms	64	70	67	68	269	$630,000
Kirk Triplett	67	68	69	66	270	378,000
Charles Howell	70	65	71	67	273	203,000
Esteban Toledo	68	67	68	70	273	203,000
Len Mattiace	67	66	74	67	274	140,000
J.J. Henry	65	71	72	67	275	126,000
Rich Beem	66	70	72	68	276	101,850
Jimmy Green	65	70	73	68	276	101,850
Neal Lancaster	65	69	70	72	276	101,850
Jim McGovern	71	68	68	69	276	101,850
Michael Muehr	65	70	70	71	276	101,850
Jose Coceres	71	66	67	73	277	73,500
Chris Riley	66	67	71	73	277	73,500
Mike Weir	69	68	72	68	277	73,500
Jonathan Kaye	66	67	72	73	278	63,000
Tom Byrum	72	69	71	67	279	56,000
Greg Chalmers	69	66	72	72	279	56,000
Robin Freeman	70	69	71	69	279	56,000
Skip Kendall	68	70	73	69	280	43,925
Greg Kraft	68	72	72	68	280	43,925
Brett Quigley	68	69	72	71	280	43,925
Dave Stockton, Jr.	70	69	67	74	280	43,925
Robert Allenby	68	70	67	76	281	33,600
Jeremy Anderson	67	70	70	74	281	33,600
Jay Don Blake	69	69	74	69	281	33,600
Luke Donald	68	69	73	72	282	25,375
Glen Hnatiuk	69	70	73	70	282	25,375
Carl Paulson	68	66	73	75	282	25,375
Nick Price	70	70	71	71	282	25,375
Mike Sposa	67	72	74	69	282	25,375
Tommy Tolles	71	70	73	68	282	25,375
Larry Mize	71	69	74	69	283	18,161.12
Brad Fabel	69	70	73	71	283	18,161.11
Lee Janzen	67	72	71	73	283	18,161.11
Joe Ogilvie	70	70	72	71	283	18,161.11
Dennis Paulson	70	70	73	70	283	18,161.11
Lee Porter	67	70	73	73	283	18,161.11
Kevin Sutherland	69	69	71	74	283	18,161.11
Phil Tataurangi	67	72	73	71	283	18,161.11
Ted Tryba	71	69	72	71	283	18,161.11
Briny Baird	68	72	70	74	284	12,600
David Duval	73	68	72	71	284	12,600
Mark O'Meara	70	71	70	73	284	12,600
Mike Reid	71	69	73	71	284	12,600
Curtis Strange	68	71	73	72	284	12,600
Chris Tidland	69	68	75	72	284	12,600
Paul Azinger	69	69	75	72	285	8,881.25
Bart Bryant	70	70	72	73	285	8,881.25
Robert Damron	72	69	70	74	285	8,881.25
Steve Flesch	70	69	73	73	285	8,881.25
Fred Funk	69	68	72	76	285	8,881.25
Paul Goydos	70	70	74	71	285	8,881.25
Mike Hulbert	70	68	75	72	285	8,881.25
Bob Tway	70	71	72	72	285	8,881.25

		SCO	RES		TOTAL	MONEY
Keith Clearwater	72	66	75	73	286	7,840
Russ Cochran	70	69	75	72	286	7,840
Danny Ellis	69	69	72	76	286	7,840
Brandt Jobe	69	70	75	72	286	7,840
Per-Ulrik Johansson	69	70	73	74	286	7,840
Jerry Kelly	67	73	74	72	286	7,840
Shigeki Maruyama	65	74	76	71	286	7,840
Ian Leggatt	73	68	71	75	287	7,455
Spike McRoy	68	69	75	75	287	7,455
Frank Nobilo	73	68	72	74	287	7,455
Willie Wood	68	72	71	76	287	7,455
Hunter Haas	70	71	76	71	288	7,245
Brian Wilson	71	68	78	71	288	7,245
Bryce Molder	66	71	76	76	289	7,105
John Riegger	67	71	72	79	289	7,105
Jeff Hart	71	69	75	77	292	6,965
Tom Scherrer	70	71	77	74	292	6,965
Gary Nicklaus	71	68	78	77	294	6,860

Invensys Classic at Las Vegas

TPC at Summerlin: Par 36-36–72; 7,243 yards
Southern Highlands Golf Course: Par 36-36–72; 7,381 yards
TPC at The Canyons: Par 36-36–72; 7,111 yards
Las Vegas, Nevada

October 10-14
purse, $4,500,000

			SCORES			TOTAL	MONEY
Bob Estes	65	66	67	68	63	329	$810,000
Tom Lehman	63	62	72	67	66	330	396,000
Rory Sabbatini	64	67	72	63	64	330	396,000
Davis Love III	69	65	68	69	61	332	198,000
Scott McCarron	68	65	65	63	71	332	198,000
Cameron Beckman	67	67	69	66	64	333	162,000
John Daly	67	62	72	69	67	337	135,562.50
Craig Parry	64	66	66	70	71	337	135,562.50
Scott Verplank	67	67	71	65	67	337	135,562.50
Chris Riley	69	65	68	68	67	337	135,562.50
Matt Gogel	69	67	68	65	69	338	108,000
Kenny Perry	71	69	67	65	66	338	108,000
Robert Allenby	66	65	71	71	67	340	81,900
Chris DiMarco	68	61	72	69	70	340	81,900
Steve Flesch	65	67	67	74	67	340	81,900
David Frost	69	67	69	66	69	340	81,900
Brian Gay	67	69	70	66	68	340	81,900
Jason Gore	66	68	70	69	68	341	65,250
Billy Mayfair	70	66	68	71	66	341	65,250
Stewart Cink	71	71	67	66	67	342	50,580
Charles Howell	66	68	72	69	67	342	50,580
Skip Kendall	66	70	69	67	70	342	50,580
Bob May	69	66	65	72	70	342	50,580
Kaname Yokoo	71	67	70	68	66	342	50,580
Woody Austin	71	67	68	69	68	343	35,887.50
Andrew Magee	67	67	66	72	71	343	35,887.50
Shigeki Maruyama	67	68	72	70	66	343	35,887.50
Kirk Triplett	69	66	70	70	68	343	35,887.50
Stuart Appleby	70	69	68	72	65	344	26,800
Russ Cochran	67	66	76	64	71	344	26,800

	SCORES					TOTAL	MONEY
John Cook	68	68	71	70	67	344	26,800
Robin Freeman	67	70	68	70	69	344	26,800
Lee Janzen	67	67	68	67	75	344	26,800
Pete Jordan	67	66	71	69	71	344	26,800
Craig Kanada	69	70	70	69	66	344	26,800
Greg Kraft	69	65	71	71	68	344	26,800
Grant Waite	70	68	69	67	70	344	26,800
Glen Day	67	68	71	68	71	345	18,450
Jeff Maggert	73	67	68	68	69	345	18,450
Joe Ogilvie	64	70	70	76	65	345	18,450
Carl Paulson	68	69	71	66	71	345	18,450
Kevin Sutherland	69	67	72	73	64	345	18,450
Bob Tway	69	68	69	70	69	345	18,450
Brian Wilson	69	69	69	68	70	345	18,450
Joel Edwards	71	63	71	71	70	346	14,850
Fulton Allem	68	69	66	69	75	347	12,240
Olin Browne	70	65	67	74	71	347	12,240
Fred Couples	63	64	72	72	76	347	12,240
Fred Funk	67	69	72	67	72	347	12,240
Paul Stankowski	69	66	71	69	72	347	12,240
Ted Tryba	68	67	73	73	66	347	12,240
Greg Chalmers	67	69	71	67	74	348	10,800
Jim Carter	65	69	73	71	71	349	10,368
Jonathan Kaye	68	69	72	73	67	349	10,368
Andrew McLardy	68	68	72	71	70	349	10,368
David Peoples	69	70	68	71	71	349	10,368
Scott Simpson	68	69	72	70	70	349	10,368
Tom Byrum	70	65	72	67	76	350	9,855
Robert Damron	67	68	71	73	71	350	9,855
Tripp Isenhour	68	68	69	72	73	350	9,855
Justin Leonard	71	68	70	70	71	350	9,855
David Morland	69	65	71	73	72	350	9,855
Jesper Parnevik	69	69	70	71	71	350	9,855
Jose Coceres	69	70	68	70	74	351	9,450
Paul Goydos	72	69	67	72	71	351	9,450
J.J. Henry	70	71	67	71	72	351	9,450
Jeff Hart	71	66	71	72	72	352	9,270
Ian Leggatt	68	67	74	73	71	353	9,180
Bob Burns	68	68	70	74	74	354	9,090
Jay Don Blake	70	68	71	71	75	355	8,910
Michael Muehr	68	66	75	73	73	355	8,910
Tom Pernice, Jr.	64	69	75	72	75	355	8,910
Brian Henninger	72	64	73	76	74	359	8,730
Stephen Ames	68	70	69	79	74	360	8,640

National Car Rental Golf Classic

Magnolia Course: Par 36-36–72; 7,190 yards
Palm Course: Par 36-36–72; 6,957 yards
Lake Buena Vista, Florida

October 18-21
purse, $3,400,000

	SCORES				TOTAL	MONEY
Jose Coceres	68	65	64	68	265	$612,000
Davis Love III	67	66	67	66	266	367,200
David Peoples	69	65	68	66	268	197,200
Jerry Smith	66	66	73	63	268	197,200
Steve Flesch	73	65	66	65	269	136,000

	SCORES			TOTAL	MONEY
Craig Perks	70	69	67	64	270	99,328.58
Danny Ellis	67	68	70	65	270	99,328.57
Skip Kendall	68	70	64	68	270	99,328.57
Scott McCarron	65	71	65	69	270	99,328.57
Jesper Parnevik	71	65	67	67	270	99,328.57
Vijay Singh	66	68	67	69	270	99,328.57
David Toms	66	68	69	67	270	99,328.57
Nick Price	70	69	67	65	271	65,733.34
Stuart Appleby	69	67	65	70	271	65,733.33
Tom Lehman	72	66	66	67	271	65,733.33
Woody Austin	70	65	69	68	272	51,000
Paul Azinger	70	69	67	66	272	51,000
John Huston	70	66	69	67	272	51,000
Billy Mayfair	68	68	68	68	272	51,000
Tiger Woods	69	67	67	69	272	51,000
Stewart Cink	65	70	71	67	273	31,053.34
Blaine McCallister	67	69	70	67	273	31,053.34
Tom Pernice, Jr.	68	68	70	67	273	31,053.34
Tommy Armour III	70	67	67	69	273	31,053.33
Robert Damron	71	66	70	66	273	31,053.33
Lee Janzen	70	67	65	71	273	31,053.33
Rocco Mediate	73	64	68	68	273	31,053.33
Bob Tway	67	69	69	68	273	31,053.33
Kaname Yokoo	66	65	71	71	273	31,053.33
Stephen Ames	69	70	67	68	274	22,610
Lee Porter	67	70	68	69	274	22,610
Briny Baird	68	69	69	69	275	19,677.50
Fred Couples	70	68	70	67	275	19,677.50
Chris DiMarco	68	70	66	71	275	19,677.50
Rocky Walcher	71	68	68	68	275	19,677.50
Robert Allenby	67	71	69	69	276	14,297
Olin Browne	71	68	68	69	276	14,297
Bob Burns	73	65	67	71	276	14,297
Jim Carter	72	66	71	67	276	14,297
Greg Kraft	70	67	69	70	276	14,297
Bernhard Langer	67	72	67	70	276	14,297
Len Mattiace	65	70	71	70	276	14,297
Michael Muehr	71	67	71	67	276	14,297
Carl Paulson	66	72	69	69	276	14,297
Mike Weir	66	71	70	69	276	14,297
Glen Day	69	69	69	70	277	9,639
John Riegger	69	68	72	68	277	9,639
Scott Verplank	68	70	70	69	277	9,639
Jay Williamson	69	67	72	69	277	9,639
Jay Don Blake	69	70	68	71	278	8,137.34
John Cook	69	69	68	72	278	8,137.34
Mark Brooks	68	69	72	69	278	8,137.33
Rory Sabbatini	69	70	69	70	278	8,137.33
Mike Sposa	72	67	69	70	278	8,137.33
Brian Wilson	66	68	73	71	278	8,137.33
Jeff Hart	68	71	70	70	279	7,684
Brian Henninger	70	68	71	70	279	7,684
Glen Hnatiuk	70	67	74	68	279	7,684
Michael Clark	72	64	73	71	280	7,276
Marco Dawson	72	65	68	75	280	7,276
Mathew Goggin	71	67	71	71	280	7,276
Charles Howell	72	67	70	71	280	7,276
Steve Lowery	65	71	70	74	280	7,276
Mark McCumber	69	66	70	75	280	7,276

	SCORES				TOTAL	MONEY
Shaun Micheel	65	70	70	75	280	7,276
Dicky Pride	70	69	71	70	280	7,276
Ted Tryba	70	68	69	73	280	7,276
Matt Kuchar	72	67	71	72	282	6,936
J.L. Lewis	69	70	72	72	283	6,868
David Morland	71	68	74	73	286	6,766
Garrett Willis	72	66	75	73	286	6,766

Buick Challenge

Callaway Gardens Resort, Mountain View Course,
Pine Mountain, Georgia
Par 36-36–72; 7,057 yards

October 25-28
purse, $3,400,000

	SCORES				TOTAL	MONEY
Chris DiMarco	67	64	71	65	267	$612,000
David Duval	67	69	68	63	267	367,200
(DiMarco defeated Duval on first playoff hole.)						
Bob Estes	71	63	69	66	269	197,200
Neal Lancaster	65	67	68	69	269	197,200
Davis Love III	68	62	69	71	270	136,000
Jeff Maggert	67	66	72	66	271	122,400
Joel Edwards	65	68	65	74	272	109,650
Per-Ulrik Johansson	65	70	68	69	272	109,650
Nick Price	70	68	69	67	274	98,600
Chris Riley	68	69	69	69	275	88,400
Vijay Singh	64	67	75	69	275	88,400
Charles Howell	68	70	68	70	276	74,800
Mark O'Meara	66	70	68	72	276	74,800
Carlos Franco	67	70	72	68	277	61,200
Shaun Micheel	67	70	70	70	277	61,200
Jeff Sluman	70	71	68	68	277	61,200
Paul Azinger	68	72	70	68	278	46,013.34
Lee Janzen	72	68	70	68	278	46,013.34
Glen Day	69	71	69	69	278	46,013.33
Brent Geiberger	69	70	70	69	278	46,013.33
Brian Henninger	70	69	69	70	278	46,013.33
Loren Roberts	68	72	69	69	278	46,013.33
Danny Ellis	65	72	69	73	279	27,965
Fred Funk	70	71	71	67	279	27,965
David Gossett	71	70	68	70	279	27,965
Skip Kendall	71	70	72	66	279	27,965
Greg Kraft	70	70	69	70	279	27,965
Steve Lowery	72	70	66	71	279	27,965
Shigeki Maruyama	71	71	70	67	279	27,965
Kenny Perry	71	70	72	66	279	27,965
Tommy Armour III	68	71	71	70	280	19,282.86
Jay Don Blake	70	72	69	69	280	19,282.86
Bill Glasson	70	70	70	70	280	19,282.86
Jesper Parnevik	73	69	67	71	280	19,282.86
Mike Sposa	65	71	73	71	280	19,282.86
David Peoples	70	71	72	67	280	19,282.85
Bob Tway	70	72	73	65	280	19,282.85
David Berganio, Jr.	69	72	71	69	281	13,600
Brad Elder	68	74	70	69	281	13,600
Steve Elkington	70	71	73	67	281	13,600
Steve Flesch	68	69	74	70	281	13,600

	SCORES				TOTAL	MONEY
Frank Lickliter	71	70	72	68	281	13,600
Spike McRoy	70	71	69	71	281	13,600
John Riegger	67	73	70	71	281	13,600
Esteban Toledo	68	69	76	68	281	13,600
Briny Baird	68	72	74	68	282	9,639
Tom Byrum	68	72	67	75	282	9,639
Jonathan Kaye	68	68	70	76	282	9,639
Kevin Sutherland	70	69	69	74	282	9,639
Stewart Cink	69	70	74	70	283	8,279
Russ Cochran	72	68	76	67	283	8,279
Bradley Hughes	71	68	71	73	283	8,279
Frank Nobilo	69	72	70	72	283	8,279
Cameron Beckman	69	71	72	72	284	7,752
Mathew Goggin	68	73	71	72	284	7,752
Blaine McCallister	70	69	74	71	284	7,752
David Sutherland	70	71	69	74	284	7,752
Grant Waite	70	71	73	70	284	7,752
Jim Carter	68	71	71	75	285	7,480
Brad Faxon	71	71	69	74	285	7,480
Peter Jacobsen	73	66	72	74	285	7,480
Harrison Frazar	67	70	74	75	286	7,276
Justin Leonard	68	74	71	73	286	7,276
Larry Mize	71	69	72	74	286	7,276
Stuart Appleby	70	71	74	72	287	7,106
Rory Sabbatini	71	71	72	73	287	7,106
J.J. Henry	68	74	73	73	288	7,004
David Frost	69	72	73	75	289	6,902
Andrew Magee	74	66	71	78	289	6,902
Jose Coceres	66	75	74	77	292	6,766
Jimmy Green	69	72	77	74	292	6,766
J.L. Lewis	67	75	75	82	299	6,664

Tour Championship

Champions Golf Club, Cypress Course, Houston, Texas
Par 36-35–71; 7,202 yards

November 1-4
purse, $5,000,000

	SCORES				TOTAL	MONEY
Mike Weir	68	66	68	68	270	$900,000
Ernie Els	69	68	65	68	270	385,000
Sergio Garcia	69	67	66	68	270	385,000
David Toms	73	66	64	67	270	385,000
(Weir won on first playoff hole.)						
Kenny Perry	70	67	65	69	271	202,500
Scott Verplank	67	65	68	71	271	202,500
Bob Estes	71	66	65	70	272	166,666.67
Jim Furyk	70	71	62	69	272	166,666.67
David Duval	69	69	63	71	272	166,666.66
Chris DiMarco	69	68	69	69	275	136,666.67
Joe Durant	73	65	67	70	275	136,666.67
Bernhard Langer	65	68	69	73	275	136,666.66
Stewart Cink	70	70	67	69	276	119,000
Tiger Woods	70	67	69	70	276	119,000
Tom Lehman	69	68	72	68	277	108,000
Davis Love III	70	72	66	69	277	108,000
Vijay Singh	70	73	68	67	278	102,000
Scott McCarron	70	70	70	69	279	100,000

	SCORES				TOTAL	MONEY
Mark Calcavecchia	71	64	69	76	280	98,000
Frank Lickliter	65	73	69	74	281	95,000
Jeff Sluman	73	70	66	72	281	95,000
Robert Allenby	76	67	67	73	283	91,000
Justin Leonard	69	66	71	77	283	91,000
Steve Stricker	74	70	72	68	284	88,000
Steve Lowery	67	70	73	75	285	86,000
Brad Faxon	68	70	70	78	286	83,000
Billy Mayfair	72	74	72	68	286	83,000
Hal Sutton	70	73	70	73	286	83,000
Scott Hoch	74	71	70	72	287	81,000

Southern Farm Bureau Classic

Annandale Golf Club, Madison, Mississippi
Par 36-36–72; 7,199 yards

November 1-4
purse, $2,400,000

	SCORES				TOTAL	MONEY
Cameron Beckman	66	69	67	67	269	$432,000
Chad Campbell	70	64	65	71	270	259,200
Fred Funk	65	69	69	68	271	163,200
Dan Forsman	68	70	65	69	272	115,200
Brett Quigley	68	69	69	67	273	96,000
Choi Kyung-ju	67	69	68	70	274	72,600
J.J. Henry	69	67	68	70	274	72,600
Carl Paulson	67	66	70	71	274	72,600
Dicky Pride	66	68	67	73	274	72,600
Loren Roberts	70	71	67	66	274	72,600
Chris Smith	70	68	69	67	274	72,600
Willie Wood	71	65	68	71	275	55,200
Neal Lancaster	69	68	70	69	276	46,400
David Peoples	74	67	66	69	276	46,400
Lee Porter	72	63	72	69	276	46,400
Russ Cochran	70	69	66	72	277	40,800
Briny Baird	71	67	71	69	278	32,480
Jim Gallagher, Jr.	72	66	72	68	278	32,480
John Huston	70	71	66	71	278	32,480
Tripp Isenhour	71	70	70	67	278	32,480
Matt Kuchar	70	69	68	71	278	32,480
Mike Sposa	68	70	70	70	278	32,480
Carlos Franco	72	66	72	69	279	21,360
David Gossett	71	70	67	71	279	21,360
Chris Tidland	71	67	72	69	279	21,360
Kirk Triplett	67	69	70	73	279	21,360
Richard Zokol	69	70	68	72	279	21,360
Tom Byrum	71	71	68	70	280	14,960
Joel Edwards	69	71	69	71	280	14,960
Jimmy Green	68	70	74	68	280	14,960
Charles Howell	71	68	68	73	280	14,960
Brandt Jobe	67	66	69	78	280	14,960
Pete Jordan	70	69	69	72	280	14,960
Jeff Maggert	68	75	67	70	280	14,960
Blaine McCallister	69	71	67	73	280	14,960
Esteban Toledo	71	68	69	72	280	14,960
Doug Barron	70	69	70	72	281	9,360
Bob Burns	68	69	72	72	281	9,360
Michael Clark	72	69	69	71	281	9,360

	SCORES				TOTAL	MONEY
John Cook	68	70	72	71	281	9,360
Glen Day	72	71	68	70	281	9,360
Jason Gore	71	71	68	71	281	9,360
Lee Janzen	72	68	69	72	281	9,360
Jerry Kelly	71	69	69	72	281	9,360
Chris Riley	68	70	72	71	281	9,360
Heath Slocum	69	65	76	71	281	9,360
Garrett Willis	72	68	69	72	281	9,360
Brad Elder	71	70	70	71	282	6,032
Brian Gay	70	70	67	75	282	6,032
Glen Hnatiuk	71	69	72	70	282	6,032
Andrew Magee	68	66	72	76	282	6,032
Steve Pate	67	74	72	69	282	6,032
Tommy Tolles	73	65	76	68	282	6,032
Richie Coughlan	68	71	74	70	283	5,520
Doug Dunakey	69	72	71	71	283	5,520
Ted Tryba	71	69	70	73	283	5,520
Keith Clearwater	70	72	70	72	284	5,352
Craig Kanada	69	68	74	73	284	5,352
Skip Kendall	69	71	72	72	284	5,352
Grant Waite	69	69	70	76	284	5,352
Jeff Brehaut	70	73	66	76	285	5,112
Scott Dunlap	72	67	66	80	285	5,112
Danny Ellis	71	71	71	72	285	5,112
Shaun Micheel	71	72	69	73	285	5,112
David Morland	68	73	73	71	285	5,112
Bob Tway	68	68	71	78	285	5,112
Ben Ferguson	70	71	73	72	286	4,896
Bradley Hughes	72	70	70	74	286	4,896
Tom Pernice, Jr.	70	71	74	71	286	4,896
Mathew Goggin	74	69	71	73	287	4,800
Mark Brooks	66	73	72	77	288	4,728
Joe Ogilvie	72	71	72	73	288	4,728
Woody Austin	71	70	72	76	289	4,632
Len Mattiace	69	73	73	74	289	4,632
Greg Kraft	71	72	75	74	292	4,560
Robin Freeman	70	71	71	81	293	4,512

Special Events

CVS/pharmacy Charity Classic

Rhode Island Country Club, Barrington, Rhode Island   July 9-10
Par 36-35–71; 6,734 yards   purse $1,100,000

	SCORES		TOTAL	MONEY
				(Team)
Nick Price/Mark Calcavecchia	60	59	119	$210,000
Brad Faxon/Gary Player	58	61	119	160,000
(Price and Calcavecchia defeated Faxon and Player on first playoff hole.)				
Davis Love III/Jay Haas	59	61	120	115,000
Tim Herron/Dudley Hart	58	62	120	115,000
Scott McCarron/David Toms	60	62	122	95,000
Jeff Sluman/Stuart Appleby	60	62	122	95,000
Peter Jacobsen/John Daly	63	62	125	85,000
Dana Quigley/Brett Quigley	63	63	126	77,500
Bill Andrade/Arnold Palmer	61	65	126	77,500
Craig Stadler/Steve Elkington	60	67	127	70,000

Fred Meyer Challenge

Reserve Vineyards and Golf Club, Fought Course, Aloha, Oregon   August 6-7
Par 36-36–72; 7,037 yards   purse $925,000

	SCORES		TOTAL	MONEY
				(Team)
Billy Andrade/Brad Faxon	60	60	120	$180,000
Fuzzy Zoeller/Jean Van de Velde	65	57	122	120,000
Bob Duval/David Duval	60	63	123	93,000
Stewart Cink/David Toms	61	62	123	93,000
Tom Lehman/Sergio Garcia	65	59	124	78,000
Steve Elkington/Craig Stadler	63	64	127	76,000
Casey Martin/Billy Mayfair	67	62	129	74,500
John Cook/Mark O'Meara	64	65	129	74,500
Fred Couples/Phil Mickelson	65	65	130	73,000
Scott McCarron/Brian Henninger	67	65	132	72,000
Arnold Palmer/Peter Jacobsen	68	67	135	71,000
Jack Nicklaus/Gary Nicklaus	71	70	141	70,000

Franklin Templeton Shootout

Doral Resort & Spa, Great White Course, Miami, Florida   November 9-11
Par 36-36–72; 7,171 yards   purse, $2,000,000

	SCORES			TOTAL	MONEY
					(Each)
Brad Faxon/Scott McCarron	64	62	57	183	$225,000
John Daly/Frank Lickliter	66	59	60	185	140,000
Stewart Cink/Raymond Floyd	65	62	60	187	82,500
Joe Durant/Lee Janzen	66	63	58	187	82,500
Olin Browne/Jeff Sluman	68	64	59	191	66,250

	SCORES			TOTAL	MONEY
					(Each)
Peter Jacobsen/Craig Stadler	68	62	61	191	66,250
Mike Hulbert/Jeff Maggert	66	67	60	193	62,500
Carlos Franco/Scott Hoch	67	66	62	195	60,000
John Cook/John Huston	71	64	61	196	57,500
Jay Haas/Corey Pavin	68	64	65	197	55,000
Per-Ulrik Johansson/Jesper Parnevik	70	67	61	198	52,500
Steve Elkington/Greg Norman	68	67	65	200	50,000

Callaway Golf Pebble Beach Invitational

Pebble Beach GL: Par 36-36–72; 6,840 yards   November 15-18
Spyglass Hills GC: Par 36-36–72; 6,859 yards   purse, $300,000
Del Monte GC: Par 36-36–72; 6,278 yards
Pebble Beach, California

	SCORES				TOTAL	MONEY
Olin Browne	66	66	68	71	271	$60,000
Todd Barranger	66	69	73	63	271	32,200
(Browne defeated Barranger on third playoff hole.)						
Brian Mogg	66	68	71	67	272	12,000
Kirk Triplett	66	72	67	67	272	12,000
Bruce Summerhays	68	67	71	66	272	12,000
Paul Stankowski	67	68	68	70	273	8,000
J.L. Lewis	70	70	66	69	275	6,750
Kevin Sutherland	69	71	67	68	275	6,750
Luke Donald	67	66	71	72	276	5,400
Beth Bauer	71	70	63	72	276	5,400
Tom Lehman	68	67	73	68	276	5,400
Todd Fischer	69	70	69	68	276	5,400
Stephen Ames	67	67	73	70	277	4,450
Jim Thorpe	71	68	71	67	277	4,450
Terry Dill	74	66	67	71	278	3,625
Mike Reid	71	68	70	69	278	3,625
Ed Fryatt	72	69	68	69	278	3,625
Matt Gogel	72	70	70	66	278	3,625
Harrison Frazar	69	69	69	72	279	2,875
Marion Dantzler	67	73	68	71	279	2,875
Jeff Gove	69	69	72	69	279	2,875
Scott Simpson	73	69	69	68	279	2,875
Bob May	70	66	74	70	280	2,550
Chris Smith	74	66	72	68	280	2,550
Brett Quigley	71	70	69	71	281	2,287.50
Sean Farren	69	71	70	71	281	2,287.50
Chad Campbell	70	71	71	69	281	2,287.50
Rick Leibovich	69	71	73	68	281	2,287.50
Mitch Lowe	70	69	70	73	282	2,097.50
Rob Boldt	72	72	67	71	282	2,097.50
Brian Claar	69	72	71	70	282	2,097.50
Jeff Quinney	70	70	73	69	282	2,097.50
Tom Purtzer	68	69	72	74	283	2,020
Michael Muehr	70	68	71	74	283	2,020
Bruce Fleisher	68	70	72	73	283	2,020
Duffy Waldorf	68	70	75	71	284	1,970
David Sutherland	70	74	69	71	284	1,970
Jim Carter	70	67	70	78	285	1,940
Bob Murphy	71	71	71	73	286	1,920
Bobby Clampett	72	71	69	75	287	1,900

UBS Warburg Cup

Ocean Course, Kiawah Island, South Carolina
Par 36-36–72; 7,296 yards

November 16-18
purse, $3,000,000

FIRST DAY
Foursomes

Bernhard Langer and Frank Nobilo (World) defeated Scott Hoch and John Cook, 2 and 1.
Jose Maria Canizares and Stewart Ginn (World) defeated Tom Watson and Loren Roberts, 1 up.
Sam Torrance and Ian Woosnam (World) tied Larry Nelson and Curtis Strange.
Nick Faldo and Isao Aoki (World) defeated Hale Irwin and Mark Calcavecchia, 2 and 1.
Gary Player and Des Smyth (World) defeated Arnold Palmer and Mark O'Meara, 3 and 2.
Dana Quigley and Raymond Floyd (US) defeated Ian Stanley and Denis Durnian, 1 up.

POINTS: Rest of the World 4½, United States 1½

SECOND DAY
Fourballs

Langer and Nobilo (World) tied Floyd and Calcavecchia.
Torrance and Woosnam (World) tied O'Meara and Cook.
Faldo and Aoki (World) tied Strange and Watson.
Hoch and Roberts (US) defeated Stanley and Durnian, 4 and 2.
Player and Smyth (World) defeated Palmer and Quigley, 2 up.
Irwin and Nelson (US) defeated Canizares and Ginn, 2 up.

POINTS: Rest of the World 2½, United States 3½

THIRD DAY
Singles

Smyth (World), defeated Roberts, 4 and 3.
Palmer (US) defeated Player, 2 and 1.
Hoch (US) defeated Aoki, 2 and 1.
O'Meara (US) defeated Ginn, 5 and 4.
Faldo (World) defeated Watson, 3 and 2.
Irwin (US) tied Langer.
Strange (US) tied Torrance.
Cook (US) defeated Canizares, 2 and 1.
Durnian (World) defeated Quigley, 1 up.
Floyd (US) tied Stanley.
Calcavecchia (US) defeated Woosnam, 1 up.
Nelson (US) defeated Nobilo, 3 and 2.

POINTS: United States 7½, Rest of the World 4½

TOTAL POINTS: United States 12½, Rest of the World 11½

(Each member of the United States team received $150,000; each member of the Rest of the World team received $100,000.)

PGA Grand Slam of Golf

Poipu Bay Resort, Kauai, Hawaii
Par 36-36–72; 7,053 yards

November 20-21
purse, $1,000,000

	SCORES		TOTAL	MONEY
Tiger Woods	67	65	132	$400,000
David Toms	68	67	135	250,000
Retief Goosen	66	71	137	200,000
David Duval	76	72	148	150,000

Office Depot Father-Son Challenge

Ocean Golf Club, Paradise Island, Bahamas
Par 36-36–72; 6,907 yards

December 1-2
purse, $919,000

	SCORES		TOTAL	MONEY
				(Won by professional)
Raymond/Robert Floyd	63	61	124	$200,000
Hale/Steve Irwin	59	66	125	105,000
Tom/Eric Weiskopf	61	65	126	80,000
Johnny/Scott Miller	64	63	127	65,000
Larry/Josh Nelson	63	65	128	55,000
Craig/Kevin Stadler	67	62	129	50,000
Hubert/Matt Green	65	65	130	48,500
Dave/Ron Stockton	65	65	130	48,500
Bob/David Charles	65	66	131	47,000
Billy/Bobby Casper	68	64	132	45,000
Tom/David Kite	66	66	132	45,000
Tom/Michael Watson	66	66	132	45,000
Lanny/Travis Wadkins	67	68	135	43,000
Lee/Tony Trevino	68	68	136	42,000

Hyundai Team Matches

Monarch Beach Golf Links, Dana Point, California
Par 34-36–70; 6,582 yards

December 8-9
purse, $1,200,000

FIRST-ROUND MATCHES

Tom Lehman and Duffy Waldorf defeated Joe Durant and Skip Kendall, 7 and 6.
Fred Couples and Mark Calcavecchia defeated David Toms and Steve Flesch, 5 and 4.

THIRD-PLACE MATCH

Durant and Kendall defeated Toms and Flesch, 2 and 1.
(Durant and Kendall received $30,000 each; Toms and Flesch received $20,000 each.)

CHAMPIONSHIP MATCH

Couples and Calcavecchia defeated Lehman and Waldorf, 1 up.
(Couples and Calcavecchia received $100,000 each; Lehman and Waldorf received $50,000 each.)

Williams World Challenge

Sherwood Country Club, Thousand Oaks, California
Par 35-35–70; 7,025 yards

December 13-16
purse, $4,100,000

	SCORES				TOTAL	MONEY
Tiger Woods	68	67	74	64	273	$1,000,000
Vijay Singh	68	66	71	71	276	500,000
Scott Hoch	70	70	72	67	279	300,000
Bernhard Langer	69	68	74	70	281	220,000
Mark O'Meara	66	74	75	66	281	220,000
Jesper Parnevik	73	65	75	70	283	180,000
Fred Couples	66	71	77	69	283	180,000
Colin Montgomerie	73	68	76	67	284	150,000
David Duval	72	70	72	71	285	146,000
Thomas Bjorn	73	80	64	68	285	146,000
David Toms	71	68	75	72	286	141,250
Lee Westwood	71	72	70	73	286	141,250
Padraig Harrington	69	74	75	71	289	137,500
Davis Love III	71	75	72	73	291	135,000
Jim Furyk	74	70	72	76	292	132,500
Scott Verplank	68	76	79	71	294	130,000
Darren Clarke	72	73	76	74	295	130,000
Mark Calcavecchia	74	71	78	76	299	130,000

Buy.com Tour

Florida Classic

Gainesville Country Club, Gainesville, Florida
Par 35-36–71; 6,936 yards

March 8-11
purse, $425,000

	SCORES				TOTAL	MONEY
Chris Couch	67	69	69	64	269	$76,500
Chad Campbell	71	65	69	65	270	45,900
Heath Slocum	66	69	71	65	271	28,900
Danny Briggs	69	70	66	67	272	17,566.67
Mike Heinen	68	67	68	69	272	17,566.67
John Patterson	73	65	64	70	272	17,566.66
Jim Benepe	69	65	73	66	273	11,505.36
Ben Crane	70	70	68	65	273	11,505.36
Jason Hill	65	70	72	66	273	11,505.36
Pat Perez	69	71	67	66	273	11,505.36
Matt Peterson	69	67	72	65	273	11,505.36
Jeff Freeman	71	68	65	69	273	11,505.35
Deane Pappas	67	66	72	68	273	11,505.35
Jason Caron	68	69	69	68	274	7,650

	SCORES				TOTAL	MONEY
Larry Rinker	68	67	70	69	274	7,650
Gene Sauers	73	66	67	68	274	7,650
Pat Bates	70	69	67	69	275	5,376.25
John Elliott	70	68	70	67	275	5,376.25
Ryuji Imada	66	70	67	72	275	5,376.25
David Kirkpatrick	69	69	72	65	275	5,376.25
Rodney Pampling	64	69	71	71	275	5,376.25
Fran Quinn	69	65	72	69	275	5,376.25
Lee Rinker	70	66	67	72	275	5,376.25
Bo Van Pelt	70	67	70	68	275	5,376.25
Paul Claxton	71	68	69	68	276	3,242.15
Mike Standly	68	70	71	67	276	3,242.15
David Gossett	70	69	69	68	276	3,242.14
Brian Kamm	68	69	70	69	276	3,242.14
Mitch Lowe	69	70	68	69	276	3,242.14
Sonny Skinner	63	72	71	70	276	3,242.14
John Wilson	68	72	66	70	276	3,242.14

Monterrey Open

Club Campestre, Garza Garcia, N.L., Mexico
Par 36-36–72; 7,090 yards

March 15-18
purse, $450,000

	SCORES				TOTAL	MONEY
Deane Pappas	67	68	67	69	271	$81,000
Keoke Cotner	68	72	68	64	272	39,600
Tim Petrovic	66	69	70	67	272	39,600
Tommy Biershenk	72	65	67	69	273	17,718.75
Chris Couch	64	70	68	71	273	17,718.75
John Kernohan	65	70	69	69	273	17,718.75
Brenden Pappas	70	67	67	69	273	17,718.75
Mike Brisky	67	70	67	70	274	13,500
Tom Kalinowski	68	66	70	70	274	13,500
Chad Campbell	68	68	71	68	275	10,350
R.W. Eaks	70	71	66	68	275	10,350
Steve Haskins	68	67	70	70	275	10,350
Richard Johnson	66	70	70	69	275	10,350
Oscar Serna	66	69	68	72	275	10,350
Ken Green	68	73	69	66	276	7,875
Matt Peterson	68	68	70	70	276	7,875
John Wilson	73	64	68	72	277	7,200
Paul Curry	71	68	67	72	278	5,287.50
John Elliott	70	71	66	71	278	5,287.50
Bobby Gage	70	70	71	67	278	5,287.50
Jay Hobby	69	71	68	70	278	5,287.50
Brian Kamm	70	70	69	69	278	5,287.50
Eric Meeks	69	69	69	71	278	5,287.50
Fran Quinn	69	69	72	68	278	5,287.50
Richard Zokol	68	71	72	67	278	5,287.50
Mike Sullivan	71	65	70	73	279	3,780
Rafael Alarcon	65	75	71	69	280	3,195
Pat Bates	69	70	70	71	280	3,195
Jason Caron	67	72	72	69	280	3,195
Michael Long	68	71	72	69	280	3,195
Pat Perez	71	68	70	71	280	3,195
Bo Van Pelt	69	72	70	69	280	3,195

Louisiana Open

Le Triomphe Country Club, Broussard, Louisiana
Par 36-36–72; 7,004 yards

March 29-April 1
purse, $450,000

	SCORES				TOTAL	MONEY
Paul Claxton	68	66	70	67	271	$81,000
Tim Petrovic	67	67	68	70	272	39,600
Steve Runge	67	65	68	72	272	39,600
Jody Bellflower	70	72	63	69	274	16,312.50
Jeff Freeman	68	69	68	69	274	16,312.50
Robert Gaus	69	73	67	65	274	16,312.50
Charles Raulerson	66	68	70	70	274	16,312.50
Jamie Rogers	69	69	67	69	274	16,312.50
Gene Sauers	67	67	70	70	274	16,312.50
Mike Heinen	68	69	68	70	275	10,800
Jason Knutzon	71	68	64	72	275	10,800
David Lebeck	61	69	73	72	275	10,800
Tim O'Neal	66	71	69	69	275	10,800
Dave Barr	72	64	67	73	276	7,875
Tommy Biershenk	70	65	70	71	276	7,875
Bobby Gage	67	68	72	69	276	7,875
Richard Zokol	72	70	65	69	276	7,875
Michael Allen	69	73	72	63	277	6,525
John Wilson	68	72	67	70	277	6,525
Brian Bateman	66	74	70	68	278	4,875
Jason Caron	70	71	70	67	278	4,875
Jim Gallagher, Jr.	73	68	65	72	278	4,875
Joel Kribel	69	67	68	74	278	4,875
Sonny Skinner	70	68	69	71	278	4,875
Phil Tataurangi	72	66	69	71	278	4,875
Jason Buha	73	64	66	76	279	3,510
Deane Pappas	69	69	69	72	279	3,510
Heath Slocum	70	71	65	73	279	3,510
Bo Van Pelt	67	72	70	70	279	3,510
Bobby Elliott	71	67	71	71	280	2,925
Brian Kamm	70	70	69	71	280	2,925
Matt Peterson	69	69	70	72	280	2,925
Chris Wollmann	68	72	71	69	280	2,925

Arkansas Classic

Diamante Country Club, Hot Springs, Arkansas
Par 36-36–72; 7,560 yards

April 19-22
purse, $450,000

	SCORES				TOTAL	MONEY
Brett Quigley	65	69	71	71	276	$81,000
John Elliott	69	71	69	70	279	48,600
Tim Petrovic	73	68	71	68	280	30,600
Pat Perez	72	68	76	66	282	21,600
Emlyn Aubrey	73	72	67	72	284	16,425
David Gossett	71	69	70	74	284	16,425
Brian Kamm	74	69	71	70	284	16,425
Jason Caron	71	72	71	71	285	13,050
Michael Long	73	70	70	72	285	13,050
Andy Morse	74	72	66	73	285	13,050
Tommy Biershenk	70	74	69	73	286	9,225

	SCORES				TOTAL	MONEY
Chad Campbell	74	70	72	70	286	9,225
Keoke Cotner	71	70	76	69	286	9,225
Paul Curry	74	72	67	73	286	9,225
Scott Gump	75	70	70	71	286	9,225
Sonny Skinner	69	71	75	71	286	9,225
Todd Barranger	72	74	68	73	287	5,500
Craig Bowden	75	68	73	71	287	5,500
Jonathan Byrd	78	67	74	68	287	5,500
Paul Claxton	74	68	73	72	287	5,500
Ryuji Imada	73	68	72	74	287	5,500
Joel Kribel	74	70	69	74	287	5,500
Rob McKelvey	74	70	72	71	287	5,500
Rodney Pampling	73	73	68	73	287	5,500
Matt Peterson	75	70	72	70	287	5,500
Patrick Burke	76	68	74	70	288	3,278.58
Ben Bates	71	71	70	76	288	3,278.57
Donnie Hammond	74	71	72	71	288	3,278.57
John Kernohan	73	70	74	71	288	3,278.57
David Kirkpatrick	71	71	70	76	288	3,278.57
Jeff Sanday	70	75	68	75	288	3,278.57
Darron Stiles	73	72	71	72	288	3,278.57

Charity Pro-Am at the Cliffs

The Cliffs Golf & Country Club, Greenville, South Carolina
Valley Course: Par 36-36–72; 7,024 yards
Keowee Vineyards Course: Par 36-35–71; 7,006 yards

April 26-29
purse, $500,000

	SCORES				TOTAL	MONEY
Jonathan Byrd	67	70	66	66	269	$90,000
Brenden Pappas	67	69	67	67	270	54,000
Matt Peterson	68	65	67	71	271	29,000
Sonny Skinner	68	68	70	65	271	29,000
R.W. Eaks	64	67	70	71	272	18,250
Don Pooley	67	70	67	68	272	18,250
Stan Utley	68	66	67	71	272	18,250
Chad Campbell	70	66	71	66	273	15,000
Jason Hill	69	67	66	71	273	15,000
Rob McMillan	69	71	67	67	274	12,500
Charles Raulerson	66	66	75	67	274	12,500
Bo Van Pelt	67	66	68	73	274	12,500
Jason Buha	68	69	67	71	275	10,000
John Rollins	67	68	69	71	275	10,000
Keoke Cotner	70	70	67	69	276	8,250
Scott Ford	65	69	71	71	276	8,250
Brad Ott	67	74	69	66	276	8,250
Todd Rose	69	69	70	68	276	8,250
Bob Friend	70	69	69	69	277	6,500
David Kirkpatrick	69	68	70	70	277	6,500
Deane Pappas	71	70	70	66	277	6,500
Jeff Freeman	69	70	69	70	278	5,200
Eric Meeks	65	69	71	73	278	5,200
Fran Quinn	65	71	70	72	278	5,200
Brian Bateman	68	73	68	70	279	3,814.29
Jay Hobby	69	67	73	70	279	3,814.29
Tim Petrovic	68	71	69	71	279	3,814.29
Mike Sullivan	69	70	69	71	279	3,814.29

		SCORES			TOTAL	MONEY
Brad Fabel	69	66	71	73	279	3,814.28
Heath Slocum	67	68	72	72	279	3,814.28
Richard Zokol	66	66	72	75	279	3,814.28

Carolina Classic

TPC at Wakefield Plantation, Raleigh, North Carolina
Par 35-36–71; 7,257 yards

May 3-6
purse, $450,000

		SCORES			TOTAL	MONEY
John Maginnes	68	65	66	70	269	$81,000
Ryuji Imada	71	64	67	69	271	48,600
Phil Tataurangi	68	66	68	71	273	30,600
Todd Fischer	69	67	67	71	274	21,600
Jim Benepe	70	69	67	69	275	18,000
Paul Claxton	72	69	66	70	277	14,568.75
David Kirkpatrick	67	72	70	68	277	14,568.75
Tim O'Neal	70	68	65	74	277	14,568.75
Willie Wood	71	67	68	71	277	14,568.75
Joel Kribel	67	69	72	70	278	11,700
Deane Pappas	72	68	66	72	278	11,700
Jonathan Byrd	72	68	68	71	279	8,550
Trevor Dodds	72	69	68	70	279	8,550
David Gossett	71	69	73	66	279	8,550
Omar Uresti	72	69	68	70	279	8,550
Mark Wurtz	67	71	70	71	279	8,550
Richard Zokol	70	71	69	69	279	8,550
Steve Haskins	70	69	70	71	280	6,075
Brad Klapprott	67	71	71	71	280	6,075
Fran Quinn	71	69	71	69	280	6,075
John Rollins	66	71	73	70	280	6,075
Guy Boros	70	70	71	70	281	4,356
Chad Campbell	68	73	72	68	281	4,356
Pat Perez	69	72	68	72	281	4,356
Jeff Sanday	70	71	69	71	281	4,356
Gene Sauers	68	73	71	69	281	4,356
Eric Meeks	68	69	72	73	282	3,600
Craig Bowden	71	71	69	72	283	3,114
John Elliott	73	69	73	68	283	3,114
Mike Heinen	67	69	77	70	283	3,114
Nick Napoleon	71	67	70	75	283	3,114
Tim Petrovic	68	72	71	72	283	3,114

Virginia Beach Open

TPC of Virginia Beach, Virginia Beach, Virginia
Par 36-36–72; 7,432 yards

May 10-13
purse, $425,000

		SCORES			TOTAL	MONEY
Trevor Dodds	65	68	73	71	277	$76,500
Deane Pappas	64	72	74	70	280	45,900
Jonathan Byrd	68	65	73	76	282	24,650
Brenden Pappas	67	70	72	73	282	24,650
David Gossett	71	69	72	71	283	17,000
Chris Couch	72	65	73	74	284	15,300

	SCORES				TOTAL	MONEY
Craig Matthew	69	70	74	72	285	12,803.13
Rodney Pampling	70	73	72	70	285	12,803.13
Mike Heinen	68	70	72	75	285	12,803.12
Heath Slocum	68	71	70	76	285	12,803.12
Paul Claxton	69	71	72	74	286	9,350
Kelly Gibson	68	68	76	74	286	9,350
David Kirkpatrick	66	67	74	79	286	9,350
Joel Kribel	75	66	71	74	286	9,350
Michael Bradley	72	68	75	72	287	6,375
John Elliott	69	70	75	73	287	6,375
Charley Hoffman	73	64	74	76	287	6,375
John Maginnes	72	69	71	75	287	6,375
Larry Rinker	69	72	75	71	287	6,375
Bobby Wadkins	72	69	75	71	287	6,375
Michael Walton	71	72	73	71	287	6,375
Ty Armstrong	74	70	73	71	288	4,250
Tom Carter	72	68	74	74	288	4,250
Ryuji Imada	67	70	76	75	288	4,250
Lee Rinker	73	70	71	74	288	4,250
Michael Allen	70	73	73	73	289	3,400
Dick Mast	70	71	72	76	289	3,400
Sonny Skinner	70	73	72	74	289	3,400
Bob Heintz	74	69	74	73	290	2,644.45
Mark Johnson	75	69	73	73	290	2,644.45
Brian Kamm	69	72	77	72	290	2,644.45
John Kernohan	71	71	74	74	290	2,644.45
Danny Briggs	74	69	73	74	290	2,644.44
Todd Fischer	70	69	72	79	290	2,644.44
Jason Knutzon	70	73	71	76	290	2,644.44
Scott Petersen	72	72	69	77	290	2,644.44
Clarence Rose	72	70	73	75	290	2,644.44

Richmond Open

Stonehenge Golf & Country Club, Richmond, Virginia
Par 35-36–71; 6,987 yards

May 17-20
purse, $425,000

	SCORES				TOTAL	MONEY
Chad Campbell	67	67	64	65	263	$76,500
Kelly Gibson	69	67	64	66	266	45,900
Darron Stiles	70	66	65	66	267	28,900
J.J. Henry	69	65	64	70	268	20,400
Ryuji Imada	71	66	64	68	269	17,000
Craig Matthew	69	69	66	68	272	14,768.75
Pat Perez	69	71	65	67	272	14,768.75
Brian Kamm	68	68	69	68	273	13,175
Jason Buha	68	69	66	71	274	11,475
Jim McGovern	66	67	70	71	274	11,475
Andrew McLardy	70	67	68	69	274	11,475
Richie Coughlan	71	65	67	72	275	8,330
Danny Ellis	69	66	71	69	275	8,330
Jeff Freeman	67	67	69	72	275	8,330
Robert Gaus	67	70	69	69	275	8,330
Max Harris	69	69	64	73	275	8,330
Tom Carter	70	69	67	70	276	5,376.25
Paul Claxton	67	68	68	73	276	5,376.25
Paul Curry	68	68	68	72	276	5,376.25

	SCORES				TOTAL	MONEY
Bobby Elliott	68	69	70	69	276	5,376.25
Gary Hallberg	70	67	65	74	276	5,376.25
Scott Hebert	73	65	68	70	276	5,376.25
D.A. Points	68	68	72	68	276	5,376.25
Jim Rutledge	72	68	69	67	276	5,376.25
Mike Brisky	69	68	69	71	277	3,116.67
Barry Cheesman	69	69	69	70	277	3,116.67
Bob Friend	70	69	67	71	277	3,116.67
Rick Price	70	66	69	72	277	3,116.67
Jamie Rogers	68	69	70	70	277	3,116.67
Bobby Wadkins	66	69	69	73	277	3,116.67
Mike Heinen	67	66	70	74	277	3,116.66
Tjaart van der Walt	66	66	71	74	277	3,116.66
Mark Wurtz	65	68	69	75	277	3,116.66

Steamtown Classic

Glenmaura National Golf Club, Moosic, Pennsylvania
Par 34-36–70; 6,933 yards

May 31-June 3
purse, $425,000

	SCORES				TOTAL	MONEY
Jason Hill	67	71	69	65	272	$76,500
Jonathan Byrd	73	66	68	68	275	37,400
Matt Peterson	68	70	65	72	275	37,400
Tim Petrovic	70	71	67	68	276	20,400
Kelly Gibson	68	71	70	68	277	14,928.13
Sonny Skinner	69	70	69	69	277	14,928.13
Jason Buha	68	68	68	73	277	14,928.12
Jeff Gove	72	67	68	70	277	14,928.12
Mark Carnevale	71	69	68	70	278	11,050
Bob Friend	70	70	67	71	278	11,050
Brian Hull	69	70	71	68	278	11,050
Brian Kamm	71	68	70	69	278	11,050
Charles Raulerson	71	72	69	67	279	7,735
John Rollins	70	71	68	70	279	7,735
Omar Uresti	73	67	70	69	279	7,735
Vic Wilk	70	72	66	71	279	7,735
Chad Wright	71	68	71	69	279	7,735
Eric Johnson	75	67	68	70	280	5,950
Geoffrey Sisk	73	71	66	70	280	5,950
Tjaart van der Walt	78	66	71	65	280	5,950
Chad Campbell	72	69	70	70	281	3,647.92
Brad Klapprott	72	69	70	70	281	3,647.92
Jim McGovern	69	70	71	71	281	3,647.92
Andy Morse	73	68	71	69	281	3,647.92
Pat Perez	73	66	72	70	281	3,647.92
Don Reese	76	67	70	68	281	3,647.92
Gene Sauers	71	73	70	67	281	3,647.92
Patrick Sheehan	72	67	72	70	281	3,647.92
Brian Bateman	71	72	67	71	281	3,647.91
Bob Heintz	72	69	67	73	281	3,647.91
Lee Rinker	72	68	70	71	281	3,647.91
Bud Still	71	70	66	74	281	3,647.91

Samsung Canadian PGA Championship

DiamondBack Golf Club, Richmond Hill, Ontario, Canada
Par 36-36–72; 7,079 yards

June 7-10
purse, $450,000

	SCORES				TOTAL	MONEY
Richard Zokol	67	68	70	66	271	$81,000
Gary Hallberg	71	67	68	68	274	48,600
Pat Perez	70	69	67	69	275	26,100
Tim Petrovic	67	72	66	70	275	26,100
Rodney Pampling	67	71	70	68	276	16,425
Omar Uresti	69	70	69	68	276	16,425
Tjaart van der Walt	70	70	71	65	276	16,425
Bob Heintz	71	70	69	67	277	13,050
David McKenzie	71	71	68	67	277	13,050
Sonny Skinner	69	72	69	67	277	13,050
Tommy Biershenk	69	72	66	71	278	10,350
Steve Haskins	71	72	69	66	278	10,350
Mike Small	72	69	69	68	278	10,350
Patrick Burke	66	75	68	70	279	7,650
Brian Hull	69	67	74	69	279	7,650
Joel Kribel	65	75	69	70	279	7,650
Stiles Mitchell	66	72	71	70	279	7,650
Jeff Sanday	65	75	72	67	279	7,650
Danny Briggs	71	71	68	70	280	5,265
Jay Delsing	71	66	73	70	280	5,265
Brian Fogt	68	72	68	72	280	5,265
Scott Gump	70	70	71	69	280	5,265
Richard Johnson	66	73	67	74	280	5,265
Chad Wright	72	71	65	72	280	5,265
Jason Enloe	71	72	68	70	281	3,870
Brenden Pappas	73	69	70	69	281	3,870
Brian Bateman	68	75	72	67	282	3,082.50
Pat Bates	68	74	70	70	282	3,082.50
Joe Daley	68	72	70	72	282	3,082.50
Scott Hebert	71	69	72	70	282	3,082.50
Jay Hobby	66	71	75	70	282	3,082.50
Eric Johnson	70	71	72	69	282	3,082.50
D.A. Points	68	73	73	68	282	3,082.50
Geoffrey Sisk	71	70	71	70	282	3,082.50

Greater Cleveland Open

Quail Hollow Country Club, Concord, Ohio
Par 36-36–72; 6,799 yards

June 14-17
purse, $425,000

	SCORES				TOTAL	MONEY
Heath Slocum	64	66	69	68	267	$76,500
Ryuji Imada	66	64	66	72	268	45,900
Jim Benepe	66	66	68	70	270	28,900
Jay Hobby	69	66	66	70	271	20,400
Mike Brisky	67	67	67	72	273	17,000
Todd Barranger	69	69	69	68	275	14,768.75
Anthony Painter	74	67	67	67	275	14,768.75
Danny Briggs	70	68	68	70	276	12,750
Darron Stiles	71	67	67	71	276	12,750
Andrew McLardy	66	70	70	71	277	11,050
Rob McMillan	69	69	65	74	277	11,050

	SCORES				TOTAL	MONEY
Paul Claxton	66	71	66	75	278	9,775
Keoke Cotner	71	69	70	69	279	6,847.23
Tim O'Neal	66	71	72	70	279	6,847.23
Rob Bradley	65	73	68	73	279	6,847.22
Ben Curtis	70	67	70	72	279	6,847.22
Bob Friend	66	70	70	73	279	6,847.22
Jeff Gove	69	69	71	70	279	6,847.22
Rob McKelvey	70	67	69	73	279	6,847.22
Jeff Sanday	68	68	72	71	279	6,847.22
Sonny Skinner	74	67	67	71	279	6,847.22
Tommy Biershenk	73	68	70	69	280	3,683.34
Stan Utley	71	69	70	70	280	3,683.34
Bobby Wadkins	71	69	70	70	280	3,683.34
Pat Bates	68	71	69	72	280	3,683.33
Jonathan Byrd	68	70	69	73	280	3,683.33
Curt Byrum	70	69	70	71	280	3,683.33
Charley Hoffman	66	71	72	71	280	3,683.33
Mike Schuchart	65	72	69	74	280	3,683.33
Chad Wright	71	68	69	72	280	3,683.33

Dayton Open

Golf Club at Yankee Trace, Centerville, Ohio
Par 36-36–72; 7,139 yards

June 21-24
purse, $425,000

	SCORES				TOTAL	MONEY
Todd Barranger	64	66	67	65	262	$76,500
Bo Van Pelt	67	67	63	66	263	45,900
Heath Slocum	65	68	66	66	265	28,900
Brian Bateman	67	65	69	65	266	18,700
Rodney Pampling	66	64	71	65	266	18,700
Tommy Biershenk	68	63	70	68	269	14,237.50
Vic Wilk	67	70	67	65	269	14,237.50
Richard Zokol	65	67	71	66	269	14,237.50
David Gossett	66	70	66	68	270	10,625
Mike Heinen	67	68	69	66	270	10,625
Darron Stiles	68	70	67	65	270	10,625
Tjaart van der Walt	68	66	68	68	270	10,625
John Wilson	69	66	69	66	270	10,625
Tim Petrovic	69	69	66	67	271	8,075
Jay Delsing	67	70	66	69	272	7,012.50
Michael Long	68	70	66	68	272	7,012.50
Matt Peterson	70	67	64	71	272	7,012.50
Tim Straub	68	67	72	65	272	7,012.50
Shane Bertsch	67	67	71	68	273	5,525
Jason Buha	67	68	68	70	273	5,525
Scott Hebert	68	67	70	68	273	5,525
Ty Armstrong	67	68	69	70	274	4,250
Jeff Gove	67	71	67	69	274	4,250
Chris Starkjohann	70	68	70	66	274	4,250
Bud Still	69	68	66	71	274	4,250
Keoke Cotner	67	72	69	67	275	3,230
Trevor Dodds	66	68	72	69	275	3,230
Bob Friend	71	68	65	71	275	3,230
Eric Johnson	69	65	72	69	275	3,230
David McKenzie	70	67	69	69	275	3,230

Knoxville Open

Fox Den Country Club, Knoxville, Tennessee
Par 36-36–72; 7,142 yards

June 28-July 1
purse, $425,000

		SCORES			TOTAL	MONEY
Heath Slocum	64	68	65	68	265	$76,500
Keoke Cotner	70	70	66	65	271	37,400
Joe Daley	70	65	66	70	271	37,400
Chris Wollmann	70	67	65	70	272	20,400
Sonny Skinner	64	70	70	69	273	16,150
Bobby Wadkins	71	68	69	65	273	16,150
Matt Peterson	68	68	68	70	274	13,706
Bo Van Pelt	66	67	70	71	274	13,706
Jonathan Byrd	71	67	69	68	275	11,475
David Gossett	68	67	68	72	275	11,475
Don Pooley	68	67	66	74	275	11,475
Pat Bates	68	71	69	68	276	8,075
Patrick Burke	70	70	64	72	276	8,075
Chris Couch	68	69	71	68	276	8,075
Tim O'Neal	68	70	69	69	276	8,075
Charles Raulerson	67	72	68	69	276	8,075
John Rollins	72	68	67	69	276	8,075
Tommy Biershenk	72	68	70	67	277	5,355
Brad Fabel	67	67	70	73	277	5,355
Jimmy Johnston	65	72	72	68	277	5,355
Jim McGovern	68	71	69	69	277	5,355
Rodney Pampling	69	69	71	68	277	5,355
John Wilson	71	65	66	75	277	5,355
Tom Carter	67	73	70	68	278	4,080
Shane Bertsche	69	72	66	72	279	3,570
John Patterson	69	71	70	69	279	3,570
Andrew Price	67	71	71	70	279	3,570
Curt Byrum	70	69	69	72	280	2,841
Chad Collins	68	70	73	69	280	2,841
Bob Heintz	70	69	68	73	280	2,841
Kevin Muncrief	69	71	71	69	280	2,841
Tim Straub	70	71	68	71	280	2,841
David White	68	72	67	73	280	2,841
Brian Kamm	68	72	73	67	280	2,841

Hershey Open

Country Club of Hershey, East Course,
Hershey, Pennsylvania
Par 36-35–71; 7,154 yards

July 5-8
purse, $425,000

		SCORES			TOTAL	MONEY
John Rollins	65	70	69	69	273	$76,500
Rodney Pampling	73	69	67	64	273	45,900
(Rollins defeated Pampling on first playoff hole.)						
Kelly Grunewald	70	71	67	67	275	24,650
Brad Klapprott	71	72	64	68	275	24,650
David Gossett	70	69	69	68	276	15,512.50
Steve Haskins	68	73	67	68	276	15,512.50
Jay Hobby	68	71	64	73	276	15,512.50
Jim McGovern	70	70	69	68	277	13,175
Deane Pappas	68	69	73	68	278	11,475

	SCORES				TOTAL	MONEY
Charles Raulerson	69	73	70	66	278	11,475
Matt Sharkey	73	65	71	69	278	11,475
Rob Bradley	68	67	73	71	279	8,606.25
Jason Dufner	70	70	70	69	279	8,606.25
Bobby Gage	71	69	72	67	279	8,606.25
David Kirkpatrick	69	70	70	70	279	8,606.25
Kevin Burton	69	70	73	68	280	6,800
Paul Claxton	70	71	69	70	280	6,800
Charley Hoffman	68	72	73	67	280	6,800
Jim Benepe	69	70	72	70	281	4,643.13
Gary Hallberg	68	69	76	68	281	4,643.13
Michael Long	69	73	70	69	281	4,643.13
John Maginnes	71	71	72	67	281	4,643.13
Arjun Atwal	71	69	69	72	281	4,643.12
Jeff Gove	71	70	68	72	281	4,643.12
Bob Heintz	71	69	69	72	281	4,643.12
Sonny Skinner	69	72	69	71	281	4,643.12
Todd Barranger	69	72	69	72	282	3,017.50
Jason Buha	72	72	67	71	282	3,017.50
Scott Hebert	72	70	70	70	282	3,017.50
Billy Judah	71	67	76	68	282	3,017.50
Tim Petrovic	69	70	72	71	282	3,017.50
Chris Wollmann	70	71	71	70	282	3,017.50

Wichita Open

Crestview Country Club, Wichita, Kansas
Par 36-36–72; 6,913 yards

July 12-15
purse, $425,000

	SCORES				TOTAL	MONEY
Jason Dufner	67	67	64	68	266	$76,500
Todd Rose	66	69	66	68	269	31,733.34
David Gossett	69	66	66	68	269	31,733.33
Jeff Gove	67	63	73	66	269	31,733.33
Scott Gutschewski	68	67	67	68	270	16,150
Billy Judah	67	70	66	67	270	16,150
Michael Allen	69	67	68	67	271	13,706.25
Pat Bates	67	66	70	68	271	13,706.25
Pat Perez	67	65	68	72	272	11,900
Scott Petersen	65	68	70	69	272	11,900
Darron Stiles	69	68	66	70	273	10,625
Todd Fischer	68	64	70	72	274	8,925
Rob McKelvey	67	70	68	69	274	8,925
Eric Meeks	67	68	67	72	274	8,925
Rob Bradley	69	66	69	71	275	6,587.50
Kevin Burton	67	69	69	70	275	6,587.50
Chad Campbell	65	68	70	72	275	6,587.50
Rob McMillan	71	69	66	69	275	6,587.50
Tim O'Neal	70	68	64	73	275	6,587.50
Mark Walker	71	67	68	69	275	6,587.50
Arjun Atwal	67	71	66	72	276	4,420
Mike Brisky	71	68	68	69	276	4,420
Brad Klapprott	68	69	72	67	276	4,420
Matt Sharkey	67	72	70	67	276	4,420
Richard Zokol	67	68	71	70	276	4,420
Jim Benepe	68	70	69	70	277	3,230
Ben Crane	70	68	68	71	277	3,230

	SCORES				TOTAL	MONEY
Bob Friend	71	69	66	71	277	3,230
Kevin Muncrief	69	70	66	72	277	3,230
Chad Wright	67	67	70	73	277	3,230

Siouxland Open

Dakota Dunes Country Club, Dakota Dunes, South Dakota
Par 36-36–72; 7,165 yards

July 19-22
purse, $425,000

	SCORES				TOTAL	MONEY
Pat Bates	67	66	70	70	273	$76,500
Matt Kuchar	70	67	71	66	274	37,400
Eric Meeks	70	67	69	68	274	37,400
Jason Buha	69	71	68	68	276	18,700
Bo Van Pelt	73	68	67	68	276	18,700
Todd Barranger	69	71	68	69	277	13,302.50
Shane Bertsch	75	67	66	69	277	13,302.50
Joe Daley	69	66	69	73	277	13,302.50
Deane Pappas	68	71	68	70	277	13,302.50
Conrad Ray	70	69	68	70	277	13,302.50
Pat Perez	69	71	69	69	278	10,200
Heath Slocum	70	70	71	67	278	10,200
Mark Johnson	67	71	70	71	279	8,216.67
John Rollins	71	66	71	71	279	8,216.67
Brian Kortan	72	66	69	72	279	8,216.66
Michael Allen	70	69	71	70	280	5,769.38
Chris Couch	66	70	75	69	280	5,769.38
Matthew Ecob	69	71	70	70	280	5,769.38
Rob McKelvey	67	70	74	69	280	5,769.38
Arjun Atwal	67	70	72	71	280	5,769.37
Emlyn Aubrey	70	69	70	71	280	5,769.37
Robert Gaus	69	66	71	74	280	5,769.37
Tyler Williamson	70	67	69	74	280	5,769.37
Brian Bateman	73	67	72	69	281	3,424.29
Craig Bowden	68	72	71	70	281	3,424.29
Jeff Freeman	69	72	71	69	281	3,424.29
David Kirkpatrick	65	71	75	70	281	3,424.29
Billy Judah	71	71	68	71	281	3,424.28
Tim O'Neal	68	71	70	72	281	3,424.28
Rick Woodson	67	69	74	71	281	3,424.28

Ozarks Open

Highland Springs Country Club, Springfield, Missouri
Par 36-36–72; 7,058 yards
(Tournament shortened to 36 holes — rain.)

July 26-29
purse, $450,000

	SCORES		TOTAL	MONEY
Steve Haskins	66	65	131	$81,000
Omar Uresti	65	67	132	48,600
Todd Barranger	65	68	133	21,600
Don Reese	66	67	133	21,600
Jamie Rogers	65	68	133	21,600
Iain Steel	65	68	133	21,600
Brenden Pappas	65	69	134	13,556.25

	SCORES				TOTAL	MONEY
Matt Peterson	66	68			134	13,556.25
Tjaart van der Walt	69	65			134	13,556.25
Tyler Williamson	67	67			134	13,556.25
Jason Dufner	66	69			135	9,900
Ryuji Imada	69	66			135	9,900
Andy Morse	67	68			135	9,900
Vic Wilk	68	67			135	9,900
Jody Bellflower	69	67			136	6,129
Shane Bertsch	66	70			136	6,129
Jason Buha	68	68			136	6,129
Kevin Burton	68	68			136	6,129
Bobby Gage	69	67			136	6,129
Sung Man Lee	65	71			136	6,129
Nick Napoleon	67	69			136	6,129
Jeff Sanday	66	70			136	6,129
Patrick Sheehan	66	70			136	6,129
Mark Wurtz	68	68			136	6,129
Rob Bradley	70	67			137	3,240
Chad Campbell	68	69			137	3,240
Trevor Dodds	69	68			137	3,240
Kuni Kuniyoshi	68	69			137	3,240
Eric Meeks	69	68			137	3,240
Charles Raulerson	67	70			137	3,240
John Rollins	68	69			137	3,240
Steve Runge	65	72			137	3,240
Rick Woodson	67	70			137	3,240
Chad Wright	68	69			137	3,240

Omaha Classic

The Champions Club, Omaha, Nebraska
Par 36-36–72; 7,059 yards

August 2-5
purse, $525,000

	SCORES				TOTAL	MONEY
Heath Slocum	64	70	66	66	266	$94,500
Rodney Pampling	66	67	69	65	267	56,700
Jeff Gove	67	64	72	67	270	35,700
Rob McKelvey	70	66	70	65	271	25,200
Scott Petersen	67	67	67	71	272	19,950
Patrick Sheehan	65	69	69	69	272	19,950
Tom Carter	68	68	68	69	273	17,587.50
Jason Dufner	69	69	68	68	274	14,700
Ryan Howison	67	73	66	68	274	14,700
Deane Pappas	67	73	68	66	274	14,700
Chad Wright	69	68	67	70	274	14,700
Pat Bates	69	69	74	63	275	9,975
Mike Brisky	71	68	68	68	275	9,975
Barry Cheesman	71	68	70	66	275	9,975
John Rollins	69	68	71	67	275	9,975
Sonny Skinner	70	68	70	67	275	9,975
Charles Warren	65	72	69	69	275	9,975
Ben Crane	74	66	69	67	276	6,390
R.W. Eaks	67	73	70	66	276	6,390
John Elliott	67	69	70	70	276	6,390
Eric Johnson	71	70	68	67	276	6,390
Billy Judah	73	66	68	69	276	6,390
Rick Price	73	66	70	67	276	6,390

	SCORES				TOTAL	MONEY
Ryan Vermeer	68	69	71	68	276	6,390
Chris Couch	70	69	66	72	277	4,200
Joe Daley	75	67	71	64	277	4,200
Matt Peterson	69	73	68	67	277	4,200
Iain Steel	73	68	62	74	277	4,200
Tyler Williamson	72	69	68	68	277	4,200
Todd Barranger	68	69	70	71	278	3,307.50
Chad Campbell	70	69	69	70	278	3,307.50
Tim Conley	67	70	70	71	278	3,307.50
Jason Knutzon	72	70	68	68	278	3,307.50
Charles Raulerson	69	73	66	70	278	3,307.50
Chris Wollmann	66	76	69	67	278	3,307.50

Fort Smith Classic

Hardscrabble Country Club, Fort Smith, Arkansas
Par 35-35–70; 6,619 yards

August 9-12
purse, $425,000

	SCORES				TOTAL	MONEY
Jay Delsing	66	66	66	65	263	$76,500
Jeff Freeman	69	69	60	65	263	45,900
(Delsing defeated Freeman on fourth playoff hole.)						
Rick Price	68	65	65	66	264	28,900
Pat Bates	66	68	68	64	266	16,734.38
Pete Morgan	69	68	68	61	266	16,734.38
Matt Peterson	64	68	68	66	266	16,734.37
Charles Raulerson	65	68	67	66	266	16,734.37
Michael Long	66	67	68	66	267	13,175
Tom Carter	66	67	71	64	268	10,625
Joe Daley	70	65	65	68	268	10,625
Kelly Gibson	69	69	65	65	268	10,625
John Morse	67	68	66	67	268	10,625
Tyler Williamson	66	67	68	67	268	10,625
Ben Crane	70	67	68	64	269	7,437.50
Mike Grob	74	62	65	68	269	7,437.50
Tim Petrovic	67	71	69	62	269	7,437.50
Fran Quinn	67	70	66	66	269	7,437.50
Tommy Biershenk	64	73	67	66	270	5,737.50
Guy Boros	72	66	66	66	270	5,737.50
Mike Brisky	70	64	68	68	270	5,737.50
Anthony Painter	69	66	67	68	270	5,737.50
Paul Claxton	68	69	68	66	271	3,885.72
David McKenzie	68	70	66	67	271	3,885.72
Vic Wilk	70	68	66	67	271	3,885.72
Kuni Kuniyoshi	69	69	65	68	271	3,885.71
Rob McKelvey	69	66	68	68	271	3,885.71
Omar Uresti	68	65	68	70	271	3,885.71
Chris Wollmann	64	73	71	63	271	3,885.71
Brian Bateman	69	67	68	68	272	2,868.75
Chip Beck	66	71	68	67	272	2,868.75
Casey Brown	68	71	70	63	272	2,868.75
Ron Whittaker	66	72	65	69	272	2,868.75

Permian Basin Open

The Club at Mission Dorado, Odessa, Texas
Par 36-36–72; 7,221 yards

August 16-19
purse, $425,000

	SCORES				TOTAL	MONEY
Chad Campbell	64	68	63	69	264	$76,500
Todd Fischer	67	63	71	67	268	45,900
Kelly Gibson	68	69	64	68	269	28,900
Tom Carter	65	67	68	70	270	17,566.67
Tim Petrovic	66	68	69	67	270	17,566.67
Eric Booker	66	68	65	71	270	17,566.66
Jonathan Byrd	66	69	68	68	271	11,935.42
Jeff Gove	66	69	66	70	271	11,935.42
Jason Hill	68	66	69	68	271	11,935.42
Anthony Painter	68	67	67	69	271	11,935.42
John Patterson	67	64	68	72	271	11,935.41
Phil Tataurangi	66	67	68	70	271	11,935.41
Danny Briggs	70	68	65	69	272	7,968.75
Bob Heintz	69	67	68	68	272	7,968.75
Rodney Pampling	65	68	66	73	272	7,968.75
Mike Sullivan	68	68	68	68	272	7,968.75
Sam Randolph	69	67	72	65	273	6,375
Mike Tschetter	66	66	71	70	273	6,375
Steven Young	69	65	69	70	273	6,375
Brian Bateman	67	69	68	70	274	4,088.50
Jorge Benedetti	68	66	69	71	274	4,088.50
Michael Long	66	70	67	71	274	4,088.50
Casey Martin	66	70	68	70	274	4,088.50
Perry Moss	70	68	68	68	274	4,088.50
Charles Raulerson	66	68	72	68	274	4,088.50
Lee Rinker	68	68	68	70	274	4,088.50
Jeff Sanday	65	68	69	72	274	4,088.50
Iain Steel	70	68	64	72	274	4,088.50
Daniel Stone	69	67	70	68	274	4,088.50
Michael Allen	66	68	70	71	275	2,720
Robert Gaus	67	70	69	69	275	2,720
Steve Gotsche	68	68	67	72	275	2,720
Steve Haskins	68	69	66	72	275	2,720
Brian Kamm	66	69	69	71	275	2,720

Utah Classic

Willow Creek Country Club, Sandy, Utah
Par 36-36–72; 7,104 yards

August 30-September 2
purse, $425,000

	SCORES				TOTAL	MONEY
David Sutherland	63	64	73	72	272	$76,500
Danny Briggs	67	66	67	73	273	45,900
Jason Hill	71	67	70	66	274	24,650
Rodney Pampling	69	70	66	69	274	24,650
John Rollins	70	69	68	68	275	14,928.13
Willie Wood	69	70	69	67	275	14,928.13
Mike Heinen	67	68	70	70	275	14,928.12
Charles Raulerson	70	66	71	68	275	14,928.12
Pat Bates	69	72	67	68	276	10,200
Jason Buha	69	68	68	71	276	10,200
Ben Crane	67	72	68	69	276	10,200

	SCORES				TOTAL	MONEY
Jeff Freeman	68	71	68	69	276	10,200
Eric Meeks	72	68	68	68	276	10,200
Jason Schultz	69	70	69	68	276	10,200
Jay Delsing	70	70	66	71	277	7,225
Sonny Skinner	69	72	67	69	277	7,225
Stan Utley	72	70	68	67	277	7,225
Tommy Biershenk	70	69	69	70	278	5,737.50
Ryuji Imada	69	72	68	69	278	5,737.50
Bo Van Pelt	70	66	71	71	278	5,737.50
Vic Wilk	68	73	70	67	278	5,737.50
Mike Brisky	71	70	67	71	279	4,114
Brian Claar	69	71	70	69	279	4,114
Jeff Gove	73	69	69	68	279	4,114
Rob McMillan	69	68	70	72	279	4,114
Charles Warren	68	73	70	68	279	4,114
Patrick Burke	69	67	71	73	280	3,145
Jin Park	68	72	68	72	280	3,145
Mike Sullivan	68	71	71	70	280	3,145
Mark Wurtz	71	68	70	71	280	3,145

Tri-Cities Open

Meadow Springs Country Club, Richland, Washington
Par 36-36–72; 6,926 yards

September 6-9
purse, $425,000

	SCORES				TOTAL	MONEY
Guy Boros	71	68	70	65	274	$76,500
Jeff Gove	70	66	71	69	276	45,900
John Rollins	70	69	65	73	277	28,900
Lee Rinker	69	68	73	68	278	14,844.65
Tjaart van der Walt	68	73	70	67	278	14,844.65
Jim Benepe	72	66	70	70	278	14,844.64
Shane Bertsch	67	72	69	70	278	14,844.64
Billy Judah	72	68	66	72	278	14,844.64
Anthony Painter	74	67	66	71	278	14,844.64
Conrad Ray	74	68	65	71	278	14,844.64
Jay Hobby	73	71	66	69	279	8,439.29
Rodney Pampling	71	71	69	68	279	8,439.29
Tim Petrovic	72	68	69	70	279	8,439.29
Steve Schneiter	68	72	69	70	279	8,439.29
Rob McKelvey	69	69	69	72	279	8,439.28
Bo Van Pelt	70	71	66	72	279	8,439.28
Chad Wright	71	69	68	71	279	8,439.28
Tommy Biershenk	71	72	69	68	280	5,737.50
Jason Dufner	70	68	69	73	280	5,737.50
Eric Meeks	71	69	71	69	280	5,737.50
Omar Uresti	69	69	72	70	280	5,737.50
Mike Brisky	74	69	70	68	281	4,114
Eric Johnson	74	65	71	71	281	4,114
John Kernohan	73	71	69	68	281	4,114
Tim O'Neal	71	71	71	68	281	4,114
Pat Perez	76	67	66	72	281	4,114
Paul Claxton	70	68	72	72	282	3,077
Michael Combs	71	73	68	70	282	3,077
Trevor Dodds	72	69	72	69	282	3,077
Sonny Skinner	71	71	70	70	282	3,077
Bret Waldman	68	74	69	71	282	3,077

Boise Open

Hillcrest Country Club, Boise, Idaho
Par 36-35–71; 6,698 yards

September 20-23
purse, $556,000

		SCORES			TOTAL	MONEY
Michael Long	66	69	67	68	270	$100,080
Tjaart van der Walt	67	67	69	68	271	60,048
Jim Benepe	68	65	71	68	272	26,688
Billy Judah	67	67	68	70	272	26,688
Rodney Pampling	69	69	67	67	272	26,688
John Rollins	73	68	65	66	272	26,688
Chad Campbell	70	68	69	66	273	17,931
Jeff Sanday	74	66	67	66	273	17,931
Brenden Pappas	70	71	68	65	274	15,568
Richard Zokol	70	69	66	69	274	15,568
Guy Boros	69	70	67	69	275	11,398
Jonathan Byrd	68	68	67	72	275	11,398
Bob Heintz	68	68	71	68	275	11,398
David McKenzie	71	69	67	68	275	11,398
David Sutherland	67	74	69	65	275	11,398
Chad Wright	69	69	66	71	275	11,398
Jeff Gove	68	68	69	71	276	8,340
Arron Oberholser	71	64	72	69	276	8,340
Don Reese	67	68	71	70	276	8,340
Bo Van Pelt	72	69	69	67	277	6,023.34
Mark Walker	71	70	69	67	277	6,023.34
Jay Hobby	71	65	71	70	277	6,023.33
Brian Kamm	71	71	66	69	277	6,023.33
Jason Knutzon	68	69	72	68	277	6,023.33
Fran Quinn	70	66	70	71	277	6,023.33
Steve Gotsche	69	71	69	69	278	4,050.86
Mike Grob	71	67	71	69	278	4,050.86
Rob McKelvey	66	74	70	68	278	4,050.86
Tim Petrovic	71	68	72	67	278	4,050.86
Steve Runge	68	72	68	70	278	4,050.86
Michael Allen	68	68	70	72	278	4,050.85
Sonny Skinner	67	72	66	73	278	4,050.85

Inland Empire Open

Empire Lakes Golf Club, Rancho Cucamonga, California
Par 36-36–72; 6,972 yards

September 27-30
purse, $425,000

		SCORES			TOTAL	MONEY
D.A. Points	65	66	68	68	267	$76,500
Rodney Pampling	67	65	67	68	267	37,400
Mark Wurtz	66	68	67	66	267	37,400
(Points defeated Wurtz on first and Pampling on third playoff hole.)						
Curt Byrum	66	68	69	65	268	17,566.67
Kevin Pendley	64	68	68	68	268	17,566.67
Jeff Gove	70	64	65	69	268	17,566.66
Craig Bowden	70	69	65	65	269	12,803.13
Chad Wright	66	67	68	68	269	12,803.13
Bobby Gage	64	68	68	69	269	12,803.12
Steve Haskins	62	70	66	71	269	12,803.12
Danny Briggs	66	65	71	68	270	8,712.50
Kelly Gibson	67	69	70	64	270	8,712.50

	SCORES				TOTAL	MONEY
Eric Meeks	67	67	66	70	270	8,712.50
Pete Morgan	68	65	68	69	270	8,712.50
Todd Murphy	63	70	70	67	270	8,712.50
Richard Zokol	64	68	69	69	270	8,712.50
Jason Hill	67	67	70	67	271	6,162.50
Jay Hobby	69	65	70	67	271	6,162.50
Matt Peterson	69	68	66	68	271	6,162.50
Brian Smock	65	69	70	67	271	6,162.50
Brian Bateman	69	66	69	68	272	4,590
Pat Bates	69	67	69	67	272	4,590
Brad Klapprott	69	69	63	71	272	4,590
Michael Long	69	67	68	68	272	4,590
Tom Carter	65	68	72	68	273	3,176.88
Sung Man Lee	72	67	68	66	273	3,176.88
Anthony Rodriguez	67	67	71	68	273	3,176.88
Steve Sear	66	72	69	66	273	3,176.88
Jason Caron	69	67	69	68	273	3,176.87
Rob McKelvey	70	68	67	68	273	3,176.87
Rob McMillan	68	69	67	69	273	3,176.87
Todd Rose	66	70	66	71	273	3,176.87

Monterey Peninsula Classic

Bayonet Golf Course, Seaside, California
Par 36-36–72; 7,110 yards

October 4-7
purse, $450,000

	SCORES				TOTAL	MONEY
Chad Campbell	69	72	70	69	280	$81,000
Deane Pappas	72	70	69	70	281	48,600
Tom Carter	74	67	68	76	285	23,400
Charley Hoffman	70	72	69	74	285	23,400
Vic Wilk	68	77	72	68	285	23,400
Tim Clark	70	70	70	76	286	16,200
Jason Caron	70	74	72	71	287	14,512.50
John Rollins	71	71	75	70	287	14,512.50
Michael Allen	73	72	75	68	288	12,150
Todd Fischer	72	71	68	77	288	12,150
Jamie Rogers	70	73	70	75	288	12,150
Dave Barr	74	74	70	71	289	9,112.50
Shane Bertsch	74	74	68	73	289	9,112.50
David McKenzie	72	73	72	72	289	9,112.50
Charles Warren	76	69	72	72	289	9,112.50
Mike Heinen	69	72	78	71	290	7,425
Eric Meeks	72	74	71	73	290	7,425
John Elliott	75	71	69	76	291	5,868
Scott Petersen	76	70	71	74	291	5,868
Jeff Quinney	74	70	72	75	291	5,868
Stan Utley	73	75	71	72	291	5,868
Tjaart van der Walt	71	71	77	72	291	5,868
Brian Kamm	74	70	73	75	292	4,500
D.A. Points	73	72	71	76	292	4,500
Brian Bateman	75	73	71	74	293	3,432.86
Jonathan Byrd	73	74	72	74	293	3,432.86
Keoke Cotner	73	75	72	73	293	3,432.86
Kelly Gibson	72	76	70	75	293	3,432.86
Jeff Sanday	75	72	74	72	293	3,432.86
Jason Schultz	73	74	71	75	293	3,432.85
Mike Springer	73	75	73	72	293	3,432.85

Gila River Classic at Wild Horse Pass Resort

Whirlwind Golf Club, Devil's Claw Course, Chandler, Arizona   October 11-14
Par 36-35–71; 7,017 yards   purse, $425,000

	SCORES				TOTAL	MONEY
Ben Crane	63	66	64	68	261	$76,500
Jason Caron	65	67	65	64	261	37,400
Bo Van Pelt	63	66	65	67	261	37,400
(Crane defeated Caron on second and Van Pelt on fourth playoff hole.)						
D.A. Points	67	67	65	64	263	20,400
Todd Fischer	66	64	66	70	266	17,000
Scott Hebert	69	67	67	64	267	13,759.38
Don Reese	67	67	64	69	267	13,759.38
Bobby Gage	66	68	69	64	267	13,759.37
John Wilson	65	69	66	67	267	13,759.37
Brian Bateman	68	67	67	66	268	10,200
Jim Benepe	68	67	68	65	268	10,200
Rob McKelvey	67	70	63	68	268	10,200
Vance Veazey	65	68	68	67	268	10,200
Pat Bates	69	68	65	67	269	6,587.50
Jason Dufner	66	64	68	71	269	6,587.50
Kelly Gibson	68	68	68	65	269	6,587.50
Ryan Howison	66	67	69	67	269	6,587.50
Billy Judah	67	68	65	69	269	6,587.50
Andy Morse	64	70	67	68	269	6,587.50
Tim O'Neal	69	66	69	65	269	6,587.50
Fran Quinn	69	63	68	69	269	6,587.50
John Elliott	68	66	65	71	270	3,995
Pete Morgan	67	71	66	66	270	3,995
Rick Price	68	66	67	69	270	3,995
Jason Schultz	66	67	68	69	270	3,995
Tjaart van der Walt	69	63	70	68	270	3,995
Vic Wilk	66	68	68	68	270	3,995
Shane Bertsch	66	70	67	68	271	3,060
Jay Hobby	70	66	67	68	271	3,060
Charles Raulerson	70	66	67	68	271	3,060

Shreveport Open

Southern Trace Country Club, Shreveport, Louisiana   October 18-21
Par 36-36–72; 6,916 yards   purse, $425,000

	SCORES				TOTAL	MONEY
Pat Bates	66	68	67	67	268	$76,500
Brian Kamm	65	68	67	69	269	45,900
Stiles Mitchell	68	68	69	66	271	24,650
Don Reese	69	67	70	65	271	24,650
Jason Caron	72	65	67	68	272	17,000
Keoke Cotner	70	68	67	68	273	14,237.50
Billy Judah	70	69	65	69	273	14,237.50
Bruce Vaughan	70	68	67	68	273	14,237.50
Brian Claar	68	67	68	71	274	12,325
Fran Quinn	67	71	69	69	276	11,475
Jason Buha	70	70	66	71	277	9,010
Jay Delsing	73	67	67	70	277	9,010
John Elliott	72	67	68	70	277	9,010
Phil Tataurangi	71	68	68	70	277	9,010

	SCORES				TOTAL	MONEY
Mark Wurtz	67	71	70	69	277	9,010
Jim McGovern	71	69	68	70	278	6,587.50
Jamie Rogers	70	68	68	72	278	6,587.50
John Rollins	71	66	72	69	278	6,587.50
Tjaart van der Walt	64	74	70	70	278	6,587.50
Jaime Gomez	68	70	72	69	279	4,951.25
Andy Morse	71	69	69	70	279	4,951.25
Tim Petrovic	69	70	71	69	279	4,951.25
John Restino	74	68	67	70	279	4,951.25
Brian Bateman	74	66	72	68	280	3,604
Bobby Elliott	74	67	69	70	280	3,604
Brad Fabel	71	69	74	66	280	3,604
Rob McKelvey	72	70	71	67	280	3,604
Vic Wilk	71	69	67	73	280	3,604
Jason Dufner	70	71	69	71	281	2,822
Kelly Gibson	71	69	67	74	281	2,822
Mike Heinen	71	68	71	71	281	2,822
Ryan Howison	74	67	72	68	281	2,822
Bo Van Pelt	69	69	73	70	281	2,822

Buy.com Tour Championship

Robert Trent Jones Golf Trail, Senator Course
at Capitol Hill, Prattville, Alabama
Par 36-36–72; 7,656 yards

October 25-28
purse, $600,000

	SCORES				TOTAL	MONEY
Pat Bates	71	72	72	69	284	$108,000
Tom Carter	72	78	69	68	287	52,800
Brenden Pappas	72	74	70	71	287	52,800
Chad Campbell	71	72	74	71	288	28,800
Ben Crane	72	76	72	69	289	21,900
Jason Dufner	73	73	74	69	289	21,900
Rodney Pampling	69	74	74	72	289	21,900
Brian Kamm	74	71	71	74	290	16,800
Tim Petrovic	70	76	71	73	290	16,800
Brett Quigley	73	74	72	71	290	16,800
John Rollins	75	74	74	67	290	16,800
Jason Buha	72	74	74	71	291	12,660
Keoke Cotner	71	76	73	71	291	12,660
Jay Delsing	71	77	74	69	291	12,660
Eric Meeks	70	76	78	68	292	10,620
Vic Wilk	74	72	76	70	292	10,620
Deane Pappas	72	76	72	73	293	8,820
Charles Raulerson	73	77	73	70	293	8,820
Don Reese	68	81	74	70	293	8,820
Tjaart van der Walt	73	75	71	74	293	8,820
Paul Claxton	73	73	74	74	294	7,320
Chris Couch	76	73	74	72	295	6,620
Rob McKelvey	72	76	77	70	295	6,620
Pat Perez	74	73	74	74	295	6,620
Tommy Biershenk	77	75	76	68	296	5,730
Jonathan Byrd	73	81	72	70	296	5,730
Bo Van Pelt	72	73	80	71	296	5,730
John Elliott	75	79	74	69	297	5,100
Kelly Gibson	73	76	75	73	297	5,100
Todd Fischer	79	74	73	72	298	4,665
Jeff Freeman	78	76	74	70	298	4,665

Canadian Tour

Panama Open Panasonic

Coronado Hotel & Resort, Coronado Beach, Panama
Par 36-36–72; 6,983 yards

January 18-21
purse, C$300,000

	SCORES				TOTAL	MONEY
Steve Runge	69	70	66	67	272	C$54,000
Jonathan Byrd	66	68	68	72	274	30,000
Chad Wright	74	70	70	62	276	21,000
Bob Friend	72	68	65	72	277	13,500
Alan Bratton	73	68	69	68	278	10,500
Ryan Dillon	70	71	70	69	280	9,000
Joe Cioe	67	70	73	71	281	8,100
Tim Straub	68	70	68	75	281	8,100
Rex Caldwell	72	68	72	70	282	7,400
Greg Gregory	72	71	68	71	282	7,400
Tim Petrovic	70	71	72	69	282	7,400
Steve Haskins	72	70	71	70	283	5,962.50
Jeff Klauk	76	69	71	67	283	5,962.50
Patrick Moore	71	72	71	69	283	5,962.50
Kenneth Staton	76	69	70	68	283	5,962.50
Rafael Alarcon	72	68	75	70	285	4,650
Steve Ford	72	69	72	72	285	4,650
Scott Petersen	71	71	71	72	285	4,650
Javier Sanchez	69	71	75	70	285	4,650
Jesus Amaya	69	72	72	73	286	3,600
Paul Claxton	73	72	73	68	286	3,600
Grant Masson	78	67	70	71	286	3,600
Rich Massey	72	75	73	67	287	2,700
Steve Scott	71	74	70	72	287	2,700
Sonny Skinner	75	70	68	74	287	2,700
Jaxon Brigman	76	71	71	70	288	2,100
Jimmy Johnston	72	75	70	71	288	2,100
Jim Rutledge	76	69	71	72	288	2,100
Dave Branshaw	73	66	77	73	289	1,725
Stephen Gangluff	67	72	70	80	289	1,725
Derek Gilchrist	73	71	72	73	289	1,725
Steve LeBrun	72	74	73	70	289	1,725
Rob McMillan	74	72	69	74	289	1,725

Myrtle Beach Open

Barefoot Resort, Fazio Course, Myrtle Beach, South Carolina
Par 35-36–71; 6,834 yards

February 22-25
purse, C$150,000

	SCORES				TOTAL	MONEY
Eamonn Brady	68	70	68	71	277	C$24,000
D.A. Points	73	65	75	67	280	9,150
Derek Gillespie	69	73	70	68	280	9,150
Aaron Barber	70	65	71	74	280	9,150

	SCORES			TOTAL	MONEY
Dave Christensen	71	67	71	71	280	9,150
Brian Kontak	72	69	72	68	281	5,400
Brian Payne	71	68	73	70	282	4,650
Jamie Neher	74	73	63	72	282	4,650
Jess Daley	70	68	72	72	282	4,650
Marty Schiene	69	67	78	70	284	4,050
Jerome Valentin	73	69	73	70	285	3,450
Chris Wall	73	71	71	70	285	3,450
Grant Masson	72	69	73	71	285	3,450
David Mathis	74	71	74	67	286	2,550
Patrick Moore	75	70	74	67	286	2,550
Joey Snyder	73	70	74	69	286	2,550
Warren Schutte	73	66	75	72	286	2,550
Jeff Bloom	72	72	70	72	286	2,550
Scott Petersen	71	72	76	68	287	1,890
Stephen Woodard	70	74	74	69	287	1,890
Jason Bohn	74	69	73	71	287	1,890
Gene Jones	73	68	73	73	287	1,890
Kevin Altenhof	67	72	74	74	287	1,890
Todd Fanning	72	71	75	70	288	1,401.67
Ray Stewart	72	70	76	70	288	1,401.67
Mike Fergin	75	69	74	70	288	1,401.67
Chris Anderson	74	72	73	69	288	1,401.67
Dave Pashko	73	74	72	69	288	1,401.67
Kenneth Staton	72	72	73	71	288	1,401.67
Steve Scott	73	73	74	68	288	1,401.67
Jerry Foltz	76	68	72	72	288	1,401.67
Rob Johnson	71	71	73	73	288	1,401.67

Barefoot Classic

Barefoot Resort, Norman Course, Myrtle Beach, South Carolina   March 1-4
Par 36-36–72; 7,035 yards   purse, C$150,000
(Fourth round cancelled — rain.)

	SCORES			TOTAL	MONEY
Aaron Barber	65	66	73	204	C$24,000
Dave Christensen	73	69	64	206	10,200
Nathan Green	70	67	69	206	10,200
Patrick Moore	70	69	67	206	10,200
Dave Branshaw	68	71	68	207	5,700
Craig Matthew	67	71	69	207	5,700
Todd Fanning	67	73	68	208	4,500
Chris Greenwood	70	71	67	208	4,500
Rich Massey	68	71	69	208	4,500
Scott Petersen	71	67	70	208	4,500
Greg Fleischer	70	71	68	209	3,300
Derek Gilchrist	71	69	69	209	3,300
Brian Payne	70	70	69	209	3,300
Marty Schiene	70	70	69	209	3,300
Duane Bock	68	73	69	210	2,325
Jace Bugg	72	69	69	210	2,325
Graham Davidson	67	70	73	210	2,325
Mark Johnson	73	66	71	210	2,325
Rob McMillan	69	71	70	210	2,325
Conrad Ray	67	71	72	210	2,325
Kevin Altenhof	71	69	71	211	1,586.67

	SCORES			TOTAL	MONEY
Dirk Ayers	71	70	70	211	1,586.67
Tim Balmer	70	72	69	211	1,586.67
Brett Bingham	72	71	68	211	1,586.67
Jess Daley	73	70	68	211	1,586.67
Scott Ford	68	71	72	211	1,586.67
Eddy Lee	68	73	70	211	1,586.67
Chris Wall	71	70	70	211	1,586.67
Steve Woods	71	71	69	211	1,586.67

South Carolina Challenge

Barefoot Resort, Love Course, Myrtle Beach, South Carolina
Par 36-36–72; 7,047 yards

March 8-11
purse, C$150,000

	SCORES				TOTAL	MONEY
Jace Bugg	72	68	71	63	274	C$24,000
Rob McMillan	68	66	73	70	277	14,400
Lewis Chitengwa	70	72	70	66	278	7,400
Scott Hend	64	74	67	73	278	7,400
Kenneth Staton	70	69	70	69	278	7,400
Paul Devenport	67	72	72	68	279	5,000
Conrad Ray	69	70	70	70	279	5,000
Steve Woods	68	71	69	71	279	5,000
Aaron Barber	70	72	68	70	280	4,350
Chris Anderson	70	69	72	70	281	3,750
Derek Gilchrist	71	67	75	68	281	3,750
Brian Guetz	72	72	73	64	281	3,750
Kris Blanks	69	69	72	72	282	2,650
David Faught	72	69	70	71	282	2,650
Doug LaBelle	72	72	68	70	282	2,650
Patrick Moore	70	67	74	71	282	2,650
Danny Norton	71	67	72	72	282	2,650
Chris Wall	69	71	73	69	282	2,650
David Mathis	70	72	75	66	283	2,025
Dave Pashko	72	69	70	72	283	2,025
Bobby Kalinowski	71	69	76	68	284	1,762.50
Grant Masson	73	70	69	72	284	1,762.50
Marty Schiene	73	71	73	67	284	1,762.50
Brian Unk	72	70	71	71	284	1,762.50
Tim Balmer	69	73	74	69	285	1,473.75
Jason Bohn	72	71	71	71	285	1,473.75
Gene Jones	73	71	73	68	285	1,473.75
Brian Payne	74	71	72	68	285	1,473.75
Tim Conley	69	72	75	70	286	1,290
Chris Greenwood	72	71	75	68	286	1,290
Matt Kuchar	72	69	73	72	286	1,290

CanAm Days Championship

Barefoot Resort, Dye Course, Myrtle Beach, South Carolina
Par 36-36–72; 7,343 yards
(First round cancelled — rain.)

March 15-18
purse, C$150,000

	SCORES			TOTAL	MONEY
Scott Ford	67	68	71	206	C$24,000
Dave Christensen	66	71	71	208	9,150
Jess Daley	73	65	70	208	9,150
David Faught	66	69	73	208	9,150
Patrick Moore	69	66	73	208	9,150
Doug LaBelle	67	70	72	209	5,400
Matt Kuchar	71	68	71	210	4,800
Jim Rutledge	70	70	70	210	4,800
Mickael Dieu	71	67	73	211	4,350
Dirk Ayers	68	73	71	212	3,750
Jaime Gomez	71	67	74	212	3,750
Bryn Parry	70	69	73	212	3,750
Chris Anderson	72	72	69	213	2,650
Aaron Barber	73	68	72	213	2,650
Lewis Chitengwa	71	72	70	213	2,650
Mark Johnson	68	69	76	213	2,650
D.A. Points	71	66	76	213	2,650
Brian Unk	72	69	72	213	2,650
Brett Bingham	69	73	72	214	1,890
Jace Bugg	68	73	73	214	1,890
Gene Jones	68	71	75	214	1,890
Craig Matthew	74	70	70	214	1,890
Drew Symons	71	70	73	214	1,890
Todd Fanning	73	70	72	215	1,509
Derek Gilchrist	69	71	75	215	1,509
Derek Gillespie	73	68	74	215	1,509
Scott Hend	68	71	76	215	1,509
Brian Payne	76	68	71	215	1,509
Jason Bohn	73	70	73	216	1,148.25
John Gudauskas	73	70	73	216	1,148.25
Rob Johnson	71	72	73	216	1,148.25
Bobby Kalinowski	71	72	73	216	1,148.25
Chris Kamin	69	72	75	216	1,148.25
Rich Massey	77	65	74	216	1,148.25
Danny Mijovic	68	72	76	216	1,148.25
Conrad Ray	70	72	74	216	1,148.25
Jason Schultz	73	71	72	216	1,148.25
Jerry Springer	72	70	74	216	1,148.25

Shell Payless Open

Gorge Vale Golf Club, Victoria, British Columbia
Par 37-34–71; 6,459 yards

June 14-17
purse, C$150,000

	SCORES				TOTAL	MONEY
Paul Devenport	66	67	71	67	271	C$24,000
Blair Piercy	65	69	69	69	272	14,400
Todd Fanning	65	70	71	67	273	9,000
Nathan Green	68	66	73	67	274	7,200
Bob Conrad	72	69	68	66	275	6,000
Jarrod Warner	72	66	74	64	276	5,400

	SCORES				TOTAL	MONEY
Steve Alker	70	70	65	72	277	4,650
Lewis Chitengwa	67	67	71	72	277	4,650
Eddie Maunder	72	70	65	70	277	4,650
Chris Locker	70	71	68	69	278	3,325
Patrick Moore	66	72	69	71	278	3,325
Mikkel Reese	71	69	68	70	278	3,325
Derek Gilchrist	68	68	73	69	278	3,325
Chris Kamin	69	72	71	66	278	3,325
Eddy Lee	69	70	70	69	278	3,325
Kris Yardley	70	67	74	68	279	2,550
Aaron Barber	71	71	66	72	280	1,969
Kenneth Staton	70	71	67	72	280	1,969
Scott Ford	68	73	69	70	280	1,969
Danny Mijovic	71	67	73	69	280	1,969
Casey Brown	68	71	68	73	280	1,969
Jorge Corral	70	68	71	71	280	1,969
Craig Matthew	73	69	68	70	280	1,969
Davidson Matyczuk	72	69	69	70	280	1,969
Brett Bingham	71	68	72	70	281	1,446
Jerry Springer	70	72	68	71	281	1,446
Steve Scott	72	66	73	70	281	1,446
David Mathis	69	71	72	69	281	1,446
Dave Branshaw	70	72	70	69	281	1,446
Dave Christensen	70	69	72	71	282	1,185
Michael Kirk	69	72	71	70	282	1,185
Ryan Dillon	72	67	72	71	282	1,185
Jonn Drewery	67	71	74	70	282	1,185
Drew Symons	71	71	69	71	282	1,185
Jace Bugg	72	66	70	74	282	1,185

Telus Vancouver Open

Point Grey Country Club, Vancouver, British Columbia
Par 36-36–72; 6,810 yards

June 21-24
purse, C$150,000

	SCORES				TOTAL	MONEY
Steve Scott	71	67	71	67	276	C$24,000
Steve Alker	66	71	70	69	276	8,400
Jess Daley	69	66	70	71	276	8,400
Scott Hend	71	71	68	66	276	8,400
Mark Slawter	69	70	69	68	276	8,400
Roger Tambellini	66	70	70	70	276	8,400
(Scott won on sixth playoff hole.)						
Kenneth Staton	72	70	66	69	277	4,950
Patrick Moore	67	69	72	70	278	4,500
Bryan Saltus	69	67	70	72	278	4,500
Dirk Ayers	70	72	70	67	279	3,750
Rich Massey	71	69	70	69	279	3,750
Zhang Lian-wei	70	69	69	71	279	3,750
Ken Duke	71	70	70	69	280	2,812.50
Andy Johnson	72	69	68	71	280	2,812.50
Rob Johnson	76	66	66	72	280	2,812.50
Chris Wall	70	69	74	67	280	2,812.50
Lewis Chitengwa	74	69	70	68	281	2,250
Matthew Lane	73	69	71	68	281	2,250
Doug McGuigan	67	69	76	69	281	2,250
Jonn Drewery	71	70	68	73	282	1,875

	SCORES				TOTAL	MONEY
Brian Payne	75	68	69	70	282	1,875
Mikkel Reese	72	70	74	66	282	1,875
Jason Bohn	73	70	71	69	283	1,650
Todd Fanning	70	71	71	71	283	1,650
Grant Masson	69	71	72	71	283	1,650
Michael Kirk	72	70	71	71	284	1,389
David Mathis	73	69	73	69	284	1,389
Joe McCormick	74	69	70	71	284	1,389
Alejandro Quiroz	72	68	71	73	284	1,389
Mario Tiziani	67	75	75	67	284	1,389

Telus Edmonton Open

Edmonton Country Club, Edmonton, Alberta
Par 35-36–71; 6,793 yards

June 28-July 1
purse, C$150,000

	SCORES				TOTAL	MONEY
Aaron Barber	68	66	65	65	264	C$24,000
Casey Brown	67	70	64	65	266	14,400
Mark Slawter	68	71	64	64	267	9,000
Jason Bohn	69	65	66	68	268	6,600
Doug McGuigan	66	66	72	64	268	6,600
Mike Belbin	68	66	69	66	269	5,400
Tim Balmer	72	67	68	64	271	4,350
Mark Brown	72	66	67	66	271	4,350
Jess Daley	69	69	70	63	271	4,350
Warren Schutte	71	65	67	68	271	4,350
Zhang Lian-wei	66	68	70	67	271	4,350
Steve Alker	67	71	69	65	272	3,037.50
Nathan Green	66	72	68	66	272	3,037.50
Eddie Maunder	66	69	71	66	272	3,037.50
Kenneth Staton	69	63	74	66	272	3,037.50
Ryan Dillon	69	67	69	68	273	2,250
Marcus Higley	66	68	73	66	273	2,250
Andy Johnson	67	70	67	69	273	2,250
Arden Knoll	66	71	68	68	273	2,250
Grant Masson	68	65	70	70	273	2,250
John Douma	72	67	68	67	274	1,762.50
Bryn Parry	68	72	67	67	274	1,762.50
Ray Stewart	70	67	68	69	274	1,762.50
Brad Sutterfield	69	69	64	72	274	1,762.50
Liam Bond	69	71	72	63	275	1,446
Michael Chavez	68	69	73	65	275	1,446
Craig Matthew	70	69	69	67	275	1,446
Davidson Matyczuk	68	68	72	67	275	1,446
Mark Wilson	71	68	69	67	275	1,446
Ken Duke	68	68	71	69	276	1,185
Derek Gillespie	70	69	69	68	276	1,185
Scott Hend	70	69	68	69	276	1,185
Wes Martin	65	72	68	71	276	1,185
Stephen Woodard	67	68	72	69	276	1,185
Zane Zwemke	71	68	66	71	276	1,185

MTS Classic

Pine Ridge Golf Club, Winnipeg, Manitoba
Par 36-35–71; 6,251 yards

July 12-15
purse, C$150,000

	SCORES				TOTAL	MONEY
Kenneth Staton	70	68	64	64	266	C$24,000
Mark Slawter	67	67	71	62	267	14,400
Tony Carolan	68	66	69	66	269	9,000
Steve Alker	69	66	68	67	270	7,200
Drew Symons	69	66	64	72	271	6,000
Darren Griff	68	71	65	68	272	5,400
Jess Daley	71	68	66	68	273	4,500
Paul Devenport	70	66	71	66	273	4,500
Brian Mogg	71	71	67	64	273	4,500
Steve Scott	70	68	69	66	273	4,500
Jace Bugg	69	66	73	66	274	2,887.50
Dave Christensen	70	67	68	69	274	2,887.50
Bob Conrad	67	68	70	69	274	2,887.50
Jonn Drewery	72	65	70	67	274	2,887.50
Derek Gilchrist	68	70	72	64	274	2,887.50
Wes Martin	70	70	72	62	274	2,887.50
Zoltan Veress	76	66	68	64	274	2,887.50
Zane Zwemke	70	69	68	67	274	2,887.50
Octavio Gonzalez	66	73	68	68	275	1,850
Ty Krieger	68	73	68	66	275	1,850
Patrick Moore	68	69	70	68	275	1,850
Andrew Smeeth	72	67	66	70	275	1,850
Mario Tiziani	67	70	69	69	275	1,850
Kris Yardley	71	66	68	70	275	1,850
Greg Fleischer	68	67	67	74	276	1,446
Doug LaBelle	69	66	70	71	276	1,446
Edward Loar	69	70	65	72	276	1,446
Danny Mijovic	69	70	69	68	276	1,446
Mark Monroe	71	70	66	69	276	1,446
Liam Bond	70	69	70	68	277	1,204.50
Chris Greenwood	71	67	70	69	277	1,204.50
Chris Wall	71	71	67	68	277	1,204.50
Brennan Webb	70	70	69	68	277	1,204.50
Bryan Wright	69	71	68	69	277	1,204.50

Ontario Open Heritage Classic

Fort Williams Country Club, Thunder Bay, Ontario
Par 36-36–72; 6,670 yards

July 19-22
purse, C$150,000

	SCORES				TOTAL	MONEY
Craig Matthew	70	66	70	66	272	C$24,000
Bob Conrad	65	69	67	71	272	14,400
(Matthew defeated Conrad on second playoff hole.)						
Steve Alker	67	69	69	70	275	9,000
Jorge Corral	72	70	68	66	276	6,200
Scott Ford	72	67	68	69	276	6,200
Derek Gilchrist	68	69	70	69	276	6,200
Carlton Forrester	68	75	63	71	277	4,800
Alex Quiroz	68	71	70	68	277	4,800
Casey Brown	69	68	71	70	278	4,050
Wes Martin	68	70	67	73	278	4,050

	SCORES				TOTAL	MONEY
Roger Tambellini	67	66	70	75	278	4,050
Edward Loar	72	66	70	71	279	3,150
Rich Massey	69	68	67	75	279	3,150
Steve Woods	70	71	69	69	279	3,150
Jess Daley	70	69	68	73	280	2,475
Ryan Dillon	70	68	71	71	280	2,475
Doug McGuigan	75	67	65	73	280	2,475
Andrew Smeeth	66	67	70	77	280	2,475
Tim Balmer	67	70	69	75	281	1,975
John Douma	70	70	71	70	281	1,975
Davidson Matyczuk	74	67	69	71	281	1,975
Tony Carolan	70	69	69	74	282	1,687.50
Michael Chavez	71	70	69	72	282	1,687.50
Kenneth Staton	70	68	72	72	282	1,687.50
Brennan Webb	69	73	66	74	282	1,687.50
Andrew Barnes	67	72	69	75	283	1,297.50
Ian Doig	70	73	68	72	283	1,297.50
Todd Fanning	70	69	72	72	283	1,297.50
Philip Jonas	72	68	70	73	283	1,297.50
Darin Osborn	71	72	68	72	283	1,297.50
Brian Payne	70	69	72	72	283	1,297.50
Mikkel Reese	71	69	74	69	283	1,297.50
Steve Scott	69	71	70	73	283	1,297.50
Chris Wall	70	73	68	72	283	1,297.50

Giant Forest Products/NRCS Classic

Timberwolf Golf Club, Sudbury, Ontario
Par 36-36–72; 7,126 yards

July 26-29
purse, C$150,000

	SCORES				TOTAL	MONEY
Derek Gilchrist	68	72	67	63	270	C$24,000
Rich Massey	70	67	67	66	270	14,400
(Gilchrist defeated Massey on second playoff hole.)						
Jason Bohn	68	70	67	68	273	9,000
Doug McGuigan	69	61	71	73	274	7,200
Steve Scott	74	64	67	70	275	6,000
Jess Daley	69	67	72	68	276	5,400
Michael Kirk	66	70	71	70	277	4,950
Jace Bugg	74	66	68	70	278	4,500
Michael Harris	72	68	68	70	278	4,500
Tony Carolan	72	72	69	66	279	3,900
Kenneth Staton	68	67	71	73	279	3,900
Scott Ford	73	68	67	72	280	2,940
Darren Griff	71	72	70	67	280	2,940
Warren Schutte	72	69	68	71	280	2,940
Mario Tiziani	71	69	71	69	280	2,940
Zane Zwemke	72	69	67	72	280	2,940
Wes Martin	70	68	71	72	281	2,250
Grant Masson	69	72	71	69	281	2,250
Mark Slawter	68	74	69	70	281	2,250
Dave Christensen	70	70	73	69	282	1,837.50
Chris Locker	69	71	72	70	282	1,837.50
Eddie Maunder	72	70	69	71	282	1,837.50
Jamie Welder	69	70	72	71	282	1,837.50
Aaron Barber	71	73	71	68	283	1,452.86
Mike Belbin	69	73	72	69	283	1,452.86

	SCORES				TOTAL	MONEY
Bob Conrad	72	73	67	71	283	1,452.86
Todd Fanning	71	71	71	70	283	1,452.86
Patrick Moore	73	68	72	70	283	1,452.86
Darin Osborn	69	73	72	69	283	1,452.86
Mikkel Reese	73	66	74	70	283	1,452.86

Telus Open

Les Quatre Domaines, Montreal, Quebec
Par 36-36–72; 7,079 yards

August 9-12
purse, C$200,000

	SCORES				TOTAL	MONEY
Paul Devenport	66	71	65	67	269	C$32,000
Ken Duke	67	64	66	72	269	19,200
(Devenport defeated Duke on second playoff hole.)						
Doug LaBelle	69	69	63	70	271	12,000
Mikkel Reese	68	69	67	68	272	9,600
Chris Greenwood	71	69	65	68	273	8,000
Jace Bugg	65	72	63	74	274	6,666.67
Dave Christensen	66	66	71	71	274	6,666.67
Michael Kirk	67	68	70	69	274	6,666.67
Chris Anderson	70	71	70	64	275	5,600
Craig Matthew	66	71	68	70	275	5,600
Perry Parker	69	73	66	69	277	4,240
Brian Payne	68	72	66	71	277	4,240
Alex Quiroz	68	71	69	69	277	4,240
Jim Rutledge	70	71	68	68	277	4,240
Mario Tiziani	70	70	68	69	277	4,240
Scott Hend	63	77	69	69	278	3,200
Steve Pleis	71	67	69	71	278	3,200
Kenneth Staton	73	69	69	67	278	3,200
Jonn Drewery	72	71	67	69	279	2,575
Scott Ford	74	65	71	69	279	2,575
Grant Masson	67	73	68	71	279	2,575
Roger Tambellini	70	66	68	75	279	2,575
Aaron Barber	69	71	69	71	280	2,060
Ryan Dillon	68	71	68	73	280	2,060
Rich Massey	69	72	66	73	280	2,060
Mark Slawter	68	70	70	72	280	2,060
Brian Unk	69	70	70	71	280	2,060
Stephen Woodard	73	71	68	68	280	2,060
Dirk Ayers	72	70	69	70	281	1,635
Dave Branshaw	69	75	72	65	281	1,635
Octavio Gonzalez	72	68	72	69	281	1,635
Michael Harris	68	70	69	74	281	1,635
Eric Lippert	70	74	72	65	281	1,635
Chris Wall	68	70	74	69	281	1,635

Eagle Creek Classic

Eagle Creek Golf Club, Ottawa, Ontario
Par 36-36–72; 7,067 yards

August 16-19
purse, C$150,000

	SCORES				TOTAL	MONEY
Mark Slawter	64	66	68	68	266	C$24,000
Chris Greenwood	65	68	67	66	266	14,400
(Slawter defeated Greenwood on first playoff hole.)						
Rich Massey	69	63	69	67	268	9,000
Todd Fanning	67	66	65	71	269	6,600
Steve Woods	66	70	68	65	269	6,600
Craig Matthew	68	67	66	69	270	5,400
Ken Duke	69	69	70	64	272	4,950
Grant Masson	66	69	71	67	273	4,500
Steve Scott	65	71	65	72	273	4,500
Chris Anderson	63	74	69	68	274	3,900
Jonn Drewery	66	69	72	67	274	3,900
Tony Carolan	72	68	69	66	275	3,037.50
Ryan Dillon	70	70	70	65	275	3,037.50
Darren Griff	68	74	67	66	275	3,037.50
Zoltan Veress	70	70	68	67	275	3,037.50
Mike Belbin	68	67	70	71	276	2,325
Bryan DeCorso	70	67	69	70	276	2,325
Steve Pleis	69	70	66	71	276	2,325
Ray Stewart	70	68	69	69	276	2,325
Paul Devenport	67	70	72	68	277	1,875
Dave Pashko	71	70	74	62	277	1,875
Bryan Wright	70	71	67	69	277	1,875
Mark Brown	67	73	69	69	278	1,687.50
Chris Locker	68	71	71	68	278	1,687.50
Steve Alker	68	69	71	71	279	1,370.63
Jason Bohn	67	69	73	70	279	1,370.63
Derek Gilchrist	67	69	72	71	279	1,370.63
Andy Johnson	69	71	69	70	279	1,370.63
Michael Kirk	68	73	70	68	279	1,370.63
Doug LaBelle	69	74	70	66	279	1,370.63
Alex Quiroz	66	74	68	71	279	1,370.63
Mikkel Reese	63	75	72	69	279	1,370.63

Aliant Cup

Clovelly Golf Course, St. John's, Newfoundland
Par 36-36–72; 6,521 yards

August 23-26
purse, C$150,000

	SCORES				TOTAL	MONEY
Brian Payne	70	71	73	67	281	C$24,000
Jason Bohn	64	65	77	76	282	14,400
John Drewery	71	69	73	71	284	7,400
Davidson Matyczuk	71	71	71	71	284	7,400
Zoltan Veress	66	71	70	77	284	7,400
Rich Massey	68	69	74	74	285	5,400
Andrew Barnes	71	69	78	68	286	4,500
Craig Marseilles	68	67	74	77	286	4,500
Brian Unk	68	73	75	70	286	4,500
Steve Woods	71	69	69	77	286	4,500
Michael Harris	70	69	75	73	287	3,450

	SCORES				TOTAL	MONEY
Kenneth Staton	69	75	70	73	287	3,450
Chris Wall	72	65	78	72	287	3,450
Mark Brown	72	66	72	78	288	2,625
Jess Daley	69	69	81	69	288	2,625
Dave Levesque	71	68	78	71	288	2,625
Roger Tambellini	70	69	76	73	288	2,625
Derek Gilchrist	69	71	79	70	289	2,175
Drew Scott	71	70	74	74	289	2,175
Dave Christensen	67	69	79	75	290	1,762.50
Octavio Gonzalez	76	68	71	75	290	1,762.50
Edward Loar	75	65	78	72	290	1,762.50
Chris Locker	70	72	75	73	290	1,762.50
Todd Pence	68	73	79	70	290	1,762.50
Bryan Wright	66	70	77	77	290	1,762.50
Brett Bingham	67	71	77	76	291	1,440
Mark Slawter	71	68	77	75	291	1,440
Zane Zwemke	70	70	78	73	291	1,440
Paul Devenport	69	72	74	77	292	1,246.50
Kent Fukushima	66	71	77	78	292	1,246.50
Michael Kirk	71	68	80	73	292	1,246.50
Bryan Saltus	77	67	77	71	292	1,246.50
Brett Taylor	74	70	76	72	292	1,246.50

Casino de Charlevoix Cup

Le Manoir Richelieu Golf Club, Pointe-au-Pic, Quebec   August 30-September 2
Par 71; 6,225 yards   purse, C$100,000

FIRST DAY
Canadian Tour

Kenneth Staton and Steve Woods defeated Andrew Barnes and Jorge Corral, 2 and 1.
Jonn Drewery and Zoltan Veress defeated Jace Bugg and Jim Almand, 1 up.
Davidson Matyczuk and Blair Piercy defeated Chris Greenwood and Dean Kennedy, 19 holes.
Eddy Lee and Chris Wall defeated Danny Mijovic and Doug McGuigan, 4 and 3.
Duane Bock and Rich Massey defeated Wes Martin and Dave Pashko, 3 and 2.
Darren Griff and Drew Symons defeated Brian Unk and Brian Payne, 19 holes.
Dave Christensen and Mikkel Reese defeated Mark Brown and David Faught, 3 and 2.
Eddie Maunder and Michael Harris defeated Scott Ford and Rob Johnson, 1 up.

Quebec Tour

Carl Desjardins and Serge Thivierge defeated Earl Lasalle and Daniel Levasseur.
Louis Bourgeois and Eric Laporte defeated Pierre-Luc Bergeron and Patrick Loiselle, 4 and 3.
Pete Bousquet and Jean-Louis Lamarre defeated Tom Bissegger and Jack Bissegger, 6 and 4.
Marc Girouard and Kevin Senecal defeated Martin Brunet and Erik Laframboise, 6 and 5.
Dave Levesque and Michel Hins defeated Michel Lapointe and Jean-Marc Tourangeau, 4 and 3.
Remi Bouchard and Chris Learmonth defeated Jean-Yves Gagnon and Nicolas Huot, 6 and 5.
Daniel Boily and Martin Genest defeated Luc Boisvert and Daniel Talbot, 5 and 4.
Jean Chatelain and Martin Plante defeated Jerome Blais and Jason Morin, 1 up.

(Each losing team received C$1,000.)

SECOND DAY
Canadian Tour

Griff and Symons defeated Christensen and Reese.
Drewery and Veress defeated Lee and Wall.
Bock and Massey defeated Maunder and Harris.
Matyczuk and Piercy defeated Staton and Woods.

Quebec Tour

Bourgeois and Laporte defeated Boily and Genest.
Girouard and Senecal defeated Bouchard and Learmonth.
Chatelain and Plante defeated Levesque and Michel Hins.
Bousquet and Lamarre defeated Desjardins and Serge Thivierge.

(Each losing team received C$2,000.)

QUARTER-FINALS

Matyczuk and Piercy defeated Massey and Bock, 2 and 1.
Griff and Symons defeated Drewery and Veress, 2 and 1.
Bousquet and Lamarre defeated Chatelain and Plante, 5 and 4.
Girouard and Senecal defeated Bourgeois and Laporte, 19 holes.

(Each losing team received C$4,000.)

SEMI-FINALS

Griff and Symons defeated Matyczuk and Piercy, 1 up.
Bousquet and Lamarre defeated Girouard and Senecal, 21 holes.

(Each losing team received C$8,000.)

FINAL

Griff and Symons defeated Bousquet and Lamarre, 19 holes.

(Griff and Symons received C$20,000; Bousquet and Lamarre received C$16,000.)

Bayer Championship

Huron Oaks Golf Course, Sarnia, Ontario
Par 35-36–71; 6,407 yards

September 13-16
purse, C$200,000

	SCORES				TOTAL	MONEY
Jason Bohn	68	71	63	58	260	C$32,000
Jace Bugg	66	67	67	62	262	19,200
Steve Scott	68	63	68	66	265	12,000
Dave Christensen	70	69	65	62	266	9,600
David Hearn	71	66	64	67	268	7,600
Steve Pleis	64	68	68	68	268	7,600
Steve Alker	66	70	71	62	269	5,800
Rich Massey	66	67	69	67	269	5,800
Craig Matthew	68	70	64	67	269	5,800
Kenneth Staton	68	67	66	68	269	5,800
Chris Wall	72	69	67	61	269	5,800
Aaron Barber	65	70	66	69	270	4,050
Jorge Corral	70	65	70	65	270	4,050
Norm Jarvis	68	67	66	69	270	4,050

	SCORES				TOTAL	MONEY
Dave Pashko	64	70	66	70	270	4,050
Rob Johnson	62	72	67	70	271	3,300
Andrew Smeeth	71	67	67	66	271	3,300
Brett Bingham	68	66	73	65	272	2,660
Derek Gillespie	67	71	65	69	272	2,660
Joel Hendry	69	69	65	69	272	2,660
Doug McGuigan	71	66	69	66	272	2,660
Brian Unk	69	72	64	67	272	2,660
David Faught	68	68	69	68	273	2,020
David Mathis	68	67	67	71	273	2,020
Joe McCormick	70	66	67	70	273	2,020
Bryn Parry	69	70	67	67	273	2,020
Brian Payne	66	69	70	68	273	2,020
Martin Price	69	71	66	67	273	2,020
Mario Tiziani	67	69	70	67	273	2,020
Wes Heffernan	65	74	68	67	274	1,660
Regan Lee	68	69	68	69	274	1,660
Zoltan Veress	67	70	71	66	274	1,660

Niagara Classic

Whirlpool Golf Club, Niagara Falls, Ontario
Par 36-36–72; 7,217 yards

September 22-23
purse, C$100,000

	SCORES		TOTAL	MONEY
Kenneth Staton	67	67	134	C$18,000
Nathan Green	66	69	135	12,000
Doug McGuigan	68	68	136	9,000
Jace Bugg	69	68	137	6,400
Dave Christensen	70	68	138	3,750
Jonn Drewery	66	72	138	3,750
Rich Massey	70	68	138	3,750
Craig Matthew	70	68	138	3,750
Paul Devenport	69	70	139	3,000
Darren Griff	70	69	139	3,000
Mario Tiziani	69	70	139	3,000
Jason Bohn	71	69	140	2,400
Steve Scott	71	69	140	2,400
Brian Unk	69	71	140	2,400
Mikkel Reese	70	71	141	2,100
Aaron Barber	73	69	142	1,850
Ken Duke	71	71	142	1,850
Derek Gilchrist	74	68	142	1,850
Brian Payne	69	73	142	1,850
Patrick Moore	71	72	143	1,550
Zoltan Veress	73	70	143	1,550
Chris Greenwood	68	76	144	1,375
Davidson Matyczuk	70	74	144	1,375
David Faught	75	70	145	1,225
Scott Ford	74	71	145	1,225
Derek Gillespie	72	73	145	1,225
Mark Slawter	72	73	145	1,225
Steve Woods	76	71	147	1,100
Todd Fanning	71	77	148	1,050

South American Tour

Rabobank Chile Masters

Brisas de Chicureo Golf Club, Santiago, Chile
Par 35-35–70; 6,733 yards

January 25-28
purse, US$100,000

	SCORES				TOTAL	MONEY
Alexandre Rocha	65	69	67	64	265	US$18,000
Dan Olsen	65	66	69	67	267	9,700
Angel Franco	66	66	68	67	267	9,700
Felipe Aguilar	66	68	72	66	272	6,400
Jesus Amaya	73	69	69	66	277	4,266.66
Donald Donahue	71	64	74	68	277	4,266.66
Raul Fretes	70	64	72	71	277	4,266.66
Rafael Gomez	73	67	71	68	279	2,500
Victor Leoni	70	71	70	68	279	2,500
Mauricio Molina	70	69	70	70	279	2,500
Guillermo Encina	68	70	70	71	279	2,500
Marco Ruiz	70	69	74	67	280	1,850
Alex Balicki	69	69	72	70	280	1,850
Rigoberto Velazquez	66	75	69	70	280	1,850
Mark Monroe	69	69	70	72	280	1,850
Alan McDonald	70	68	76	67	281	1,550
Richard Terga	70	70	68	73	281	1,550
Ramon Franco	74	72	69	67	282	1,250
Esteban Isasi	70	70	74	68	282	1,250
Jeffrey Peck	71	72	70	69	282	1,250
Benjamin Finley	71	66	72	73	282	1,250
Alvaro Ortiz	69	78	69	67	283	990
Travis Perkins	66	75	69	73	283	990
Damian Hale	69	69	74	72	284	900
Fredrick Mansson	71	71	70	72	284	900
*Hugo Leon	70	71	72	72	285	
Cristian Leon	68	72	73	73	286	800
David Schuster	69	72	72	73	286	800
*Gabriel Tumani	72	70	71	73	286	
Pedro Martinez	70	74	69	73	286	800

Mexico Masters

Atlas Country Club, Guadalajara, Mexico
Par 36-36–72; 7,112 yards

February 8-11
purse, US$100,000

	SCORES				TOTAL	MONEY
Raul Fretes	68	64	70	74	276	US$18,000
Matt Kuchar	72	66	67	71	276	11,400
(Fretes defeated Kuchar on fifth playoff hole.)						
Adam Armagost	70	66	70	71	277	8,000
Jorge Perez	72	69	71	67	279	5,800
Oscar Serna	71	72	68	68	279	5,800
Alex Balicki	75	71	69	67	282	3,800

	SCORES				TOTAL	MONEY
Travis Perkins	68	66	73	75	282	3,800
Angel Franco	70	73	71	70	284	2,600
Cesar Perez	78	68	68	70	284	2,600
Miguel Suarez	73	70	70	71	284	2,600
Octavio Gonzalez	76	69	67	73	285	2,200
Alejandro Quiroz	73	72	71	70	286	1,950
Pedro Martinez	68	69	74	75	286	1,950
Marco Ruiz	72	72	71	72	287	1,800
Paul Antenucci	71	72	73	72	288	1,550
Grant Masson	71	76	68	73	288	1,550
Jose Trauwitz	72	72	70	74	288	1,550
Alexis Noudeu	71	72	70	75	288	1,550
Dan Olsen	74	71	73	71	289	1,200
Jesus Amaya	72	75	68	74	289	1,200
Juan Brito	68	72	71	78	289	1,200
Alan McDonald	74	70	74	72	290	1,020
Damian Hale	74	71	76	70	291	900
Alvaro Ortiz	76	71	73	71	291	900
Bryant Mackellar	70	73	75	73	291	900
Eduardo Pesenti	72	74	69	76	291	900
Miguel Martinez	71	75	75	71	292	780
David Deanda	72	72	75	73	292	780
Rafael Alarcon	74	73	75	71	293	690
Jesus Torres	74	72	75	72	293	690
Sixto Torres	73	74	73	73	293	690
Alexandre Rocha	76	70	73	74	293	690
Rafael Gomez	75	72	71	75	293	690
Martin Stanovich	70	76	71	76	293	690

PGA Championship of Latin America

Isla Navidad Country Club, Manzanillo, Mexico
Par 36-36—72; 6,943 yards

February 15-18
purse, US$200,000

	SCORES				TOTAL	MONEY
Angel Romero	66	70	70	63	269	US$36,000
Jose Trauwitz	71	62	71	71	275	22,800
Dave Bishop	72	71	66	67	276	14,400
Adam Armagost	68	70	67	71	276	14,400
Donald Donahue	71	72	70	74	277	8,533.33
Ramon Franco	73	69	69	66	277	8,533.33
Octavio Gonzalez	74	66	69	68	277	8,533.33
Ron Philo	69	75	66	68	278	5,600
Paul Antenucci	74	66	69	70	279	5,200
Eduardo Pesenti	73	69	70	68	280	4,120
Richard Terga	72	70	69	69	280	4,120
Alejandro Quiroz	70	72	69	69	280	4,120
Gregory Boyette	70	73	68	69	280	4,120
Jesus Amaya	69	69	72	70	280	4,120
Jaime Gomez	68	78	71	64	281	3,100
Angel Franco	71	74	69	67	281	3,100
Rob Corcoran	70	75	67	69	281	3,100
Manuel Inman	71	70	70	70	281	3,100
Grant Masson	74	72	71	65	282	2,232
Warren Jurkowitz	72	71	70	69	282	2,232
Alex Balicki	69	70	71	72	282	2,232
Matt Kuchar	70	71	69	72	282	2,232

	SCORES				TOTAL	MONEY
Carlos Pelaez	68	71	68	75	282	2,232
Jorge Perez	73	71	71	68	283	1,720
Raul Fretes	76	70	69	68	283	1,720
Pedro Martinez	70	75	68	70	283	1,720
Marco Ruiz	71	71	70	71	283	1,720
Travis Perkins	75	71	72	66	284	1,420
Shannon Sykora	74	70	71	69	284	1,420
Martin Stanovich	73	72	69	70	284	1,420
Jesus Torres	72	73	69	70	284	1,420
Rafael Alarcon	71	70	72	71	284	1,420
Damian Hale	70	70	69	75	284	1,420

Sao Paulo Brazil Open

Sao Paulo Golf Club, Sao Paulo, Brazil
Par 35-36–71; 6,646 yards
(Shortened to 54 holes and extended to Monday — rain.)

March 22-26
purse, £470,000

	SCORES			TOTAL	MONEY
Darren Fichardt	67	61	67	195	£78,242.36
Richard Johnson	68	67	75	200	35,006.68
Jose Coceres	68	64	68	200	35,006.68
Brett Rumford	66	65	69	200	35,006.68
Raphael Jacquelin	66	70	65	201	18,167.88
Nic Henning	70	64	67	201	18,167.88
Anthony Wall	71	67	64	202	14,083.63
Simon Hurley	69	69	65	203	10,069.79
Neil Cheetham	69	67	67	203	10,069.79
Matthew Blackey	67	68	68	203	10,069.79
Christopher Hanell	68	65	70	203	10,069.79
Robin Byrd	68	69	67	204	8,074.61
Gustavo Rojas	67	68	70	205	7,370.43
Daren Lee	68	68	69	205	7,370.43
Philip Walton	69	66	71	206	6,347.02
Kenneth Ferrie	70	67	69	206	6,347.02
Thomas Gogele	70	67	69	206	6,347.02
Massimo Florioli	69	68	69	206	6,347.02
Tomas Jesus Munoz	71	66	69	206	6,347.02
Peter Fowler	70	70	67	207	5,170.70
Warren Bennett	70	68	69	207	5,170.70
Carlos Rodiles	69	71	67	207	5,170.70
Eduardo Pesenti	71	69	67	207	5,170.70
Diego Borrego	68	67	72	207	5,170.70
Benoit Teilleria	70	68	69	207	5,170.70
Alexandre Rocha	74	69	64	207	5,170.70
Thomas Levet	67	71	70	208	4,389.40
Per Nyman	65	73	70	208	4,389.40
Jorge Berendt	75	66	67	208	4,389.40
Angel Romero	70	69	69	208	4,389.40
Mark Roe	67	70	72	209	3,552.20
Jesus Amaya	69	70	70	209	3,552.20
Andrew Beal	68	73	68	209	3,552.20
Olle Karlsson	70	71	68	209	3,552.20
Christophe Pottier	72	71	66	209	3,552.20
Johan Skold	70	65	74	209	3,552.20
Erol Simsek	67	71	71	209	3,552.20
Hank Kuehne	67	69	73	209	3,552.20

	SCORES			TOTAL	MONEY
Carl Pettersson	74	69	66	209	3,552.20
Bradford Vaughan	72	67	71	210	2,769.78
Christophe Ravetto	69	69	72	210	2,769.78
Henrik Stenson	75	67	68	210	2,769.78
Joakim Haeggman	70	70	70	210	2,769.78
Francisco Cea	70	69	71	210	2,769.78
Jose Aderbal	67	71	72	210	2,769.78
Adam Armagost	69	71	70	210	2,769.78
Marten Olander	68	70	73	211	2,112.54
Stephen Scahill	73	68	70	211	2,112.54
Paul Streeter	71	68	72	211	2,112.54
Andrew Raitt	73	67	71	211	2,112.54
Gary Clark	69	71	71	211	2,112.54
Mauricio Molina	70	69	72	211	2,112.54
Shannon Sykora	73	69	69	211	2,112.54
Gregory Havret	73	66	73	212	1,596.14
Ricardo Gonzalez	70	67	75	212	1,596.14
Han Lee	71	68	73	212	1,596.14
Rafael Barcellos	75	65	72	212	1,596.14
Santiago Luna	67	72	74	213	1,197.11
Marc Pendaries	69	73	71	213	1,197.11
Felix Lubenau	73	69	71	213	1,197.11
Scott Drummond	70	73	70	213	1,197.11
Henrik Bjornstad	71	68	74	213	1,197.11
Paul Eales	72	71	70	213	1,197.11
Marcello Santi	73	70	70	213	1,197.11
Charles Challen	69	74	70	213	1,197.11
Rodolfo Gonzalez	71	72	70	213	1,197.11
Sebastian Fernandez	72	71	70	213	1,197.11
Van Phillips	75	68	71	214	818.98
Simon Khan	73	70	71	214	818.98
Michael Jonzon	68	69	77	214	818.98
Marco Bernardini	68	70	76	214	818.98
Gustavo Acosta	70	73	71	214	818.98
Jeremy Robinson	72	71	72	215	698.55
Paul Dwyer	70	69	76	215	698.55
Erik Andersson	69	73	73	215	698.55
Hennie Otto	72	69	75	216	694.79
Jose Priscilo Diniz	73	70	74	217	692.91
Peter Hanson	72	71	75	218	690.10
Sergio Brasil	72	70	76	218	690.10

Open de Argentina

Jockey Club, Red Course, Buenos Aires, Argentina
Par 35-35–70; 6,646 yards

March 29-April 1
purse, US$700,000

	SCORES				TOTAL	MONEY
Angel Cabrera	67	65	69	67	268	£81,626.08
Carl Pettersson	65	69	67	69	270	54,415.05
Graeme Storm	68	66	69	69	272	30,660.50
Matthew Blackey	66	70	71	67	274	19,273.02
Mark Mouland	69	68	69	68	274	19,273.02
Henrik Bjornstad	70	70	66	68	274	19,273.02
Costantino Rocca	71	67	65	71	274	19,273.02
Nic Henning	70	69	71	65	275	10,089.56
Olle Karlsson	65	69	72	69	275	10,089.56

	SCORES				TOTAL	MONEY
Vicente Fernandez	69	72	65	69	275	10,089.56
Daren Lee	72	66	67	70	275	10,089.56
Hennie Otto	70	67	68	70	275	10,089.56
Ruben Alvarez	71	72	66	67	276	7,219.42
Christopher Hanell	70	69	69	68	276	7,219.42
Angel Franco	64	72	71	69	276	7,219.42
Anthony Wall	68	70	68	70	276	7,219.42
Ricardo Gonzalez	70	64	69	73	276	7,219.42
Thomas Levet	69	70	70	68	277	5,897.01
Paul Eales	69	69	70	69	277	5,897.01
Jose Manuel Lara	65	71	71	70	277	5,897.01
*Matias Anselmo	73	64	70	70	277	
Eduardo Romero	70	66	69	72	277	5,897.01
Tomas Jesus Munoz	69	66	67	75	277	5,897.01
Massimo Florioli	71	68	70	69	278	5,314.16
Simon Hurley	73	64	70	71	278	5,314.16
Martin Lonardi	72	70	73	64	279	4,506.02
Miguel Fernandez	73	69	71	66	279	4,506.02
Diego Borrego	69	72	71	67	279	4,506.02
Mikael Lundberg	66	72	72	69	279	4,506.02
Darren Fichardt	68	72	70	69	279	4,506.02
Francisco Cea	69	70	70	70	279	4,506.02
Johan Skold	73	68	66	72	279	4,506.02
Julio Zapata	69	69	68	73	279	4,506.02
Craig Hainline	71	70	70	69	280	3,624.41
Erol Simsek	65	71	71	73	280	3,624.41
Dave Bishop	67	71	69	73	280	3,624.41
Jorge Berendt	70	65	69	76	280	3,624.41
Mauricio Molina	70	69	66	75	280	3,624.41
Mark Roe	73	65	75	68	281	3,036.67
Nicolas Colsaerts	75	67	71	68	281	3,036.67
Gustavo Rojas	72	70	69	70	281	3,036.67
Van Phillips	71	71	69	70	281	3,036.67
John Wade	73	67	70	71	281	3,036.67
Richard Johnson	65	71	73	72	281	3,036.67
Stephen Scahill	69	67	73	72	281	3,036.67
Horacio Carbonetti	71	67	70	73	281	3,036.67
Ariel Licera	67	71	76	68	282	2,253.01
Jonathan Lomas	70	72	72	68	282	2,253.01
Marcello Santi	72	69	72	69	282	2,253.01
Jesus Amaya	71	70	70	71	282	2,253.01
Simon Hurd	72	69	70	71	282	2,253.01
Alexandre Rocha	74	68	69	71	282	2,253.01
Andrew Raitt	70	68	70	74	282	2,253.01
Raphael Jacquelin	72	71	65	74	282	2,253.01
Dennis Edlund	71	70	72	70	283	1,626.09
Hank Kuehne	72	71	69	71	283	1,626.09
Ramon Franco	68	74	69	72	283	1,626.09
Michael Jonzon	72	67	71	73	283	1,626.09
Gary Clark	69	69	70	75	283	1,626.09
Carlos Rodiles	73	67	75	69	284	1,297.93
Gregory Havret	72	70	72	70	284	1,297.93
Kenneth Ferrie	70	72	71	71	284	1,297.93
Simon Khan	70	71	71	72	284	1,297.93
Roberto Coceres	70	71	71	72	284	1,297.93
Ariel Canete	73	65	72	74	284	1,297.93
Eduardo Argiro	69	70	75	71	285	1,102.01
Olivier Edmond	70	73	69	73	285	1,102.01
Donald Donahue	74	69	76	67	286	1,004.06

	SCORES				TOTAL	MONEY
Thomas Gogele	75	68	67	76	286	1,004.06
Cesar Monasterio	74	66	75	72	287	855.89
Damian Hale	72	71	72	72	287	855.89
Esteban Isasi	72	69	71	75	287	855.89
Tim Hegna	73	70	73	72	288	732.59
Steven Richardson	72	71	72	74	289	730.72
Fredrik Andersson	69	74	77	70	290	727.91
Christian Cevaer	69	72	76	73	290	727.91
Andrew Beal	72	71	76	72	291	724.16
Adan Sowa	72	71	75	73	291	724.16
*Fernando Chiesa	70	73	72	76	291	
Simon Dyson	72	71	75	74	292	721.35
Philip Walton	72	70	79	73	294	719.47

Movilnet Venezuela Open

Lagunita Golf Club, Caracas, Venezuela
Par 35-35–70; 6,842 yards

November 15-18
purse, US$120,000

	SCORES				TOTAL	MONEY
Rafael Alarcon	71	68	66	63	268	US$21,600
Alexandre Rocha	64	72	71	62	269	13,680
Rafael Gomez	68	67	66	69	270	9,600
Gustavo Acosta	71	66	66	69	272	6,960
Jon Levitt	71	67	65	69	272	6,960
Roberto Coceres	69	66	71	68	274	5,040
Mauricio Molina	69	65	73	68	275	3,360
Todd Sapere	66	69	71	69	275	3,360
Rodolfo Gonzalez	70	67	68	70	275	3,360
Donald Donahue	67	71	67	70	275	3,360
*Jonathan Vegas	68	74	69	65	276	
Rigoberto Velazquez	68	68	66	74	276	2,640
Steve Woods	67	67	75	68	277	2,400
Landry Mahan	73	69	69	67	278	2,100
Fredrik Mansson	68	69	71	70	278	2,100
Sean Quinlivan	67	69	70	72	278	2,100
Carlos Larrain	67	66	72	73	278	2,100
Pablo Del Grosso	70	70	71	68	279	1,740
Alex Balicki	69	69	70	71	279	1,740
Adam Adams	72	69	72	67	280	1,386
Ramon Franco	71	72	69	68	280	1,386
Federico Sauce	73	69	69	69	280	1,386
Markus Westerberg	71	72	68	69	280	1,386
Bob Jacobson	73	70	69	69	281	1,152
Victor Leoni	73	71	68	70	282	988
Mauricio Asbun	67	72	72	71	282	988
Pedro Martinez	69	70	72	71	282	988
Hiroshi Matsuo	71	70	69	72	282	988
Shannon Sykora	73	70	67	72	282	988
Brian Cooper	69	70	70	73	282	988

Litoral Open

Rosario Golf Club, Rosario, Argentina
Par 35-36–71; 6,519 yards

November 22-25
purse, US$60,000

	SCORES				TOTAL	MONEY
Marco Ruiz	71	72	69	66	278	US$12,600
Ariel Canete	72	73	66	67	278	5,425
Rafael Gomez	71	71	67	69	278	5,425
Gustavo Acosta	71	71	66	70	278	5,425
Rodolfo Gonzalez	67	69	68	74	278	5,425
(Ruiz won in playoff.)						
Angel Cabrera	73	69	71	66	279	2,275
Sebastian Fernandez	68	68	74	69	279	2,275
Hiroshi Matsuo	67	71	70	71	279	2,275
Ricardo Gonzalez	69	70	69	71	279	2,275
Adam Armagost	72	67	71	70	280	1,680
Cesar Monasterio	69	68	72	72	281	1,540
Daniel Nunez	69	72	72	69	282	1,330
Mark Monroe	67	72	72	71	282	1,330
Julio Zapata	70	72	68	72	282	1,330
Pablo Del Grosso	71	73	72	67	283	1,155
Landry Mahan	70	69	72	72	283	1,155
Mauricio Molina	70	73	73	68	284	980
Adan Sowa	71	73	70	70	284	980
Amalio Britez	71	67	72	74	284	980
Gustavo Piovano	78	67	71	70	286	749
Will Burnitz	70	71	73	72	286	749
Fabian Gomez	74	70	70	72	286	749
Jose Cantero	70	68	75	73	286	749
Roberto Coceres	70	72	72	73	287	616
Nicolas Sedler	74	66	72	75	287	616
Martin Lonardi	70	70	70	77	287	616
Pablo Alderete	70	69	76	73	288	536.66
Miguel Rodriguez	69	75	71	73	288	536.66
Markus Westerberg	69	73	70	76	288	536.66
Victor Leoni	75	69	77	68	289	476
Ariel Licera	75	70	74	70	289	476
Jon Levitt	73	72	74	70	289	476
Eduardo Romero	73	70	75	71	289	476
Miguel Fernandez	71	71	75	72	289	476

Chevrolet Brazil Open

Sao Paulo Golf Club, Sao Paulo, Brazil
Par 35-36–71; 6,450 yards

November 29-December 2
purse, US$110,000

	SCORES				TOTAL	MONEY
Carlos Franco	69	67	70	67	273	US$18,000
Miguel Guzman	70	66	71	70	277	11,400
Gustavo Acosta	68	70	72	68	278	7,200
Carlos Dluhosch	71	68	68	71	278	7,200
Daniel Nunez	67	72	69	71	279	5,200
Ramon Franco	67	72	71	70	280	3,250
Chris Moody	68	73	69	70	280	3,250
Tim Hegna	69	67	73	71	280	3,250
Pedro Martinez	68	69	72	71	280	3,250
Juan Abbate	69	69	75	68	281	2,200

		SCORES			TOTAL	MONEY
Hiroshi Matsuo	68	69	71	73	281	2,200
Bob Jacobson	65	68	70	78	281	2,200
Donald Donahue	69	67	75	71	282	1,850
Rafael Barcellos	69	70	71	72	282	1,850
Eric Giraud	75	68	71	69	283	1,550
Angel Romero	65	70	77	71	283	1,550
Alexandre Rocha	68	69	73	73	283	1,550
Rafael Gonzalez	75	68	66	74	283	1,550
Markus Westerberg	69	73	74	68	284	1,300
Felizardo Ruberlei	74	68	75	68	285	1,040
Shannon Sykora	66	76	75	68	285	1,040
Joao Corteiz	70	72	73	70	285	1,040
Jim Johnson	68	73	72	72	285	1,040
Pablo Del Grosso	68	74	70	73	285	1,040
Jonas Runnquist	70	71	76	69	286	804
Luiz Martins	72	69	74	71	286	804
Jose Aderbal	70	72	71	73	286	804
Erik Andersson	71	69	72	74	286	804
Landry Mahan	71	70	70	75	286	804
Jesus Amaya	71	71	77	68	287	700
Esteban Isasi	71	69	78	69	287	700
Mauricio Asbun	73	71	72	71	287	700
*Rodrigo Lacerda	70	68	70	79	287	700

Telefonica Masters Tournament

Olivos Golf Club, Buenos Aires, Argentina
Par 36-35–71; 6,705 yards

December 6-9
purse, US$100,000

		SCORES			TOTAL	MONEY
Angel Cabrera	66	65	72	69	272	US$12,600
Eduardo Romero	68	68	68	70	274	7,980
Vicente Fernandez	66	71	70	70	277	5,600
Jorge Berendt	67	72	70	69	278	4,060
Carlos Franco	68	69	67	74	278	4,060
Roberto Coceres	69	74	68	68	279	2,940
Gustavo Rojas	70	71	72	67	280	2,053.33
Marco Ruiz	69	68	71	72	280	2,053.33
Hiroshi Matsuo	65	73	69	73	280	2,053.33
Jean Yvet	73	70	73	66	282	1,487.50
Landry Mahan	65	73	73	71	282	1,487.50
Rafael Gomez	66	72	73	71	282	1,487.50
Brian Payne	72	68	69	73	282	1,487.50
Scott Dunlap	69	73	70	72	284	1,225
Martin Lonardi	69	70	70	75	284	1,225
Mauricio Molina	69	74	74	69	286	980
Rodolfo Gonzalez	72	72	73	69	286	980
Damian Hale	70	72	74	70	286	980
Daniel Vancsik	74	70	72	70	286	980
Ariel Canete	70	70	71	75	286	980
Miguel Guzman	68	74	77	68	287	770
Jose Cantero	68	75	76	69	288	646.80
Miguel Fernandez	72	72	75	69	288	646.80
Cesar Monasterio	69	75	74	70	288	646.80
Cesar Costilla	71	73	73	71	288	646.80
Bob Jacobson	72	71	73	72	288	646.80
Alex Balicki	68	74	77	70	289	528.50

	SCORES				TOTAL	MONEY
Sean Quinlivan	71	73	72	73	289	528.50
Alberto Giannone	75	70	71	73	289	528.50
Jim Johnson	72	69	72	76	289	528.50

Baviera Paraguay Open

Paraguay Yacht & Golf Club, Asuncion, Paraguay   December 13-16
Par 37-34–71; 6,534 yards   purse, US$50,000

	SCORES				TOTAL	MONEY
Raul Fretes	67	68	73	71	279	US$9,000
Ruberlei Felizardo	72	64	74	70	280	5,700
Angel Franco	71	71	70	70	282	4,000
Marco Ruiz	68	66	75	74	283	2,900
David Schuster	69	68	71	75	283	2,900
Pablo Del Grosso	73	71	70	70	284	2,100
Landry Mahan	73	69	74	69	285	1,466.66
Hector Ortega	71	72	73	69	285	1,466.66
Sean Quinlivan	74	68	70	73	285	1,466.66
Bob Jacobson	73	69	73	71	286	1,150
Markus Westerberg	75	71	68	72	286	1,150
*Fabrizio Zanotti	72	68	75	72	287	
Alan McDonald	69	69	73	76	287	1,000
Damian Halex	71	70	74	73	288	1,000
Jose Trauwitzx	71	73	75	70	289	1,000
Pedro Martinez	73	69	76	71	289	1,000
Brooks Roberts	71	72	71	75	289	1,000
Miguel Guzman	70	75	75	70	290	650
Ramon Franco	74	70	74	72	290	650
Eladio Franco	72	76	69	73	290	650
Daniel Barbetti	71	71	70	78	290	650
Esteban Isasi	67	69	72	82	290	650
Eric Giraudx	71	76	75	69	291	650
Brian De Alexandris	75	71	74	71	291	650
Jim Johnson	73	73	72	73	291	650
Carlos Franco	73	72	71	75	291	650
Gustavo Acosta	71	70	71	79	291	650
Marvin King	77	71	71	73	292	383.33
Victor Leoni	70	74	74	74	292	383.33
Miguel Fernandez	73	73	68	78	292	383.33

European Tours

Alfred Dunhill Championship
See African Tours chapter.

Mercedes-Benz South African Open
See African Tours chapter.

Heineken Classic
See Australasian Tour chapter.

Greg Norman Holden International
See Australasian Tour chapter.

Carlsberg Malaysian Open
See Asia/Japan Tours chapter.

Caltex Singapore Masters
See Asia/Japan Tours chapter.

Dubai Desert Classic

Emirates Golf Club, Dubai, United Arab Emirates
Par 35-37–72; 7,127 yards

March 1-4
purse, £1,000,000

	SCORES				TOTAL	MONEY
Thomas Bjorn	64	66	67	69	266	£166,660
Tiger Woods	64	64	68	72	268	86,855
Padraig Harrington	66	69	64	69	268	86,855
Ian Woosnam	69	68	64	69	270	46,200
Mathias Gronberg	68	68	66	68	270	46,200
Jeev Milkha Singh	67	66	67	71	271	32,500
Brian Davis	69	65	67	70	271	32,500
Trevor Immelman	66	73	68	65	272	25,000
Elliot Boult	69	69	70	65	273	20,266.67
Paul McGinley	70	64	67	72	273	20,266.67
Angel Cabrera	66	70	65	72	273	20,266.67
Eamonn Darcy	68	67	70	69	274	15,480
Jean-Francois Remesy	68	68	68	70	274	15,480
Anders Hansen	70	66	67	71	274	15,480
Richard Green	67	73	67	67	274	15,480
Greg Owen	70	68	67	69	274	15,480
Andrew Oldcorn	71	66	68	70	275	12,700
David Lynn	70	71	66	68	275	12,700
Lee Westwood	66	70	69	70	275	12,700
Retief Goosen	70	68	67	70	275	12,700
Gary Emerson	70	67	65	74	276	10,700
Colin Montgomerie	69	70	65	72	276	10,700
Russell Claydon	67	70	71	68	276	10,700
Phillip Price	66	72	69	69	276	10,700
Ricardo Gonzalez	71	67	69	69	276	10,700

	SCORES				TOTAL	MONEY
Paul Lawrie	70	67	71	68	276	10,700
John Bickerton	68	67	70	71	276	10,700
Jamie Spence	72	66	68	71	277	8,900
Soren Hansen	69	69	68	71	277	8,900
Rolf Muntz	71	69	66	71	277	8,900
Dean Robertson	69	68	69	71	277	8,900
Thongchai Jaidee	73	67	68	69	277	8,900
Anders Forsbrand	71	67	72	68	278	7,010
Tony Johnstone	71	69	63	75	278	7,010
Warren Bennett	70	69	69	70	278	7,010
Sven Struver	71	68	68	71	278	7,010
John Senden	68	71	67	72	278	7,010
Tjaart van der Walt	68	72	70	68	278	7,010
Nicolas Colsaerts	70	70	65	73	278	7,010
Jarrod Moseley	69	70	70	69	278	7,010
Andrew Coltart	70	69	70	69	278	7,010
Yeh Wei-tze	70	70	67	71	278	7,010
Des Smyth	69	69	68	73	279	5,600
David Howell	69	69	72	69	279	5,600
Carl Suneson	69	72	65	73	279	5,600
Tobias Dier	68	72	67	72	279	5,600
Ignacio Garrido	68	73	67	72	280	4,800
Roger Wessels	70	70	70	70	280	4,800
Bradley Dredge	70	65	73	72	280	4,800
Robert Coles	68	70	68	74	280	4,800
Zhang Lian-wei	70	69	70	72	281	4,000
Carlos Rodiles	67	70	72	72	281	4,000
Raymond Russell	68	69	72	72	281	4,000
Marco Bernardini	70	70	70	71	281	4,000
Steve Webster	71	70	68	73	282	3,300
Kang Wook-soon	72	69	71	70	282	3,300
Fredrik Jacobson	70	71	66	75	282	3,300
Mark Roe	71	69	71	72	283	2,650
Ross Bain	71	69	71	72	283	2,650
Jose Manuel Lara	66	72	68	77	283	2,650
Jean Hugo	70	67	71	75	283	2,650
Michele Reale	72	69	70	72	283	2,650
Gary Evans	70	66	72	75	283	2,650
Darren Clarke	71	69	70	73	283	2,650
Peter Lonard	68	71	72	72	283	2,650
Thomas Levet	73	68	72	71	284	2,150
Diego Borrego	72	69	73	70	284	2,150
Mark McNulty	66	74	71	74	285	1,910
Johan Rystrom	69	70	72	74	285	1,910
Christopher Hanell	71	70	69	75	285	1,910
Costantino Rocca	70	71	70	75	286	1,494.99
Raphael Jacquelin	67	72	71	76	286	1,494.99
Per Haugsrud	70	71	77	68	286	1,494.99
Peter Mitchell	68	72	73	73	286	1,494.99
Thomas Gogele	69	70	73	74	286	1,494.99
Lucas Parsons	70	70	73	73	286	1,494.99
Maarten Lafeber	70	69	74	74	287	1,486.51
Justin Rose	71	70	71	75	287	1,486.51
Daren Lee	71	70	70	76	287	1,486.51
Joakim Haeggman	71	67	77	73	288	1,481.79
Jarmo Sandelin	69	72	72	75	288	1,481.79
Ian Poulter	71	69	72	77	289	1,478.96

Qatar Masters

Doha Golf Club, Doha, Qatar
Par 36-36–72; 6,500 yards

March 8-11
purse, US$750,000

	SCORES				TOTAL	MONEY
Tony Johnstone	68	70	66	70	274	£84,889.65
Robert Karlsson	63	70	70	73	276	56,590.83
Elliot Boult	68	67	72	71	278	31,884.55
Olivier Edmond	65	70	71	73	279	23,531.41
Dean Robertson	67	69	68	75	279	23,531.41
John Senden	69	73	68	71	281	16,553.48
Angel Cabrera	66	70	67	78	281	16,553.48
Anders Hansen	71	69	71	71	282	10,492.36
Steve Webster	71	70	73	68	282	10,492.36
Ricardo Gonzalez	67	71	70	74	282	10,492.36
Greg Owen	69	71	69	73	282	10,492.36
David Higgins	70	72	72	68	282	10,492.36
Ian Woosnam	71	70	71	71	283	7,203.49
Maarten Lafeber	69	73	68	73	283	7,203.49
Paul McGinley	71	67	71	74	283	7,203.49
Rolf Muntz	70	69	74	70	283	7,203.49
Fredrik Jacobson	70	71	69	73	283	7,203.49
David Carter	69	71	74	69	283	7,203.49
Martin Maritz	70	69	70	74	283	7,203.49
Roger Chapman	72	71	72	69	284	5,925.30
Jarrod Moseley	67	74	75	68	284	5,925.30
David Lynn	67	71	70	76	284	5,925.30
Thomas Bjorn	69	71	70	75	285	5,373.51
Daren Lee	67	72	75	71	285	5,373.51
Lucas Parsons	73	70	68	74	285	5,373.51
Marco Bernardini	66	73	71	75	285	5,373.51
Eamonn Darcy	69	68	72	77	286	4,385.96
Des Smyth	71	71	68	76	286	4,385.96
Soren Kjeldsen	70	71	71	74	286	4,385.96
Carl Suneson	69	71	73	73	286	4,385.96
Mathias Gronberg	68	72	70	76	286	4,385.96
Paul Lawrie	68	70	69	79	286	4,385.96
Peter Lonard	69	74	72	71	286	4,385.96
Van Phillips	67	72	75	72	286	4,385.96
Carl Pettersson	70	69	75	72	286	4,385.96
David Howell	68	71	73	75	287	3,514.43
Zhang Lian-wei	70	70	70	77	287	3,514.43
Brian Davis	71	67	72	77	287	3,514.43
Thomas Gogele	71	71	70	75	287	3,514.43
Roger Wessels	66	73	74	74	287	3,514.43
Craig Hainline	70	73	69	76	288	3,005.09
Trevor Immelman	70	68	73	77	288	3,005.09
Neil Cheetham	69	71	73	75	288	3,005.09
Stephen Dodd	68	73	75	72	288	3,005.09
Ignacio Garrido	72	68	70	78	288	3,005.09
Mark Roe	72	70	70	77	289	2,190.16
Jean-Francois Remesy	71	70	67	81	289	2,190.16
Fredrik Henge	72	71	71	75	289	2,190.16
Richard Johnson	69	70	73	77	289	2,190.16
Johan Rystrom	68	71	73	77	289	2,190.16
Jorge Berendt	71	71	72	75	289	2,190.16
Massimo Scarpa	66	73	73	77	289	2,190.16
Bradley Dredge	72	71	69	77	289	2,190.16
Mark Pilkington	63	79	72	75	289	2,190.16

	SCORES				TOTAL	MONEY
Andrew Coltart	71	69	75	74	289	2,190.16
Matthew Blackey	70	72	75	72	289	2,190.16
Russell Claydon	69	74	72	75	290	1,553.48
Henrik Nystrom	67	71	75	77	290	1,553.48
Tom Gillis	67	76	75	73	291	1,298.81
Gregory Havret	71	69	73	78	291	1,298.81
Soren Hansen	67	73	75	76	291	1,298.81
Jeremy Robinson	71	69	73	78	291	1,298.81
Michele Reale	70	73	73	75	291	1,298.81
Jonathan Lomas	71	72	74	74	291	1,298.81
Markus Brier	66	70	73	82	291	1,298.81
Patrik Sjoland	69	74	71	77	291	1,298.81
Sven Struver	70	73	76	73	292	996.60
Kenneth Ferrie	68	74	75	75	292	996.60
Henrik Stenson	70	70	70	82	292	996.60
Tobias Dier	71	70	72	79	292	996.60
Marc Farry	71	70	72	80	293	763.69
Massimo Florioli	71	70	74	79	294	761.79
Santiago Luna	73	70	77	75	295	758.94
Barry Lane	68	75	77	75	295	758.94
Raphael Jacquelin	69	71	75	81	296	756.08
Hennie Otto	71	72	71		DQ	

Madeira Island Open

Santo da Serra Golf Club, Madeira, Portugal
Par 36-36–72; 6,661 yards

March 15-18
purse, £350,000

	SCORES				TOTAL	MONEY
Des Smyth	66	70	68	66	270	£58,181.31
John Bickerton	67	67	69	69	272	38,789.66
Massimo Florioli	68	68	65	73	274	16,582.88
Stephen Dodd	71	67	66	70	274	16,582.88
Massimo Scarpa	69	68	70	67	274	16,582.88
Niclas Fasth	69	63	72	70	274	16,582.88
Pehr Magnebrant	70	70	69	66	275	9,600.61
David Lynn	68	71	64	72	275	9,600.61
Jose Manuel Lara	68	68	71	69	276	7,401.20
Craig Hainline	69	70	65	72	276	7,401.20
Gary Emerson	69	67	72	70	278	5,847.65
Peter Mitchell	72	70	70	66	278	5,847.65
Gary Clark	71	68	71	68	278	5,847.65
Jarmo Sandelin	69	69	73	67	278	5,847.65
Andrew Oldcorn	67	69	69	74	279	4,631.57
Peter Fowler	69	68	71	71	279	4,631.57
Steve Webster	74	68	68	69	279	4,631.57
Simon Khan	68	73	69	69	279	4,631.57
Francis Valera	73	65	70	71	279	4,631.57
Graeme Storm	71	71	68	69	279	4,631.57
Santiago Luna	70	72	67	71	280	3,787.88
Eric Carlberg	69	72	70	69	280	3,787.88
Fredrik Henge	70	68	69	73	280	3,787.88
Stuart Little	72	66	70	72	280	3,787.88
Jeremy Robinson	68	72	69	71	280	3,787.88
Ian Garbutt	71	67	72	70	280	3,787.88
Philip Golding	67	72	69	73	281	3,368.94
Gary Orr	71	72	70	68	281	3,368.94

	SCORES				TOTAL	MONEY
Malcolm Mackenzie	66	73	70	73	282	3,107.11
Simon Hurd	73	69	67	73	282	3,107.11
Alastair Forsyth	69	75	69	69	282	3,107.11
Marten Olander	75	68	70	70	283	2,560.16
Henrik Stenson	70	66	73	74	283	2,560.16
Thomas Gogele	72	72	71	68	283	2,560.16
Andrew Beal	73	70	70	70	283	2,560.16
Russell Claydon	70	72	72	69	283	2,560.16
Birgir Hafthorsson	69	71	74	69	283	2,560.16
Markus Brier	68	68	71	76	283	2,560.16
David Carter	68	74	70	71	283	2,560.16
Nic Henning	73	71	69	70	283	2,560.16
Mark Mouland	70	69	70	75	284	2,024.86
Philip Walton	67	75	70	72	284	2,024.86
Marc Pendaries	70	71	68	75	284	2,024.86
Greg Owen	69	74	71	70	284	2,024.86
Johan Skold	67	71	75	71	284	2,024.86
Lee James	72	68	71	73	284	2,024.86
Seve Ballesteros	71	68	70	76	285	1,571.01
Shaun Webster	72	71	71	71	285	1,571.01
Hennie Otto	68	71	74	72	285	1,571.01
John Hawksworth	71	73	71	70	285	1,571.01
Simon Hurley	70	73	69	73	285	1,571.01
Matthew Blackey	68	75	71	71	285	1,571.01
Hank Kuehne	67	76	71	71	285	1,571.01
Richard Bland	70	73	73	70	286	1,159.06
Robin Byrd	71	70	73	72	286	1,159.06
Dennis Edlund	74	70	67	75	286	1,159.06
Raimo Sjoberg	68	73	73	72	286	1,159.06
Stephen Scahill	68	74	73	71	286	1,159.06
Wayne Riley	71	72	73	71	287	977.52
Soren Kjeldsen	70	70	71	76	287	977.52
Jose Romero	74	67	72	74	287	977.52
Jean-Francois Lucquin	71	71	73	73	288	855.33
Jorge Berendt	68	72	75	73	288	855.33
Stuart Cage	69	70	73	76	288	855.33
Benoit Teilleria	72	67	76	73	288	855.33
David Howell	70	73	72	74	289	700.77
Gregory Havret	69	75	72	73	289	700.77
Fredrik Andersson	72	72	72	73	289	700.77
Iain Pyman	75	69	74	71	289	700.77
Marcus Knight	70	72	73	74	289	700.77
Sam Walker	74	70	75	71	290	523.67
Steven Richardson	72	71	75	73	291	519.86
Antonio Sobrinho	72	71	75	73	291	519.86
Dean Robertson	69	72	79	71	291	519.86
Mats Lanner	73	71	75	73	292	515.10
Kenneth Ferrie	72	72	71	77	292	515.10
Robert Jan Derksen	73	71	77	72	293	511.29
Ulrik Gustafsson	70	72	75	76	293	511.29
Paul Sherman	72	71	81	75	299	508.44
Paddy Gribben	70	71	73		DQ	

Sao Paulo Brazil Open

See American Tours chapter.

Open de Argentina
See American Tours chapter.

Moroccan Open

Royal Golf Dar-es-Salam, Red Course, Rabat, Morocco   April 12-15
Par 36-37–73; 7,359 yards   purse, £400,000

	SCORES			TOTAL	MONEY
Ian Poulter	71	67	69	70	277	£66,660
David Lynn	72	72	68	67	279	44,440
Peter Lonard	71	75	66	68	280	25,040
Thomas Levet	73	68	70	71	282	18,480
Stephen Gallacher	72	72	70	68	282	18,480
Greg Owen	73	70	70	70	283	13,000
Gary Evans	70	75	66	72	283	13,000
Peter Hanson	73	71	68	72	284	8,580
Paul McGinley	67	75	70	72	284	8,580
Federico Bisazza	72	71	69	72	284	8,580
Hank Kuehne	71	71	71	71	284	8,580
Robert Karlsson	70	71	70	74	285	6,880
Gary Emerson	73	72	68	73	286	6,280
Paolo Quirici	73	69	71	73	286	6,280
Kenneth Ferrie	72	73	75	67	287	5,520
Craig Hainline	68	72	73	74	287	5,520
Olivier Edmond	71	72	70	74	287	5,520
Sam Walker	69	76	67	75	287	5,520
Andrew Sherborne	72	72	70	74	288	4,664
Peter Fowler	74	72	68	74	288	4,664
Andrew Marshall	72	74	71	71	288	4,664
Jean Hugo	71	74	70	73	288	4,664
Christophe Pottier	73	69	71	75	288	4,664
Wayne Riley	71	74	73	71	289	3,920
Soren Kjeldsen	71	72	71	75	289	3,920
Jean-Francois Lucquin	73	73	70	73	289	3,920
Carl Suneson	74	71	72	72	289	3,920
Bradley Dredge	70	76	70	73	289	3,920
Andrew Coltart	75	72	71	71	289	3,920
Simon Dyson	72	73	72	72	289	3,920
Roger Chapman	72	74	68	76	290	2,900
Raphael Jacquelin	71	75	70	74	290	2,900
Bradford Vaughan	76	71	73	70	290	2,900
Hennie Otto	74	70	72	74	290	2,900
Trevor Immelman	74	74	71	71	290	2,900
Henrik Bjornstad	71	74	69	76	290	2,900
Simon Hurley	77	69	71	73	290	2,900
Gregory Havret	73	70	72	75	290	2,900
Raimo Sjoberg	74	70	72	74	290	2,900
Michael Jonzon	68	75	72	75	290	2,900
Erol Simsek	71	75	72	72	290	2,900
Tobias Dier	71	75	73	71	290	2,900
Anders Forsbrand	73	71	73	74	291	2,200
Graham Rankin	73	75	70	73	291	2,200
Massimo Florioli	74	69	72	76	291	2,200
Gustavo Rojas	75	70	72	74	291	2,200
Francis Valera	73	74	70	74	291	2,200
Marc Farry	71	74	70	77	292	1,760
Elliot Boult	75	72	73	72	292	1,760

	SCORES				TOTAL	MONEY
Justin Rose	75	71	69	77	292	1,760
Massimo Scarpa	72	73	72	75	292	1,760
Nic Henning	76	70	72	74	292	1,760
James McLean	74	68	74	76	292	1,760
Mark Roe	76	72	74	71	293	1,274.28
Jean-Francois Remesy	72	74	73	74	293	1,274.28
Jose Romero	73	72	75	73	293	1,274.28
Didier de Vooght	72	71	74	76	293	1,274.28
Paul Streeter	72	76	71	74	293	1,274.28
Gary Clark	76	72	71	74	293	1,274.28
David Park	69	73	74	77	293	1,274.28
*Abdelkader El Hali	74	74	70	75	293	
Malcolm Mackenzie	72	70	73	79	294	1,060
Raymond Russell	71	75	76	72	294	1,060
*Nick Dougherty	76	69	73	76	294	
Johan Rystrom	73	73	74	75	295	920
Andrew Beal	76	71	73	75	295	920
Stephen Dodd	75	73	70	77	295	920
Adam Mednick	73	75	73	74	295	920
John Bickerton	74	70	75	76	295	920
Philip Walton	71	71	75	79	296	725.05
Peter Mitchell	75	72	74	75	296	725.05
Markus Brier	74	74	75	73	296	725.05
Matthew Blackey	73	72	76	75	296	725.05
Nils Roerbaek	73	75	75	74	297	597.40
Dennis Edlund	76	71	71	79	297	597.40
John Wade	75	71	74	78	298	592.70
Russell Claydon	78	70	74	76	298	592.70
Alastair Forsyth	73	72	79	74	298	592.70
Andrew Raitt	72	74	77	76	299	588.01
Benoit Teilleria	74	73	70	82	299	588.01
Neil Cheetham	68	76	74	82	300	584.26
Juan Vizcaya	76	72	79	73	300	584.26
Roger Winchester	75	73	75	78	301	581.44
Pascal Edmond	72	76	73	81	302	579.56
Ross Drummond	72	76	75	81	304	577.68

Via Digital Open de Espana

El Saler, Valencia, Spain
Par 36-36–72; 6,952 yards

April 19-22
purse, £743,000

	SCORES				TOTAL	MONEY
Robert Karlsson	68	68	71	70	277	£123,839.78
Jean-Francois Remesy	66	72	75	66	279	82,557.79
Miguel Angel Jimenez	71	69	70	70	280	41,833.08
Soren Hansen	68	71	70	71	280	41,833.08
Peter Mitchell	71	72	71	67	281	26,600.78
Joakim Haeggman	70	71	71	69	281	26,600.78
Gustavo Rojas	72	69	74	66	281	26,600.78
Raphael Jacquelin	74	71	72	65	282	18,575.97
Malcolm Mackenzie	72	67	74	70	283	13,173.02
Justin Rose	70	73	72	68	283	13,173.02
Gary Emerson	71	69	71	72	283	13,173.02
Domingo Hospital	70	74	70	69	283	13,173.02
Jean Hugo	70	72	69	72	283	13,173.02
Stephen Scahill	70	68	74	71	283	13,173.02

A few weeks after the U.S. Open, Retief Goosen took the first of two European titles in the Scottish Open at Loch Lomond.

HOLE	1	2	3	4	5	6	7	8	9	10	11	12	13	14	15	16	17	18	TOTAL
PAR	4	3	5	4	4	4	4	3	5	4	3	5	4	3	4	5	4	4	216
9 MCGINLEY	9	9	10	9	8	8	8	7	8	8	8	10	10	10	10	11	11		
7 GRONBERG	8	7	7	7	7	7	8	8	8	8	8	9	9	8	8	9	9		
6 CLARKE	6	6	7	7	8	8	9	10	10	10	10	10	10	10	9	9			
6 HARRINGTON	6	5	5	5	6	6	6	7	8	9	9	10	9	9	10	11	11		20 8
5 LANGER	6	6	6	6	6	5	5	5	5	5	6	5	6	5	7	7	8		20 6
3 SCOTT	3	4	5	5	6	6	5	6	5	6	7	8	8	9	10	10	10	10	20
5 KARLSSON	5	5	6	7	6	7	5	5	6	6	6	7	7	7	9	8	8		
2 HO...L	3	3	3	5	5	5	5	5	5	5	5	5	5	6	7	7	7		20
4 MO...RIE	4	4	6	6	6	5	4	4	5	5	6	6	6	7	7	8	9	8	2
1 GOO...	1	1	2	2	2	2	2	3	3	3	4	4	5	7	7	7			
3 JO...	3	3	3	3	3	4	5	5	6	6	5	5	5	5	6	7	7	8	

Padraig Harrington ended the European season with a victory in Spain — his only win of the year — and was second to Goosen on the Order of Merit.

Darren Clarke won in Europe, Africa, Japan.   Ernie Els was No. 6 in world money.

Michael C. Cohen

Colin Montgomerie posted three wins.

Stuart Franklin/Allsport

Ian Woosnam rose to No. 18 on Order of Merit.

Michael C. Cohen

Bernhard Langer won two in Europe.

Ross Kinnaird/Allsport

Lee Westwood fell from No. 4 to 29 in world.

Thomas Bjorn was No. 7 on Order of Merit.

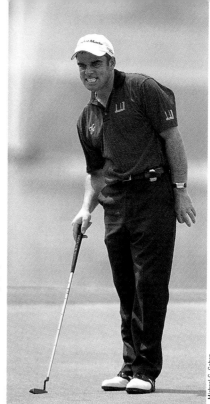

Paul McGinley was European No. 8.

Niclas Fasth climbed to No. 10 in Europe.

Paul Lawrie won Dunhill event.

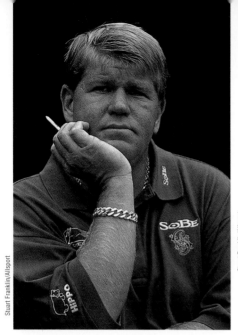

John Daly won in Germany.

Miguel Angel Jimenez was off-form.

Angel Cabrera took two titles.

Michael Campbell was No. 12 in Europe.

Jose Maria Olazabal won twice.

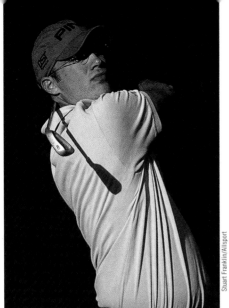

There were two French winners — Greg Havret (left) and Thomas Levet (right).

David Howell was Europe's No. 14.

Nick Dougherty, age 19, qualified.

Adam Scott won in South Africa.

Paul Casey won at Gleneagles.

Cisco World Match Play

Andrew Redington/Allsport

Ian Woosnam's revival was confirmed in his Cisco World Match Play victory.

Andrew Redington/Allsport

Padraig Harrington lost in the final.

Andrew Redington/Allsport

Sam Torrance won two matches.

Around The World

Toshimitsu Izawa took five Japan titles.

Hidemichi Tanaka won twice in Japan.

Aaron Baddeley won in Australia.

Mark McNulty won the S.A. Masters and Open.

Thaworn Wiratchant won two in a row.

Charlie Wi took three Asian titles.

Thongchai Jaidee was an Asian star.

Eight worldwide victories aside, Annika Sorenstam's best number was 59 in Phoenix.

Karrie Webb's five wins included the U.S. Women's Open and McDonald's LPGA Championship.

Lorie Kane posted two victories.

Se Ri Pak had the British title among her five, as she was second on the money list.

Maria Hjorth was the LPGA's No. 5 money winner.

Mi Hyun Kim was eighth on LPGA list.

Dottie Pepper was seventh on money list.

Laura Davies had three worldwide titles.

Laura Diaz was a top-10 money winner.

Catriona Matthew won in Hawaii.

Raquel Carriedo led the European women.

Betsy King added to her LPGA victories.

Sophie Gustafson won in Australia.

Rosie Jones was sixth on the LPGA.

Yuri Fudoh was No. 1 in Japan.

Senior Tours

Allen Doyle won four times — two official — and earned over $2.9 million.

Bruce Fleisher counted the U.S. Senior Open among his three titles.

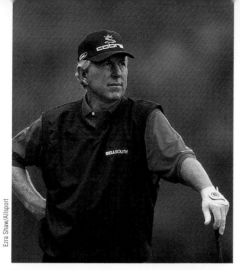

Hale Irwin was third with $2.4 million.

Larry Nelson posted five victories.

Gil Morgan won two titles.

Tom Watson was Senior PGA champion.

Jim Thorpe had consecutive wins.

Doug Tewell won a major.

Ian Stanley took the British title.

Bruce Lietzke won twice as a rookie.

Tom Kite had one victory.

	SCORES				TOTAL	MONEY
Jarmo Sandelin	70	66	76	71	283	13,173.02
Warren Bennett	69	70	75	70	284	9,319.83
Sergio Garcia	69	73	71	71	284	9,319.83
Steve Webster	69	70	73	72	284	9,319.83
Jonathan Lomas	70	69	74	71	284	9,319.83
Peter Lonard	71	72	72	69	284	9,319.83
Andrew Raitt	67	68	79	70	284	9,319.83
Carl Pettersson	67	69	74	74	284	9,319.83
Gordon Brand, Jr.	71	72	73	69	285	7,281.78
Miguel Angel Martin	70	71	70	74	285	7,281.78
Soren Kjeldsen	71	69	71	74	285	7,281.78
Gregory Havret	75	70	71	69	285	7,281.78
Thomas Gogele	68	72	76	69	285	7,281.78
Olle Karlsson	72	71	74	68	285	7,281.78
Greg Owen	70	73	73	69	285	7,281.78
Andrew Coltart	69	68	79	69	285	7,281.78
Dean Robertson	71	70	71	73	285	7,281.78
Andrew Oldcorn	64	73	78	71	286	5,372.17
Jose Manuel Lara	70	73	70	73	286	5,372.17
David Gilford	71	71	73	71	286	5,372.17
Desvonde Botes	69	71	77	69	286	5,372.17
Nicolas Colsaerts	76	69	74	67	286	5,372.17
Jarrod Moseley	70	74	72	70	286	5,372.17
Ian Garbutt	68	74	73	71	286	5,372.17
Nicolas Vanhootegem	75	70	72	69	286	5,372.17
Darren Clarke	67	68	72	79	286	5,372.17
Raymond Russell	72	69	76	69	286	5,372.17
Des Smyth	70	72	75	70	287	4,086.71
Jesus Maria Arruti	73	68	74	72	287	4,086.71
Neil Cheetham	73	71	74	69	287	4,086.71
Peter O'Malley	73	69	75	70	287	4,086.71
Fredrik Jacobson	72	72	73	70	287	4,086.71
Stephen Gallacher	72	72	69	74	287	4,086.71
Christopher Hanell	71	73	69	74	287	4,086.71
Anders Forsbrand	76	69	73	70	288	2,897.85
Sven Struver	72	72	74	70	288	2,897.85
Michele Reale	73	71	76	68	288	2,897.85
Gary Evans	71	74	74	69	288	2,897.85
Phillip Price	70	74	71	73	288	2,897.85
Christian Cevaer	76	69	74	69	288	2,897.85
Van Phillips	74	70	72	72	288	2,897.85
David Lynn	69	75	73	71	288	2,897.85
Graeme Storm	70	71	75	72	288	2,897.85
David Howell	72	72	75	70	289	2,043.36
Anders Hansen	75	69	72	73	289	2,043.36
Diego Borrego	69	72	74	74	289	2,043.36
Ignacio Garrido	71	73	75	70	289	2,043.36
Markus Brier	75	70	73	71	289	2,043.36
Simon Dyson	72	71	75	71	289	2,043.36
Andrew Sherborne	73	68	73	76	290	1,563.04
Graham Rankin	67	72	74	77	290	1,563.04
Raul Ballesteros	70	73	72	75	290	1,563.04
John Bickerton	71	67	77	75	290	1,563.04
Erol Simsek	74	69	79	68	290	1,563.04
Mikael Lundberg	69	76	73	72	290	1,563.04
Alastair Forsyth	72	72	78	68	290	1,563.04
Santiago Luna	73	71	76	71	291	1,111.77
John Senden	74	71	75	71	291	1,111.77
Patrik Sjoland	74	71	75	71	291	1,111.77

	SCORES				TOTAL	MONEY
Daren Lee	71	71	78	71	291	1,111.77
Carlos Rodiles	67	77	76	72	292	1,105.27
Fernando Roca	71	73	71	77	292	1,105.27
Fredrik Andersson	70	74	75	73	292	1,105.27
Mark Mouland	74	71	76	72	293	1,101.55
Johan Rystrom	72	72	78	72	294	1,098.77
Francis Valera	69	72	77	76	294	1,098.77
Juan Quiros	72	73	78	72	295	1,095.98
*Tom Whitehouse	71	74	79	74	298	
Brian Davis	72	73	81	76	302	1,094.12

Algarve Open de Portugal

Quinta do Lago, Algarve, Portugal
Par 36-36–72; 7,099 yards

April 26-29
purse, £634,388

	SCORES				TOTAL	MONEY
Phillip Price	72	67	70	64	273	£104,330.08
Padraig Harrington	64	70	71	70	275	54,371.71
Sven Struver	70	70	65	70	275	54,371.71
Ignacio Garrido	69	68	70	70	277	26,584.37
Stephen Scahill	70	69	66	72	277	26,584.37
Alastair Forsyth	68	68	72	69	277	26,584.37
Alex Cejka	70	73	70	65	278	17,215.15
Brett Rumford	74	68	67	69	278	17,215.15
David Howell	67	70	69	73	279	11,414.17
Warren Bennett	70	70	70	69	279	11,414.17
David Gilford	66	70	69	74	279	11,414.17
Russell Claydon	70	72	71	66	279	11,414.17
Niclas Fasth	66	72	68	73	279	11,414.17
Simon Dyson	69	69	67	74	279	11,414.17
Brian Davis	71	71	73	65	280	8,638.88
Elliot Boult	67	73	69	71	280	8,638.88
Roger Wessels	73	68	66	73	280	8,638.88
Mikael Lundberg	70	72	69	69	280	8,638.88
Santiago Luna	71	70	72	68	281	7,100.69
Anders Hansen	68	71	69	73	281	7,100.69
Maarten Lafeber	72	71	71	67	281	7,100.69
Richard Green	71	72	69	69	281	7,100.69
Trevor Immelman	68	73	67	73	281	7,100.69
David Park	70	71	69	71	281	7,100.69
Patrik Sjoland	67	72	70	72	281	7,100.69
*Nick Dougherty	71	72	71	67	281	
Roger Chapman	68	70	72	72	282	5,483.81
Greg Turner	69	74	69	70	282	5,483.81
Hennie Otto	71	73	70	68	282	5,483.81
Henrik Stenson	70	73	68	71	282	5,483.81
Nicolas Colsaerts	71	70	70	71	282	5,483.81
Jeremy Robinson	71	68	72	71	282	5,483.81
Paolo Quirici	73	71	71	67	282	5,483.81
Joakim Haeggman	68	72	68	74	282	5,483.81
Markus Brier	70	72	69	71	282	5,483.81
Andrew Coltart	75	68	68	71	282	5,483.81
Malcolm Mackenzie	70	72	68	73	283	4,194.24
Soren Kjeldsen	73	70	69	71	283	4,194.24
Desvonde Botes	73	69	71	70	283	4,194.24
Gregory Havret	71	72	75	65	283	4,194.24

	SCORES			TOTAL	MONEY
Robin Byrd	72	71	67 73	283	4,194.24
Paul McGinley	71	69	70 73	283	4,194.24
Ricardo Gonzalez	68	71	68 76	283	4,194.24
Anders Forsbrand	70	69	71 74	284	3,192.63
Ian Woosnam	74	70	69 71	284	3,192.63
Peter Fowler	71	69	71 73	284	3,192.63
Steve Webster	69	74	70 71	284	3,192.63
Francisco Cea	71	73	66 74	284	3,192.63
Jarmo Sandelin	72	71	69 72	284	3,192.63
Henrik Nystrom	72	71	71 70	284	3,192.63
John Bickerton	69	73	70 72	284	3,192.63
David Higgins	66	77	72 69	284	3,192.63
Mark Mouland	70	70	73 72	285	2,199.96
Justin Rose	70	71	74 70	285	2,199.96
Massimo Scarpa	76	66	74 69	285	2,199.96
Gustavo Rojas	72	69	70 74	285	2,199.96
Bradley Dredge	72	71	71 71	285	2,199.96
Raymond Russell	72	71	69 73	285	2,199.96
Matthew Blackey	68	75	71 71	285	2,199.96
Mark Davis	70	74	72 70	286	1,627.61
Justin Hobday	70	70	76 70	286	1,627.61
Paul Eales	74	70	69 73	286	1,627.61
Johan Rystrom	71	73	74 68	286	1,627.61
Mathias Gronberg	72	71	74 69	286	1,627.61
Tomas Jesus Munoz	68	75	70 73	286	1,627.61
David Lynn	66	75	76 69	286	1,627.61
Manuel Pinero	75	68	72 72	287	1,255.77
Domingo Hospital	70	73	72 72	287	1,255.77
Jorge Berendt	68	75	68 76	287	1,255.77
Paul Streeter	72	72	68 75	287	1,255.77
Hank Kuehne	71	69	73 74	287	1,255.77
Andrew Oldcorn	70	74	72 72	288	937.13
Ian Poulter	67	76	75 70	288	937.13
Roger Winchester	69	74	71 74	288	937.13
Kenneth Ferrie	68	74	70 77	289	933.37
*Nuno Campino	72	71	74 72	289	
*David Price	70	73	72 74	289	
Shaun Webster	70	74	71 75	290	929.62
Christian Cevaer	71	70	76 73	290	929.62
Andrew Raitt	70	74	73 73	290	929.62
Craig Hainline	72	69	73 77	291	925.86
Jose Rivero	70	74	76 73	293	923.98

Novotel Perrier Open de France

Lyon Golf Club, Villette d'Anthon, France
Par 34-36–70; 7,175 yards

May 3-6
purse, £818,607

	SCORES			TOTAL	MONEY
Jose Maria Olazabal	66	69	66 67	268	£134,624.11
Costantino Rocca	68	69	64 69	270	60,234.75
Greg Turner	69	67	67 67	270	60,234.75
Paul Eales	66	69	67 68	270	60,234.75
Gregory Havret	67	67	69 68	271	34,249.43
Marc Farry	68	65	71 68	272	28,271.93
Anders Hansen	66	68	70 69	273	20,840.45
Paul McGinley	72	67	69 65	273	20,840.45

	SCORES				TOTAL	MONEY
Ian Garbutt	68	71	70	64	273	20,840.45
Alex Cejka	67	70	70	67	274	13,362.81
Neil Cheetham	67	69	66	72	274	13,362.81
Jorge Berendt	66	71	69	68	274	13,362.81
Paul Lawrie	71	67	67	69	274	13,362.81
John Bickerton	70	67	66	71	274	13,362.81
Paddy Gribben	68	68	68	70	274	13,362.81
James McLean	65	71	69	69	274	13,362.81
Soren Kjeldsen	70	68	71	66	275	9,362.05
Stephen Leaney	72	67	66	70	275	9,362.05
Anthony Wall	69	68	67	71	275	9,362.05
Desvonde Botes	67	68	71	69	275	9,362.05
Domingo Hospital	69	67	66	73	275	9,362.05
Roger Winchester	66	69	72	68	275	9,362.05
Joakim Haeggman	68	70	67	70	275	9,362.05
Peter O'Malley	72	67	70	66	275	9,362.05
Mark Pilkington	70	66	69	70	275	9,362.05
Brett Rumford	68	70	69	68	275	9,362.05
Anders Forsbrand	65	70	70	71	276	7,067.98
Eduardo Romero	67	73	68	68	276	7,067.98
Philip Walton	68	71	68	69	276	7,067.98
Richard Green	68	69	70	69	276	7,067.98
Hennie Walters	69	68	70	69	276	7,067.98
Russell Claydon	68	68	68	72	276	7,067.98
Diego Borrego	69	68	69	70	276	7,067.98
Tobias Dier	69	71	70	66	276	7,067.98
Andrew Marshall	66	71	70	70	277	5,977.49
Fredrik Andersson	68	71	69	69	277	5,977.49
Peter Hanson	71	65	72	70	278	5,492.83
Shaun Webster	68	71	65	74	278	5,492.83
Jonathan Lomas	65	72	69	72	278	5,492.83
Robert Coles	67	69	71	71	278	5,492.83
Mark Roe	72	67	71	69	279	4,281.18
Mark Davis	67	68	77	67	279	4,281.18
John Senden	69	68	72	70	279	4,281.18
Peter Baker	69	68	71	71	279	4,281.18
Henrik Bjornstad	72	68	63	76	279	4,281.18
Per Nyman	68	72	75	64	279	4,281.18
Ricardo Gonzalez	70	68	69	72	279	4,281.18
Ignacio Garrido	68	69	71	71	279	4,281.18
Christian Cevaer	69	71	67	72	279	4,281.18
Daren Lee	64	71	68	76	279	4,281.18
Nic Henning	73	66	70	70	279	4,281.18
Warren Bennett	65	73	75	67	280	3,150.30
Olivier Edmond	70	69	71	70	280	3,150.30
Andrew Raitt	69	71	72	68	280	3,150.30
*Francois Delamontagne	72	68	71	69	280	
Ross Drummond	67	72	72	70	281	2,552.55
Jose Rivero	68	70	71	72	281	2,552.55
Gary Murphy	70	69	73	69	281	2,552.55
Jeremy Robinson	67	69	74	71	281	2,552.55
Olle Karlsson	70	69	69	73	281	2,552.55
Miguel Angel Martin	71	69	68	74	282	2,100.20
Gary Evans	68	67	76	71	282	2,100.20
Tomas Jesus Munoz	69	70	71	72	282	2,100.20
David Park	70	68	74	70	282	2,100.20
Erol Simsek	67	72	72	71	282	2,100.20
Jarrod Moseley	63	75	74	71	283	1,777.09
Van Phillips	68	72	72	71	283	1,777.09

	SCORES				TOTAL	MONEY
Nicolas Joakimides	67	73	68	75	283	1,777.09
Garry Houston	66	71	76	71	284	1,460.20
Elliot Boult	69	70	70	75	284	1,460.20
Hennie Otto	69	70	75	70	284	1,460.20
Jamie Spence	69	70	69	76	284	1,460.20
Barry Lane	71	68	74	72	285	1,208.86
Justin Hobday	67	72	73	73	285	1,208.86
Thomas Gogele	69	70	74	73	286	1,206.06
Massimo Florioli	68	72	72	75	287	1,204.20
Michele Reale	69	70	78	71	288	1,202.33
Trevor Immelman	71	69	77	75	292	1,198.61
Lionel Alexandre	69	70	80	73	292	1,198.61
Chris Benians	69	71	76	76	292	1,198.61

Benson and Hedges International Open

The De Vere Belfry, Wishaw, England
Par 36-36–72; 7,118 yards

May 10-13
purse, £1,000,000

	SCORES				TOTAL	MONEY
Henrik Stenson	66	68	71	70	275	£166,660
Paul McGinley	66	72	70	70	278	86,855
Angel Cabrera	70	70	69	69	278	86,855
Olle Karlsson	69	71	68	73	281	50,000
Desvonde Botes	69	69	72	72	282	42,400
Richard Green	72	70	70	71	283	35,000
Eduardo Romero	70	74	66	74	284	23,160
David Howell	69	70	73	72	284	23,160
Raphael Jacquelin	68	74	72	70	284	23,160
Thomas Bjorn	69	68	75	72	284	23,160
Retief Goosen	71	68	74	71	284	23,160
Colin Montgomerie	73	69	71	72	285	15,150
Ian Garbutt	72	70	72	71	285	15,150
Phillip Price	70	74	67	74	285	15,150
Jorge Berendt	75	67	70	73	285	15,150
Patrik Sjoland	69	73	71	72	285	15,150
*Nick Dougherty	72	72	70	71	285	
Paul Casey	72	73	71	69	285	15,150
Padraig Harrington	68	72	76	70	286	11,537.50
Richard Johnson	73	71	74	68	286	11,537.50
Jarrod Moseley	70	69	72	75	286	11,537.50
Johan Rystrom	72	70	75	69	286	11,537.50
Diego Borrego	68	73	74	71	286	11,537.50
Paul Lawrie	70	71	74	71	286	11,537.50
Brett Rumford	72	71	71	72	286	11,537.50
Aaron Baddeley	69	72	69	76	286	11,537.50
Jeev Milkha Singh	72	69	71	75	287	9,050
Jose Manuel Lara	72	73	69	73	287	9,050
Jose Maria Olazabal	67	75	72	73	287	9,050
Sven Struver	74	66	75	72	287	9,050
Miguel Angel Jimenez	72	70	71	74	287	9,050
Peter Mitchell	76	69	69	73	287	9,050
Darren Clarke	69	76	68	74	287	9,050
Robert Coles	70	73	74	70	287	9,050
Costantino Rocca	73	71	74	70	288	7,100
Jose Rivero	72	67	76	73	288	7,100
Mark McNulty	70	74	73	71	288	7,100

	SCORES				TOTAL	MONEY
Elliot Boult	68	73	77	70	288	7,100
Nick O'Hern	70	75	71	72	288	7,100
Russell Claydon	71	68	74	75	288	7,100
Markus Brier	73	72	71	72	288	7,100
David Gilford	68	73	73	75	289	5,400
Steve Webster	71	73	69	76	289	5,400
Anthony Wall	69	72	76	72	289	5,400
Peter Baker	71	71	75	72	289	5,400
Henrik Bjornstad	72	72	71	74	289	5,400
Robert Karlsson	71	73	72	73	289	5,400
Jonathan Lomas	72	72	70	75	289	5,400
Dean Robertson	71	70	72	76	289	5,400
Henrik Nystrom	70	70	71	78	289	5,400
Stephen Gallacher	69	74	72	74	289	5,400
Jean-Francois Remesy	71	70	73	76	290	3,900
Soren Kjeldsen	71	74	72	73	290	3,900
Paul Eales	73	72	73	72	290	3,900
Francisco Cea	70	72	72	76	290	3,900
Marco Bernardini	73	70	73	74	290	3,900
Eamonn Darcy	75	67	75	74	291	2,914.29
Bernhard Langer	72	69	73	77	291	2,914.29
Ian Woosnam	71	69	74	77	291	2,914.29
Marc Farry	70	75	69	77	291	2,914.29
Fredrik Henge	70	72	74	75	291	2,914.29
Jean Van de Velde	72	73	74	72	291	2,914.29
Lee Westwood	73	68	76	74	291	2,914.29
Jean Hugo	69	76	73	74	292	2,350
Pierre Fulke	75	68	77	72	292	2,350
Ricardo Gonzalez	71	70	80	71	292	2,350
Graeme Storm	76	68	73	75	292	2,350
Peter Hanson	73	72	75	73	293	1,865.95
Gregory Havret	72	72	71	78	293	1,865.95
Stephen Dodd	73	72	77	71	293	1,865.95
Nicolas Vanhootegem	68	73	76	76	293	1,865.95
David Lynn	72	73	74	74	293	1,865.95
Santiago Luna	72	73	73	76	294	1,496.05
Carl Suneson	74	70	73	77	294	1,496.05
Greg Owen	72	72	75	75	294	1,496.05
Steen Tinning	75	68	79	74	296	1,492.31
Gary Emerson	69	73	83	73	298	1,490.45
David Carter	74	70	77	80	301	1,488.58

Deutsche Bank - SAP Open

St. Leon-Rot, Heidelberg, Germany
Par 36-36–72; 7,207 yards

May 17-20
purse, £1,680,642

	SCORES				TOTAL	MONEY
Tiger Woods	69	68	63	66	266	£278,024.91
Michael Campbell	62	65	73	70	270	185,349.94
Soren Kjeldsen	70	67	69	65	271	93,913.73
Peter O'Malley	71	68	63	69	271	93,913.73
Padraig Harrington	70	69	64	70	273	59,719.75
Andrew Coltart	68	69	68	68	273	59,719.75
Mikael Lundberg	69	69	69	66	273	59,719.75
Nick O'Hern	69	69	66	70	274	39,535.14
Henrik Stenson	71	68	63	72	274	39,535.14

	SCORES				TOTAL	MONEY
Richard Green	68	69	69	69	275	29,901.58
Colin Montgomerie	70	66	69	70	275	29,901.58
Paul McGinley	69	65	72	69	275	29,901.58
John Bickerton	69	67	73	66	275	29,901.58
Eduardo Romero	66	67	66	77	276	23,048.27
Peter Baker	71	70	68	67	276	23,048.27
Miguel Angel Jimenez	69	69	68	70	276	23,048.27
Phillip Price	71	70	66	69	276	23,048.27
Ricardo Gonzalez	73	67	68	68	276	23,048.27
Retief Goosen	72	68	64	72	276	23,048.27
Warren Bennett	68	70	67	73	278	19,142.02
Greg Turner	71	71	69	67	278	19,142.02
Angel Cabrera	69	70	68	71	278	19,142.02
Peter Lonard	70	71	68	69	278	19,142.02
Darren Fichardt	71	69	70	69	279	17,098.53
Thomas Levet	74	67	72	66	279	17,098.53
Darren Clarke	76	67	69	67	279	17,098.53
Gustavo Rojas	66	72	69	72	279	17,098.53
Miguel Angel Martin	69	70	69	72	280	13,901.25
Ian Woosnam	66	72	73	69	280	13,901.25
Justin Rose	70	69	73	68	280	13,901.25
Paul Eales	68	71	66	75	280	13,901.25
Ernie Els	66	71	72	71	280	13,901.25
Mathias Gronberg	69	68	72	71	280	13,901.25
Greg Owen	68	70	72	70	280	13,901.25
Patrik Sjoland	71	70	70	69	280	13,901.25
Daren Lee	70	68	69	73	280	13,901.25
Mark McNulty	69	73	68	71	281	11,009.79
Peter Mitchell	74	67	73	67	281	11,009.79
Robert Karlsson	71	71	69	70	281	11,009.79
Paul Lawrie	72	70	69	70	281	11,009.79
Dean Robertson	69	68	72	72	281	11,009.79
Lucas Parsons	66	75	68	72	281	11,009.79
Anders Hansen	74	69	70	69	282	9,341.64
Carl Suneson	67	76	70	69	282	9,341.64
Niclas Fasth	74	69	71	68	282	9,341.64
Adam Scott	74	68	70	70	282	9,341.64
Bernhard Langer	72	71	70	70	283	7,840.30
Anthony Wall	72	71	69	71	283	7,840.30
Steen Tinning	70	70	68	75	283	7,840.30
Soren Hansen	70	73	66	74	283	7,840.30
Andrew Raitt	70	69	75	69	283	7,840.30
Malcolm Mackenzie	71	69	69	75	284	6,172.15
John Senden	70	71	72	71	284	6,172.15
Jarrod Moseley	72	71	68	73	284	6,172.15
Ian Garbutt	73	70	70	71	284	6,172.15
Lee Westwood	66	71	70	77	284	6,172.15
Jean-Francois Remesy	75	66	75	69	285	4,754.23
Jose Maria Olazabal	70	71	71	73	285	4,754.23
Olivier Edmond	71	67	71	76	285	4,754.23
Jarmo Sandelin	70	69	70	76	285	4,754.23
Christopher Hanell	70	73	70	72	285	4,754.23
Tobias Dier	71	71	74	69	285	4,754.23
Marc Farry	70	70	73	73	286	3,836.74
Brian Davis	70	69	71	76	286	3,836.74
Jamie Spence	71	71	72	72	286	3,836.74
Gary Orr	71	71	71	73	286	3,836.74
David Park	73	69	75	69	286	3,836.74
Diego Borrego	71	72	73	71	287	3,252.89

	SCORES				TOTAL	MONEY
Christian Cevaer	72	69	75	71	287	3,252.89
Eamonn Darcy	71	72	74	71	288	2,682.84
Des Smyth	74	69	71	74	288	2,682.84
Alex Cejka	73	68	73	74	288	2,682.84
Emanuele Canonica	72	71	69	77	289	2,497.59
Thomas Bjorn	67	75	71	76	289	2,497.59
Mikko Ilonen	71	72	72	77	292	2,494.81

Volvo PGA Championship

Wentworth Club, Surrey, England
Par 35-37–72; 7,047 yards

May 25-28
purse, £2,000,000

	SCORES				TOTAL	MONEY
Andrew Oldcorn	66	66	69	71	272	£333,330
Angel Cabrera	63	71	72	68	274	222,220.03
Nick Faldo	72	66	70	67	275	125,199.99
Phillip Price	65	69	72	71	277	84,933.34
Mathias Gronberg	71	69	72	65	277	84,933.34
Michael Campbell	70	70	67	70	277	84,933.34
Vijay Singh	73	65	70	70	278	60,000
Peter Baker	67	72	75	65	279	44,933.34
Darren Clarke	72	69	68	70	279	44,933.34
Gary Orr	74	67	69	69	279	44,933.34
Jose Maria Olazabal	72	68	67	73	280	34,466.66
Steve Webster	67	68	72	73	280	34,466.66
Dean Robertson	68	68	75	69	280	34,466.66
John Senden	71	67	72	71	281	29,400
Niclas Fasth	69	68	69	75	281	29,400
Simon Dyson	68	72	72	69	281	29,400
Richard Green	73	68	70	71	282	25,400
Anthony Wall	70	70	72	70	282	25,400
Colin Montgomerie	73	69	69	71	282	25,400
Paul Lawrie	69	68	72	73	282	25,400
Ian Woosnam	71	68	73	71	283	22,000
Anders Hansen	71	70	72	70	283	22,000
Stephen Leaney	70	64	74	75	283	22,000
Gary Emerson	70	69	71	73	283	22,000
Mikael Lundberg	67	72	70	74	283	22,000
Raphael Jacquelin	69	68	74	73	284	18,700
Thomas Levet	72	71	72	69	284	18,700
Peter O'Malley	69	71	71	73	284	18,700
Paul McGinley	66	74	73	71	284	18,700
Ian Garbutt	71	71	70	72	284	18,700
Diego Borrego	72	70	69	73	284	18,700
Soren Kjeldsen	71	66	72	76	285	15,085.71
Justin Rose	72	69	73	71	285	15,085.71
Joakim Haeggman	68	73	74	70	285	15,085.71
Greg Owen	69	74	68	74	285	15,085.71
Markus Brier	72	71	71	71	285	15,085.71
Andrew Coltart	68	69	71	77	285	15,085.71
Adam Scott	70	69	74	72	285	15,085.71
Henrik Stenson	76	66	71	73	286	12,400
Ernie Els	70	72	68	76	286	12,400
Rolf Muntz	71	67	74	74	286	12,400
Thomas Bjorn	68	69	72	77	286	12,400
Henrik Nystrom	69	72	72	73	286	12,400

	SCORES				TOTAL	MONEY
Christopher Hanell	72	71	72	71	286	12,400
Eamonn Darcy	72	71	71	73	287	9,200
Des Smyth	70	68	75	74	287	9,200
Padraig Harrington	67	75	69	76	287	9,200
Carlos Rodiles	69	70	78	70	287	9,200
Steen Tinning	70	73	73	71	287	9,200
Jonathan Lomas	72	67	73	75	287	9,200
Nicolas Vanhootegem	69	71	72	75	287	9,200
David Lynn	72	71	75	69	287	9,200
Patrik Sjoland	70	73	74	70	287	9,200
John Bickerton	69	71	76	71	287	9,200
Paul Broadhurst	69	74	73	72	288	6,600
David Higgins	72	71	74	71	288	6,600
Alastair Forsyth	67	73	75	73	288	6,600
Miguel Angel Martin	69	70	75	75	289	5,600
Damian McGrane	68	72	70	79	289	5,600
Nick O'Hern	66	71	78	74	289	5,600
Soren Hansen	71	70	73	75	289	5,600
Raymond Russell	72	69	76	72	289	5,600
Warren Bennett	71	68	76	75	290	4,700
Jean Hugo	72	70	75	73	290	4,700
Emanuele Canonica	71	70	72	77	290	4,700
Peter Lonard	71	71	72	76	290	4,700
Robert Karlsson	72	70	73	76	291	4,000
Alex Cejka	73	70	75	73	291	4,000
Pierre Fulke	71	70	79	71	291	4,000
Gary Evans	71	71	77	74	293	3,650
Jarmo Sandelin	71	72	73	78	294	3,000.16
Jeev Milkha Singh	76	67	76	80	299	2,998.32

Victor Chandler British Masters

Woburn Golf & Country Club, Milton Keynes, England   May 31-June 3
Par 36-36–72; 7,214 yards   purse, £1,250,000

	SCORES				TOTAL	MONEY
Thomas Levet	69	69	67	69	274	£208,330
David Howell	68	65	68	73	274	93,210.01
Robert Karlsson	66	67	69	72	274	93,210.01
Mathias Gronberg	69	70	67	68	274	93,210.01
(Levet defeated Howell and Karlsson on first, Gronberg on third playoff hole.)						
Olle Karlsson	71	70	68	69	278	53,000
Ricardo Gonzalez	70	73	67	69	279	40,625
Niclas Fasth	74	69	66	70	279	40,625
Anthony Wall	70	68	69	73	280	29,625
Lee Westwood	69	70	67	74	280	29,625
Roger Wessels	70	68	72	71	281	25,000
Malcolm Mackenzie	70	70	66	76	282	21,541.67
Fredrik Jacobson	70	71	75	66	282	21,541.67
Erol Simsek	68	73	73	68	282	21,541.67
Mark Mouland	70	73	72	68	283	16,640.63
Ian Woosnam	69	73	72	69	283	16,640.63
Warren Bennett	70	72	72	69	283	16,640.63
Sven Struver	68	73	71	71	283	16,640.63
Richard Green	73	71	70	69	283	16,640.63
Jean Hugo	72	72	70	69	283	16,640.63
Rolf Muntz	72	70	70	71	283	16,640.63

	SCORES				TOTAL	MONEY
Adam Scott	67	74	71	71	283	16,640.63
Mark McNulty	70	66	76	72	284	13,375
Greg Turner	70	72	73	69	284	13,375
Stephen Leaney	72	72	73	67	284	13,375
Justin Rose	70	70	73	71	284	13,375
Peter Mitchell	72	69	74	69	284	13,375
John Senden	71	69	78	67	285	11,125
Colin Montgomerie	68	71	74	72	285	11,125
Thomas Bjorn	69	75	69	72	285	11,125
David Park	72	71	71	71	285	11,125
John Bickerton	69	73	72	71	285	11,125
David Carter	76	66	72	71	285	11,125
Paul Casey	71	69	69	76	285	11,125
Sandy Lyle	69	72	72	73	286	8,750
Brian Davis	70	74	66	76	286	8,750
Nick O'Hern	69	70	72	75	286	8,750
Steen Tinning	72	72	71	71	286	8,750
Alex Cejka	71	71	71	73	286	8,750
Peter O'Malley	71	71	71	73	286	8,750
Jorge Berendt	70	71	72	73	286	8,750
Greg Owen	68	74	73	71	286	8,750
Mark Roe	73	70	72	72	287	7,125
David Gilford	72	72	71	72	287	7,125
Ian Garbutt	71	73	72	71	287	7,125
Darren Clarke	70	72	71	74	287	7,125
Michael Campbell	74	70	69	74	287	7,125
Sam Torrance	72	72	66	78	288	5,750
Fredrik Henge	70	72	74	72	288	5,750
Gary Evans	74	69	73	72	288	5,750
Markus Brier	72	72	70	74	288	5,750
Andrew Coltart	70	68	75	75	288	5,750
Christopher Hanell	74	70	76	68	288	5,750
Peter Fowler	71	69	77	72	289	4,500
Patrik Sjoland	71	73	69	76	289	4,500
Dean Robertson	72	70	70	77	289	4,500
Simon Dyson	73	71	71	74	289	4,500
Des Smyth	72	72	71	75	290	3,375
Ian Poulter	72	70	74	74	290	3,375
Carlos Rodiles	72	70	76	72	290	3,375
Per Haugsrud	72	71	72	75	290	3,375
Jarrod Moseley	73	71	74	72	290	3,375
Jeremy Robinson	72	72	71	75	290	3,375
Thomas Gogele	70	72	73	75	290	3,375
Russell Claydon	73	70	69	78	290	3,375
David Lynn	69	74	73	74	290	3,375
Andrew Oldcorn	71	73	74	73	291	2,687.50
Massimo Scarpa	72	71	76	72	291	2,687.50
Marco Bernardini	68	74	79	71	292	2,500
Costantino Rocca	72	70	73	78	293	2,375
Elliot Boult	73	71	70	81	295	2,290
Neil Cheetham	73	71	73	79	296	1,875.14
Darren Fichardt	74	68	80	75	297	1,873.33
Eamonn Darcy	68	75	77	78	298	1,871.52
Tony Johnstone	72	72	76	78	298	1,871.52

Compass Group English Open

Marriott Forest of Arden Hotel, Warwickshire, England
Par 36-36–72; 7,182 yards

June 7-10
purse, £800,000

	SCORES			TOTAL	MONEY
Peter O'Malley	70	69	70	66	275	£133,330.01
Raphael Jacquelin	73	67	66	70	276	88,879.99
Adam Scott	67	70	67	73	277	50,080
Jean Hugo	70	68	68	73	279	40,000
Steve Webster	73	69	73	66	281	26,480
Darren Clarke	74	72	67	68	281	26,480
Lee Westwood	77	67	68	69	281	26,480
Retief Goosen	75	71	65	70	281	26,480
Ian Poulter	72	71	69	70	282	17,920
Paul McGinley	73	69	70	71	283	16,000
Greg Owen	77	70	66	71	284	14,720
Jorge Berendt	72	72	73	68	285	12,660
Massimo Scarpa	70	69	74	72	285	12,660
David Lynn	74	70	70	71	285	12,660
Paul Casey	73	72	72	68	285	12,660
Roger Chapman	75	70	69	72	286	10,034.29
Jeremy Robinson	75	67	71	73	286	10,034.29
Ian Garbutt	72	77	69	68	286	10,034.29
Paul Lawrie	70	77	69	70	286	10,034.29
Raymond Russell	76	69	68	73	286	10,034.29
John Bickerton	79	70	64	73	286	10,034.29
Alastair Forsyth	73	72	68	73	286	10,034.29
Costantino Rocca	69	73	73	72	287	8,560
Anthony Wall	70	75	69	73	287	8,560
Marco Bernardini	68	72	69	78	287	8,560
Andrew Oldcorn	67	76	73	72	288	7,360
David Gilford	74	71	73	70	288	7,360
Justin Rose	72	67	70	79	288	7,360
Peter Baker	77	68	71	72	288	7,360
Jonathan Lomas	71	78	71	68	288	7,360
Stephen Dodd	72	70	73	73	288	7,360
Francisco Cea	72	74	70	72	288	7,360
Barry Lane	74	74	72	69	289	6,280
Tobias Dier	73	71	73	72	289	6,280
David Howell	69	76	72	73	290	5,680
Anders Hansen	77	71	75	67	290	5,680
Dennis Edlund	77	69	71	73	290	5,680
Phillip Price	74	75	70	71	290	5,680
Stephen Gallacher	74	71	72	73	290	5,680
David J. Russell	76	70	70	75	291	4,960
Warren Bennett	73	74	75	69	291	4,960
Steen Tinning	72	73	70	76	291	4,960
Nic Henning	73	71	74	73	291	4,960
Mark McNulty	70	76	72	74	292	4,080
Brian Davis	73	74	73	72	292	4,080
Nick O'Hern	73	76	72	71	292	4,080
Carl Suneson	75	73	75	69	292	4,080
Gary Evans	74	69	72	77	292	4,080
David Carter	74	73	73	72	292	4,080
David Higgins	76	73	71	72	292	4,080
Peter Hanson	74	71	73	75	293	3,200
Peter Mitchell	71	73	73	76	293	3,200
Johan Rystrom	71	75	74	73	293	3,200
Mark Pilkington	76	70	73	74	293	3,200

	SCORES				TOTAL	MONEY
Greg Turner	72	75	75	72	294	2,640
Roger Wessels	73	73	72	76	294	2,640
Gary Orr	76	71	75	72	294	2,640
Gordon Brand, Jr.	76	73	71	75	295	2,280
Sandy Lyle	77	72	74	72	295	2,280
Philip Walton	75	72	76	72	295	2,280
Paolo Quirici	73	74	74	74	295	2,280
Wayne Riley	78	71	74	74	297	2,000
Peter Fowler	73	71	74	79	297	2,000
Hennie Otto	71	73	77	76	297	2,000
Marc Farry	74	66	81	77	298	1,645
Stephen Leaney	71	77	73	77	298	1,645
Paul Broadhurst	76	73	77	72	298	1,645
Gary Emerson	73	74	74	77	298	1,645
Bradley Dredge	72	76	74	76	298	1,645
Francis Valera	77	72	72	77	298	1,645
Tony Johnstone	77	71	75	76	299	1,197.07
Graham Rankin	72	73	74	80	299	1,197.07
Andrew Marshall	74	74	74	77	299	1,197.07
Neil Cheetham	76	71	75	77	299	1,197.07
Yeh Wei-tze	73	74	75	78	300	1,192.59
Robert Coles	75	72	77	77	301	1,190.80

Great North Open

De Vere Slaley Hall, Northumberland, England
Par 36-36–72; 7,088 yards

June 21-24
purse, £800,000

	SCORES				TOTAL	MONEY
Andrew Coltart	68	68	69	72	277	£133,330
Stephen Gallacher	76	67	67	68	278	69,480.02
Paul Casey	71	66	72	69	278	69,480.02
Steve Webster	73	68	71	67	279	33,973.34
Bradley Dredge	69	67	72	71	279	33,973.34
Daren Lee	66	74	69	70	279	33,973.34
Ian Poulter	73	68	73	66	280	24,000
Peter Fowler	71	71	70	69	281	14,506.67
Jamie Spence	68	70	70	73	281	14,506.67
Gregory Havret	73	68	70	70	281	14,506.67
Soren Hansen	71	70	72	68	281	14,506.67
Andrew Beal	72	69	68	72	281	14,506.67
Christophe Pottier	76	69	70	66	281	14,506.67
Dean Robertson	73	70	69	69	281	14,506.67
Lucas Parsons	71	69	69	72	281	14,506.67
Scott Gardiner	69	71	69	72	281	14,506.67
Justin Rose	70	70	72	70	282	10,346.67
Gary Evans	70	74	69	69	282	10,346.67
Fredrik Jacobson	73	69	69	71	282	10,346.67
Warren Bennett	72	71	69	71	283	9,056
Richard Green	75	64	72	72	283	9,056
Carlos Rodiles	72	70	73	68	283	9,056
Jean Hugo	75	71	68	69	283	9,056
Brett Rumford	74	71	66	72	283	9,056
Gordon Brand, Jr.	70	74	69	71	284	7,480
Roger Chapman	69	72	72	71	284	7,480
Elliot Boult	74	70	69	71	284	7,480
Marcello Santi	72	72	72	68	284	7,480

	SCORES			TOTAL	MONEY
Per Nyman	72 72 70 70			284	7,480
Olle Karlsson	74 65 72 73			284	7,480
Jonathan Lomas	73 70 71 70			284	7,480
Nicolas Vanhootegem	72 66 72 74			284	7,480
Andrew Oldcorn	69 72 71 73			285	5,933.33
Greg Turner	69 74 73 69			285	5,933.33
Paul Nilbrink	75 71 70 69			285	5,933.33
Henrik Bjornstad	73 72 68 72			285	5,933.33
Robin Byrd	73 71 71 70			285	5,933.33
Carl Watts	73 71 73 68			285	5,933.33
Mark Roe	72 70 75 69			286	4,880
David Gilford	73 70 73 70			286	4,880
Garry Houston	74 70 69 73			286	4,880
Fredrik Henge	76 69 68 73			286	4,880
Nicolas Colsaerts	71 73 69 73			286	4,880
Massimo Scarpa	73 71 68 74			286	4,880
Roger Wessels	71 75 70 70			286	4,880
*Nick Dougherty	70 73 72 71			286	
Peter Baker	70 71 77 69			287	4,160
Greg Owen	72 70 72 73			287	4,160
Mats Lanner	74 68 71 75			288	3,600
Barry Lane	76 69 74 69			288	3,600
Scott Drummond	75 71 74 68			288	3,600
Francis Valera	76 70 70 72			288	3,600
Erol Simsek	74 69 74 71			288	3,600
John Wade	74 67 76 72			289	2,800
Marc Pendaries	71 71 74 73			289	2,800
Hennie Otto	74 71 71 73			289	2,800
Francisco Cea	75 70 71 73			289	2,800
David Carter	74 68 70 77			289	2,800
Brian Davis	75 71 74 70			290	2,280
Shaun Webster	71 73 72 74			290	2,280
Michael Archer	75 71 75 69			290	2,280
Richard Bland	72 70 72 76			290	2,280
Mark James	74 71 76 70			291	1,960
Ross McFarlane	74 71 71 75			291	1,960
Craig Hainline	73 73 71 74			291	1,960
Simon Dyson	72 68 77 74			291	1,960
Jeremy Robinson	70 73 75 74			292	1,640
David Lynn	75 70 74 73			292	1,640
Mark Pilkington	71 73 74 74			292	1,640
Iain Pyman	74 72 74 72			292	1,640
Mattias Nilsson	73 70 74 76			293	1,335.02
Massimo Florioli	75 70 74 74			293	1,335.02
Gordon J. Brand	71 74 77 73			295	1,198.20
David Orr	72 71 79 76			298	1,196.36
Paul Eales	74 71 80 78			303	1,194.52

Murphy's Irish Open

Fota Island Golf Club, Cork, Ireland
Par 36-35–71; 6,927 yards

June 28-July 1
purse, £969,732

	SCORES			TOTAL	MONEY
Colin Montgomerie	63 69 68 66			266	£161,618
Padraig Harrington	67 72 68 64			271	72,311.72
Darren Clarke	70 72 65 64			271	72,311.72

		SCORES			TOTAL	MONEY
Niclas Fasth	68	71	69	63	271	72,311.72
Thomas Bjorn	66	69	72	66	273	41,116.65
Gary Emerson	68	70	67	69	274	29,091.97
Robert Karlsson	71	69	67	67	274	29,091.97
Adam Scott	68	69	66	71	274	29,091.97
David Howell	68	70	71	66	275	17,681.45
Barry Lane	68	67	72	68	275	17,681.45
Ian Poulter	69	69	71	66	275	17,681.45
Steen Tinning	69	68	72	66	275	17,681.45
Thomas Levet	68	67	72	68	275	17,681.45
Andrew Coltart	67	71	69	68	275	17,681.45
Gordon Brand, Jr.	68	69	71	68	276	13,110.78
Ian Woosnam	73	69	70	64	276	13,110.78
Steve Webster	67	71	72	66	276	13,110.78
Anthony Wall	67	67	71	71	276	13,110.78
Justin Rose	70	70	69	67	276	13,110.78
Mark Mouland	71	70	67	69	277	10,828.68
Marc Farry	72	65	71	69	277	10,828.68
John Senden	67	70	71	69	277	10,828.68
Ian Garbutt	70	71	69	67	277	10,828.68
Gary Evans	66	70	73	68	277	10,828.68
Massimo Scarpa	67	73	67	70	277	10,828.68
Gregory Havret	69	71	69	69	278	9,357.92
Christophe Pottier	70	69	72	67	278	9,357.92
Peter Lonard	73	68	71	66	278	9,357.92
Carl Pettersson	68	72	72	66	278	9,357.92
Phillip Price	75	65	73	66	279	8,048.78
Jorge Berendt	68	73	71	67	279	8,048.78
Paul Lawrie	71	66	72	70	279	8,048.78
David Lynn	71	65	75	68	279	8,048.78
Raymond Russell	71	69	71	68	279	8,048.78
Soren Kjeldsen	69	73	72	66	280	6,497.21
Stephen Leaney	71	70	70	69	280	6,497.21
Andrew Beal	70	70	68	72	280	6,497.21
Jonathan Lomas	72	70	70	68	280	6,497.21
Ignacio Garrido	68	72	68	72	280	6,497.21
Gary Orr	72	69	70	69	280	6,497.21
Dean Robertson	67	70	73	70	280	6,497.21
John Bickerton	67	72	69	72	280	6,497.21
Simon Dyson	70	72	69	69	280	6,497.21
Sandy Lyle	68	72	70	71	281	5,236.55
Costantino Rocca	70	72	70	69	281	5,236.55
Peter O'Malley	71	70	69	71	281	5,236.55
Stephen Dodd	69	72	71	69	281	5,236.55
Jean-Francois Remesy	69	73	69	71	282	4,266.82
Fredrik Henge	65	70	70	77	282	4,266.82
Henrik Bjornstad	66	74	67	75	282	4,266.82
Paul McGinley	69	73	66	74	282	4,266.82
Henrik Nystrom	70	72	71	69	282	4,266.82
Mikael Lundberg	69	72	73	68	282	4,266.82
Peter Fowler	73	69	70	71	283	3,394.06
Warren Bennett	72	67	72	72	283	3,394.06
Sven Struver	67	74	68	74	283	3,394.06
Raphael Jacquelin	68	71	73	72	284	2,957.68
Francisco Cea	70	71	72	71	284	2,957.68
Darren Lee	70	70	73	72	285	2,812.22
Andrew Oldcorn	73	69	73	71	286	2,618.28
Fredrik Jacobson	70	72	70	74	286	2,618.28
Yeh Wei-tze	72	70	75	69	286	2,618.28
Eamonn Darcy	65	75	72	75	287	2,424.33

	SCORES				TOTAL	MONEY
Carlos Rodiles	71	71	74	72	288	2,230.38
Raul Ballesteros	70	71	74	73	288	2,230.38
Erol Simsek	68	72	73	75	288	2,230.38
Thomas Gogele	70	72	72	75	289	1,987.95
Marco Bernardini	72	70	69	78	289	1,987.95
Patrik Sjoland	73	68	70	80	291	1,842.49
Graham Rankin	70	70	74	81	295	1,775.82

Smurfit European Open

The K Club, Dublin, Ireland
Par 35-37–72; 7,227 yards

July 5-8
purse, £2,000,000

	SCORES				TOTAL	MONEY
Darren Clarke	68	68	71	66	273	£333,330
Ian Woosnam	69	66	73	68	276	149,140.02
Padraig Harrington	70	67	69	70	276	149,140.02
Thomas Bjorn	73	71	65	67	276	149,140.02
Mark Mouland	70	71	68	68	277	84,800.02
Henrik Bjornstad	67	68	70	73	278	65,000
Retief Goosen	69	70	73	66	278	65,000
Bernhard Langer	71	70	69	69	279	42,900
Phillip Price	70	72	70	67	279	42,900
Ricardo Gonzalez	69	70	70	70	279	42,900
Dean Robertson	70	72	69	68	279	42,900
Miguel Angel Martin	71	71	67	71	280	29,050
Costantino Rocca	70	69	69	72	280	29,050
Raphael Jacquelin	70	70	72	68	280	29,050
Richard Green	70	70	70	70	280	29,050
Thomas Levet	72	68	69	71	280	29,050
Mathias Gronberg	68	70	73	69	280	29,050
Paul Lawrie	70	72	68	70	280	29,050
Darren Lee	70	70	71	69	280	29,050
Colin Montgomerie	68	72	69	72	281	23,266.67
Gary Evans	73	67	72	69	281	23,266.67
Paul Casey	69	68	71	73	281	23,266.67
Sven Struver	75	70	69	68	282	20,200
Stephen Leaney	71	69	71	71	282	20,200
Trevor Immelman	74	68	70	70	282	20,200
Robert Karlsson	72	70	69	71	282	20,200
Roger Wessels	69	72	69	72	282	20,200
Jarmo Sandelin	69	71	65	77	282	20,200
Michael Campbell	67	70	71	74	282	20,200
David Howell	69	71	71	72	283	16,900
Anders Hansen	74	68	71	70	283	16,900
Olle Karlsson	72	73	69	69	283	16,900
Christopher Hanell	72	72	70	69	283	16,900
Anders Forsbrand	73	72	66	73	284	14,400
Marc Farry	70	75	70	69	284	14,400
Maarten Lafeber	67	72	73	72	284	14,400
Angel Cabrera	71	73	66	74	284	14,400
Andrew Coltart	72	71	69	72	284	14,400
Mikael Lundberg	67	65	72	80	284	14,400
Mark Roe	72	72	71	70	285	12,200
Jonathan Lomas	76	69	71	69	285	12,200
Peter O'Malley	71	73	72	69	285	12,200
Massimo Scarpa	67	71	73	74	285	12,200
Brett Rumford	68	77	73	67	285	12,200

	SCORES				TOTAL	MONEY
Eamonn Darcy	75	69	72	70	286	9,800
John Senden	71	74	70	71	286	9,800
Soren Hansen	71	69	70	76	286	9,800
Joakim Haeggman	72	72	70	72	286	9,800
Rolf Muntz	71	71	71	73	286	9,800
Peter Lonard	73	71	71	71	286	9,800
Niclas Fasth	69	75	68	74	286	9,800
Brian Davis	70	70	72	75	287	7,200
Stephen Dodd	73	72	68	74	287	7,200
Markus Brier	73	70	70	74	287	7,200
Raymond Russell	72	73	68	74	287	7,200
Alastair Forsyth	70	75	75	67	287	7,200
Scott Gardiner	74	70	70	73	287	7,200
Eduardo Romero	72	72	70	74	288	5,700
Greg Turner	71	74	73	70	288	5,700
Steen Tinning	72	73	71	72	288	5,700
Greg Owen	70	69	71	78	288	5,700
Santiago Luna	72	73	71	73	289	4,700
Warren Bennett	70	73	74	72	289	4,700
Ian Garbutt	71	69	73	76	289	4,700
Lee Westwood	71	74	73	71	289	4,700
Stephen Gallacher	74	69	74	72	289	4,700
Adam Scott	75	70	71	73	289	4,700
Gordon Brand, Jr.	71	73	71	75	290	3,304.14
Jean-Francois Remesy	71	72	75	72	290	3,304.14
Jamie Spence	71	74	70	75	290	3,304.08
Gregory Havret	76	68	72	74	290	3,304.14
Olivier Edmond	71	73	71	75	290	3,304.14
Alex Cejka	72	71	73	74	290	3,304.14
Des Terblanche	70	72	74	74	290	3,304.14
Alan McLean	73	71	71	75	290	3,304.14
Damian McGrane	73	72	72	74	291	2,988.50
Paul Broadhurst	78	67	68	78	291	2,988.50
Nicolas Vanhootegem	73	72	71	75	291	2,988.50
Simon Dyson	73	69	75	74	291	2,988.50
Roger Chapman	75	70	66	81	292	2,983.08
Paul Eales	71	72	74	75	292	2,983.08
Steve Webster	72	69	79	73	293	2,978.57
David Carter	72	73	69	79	293	2,978.57
Yeh Wei-tze	73	70	77	73	293	2,978.57
Richard Johnson	74	71	75	74	294	2,974.96
David Gilford	75	69	74	77	295	2,972.25
Marco Bernardini	74	70	74	77	295	2,972.25
Gary Emerson	71	73	72	80	296	2,969.54
Wayne Riley	75	70	77	79	301	2,967.73
Ian Poulter	71	74	78	79	302	2,965.93
Stephen Scahill	71	73	76	83	303	2,964.12

Scottish Open at Loch Lomond

Loch Lomond Golf Club, Glasgow, Scotland
Par 36-35–71; 7,050 yards

July 12-15
purse, £2,200,000

	SCORES				TOTAL	MONEY
Retief Goosen	62	69	66	71	268	£366,660
Thomas Bjorn	68	67	69	67	271	244,440
Barry Lane	70	65	69	68	272	104,500

	SCORES				TOTAL	MONEY
Paul McGinley	68	67	67	70	272	104,500
John Daly	68	68	66	70	272	104,500
Adam Scott	65	68	67	72	272	104,500
Darren Clarke	69	67	68	69	273	66,000
Jesper Parnevik	71	69	65	70	275	52,140
Mathias Gronberg	73	70	65	67	275	52,140
Jose Coceres	69	72	69	66	276	44,000
*Michael Hoey	71	71	71	64	277	
Greg Owen	72	68	68	69	277	39,160
Brett Rumford	73	65	71	68	277	39,160
Sergio Garcia	69	69	69	71	278	31,114.28
Soren Hansen	72	71	64	71	278	31,114.28
Geoff Ogilvy	69	73	69	67	278	31,114.28
Fredrik Jacobson	69	70	68	71	278	31,114.28
Niclas Fasth	67	71	66	74	278	31,114.28
Tom Lehman	70	66	74	68	278	31,114.28
Daren Lee	70	67	73	68	278	31,114.28
Jose Maria Olazabal	70	73	65	71	279	24,231.43
Anders Hansen	69	71	70	69	279	24,231.43
Ian Poulter	69	72	71	67	279	24,231.43
Ricardo Gonzalez	74	69	68	68	279	24,231.43
Peter Lonard	69	71	71	68	279	24,231.43
John Bickerton	72	69	71	67	279	24,231.43
Simon Dyson	69	73	68	69	279	24,231.43
Greg Chalmers	70	66	75	69	280	18,944.44
Steve Webster	69	70	69	72	280	18,944.44
Anthony Wall	67	70	70	73	280	18,944.44
Carlos Rodiles	68	73	69	70	280	18,944.44
Colin Montgomerie	70	67	69	74	280	18,944.44
Richard Johnson	73	70	67	70	280	18,944.44
Johan Rystrom	73	69	68	70	280	18,944.44
Angel Cabrera	68	74	70	68	280	18,944.44
Dean Robertson	73	69	70	68	280	18,944.44
Jeev Milkha Singh	71	71	70	69	281	15,400
Sven Struver	73	69	66	73	281	15,400
Justin Rose	67	70	72	72	281	15,400
Carl Pettersson	69	71	68	73	281	15,400
Nick Faldo	70	73	69	70	282	13,200
Raphael Jacquelin	70	67	76	69	282	13,200
Miguel Angel Jimenez	70	72	68	72	282	13,200
Peter O'Malley	72	71	69	70	282	13,200
David Lynn	68	75	67	72	282	13,200
David Carter	70	69	72	71	282	13,200
Warren Bennett	71	68	75	69	283	11,220
John Senden	69	72	73	69	283	11,220
Colin Gillies	69	69	72	73	283	11,220
Thomas Levet	72	67	72	73	284	9,900
Jarrod Moseley	65	75	68	76	284	9,900
Christian Cevaer	70	73	73	68	284	9,900
Emanuele Canonica	71	70	71	73	285	8,360
Ian Garbutt	68	74	72	71	285	8,360
Andrew Coltart	72	70	73	70	285	8,360
Erol Simsek	69	74	70	72	285	8,360
Gary Orr	69	71	72	74	286	7,040
Michael Campbell	71	68	74	73	286	7,040
David Howell	70	69	72	76	287	6,490
Peter Baker	72	69	73	73	287	6,490
Andrew Oldcorn	71	69	78	70	288	5,940
Thomas Gogele	68	70	78	72	288	5,940

	SCORES				TOTAL	MONEY
Diego Borrego	72	67	72	77	288	5,940
Andrew McLardy	71	70	75	73	289	5,390
Jamie Spence	73	70	72	74	289	5,390
Stephen Scahill	73	69	75	73	290	5,060
Greg Norman	68	71	74	78	291	4,840
Mark Mouland	70	67	78	77	292	4,620
Sandy Lyle	72	70	74	78	294	4,400
Bradley Dredge	73	69	76	77	295	4,180
Bernhard Langer	70	69			WD	4,020

British Open Championship

Royal Lytham & St. Annes Golf Club, Lancashire, England
Par 35-36–71; 6,905 yards

July 19-22
purse, £3,300,000

	SCORES				TOTAL	MONEY
David Duval	69	73	65	67	274	£600,000
Niclas Fasth	69	69	72	67	277	360,000
Bernhard Langer	71	69	67	71	278	141,666.67
Ian Woosnam	72	68	67	71	278	141,666.67
Miguel Angel Jimenez	69	72	67	70	278	141,666.67
Billy Mayfair	69	72	67	70	278	141,666.67
Ernie Els	71	71	67	69	278	141,666.67
Darren Clarke	70	69	69	70	278	141,666.67
Sergio Garcia	70	72	67	70	279	63,750
Jesper Parnevik	69	68	71	71	279	63,750
Mikko Ilonen	68	75	70	66	279	63,750
Kevin Sutherland	75	69	68	67	279	63,750
Des Smyth	74	65	70	71	280	40,062.50
Loren Roberts	70	70	70	70	280	40,062.50
Raphael Jacquelin	71	68	69	72	280	40,062.50
Colin Montgomerie	65	70	73	72	280	40,062.50
Billy Andrade	69	70	70	71	280	40,062.50
Vijay Singh	70	70	71	69	280	40,062.50
Alex Cejka	69	69	69	73	280	40,062.50
Retief Goosen	74	68	67	71	280	40,062.50
Nick Price	73	67	68	73	281	32,500
Davis Love III	73	67	74	67	281	32,500
Greg Owen	69	68	72	73	282	30,500
Michael Campbell	71	72	71	68	282	30,500
Eduardo Romero	70	68	72	73	283	27,500
Tiger Woods	71	68	73	71	283	27,500
Bob Estes	74	70	73	66	283	27,500
Joe Ogilvie	69	68	71	75	283	27,500
Barry Lane	70	72	72	70	284	25,000
Stewart Cink	71	72	72	70	285	21,500
Justin Rose	69	72	74	70	285	21,500
Scott Verplank	71	72	70	72	285	21,500
Phillip Price	74	69	71	71	285	21,500
Nicolas Vanhootegem	72	68	70	75	285	21,500
Phil Mickelson	70	72	72	71	285	21,500
*David Dixon	70	71	70	74	285	
Frank Lickliter	71	71	73	71	286	16,300
Dudley Hart	74	69	69	74	286	16,300
Toru Taniguchi	72	69	72	73	286	16,300
Andrew Coltart	75	68	70	73	286	16,300
Padraig Harrington	75	66	74	71	286	16,300

	SCORES				TOTAL	MONEY
Mark O'Meara	70	69	72	76	287	13,500
Steve Stricker	71	69	72	75	287	13,500
Richard Green	71	70	72	74	287	13,500
J.P. Hayes	69	71	74	73	287	13,500
Paul Lawrie	72	70	69	76	287	13,500
Brad Faxon	68	71	74	75	288	10,628.57
Peter Lonard	72	70	74	72	288	10,628.57
Robert Allenby	73	71	71	73	288	10,628.57
Lee Westwood	73	70	71	74	288	10,628.57
Chris DiMarco	68	74	72	74	288	10,628.57
Adam Scott	73	71	70	74	288	10,628.57
Matt Gogel	73	70	71	74	288	10,628.57
Jose Maria Olazabal	69	74	73	73	289	8,942.85
Paul Curry	72	71	71	75	289	8,942.85
Mark Calcavecchia	72	70	72	75	289	8,942.85
Carlos Franco	71	71	73	74	289	8,942.85
Paul McGinley	69	72	72	76	289	8,942.85
Duffy Waldorf	70	73	69	77	289	8,942.85
Rory Sabbatini	70	69	76	74	289	8,942.85
Stuart Appleby	69	75	72	74	290	8,500
Gordon Brand, Jr.	70	72	75	74	291	8,400
Brandel Chamblee	72	69	74	76	291	8,400
Pierre Fulke	69	67	72	83	291	8,400
Neil Cheetham	72	72	73	78	295	8,300
Alexandre Balicki	69	75	75	77	296	8,225
Thomas Levet	72	72	77	75	296	8,225
David Smail	71	72	76	79	298	8,150
Sandy Lyle	72	71	77	81	301	8,075
Scott Henderson	75	69	81	76	301	8,075

Out of Final 36 Holes

Steve Flesch	74	71		145	1,300
Soren Kjeldsen	73	72		145	1,300
Justin Leonard	74	71		145	1,300
Stephen Leaney	76	69		145	1,300
Gary Birch	75	70		145	1,300
Jean Hugo	73	72		145	1,300
Joe Durant	75	70		145	1,300
Peter O'Malley	71	74		145	1,300
Mathias Gronberg	75	70		145	1,300
Fredrik Jacobson	74	71		145	1,300
Markus Brier	74	71		145	1,300
John Bickerton	74	71		145	1,300
Nick Faldo	75	71		146	1,100
Corey Pavin	71	75		146	1,100
Bradford Vaughan	72	74		146	1,100
Shigeki Maruyama	75	71		146	1,100
Taichi Teshima	74	72		146	1,100
Soren Hansen	71	75		146	1,100
Dinesh Chand	75	71		146	1,100
Robert Karlsson	75	71		146	1,100
Robert Coles	73	73		146	1,100
Mark Brooks	73	73		146	1,100
Matthew Cort	77	69		146	1,100
David Howell	74	73		147	1,100
Mark Wiebe	73	74		147	1,100
Olle Karlsson	72	75		147	1,100
Scott Hoch	75	72		147	1,100

	SCORES		TOTAL	MONEY
Mark Pilkington	77	70	147	1,100
Tom Lehman	75	72	147	1,100
David Toms	74	73	147	1,100
Aaron Baddeley	75	72	147	1,100
*Stuart Wilson	77	70	147	
David Frost	74	74	148	1,100
Nobuhito Sato	76	72	148	1,100
Jose Coceres	71	77	148	1,100
Gary Orr	73	75	148	1,100
Jeff Maggert	72	76	148	1,100
John Daly	72	76	148	1,100
Daren Lee	76	72	148	1,100
Dennis Paulson	78	70	148	1,100
Brian Gay	72	76	148	1,100
Seve Ballesteros	78	71	149	1,000
Bob Charles	75	74	149	1,000
Tony Jacklin	75	74	149	1,000
Andrew Oldcorn	73	76	149	1,000
Steve Elkington	77	72	149	1,000
Mark McNulty	70	79	149	1,000
Fred Couples	71	78	149	1,000
*Michael Hoey	73	76	149	
Bob May	77	72	149	1,000
*Jeff Quinney	76	73	149	
Carl Paulson	72	77	149	1,000
Naomichi Ozaki	77	73	150	1,000
Mike Weir	78	72	150	1,000
Dean Wilson	72	78	150	1,000
Simon Dyson	77	73	150	1,000
Shingo Katayama	75	75	150	1,000
*Matthew Griffiths	73	77	150	
Nathan Green	75	75	150	1,000
Mark Roe	73	78	151	1,000
Jerry Kelly	74	77	151	1,000
Geoff Ogilvy	76	75	151	1,000
Steve Jones	74	77	151	1,000
John Huston	76	75	151	1,000
Thomas Bjorn	76	75	151	1,000
Brett Rumford	73	78	151	1,000
Roger Chapman	76	76	152	900
Tom Watson	74	78	152	900
Greg Turner	79	73	152	900
Jim Furyk	77	75	152	900
Henrik Stenson	75	77	152	900
Jean Van de Velde	77	75	152	900
Mark Sanders	79	73	152	900
Graham Rankin	79	75	154	900
Juan Carlos Aguero	77	77	154	900
Hidemichi Tanaka	76	78	154	900
*John Kemp	76	78	154	
Wayne Riley	78	77	155	900
Angel Cabrera	80	75	155	900
Matthew McGuire	71	85	156	900
Toshiaki Odate	76	80	156	900
Gary Player	77	82	159	900
Simon Vale	85	74	159	900
Stuart Callan	78	82	160	900
Chris Perry	78		WD	900
Rocco Mediate	74		WD	900

TNT Open

Noordwijkse Golf Club, Noordwijk, The Netherlands

Par 35-36–71; 6,741 yards

July 26-29

purse, £1,097,507

	SCORES				TOTAL	MONEY
Bernhard Langer	69	67	67	66	269	£182,917.91
Warren Bennett	68	67	67	67	269	121,945.27
(Langer defeated Bennett on first playoff hole.)						
Miguel Angel Jimenez	71	65	71	66	273	68,703.97
Barry Lane	71	67	66	70	274	46,607.48
Anders Hansen	69	67	75	63	274	46,607.48
Raymond Russell	68	68	69	69	274	46,607.48
Greg Turner	68	65	71	71	275	30,181.45
Ricardo Gonzalez	67	65	75	68	275	30,181.45
Andrew Oldcorn	70	65	72	69	276	22,242.82
Padraig Harrington	67	67	71	71	276	22,242.82
Stephen Leaney	71	67	70	68	276	22,242.82
Ian Garbutt	69	71	71	66	277	18,273.50
Ernie Els	68	70	75	64	277	18,273.50
Raphael Jacquelin	68	71	69	70	278	15,163.89
Peter Baker	66	68	74	70	278	15,163.89
Henrik Bjornstad	73	64	72	69	278	15,163.89
Roger Winchester	72	66	72	68	278	15,163.89
Peter O'Malley	73	68	69	68	278	15,163.89
Gary Evans	69	71	69	69	278	15,163.89
Steve Webster	71	69	71	68	279	12,593.90
Bradley Dredge	70	70	71	68	279	12,593.90
Dean Robertson	66	68	72	73	279	12,593.90
Scott Gardiner	68	73	71	67	279	12,593.90
Philip Walton	69	68	70	73	280	11,084.83
John Senden	69	70	69	72	280	11,084.83
Desvonde Botes	69	70	70	71	280	11,084.83
Tomas Jesus Munoz	74	67	65	74	280	11,084.83
Des Terblanche	69	71	74	66	280	11,084.83
Roger Chapman	70	69	72	70	281	9,767.82
Joakim Haeggman	70	69	71	71	281	9,767.82
Michael Jonzon	68	68	76	69	281	9,767.82
Peter Fowler	69	71	72	70	282	8,162.71
Mark McNulty	71	67	72	72	282	8,162.71
Darren Fichardt	68	66	70	78	282	8,162.71
Peter Hanson	70	69	72	71	282	8,162.71
Jamie Spence	69	70	70	73	282	8,162.71
Soren Hansen	70	71	70	71	282	8,162.71
Rolf Muntz	71	68	71	72	282	8,162.71
Richard Sterne	67	67	73	75	282	8,162.71
Jarrod Moseley	67	73	74	69	283	6,694.80
Per Nyman	73	67	69	74	283	6,694.80
Paul McGinley	71	70	67	75	283	6,694.80
Christian Cevaer	70	67	72	74	283	6,694.80
David Higgins	70	71	67	75	283	6,694.80
Gregory Havret	72	69	72	71	284	4,938.78
Jonathan Lomas	70	68	76	70	284	4,938.78
Stephen Dodd	70	71	72	71	284	4,938.78
Gary Orr	71	68	72	73	284	4,938.78
David Park	68	72	74	70	284	4,938.78
Fredrik Andersson	71	68	73	72	284	4,938.78
Andrew Coltart	66	69	79	70	284	4,938.78
Daren Lee	72	68	70	74	284	4,938.78
John Bickerton	70	69	73	72	284	4,938.78

	SCORES				TOTAL	MONEY
Alastair Forsyth	70	71	71	72	284	4,938.78
Aaron Baddeley	72	69	74	69	284	4,938.78
Jose Manuel Carriles	68	72	73	72	285	3,374.84
Paolo Quirici	67	72	73	73	285	3,374.84
Darren Clarke	68	70	73	74	285	3,374.84
Graeme Storm	71	68	71	75	285	3,374.84
Mikael Lundberg	67	72	69	78	286	3,018.15
Olle Karlsson	67	70	74	75	286	3,018.15
*Niels Boysen	64	75	77	71	287	
Mark Roe	69	69	73	77	288	2,743.77
Carl Suneson	69	70	76	73	288	2,743.77
Christophe Pottier	68	72	73	75	288	2,743.77
Hennie Otto	71	70	74	74	289	2,414.52
Joost Steenkamer	75	64	75	75	289	2,414.52
Marco Bernardini	69	71	72	77	289	2,414.52
Eamonn Darcy	70	71	76	73	290	2,140.14
Elliot Boult	74	63	75	78	290	2,140.14
Gordon Brand, Jr.	72	69	77	73	291	1,999.90

Volvo Scandinavian Masters

Barseback Golf & Country Club, Malmo, Sweden August 2-5
Par 35-37–72; 7,323 yards purse, £1,104,674

	SCORES				TOTAL	MONEY
Colin Montgomerie	66	69	69	70	274	£184,112.33
Ian Poulter	70	65	68	72	275	95,947.07
Lee Westwood	67	67	69	72	275	95,947.07
Warren Bennett	67	70	69	70	276	40,298.51
Dennis Edlund	69	67	71	69	276	40,298.51
Joakim Haeggman	71	67	70	68	276	40,298.51
Jarmo Sandelin	68	74	68	66	276	40,298.51
Adam Scott	69	72	67	68	276	40,298.51
Peter Hanson	70	72	66	69	277	21,541.14
Soren Hansen	66	73	68	70	277	21,541.14
Peter Hedblom	66	70	68	73	277	21,541.14
Thomas Bjorn	68	72	67	70	277	21,541.14
Fredrik Andersson	69	71	71	67	278	16,975.16
Niclas Fasth	67	69	72	70	278	16,975.16
Michael Campbell	69	70	70	69	278	16,975.16
Anders Forsbrand	72	69	67	71	279	14,084.59
Tony Johnstone	71	69	70	69	279	14,084.59
Johan Rystrom	67	72	71	69	279	14,084.59
Olivier Edmond	68	74	68	69	279	14,084.59
Darren Clarke	66	70	70	73	279	14,084.59
Peter Lonard	71	68	69	71	279	14,084.59
Roger Chapman	69	69	72	70	280	12,151.41
Raphael Jacquelin	68	75	68	69	280	12,151.41
Steve Webster	71	68	70	71	280	12,151.41
Wayne Riley	71	68	71	71	281	10,991.51
Thomas Levet	67	72	67	75	281	10,991.51
Ian Garbutt	71	71	69	70	281	10,991.51
Pierre Fulke	68	71	71	71	281	10,991.51
Costantino Rocca	68	72	71	71	282	9,184.57
Brian Davis	71	71	69	71	282	9,184.57
Anthony Wall	63	76	71	72	282	9,184.57
Jarrod Moseley	70	71	66	75	282	9,184.57

	SCORES				TOTAL	MONEY
Peter O'Malley	70	71	68	73	282	9,184.57
Paul Lawrie	69	71	65	77	282	9,184.57
Carl Pettersson	74	68	70	70	282	9,184.57
David Howell	73	70	66	74	283	6,959.45
Jesper Parnevik	71	72	69	71	283	6,959.45
Anders Hansen	71	72	70	70	283	6,959.45
Soren Kjeldsen	69	72	71	71	283	6,959.45
Fredrik Henge	71	69	69	74	283	6,959.45
Peter Baker	72	70	72	69	283	6,959.45
Carl Suneson	68	74	72	69	283	6,959.45
Alex Cejka	73	70	70	70	283	6,959.45
Ignacio Garrido	71	71	72	69	283	6,959.45
Raymond Russell	70	74	71	68	283	6,959.45
Stephen Gallacher	70	70	69	74	283	6,959.45
Desvonde Botes	71	68	72	73	284	5,081.50
Paul Broadhurst	71	73	69	71	284	5,081.50
Per-Ulrik Johansson	72	72	68	72	284	5,081.50
Christian Cevaer	71	69	73	71	284	5,081.50
Steven Richardson	74	66	72	72	284	5,081.50
Christopher Hanell	70	72	72	70	284	5,081.50
Gordon Brand, Jr.	72	71	72	70	285	3,774.30
Mark Roe	72	71	71	71	285	3,774.30
Mark McNulty	70	71	70	74	285	3,774.30
Jamie Spence	69	74	70	72	285	3,774.30
Gary Evans	72	71	72	70	285	3,774.30
Bradley Dredge	68	74	73	70	285	3,774.30
Ian Woosnam	70	74	73	69	286	2,761.68
Marc Farry	71	72	71	72	286	2,761.68
Richard Green	69	74	70	73	286	2,761.68
Steen Tinning	73	71	73	69	286	2,761.68
Peter Mitchell	72	70	72	72	286	2,761.68
Ricardo Gonzalez	71	73	75	67	286	2,761.68
Fredrik Jacobson	71	73	71	71	286	2,761.68
Greg Owen	73	71	70	72	286	2,761.68
David Carter	70	70	73	73	286	2,761.68
Hennie Otto	69	74	74	70	287	1,994.55
Henrik Bjornstad	73	70	71	73	287	1,994.55
Nicolas Colsaerts	71	71	73	72	287	1,994.55
Olle Karlsson	71	73	73	70	287	1,994.55
Greg Turner	72	72	74	70	288	1,654.25
Carlos Rodiles	72	71	71	74	288	1,654.25
Marcus Norgren	73	69	74	73	289	1,646.88
Gregory Havret	67	73	75	74	289	1,646.88
Roger Winchester	75	69	69	76	289	1,646.88
Van Phillips	70	74	72	73	289	1,646.88
Stephen Scahill	72	67	73	77	289	1,646.88
Michael Jonzon	71	70	74	74	289	1,646.88
Henrik Stenson	70	74	74	72	290	1,640.44
Des Terblanche	70	72	77	73	292	1,638.60
Tomas Jesus Munoz	70	74	73	76	293	1,636.76
*Niklas Lemke	72	72	75	75	294	

Celtic Manor Resort Wales Open

Celtic Manor Resort, Newport, Wales
Par 36-36–72; 7,324 yards
(Shortened to 36 holes — rain.)

August 9-12
purse, £750,000

	SCORES		TOTAL	MONEY
Paul McGinley	67	71	138	£125,000
Paul Lawrie	67	71	138	65,140
Daren Lee	69	69	138	65,140
(McGinley defeated Lawrie on second and Lee on fifth playoff hole.)				
Anders Forsbrand	72	67	139	31,850
Mark Pilkington	68	71	139	31,850
Jamie Donaldson	68	71	139	31,850
Anders Hansen	72	68	140	22,500
Steve Webster	74	67	141	14,887.50
Nick O'Hern	70	71	141	14,887.50
Thomas Levet	71	70	141	14,887.50
Roger Wessels	68	73	141	14,887.50
Gary Orr	67	74	141	14,887.50
Nic Henning	73	68	141	14,887.50
Kevin Spurgeon	72	70	142	10,362.50
Sven Struver	72	70	142	10,362.50
Jarrod Moseley	70	72	142	10,362.50
Phillip Price	70	72	142	10,362.50
Simon Dyson	73	69	142	10,362.50
Scott Gardiner	69	73	142	10,362.50
Santiago Luna	72	71	143	7,580.77
Warren Bennett	72	71	143	7,580.77
Soren Kjeldsen	70	73	143	7,580.77
John Senden	72	71	143	7,580.77
Graham Rankin	68	75	143	7,580.77
Ian Poulter	71	72	143	7,580.77
Jean Hugo	72	71	143	7,580.77
Jeremy Robinson	73	70	143	7,580.77
Jonathan Lomas	73	70	143	7,580.77
Ignacio Garrido	72	71	143	7,580.77
Simon Hurd	69	74	143	7,580.77
David Higgins	73	70	143	7,580.77
Alastair Forsyth	72	71	143	7,580.77
Andrew Oldcorn	69	75	144	4,804.69
Mark Roe	70	74	144	4,804.69
Marc Farry	71	73	144	4,804.69
Mark McNulty	77	67	144	4,804.69
Trevor Immelman	72	72	144	4,804.69
Justin Rose	71	73	144	4,804.69
Fredrik Henge	72	72	144	4,804.69
Roger Winchester	68	76	144	4,804.69
Per Nyman	72	72	144	4,804.69
Alex Cejka	74	70	144	4,804.69
Des Terblanche	77	67	144	4,804.69
David Lynn	69	75	144	4,804.69
Michael Jonzon	70	74	144	4,804.69
John Bickerton	71	73	144	4,804.69
Paul Casey	74	70	144	4,804.69
Carl Pettersson	74	70	144	4,804.69
Ian Woosnam	73	72	145	2,580
Jeev Milkha Singh	75	70	145	2,580
Barry Lane	71	74	145	2,580
Anthony Wall	72	73	145	2,580

	SCORES			TOTAL	MONEY
Dennis Edlund	72	73		145	2,580
Thomas Gogele	70	75		145	2,580
Olivier Edmond	75	70		145	2,580
Gary Evans	72	73		145	2,580
Jorge Berendt	74	71		145	2,580
Tomas Jesus Munoz	70	75		145	2,580
Markus Brier	72	73		145	2,580
Fredrik Andersson	72	73		145	2,580
David Carter	70	75		145	2,580
Stephen Gallacher	74	71		145	2,580
Marco Bernardini	73	72		145	2,580
*Craig Williams	74	71		145	
Wayne Riley	70	76		146	1,306.49
Gary Murphy	71	75		146	1,306.49
Maarten Lafeber	72	74		146	1,306.49
Richard Green	73	73		146	1,306.49
Marcus Higley	70	76		146	1,306.49
Garry Houston	73	73		146	1,306.49
Desvonde Botes	73	73		146	1,306.49
Simon Hurley	75	71		146	1,306.49
Andrew Beal	74	72		146	1,306.49
Massimo Scarpa	74	72		146	1,306.49
Steven Richardson	74	72		146	1,306.49
Sion Bebb	72	74		146	1,306.49
Stephen Scahill	72	74		146	1,306.49
Bradley Dredge	73	73		146	1,306.49
David Park	72	74		146	1,306.49
Jarmo Sandelin	71	75		146	1,306.49
Erol Simsek	72	74		146	1,306.49

North West of Ireland Open

Slieve Russell Hotel Golf & Country Club,
Co. Cavan, Ireland
Par 36-36–72; 7,061 yards

August 16-19
purse, £219,225

	SCORES				TOTAL	MONEY
Tobias Dier	66	68	66	71	271	£36,535.49
Stephen Dodd	67	68	68	69	272	24,352.82
Mark Pilkington	68	69	69	68	274	13,723.51
Mattias Eliasson	67	70	72	68	277	10,128.22
James Hepworth	68	69	72	68	277	10,128.22
Peter Hanson	75	65	67	71	278	5,509.87
Peter Hedblom	71	67	70	70	278	5,509.87
David Higgins	69	71	69	69	278	5,509.87
Domingo Hospital	70	69	73	66	278	5,509.87
Andreas Ljunggren	72	71	66	69	278	5,509.87
Graeme Storm	69	73	70	66	278	5,509.87
Robert Jan Derksen	68	68	69	74	279	3,393.61
Kenneth Ferrie	70	68	73	68	279	3,393.61
Jesus Maria Arruti	65	72	70	72	279	3,393.61
Johan Skold	71	69	69	70	279	3,393.61
Joakim Rask	71	72	68	68	279	3,393.61
Christian Cevaer	74	69	67	70	280	2,893.78
Jamie Donaldson	69	69	72	70	280	2,893.78
Niels Kraaij	72	71	71	67	281	2,385.17
Damian McGrane	70	70	72	69	281	2,385.17

	SCORES				TOTAL	MONEY
Grant Dodd	68	70	75	68	281	2,385.17
Graham Rankin	71	70	70	70	281	2,385.17
Renaud Guillard	76	68	67	70	281	2,385.17
Trevor Immelman	71	71	70	69	281	2,385.17
Jeremy Robinson	73	71	68	69	281	2,385.17
Johan Rystrom	71	73	67	70	281	2,385.17
Andrew Raitt	74	68	67	72	281	2,385.17
Michael Jonzon	68	70	71	72	281	2,385.17
Klas Eriksson	72	69	71	70	282	1,885.34
Gary Murphy	72	70	73	67	282	1,885.34
Kalle Brink	72	70	71	69	282	1,885.34
Gary Evans	72	72	68	70	282	1,885.34
Matthew Blackey	70	69	71	72	282	1,885.34
Peter Fowler	72	71	74	66	283	1,622.27
Euan Little	74	70	68	71	283	1,622.27
Simon Hurley	71	71	70	71	283	1,622.27
Raimo Sjoberg	72	71	73	67	283	1,622.27
Greig Hutcheon	68	72	74	70	284	1,424.97
Alberto Binaghi	71	70	71	72	284	1,424.97
Philip Golding	74	69	70	71	284	1,424.97
Mattias Nilsson	72	68	73	71	284	1,424.97
Didier de Vooght	74	70	67	73	284	1,424.97
Des Smyth	72	72	72	69	285	1,183.82
Robin Byrd	73	68	72	72	285	1,183.82
Miles Tunnicliff	72	71	71	71	285	1,183.82
Gianluca Baruffaldi	72	68	74	71	285	1,183.82
Robert Coles	74	70	71	70	285	1,183.82
Birgir Hafthorsson	72	72	72	69	285	1,183.82
Paul Nilbrink	72	71	69	74	286	920.75
Craig Hainline	72	70	71	73	286	920.75
Chris Gane	75	67	69	75	286	920.75
Dennis Edlund	69	69	75	73	286	920.75
Simon Khan	73	66	76	71	286	920.75
Alan McLean	71	73	72	70	286	920.75
Knud Storgaard	70	72	73	72	287	667.07
Michele Reale	70	70	71	76	287	667.07
Federico Bisazza	75	69	69	74	287	667.07
Gianluca Pietrobono	71	71	77	68	287	667.07
Carlos Larrain	74	68	73	72	287	667.07
Sebastien Delagrange	70	74	72	71	287	667.07
Nic Henning	71	73	68	75	287	667.07
Eric Carlberg	70	74	70	74	288	515.18
Patrik Gottfridson	71	73	72	72	288	515.18
Marcello Santi	73	69	72	74	288	515.18
Jose Romero	71	71	74	72	288	515.18
Francis Howley	75	68	75	70	288	515.18
Simon Wakefield	69	71	73	75	288	515.18
Pasi Purhonen	74	67	74	74	289	427.49
Ian Hutchings	75	68	72	74	289	427.49
Andrew Marshall	67	74	74	75	290	347
Mads Vibe-Hastrup	71	70	78	71	290	347
Wolfgang Huget	70	72	73	75	290	347
Thomas Norret	73	70	76	71	290	347
Jorge Berendt	72	72	72	75	291	320.38
Dominique Nouailhac	70	71	74	76	291	320.38
John Mellor	75	67	74	75	291	320.38
Kariem Baraka	73	70	77	71	291	320.38
Marten Olander	73	71	79	69	292	313.81
Garry Houston	74	70	76	72	292	313.81

	SCORES				TOTAL	MONEY
Stuart Little	70	74	75	73	292	313.81
John Dignam	69	75	74	75	293	309.11
David Dixon	71	71	77	74	293	309.11
Marco Bernardini	72	69	72	82	295	306.29
Roger Winchester	73	70	78	75	296	304.41
Andrew Butterfield	75	68	80	74	297	302.53

Gleneagles Scottish PGA Championship

Gleneagles Hotel, Perth, Scotland
Par 36-36–72; 7,060 yards

August 23-26
purse, £1,000,000

	SCORES				TOTAL	MONEY
Paul Casey	69	69	67	69	274	£166,660
Alex Cejka	71	67	66	71	275	111,110
David Howell	70	71	66	70	277	62,600
Gary Evans	66	67	77	68	278	42,466.67
Christian Cevaer	72	71	69	66	278	42,466.67
Carl Pettersson	75	66	70	67	278	42,466.67
Peter Hanson	74	64	69	72	279	24,350
Jonathan Lomas	66	74	70	69	279	24,350
Des Terblanche	73	70	70	66	279	24,350
Stephen Gallacher	67	71	69	72	279	24,350
Mark Mouland	65	70	73	72	280	15,614.29
Andrew Oldcorn	70	67	73	70	280	15,614.29
Des Smyth	71	71	68	70	280	15,614.29
Justin Rose	67	71	68	74	280	15,614.29
Peter O'Malley	68	72	70	70	280	15,614.29
Stephen Scahill	69	74	69	68	280	15,614.29
David Higgins	67	71	70	72	280	15,614.29
Roger Chapman	72	70	70	69	281	12,225
Gary Murphy	68	69	70	74	281	12,225
Roger Wessels	69	72	68	72	281	12,225
Paul Lawrie	75	69	69	68	281	12,225
Malcolm Mackenzie	75	66	70	71	282	10,400
Mark Roe	73	71	69	69	282	10,400
Greg Turner	69	67	75	71	282	10,400
Paul Broadhurst	68	69	73	72	282	10,400
Johan Rystrom	72	69	67	74	282	10,400
David Lynn	69	70	72	71	282	10,400
Simon Dyson	69	70	69	74	282	10,400
Robert Karlsson	70	69	70	74	283	8,450
Stephen Dodd	73	70	70	70	283	8,450
Ian Garbutt	70	72	70	71	283	8,450
Nicolas Vanhootegem	73	65	69	76	283	8,450
Jarmo Sandelin	72	66	72	73	283	8,450
Jamie Donaldson	69	71	71	72	283	8,450
Peter Fowler	66	68	78	72	284	7,400
Carlos Rodiles	69	67	75	73	284	7,400
Mark James	72	71	70	72	285	6,200
Sam Torrance	68	74	70	73	285	6,200
Brian Davis	72	72	69	72	285	6,200
Anthony Wall	69	74	70	72	285	6,200
Jamie Spence	71	68	72	74	285	6,200
Russell Claydon	70	72	74	69	285	6,200
Rolf Muntz	69	72	74	70	285	6,200
Andrew Raitt	73	67	72	73	285	6,200

	SCORES				TOTAL	MONEY
Dean Robertson	72	69	73	71	285	6,200
Nick Dougherty	70	74	70	71	285	6,200
Ross Drummond	71	72	71	72	286	4,800
Soren Kjeldsen	71	68	71	76	286	4,800
Trevor Immelman	71	73	70	72	286	4,800
Colin Gillies	74	66	70	76	286	4,800
Wayne Riley	69	72	72	74	287	3,900
Warren Bennett	67	75	72	73	287	3,900
David Park	73	70	70	74	287	3,900
Mark Pilkington	72	69	74	72	287	3,900
Raymond Russell	71	70	68	78	287	3,900
Eamonn Darcy	73	69	73	73	288	3,020
Anders Forsbrand	68	70	80	70	288	3,020
Shaun Webster	70	72	74	72	288	3,020
Olivier Edmond	68	74	73	73	288	3,020
Robert Arnott	74	66	71	77	288	3,020
Brian Marchbank	75	69	71	74	289	2,600
Desvonde Botes	71	70	74	74	289	2,600
Daren Lee	72	71	74	72	289	2,600
Santiago Luna	71	72	74	73	290	2,250
Garry Houston	74	70	71	75	290	2,250
John Senden	72	70	70	78	290	2,250
Olle Karlsson	72	72	73	73	290	2,250
David Gilford	74	70	74	73	291	1,910
Graham Rankin	74	70	73	74	291	1,910
Mathias Gronberg	73	71	75	72	291	1,910
Sandy Lyle	72	71	75	74	292	1,498.79
Jean Hugo	73	71	72	76	292	1,498.79
Neil Cheetham	74	70	72	77	293	1,495.94
Gregory Havret	69	73	75	77	294	1,493.09
Paul Eales	70	74	78	72	294	1,493.09
Roger Winchester	73	70	79	73	295	1,490.24
Craig Hainline	72	72	75	77	296	1,487.39
Soren Hansen	74	69	77	76	296	1,487.39
Van Phillips	75	69	77	75	296	1,487.39

BMW International Open

Golfclub Munchen Nord-Eichenreid,
Munich, Germany
Par 36-36–72; 6,914 yards

August 30-September 2
purse, £1,136,112

	SCORES				TOTAL	MONEY
John Daly	63	64	68	66	261	£189,352.10
Padraig Harrington	69	63	62	68	262	126,234.73
Thomas Levet	70	66	64	68	268	71,120.65
Raymond Russell	68	66	66	69	269	48,246.92
Dean Robertson	64	69	69	67	269	48,246.92
Christopher Hanell	71	65	66	67	269	48,246.92
Sergio Garcia	67	67	69	67	270	29,311.71
Justin Rose	67	69	68	66	270	29,311.71
Paul Casey	69	67	69	65	270	29,311.71
Soren Kjeldsen	65	70	71	65	271	21,055.95
Paul McGinley	70	66	68	67	271	21,055.95
David Carter	69	66	68	68	271	21,055.95
Jose Maria Olazabal	70	62	70	70	272	17,458.26
Raphael Jacquelin	68	67	70	67	272	17,458.26

	SCORES				TOTAL	MONEY
Colin Montgomerie	69	69	68	66	272	17,458.26
Bernhard Langer	67	69	69	68	273	14,746.74
Warren Bennett	69	68	69	67	273	14,746.74
Peter O'Malley	71	67	66	69	273	14,746.74
Thomas Bjorn	65	67	65	76	273	14,746.74
Carl Pettersson	66	69	70	68	273	14,746.74
Alex Cejka	69	66	69	70	274	13,008.49
Ricardo Gonzalez	67	68	69	70	274	13,008.49
Sandy Lyle	69	71	71	65	276	11,474.74
Stephen Dodd	69	70	69	68	276	11,474.74
Fredrik Jacobson	68	66	68	74	276	11,474.74
Fredrik Andersson	69	68	69	70	276	11,474.74
Retief Goosen	68	69	68	71	276	11,474.74
Mikael Lundberg	72	68	70	66	276	11,474.74
Adam Scott	67	64	77	68	276	11,474.74
Greg Turner	69	70	71	67	277	9,137.59
Anders Hansen	69	69	70	69	277	9,137.59
Steen Tinning	74	66	69	68	277	9,137.59
Johan Rystrom	67	70	70	70	277	9,137.59
Russell Claydon	70	70	72	65	277	9,137.59
Paul Lawrie	70	70	69	68	277	9,137.59
Stephen Gallacher	67	70	68	72	277	9,137.59
Mark Mouland	68	68	70	72	278	7,157.51
Ian Woosnam	69	67	71	71	278	7,157.51
Barry Lane	69	69	70	70	278	7,157.51
John Senden	68	67	70	73	278	7,157.51
Gregory Havret	68	70	70	70	278	7,157.51
Jorge Berendt	69	67	71	71	278	7,157.51
Robert Coles	72	66	68	72	278	7,157.51
Markus Brier	72	68	70	68	278	7,157.51
Brett Rumford	68	68	69	73	278	7,157.51
Desvonde Botes	70	70	69	70	279	5,339.73
Carl Suneson	72	68	70	69	279	5,339.73
Roger Wessels	66	70	72	71	279	5,339.73
Gary Orr	68	69	71	71	279	5,339.73
Mikko Ilonen	71	68	68	72	279	5,339.73
Alastair Forsyth	68	66	74	71	279	5,339.73
Nick Dougherty	71	68	68	72	279	5,339.73
Maarten Lafeber	72	68	71	69	280	3,797.86
Richard Green	63	69	75	73	280	3,797.86
Joakim Haeggman	67	71	71	71	280	3,797.86
Robert Karlsson	70	68	71	71	280	3,797.86
Ignacio Garrido	68	72	71	69	280	3,797.86
Stephen Scahill	71	66	71	72	280	3,797.86
Graeme Storm	71	69	68	72	280	3,797.86
Andrew Oldcorn	67	69	70	75	281	2,840.28
Eduardo Romero	71	67	71	72	281	2,840.28
Peter Mitchell	68	70	72	71	281	2,840.28
Greg Owen	69	67	74	71	281	2,840.28
David Park	68	71	74	68	281	2,840.28
Niclas Fasth	67	71	71	72	281	2,840.28
John Bickerton	67	68	72	74	281	2,840.28
Tony Johnstone	66	71	72	73	282	2,048.90
Marc Farry	67	67	75	73	282	2,048.90
Brian Davis	68	68	74	72	282	2,048.90
Trevor Immelman	70	69	69	74	282	2,048.90
Pierre Fulke	69	71	72	70	282	2,048.90
David Lynn	70	69	70	73	282	2,048.90
Jonathan Lomas	66	71	74	72	283	1,700.38

	SCORES				TOTAL	MONEY
Soren Hansen	68	70	78	68	284	1,698.49
Mark James	72	67	74	72	285	1,696.59
Jarmo Sandelin	69	71	70	76	286	1,694.70
Andrew Coltart	69	71	74	73	287	1,692.81
Sven Struver	71	69	76	73	289	1,690.91
Patrik Sjoland	74	66	78	76	294	1,689.02

Omega European Masters

Crans-sur-Sierre Golf Club, Crans-sur-Sierre, Switzerland September 6-9
Par 36-35–71; 6,857 yards purse, £939,696

	SCORES				TOTAL	MONEY
Ricardo Gonzalez	65	67	68	68	268	£156,616.09
Soren Hansen	70	65	68	68	271	104,406.55
Craig Stadler	69	69	67	68	273	52,904.92
Gary Orr	67	66	71	69	273	52,904.92
Fredrik Jacobson	68	71	65	70	274	39,843.13
Stephen Scahill	67	67	68	74	276	30,540.14
Greg Owen	68	67	68	73	276	30,540.14
Gordon Brand, Jr.	66	71	71	69	277	22,270.81
Peter Fowler	69	71	69	68	277	22,270.81
Eduardo Romero	72	67	71	68	278	17,415.71
David Gilford	67	66	72	73	278	17,415.71
Raphael Jacquelin	68	70	72	68	278	17,415.71
Francis Valera	69	72	67	71	279	14,440
Markus Brier	69	67	70	73	279	14,440
Jamie Donaldson	71	72	66	70	279	14,440
Greg Turner	67	71	71	71	280	11,786.48
Stephen Leaney	67	71	72	70	280	11,786.48
Jeremy Robinson	70	72	70	68	280	11,786.48
Peter O'Malley	68	71	67	74	280	11,786.48
Ernie Els	71	72	68	69	280	11,786.48
Lee Westwood	70	69	69	72	280	11,786.48
Steven O'Hara	74	64	71	71	280	11,786.48
Mark Mouland	69	72	72	68	281	8,927.12
Barry Lane	72	69	69	71	281	8,927.12
Brian Davis	68	71	71	71	281	8,927.12
Jose Manuel Carriles	73	68	70	70	281	8,927.12
Paul Eales	68	69	70	74	281	8,927.12
Joakim Haeggman	71	68	73	69	281	8,927.12
David Park	69	71	70	71	281	8,927.12
Fredrik Andersson	68	70	70	73	281	8,927.12
Dean Robertson	66	70	74	71	281	8,927.12
David Carter	73	67	69	72	281	8,927.12
Adam Scott	69	69	72	71	281	8,927.12
Justin Rose	69	69	72	72	282	7,047.72
Mathias Gronberg	70	72	68	72	282	7,047.72
Christopher Hanell	69	71	70	72	282	7,047.72
Sam Torrance	72	71	71	69	283	5,920.09
Gary Murphy	69	69	72	73	283	5,920.09
Elliot Boult	70	72	71	70	283	5,920.09
Thomas Gogele	66	75	71	71	283	5,920.09
Johan Rystrom	69	74	69	71	283	5,920.09
Alex Cejka	70	72	69	72	283	5,920.09
David Lynn	68	70	73	72	283	5,920.09
David Higgins	71	70	71	71	283	5,920.09

	SCORES				TOTAL	MONEY
Paul Casey	76	67	65	75	283	5,920.09
Nick Faldo	70	72	70	72	284	4,416.57
Marc Farry	70	70	71	73	284	4,416.57
Trevor Immelman	70	69	72	73	284	4,416.57
Miguel Angel Jimenez	73	68	73	70	284	4,416.57
Olle Karlsson	71	69	70	74	284	4,416.57
Emanuele Canonica	70	72	70	72	284	4,416.57
Van Phillips	69	69	74	72	284	4,416.57
Mark James	71	70	71	73	285	3,288.94
Santiago Luna	71	70	69	75	285	3,288.94
Warren Bennett	68	69	74	74	285	3,288.94
Shaun Webster	69	71	69	76	285	3,288.94
Stephen Gallacher	71	69	74	71	285	3,288.94
Sandy Lyle	72	70	71	73	286	2,584.17
Jean Hugo	72	68	74	72	286	2,584.17
Russell Claydon	72	71	72	71	286	2,584.17
Christian Cevaer	71	71	72	72	286	2,584.17
Henrik Nystrom	66	73	75	72	286	2,584.17
Graeme Storm	71	72	68	75	286	2,584.17
Roger Chapman	72	70	71	74	287	2,067.33
David Howell	71	72	73	71	287	2,067.33
Anders Hansen	73	69	70	75	287	2,067.33
Roger Winchester	71	71	76	69	287	2,067.33
Ian Garbutt	72	69	73	73	287	2,067.33
Carlos Rodiles	71	72	70	75	288	1,785.42
Wayne Riley	74	67	73	75	289	1,563.03
Gary Emerson	71	72	71	75	289	1,563.03
Ignacio Garrido	67	72	75	76	290	1,407.67
Maarten Lafeber	72	71	77	71	291	1,403.91
Peter Mitchell	71	71	71	78	291	1,403.91
Nic Henning	72	66	74	79	291	1,403.91
Seve Ballesteros	72	71	76	74	293	1,400.15
Philip Walton	68	73	74	80	295	1,398.27
Massimo Scarpa	70	73	78	77	298	1,396.39
Kim Felton	70	73	77	79	299	1,394.51

Trophee Lancome

Saint-Nom-La-Breteche, Paris, France
Par 36-35–71; 6,903 yards

September 20-23
purse, £900,000

	SCORES				TOTAL	MONEY
Sergio Garcia	68	65	68	65	266	£150,000
Retief Goosen	64	71	65	67	267	100,000
Jean Hugo	66	68	69	66	269	56,340
Gary Emerson	66	70	66	69	271	45,000
Niclas Fasth	69	66	66	71	272	38,160
Raphael Jacquelin	68	71	68	66	273	29,250
Anthony Wall	68	65	70	70	273	29,250
Ian Woosnam	68	71	69	66	274	20,220
Trevor Immelman	70	72	67	65	274	20,220
Henrik Nystrom	70	66	69	69	274	20,220
Steve Webster	66	68	71	70	275	15,510
Phillip Price	70	67	66	72	275	15,510
Adam Scott	69	70	65	71	275	15,510
Mark Mouland	75	67	69	65	276	12,435
Sven Struver	69	68	70	69	276	12,435

	SCORES				TOTAL	MONEY
Shaun Webster	67	68	69	72	276	12,435
David Lynn	70	71	64	71	276	12,435
Andrew Coltart	66	71	66	73	276	12,435
Graeme Storm	71	65	69	71	276	12,435
Richard Johnson	70	72	67	68	277	10,470
Greg Owen	68	70	73	66	277	10,470
John Bickerton	68	71	71	67	277	10,470
Malcolm Mackenzie	69	70	70	69	278	9,090
Paul Eales	69	70	69	70	278	9,090
Russell Claydon	68	73	69	68	278	9,090
Jonathan Lomas	69	71	70	68	278	9,090
Markus Brier	73	66	67	72	278	9,090
Dean Robertson	69	71	66	72	278	9,090
David Carter	72	67	68	71	278	9,090
Mark Roe	66	66	75	72	279	7,132.50
Mark McNulty	71	68	68	72	279	7,132.50
Jarrod Moseley	71	71	70	67	279	7,132.50
Per Nyman	74	67	73	65	279	7,132.50
Jorge Berendt	69	68	68	74	279	7,132.50
Christian Cevaer	73	67	67	72	279	7,132.50
Angel Cabrera	72	68	67	72	279	7,132.50
Gary Orr	66	73	71	69	279	7,132.50
Santiago Luna	71	68	68	73	280	5,850
Thomas Levet	68	72	71	69	280	5,850
Emanuele Canonica	72	67	71	70	280	5,850
Diego Borrego	70	71	69	70	280	5,850
Fredrik Andersson	71	68	70	71	280	5,850
Jose Rivero	71	71	67	72	281	4,860
Graham Rankin	69	72	68	72	281	4,860
Joakim Haeggman	69	71	70	71	281	4,860
Van Phillips	70	68	72	71	281	4,860
Brett Rumford	70	72	69	70	281	4,860
Scott Gardiner	66	73	70	72	281	4,860
Peter Hanson	71	68	69	74	282	3,870
Peter Baker	67	72	71	72	282	3,870
Jeremy Robinson	71	69	75	67	282	3,870
Massimo Scarpa	69	72	67	74	282	3,870
Robert Coles	67	70	69	76	282	3,870
Eduardo Romero	67	72	69	75	283	2,760
Jean Van de Velde	70	69	71	73	283	2,760
Carl Suneson	69	72	72	70	283	2,760
Robert Karlsson	67	72	72	72	283	2,760
Bradley Dredge	71	71	70	71	283	2,760
Fredrik Jacobson	71	67	68	77	283	2,760
Erol Simsek	69	72	70	72	283	2,760
Mikael Lundberg	66	73	73	71	283	2,760
Simon Dyson	69	68	70	76	283	2,760
Gordon Brand, Jr.	71	69	71	73	284	2,205
Andrew Oldcorn	71	67	72	74	284	2,205
Barry Lane	72	69	71	73	285	1,848.33
Maarten Lafeber	71	71	72	71	285	1,848.33
Stephen Leaney	70	72	69	74	285	1,848.33
Garry Houston	69	68	76	72	285	1,848.33
Peter Mitchell	71	71	70	73	285	1,848.33
Ian Garbutt	73	69	73	70	285	1,848.33
Raymond Russell	75	67	69	75	286	1,349.04
Carl Pettersson	70	71	68	77	286	1,349.04
Olivier David	71	71	69	76	287	1,346.22
David Gilford	68	73	72	75	288	1,344.34

	SCORES				TOTAL	MONEY
Nicolas Colsaerts	68	73	73	76	290	1,342.47
David Howell	71	71	74	76	292	1,339.65
Olivier Edmond	73	69	75	75	292	1,339.65
Marc Pendaries	73	69	76	77	295	1,336.84

Linde German Masters

Gut Larchenhof, Cologne, Germany
Par 36-36–72; 7,289 yards

October 4-7
purse, £1,672,271

	SCORES				TOTAL	MONEY
Bernhard Langer	67	64	68	67	266	£278,711.98
Fredrik Jacobson	67	66	67	67	267	145,246.10
John Daly	71	67	64	65	267	145,246.10
Roger Chapman	67	69	67	66	269	77,258.96
Greg Owen	65	68	67	69	269	77,258.96
Gary Orr	70	67	66	67	270	54,348.84
David Lynn	68	66	68	68	270	54,348.84
Ian Woosnam	69	68	66	68	271	39,632.84
Paul McGinley	70	67	68	66	271	39,632.84
Robert Karlsson	67	69	69	68	273	29,097.53
Gary Evans	71	65	66	71	273	29,097.53
Roger Wessels	67	70	65	71	273	29,097.53
Raymond Russell	71	67	67	68	273	29,097.53
Retief Goosen	68	68	67	70	273	29,097.53
Marc Farry	72	65	66	71	274	23,077.35
Steve Webster	70	68	65	71	274	23,077.35
Ian Poulter	67	69	67	71	274	23,077.35
Colin Montgomerie	70	70	68	66	274	23,077.35
Anders Forsbrand	73	69	64	69	275	19,231.13
Padraig Harrington	70	67	67	71	275	19,231.13
Barry Lane	68	70	68	69	275	19,231.13
Peter O'Malley	69	70	66	70	275	19,231.13
Markus Brier	70	70	65	70	275	19,231.13
Michael Campbell	72	68	68	67	275	19,231.13
Trevor Immelman	68	72	69	67	276	15,886.58
Miguel Angel Jimenez	68	69	68	71	276	15,886.58
Jean Hugo	70	72	68	66	276	15,886.58
Roger Winchester	68	70	72	66	276	15,886.58
Van Phillips	68	69	72	67	276	15,886.58
Niclas Fasth	72	69	68	67	276	15,886.58
Paul Casey	72	69	67	68	276	15,886.58
Warren Bennett	68	66	71	72	277	12,263.33
Anders Hansen	70	68	70	69	277	12,263.33
Soren Kjeldsen	70	67	72	68	277	12,263.33
Stephen Leaney	67	66	67	77	277	12,263.33
Pierre Fulke	67	70	69	71	277	12,263.33
Darren Clarke	68	67	71	71	277	12,263.33
Rolf Muntz	70	71	70	66	277	12,263.33
Jarmo Sandelin	67	69	70	71	277	12,263.33
Mikko Ilonen	69	67	72	69	277	12,263.33
Mark McNulty	68	72	70	68	278	9,866.40
John Senden	66	72	68	72	278	9,866.40
Carl Suneson	70	69	68	71	278	9,866.40
Ricardo Gonzalez	66	70	73	69	278	9,866.40
David Carter	73	68	67	70	278	9,866.40
David Howell	70	70	69	70	279	7,023.54

		SCORES			TOTAL	MONEY
Maarten Lafeber	72	68	72	67	279	7,023.54
Anthony Wall	71	69	70	69	279	7,023.54
Justin Rose	72	66	68	73	279	7,023.54
Henrik Stenson	67	69	73	70	279	7,023.54
Jean Van de Velde	73	68	67	71	279	7,023.54
Jonathan Lomas	69	68	71	71	279	7,023.54
Ian Garbutt	74	65	70	70	279	7,023.54
Mathias Gronberg	67	74	69	69	279	7,023.54
Paul Lawrie	71	70	67	71	279	7,023.54
Wolfgang Huget	70	68	70	71	279	7,023.54
Nick Dougherty	69	72	66	72	279	7,023.54
Jean-Francois Remesy	68	70	72	70	280	4,849.59
Thomas Levet	71	71	69	69	280	4,849.59
Lucas Parsons	69	70	69	72	280	4,849.59
Santiago Luna	71	69	70	71	281	4,013.45
Des Smyth	71	71	72	67	281	4,013.45
Brian Davis	67	74	69	71	281	4,013.45
Alex Cejka	74	67	67	73	281	4,013.45
Ignacio Garrido	72	70	70	69	281	4,013.45
Henrik Nystrom	65	73	70	73	281	4,013.45
Stephen Gallacher	72	70	72	67	281	4,013.45
Tony Johnstone	71	71	71	69	282	3,260.93
Jose Maria Olazabal	69	71	68	74	282	3,260.93
Jochen Lupprian	70	70	70	73	283	2,613.95
Marcel Siem	72	70	71	70	283	2,613.95
Massimo Scarpa	72	68	74	69	283	2,613.95
Andrew Coltart	72	69	72	70	283	2,613.95
Nick Cassini	73	68	70	72	283	2,613.95
Lee Westwood	72	70	69	73	284	2,500.05
Adam Scott	70	71	73	70	284	2,500.05
Emanuele Canonica	70	71	71	73	285	2,497.26
Darren Fichardt	68	74	75	69	286	2,494.47
Gary Emerson	71	71	70	74	286	2,494.47
Gordon Brand, Jr.	70	69	73	75	287	2,491.69
Mark James	72	70	72	80	294	2,489.83

Cisco World Match Play

Wentworth Club, West Course, Surrey, England
Par 434 534 444–35; 345 434 455–37–72; 7,047 yards

October 11-14
purse, £1,000,000

FIRST ROUND

Thomas Bjorn defeated Adam Scott, 4 and 3

Bjorn	3 3 5	4 2 3	4 4 3	31	4 3 3	4 2 4	4 5 5	34 65
Scott	4 4 4	4 3 4	4 3 4	34	3 4 4	4 3 4	3 4 4	33 67

Bjorn leads, 2 up

Bjorn	4 3 4	4 2 W	4 4 4	X	2 4 4	4 3 4		
Scott	3 3 4	4 3 C	5 5 4	X	3 4 4	3 2 4		

Ian Woosnam defeated Retief Goosen, 4 and 3

Goosen	4 3 4	4 3 4	4 4 5	35	4 4 5	3 3 4	4 4 4	35 70
Woosnam	5 2 4	5 2 4	4 4 3	33	3 4 4	3 3 3	4 4 4	32 65

Woosnam leads, 4 up

Goosen	4 3 5	4 3 4	3 4 4	34	3 3 4	4 2 4		
Woosnam	4 4 4	5 2 3	C 3 5	X	3 4 4	3 2 4		

Padraig Harrington defeated Nick Faldo, 9 and 8

Harrington	3 2 4	4 3 3	4 4 3	30	2 4 4	4 3 3	4 5 4	33	63
Faldo	5 4 5	4 3 5	4 4 4	38	3 3 4	4 3 3	5 4 5	34	72

Harrington leads, 6 up

Harrington	4 3 4	3 3 4	4 3 4	32	3	
Faldo	4 3 5	4 3 4	4 4 4	35	3	

Sam Torrance defeated Seve Ballesteros, 3 and 2

Torrance	4 2 4	4 3 4	4 4 5	34	3 3 5	4 3 4	4 5 4	35	69
Ballesteros	4 2 5	4 2 3	5 4 4	33	4 3 5	4 3 3	4 4 5	35	68

Ballesteros leads, 1 up

Torrance	4 3 5	4 3 4	4 4 4	35	3 4 4	4 4 4	3
Ballesteros	4 4 4	6 3 4	5 5 5	40	3 4 6	3 3 4	4

SECOND ROUND

Lee Westwood defeated Thomas Bjorn, 1 up

Westwood	4 3 4	4 3 4	4 3 3	32	3 4 5	3 3 4	4 6 4	36	68
Bjorn	4 3 4	3 4 4	3 3 4	32	2 4 4	4 2 5	4 4 4	33	65

Bjorn leads, 2 up

Westwood	3 3 4	3 2 4	4 4 4	31	3 4 4	4 2 3	4 4 4	32	63
Bjorn	3 3 4	4 3 4	4 4 3	32	3 4 4	4 2 5	4 4 5	35	67

Ian Woosnam defeated Colin Montgomerie, 4 and 3

Montgomerie	3 3 3	4 3 5	3 4 5	33	3 4 4	4 3 4	4 4 4	34	67
Woosnam	4 2 4	3 2 4	5 4 4	32	3 4 4	3 2 4	4 4 5	33	65

Woosnam leads, 3 up

Montgomerie	4 3 4	4 4 3	3 4 5	34	3 4 4	5 3 5	
Woosnam	4 3 4	4 3 5	4 3 4	34	4 4 4	5 3 4	

Padraig Harrington defeated Darren Clarke, 5 and 4

Clarke	5 2 4	5 3 4	3 4 5	35	3 4 4	5 3 4	4 5 4	36	71
Harrington	4 3 4	4 3 4	4 3 4	33	3 5 4	4 3 4	4 5 4	36	69

Harrington leads, 2 up

Clarke	4 3 4	5 3 4	4 4 3	34	3 3 5	4 3	
Harrington	4 3 4	3 3 3	3 3 4	30	3 4 4	4 3	

Sam Torrance defeated Vijay Singh, 1 up

Singh	5 3 4	3 3 4	3 4 4	33	3 3 3	3 3 4	4 5 5	33	66
Torrance	4 3 4	4 3 4	4 4 4	34	2 4 4	4 3 4	4 4 5	34	68

Singh leads, 2 up

Singh	3 3 3	4 3 3	4 4 4	31	4 4 4	4 3 4	4 5 5	37	68
Torrance	4 3 3	3 3 3	3 4 4	30	3 4 4	5 2 5	3 4 5	35	65

SEMI-FINALS

Ian Woosnam defeated Lee Westwood, 10 and 9

Westwood	5 3 4	5 3 4	4 5 4	37	3 4 5	4 3 4	4 4 5	36	73
Woosnam	4 3 4	4 3 3	3 4 4	32	2 5 4	3 3 4	4 4 5	34	66

Woosnam leads, 7 up

Westwood	4 3 4	5 3 4	4 4 4	35	
Woosnam	4 3 4	4 3 3	4 3 4	32	

Padraig Harrington defeated Sam Torrance, 4 and 3

Harrington	4 3 4	4 3 3	4 4 4	33	3 3 4	4 3 5	3 4 4	33	66
Torrance	4 3 4	4 2 3	4 4 4	32	3 3 4	4 3 4	5 5 4	35	67

Match all-square

Harrington	3 3 3	4 3 4	4 4 4	32	3 4 4	4 3 5
Torrance	4 3 5	5 4 4	3 3 4	35	3 4 4	5 4 5

FINAL

Ian Woosnam defeated Padraig Harrington, 2 and 1

Woosnam	4 2 3	4 2 3	3 3 4	28	3 4 5	4 3 3	4 6 4	36	64
Harrington	3 2 4	4 3 4	3 3 5	31	2 3 4	3 3 4	3 4 4	30	61

Harrington leads, 2 up

Woosnam	4 4 4	4 3 4	3 3 W	X	3 3 4	3 3 4	4 4
Harrington	5 3 3	4 3 4	5 3 C	X	3 4 5	5 3 4	4 4

PRIZE MONEY: Woosnam £250,000; Harrington £120,000; Westwood, Torrance £85,000 each; Bjorn, Montgomerie, Clarke, Singh £65,000 each; Scott, Goosen, Faldo, Ballesteros £50,000 each.

LEGEND: C—conceded hole to opponent; W—won hole by concession without holing out; X—no total score.

Cannes Open

Cannes-Mougins Golf Club, Cannes, France
Par 36-36–72; 6,830 yards

October 11-14
purse, £343,971

	SCORES				TOTAL	MONEY
Jorge Berendt	67	66	67	68	268	£57,319.55
Jean Van de Velde	70	66	68	65	269	38,208.90
Santiago Luna	70	66	68	68	272	17,769.06
Thomas Levet	69	66	69	68	272	17,769.06
Andrew Marshall	65	68	69	70	272	17,769.06
Warren Bennett	66	66	70	71	273	10,317.52
Johan Rystrom	67	71	69	66	273	10,317.52
Ignacio Garrido	69	67	67	70	273	10,317.52
Henrik Bjornstad	65	68	70	71	274	7,703.75
Shaun Webster	68	72	67	68	275	6,164.72
Paul Eales	67	70	68	70	275	6,164.72
Fredrik Andersson	70	68	67	70	275	6,164.72
Matthew Blackey	69	70	66	70	275	6,164.72
Raphael Jacquelin	69	65	71	71	276	4,952.41
Carl Suneson	68	67	71	70	276	4,952.41
Bradley Dredge	68	67	71	70	276	4,952.41
David Park	64	75	71	66	276	4,952.41
Van Phillips	67	69	69	72	277	4,140.76
Lucas Parsons	62	73	72	70	277	4,140.76
Richard Sterne	71	71	68	67	277	4,140.76
Steven O'Hara	67	69	71	70	277	4,140.76
Martin Maritz	71	69	68	69	277	4,140.76
Jeremy Robinson	66	76	71	65	278	3,576.74
Roger Winchester	69	69	68	72	278	3,576.74
Jose Romero	70	68	71	69	278	3,576.74
Roger Wessels	66	70	73	69	278	3,576.74
Paddy Gribben	71	69	67	71	278	3,576.74
Wayne Riley	66	69	75	69	279	2,910.40
Garry Houston	71	68	68	72	279	2,910.40
Tomas Jesus Munoz	71	71	67	70	279	2,910.40
Des Terblanche	72	68	72	67	279	2,910.40
Robert Coles	68	70	73	68	279	2,910.40
David Higgins	70	72	69	68	279	2,910.40
Simon Dyson	71	67	71	70	279	2,910.40
David Dixon	69	69	70	71	279	2,910.40
Lionel Alexandre	68	69	70	73	280	2,441.81
Fredrik Henge	67	68	74	71	280	2,441.81

	SCORES			TOTAL	MONEY
Gregory Havret	72	70	70	68	280	2,441.81
Anders Forsbrand	68	74	71	68	281	1,960.33
Mark Mouland	71	67	69	74	281	1,960.33
Marc Farry	71	70	71	69	281	1,960.33
Jean-Francois Remesy	69	70	71	71	281	1,960.33
Thomas Gogele	73	67	71	70	281	1,960.33
Stephen Dodd	67	71	71	72	281	1,960.33
Mark Pilkington	68	69	75	69	281	1,960.33
Frederic Cupillard	70	67	72	72	281	1,960.33
Daren Lee	69	69	73	70	281	1,960.33
Christopher Hanell	71	69	72	69	281	1,960.33
Scott Gardiner	68	70	68	75	281	1,960.33
Peter Fowler	72	69	71	70	282	1,478.84
Nicolas Vanhootegem	71	69	70	72	282	1,478.84
Henrik Nystrom	72	69	71	70	282	1,478.84
Emanuele Canonica	71	68	71	73	283	1,238.10
Nicolas Kalouguine	71	71	71	70	283	1,238.10
Erol Simsek	70	67	72	74	283	1,238.10
Graeme Storm	70	69	70	74	283	1,238.10
Jose Manuel Carriles	69	73	71	71	284	1,014.56
Peter Hanson	69	71	75	69	284	1,014.56
Paul Broadhurst	70	68	70	76	284	1,014.56
Russell Claydon	71	70	73	70	284	1,014.56
Domingo Hospital	71	71	74	71	287	894.19
Marcello Santi	70	71	71	75	287	894.19
Michele Reale	71	69	76	71	287	894.19
Gary Evans	70	67	70	81	288	808.21
Alastair Forsyth	69	72	74	73	288	808.21
Gustavo Rojas	72	69	70	78	289	756.62
Robin Byrd	72	67	75	76	290	722.23
Olivier Edmond	70	72	72	77	291	687.83
Patrik Sjoland	72	69	81	71	293	653.44
Bertrand Cornut	71	70	76	78	295	630.82

Dunhill Links Championship

St. Andrews Old Course: Par 36-36–72; 7,115 yards
Carnoustie Championship Course: Par 36-36–72; 7,361 yards
Kingsbarns Golf Links: Par 36-36–72; 7,126 yards
St. Andrews, Scotland
(Tournament extended until Monday due to rain.)

October 18-22
purse, £3,355,748

	SCORES			TOTAL	MONEY
Paul Lawrie	71	68	63	68	270	£551,040.11
Ernie Els	65	70	68	68	271	367,357.76
David Howell	67	68	69	68	272	206,970.64
Jean Hugo	68	70	69	66	273	165,312.05
Padraig Harrington	67	67	72	69	275	109,436.55
Colin Montgomerie	71	68	69	67	275	109,436.55
Peter O'Malley	71	67	68	69	275	109,436.55
Paul Casey	69	70	66	70	275	109,436.55
Paul McGinley	67	64	71	74	276	64,471.72
Mathias Gronberg	68	70	71	67	276	64,471.72
Retief Goosen	69	69	69	69	276	64,471.72
Jamie Donaldson	68	66	74	68	276	64,471.72
Brian Davis	65	68	72	72	277	49,758.92
Thomas Bjorn	70	67	71	69	277	49,758.92

	SCORES				TOTAL	MONEY
Mark Pilkington	69	69	71	68	277	49,758.92
Brett Rumford	72	67	68	70	277	49,758.92
Justin Rose	69	68	74	67	278	40,005.51
Wayne Smith	71	74	67	66	278	40,005.51
Emanuele Canonica	66	74	69	69	278	40,005.51
David Lynn	71	69	69	69	278	40,005.51
Greg Owen	70	67	72	69	278	40,005.51
Patrik Sjoland	71	66	72	69	278	40,005.51
Lucas Parsons	72	68	69	69	278	40,005.51
Darren Clarke	72	67	70	70	279	34,384.90
John Bickerton	69	70	69	71	279	34,384.90
David Dixon	69	70	72	68	279	34,384.90
Jarrod Moseley	67	70	71	72	280	31,905.22
Ricardo Gonzalez	67	70	72	71	280	31,905.22
Eduardo Romero	70	71	72	68	281	27,937.73
Raphael Jacquelin	72	68	74	67	281	27,937.73
Miguel Angel Jimenez	70	70	69	72	281	27,937.73
James Kingston	74	67	70	70	281	27,937.73
Daren Lee	68	70	71	72	281	27,937.73
David Carter	71	73	69	68	281	27,937.73
Anders Forsbrand	71	64	76	71	282	22,482.44
Barry Lane	68	72	74	68	282	22,482.44
Robert Karlsson	70	70	73	69	282	22,482.44
Ian Garbutt	72	69	68	73	282	22,482.44
Ignacio Garrido	67	72	74	69	282	22,482.44
Henrik Nystrom	70	66	74	72	282	22,482.44
Nick Dougherty	68	68	73	73	282	22,482.44
Adam Scott	72	68	75	67	282	22,482.44
Soren Kjeldsen	68	72	71	73	284	18,184.32
Jonathan Lomas	67	73	72	72	284	18,184.32
Graeme Storm	71	74	70	69	284	18,184.32
Brett Quigley	68	69	73	74	284	18,184.32
Scott Gardiner	72	67	75	70	284	18,184.32
Tony Johnstone	67	66	80	72	285	15,208.70
Gary Orr	75	67	71	72	285	15,208.70
Van Phillips	75	68	69	73	285	15,208.70
Fredrik Jacobson	73	66	75	71	285	15,208.70
Maarten Lafeber	71	74	70	71	286	12,563.71
Roger Wessels	72	69	73	72	286	12,563.71
Mikael Lundberg	74	68	72	72	286	12,563.71
Simon Dyson	70	72	71	73	286	12,563.71
Jorge Berendt	70	72	73	72	287	10,359.56
Peter Lonard	71	68	76	72	287	10,359.56
Markus Brier	70	72	69	76	287	10,359.56
Jean-Francois Remesy	72	74	69	73	288	9,422.79
Omar Sandys	65	71	74	78	288	9,422.79
Steve Webster	70	70	75	75	290	8,596.72
David Smail	70	70	75	75	290	8,596.72
Jamie Spence	69	74	72	75	290	8,596.72
Sam Torrance	69	70	76	76	291	7,934.98

Telefonica Open de Madrid

Club de Campo, Madrid, Spain
Par 36-35–71; 6,957 yards

October 25-28
purse, £875,438

	SCORES				TOTAL	MONEY
Retief Goosen	66	64	66	68	264	£145,904.20
Steve Webster	68	62	68	66	264	97,267.38
(Goosen defeated Webster on third playoff hole.)						
Brian Davis	66	64	73	62	265	49,287.14
Diego Borrego	69	65	64	67	265	49,287.14
Markus Brier	67	68	66	66	267	37,118.56
Jeev Milkha Singh	72	67	65	64	268	24,599.80
Anders Hansen	68	69	65	66	268	24,599.80
Darren Clarke	67	69	65	67	268	24,599.80
Robert Coles	66	69	69	64	268	24,599.80
Thomas Bjorn	68	71	66	64	269	16,808.40
Angel Cabrera	68	69	65	67	269	16,808.40
Richard Green	69	67	65	69	270	13,853.80
Van Phillips	68	67	69	66	270	13,853.80
David Lynn	68	66	68	68	270	13,853.80
John Bickerton	69	67	68	66	270	13,853.80
Jose Maria Olazabal	69	67	68	67	271	11,363.18
Carlos Rodiles	65	70	67	69	271	11,363.18
Gary Emerson	70	68	68	65	271	11,363.18
Phillip Price	66	69	67	69	271	11,363.18
Greg Owen	67	70	66	68	271	11,363.18
Barry Lane	66	72	66	68	272	9,761.13
Richard Johnson	73	65	67	67	272	9,761.13
Ignacio Garrido	70	67	71	64	272	9,761.13
Bradley Dredge	70	68	65	69	272	9,761.13
Padraig Harrington	63	72	69	69	273	8,447.97
Jose Manuel Carriles	72	68	69	64	273	8,447.97
Fredrik Andersson	69	65	71	68	273	8,447.97
Henrik Nystrom	67	67	72	67	273	8,447.97
Stephen Gallacher	64	70	70	69	273	8,447.97
David Higgins	67	62	69	75	273	8,447.97
Des Smyth	65	73	67	69	274	7,134.82
Miguel Angel Jimenez	65	67	70	72	274	7,134.82
Ian Garbutt	69	71	70	64	274	7,134.82
Alastair Forsyth	69	67	71	67	274	7,134.82
Eduardo Romero	70	67	72	66	275	6,303.15
Maarten Lafeber	71	69	68	67	275	6,303.15
Roger Winchester	71	65	72	67	275	6,303.15
Carl Pettersson	70	70	67	68	275	6,303.15
Santiago Luna	72	68	67	69	276	5,340.17
David Howell	70	69	65	72	276	5,340.17
Mark McNulty	70	69	69	68	276	5,340.17
Peter Mitchell	70	69	68	69	276	5,340.17
Johan Rystrom	67	67	71	71	276	5,340.17
Emanuele Canonica	70	70	67	69	276	5,340.17
Brett Rumford	71	69	66	70	276	5,340.17
Henrik Bjornstad	70	69	72	66	277	4,464.73
Thomas Gogele	68	68	73	68	277	4,464.73
Stephen Dodd	71	65	72	69	277	4,464.73
Wayne Riley	71	67	66	74	278	3,589.29
Mark Roe	67	70	70	71	278	3,589.29
Darren Fichardt	72	68	66	72	278	3,589.29
Paul Broadhurst	72	68	69	69	278	3,589.29
Gary Orr	70	68	68	72	278	3,589.29

	SCORES				TOTAL	MONEY
Matthew Blackey	72	67	72	67	278	3,589.29
Nick Dougherty	71	67	71	69	278	3,589.29
Andrew Marshall	66	68	77	68	279	2,888.94
Juan Quiros	70	70	70	70	280	2,407.45
Alvaro Salto	69	68	73	70	280	2,407.45
Marc Farry	67	71	71	71	280	2,407.45
Henrik Stenson	71	68	70	71	280	2,407.45
Olle Karlsson	71	69	70	70	280	2,407.45
Rolf Muntz	71	69	72	68	280	2,407.45
David Park	68	69	74	69	280	2,407.45
Paul Casey	69	70	72	69	280	2,407.45
Jean-Francois Remesy	70	68	73	70	281	1,838.42
Soren Hansen	69	69	72	71	281	1,838.42
Michele Reale	68	70	72	71	281	1,838.42
Fernando Roca	67	68	76	70	281	1,838.42
Graeme Storm	66	72	73	70	281	1,838.42
Lucas Parsons	69	70	70	73	282	1,600.80
Mark Pilkington	70	69	74	72	285	1,313.16
Mark James	69	71	72	80	292	1,311.28

Atlanet Italian Open

Is Molas Golf, Sardinia, Italy
Par 35-37–72; 7,013 yards

November 1-4
purse, £621,760

	SCORES				TOTAL	MONEY
Gregory Havret	65	66	68	69	268	£103,622.37
Bradley Dredge	69	66	65	69	269	69,083.65
Mark Roe	63	69	73	66	271	29,533.56
Shaun Webster	70	67	66	68	271	29,533.56
Ian Poulter	67	69	68	67	271	29,533.56
Diego Borrego	70	66	65	70	271	29,533.56
Steve Webster	68	67	68	69	272	17,098.37
Henrik Stenson	67	70	68	67	272	17,098.37
David Howell	71	66	68	68	273	11,701.51
Trevor Immelman	70	67	65	71	273	11,701.51
Michele Reale	63	73	68	69	273	11,701.51
Markus Brier	70	66	70	67	273	11,701.51
Fredrik Andersson	65	72	67	69	273	11,701.51
Sven Struver	66	68	64	76	274	9,139.86
Stephen Dodd	70	68	68	68	274	9,139.86
Mikko Ilonen	68	71	66	69	274	9,139.86
Warren Bennett	70	71	68	66	275	7,637.27
Silvio Grappasonni	70	65	69	71	275	7,637.27
Richard Green	72	69	66	68	275	7,637.27
Anthony Wall	66	71	72	66	275	7,637.27
Jean Van de Velde	67	65	74	69	275	7,637.27
Jonathan Lomas	68	72	70	65	275	7,637.27
Santiago Luna	69	70	68	69	276	6,373.03
Jeremy Robinson	70	68	70	68	276	6,373.03
Carl Suneson	73	68	69	66	276	6,373.03
Nicolas Vanhootegem	70	69	68	69	276	6,373.03
Robert Coles	72	68	69	67	276	6,373.03
Raymond Russell	66	70	70	70	276	6,373.03
Johan Rystrom	66	70	71	70	277	5,533.66
Gary Evans	70	70	66	71	277	5,533.66
Patrik Sjoland	69	71	66	71	277	5,533.66

	SCORES				TOTAL	MONEY
Ronan Rafferty	68	69	69	72	278	4,756.46
Eduardo Romero	66	70	75	67	278	4,756.46
Richard Johnson	70	70	70	68	278	4,756.46
Marcello Santi	68	74	69	67	278	4,756.46
Massimo Scarpa	70	69	64	75	278	4,756.46
Stephen Gallacher	67	71	69	71	278	4,756.46
Roger Chapman	67	69	72	71	279	3,979.26
Peter Hanson	71	66	70	72	279	3,979.26
Robin Byrd	68	72	68	71	279	3,979.26
Olle Karlsson	72	70	66	71	279	3,979.26
Christian Cevaer	69	66	71	73	279	3,979.26
Lucas Parsons	68	71	68	72	279	3,979.26
Stefano Soffietti	68	73	68	71	280	3,295.32
Henrik Bjornstad	71	68	70	71	280	3,295.32
Steven Richardson	67	73	72	68	280	3,295.32
Tony Edlund	69	73	70	68	280	3,295.32
Peter Lonard	69	70	69	72	280	3,295.32
Alastair Forsyth	70	70	71	70	281	2,922.27
Malcolm Mackenzie	70	70	73	69	282	2,487.04
Mark Mouland	70	71	70	71	282	2,487.04
Elliot Boult	71	70	74	67	282	2,487.04
Roger Winchester	73	68	70	71	282	2,487.04
Angel Cabrera	72	68	67	75	282	2,487.04
Mark Pilkington	69	69	72	72	282	2,487.04
Alessandro Tadini	71	69	69	74	283	1,844.55
Paul Broadhurst	70	72	71	70	283	1,844.55
Emanuele Canonica	71	70	71	71	283	1,844.55
David Park	72	67	73	71	283	1,844.55
Gianluca Pietrobono	67	70	74	72	283	1,844.55
Daren Lee	72	69	72	70	283	1,844.55
Dennis Edlund	70	71	74	69	284	1,554.40
Simon Hurd	73	69	72	70	284	1,554.40
Luca Bernardini	70	72	70	72	284	1,554.40
Neil Cheetham	70	70	72	73	285	1,398.96
Eduardo De La Riva	72	68	75	70	285	1,398.96
Paolo Terreni	73	69	71	73	286	1,217.09
Stefano Reale	71	70	73	72	286	1,217.09
Thomas Gogele	70	71	74	71	286	1,217.09
Nic Henning	74	68	70	74	286	1,217.09
*Andrea Romano	69	71	79	70	289	
Paul Eales	73	69	74	75	291	932.64
*Michele Rigone	75	67	76	73	291	

Volvo Masters Andalucia

Montecastillo Hotel & Golf Resort, Jerez, Spain
Par 36-36—72; 7,069 yards
(Shortened to 54 holes — wind.)

November 8-11
purse, £2,000,000

	SCORES			TOTAL	MONEY
Padraig Harrington	67	71	66	204	£333,330
Paul McGinley	66	69	70	205	222,220.02
Adam Scott	67	74	65	206	125,199.97
Robert Karlsson	71	68	68	207	84,933.34
Darren Clarke	70	68	69	207	84,933.34
Mathias Gronberg	70	67	70	207	84,933.34
Tony Johnstone	69	72	67	208	51,600

	SCORES			TOTAL	MONEY
Bernhard Langer	69	70	69	208	51,600
Colin Montgomerie	71	69	68	208	51,600
Retief Goosen	68	75	66	209	38,000
David Howell	69	73	67	209	38,000
Greg Turner	72	70	68	210	31,150
Dean Robertson	69	72	69	210	31,150
Gary Evans	69	71	70	210	31,150
Roger Wessels	70	70	70	210	31,150
Peter Lonard	65	78	68	211	27,400
Phillip Price	70	73	68	211	27,400
Angel Cabrera	69	73	69	211	27,400
Jose Maria Olazabal	69	70	72	211	27,400
Steve Webster	70	71	71	212	25,400
Soren Hansen	72	73	68	213	23,800
Charlie Wi	70	72	71	213	23,800
Niclas Fasth	72	67	74	213	23,800
David Lynn	71	71	72	214	21,600
Ricardo Gonzalez	71	76	67	214	21,600
Paul Lawrie	74	73	67	214	21,600
Carl Pettersson	70	74	71	215	19,800
John Bickerton	73	75	67	215	19,800
Nick O'Hern	69	72	74	215	19,800
Miguel Angel Jimenez	70	74	72	216	18,000
Brian Davis	68	75	73	216	18,000
Michael Campbell	73	72	71	216	18,000
Stephen Gallacher	70	76	71	217	16,500
Anthony Wall	72	71	74	217	16,500
Jean Hugo	72	72	74	218	13,266.66
Mark Mouland	70	74	74	218	13,266.66
Soren Kjeldsen	70	75	73	218	13,266.66
Thomas Levet	69	76	73	218	13,266.66
Mark McNulty	69	74	75	218	13,266.66
Richard Green	72	71	75	218	13,266.66
Barry Lane	71	75	72	218	13,266.66
Raphael Jacquelin	72	74	72	218	13,266.66
Greg Owen	73	76	69	218	13,266.66
Pierre Fulke	73	72	74	219	10,000
Andrew Coltart	70	76	73	219	10,000
Thomas Bjorn	73	69	77	219	10,000
Mikael Lundberg	73	74	72	219	10,000
Fredrik Jacobson	73	77	69	219	10,000
Ian Poulter	64	81	76	221	8,450
Ian Garbutt	71	76	74	221	8,450
Paul Casey	76	74	71	221	8,450
Lee Westwood	69	76	77	222	7,650
Anders Hansen	69	74	79	222	7,650
Sven Struver	72	79	71	222	7,650
Raymond Russell	70	77	76	223	7,200
Justin Rose	69	83	72	224	6,900
Henrik Stenson	81	73	70	224	6,900
Brett Rumford	70	81	74	225	6,500
Peter O'Malley	77	74	74	225	6,500
Gregory Havret	70	79	77	226	6,200
Olle Karlsson	72	79	76	227	6,000
Daren Lee	75	78	75	228	5,800
Seve Ballesteros	79	80	71	230	5,650
Ian Woosnam	74	77		DQ	5,366.67
Warren Bennett	72	78		WD	5,366.67
Gary Orr	77	80		WD	5,366.67

Challenge Tour

Tusker Kenya Open

Muthaiga Golf Club, Nairobi, Kenya
Par 36-35–71; 6,825 yards

March 1-4
purse, £75,000

	SCORES				TOTAL	MONEY
Ashley Roestoff	73	65	68	65	271	£12,495.05
Andrew Sherborne	66	67	68	70	271	8,325.03
(Roestoff defeated Sherborne on first playoff hole.)						
Alvaro Salto	69	69	66	69	273	4,695.02
Mark Foster	69	70	67	69	275	3,750.02
Jean-Francois Lucquin	68	68	71	69	276	3,180.01
Niels Kraaij	67	76	66	68	277	2,398.76
Philip Golding	76	64	67	70	277	2,398.76
Massimo Florioli	68	69	71	69	277	2,398.76
Thomas Havemann	69	72	65	71	277	2,398.76
Fredrik Widmark	73	68	66	70	277	2,398.76
Lee Slattery	72	67	69	69	277	2,398.76
Thomas Besancenez	71	66	70	71	278	1,539.38
Andre Bossert	73	67	69	69	278	1,539.38
Alan McLean	65	69	71	73	278	1,539.38
Jamie Donaldson	72	68	69	69	278	1,539.38
Simon Hurd	73	69	65	72	279	1,031.26
Benoit Teilleria	70	71	71	67	279	1,031.26
Sam Walker	68	68	67	76	279	1,031.26
Thabang Simon	70	70	69	70	279	1,031.26
Sebastien Delagrange	71	69	72	68	280	885.00
Bradford Vaughan	70	70	67	75	282	802.51
Chris Gane	70	70	74	68	282	802.51
Andrew Butterfield	74	67	69	72	282	802.51
Gary Clark	71	71	71	69	282	802.51
Wallie Coetsee	67	71	75	70	283	712.50
Felix Lubenau	70	70	71	72	283	712.50
Michael Archer	75	66	68	74	283	712.50
Nils Rorbaek	68	74	71	71	284	635.63
Adam Mednick	71	69	71	73	284	635.63
Didier de Vooght	71	72	68	73	284	635.63
Johan Skold	67	75	68	74	284	635.63

Stanbic Zambia Open

See African Tours chapter.

Segura Viudas Challenge de Espana

Club de Golf Villamartin, Alicante, Spain
Par 36-36–72; 6,705 yards

March 29-April 1
purse, £54,589

	SCORES				TOTAL	MONEY
Euan Little	72	69	68	68	277	£9,364.40
Jesus Maria Arruti	71	75	68	64	278	6,239.19

	SCORES				TOTAL	MONEY
Mark Foster	69	73	72	65	279	3,164.56
Carlos Larrain	69	69	69	72	279	3,164.56
Stuart Little	69	70	74	67	280	2,284.89
Ricardo Jimenez	70	72	68	70	280	2,284.89
Emilio Rodriguez	70	74	70	67	281	1,858.64
Jose Rozadilla	71	70	73	67	281	1,858.64
Joakim Rask	70	71	71	69	281	1,858.64
Patrik Gottfridson	70	72	71	69	282	1,512.02
Birgir Hafthorsson	72	72	70	68	282	1,512.02
Robert Jan Derksen	72	74	70	67	283	963.28
Jose Manuel Carriles	73	73	69	68	283	963.28
Graeme van der Nest	72	71	70	70	283	963.28
Andre Bossert	70	71	69	73	283	963.28
Andrew Butterfield	75	68	71	69	283	963.28
Simon Wakefield	74	69	72	68	283	963.28
Dominique Nouailhac	70	72	70	71	283	963.28
Lee James	73	71	69	70	283	963.28
Kalle Vainola	71	70	72	71	284	637.03
Daniel Westermark	69	74	69	72	284	637.03
Juan Carlos Aguero	69	73	73	69	284	637.03
Luis Claverie	73	73	68	71	285	569.58
Ivo Giner	71	70	72	72	285	569.58
Fredrik Widmark	72	73	72	68	285	569.58
Juan Quiros	68	76	70	72	286	517.12
Martin Erlandsson	71	72	73	70	286	517.12
Thomas Norret	70	72	68	76	286	517.12
Greig Hutcheon	70	73	70	74	287	462.32
Michael Archer	71	74	71	71	287	462.32
Eduardo De La Riva	68	75	72	72	287	462.32
Mikael Piltz	70	70	76	71	287	462.32

Open Golf Montecchia - PGA Triveneta

Golf Club Montecchia, Padova, Italy
Par 36-36–72; 6,926 yards

April 26-29
purse, £74,763

	SCORES				TOTAL	MONEY
Andrew Sherborne	70	66	67	66	269	£11,894.10
Marc Pendaries	69	70	66	68	273	6,196.33
Stuart Little	65	72	70	66	273	6,196.33
Simon Hurd	69	68	67	70	274	3,568.23
Euan Little	71	67	72	65	275	2,785.60
Lionel Alexandre	68	67	68	72	275	2,785.60
Andrew Marshall	70	66	72	67	275	2,785.60
Mattias Eliasson	72	68	70	67	277	2,174.24
Ian Hutchings	71	72	68	66	277	2,174.24
Gary Clark	71	66	66	74	277	2,174.24
Patrik Gottfridson	70	69	66	73	278	1,686.58
Michael Archer	71	67	72	68	278	1,686.58
Federico Bisazza	71	68	70	69	278	1,686.58
Alberto Binaghi	71	68	69	71	279	1,186.44
Marcel Siem	71	71	68	69	279	1,186.44
Raimo Sjoberg	69	74	69	67	279	1,186.44
Benoit Teilleria	69	68	72	70	279	1,186.44
Jean-Francois Lucquin	72	70	68	70	280	887.30
Mattias Nilsson	73	68	68	71	280	887.30
Iain Pyman	73	65	69	73	280	887.30

	SCORES			TOTAL	MONEY
Alvaro Salto	73	70	69	69	281	738.62
Eric Carlberg	69	69	72	71	281	738.62
Dennis Edlund	72	71	67	71	281	738.62
Jesus Maria Arruti	71	68	68	74	281	738.62
Adam Mednick	71	69	67	74	281	738.62
James Hepworth	70	71	71	69	281	738.62
Damian McGrane	73	70	71	68	282	582.81
Knud Storgaard	71	69	68	74	282	582.81
Martin Erlandsson	69	71	70	72	282	582.81
Paul Nilbrink	71	71	69	71	282	582.81
Richard Gillot	75	68	71	68	282	582.81
Andrew Beal	74	69	72	67	282	582.81
Simon Khan	71	72	67	72	282	582.81
Bjorn Pettersson	70	68	70	74	282	582.81
Mike Capone	69	72	73	68	282	582.81

Credit Suisse Private Banking Open

Golf Club Patriziale, Ascona, Switzerland
Par 36-35–71; 6,488 yards

May 3-6
purse, £66,568

	SCORES			TOTAL	MONEY
Greig Hutcheon	66	70	64	66	266	£10,873.82
Jesus Maria Arruti	68	68	67	64	267	5,664.64
Kariem Baraka	70	69	66	62	267	5,664.64
Kalle Vainola	68	67	66	68	269	3,262.15
Stuart Little	65	72	69	64	270	2,652.12
Gary Clark	63	73	66	68	270	2,652.12
Damian McGrane	68	69	70	64	271	2,157.37
Peter Lawrie	70	68	67	66	271	2,157.37
Ashley Roestoff	65	69	67	70	271	2,157.37
Gianluca Baruffaldi	65	71	67	69	272	1,755.03
Pascal Edmond	64	70	70	68	272	1,755.03
Pehr Magnebrant	68	68	65	72	273	1,339.11
Adam Mednick	71	69	69	64	273	1,339.11
Simon Wakefield	68	71	67	67	273	1,339.11
Federico Bisazza	67	68	70	68	273	1,339.11
Jean Pierre Cixous	69	68	68	69	274	962.33
Iain Pyman	71	68	68	67	274	962.33
Paul Dwyer	69	68	71	67	275	831.85
Ivo Giner	69	70	66	70	275	831.85
Patrik Gottfridson	67	71	69	69	276	725.83
Richard Dinsdale	68	68	73	67	276	725.83
Lee James	66	66	72	72	276	725.83
Jamie Donaldson	66	73	69	68	276	725.83
Jean-Francois Lucquin	68	72	69	68	277	639.38
Olivier David	71	69	66	71	277	639.38
Lorne Kelly	69	66	72	70	277	639.38
Peter Malmgren	69	71	70	68	278	554.56
Steve Rey	67	68	70	73	278	554.56
Chris Gane	67	72	68	71	278	554.56
Morten Orveland	68	69	68	73	278	554.56
Mattias Nilsson	71	68	68	71	278	554.56
Nicolas Marin	70	70	70	68	278	554.56

Austrian Open

Golf Club Murhof, Graz, Austria
Par 36-36–72; 6,883 yards

May 17-20
purse, £55,600

	SCORES				TOTAL	MONEY
Chris Gane	73	65	64	68	270	£9,267.50
Andrew Marshall	71	67	63	70	271	6,172.15
Didier de Vooght	68	67	65	72	272	3,477.16
Hennie Walters	69	69	68	67	273	2,322.90
Massimo Florioli	67	67	71	68	273	2,322.90
Simon Wakefield	68	70	68	67	273	2,322.90
Jamie Donaldson	71	63	66	73	273	2,322.90
Mattias Eliasson	70	68	69	67	274	1,834.96
Robert Jan Derksen	68	69	68	70	275	1,498.55
Mark Foster	70	66	67	72	275	1,498.55
Michael Archer	65	70	71	69	275	1,498.55
Sam Walker	75	68	67	65	275	1,498.55
Roberto Zappa	70	66	68	72	276	1,195.51
Stuart Little	72	66	69	70	277	1,028.69
Ivo Giner	67	67	68	75	277	1,028.69
Andrew Sherborne	73	69	68	68	278	764.57
Kenneth Ferrie	74	66	67	71	278	764.57
Richard Dinsdale	71	69	68	70	278	764.57
Markus Brier	73	69	68	68	278	764.57
Alberto Binaghi	75	65	71	68	279	630.19
Jean-Francois Lucquin	73	70	65	71	279	630.19
Carl Richardson	70	70	69	70	279	630.19
Garry Houston	69	70	69	72	280	546.04
Simon Vale	70	67	74	69	280	546.04
Pasi Purhonen	75	68	69	68	280	546.04
Andre Bossert	71	70	73	66	280	546.04
Ashley Roestoff	69	72	66	73	280	546.04
Ulf Wendling	73	69	70	69	281	471.25
Richard Bland	70	68	70	73	281	471.25
Gary Clark	68	69	71	73	281	471.25
Lee James	72	71	70	68	281	471.25

5th Aa Saint Omer Open

Aa Saint Omer Golf Club, Lumbres, France
Par 38-35–73; 6,884 yards

May 24-27
purse, £93,353

	SCORES				TOTAL	MONEY
Sebastien Delagrange	63	67	70	72	272	£15,554.79
Jamie Donaldson	70	70	68	65	273	10,369.86
Franck Aumonier	69	71	64	70	274	5,843.91
Pehr Magnebrant	68	69	67	71	275	4,085.76
Benn Barham	72	69	67	67	275	4,085.76
Iain Pyman	67	68	67	73	275	4,085.76
Johan Skold	68	68	67	73	276	3,342.05
Knud Storgaard	66	67	70	74	277	3,080.66
Alvaro Salto	70	70	70	68	278	2,515.87
Neil Reilly	71	68	68	71	278	2,515.87
Gary Clark	73	69	65	71	278	2,515.87
Sam Walker	71	64	72	71	278	2,515.87
Peter Fowler	66	71	72	70	279	1,913.74
Sion Bebb	70	71	66	72	279	1,913.74

	SCORES				TOTAL	MONEY
Robert Jan Derksen	71	69	70	70	280	1,274.94
Mark Foster	67	69	70	74	280	1,274.94
Garry Houston	73	68	70	69	280	1,274.94
Peter Hanson	70	70	71	69	280	1,274.94
Mattias Nilsson	73	67	69	71	280	1,274.94
Simon Khan	71	70	67	72	280	1,274.94
Mark Pilkington	71	70	68	71	280	1,274.94
Nils Roerbaek	73	69	69	70	281	933.53
Jean-Francois Lucquin	70	69	73	69	281	933.53
Adam Mednick	68	72	69	72	281	933.53
Paul Dwyer	74	67	70	70	281	933.53
Dominique Nouailhac	69	69	66	77	281	933.53
Matthew Blackey	67	71	69	74	281	933.53
Christophe Pottier	72	69	69	72	282	816.84
Andrew Butterfield	71	70	68	73	282	816.84
Greig Hutcheon	70	71	71	71	283	737.49
Michael Archer	70	72	72	69	283	737.49
Dennis Edlund	70	71	71	71	283	737.49
Jesus Maria Arruti	70	71	69	73	283	737.49
Jean Pierre Cixous	69	71	67	76	283	737.49

NCC Open

Soderasens Golf Club, Billesholm, Sweden
Par 35-36–71; 6,617 yards

May 31-June 3
purse, £60,000

	SCORES				TOTAL	MONEY
Benn Barham	71	67	63	72	273	£9,353.87
Paul Dwyer	73	67	69	66	275	6,235.69
Hennie Walters	71	67	68	71	277	2,896.44
Grant Hamerton	70	67	72	68	277	2,896.44
Simon Wakefield	69	70	67	71	277	2,896.44
Ulrik Gustafsson	71	68	67	72	278	2,096.20
Ian Hutchings	74	67	68	69	278	2,096.20
Viktor Gustavsson	68	70	73	68	279	1,709.89
Marten Olander	69	69	66	75	279	1,709.89
Johan Skold	70	64	73	72	279	1,709.89
Jonas Karlsson	70	71	71	68	280	1,055.82
Klas Eriksson	70	71	70	69	280	1,055.82
Michael Archer	71	71	69	69	280	1,055.82
Stuart Little	71	67	68	74	280	1,055.82
Mattias Nilsson	70	69	74	67	280	1,055.82
Dennis Edlund	70	71	70	69	280	1,055.82
Mikael Piltz	71	69	70	70	280	1,055.82
Ben Mason	72	70	71	67	280	1,055.82
Lars Storm	71	71	70	69	281	626.71
Nils Rorbaek	71	70	69	71	281	626.71
Mikko Manerus	72	69	71	69	281	626.71
Raimo Sjoberg	74	66	69	72	281	626.71
Gary Clark	71	69	68	73	281	626.71
Johan Moller	72	69	69	71	281	626.71
Fredrik Orest	72	70	68	72	282	524.75
Eric Carlberg	70	71	72	69	282	524.75
Pasi Purhonen	67	73	73	69	282	524.75
Joakim Rask	73	68	67	74	282	524.75
Ralph Miller	73	68	73	69	283	449.92
Patrik Gottfridson	69	70	69	75	283	449.92

	SCORES				TOTAL	MONEY
Per Larsson	69	70	71	73	283	449.92
Euan Little	72	70	69	72	283	449.92
Adam Mednick	68	74	67	74	283	449.92
Ola Eliasson	72	69	69	73	283	449.92

Nykredit Danish Open

Aalborg Golf Club, Aalborg, Denmark
Par 36-35–71; 6,649 yards

June 7-10
purse, £65,658

	SCORES				TOTAL	MONEY
Sebastien Delagrange	65	69	75	73	282	£10,941.06
Peter Malmgren	76	73	69	66	284	7,294.04
Jean-Francois Lucquin	73	71	71	70	285	3,696.56
Ulrik Gustafsson	67	71	74	73	285	3,696.56
Paul Nilbrink	70	73	74	69	286	2,370.27
Greig Hutcheon	74	69	74	69	286	2,370.27
Mads Vibe-Hastrup	74	67	70	75	286	2,370.27
Wolfgang Huget	72	72	71	71	286	2,370.27
Magnus Persson	71	76	69	70	286	2,370.27
James Hepworth	75	73	70	69	287	1,838.43
Paul Dwyer	73	72	72	71	288	1,621.76
Didier de Vooght	75	71	72	70	288	1,621.76
Andreas Ljunggren	74	74	71	70	289	1,411.65
Michael Jorgensen	72	74	76	68	290	973.62
Gary Clark	74	75	73	68	290	973.62
Birgir Hafthorsson	74	74	74	68	290	973.62
Kalle Vainola	73	73	69	75	290	973.62
Raimo Sjoberg	75	72	72	71	290	973.62
Luis Claverie	73	76	71	70	290	973.62
Miles Tunnicliff	72	74	73	71	290	973.62
Kariem Baraka	67	75	72	77	291	679.56
Martin Erlandsson	71	75	69	76	291	679.56
Alberto Binaghi	71	75	75	70	291	679.56
Tony Edlund	77	72	72	70	291	679.56
Pehr Magnebrant	75	72	72	72	291	679.56
Thomas Havemann	73	73	73	72	291	679.56
Robert Jan Derksen	73	75	70	74	292	574.51
Knut Ekjord	78	70	72	72	292	574.51
Chris Gane	73	75	72	72	292	574.51
Knud Storgaard	76	73	73	70	292	574.51

Galeria Kaufhof Pokal Challenge

Rittergut Birkhof Golf Club, Korschenbroich, Germany
Par 37-36–73; 6,826 yards

June 14-17
purse, £55,853

	SCORES				TOTAL	MONEY
Wolfgang Huget	70	64	69	67	270	£8,716.15
Tino Schuster	65	68	73	67	273	5,810.77
Alex Cejka	67	70	69	68	274	2,702.46
Sam Walker	74	69	63	68	274	2,702.46
Ben Mason	69	67	71	67	274	2,702.46
Pasi Purhonen	68	70	71	66	275	2,035.31
Andrew Marshall	70	68	69	69	276	1,799.86

	SCORES				TOTAL	MONEY
Mads Vibe-Hastrup	67	71	69	69	276	1,799.86
Robert McGuirk	65	70	71	72	278	1,410.07
Stephan Wittkop	70	71	68	69	278	1,410.07
Iain Pyman	71	72	66	69	278	1,410.07
Thomas Havemann	70	67	70	71	278	1,410.07
Simon Hurd	68	71	71	69	279	1,020.27
Mikael Piltz	66	71	73	69	279	1,020.27
Sebastien Delagrange	71	67	74	67	279	1,020.27
Klas Eriksson	71	69	73	67	280	810.98
Robert Jan Derksen	68	74	68	71	281	627.86
Ulf Wendling	68	74	70	69	281	627.86
Mark Hilton	69	65	74	73	281	627.86
Euan Little	69	74	69	69	281	627.86
Olivier David	67	75	70	69	281	627.86
Jesus Maria Arruti	71	72	71	67	281	627.86
Carl Richardson	70	70	73	68	281	627.86
*Christian Reimbold	63	78	72	68	281	
Kalle Brink	73	65	71	73	282	504.90
Raul Quiros	67	69	76	70	282	504.90
Adam Mednick	68	72	72	70	282	504.90
Ian Kennedy	70	67	70	75	282	504.90
Alberto Binaghi	69	72	69	73	283	431.65
Andrew Butterfield	67	71	74	71	283	431.65
Francis Howley	77	66	69	71	283	431.65
Federico Bisazza	68	66	79	70	283	431.65
Sigi Beretzki	69	69	72	73	283	431.65
Sandeep Grewal	69	71	74	69	283	431.65

DEXIA-BIL Luxembourg Open

Kikuoka Country Club, Canach, Luxembourg
Par 36-36–72; 7,067 yards

June 21-24
purse, £55,244

	SCORES				TOTAL	MONEY
Grant Hamerton	66	67	69	69	271	£15,000
Mark Foster	69	71	70	64	274	6,706
Marcel Siem	70	70	65	69	274	6,706
Sam Walker	70	64	71	69	274	6,706
Mads Vibe-Hastrup	71	61	69	74	275	3,658.50
Jamie Donaldson	69	69	68	69	275	3,658.50
Klas Eriksson	74	67	66	69	276	2,862
Didier de Vooght	67	71	68	70	276	2,862
Paul Dwyer	68	67	71	70	276	2,862
Benn Barham	70	68	69	69	276	2,862
Ulf Wendling	70	71	68	69	278	1,942.20
Stuart Little	71	69	69	69	278	1,942.20
Richard Dinsdale	68	70	68	72	278	1,942.20
Federico Bisazza	71	68	67	72	278	1,942.20
Martin Maritz	68	71	69	70	278	1,942.20
Marc Cayeux	71	67	71	71	280	1,327.50
Miles Tunnicliff	68	74	68	70	280	1,327.50
Patrick Platz	71	70	69	71	281	1,071
Alberto Binaghi	68	72	70	71	281	1,071
Simon Hurd	68	73	67	73	281	1,071
James Hepworth	71	71	73	66	281	1,071
Dominique Nouailhac	68	72	67	74	281	1,071
Fredrik Orest	68	71	69	74	282	897.75

	SCORES				TOTAL	MONEY
Hayo Bensdorp	70	66	74	72	282	897.75
Sam Little	67	75	68	72	282	897.75
Luis Claverie	66	70	71	75	282	897.75
Damian McGrane	71	69	72	71	283	787.50
Mark Hilton	69	73	70	71	283	787.50
Greig Hutcheon	67	73	70	73	283	787.50
Fredrik Widmark	73	68	75	67	283	787.50

Open des Volcans

Golf des Volcans, Clermont-Ferrand, France
Par 36-36–72; 6,874 yards

June 28-July 1
purse, £55,744

	SCORES				TOTAL	MONEY
Scott Drummond	66	70	69	66	271	£9,242.76
Marc Pendaries	66	68	67	71	272	6,157.80
Benn Barham	72	68	65	69	274	3,465.76
Greig Hutcheon	67	72	67	70	276	2,772.83
Dennis Edlund	71	65	70	71	277	2,351.36
Andrew Sherborne	70	68	69	71	278	2,157.26
Iain Pyman	69	68	70	72	279	1,907.71
Peter Lawrie	73	70	66	70	279	1,907.71
Carlos Larrain	76	67	70	67	280	1,375.32
Younes El Hassani	70	70	72	68	280	1,375.32
Eric Giraud	67	69	70	74	280	1,375.32
Benoit Teilleria	69	72	70	69	280	1,375.32
Ian Hutchings	69	74	66	71	280	1,375.32
Andreas Ljunggren	69	70	69	72	280	1,375.32
Peter Hedblom	68	73	67	73	281	804.12
Robin Byrd	71	71	71	68	281	804.12
Alberto Binaghi	73	69	72	67	281	804.12
Jean Marc De Polo	74	70	69	68	281	804.12
Paul Dwyer	69	70	72	70	281	804.12
Ilya Goroneskoul	66	74	70	72	282	605.59
Marten Olander	71	73	68	70	282	605.59
Andrew Marshall	73	70	69	70	282	605.59
Paolo Terreni	71	68	69	74	282	605.59
Richard Bland	67	68	69	78	282	605.59
Massimo Florioli	75	68	70	70	283	518.52
Federico Bisazza	74	68	71	70	283	518.52
Mattias Nilsson	71	71	68	73	283	518.52
Simon McCarthy	74	70	70	69	283	518.52
Frederic Cupillard	71	68	70	75	284	433.25
Gary Clark	71	68	70	75	284	433.25
Marcel Siem	65	76	69	74	284	433.25
Birgir Hafthorsson	72	72	67	73	284	433.25
Franck Aumonier	68	71	73	72	284	433.25
Amine Joudar	76	68	69	71	284	433.25
Ulrik Gustafsson	70	70	74	70	284	433.25
Gianluca Baruffaldi	72	72	68	72	284	433.25

Challenge Total Fina Elf

Joyenval Golf Club, Chambourcy, France
Par 36-36–72; 6,842 yards

July 5-8
purse, £74,440

	SCORES				TOTAL	MONEY
Kenneth Ferrie	71	65	63	69	268	£12,238.14
Andrew Marshall	68	70	64	67	269	8,156.75
Marten Olander	73	65	66	68	272	4,589.69
David Drysdale	68	66	67	72	273	3,672.04
Frederic Cupillard	71	65	69	70	275	3,113.89
Andrew Sherborne	68	70	71	67	276	2,535.55
Alvaro Salto	67	67	70	72	276	2,535.55
Marcello Santi	71	68	69	68	276	2,535.55
Fredrik Widmark	67	73	70	66	276	2,535.55
Philip Golding	70	70	68	69	277	2,056.34
Mark Foster	68	72	69	69	278	1,813.99
Didier de Vooght	72	67	68	71	278	1,813.99
Andreas Lindberg	68	69	70	72	279	1,150.27
Robin Byrd	70	70	71	68	279	1,150.27
Amine Joudar	70	68	72	69	279	1,150.27
Jesus Maria Arruti	67	68	71	73	279	1,150.27
Christophe Pottier	66	69	69	75	279	1,150.27
Grant Hamerton	70	68	73	68	279	1,150.27
Simon Khan	67	69	71	72	279	1,150.27
Gary Clark	67	70	70	72	279	1,150.27
Chris Gane	69	69	70	72	280	785.82
Andre Bossert	66	70	71	73	280	785.82
Federico Bisazza	71	68	68	73	280	785.82
Sebastien Delagrange	69	67	71	73	280	785.82
Thomas Besancenez	70	70	72	69	281	697.69
Massimo Florioli	68	72	73	68	281	697.69
Sam Walker	68	68	74	71	281	697.69
Gary Murphy	71	69	71	71	282	631.59
Lee James	70	70	72	70	282	631.59
Wolfgang Huget	72	66	72	72	282	631.59

Volvo Finnish Open

Espoo Golf Club, Helsinki, Finland
Par 36-36–72; 6,730 yards

July 12-15
purse, £48,007

	SCORES				TOTAL	MONEY
Peter Hedblom	66	69	69	70	274	£7,999.33
Mads Vibe-Hastrup	69	68	71	66	274	5,328.88
(Hedblom defeated Vibe-Hastrup on fourth playoff hole.)						
Tim Milford	73	68	70	64	275	3,004.10
Mikael Piltz	68	72	71	67	278	2,400.40
Mattias Eliasson	73	70	68	68	279	1,951.52
Pauli Hughes	71	66	70	72	279	1,951.52
Michael Archer	70	66	73	71	280	1,651.47
Jamie Little	70	73	71	66	280	1,651.47
David Lindqvist	69	72	71	69	281	1,293.81
Johan Annerfelt	74	67	71	69	281	1,293.81
Per G. Nyman	68	73	73	67	281	1,293.81
Philip Golding	73	67	70	71	281	1,293.81
Robert Jan Derksen	71	70	74	67	282	888.15
Ulrik Gustafsson	70	67	72	73	282	888.15

	SCORES				TOTAL	MONEY
Dennis Edlund	73	70	71	68	282	888.15
David Drysdale	72	68	74	68	282	888.15
Magnus Persson	72	70	72	69	283	588.10
Kalle Vainola	75	67	72	69	283	588.10
Simon Hurley	77	67	68	71	283	588.10
Marcel Siem	70	70	74	69	283	588.10
Per Nyman	69	70	75	69	283	588.10
Joakim Rask	69	71	73	70	283	588.10
Christian Nilsson	69	74	71	70	284	471.44
Ralf Geilenberg	74	66	73	71	284	471.44
*Panu Kylliainen	73	71	68	72	284	
Sean Whiffin	71	70	70	73	284	471.44
Richard Dinsdale	69	73	71	71	284	471.44
David Dupart	70	71	75	68	284	471.44
Mark Hilton	74	68	70	73	285	412.87
Christophe Pottier	70	71	71	73	285	412.87
Sam Walker	70	70	74	71	285	412.87

Gunther Hamburg Classics

Treudelberg Golf & Country Club, Hamburg, Germany
Par 36-36–72; 6,727 yards

July 19-22
purse, £170,600

	SCORES				TOTAL	MONEY
Peter Hanson	66	64	69	66	265	£28,429.38
Robert Jan Derksen	66	69	65	68	268	18,954.95
Greig Hutcheon	70	68	67	65	270	8,263.47
Simon Hurley	70	62	70	68	270	8,263.47
Peter Hedblom	69	66	66	69	270	8,263.47
Andre Bossert	68	66	69	67	270	8,263.47
Klas Eriksson	67	68	67	69	271	5,641.20
Scott Drummond	69	68	65	69	271	5,641.20
Michael Archer	66	65	69	71	271	5,641.20
Hennie Walters	70	66	70	66	272	4,401.50
Andrew Marshall	68	67	68	69	272	4,401.50
Mads Vibe-Hastrup	71	66	67	68	272	4,401.50
Andrew Sherborne	70	67	71	65	273	2,874.62
Kalle Vainola	73	67	65	68	273	2,874.62
Philip Golding	69	64	72	68	273	2,874.62
Ian Hutchings	67	70	66	70	273	2,874.62
Christophe Pottier	71	68	68	66	273	2,874.62
Gianluca Baruffaldi	72	68	63	70	273	2,874.62
Mark Foster	69	66	70	69	274	1,978.97
Alberto Binaghi	69	71	66	68	274	1,978.97
Andrew Butterfield	67	66	68	73	274	1,978.97
Simon Wakefield	69	69	67	69	274	1,978.97
Paddy Gribben	73	66	68	68	275	1,791.31
Birgir Hafthorsson	72	68	69	67	276	1,646.30
Kariem Baraka	71	69	67	69	276	1,646.30
Sam Walker	67	71	71	67	276	1,646.30
Jamie Donaldson	67	73	69	67	276	1,646.30
Marc Pendaries	69	68	69	71	277	1,389.18
Mattias Nilsson	72	68	67	70	277	1,389.18
Johan Skold	72	66	70	69	277	1,389.18
Dominique Nouailhac	66	74	71	66	277	1,389.18
Joakim Rask	70	70	71	66	277	1,389.18
Iain Pyman	68	68	68	73	277	1,389.18
Bjorn Pettersson	69	70	70	68	277	1,389.18

Charles Church Challenge Tour Championship

Bowood Golf & Country Club, Wiltshire, England
Par 36-36–72; 7,317 yards

July 26-29
purse, £130,000

	SCORES				TOTAL	MONEY
Mark Foster	67	70	71	69	277	£21,660
Philip Golding	67	69	73	70	279	11,283
Sebastien Delagrange	71	68	70	70	279	11,283
Francesco Guermani	68	70	72	70	280	6,500
Andrew Marshall	67	70	68	76	281	4,878.25
Richard Bland	70	71	66	74	281	4,878.25
Mattias Nilsson	71	67	68	75	281	4,878.25
Lee James	72	70	72	67	281	4,878.25
John Wade	71	70	71	70	282	3,503.50
Per Larsson	71	69	70	72	282	3,503.50
Peter Hedblom	75	67	71	69	282	3,503.50
Gary Clark	71	69	74	68	282	3,503.50
Iain Pyman	71	70	67	75	283	2,795
Robert Jan Derksen	72	69	73	70	284	2,405
John Wells	69	72	69	74	284	2,405
Marten Olander	71	71	71	72	285	1,692.17
Simon Hurley	69	71	73	72	285	1,692.17
Jean-Francois Lucquin	67	74	72	72	285	1,692.17
Joakim Rask	70	70	73	72	285	1,692.17
Matthew Cort	68	68	75	74	285	1,692.17
Kariem Baraka	73	69	74	69	285	1,692.17
Gary Murphy	70	72	70	74	286	1,259.38
Mattias Eliasson	69	72	76	69	286	1,259.38
Knud Storgaard	71	72	70	73	286	1,259.38
Hennie Walters	71	72	71	72	286	1,259.38
Alberto Binaghi	67	73	74	72	286	1,259.38
Dominique Nouailhac	65	76	72	73	286	1,259.38
Thomas Havemann	68	70	74	74	286	1,259.38
Mads Vibe-Hastrup	73	67	70	76	286	1,259.38
Klas Eriksson	72	70	72	73	287	1,001
Denny Lucas	67	73	75	72	287	1,001
Ian Hutchings	69	72	71	75	287	1,001
Carl Watts	73	70	71	73	287	1,001
Johan Skold	69	73	68	77	287	1,001
Carlos Larrain	73	70	73	71	287	1,001
Ashley Roestoff	72	71	68	76	287	1,001

BMW Russian Open

Moscow Golf & Country Club, Moscow, Russia
Par 36-36–72; 7,064 yards

August 2-5
purse, £100,000

	SCORES				TOTAL	MONEY
Jamie Donaldson	65	66	71	68	270	£16,660
Michael Archer	65	72	67	69	273	8,680
Mikael Piltz	69	67	67	70	273	8,680
Gary Clark	70	70	64	71	275	4,376.67
Benn Barham	71	69	67	68	275	4,376.67
Gianluca Pietrobono	68	68	69	70	275	4,376.67
Marc Pendaries	67	69	69	71	276	3,306.67
Damien McGrane	68	70	66	72	276	3,306.67
Andre Bossert	63	74	70	69	276	3,306.67

	SCORES				TOTAL	MONEY
Richard Bland	73	64	68	72	277	2,580
Dominique Nouailhac	67	69	70	71	277	2,580
Ashley Roestoff	70	69	68	70	277	2,580
Lee James	70	71	72	65	278	1,850
Benoit Teilleria	69	71	70	68	278	1,850
Leif Westerberg	69	71	69	69	278	1,850
Bjorn Pettersson	68	70	67	73	278	1,850
Adam Mednick	68	66	76	69	279	1,316.67
Daniel Chopra	67	68	68	76	279	1,316.67
Fredrik Widmark	70	68	72	69	279	1,316.67
Andrew Sherborne	68	71	70	71	280	1,112.50
Mark Foster	69	67	71	73	280	1,112.50
Martin Erlandsson	68	69	73	70	280	1,112.50
Alan McLean	69	72	69	70	280	1,112.50
Didier de Vooght	70	69	74	68	281	1,010
Hennie Walters	71	68	70	73	282	965
Gary Birch, Jr.	73	68	70	71	282	965
Marten Olander	69	70	73	71	283	850
Scott Drummond	69	71	72	71	283	850
Philip Golding	69	71	68	75	283	850
Chris Gane	70	71	69	73	283	850
Lee Thompson	71	70	72	70	283	850
Andre Cruse	71	69	68	75	283	850

Talma Finnish Challenge

Talma Golf Club, Talma, Finland
Par 36-36–72; 6,747 yards

August 9-12
purse, £92,966

	SCORES				TOTAL	MONEY
Klas Eriksson	69	72	66	65	272	£15,494.46
Gary Clark	70	69	69	68	276	10,325.51
Niels Kraaij	72	70	67	68	277	5,227.83
Alberto Binaghi	72	65	72	68	277	5,227.83
Per Larsson	71	68	71	68	278	3,941.79
Marten Olander	68	71	70	70	279	3,616.41
Pasi Purhonen	69	71	74	66	280	3,074.10
Miles Tunnicliff	73	70	72	65	280	3,074.10
Simon Khan	72	69	70	69	280	3,074.10
Hennie Walters	71	73	71	66	281	2,500.81
Joakim Rask	69	72	72	68	281	2,500.81
Steve Rey	72	71	71	68	282	1,814.71
Johan Edfors	73	72	67	70	282	1,814.71
Didier de Vooght	70	71	70	71	282	1,814.71
Andre Bossert	73	71	71	67	282	1,814.71
Fredrik Widmark	71	73	72	66	282	1,814.71
*Tuomas Tuovinen	69	76	70	67	282	
Fredrik Orest	71	74	69	69	283	1,163.94
Mattias Eliasson	70	71	70	72	283	1,163.94
Ian Hutchings	68	74	70	71	283	1,163.94
Jean Pierre Cixous	69	76	71	67	283	1,163.94
Andreas Ljunggren	74	71	66	72	283	1,163.94
Paul Nilbrink	71	74	67	72	284	915.06
Stuart Little	70	70	71	73	284	915.06
Chris Gane	72	70	72	70	284	915.06
Richard Bland	73	67	72	72	284	915.06
Christophe Pottier	74	69	70	71	284	915.06

	SCORES				TOTAL	MONEY
Adam Mednick	71	73	73	67	284	915.06
Andre Cruse	72	73	68	71	284	915.06
Knut Ekjord	74	71	72	68	285	785.57
Lorne Kelly	74	70	71	70	285	785.57

North West of Ireland Open

See PGA European Tour section.

Rolex Trophy

Geneve Golf Club, Geneva, Switzerland
Par 36-36–72; 6,875 yards

August 23-26
purse, £64,825

	SCORES				TOTAL	MONEY
Stuart Little	66	67	69	69	271	£7,920.86
Andre Bossert	68	68	68	69	273	5,211.09
Greig Hutcheon	67	71	69	67	274	3,626.92
Peter Hedblom	68	70	68	68	274	3,626.92
Grant Hamerton	71	65	66	72	274	3,626.92
Scott Drummond	71	69	68	67	275	2,487.42
Simon Wakefield	65	67	71	72	275	2,487.42
Wolfgang Huget	67	69	68	71	275	2,487.42
Mark Foster	68	68	68	72	276	2,042.75
Alberto Binaghi	72	67	70	67	276	2,042.75
Andrew Marshall	66	67	71	72	276	2,042.75
Michael Archer	72	68	67	69	276	2,042.75
Simon Hurley	69	70	70	69	278	1,750.93
Chris Gane	71	74	63	70	278	1,750.93
Mads Vibe-Hastrup	65	69	73	71	278	1,750.93
Benn Barham	72	70	67	70	279	1,584.17
Alvaro Salto	71	69	67	73	280	1,479.95
Lee James	67	72	68	73	280	1,479.95
Euan Little	72	69	67	74	282	1,396.57
Philip Golding	75	68	66	73	282	1,396.57

Skandia PGA Open

Bokskogens Golf Club, Bara, Sweden
Par 36-36–72; 6,894 yards

August 23-26
purse, £56,241

	SCORES				TOTAL	MONEY
Christophe Pottier	69	69	64	70	272	£9,061.13
Joakim Rask	68	69	70	66	273	6,040.30
Bjorn Pettersson	72	69	68	66	275	3,394.61
Johan Annerfelt	70	66	71	70	277	2,511.81
Pasi Purhonen	68	71	67	71	277	2,511.81
Magnus Persson	70	69	70	69	278	2,030.65
Hampus Von Post	68	73	69	68	278	2,030.65
Thomas Besancenez	71	69	69	70	279	1,723.47
Johan Moller	71	68	71	69	279	1,723.47
Grant Dodd	69	71	68	72	280	1,402.70
Pehr Magnebrant	69	69	69	73	280	1,402.70
Thomas Norret	74	67	69	70	280	1,402.70

	SCORES				TOTAL	MONEY
Klas Eriksson	69	73	69	70	281	916.10
Peter Malmgren	70	73	70	68	281	916.10
Marcus Norgren	66	74	72	69	281	916.10
Ian Hutchings	71	68	71	71	281	916.10
Johan Skold	67	73	71	70	281	916.10
Peter Gustafsson	71	71	72	67	281	916.10
David Lindqvist	69	68	73	72	282	586.50
Mats Hallberg	69	73	67	73	282	586.50
Per Nyman	70	73	72	67	282	586.50
Michael Jonzon	69	71	71	71	282	586.50
Leif Westerberg	69	73	72	68	282	586.50
Fredrik Widmark	69	67	73	73	282	586.50
Lorne Kelly	67	72	70	73	282	586.50
Ben Mason	66	70	73	73	282	586.50
Ove Sellberg	70	71	72	70	283	449.90
Viktor Gustavsson	69	72	73	69	283	449.90
Per Larsson	71	70	71	71	283	449.90
Jamie Little	68	73	71	71	283	449.90
Sam Little	69	75	73	66	283	449.90
Raimo Sjoberg	71	71	72	69	283	449.90
Nicolas Joakimides	71	71	71	70	283	449.90
Lee Thompson	68	74	72	69	283	449.90

Formby Hall Challenge

Formby Hall Golf Club, Merseyside, England
Par 35-37–72; 6,951 yards

August 30-September 2
purse, £55,000

	SCORES				TOTAL	MONEY
Sam Little	71	72	64	69	276	£9,160
Grant Hamerton	65	72	70	70	277	6,110
Damien McGrane	65	68	70	76	279	3,441
Paul Sherman	71	66	70	73	280	2,407.17
Olivier David	69	69	70	72	280	2,407.17
Richard Dinsdale	68	72	70	70	280	2,407.17
Philip Golding	70	69	72	70	281	1,818.67
Gary Clark	69	73	64	75	281	1,818.67
Lee Thompson	67	68	74	72	281	1,818.67
Ben Mason	71	73	69	70	283	1,540
Hennie Walters	69	71	70	74	284	1,243
Simon Khan	71	69	73	71	284	1,243
Hampus Von Post	71	72	72	69	284	1,243
Matthew Ellis	72	71	68	73	284	1,243
Chris Gane	72	70	71	72	285	861.67
Craig Cowper	70	69	69	77	285	861.67
David Dixon	70	75	66	74	285	861.67
Sam Walker	72	70	68	76	286	720.50
*Tom Whitehouse	73	69	68	76	286	
Stephen Field	74	69	72	72	287	625.90
Carl Watts	71	71	70	75	287	625.90
Paul Streeter	72	72	71	72	287	625.90
Carl Richardson	69	75	72	71	287	625.90
Edward Rush	71	69	71	76	287	625.90
Mattias Eliasson	70	70	72	76	288	514.25
Johan Annerfelt	70	72	73	73	288	514.25
Ralf Geilenberg	70	74	72	72	288	514.25
Lee James	69	73	72	74	288	514.25

	SCORES				TOTAL	MONEY
Simon Griffiths	75	70	68	75	288	514.25
Darren Leng	70	75	73	70	288	514.25

Muermans Real Estate Challenge

Herkenbosch Golf & Country Club, Roermond, Netherlands
Par 34-36–70; 6,715 yards

September 5-8
purse, £75,175

	SCORES				TOTAL	MONEY
Dominique Nouailhac	68	64	65	64	261	£12,529.29
Tony Edlund	66	66	66	67	265	8,350.77
Kariem Baraka	67	67	66	66	266	4,694.72
Marten Olander	67	64	70	66	267	3,758.79
Andrew Marshall	68	67	64	69	268	2,612.36
Mattias Nilsson	70	65	67	66	268	2,612.36
Simon Wakefield	68	68	65	67	268	2,612.36
Federico Bisazza	68	65	68	67	268	2,612.36
Fredrik Widmark	66	71	70	61	268	2,612.36
Sam Walker	68	64	67	69	268	2,612.36
Alberto Binaghi	67	63	67	72	269	1,856.84
Frederic Cupillard	67	69	69	64	269	1,856.84
Dennis Edlund	68	69	65	68	270	1,541.10
Miles Tunnicliff	68	67	67	68	270	1,541.10
Robert Jan Derksen	63	66	72	70	271	1,090.05
Philip Golding	68	66	69	68	271	1,090.05
Stuart Little	69	63	69	70	271	1,090.05
Ivo Giner	70	68	67	66	271	1,090.05
Paddy Gribben	71	64	66	70	271	1,090.05
Michael Archer	71	66	68	67	272	851.99
Jesus Maria Arruti	69	64	70	69	272	851.99
Grant Hamerton	70	67	67	68	272	851.99
Renaud Guillard	66	71	64	72	273	749.88
Didier de Vooght	72	66	66	69	273	749.88
Alan McLean	68	67	69	69	273	749.88
Lee Thompson	67	66	73	67	273	749.88
Klas Eriksson	70	67	68	69	274	648.01
Richard Bland	69	68	71	66	274	648.01
Olivier David	68	68	70	68	274	648.01
Jean Pierre Cixous	67	68	70	69	274	648.01
Michael Jonzon	69	66	68	71	274	648.01

Telia Grand Prix

Bro Balsta Golf Club, Stockholm, Sweden
Par 37-36–73; 7,111 yards

September 13-16
purse, £71,334

	SCORES				TOTAL	MONEY
Jamie Donaldson	66	69	65	70	270	£11,888.95
Magnus Persson	66	69	66	69	270	7,925.97
(Donaldson defeated Persson on third playoff hole.)						
Klas Eriksson	67	71	67	67	272	4,010
Hampus Von Post	69	66	68	69	272	4,010
Robert Jan Derksen	64	69	70	70	273	2,899.77
Grant Hamerton	69	67	66	71	273	2,899.77
Mark Foster	64	69	74	67	274	2,268.45

	SCORES				TOTAL	MONEY
Miles Tunnicliff	71	66	68	69	274	2,268.45
Johan Skold	67	69	67	71	274	2,268.45
Mads Vibe-Hastrup	71	65	69	69	274	2,268.45
Gary Murphy	68	67	69	71	275	1,400.20
Kalle Brink	72	68	67	68	275	1,400.20
Patrik Gottfridson	66	66	71	72	275	1,400.20
Per Larsson	67	67	67	74	275	1,400.20
Christophe Pottier	70	67	71	67	275	1,400.20
Benn Barham	69	66	69	71	275	1,400.20
Leif Westerberg	73	67	68	67	275	1,400.20
Kalle Vainola	69	71	68	68	276	866.72
Marten Olander	68	69	71	68	276	866.72
Daniel Chopra	66	69	68	73	276	866.72
Bjorn Pettersson	67	70	69	70	276	866.72
Alvaro Salto	74	65	67	71	277	777.55
Gianluca Baruffaldi	71	69	71	67	278	722.86
Adam Mednick	69	71	68	70	278	722.86
Gary Clark	68	72	67	71	278	722.86
Stuart Little	69	66	70	74	279	666.98
Mikael Piltz	70	68	68	73	279	666.98
Peter Malmgren	67	67	69	77	280	596.36
Scott Drummond	70	68	69	73	280	596.36
Euan Little	68	71	70	71	280	596.36
Mattias Nilsson	68	71	68	73	280	596.36
Simon Wakefield	67	71	69	73	280	596.36

PGA of Austria Masters

Eichenheim Golf Club, Kitzbuhel, Austria
Par 36-35–71; 6,567 yards

September 27-30
purse, £85,317

	SCORES				TOTAL	MONEY
Iain Pyman	69	65	61	73	268	£14,217.45
Daniel Chopra	67	68	70	64	269	9,476.21
Robert McGuirk	68	70	68	64	270	4,404.85
Andre Bossert	68	68	66	68	270	4,404.85
Steven O'Hara	68	67	67	68	270	4,404.85
Peter Lawrie	68	68	70	65	271	3,318.84
Mattias Eliasson	68	70	70	64	272	3,054.36
Andrew Marshall	70	68	69	66	273	2,499.79
Marcello Santi	66	71	67	69	273	2,499.79
Dominique Nouailhac	71	68	71	63	273	2,499.79
Thomas Havemann	69	69	67	68	273	2,499.79
Michael Archer	70	68	68	68	274	1,923.90
Marcel Siem	65	70	67	72	274	1,923.90
Thomas Norret	67	71	66	71	275	1,663.69
Ulf Wendling	70	69	68	69	276	1,281.89
Alberto Binaghi	69	72	66	69	276	1,281.89
Chris Gane	66	71	72	67	276	1,281.89
Charles Challen	66	74	67	69	276	1,281.89
Pasi Purhonen	71	69	66	71	277	1,032.34
Grant Hamerton	63	70	75	69	277	1,032.34
Marc Pendaries	66	69	73	70	278	964.08
Massimo Florioli	68	70	72	69	279	866.82
Miles Tunnicliff	71	68	70	70	279	866.82
Pehr Magnebrant	71	68	69	71	279	866.82
Johan Skold	69	70	69	71	279	866.82

	SCORES				TOTAL	MONEY
Lee Thompson	70	70	69	70	279	866.82
Magnus Persson	66	72	70	72	280	715.45
Alvaro Salto	70	69	71	70	280	715.45
Kalle Brink	69	70	70	71	280	715.45
Marten Olander	68	73	71	68	280	715.45
Simon Hurley	67	72	71	70	280	715.45
Simon Hurd	72	68	70	70	280	715.45
David Patrick	70	70	69	71	280	715.45

San Paolo Vita & Asset Management Open

Margara Golf Club, Margara, Italy
Par 36-36–72; 6,780 yards

October 3-6
purse, £77,420

	SCORES				TOTAL	MONEY
Mads Vibe-Hastrup	65	68	69	65	267	£12,901.27
Alberto Binaghi	66	68	65	69	268	6,718.51
Pehr Magnebrant	68	70	64	66	268	6,718.51
Peter Fowler	67	68	65	70	270	3,871
Klas Eriksson	64	70	67	70	271	2,690.34
Mark Foster	66	66	67	72	271	2,690.34
Richard Bland	70	65	69	67	271	2,690.34
Peter Hedblom	68	66	71	66	271	2,690.34
Gary Clark	70	67	68	66	271	2,690.34
Federico Bisazza	69	69	69	64	271	2,690.34
Stefano Reale	71	69	69	63	272	1,912.27
Grant Hamerton	69	70	66	67	272	1,912.27
Robert Jan Derksen	68	65	73	67	273	1,509.69
Miles Tunnicliff	66	66	70	71	273	1,509.69
Matthew Blackey	71	69	67	66	273	1,509.69
Peter Malmgren	67	66	68	73	274	1,099.36
Mattias Eliasson	70	68	67	69	274	1,099.36
Dominique Nouailhac	69	69	68	68	274	1,099.36
Philip Golding	73	67	68	67	275	898.07
Massimo Florioli	70	69	69	67	275	898.07
Andrew Butterfield	68	71	67	69	275	898.07
Daniel Chopra	72	67	68	68	275	898.07
Silvio Grappasonni	70	66	70	70	276	760.26
Andrew Marshall	70	69	71	66	276	760.26
Ian Hutchings	72	66	68	70	276	760.26
Christophe Pottier	71	69	71	65	276	760.26
Andreas Ljunggren	69	71	70	66	276	760.26
Andrew Sherborne	67	71	67	72	277	647.23
Gary Murphy	71	66	74	66	277	647.23
Hennie Walters	70	66	70	71	277	647.23
Thomas Besancenez	69	68	74	66	277	647.23
Didier de Vooght	72	68	71	66	277	647.23

Hardelot Challenge de France

Hardelot Golf Club, Hardelot, France
Par 36-35–71; 6,458 yards

October 11-14
purse, £75,600

	SCORES				TOTAL	MONEY
Marten Olander	68	68	62	70	268	£12,597.91
Scott Drummond	64	68	67	70	269	8,396.54
Magnus Persson	69	66	67	68	270	3,903.35
Gary Murphy	72	62	66	70	270	3,903.35
Andrew Butterfield	66	71	66	67	270	3,903.35
Klas Eriksson	67	67	69	68	271	2,940.83
Chris Gane	67	70	68	67	272	2,404.07
Miles Tunnicliff	69	65	68	70	272	2,404.07
Simon Khan	68	68	66	70	272	2,404.07
Jamie Donaldson	67	68	64	73	272	2,404.07
Kenneth Ferrie	72	67	67	67	273	1,631.44
Peter Lawrie	72	65	66	70	273	1,631.44
Greig Hutcheon	66	66	70	71	273	1,631.44
Gianluca Baruffaldi	71	66	69	67	273	1,631.44
Federico Bisazza	67	70	62	74	273	1,631.44
Robert McGuirk	69	70	68	67	274	984.06
Stuart Little	67	67	72	68	274	984.06
Simon Hurd	70	69	69	66	274	984.06
Simon Wakefield	68	67	70	69	274	984.06
Mads Vibe-Hastrup	71	66	66	71	274	984.06
Tino Schuster	66	71	67	70	274	984.06
Ian Hutchings	68	71	66	70	275	793.80
Adam Mednick	73	66	65	71	275	793.80
Lee James	72	66	65	72	275	793.80
Ilya Goroneskoul	69	68	67	72	276	706.86
Jean-Francois Lucquin	69	68	69	70	276	706.86
Didier de Vooght	68	70	69	69	276	706.86
Gary Clark	70	66	70	70	276	706.86
Damien McGrane	68	70	67	72	277	613.87
Xavier Lazurowicz	67	72	67	71	277	613.87
Jesus Maria Arruti	69	70	67	71	277	613.87
Andre Bossert	69	69	66	73	277	613.87
Benoit Teilleria	68	72	68	69	277	613.87

Terme Euganee International Open Padova

Padova Golf Club, Valsansibio, Italy
Par 36-36–72; 6,620 yards

October 18-21
purse, £71,283

	SCORES				TOTAL	MONEY
Chris Gane	70	64	65	66	265	£11,880.57
Philip Golding	66	63	68	69	266	6,185.02
Mattias Nilsson	64	67	70	65	266	6,185.02
Mattias Eliasson	70	66	65	66	267	3,564.17
Federico Bisazza	68	65	67	68	268	3,022.42
Silvio Grappasonni	67	66	70	67	270	2,279.88
Martin Erlandsson	68	67	66	69	270	2,279.88
Richard Bland	67	68	67	68	270	2,279.88
Stefano Reale	65	66	74	65	270	2,279.88
Dennis Edlund	67	71	65	67	270	2,279.88
Ian Hutchings	67	67	68	68	270	2,279.88
Marcello Santi	70	67	67	67	271	1,534.97

	SCORES				TOTAL	MONEY
Kariem Baraka	67	68	72	64	271	1,534.97
Paddy Gribben	68	69	65	69	271	1,534.97
Magnus Persson	71	63	72	66	272	1,071.03
Peter Hanson	68	69	69	66	272	1,071.03
Simon Khan	66	72	70	64	272	1,071.03
Simon Hurd	69	69	67	67	272	1,071.03
Miles Tunnicliff	70	66	65	72	273	811.21
Andre Bossert	67	72	68	66	273	811.21
Tony Edlund	66	73	66	68	273	811.21
Johan Skold	64	68	68	73	273	811.21
Bjorn Pettersson	66	68	69	70	273	811.21
Gary Murphy	68	72	70	64	274	666.50
Alberto Binaghi	65	71	70	68	274	666.50
Andrew Marshall	69	70	65	70	274	666.50
Sam Little	71	67	70	66	274	666.50
Gary Clark	66	68	72	68	274	666.50
Dominique Nouailhac	71	67	68	68	274	666.50
Gianluca Baruffaldi	71	69	71	64	275	584.52
Fredrik Widmark	69	67	70	69	275	584.52

Challenge Tour Grand Final

Golf du Medoc, Bordeaux, France
Par 35-36–71; 6,918 yards

November 1-4
purse, £124,351

	SCORES				TOTAL	MONEY
Richard Bland	69	68	66	63	266	£21,139.81
Philip Golding	69	71	65	66	271	14,300.46
Gary Clark	70	68	68	66	272	7,243.49
Andrew Marshall	69	68	65	70	272	7,243.49
Didier de Vooght	71	65	69	69	274	5,191.69
Ashley Roestoff	71	68	66	69	274	5,191.69
Scott Drummond	70	69	68	68	275	4,414.49
Mark Foster	69	70	67	69	275	4,414.49
Stuart Little	69	66	72	69	276	3,730.55
Grant Hamerton	71	66	70	69	276	3,730.55
Jamie Donaldson	71	68	69	70	278	3,005.17
Michael Archer	68	73	67	70	278	3,005.17
Ian Hutchings	69	71	68	70	278	3,005.17
Peter Hedblom	74	68	69	68	279	2,129.52
Marten Olander	72	70	69	68	279	2,129.52
Simon Wakefield	71	69	70	69	279	2,129.52
Andre Bossert	71	67	71	70	279	2,129.52
Miles Tunnicliff	69	68	74	69	280	1,585.49
Kariem Baraka	69	72	70	69	280	1,585.49
Joakim Rask	67	75	69	69	280	1,585.49
Mads Vibe-Hastrup	71	73	67	69	280	1,585.49
Alberto Binaghi	70	70	70	71	281	1,430.05
Benn Barham	69	72	71	70	282	1,305.69
Dominique Nouailhac	69	72	70	71	282	1,305.69
Sebastien Delagrange	71	71	69	71	282	1,305.69
Iain Pyman	72	65	73	73	283	1,196.89
Mattias Nilsson	69	67	73	74	283	1,196.89
Andrew Sherborne	75	70	72	67	284	1,119.17
Chris Gane	74	69	72	69	284	1,119.17
Greig Hutcheon	76	68	68	72	284	1,119.17

Asia/Japan Tours

Asian PGA Davidoff Tour

Thailand Masters

Windmill Park Country Club, Bangkok, Thailand
Par 36-36–72; 6,876 yards

February 1-4
purse, US$200,000

	SCORES				TOTAL	MONEY
Kang Wook-soon	67	65	66	66	264	US$32,300
Thongchai Jaidee	64	66	68	71	269	22,260
Chawalit Plaphol	64	68	68	70	270	11,200
Jyoti Randhawa	64	68	71	67	270	11,200
Eric Meeks	67	64	71	69	271	8,000
Mardan Mamat	67	67	71	67	272	7,000
Jim Rutledge	73	62	69	69	273	5,500
Satoshi Oide	68	69	68	68	273	5,500
Prayad Marksaeng	66	72	67	69	274	4,460
Olle Nordberg	69	69	69	68	275	4,000
Andrew Pitts	69	68	72	67	276	3,440
Mike Cunning	69	70	67	70	276	3,440
Will Yanagisawa	67	74	64	71	276	3,440
Ted Oh	70	67	73	67	277	3,060
*Chan Wongluekiet	70	69	69	69	277	
*Prom Meesawat	65	74	69	69	277	
Sanchai Senaprom	71	67	70	70	278	2,704
David Gleeson	72	67	70	69	278	2,704
Charlie Wi	69	71	66	72	278	2,704
Chung Joon	68	71	69	70	278	2,704
Lu Chien-soon	63	72	71	72	278	2,704
James Stewart	72	70	71	66	279	2,370
Hsieh Yu-shu	69	72	72	66	279	2,370
Gilberto Morales	66	70	71	73	280	2,220
Greg Hanrahan	66	71	74	69	280	2,220
Jeff Burns	68	72	74	66	280	2,220
Shin Yong-jin	70	68	76	67	281	1,950
Suppacheep Meesom	72	70	68	71	281	1,950
Zaw Moe	69	70	72	70	281	1,950
Gary Rusnak	68	71	73	68	281	1,950
Udorn Duangdecha	68	72	69	72	281	1,950
Harmeet Kahlon	68	74	66	73	281	1,950

London Myanmar Open

Yangon Golf Club, Yangon, Myanmar
Par 36-36–72; 7,011 yards

February 8-11
purse, US$200,000

	SCORES				TOTAL	MONEY
Anthony Kang	74	71	71	66	282	US$32,300
Charlie Wi	72	73	71	68	284	22,260
Eric Meeks	71	70	75	69	285	12,400

	SCORES				TOTAL	MONEY
Lu Wen-teh	78	72	69	67	286	9,000
Mark Mouland	70	73	71	72	286	9,000
Sushi Ishigaki	75	69	70	73	287	6,000
Gary Rusnak	73	72	72	70	287	6,000
Thongchai Jaidee	72	74	71	70	287	6,000
Satoshi Oide	72	69	74	73	288	4,230
Ted Oh	68	74	72	74	288	4,230
Olle Nordberg	72	72	73	72	289	3,440
Amritinder Singh	73	73	71	72	289	3,440
Kyi Hla Han	73	74	74	68	289	3,440
Park No-seok	72	73	70	75	290	3,000
Ahmad Bateman	69	76	74	71	290	3,000
Zaw Moe	72	68	76	75	291	2,760
Song Byung-joo	75	69	69	78	291	2,760
Jim Rutledge	72	73	74	73	292	2,530
Tsai Chi-huang	72	74	72	74	292	2,530
Danny Zarate	75	71	73	74	293	2,250
Tatsuya Kihara	73	72	77	71	293	2,250
Zaw Paing Oo	72	73	76	72	293	2,250
Nam Young-woo	73	75	72	73	293	2,250
Mike Cunning	75	76	74	68	293	2,250
Kang Wook-soon	74	76	73	70	293	2,250
Ryuichi Tayasu	74	71	73	76	294	1,920
Lin Wen-tang	74	72	76	72	294	1,920
Harmeet Kahlon	74	72	73	75	294	1,920
David Gleeson	78	73	72	71	294	1,920
Win Naing Tun	75	73	73	73	294	1,920

Carlsberg Malaysian Open

Saujana Golf & Country Club, Kuala Lumpur, Malaysia
Par 36-36–72; 6,945 yards

February 15-18
purse, US$910,000

	SCORES				TOTAL	MONEY
Vijay Singh	68	70	68	68	274	US$151,660
Padraig Harrington	70	66	68	70	274	101,110
(Singh defeated Harrington on third playoff hole.)						
Ahmad Bateman	72	69	68	67	276	51,233
Charlie Wi	70	70	67	69	276	51,233
Soren Hansen	69	70	70	69	278	38,584
Wang Ter-chang	69	71	68	71	279	31,850
Thongchai Jaidee	75	67	68	70	280	21,075.60
Desvonde Botes	72	67	71	70	280	21,075.60
Michael Campbell	69	67	71	73	280	21,075.60
Carl Pettersson	72	69	67	72	280	21,075.60
Maarten Lafeber	67	72	69	72	280	21,075.60
Olle Karlsson	73	65	72	71	281	15,151.50
Mardan Mamat	70	70	70	71	281	15,151.50
Thammanoon Sriroj	71	67	72	72	282	13,104
Jean Hugo	75	69	73	65	282	13,104
Soren Kjeldsen	70	69	72	71	282	13,104
John Daly	72	72	69	69	282	13,104
Patrik Sjoland	75	65	68	75	283	10,647
Jose Manuel Lara	75	68	71	69	283	10,647
Ignacio Garrido	72	69	73	69	283	10,647
Justin Hobday	69	69	71	74	283	10,647
Yang Yong-eun	72	70	67	74	283	10,647

	SCORES				TOTAL	MONEY
Henrik Nystrom	71	71	70	71	283	10,647
Robert Coles	68	73	71	71	283	10,647
Kang Wook-soon	72	65	75	72	284	8,918
Clay Devers	75	67	67	75	284	8,918
Alex Cejka	75	69	69	71	284	8,918
Gerald Rosales	72	69	74	69	284	8,918
Robert Huxtable	71	71	67	75	284	8,918
John Bickerton	74	70	72	69	285	7,689.50
Garry Houston	76	70	72	67	285	7,689.50
Jean-Francois Remesy	72	74	71	68	285	7,689.50
Des Terblanche	69	75	73	68	285	7,689.50
Felix Casas	72	69	73	72	286	6,370
Gustavo Rojas	75	70	74	67	286	6,370
Kyi Hla Han	72	71	71	72	286	6,370
Wayne Riley	73	71	70	72	286	6,370
Anders Hansen	70	71	74	71	286	6,370
Stephen Scahill	75	71	71	69	286	6,370
Tjaart van der Walt	75	71	72	68	286	6,370
Tobias Dier	71	74	71	70	286	6,370
Elliot Boult	72	66	71	78	287	5,187
Arjun Atwal	71	69	75	72	287	5,187
Fredrik Andersson	74	70	72	71	287	5,187
Anthony Kang	71	73	72	71	287	5,187
Costantino Rocca	69	76	69	73	287	5,187
Ted Purdy	72	69	72	75	288	4,368
Mikael Lundberg	72	70	75	71	288	4,368
Erol Simsek	74	71	72	71	288	4,368
Thomas Levet	72	72	74	70	288	4,368
Joakim Haeggman	75	69	71	74	289	3,287.38
Andrew Raitt	73	70	72	74	289	3,287.38
Danny Zarate	71	71	74	73	289	3,287.38
Simon Yates	72	72	70	75	289	3,287.38
Jim Rutledge	74	72	70	73	289	3,287.38
Marc Farry	74	72	72	71	289	3,287.38
Robert Floyd	72	73	70	74	289	3,287.38
Zhang Lian-wei	71	75	71	72	289	3,287.38
Chawalit Plaphol	74	71	72	73	290	2,639
Gary Evans	70	72	75	74	291	2,548
Hong Chia-yuh	74	71	74	73	292	2,275
Amandeep Johl	75	71	73	73	292	2,275
Rodrigo Cuello	74	72	71	75	292	2,275
Graeme Storm	71	73	72	76	292	2,275
Holden Kim	73	73	74	72	292	2,275
Mark Pilkington	78	68	71	76	293	1,956.50
R. Nachimuthu	74	71	75	73	293	1,956.50
S. Murthy	72	71	79	72	294	1,820
Hsieh Yu-shu	76	67	78	74	295	1,729
Peter Mitchell	71	74	78	73	296	1,666
Frankie Minoza	77	68	77	75	297	1,365.03
Zaw Moe	69	72	78	79	298	1,362.25
Stephen Dodd	70	73	80	79	302	1,359.47

Caltex Singapore Masters

Singapore Island Country Club, Singapore
Par 35-36–71; 6,751 yards

February 22-25
purse, US$850,000

	SCORES				TOTAL	MONEY
Vijay Singh	64	63	68	68	263	US$141,660
Warren Bennett	63	69	65	68	265	94,440
Maarten Lafeber	64	67	70	65	266	47,855
Colin Montgomerie	66	67	65	68	266	47,855
Anders Hansen	69	64	69	65	267	32,895
Padraig Harrington	63	67	71	66	267	32,895
Frankie Minoza	64	61	71	72	268	23,375
Mikael Lundberg	69	64	64	71	268	23,375
Prayad Marksaeng	67	63	69	70	269	19,040
Clay Devers	70	65	70	65	270	17,000
Andrew Pitts	71	67	67	66	271	14,648.33
Lin Keng-chi	67	69	64	71	271	14,648.33
Hong Chia-yuh	66	71	65	69	271	14,648.33
Tom Gillis	69	66	70	67	272	12,495
Yang Yong-eun	67	66	72	67	272	12,495
Stephen Dodd	69	66	66	71	272	12,495
Chawalit Plaphol	67	66	70	70	273	10,285
Henrik Nystrom	67	66	70	70	273	10,285
Gary Orr	68	68	67	70	273	10,285
Gerald Rosales	68	69	70	66	273	10,285
Robert Coles	68	69	69	67	273	10,285
Costantino Rocca	67	69	68	69	273	10,285
Anthony Wall	64	71	65	73	273	10,285
Carlos Rodiles	72	67	66	69	274	8,585
Zaw Moe	68	67	68	71	274	8,585
Ignacio Garrido	70	68	69	67	274	8,585
Jeev Milkha Singh	68	68	67	71	274	8,585
Andrew Coltart	68	71	65	70	274	8,585
Thongchai Jaidee	73	66	66	70	275	6,856.67
Gustavo Rojas	70	67	69	69	275	6,856.67
Steen Tinning	67	68	70	70	275	6,856.67
Anthony Kang	66	69	71	69	275	6,856.67
Stephen Scahill	68	70	70	67	275	6,856.67
Ted Purdy	67	70	70	68	275	6,856.67
Henrik Bjornstad	68	70	68	69	275	6,856.67
Yeh Wei-tze	68	70	66	71	275	6,856.67
Jose Manuel Lara	67	72	70	66	275	6,856.67
Mark Mouland	66	66	71	73	276	5,525
Gerry Norquist	69	68	71	68	276	5,525
Eric Meeks	68	70	67	71	276	5,525
Justin Hobday	67	71	70	68	276	5,525
Gary Rusnak	67	71	67	71	276	5,525
Olivier Edmond	67	64	76	70	277	4,845
Richard Green	65	71	70	71	277	4,845
Massimo Scarpa	66	72	70	69	277	4,845
Charlie Wi	69	67	73	69	278	4,165
Ahmad Bateman	70	69	75	64	278	4,165
David Howell	69	69	73	67	278	4,165
Alex Cejka	68	69	71	70	278	4,165
Arjun Atwal	69	69	68	72	278	4,165
Kang Wook-soon	72	67	71	69	279	2,941
Graeme Storm	71	67	70	71	279	2,941
Boonchu Ruangkit	71	67	67	74	279	2,941
Unho Park	70	68	73	68	279	2,941

	SCORES				TOTAL	MONEY
Jorge Berendt	69	68	71	71	279	2,941
Raymond Russell	69	69	72	69	279	2,941
Paul Eales	68	69	72	70	279	2,941
Madasaamy Murugiah	68	70	71	70	279	2,941
Mark Pilkington	67	70	70	72	279	2,941
Des Terblanche	66	72	72	69	279	2,941
Pablo Del Olmo	69	64	72	75	280	2,082.50
Paul Streeter	71	66	72	71	280	2,082.50
Peter Mitchell	71	68	71	70	280	2,082.50
Wang Ter-chang	70	69	72	69	280	2,082.50
Olle Nordberg	70	69	69	72	280	2,082.50
Rafael Ponce	69	70	72	69	280	2,082.50
Amandeep Johl	72	67	72	70	281	1,742.50
Ted Oh	69	68	74	70	281	1,742.50
James Kingston	72	67	72	71	282	1,587.50
Daisuke Maruyama	69	70	72	71	282	1,587.50
Elliot Boult	69	69	74	71	283	1,275.35
Lam Chih-bing	69	70	74	71	284	1,269.85
Shin Yong-jin	69	70	73	72	284	1,269.85
Aaron Meeks	67	71	71	75	284	1,269.85
Haruyuki Tsujimura	70	69	71	76	286	1,264.36
Raul Ballesteros	71	68	72	76	287	1,261.61

Wills Indian Open

Classic Golf Resort, New Delhi, India
Par 36-36–72; 7,084 yards

March 15-18
purse, US$300,000

	SCORES				TOTAL	MONEY
Thongchai Jaidee	67	69	69	66	271	US$50,010
Ross Bain	71	67	68	66	272	33,000
Chris Williams	68	68	72	68	276	16,800
Arjun Atwal	71	71	68	66	276	16,800
James Kingston	70	69	73	65	277	11,400
David Gleeson	68	74	69	66	277	11,400
Adam Spring	71	67	72	68	278	7,590
Craig Kamps	72	71	67	68	278	7,590
Greg Hanrahan	74	68	70	67	279	5,520
Arjun Singh	69	71	71	68	279	5,520
Andrew Pitts	68	76	68	67	279	5,520
Gerald Rosales	69	69	70	72	280	4,890
Hong Chia-yuh	71	73	68	68	280	4,890
Prayad Marksaeng	68	73	69	71	281	4,680
Brad Kennedy	70	69	74	69	282	4,260
Jeff Burns	67	69	73	73	282	4,260
Jyoti Randhawa	67	69	72	74	282	4,260
Simon Yates	74	70	67	71	282	4,260
Nico van Rensburg	68	71	69	74	282	4,260
Robert Huxtable	69	72	72	69	282	4,260
Chawalit Plaphol	70	71	74	68	283	3,720
Vivek Bhandari	67	71	74	71	283	3,720
Taimur Hussain	70	71	70	72	283	3,720
Felix Casas	73	68	74	69	284	3,060
Thammanoon Sriroj	76	69	70	69	284	3,060
Chen Yuan-chi	71	70	71	72	284	3,060
Shinichi Akiba	71	71	72	70	284	3,060
Indrajit Bhalotia	70	71	71	72	284	3,060

	SCORES				TOTAL	MONEY
Mike Cunning	70	74	71	69	284	3,060
Stephen Lindskog	70	74	70	70	284	3,060
Chung Joon	70	74	69	71	284	3,060

Maekyung LG Fashion Open

Nam Seoul Country Club, Seoul, Korea
Par 36-36–72; 6,796 yards

April 26-29
purse, US$350,000

	SCORES				TOTAL	MONEY
Choi Gwang-soo	65	69	68	69	271	$51,813.47
*Kim Dae-sub	69	69	68	66	272	
Arjun Atwal	71	70	65	66	272	31,502.59
Hwang Sung-ha	70	69	66	69	274	17,431.53
Amandeep Johl	73	63	69	71	276	11,815.94
Chung Chun-hsing	74	70	71	61	276	11,815.94
Zaw Moe	66	71	69	70	276	11,815.94
Andrew Pitts	68	70	69	70	277	7,416.73
Yoo Jae-chul	68	71	71	67	277	7,416.73
Prayad Marksaeng	68	74	69	67	278	5,803.11
Lin Chie-hsiang	73	64	70	73	280	4,757.32
Thammanoon Sriroj	69	66	72	73	280	4,757.32
Shin Yong-jin	70	68	75	67	280	4,757.32
Mardan Mamat	74	69	67	70	280	4,757.32
Kim Wan-tae	69	71	71	69	280	4,757.32
Kang Wook-soon	72	72	69	67	280	4,757.32
Aaron Meeks	65	73	70	72	280	4,757.32
Hur Suk-ho	66	66	75	74	281	4,047
Nam Young-woo	72	69	71	69	281	4,047
Jun Tae-hyun	68	73	71	69	281	4,047
Ted Oh	69	77	66	69	281	4,047
Choi Sang-ho	72	68	73	69	282	3,693.56
Yang Yong-eun	73	72	69	68	282	3,693.56
*Kwon Ki-taek	71	68	72	72	283	
Kim Jong-duk	71	71	66	75	283	3,282.01
Anthony Kang	69	73	71	70	283	3,282.01
Arjun Singh	68	74	70	71	283	3,282.01
Yeh Wei-tze	67	74	70	72	283	3,282.01
Kwon Oh-chul	68	75	68	72	283	3,282.01
Thongchai Jaidee	76	68	69	71	284	2,695.78
Park Nam-sin	73	69	74	68	284	2,695.78
Clay Devers	75	70	70	69	284	2,695.78
Mike Cunning	70	70	71	73	284	2,695.78
Mo Joong-kyung	73	71	72	68	284	2,695.78

Macau Open

Macau Golf & Country Club, Macau
Par 35-36–71; 6,622 yards

May 3-6
purse, US$250,000

	SCORES				TOTAL	MONEY
Zhang Lian-wei	70	64	71	68	273	$40,375
Simon Yates	70	68	66	70	274	27,825
Yeh Wei-tze	67	72	65	72	276	15,500
Thongchai Jaidee	72	67	69	69	277	11,250

	SCORES				TOTAL	MONEY
Lin Chie-hsiang	68	74	66	69	277	11,250
John Daly	72	68	69	69	278	8,125
Taimur Hussain	72	70	66	70	278	8,125
Anthony Kang	72	65	67	75	279	6,250
Tsai Chi-huang	68	67	70	75	280	5,287.50
Liang Wen-chong	74	68	69	69	280	5,287.50
Hong Chia-yuh	71	70	70	70	281	4,300
Thaworn Wiratchant	70	70	69	72	281	4,300
Arjun Singh	74	71	68	68	281	4,300
Charlie Wi	73	69	69	71	282	3,750
Dominique Boulet	68	71	73	70	282	3,750
Ted Purdy	71	67	74	71	283	3,306.25
Chang Tse-peng	75	69	72	67	283	3,306.25
Ted Oh	75	69	72	67	283	3,306.25
Thammanoon Sriroj	70	71	71	71	283	3,306.25
Yang Yong-eun	76	66	74	68	284	2,737.50
Hsu Mong-nan	74	68	73	69	284	2,737.50
Sammy Daniels	74	69	69	72	284	2,737.50
Sushi Ishigaki	72	71	68	73	284	2,737.50
Jyoti Randhawa	69	71	69	75	284	2,737.50
Scott Kammann	71	72	70	71	284	2,737.50
Gaurav Ghei	72	72	69	71	284	2,737.50
Prayad Marksaeng	71	73	71	69	284	2,737.50
Mike Cunning	76	68	70	71	285	2,250
Scott Taylor	68	69	79	69	285	2,250
Yasunobu Kuramoto	72	69	71	73	285	2,250
Olle Nordberg	70	73	71	71	285	2,250
Andrew Pitts	68	73	72	72	285	2,250

SK Telecom Open

Il Dong Lake Golf Club, Koyang, Korea
Par 36-36–72; 7,021 yards

May 17-20
purse, US$300,000

	SCORES				TOTAL	MONEY
Charlie Wi	69	72	69	71	281	US$48,450
Simon Yates	69	72	69	71	281	25,995
Kang Wook-soon	70	73	68	70	281	25,995
(Wi defeated Yates on fifth and Kang on seventh playoff hole.)						
Lin Chie-hsiang	70	74	70	68	282	15,000
Yang Yong-nam	74	69	71	69	283	9,750
Yang Yong-eun	71	71	72	69	283	9,750
Arjun Atwal	69	72	71	71	283	9,750
Greg Hanrahan	71	73	70	69	283	9,750
*Kim Dae-sub	73	70	71	70	284	
Naoto Fukasawa	70	70	73	71	284	5,634
Clay Devers	70	71	72	71	284	5,634
Anthony Kang	74	73	70	67	284	5,634
Nam Young-woo	70	74	69	71	284	5,634
Thammanoon Sriroj	69	75	71	69	284	5,634
Thongchai Jaidee	74	72	71	68	285	4,410
Thaworn Wiratchant	71	72	71	71	285	4,410
Olle Nordberg	71	74	71	69	285	4,410
Taimur Hussain	70	73	73	70	286	4,050
Chawalit Plaphol	76	69	72	70	287	3,675
Kong Young-joon	73	70	73	71	287	3,675
Scott Kammann	71	75	69	72	287	3,675

	SCORES			TOTAL	MONEY
Lee In-woo	71	77	69	70	287	3,675
James Stewart	75	72	69	72	288	3,375
Lee Jun-young	71	75	70	72	288	3,375
Lien Yung-sheng	77	68	70	74	289	2,838
Kim Kyung-min	72	71	77	69	289	2,838
Shin Yong-jin	76	71	68	74	289	2,838
Sushi Ishigaki	77	72	71	69	289	2,838
Chung Joon	72	72	71	74	289	2,838
Shinnosuke Sakagami	74	73	73	69	289	2,838
Vivek Bhandari	73	73	74	69	289	2,838
Lee Yong-kun	73	73	72	71	289	2,838
Cho Do-hyun	74	75	70	70	289	2,838
Suk Jong-yul	71	77	71	70	289	2,838

Alcatel Singapore Open

Jurong Country Club, Singapore
Par 35-37–72; 6,800 yards

June 21-24
purse, US$300,000

	SCORES			TOTAL	MONEY
Thaworn Wiratchant	68	69	68	67	272	$48,450
Hsieh Yu-shu	72	66	68	67	273	33,390
Charlie Wi	68	71	65	71	275	16,800
Clay Devers	65	72	69	69	275	16,800
James Kingston	67	68	69	72	276	11,250
Chris Williams	67	71	71	67	276	11,250
Hendrik Buhrmann	70	65	73	70	278	7,730
Liang Wen-chong	72	69	68	69	278	7,730
Will Yanagisawa	69	70	70	69	278	7,730
Thammanoon Sriroj	72	65	70	72	279	5,370
Mardan Mamat	71	68	70	70	279	5,370
Kim Felton	69	68	69	73	279	5,370
Amandeep Johl	68	69	73	69	279	5,370
Lin Wen-ko	70	66	77	67	280	4,145
Arjun Singh	74	67	72	67	280	4,145
Simon Yates	71	68	70	71	280	4,145
Pablo Del Olmo	69	69	76	66	280	4,145
Yasunobu Kuramoto	67	70	71	72	280	4,145
Lu Wen-teh	71	71	65	73	280	4,145
Wallie Coetsee	65	70	72	74	281	3,600
Craig Kamps	71	67	75	69	282	3,240
Jason Dawes	71	67	74	70	282	3,240
Jamnian Chitprasong	72	68	69	73	282	3,240
Yang Yong-eun	70	69	74	69	282	3,240
Adrian Percey	73	69	67	73	282	3,240
Park Do-kyu	70	69	70	73	282	3,240
Marciano Pucay	71	70	72	69	282	3,240
Grant Muller	75	66	73	69	283	2,660
Scott Taylor	71	66	74	72	283	2,660
Chung Chun-hsing	73	69	69	72	283	2,660
Gerald Rosales	71	70	74	68	283	2,660
Terry Noe	72	70	68	73	283	2,660
Shinnosuke Sakagami	71	71	70	71	283	2,660

Volvo Masters of Malaysia

Kota Permai Golf and Country Club,
Kuala Lumpur, Malaysia
Par 36-36–72; 6,962 yards

August 9-12
purse, US$275,000

	SCORES				TOTAL	MONEY
Thaworn Wiratchant	69	67	67	68	271	US$44,412.50
Scott Kammann	67	67	69	71	274	30,607.50
James Kingston	71	67	68	69	275	17,050
Simon Yates	69	69	69	69	276	11,458.33
Zhang Lian-wei	66	70	68	72	276	11,458.33
Thongchai Jaidee	68	71	68	69	276	11,458.33
Lu Chien-soon	71	67	71	68	277	7,085.83
Kyi Hla Han	67	70	70	70	277	7,085.83
Liang Wen-chong	69	72	69	67	277	7,085.83
Boonchu Ruangkit	72	68	71	68	279	4,922.50
Tsai Chi-huang	72	69	69	69	279	4,922.50
Marciano Pucay	70	72	68	69	279	4,922.50
Yeh Wei-tze	69	73	69	68	279	4,922.50
Amandeep Johl	70	68	72	70	280	3,877.50
Vivek Bhandari	73	68	69	70	280	3,877.50
Daniel Chopra	71	71	68	70	280	3,877.50
Periasamy Gunasegaran	70	71	65	74	280	3,877.50
Anthony Kang	67	72	67	74	280	3,877.50
Mo Joong-kyung	70	69	71	71	281	3,355
Hendrik Buhrmann	67	71	72	71	281	3,355
Zaw Moe	70	69	68	75	282	2,928.75
Mike Cunning	71	70	70	71	282	2,928.75
Thammanoon Sriroj	72	70	67	73	282	2,928.75
Ted Oh	71	71	68	72	282	2,928.75
Arjun Singh	67	71	71	73	282	2,928.75
Sushi Ishigaki	69	72	75	66	282	2,928.75
Prayad Marksaeng	63	72	74	73	282	2,928.75
Arjun Atwal	71	73	71	67	282	2,928.75
Kazuhiro Shimizu	71	68	72	72	283	2,365
Jyoti Randhawa	67	69	73	74	283	2,365
Lu Wen-teh	69	70	72	72	283	2,365
Rick Gibson	69	71	68	75	283	2,365
Olle Nordberg	69	72	73	69	283	2,365
Andrew Pitts	70	74	71	68	283	2,365

Acer Taiwan Open

Sunrise Golf & Country Club, Taipei, Taiwan
Par 36-36–72; 7,062 yards
(Fourth round cancelled — rain.)

August 30-September 2
purse, US$300,000

	SCORES			TOTAL	MONEY
Andrew Pitts	64	65	68	197	US$50,000
Mardan Mamat	71	65	67	203	33,090
Ted Oh	68	66	70	204	18,325
Aaron Meeks	69	69	67	205	12,275
Thongchai Jaidee	66	71	68	205	12,275
Arjun Atwal	65	72	68	205	12,275
Daniel Chopra	71	63	72	206	6,879
*Kao Bo-song	68	69	69	206	

	SCORES			TOTAL	MONEY
Thammanoon Sriroj	68	70	68	206	6,879
Thaworn Wiratchant	67	70	69	206	6,879
Scott Hoch	68	72	66	206	6,879
Gary Rusnak	64	72	70	206	6,879
Charlie Wi	67	68	72	207	4,855
Prayad Marksaeng	70	70	67	207	4,855
Chung Chun-hsing	72	71	64	207	4,855
Jeev Milkha Singh	69	68	72	209	4,320
Sushi Ishigaki	72	70	67	209	4,320
Boonchu Ruangkit	74	65	71	210	3,592.50
Anthony Kang	73	69	68	210	3,592.50
Lu Chien-soon	69	69	72	210	3,592.50
Ho Chia-feng	67	69	74	210	3,592.50
*Cheng Chen-liang	69	70	71	210	
Lin Chie-hsiang	70	71	69	210	3,592.50
Yeh Chang-ting	68	71	71	210	3,592.50
Clay Devers	68	71	71	210	3,592.50
Brad Lamb	69	72	69	210	3,592.50
Jim Rutledge	72	68	71	211	3,105
Robert Huxtable	70	68	73	211	3,105
Chang Tse-peng	70	69	73	212	2,835
*Lu Tze-shyan	70	70	72	212	
Scott Taylor	68	70	74	212	2,835
Hsieh Yu-shu	63	72	77	212	2,835
Jyoti Randhawa	68	76	68	212	2,835

Mercuries Masters

Taiwan Golf & Country Club, Taipei, Taiwan
Par 36-36–72; 6,950 yards

September 6-9
purse, US$300,000

	SCORES				TOTAL	MONEY
Daniel Chopra	71	69	73	71	284	US$69,565.22
Vivek Bhandari	70	74	72	69	285	41,739.13
Arjun Singh	72	70	74	71	287	20,869.57
Chung Chun-hsing	73	73	68	73	287	20,869.57
Thongchai Jaidee	71	72	73	72	288	12,173.91
Hendrik Buhrmann	72	77	69	70	288	12,173.91
Chen Yuan-chi	73	72	73	71	289	7,791.30
Hsu Mong-nan	72	72	69	76	289	7,791.30
Yeh Wei-tze	71	74	69	75	289	7,791.30
Chang Tse-peng	73	69	72	76	290	5,576.81
Thammanoon Sriroj	70	71	74	75	290	5,576.81
James Kingston	70	76	74	70	290	5,576.81
Andrew Pitts	79	67	69	76	291	4,660.87
Arjun Atwal	72	73	74	72	291	4,660.87
David Gleeson	81	67	73	71	292	3,979.13
Scott Taylor	74	69	71	78	292	3,979.13
Gerald Rosales	72	70	73	77	292	3,979.13
Chen Liang-hsi	72	72	75	73	292	3,979.13
Hsieh Chin-sheng	72	73	74	73	292	3,979.13
Hsieh Yu-shu	74	70	76	73	293	3,501.45
Jim Rutledge	74	71	76	72	293	3,501.45
Kang Wook-soon	70	72	77	74	293	3,501.45
Gary Rusnak	72	73	76	73	294	3,304.35
Jyoti Randhawa	72	73	73	76	294	3,304.35
Lin Chie-hsiang	70	71	79	75	295	3,200

	SCORES				TOTAL	MONEY
Nico van Rensburg	77	73	73	73	296	3,095.65
Hong Chia-yuh	75	75	73	73	296	3,095.65
Hsieh Min-nan	69	77	76	75	297	2,956.52
Jeff Burns	72	77	74	74	297	2,956.52
Craig Kamps	73	68	77	80	298	2,718.84
Mardan Mamat	76	71	70	81	298	2,718.84
Lu Wen-teh	75	73	77	73	298	2,718.84
Rodrigo Cuello	73	74	71	80	298	2,718.84
Chang Chin-kuo	74	76	73	75	298	2,718.84
Chawalit Plaphol	71	78	72	77	298	2,718.84

Kolon Cup Korean Open

Seoul Country Club, Seoul, Korea   September 13-16
Par 36-36–72; 6,374 yards   purse, US$350,000

	SCORES				TOTAL	MONEY
*Kim Dae-sub	66	67	70	69	272	
Park Do-kyu	66	71	68	70	275	US$54,669
*Kwon Ki-taek	68	70	70	69	277	
James Kingston	69	71	71	66	277	30,372
Hwang Sung-ha	72	69	70	67	278	21,260
Hur Suk-ho	70	70	67	72	279	13,667
Kim Jin-young	68	74	67	70	279	13,667
Arjun Atwal	70	67	72	71	280	7,444
Lu Wen-teh	73	68	71	68	280	7,444
Mike Cunning	71	68	70	71	280	7,444
Pablo Del Olmo	72	68	70	70	280	7,444
Cho Chul-sang	69	69	70	72	280	7,444
Kim Jong-myung	71	71	71	67	280	7,444
Paul Lawrie	70	71	70	69	280	7,444
Thongchai Jaidee	68	72	73	67	280	7,444
Greg Hanrahan	70	72	68	70	280	7,444
Andrew Pitts	72	66	66	77	281	3,523
Justin Hobday	73	69	70	69	281	3,523
Chawalit Plaphol	69	69	69	74	281	3,523
Shin Yong-jin	71	70	73	67	281	3,523
Jang Ik-jae	70	70	71	70	281	3,523
Taimur Hussain	72	71	71	67	281	3,523
Adrian Percey	70	71	71	69	281	3,523
Hendrik Buhrmann	70	71	69	71	281	3,523
Charlie Wi	70	68	73	71	282	2,680
David Gleeson	71	68	71	72	282	2,680
Simon Yates	71	69	70	72	282	2,680
Gerald Rosales	73	70	70	69	282	2,680
Liang Wen-chong	72	70	68	72	282	2,680
Gary Rusnak	71	71	69	71	282	2,680
Lee Boo-young	71	72	71	68	282	2,680
Ted Oh	67	73	73	69	282	2,680

Shin Han Dong Hae Open

Kaya Golf & Country Club, Pusan, Korea
Par 36-36–72; 7,045 yards

September 20-23
purse, US$400,000

	SCORES				TOTAL	MONEY
Charlie Wi	66	70	70	70	276	US$60,195
Yang Yong-eun	65	66	73	73	277	29,345
Vivek Bhandari	69	71	71	66	277	29,345
Andrew Pitts	69	69	70	70	278	16,553
Mike Cunning	69	71	71	68	279	13,167
Park Young-soo	69	73	71	66	279	13,167
Park Boo-won	67	69	74	70	280	10,534
Park Do-kyu	62	70	79	70	281	9,029
Kim Hyung-tae	70	71	74	67	282	6,489
Lee Kun-hee	69	72	68	73	282	6,489
Kang Wook-soon	67	73	71	71	282	6,489
Park No-seok	65	76	71	70	282	6,489
Lee Jun-young	71	69	70	73	283	4,213
Choi Gwang-soo	71	71	71	70	283	4,213
Choi Sang-ho	68	71	72	72	283	4,213
Pablo Del Olmo	64	72	78	69	283	4,213
James Kingston	66	77	74	66	283	4,213
Amritinder Singh	72	71	73	68	284	3,141
Chawalit Plaphol	71	71	73	69	284	3,141
Song Byung-joo	72	71	70	71	284	3,141
Kim Wan-tae	67	72	74	71	284	3,141
Lee Boo-young	69	74	72	70	285	2,671
Yoo Jong-koo	68	74	72	71	285	2,671
Kwon Jong-kil	71	69	76	70	286	2,445
Yoo Jae-chul	72	70	74	70	286	2,445
Bong Tae-ha	70	71	73	72	286	2,445
Shin Yong-jin	70	74	71	71	286	2,445
Park Sang-soo	69	72	74	72	287	2,276
*Chung Ji-ho	68	72	72	75	287	
Kim Yong-soo	70	73	70	74	287	2,276

Volvo China Open

Shanghai Silport Golf Club, Shanghai, China
Par 36-36–72; 7,062 yards

October 18-21
purse, US$400,000

	SCORES				TOTAL	MONEY
Charlie Wi	68	67	69	68	272	US$72,000
Thongchai Jaidee	70	70	67	66	273	44,520
Andrew Pitts	66	69	73	69	277	24,800
Sushi Ishigaki	69	68	68	74	279	19,000
Boonchu Ruangkit	71	70	68	72	281	14,000
Harmeet Kahlon	72	71	69	69	281	14,000
Rodrigo Cuello	74	68	72	68	282	9,353.33
Brad Kennedy	71	70	68	73	282	9,353.33
Danny Zarate	71	72	69	70	282	9,353.33
Anthony Kang	71	67	71	74	283	6,516.67
Thammanoon Sriroj	75	68	70	70	283	6,516.67
Choi Gwang-soo	73	68	70	72	283	6,516.67
Lu Wen-teh	73	70	68	72	283	6,516.67
Simon Yates	71	71	68	73	283	6,516.67
Amandeep Johl	71	72	70	70	283	6,516.67

	SCORES				TOTAL	MONEY
Stephen Lindskog	73	72	67	72	284	5,290
Hong Chia-yuh	70	73	73	68	284	5,290
Chawalit Plaphol	71	73	70	70	284	5,290
Arjun Singh	71	75	67	71	284	5,290
Taimur Hussain	74	71	72	68	285	4,680
Chen Yuan-chi	74	72	69	70	285	4,680
Rick Gibson	66	75	70	74	285	4,680
Park No-seok	77	69	71	69	286	4,380
Rafael Ponce	71	71	71	73	286	4,380
Derek Fung	71	68	74	74	287	4,080
Mardan Mamat	71	74	67	75	287	4,080
Zheng Wen-gen	72	75	66	74	287	4,080
Tadaaki Kimura	74	68	71	75	288	3,497.14
Aaron Meeks	69	69	74	76	288	3,497.14
Scott Taylor	74	71	73	70	288	3,497.14
Pablo Del Olmo	77	71	70	70	288	3,497.14
Hwang Sung-ha	74	71	71	72	288	3,497.14
Liang Wen-chong	74	72	73	69	288	3,497.14
Richard Best	72	74	68	74	288	3,497.14

BMW Asian Open

Westin Resort, Ta Shee, Taiwan
Par 36-36–72; 7,104 yards

November 22-25
purse, US$1,500,000

	SCORES				TOTAL	MONEY
Jarmo Sandelin	72	66	72	68	278	US$242,200
Jose Maria Olazabal	70	70	72	67	279	129,920
Thongchai Jaidee	74	70	68	67	279	129,920
Carl Pettersson	72	68	69	72	281	67,440
Barry Lane	70	73	69	69	281	67,440
Miguel Angel Jimenez	70	69	70	73	282	48,687.50
Michael Campbell	72	73	71	66	282	48,687.50
Vijay Singh	71	69	73	70	283	33,585
Stephen Dodd	72	69	70	72	283	33,585
Brian Davis	72	70	69	72	283	33,585
Charlie Wi	76	68	68	72	284	25,735
Rolf Muntz	72	70	73	69	284	25,735
Stephen Scahill	70	71	74	69	284	25,735
Steve Webster	76	71	70	68	285	22,885
Soren Kjeldsen	75	68	71	72	286	21,085
Ted Oh	72	73	72	69	286	21,085
Jyoti Randhawa	71	75	71	69	286	21,085
Anders Forsbrand	76	66	78	67	287	17,335
Kim Felton	76	70	72	69	287	17,335
Adrian Percey	74	70	71	72	287	17,335
Thomas Levet	71	70	69	77	287	17,335
Unho Park	71	71	72	73	287	17,335
Jamie Spence	69	72	72	74	287	17,335
Philip Golding	73	73	70	71	287	17,335
Gary Evans	70	74	72	71	287	17,335
Christian Cevaer	75	68	76	69	288	13,885
James Kingston	76	69	70	73	288	13,885
Nick Faldo	73	70	74	71	288	13,885
Gregory Havret	77	71	71	69	288	13,885
Wang Ter-chang	73	73	69	73	288	13,885
Tony Johnstone	69	75	74	70	288	13,885
Kyi Hla Han	71	78	69	70	288	13,885

	SCORES				TOTAL	MONEY
Arjun Atwal	76	70	73	70	289	11,935
Klas Eriksson	74	74	71	70	289	11,935
Hendrik Buhrmann	72	75	68	74	289	11,935
Johan Rystrom	78	65	74	73	290	11,185
Stephen Lindskog	74	72	71	73	290	11,185
Neil Reilly	76	71	72	72	291	10,435
Soren Hansen	77	72	71	71	291	10,435
Sebastien Delagrange	68	77	72	74	291	10,435
Jonathan Lomas	80	69	68	75	292	9,235
Hsieh Yu-shu	79	70	67	76	292	9,235
Des Terblanche	74	71	72	75	292	9,235
Choi Kwang-soo	75	73	71	73	292	9,235
Jean-Francois Remesy	74	75	72	71	292	9,235
Craig Cowper	77	70	70	76	293	7,735
Raphael Jacquelin	73	71	77	72	293	7,735
Henrik Bjornstad	74	72	74	73	293	7,735
Chen Yuan-chi	75	73	73	72	293	7,735
Yeh Wei-tze	74	75	76	68	293	7,735
Patrik Sjoland	77	72	74	71	294	6,385
Shinichi Akiba	74	72	74	74	294	6,385
Elliot Boult	73	75	73	73	294	6,385
Gregory Hanrahan	71	76	75	72	294	6,385
Aaron Meeks	77	71	74	73	295	5,335
Lu Wen-teh	74	74	74	73	295	5,335
Francis Quinn	75	74	71	75	295	5,335
Chung Chun-hsing	74	71	77	74	296	4,510
Scott Drummond	76	73	76	71	296	4,510
Arjun Singh	74	73	72	77	296	4,510
Gary Clark	69	75	76	76	296	4,510
Mark James	77	72	76	72	297	3,835
Lin Chie-hsiang	77	72	72	76	297	3,835
Malcolm Mackenzie	74	73	78	72	297	3,835
Lee Thompson	75	73	76	73	297	3,835
David Gleeson	73	74	75	75	297	3,835
Marc Farry	76	69	75	78	298	3,235
Tobias Dier	74	73	75	76	298	3,235
Ian Poulter	71	77	72	78	298	3,235
James Stewart	76	71	78	74	299	2,323
Simon Dyson	73	74	77	75	299	2,323
Mike Cunning	78	71	77	74	300	1,200
Craig Kamps	75	74	77	74	300	1,200
Nico van Rensburg	71	76	75	78	300	1,200
Rafael Ponce	72	77	76	75	300	1,200
Dominique Nouailhac	80	67	76	78	301	1,200
Rodrigo Cuello	74	73	78	76	301	1,200
Lu Chien-soon	75	73	75	78	301	1,200
Danny Zarate	77	70	80	78	305	1,200
Hsieh Min-nan	73	76	78	79	306	1,200

Omega Hong Kong Open

Hong Kong Golf Club, Hong Kong
Par 35-36–71; 6,697 yards

November 29-December 2
purse, US$700,000

	SCORES				TOTAL	MONEY
Jose Maria Olazabal	65	69	64	64	262	US$113,000
Henrik Bjornstad	66	69	61	67	263	77,870
Adam Scott	64	67	66	67	264	43,360

	SCORES				TOTAL	MONEY
Mark Foster	66	65	67	67	265	34,960
Carl Pettersson	67	64	68	67	266	27,960
Anders Forsbrand	67	64	68	68	267	20,960
Andrew Marshall	68	66	68	65	267	20,960
Mark Pilkington	69	68	62	68	267	20,960
Yeh Wei-tze	66	63	72	67	268	13,577.25
Simon Dyson	67	64	70	67	268	13,577.25
Brian Davis	70	67	64	67	268	13,577.25
Jarmo Sandelin	68	70	66	64	268	13,577.25
Gary Evans	70	66	65	68	269	10,712
Michael Campbell	66	69	68	66	269	10,712
Thongchai Jaidee	67	70	67	65	269	10,712
Simon Yates	66	66	70	68	270	9,217.50
Andrew Pitts	68	67	70	65	270	9,217.50
Thomas Levet	70	67	66	67	270	9,217.50
Zhang Lian-wei	67	67	68	68	270	9,217.50
Christian Cevaer	68	69	67	67	271	8,360
Des Terblanche	70	63	69	70	272	7,730
Marten Olander	68	65	71	68	272	7,730
Thaworn Wiratchant	70	66	68	68	272	7,730
Stephen Scahill	68	67	68	69	272	7,730
Stephen Lindskog	66	70	68	68	272	7,730
Rolf Muntz	69	65	67	72	273	6,373.75
Liang Wen-chong	69	66	73	65	273	6,373.75
Paul McGinley	65	66	74	68	273	6,373.75
Aaron Meeks	71	66	68	68	273	6,373.75
Jean-Francois Remesy	67	68	68	70	273	6,373.75
Nick O'Hern	67	68	67	71	273	6,373.75
Thammanoon Sriroj	69	69	66	69	273	6,373.75
Mark Mouland	67	71	65	70	273	6,373.75
Anthony Kang	71	64	69	70	274	5,140
Zaw Moe	66	64	71	73	274	5,140
Johan Rystrom	67	67	73	67	274	5,140
Matthew Cort	66	67	71	70	274	5,140
Boonchu Ruangkit	69	68	68	69	274	5,140
Robert Coles	70	69	70	65	274	5,140
Patrik Sjoland	66	73	68	67	274	5,140
Jean van de Velde	71	66	69	69	275	4,090
Gerald Rosales	70	66	67	72	275	4,090
Jonathan Lomas	72	67	67	69	275	4,090
Anthony Wall	66	67	72	70	275	4,090
Arjun Singh	70	67	67	71	275	4,090
Gregory Havret	71	67	66	71	275	4,090
Barry Lane	66	69	73	67	275	4,090
Arjun Atwal	70	69	68	68	275	4,090
Peter Fowler	67	66	71	72	276	3,390
Sushi Ishigaki	70	67	71	68	276	3,390
Jamie Donaldson	72	66	70	69	277	2,970
Jyoti Randhawa	70	67	71	69	277	2,970
Wang Ter-chang	67	69	71	70	277	2,970
Chris Williams	66	71	68	72	277	2,970
Stephen Dodd	71	65	72	70	278	2,410
Lam Chih-bing	71	67	65	75	278	2,410
Soren Hansen	68	70	71	69	278	2,410
Christophe Pottier	68	70	71	69	278	2,410
Klas Eriksson	72	66	69	72	279	1,815
Emanuelle Canonica	71	67	70	71	279	1,815
Tobias Dier	68	68	72	71	279	1,815
Gary Rusnak	71	68	67	73	279	1,815

	SCORES				TOTAL	MONEY
Yeh Chang-ting	70	68	67	74	279	1,815
Pablo Del Olmo	67	69	72	71	279	1,815
Simon Khan	68	69	71	71	279	1,815
Greg Hanrahan	69	69	69	72	279	1,815
Philip Golding	69	70	68	72	279	1,815
James Stewart	65	71	71	72	279	1,815
Choi Gwang-soo	69	65	72	74	280	1,161.63
Amandeep Johl	73	66	72	69	280	1,161.63
Lu Wen-teh	71	68	71	70	280	1,161.63
Kim Felton	69	68	68	75	280	1,161.63
Vivek Bhandari	70	69	73	68	280	1,161.63
Danny Zarate	68	70	71	71	280	1,161.63
Justin Hobday	71	67	69	74	281	1,037.05
Fran Quinn	70	69	71	71	281	1,037.05
Jamie Spence	72	67	70	73	282	1,033.11
Charlie Wi	69	70	74	71	284	1,030.47
Gaurav Ghei	74	63	79	71	287	1,027.85

Japan Tour

Token Corporation Cup

Tado Country Club, Mie
Par 35-36–71; 6,968 yards
(Shortened to 54 holes — snow.)

March 8-11
purse, ¥100,000,000

	SCORES			TOTAL	MONEY
Shingo Katayama	69	63	73	205	¥15,000,000
Tsuneyuki Nakajima	74	63	70	207	7,500,000
Shinichi Yokota	69	68	71	208	5,100,000
Shusaku Sugimoto	70	70	69	209	3,300,000
Jeev Milkha Singh	73	69	67	209	3,300,000
Hirofumi Miyase	69	68	73	210	2,487,500
Dean Wilson	73	65	72	210	2,487,500
Kim Felton	73	69	68	210	2,487,500
Hisayuki Sasaki	68	71	72	211	1,965,000
Toru Taniguchi	69	68	74	211	1,965,000
Kazuhiro Kinjo	68	69	74	211	1,965,000
Hideki Kase	71	70	71	212	1,410,000
Kiyoshi Murota	67	70	75	212	1,410,000
Hsieh Chin-sheng	67	72	73	212	1,410,000
David Smail	67	72	73	212	1,410,000
Takao Nogami	71	69	72	212	1,410,000
Tsuyoshi Yoneyama	72	69	72	213	977,500
Taichi Teshima	71	69	73	213	977,500
Tetsuji Hiratsuka	67	70	76	213	977,500
Lin Keng-chi	71	69	73	213	977,500
Hiroo Kawai	69	72	72	213	977,500
Kiyoshi Miyazato	73	66	74	213	977,500

	SCORES			TOTAL	MONEY
Hiroshi Goda	72	69	73	214	681,000
Anthony Gilligan	72	68	74	214	681,000
Katsunori Kuwabara	72	68	74	214	681,000
Hiroyuki Fujita	70	72	72	214	681,000
Hidemasa Hoshino	71	69	74	214	681,000
Takashi Kanemoto	73	69	73	215	555,000
Go Higaki	69	72	74	215	555,000
Tetsuya Haraguchi	72	69	74	215	555,000

Dydo Drinco Shizuoka Open

Shizuoka Country Club, Hamaoka, Shizuoka
Par 36-36–72; 6,897 yards

March 15-18
purse, ¥100,000,000

	SCORES				TOTAL	MONEY
Eiji Mizoguchi	68	68	66	77	279	¥20,000,000
Frankie Minoza	68	73	70	68	279	10,000,000
(Mizoguchi defeated Minoza on first playoff hole.)						
Tsukasa Watanabe	70	67	71	72	280	4,800,000
Katsuyoshi Tomori	70	67	70	73	280	4,800,000
Hidemichi Tanaka	70	68	71	71	280	4,800,000
Dean Wilson	72	67	64	77	280	4,800,000
Toru Suzuki	73	66	71	71	281	3,056,666
Steven Conran	70	68	70	73	281	3,056,666
Wang Ter-chang	71	70	71	69	281	3,056,666
Masayuki Kawamura	71	70	69	72	282	2,420,000
Anthony Gilligan	72	69	71	70	282	2,420,000
Toru Taniguchi	69	74	68	71	282	2,420,000
Tsuneyuki Nakajima	71	68	70	74	283	1,795,000
Kazuhiro Kinjo	74	70	67	72	283	1,795,000
Tomohiro Kondou	68	67	73	75	283	1,795,000
Brendan Jones	71	73	69	70	283	1,795,000
Hisayuki Sasaki	71	69	72	72	284	1,344,000
Hiroyuki Fujita	69	73	69	73	284	1,344,000
Taichi Teshima	72	69	70	73	284	1,344,000
Masashi Shimada	70	70	66	78	284	1,344,000
Masanori Kobayashi	72	67	71	74	284	1,344,000
Mitsuo Harada	71	70	72	72	285	940,000
Kosaku Makisaka	71	68	71	75	285	940,000
Kazuhiko Hosokawa	71	67	73	74	285	940,000
Lin Keng-chi	71	69	69	76	285	940,000
Hiroo Kawai	72	67	67	79	285	940,000
Kenny Druce	71	71	69	74	285	940,000
Kiyoshi Maita	69	72	69	76	286	656,250
Tatsuya Shiraishi	72	72	68	74	286	656,250
Koki Idoki	68	72	72	74	286	656,250
Satoshi Oide	71	68	73	74	286	656,250
Toshiaki Odate	71	69	69	77	286	656,250
Hidezumi Shirakata	69	74	70	73	286	656,250
Jun Kikuchi	72	71	69	74	286	656,250
Takao Nogami	71	70	71	74	286	656,250

Tsuruya Open

Sports Shinko Country Club, Kawanishi, Hyogo
Par 36-36–72; 6,847 yards

April 12-15
purse, ¥100,000,000

	SCORES				TOTAL	MONEY
Hidemichi Tanaka	71	69	68	66	274	¥20,000,000
Masayuki Kawamura	68	63	72	73	276	10,000,000
Kiyoshi Murota	68	73	67	70	278	6,800,000
Tsukasa Watanabe	69	68	74	68	279	4,800,000
Satoshi Oide	67	72	71	71	281	3,487,500
Eiji Mizoguchi	70	68	71	72	281	3,487,500
Hidezumi Shirakata	69	70	72	70	281	3,487,500
Todd Hamilton	70	67	70	74	281	3,487,500
Satoshi Higashi	71	71	70	70	282	2,420,000
Tsuyoshi Yoneyama	73	68	69	72	282	2,420,000
Kenichi Kuboya	71	68	75	68	282	2,420,000
Frankie Minoza	69	74	67	72	282	2,420,000
Scott Laycock	67	72	70	73	282	2,420,000
Masashi Ozaki	73	70	68	72	283	1,573,333
Hirofumi Miyase	72	70	70	71	283	1,573,333
Taichi Teshima	71	68	73	71	283	1,573,333
David Smail	70	70	74	69	283	1,573,333
Ryusaku Watanabe	71	72	70	70	283	1,573,333
Tetsuya Haraguchi	68	71	73	71	283	1,573,333
Yoshimitsu Fukuzawa	73	70	71	70	284	1,100,000
Shoichi Kuwabara	71	70	70	73	284	1,100,000
Nozomi Kawahara	69	71	71	73	284	1,100,000
Brian Watts	70	68	73	73	284	1,100,000
Brendan Jones	70	72	72	70	284	1,100,000
Hajime Meshiai	70	70	71	74	285	840,000
Toru Taniguchi	69	69	71	76	285	840,000
Takao Nogami	70	70	71	74	285	840,000
Kim Jong-duk	69	72	74	70	285	840,000
Saburo Fujiki	67	71	74	74	286	651,666
Tetsu Nishikawa	71	71	73	71	286	651,666
Steven Conran	67	72	73	74	286	651,666
Tatsuya Mitsuhashi	70	74	72	70	286	651,666
Katsumune Imai	72	68	72	74	286	651,666
Tatsuhiko Ichihara	68	72	75	71	286	651,666
*Masao Nakajima	72	70	70	74	286	

Kirin Open

Ibaragi Golf Club, East Course, Ina, Ibaragi
Par 35-36–71; 7,049 yards

April 19-22
purse, ¥100,000,000

	SCORES				TOTAL	MONEY
Shingo Katayama	64	70	70	67	271	¥20,000,000
Hajime Meshiai	68	72	73	64	277	11,000,000
Tsuneyuki Nakajima	70	66	72	70	278	5,683,333
Toshimitsu Izawa	68	71	68	71	278	5,683,333
Shigemasa Higaki	73	68	69	68	278	5,683,333
Kiyoshi Murota	65	71	72	71	279	2,781,250
Keiichiro Fukabori	71	69	69	70	279	2,781,250
Toru Taniguchi	70	67	70	72	279	2,781,250
Brendan Jones	71	71	69	68	279	2,781,250
Masahiro Kuramoto	70	67	71	72	280	1,840,000

	SCORES				TOTAL	MONEY
Kenny Druce	71	68	71	70	280	1,840,000
Yeh Wei-tze	71	68	72	70	281	1,560,000
Nobuhito Sato	70	68	76	68	282	1,420,000
*Andrew Buckle	70	70	70	72	282	
Seiki Okuda	71	70	73	69	283	1,270,000
Tomohiro Kondou	66	71	75	71	283	1,270,000
Kiyoshi Maita	73	69	69	73	284	1,095,000
Hirofumi Miyase	70	70	73	71	284	1,095,000
Shinichi Yokota	72	70	73	69	284	1,095,000
Brian Watts	71	69	70	74	284	1,095,000
Tateo Ozaki	72	70	74	69	285	924,600
Kazuhiko Hosokawa	72	69	73	71	285	924,600
Peter Senior	64	72	74	75	285	924,600
Thongchai Jaidee	75	68	75	67	285	924,600
Mahal Pearce	72	70	71	72	285	924,600
Masashi Ozaki	72	69	73	72	286	830,000
Nobuo Serizawa	69	72	76	69	286	830,000
Satoshi Higashi	71	71	74	70	286	830,000
Tetsuji Hiratsuka	72	68	70	76	286	830,000
Thammanoon Sriroj	73	68	73	72	286	830,000

Chunichi Crowns

Nagoya Golf Club, Wago Course, Togo, Aichi
Par 35-35–70; 6,511 yards

April 26-29
purse, ¥110,000,000

	SCORES				TOTAL	MONEY
Darren Clarke	66	67	67	67	267	¥22,000,000
Keiichiro Fukabori	69	69	67	66	271	9,240,000
Shinichi Yokota	64	70	68	69	271	9,240,000
Tsukasa Watanabe	69	68	65	70	272	4,840,000
Dean Wilson	62	70	69	71	272	4,840,000
Shingo Katayama	69	68	73	63	273	3,960,000
Toru Suzuki	70	65	71	68	274	3,362,333
Hiroyuki Fujita	65	69	71	69	274	3,362,333
Kenichi Kuboya	72	66	69	67	274	3,362,333
Taichi Teshima	72	68	72	63	275	2,772,000
David Smail	70	67	68	70	275	2,772,000
Shoichi Yamamoto	72	65	69	70	276	2,222,000
Mitsutaka Kusakabe	66	66	73	71	276	2,222,000
Lin Keng-chi	71	67	70	68	276	2,222,000
Kiyoshi Maita	72	67	71	67	277	1,837,000
Frankie Minoza	68	66	75	68	277	1,837,000
Nobuo Serizawa	71	66	70	71	278	1,523,500
Toshimitsu Izawa	72	70	71	65	278	1,523,500
Hsieh Chin-sheng	72	70	67	69	278	1,523,500
Shigemasa Higaki	69	64	72	73	278	1,523,500
Masashi Ozaki	75	68	68	68	279	1,100,000
Tsuyoshi Yoneyama	72	68	71	68	279	1,100,000
Eiji Mizoguchi	68	64	77	70	279	1,100,000
Toru Taniguchi	65	71	74	69	279	1,100,000
Takashi Kanemoto	71	69	69	70	279	1,100,000
Todd Hamilton	68	71	70	70	279	1,100,000
*Yusaku Miyazato	67	69	73	70	279	
Tateo Ozaki	70	70	70	70	280	836,000
Katsuyoshi Tomori	70	70	71	69	280	836,000
Tetsuji Hiratsuka	75	68	69	68	280	836,000
Shusaku Sugimoto	70	66	74	70	280	836,000

Fujisankei Classic

Kawana Hotel Golf Course, Fuji Course, Ito, Shizuoka
Par 35-36–71; 6,694 yards

May 3-6
purse, ¥110,000,000

	SCORES				TOTAL	MONEY
Frankie Minoza	71	68	71	66	276	¥22,000,000
Tsukasa Watanabe	70	69	69	69	277	11,000,000
Tetsuji Hiratsuka	71	68	72	67	278	6,380,000
Lin Keng-chi	70	66	67	75	278	6,380,000
Tomohiro Kondou	66	73	71	70	280	4,400,000
Jeev Milkha Singh	76	68	70	67	281	3,960,000
Ikuo Shirahama	72	70	68	72	282	3,362,333
Yeh Chang-ting	73	67	71	71	282	3,362,333
Todd Hamilton	75	69	71	67	282	3,362,333
Nobuo Serizawa	75	68	68	72	283	2,059,200
Yoshinori Mizumaki	73	68	71	71	283	2,059,200
Masahiro Kuramoto	75	68	72	68	283	2,059,200
Katsuyoshi Tomori	72	71	66	74	283	2,059,200
Toshiaki Odate	68	71	73	71	283	2,059,200
Craig Warren	74	69	71	69	283	2,059,200
Keiichiro Fukabori	75	65	72	71	283	2,059,200
Nobuhito Sato	75	69	70	69	283	2,059,200
Taichi Teshima	74	66	73	70	283	2,059,200
Mamoru Osanai	77	66	68	72	283	2,059,200
Tatsuo Takasaki	75	69	68	72	284	1,342,000
Tsuyoshi Yoneyama	71	65	74	74	284	1,342,000
Dean Wilson	71	68	72	74	285	1,210,000
Satoshi Higashi	74	70	72	70	286	952,285
Toru Suzuki	73	69	67	77	286	952,285
Takashi Kanemoto	73	71	67	75	286	952,285
Kim Jong-duk	72	71	68	75	286	952,285
Brendan Jones	75	71	71	69	286	952,285
Andre Stolz	73	71	72	70	286	952,285
Andrew Bonhomme	76	70	69	71	286	952,285
Taisuke Kitajima	75	68	74	70	287	729,666
Hiroyuki Fujita	70	71	68	78	287	729,666
Shinichi Yokota	75	69	73	70	287	729,666

Japan PGA Championship

Queen's Hill Golf Club, Maebaru, Fukuoka
Par 36-35–71; 7,002 yards

May 10-13
purse, ¥110,000,000

	SCORES				TOTAL	MONEY
Dean Wilson	68	68	71	74	281	¥22,000,000
Hideki Kase	71	75	72	67	285	11,000,000
Hsieh Chin-sheng	68	74	74	71	287	7,480,000
Satoshi Higashi	68	74	73	73	288	5,280,000
Eduardo Herrera	75	74	71	69	289	4,400,000
Masahiro Kuramoto	73	72	73	72	290	3,648,333
Keiichiro Fukabori	70	71	76	73	290	3,648,333
Taichi Teshima	70	75	73	72	290	3,648,333
Hiroyuki Fujita	75	68	74	74	291	2,662,000
Shinichi Yokota	72	76	71	72	291	2,662,000
Kenichi Kuboya	68	79	73	71	291	2,662,000
Naotoshi Nakamura	74	70	75	72	291	2,662,000
Katsuya Nakagawa	74	73	72	72	291	2,662,000

	SCORES				TOTAL	MONEY
Nobuo Serizawa	75	73	73	71	292	1,837,000
Hajime Meshiai	73	68	76	75	292	1,837,000
Richard Backwell	76	71	74	71	292	1,837,000
Lin Keng-chi	73	73	72	74	292	1,837,000
Takashi Kanemoto	73	71	75	74	293	1,386,000
Nozomi Kawahara	75	71	75	72	293	1,386,000
Shigemasa Higaki	73	72	74	74	293	1,386,000
Shingo Katayama	73	74	75	71	293	1,386,000
Frankie Minoza	73	75	71	74	293	1,386,000
Kiyoshi Murota	73	74	73	74	294	998,800
Eiji Mizoguchi	75	72	74	73	294	998,800
Toshikazu Sugihara	77	71	73	73	294	998,800
Toshiaki Odate	76	72	74	72	294	998,800
Scott Laycock	74	72	74	74	294	998,800
Kazuhiro Takami	73	76	72	74	295	737,000
Masayuki Kawamura	75	73	76	71	295	737,000
Shoichi Kuwabara	76	71	71	77	295	737,000
Toru Taniguchi	69	77	74	75	295	737,000
Kosaku Makisaka	71	75	71	78	295	737,000
Kazuhiko Hosokawa	70	75	77	73	295	737,000
Shusaku Sugimoto	74	73	74	74	295	737,000

Munsingwear Open KSB Cup

Rokko Kokusai Golf Club, Kobe, Hyogo
Par 36-36–72; 7,158 yards

May 17-20
purse, ¥120,000,000

	SCORES				TOTAL	MONEY
Dinesh Chand	69	68	67	67	271	¥24,000,000
Toshimitsu Izawa	68	70	68	67	273	12,000,000
Taichi Teshima	71	66	68	73	278	8,160,000
Toru Taniguchi	68	70	69	72	279	5,760,000
David Smail	72	70	73	65	280	4,600,000
Shoichi Yamamoto	69	68	73	71	281	4,320,000
Nobuo Serizawa	68	71	70	73	282	3,668,000
Masahiro Kuramoto	72	69	71	70	282	3,668,000
Eiji Mizoguchi	71	72	70	69	282	3,668,000
Anthony Gilligan	71	69	74	69	283	2,475,428
Mitsutaka Kusakabe	72	70	73	68	283	2,475,428
Hidemichi Tanaka	72	69	73	69	283	2,475,428
Shinichi Yokota	68	70	72	73	283	2,475,428
Katsumasa Miyamoto	71	72	71	69	283	2,475,428
Tatsuya Mitsuhashi	69	72	69	73	283	2,475,428
Scott Laycock	67	71	72	73	283	2,475,428
Satoshi Higashi	72	71	71	70	284	1,662,000
Richard Backwell	70	71	72	71	284	1,662,000
Zaw Moe	70	73	73	68	284	1,662,000
Lin Keng-chi	72	72	72	68	284	1,662,000
Hideki Kase	75	67	74	69	285	1,200,000
Koki Idoki	71	68	70	76	285	1,200,000
Hsieh Chin-sheng	69	74	68	74	285	1,200,000
Jun Kikuchi	73	71	69	72	285	1,200,000
Kiyoshi Miyazato	70	69	72	74	285	1,200,000
Dean Wilson	74	68	70	73	285	1,200,000
Seiki Okuda	73	71	72	70	286	845,142
Yasunori Ida	75	65	73	73	286	845,142
Hidezumi Shirakata	71	71	74	70	286	845,142

	SCORES				TOTAL	MONEY
Steven Conran	70	72	77	67	286	845,142
Lu Chien-soon	72	70	72	72	286	845,142
Shane Tait	68	69	75	74	286	845,142
Andrew Pitts	72	72	70	72	286	845,142

Diamond Cup

Oarai Golf Club, Oarai, Ibaraki
Par 36-36–72; 7,160 yards

May 24-27
purse, ¥100,000,000

	SCORES				TOTAL	MONEY
Toshimitsu Izawa	77	68	64	68	277	¥20,000,000
Yuji Igarashi	73	68	68	68	277	8,400,000
Hiroyuki Fujita	69	66	72	70	277	8,400,000
(Izawa defeated Igarashi and Fujita on first playoff hole.)						
Mitsuo Harada	74	68	68	68	278	4,800,000
Tsukasa Watanabe	72	71	69	67	279	4,000,000
Kosaku Makisaka	70	69	71	70	280	3,600,000
Tsuneyuki Nakajima	73	68	74	66	281	3,300,000
Masashi Ozaki	72	70	68	72	282	2,727,500
Satoshi Higashi	70	69	72	71	282	2,727,500
Katsuyoshi Tomori	74	70	69	69	282	2,727,500
Eduardo Herrera	69	69	71	73	282	2,727,500
Brendan Jones	74	67	73	69	283	2,220,000
Toru Taniguchi	74	66	74	70	284	1,795,000
Taichi Teshima	71	72	70	71	284	1,795,000
David Smail	76	68	71	69	284	1,795,000
Dinesh Chand	75	69	69	71	284	1,795,000
Toru Suzuki	72	69	72	72	285	1,426,666
Shigemasa Higaki	70	72	72	71	285	1,426,666
Takashi Iwamoto	71	72	70	72	285	1,426,666
Koki Idoki	70	71	73	72	286	1,140,000
Anthony Gilligan	71	74	67	74	286	1,140,000
Keiichiro Fukabori	72	72	71	71	286	1,140,000
Zaw Moe	72	72	72	70	286	1,140,000
Tsuyoshi Yoneyama	72	72	72	71	287	880,000
Takeshi Sakiyama	73	69	76	69	287	880,000
Koji Yamamoto	74	71	75	67	287	880,000
Andrew Bonhomme	69	73	76	69	287	880,000
Kazuhiro Takami	74	69	77	68	288	670,000
Seiki Okuda	72	71	74	71	288	670,000
Daisuke Maruyama	74	67	73	74	288	670,000
Lin Keng-chi	72	70	72	74	288	670,000
Tatsuhiko Takahashi	73	72	73	70	288	670,000
Tetsuya Haraguchi	71	70	75	72	288	670,000
Prayad Marksaeng	71	69	75	73	288	670,000

JCB Classic Sendai

Omotezao Kokusai Golf Club, Shibata, Miyagi
Par 36-35–71; 6,659 yards

May 31-June 3
purse, ¥100,000,000

	SCORES				TOTAL	MONEY
Toshiaki Odate	67	69	68	71	275	¥20,000,000
Taichi Teshima	68	70	69	70	277	10,000,000

	SCORES				TOTAL	MONEY
Lin Keng-chi	70	71	70	67	278	6,800,000
Prayad Marksaeng	71	72	67	69	279	4,800,000
Masashi Ozaki	73	69	70	68	280	3,800,000
Hiroyuki Fujita	70	72	68	70	280	3,800,000
Hajime Meshiai	72	70	72	67	281	3,175,000
Zaw Moe	69	70	73	69	281	3,175,000
Kosaku Makisaka	72	67	71	72	282	2,820,000
*Yusaku Miyazato	71	72	70	69	282	
Tetsuji Hiratsuka	74	66	74	69	283	2,520,000
Taku Sugaya	72	70	69	72	283	2,520,000
Yeh Chang-ting	75	69	67	73	284	2,220,000
Ikuo Shirahama	69	73	70	73	285	1,686,666
Nobuo Serizawa	71	67	73	74	285	1,686,666
Satoshi Higashi	75	70	69	71	285	1,686,666
Shoichi Yamamoto	69	72	70	74	285	1,686,666
Mamoru Osanai	71	72	73	69	285	1,686,666
Brendan Jones	69	75	73	68	285	1,686,666
Toshikazu Sugihara	69	70	74	73	286	1,260,000
Takeshi Sakiyama	70	73	74	69	286	1,260,000
Keiichiro Fukabori	71	68	71	76	286	1,260,000
Yoshinori Mizumaki	66	75	75	71	287	940,000
Richard Backwell	72	71	73	71	287	940,000
Nobuhito Sato	72	71	71	73	287	940,000
Shigemasa Higaki	75	70	72	70	287	940,000
Akinori Tani	69	74	70	74	287	940,000
Kim Jong-duk	70	73	73	71	287	940,000
Saburo Fujiki	67	68	75	78	288	720,000
Akihito Yokoyama	74	68	69	77	288	720,000
Taisuke Kitajima	72	71	73	72	288	720,000
Kazuhiro Shimizu	72	72	73	71	288	720,000

Tamanoi Yomiuri Open

Yomiuri Country Club, Nishinomiya, Hyogo
Par 36-36–72; 7,030 yards

June 14-17
purse, ¥90,000,000

	SCORES				TOTAL	MONEY
Yoshimitsu Fukuzawa	64	70	70	68	272	¥18,000,000
Toru Suzuki	68	66	72	66	272	9,000,000
(Fukuzawa defeated Suzuki on first playoff hole.)						
Kiyoshi Miyazato	69	68	67	69	273	6,120,000
Tsuneyuki Nakajima	73	66	68	68	275	2,993,625
Koki Idoki	68	67	73	67	275	2,993,625
Naoki Hattori	65	73	72	65	275	2,993,625
Keiichiro Fukabori	65	71	69	70	275	2,993,625
Taichi Teshima	67	70	67	71	275	2,993,625
Katsumasa Miyamoto	65	68	68	74	275	2,993,625
Yui Ueda	70	67	68	70	275	2,993,625
Prayad Marksaeng	72	69	66	68	275	2,993,625
Kiyoshi Murota	70	68	68	70	276	1,908,000
Tomohiro Kondou	69	69	70	68	276	1,908,000
Masashi Ozaki	69	67	71	70	277	1,548,000
Eiji Mizoguchi	70	72	67	68	277	1,548,000
Kim Jong-duk	70	68	70	69	277	1,548,000
Yasunori Ida	72	72	68	66	278	1,323,000
Kazuhiko Hosokawa	71	69	67	71	278	1,323,000
Akihito Yokoyama	73	71	68	67	279	1,098,000

	SCORES				TOTAL	MONEY
Mitsuo Harada	72	69	70	68	279	1,098,000
Kazuhiro Kinjo	69	67	71	72	279	1,098,000
Shinichi Yokota	68	70	70	71	279	1,098,000
Hirofumi Miyase	68	71	69	72	280	862,000
Kenny Druce	68	73	68	71	280	862,000
Ikuo Shirahama	70	70	73	68	281	720,000
Naoya Sugiyama	68	73	66	74	281	720,000
Yuji Igarashi	68	71	69	73	281	720,000
Zaw Moe	72	69	70	70	281	720,000
Kazumasa Sakaitani	71	69	71	70	281	720,000
Hidemasa Hoshino	71	70	71	69	281	720,000

Mizuno Open

Setonaikai Golf Club, Kasaoka, Okayama

June 21-24

Par 36-36–72; 7,214 yards

purse, ¥100,000,000

	SCORES				TOTAL	MONEY
Hidemichi Tanaka	66	69	68	69	272	¥20,000,000
Eduardo Herrera	73	67	68	67	275	10,000,000
Kenichi Kuboya	68	66	73	69	276	6,800,000
Jeev Milkha Singh	70	66	72	69	277	4,800,000
Tetsuji Hiratsuka	69	69	71	69	278	3,487,500
Kazumasa Sakaitani	70	66	71	71	278	3,487,500
Tomohiro Kondou	71	70	67	70	278	3,487,500
Christian Pena	69	71	68	70	278	3,487,500
Masashi Ozaki	70	67	75	67	279	2,420,000
Taichi Teshima	75	67	70	67	279	2,420,000
Zaw Moe	75	61	75	68	279	2,420,000
David Smail	70	69	73	67	279	2,420,000
Mitsuhiro Tateyama	71	66	72	70	279	2,420,000
Hiroshi Tominaga	71	67	71	71	280	1,770,000
Shane Tait	71	72	72	65	280	1,770,000
Yoshinori Mizumaki	70	70	72	69	281	1,520,000
Nobuhito Sato	72	68	69	72	281	1,520,000
Kenny Druce	69	70	71	71	281	1,520,000
Akihito Yokoyama	70	70	70	72	282	1,300,000
Lu Chien-soon	72	71	70	69	282	1,300,000
Hideki Kase	74	68	71	70	283	1,000,000
Tsuneyuki Nakajima	70	70	72	71	283	1,000,000
Kiyoshi Murota	71	68	73	71	283	1,000,000
Hajime Meshiai	71	72	73	67	283	1,000,000
Shigeru Nonaka	72	70	71	70	283	1,000,000
Taku Sugaya	66	70	76	71	283	1,000,000
Shoichi Yamamoto	73	67	73	71	284	721,666
Hiroyuki Fujita	70	73	68	73	284	721,666
Shusaku Sugimoto	71	71	73	69	284	721,666
Tetsuya Haraguchi	71	69	72	72	284	721,666
Yui Ueda	72	69	73	70	284	721,666
Katsumune Imai	73	69	73	69	284	721,666

Japan Tour Championship Iiyama Cup

Hourai Country Club, Nishinasuno, Tochigi
Par 36-36–72; 7,090 yards

June 28-July 1
purse, ¥120,000,000

	SCORES				TOTAL	MONEY
Katsumasa Miyamoto	69	67	68	69	273	¥24,000,000
Eduardo Herrera	68	68	72	72	280	10,000,000
Jeev Milkha Singh	66	70	68	76	280	10,000,000
Hidemichi Tanaka	69	70	68	74	281	5,280,000
Dean Wilson	69	71	68	73	281	5,280,000
Kiyoshi Murota	72	69	67	74	282	4,320,000
Kazuhiro Takami	67	71	71	74	283	3,810,000
Hajime Meshiai	65	72	73	73	283	3,810,000
Yoshinori Mizumaki	67	74	69	74	284	3,144,000
Toshikazu Sugihara	69	68	71	76	284	3,144,000
Kosaku Makisaka	66	72	70	76	284	3,144,000
Anthony Gilligan	70	71	70	74	285	2,256,000
Mitsutaka Kusakabe	65	73	75	72	285	2,256,000
Hsieh Chin-sheng	65	67	79	74	285	2,256,000
Keiichiro Fukabori	73	69	68	75	285	2,256,000
Shigemasa Higaki	70	72	71	72	285	2,256,000
Masashi Ozaki	71	70	69	76	286	1,612,800
Katsumune Imai	71	71	72	72	286	1,612,800
Prayad Marksaeng	69	71	70	76	286	1,612,800
Shane Tait	73	66	73	74	286	1,612,800
Brendan Jones	65	68	74	79	286	1,612,800
Tsuneyuki Nakajima	68	70	76	73	287	1,156,800
Toshimitsu Izawa	67	74	69	77	287	1,156,800
Hiroyuki Fujita	70	72	72	73	287	1,156,800
Kazuhiko Hosokawa	67	69	70	81	287	1,156,800
Charlie Wi	69	71	73	74	287	1,156,800
Satoshi Higashi	66	75	73	74	288	826,500
Yasunori Ida	69	72	71	76	288	826,500
Shigeru Nonaka	70	70	74	74	288	826,500
Tetsuji Hiratsuka	72	68	68	80	288	826,500
Lin Keng-chi	69	69	73	77	288	826,500
Steven Conran	70	69	72	77	288	826,500
Yoshinobu Tsukada	71	70	73	74	288	826,500
Thongchai Jaidee	67	70	71	80	288	826,500

Jyuken Sangyo Open Hiroshima

Hiroshima Country Club, Higashi, Hiroshima
Par 36-36–72; 6,950 yards
(Second round cancelled — rain.)

July 5-8
purse, ¥90,000,000

	SCORES			TOTAL	MONEY
Keiichiro Fukabori	67	67	69	203	¥13,500,000
Masashi Ozaki	72	66	65	203	6,750,000
(Fukabori defeated Ozaki on first playoff hole.)					
Toru Taniguchi	71	66	68	205	3,915,000
Jeev Milkha Singh	70	66	69	205	3,915,000
Hidemichi Tanaka	72	65	69	206	2,263,950
Kosaku Makisaka	70	66	70	206	2,263,950
Yeh Chang-ting	70	68	68	206	2,263,950
Shingo Katayama	69	68	69	206	2,263,950
Boonchu Ruangkit	68	68	70	206	2,263,950

	SCORES			TOTAL	MONEY
Nobuhito Sato	70	65	72	207	1,768,500
Eduardo Herrera	69	68	71	208	1,431,000
Shigeru Nonaka	71	68	69	208	1,431,000
Kazuhiko Hosokawa	68	73	67	208	1,431,000
Kenichi Kuboya	71	69	68	208	1,431,000
Takeshi Sakiyama	69	68	72	209	913,500
Zaw Moe	72	70	67	209	913,500
Tetsuji Hiratsuka	68	72	69	209	913,500
Jun Kikuchi	72	68	69	209	913,500
Yasuharu Imano	71	68	70	209	913,500
Dinesh Chand	66	71	72	209	913,500
Masanori Kobayashi	67	72	70	209	913,500
Lu Chien-soon	70	67	72	209	913,500
Andrew Bonhomme	71	71	67	209	913,500
Masanari Kato	77	67	66	210	621,000
Kenny Druce	71	66	73	210	621,000
Masayuki Kawamura	74	68	69	211	526,500
Katsunori Kuwabara	71	70	70	211	526,500
Taku Sugaya	69	72	70	211	526,500
Chen Tze-chung	72	72	67	211	526,500
Prayad Marksaeng	70	71	70	211	526,500

Aiful Cup

Ajigasawa Kogen Golf Club, Aomori
Par 36-36–72; 7,074 yards

July 12-15
purse, ¥90,000,000

	SCORES				TOTAL	MONEY
Lin Keng-chi	68	67	67	68	270	¥18,000,000
Toru Suzuki	66	66	67	71	270	9,000,000
(Lin defeated Suzuki on second playoff hole.)						
Taku Sugaya	66	69	69	67	271	4,680,000
Katsumasa Miyamoto	68	68	67	68	271	4,680,000
Prayad Marksaeng	67	67	68	69	271	4,680,000
Lam Chih-bing	67	70	70	65	272	3,240,000
Tomohiro Kondou	69	70	69	65	273	2,970,000
Takenori Hiraishi	68	66	68	73	275	2,454,750
Zaw Moe	68	68	72	67	275	2,454,750
Kenichi Kuboya	67	72	67	69	275	2,454,750
Katsumune Imai	70	69	69	67	275	2,454,750
Tsuneyuki Nakajima	69	67	69	71	276	1,750,500
Tsukasa Watanabe	66	67	71	72	276	1,750,500
Yeh Chang-ting	67	68	70	71	276	1,750,500
Tetsuji Hiratsuka	68	67	75	66	276	1,750,500
Katsunari Takahashi	68	71	69	69	277	1,327,500
Tetsu Nishikawa	69	70	70	68	277	1,327,500
Yoshiaki Mano	70	70	67	70	277	1,327,500
Todd Hamilton	72	68	68	69	277	1,327,500
Hidezumi Shirakata	70	70	70	68	278	960,000
Yasuharu Imano	73	67	70	68	278	960,000
Kazumasa Sakaitani	70	69	70	69	278	960,000
Yoshinaga Tomokazu	68	71	71	68	278	960,000
Christian Pena	73	67	71	67	278	960,000
Wang Ter-chang	66	68	73	71	278	960,000
Kazuhiro Takami	69	68	71	71	279	651,375
Hajime Meshiai	69	67	73	70	279	651,375
Hsieh Chin-sheng	69	67	69	74	279	651,375
Shinichi Yokota	69	69	68	73	279	651,375

	SCORES				TOTAL	MONEY
Jun Kikuchi	69	68	74	68	279	651,375
Hidemasa Hoshino	67	70	72	70	279	651,375
Kiyoshi Miyazato	73	64	70	72	279	651,375
S.K. Ho	73	66	71	69	279	651,375

NST Niigata Open

Nakajo Golf Club, Nakajo, Niigata
Par 36-36–72; 7,029 yards

July 26-29
purse, ¥50,000,000

	SCORES				TOTAL	MONEY
Go Higaki	66	67	65	66	264	¥10,000,000
Scott Laycock	64	72	68	66	270	5,000,000
Yuji Igarashi	67	69	69	70	275	2,400,000
Kazuhiro Kinjo	67	69	67	72	275	2,400,000
Daisuke Maruyama	70	68	70	67	275	2,400,000
Katsumune Imai	69	69	69	68	275	2,400,000
Takenori Hiraishi	67	69	72	69	277	1,587,500
Tomohiro Kondou	71	71	70	65	277	1,587,500
Gregory Meyer	71	73	65	69	278	1,360,000
Andrew Bonhomme	73	67	67	71	278	1,360,000
Taisuke Kitajima	72	69	69	69	279	952,857
Hidezumi Shirakata	70	67	70	72	279	952,857
Yeh Chang-ting	70	71	68	70	279	952,857
Tatsuhiko Takahashi	68	70	71	70	279	952,857
Akinori Tani	69	68	70	72	279	952,857
Tajima Soushi	71	69	70	69	279	952,857
Lu Chien-soon	68	71	71	69	279	952,857
Kosaku Makisaka	69	70	68	73	280	650,000
Shinichi Yokota	71	69	70	70	280	650,000
Yoshiaki Mano	71	69	70	70	280	650,000
Kazuhiro Shimizu	72	71	69	68	280	650,000
Takeshi Sakiyama	71	71	71	68	281	495,000
Kazuhiko Hosokawa	70	74	69	68	281	495,000
Jun Kikuchi	73	68	68	72	281	495,000
Takashi Kamiyama	71	69	69	72	281	495,000
Hiroshi Goda	71	71	69	71	282	410,000
Katsumi Kubo	73	69	69	71	282	410,000
Hidemasa Hoshino	67	73	68	74	282	410,000
Takeshi Kibamoto	69	72	72	70	283	333,000
Makoto Inoue	71	73	69	70	283	333,000
Takashi Iwamoto	68	75	68	72	283	333,000
Kenny Druce	68	76	67	72	283	333,000
Hong Chia-yuh	73	71	70	69	283	333,000

Sun Chlorella Classic

Sapporo Bay Golf Club, Ishikari, Hokkaido
Par 36-36–72; 6,958 yards

August 2-5
purse, ¥110,000,000

	SCORES				TOTAL	MONEY
Hiroyuki Fujita	71	73	71	68	283	¥22,000,000
Katsuyoshi Tomori	69	73	74	67	283	11,000,000
(Fujita defeated Tomori on first playoff hole.)						
Hajime Meshiai	71	72	68	73	284	5,720,000

	SCORES				TOTAL	MONEY
Yasunori Ida	73	75	64	72	284	5,720,000
Katsumune Imai	71	72	72	69	284	5,720,000
Hiroshi Goda	71	69	75	70	285	3,795,000
Shingo Katayama	75	74	69	67	285	3,795,000
Takenori Hiraishi	74	71	72	69	286	3,228,500
Andrew Bonhomme	74	72	67	73	286	3,228,500
Masashi Ozaki	71	76	69	71	287	2,772,000
Takao Nogami	71	75	73	68	287	2,772,000
Hidemichi Tanaka	76	70	72	70	288	2,139,500
Jun Kikuchi	69	75	73	71	288	2,139,500
Takashi Kamiyama	72	70	73	73	288	2,139,500
Andre Stolz	73	74	71	70	288	2,139,500
Nobuhito Sato	75	76	70	68	289	1,529,000
Zaw Moe	76	72	74	67	289	1,529,000
Yeh Chang-ting	72	72	72	73	289	1,529,000
Masanori Kobayashi	72	74	75	68	289	1,529,000
Takashi Iwamoto	70	73	74	72	289	1,529,000
Scott Laycock	71	72	74	72	289	1,529,000
Ikuo Shirahama	74	76	71	69	290	1,008,857
Kazuhiro Takami	78	73	70	69	290	1,008,857
Keiichiro Fukabori	74	76	71	69	290	1,008,857
Shigemasa Higaki	77	72	72	69	290	1,008,857
Kazumasa Sakaitani	74	73	74	69	290	1,008,857
Yui Ueda	72	76	72	70	290	1,008,857
Nobuhiro Masuda	71	74	72	73	290	1,008,857
Toru Nakamura	74	76	68	73	291	688,875
Craig Warren	76	73	73	69	291	688,875
Hsieh Chin-sheng	72	77	70	72	291	688,875
Hidezumi Shirakata	78	70	72	71	291	688,875
Mamoru Osanai	74	75	70	72	291	688,875
Tajima Soushi	74	69	73	75	291	688,875
Boonchu Ruangkit	73	72	74	72	291	688,875
Shane Tait	73	73	75	70	291	688,875

Hisamitsu-KBC Augusta

Keya Golf Club, Shima, Fukuoka
Par 36-36–72; 7,154 yards

August 23-26
purse, ¥90,000,000

	SCORES				TOTAL	MONEY
Takenori Hiraishi	67	69	68	69	273	¥18,000,000
Hideki Kase	68	69	68	68	273	7,580,000
Shigemasa Higaki	69	71	69	64	273	7,580,000
(Hiraishi defeated Kase and Higaki on fourth playoff hole.)						
Toshimitsu Izawa	74	69	65	68	276	3,060,000
Kazumasa Sakaitani	66	70	69	71	276	3,060,000
Kiyoshi Maita	69	65	71	72	277	2,985,000
Anthony Gilligan	69	71	67	70	277	2,985,000
Tetsuji Hiratsuka	73	71	68	65	277	2,985,000
Taichi Teshima	68	69	70	71	278	2,358,000
Zaw Moe	69	71	68	70	278	2,358,000
Katsumasa Miyamoto	69	67	73	69	278	2,358,000
Nobuo Serizawa	71	71	67	71	280	1,750,500
Masahiro Kuramoto	70	72	68	70	280	1,750,500
Hidezumi Shirakata	72	72	65	71	280	1,750,500
Kazuhiko Hosokawa	69	72	68	71	280	1,750,500
Seiki Okuda	72	72	69	68	281	1,368,000

	SCORES				TOTAL	MONEY
Katsuyoshi Tomori	69	71	71	70	281	1,368,000
Christian Pena	69	71	69	72	281	1,368,000
Keiichiro Fukabori	65	72	70	75	282	1,130,000
Lin Keng-chi	66	71	71	74	282	1,130,000
Tatsuhiko Takahashi	71	71	71	69	282	1,130,000
Tetsu Nishikawa	73	68	70	72	283	918,000
Toru Suzuki	73	71	69	70	283	918,000
Kazuhiro Kinjo	68	70	74	71	283	918,000
Katsunari Takahashi	70	72	73	69	284	756,000
Kazuhiro Takami	71	71	69	73	284	756,000
Koki Idoki	76	68	70	70	284	756,000
Nobuhito Sato	70	69	69	76	284	756,000
Akihito Yokoyama	71	72	70	72	285	614,250
Hirofumi Miyase	72	69	72	72	285	614,250
Dinesh Chand	71	67	76	71	285	614,250
Lu Chien-soon	69	74	72	70	285	614,250

Japan PGA Match Play

Nidom Classic Course, Tomakomai, Hokkaido
Par 36-36–72; 6,958 yards

August 30-September 2
purse, ¥80,000,000

FIRST ROUND

Tsuyoshi Yoneyama defeated Shingo Katayama, 2 and 1.
Kenichi Kuboya defeated Tsukasa Watanabe, 22 holes.
Hirofumi Miyase defeated Hideki Kase, 2 up.
Hiroyuki Fujita defeated Satoshi Higashi, 6 and 5.
Keiichiro Fukabori defeated Kosaku Makisaka, 2 up.
Dean Wilson defeated Katsuyoshi Tomori, 5 and 3.
Toru Suzuki defeated Tsuneyuki Nakajima, 4 and 2.
Hajime Meshiai defeated Yasuharu Imano, 2 up.
Toru Taniguchi defeated Nobuo Serizawa, 21 holes.
Naomichi Ozaki defeated Eiji Mizoguchi, 5 and 3.
Kazuhiko Hosokawa defeated Nobuhito Sato, 1 up.
Lin Keng-chi defeated Shinichi Yokota, 4 and 2.
Hidemichi Tanaka defeated Dinesh Chand, 21 holes.
Frankie Minoza defeated Toshiaki Odate, 3 and 1.
Eduardo Herrera defeated Shigemasa Higaki, 2 up.
Taichi Teshima defeated Kiyoshi Murota, 2 and 1.

(Each losing player received ¥400,000.)

SECOND ROUND

Yoneyama defeated Kuboya, 2 and 1.
Fujita defeated Miyase, 20 holes.
Wilson defeated Fukabori, 4 and 3.
Suzuki defeated Meshiai, 4 and 3.
Taniguchi defeated Ozaki, 1 up.
Lin defeated Hosokawa, 2 and 1.
Minoza defeated Tanaka, 3 and 2.
Herrera defeated Teshima, 2 and 1.

(Each losing player received ¥800,000.)

QUARTER-FINALS

Fujita defeated Yoneyama, 2 and 1.
Wilson defeated Suzuki, 6 and 4.
Lin defeated Taniguchi, 3 and 2.
Minoza defeated Herrera, 2 and 1.

(Each losing player received ¥1,800,000.)

SEMI-FINALS

Wilson defeated Fujita, 4 and 3.
Lin defeated Minoza, 3 and 2.

THIRD-FOURTH PLACE PLAYOFF

Fujita defeated Minoza, 3 and 1.

(Fujita received ¥9,000,000; Minoza received ¥6,000,000.)

FINAL

Wilson defeated Lin, 2 and 1.

(Wilson received ¥30,000,000; Lin received ¥15,000,000.)

Suntory Open

Sobu Country Club, Inzai, Chiba   September 6-9
Par 35-36–71; 7,166 yards   purse, ¥90,000,000

	SCORES				TOTAL	MONEY
Shingo Katayama	66	68	68	66	268	¥18,000,000
Nobuo Serizawa	70	65	68	68	271	6,480,000
Keiichiro Fukabori	69	68	68	66	271	6,480,000
Darren Clarke	68	68	67	68	271	6,480,000
Masashi Ozaki	69	66	68	69	272	3,600,000
Katsunori Kuwabara	69	66	69	70	274	3,105,000
Dinesh Chand	68	68	67	71	274	3,105,000
Katsumasa Miyamoto	70	65	70	70	275	2,745,000
Katsuyoshi Tomori	66	70	69	71	276	2,448,000
Scott Laycock	66	69	71	70	276	2,448,000
Toru Taniguchi	69	68	72	69	278	1,773,000
Yui Ueda	70	67	70	71	278	1,773,000
Katsumune Imai	66	71	71	70	278	1,773,000
Prayad Marksaeng	71	69	70	68	278	1,773,000
Christian Pena	72	68	69	69	278	1,773,000
Dean Wilson	72	69	67	70	278	1,773,000
Mitsutaka Kusakabe	72	67	66	74	279	1,246,500
Steven Conran	71	71	69	68	279	1,246,500
Kazumasa Sakaitani	69	71	66	73	279	1,246,500
Jeev Milkha Singh	71	67	72	69	279	1,246,500
Tsuneyuki Nakajima	72	69	71	68	280	990,000
Shoichi Yamamoto	67	73	67	73	280	990,000
Toru Morita	69	71	70	70	280	990,000
Kiyoshi Murota	69	72	71	69	281	738,000
Nobumitsu Yuhara	68	70	71	72	281	738,000
Akihito Yokoyama	70	70	73	68	281	738,000
Takashi Kanemoto	72	70	71	68	281	738,000

	SCORES				TOTAL	MONEY
Mitsuhiro Tateyama	71	67	73	70	281	738,000
Tatsuhiko Takahashi	69	69	72	71	281	738,000
Yoshinobu Tsukada	69	69	73	70	281	738,000

ANA Open

Sapporo Golf Club, Wattsu Course,
Kitahiroshima, Hokkaido
Par 36-36–72; 7,063 yards

September 13-16
purse, ¥100,000,000

	SCORES				TOTAL	MONEY
Lin Keng-chi	66	70	66	71	273	¥20,000,000
Tsuneyuki Nakajima	70	71	67	67	275	5,400,000
Kazuhiro Kinjo	77	66	66	66	275	5,400,000
Shane Tait	64	73	69	70	276	4,800,000
Scott Laycock	69	68	69	71	277	4,000,000
Hajime Meshiai	70	76	68	64	278	3,600,000
Kiyoshi Maita	70	69	70	71	280	3,350,000
Kiyoshi Murota	74	70	68	69	281	2,626,000
Eduardo Herrera	65	74	70	72	281	2,626,000
Mamoru Osanai	69	73	70	69	281	2,626,000
Frankie Minoza	73	70	70	68	281	2,626,000
Kenneth Druce	70	68	70	73	281	2,626,000
Masashi Ozaki	68	75	70	69	282	1,740,000
Yoshinori Mizumaki	69	72	73	68	282	1,740,000
Toru Suzuki	70	71	71	70	282	1,740,000
Zaw Moe	67	71	74	70	282	1,740,000
Brendan Jones	74	69	70	69	282	1,740,000
Katsumasa Miyamoto	70	70	72	71	283	1,420,000
Nobumitsu Yuhara	68	72	71	73	284	1,140,000
Hidezumi Shirakata	70	74	70	70	284	1,140,000
Shigemasa Higaki	73	71	70	70	284	1,140,000
Jun Kikuchi	71	70	71	72	284	1,140,000
Mitsuhiro Tateyama	74	68	68	74	284	1,140,000
Andrew Bonhomme	72	69	72	71	284	1,140,000
Naomichi Ozaki	70	69	73	73	285	761,250
Toshimitsu Izawa	73	72	70	70	285	761,250
Takashi Kanemoto	72	72	71	70	285	761,250
Yasuharu Imano	71	71	71	72	285	761,250
Dinesh Chand	69	72	69	75	285	761,250
Ichihara Koudai	69	71	73	72	285	761,250
Gerry Norquist	69	75	70	71	285	761,250
Christian Pena	71	69	72	73	285	761,250

Mitsui Sumitomo Visa Taiheiyo Masters

Taiheiyo Club, Gotemba Course, Gotemba, Shizuoka
Par 36-36–72; 7,232 yards

September 20-23
purse, ¥140,000,000

	SCORES				TOTAL	MONEY
Toshimitsu Izawa	66	67	68	69	270	¥28,000,000
Shigeru Nonaka	74	65	66	67	272	14,000,000
*Yusaku Miyazato	71	67	67	67	272	
Masashi Ozaki	66	67	69	73	275	7,280,000
Takenori Hiraishi	69	68	68	70	275	7,280,000

	SCORES				TOTAL	MONEY
Kenichi Kuboya	69	65	72	69	275	7,280,000
Katsumasa Miyamoto	68	68	70	70	276	4,643,333
David Smail	68	67	76	65	276	4,643,333
Todd Hamilton	68	68	70	70	276	4,643,333
Hajime Meshiai	69	69	69	70	277	3,388,000
Masayuki Kawamura	65	70	71	71	277	3,388,000
Mitsutaka Kusakabe	68	72	68	69	277	3,388,000
Toru Taniguchi	67	70	70	70	277	3,388,000
Tetsuji Hiratsuka	65	68	71	73	277	3,388,000
Naomichi Ozaki	70	69	71	68	278	2,408,000
Nobuhito Sato	67	66	75	70	278	2,408,000
Scott Laycock	67	72	70	69	278	2,408,000
Seiki Okuda	68	67	69	75	279	1,881,600
Katsuyoshi Tomori	66	70	69	74	279	1,881,600
Koki Idoki	70	67	70	72	279	1,881,600
Katsunori Kuwabara	71	69	71	68	279	1,881,600
Nakata Norihiko	66	70	71	72	279	1,881,600
Nobuo Serizawa	69	68	71	72	280	1,284,000
Kazuhiro Takami	70	67	71	72	280	1,284,000
Tsuyoshi Yoneyama	68	71	69	72	280	1,284,000
Kazuhiko Hosokawa	66	67	74	73	280	1,284,000
Kazumasa Sakaitani	68	70	68	74	280	1,284,000
Hidemasa Hoshino	65	71	75	69	280	1,284,000
Christian Pena	64	71	68	77	280	1,284,000
Tsuneyuki Nakajima	68	71	69	73	281	894,000
Tsukasa Watanabe	65	67	74	75	281	894,000
Jun Kikuchi	70	69	68	74	281	894,000
Yasuharu Imano	70	67	72	72	281	894,000
Mamoru Osanai	71	69	71	70	281	894,000
Yoshiaki Mano	69	68	74	70	281	894,000
Frankie Minoza	69	69	70	73	281	894,000

Acom International

Ishioka Golf Club, Ogawa, Ibaraki
Par 36-35–71; 7,046 yards

September 27-30
purse, ¥110,000,000

	SCORES				TOTAL	MONEY
Kazuhiko Hosokawa	68	63	65	71	267	¥22,000,000
Toru Taniguchi	67	64	69	69	269	6,424,000
Nobuhito Sato	69	66	69	65	269	6,424,000
Shinichi Yokota	68	67	66	68	269	6,424,000
Katsumune Imai	66	66	68	69	269	6,424,000
Scott Laycock	69	65	70	65	269	6,424,000
Takashi Kanemoto	65	67	68	70	270	3,630,000
Shingo Katayama	67	67	67	71	272	3,228,500
Kiyoshi Miyazato	62	69	72	69	272	3,228,500
David Smail	65	67	70	71	273	2,662,000
Hidemasa Hoshino	68	68	65	72	273	2,662,000
Todd Hamilton	69	66	69	69	273	2,662,000
Kenichi Kuboya	69	66	66	73	274	2,112,000
Kim Jong-duk	66	70	71	67	274	2,112,000
Masashi Ozaki	68	66	72	69	275	1,727,000
Eduardo Herrera	66	67	70	72	275	1,727,000
Shigeru Nonaka	67	65	72	71	275	1,727,000
Takashi Kamiyama	69	71	68	67	275	1,727,000
Tsuyoshi Yoneyama	67	66	70	73	276	1,430,000

	SCORES				TOTAL	MONEY
Masashi Shimada	66	74	66	70	276	1,430,000
Toshimitsu Izawa	70	68	69	70	277	1,254,000
Nozomi Kawahara	65	71	70	71	277	1,254,000
Hidemichi Tanaka	67	70	70	71	278	1,048,666
Hiroyuki Fujita	72	67	68	71	278	1,048,666
Tomohiro Kondou	68	71	69	70	278	1,048,666
Nobumitsu Yuhara	72	68	67	72	279	880,000
Takenori Hiraishi	68	71	70	70	279	880,000
Shoichi Yamamoto	72	66	71	70	279	880,000
Shusaku Sugimoto	70	71	71	67	279	880,000
Richard Backwell	71	67	72	70	280	683,833
Taichi Teshima	69	69	70	72	280	683,833
Tetsuya Haraguchi	70	69	68	73	280	683,833
Yui Ueda	69	68	70	73	280	683,833
Tatsuhiko Ichihara	72	65	73	70	280	683,833
Shane Tait	71	69	71	69	280	683,833

Georgia Tokai Classic

Miyoshi Country Club, Miyoshi, Aichi
Par 36-36–72; 7,075 yards

October 4-7
purse, ¥120,000,000

	SCORES				TOTAL	MONEY
Toshimitsu Izawa	65	68	70	69	272	¥24,000,000
Lin Keng-chi	70	66	69	69	274	10,080,000
Tomohiro Kondou	69	68	69	68	274	10,080,000
Nozomi Kawahara	67	68	69	71	275	5,280,000
Shingo Katayama	67	71	69	68	275	5,280,000
Kiyoshi Maita	67	72	70	67	276	4,320,000
Shigeru Nonaka	69	68	73	67	277	3,810,000
Daisuke Maruyama	68	68	73	68	277	3,810,000
Hidemichi Tanaka	68	68	69	73	278	3,334,000
Seiki Okuda	68	72	67	72	279	2,317,333
Toru Suzuki	69	72	67	71	279	2,317,333
Kazuhiko Hosokawa	71	69	69	70	279	2,317,333
Shinichi Yokota	73	65	70	71	279	2,317,333
Kazumasa Sakaitani	71	67	70	71	279	2,317,333
Mitsuhiro Tateyama	65	73	71	70	279	2,317,333
Shusaku Sugimoto	66	70	72	71	279	2,317,333
Katsumune Imai	71	70	68	70	279	2,317,333
Yoshikazu Haku	68	67	73	71	279	2,317,333
Go Higaki	68	71	72	69	280	1,608,000
Naomichi Ozaki	69	68	72	72	281	1,320,000
Toru Taniguchi	71	70	69	71	281	1,320,000
Hiroyuki Fujita	70	69	69	73	281	1,320,000
Nobuhito Sato	64	71	75	71	281	1,320,000
Taichi Teshima	69	71	74	67	281	1,320,000
Katsuyoshi Tomori	71	69	72	70	282	936,000
Katsunori Kuwabara	71	69	70	72	282	936,000
Terry Price	70	70	70	72	282	936,000
Naoya Sugiyama	69	71	72	70	282	936,000
Mitsutaka Kusakabe	71	72	68	71	282	936,000
Tetsuji Hiratsuka	73	67	71	71	282	936,000
Shane Tait	68	69	74	71	282	936,000

Japan Open

Tokyo Golf Club, Sayama, Saitama
Par 36-35–71; 6,908 yards

October 11-14
purse, ¥120,000,000

	SCORES				TOTAL	MONEY
Taichi Teshima	68	72	67	70	277	¥24,000,000
Tsuyoshi Yoneyama	74	72	67	68	281	13,200,000
Katsuyoshi Tomori	67	72	70	73	282	7,710,000
Toshimitsu Izawa	68	73	70	71	282	7,710,000
Nobuhito Sato	66	73	73	71	283	5,040,000
Satoshi Higashi	72	71	69	72	284	4,080,000
Lin Keng-chi	69	70	76	70	285	3,288,000
Katsumasa Miyamoto	68	71	72	74	285	3,288,000
*Yusaku Miyazato	73	70	68	74	285	
Shingo Katayama	71	72	68	75	286	2,694,000
Kiyoshi Maita	70	71	73	73	287	1,998,000
Keiichiro Fukabori	70	70	70	77	287	1,998,000
Takashi Kanemoto	74	71	70	72	287	1,998,000
Frankie Minoza	69	74	70	74	287	1,998,000
Hidemichi Tanaka	74	70	70	74	288	1,524,000
Shinichi Akiba	69	71	74	74	288	1,524,000
Ikuo Shirahama	69	68	73	79	289	1,344,000
Tsuneyuki Nakajima	70	70	72	77	289	1,344,000
Nobumitsu Yuhara	74	73	70	72	289	1,344,000
Naoki Hattori	71	70	73	76	290	1,224,000
Masashi Ozaki	70	73	74	74	291	1,152,000
Shinichi Yokota	72	70	75	74	291	1,152,000
Kiyoshi Murota	70	71	74	77	292	1,062,000
Atsushi Takamatsu	73	71	74	74	292	1,062,000
Hidezumi Shirakata	72	75	73	72	292	1,062,000
Nozomi Kawahara	69	76	74	73	292	1,062,000
Tatsuhiko Takahashi	73	74	74	71	292	1,062,000
Hirofumi Miyase	69	76	72	76	293	972,000
Yeh Chang-ting	72	70	78	73	293	972,000
Jeev Milkha Singh	74	71	73	75	293	972,000

Bridgestone Open

Sodegaura Country Club, Yokoshiba, Chiba
Par 36-36–72; 7,178 yards

October 18-21
purse, ¥110,000,000

	SCORES				TOTAL	MONEY
Toshimitsu Izawa	71	67	67	69	274	¥22,000,000
Masashi Ozaki	70	68	69	68	275	11,000,000
Scott Laycock	70	68	69	69	276	7,480,000
Hidemichi Tanaka	72	71	67	67	277	5,280,000
*Yusaku Miyazato	73	66	73	65	277	
Tsuneyuki Nakajima	69	66	73	70	278	3,836,250
Hirofumi Miyase	73	65	70	70	278	3,836,250
Tomohiro Kondou	69	72	69	68	278	3,836,250
Dean Wilson	71	69	71	67	278	3,836,250
Naomichi Ozaki	71	70	69	69	279	2,992,000
Dinesh Chand	73	68	66	72	279	2,992,000
Shusaku Sugimoto	72	70	72	66	280	2,552,000
Kang Wook-soon	70	71	71	68	280	2,552,000
Kiyoshi Murota	75	68	70	68	281	2,038,666
Tsukasa Watanabe	71	68	69	73	281	2,038,666

	SCORES				TOTAL	MONEY
Nobuhito Sato	71	73	70	67	281	2,038,666
Tateo Ozaki	72	66	73	71	282	1,529,000
Ryoken Kawagishi	70	68	74	70	282	1,529,000
Shigeki Maruyama	76	67	69	70	282	1,529,000
Katsunori Kuwabara	74	68	71	69	282	1,529,000
Frankie Minoza	72	66	73	71	282	1,529,000
Brian Watts	73	70	71	68	282	1,529,000
Yoshinori Mizumaki	69	72	76	66	283	984,500
Anthony Gilligan	69	71	69	74	283	984,500
Nozomi Kawahara	73	71	74	65	283	984,500
Shinichi Yokota	70	66	75	72	283	984,500
Jun Kikuchi	70	73	71	69	283	984,500
Yasuharu Imano	70	73	69	71	283	984,500
Prayad Marksaeng	72	68	73	70	283	984,500
Shane Tait	74	69	69	71	283	984,500

Philip Morris Championship

ABC Golf Club, Tojo, Hyogo
Par 36-36–72; 7,176 yards

October 25-28
purse, ¥200,000,000

	SCORES				TOTAL	MONEY
Toshimitsu Izawa	67	67	66	72	272	¥40,000,000
Hidemichi Tanaka	70	68	67	68	273	16,800,000
Toru Taniguchi	69	69	67	68	273	16,800,000
Nobuhito Sato	65	67	68	74	274	8,800,000
Shingo Katayama	69	67	70	68	274	8,800,000
Kiyoshi Maita	69	68	72	66	275	7,200,000
Tateo Ozaki	72	67	68	69	276	6,600,000
Hajime Meshiai	67	70	70	70	277	6,100,000
Taichi Teshima	71	71	65	71	278	5,240,000
Katsumasa Miyamoto	73	69	70	66	278	5,240,000
Dinesh Chand	67	71	67	73	278	5,240,000
Keiichiro Fukabori	68	69	74	68	279	3,890,000
Mamoru Osanai	67	71	70	71	279	3,890,000
Brian Watts	69	70	70	70	279	3,890,000
Kim Jong-duk	68	65	74	72	279	3,890,000
Katsuyoshi Tomori	68	71	71	70	280	2,950,000
Shinichi Yokota	69	69	72	70	280	2,950,000
Chen Tze-chung	66	68	72	74	280	2,950,000
Scott Laycock	71	70	71	68	280	2,950,000
Masashi Ozaki	68	71	71	71	281	2,200,000
Shoichi Yamamoto	66	76	70	69	281	2,200,000
Taku Sugaya	75	68	70	68	281	2,200,000
David Smail	69	69	70	73	281	2,200,000
Hidemasa Hoshino	72	69	64	76	281	2,200,000
Hideki Kase	72	67	72	71	282	1,680,000
Hirofumi Miyase	72	68	69	73	282	1,680,000
Yeh Chang-ting	70	70	71	71	282	1,680,000
Go Higaki	69	71	71	71	282	1,680,000
Tsuyoshi Yoneyama	67	72	73	71	283	1,365,000
Masashi Shimada	70	71	72	70	283	1,365,000
Tetsuji Hiratsuka	72	69	73	69	283	1,365,000
Shusaku Sugimoto	67	73	71	72	283	1,365,000

Ube Kosan Open

Ube Country Club, Ebataike Course,
Ajisu, Yamaguchi
Par 36-36—72; 6,859 yards

November 1-4
purse, ¥140,000,000

		SCORES			TOTAL	MONEY
Dean Wilson	65	67	68	67	267	¥28,000,000
Taichi Teshima	71	61	67	69	268	14,000,000
Hajime Meshiai	68	63	70	69	270	9,520,000
Todd Hamilton	65	65	71	70	271	6,720,000
Tsuneyuki Nakajima	70	67	65	70	272	5,086,666
Mitsuo Harada	68	70	67	67	272	5,086,666
Keiichiro Fukabori	69	66	67	70	272	5,086,666
Nozomi Kawahara	70	62	73	68	273	4,109,000
Scott Laycock	67	66	74	66	273	4,109,000
Naomichi Ozaki	64	69	72	69	274	3,248,000
Katsuyoshi Tomori	65	71	69	69	274	3,248,000
Yasuharu Imano	68	66	69	71	274	3,248,000
David Smail	67	67	69	71	274	3,248,000
Katsunori Kuwabara	68	66	69	72	275	2,408,000
Yeh Chang-ting	70	67	68	70	275	2,408,000
Christian Pena	70	65	72	68	275	2,408,000
Nobumitsu Yuhara	69	68	71	68	276	1,711,500
Toru Suzuki	65	70	72	69	276	1,711,500
Eiji Mizoguchi	68	69	68	71	276	1,711,500
Toshikazu Sugihara	69	67	68	72	276	1,711,500
Daisuke Maruyama	64	72	71	69	276	1,711,500
Shigemasa Higaki	72	67	68	69	276	1,711,500
Shingo Katayama	67	65	74	70	276	1,711,500
Steven Conran	68	71	69	68	276	1,711,500
Tateo Ozaki	65	75	67	70	277	1,232,000
Kiyoshi Murota	66	71	66	74	277	1,232,000
Masashi Ozaki	68	72	68	70	278	1,092,000
Kiyoshi Maita	67	70	65	76	278	1,092,000
Kenichi Kuboya	65	69	69	75	278	1,092,000
Hideki Kase	67	71	70	71	279	928,666
Ikuo Shirahama	69	70	69	71	279	928,666
Jun Kikuchi	68	70	72	69	279	928,666

Dunlop Phoenix

Phoenix Country Club, Miyazaki
Par 36-35—71; 6,856 yards

November 8-11
purse, ¥200,000,000

		SCORES			TOTAL	MONEY
David Duval	65	67	68	69	269	¥40,000,000
Taichi Teshima	68	67	69	65	269	20,000,000
(Duval defeated Teshima on first playoff hole.)						
Shingo Katayama	71	65	70	68	274	11,600,000
Scott Laycock	73	68	66	67	274	11,600,000
Tsuneyuki Nakajima	68	69	69	69	275	6,975,000
Katsunori Kuwabara	69	68	67	71	275	6,975,000
Yeh Chang-ting	69	70	69	67	275	6,975,000
Dean Wilson	67	70	68	70	275	6,975,000
David Smail	69	69	70	68	276	5,640,000
Jerry Kelly	70	66	67	74	277	5,040,000
David Gossett	68	66	74	69	277	5,040,000

	SCORES				TOTAL	MONEY
Shigemasa Higaki	69	71	67	71	278	3,640,000
Hidemichi Tanaka	71	69	69	69	278	3,640,000
Toshimitsu Izawa	70	69	73	66	278	3,640,000
Toru Taniguchi	70	71	68	69	278	3,640,000
Aaron Baddeley	69	66	72	71	278	3,640,000
Naomichi Ozaki	68	71	67	72	278	3,640,000
Hiroyuki Fujita	69	70	72	68	279	2,760,000
Hirofumi Miyase	66	75	70	68	279	2,760,000
Tetsuji Hiratsuka	72	65	73	71	281	2,280,000
Keng-Chi Lin	69	72	69	71	281	2,280,000
Masashi Shimada	69	73	70	69	281	2,280,000
Kiyoshi Maita	70	72	68	71	281	2,280,000
Tetsuya Haraguchi	69	71	73	69	282	1,880,000
Kaname Yokoo	71	70	69	73	283	1,720,000
Masashi Ozaki	72	73	71	67	283	1,720,000
Katsumasa Miyamoto	68	74	69	72	283	1,720,000
Geoff Ogilvy	70	75	70	69	284	1,440,000
Hidezumi Shirakata	70	72	73	69	284	1,440,000
Hisayuki Sasaki	73	69	70	72	284	1,440,000
Go Higaki	71	66	74	73	284	1,440,000

WGC EMC World Cup

The Taiheiyo Club, Gotemba Course, Gotemba, Shizuoka
Par 36-36–72; 7,232 yards

November 15-18
purse, US$3,000,000

	INDIVIDUAL SCORES				TOTAL
SOUTH AFRICA—$1,000,000					
Ernie Els/Retief Goosen	64	71	63	66	264
DENMARK—$316,666					
Thomas Bjorn/Soren Hansen	65	69	65	65	264
UNITED STATES—$316,666					
Tiger Woods/David Duval	66	68	63	67	264
NEW ZEALAND—$316,666					
David Smail/Michael Campbell	63	66	65	70	264

(Els/Goosen won on second playoff hole.)

	INDIVIDUAL SCORES				TOTAL
ENGLAND—$115,000					
Ian Poulter/Paul Casey	65	72	63	67	267
CANADA—$95,000					
Mike Weir/Ian Leggatt	62	73	66	67	268
SPAIN—$95,000					
Sergio Garcia/Miguel Angel Jimenez	63	71	65	69	268
FIJI—$70,000					
Vijay Singh/Dinesh Chand	66	69	66	68	269
ARGENTINA—$70,000					
Angel Cabrera/Eduardo Romero	67	68	63	71	269
FRANCE—$70,000					
Thomas Levet/Raphael Jacquelin	67	68	63	71	269

SCOTLAND—$50,000
Andrew Coltart/Dean Robertson   62   71   66   71   270

WALES—$50,000
Phillip Price/Mark Mouland   66   71   62   71   270

JAPAN—$50,000
Toshimitsu Izawa/Shigeki Maruyama   64   69   65   72   270

AUSTRALIA—$39,500
Adam Scott/Aaron Baddeley   66   70   64   71   271

IRELAND—$39,500
Padraig Harrington/Paul McGinley   64   72   64   71   271

SWEDEN—$38,000
Niclas Fasth/Robert Karlsson   62   73   66   71   272

CHINA—$36,000
Zhang Lian-wei/Liang Wen-chong   67   69   68   70   274

MEXICO—$36,000
Octavio Gonzalez/Alejandro Quiroz   66   71   67   70   274

NORWAY—$36,000
Per Haugsrud/Henrik Bjornstad   67   72   61   74   274

ZIMBABWE—$34,000
Mark McNulty/Tony Johnstone   66   74   66   72   278

PARAGUAY—$33,000
Carlos Franco/Angel Franco   68   72   66   75   281

HOLLAND—$32,000
Maarten Lefeber/Robert Jan Derksen   70   72   64   76   282

MALAYSIA—$31,000
Danny Chia/Periasamy Gunasegaran   66   80   68   71   285

PHILIPPINES—$30,000
Rodrigo Cuello/Danny Zarate   67   75   73   74   289

Casio World Open

Ibusuki Golf Club, Kaimon, Kagoshima   November 22-25
Par 36-36–72; 7,105 yards   purse, ¥140,000,000

	SCORES				TOTAL	MONEY
Kiyoshi Murota	65	68	63	68	264	¥28,000,000
Dinesh Chand	70	66	64	66	266	14,000,000
Sergio Garcia	69	65	66	67	267	9,520,000
Shingo Katayama	70	64	68	73	275	6,160,000
Brendan Jones	64	70	68	73	275	6,160,000
Masashi Ozaki	65	69	72	70	276	4,643,333
Nobuhito Sato	67	71	69	69	276	4,643,333
Zaw Moe	72	68	68	68	276	4,643,333
Hideki Kase	71	69	68	69	277	3,808,000
Christian Pena	67	75	69	66	277	3,808,000
Tsuneyuki Nakajima	74	64	70	71	279	3,108,000

		SCORES			TOTAL	MONEY
Tsukasa Watanabe	71	67	68	73	279	3,108,000
Mamoru Osanai	66	74	69	70	279	3,108,000
Satoshi Higashi	68	71	71	71	281	2,202,666
Toru Suzuki	70	72	68	71	281	2,202,666
Toru Taniguchi	70	68	73	70	281	2,202,666
Taichi Teshima	70	72	67	72	281	2,202,666
Steven Conran	67	71	71	72	281	2,202,666
Go Higaki	70	67	72	72	281	2,202,666
Hirofumi Miyase	67	71	69	75	282	1,493,333
Ryoken Kawagishi	68	71	74	69	282	1,493,333
Kenichi Kuboya	76	67	67	72	282	1,493,333
Mitsuhiro Tateyama	71	70	68	73	282	1,493,333
Hidemasa Hoshino	71	69	73	69	282	1,493,333
Per Haugsrud	72	69	71	70	282	1,493,333
Nobuo Serizawa	73	69	71	70	283	1,038,000
Masahiro Kuramoto	69	70	72	72	283	1,038,000
Shigemasa Higaki	71	71	67	74	283	1,038,000
Tatsuya Mitsuhashi	72	70	67	74	283	1,038,000
Katsumune Imai	72	66	72	73	283	1,038,000
Tomohiro Kondou	74	68	69	72	283	1,038,000
Kim Jong-duk	72	67	73	71	283	1,038,000

Nippon Series JT Cup

Tokyo Yomiuri Country Club, Tokyo
Par 35-35–70; 6,958 yards

November 29-December 2
purse, ¥90,000,000

		SCORES			TOTAL	MONEY
Katsumasa Miyamoto	72	64	66	66	268	¥30,000,000
Tsuneyuki Nakajima	66	71	66	66	269	10,000,000
Toshimitsu Izawa	71	65	65	68	269	10,000,000
Takenori Hiraishi	69	64	70	67	270	4,263,333
Keiichiro Fukabori	67	64	67	72	270	4,263,333
Toru Taniguchi	64	71	67	68	270	4,263,333
Shigeki Maruyama	68	70	68	66	272	2,950,000
Masashi Ozaki	72	69	64	68	273	2,600,000
Dinesh Chand	68	72	66	68	274	2,250,000
Kiyoshi Murota	73	69	65	69	276	1,840,000
Taichi Teshima	71	69	69	67	276	1,840,000
Shinichi Yokota	71	69	69	68	277	1,550,000
Scott Laycock	71	72	65	69	277	1,550,000
Katsuyoshi Tomori	71	68	68	71	278	1,300,000
Lin Keng-chi	71	67	68	72	278	1,300,000
Go Higaki	75	68	67	68	278	1,300,000
Kazuhiko Hosokawa	70	71	65	73	279	1,110,000
Hajime Meshiai	70	72	68	71	281	928,000
Eiji Mizoguchi	69	70	72	70	281	928,000
Shingo Katayama	72	75	70	64	281	928,000
David Smail	71	71	72	67	281	928,000
Frankie Minoza	70	65	72	74	281	928,000
Hiroyuki Fujita	71	69	71	71	282	775,000
Nobuhito Sato	76	64	71	71	282	775,000
Yoshimitsu Fukuzawa	77	71	65	73	288	738,000
Toshiaki Odate	73	71	71	74	291	500,000

Australasian Tour

WGC Accenture Match Play

Metropolitan Golf Club, South Oakleigh, Victoria
Par 36-36–72; 7,066 yards

January 3-7
purse, US$5,000,000

FIRST ROUND

Ernie Els defeated Greg Kraft, 3 and 2.
Hidemichi Tanaka defeated Bernhard Langer, 19 holes.
Jean Van de Velde defeated Duffy Waldorf, 19 holes.
Retief Goosen defeated Steve Lowery, 2 and 1.
Craig Stadler defeated John Huston, 4 and 2.
Craig Parry defeated Dennis Paulson, 21 holes.
David Toms defeated Hirofumi Miyase, 1 up.
Andrew Coltart defeated Phillip Price, 3 and 2.
Tom Lehman defeated Greg Chalmers, 2 and 1.
Jeff Sluman defeated Naomichi Ozaki, 3 and 2.
Chris Perry defeated Jonathan Kaye, 1 up.
Brad Faxon defeated Jose Coceres, 3 and 2.
Michael Campbell defeated Mathias Gronberg, 4 and 3.
Toshimitsu Izawa defeated Steve Pate, 19 holes.
Glen Day defeated Kirk Triplett, 3 and 1.
Pierre Fulke defeated Fred Funk, 5 and 4.
Nick O'Hern defeated Hal Sutton, 21 holes.
Tim Herron defeated Franklin Langham, 2 and 1.
Robert Allenby defeated Nobuhito Sato, 2 and 1.
Dudley Hart defeated Skip Kendall, 6 and 5.
Justin Leonard defeated Patrik Sjoland, 6 and 5.
Gary Orr defeated Paul McGinley, 2 and 1.
Steve Stricker defeated Padraig Harrington, 2 and 1.
Scott Verplank defeated Brent Geiberger, 19 holes.
Vijay Singh defeated Kevin Sutherland, 4 and 2.
Toru Taniguchi defeated Bob Estes, 3 and 2.
Stuart Appleby defeated Kenny Perry, 1 up.
Per-Ulrik Johansson defeated Steve Flesch, 5 and 4.
Mark McNulty defeated Stewart Cink, 1 up.
Paul Lawrie defeated Chris DiMarco, 5 and 4.
Bob May defeated Tom Scherrer, 2 and 1.
Shigeki Maruyama defeated Scott Dunlap, 2 and 1.

(Each losing player received US$25,000.)

SECOND ROUND

Els defeated Tanaka, 1 up.
Van de Velde defeated Goosen, 4 and 3.
Stadler defeated Parry, 7 and 6.
Coltart defeated Toms, 3 and 2.
Lehman defeated Sluman, 3 and 2.
Faxon defeated Perry, 1 up.
Campbell defeated Izawa, 5 and 4.
Fulke defeated Day, 20 holes.
O'Hern defeated Herron, 5 and 3.
Hart defeated Allenby, 5 and 4.
Leonard defeated Orr, 20 holes.

Stricker defeated Verplank, 3 and 2.
Taniguchi defeated Singh, 1 up.
Appleby defeated Johansson, 4 and 3.
McNulty defeated Lawrie, 5 and 4.
Maruyama defeated May, 22 holes.

(Each losing player received US$50,000.)

THIRD ROUND

Els defeated Van de Velde, 19 holes.
Stadler defeated Colbert, 19 holes.
Faxon defeated Lehman, 1 up.
Fulke defeated Campbell, 1 up.
O'Hern defeated Hart, 5 and 4.
Stricker defeated Leonard, 6 and 5.
Taniguchi defeated Appleby, 2 and 1.
Maruyama defeated McNulty, 4 and 3.

(Each losing player received US$75,000.)

QUARTER-FINALS

Els defeated Stadler, 1 up.
Fulke defeated Faxon, 19 holes.
Stricker defeated O'Hern, 20 holes.
Taniguchi defeated Maruyama, 2 and 1.

(Each losing player received US$150,000.)

SEMI-FINALS

Fulke defeated Els, 2 and 1.
Striker defeated Taniguchi, 2 and 1.

THIRD-PLACE MATCH

Taniguchi defeated Els, 4 and 3.

(Taniguchi received US$400,000; Els received US$300,000.)

FINAL

Stricker defeated Fulke, 2 and 1.

(Stricker received US$1,000,000; Fulke received US$500,000.)

Victorian Open

Cranbourne Golf Club, Melbourne, Victoria
Par 36-36–72; 6,677 yards

January 11-14
purse, A$250,000

	SCORES				TOTAL	MONEY
Scott Laycock	67	68	70	65	270	A$45,000
Richard Green	70	70	68	65	273	25,500
James McLean	69	70	71	64	274	16,875
Jon Riley	69	72	70	66	277	9,250
Euan Walters	67	68	75	67	277	9,250
Michael Long	71	67	71	68	277	9,250
Scott Hend	68	69	71	69	277	9,250

	SCORES				TOTAL	MONEY
David Diaz	70	70	69	68	277	9,250
Doug LaBelle	72	68	71	67	278	5,875
David Podlich	65	68	72	73	278	5,875
David Gossett	66	69	72	71	278	5,875
Scott Gardiner	67	67	70	74	278	5,875
Wayne Perske	72	70	70	67	279	4,087.50
Richard Lee	70	73	68	68	279	4,087.50
Mark Wilson	68	70	71	70	279	4,087.50
Scott Wearne	67	72	71	69	279	4,087.50
Nathan Gatehouse	71	72	70	67	280	3,020.83
Stephen Leaney	66	71	75	68	280	3,020.83
*Andrew Buckle	70	67	73	70	280	
Peter Lonard	67	71	71	71	280	3,020.83
Kim Felton	72	69	72	68	281	2,500
Steve Collins	71	70	71	69	281	2,500
Tony Carolan	74	65	73	69	281	2,500
Ed Stedman	71	73	68	69	281	2,500
Alan Patterson	74	67	70	70	281	2,500
Gavin Coles	67	71	70	73	281	2,500
Marcus Wheelhouse	68	73	75	66	282	1,880
Danny Willersdorf	66	75	74	67	282	1,880
Chris Gaunt	69	71	73	69	282	1,880
Gary Simpson	67	69	75	71	282	1,880
Marcus Cain	71	67	73	71	282	1,880

TelstraSaturn New Zealand Open

Grange Golf Club, Auckland, New Zealand
Par 35-35–70; 6,472 yards

January 18-21
purse, NZ$500,000

	SCORES				TOTAL	MONEY
David Smail	66	68	69	70	273	A$72,189
Michael Campbell	71	72	66	66	275	25,817.59
Nathan Gatehouse	66	71	70	68	275	25,817.59
Steve Alker	67	70	69	69	275	25,817.59
Roger Chapman	72	66	68	69	275	25,817.59
Brett Ogle	68	72	67	69	276	14,437.80
David Armstrong	75	66	70	66	277	10,828.35
Mark Brown	75	67	69	66	277	10,828.35
Kenny Druce	74	69	67	67	277	10,828.35
James McLean	74	68	67	68	277	10,828.35
Greg Turner	74	66	68	69	277	10,828.35
Craig Jones	67	70	73	68	278	7,352.58
Peter O'Malley	69	66	73	70	278	7,352.58
Euan Walters	68	70	69	71	278	7,352.58
David Gossett	67	75	69	68	279	6,095.96
Bob Charles	68	68	73	70	279	6,095.96
*Eddie Lee	72	68	69	70	279	
Nathan Green	71	72	74	63	280	4,717.35
Adam Henwood	71	69	72	68	280	4,717.35
Rodney Pampling	70	71	69	70	280	4,717.35
Leigh McKechnie	71	72	66	71	280	4,717.35
Michael Long	74	69	69	69	281	3,856.76
Cameron Percy	70	70	71	70	281	3,856.76
Martin Doyle	74	65	71	71	281	3,856.76
Paul Sheehan	65	72	72	72	281	3,856.76
Mark Wilson	70	73	66	72	281	3,856.76

	SCORES				TOTAL	MONEY
David Bransdon	68	69	70	74	281	3,856.76
Adrian Percey	71	72	71	68	282	2,855.47
Martin Pettigrew	68	73	72	69	282	2,855.47
Andrew Tschudin	74	69	70	69	282	2,855.47
David Podlich	73	70	69	70	282	2,855.47
Brad Andrews	72	67	67	76	282	2,855.47

Canon Challenge

Castle Hill Country Club, Sydney, New South Wales
Par 36-36–72; 6,766 yards

January 25-28
purse, A$550,000

	SCORES				TOTAL	MONEY
David Smail	69	64	69	67	269	A$99,000
David Gossett	67	68	67	68	270	56,100
Justin Cooper	71	69	65	66	271	31,762.50
Tod Power	69	69	63	70	271	31,762.50
Paul Gow	60	69	74	69	272	22,000
Doug LaBelle	69	69	68	67	273	18,700
Peter Lonard	71	65	67	70	273	18,700
Kenny Druce	66	68	72	68	274	14,850
Richard Backwell	71	67	68	68	274	14,850
Peter Senior	70	70	66	68	274	14,850
David Podlich	71	71	67	66	275	10,230
Scott Wearne	71	71	66	67	275	10,230
Nathan Green	69	69	69	68	275	10,230
Martin Doyle	71	70	64	70	275	10,230
Jim Benepe	66	69	68	72	275	10,230
David Armstrong	70	70	67	69	276	7,223.33
Gavin Coles	71	66	69	70	276	7,223.33
Adam Le Vesconte	68	72	65	71	276	7,223.33
Nick O'Hern	68	71	71	67	277	5,864.37
Stephen Leaney	65	70	71	71	277	5,864.37
Martyn Roberts	68	70	68	71	277	5,864.37
Scott Gardiner	67	69	68	73	277	5,864.37
Richard Lee	71	70	69	68	278	4,939
Rodney Pampling	69	66	73	70	278	4,939
Anthony Gilligan	68	69	69	72	278	4,939
Tony Carolan	71	66	69	72	278	4,939
James McLean	71	68	67	72	278	4,939
Paul Devenport	68	71	68	72	279	3,987.50
Thomas Gogele	66	72	64	77	279	3,987.50
Peter O'Malley	70	68	74	68	280	3,443
Brad Andrews	74	68	69	69	280	3,443
Shane Tait	72	67	70	71	280	3,443
Andre Stolz	68	69	70	73	280	3,443
Wayne Smith	69	71	67	73	280	3,443

Heineken Classic

The Vines Resort, Perth, Western Australia
Par 36-36–72; 7,101 yards

February 1-4
purse, A$1,750,000

	SCORES				TOTAL	MONEY
Michael Campbell	69	70	67	64	270	A$315,000
David Smail	71	72	66	66	275	178,500
Nick O'Hern	66	69	69	72	276	118,125
Jarrod Moseley	70	70	70	67	277	68,250
Steen Tinning	69	66	72	70	277	68,250
Paul Devenport	71	68	69	69	277	68,250
Dean Robertson	65	74	68	70	277	68,250
Ian Garbutt	78	66	68	68	280	47,250
Thomas Bjorn	67	71	73	69	280	47,250
Robert Karlsson	72	66	72	70	280	47,250
Henrik Nystrom	75	69	70	68	282	32,550
Fredrik Jacobson	71	72	70	69	282	32,550
Kenny Druce	72	72	66	72	282	32,550
Greg Turner	70	71	69	72	282	32,550
Peter Lonard	70	71	66	75	282	32,550
Brett Rumford	72	70	71	70	283	22,983.33
Greg Norman	66	73	70	74	283	22,983.33
Craig Parry	70	70	69	74	283	22,983.33
Soren Hansen	76	69	71	68	284	18,659.37
Nathan Green	72	70	72	70	284	18,659.37
David Carter	73	70	71	70	284	18,659.37
Phillip Price	75	70	69	70	284	18,659.37
Christopher Hanell	74	70	72	69	285	14,136.11
Scott Gardiner	71	72	71	71	285	14,136.11
Paul Broadhurst	74	69	70	72	285	14,136.11
Justin Rose	70	75	68	72	285	14,136.11
Anthony Gilligan	71	73	69	72	285	14,136.11
Pierre Fulke	67	76	69	73	285	14,136.11
Markus Brier	71	73	68	73	285	14,136.11
David Howell	72	73	66	74	285	14,136.11
Brendan Jones	72	70	69	74	285	14,136.11
Scott Laycock	67	74	74	71	286	10,675
John Wade	73	70	70	73	286	10,675
Sven Struver	72	71	73	71	287	9,450
Gary Evans	72	73	71	71	287	9,450
Lucas Parsons	72	73	70	72	287	9,450
Wayne Smith	69	73	72	73	287	9,450
Andrew Tschudin	73	68	71	75	287	9,450
Richard Green	69	76	74	69	288	7,700
Shane Tait	67	72	77	72	288	7,700
Michael Long	71	72	73	72	288	7,700
Andre Stolz	73	71	70	74	288	7,700
John Bickerton	74	66	73	75	288	7,700
Ignacio Garrido	68	75	76	70	289	6,125
Anthony Painter	70	72	73	74	289	6,125
Bradley King	69	74	70	76	289	6,125
Gerry Norquist	71	74	68	76	289	6,125
Matthew Ecob	73	72	75	70	290	4,506.25
Stephen Scahill	74	70	75	71	290	4,506.25
Joakim Haeggman	73	71	75	71	290	4,506.25
Richard Johnson	77	68	71	74	290	4,506.25
Martyn Roberts	73	72	70	75	290	4,506.25
Peter Senior	69	72	73	76	290	4,506.25
David Lynn	72	73	73	73	291	3,797.50

	SCORES				TOTAL	MONEY
Matthew Lane	72	73	73	73	291	3,797.50
Marcus Cain	71	73	72	75	291	3,797.50
Jeff Wagner	77	68	71	75	291	3,797.50
Rodney Pampling	76	69	76	71	292	3,710
Maarten Lafeber	70	73	75	75	293	3,675
John Senden	76	68	77	73	294	3,605
Rolf Muntz	72	72	72	78	294	3,605
Roger Chapman	73	67	74	80	294	3,605
Stuart Bouvier	73	71	78	73	295	3,535
Niclas Fasth	73	72	79	72	296	3,482.50
Roger Winchester	72	73	74	77	296	3,482.50
Henrik Stenson	69	74	76	78	297	3,430
James McLean	74	67	86	71	298	3,342.50
Charles Howell	70	73	77	78	298	3,342.50
Robert Floyd	75	69	75	79	298	3,342.50
Justin Cooper	74	70	70	84	298	3,342.50

Greg Norman Holden International

The Lakes Golf Club, Sydney, New South Wales
Par 36-37–73; 6,904 yards

February 8-11
purse, A$2,000,000

	SCORES				TOTAL	MONEY
Aaron Baddeley	67	68	68	68	271	A$360,000
Sergio Garcia	64	69	70	68	271	204,000
(Baddeley defeated Garcia on first playoff hole.)						
Ian Poulter	70	69	65	68	272	135,000
Greg Norman	66	68	71	68	273	96,000
Nick O'Hern	70	69	72	65	276	80,000
Jarrod Moseley	72	68	66	71	277	68,000
Peter Lonard	74	66	66	71	277	68,000
Carlos Rodiles	70	72	69	67	278	49,200
Craig Parry	69	68	71	70	278	49,200
Robert Karlsson	74	69	68	67	278	49,200
Phillip Price	66	69	74	69	278	49,200
Scott Gardiner	71	72	66	69	278	49,200
Steve Alker	66	72	71	70	279	32,700
David Smail	71	68	71	69	279	32,700
Rodney Pampling	70	71	69	69	279	32,700
Pierre Fulke	65	71	73	70	279	32,700
Marc Farry	68	70	73	69	280	23,525
Peter Baker	71	68	70	71	280	23,525
David Park	71	72	72	65	280	23,525
David Carter	68	74	72	66	280	23,525
Stephen Leaney	71	71	68	71	281	19,680
Kenny Druce	72	69	71	69	281	19,680
Justin Rose	75	69	66	71	281	19,680
Fredrik Jacobson	68	74	72	67	281	19,680
Daren Lee	66	71	76	68	281	19,680
Anders Hansen	75	69	72	66	282	15,040
David Bransdon	70	73	66	73	282	15,040
Joakim Haeggman	70	70	73	69	282	15,040
Raymond Russell	71	71	71	69	282	15,040
Adam Scott	70	67	74	71	282	15,040
Roger Chapman	70	70	70	73	283	11,425
Soren Hansen	67	72	72	72	283	11,425
John Senden	69	72	72	70	283	11,425

	SCORES				TOTAL	MONEY
Matthew Lane	72	70	71	70	283	11,425
Peter O'Malley	68	74	71	70	283	11,425
Niclas Fasth	70	70	70	73	283	11,425
Dean Robertson	75	68	69	71	283	11,425
John Bickerton	72	72	69	70	283	11,425
Marcus Norgren	70	72	75	68	285	8,400
Soren Kjeldsen	72	68	73	72	285	8,400
Ian Garbutt	71	72	74	68	285	8,400
David Lynn	70	71	70	74	285	8,400
Charles Howell	75	68	69	73	285	8,400
Nathan Green	67	69	77	72	285	8,400
James McLean	69	67	75	74	285	8,400
Brett Rumford	72	67	74	73	286	6,800
Tim Elliott	71	73	73	70	287	5,466.66
Shane Tait	70	68	74	75	287	5,466.66
Elliot Boult	74	70	70	73	287	5,466.66
Paolo Quirici	70	73	71	73	287	5,466.66
Bob Friend	72	71	75	69	287	5,466.66
Andrew Raitt	72	72	69	74	287	5,466.66
Wayne Riley	74	70	72	72	288	4,372
Anthony Wall	70	71	77	70	288	4,372
Marcus Cain	72	69	73	74	288	4,372
Greg Owen	69	72	74	73	288	4,372
Terry Price	71	72	74	71	288	4,372
Richard Johnson	75	69	72	73	289	4,240
Scott Laycock	74	70	69	77	290	4,160
Gary Evans	72	72	70	76	290	4,160
Lucas Parsons	74	65	76	75	290	4,160
Stephen Collins	68	73	75	75	291	4,060
Roger Wessels	73	69	73	76	291	4,060
Rodger Davis	71	72	73	76	292	3,960
Henrik Stenson	76	68	72	76	292	3,960
Philip Tataurangi	75	69	72	76	292	3,960
Andre Stolz	74	70	75	74	293	3,860
Anthony Painter	75	68	75	75	293	3,860
Maarten Lafeber	70	72	75	77	294	3,800
Adrian Percey	70	74	71	80	295	3,760
John Wade	71	72	78	76	297	3,700
Martyn Roberts	78	66	77	76	297	3,700

Ericsson Masters

Huntingdale Golf Club, Melbourne, Victoria
Par 36-36–72; 6,814 yards

February 15-18
purse, A$1,000,000

	SCORES				TOTAL	MONEY
Colin Montgomerie	72	67	70	69	278	A$180,000
Nathan Green	68	73	67	71	279	102,000
Rodney Pampling	69	70	71	70	280	51,833.33
Peter O'Malley	68	72	69	71	280	51,833.33
Brett Rumford	67	73	64	76	280	51,833.33
Peter Lonard	70	68	70	73	281	36,000
*Michael Cocking	65	75	68	73	281	
David Podlich	69	71	73	69	282	28,250
Adam Scott	71	66	72	73	282	28,250
Jim Benepe	70	70	67	75	282	28,250
Anthony Painter	69	71	67	75	282	28,250

	SCORES				TOTAL	MONEY
Andrew Tschudin	69	73	74	67	283	17,200
Steven Conran	74	69	71	69	283	17,200
John Wade	71	71	71	70	283	17,200
Scott Laycock	73	70	69	71	283	17,200
Nick O'Hern	70	73	69	71	283	17,200
Craig Parry	67	72	70	74	283	17,200
Aaron Baddeley	72	72	65	74	283	17,200
Marcus Cain	70	71	72	71	284	10,930
Mark Wilson	73	66	72	73	284	10,930
Brad Lamb	68	76	67	73	284	10,930
Steve Alker	72	69	69	74	284	10,930
Rodger Davis	69	70	69	76	284	10,930
Richard Green	71	72	70	72	285	9,275
Richard Backwell	73	67	72	73	285	9,275
Ed Stedman	72	69	71	73	285	9,275
Gary Simpson	71	69	71	74	285	9,275
Scott Hend	73	67	75	71	286	7,275
Brendan Jones	73	69	72	72	286	7,275
Matthew Ecob	70	69	73	74	286	7,275
Bradley King	70	68	69	79	286	7,275

Australasian Tour Championship

Concord Golf Club, Sydney, New South Wales
Par 35-36–71; 6,613 yards

February 22-25
purse, A$1,500,000

	SCORES				TOTAL	MONEY
Peter Lonard	67	67	69	66	269	A$270,000
Nathan Green	71	65	67	67	270	153,000
Marcus Norgren	72	70	66	64	272	86,625
Jim Benepe	71	71	65	65	272	86,625
Brett Rumford	72	66	70	66	274	60,000
Nick O'Hern	70	65	72	68	275	46,500
Geoff Ogilvy	70	68	68	69	275	46,500
David Smail	69	67	70	69	275	46,500
Anthony Painter	69	67	68	71	275	46,500
Mark Allen	71	66	73	66	276	33,500
Mark Wilson	75	67	68	66	276	33,500
Scott Gardiner	71	70	63	72	276	33,500
Gary Simpson	71	71	73	62	277	22,600
Jarrod Moseley	69	71	70	67	277	22,600
Richard Lee	70	64	75	68	277	22,600
John Senden	72	69	68	68	277	22,600
Aaron Baddeley	62	71	74	70	277	22,600
Scott Laycock	68	70	69	70	277	22,600
Steve Alker	72	68	68	70	278	16,537.50
Stephen Leaney	67	68	72	71	278	16,537.50
Marcus Cain	68	72	70	69	279	15,600
Shane Tait	72	66	74	68	280	15,150
Matthew Ecob	68	70	73	69	280	15,150
Craig Warren	74	66	74	67	281	12,042.85
Peter O'Malley	70	69	74	68	281	12,042.85
Paul Sheehan	76	65	71	69	281	12,042.85
Clark Dennis	74	68	70	69	281	12,042.85
Shigemasa Higaki	72	66	72	71	281	12,042.85
Andrew Bonhomme	71	69	69	72	281	12,042.85
James McLean	67	71	70	73	281	12,042.85

Australian PGA Championship

Royal Queensland Golf Club, Brisbane, Queensland
Par 35-37–72; 7,028 yards

November 15-18
purse, A$1,000,000

	SCORES				TOTAL	MONEY
Robert Allenby	65	69	70	69	273	A$180,000
Geoff Ogilvy	71	66	68	69	274	102,000
Gareth Paddison	68	70	70	69	277	57,750
Craig Parry	70	65	70	72	277	57,750
Mathew Goggin	66	71	70	71	278	40,000
Greg Norman	68	73	72	66	279	36,800
Leigh McKechnie	71	70	69	70	280	30,500
Richard Lee	68	67	74	71	280	30,500
Anthony Painter	70	68	72	71	281	26,000
David Gleeson	70	69	68	74	281	26,000
Nathan Green	71	72	72	67	282	19,250
Scott Gardiner	70	70	74	68	282	19,250
Michael Wright	71	71	71	69	282	19,250
Nick O'Hern	68	70	70	74	282	19,250
Brett Ogle	73	68	73	69	283	14,466.66
Steven Conran	71	71	71	70	283	14,466.66
Tony Carolan	72	70	69	72	283	14,466.66
Gavin Coles	68	72	75	69	284	10,607.14
Andrew Bonhomme	72	69	74	69	284	10,607.14
Peter Senior	71	68	74	71	284	10,607.14
David Hill	71	67	73	73	284	10,607.14
Grant Dodd	71	70	70	73	284	10,607.14
David Diaz	71	68	70	75	284	10,607.14
Marcus Cain	68	73	68	75	284	10,607.14
Chris Riley	72	71	73	69	285	7,766.66
Andre Stolz	74	69	73	69	285	7,766.66
Andrew Tschudin	69	70	75	71	285	7,766.66
Stephen Leaney	70	70	72	73	285	7,766.66
Martyn Roberts	68	74	69	74	285	7,766.66
Peter Lonard	70	66	70	79	285	7,766.66

Holden Australian Open

Grand Golf Club, Gold Coast
Par 36-36–72; 6,624 yards

November 22-25
purse, A$1,500,000

	SCORES				TOTAL	MONEY
Stuart Appleby	69	70	67	65	271	A$270,000
Scott Laycock	69	66	71	68	274	153,000
Ernie Els	66	70	73	67	276	101,250
Rodney Pampling	66	70	75	67	278	72,000
Peter Lonard	68	72	73	67	280	60,000
Brett Rumford	73	67	73	68	281	51,000
Geoff Ogilvy	71	65	74	71	281	51,000
Richard Green	72	73	71	66	282	43,500
Craig Parry	72	72	72	67	283	37,000
Charles Howell	75	71	70	67	283	37,000
Stephen Leaney	77	69	69	68	283	37,000
Adam Scott	73	70	71	70	284	30,000
Matthew Ecob	73	70	73	69	285	25,500
Scott Gardiner	69	75	71	70	285	25,500

	SCORES				TOTAL	MONEY
Richard Lee	73	72	69	71	285	25,500
Craig Jones	72	73	72	69	286	17,692.50
Paul Gow	73	72	71	70	286	17,692.50
Gavin Coles	74	72	70	70	286	17,692.50
Marcus Cain	69	69	77	71	286	17,692.50
Greg Chalmers	71	67	76	72	286	17,692.50
Thomas Bjorn	76	67	70	73	286	17,692.50
*Chris Campbell	73	68	77	69	287	
Robert Allenby	71	73	73	70	287	15,300
*James Nitties	74	70	69	74	287	
Brad Kennedy	70	76	72	70	288	13,075
Michael Long	72	74	72	70	288	13,075
Brett Ogle	68	70	79	71	288	13,075
Gareth Paddison	71	75	71	71	288	13,075
Leigh McKechnie	72	73	71	72	288	13,075
John Sutherland	72	73	71	72	288	13,075

African Tours

Nashua Nedtel Cellular Masters

Wild Coast Sun Country Club, Port Edward, Natal
Par 35-35–70; 6,351 yards

January 11-14
purse, R1,000,000

	SCORES				TOTAL	MONEY
Mark McNulty	64	67	70	73	274	R158,000
Retief Goosen	67	73	68	67	275	92,100
Des Terblanche	62	71	69	73	275	92,100
Roger Wessels	64	75	69	69	277	45,200
Bradford Vaughan	69	70	69	69	277	45,200
Mark Hilton	66	74	68	70	278	32,450
Bobby Lincoln	70	68	69	71	278	32,450
David Park	69	74	66	70	279	21,933.33
Lee Slattery	71	69	68	71	279	21,933.33
Hugh Baiocchi	65	69	71	74	279	21,933.33
Andre Cruse	65	74	69	72	280	17,300
Sean Ludgater	67	69	71	73	280	17,300
Nico van Rensburg	68	71	73	69	281	14,033.33
Ashley Roestoff	72	70	69	70	281	14,033.33
Michael du Toit	64	71	75	71	281	14,033.33
Trevor Immelman	71	69	69	72	281	14,033.33
Marc Cayeux	66	68	73	74	281	14,033.33
John Mashego	67	70	68	76	281	14,033.33
Michael Archer	72	70	71	69	282	11,800
Titch Moore	68	68	71	75	282	11,800
Richard Kaplan	68	73	66	75	282	11,800
Darren Fichardt	67	72	73	71	283	10,950
Brenden Pappas	71	72	68	72	283	10,950
Jean Hugo	67	70	75	72	284	10,500
Trevor Case	67	73	72	73	285	9,450
Martin Maritz	73	69	70	73	285	9,450
Nic Henning	70	73	69	73	285	9,450
Trevor Dodds	76	68	68	73	285	9,450
Michael Kirk	70	73	67	75	285	9,450
Grant Muller	71	72	66	76	285	9,450

Alfred Dunhill Championship

Houghton Golf Club, Johannesburg, South Africa
Par 36-36–72; 7,309 yards

January 18-21
purse, £500,000

	SCORES				TOTAL	MONEY
Adam Scott	67	66	65	69	267	R913,539.41
Justin Rose	66	67	66	69	268	664,917.93
Nick Faldo	68	65	68	68	269	342,577.27
Dean Robertson	62	70	67	70	269	342,577.27
Anthony Wall	69	64	70	67	270	239,370.45
Malcolm Mackenzie	68	68	67	68	271	204,679.08
Brian Davis	69	70	69	64	272	156,400.26
Retief Goosen	73	68	67	64	272	156,400.26
Sven Struver	71	70	69	63	273	124,888.93

		SCORES			TOTAL	MONEY
Greg Owen	66	70	69	69	274	104,459.57
Ricardo Gonzalez	69	64	70	71	274	104,459.57
Michael Kirk	68	66	69	71	274	104,459.57
Steve Webster	66	70	72	67	275	85,957.50
Jeev Milkha Singh	70	66	69	70	275	85,957.50
Bradley Dredge	67	68	68	72	275	85,957.50
Carl Suneson	70	67	72	67	276	73,545.70
Brenden Pappas	68	67	73	68	276	73,545.70
Jonathan Lomas	72	67	69	68	276	73,545.70
Mathias Gronberg	66	70	71	69	276	73,545.70
Paul McGinley	67	71	68	70	276	73,545.70
Sean Ludgater	69	67	71	70	277	65,046.31
Nic Henning	68	69	69	71	277	65,046.31
David Faught	72	67	71	68	278	54,812.36
Anders Hansen	71	68	71	68	278	54,812.36
David Higgins	69	70	71	68	278	54,812.36
Mark McNulty	67	70	72	69	278	54,812.36
Andrew Raitt	71	68	70	69	278	54,812.36
Ashley Roestoff	66	70	72	70	278	54,812.36
Markus Brier	69	69	70	70	278	54,812.36
Bobby Lincoln	69	68	70	71	278	54,812.36
Peter Baker	73	66	67	72	278	54,812.36
Des Terblanche	68	65	72	73	278	54,812.36
Marco Bernardini	73	68	72	66	279	46,833.35
Ian Garbutt	68	71	73	68	280	42,207.83
Trevor Immelman	75	66	71	68	280	42,207.83
Alastair Forsyth	68	66	77	69	280	42,207.83
Bradford Vaughan	70	71	70	69	280	42,207.83
Justin Hobday	70	67	73	70	280	42,207.83
Stephen Dodd	69	70	70	71	280	42,207.83
Paul Broadhurst	66	70	71	73	280	42,207.83
Van Phillips	69	72	73	67	281	33,534.99
Gregory Havret	71	68	74	68	281	33,534.99
Bradley Davison	71	70	72	68	281	33,534.99
Simon Dyson	69	66	77	69	281	33,534.99
Craig Kamps	67	74	71	69	281	33,534.99
Raphael Jacquelin	71	68	70	72	281	33,534.99
David Howell	71	69	69	72	281	33,534.99
Peter Hanson	73	65	69	74	281	33,534.99
Mikael Lundberg	71	70	72	69	282	26,596.72
Chris Williams	72	67	73	70	282	26,596.72
Jamie Spence	69	69	73	71	282	26,596.72
Adilson da Silva	69	69	71	73	282	26,596.72
Jean Hugo	71	67	76	69	283	19,369.34
Neil Cheetham	70	67	76	70	283	19,369.34
Paul Eales	65	74	73	71	283	19,369.34
Mark Hilton	72	68	72	71	283	19,369.34
Brett Liddle	70	70	72	71	283	19,369.34
Ian Poulter	67	72	72	72	283	19,369.34
Marco Gortana	68	72	71	72	283	19,369.34
Olivier Edmond	70	68	72	73	283	19,369.34
Tony Johnstone	69	68	71	75	283	19,369.34
Deane Pappas	69	70	67	77	283	19,369.34
Robert Coles	75	66	76	67	284	13,041.40
James Kingston	74	66	74	70	284	13,041.40
Steen Tinning	71	68	74	71	284	13,041.40
Darren Fichardt	72	65	75	72	284	13,041.40
Ian Palmer	69	72	71	72	284	13,041.40
Hennie Walters	69	71	71	73	284	13,041.40

	SCORES				TOTAL	MONEY
Doug McGuigan	70	66	74	74	284	13,041.40
Johan Rystrom	71	69	70	74	284	13,041.40
Richard Johnson	68	72	68	76	284	13,041.40
Don Gammon	72	69	72	72	285	8,650
Titch Moore	69	71	75	72	287	8,591.75
Michele Reale	73	68	73	73	287	8,591.75
Ryan Dreyer	71	66	75	75	287	8,591.75
Warren Bennett	69	68	72	78	287	8,591.75
Desvonde Botes	72	69	75	72	288	8,522.50
Erol Simsek	67	71	74	76	288	8,522.50
Ulrich van den Berg	69	70	77	73	289	8,488
Nicolas Colsaerts	70	69	73	78	290	8,465
Simon McCarthy	69	71	74	77	291	8,442

Mercedes-Benz South African Open

East London Golf Club, East London, South Africa   January 25-28
Par 36-36–72; 6,847 yards   purse, US$1,000,000

	SCORES				TOTAL	MONEY
Mark McNulty	69	71	69	71	280	R1,248,029
Justin Rose	72	69	68	72	281	905,510
Thomas Bjorn	72	67	71	72	282	465,353.40
Roger Wessels	67	69	72	74	282	465,353.40
Mikael Lundberg	71	67	73	72	283	299,999.40
Hennie Otto	65	70	71	77	283	299,999.40
Malcolm Mackenzie	76	68	77	63	284	209,448.40
Bradford Vaughan	71	74	70	69	284	209,448.40
Johan Rystrom	71	71	75	68	285	133,520.54
Desvonde Botes	70	71	74	70	285	133,520.54
Arjun Atwal	72	70	72	71	285	133,520.54
Tobias Dier	71	66	76	72	285	133,520.54
Stephen Gallacher	70	71	71	73	285	133,520.54
Justin Hobday	70	70	70	75	285	133,520.54
Simon Dyson	69	72	69	75	285	133,520.54
Peter Baker	72	73	75	66	286	99,369.88
Brian Davis	73	70	74	69	286	99,369.88
Martin Maritz	69	71	74	72	286	99,369.88
Ignacio Garrido	66	73	73	74	286	99,369.88
David Howell	71	67	73	75	286	99,369.88
Erol Simsek	72	70	75	70	287	84,251.80
Michael Archer	71	73	71	72	287	84,251.80
Paul McGinley	71	72	70	74	287	84,251.80
Retief Goosen	71	68	73	75	287	84,251.80
Bradley Dredge	67	70	74	76	287	84,251.80
David Lynn	72	72	75	69	288	69,448.05
David Park	74	68	76	70	288	69,448.05
Bruce Vaughan	70	71	74	73	288	69,448.05
James Kingston	68	74	73	73	288	69,448.05
Trevor Immelman	72	73	69	74	288	69,448.05
Jeev Milkha Singh	71	71	70	76	288	69,448.05
Markus Brier	70	73	68	77	288	69,448.05
Greg Owen	67	69	74	78	288	69,448.05
Trevor Dodds	70	73	75	71	289	59,055
Shaun Webster	72	71	75	71	289	59,055
Rolf Muntz	75	69	73	72	289	59,055
Grant Muller	69	73	72	75	289	59,055

	SCORES				TOTAL	MONEY
Daren Lee	75	70	76	69	290	50,393.60
Carl Pettersson	72	73	75	70	290	50,393.60
Bradley Davison	71	73	74	72	290	50,393.60
Wayne Bradley	71	74	73	72	290	50,393.60
Paul Eales	71	72	74	73	290	50,393.60
Doug McGuigan	74	69	70	77	290	50,393.60
Alastair Forsyth	74	70	69	77	290	50,393.60
Sven Struver	70	73	77	71	291	40,157.40
David Higgins	70	73	77	71	291	40,157.40
Ashley Roestoff	72	73	75	71	291	40,157.40
Derek Crawford	70	73	76	72	291	40,157.40
Andre Cruse	70	74	73	74	291	40,157.40
Nasho Kamungeremu	69	71	72	79	291	40,157.40
Peter Hanson	72	72	78	70	292	33,070.80
Wayne Riley	69	71	79	73	292	33,070.80
Brenden Pappas	68	72	73	79	292	33,070.80
Ian Poulter	72	70	79	72	293	27,559
*Jaco van der Merwe	72	72	76	73	293	
Michele Reale	71	74	75	73	293	27,559
Dean van Staden	75	70	73	75	293	27,559
Paolo Quirici	67	73	75	78	293	27,559
Matthew Wilcox	70	71	81	72	294	22,834.60
Jean-Francois Remesy	70	74	78	72	294	22,834.60
Deane Pappas	72	70	79	73	294	22,834.60
Gary Emerson	75	70	74	75	294	22,834.60
Mathias Gronberg	76	69	73	76	294	22,834.60
*Jaco Van Zyl	75	67	72	80	294	
Ted Hendriks	72	73	75	75	295	19,291.30
Raphael Jacquelin	71	71	76	77	295	19,291.30
Wallie Coetsee	72	73	71	79	295	19,291.30
Bobby Lincoln	70	69	76	80	295	19,291.30
Richard Kaplan	72	72	80	72	296	16,929.10
Lindani Ndwandwe	73	71	74	78	296	16,929.10
Ian Kennedy	72	72	79	74	297	15,748
Chris Davison	71	74	79	76	300	14,960.60

Dimension Data Pro-Am

Gary Player Country Club: Par 36-36–72; 6,958 yards
Lost City Golf Course: Par 36-36–72; 6,983 yards
Sun City, South Africa

February 1-4
purse, R2,000,000

	SCORES				TOTAL	MONEY
Darren Clarke	71	63	69	71	274	R317,000
Tjaart van der Walt	70	69	71	66	276	184,100
Retief Goosen	70	69	68	69	276	184,100
Titch Moore	71	68	71	69	279	83,533.33
Bradford Vaughan	68	69	71	71	279	83,533.33
Nick Price	74	67	67	71	279	83,533.33
Bruce Vaughan	65	68	74	73	280	58,200
Nic Henning	71	69	73	68	281	45,200
Hennie Otto	71	70	68	72	281	45,200
Graeme Storm	70	71	72	69	282	35,533.33
Martin Maritz	69	69	71	73	282	35,533.33
Ian Palmer	70	70	70	72	282	35,533.33
Mathias Gronberg	73	70	70	70	283	28,400
Trevor Immelman	73	69	74	67	283	28,400

	SCORES				TOTAL	MONEY
Brett Liddle	70	71	72	70	283	28,400
Justin Hobday	66	71	73	73	283	28,400
Jeev Milkha Singh	71	68	69	75	283	28,400
Doug McGuigan	73	69	72	70	284	23,850
Marco Gortana	71	71	70	72	284	23,850
Gavin Levenson	70	68	73	73	284	23,850
Ashley Roestoff	72	70	66	76	284	23,850
Deane Pappas	69	76	68	72	285	21,400
Andrew Coltart	73	71	70	71	285	21,400
Kevin Stone	69	70	73	73	285	21,400
Trevor Dodds	71	74	68	73	286	18,175
Paul McGinley	70	70	73	73	286	18,175
Ian Hutchings	72	71	73	70	286	18,175
Lee Westwood	71	70	71	74	286	18,175
Shaun Webster	75	71	71	69	286	18,175
Simon Hurd	70	71	76	69	286	18,175
Lee Slattery	71	71	70	74	286	18,175
Nasho Kamungeremu	72	74	72	68	286	18,175

South African PGA Championship

Woodhill Country Club, Pretoria, South Africa
Par 36-36–72; 7,382 yards

February 8-11
purse, R1,000,000

	SCORES				TOTAL	MONEY
Deane Pappas	68	67	67	67	269	R158,500
Don Gammon	66	67	72	67	272	115,000
Hendrik Buhrmann	70	69	69	65	273	48,600
Alan McLean	69	67	70	67	273	48,600
Nic Henning	70	69	67	67	273	48,600
Martin Maritz	68	69	65	71	273	48,600
Bruce Vaughan	68	65	72	69	274	29,100
Darren Fichardt	68	70	70	68	276	24,100
Steve van Vuuren	69	72	66	70	277	19,266.66
Chris Williams	66	67	72	72	277	19,266.66
Sammy Daniels	68	67	67	75	277	19,266.66
Wallie Coetsee	66	70	68	74	278	16,600
James Hepworth	69	68	73	69	279	13,671.42
Jaco Olver	68	70	72	69	279	13,671.42
Titch Moore	72	68	70	69	279	13,671.42
Jamie Donaldson	69	73	68	69	279	13,671.42
Callie Swart	70	68	70	71	279	13,671.42
De Wet Basson	69	66	72	72	279	13,671.42
Ulrich van den Berg	65	69	73	72	279	13,671.42
Peter Lawrie	68	72	75	65	280	11,175
Andre Bossert	72	70	66	72	280	11,175
Phillip Sanderson	69	68	69	74	280	11,175
Stefaan van den Heever	68	68	69	75	280	11,175
Andre Cruse	69	71	75	66	281	10,400
Dawie Stander	69	72	73	68	282	9,650
Trevor Immelman	68	71	73	70	282	9,650
Gavin Levenson	72	71	69	70	282	9,650
Brenden Pappas	72	71	68	71	282	9,650
Bobby Lincoln	71	72	72	68	283	8,112.50
Bradford Vaughan	71	71	71	70	283	8,112.50
Marco Gortana	70	71	71	71	283	8,112.50
Craig Kamps	70	73	69	71	283	8,112.50

	SCORES				TOTAL	MONEY
Mark Hilton	70	72	69	72	283	8,112.50
Kevin Stone	68	70	72	73	283	8,112.50
Derek Crawford	67	69	73	74	283	8,112.50
Michael Green	69	71	69	74	283	8,112.50

Investec Royal Swazi Sun Open

Royal Swazi Sun Country Club, Mbabane, Swaziland
Par 36-36–72; 6,745 yards

February 15-18
purse, R500,000

	SCORES				TOTAL	MONEY
Bradford Vaughan	67	67	65	64	263	R79,000
Trevor Immelman	70	70	66	65	271	46,050
Mark Hilton	67	65	70	69	271	46,050
Simon Hurd	68	69	67	69	273	22,600
Doug McGuigan	68	69	67	69	273	22,600
Jamie Donaldson	71	67	71	65	274	14,916.66
Chris Williams	67	72	67	68	274	14,916.66
Peter Wilson	63	71	70	70	274	14,916.66
Murray Urquhart	68	64	71	72	275	10,300
Andre Bossert	66	68	68	73	275	10,300
Ashley Roestoff	69	70	71	66	276	7,920
Omar Sandys	67	68	73	68	276	7,920
Wayne Bradley	69	70	68	69	276	7,920
Brett Liddle	71	65	70	70	276	7,920
Titch Moore	69	68	68	71	276	7,920
Bobby Lincoln	71	69	69	68	277	6,150
Ulrich van den Berg	69	68	71	69	277	6,150
Jaco Olver	65	74	69	69	277	6,150
Wallie Coetsee	70	69	69	69	277	6,150
Sean Farrell	68	69	70	70	277	6,150
Ian Palmer	73	65	68	71	277	6,150
Hennie Otto	67	68	67	75	277	6,150
John Mashego	68	69	72	69	278	5,025
Alan McLean	69	68	72	69	278	5,025
Kevin Stone	69	66	76	67	278	5,025
Andre Cruse	69	70	69	70	278	5,025
Bradley Davison	70	71	67	70	278	5,025
Jaco Rall	71	69	66	72	278	5,025
Mark Murless	74	69	68	68	279	4,500
Vaughn Groenewald	69	73	67	71	280	4,150
Warrick Druian	69	71	72	68	280	4,150
Ian Kennedy	71	70	71	68	280	4,150
Marco Gortana	68	68	72	72	280	4,150
Bruce Vaughan	66	68	73	73	280	4,150

Sunshine Tour Championship

Leopard Creek Country Club, Nelspruit, South Africa
Par 35-36–71; 7,079 yards

February 22-25
purse, R2,000,000

	SCORES				TOTAL	MONEY
Darren Fichardt	66	69	67	68	270	R317,140
Hennie Otto	69	68	70	67	274	230,140
Grant Muller	64	72	67	72	275	138,340

	SCORES				TOTAL	MONEY
Bradford Vaughan	65	74	70	67	276	98,340
Wallie Coetsee	72	66	70	69	277	70,340
Doug McGuigan	65	71	71	70	277	70,340
Mark Hilton	70	67	68	72	277	70,340
*Richard Sterne	69	69	70	70	278	
Ernie Els	73	71	70	65	279	41,090
David Faught	68	72	69	70	279	41,090
Roger Wessels	69	67	71	72	279	41,090
Trevor Immelman	67	68	69	75	279	41,090
Marco Gortana	70	66	72	72	280	33,340
Hendrik Buhrmann	70	68	71	72	281	30,340
Deane Pappas	69	71	68	73	281	30,340
Don Gammon	69	72	71	70	282	28,340
Simon Hurd	69	72	73	69	283	26,840
*Jaco van der Merwe	69	73	71	70	283	
Bruce Vaughan	71	67	74	71	283	26,840
Mark McNulty	72	72	71	69	284	24,840
Derek Crawford	68	72	72	72	284	24,840
Jaco Olver	72	70	74	69	285	22,180
Wayne Bradley	69	74	73	69	285	22,180
Martin Maritz	70	74	70	71	285	22,180
Alan McLean	68	71	73	73	285	22,180
Bobby Lincoln	67	73	70	75	285	22,180
Michael Archer	71	71	70	74	286	19,740
Titch Moore	70	73	68	75	286	19,740
Steve van Vuuren	69	68	69	80	286	19,740
Lee Slattery	72	74	71	70	287	17,690
Ian Hutchings	67	74	72	74	287	17,690
Michael du Toit	70	72	70	75	287	17,690
Keith Horne	66	67	76	78	287	17,690

Stanbic Zambia Open

Lusaka Golf Club, Lusaka, Zambia
Par 35-38–73; 7,226 yards

March 8-11
purse, £50,000

	SCORES				TOTAL	MONEY
Mark Foster	70	70	70	68	278	R87,361.88
Stuart Little	69	71	68	71	279	53,544.37
Jaco Olver	71	72	72	64	279	53,544.37
Euan Little	69	71	72	68	280	30,999.37
Roger Beames	71	71	70	68	280	30,999.37
Ulrich van den Berg	67	73	72	69	281	22,545
Graeme van der Nest	68	68	73	73	282	15,030
Lee James	74	71	68	69	282	15,030
Andre Cruse	69	73	72	68	282	15,030
Titch Moore	76	70	70	67	283	12,399.75
Andrew Marshall	73	69	69	73	284	9,863.44
Mattias Nilsson	67	71	73	73	284	9,863.44
Andre Bossert	70	75	69	70	284	9,863.44
Lee Thompson	72	71	68	73	284	9,863.44
Ashley Roestoff	73	70	70	71	284	9,863.44
Mike Capone	72	70	69	73	284	9,863.44
Wallie Coetsee	69	69	72	75	285	6,556.84
Marc Cayeux	72	72	67	74	285	6,556.84
Craig Cowper	75	67	73	70	285	6,556.84
Sam Walker	71	72	72	70	285	6,556.84

	SCORES				TOTAL	MONEY
Jamie Donaldson	70	71	74	70	285	6,556.84
Tyrol Auret	71	71	69	74	285	6,556.84
Fredrik Orest	73	70	72	71	286	5,072.62
Marten Olander	74	72	65	75	286	5,072.62
Philip Archer	70	72	72	72	286	5,072.62
Ulrik Gustafsson	73	69	71	73	286	5,072.62
Olivier David	71	69	76	70	286	5,072.62
James Hepworth	69	72	71	74	286	5,072.62
Jean-Charles Clugnac	73	72	72	69	286	5,072.62
Sean Farrell	68	75	72	72	287	4,509
Michael Green	73	71	73	70	287	4,509
Han Lee	71	70	75	71	287	4,509

Cock of the North

Ndola Golf Club, Ndola, Zambia
Par 37-36–73; 7,079 yards

March 16-18
purse, R200,000

	SCORES			TOTAL	MONEY
Sean Farrell	71	72	66	209	R31,400
Graeme van der Nest	70	73	70	213	23,000
*Madiliso Muthiya	72	72	71	215	
Mike Lamb	70	72	73	215	12,266.66
Andre Cruse	70	72	73	215	12,266.66
Nasho Kamungeremu	72	69	74	215	12,266.66
Bafana Hlophe	75	73	68	216	5,700
John Bele	70	74	72	216	5,700
Tyrol Auret	74	70	72	216	5,700
Brett Liddle	71	71	74	216	5,700
Jacob Okello	77	70	70	217	3,960
Bobby Lincoln	71	75	71	217	3,960
Gerry Coetzee	71	71	75	217	3,960
Thabang Simon	73	71	74	218	3,480
Schalk van der Merwe	71	72	75	218	3,480
Douglas Wood	72	77	70	219	3,200
Shane Pringle	73	75	71	219	3,200
James Loughnane	77	71	72	220	3,020
Nathan Main	74	74	74	222	2,850
Grant White	74	74	74	222	2,850
Josef Fourie	76	75	72	223	2,600
Peter Njiru	70	78	75	223	2,600
Theo Dauwa	71	73	79	223	2,600
Charan Thethy	75	74	76	225	2,240
Kelvin Phiri	77	73	75	225	2,240
Anil Shah	71	77	77	225	2,240
John Mashego	72	76	77	225	2,240
Jonathan Drummond	77	75	73	225	2,240
Barry Painting	74	76	76	226	2,000
John Nkandu	74	77	76	227	1,940

FNB Botswana Open

Gaborone Golf Club, Gaborone, Botswana
Par 36-35–71; 6,814 yards

March 29-31
purse, R210,000

	SCORES			TOTAL	MONEY
Marc Cayeux	66	63	68	197	R33,099.53
Hendrik Buhrmann	68	68	63	199	20,555.44
Grant Muller	66	68	65	199	20,555.44
Sean Ludgater	68	65	68	201	12,438.68
*Madiliso Muthiya	65	67	69	201	
Sean Farrell	69	67	66	202	7,941.07
Omar Sandys	70	65	67	202	7,941.07
Warren Abery	66	68	68	202	7,941.07
Mike Lamb	67	69	67	203	4,570.68
Ashley Roestoff	68	68	67	203	4,570.68
James Kingston	69	66	68	203	4,570.68
Andre van Staden	65	69	69	203	4,570.68
Chris Williams	66	67	70	203	4,570.68
Craig Kamps	67	68	69	204	3,591.05
Wayne Bradley	67	68	69	204	3,591.05
Andre Cruse	68	66	70	204	3,591.05
Nasho Kamungeremu	71	66	68	205	3,183.45
Mark Murless	71	65	69	205	3,183.45
Michael Green	68	67	70	205	3,183.45
Bobby Lincoln	71	68	67	206	2,898.84
Douglas McCabe	71	65	70	206	2,898.84
Ulrich van den Berg	71	70	66	207	2,688.02
Warrick Druian	68	68	71	207	2,688.02
Titch Moore	69	71	68	208	2,171.49
Christopher Joseph	69	71	68	208	2,171.49
Steve van Vuuren	69	70	69	208	2,171.49
Wilhelm Winsnes	70	69	69	208	2,171.49
Shane Pringle	70	69	69	208	2,171.49
Schalk van der Merwe	70	68	70	208	2,171.49
Josef Fourie	69	68	71	208	2,171.49
Callie Swart	72	64	72	208	2,171.49
Jaco Van Zyl	68	68	72	208	2,171.49
Keith Horne	66	68	74	208	2,171.49

Royal Swazi Sun Classic

Royal Swazi Sun Country Club, Mbabane, Swaziland
Par 36-36–72; 6,745 yards

April 20-22
purse, R200,000

	SCORES			TOTAL	MONEY
Titch Moore	65	70	65	200	R31,400
Keith Horne	64	68	68	200	23,000
(Moore defeated Horne on second playoff hole.)					
Marc Cayeux	67	67	67	201	13,900
Warren Abery	67	66	68	201	13,900
Jaco Van Zyl	70	65	69	204	8,000
Ulrich van den Berg	70	65	69	204	8,000
John Mashego	69	71	65	205	5,600
Steve van Vuuren	70	67	68	205	5,600
John Bele	73	71	63	207	4,246.66
Hennie Walters	69	68	70	207	4,246.66
Bradford Vaughan	67	69	71	207	4,246.66

	SCORES			TOTAL	MONEY
Michael Green	68	70	70	208	3,566.66
Mike Lamb	67	71	70	208	3,566.66
Ryan Reid	68	69	71	208	3,566.66
Andre Cruse	71	69	69	209	3,140
Alan Michell	69	69	71	209	3,140
Michiel Bothma	65	72	72	209	3,140
Shane Pringle	74	70	66	210	2,470
Hendrik Buhrmann	72	71	67	210	2,470
Damian Dunford	70	72	68	210	2,470
Schalk van der Merwe	72	70	68	210	2,470
Douglas Wood	71	70	69	210	2,470
Mark Murless	66	74	70	210	2,470
Bobby Lincoln	70	70	70	210	2,470
Omar Sandys	69	71	70	210	2,470
Sean Farrell	68	71	71	210	2,470
Gerry Coetzee	67	71	72	210	2,470
Christopher Joseph	72	70	69	211	1,970
Bradley Davison	71	69	71	211	1,970
Brett Liddle	72	70	70	212	1,820
Ian Kennedy	70	71	71	212	1,820
Henk Alberts	68	72	72	212	1,820

Pietersburg Industrelek Classic

Pietersburg Golf Club, Pietersburg, South Africa
Par 36-36–72; 7,090 yards

May 10-12
purse, R200,000

	SCORES			TOTAL	MONEY
Ryan Reid	74	67	63	204	R31,400
Naithen Moore	67	69	70	206	23,000
David Owen	67	72	68	207	16,000
Christopher Joseph	71	70	67	208	8,450
Nico van Rensburg	70	70	68	208	8,450
Bradley Davison	68	68	72	208	8,450
Keith Horne	67	66	75	208	8,450
Mike Michell	67	74	69	210	4,206.66
Grant Muller	70	70	70	210	4,206.66
Michiel Bothma	69	71	70	210	4,206.66
Wilhelm Winsnes	69	71	70	210	4,206.66
Don Gammon	68	71	71	210	4,206.66
Shane Pringle	67	71	72	210	4,206.66
Schalk van der Merwe	70	73	68	211	3,144
Steve van Vuuren	73	69	69	211	3,144
Jaco Van Zyl	67	71	73	211	3,144
Philip van den Berg	67	71	73	211	3,144
Sean Pappas	67	70	74	211	3,144
Bafana Hlophe	71	69	72	212	2,800
John Bele	71	73	69	213	2,550
Mark Murless	71	71	71	213	2,550
Jaco Olver	70	71	72	213	2,550
Callie Swart	66	74	73	213	2,550
Warren Abery	72	72	70	214	2,160
Henk Alberts	71	73	70	214	2,160
Wallie Coetsee	74	69	71	214	2,160
Sean Ludgater	69	74	71	214	2,160
Marc Cayeux	73	67	74	214	2,160
Wayne Bradley	74	69	72	215	1,790

	SCORES			TOTAL	MONEY
Vaughn Groenewald	73	69	73	215	1,790
Andre van Staden	70	72	73	215	1,790
Richard Fulford	69	72	74	215	1,790
Mike Lamb	74	67	74	215	1,790
Chris Williams	68	72	75	215	1,790

Goldfields Powerade Classic

Oppenheimer Park Golf Club, Welkom, South Africa   September 7-9
Par 36-36–72; 7,105 yards   purse, R200,000

	SCORES			TOTAL	MONEY
Callie Swart	67	74	66	207	R31,400
Ryan Reid	67	71	70	208	23,000
Naithen Moore	68	76	65	209	13,900
James du Plessis	72	69	68	209	13,900
Marc Cayeux	70	71	69	210	6,800
Mark Murless	71	70	69	210	6,800
Titch Moore	68	72	70	210	6,800
Andre Cruse	72	68	70	210	6,800
Warren Abery	70	69	72	211	4,600
Ian Hutchings	74	69	69	212	3,860
Keith Horne	76	65	71	212	3,860
Phillip Sanderson	67	73	72	212	3,860
Dean Lambert	71	69	72	212	3,860
Richard Fulford	76	67	70	213	3,144
Andy Bean	71	70	72	213	3,144
Graeme van der Nest	72	69	72	213	3,144
Ian Palmer	69	70	74	213	3,144
Jaco Van Zyl	68	68	77	213	3,144
Damian Dunford	75	69	70	214	2,700
Tyrol Auret	71	71	72	214	2,700
Omar Sandys	69	72	73	214	2,700
Johan Kruger	74	69	72	215	2,324
Richard Kaplan	70	73	72	215	2,324
Dean van Staden	72	70	73	215	2,324
Gerry Coetzee	72	70	73	215	2,324
Jaco Olver	72	68	75	215	2,324
Travis Fraser	69	75	72	216	1,944
Sean Ludgater	73	71	72	216	1,944
Mike Lamb	74	70	72	216	1,944
Sean Farrell	74	69	73	216	1,944
Robert Oosthuizen	69	74	73	216	1,944

Bloemfontein Classic

Schoeman Park Golf Club, Bloemfontein, South Africa   September 11-13
Par 36-36–72; 7,152 yards   purse, R200,000

	SCORES			TOTAL	MONEY
Andre Cruse	70	70	67	207	R31,400
Steve van Vuuren	67	70	71	208	23,000
Dean van Staden	67	71	71	209	13,900
Patrick O'Brien	68	68	73	209	13,900
Henk Alberts	71	69	70	210	7,333

	SCORES			TOTAL	MONEY
Michiel Bothma	72	67	71	210	7,333
Jaco Van Zyl	69	68	73	210	7,333
Gerry Coetzee	72	71	68	211	4,666
Ian Hutchings	71	70	70	211	4,666
Ulrich van den Berg	71	68	72	211	4,666
Sean Farrell	70	73	69	212	3,746
Michael Green	71	70	71	212	3,746
Omar Sandys	70	70	72	213	3,746
Wallie Coetsee	71	70	72	213	3,330
Bobby Lincoln	72	68	73	214	3,330
Richard Kaplan	74	69	71	214	2,965
Travis Fraser	68	73	73	214	2,965
Ian Palmer	71	69	74	214	2,965
Titch Moore	70	68	76	214	2,965
Dean Lambert	67	76	72	215	2,650
Robert Oosthuizen	72	69	74	215	2,650
Mike Lamb	72	71	73	216	2,406
Alan Michell	71	70	75	216	2,406
John Bele	65	75	76	216	2,406
Bradley Davison	74	72	71	217	2,017
Sean Ludgater	70	76	71	217	2,017
Vaughn Groenewald	72	74	71	217	2,017
Wayne Bradley	70	75	72	217	2,017
David Owen	73	72	72	217	2,017
Shane Howe	72	70	75	217	2,017
Mark Murless	71	71	75	217	2,017

Randfontein Classic

Randfontein Country Club, Johannesburg, South Africa
Par 36-36–72; 6,630 yards

September 26-28
purse, R200,000

	SCORES			TOTAL	MONEY
James Kingston	67	72	66	205	R31,400
Sean Ludgater	69	70	66	205	19,500
Andre Cruse	68	71	66	205	19,500
(Kingston defeated Ludgater and Cruse on first playoff hole.)					
Naithen Moore	67	71	68	206	11,600
Nic Henning	67	73	68	208	6,800
Roger Wessels	72	68	68	208	6,800
Grant Muller	67	72	69	208	6,800
Ulrich van den Berg	70	69	69	208	6,800
Rudy Whitfield	70	71	68	209	4,120
Marc Cayeux	71	67	71	209	4,120
Patrick O'Brien	70	68	71	209	4,120
Ashley Roestoff	66	71	72	209	4,120
Nico van Rensburg	68	73	69	210	3,340
Dean Lambert	68	72	70	210	3,340
Michael Green	70	70	70	210	3,340
Richard Sterne	69	70	71	210	3,340
Keith Horne	69	74	69	212	2,906.66
Henk Alberts	69	71	72	212	2,906.66
Darren Fichardt	68	72	72	212	2,906.66
Dean van Staden	70	74	69	213	2,550
Johan Kruger	71	70	72	213	2,550
Wayne Bradley	68	73	72	213	2,550
Desvonde Botes	72	68	73	213	2,550

	SCORES			TOTAL	MONEY
Brett Liddle	71	72	71	214	2,200
Tyrol Auret	70	73	71	214	2,200
Wayne de Haas	72	71	71	214	2,200
Jaco Olver	70	71	73	214	2,200
Bradford Vaughan	69	75	71	215	1,850
Vaughn Groenewald	70	74	71	215	1,850
Gregory Jacobs	72	71	72	215	1,850
James du Plessis	69	74	72	215	1,850
Jason Lipshitz	69	73	73	215	1,850
Mark Murless	71	68	76	215	1,850

Bearing Man Highveld Classic

Witbank Golf Club, Witbank, South Africa
Par 36-36–72; 6,702 yards

October 5-7
purse, R200,000

	SCORES			TOTAL	MONEY
Justin Hobday	69	69	65	203	R31,400
Marc Cayeux	64	68	71	203	23,000
(Hobday defeated Cayeux on second playoff hole.)					
Hendrik Buhrmann	68	66	70	204	16,000
Omar Sandys	74	68	63	205	9,266.66
Richard Sterne	71	68	66	205	9,266.66
Sean Pappas	72	67	66	205	9,266.66
Dean van Staden	71	68	67	206	5,000
Lindani Ndwandwe	67	71	68	206	5,000
Titch Moore	67	71	68	206	5,000
Jaco Van Zyl	69	68	69	206	5,000
Bradford Vaughan	67	73	67	207	3,506.66
Don Gammon	67	71	69	207	3,506.66
Mark Murless	69	69	69	207	3,506.66
Jason Vaughan	69	68	70	207	3,506.66
Leonard Loxton	69	66	72	207	3,506.66
Grant Muller	70	65	72	207	3,506.66
Sean Farrell	71	71	66	208	2,753.33
Richard Fulford	71	69	68	208	2,753.33
Sean Ludgater	73	67	68	208	2,753.33
Ryan Reid	69	70	69	208	2,753.33
Thabang Simon	69	70	69	208	2,753.33
Andre Cruse	69	68	71	208	2,753.33
Wallie Coetsee	73	69	67	209	2,280
Ulrich van den Berg	70	70	69	209	2,280
Wayne Bradley	68	71	70	209	2,280
Chris Williams	72	66	71	209	2,280
Martin Maritz	70	73	67	210	2,006.66
Henk Alberts	72	68	70	210	2,006.66
Nicholas Lawrence	68	69	73	210	2,006.66
Alan Michell	71	70	70	211	1,820
Wilhelm Winsnes	68	72	71	211	1,820
Rudy Whitfield	66	73	72	211	1,820

Atlantic Beach Classic

Atlantic Beach Golf & Country Estate,
Cape Town, South Africa
Par 36-37–73; 6,687 yards

October 10-12
purse, R200,000

	SCORES			TOTAL	MONEY
James Kingston	72	69	72	213	R31,400
Wallie Coetsee	72	71	77	220	19,500
Justin Hobday	75	68	77	220	19,500
Andre Cruse	78	72	72	222	11,800
Nicholas Lawrence	76	70	77	223	7,333
Alan McLean	76	70	77	223	7,333
Chris Williams	76	70	77	223	7,333
Ian Kennedy	74	75	76	225	4,666
Ryan Reid	78	71	76	225	4,666
Lindani Ndwandwe	78	69	78	225	4,666
Ulrich van den Berg	78	75	73	226	3,437
Michael Green	76	75	75	226	3,437
Ben Fouchee	76	73	77	226	3,437
Alan Michell	76	71	79	226	3,437
Sammy Daniels	75	71	80	226	3,437
Shane Pringle	74	69	83	226	3,437
Keith Horne	70	73	83	226	3,437
Gerry Coetzee	75	73	79	227	2,850
Schalk van der Merwe	71	75	81	227	2,850
Sean Ludgater	79	71	78	228	2,600
David Owen	75	72	81	228	2,600
Teddy Webber	76	70	82	228	2,600
Adilson da Silva	79	74	76	229	2,360
Brett Liddle	79	71	79	229	2,360
Steve van Vuuren	80	72	78	230	2,084
Vaughn Groenewald	75	73	82	230	2,084
Mike Lamb	74	74	82	230	2,084
Wayne Bradley	76	71	83	230	2,084
Andrew Rose	76	71	83	230	2,084
Bobby Lincoln	79	72	80	231	1,880

Western Cape Classic

Rondebosch Golf Club, Cape Town, South Africa
Par 36-36–72; 6,633 yards

October 18-20
purse, R200,000

	SCORES			TOTAL	MONEY
Lindani Ndwandwe	66	70	71	207	R31,400
Richard Kaplan	66	72	70	208	23,000
Keith Horne	70	72	69	211	12,266
Clinton Whitelaw	71	70	70	211	12,266
Gerry Coetzee	66	73	72	211	12,266
Alan Michell	69	73	71	213	6,500
Alan McLean	71	68	74	213	6,500
Brett Liddle	63	77	74	214	5,200
Bobby Lincoln	72	73	70	215	4,400
Callie Swart	70	70	75	215	4,400
Don Gammon	73	73	70	216	3,437
Ryan Reid	73	72	71	216	3,437
Gary Birch, Jr.	70	74	72	216	3,437
Wallie Coetsee	74	70	72	216	3,437

	SCORES			TOTAL	MONEY
Sean Ludgater	74	70	72	216	3,437
Wilhelm Winsnes	70	73	73	216	3,437
Tony Louw	72	71	73	216	3,437
Marc Cayeux	75	71	71	217	2,602
Chris Williams	75	71	71	217	2,602
James du Plessis	72	72	73	217	2,602
Jason Vaughan	72	71	74	217	2,602
Bradley Davison	72	71	74	217	2,602
Steve van Vuuren	72	70	75	217	2,602
Richard Fulford	72	69	76	217	2,602
Patrick O'Brien	69	76	73	218	2,160
Richard Michelmore	72	73	73	218	2,160
Warren Abery	70	71	77	218	2,160
Chris Davison	72	73	74	219	1,910
Bafana Hlophe	71	73	75	219	1,910
Mark Murless	67	76	76	219	1,910
Christiaan Petersson	70	70	79	219	1,910

Vodacom Trophy

Zwartkop Country Club, Centurion, South Africa
Par 36-36–72; 7,226 yards

October 25-27
purse, R200,000

	SCORES			TOTAL	MONEY
Ulrich van den Berg	68	66	64	198	R31,400
Jaco Van Zyl	70	65	65	200	23,000
Gary Birch, Jr.	68	69	64	201	12,266.66
Roger Wessels	69	67	65	201	12,266.66
Martin Maritz	67	69	65	201	12,266.66
Don Gammon	71	66	66	203	7,000
Bradford Vaughan	71	68	65	204	5,266.66
Michael Green	69	68	67	204	5,266.66
Nic Henning	69	67	68	204	5,266.66
Sammy Daniels	71	68	66	205	3,960
Sean Farrell	67	69	69	205	3,960
Chris Williams	66	67	72	205	3,960
Alan McLean	69	68	69	206	3,560
Wallie Coetsee	70	69	68	207	3,266.66
Michiel Bothma	70	67	70	207	3,266.66
Bobby Lincoln	69	66	72	207	3,266.66
Dean Lambert	72	70	66	208	2,753.33
Jaco Olver	73	68	67	208	2,753.33
Ryan Reid	70	70	68	208	2,753.33
Richard Kaplan	71	68	69	208	2,753.33
Justin Hobday	74	63	71	208	2,753.33
Damian Dunford	67	66	75	208	2,753.33
Ian Hutchings	74	67	68	209	2,320
Keith Horne	69	71	69	209	2,320
Hendrik Buhrmann	68	71	70	209	2,320
Ashley Roestoff	74	68	68	210	1,948.57
Andre Cruse	67	74	69	210	1,948.57
Callie Swart	69	71	70	210	1,948.57
David Owen	70	70	70	210	1,948.57
Mark Murless	70	69	71	210	1,948.57
Christiaan Petersson	70	69	71	210	1,948.57
Lindani Ndwandwe	72	66	72	210	1,948.57

Graceland Challenge

Graceland Country Club, Secunda, South Africa
Par 36-36–72; 7,114 yards

November 8-10
purse, R200,000

	SCORES			TOTAL	MONEY
Warren Abery	69	70	66	205	R31,400
Richard Sterne	66	68	74	208	23,000
Justin Hobday	68	70	71	209	16,000
Wayne Bradley	69	73	68	210	10,400
Wallie Coetsee	73	68	69	210	10,400
Ian Palmer	75	70	66	211	6,500
Craig Kamps	69	71	71	211	6,500
Grant Muller	74	71	67	212	4,091.42
Jaco Olver	70	73	69	212	4,091.42
Nico van Rensburg	71	71	70	212	4,091.42
Bobby Lincoln	68	72	72	212	4,091.42
Andre Cruse	67	73	72	212	4,091.42
Michiel Bothma	67	73	72	212	4,091.42
Adilson da Silva	67	70	75	212	4,091.42
Graeme van der Nest	71	71	71	213	3,260
Sammy Daniels	71	72	71	214	3,020
David Owen	70	72	72	214	3,020
Bradford Vaughan	68	72	74	214	3,020
Nic Henning	74	71	70	215	2,422.22
Andy Bean	72	73	70	215	2,422.22
Andrew Rose	70	75	70	215	2,422.22
Alan Michell	72	72	71	215	2,422.22
Gary Birch, Jr.	76	68	71	215	2,422.22
Marc Cayeux	74	69	72	215	2,422.22
Dean Lambert	71	71	73	215	2,422.22
Richard Fulford	73	69	73	215	2,422.22
Jesper Nielsen	67	70	78	215	2,422.22
Darren Fichardt	74	70	72	216	1,970
Bradley Davison	69	75	72	216	1,970
Nicholas Lawrence	70	75	72	217	1,790
Leonard Loxton	73	70	74	217	1,790
Thabang Simon	70	72	75	217	1,790
Joachim Backstrom	74	68	75	217	1,790

Hassan II Trophy

Dar-es-Salam Golf Club, Red Course, Rabat, Morocco
Par 36-37–73; 7,300 yards

November 8-11
purse, US$354,600

	SCORES				TOTAL	MONEY
Joakim Haeggman	67	70	75	72	284	US$80,000
Santiago Luna	71	73	67	74	285	34,000
Mark Roe	71	69	71	74	285	34,000
Olivier Edmond	73	69	72	72	286	19,500
Jean Van de Velde	69	71	75	71	286	19,500
Carl Suneson	73	71	72	71	287	16,000
Marc Farry	73	73	73	71	290	14,500
Christophe Pottier	72	72	72	74	290	14,500
Henrik Nystrom	69	74	73	75	291	13,000
Gustavo Rojas	68	76	74	75	293	11,000
Roger Chapman	72	74	74	73	293	11,000
Peter Hedblom	72	79	70	72	293	11,000

	SCORES			TOTAL	MONEY
Ignacio Garrido	77	76	71	70	294	9,500
Jorge Berendt	72	75	76	72	295	9,000
Younes El Hassani	77	71	73	77	298	8,600
Ronan Rafferty	78	74	74	74	300	8,500
Amine Joudar	72	81	73	76	302	8,400
Billy Casper	74	74	78	77	303	8,300
X. Barrazza	78	74	76	79	307	8,200
D. Dupin	76	77	82	75	310	8,100
R. El Hali	76	81	80	79	316	8,000

Platinum Classic

Mooinooi Golf Club, Rustenburg, Namibia
Par 36-36–72; 6,797 yards

November 16-18
purse, R440,000

	SCORES			TOTAL	MONEY
Roger Wessels	68	69	64	201	R69,520
Des Terblanche	68	65	72	205	50,600
Richard Sterne	73	69	65	207	26,026
Marc Cayeux	70	69	68	207	26,026
Dean Lambert	73	70	66	209	15,576
Darren Fichardt	68	73	68	209	15,576
James Kingston	69	70	70	209	15,576
Josef Fourie	70	71	69	210	9,207
Lee Slattery	70	71	69	210	9,207
Hendrik Buhrmann	73	67	70	210	9,207
Craig Kamps	69	71	70	210	9,207
Chris Williams	71	72	68	211	6,482.66
Thabang Simon	71	71	69	211	6,482.66
Alan McLean	70	72	69	211	6,482.66
Dean van Staden	71	70	70	211	6,482.66
Sammy Daniels	69	70	72	211	6,482.66
James Loughnane	69	69	73	211	6,482.66
Desvonde Botes	69	70	73	212	5,632
Brett Liddle	74	70	69	213	4,909.14
Gary Birch, Jr.	70	74	69	213	4,909.14
Andre Cruse	73	70	70	213	4,909.14
Nicholas Lawrence	72	71	70	213	4,909.14
Graeme van der Nest	72	71	70	213	4,909.14
Nasho Kamungeremu	69	71	73	213	4,909.14
Michiel Bothma	70	70	73	213	4,909.14
Warren Abery	78	67	69	214	4,092
Don Gammon	70	73	71	214	4,092
Ryan Reid	72	71	71	214	4,092
Phillip Sanderson	70	71	73	214	4,092
Gary Thain	75	66	73	214	4,092

CABS/Old Mutual Zimbabwe Open

Chapman Golf Club, Harare, Zimbabwe
Par 36-36–72; 7,198 yards

November 22-25
purse, R1,000,000

	SCORES				TOTAL	MONEY
Darren Fichardt	68	69	69	69	275	R158,500
Bradford Vaughan	72	71	68	67	278	92,050

	SCORES				TOTAL	MONEY
Mark Murless	70	68	71	69	278	92,050
Michael Green	70	70	70	69	279	41,766.66
Jean Hugo	68	69	72	70	279	41,766.66
Nicholas Lawrence	69	71	69	70	279	41,766.66
Sean Farrell	72	68	73	68	281	23,350
Bradley Davison	71	69	72	69	281	23,350
Richard Sterne	72	66	70	73	281	23,350
Andre van Staden	71	68	69	73	281	23,350
Marc Cayeux	67	71	76	68	282	14,725
Josef Fourie	72	73	69	68	282	14,725
Lee Slattery	72	71	70	69	282	14,725
Callie Swart	74	71	68	69	282	14,725
Tyrol Auret	72	74	67	69	282	14,725
Nic Henning	68	73	70	71	282	14,725
Grant Muller	75	68	68	71	282	14,725
Ian Hutchings	69	69	71	73	282	14,725
Steve van Vuuren	69	73	71	70	283	11,700
Naithen Moore	72	72	69	70	283	11,700
Chris Williams	72	72	69	70	283	11,700
Gerry Coetzee	72	69	71	72	284	10,850
Barry Painting	72	71	69	72	284	10,850
Ashley Roestoff	71	72	73	69	285	10,100
Sean Ludgater	71	71	73	70	285	10,100
Warren Abery	72	72	69	72	285	10,100
Wallie Coetsee	75	71	70	70	286	9,350
Brett Liddle	75	71	67	73	286	9,350
Jaco Olver	71	75	69	72	287	8,900
Simon Cooke	70	72	74	72	288	8,100
Leonard Loxton	70	73	73	72	288	8,100
Shane Pringle	68	74	73	73	288	8,100
Simon Hurd	74	73	68	73	288	8,100
Mike Lamb	78	68	68	74	288	8,100
Andre Cruse	76	69	68	75	288	8,100

PriceWaterhouseCoopers Nelson Mandela Invitational

Pecanwood Golf & Country Club, Hartebespoortdam, South Africa   November 24-25
Par 36-36–72; 7,150 yards   purse, R250,000

	SCORES		TOTAL	MONEY
Simon Hobday/Martin Maritz	61	62	123	R250,000
Retief Goosen/Allan Henning	66	62	128	
Solly Sepeng/David Frost	63	65	128	
John Fourie/Roger Wessels	65	64	129	
Gary Player/Rory Sabbatini	66	64	130	
Joe Dlamini/Andrew Coltart	67	65	132	
Tommy Horton/Lindani Ndwandwe	66	66	132	
Gabriel Putsoe/Trevor Immelman	68	65	133	

Nedbank Golf Challenge

Gary Player Country Club, Sun City, South Africa
Par 36-36–72; 7,738 yards

November 29-December 2
purse, US$4,060,000

	SCORES				TOTAL	MONEY
Sergio Garcia	68	71	66	63	268	$2,000,000
Ernie Els	67	66	66	69	268	300,000
(Garcia defeated Els on first playoff hole.)						
Bernhard Langer	68	67	67	69	271	250,000
Mike Weir	68	67	69	68	272	225,000
Lee Westwood	69	65	70	71	275	200,000
Padraig Harrington	70	72	61	73	276	175,000
Nick Price	68	71	70	70	279	160,000
Retief Goosen	68	68	74	71	281	150,000
Thomas Bjorn	71	72	68	70	281	150,000
Colin Montgomerie	68	69	72	73	282	150,000
Darren Clarke	75	68	74	76	293	150,000
Jim Furyk	71	67			DQ	150,000

Vodacom Players Championship

Royal Cape Golf Club, Cape Town, South Africa
Par 36-36–72; 6,693 yards

December 6-9
purse, R2,000,000

	SCORES				TOTAL	MONEY
Ernie Els	70	68	70	65	273	R317,000
Martin Maritz	67	67	73	67	274	137,500
Trevor Immelman	69	69	69	67	274	137,500
Alan McLean	68	64	70	72	274	137,500
Retief Goosen	69	66	67	72	274	137,500
Bradford Vaughan	68	66	71	71	276	64,200
Omar Sandys	66	70	69	71	276	64,200
Darren Fichardt	69	71	65	72	277	48,200
Titch Moore	67	70	69	72	278	40,200
Nic Henning	72	68	64	74	278	40,200
Roger Wessels	74	67	66	72	279	33,200
Stephen Browne	67	70	68	74	279	33,200
Callie Swart	68	69	68	74	279	33,200
Craig Kamps	73	70	72	65	280	27,200
James Kingston	71	72	70	67	280	27,200
Douglas McCabe	73	71	69	67	280	27,200
Jesper Nielsen	72	67	72	69	280	27,200
Des Terblanche	67	66	72	75	280	27,200
Doug McGuigan	70	67	77	67	281	23,050
Craig Lile	67	74	70	70	281	23,050
Brenden Pappas	66	74	70	71	281	23,050
James du Plessis	70	69	68	74	281	23,050
Andrew Rose	71	72	71	68	282	20,500
Ashley Roestoff	70	70	73	69	282	20,500
Gary Birch, Jr.	69	72	71	70	282	20,500
Justin Hobday	71	68	69	74	282	20,500
Dean van Staden	72	70	74	67	283	17,840
David Faught	70	71	74	68	283	17,840
Ulrich van den Berg	70	71	71	71	283	17,840
Deane Pappas	71	67	71	74	283	17,840
Jean Hugo	68	66	73	76	283	17,840

Ernie Els Invitational

Fancourt Golf Club, George, South Africa   December 18-19
Outeniqua Golf Course: Par 36-36–72; 6,911 yards   purse, R263,000
Montagu Golf Course: Par 36-36–72; 5746 yards

	SCORES		TOTAL	MONEY
John Bland	62	63	125	R25,000
Jean Hugo	67	62	129	20,000
Ian Hutchings	66	68	134	13,500
Trevor Immelman	68	66	134	13,500
Chris Davison	65	70	135	11,000
Ernie Els	68	68	136	5,000
Keith Horne	69	68	137	5,000
Titch Moore	70	67	137	5,000
Bradford Vaughan	70	67	137	5,000
Craig Kamps	71	67	138	5,000
Wallie Coetsee	68	70	138	5,000
Bobby Lincoln	69	69	138	5,000
Martin Maritz	65	73	138	5,000
Grant Muller	70	68	138	5,000
Des Terblanche	66	72	138	5,000
Doug McGuigan	68	71	139	5,000
Wayne Bradley	71	69	140	5,000
Hendrik Buhrmann	68	72	140	5,000
Ashley Roestoff	72	68	140	5,000
Schalk van der Merwe	66	74	140	5,000
Sammy Daniels	68	73	141	5,000
Gavin Levenson	68	73	141	5,000
De Wet Basson	69	73	142	5,000
Ian Palmer	69	73	142	5,000
Sean Pappas	74	69	143	5,000
Richard Sterne	70	73	143	5,000
Nico van Rensburg	72	71	143	5,000
Nic Henning	72	72	144	5,000
Richard Kaplan	74	70	144	5,000
Don Gammon	72	73	145	5,000
Lindani Ndwandwe	74	71	145	5,000

Senior Tours

MasterCard Championship

Hualalai Golf Club, Kaupulehu-Kona, Hawaii
Par 36-36–72; 7,053 yards

January 19-21
purse, $1,400,000

	SCORES			TOTAL	MONEY
Larry Nelson	67	64	66	197	$240,000
Jim Thorpe	67	66	65	198	143,000
Ed Dougherty	68	69	65	202	107,000
Bruce Fleisher	66	66	70	202	107,000
Gary McCord	68	70	66	204	71,000
Leonard Thompson	66	68	70	204	71,000
Allen Doyle	69	70	66	205	57,000
Doug Tewell	70	66	70	206	48,000
Tom Watson	68	67	71	206	48,000
Dave Eichelberger	67	70	71	208	39,500
Fred Gibson	64	72	72	208	39,500
Hale Irwin	69	73	68	210	31,625
Tom Kite	68	72	70	210	31,625
Gil Morgan	72	71	67	210	31,625
Dave Stockton	71	72	67	210	31,625
Jim Ahern	71	70	70	211	26,250
Dana Quigley	72	71	68	211	26,250
Tom Jenkins	70	72	70	212	23,250
John Mahaffey	70	69	73	212	23,250
Graham Marsh	74	70	70	214	21,000
Hubert Green	73	71	71	215	19,750
David Graham	69	78	69	216	17,750
John Jacobs	74	74	68	216	17,750
Lee Trevino	70	73	73	216	17,750
Vicente Fernandez	72	74	71	217	15,375
Tom McGinnis	70	76	71	217	15,375
Joe Inman	71	72	75	218	13,750
Jack Nicklaus	76	73	69	218	13,750
Lanny Wadkins	74	69	75	218	13,750
George Archer	77	74	68	219	12,750
Bob Duval	71	76	73	220	12,500
Tom Wargo	74	73	76	223	12,250

Royal Caribbean Classic

Crandon Park Golf Club, Key Biscayne, Florida
Par 35-36–71; 7,167 yards

February 2-4
purse, $1,400,000

	POINTS			TOTAL	MONEY
Larry Nelson	6	15	8	29	$210,000
Isao Aoki	8	9	11	28	123,200
Bob Eastwood	14	0	12	26	92,400
Tom Jenkins	4	8	14	26	92,400
Dana Quigley	5	8	12	25	67,200
Allen Doyle	9	2	13	24	50,400
Tom Kite	8	13	3	24	50,400

	POINTS			TOTAL	MONEY
Doug Tewell	5	4	15	24	50,400
Bob Gilder	7	15	1	23	37,800
Vicente Fernandez	8	7	8	23	37,800
Leonard Thompson	6	13	3	22	32,200
Bruce Fleisher	4	10	8	22	32,200
Terry Mauney	1	10	10	21	26,600
Walter Hall	10	7	4	21	26,600
Andy North	11	2	8	21	26,600
Jim Ahern	5	7	8	20	21,735
Steve Veriato	4	10	6	20	21,735
Ed Dougherty	6	12	2	20	21,735
John Bland	10	4	6	20	21,735
Howard Twitty	1	9	9	19	17,360
Gil Morgan	4	9	6	19	17,360
John Jacobs	7	12	0	19	17,360
Mike McCullough	-1	6	13	18	14,028
David Lundstrom	-2	8	12	18	14,028
Terry Dill	7	8	3	18	14,028
Stewart Ginn	5	8	5	18	14,028
Dave Eichelberger	8	6	4	18	14,028
Jerry McGee	-4	14	7	17	11,900
George Archer	8	6	3	17	11,900
Sammy Rachels	6	6	4	16	10,780
Bobby Walzel	9	2	5	16	10,780
Bob Duval	-1	3	13	15	9,870
Raymond Floyd	1	5	9	15	9,870
Jose Maria Canizares	6	6	2	14	8,610
Hugh Baiocchi	2	12	0	14	8,610
Jim Thorpe	6	11	-3	14	8,610
John Schroeder	2	8	4	14	8,610
Bob Charles	4	7	2	13	7,280
Rex Caldwell	11	1	1	13	7,280
Jim Albus	0	6	7	13	7,280
Ted Goin	7	2	4	13	7,280

ACE Group Classic

Pelican Marsh Golf Club, Naples, Florida
Par 36-36–72; 6,960 yards

February 9-11
purse, $1,400,000

	SCORES			TOTAL	MONEY
Gil Morgan	71	67	66	204	$210,000
Dana Quigley	69	70	67	206	123,200
Stewart Ginn	71	72	66	209	100,800
Tom Kite	72	70	68	210	84,000
Jose Maria Canizares	68	73	70	211	57,866.67
Dave Stockton	74	70	67	211	57,866.67
Allen Doyle	72	69	70	211	57,866.66
Vicente Fernandez	74	71	67	212	36,960
Bruce Fleisher	74	69	69	212	36,960
Larry Nelson	72	69	71	212	36,960
Gary Player	74	71	67	212	36,960
Bobby Walzel	75	66	71	212	36,960
Bob Gilder	73	68	72	213	25,900
Graham Marsh	71	71	71	213	25,900
Bruce Summerhays	70	71	72	213	25,900
Doug Tewell	72	69	72	213	25,900

	SCORES			TOTAL	MONEY
John Bland	70	69	75	214	19,796
Ed Dougherty	74	72	68	214	19,796
Walter Hall	74	72	68	214	19,796
Mike McCullough	69	70	75	214	19,796
Steven Veriato	72	69	73	214	19,796
Terry Dill	71	72	72	215	14,396.67
Raymond Floyd	76	68	71	215	14,396.67
Bob Murphy	74	69	72	215	14,396.67
Sammy Rachels	75	70	70	215	14,396.67
Bob Eastwood	76	67	72	215	14,396.66
Hubert Green	71	71	73	215	14,396.66
George Archer	77	64	75	216	11,340
Jim Colbert	78	68	70	216	11,340
Jim Dent	73	70	73	216	11,340
Tom Watson	73	69	74	216	11,340
Isao Aoki	71	74	72	217	9,870
Tom Wargo	73	72	72	217	9,870
Jim Thorpe	76	71	71	218	7,793.34
Howard Twitty	75	74	69	218	7,793.34
Larry Ziegler	76	73	69	218	7,793.34
Jim Ahern	70	70	78	218	7,793.33
Jim Albus	75	68	75	218	7,793.33
Hugh Baiocchi	70	75	73	218	7,793.33
Joe Inman	73	73	72	218	7,793.33
Tom Jenkins	74	71	73	218	7,793.33
Leonard Thompson	72	70	76	218	7,793.33

Verizon Classic

TPC of Tampa Bay, Lutz, Florida
Par 35-36–71; 6,638 yards

February 16-18
purse, $1,400,000

	SCORES			TOTAL	MONEY
Bob Gilder	70	68	67	205	$210,000
Bruce Fleisher	69	69	70	208	93,800
Raymond Floyd	68	73	67	208	93,800
Gil Morgan	71	67	70	208	93,800
Bobby Walzel	70	68	70	208	93,800
Allen Doyle	69	73	67	209	50,400
Larry Nelson	75	67	67	209	50,400
Christy O'Connor, Jr.	71	69	69	209	50,400
Jose Maria Canizares	70	68	72	210	33,600
Hale Irwin	70	66	74	210	33,600
Tom Jenkins	71	70	69	210	33,600
Dana Quigley	74	65	71	210	33,600
Leonard Thompson	70	69	71	210	33,600
Doug Johnson	72	67	72	211	25,200
Terry Mauney	70	70	71	211	25,200
Tom Wargo	71	69	71	211	25,200
Doug Tewell	67	72	73	212	21,046.67
Tom Watson	73	70	69	212	21,046.67
Mike McCullough	70	69	73	212	21,046.66
Mike Hill	70	71	72	213	16,870
Jack Nicklaus	67	71	75	213	16,870
Dave Stockton	71	71	71	213	16,870
Bruce Summerhays	71	71	71	213	16,870
George Archer	71	72	71	214	14,000

	SCORES			TOTAL	MONEY
Hugh Baiocchi	72	67	75	214	14,000
Steven Veriato	71	71	72	214	14,000
John Bland	71	76	68	215	11,900
John Mahaffey	73	73	69	215	11,900
Walter Morgan	70	72	73	215	11,900
Gary Player	72	70	73	215	11,900
Jim Dent	77	69	71	217	9,450
Dale Douglass	70	79	68	217	9,450
Vicente Fernandez	70	73	74	217	9,450
Walter Hall	73	72	72	217	9,450
Jim Holtgrieve	69	72	76	217	9,450
Steve Stull	70	73	74	217	9,450
Tommy Aaron	74	72	72	218	7,280
Bob Charles	76	70	72	218	7,280
Bob Dickson	72	73	73	218	7,280
Ed Dougherty	75	72	71	218	7,280
Graham Marsh	78	72	68	218	7,280
Lanny Wadkins	77	73	68	218	7,280

Mexico Senior Classic

LaVista Country Club, Puebla, Mexico
Par 36-36–72; 7,091 yards

February 23-25
purse, $1,500,000

	SCORES			TOTAL	MONEY
Mike McCullough	68	68	68	204	$225,000
Jim Colbert	74	62	69	205	120,000
Bob Eastwood	65	71	69	205	120,000
Hugh Baiocchi	68	74	64	206	81,000
Bobby Walzel	66	72	68	206	81,000
Jim Albus	76	66	66	208	57,000
Jose Maria Canizares	72	68	68	208	57,000
Edward Brooks	71	70	68	209	48,000
Ed Dougherty	65	73	72	210	42,000
Jerry Bruner	72	74	65	211	34,500
George Burns	72	70	69	211	34,500
Stewart Ginn	76	67	68	211	34,500
Bruce Summerhays	70	70	71	211	34,500
Walter Hall	68	69	75	212	24,775
Lon Hinkle	72	71	69	212	24,775
Tom Jenkins	72	67	73	212	24,775
John Mahaffey	73	76	63	212	24,775
Walter Morgan	72	70	70	212	24,775
John Schroeder	72	70	70	212	24,775
Bob Charles	71	70	72	213	17,610
Jim Holtgrieve	71	71	71	213	17,610
Jerry McGee	71	75	67	213	17,610
Sammy Rachels	72	71	70	213	17,610
Steve Veriato	69	72	72	213	17,610
Bob Dickson	72	71	71	214	14,300
Bob Murphy	71	70	73	214	14,300
Bob Wynn	72	74	68	214	14,300
Bob Betley	73	73	69	215	11,880
John Bland	75	74	66	215	11,880
Dick Lotz	68	70	77	215	11,880
Graham Marsh	73	71	71	215	11,880
Rod Murray	75	68	72	215	11,880
Bill Brask	73	70	73	216	9,675

	SCORES			TOTAL	MONEY
John Jacobs	74	72	70	216	9,675
Christy O'Connor, Jr.	75	69	72	216	9,675
Michael Zinni	77	70	69	216	9,675
Bobby Cole	72	70	75	217	8,250
Babe Hiskey	70	75	72	217	8,250
Rocky Thompson	75	72	70	217	8,250
Tony Peterson	69	77	72	218	7,350
Paul Reed	75	72	71	218	7,350
Larry Ziegler	73	70	75	218	7,350

Toshiba Senior Classic

Newport Beach Country Club, Newport Beach, California
Par 35-36–71; 6,584 yards

March 2-4
purse, $1,400,000

	SCORES			TOTAL	MONEY
Jose Maria Canizares	65	70	67	202	$210,000
Gil Morgan	68	70	64	202	123,200
(Canizares defeated Morgan on ninth playoff hole.)					
Allen Doyle	68	69	66	203	100,800
John Bland	68	67	69	204	69,066.67
Hale Irwin	67	69	68	204	69,066.67
Dave Stockton	65	70	69	204	69,066.66
Walter Hall	70	69	66	205	47,600
Larry Nelson	70	63	72	205	47,600
Lee Trevino	68	72	66	206	39,200
Tom Kite	69	66	72	207	35,000
Terry Mauney	67	63	77	207	35,000
Jim Ahern	68	71	69	208	26,133.34
Tom Watson	73	68	67	208	26,133.34
Jim Colbert	67	71	70	208	26,133.33
Bruce Fleisher	65	71	72	208	26,133.33
Bob Gilder	65	66	77	208	26,133.33
Dana Quigley	65	71	72	208	26,133.33
Mike McCullough	71	67	71	209	19,145
Sammy Rachels	73	69	67	209	19,145
John Schroeder	68	74	67	209	19,145
Bruce Summerhays	68	71	70	209	19,145
George Archer	68	73	69	210	14,728
Terry Dill	70	71	69	210	14,728
Bob Eastwood	70	71	69	210	14,728
Dave Eichelberger	70	68	72	210	14,728
Gary McCord	70	67	73	210	14,728
Hugh Baiocchi	70	69	72	211	11,620
Bob Charles	72	68	71	211	11,620
Dale Douglass	69	69	73	211	11,620
John Mahaffey	68	72	71	211	11,620
Mike Smith	70	71	70	211	11,620
Ed Dougherty	70	69	73	212	9,240
Vicente Fernandez	71	69	72	212	9,240
Stewart Ginn	69	70	73	212	9,240
Doug Tewell	72	70	70	212	9,240
Tom Wargo	70	72	70	212	9,240
Raymond Floyd	69	69	75	213	7,560
Al Geiberger	71	72	70	213	7,560
Ted Goin	70	70	73	213	7,560
Bobby Walzel	69	74	70	213	7,560

SBC Senior Classic

Valencia Country Club, Valencia, California
Par 36-36–72; 6,575 yards

March 9-11
purse, $1,400,000

	SCORES			TOTAL	MONEY
Jim Colbert	67	67	70	204	$210,000
Jose Maria Canizares	65	70	70	205	123,200
Ed Dougherty	67	72	67	206	84,000
Gary McCord	73	65	68	206	84,000
Larry Nelson	70	64	72	206	84,000
Bob Eastwood	67	71	70	208	50,400
Tom Kite	69	71	68	208	50,400
Walter Morgan	73	71	64	208	50,400
Jim Ahern	68	67	74	209	35,000
Bob Gilder	71	71	67	209	35,000
Stewart Ginn	70	69	70	209	35,000
John Mahaffey	72	72	65	209	35,000
Hugh Baiocchi	69	70	71	210	23,820
Don Bies	70	69	71	210	23,820
Allen Doyle	72	68	70	210	23,820
Hale Irwin	67	72	71	210	23,820
Tom Jenkins	69	71	70	210	23,820
Graham Marsh	69	67	74	210	23,820
Dana Quigley	68	73	69	210	23,820
Lanny Wadkins	70	69	72	211	18,480
Roy Vucinich	74	69	69	212	16,333.34
Gil Morgan	68	74	70	212	16,333.33
Sammy Rachels	73	70	69	212	16,333.33
George Archer	72	73	68	213	13,685
Bob Charles	65	74	74	213	13,685
Bruce Fleisher	67	74	72	213	13,685
John Schroeder	75	69	69	213	13,685
Terry Dill	73	70	71	214	11,620
Dave Eichelberger	76	71	67	214	11,620
Fred Gibson	68	76	70	214	11,620
Mike McCullough	71	72	72	215	10,080
Gary Player	72	72	71	215	10,080
Jim Thorpe	66	75	74	215	10,080
Vicente Fernandez	70	72	74	216	8,428
Jim Holtgrieve	68	76	72	216	8,428
Bob Ralston	71	69	76	216	8,428
Doug Tewell	73	69	74	216	8,428
Leonard Thompson	70	73	73	216	8,428
Bill Brask	74	72	71	217	6,580
Jim Dent	75	72	70	217	6,580
Raymond Floyd	73	73	71	217	6,580
Joe Inman	73	73	71	217	6,580
Mike Smith	74	68	75	217	6,580
Bruce Summerhays	70	74	73	217	6,580
Howard Twitty	71	73	73	217	6,580

Siebel Classic in Silicon Valley

Coyote Creek Golf Club, San Jose, California
Par 36-36–72; 6,927 yards

March 16-18
purse, $1,400,000

	SCORES			TOTAL	MONEY
Hale Irwin	71	70	65	206	$210,000
Allen Doyle	72	70	69	211	112,000
Tom Watson	77	67	67	211	112,000
Jack Nicklaus	68	74	71	213	84,000
Jim Colbert	68	76	70	214	57,866.67
Mike McCullough	75	69	70	214	57,866.67
Sammy Rachels	71	71	72	214	57,866.66
Tom Jenkins	72	70	73	215	42,000
Gary Player	74	71	70	215	42,000
Ed Dougherty	76	72	68	216	31,080
Mark Hayes	72	70	74	216	31,080
Graham Marsh	74	70	72	216	31,080
Andy North	72	74	70	216	31,080
Rocky Thompson	73	71	72	216	31,080
John Bland	72	70	75	217	23,800
Larry Nelson	71	74	72	217	23,800
Bruce Summerhays	72	73	72	217	23,800
Bob Eastwood	74	73	71	218	17,560
Dave Eichelberger	70	78	70	218	17,560
John Mahaffey	69	76	73	218	17,560
Gary McCord	72	77	69	218	17,560
Christy O'Connor, Jr.	72	72	74	218	17,560
Mike Smith	75	70	73	218	17,560
Jim Thorpe	70	76	72	218	17,560
Hugh Baiocchi	76	70	73	219	11,935
Bill Brask	76	70	73	219	11,935
Jose Maria Canizares	77	72	70	219	11,935
Terry Dill	73	76	70	219	11,935
J.C. Snead	66	80	73	219	11,935
Dave Stockton	69	75	75	219	11,935
Leonard Thompson	71	73	75	219	11,935
Tom Wargo	74	71	74	219	11,935
Bruce Fleisher	75	71	74	220	8,820
Ted Goin	75	73	72	220	8,820
Joe Inman	72	77	71	220	8,820
John Jacobs	71	76	73	220	8,820
David Lundstrom	76	71	73	220	8,820
Jesse Patino	70	77	74	221	7,420
John Schroeder	76	71	74	221	7,420
Steven Veriato	74	72	75	221	7,420

Emerald Coast Classic

The Moors Golf Club, Milton, Florida
Par 35-35–70; 6,784 yards

March 23-25
purse, $1,400,000

	SCORES			TOTAL	MONEY
Mike McCullough	67	68	65	200	$210,000
Andy North	67	68	65	200	123,200
(McCullough defeated North on first playoff hole.)					
Jim Ahern	69	64	70	203	100,800
Jose Maria Canizares	68	68	68	204	75,600

	SCORES			TOTAL	MONEY
John Schroeder	65	67	72	204	75,600
Bruce Fleisher	70	66	70	206	43,400
Graham Marsh	72	66	68	206	43,400
Gary McCord	71	68	67	206	43,400
Gil Morgan	71	69	66	206	43,400
Larry Nelson	69	67	70	206	43,400
Tom Wargo	68	70	68	206	43,400
Bruce Summerhays	73	65	69	207	29,400
Leonard Thompson	70	67	70	207	29,400
John Bland	71	69	68	208	25,900
Sammy Rachels	69	68	71	208	25,900
Ed Dougherty	70	70	69	209	21,084
Dave Eichelberger	69	69	71	209	21,084
Bob Gilder	69	70	70	209	21,084
Terry Mauney	72	68	69	209	21,084
Jerry McGee	71	68	70	209	21,084
Bob Duval	70	70	70	210	15,166.67
Bob Eastwood	71	69	70	210	15,166.67
John Jacobs	69	72	69	210	15,166.67
Rocky Thompson	71	70	69	210	15,166.67
Bill Brask	71	68	71	210	15,166.66
Mike Smith	66	72	72	210	15,166.66
George Burns	70	71	70	211	11,120
Jim Dent	70	74	67	211	11,120
Walter Hall	68	72	71	211	11,120
Mike Hill	68	71	72	211	11,120
Joe Inman	70	72	69	211	11,120
Gary Player	67	72	72	211	11,120
Jim Thorpe	71	69	71	211	11,120
Allen Doyle	70	73	69	212	8,610
Tom Jenkins	68	72	72	212	8,610
Dana Quigley	70	71	71	212	8,610
Bobby Walzel	67	77	68	212	8,610
Fred Gibson	73	70	70	213	7,560
Lee Trevino	72	70	71	213	7,560
Hugh Baiocchi	71	69	74	214	6,580
Jim Colbert	68	72	74	214	6,580
Kurt Cox	71	70	73	214	6,580
Jim Holtgrieve	73	70	71	214	6,580
Walter Morgan	74	68	72	214	6,580

Liberty Mutual Legends of Golf

World Golf Village, The King & The Bear Course,
St. Augustine, Florida
Par 36-36–72; 7,048 yards
(Shortened to 36 holes — rain.)

March 29-April 1
purse, $1,800,000

	SCORES		TOTAL	MONEY
				(Each)
Jim Colbert/Andy North	59	65	124	$170,000
Bruce Fleisher/David Graham	65	62	127	100,000
Doug Tewell/Leonard Thompson	63	66	129	75,000
Hubert Green/Gil Morgan	65	67	132	38,833.33
Jim Albus/Simon Hobday	65	67	132	38,833.33
John Bland/Graham Marsh	64	68	132	38,833.33
Gibby Gilbert/J.C. Snead	66	67	133	18,375
Jim Thorpe/Bob Gilder	66	67	133	18,375

	SCORES				TOTAL	MONEY (Each)
George Archer/Jim Dent	64	69			133	18,375
Tommy Aaron/Don Bies	62	71			133	18,375
Harold Henning/Chi Chi Rodriguez	68	67			135	13,062.50
Orville Moody/Jimmy Powell	66	69			135	13,062.50
Jack Nicklaus/Arnold Palmer	66	69			135	13,062.50
John Mahaffey/Tom Wargo	63	72			135	13,062.50
Butch Baird/Bobby Nichols	68	68			136	11,000
Mike Hill/Lee Trevino	67	70			137	10,500
Charles Coody/Dale Douglass	69	69			138	10,000
Tony Jacklin/Larry Laoretti	68	71			139	9,500
Al Geiberger/Tom Shaw	68	72			140	9,000
Larry Mowry/Ken Still	72	69			141	8,500
Miller Barber/Jim Ferree	71	71			142	7,750
Bud Allin/Jerry Heard	69	73			142	7,750
Bruce Devlin/Larry Ziegler	70	74			144	7,000
Tommy Jacobs/Bob Toski	72	74			146	6,500
Lee Elder/Doug Sanders	75	72			147	6,000
Johnny Pott/Mason Rudolph	74	74			148	5,250
Calvin Peete	70	78			148	5,250
Gay Brewer/Billy Casper	76	74			150	4,375
Lou Graham/Don Massengale	76	74			150	4,375

The Countrywide Tradition

Golf Club at Desert Mountain, Cochise Course,
Scottsdale, Arizona
Par 36-36–72; 6,961 yards

April 12-15
purse, $1,700,000

	SCORES				TOTAL	MONEY
Doug Tewell	66	67	70	62	265	$255,000
Mike McCullough	67	69	69	69	274	149,600
Hale Irwin	70	68	70	67	275	122,400
Gil Morgan	69	69	73	66	277	102,000
Larry Nelson	72	64	69	75	280	74,800
J.C. Snead	70	71	69	70	280	74,800
John Bland	73	66	71	71	281	54,400
Bruce Fleisher	71	67	72	71	281	54,400
Howard Twitty	73	68	69	71	281	54,400
Allen Doyle	71	66	73	72	282	42,500
Hubert Green	70	69	72	71	282	42,500
Jim Ahern	69	74	66	74	283	33,575
Bill Brask	71	79	65	68	283	33,575
Jose Maria Canizares	69	73	71	70	283	33,575
Walter Hall	72	70	71	70	283	33,575
Terry Dill	68	72	71	73	284	27,200
Raymond Floyd	76	71	68	69	284	27,200
John Jacobs	69	71	70	74	284	27,200
Stewart Ginn	71	70	75	69	285	21,182
Jim Holtgrieve	68	72	72	73	285	21,182
Gary Player	72	72	72	69	285	21,182
Jim Thorpe	69	77	66	73	285	21,182
Tom Wargo	67	69	71	78	285	21,182
Bob Dickson	75	72	70	69	286	16,252
Ed Dougherty	70	70	74	72	286	16,252
Tom Kite	72	72	68	74	286	16,252
Bruce Summerhays	76	70	70	70	286	16,252
Bobby Walzel	71	73	71	71	286	16,252

	SCORES				TOTAL	MONEY
Jim Colbert	72	70	69	76	287	12,852
Vicente Fernandez	76	73	68	70	287	12,852
Bob Gilder	68	73	72	74	287	12,852
Jerry McGee	70	73	70	74	287	12,852
Jack Nicklaus	73	73	70	71	287	12,852
Dave Eichelberger	75	72	67	74	288	10,455
Terry Mauney	77	69	69	73	288	10,455
Andy North	73	73	73	69	288	10,455
Dana Quigley	78	71	66	73	288	10,455
Tom Jenkins	70	70	75	74	289	9,180
DeWitt Weaver	72	73	69	75	289	9,180
Hugh Baiocchi	77	70	73	70	290	8,330
Dale Douglass	70	71	76	73	290	8,330
John Schroeder	70	76	72	72	290	8,330

Las Vegas Senior Classic

TPC at Summerlin, Las Vegas, Nevada   April 20-22
Par 36-36–72; 6,963 yards   purse, $1,400,000

	SCORES			TOTAL	MONEY
Bruce Fleisher	70	68	70	208	$210,000
Jose Maria Canizares	68	73	70	211	86,240
Vicente Fernandez	69	70	72	211	86,240
Walter Hall	72	67	72	211	86,240
Hale Irwin	72	69	70	211	86,240
Doug Tewell	74	66	71	211	86,240
Larry Nelson	69	72	71	212	50,400
Allen Doyle	72	71	70	213	38,500
Tom Jenkins	71	72	70	213	38,500
Jerry McGee	69	67	77	213	38,500
Dave Stockton	73	69	71	213	38,500
Walter Morgan	71	72	71	214	29,400
Howard Twitty	72	67	75	214	29,400
Stewart Ginn	68	75	72	215	25,900
Bruce Summerhays	73	71	71	215	25,900
Dana Quigley	72	71	73	216	21,735
J.C. Snead	71	74	71	216	21,735
Steve Stull	73	71	72	216	21,735
DeWitt Weaver	71	72	73	216	21,735
Terry Dill	74	71	72	217	18,480
Jim Colbert	75	72	71	218	15,925
David Graham	76	67	75	218	15,925
Mark Hayes	74	70	74	218	15,925
Jim Thorpe	71	74	73	218	15,925
Jim Ahern	72	73	74	219	12,200
John Bland	73	76	70	219	12,200
Dale Douglass	75	71	73	219	12,200
Bob Eastwood	74	72	73	219	12,200
John Mahaffey	71	72	76	219	12,200
John Schroeder	74	71	74	219	12,200
Bobby Walzel	71	73	75	219	12,200
Isao Aoki	75	72	73	220	9,030
Hugh Baiocchi	68	75	77	220	9,030
Bob Duval	71	78	71	220	9,030
Gibby Gilbert	73	72	75	220	9,030
John Jacobs	77	75	68	220	9,030

	SCORES			TOTAL	MONEY
Leonard Thompson	73	72	75	220	9,030
Frank Conner	75	70	76	221	7,000
Fred Gibson	75	76	70	221	7,000
Hubert Green	72	74	75	221	7,000
Joe Inman	76	71	74	221	7,000
Mike McCullough	73	72	76	221	7,000
Andy North	73	75	73	221	7,000

Bruno's Memorial Classic

Greystone Golf & Country Club, Hoover, Alabama   April 27-29
Par 36-36–72; 6,992 yards   purse, $1,400,000

	SCORES			TOTAL	MONEY
Hale Irwin	65	65	65	195	$210,000
Stewart Ginn	67	65	67	199	123,200
Allen Doyle	67	66	68	201	92,400
Tom Kite	67	66	68	201	92,400
Gil Morgan	67	63	72	202	67,200
Sammy Rachels	67	68	68	203	56,000
Jim Thorpe	69	67	68	204	50,400
Jim Ahern	66	69	70	205	42,000
Jose Maria Canizares	65	72	68	205	42,000
Graham Marsh	71	67	68	206	35,000
Dave Stockton	71	65	70	206	35,000
Bob Gilder	70	67	70	207	29,400
Joe Inman	69	69	69	207	29,400
Vicente Fernandez	72	69	67	208	25,200
Raymond Floyd	69	71	68	208	25,200
Tom Jenkins	70	71	67	208	25,200
Jim Dent	71	68	70	209	21,700
Lee Trevino	71	70	68	209	21,700
Bob Charles	72	71	67	210	15,773.34
Bruce Fleisher	73	72	65	210	15,773.34
Bruce Summerhays	74	69	67	210	15,773.34
Hugh Baiocchi	70	70	70	210	15,773.33
Jim Colbert	71	66	73	210	15,773.33
Al Geiberger	70	69	71	210	15,773.33
David Graham	69	68	73	210	15,773.33
Bob Murphy	68	70	72	210	15,773.33
Mike Smith	70	70	70	210	15,773.33
Hubert Green	67	70	74	211	11,088
Walter Hall	67	71	73	211	11,088
Mike Hill	70	68	73	211	11,088
Mike McCullough	69	66	76	211	11,088
Dana Quigley	68	71	72	211	11,088
John Bland	70	74	68	212	8,820
David Lundstrom	74	69	69	212	8,820
Jerry McGee	69	72	71	212	8,820
Doug Tewell	72	71	69	212	8,820
Bobby Walzel	71	71	70	212	8,820
George Archer	69	73	71	213	6,580
Don Bies	72	70	71	213	6,580
Dave Eichelberger	74	71	68	213	6,580
John Jacobs	71	72	70	213	6,580
Gene Littler	67	73	73	213	6,580
John Mahaffey	72	68	73	213	6,580

	SCORES			TOTAL	MONEY
Dick Mast	72	74	67	213	6,580
Terry Mauney	69	71	73	213	6,580
Jimmy Powell	69	73	71	213	6,580

Home Depot Invitational

TPC at Piper Glen, Charlotte, North Carolina   May 4-6
Par 36-36–72; 6,820 yards   purse, $1,300,000

	SCORES			TOTAL	MONEY
Bruce Fleisher	66	67	68	201	$195,000
John Bland	68	70	66	204	114,400
Jim Colbert	64	68	73	205	78,000
Larry Nelson	71	68	66	205	78,000
Jim Thorpe	69	70	66	205	78,000
Allen Doyle	68	68	70	206	49,400
Joe Inman	68	65	73	206	49,400
Walter Hall	72	65	70	207	39,000
Dana Quigley	71	69	67	207	39,000
Bob Gilder	69	70	69	208	27,114.29
David Lundstrom	73	65	70	208	27,114.29
Graham Marsh	68	71	69	208	27,114.29
J.C. Snead	69	67	72	208	27,114.29
Mike Hill	69	66	73	208	27,114.28
Sammy Rachels	71	65	72	208	27,114.28
Rocky Thompson	68	67	73	208	27,114.28
Jim Ahern	69	69	71	209	17,831.67
Don Bies	71	67	71	209	17,831.67
Vicente Fernandez	68	70	71	209	17,831.67
Doug Tewell	68	71	70	209	17,831.67
Tom Jenkins	69	67	73	209	17,831.66
Howard Twitty	69	68	72	209	17,831.66
Gary McCord	67	71	72	210	13,975
Mike Smith	70	71	69	210	13,975
Ed Dougherty	68	71	72	211	12,122.50
Jim Holtgrieve	72	71	68	211	12,122.50
John Schroeder	74	67	70	211	12,122.50
Leonard Thompson	67	72	72	211	12,122.50
Dave Eichelberger	73	71	68	212	10,270
Terry Mauney	72	68	72	212	10,270
Steven Veriato	71	71	70	212	10,270
Gibby Gilbert	75	70	68	213	8,970
Simon Hobday	70	71	72	213	8,970
Walter Morgan	72	69	72	213	8,970
Kurt Cox	73	69	72	214	7,800
Bob Duval	73	73	68	214	7,800
John Jacobs	72	71	71	214	7,800
Bob Charles	73	71	71	215	6,370
Frank Conner	72	74	69	215	6,370
Charles Coody	70	70	75	215	6,370
Mark Hayes	72	69	74	215	6,370
Tom McGinnis	71	69	75	215	6,370
Andy North	71	72	72	215	6,370
Larry Ziegler	68	74	73	215	6,370

Enterprise Rent-A-Car Match Play

Boone Valley Golf Club, Augusta, Missouri
Par 36-36–72; 6,731 yards

May 10-13
purse, $2,000,000

QUALIFYING ROUNDS

Tom Watson	70	66	136	
Hale Irwin	68	68	136	
Dave Stockton	67	69	136	
Bob Charles	72	64	136	
Leonard Thompson	70	68	138	
Bob Gilder	70	69	139	
Jim Thorpe	71	68	139	
Tom Kite	73	66	139	
John Jacobs	72	68	140	
Gil Morgan	67	73	140	
Bruce Summerhays	71	69	140	
Vicente Fernandez	73	67	140	
Ted Goin	74	66	140	
Terry Mauney	75	66	141	
Allen Doyle	73	68	141	
Lanny Wadkins	70	71	141	
Mike Hill	72	69	141	$31,000
Tom Jenkins	69	72	141	31,000
Dave Eichelberger	75	67	142	24,920
Bruce Fleisher	74	68	142	24,920
Babe Hiskey	71	71	142	24,920
Larry Nelson	73	69	142	24,920
J.C. Snead	72	70	142	24,920
Bill Brask	70	73	143	19,120
Jim Dent	74	69	143	19,120
Walter Morgan	73	70	143	19,120
Jesse Patino	71	72	143	19,120
Mike Smith	72	71	143	19,120
Sammy Rachels	73	71	144	14,485.72
Jerry Tucker	70	74	144	14,485.72
Bobby Walzel	75	69	144	14,485.72
Ed Dougherty	71	73	144	14,485.71
Walter Hall	73	71	144	14,485.71
Jerry McGee	72	72	144	14,485.71
Howard Twitty	73	71	144	14,485.71
Frank Conner	72	73	145	10,833.34
DeWitt Weaver	75	70	145	10,833.34
Hugh Baiocchi	71	74	145	10,833.33
Mark Hayes	73	72	145	10,833.33
John Mahaffey	71	74	145	10,833.33
Dana Quigley	72	73	145	10,833.33

THIRD ROUND

Hale Irwin defeated Lanny Wadkins, 4 and 3.
Gil Morgan defeated Tom Kite, 19 holes.
Ted Goin defeated Bob Charles, 23 holes.
Leonard Thompson defeated John Jacobs, 3 and 2.
Terry Mauney defeated Dave Stockton, 1 up.
Vicente Fernandez defeated Jim Thorpe, 1 up.
Allen Doyle defeated Tom Watson, 20 holes.
Bob Gilder defeated Bruce Summerhays, 1 up.

(Each losing player received $43,500.)

QUARTER-FINALS

Irwin defeated Morgan, 5 and 4.
Thompson defeated Goin, 19 holes.
Fernandez defeated Mauney, 2 up.
Gilder defeated Doyle, 2 and 1.

(Each losing player received $78,000.)

SEMI-FINALS

Thompson defeated Irwin, 4 and 3.
Fernandez defeated Gilder, 6 and 5.

PLAYOFF FOR THIRD-FOURTH PLACE

Irwin defeated Gilder.

(Irwin received $144,000; Gilder received $120,000.)

FINAL

Thompson defeated Fernandez, 1 up.

(Thompson received $300,000; Fernandez received $176,000.)

TD Waterhouse Championship

Tiffany Greens Golf Club, Kansas City, Missouri
Par 36-36–72; 6,888 yards

May 18-20
purse, $1,500,000

	SCORES			TOTAL	MONEY
Ed Dougherty	62	66	66	194	$225,000
Hugh Baiocchi	66	67	69	202	110,000
Walter Morgan	68	70	64	202	110,000
Dana Quigley	65	68	69	202	110,000
Dave Eichelberger	67	68	68	203	72,000
Joe Inman	71	64	70	205	54,000
Dick Mast	70	66	69	205	54,000
Bruce Summerhays	67	68	70	205	54,000
Bob Gilder	66	70	70	206	39,000
Walter Hall	68	68	70	206	39,000
Gil Morgan	69	71	66	206	39,000
Bob Eastwood	68	68	71	207	30,500
Jim Thorpe	68	73	66	207	30,500
Yoshitaka Yamamoto	72	66	69	207	30,500
Jim Dent	68	67	73	208	23,325
Ted Goin	64	72	72	208	23,325
Doug Johnson	70	68	70	208	23,325
Graham Marsh	67	68	73	208	23,325
Sammy Rachels	66	68	74	208	23,325
Roy Vucinich	70	68	70	208	23,325
Isao Aoki	70	69	70	209	16,650
Stewart Ginn	70	67	72	209	16,650
Tom Jenkins	68	68	73	209	16,650
Jesse Patino	69	71	69	209	16,650
Doug Tewell	69	69	71	209	16,650
Allen Doyle	71	68	71	210	12,750
Hale Irwin	73	69	68	210	12,750

	SCORES			TOTAL	MONEY
Mike McCullough	69	68	73	210	12,750
Lee Trevino	71	70	69	210	12,750
Howard Twitty	72	66	72	210	12,750
Larry Ziegler	67	72	71	210	12,750
Bill Brask	70	68	73	211	9,675
George Burns	71	73	67	211	9,675
Jim Colbert	71	71	69	211	9,675
Vicente Fernandez	65	77	69	211	9,675
John Jacobs	71	70	70	211	9,675
Andy North	69	75	67	211	9,675
Rex Caldwell	67	72	73	212	7,500
Bobby Cole	71	70	71	212	7,500
Barry Jaeckel	70	71	71	212	7,500
David Lundstrom	71	71	70	212	7,500
Rocky Thompson	67	72	73	212	7,500
Tom Watson	70	74	68	212	7,500

Senior PGA Championship

Ridgewood Country Club, Paramus, New Jersey
Par 36-36–72; 6,904 yards

May 24-27
purse, $2,000,000

	SCORES				TOTAL	MONEY
Tom Watson	72	69	66	67	274	$360,000
Jim Thorpe	67	69	71	68	275	216,000
Bob Gilder	68	69	70	70	277	136,000
Allen Doyle	70	70	68	70	278	96,000
Stewart Ginn	73	68	71	69	281	71,000
Hale Irwin	69	75	71	66	281	71,000
Bruce Fleisher	70	69	72	71	282	62,000
Gary Player	70	73	71	69	283	56,000
Doug Tewell	70	75	69	69	283	56,000
Walter Hall	73	73	69	69	284	48,000
Bruce Summerhays	73	69	75	67	284	48,000
Jack Nicklaus	68	75	71	71	285	42,000
Bob Murphy	71	72	73	70	286	37,500
Howard Twitty	71	70	73	72	286	37,500
Dana Quigley	70	71	75	71	287	33,000
Lanny Wadkins	73	75	71	68	287	33,000
John Bland	74	73	70	71	288	28,000
Terry Dill	73	73	71	71	288	28,000
Seiji Ebihara	74	71	74	69	288	28,000
Isao Aoki	71	76	73	69	289	22,000
Joe Inman	74	74	67	74	289	22,000
Tom Wargo	71	75	72	71	289	22,000
Mark Hayes	72	76	73	69	290	17,500
Tom Kite	72	77	71	70	290	17,500
Vicente Fernandez	71	74	73	73	291	15,500
Fred Gibson	73	74	71	73	291	15,500
Frank Conner	71	74	71	76	292	12,000
Rodger Davis	75	73	74	70	292	12,000
Dale Douglass	71	75	74	72	292	12,000
John Grace	72	74	73	73	292	12,000
Hubert Green	73	75	72	72	292	12,000
Doug Johnson	69	79	74	70	292	12,000
Graham Marsh	76	74	71	71	292	12,000
Walter Morgan	71	75	74	72	292	12,000

	SCORES				TOTAL	MONEY
Larry Nelson	68	76	76	72	292	12,000
Jim Colbert	69	78	76	70	293	8,825
Jim Dent	71	76	71	75	293	8,825
Tom Jenkins	75	75	73	70	293	8,825
Roy Vucinich	71	77	75	70	293	8,825
Jim Ahern	74	75	74	71	294	6,600
Hugh Baiocchi	74	72	76	72	294	6,600
Bill Brask	72	71	78	73	294	6,600
Ed Brooks	70	77	71	76	294	6,600
Dave Eichelberger	75	72	77	70	294	6,600
Raymond Floyd	79	70	74	71	294	6,600
John Jacobs	72	75	74	73	294	6,600
John Schroeder	74	73	74	73	294	6,600
Steve Stull	74	75	72	73	294	6,600

BellSouth Senior Classic at Opryland

Springhouse Golf Club, Nashville, Tennessee
Par 36-36–72; 6,783 yards

June 1-3
purse, $1,600,000

	SCORES			TOTAL	MONEY
Sammy Rachels	66	70	63	199	$240,000
Hale Irwin	69	68	66	203	140,800
Bruce Fleisher	71	67	66	204	105,600
Tom Kite	67	71	66	204	105,600
Allen Doyle	66	71	68	205	70,400
Gil Morgan	72	69	64	205	70,400
Dana Quigley	68	69	70	207	54,400
Leonard Thompson	70	66	71	207	54,400
Jim Ahern	68	73	68	209	38,400
Jose Maria Canizares	68	71	70	209	38,400
Mike Hill	69	68	72	209	38,400
Terry Mauney	67	70	72	209	38,400
Howard Twitty	67	70	72	209	38,400
David Graham	69	69	72	210	29,600
Doug Tewell	69	72	69	210	29,600
Tom Wargo	67	69	75	211	27,200
John Schroeder	69	74	69	212	24,053.34
John Bland	73	70	69	212	24,053.33
Mike Smith	71	69	72	212	24,053.33
Frank Conner	72	68	73	213	18,784
Bob Eastwood	70	74	69	213	18,784
Dave Eichelberger	71	69	73	213	18,784
Tom Jenkins	71	72	70	213	18,784
Andy North	68	69	76	213	18,784
Charles Coody	72	71	71	214	14,266.67
David Lundstrom	73	74	67	214	14,266.67
Larry Nelson	74	75	65	214	14,266.67
Lee Trevino	71	72	71	214	14,266.67
Jim Holtgrieve	74	68	72	214	14,266.66
Dick Mast	71	69	74	214	14,266.66
Isao Aoki	71	73	71	215	11,520
Hugh Baiocchi	72	70	73	215	11,520
Joe Inman	67	74	74	215	11,520
Bob Charles	69	74	73	216	9,080
Rodger Davis	77	68	71	216	9,080
Ed Dougherty	74	69	73	216	9,080

	SCORES			TOTAL	MONEY
Gibby Gilbert	73	72	71	216	9,080
Mark Hayes	72	73	71	216	9,080
John Jacobs	72	71	73	216	9,080
J.C. Snead	70	72	74	216	9,080
Bruce Summerhays	71	73	72	216	9,080

NFL Golf Classic

Upper Montclair Country Club, Clifton, New Jersey   June 8-10
Par 36-36–72; 6,816 yards   purse, $1,200,000

	SCORES			TOTAL	MONEY
John Schroeder	69	70	68	207	$180,000
Allen Doyle	73	66	68	207	105,600
(Schroeder defeated Doyle on second playoff hole.)					
Hugh Baiocchi	71	70	67	208	79,200
Mike Smith	69	70	69	208	79,200
Raymond Floyd	71	69	69	209	52,800
Roy Vucinich	71	67	71	209	52,800
Walter Hall	72	70	68	210	40,800
Terry Mauney	70	70	70	210	40,800
Bruce Summerhays	70	72	69	211	33,600
Jim Colbert	68	73	72	213	27,600
Dave Eichelberger	74	70	69	213	27,600
Jim Holtgrieve	65	72	76	213	27,600
Tom Watson	74	68	71	213	27,600
John Bland	68	72	74	214	20,400
Bob Dickson	71	73	70	214	20,400
Tom Jenkins	75	68	71	214	20,400
Walter Zembriski	74	72	68	214	20,400
Larry Ziegler	69	67	78	214	20,400
Rex Caldwell	73	72	70	215	14,194.29
John Jacobs	74	70	71	215	14,194.29
Sammy Rachels	72	70	73	215	14,194.29
Tom Wargo	71	73	71	215	14,194.29
Jim Albus	72	70	73	215	14,194.28
Ted Goin	68	71	76	215	14,194.28
Tom Shaw	70	69	76	215	14,194.28
Lee Trevino	71	71	74	216	11,400
George Burns	72	72	73	217	9,740
Terry Dill	75	70	72	217	9,740
Terry Florence	71	73	73	217	9,740
Barry Jaeckel	73	71	73	217	9,740
Dave Stockton	71	71	75	217	9,740
Jim Thorpe	75	71	71	217	9,740
Ed Dougherty	73	74	71	218	7,400
Fred Gibson	74	72	72	218	7,400
Hubert Green	79	65	74	218	7,400
Gary McCord	77	72	69	218	7,400
Mike McCullough	72	72	74	218	7,400
Dana Quigley	70	78	70	218	7,400
Bill Brask	72	70	77	219	6,120
Jim Dent	76	73	70	219	6,120
Walter Morgan	74	74	71	219	6,120

Instinet Classic

TPC at Jasna Polana, Princeton, New Jersey
Par 36-36–72; 6,893 yards

June 15-17
purse, $1,500,000

	SCORES			TOTAL	MONEY
Gil Morgan	63	69	69	201	$225,000
Tom Jenkins	65	71	67	203	120,000
J.C. Snead	71	67	65	203	120,000
Jim Thorpe	68	68	68	204	90,000
Kurt Cox	69	69	67	205	72,000
Terry Mauney	67	69	70	206	51,000
Dana Quigley	67	70	69	206	51,000
Doug Tewell	71	67	68	206	51,000
Rocky Thompson	70	67	69	206	51,000
David Lundstrom	67	69	72	208	39,000
John Bland	69	66	74	209	30,900
Bob Charles	67	68	74	209	30,900
Joe Inman	70	71	68	209	30,900
Graham Marsh	70	71	68	209	30,900
Steven Veriato	73	68	68	209	30,900
Mike Hill	68	69	73	210	24,000
Tom McGinnis	72	70	68	210	24,000
Bruce Summerhays	65	72	73	210	24,000
Bob Gilder	68	70	73	211	19,237.50
Walter Hall	71	68	72	211	19,237.50
Sammy Rachels	67	70	74	211	19,237.50
Tom Wargo	69	68	74	211	19,237.50
Hugh Baiocchi	68	69	75	212	14,700
Bruce Fleisher	68	71	73	212	14,700
Al Geiberger	71	70	71	212	14,700
Hubert Green	71	73	68	212	14,700
Mark Hayes	69	72	71	212	14,700
John Jacobs	73	68	71	212	14,700
Jim Albus	71	71	71	213	11,850
Ed Dougherty	71	71	71	213	11,850
Gary McCord	66	76	71	213	11,850
Jim Colbert	74	71	69	214	10,800
Dale Douglass	72	73	70	215	9,250
Tom Elfers	71	74	70	215	9,250
Gibby Gilbert	71	72	72	215	9,250
Jim Holtgrieve	71	73	71	215	9,250
Jesse Patino	75	68	72	215	9,250
Jay Sigel	67	75	73	215	9,250
Terry Dill	70	72	74	216	7,500
Ted Goin	73	69	74	216	7,500
Jerry McGee	74	68	74	216	7,500
Jimmy Powell	66	76	74	216	7,500

FleetBoston Classic

Nashawtuc Country Club, Concord, Massachusetts
Par 36-36–72; 6,787 yards

June 22-24
purse, $1,400,000

	SCORES			TOTAL	MONEY
Larry Nelson	65	69	67	201	$210,000
Bruce Fleisher	71	67	66	204	123,200
Mike Hill	67	66	72	205	92,400

	SCORES			TOTAL	MONEY
Tom Kite	70	68	67	205	92,400
Allen Doyle	66	69	71	206	61,600
Dana Quigley	69	69	68	206	61,600
J.C. Snead	70	68	69	207	44,800
Doug Tewell	70	70	67	207	44,800
Leonard Thompson	70	70	67	207	44,800
Vicente Fernandez	69	69	70	208	33,600
John Mahaffey	70	69	69	208	33,600
Mike McCullough	70	65	73	208	33,600
Isao Aoki	70	70	69	209	24,500
John Bland	71	69	69	209	24,500
Jose Maria Canizares	69	67	73	209	24,500
Walter Hall	70	70	69	209	24,500
Hale Irwin	67	71	71	209	24,500
Jim Thorpe	67	72	70	209	24,500
Dave Eichelberger	67	69	74	210	19,110
Tom Jenkins	69	69	72	210	19,110
Dick Mast	68	70	73	211	16,800
Howard Twitty	70	72	69	211	16,800
Sammy Rachels	72	72	68	212	15,050
Tom Wargo	69	72	71	212	15,050
Hugh Baiocchi	71	72	70	213	13,346.67
Bob Charles	73	69	71	213	13,346.67
Bob Murphy	69	70	74	213	13,346.66
Gibby Gilbert	70	71	73	214	10,850
Tom McGinnis	69	70	75	214	10,850
Andy North	74	70	70	214	10,850
Jesse Patino	69	74	71	214	10,850
Gary Player	72	72	70	214	10,850
Mike Smith	72	69	73	214	10,850
Ed Dougherty	72	72	71	215	9,030
Al Geiberger	75	69	71	215	9,030
Jim Albus	71	72	73	216	6,731.67
Bill Brask	73	70	73	216	6,731.67
Rex Caldwell	74	71	71	216	6,731.67
Jim Colbert	70	72	74	216	6,731.67
Jim Dent	72	71	73	216	6,731.67
Terry Mauney	71	75	70	216	6,731.67
Jerry McGee	74	69	73	216	6,731.67
Dave Stockton	74	75	67	216	6,731.67
Hubert Green	70	70	76	216	6,731.66
Mark Hayes	69	71	76	216	6,731.66
John Jacobs	69	73	74	216	6,731.66
Lee Trevino	73	68	75	216	6,731.66

U.S. Senior Open

Salem Country Club, Peabody, Massachusetts
Par 35-35–70; 6,709 yards

June 28-July 1
purse, $2,400,000

	SCORES				TOTAL	MONEY
Bruce Fleisher	69	71	72	68	280	$430,000
Isao Aoki	71	68	69	73	281	209,799
Gil Morgan	70	70	71	70	281	209,799
Jim Colbert	75	67	67	73	282	96,655
Allen Doyle	78	67	68	69	282	96,655
Jack Nicklaus	71	72	69	70	282	96,655

	SCORES			TOTAL	MONEY
Jim Ahern	72	70	71	71	284	65,735
John Mahaffey	78	69	69	68	284	65,735
Larry Nelson	74	67	68	75	284	65,735
Dave Stockton	73	70	74	67	284	65,735
Bob Gilder	74	69	69	73	285	49,436
Hale Irwin	73	70	69	73	285	49,436
Dana Quigley	71	70	70	74	285	49,436
Jay Sigel	77	72	64	72	285	49,436
Tom Kite	73	70	74	69	286	42,416
Raymond Floyd	72	70	73	72	287	38,177
Ted Goin	75	70	74	68	287	38,177
Tom Watson	74	73	70	70	287	38,177
Walter Hall	71	74	70	73	288	33,042
Leonard Thompson	72	77	69	70	288	33,042
Ed Brooks	74	72	72	71	289	27,788
Jim Holtgrieve	76	68	73	72	289	27,788
Bruce Summerhays	73	76	68	72	289	27,788
Jim Thorpe	77	65	74	73	289	27,788
Gary McCord	74	70	73	73	290	23,746
Bill Brask	73	74	72	72	291	20,807
Tom Jenkins	76	70	77	68	291	20,807
Tom McGinnis	76	71	71	73	291	20,807
Hugh Baiocchi	75	70	72	75	292	16,717
Terry Florence	77	71	70	74	292	16,717
Hubert Green	73	70	72	77	292	16,717
Wayne McDonald	73	71	73	75	292	16,717
J.C. Snead	76	72	72	72	292	16,717
Jim Barker	72	73	72	76	293	14,033
Jim Dent	76	73	70	74	293	14,033
Fred Gibson	72	75	71	75	293	14,033
Bob Murphy	78	69	73	73	293	14,033
Daniel Nishimoto	73	72	74	74	293	14,033
Doug Tewell	72	74	73	74	293	14,033
John Jacobs	74	71	76	73	294	11,891
Graham Marsh	72	75	74	73	294	11,891
Jack Sommers	74	75	74	71	294	11,891
*Paul Simson	74	74	73	73	294	

Farmers Charity Classic

Egypt Valley Country Club, Ada, Michigan
Par 36-36–72; 6,960 yards

July 6-8
purse, $1,400,000

	SCORES			TOTAL	MONEY
Larry Nelson	67	67	68	202	$210,000
Jim Ahern	70	67	66	203	123,200
Walter Hall	68	69	67	204	92,400
Dana Quigley	68	70	66	204	92,400
Terry Mauney	69	69	68	206	67,200
Bob Gilder	65	69	73	207	56,000
Jose Maria Canizares	69	70	69	208	47,600
Dick Mast	68	71	69	208	47,600
Mike Hill	67	72	70	209	36,400
John Jacobs	69	71	69	209	36,400
Lee Trevino	69	72	68	209	36,400
Jim Holtgrieve	70	67	73	210	27,650
Tom McGinnis	71	69	70	210	27,650

	SCORES				TOTAL	MONEY
Jay Overton	71	68	71		210	27,650
Tom Wargo	72	71	67		210	27,650
Jim Dent	67	72	72		211	22,400
Allen Doyle	70	71	70		211	22,400
Jay Sigel	71	71	69		211	22,400
Bruce Summerhays	72	69	71		212	19,110
Rocky Thompson	70	73	69		212	19,110
Bill Brask	73	72	68		213	15,166.67
Jim Colbert	76	70	67		213	15,166.67
Ed Dougherty	71	71	71		213	15,166.67
Ted Goin	73	69	71		213	15,166.67
Rodger Davis	68	71	74		213	15,166.66
John Schroeder	75	67	71		213	15,166.66
Isao Aoki	74	70	70		214	11,900
Terry Dill	72	72	70		214	11,900
Vicente Fernandez	69	69	76		214	11,900
Harold Henning	69	75	70		214	11,900
Kurt Cox	74	72	69		215	9,047.50
Lon Hinkle	70	74	71		215	9,047.50
Babe Hiskey	74	72	69		215	9,047.50
Mike McCullough	73	71	71		215	9,047.50
Tony Peterson	71	72	72		215	9,047.50
Dave Stockton	72	73	70		215	9,047.50
Jerry Tucker	76	67	72		215	9,047.50
Howard Twitty	69	71	75		215	9,047.50
Danny Edwards	73	73	70		216	7,000
Stewart Ginn	72	74	70		216	7,000
Walter Morgan	72	73	71		216	7,000
Sammy Rachels	74	74	68		216	7,000

Ford Senior Players Championship

TPC of Michigan, Dearborn, Michigan
Par 36-36–72; 6,986 yards

July 12-15
purse, $2,500,000

	SCORES				TOTAL	MONEY
Allen Doyle	67	69	70	67	273	$375,000
Doug Tewell	74	66	67	66	273	220,000
(Doyle defeated Tewell on first playoff hole.)						
Hale Irwin	70	65	75	66	276	180,000
Ed Dougherty	67	70	68	73	278	135,000
Bruce Fleisher	69	69	72	68	278	135,000
Raymond Floyd	67	73	69	70	279	95,000
Mike McCullough	69	73	68	69	279	95,000
Jay Sigel	68	70	70	72	280	75,000
Tom Watson	67	68	72	73	280	75,000
Jim Albus	72	70	72	68	282	60,000
Tom Kite	71	68	71	72	282	60,000
Bobby Walzel	75	74	66	67	282	60,000
Gil Morgan	72	68	69	74	283	50,000
Hugh Baiocchi	71	67	74	72	284	46,250
Gary McCord	74	74	67	69	284	46,250
J.C. Snead	69	74	70	72	285	42,500
Vicente Fernandez	71	69	78	68	286	37,583.34
Isao Aoki	69	69	73	75	286	37,583.33
Joe Inman	72	70	71	73	286	37,583.33
Hubert Green	77	69	73	68	287	31,000

	SCORES				TOTAL	MONEY
Mike Hill	77	72	68	70	287	31,000
John Jacobs	74	68	72	73	287	31,000
Dave Eichelberger	69	73	74	72	288	26,250
Graham Marsh	75	70	70	73	288	26,250
Dana Quigley	72	72	72	72	288	26,250
Jose Maria Canizares	74	70	71	74	289	23,250
Jim Thorpe	75	72	75	67	289	23,250
Jim Ahern	74	73	68	75	290	20,750
Leonard Thompson	74	73	70	73	290	20,750
Tom Wargo	75	72	71	72	290	20,750
Jim Dent	79	71	68	73	291	17,250
Tom Jenkins	73	72	74	72	291	17,250
Bob Murphy	77	73	72	69	291	17,250
Larry Nelson	67	70	78	76	291	17,250
John Schroeder	77	73	71	70	291	17,250
Lee Trevino	72	71	75	74	292	14,625
Steven Veriato	79	71	72	70	292	14,625
George Archer	77	73	70	73	293	13,500
Jim Colbert	77	73	72	71	293	13,500
Roy Vucinich	75	72	72	75	294	12,750

SBC Senior Open

Kemper Lakes Golf Club, Long Grove, Illinois
Par 36-36–72; 6,951 yards
(Event extended to Monday due to darkness.)

July 20-23
purse, $1,400,000

	SCORES			TOTAL	MONEY
Dana Quigley	65	66	69	200	$210,000
Jay Sigel	72	63	70	205	123,200
Ed Dougherty	69	72	66	207	92,400
Tom Kite	70	73	64	207	92,400
Bob Gilder	68	68	72	208	61,600
Hale Irwin	69	68	71	208	61,600
Jim Ahern	69	70	70	209	42,700
Gary McCord	65	73	71	209	42,700
Jimmy Powell	70	71	68	209	42,700
Yoshitaka Yamamoto	70	66	73	209	42,700
Walter Hall	71	65	74	210	32,200
Bobby Walzel	71	66	73	210	32,200
Allen Doyle	71	71	69	211	25,900
Bruce Fleisher	71	70	70	211	25,900
Stewart Ginn	74	68	69	211	25,900
Joe Inman	71	70	70	211	25,900
Jose Maria Canizares	74	67	71	212	19,796
John Mahaffey	69	75	68	212	19,796
John Schroeder	71	71	70	212	19,796
Jim Thorpe	70	69	73	212	19,796
Steve Veriato	69	69	74	212	19,796
Jim Dent	71	70	72	213	15,820
Hubert Green	71	71	71	213	15,820
Bruce Lietzke	74	66	74	214	14,000
David Lundstrom	71	72	71	214	14,000
J.C. Snead	73	68	73	214	14,000
John Bland	70	72	73	215	11,620
Rodger Davis	74	70	71	215	11,620
Fred Gibson	68	75	72	215	11,620

	SCORES			TOTAL	MONEY
Tom Jenkins	72	69	74	215	11,620
Mike Smith	71	73	71	215	11,620
Kurt Cox	69	74	73	216	9,450
Bruce Summerhays	73	71	72	216	9,450
Doug Tewell	75	70	71	216	9,450
Leonard Thompson	71	74	71	216	9,450
John Jacobs	72	72	73	217	8,190
Mike McCullough	79	65	73	217	8,190
Danny Edwards	69	75	74	218	7,140
Dave Eichelberger	71	74	73	218	7,140
Raymond Floyd	69	72	77	218	7,140
Jack Sommers	71	73	74	218	7,140
Howard Twitty	74	72	72	218	7,140

State Farm Senior Classic

Hayfields Country Club, Hunt Valley, Maryland
Par 36-36–72; 6,852 yards

July 27-29
purse, $1,450,000

	SCORES			TOTAL	MONEY
Allen Doyle	73	65	67	205	$217,500
Bruce Fleisher	71	65	69	205	127,600
(Doyle defeated Fleisher on third playoff hole.)					
Jim Thorpe	67	69	70	206	104,400
Mike McCullough	71	68	69	208	87,000
Tom Kite	72	67	70	209	69,600
Jim Ahern	71	68	71	210	52,200
Mike Smith	73	65	72	210	52,200
Bruce Summerhays	73	68	69	210	52,200
Bruce Lietzke	71	71	69	211	40,600
Rex Caldwell	71	70	72	213	33,350
Stewart Ginn	76	67	70	213	33,350
Dick Mast	75	68	70	213	33,350
Dana Quigley	73	70	70	213	33,350
Bob Gilder	69	72	73	214	22,601.88
Terry Mauney	71	71	72	214	22,601.88
Tom McGinnis	70	73	71	214	22,601.88
Jay Overton	71	72	71	214	22,601.88
George Burns	68	71	75	214	22,601.87
Jim Dent	73	68	73	214	22,601.87
Jim Holtgrieve	69	72	73	214	22,601.87
Doug Johnson	66	72	76	214	22,601.87
Hugh Baiocchi	73	69	73	215	15,623.75
Ed Dougherty	72	72	71	215	15,623.75
Joe Inman	73	70	72	215	15,623.75
Roy Vucinich	78	69	68	215	15,623.75
Jose Maria Canizares	68	74	74	216	12,905
Dave Eichelberger	74	69	73	216	12,905
John Jacobs	74	71	71	216	12,905
Bob Murphy	76	70	70	216	12,905
Danny Edwards	70	75	72	217	9,227.28
Fred Gibson	70	75	72	217	9,227.28
Steve Stull	77	70	70	217	9,227.28
Jim Albus	74	71	72	217	9,227.27
Bill Brask	70	69	78	217	9,227.27
Frank Conner	73	70	74	217	9,227.27
Ken Corliss	79	67	71	217	9,227.27

	SCORES			TOTAL	MONEY
Walter Hall	72	69	76	217	9,227.27
Graham Marsh	71	71	75	217	9,227.27
Dwight Nevil	74	71	72	217	9,227.27
Bobby Walzel	71	73	73	217	9,227.27

Lightpath Long Island Classic

Meadow Brook Club, Jericho, New York
Par 36-36–72; 6,842 yards

August 3-5
purse, $1,700,000

	SCORES			TOTAL	MONEY
Bobby Wadkins	65	69	68	202	255,000
Allen Doyle	68	66	69	203	136,000
Larry Nelson	69	65	69	203	136,000
Walter Hall	69	67	68	204	91,800
Jay Sigel	66	64	74	204	91,800
Mike McCullough	69	69	67	205	68,000
Jose Maria Canizares	68	68	70	206	49,640
Dave Eichelberger	70	69	67	206	49,640
Bruce Fleisher	69	69	68	206	49,640
John Jacobs	67	66	73	206	49,640
Jim Thorpe	69	65	72	206	49,640
Joe Inman	65	69	73	207	35,700
Tom Jenkins	70	70	67	207	35,700
Gil Morgan	72	68	68	208	31,450
Steven Veriato	66	70	72	208	31,450
George Archer	69	72	68	209	25,602
John Bland	70	67	72	209	25,602
Bob Eastwood	72	69	68	209	25,602
Walter Morgan	68	74	67	209	25,602
J.C. Snead	65	74	70	209	25,602
John Mahaffey	71	69	70	210	17,995.72
Bruce Summerhays	68	72	70	210	17,995.72
Leonard Thompson	69	71	70	210	17,995.72
Hale Irwin	70	70	70	210	17,995.71
Jesse Patino	67	71	72	210	17,995.71
Bobby Walzel	69	70	71	210	17,995.71
Larry Ziegler	69	69	72	210	17,995.71
Bob Gilder	71	69	71	211	13,464
Stewart Ginn	68	69	74	211	13,464
Andy North	69	70	72	211	13,464
Mike Smith	70	70	71	211	13,464
Yoshitaka Yamamoto	73	68	70	211	13,464
Ed Dougherty	73	70	69	212	10,965
Bobby Heins	70	72	70	212	10,965
David Lundstrom	69	69	74	212	10,965
Howard Twitty	69	71	72	212	10,965
Bill Brask	72	71	70	213	8,840
Jim Colbert	70	68	75	213	8,840
Fred Gibson	70	73	70	213	8,840
Ted Goin	74	69	70	213	8,840
Doug Johnson	72	70	71	213	8,840
Rocky Thompson	73	69	71	213	8,840

3M Championship

TPC of the Twin Cities, Blaine, Minnesota
Par 36-36–72; 6,909 yards

August 10-12
purse, $1,750,000

	SCORES			TOTAL	MONEY
Bruce Lietzke	72	66	69	207	$262,500
Doug Tewell	69	73	67	209	154,000
Jose Maria Canizares	70	66	74	210	96,250
Bruce Fleisher	72	67	71	210	96,250
Hale Irwin	68	68	74	210	96,250
Gil Morgan	72	68	70	210	96,250
Jim Ahern	70	71	70	211	56,000
Tom Jenkins	71	69	71	211	56,000
Bobby Wadkins	71	68	72	211	56,000
Ed Dougherty	70	71	71	212	40,250
Jim Holtgrieve	74	67	71	212	40,250
Tom Kite	70	75	67	212	40,250
Tom Watson	73	70	69	212	40,250
Mike McCullough	66	72	75	213	31,500
Dana Quigley	73	70	70	213	31,500
John Schroeder	71	70	72	213	31,500
Rex Caldwell	69	73	72	214	26,308.34
Jim Dent	70	72	72	214	26,308.33
John Mahaffey	73	69	72	214	26,308.33
Jim Albus	76	70	69	215	21,087.50
Walter Hall	71	74	70	215	21,087.50
Andy North	74	69	72	215	21,087.50
Mike Smith	71	70	74	215	21,087.50
John Bland	73	72	71	216	15,640.63
Terry Dill	76	70	70	216	15,640.63
Bob Eastwood	73	74	69	216	15,640.63
Leonard Thompson	73	73	70	216	15,640.63
Danny Edwards	70	71	75	216	15,640.62
John Jacobs	69	73	74	216	15,640.62
Steven Veriato	72	72	72	216	15,640.62
Larry Ziegler	74	71	71	216	15,640.62
Hugh Baiocchi	74	71	72	217	11,050
Jim Colbert	77	67	73	217	11,050
Ted Goin	70	71	76	217	11,050
Terry Mauney	75	70	72	217	11,050
Bruce Summerhays	75	73	69	217	11,050
Howard Twitty	75	70	72	217	11,050
Bobby Walzel	75	72	70	217	11,050
George Burns	72	75	71	218	8,050
Bob Dickson	71	73	74	218	8,050
Fred Gibson	73	72	73	218	8,050
Joe Inman	72	74	72	218	8,050
Graham Marsh	73	73	72	218	8,050
J.C. Snead	72	73	73	218	8,050
Jim Thorpe	73	73	72	218	8,050
DeWitt Weaver	71	74	73	218	8,050

Novell Utah Showdown

Park Meadows Golf Club, Park City, Utah
Par 36-36–72; 7,167 yards

August 17-19
purse, $1,500,000

	SCORES			TOTAL	MONEY
Steven Veriato	68	68	68	204	$225,000
Tom Jenkins	69	68	68	205	100,500
Bruce Lietzke	65	71	69	205	100,500
Graham Marsh	67	70	68	205	100,500
Jesse Patino	68	70	67	205	100,500
Walter Hall	69	69	68	206	57,000
Bruce Summerhays	67	65	74	206	57,000
Jim Thorpe	71	69	67	207	45,000
Howard Twitty	65	71	71	207	45,000
John Jacobs	64	71	74	209	37,500
Mike Smith	63	70	76	209	37,500
Frank Conner	70	69	71	210	28,000
Bruce Fleisher	68	70	72	210	28,000
Stewart Ginn	68	69	73	210	28,000
Andy North	67	71	72	210	28,000
Jay Overton	73	66	71	210	28,000
Dana Quigley	72	66	72	210	28,000
Vicente Fernandez	70	68	73	211	19,890
Mark Hayes	68	72	71	211	19,890
Terry Mauney	70	68	73	211	19,890
Mike McCullough	69	71	71	211	19,890
Jay Sigel	74	69	68	211	19,890
Ed Dougherty	68	70	74	212	14,700
Dave Eichelberger	74	68	70	212	14,700
Bob Gilder	69	71	72	212	14,700
Jim Holtgrieve	69	72	71	212	14,700
Jerry McGee	73	68	71	212	14,700
Yoshitaka Yamamoto	71	71	70	212	14,700
Hugh Baiocchi	70	71	72	213	10,185
Fred Gibson	69	73	71	213	10,185
Gibby Gilbert	71	72	70	213	10,185
David Lundstrom	69	71	73	213	10,185
John Mahaffey	73	68	72	213	10,185
Gil Morgan	69	73	71	213	10,185
Walter Morgan	73	67	73	213	10,185
J.C. Snead	68	70	75	213	10,185
Dave Stockton	72	67	74	213	10,185
Lee Trevino	73	70	70	213	10,185
Bob Charles	72	72	70	214	7,800
Ted Goin	70	73	71	214	7,800

AT&T Canada Senior Open

Mississauga Golf & Country Club, Mississauga,
Ontario, Canada
Par 36-36–72; 6,850 yards

August 23-26
purse, $1,600,000

	SCORES				TOTAL	MONEY
Walter Hall	68	66	65	70	269	$240,000
Ed Dougherty	66	71	67	65	269	140,800
(Hall defeated Dougherty on first playoff hole.)						
Bruce Fleisher	69	66	67	68	270	115,200

	SCORES				TOTAL	MONEY
Vicente Fernandez	68	69	66	68	271	96,000
Jim Thorpe	63	69	68	72	272	76,800
Tom Kite	66	70	66	71	273	64,000
Danny Edwards	67	69	67	71	274	57,600
Allen Doyle	69	69	67	70	275	48,000
Jesse Patino	69	70	65	71	275	48,000
Ted Goin	70	70	69	67	276	36,800
Hale Irwin	68	72	70	66	276	36,800
Mike McCullough	67	68	69	72	276	36,800
Doug Tewell	70	69	68	69	276	36,800
Bob Charles	70	69	69	69	277	28,000
Graham Marsh	69	68	73	67	277	28,000
Tom McGinnis	66	72	70	69	277	28,000
Dana Quigley	70	69	70	68	277	28,000
Dale Douglass	71	68	71	68	278	22,560
Andy North	70	68	70	70	278	22,560
John Schroeder	76	66	70	66	278	22,560
George Archer	67	70	72	70	279	17,333.34
Bobby Wadkins	70	71	69	69	279	17,333.34
Hugh Baiocchi	69	70	68	72	279	17,333.33
George Burns	72	73	65	69	279	17,333.33
Bob Gilder	71	69	67	72	279	17,333.33
Jim Holtgrieve	67	72	70	70	279	17,333.33
Rex Caldwell	71	74	66	69	280	13,600
Bob Dickson	69	73	68	70	280	13,600
John Jacobs	68	69	70	73	280	13,600
Walter Morgan	70	71	71	68	280	13,600
Tom Jenkins	73	68	67	73	281	11,520
Mike Smith	69	66	72	74	281	11,520
Howard Twitty	67	68	72	74	281	11,520
Ed Brooks	69	70	71	72	282	10,080
Gibby Gilbert	69	69	74	70	282	10,080
Tony Peterson	71	69	71	71	282	10,080
Fred Gibson	70	69	70	74	283	9,120
Jim Colbert	71	69	71	73	284	8,640
Lon Hinkle	75	69	70	70	284	8,640
Don Bies	71	75	68	72	286	7,680
Terry Mauney	71	73	73	69	286	7,680
Tom Shaw	75	74	67	70	286	7,680
Kermit Zarley	71	73	68	74	286	7,680

Kroger Senior Classic

Golf Center at Kings Island, Grizzly Course,
Mason, Ohio
Par 35-35–70; 6,639 yards
(Final round cancelled — rain.)

August 31-September 2
purse, $1,500,000

	SCORES		TOTAL	MONEY
Jim Thorpe	65	65	130	$225,000
Tom Jenkins	67	63	130	132,000
(Thorpe defeated Jenkins on first playoff hole.)				
Dana Quigley	66	66	132	108,000
Hale Irwin	66	68	134	69,000
Don Pooley	68	66	134	69,000
John Schroeder	71	63	134	69,000
Bruce Summerhays	69	65	134	69,000

	SCORES			TOTAL	MONEY
John Bland	70	65		135	43,000
Vicente Fernandez	68	67		135	43,000
Gary McCord	68	67		135	43,000
Jim Colbert	69	67		136	30,000
Ed Dougherty	68	68		136	30,000
Bruce Lietzke	71	65		136	30,000
Graham Marsh	70	66		136	30,000
Larry Nelson	65	71		136	30,000
Sammy Rachels	70	66		136	30,000
Hugh Baiocchi	68	69		137	21,210
Jose Maria Canizares	69	68		137	21,210
Gibby Gilbert	70	67		137	21,210
John Mahaffey	66	71		137	21,210
Bobby Wadkins	70	67		137	21,210
John Jacobs	70	68		138	15,085.72
Gil Morgan	71	67		138	15,085.72
Howard Twitty	70	68		138	15,085.72
Al Geiberger	68	70		138	15,085.71
Dick Mast	70	68		138	15,085.71
Bob Murphy	66	72		138	15,085.71
Jay Overton	68	70		138	15,085.71
Allen Doyle	69	70		139	11,340
Ted Goin	69	70		139	11,340
Hubert Green	69	70		139	11,340
David Lundstrom	68	71		139	11,340
Tom McGinnis	71	68		139	11,340
Terry Mauney	73	67		140	7,719.24
Isao Aoki	69	71		140	7,719.23
Bob Charles	72	68		140	7,719.23
Jim Dent	67	73		140	7,719.23
Dale Douglass	71	69		140	7,719.23
Walter Hall	69	71		140	7,719.23
Mark Hayes	68	72		140	7,719.23
Mike Hill	70	70		140	7,719.23
Mike McCullough	73	67		140	7,719.23
J.C. Snead	71	69		140	7,719.23
Leonard Thompson	72	68		140	7,719.23
Roy Vucinich	68	72		140	7,719.23
Tom Wargo	70	70		140	7,719.23

Allianz Championship

Glen Oak Country Club, West Des Moines, Iowa
Par 35-36–71; 6,786 yards

September 7-9
purse, $1,750,000

	SCORES			TOTAL	MONEY
Jim Thorpe	68	65	66	199	$262,500
Gil Morgan	65	71	65	201	154,000
Bruce Lietzke	69	66	67	202	126,000
Bruce Summerhays	71	67	65	203	86,333.34
Isao Aoki	69	65	69	203	86,333.33
Tom Kite	68	66	69	203	86,333.33
Gary McCord	71	68	65	204	56,000
Dana Quigley	70	69	65	204	56,000
Dave Stockton	68	68	68	204	56,000
Allen Doyle	71	65	69	205	43,750
Don Pooley	72	66	67	205	43,750

	SCORES			TOTAL	MONEY
Stewart Ginn	72	67	67	206	32,666.67
Larry Nelson	73	66	67	206	32,666.67
Jay Sigel	69	72	65	206	32,666.67
Bobby Wadkins	69	71	66	206	32,666.67
John Jacobs	70	67	69	206	32,666.66
Sammy Rachels	72	66	68	206	32,666.66
Ed Dougherty	69	70	68	207	26,250
Vicente Fernandez	68	71	69	208	22,443.75
Fred Gibson	72	67	69	208	22,443.75
Bob Gilder	68	69	71	208	22,443.75
Graham Marsh	70	70	68	208	22,443.75
Hugh Baiocchi	70	68	71	209	17,535
Ted Goin	70	69	70	209	17,535
Tom Jenkins	70	68	71	209	17,535
Leonard Thompson	72	70	67	209	17,535
Bobby Walzel	67	70	72	209	17,535
John Bland	71	71	68	210	14,175
Bruce Fleisher	73	71	66	210	14,175
John Mahaffey	69	72	69	210	14,175
Mike McCullough	68	71	71	210	14,175
Jim Ahern	74	70	67	211	12,337.50
Doug Johnson	70	68	73	211	12,337.50
David Graham	71	72	69	212	10,762.50
Joe Inman	71	70	71	212	10,762.50
Tom McGinnis	71	71	70	212	10,762.50
Andy North	77	69	66	212	10,762.50
James Mason	71	72	70	213	9,275
J.C. Snead	72	74	67	213	9,275
Howard Twitty	70	71	72	213	9,275

SAS Championship

Prestonwood Country Club, Cary, North Carolina
Par 36-36–72; 7,137 yards

September 21-23
purse, $1,600,000

	SCORES			TOTAL	MONEY
Bruce Lietzke	69	66	66	201	$240,000
Allen Doyle	69	69	66	204	128,000
Gary McCord	69	68	67	204	128,000
Doug Tewell	66	72	67	205	86,400
Bobby Wadkins	68	67	70	205	86,400
Bruce Fleisher	67	70	69	206	54,400
Hale Irwin	73	68	65	206	54,400
Larry Nelson	65	71	70	206	54,400
Jay Overton	66	69	71	206	54,400
Bob Gilder	71	69	67	207	40,000
Dana Quigley	70	68	69	207	40,000
Jim Albus	68	71	69	208	30,720
Isao Aoki	66	72	70	208	30,720
John Bland	68	73	67	208	30,720
Jose Maria Canizares	74	66	68	208	30,720
Gil Morgan	71	67	70	208	30,720
John Jacobs	68	71	70	209	22,624
Don Pooley	68	73	68	209	22,624
John Schroeder	72	65	72	209	22,624
Leonard Thompson	71	68	70	209	22,624
Jim Thorpe	73	72	64	209	22,624

	SCORES			TOTAL	MONEY
Jim Colbert	68	71	71	210	16,832
Fred Gibson	73	67	70	210	16,832
Walter Hall	71	74	65	210	16,832
Tom Kite	69	69	72	210	16,832
Tom McGinnis	72	70	68	210	16,832
Vicente Fernandez	73	72	66	211	12,986.67
Graham Marsh	73	72	66	211	12,986.67
Terry Mauney	74	68	69	211	12,986.67
Bruce Summerhays	74	70	67	211	12,986.67
Bob Charles	73	68	70	211	12,986.66
Joe Inman	71	69	71	211	12,986.66
Ed Dougherty	73	70	69	212	10,080
Terry Florence	72	69	71	212	10,080
Ted Goin	72	71	69	212	10,080
Jerry McGee	71	71	70	212	10,080
Dave Stockton	73	73	66	212	10,080
Jim Ahern	72	71	70	213	8,160
Dave Eichelberger	76	65	72	213	8,160
Tom Jenkins	70	72	71	213	8,160
Andy North	68	71	74	213	8,160
Bobby Walzel	71	70	72	213	8,160

Gold Rush Classic

Serrano Country Club, El Dorado Hills, California
Par 36-36–72; 6,776 yards

September 28-30
purse, $1,300,000

	SCORES			TOTAL	MONEY
Tom Kite	65	62	67	194	$195,000
Allen Doyle	65	67	63	195	114,400
Ed Dougherty	67	65	66	198	93,600
Don Pooley	66	68	65	199	64,133.34
Walter Hall	66	67	66	199	64,133.33
Bruce Lietzke	67	65	67	199	64,133.33
Jim Thorpe	68	64	68	200	46,800
Gary McCord	70	64	67	201	41,600
Jim Colbert	68	66	69	203	35,100
Bruce Fleisher	68	68	67	203	35,100
John Jacobs	67	70	67	204	28,600
Dana Quigley	68	70	66	204	28,600
Steven Veriato	66	68	70	204	28,600
Ray Arinno	70	68	67	205	22,100
John Mahaffey	66	68	71	205	22,100
Gil Morgan	68	68	69	205	22,100
Doug Tewell	69	70	66	205	22,100
Leonard Thompson	70	70	65	205	22,100
Hugh Baiocchi	72	70	64	206	16,198
Vicente Fernandez	73	64	69	206	16,198
Stewart Ginn	67	68	71	206	16,198
Dick Mast	68	68	70	206	16,198
John Schroeder	65	70	71	206	16,198
Graham Marsh	71	70	66	207	12,707.50
Mark McCumber	69	69	69	207	12,707.50
Sammy Rachels	67	69	71	207	12,707.50
Rocky Thompson	68	67	72	207	12,707.50
Gibby Gilbert	70	72	66	208	11,050
Jay Sigel	71	69	68	208	11,050

	SCORES			TOTAL	MONEY
Jim Ahern	69	70	70	209	9,386
Bill Brask	70	67	72	209	9,386
Jim Holtgrieve	68	74	67	209	9,386
Walter Morgan	73	68	68	209	9,386
Bobby Walzel	73	70	66	209	9,386
Bob Charles	68	70	72	210	7,637.50
Al Geiberger	73	71	66	210	7,637.50
Ted Goin	71	66	73	210	7,637.50
Terry Mauney	71	69	70	210	7,637.50
Tom Jenkins	69	73	69	211	6,630
Jerry McGee	71	71	69	211	6,630
Bobby Wadkins	70	72	69	211	6,630

Turtle Bay Championship

The Palmer Course at Turtle Bay, Kahuku, Hawaii
Par 36-36–72; 6,795 yards

October 5-7
purse, $1,500,000

	SCORES			TOTAL	MONEY
Hale Irwin	69	68	68	205	$225,000
John Jacobs	68	71	69	208	132,000
Allen Doyle	73	69	68	210	99,000
Terry Mauney	68	75	67	210	99,000
Hubert Green	69	70	72	211	66,000
Mike McCullough	71	73	67	211	66,000
Isao Aoki	69	73	70	212	48,000
Walter Hall	70	72	70	212	48,000
Bruce Summerhays	73	71	68	212	48,000
Jay Sigel	78	70	65	213	39,000
George Archer	69	72	73	214	31,875
Fred Gibson	68	76	70	214	31,875
Don Pooley	69	71	74	214	31,875
Howard Twitty	73	74	67	214	31,875
Hugh Baiocchi	71	73	71	215	22,650
Ed Brooks	72	73	70	215	22,650
Bob Gilder	74	72	69	215	22,650
Stewart Ginn	71	71	73	215	22,650
Dick Mast	69	72	74	215	22,650
Jay Overton	71	71	73	215	22,650
Jim Thorpe	73	71	71	215	22,650
Bob Charles	74	72	70	216	15,425
Danny Edwards	72	73	71	216	15,425
Vicente Fernandez	70	74	72	216	15,425
Ted Goin	73	71	72	216	15,425
John Schroeder	72	70	74	216	15,425
Bobby Walzel	70	72	74	216	15,425
Bill Holstead	71	75	71	217	12,750
Tom McGinnis	80	68	69	217	12,750
Jim Albus	72	73	73	218	10,830
Joe Inman	72	75	71	218	10,830
Walter Morgan	72	75	71	218	10,830
Jesse Patino	73	74	71	218	10,830
Bobby Wadkins	73	73	72	218	10,830
Dick Lotz	77	75	67	219	8,812.50
Graham Marsh	70	76	73	219	8,812.50
Bob Murphy	73	74	72	219	8,812.50
Roy Vucinich	70	74	75	219	8,812.50

	SCORES			TOTAL	MONEY
Dave Eichelberger	76	73	71	220	7,050
Mark Hayes	71	76	73	220	7,050
James Mason	72	75	73	220	7,050
Dick McClean	73	74	73	220	7,050
Dana Quigley	73	75	72	220	7,050
Rocky Thompson	74	75	71	220	7,050
DeWitt Weaver	73	76	71	220	7,050

The Transamerica

Silverado Country Club, South Course, Napa, California October 12-14
Par 35-37–72; 6,640 yards purse, $1,300,000

	SCORES			TOTAL	MONEY
Sammy Rachels	70	63	69	202	$195,000
Raymond Floyd	70	69	64	203	104,000
Doug Tewell	71	66	66	203	104,000
Allen Doyle	67	66	71	204	59,800
Bob Gilder	70	65	69	204	59,800
Hale Irwin	68	71	65	204	59,800
John Mahaffey	71	62	71	204	59,800
Jim Colbert	71	65	69	205	34,320
Bruce Fleisher	73	64	68	205	34,320
Ted Goin	70	64	71	205	34,320
Graham Marsh	73	67	65	205	34,320
Don Pooley	69	68	68	205	34,320
Terry Mauney	69	69	68	206	26,000
Tom Jenkins	68	71	68	207	24,700
Gary McCord	72	69	67	208	22,100
Dave Stockton	73	66	69	208	22,100
Jim Thorpe	70	68	70	208	22,100
Stewart Ginn	73	69	67	209	18,330
Hubert Green	74	66	69	209	18,330
Larry Nelson	72	69	68	209	18,330
Vicente Fernandez	75	68	67	210	14,083.34
Rocky Thompson	69	71	70	210	14,083.34
Jim Ahern	72	68	70	210	14,083.33
Rodger Davis	73	67	70	210	14,083.33
John Schroeder	73	67	70	210	14,083.33
Steven Veriato	73	68	69	210	14,083.33
Jose Maria Canizares	71	68	72	211	11,830
Hugh Baiocchi	72	69	71	212	10,075
Terry Dill	73	69	70	212	10,075
Walter Hall	70	70	72	212	10,075
John Jacobs	73	69	70	212	10,075
Jay Sigel	76	70	66	212	10,075
Leonard Thompson	72	69	71	212	10,075
Bob Murphy	71	68	74	213	8,580
Walter Morgan	71	71	72	214	7,995
Bruce Summerhays	74	70	70	214	7,995
Jim Albus	76	67	72	215	6,890
John Bland	70	69	76	215	6,890
Jim Holtgrieve	71	70	74	215	6,890
Dick Mast	75	71	69	215	6,890
Tom McGinnis	76	68	71	215	6,890

SBC Championship

Dominion Country Club, San Antonio, Texas
Par 36-36–72; 6,813 yards

October 19-21
purse, $1,400,000

	SCORES			TOTAL	MONEY
Larry Nelson	67	69	63	199	$210,000
Bob Gilder	68	67	66	201	112,000
Gary McCord	63	71	67	201	112,000
Doug Tewell	67	68	68	203	84,000
Raymond Floyd	70	69	67	206	57,866.67
Bobby Wadkins	65	72	69	206	57,866.67
Bruce Fleisher	66	69	71	206	57,866.66
Fred Gibson	70	68	69	207	40,133.34
Jim Barker	71	65	71	207	40,133.33
Bob Murphy	68	66	73	207	40,133.33
Allen Doyle	68	70	70	208	28,840
John Jacobs	71	69	68	208	28,840
Tom Jenkins	72	68	68	208	28,840
Bruce Lietzke	67	72	69	208	28,840
Dana Quigley	71	68	69	208	28,840
Hale Irwin	72	70	67	209	20,463.34
Mike Smith	67	75	67	209	20,463.34
Tom Kite	69	70	70	209	20,463.33
Gil Morgan	70	72	67	209	20,463.33
Sammy Rachels	70	72	67	209	20,463.33
Leonard Thompson	71	67	71	209	20,463.33
Jose Maria Canizares	73	68	69	210	15,085
Ed Dougherty	74	69	67	210	15,085
Jim Thorpe	68	72	70	210	15,085
DeWitt Weaver	70	69	71	210	15,085
Jim Albus	69	69	73	211	13,020
Jay Sigel	72	68	71	211	13,020
John Bland	72	70	70	212	11,088
Bob Charles	70	70	72	212	11,088
Graham Marsh	71	70	71	212	11,088
Terry Mauney	68	72	72	212	11,088
Gary Player	72	69	71	212	11,088
George Archer	71	69	73	213	9,030
Vicente Fernandez	72	67	74	213	9,030
Mike Hill	71	73	69	213	9,030
Lanny Wadkins	68	70	75	213	9,030
Terry Dill	68	75	71	214	7,280
Bob Eastwood	71	73	70	214	7,280
Walter Hall	77	64	73	214	7,280
Mike McCullough	73	71	70	214	7,280
Bruce Summerhays	75	69	70	214	7,280
Rocky Thompson	73	69	72	214	7,280

Senior Tour Championship

Gaillardia Golf & Country Club, Oklahoma City, Oklahoma
Par 36-36–72; 7,249 yards

October 25-28
purse, $2,500,000

	SCORES				TOTAL	MONEY
Bob Gilder	67	68	69	73	277	$440,000
Doug Tewell	71	70	68	69	278	254,000
Bruce Lietzke	71	63	69	76	279	213,000

		SCORES			TOTAL	MONEY
Tom Watson	71	66	74	71	282	176,000
Gil Morgan	70	66	72	76	284	128,500
Larry Nelson	75	69	69	71	284	128,500
Walter Hall	74	68	67	76	285	89,000
Hale Irwin	72	68	70	75	285	89,000
Tom Jenkins	70	72	71	72	285	89,000
Tom Kite	68	68	73	76	285	89,000
John Schroeder	72	71	70	73	286	64,333.34
Gary McCord	75	67	69	75	286	64,333.33
Jim Thorpe	72	72	69	73	286	64,333.33
Leonard Thompson	75	71	74	67	287	55,000
Mike McCullough	73	71	67	77	288	52,000
Vicente Fernandez	72	73	69	75	289	47,500
Sammy Rachels	71	75	72	71	289	47,500
John Bland	70	73	71	77	291	40,500
Jose Maria Canizares	70	68	75	78	291	40,500
Bruce Fleisher	70	70	73	78	291	40,500
Bruce Summerhays	69	76	72	76	293	36,000
Jim Ahern	69	75	75	76	295	33,000
Allen Doyle	73	74	72	76	295	33,000
Dana Quigley	74	70	71	81	296	30,000
Jim Colbert	74	71	75	77	297	29,000
Ed Dougherty	74	76	73	76	299	26,500
Terry Mauney	74	75	70	80	299	26,500
Stewart Ginn	73	70	78	80	301	25,000
John Jacobs	77	73	78	77	305	24,500
Hugh Baiocchi	75	77	78	77	307	24,000

Senior Slam

World Golf Village, The Slammer & The Squire Course,   November 10-11
St. Augustine, Florida   purse, $600,000
Par 36-36–72; 6,910 yards

	SCORES		TOTAL	MONEY
Allen Doyle	67	67	134	$300,000
Tom Watson	70	66	136	150,000
Bruce Fleisher	72	65	137	100,000
Doug Tewell	71	67	138	50,000

Hyundai Team Matches

Monarch Beach Golf Links, Dana Point, California   December 8-9
Par 34-36–70; 6,548 yards   purse, $1,200,000

FIRST-ROUND MATCHES

Tom Watson and Andy North defeated Arnold Palmer and Bruce Fleisher, 5 and 3.
Allen Doyle and Dana Quigley defeated Tim Kite and Gary McCord, 5 and 4.

THIRD-PLACE MATCH

Palmer and Fleisher defeated Kite and McCord, 1 up.
(Palmer and Fleisher received $30,000 each; Kite and McCord received $20,000 each.)

CHAMPIONSHIP MATCH

Doyle and Quigley defeated Watson and North, 1 up, 21 holes.
(Doyle and Quigley received $100,000 each; Watson and North received $50,000
each.)

European Seniors Tour

Royal Westmoreland Barbados Open

Royal Westmoreland Golf Club, St. James, Barbados
Par 36-36–72; 6,674 yards

March 29-31
purse, £125,000

	SCORES			TOTAL	MONEY
Priscillo Diniz	64	67	69	200	£21,100
David Creamer	66	67	70	203	14,100
John Morgan	71	67	68	206	9,300
George Burns	67	72	69	208	6,300
Jay Dolan III	68	73	68	209	5,650
Nick Job	67	74	69	210	4,890
Denis O'Sullivan	69	69	72	210	4,890
Alan Tapie	70	73	68	211	4,115
Delroy Cambridge	69	71	71	211	4,115
Noel Ratcliffe	69	71	72	212	3,560
Maurice Bembridge	74	70	69	213	2,684
David Oakley	68	71	74	213	2,684
Jeff Van Wagenen	70	69	74	213	2,684
Bobby Verwey	72	72	69	213	2,684
John Grace	70	71	72	213	2,684
Bill Hardwick	72	70	72	214	1,800
Bob Lendzion	75	69	70	214	1,800
John McTear	69	71	74	214	1,800
Denis Durnian	73	72	70	215	1,436.67
Peter Dawson	73	70	72	215	1,436.67
Jerry Bruner	73	72	70	215	1,436.67
Jay Horton	74	69	73	216	1,280
Brian Huggett	69	75	73	217	1,124
Tommy Price	72	69	76	217	1,124
John Tolhurst	74	70	73	217	1,124
David Good	72	73	72	217	1,124
Tony Peterson	71	71	75	217	1,124
Bernard Gallacher	70	76	72	218	950
Randall Vines	73	73	72	218	950
Kurt Cox	74	68	76	218	950
Alberto Croce	70	76	72	218	950
Jim Rhodes	74	71	73	218	950
Ian Stanley	75	72	71	218	950

Beko Classic

Gloria Golf Resort, Antalya, Turkey
Par 36-36–72; 6,515 yards

May 3-5
purse, US$330,000

	SCORES			TOTAL	MONEY
Noel Ratcliffe	69	73	67	209	£38,280.18
Terry Gale	68	72	70	210	25,527.78
Mike Miller	75	63	73	211	11,856.29
Malcolm Gregson	68	70	73	211	11,856.29
Ian Stanley	70	70	71	211	11,856.29
Barry Andrew Vivian	68	73	70	211	11,856.29
Bob Shearer	67	74	71	212	7,842.92
Bob Lendzion	72	72	68	212	7,842.92
John Grace	73	70	69	212	7,842.92
Jay Horton	71	71	71	213	5,675.39
Bobby Verwey	69	72	72	213	5,675.39
Seiji Ebihara	67	77	69	213	5,675.39
Delroy Cambridge	72	70	71	213	5,675.39
Brian Huggett	71	70	73	214	3,488.73
Bill Hardwick	71	72	71	214	3,488.73
Graham Burroughs	72	70	72	214	3,488.73
Craig Defoy	75	67	72	214	3,488.73
Trevor Downing	72	72	70	214	3,488.73
David Good	73	71	70	214	3,488.73
Maurice Bembridge	74	69	72	215	2,429.85
Peter Dawson	73	71	71	215	2,429.85
Alan Tapie	69	73	73	215	2,429.85
Jim Rhodes	72	72	71	215	2,429.85
Peter Townsend	73	71	72	216	2,075.61
Simon Owen	72	73	71	216	2,075.61
Ray Carrasco	72	75	69	216	2,075.61
Brian Waites	73	70	74	217	1,907.12
David Creamer	68	74	75	217	1,907.12
Bernard Gallacher	69	77	72	218	1,815.21
David Oakley	70	77	71	218	1,815.21

AIB Irish Seniors Open

Powerscourt Golf Club, Dublin, Ireland
Par 36-36–72; 6,589 yards

May 11-13
purse, £197,463

	SCORES			TOTAL	MONEY
Seiji Ebihara	65	71	71	207	£32,897.34
Simon Owen	68	65	75	208	21,938.14
Denis Durnian	71	67	71	209	12,134.10
Bernard Gallacher	69	68	72	209	12,134.10
Neil Coles	69	71	70	210	7,636.88
Alan Tapie	69	72	69	210	7,636.88
Jeff Van Wagenen	70	72	68	210	7,636.88
Delroy Cambridge	67	70	73	210	7,636.88
Peter Dawson	71	70	70	211	5,614.53
Alberto Croce	74	68	69	211	5,614.53
Bob Lendzion	70	73	68	211	5,614.53
David Oakley	70	69	73	212	3,983.81
Jerry Bruner	68	70	74	212	3,983.81
Tommy Price	72	69	71	212	3,983.81
Priscillo Diniz	71	74	67	212	3,983.81

	SCORES			TOTAL	MONEY
Noel Ratcliffe	69	77	67	213	2,234.92
Malcolm Gregson	69	75	69	213	2,234.92
Bill Hardwick	70	70	73	213	2,234.92
Norman Wood	66	73	74	213	2,234.92
Roberto Bernardini	68	73	72	213	2,234.92
John McTear	68	71	74	213	2,234.92
Jay Dolan III	71	70	72	213	2,234.92
David Creamer	73	69	71	213	2,234.92
John Grace	67	72	74	213	2,234.92
John Tolhurst	73	70	70	213	2,234.92
George Burns	68	72	73	213	2,234.92
Terry Gale	72	69	74	215	1,638.95
John Irwin	72	74	69	215	1,638.95
Manuel Ballesteros	71	73	72	216	1,540.21
Tommy Horton	75	71	70	216	1,540.21
John Morgan	71	72	73	216	1,540.21

De Vere PGA Seniors' Championship

De Vere Carden Park, Chester, England
Par 36-36–72; 6,583 yards

May 31-June 3
purse, £200,000

	SCORES				TOTAL	MONEY
Ian Stanley	71	66	68	73	278	£33,320
Maurice Bembridge	65	75	68	72	280	22,220
Barry Vivian	72	71	69	72	284	14,680
Simon Owen	68	69	72	76	285	9,300
Jeff Van Wagenen	75	71	70	69	285	9,300
David Ojala	72	69	72	73	286	8,000
Peter Townsend	71	71	75	70	287	6,826.67
Craig Defoy	70	74	71	72	287	6,826.67
David Good	72	74	71	70	287	6,826.67
Steve Wild	68	74	70	76	288	5,410
Iain Clark	74	69	73	72	288	5,410
Bernard Gallacher	73	71	73	72	289	4,246.67
Jim Farmer	68	72	73	76	289	4,246.67
Bobby Verwey	72	71	73	73	289	4,246.67
Nick Job	68	71	74	77	290	2,884
John Morgan	71	74	73	72	290	2,884
Bill Hardwick	73	72	68	77	290	2,884
Lawrence Farmer	72	70	74	74	290	2,884
Jay Horton	76	69	71	74	290	2,884
Alberto Croce	73	72	75	71	291	2,166.67
Jim Rhodes	72	75	70	74	291	2,166.67
Ross Metherell	70	75	70	76	291	2,166.67
Neil Coles	72	72	73	75	292	1,880
David Huish	72	75	72	73	292	1,880
Denis O'Sullivan	72	71	71	78	292	1,880
Noel Ratcliffe	76	71	72	74	293	1,623.34
Ray Carrasco	72	71	70	80	293	1,623.34
J.R. Delich	69	71	76	77	293	1,623.34
Michael Steadman	67	75	76	75	293	1,623.34
Paul Herbert	77	68	72	76	293	1,623.34
Seiji Ebihara	71	73	70	79	293	1,623.34

Wales Seniors Open

Royal St. David's Golf Club, Harlech, Wales
Par 36-35–71; 6,475 yards

June 8-10
purse, £500,000

	SCORES			TOTAL	MONEY
Denis Durnian	74	65	69	208	£83,300
Jay Horton	71	69	69	209	55,550
Bernard Gallacher	70	67	74	211	36,700
Keith MacDonald	71	72	69	212	23,250
Priscillo Diniz	72	72	68	212	23,250
David Vaughan	71	68	74	213	17,800
Terry Gale	72	68	73	213	17,800
Paul Leonard	68	69	76	213	17,800
John Grace	71	72	70	213	17,800
John Morgan	72	71	71	214	10,735.71
Simon Owen	70	70	74	214	10,735.71
Alan Tapie	76	63	75	214	10,735.71
Alberto Croce	74	69	71	214	10,735.71
Bob Lendzion	69	74	71	214	10,735.71
Jerry Bruner	75	68	71	214	10,735.71
Seiji Ebihara	72	72	70	214	10,735.71
Peter Dawson	71	70	74	215	6,180
Bob Shearer	74	69	72	215	6,180
Ray Carrasco	71	72	72	215	6,180
David Good	75	70	70	215	6,180
Hank Woodrome	71	72	72	215	6,180
Joe McDermott	77	69	70	216	5,025
Gordon MacDonald	68	75	73	216	5,025
Noel Ratcliffe	74	72	71	217	4,437.50
Liam Higgins	72	73	72	217	4,437.50
Jim Rhodes	69	73	75	217	4,437.50
Ian Stanley	70	75	72	217	4,437.50
Neil Coles	73	71	74	218	3,800
David Oakley	73	72	73	218	3,800
Eddie Polland	74	72	72	218	3,800
John McTear	72	74	72	218	3,800
Jeff Van Wagenen	76	69	73	218	3,800
David Creamer	74	71	73	218	3,800
Barry Vivian	77	69	72	218	3,800

Microlease Jersey Seniors Masters

La Moye Golf Club, Jersey
Par 36-36–72; 6,581 yards

June 15-17
purse, £110,000

	SCORES			TOTAL	MONEY
Seiji Ebihara	69	73	71	213	£16,819.11
Denis Durnian	69	70	74	213	9,313.15
Delroy Cambridge	69	71	73	213	9,313.15
(Ebihara defeated Cambridge on first and Durnian on third playoff hole.)					
David Huish	72	73	69	214	4,293.11
Denis O'Sullivan	73	70	71	214	4,293.11
David Good	72	74	68	214	4,293.11
Barry Vivian	69	71	74	214	4,293.11
Neil Coles	71	69	75	215	3,442.56
Maurice Bembridge	72	73	71	216	2,870.48

	SCORES			TOTAL	MONEY
Mike Miller	72	72	72	216	2,870.48
John Grace	69	72	75	216	2,870.48
John Morgan	73	71	73	217	2,256.38
Malcolm Gregson	75	75	67	217	2,256.38
Randall Vines	73	73	72	218	1,817.20
Priscillo Diniz	70	75	73	218	1,817.20
Bernard Gallacher	74	73	72	219	1,198.01
Peter Townsend	75	71	73	219	1,198.01
Simon Owen	69	74	76	219	1,198.01
Terry Gale	75	75	69	219	1,198.01
Alan Tapie	70	77	72	219	1,198.01
Manuel Sanchez	75	72	72	219	1,198.01
Jay Horton	71	76	72	219	1,198.01
Bobby Verwey	71	69	79	219	1,198.01
Raymond Kane	72	75	72	219	1,198.01
Antonio Garrido	76	74	70	220	832.16
Peter Dawson	74	73	73	220	832.16
Bob Shearer	71	75	74	220	832.16
Kenny Stevenson	71	76	73	220	832.16
Craig Defoy	71	73	76	220	832.16
Jim Rhodes	74	74	72	220	832.16
Peter Ward	71	76	73	220	832.16

Palmerston Trophy Berlin

Sporting Club Berlin, Faldo Course, Berlin, Germany
Par 36-36–72; 6,635 yards

June 22-24
purse, £122,766

	SCORES			TOTAL	MONEY
Denis O'Sullivan	71	72	69	212	£21,785.71
Eddie Polland	72	72	72	216	12,107.14
Seiji Ebihara	70	75	71	216	12,107.14
David Good	74	73	70	217	6,500
Ray Carrasco	74	72	72	218	5,073.57
Denis Durnian	72	74	72	218	5,073.57
Bernard Gallacher	71	74	73	218	5,073.57
Bill Hardwick	73	77	68	218	5,073.57
Jerry Bruner	71	75	73	219	4,090.71
Malcolm Gregson	73	74	73	220	3,238.75
John Morgan	74	74	72	220	3,238.75
David Oakley	72	73	75	220	3,238.75
Jeff Van Wagenen	79	69	72	220	3,238.75
Bob Shearer	72	78	71	221	2,360.36
Geoff Parslow	72	72	77	221	2,360.36
Delroy Cambridge	77	69	76	222	1,875.24
Peter Dawson	74	74	74	222	1,875.24
Silvano Locatelli	72	77	73	222	1,875.24
John Irwin	72	73	78	223	1,429.43
John Grace	77	74	72	223	1,429.43
Nick Job	75	75	73	223	1,429.43
Maurice Bembridge	76	74	73	223	1,429.43
Jay Horton	73	75	75	223	1,429.43
Terry Gale	76	72	76	224	1,163.75
Bob Lendzion	76	77	71	224	1,163.75
Alan Tapie	76	73	75	224	1,163.75
Jim Rhodes	75	73	76	224	1,163.75
Hank Woodrome	75	75	75	225	1,023

	SCORES			TOTAL	MONEY
Brad Franks	75	76	74	225	1,023
Simon Owen	74	78	73	225	1,023
Keith MacDonald	74	77	74	225	1,023
Alberto Croce	72	75	78	225	1,023

Lawrence Batley Seniors

Huddersfield Golf Club, West Yorkshire, England
Par 36-35–71; 6,447 yards

June 28-30
purse, £120,000

	SCORES			TOTAL	MONEY
Nick Job	69	72	63	204	£20,000
Denis Durnian	71	71	67	209	13,320
Neil Coles	73	67	70	210	9,050
Ian Stanley	70	73	68	211	6,040
Bob Shearer	74	71	67	212	4,946.66
John McTear	68	75	69	212	4,946.66
Jeff Van Wagenen	71	72	69	212	4,946.66
Maurice Bembridge	66	73	74	213	4,120
Brian Waites	72	71	71	214	3,520
Craig Defoy	70	75	69	214	3,520
Malcolm Gregson	69	72	74	215	2,645
Jim Rhodes	72	71	72	215	2,645
Denis O'Sullivan	70	72	73	215	2,645
David Good	74	71	70	215	2,645
Liam Higgins	72	67	77	216	1,640
Peter Townsend	70	74	72	216	1,640
David Oakley	75	73	68	216	1,640
Alberto Croce	72	72	72	216	1,640
Jay Dolan III	71	68	77	216	1,640
David Creamer	72	73	71	216	1,640
Seiji Ebihara	72	72	72	216	1,640
John Morgan	74	73	70	217	1,220
Jerry Bruner	69	75	73	217	1,220
Antonio Garrido	70	76	72	218	1,110
J.R. Delich	77	69	72	218	1,110
Geoff Parslow	71	73	74	218	1,110
Manuel Sanchez	71	77	71	219	1,010
John Tolhurst	73	73	73	219	1,010
Delroy Cambridge	73	73	73	219	1,010
Bernard Gallacher	74	75	71	220	902
Simon Owen	70	74	76	220	902
Alan Tapie	78	73	69	220	902
David Huish	80	72	68	220	902
Tommy Price	71	74	75	220	902

STC Scandinavian International

Kungsangen Golf Club, Stockholm, Sweden
Par 36-35–71; 6,322 yards

July 13-15
purse, £225,000

	SCORES			TOTAL	MONEY
Denis O'Sullivan	73	67	65	205	£37,485
Maurice Bembridge	70	66	70	206	24,997.50
Mike Miller	72	70	67	209	13,826.25

	SCORES			TOTAL	MONEY
John Morgan	70	72	67	209	13,826.25
Eddie Polland	68	71	71	210	9,787.50
Roberto Bernardini	72	70	70	212	9,000
Bill Hardwick	70	71	72	213	7,680
Ian Stanley	68	71	74	213	7,680
Bob Lendzion	69	72	72	213	7,680
Tommy Horton	71	73	70	214	5,820
Keith MacDonald	71	72	71	214	5,820
Simon Owen	71	71	72	214	5,820
Alan Tapie	67	72	76	215	4,522.50
Manuel Sanchez	75	70	70	215	4,522.50
Bernard Gallacher	70	72	74	216	3,502.50
Paul Leonard	70	75	71	216	3,502.50
Delroy Cambridge	72	70	74	216	3,502.50
Alberto Croce	75	69	73	217	2,760
Bobby Verwey	70	69	78	217	2,760
David Good	69	77	71	217	2,760
Nick Job	74	75	69	218	2,175
Leonard Owens	70	73	75	218	2,175
Peter Dawson	70	75	73	218	2,175
Arnold O'Connor	72	71	75	218	2,175
Craig Defoy	70	71	77	218	2,175
Jerry Bruner	74	72	72	218	2,175
Denis Durnian	74	73	72	219	1,777.50
Bob Shearer	75	70	74	219	1,777.50
Jan Bjornsson	76	70	73	219	1,777.50
Gordon MacDonald	75	70	74	219	1,777.50
Jeff Van Wagenen	71	74	74	219	1,777.50
David Creamer	72	74	73	219	1,777.50

Senior British Open

Royal County Down Golf Club, Northern Ireland

Par 35-36–71; 6,614 yards

July 26-29

purse, £500,000

	SCORES				TOTAL	MONEY
Ian Stanley	70	69	70	69	278	£79,000
Bob Charles	69	69	72	68	278	50,200
(Stanley defeated Charles on first playoff hole.)						
John Morgan	69	70	72	70	281	26,450
Jack Nicklaus	70	72	70	69	281	26,450
Bobby Verwey	74	69	69	72	284	19,500
Brian Huggett	69	71	72	73	285	16,850
Simon Owen	71	69	72	73	285	16,850
Bernard Gallacher	69	71	77	69	286	15,000
Barry Vivian	72	74	72	69	287	12,550
Noel Ratcliffe	70	75	73	69	287	12,550
Dave Stockton	71	71	71	74	287	12,550
David Oakley	70	68	72	78	288	10,300
John Bland	68	69	76	76	289	8,650
Eddie Polland	75	74	70	70	289	8,650
Peter Dawson	73	71	70	76	290	6,600
David Huish	75	71	71	73	290	6,600
Russell Weir	73	67	71	79	290	6,600
Gary Player	72	73	70	76	291	5,300
John Grace	77	70	67	77	291	5,300
David Good	75	74	71	71	291	5,300

	SCORES				TOTAL	MONEY
Nick Job	75	69	71	77	292	4,800
Maurice Bembridge	74	72	74	73	293	4,400
Tommy Price	73	71	72	77	293	4,400
Seiji Ebihara	74	75	71	73	293	4,400
Terry Gale	74	72	72	75	293	4,400
Kenny Stevenson	72	72	76	73	293	4,400
Neil Coles	74	72	73	75	294	3,950
Ray Carrasco	74	76	70	74	294	3,950
Katsunari Takahashi	77	73	68	76	294	3,950
David Creamer	75	74	69	76	294	3,950

De Vere Hotels Seniors Classic

De Vere Slaley Hall, Priestman Course, Hexham, England   August 3-5
Par 36-36–72; 6,730 yards   purse, £150,000

	SCORES			TOTAL	MONEY
Noel Ratcliffe	67	71	67	205	£25,000
Simon Owen	65	70	71	206	13,800
Jerry Bruner	70	67	69	206	13,800
Seiji Ebihara	68	70	69	207	7,500
Denis Durnian	70	68	70	208	6,550
Graham Burroughs	69	69	71	209	6,000
Nick Job	69	72	69	210	5,120
John Irwin	70	71	69	210	5,120
Delroy Cambridge	74	65	71	210	5,120
Denis O'Sullivan	70	71	70	211	3,705
John McTear	74	68	69	211	3,705
John Grace	71	72	68	211	3,705
Barry Vivian	73	70	68	211	3,705
Jim Rhodes	69	72	71	212	2,685
David Good	72	72	68	212	2,685
Maurice Bembridge	73	68	72	213	2,320
Bernard Gallacher	73	70	71	214	1,757.14
Peter Dawson	70	70	74	214	1,757.14
Bob Shearer	73	73	68	214	1,757.14
David Oakley	74	70	70	214	1,757.14
Joe McDermott	72	68	74	214	1,757.14
Ian Stanley	71	70	73	214	1,757.14
Trevor Downing	69	69	76	214	1,757.14
Peter Townsend	72	73	70	215	1,308
Paul Leonard	69	71	75	215	1,308
Eddie Polland	71	72	72	215	1,308
Lawrence Farmer	75	67	73	215	1,308
Tommy Price	70	69	76	215	1,308
Manuel Ballesteros	74	71	71	216	1,140
Antonio Garrido	73	71	72	216	1,140
Bill Hardwick	77	67	72	216	1,140
Barry Sandry	75	67	74	216	1,140
Paul Van Biljon	75	71	70	216	1,140

Bad Ragaz PGA Seniors Open

Bad Ragaz Golf Club, Zurich, Switzerland
Par 35-35–70; 6,232 yards

August 10-12
purse, £125,000

	SCORES			TOTAL	MONEY
David Huish	70	64	64	198	£20,825
David Good	65	67	66	198	13,887.50
(Huish defeated Good on first playoff hole.)					
Bob Lendzion	66	67	67	200	7,681.25
John Irwin	68	70	62	200	7,681.25
Trevor Downing	68	70	63	201	5,218.75
John Grace	67	70	64	201	5,218.75
Malcolm Gregson	68	68	66	202	4,450
Denis O'Sullivan	72	65	65	202	4,450
Bernard Gallacher	67	70	66	203	3,250
Keith MacDonald	69	68	66	203	3,250
Bob Shearer	68	70	65	203	3,250
David Oakley	63	67	73	203	3,250
John McTear	70	69	64	203	3,250
Simon Owen	68	70	66	204	1,972.50
Alberto Croce	71	69	64	204	1,972.50
Priscillo Diniz	68	67	69	204	1,972.50
Barry Vivian	67	69	68	204	1,972.50
Delroy Cambridge	69	69	66	204	1,972.50
Maurice Bembridge	68	71	66	205	1,475
Eddie Polland	69	72	64	205	1,475
Ray Carrasco	70	69	67	206	1,259.38
Ian Stanley	69	68	69	206	1,259.38
John Fourie	68	73	65	206	1,259.38
Bobby Verwey	72	68	66	206	1,259.38
Nick Job	70	67	70	207	1,043.75
John Morgan	65	73	69	207	1,043.75
Liam Higgins	65	69	73	207	1,043.75
Alan Tapie	69	68	70	207	1,043.75
Jeff Van Wagenen	68	69	70	207	1,043.75
David Creamer	68	70	69	207	1,043.75

Energis Senior Masters

Wentworth Club, Edinburgh Course, Surrey, England
Par 36-36–72; 6,690 yards

August 17-19
purse, £225,000

	SCORES			TOTAL	MONEY
David Oakley	68	69	71	208	£37,485
Malcolm Gregson	71	71	69	211	24,997.50
Craig Defoy	72	69	71	212	13,826.25
Hank Woodrome	71	70	71	212	13,826.25
Noel Ratcliffe	68	75	70	213	9,393.75
Simon Owen	72	71	70	213	9,393.75
Tommy Horton	74	72	68	214	7,680
John Morgan	75	66	73	214	7,680
Delroy Cambridge	72	70	72	214	7,680
Renato Campagnoli	74	69	72	215	5,557.50
Bob Lendzion	74	69	72	215	5,557.50
John McTear	69	73	73	215	5,557.50
Barry Vivian	72	72	71	215	5,557.50
David Creamer	71	75	70	216	3,862.50

	SCORES			TOTAL	MONEY
John Grace	72	73	71	216	3,862.50
David Good	70	74	72	216	3,862.50
Rodger Davis	72	72	73	217	3,082.50
Ross Metherell	71	73	73	217	3,082.50
Silvano Locatelli	73	72	73	218	2,452.50
Jim Rhodes	71	72	75	218	2,452.50
David Huish	70	76	72	218	2,452.50
Jerry Bruner	76	70	72	218	2,452.50
John Fourie	70	76	72	218	2,452.50
Manuel Ballesteros	76	70	73	219	1,938.75
Brian Waites	75	67	77	219	1,938.75
Keith MacDonald	71	74	74	219	1,938.75
Bob Shearer	72	74	73	219	1,938.75
Ray Carrasco	79	66	74	219	1,938.75
Terry Gale	70	73	76	219	1,938.75
Eddie Polland	72	75	73	220	1,710
Ian Stanley	74	71	75	220	1,710
Bobby Verwey	74	69	77	220	1,710

Legends in Golf

Crayestein Golf Club, Dordrecht, Netherlands
Par 36-35–71; 6,165 yards

August 24-26
purse, £110,880

	SCORES			TOTAL	MONEY
David Good	69	66	69	204	£16,948.94
Jerry Bruner	66	68	70	204	11,278.17
(Good defeated Bruner on first playoff hole.)					
Delroy Cambridge	69	67	69	205	7,413.18
David Creamer	67	69	70	206	4,986.47
John Irwin	72	67	68	207	4,498.60
David Oakley	70	69	69	208	4,118.43
Maurice Bembridge	71	69	69	209	3,484.83
Mike Miller	69	71	69	209	3,484.83
Keith MacDonald	72	67	70	209	3,484.83
Bill Hardwick	70	70	70	210	2,478.98
Denis O'Sullivan	72	71	67	210	2,478.98
Priscillo Diniz	73	69	68	210	2,478.98
David Ojala	69	72	69	210	2,478.98
Paul Leonard	70	70	71	211	1,731.85
T.R. Jones	68	69	74	211	1,731.85
David Huish	68	71	72	211	1,731.85
Silvano Locatelli	72	69	71	212	1,241.87
Jay Horton	69	67	76	212	1,241.87
Tommy Price	71	75	66	212	1,241.87
Hank Woodrome	68	71	73	212	1,241.87
Barry Vivian	70	73	69	212	1,241.87
Denis Durnian	70	74	69	213	940.27
Peter Townsend	71	72	70	213	940.27
Pat Kaylor	73	70	70	213	940.27
Ross Metherell	71	72	70	213	940.27
Seiji Ebihara	76	68	69	213	940.27
Alberto Croce	70	72	72	214	811.01
Jeff Van Wagenen	72	71	71	214	811.01
Trevor Downing	73	68	73	214	811.01
Jay Dolan	73	71	70	214	811.01

Scottish Seniors Open

Roxburghe Golf Club, Kelso, Scotland
Par 36-36–72; 6,865 yards

August 31-September 2
purse, £150,000

	SCORES			TOTAL	MONEY
David Oakley	65	70	75	210	£24,990
Keith MacDonald	71	67	72	210	16,665
(Oakley defeated MacDonald on second playoff hole.)					
Russell Weir	70	71	70	211	9,217.50
Seiji Ebihara	68	74	69	211	9,217.50
Nick Job	70	71	71	212	5,801.25
John Morgan	69	71	72	212	5,801.25
Jim Rhodes	71	72	69	212	5,801.25
Denis O'Sullivan	68	72	72	212	5,801.25
Rodger Davis	67	71	75	213	4,080
Craig Defoy	70	69	74	213	4,080
John Chillas	73	70	70	213	4,080
Delroy Cambridge	71	72	70	213	4,080
Terry Gale	69	74	71	214	2,860
Ian Stanley	69	73	72	214	2,860
Priscillo Diniz	71	70	73	214	2,860
Tommy Horton	75	72	68	215	1,877.14
Mike Miller	72	72	71	215	1,877.14
Peter Townsend	73	75	67	215	1,877.14
Eddie Polland	71	71	73	215	1,877.14
Lawrence Farmer	73	72	70	215	1,877.14
John Fourie	74	73	68	215	1,877.14
David Good	74	70	71	215	1,877.14
Bernard Gallacher	71	71	74	216	1,410
Tommy Price	69	73	74	216	1,410
John Irwin	68	74	74	216	1,410
Peter Dawson	69	73	75	217	1,265
Alan Tapie	70	74	73	217	1,265
Bill Hardwick	70	76	71	217	1,265
Randall Vines	74	69	75	218	1,170
Jerry Bruner	71	74	73	218	1,170
Jeff Van Wagenen	70	76	72	218	1,170

STC Bovis Lend Lease European Invitational

Woburn Golf & Country Club, Milton Keynes, England
Par 34-38–72; 6,800 yards

September 7-9
purse, £225,000

	SCORES			TOTAL	MONEY
Bob Shearer	70	71	67	208	£37,485
Noel Ratcliffe	69	72	68	209	24,997.50
Bob Charles	71	70	69	210	12,480
Jerry Bruner	72	69	69	210	12,480
Seiji Ebihara	68	72	70	210	12,480
Denis Durnian	74	70	67	211	8,010
John McTear	74	70	67	211	8,010
David Creamer	71	70	70	211	8,010
David Good	68	72	71	211	8,010
Tommy Horton	69	73	70	212	6,345
Rodger Davis	75	69	69	213	5,557.50
Delroy Cambridge	67	72	74	213	5,557.50
Tommy Price	68	74	72	214	4,770

	SCORES			TOTAL	MONEY
Bernard Gallacher	74	72	69	215	4,050
John Morgan	69	75	71	215	4,050
Simon Owen	78	67	71	216	3,099.37
Maurice Bembridge	73	73	70	216	3,099.37
Alan Tapie	73	73	70	216	3,099.37
Roberto Bernardini	72	72	72	216	3,099.37
Nick Job	73	73	71	217	2,437.50
Jan Bjornsson	71	70	76	217	2,437.50
Jim Rhodes	71	73	73	217	2,437.50
Keith MacDonald	75	73	70	218	2,006.25
Russell Weir	70	73	75	218	2,006.25
Peter Townsend	77	68	73	218	2,006.25
Silvano Locatelli	73	76	69	218	2,006.25
Glenn MacDonald	69	75	74	218	2,006.25
John Chillas	70	76	72	218	2,006.25
Manuel Ballesteros	75	73	71	219	1,642.50
Antonio Garrido	70	72	77	219	1,642.50
Malcolm Gregson	71	75	73	219	1,642.50
Kenny Stevenson	73	74	72	219	1,642.50
Ian Stanley	72	74	73	219	1,642.50
Jeff Van Wagenen	75	72	72	219	1,642.50
John Grace	75	70	74	219	1,642.50
Barry Vivian	71	74	74	219	1,642.50

TEMES Seniors Open

Glyfada Golf Club, Athens, Greece
Par 36-36–72; 6,699 yards

September 21-23
purse, £126,000

	SCORES			TOTAL	MONEY
Russell Weir	66	68	68	202	£20,991.60
David Good	68	67	68	203	13,998.60
Delroy Cambridge	69	68	69	206	9,248.40
Peter Dawson	75	65	68	208	6,237
Simon Owen	68	68	73	209	5,481
Bernard Gallacher	73	66	71	210	4,126.50
John Morgan	69	72	69	210	4,126.50
Renato Campagnoli	75	68	67	210	4,126.50
Jim Rhodes	70	70	70	210	4,126.50
Ian Stanley	71	67	72	210	4,126.50
John Chillas	71	70	69	210	4,126.50
Denis Durnian	73	66	72	211	2,424.24
Ian Mosey	72	70	69	211	2,424.24
Peter Townsend	72	64	75	211	2,424.24
Eddie Polland	72	68	71	211	2,424.24
Jerry Bruner	69	72	70	211	2,424.24
Tommy Horton	70	71	71	212	1,557.36
Bill Hardwick	72	71	69	212	1,557.36
Craig Defoy	73	67	72	212	1,557.36
Ross Metherell	73	72	67	212	1,557.36
Priscillo Diniz	72	68	72	212	1,557.36
Keith MacDonald	72	69	72	213	1,212.75
Manuel Sanchez	73	70	70	213	1,212.75
Steve Wild	71	72	70	213	1,212.75
Trevor Downing	74	70	69	213	1,212.75
Noel Ratcliffe	69	71	74	214	1,048.95
Paul Leonard	69	69	76	214	1,048.95

	SCORES			TOTAL	MONEY
Geoff Parslow	73	72	69	214	1,048.95
Barry Vivian	69	70	75	214	1,048.95
Maurice Bembridge	72	72	71	215	982.80

Dan Technology Senior Tournament of Champions

Mere Golf & Country Club, Knutsford, England　　　　　　October 5-7
Par 36-35–71; 6,583 yards　　　　　　　　　　　　　　purse, £150,000

	SCORES			TOTAL	MONEY
Delroy Cambridge	69	67	69	205	£24,310.42
Jerry Bruner	69	69	68	206	15,925.42
Mike Miller	68	74	65	207	7,640.42
Bill Hardwick	67	69	71	207	7,640.42
Priscillo Diniz	70	69	68	207	7,640.42
Paul Leonard	67	72	69	208	5,755.42
Bob Lendzion	67	70	72	209	5,230.42
Ian Mosey	64	71	75	210	4,622.92
Peter Dawson	66	75	69	210	4,622.92
David Creamer	72	69	70	211	4,075.42
Nick Job	75	69	68	212	3,632.92
Ian Stanley	73	69	70	212	3,632.92
Denis Durnian	70	69	74	213	3,105.42
John Morgan	74	70	69	213	3,105.42
John McTear	70	74	69	213	3,105.42
Bernard Gallacher	71	71	72	214	2,554.42
Tommy Horton	73	73	68	214	2,554.42
Simon Owen	74	70	70	214	2,554.42
Eddie Polland	71	71	72	214	2,554.42
David Good	74	69	71	214	2,554.42
Noel Ratcliffe	70	74	71	215	2,070.42
Brian Huggett	73	72	70	215	2,070.42
Craig Defoy	71	68	76	215	2,070.42
Keith MacDonald	74	72	70	216	1,686.67
Jim Rhodes	73	73	70	216	1,686.67
Jay Horton	69	74	73	216	1,686.67
John Irwin	72	73	71	216	1,686.67
Alan Tapie	72	70	75	217	1,465.42
David Oakley	75	73	69	217	1,465.42
Malcolm Gregson	74	75	69	218	1,405.42
David Huish	73	72	73	218	1,405.42
Jeff Van Wagenen	77	70	71	218	1,405.42

Tunisian Seniors Open

Port El Kantaoui Golf Club, Port El Kantaoui, Tunisia　　　　October 17-19
Par 36-36–72; 6,772 yards　　　　　　　　　　　　　　purse, £100,000

	SCORES			TOTAL	MONEY
Simon Owen	69	73	66	208	£16,660
Bob Lendzion	67	69	72	208	10,330
(Owen defeated Lendzion on second playoff hole.)					
Bill Hardwick	71	73	66	210	6,380
Noel Ratcliffe	69	70	72	211	4,266.67
Lawrence Farmer	70	70	71	211	4,266.67

	SCORES			TOTAL	MONEY
Jerry Bruner	71	69	71	211	4,266.67
John Morgan	72	69	71	212	2,940
Jim Rhodes	68	68	76	212	2,940
John Chillas	69	73	70	212	2,940
David Good	69	69	74	212	2,940
John Irwin	68	73	71	212	2,940
Mike Miller	70	74	69	213	1,916.67
Jeff Van Wagenen	72	70	71	213	1,916.67
Priscillo Diniz	67	70	76	213	1,916.67
Brian Waites	73	69	72	214	1,310
Keith MacDonald	71	73	70	214	1,310
Renato Campagnoli	69	73	72	214	1,310
Silvano Locatelli	71	72	71	214	1,310
Pat Kaylor	71	71	72	214	1,310
Maurice Bembridge	72	69	74	215	986
Graham Burroughs	71	71	73	215	986
Eddie Polland	73	71	71	215	986
Denis O'Sullivan	71	71	73	215	986
John Fourie	75	68	72	215	986
Tommy Horton	71	72	73	216	890
Ian Mosey	72	71	73	216	890
Antonio Garrido	73	72	72	217	830
Russell Weir	75	68	74	217	830
Malcolm Gregson	73	70	74	217	830
Glenn MacDonald	70	76	71	217	830

SSL International/Sodexho Match Play

Le Meridien Penina Golf & Resort, Portimao, Portugal
Par 35-38–73; 6,643 yards

October 24-27
purse, £100,000

FIRST ROUND

Ian Stanley defeated Jay Horton, 3 and 1.
David Creamer defeated Hank Woodrome, 1 up.
Jim Rhodes defeated Peter Cowen, 4 and 3.
Denis O'Sullivan defeated John McTear, 3 and 2.
David Good defeated Maurice Bembridge, 6 and 5.
Priscillo Diniz defeated Russell Weir, 5 and 4.
Tommy Horton defeated Bobby Verwey, 1 up.
David Oakley defeated Mike Miller, 4 and 3.
Peter Dawson defeated Noel Ratcliffe, 2 and 1.
Jeff Van Wagenen defeated Barry Vivian, 4 and 3.
Bill Hardwick defeated Peter Townsend, 3 and 2.
Delroy Cambridge defeated Keith MacDonald, 2 and 1.
Craig Defoy defeated John Morgan, 1 up.
Paul Leonard defeated Nick Job, 2 and 1.
Jerry Bruner defeated David Huish, 4 and 3.
Denis Durnian defeated Eddie Polland, 1 up.

(Each losing player received £1,125.)

SECOND ROUND

Stanley defeated Creamer, 2 and 1.
Rhodes defeated O'Sullivan, 2 and 1.
Diniz defeated Good, 2 and 1.
Oakley defeated Horton, 19 holes.

Dawson defeated Van Wagenen, 4 and 3.
Cambridge defeated Hardwick, 19 holes.
Defoy defeated Leonard, 1 up.
Bruner defeated Durnian, 2 and 1.

(Each losing player received £2,500.)

QUARTER-FINALS

Rhodes defeated Stanley, 1 up.
Oakley defeated Diniz, 3 and 2.
Dawson defeated Cambridge, 7 and 6.
Defoy defeated Bruner, 2 and 1.

(Each losing player received £5,000.)

SEMI-FINALS

Rhodes defeated Oakley, 3 and 2.
Defoy defeated Dawson, 21 holes.

(Each losing player received £7,500.)

FINAL

Rhodes defeated Defoy, 2 up.

(Rhodes received £16,000; Defoy received £11,000.)

European Seniors Tour Championship

PGA Golf de Catalunya, Girona, Spain
Par 36-36–72; 6,866 yards

November 2-4
purse, £225,000

	SCORES			TOTAL	MONEY
Jerry Bruner	73	69	68	210	£37,000
David Good	72	68	71	211	24,750
Denis Durnian	71	68	74	213	12,443.33
Tommy Horton	71	70	72	213	12,443.33
Peter Dawson	69	76	68	213	12,443.33
Steve Wild	70	76	68	214	8,330
Ian Stanley	72	72	70	214	8,330
Barry Vivian	73	70	71	214	8,330
Jim Rhodes	71	70	74	215	7,020
Nick Job	74	70	72	216	6,345
Mike Miller	68	74	75	217	5,043.75
Silvano Locatelli	72	71	74	217	5,043.75
David Oakley	73	73	71	217	5,043.75
Delroy Cambridge	74	71	72	217	5,043.75
John Morgan	74	72	72	218	3,505
John Chillas	71	76	71	218	3,505
David Creamer	72	70	76	218	3,505
Neil Coles	79	67	73	219	2,760
Alberto Croce	74	71	74	219	2,760
David Huish	73	69	77	219	2,760
Bernard Gallacher	76	72	72	220	2,220
Bob Shearer	71	73	76	220	2,220
Malcolm Gregson	73	72	75	220	2,220
Paul Leonard	75	74	71	220	2,220

	SCORES			TOTAL	MONEY
Bobby Verwey	77	70	73	220	2,220
Maurice Bembridge	75	70	76	221	1,898.33
Lawrence Farmer	71	77	73	221	1,898.33
Priscillo Diniz	76	73	72	221	1,898.33
Antonio Garrido	74	73	75	222	1,765
Keith MacDonald	74	72	76	222	1,765

Japan Senior Tour

ANA Ishigaki Senior

Ishigaki Golf Club, Ishigaki, Okinawa
Par 36-36–72; 6,537 yards

February 3-4
purse, ¥5,500,000

	SCORES		TOTAL	MONEY
Fujio Kobayashi	67	65	132	¥300,000
Hsieh Min-nan	67	66	133	260,000
Wataru Horiguchi	67	66	133	260,000
Koichi Uehara	66	68	134	225,000
Shigeru Uchida	71	63	134	225,000
Minoru Nakamura	65	70	135	200,000
Hisao Inoue	65	70	135	200,000
Teruo Suzumura	66	69	135	200,000
Seiichi Kanai	70	67	137	180,000
Masaru Sato	67	71	138	163,333
Hiroshi Tahara	66	72	138	163,333
Kanae Nobechi	67	71	138	163,333
Seiji Ogawa	71	68	139	155,000
Tetsuhiro Ueda	70	69	139	155,000
Shogo Fujii	69	71	140	150,000
Motomu Mentona	70	70	140	150,000
Noboru Sugai	71	70	141	145,000
Masaru Amano	73	69	142	140,000
Seiji Ebihara	72	70	142	140,000
Shigeru Kawamata	69	73	142	140,000
Koji Nakajima	70	72	142	140,000
Mitoshi Tomita	72	70	142	140,000
Ichiro Ino	68	75	143	130,000
Shoji Kikuchi	70	73	143	130,000
Namio Takasu	69	74	143	130,000
Myosuke Ota	70	73	143	130,000
Hideyo Sugimoto	73	71	144	126,666
Isao Matsui	72	72	144	126,666
Toshiki Matsui	72	72	144	126,666
Kesahiko Uchida	72	73	145	120,000
Hiroshi Kazaki	71	74	145	120,000

Castle Hill Senior Open

Castle Hill County Club, Hoi-gun, Aichi
Par 36-36–72; 6,716 yards

May 18-20
purse, ¥30,000,000

	SCORES			TOTAL	MONEY
Noboru Sugai	67	73	71	211	¥5,400,000
Fujio Kobayashi	74	70	67	211	2,700,000
(Sugai defeated Kobayashi on first playoff hole.)					
Hsieh Min-nan	73	70	70	213	1,575,000
Katsuji Hasegawa	71	68	74	213	1,575,000
Yasuzo Hagiwara	72	69	73	214	1,125,000
Hisao Inoue	72	71	71	214	1,125,000
Seiji Ogawa	76	70	69	215	825,000
Yasuo Sone	71	71	73	215	825,000
Seiji Ebihara	70	71	75	216	645,000
Fumio Tanaka	69	72	75	216	645,000
Ichiro Teramoto	69	73	75	216	645,000
Shigeru Kawamata	73	77	67	217	515,000
Yukio Noguchi	72	73	72	217	515,000
Tatsuo Fujima	69	73	75	217	515,000
Namio Takasu	69	71	79	219	435,000
Katsunari Takahashi	68	78	73	219	435,000
Hiroshi Kazami	73	74	73	220	345,000
Tadao Nakamura	75	70	75	220	345,000
Yurio Akitomi	70	74	76	220	345,000
Tadami Ueno	72	72	76	220	345,000
Motomasa Aoki	75	72	74	221	250,285
Yoshiharu Nakase	73	72	76	221	250,285
Yoshimi Watanabe	72	74	75	221	250,285
Ryosuke Ota	76	76	69	221	250,285
Toshihiko Kikuichi	72	75	74	221	250,285
Norihiko Matsumoto	75	71	75	221	250,285
Mitsuo Iwata	77	72	72	221	250,285
Seiichi Kanai	79	70	73	222	211,800
Masaji Kusakabe	74	71	77	222	211,800
Shuichi Sano	74	73	75	222	211,800
Hiroshi Ishii	73	71	78	222	211,800
Takayoshi Nishikawa	70	74	78	222	211,800

Asahi Ryokuken Cup

Ito Golf Club, Fukuoka
Par 36-36–72; 6,769 yards

June 2-3
purse, ¥10,000,000

	SCORES		TOTAL	MONEY
Noboru Sugai	72	67	139	¥2,000,000
Teruo Suzumura	71	69	140	750,000
Yurio Akitomi	70	73	143	450,000
Takaaki Kono	73	71	144	285,000
Hsieh Min-nan	71	73	144	285,000
Katsuji Hasegawa	70	74	144	285,000
Kunio Koike	72	72	144	285,000
Hisao Inoue	71	74	145	225,000
Makoto Nanbu	73	72	145	225,000
Koichi Uehara	72	74	146	203,333
Masaji Kusakabe	71	75	146	203,333

	SCORES		TOTAL	MONEY
Tadami Ueno	73	73	146	203,333
Eiichi Itai	69	78	147	190,000
Koji Nakajima	74	73	147	190,000
Tadao Nakamura	72	75	147	190,000
Yukio Noguchi	72	75	147	190,000
Shigemi Nakazono	73	74	147	190,000
Norihiko Matsumoto	72	75	147	190,000
*Toshio Kanai	74	73	147	
*Makie Bito	72	75	147	
*Nobuhiro Kawasaki	74	73	147	
Masaru Amano	76	72	148	170,000
Kikuo Arai	75	73	148	170,000
Yoshihisa Iwashita	77	71	148	170,000
Seiichi Kanai	73	75	148	170,000
*Shigenobu Dokawa	71	77	148	
Motomasa Aoki	72	77	149	160,000
Shigeru Uchida	75	74	149	160,000
Hisataka Fujii	73	76	149	160,000
Hiroshi Kazami	76	74	150	160,000
Tetsuhiro Ueda	75	75	150	160,000
Tadayoshi Bandoh	73	77	150	160,000
Reiji Bando	80	70	150	160,000
Mineyuki Yoshimatsu	76	74	150	160,000
*Keiichi Shimoda	79	71	150	

Old Man Par Senior Open

Southern Cross Golf Club, Shizuoka
Par 35-35–70; 6,061 yards

July 27-28
purse, ¥5,840,000

	SCORES		TOTAL	MONEY
Motomasa Aoki	63	69	132	¥1,200,000
Kikuo Arai	66	67	133	433,333
Shigeru Kawamata	70	63	133	433,333
Fujio Kobayashi	69	64	133	433,333
Masaru Amano	69	65	134	250,000
Koichi Uehara	67	68	135	177,500
Masaji Kusakabe	68	67	135	177,500
Hiroshi Kaihaya	66	70	136	145,000
Mamoru Kondo	69	67	136	145,000
Mitoshi Tomita	70	66	136	145,000
Masao Kikuchi	69	68	137	136,250
Koji Nakajima	67	70	137	136,250
*Daitou Memoto	68	69	137	
Seiji Ogawa	72	66	138	127,500
Yukio Noguchi	72	66	138	127,500
Isao Matsui	68	70	138	127,500
Toshiki Matsui	69	69	138	127,500
Tadao Furuichi	75	63	138	127,500
Tooru Kurihara	71	68	139	118,750
Wataru Horiguchi	68	71	139	118,750
*Naoki Inoue	69	70	139	
Tadao Nakamura	73	67	140	115,000
*Ono Susumu	70	70	140	
Kesahiko Uchida	71	70	141	108,750
Seiichi Kanai	72	69	141	108,750
Norihiko Matsumoto	72	69	141	108,750

	SCORES		TOTAL	MONEY
Kenichi Tsurumoto	71	70	141	108,750
*Nakakita Shouji	73	68	141	
*Hideaki Nakaema	69	72	141	
*Keizo Sugita	72	69	141	

Fancl Senior Classic

Susono Country Club, Shizuoka
Par 36-36–72; 6,770 yards

August 10-12
purse, ¥60,000,000

	SCORES			TOTAL	MONEY
Katsunari Takahashi	69	68	66	201	¥15,000,000
Shuichi Sano	70	68	69	207	6,900,000
Yasuzo Hagiwara	71	71	69	211	3,600,000
Teiji Sano	73	68	71	212	2,400,000
Tatsuo Fujima	69	74	70	213	1,747,500
Wataru Horiguchi	72	73	68	213	1,747,500
Yasuo Sone	71	70	72	213	1,747,500
Toshiharu Morimoto	69	72	72	213	1,747,500
Kikuo Arai	68	72	74	214	1,218,000
Toyotake Nakao	71	70	73	214	1,218,000
Fujio Kobayashi	70	71	74	215	942,000
Yukio Noguchi	69	72	74	215	942,000
Katsuji Hasegawa	75	70	70	215	942,000
Hisao Inoue	71	75	69	215	942,000
Teruo Sugihara	71	74	70	215	942,000
Seiichi Kanai	71	70	75	216	720,000
Katsumi Nanjo	75	67	74	216	720,000
Yurio Akitomi	69	73	74	216	720,000
Seiji Ebihara	72	74	71	217	609,000
Noboru Sugai	71	70	76	217	609,000
Toshihiko Kikuichi	71	70	76	217	609,000
Hisashi Suzumura	70	71	76	217	609,000
Koichi Uehara	72	74	72	218	483,000
Fumio Tanaka	75	69	74	218	483,000
Tadao Nakamura	73	73	72	218	483,000
Tadami Ueno	72	74	72	218	483,000
Hiroshi Oku	75	72	71	218	483,000
Mitoshi Tomita	71	76	71	218	483,000
Hiroshi Kazami	69	74	76	219	405,000
Koji Nakajima	73	73	73	219	405,000

HTD Senior Classic

Mitsui Kanko Iris Golf Club, Hokkaido
Par 36-36–72; 6,464 yards

September 8-9
purse, ¥10,000,000

	SCORES		TOTAL	MONEY
Fujio Kobayashi	65	69	134	¥2,500,000
Hisao Inoue	68	68	136	1,200,000
Katsuji Hasegawa	71	67	138	750,000
Katsunari Takahashi	71	68	139	550,000
Koichi Uehara	65	75	140	450,000
Fumio Tanaka	69	72	141	300,000
Kikuo Arai	70	72	142	236,666

	SCORES		TOTAL	MONEY
Seiichi Kanai	73	69	142	236,666
Haruo Yasuda	71	71	142	236,666
Toru Nakayama	72	72	144	210,000
Seiji Ogawa	68	77	145	191,666
Noboru Sugai	71	74	145	191,666
Yukio Noguchi	74	71	145	191,666
Yasuo Sone	74	72	146	180,000
Masaru Amano	74	73	147	173,000
Teruo Sugihara	74	73	147	173,000
Mitsuo Iwata	73	74	147	173,000
*Minoru Saito	76	72	148	
Mamoru Omodera	73	76	149	169,000
*Yoichi Sato	75	74	149	
Tetsuhiro Ueda	76	74	150	167,000
Namio Takasu	72	79	151	165,000
*Masaru Kiyokobu	74	77	151	
Isao Matsui	77	75	152	162,000
Kunio Koike	73	79	152	162,000
*Hideshi Doi	77	75	152	
Ichiro Ino	77	76	153	158,000
Kanae Nobechi	74	79	153	158,000
*Shinzo Yoshida	76	77	153	
*Iwao Yang	72	83	155	
*Yasuhiro Shirato	73	82	155	

Fujita Kanko Open

Cameria Hills Country Club, Chiba
Par 36-36–72; 6,703 yards

September 14-15
purse, ¥20,000,000

	SCORES		TOTAL	MONEY
Yasuzo Hagiwara	68	66	134	¥3,600,000
Norihiko Matsumoto	64	70	134	1,800,000
(Hagiwara defeated Matsumoto on second playoff hole.)				
Koichi Uehara	67	68	135	1,200,000
Seiji Ebihara	70	66	136	800,000
Fujio Kobayashi	70	66	136	800,000
Hisao Inoue	69	67	136	800,000
Shuichi Sano	70	68	138	497,500
Noboru Sugai	67	71	138	497,500
Katsunari Takahashi	69	69	138	497,500
Katsuji Hasegawa	66	72	138	497,500
Fumio Tanaka	67	72	139	400,000
Namio Takasu	72	68	140	343,333
Yukio Noguchi	69	71	140	343,333
Mitsuo Iwata	71	69	140	343,333
Kikuo Arai	71	70	141	260,000
Masaji Kusakabe	71	70	141	260,000
Renkyoku Sugiyama	69	72	141	260,000
Haruo Yasuda	71	70	141	260,000
Takayoshi Nishikawa	71	70	141	260,000
Yoshiharu Nakase	71	71	142	180,000
Toru Nakayama	71	71	142	180,000
Yurio Akitomi	70	72	142	180,000
Takashi Miyoshi	71	71	142	180,000
Toshiharu Morimoto	72	70	142	180,000
Yoshiki Watanabe	68	75	143	154,000

	SCORES				TOTAL	MONEY
Koji Okuno	71	72			143	154,000
Yasuo Sone	70	73			143	154,000
Toyotake Nakao	71	72			143	154,000
Kenjiro Ewama	70	74			144	139,500
Takaaki Kono	74	70			144	139,500
Tatsuo Fujima	73	71			144	139,500
Toshihiko Kikuichi	75	69			144	139,500

Japan PGA Senior Championship

Biglayzac Country Club, Miyagi
Par 36-36–72; 6,834 yards

October 4-7
purse, ¥30,000,000

	SCORES				TOTAL	MONEY
Yasuhiro Miyamoto	69	71	75	69	284	¥5,400,000
Masaru Amano	73	70	72	74	289	1,762,500
Kikuo Arai	73	70	74	72	289	1,762,500
Seiji Ebihara	74	72	72	71	289	1,762,500
Noboru Sugai	70	75	72	72	289	1,762,500
Fumio Tanaka	75	71	72	72	290	847,500
Yurio Akitomi	73	75	72	70	290	847,500
Hisao Inoue	70	72	72	76	290	847,500
Toyotake Nakao	69	74	75	72	290	847,500
Masayuki Ohno	75	75	69	72	291	622,500
Katsuji Hasegawa	73	72	72	74	291	622,500
Motomasa Aoki	79	70	69	74	292	467,500
Katsunari Takahashi	70	71	79	72	292	467,500
Junji Hashizoe	76	70	77	69	292	467,500
Shimon Yakamatsu	75	70	72	75	292	467,500
Toshiki Matsui	76	72	71	73	292	467,500
Tadao Furuichi	72	74	73	73	292	467,500
Fujio Kobayashi	75	71	73	74	293	299,000
Shuichi Sano	72	69	78	74	293	299,000
Haruo Yasuda	74	73	71	75	293	299,000
Takashi Miyoshi	73	77	69	74	293	299,000
Toshiharu Morimoto	71	72	75	75	293	299,000
Mitsuo Iwata	71	75	70	77	293	299,000
Koji Okuno	72	70	75	77	294	243,000
Koichi Uehara	72	74	77	72	295	225,000
Masaji Kusakabe	74	74	73	74	295	225,000
Yasuzo Hagiwara	75	74	77	69	295	225,000
Takayoshi Nishikawa	72	74	75	74	295	225,000
Naoto Matsushita	73	76	73	74	296	210,000
Tatsuo Fujima	72	73	81	71	297	195,000
Wataru Horiguchi	78	71	73	75	297	195,000
Tadami Ueno	74	76	76	71	297	195,000
Masamitsu Oguri	74	74	75	74	297	195,000

Komatsu Open

Katayamazu Golf Club, Ishikawa
Par 36-36–72; 6,721 yards

October 19-21
purse, ¥40,000,000

	SCORES			TOTAL	MONEY
Katsunari Takahashi	70	71	70	211	¥8,000,000
Seiichi Kanai	71	69	71	211	4,000,000
(Takahashi defeated Kanai on third playoff hole.)					
Motomasa Aoki	74	70	69	213	2,013,333
Seiji Ebihara	71	71	71	213	2,013,333
Hisao Inoue	69	72	72	213	2,013,333
Koichi Uehara	69	72	73	214	1,260,000
Toshiyuki Misawa	72	71	71	214	1,260,000
Yurio Akitomi	69	76	70	215	986,000
Hiroaki Uenishi	67	73	75	215	986,000
Kikuo Arai	73	74	69	216	812,000
Eitaro Deguchi	70	70	76	216	812,000
Noboru Sugai	73	74	70	217	728,000
Shigeru Kawamata	72	73	73	218	625,333
Akira Yabe	73	73	72	218	625,333
Hiroshi Ishii	73	71	74	218	625,333
Mitoshi Tomita	75	72	72	219	550,000
Toyotake Nakao	74	74	71	219	550,000
Katsuji Hasegawa	75	71	74	219	550,000
Haruo Yasuda	70	70	80	220	500,000
Yoshimi Watanabe	75	70	75	220	500,000
Tomishige Ikeda	72	76	73	221	440,000
Namio Takasu	72	76	73	221	440,000
Yoshitaka Yamamoto	75	73	73	221	440,000
Seiji Kusakabe	75	70	77	222	340,000
Shoichi Sato	77	71	74	222	340,000
Yoshiharu Nakase	76	75	71	222	340,000
Yukio Noguchi	73	71	78	222	340,000
Yasuo Sone	75	72	75	222	340,000
Norihiko Matsumoto	73	77	72	222	340,000
Mitsuo Iwata	71	75	76	222	340,000

Japan Senior Open Championship

Dazaifu Golf Club, Fukuoka
Par 36-36–72; 6,854 yards

October 25-28
purse, ¥50,000,000

	SCORES				TOTAL	MONEY
Fujio Kobayashi	71	72	71	72	286	¥10,000,000
Katsunari Takahashi	75	70	67	74	286	4,687,500
Terry Gale	72	75	67	72	286	4,687,500
(Kobayashi defeated Takahashi and Gale on first playoff hole.)						
Hisao Inoue	71	68	74	74	287	2,550,000
Hsieh Min-nan	72	73	74	71	290	1,745,000
Katsuji Hasegawa	71	75	70	74	290	1,745,000
Tadami Ueno	74	73	71	72	290	1,745,000
Wataru Horiguchi	69	72	72	78	291	1,305,000
Masaru Amano	75	74	71	72	292	935,750
Noboru Sugai	73	72	73	74	292	935,750
Yukio Noguchi	74	73	72	73	292	935,750
Tadao Furuichi	71	73	75	73	292	935,750

	SCORES			TOTAL	MONEY
Seiji Ogawa	75	75	69	74	293	625,000
Sadao Sakashita	73	73	74	73	293	625,000
Shuichi Sano	74	75	71	73	293	625,000
Toshihiko Kikuichi	75	75	73	70	293	625,000
Norihiko Matsumoto	74	70	73	76	293	625,000
Seiji Ebihara	76	71	71	76	294	535,000
Kikuo Arai	79	70	70	76	295	482,500
Koichi Uehara	71	73	76	75	295	482,500
Yurio Akitomi	76	74	71	74	295	482,500
Toshiharu Morimoto	72	75	69	79	295	482,500
Tomishige Ikeda	78	70	74	74	296	433,400
Yasushi Taki	73	76	72	75	296	433,400
Tatsuo Fujima	73	75	75	73	296	433,400
Toyotake Nakao	72	79	69	76	296	433,400
Yasuhiro Miyamoto	74	71	76	75	296	433,400
*Tetsuo Sakata	73	75	74	74	296	
Motomasa Aoki	75	72	73	77	297	395,000
Fumio Tanaka	73	74	75	75	297	395,000
Toru Nakayama	73	74	74	76	297	395,000

Takanosu Senior Open

Takanosu Golf Club, Hiroshima
Par 36-36–72; 6,730 yards

November 21-22
purse, ¥10,000,000

	SCORES		TOTAL	MONEY
Tadami Ueno	68	71	139	¥2,000,000
Seiji Ebihara	68	72	140	800,000
Katsuji Hasegawa	69	72	141	500,000
Katsunari Takahashi	74	68	142	300,000
Yasuo Sone	72	70	142	300,000
Katsumasa Iwao	70	72	142	300,000
Tomishige Ikeda	73	70	143	136,250
Junji Hashizoe	72	71	143	136,250
Yukio Noguchi	70	73	143	136,250
Hisao Inoue	68	75	143	136,250
Yasuhiro Daio	71	72	143	136,250
Ichiro Teramoto	73	70	143	136,250
Takayoshi Nishikawa	68	75	143	136,250
Katsumi Hara	72	71	143	136,250
Motomasa Aoki	73	71	144	110,000
Seiichi Kanai	72	72	144	110,000
Fumio Tanaka	71	73	144	110,000
Toru Nakayama	74	70	144	110,000
Tetsuhiro Ueda	73	71	144	110,000
Takafumi Ogawa	72	72	144	110,000
Yasuzo Hagiwara	73	72	145	105,000
Toyotake Nakao	70	75	145	105,000
Reiji Bando	72	73	145	105,000
Toshiki Matsui	68	77	145	105,000
Yasuhiro Miyamoto	73	72	145	105,000
Eiichi Itai	72	74	146	102,000
Toshihiko Kikuichi	76	70	146	102,000
Norihiko Matsumoto	71	69	147	101,428
Shigeru Kawamata	76	71	147	101,428
Hisao Jitsukata	77	70	147	101,428
Hiroshi Kazami	74	73	147	101,428

	SCORES		TOTAL	MONEY
Namio Takasu	74	73	147	101,428
Yurio Akitomi	74	73	147	101,428
Hiroshi Ishii	72	75	147	101,428
Hiroshi Yaminaka	75	72	147	101,428
*Yurio Saiki	75	72	147	

N. Cup Senior Open

Central Golf Club, Ibaragi
Par 37-36–73; 6,931 yards

November 28-29
purse, ¥15,000,000

	SCORES		TOTAL	MONEY
Seiji Ebihara	68	67	135	¥2,500,000
Yukio Noguchi	68	69	137	1,250,000
Isao Aoki	69	70	139	1,000,000
Teiji Sano	70	71	141	800,000
Haruo Yasuda	71	71	142	700,000
Noboru Sugai	73	70	143	516,666
Tatsuo Fujima	71	72	143	516,666
Toshiyuki Misawa	70	73	143	516,666
Koichi Uehara	71	73	144	330,000
Fujio Kobayashi	71	73	144	330,000
Katsuji Hasegawa	73	71	144	330,000
Toshimoto Mouri	71	73	144	330,000
Kikuo Arai	73	72	145	227,500
Seiji Ogawa	71	74	145	227,500
Masaji Kusakabe	68	77	145	227,500
Koji Nakajima	68	77	145	227,500
Toru Nakayama	71	75	146	180,000
Mitoyoshi Maruyama	74	72	146	180,000
Hisao Inoue	73	73	146	180,000
Toshihiko Kikuichi	73	73	146	180,000
Tadao Furuichi	72	74	146	180,000
Motomasa Aoki	75	72	147	145,000
Norihiko Matsumoto	73	74	147	145,000
*Saburo Murata	75	72	147	
Masaru Amano	72	76	148	116,000
Seiichi Kanai	74	74	148	116,000
Shigeru Kawamata	77	71	148	116,000
Hiroshi Kazaki	73	75	148	116,000
Wataru Horiguchi	76	72	148	116,000
Mitsutaka Kono	74	75	149	100,000
Fumio Tanaka	74	75	149	100,000
Yasuhiro Miyamoto	74	75	149	100,000

Women's Tours

YourLife Vitamins LPGA Classic

Grand Cypress Resort, Orlando, Florida
Par 36-36–72; 6,220 yards

January 12-14
purse, $1,000,000

	SCORES			TOTAL	MONEY
Se Ri Pak	71	68	64	203	$150,000
Penny Hammel	67	72	68	207	80,513
Carin Koch	69	68	70	207	80,513
Lorie Kane	70	70	69	209	52,836
Brandie Burton	71	70	69	210	42,772
Janice Moodie	71	73	67	211	30,360
Dawn Coe-Jones	72	70	69	211	30,360
Leta Lindley	71	71	69	211	30,360
Kelly Robbins	70	74	68	212	23,651
Cristie Kerr	73	70	70	213	16,893
Chris Johnson	72	71	70	213	16,893
Joanne Morley	71	71	71	213	16,893
Mardi Lunn	72	69	72	213	16,893
Nancy Scranton	71	69	73	213	16,893
Mi Hyun Kim	72	67	74	213	16,893
Kellee Booth	68	71	74	213	16,893
Michelle McGann	72	73	69	214	11,353
Pat Hurst	72	73	69	214	11,353
Dottie Pepper	71	74	69	214	11,353
Wendy Ward	71	74	69	214	11,353
Grace Park	69	76	69	214	11,353
Tammie Green	74	70	70	214	11,353
Michele Redman	71	73	70	214	11,353
Heather Zakhar	69	73	72	214	11,353
Vicki Goetze-Ackerman	75	69	71	215	9,309
Jane Geddes	73	69	73	215	9,309
Beth Daniel	74	74	68	216	7,972
Sara Sanders	77	69	70	216	7,972
Mhairi McKay	71	75	70	216	7,972
Jill McGill	77	67	72	216	7,972
Leigh Ann Mills	68	76	72	216	7,972
Danielle Ammaccapane	72	69	75	216	7,972
Susie Redman	70	71	75	216	7,972

Subaru Memorial of Naples

The Club at the Strand, Naples, Florida
Par 36-36–72; 6,328 yards

January 18-21
purse, $1,000,000

	SCORES				TOTAL	MONEY
Sophie Gustafson	68	64	70	70	272	$150,000
Karrie Webb	68	70	68	69	275	93,093
Dottie Pepper	68	69	72	67	276	67,933
Marisa Baena	68	71	72	66	277	52,836
Laura Davies	69	75	68	66	278	31,500
Jean Bartholomew	67	70	75	66	278	31,500
Michele Redman	72	71	68	67	278	31,500

		SCORES			TOTAL	MONEY
Juli Inkster	69	70	69	70	278	31,500
Vicki Goetze-Ackerman	67	71	70	70	278	31,500
Lorie Kane	72	69	71	67	279	18,702
Laura Diaz	67	70	73	69	279	18,702
Brandie Burton	67	69	74	69	279	18,702
Meg Mallon	68	69	72	70	279	18,702
Alison Nicholas	73	70	69	68	280	15,208
Danielle Ammaccapane	69	70	71	70	280	15,208
Dina Ammaccapane	69	72	69	71	281	13,195
Beth Daniel	68	70	71	72	281	13,195
Heather Bowie	67	70	72	72	281	13,195
Mi Hyun Kim	64	70	75	73	282	12,189
Nancy Scranton	69	69	74	71	283	11,182
Kristi Albers	69	69	73	72	283	11,182
Pat Hurst	68	69	72	74	283	11,182
Laurel Kean	72	68	73	71	284	9,735
Cindy Figg-Currier	68	73	71	72	284	9,735
Helen Alfredsson	70	71	70	73	284	9,735
Kelli Kuehne	66	74	70	74	284	9,735
Janice Moodie	69	70	76	70	285	8,084
Jill McGill	69	70	76	70	285	8,084
Jackie Gallagher-Smith	73	71	69	72	285	8,084
Val Skinner	72	70	71	72	285	8,084
Susan Ginter	71	70	72	72	285	8,084
Wendy Doolan	65	76	72	72	285	8,084
Rachel Teske	69	71	73	72	285	8,084

The Office Depot

Doral Golf Resort & Spa, Miami, Florida
Blue Monster Course: Par 36-36–72; 6,388 yards
Red Course: Par 35-35–70; 5,842 yards

January 25-28
purse, $825,000

		SCORES			TOTAL	MONEY
Grace Park	70	69	70	71	280	$123,750
Karrie Webb	69	72	69	71	281	76,801
Karen Weiss	76	69	67	70	282	49,817
Jennifer Rosales	70	72	70	70	282	49,817
Jackie Gallagher-Smith	66	74	72	71	283	35,286
Kellee Booth	70	69	73	72	284	26,776
Meg Mallon	74	69	68	73	284	26,776
Laura Diaz	67	74	69	75	285	20,549
Michele Redman	73	69	67	76	285	20,549
Emilee Klein	71	69	71	75	286	16,605
Vicki Goetze-Ackerman	68	72	70	76	286	16,605
Wendy Doolan	73	68	77	69	287	13,284
Heather Bowie	73	68	75	71	287	13,284
Kelli Kuehne	72	71	71	73	287	13,284
Janice Moodie	73	69	72	73	287	13,284
Dawn Coe-Jones	74	71	71	72	288	10,378
Sophie Gustafson	72	71	73	72	288	10,378
Donna Andrews	73	72	69	74	288	10,378
Juli Inkster	70	74	68	76	288	10,378
Barb Mucha	71	67	73	77	288	10,378
Kelly Robbins	76	70	72	71	289	8,410
Amy Fruhwirth	73	71	73	72	289	8,410
Laura Davies	72	71	73	73	289	8,410

	SCORES				TOTAL	MONEY
Michelle McGann	70	71	73	75	289	8,410
Tammie Green	68	72	72	77	289	8,410
Gail Graham	74	76	72	68	290	7,057
Pat Hurst	77	71	72	70	290	7,057
Liselotte Neumann	76	73	70	71	290	7,057
Kathryn Marshall	71	75	72	72	290	7,057
Nancy Scranton	69	72	74	75	290	7,057

Takefuji Classic

Kona Country Club, Kailua-Kona, Hawaii
Par 36-36–72; 6,257 yards

February 8-10
purse, $850,000

	SCORES			TOTAL	MONEY
Lorie Kane	70	69	66	205	$127,500
Annika Sorenstam	70	67	70	207	79,129
Cristie Kerr	70	69	69	208	57,743
Maria Hjorth	67	75	67	209	40,633
Pat Hurst	70	70	69	209	40,633
Karrie Webb	70	69	71	210	29,940
Nancy Harvey	70	71	70	211	23,738
Wendy Ward	72	68	71	211	23,738
Emilee Klein	68	73	71	212	17,352
Marnie McGuire	73	68	71	212	17,352
Nancy Scranton	68	73	71	212	17,352
Sherri Turner	71	69	72	212	17,352
Helen Alfredsson	70	71	72	213	12,891
Dorothy Delasin	70	70	73	213	12,891
Sophie Gustafson	68	72	73	213	12,891
Leta Lindley	73	70	70	213	12,891
Heather Bowie	72	72	70	214	10,538
Eva Dahllof	74	73	67	214	10,538
Moira Dunn	69	73	72	214	10,538
A.J. Eathorne	69	70	75	214	10,538
Mi Hyun Kim	71	72	72	215	9,055
Jill McGill	73	72	70	215	9,055
Charlotta Sorenstam	76	68	71	215	9,055
Heather Daly-Donofrio	72	72	72	216	7,972
Laura Diaz	73	68	75	216	7,972
Hiromi Kobayashi	72	71	73	216	7,972
Janice Moodie	74	71	71	216	7,972
Marisa Baena	73	73	71	217	6,826
Tina Barrett	78	66	73	217	6,826
Audra Burks	71	74	72	217	6,826
Akiko Fukushima	73	72	72	217	6,826
Carin Koch	73	73	71	217	6,826

Cup Noodles Hawaiian Ladies Open

Kapolei Golf Course, Kapolei, Oahu, Hawaii
Par 36-36–72; 6,100 yards

February 15-17
purse, $750,000

	SCORES			TOTAL	MONEY
Catriona Matthew	67	71	72	210	$112,500
Annika Sorenstam	74	69	70	213	69,819

	SCORES			TOTAL	MONEY
Danielle Ammaccapane	75	70	69	214	40,884
Nancy Scranton	76	64	74	214	40,884
Wendy Ward	74	67	73	214	40,884
Michelle McGann	73	72	70	215	22,769
Michele Redman	73	71	71	215	22,769
Leslie Spalding	71	74	70	215	22,769
Dina Ammaccapane	73	71	72	216	14,215
Brandie Burton	72	71	73	216	14,215
Vicki Fergon	73	73	70	216	14,215
Vicki Goetze-Ackerman	71	69	76	216	14,215
Cindy Schreyer	72	74	70	216	14,215
Karrie Webb	77	69	70	216	14,215
Jenny Lidback	75	72	70	217	9,686
Mhairi McKay	71	76	70	217	9,686
Janice Moodie	74	73	70	217	9,686
Grace Park	74	70	73	217	9,686
Kelly Robbins	76	72	69	217	9,686
Shani Waugh	77	69	71	217	9,686
Kellee Booth	73	72	73	218	7,645
Hee-Won Han	69	77	72	218	7,645
Becky Iverson	73	71	74	218	7,645
Lorie Kane	77	73	68	218	7,645
Jill McGill	76	71	71	218	7,645
Akiko Fukushima	75	73	71	219	6,641
Cathy Johnston-Forbes	78	72	69	219	6,641
Kelli Kuehne	74	71	74	219	6,641
Leta Lindley	74	73	72	219	6,641
Jackie Gallagher-Smith	72	75	73	220	5,660
Mi Hyun Kim	76	73	71	220	5,660
Liselotte Neumann	75	75	70	220	5,660
Karen Pearce	72	74	74	220	5,660
Charlotta Sorenstam	76	70	74	220	5,660
Angela Stanford	78	71	71	220	5,660

Welch's/Circle K Championship

Randolph North Golf Course, Tucson, Arizona
Par 35-37–72; 6,222 yards

March 8-11
purse, $750,000

	SCORES				TOTAL	MONEY
Annika Sorenstam	65	68	67	65	265	$112,500
Michelle McGann	70	66	71	64	271	48,118
Laura Diaz	68	69	68	66	271	48,118
Dottie Pepper	67	67	70	67	271	48,118
Se Ri Pak	68	67	67	69	271	48,118
Grace Park	68	68	70	67	273	26,418
Nancy Scranton	71	67	72	66	276	20,945
Juli Inkster	70	69	70	67	276	20,945
*Lorena Ochoa	66	74	71	65	276	
Danielle Ammaccapane	72	70	70	65	277	14,223
Jennifer Rosales	68	70	70	69	277	14,223
Jill McGill	69	68	71	69	277	14,223
Lorie Kane	67	67	74	69	277	14,223
Emilee Klein	66	70	71	70	277	14,223
Becky Iverson	69	69	68	71	277	14,223
Kris Tschetter	71	67	71	69	278	9,899
Janice Moodie	72	70	66	70	278	9,899

	SCORES				TOTAL	MONEY
Helen Alfredsson	70	66	71	71	278	9,899
Brandie Burton	67	67	72	72	278	9,899
Marcy Newton	69	71	69	69	278	9,899
Cindy Schreyer	70	72	71	66	279	7,830
Gloria Park	71	71	69	68	279	7,830
Heather Bowie	69	70	71	69	279	7,830
Michelle Ellis	69	70	71	69	279	7,830
Deb Richard	69	66	70	74	279	7,830
Jen Hanna	63	68	72	76	279	7,830
Maria Hjorth	69	69	72	70	280	6,427
Akiko Fukushima	67	71	71	71	280	6,427
Mi Hyun Kim	70	67	72	71	280	6,427
Michele Redman	66	71	69	74	280	6,427
Dorothy Delasin	67	68	70	75	280	6,427

Standard Register Ping

Moon Valley Country Club, Phoenix, Arizona
Par 36-36–72; 6,459 yards

March 15-18
purse, $1,000,000

	SCORES				TOTAL	MONEY
Annika Sorenstam	65	59	69	68	261	$150,000
Se Ri Pak	65	68	63	67	263	93,093
Dottie Pepper	68	67	73	67	275	60,384
Yu Ping Lin	72	65	68	70	275	60,384
Dorothy Delasin	69	69	70	68	276	38,998
Akiko Fukushima	70	66	71	69	276	38,998
Vicki Goetze-Ackerman	73	68	71	65	277	21,197
Rosie Jones	70	69	72	66	277	21,197
Michelle McGann	72	70	68	67	277	21,197
Rachel Teske	67	70	73	67	277	21,197
Karrie Webb	73	69	67	68	277	21,197
Pat Hurst	69	64	76	68	277	21,197
Lorie Kane	67	70	71	69	277	21,197
Kris Tschetter	63	69	75	70	277	21,197
Michele Redman	71	68	70	69	278	14,090
Jackie Gallagher-Smith	68	72	68	70	278	14,090
Meg Mallon	71	71	70	67	279	12,831
Kelly Robbins	69	70	73	67	279	12,831
Karen Weiss	71	69	77	63	280	11,080
Catriona Matthew	73	69	67	71	280	11,080
Mi Hyun Kim	68	67	74	71	280	11,080
Nancy Scranton	68	70	70	72	280	11,080
Laura Diaz	67	66	74	73	280	11,080
Heather Zakhar	73	70	74	64	281	9,611
Wendy Ward	71	69	71	70	281	9,611
Hiromi Kobayashi	66	75	75	66	282	8,259
Juli Inkster	73	70	71	68	282	8,259
Sophie Gustafson	71	70	69	72	282	8,259
Michelle Ellis	66	72	72	72	282	8,259
Kellee Booth	72	68	69	73	282	8,259
Sherri Steinhauer	69	66	74	73	282	8,259
Marcy Newton	73	67	71	71	282	8,259

Nabisco Championship

Mission Hills Country Club, Rancho Mirage, California
Par 36-36–72; 6,520 yards

March 22-25
purse, $1,500,000

	SCORES				TOTAL	MONEY
Annika Sorenstam	72	70	70	69	281	$225,000
Karrie Webb	73	72	70	69	284	87,557
Janice Moodie	72	72	70	70	284	87,557
Dottie Pepper	71	71	71	71	284	87,557
Akiko Fukushima	74	68	70	72	284	87,557
Rachel Teske	72	73	66	73	284	87,557
Sophie Gustafson	72	74	70	69	285	41,891
Brandie Burton	74	69	72	70	285	41,891
Laura Diaz	71	74	69	72	286	33,589
Pat Hurst	70	68	74	74	286	33,589
Laura Davies	71	73	75	68	287	25,957
Dorothy Delasin	73	70	74	70	287	25,957
Se Ri Pak	73	69	73	72	287	25,957
Tina Barrett	71	73	70	73	287	25,957
Mi Hyun Kim	74	71	70	73	288	20,736
Carin Koch	70	69	75	74	288	20,736
Juli Inkster	70	75	68	75	288	20,736
Liselotte Neumann	70	74	74	71	289	18,220
Jeong Jang	74	71	71	73	289	18,220
Michele Redman	71	72	71	75	289	18,220
Jill McGill	75	71	70	74	290	16,711
*Lorena Ochoa	72	71	74	73	290	
Becky Iverson	75	70	72	74	291	15,955
Maria Hjorth	73	72	75	72	292	14,540
Tammie Green	72	73	75	72	292	14,540
Kelly Robbins	75	72	72	73	292	14,540
Penny Hammel	70	75	72	75	292	14,540
Meg Mallon	74	71	78	70	293	12,063
Grace Park	75	75	72	71	293	12,063
Dina Ammaccapane	74	74	73	72	293	12,063
Rosie Jones	73	73	75	72	293	12,063
Alison Nicholas	71	75	75	72	293	12,063
Stefania Croce	74	72	73	74	293	12,063
Emilee Klein	72	74	72	75	293	12,063

Office Depot Hosted by Amy Alcott

Wilshire Country Club, Los Angeles, California
Par 35-36–71; 6,349 yards

April 12-14
purse, $800,000

	SCORES			TOTAL	MONEY
Annika Sorenstam	71	73	66	210	$120,000
Mi Hyun Kim	70	75	65	210	74,474
(Sorenstam defeated Kim on first playoff hole.)					
Pat Hurst	67	67	77	211	54,346
Michele Redman	71	70	71	212	42,269
Dina Ammaccapane	69	73	71	213	31,198
Liselotte Neumann	70	67	76	213	31,198
Janice Moodie	74	73	67	214	21,201
Juli Inkster	72	74	68	214	21,201
Kristi Albers	69	72	73	214	21,201
Dorothy Delasin	71	74	70	215	14,894

	SCORES			TOTAL	MONEY
Pearl Sinn	74	70	71	215	14,894
Charlotta Sorenstam	71	73	71	215	14,894
Kathryn Marshall	75	67	73	215	14,894
Penny Hammel	70	78	68	216	10,638
Rosie Jones	72	75	69	216	10,638
Dottie Pepper	71	75	70	216	10,638
Michelle McGann	69	77	70	216	10,638
Michelle Estill	72	73	71	216	10,638
Brandie Burton	71	73	72	216	10,638
Luciana Bemvenuti	72	71	73	216	10,638
*Candie Kung	74	74	69	217	
Mhairi McKay	77	68	72	217	8,466
Danielle Ammaccapane	72	73	72	217	8,466
Vicki Goetze-Ackerman	74	70	73	217	8,466
Heather Bowie	75	72	71	218	7,205
Wendy Doolan	71	76	71	218	7,205
Mardi Lunn	75	71	72	218	7,205
Betsy King	75	70	73	218	7,205
Marianne Morris	74	71	73	218	7,205
Angela Stanford	76	66	76	218	7,205

Longs Drugs Challenge

Twelve Bridges Golf Club, Lincoln, California
Par 36-36–72; 6,388 yards
(Shortened to 54 holes — rain.)

April 19-22
purse, $800,000

	SCORES			TOTAL	MONEY
Se Ri Pak	66	71	71	208	$120,000
Laura Diaz	70	72	68	210	74,474
Michele Redman	68	70	73	211	54,346
Rosie Jones	74	68	70	212	34,888
Denise Killeen	72	69	71	212	34,888
Karen Weiss	70	71	71	212	34,888
Becky Morgan	73	73	67	213	22,342
Mi Hyun Kim	73	69	71	213	22,342
Pat Hurst	70	75	69	214	15,699
Nancy Scranton	72	71	71	214	15,699
Cindy Figg-Currier	72	71	71	214	15,699
Helen Alfredsson	71	72	71	214	15,699
Luciana Bemvenuti	70	73	71	214	15,699
Kathryn Marshall	74	72	69	215	12,076
Tina Fischer	71	72	72	215	12,076
Michelle Murphy	75	73	68	216	10,265
Liselotte Neumann	73	73	70	216	10,265
Vicki Goetze-Ackerman	71	72	73	216	10,265
Mhairi McKay	70	73	73	216	10,265
Carin Koch	75	74	68	217	8,493
Penny Hammel	76	72	69	217	8,493
Kelli Kuehne	72	75	70	217	8,493
Barb Mucha	72	74	71	217	8,493
Rachel Teske	69	72	76	217	8,493
Pearl Sinn	76	72	70	218	6,843
Alicia Dibos	75	73	70	218	6,843
Dorothy Delasin	75	72	71	218	6,843
Leta Lindley	73	72	73	218	6,843
Amy Fruhwirth	71	74	73	218	6,843

	SCORES			TOTAL	MONEY
Cindy Flom	70	74	74	218	6,843
Patricia Meunier-Lebouc	70	72	76	218	6,843

Kathy Ireland Championship Honoring Harvey Penick

Onion Creek Club, Austin, Texas   April 26-29
Par 35-35–70; 6,067 yards   purse, $900,000

	SCORES				TOTAL	MONEY
Rosie Jones	66	67	68	67	268	$135,000
Mi Hyun Kim	70	68	64	66	268	83,783
(Jones defeated Kim on first playoff hole.)						
Marisa Baena	70	67	64	68	269	61,139
Dottie Pepper	71	66	68	67	272	47,553
Lorie Kane	67	68	68	72	275	38,494
Dorothy Delasin	70	69	71	67	277	25,814
Patricia Meunier-Lebouc	72	70	67	68	277	25,814
Mhairi McKay	67	72	69	69	277	25,814
Catriona Matthew	70	67	71	69	277	25,814
Hee-Won Han	75	69	67	67	278	18,146
Jane Crafter	69	73	68	68	278	18,146
Cindy Schreyer	73	69	67	70	279	14,554
Maria Hjorth	72	70	67	70	279	14,554
Barb Mucha	70	70	69	70	279	14,554
Leslie Spalding	71	70	67	71	279	14,554
Heather Bowie	69	70	74	67	280	11,384
Alison Nicholas	70	72	70	68	280	11,384
Michele Redman	68	70	72	70	280	11,384
Jenny Lidback	72	69	67	72	280	11,384
Michelle McGann	68	69	71	72	280	11,384
Moira Dunn	76	67	71	67	281	10,026
Carin Koch	66	72	74	70	282	9,369
Leta Lindley	67	70	74	71	282	9,369
Marianne Morris	70	74	73	66	283	8,033
Tina Barrett	66	72	76	69	283	8,033
Helen Dobson	70	72	71	70	283	8,033
Sophie Gustafson	71	69	73	70	283	8,033
Betsy King	73	70	69	71	283	8,033
Yu Ping Lin	68	72	72	71	283	8,033
Pearl Sinn	68	73	70	72	283	8,033

Chick-fil-A Charity Championship

Eagle's Landing Country Club, Stockbridge, Georgia   May 4-6
Par 36-36–72; 6,218 yards   purse, $1,200,000

	SCORES			TOTAL	MONEY
Annika Sorenstam	70	66	67	203	$180,000
Sophie Gustafson	70	65	68	203	111,711
(Sorenstam defeated Gustafson on second playoff hole.)					
Dottie Pepper	66	74	64	204	72,461
Beth Daniel	67	68	69	204	72,461
Catriona Matthew	71	65	69	205	51,326
Kelly Robbins	70	70	66	206	38,947
Sara Sanders	66	73	67	206	38,947

	SCORES			TOTAL	MONEY
Vicki Goetze-Ackerman	68	72	67	207	28,381
Kathryn Marshall	67	72	68	207	28,381
Nancy Scranton	69	68	70	207	28,381
Sherri Steinhauer	68	70	70	208	21,335
Juli Inkster	68	70	70	208	21,335
Heather Bowie	67	70	71	208	21,335
Hiromi Kobayashi	70	73	66	209	16,665
Cindy Figg-Currier	71	71	67	209	16,665
Betsy King	71	68	70	209	16,665
Emilee Klein	67	72	70	209	16,665
Silvia Cavalleri	67	71	71	209	16,665
Janice Moodie	73	71	66	210	13,032
Pamela Kerrigan	71	72	67	210	13,032
Mhairi McKay	73	69	68	210	13,032
Michelle McGann	69	70	71	210	13,032
Leta Lindley	68	70	72	210	13,032
Heather Daly-Donofrio	69	66	75	210	13,032
Karen Stupples	69	74	68	211	11,170
Laura Diaz	69	71	71	211	11,170
Sherri Turner	75	70	67	212	10,083
Lorie Kane	69	75	68	212	10,083
Jean Bartholomew	71	69	72	212	10,083
Gloria Park	71	70	71	212	10,083

Electrolux USA Championship

Legends Club of Tennessee, Ironhorse Course,   May 10-13
Franklin, Tennessee   purse, $800,000
Par 36-36–72; 6,425 yards

	SCORES				TOTAL	MONEY
Juli Inkster	73	67	69	65	274	$120,000
Catriona Matthew	66	71	69	69	275	74,474
Annika Sorenstam	69	67	70	70	276	54,346
Nancy Scranton	69	69	72	67	277	42,269
Sherri Turner	65	74	70	69	278	31,198
Jackie Gallagher-Smith	70	67	72	69	278	31,198
Tracy Hanson	67	67	73	72	279	22,342
Pat Hurst	64	71	70	74	279	22,342
Heather Bowie	72	69	71	68	280	15,699
Kris Tschetter	75	69	67	69	280	15,699
Wendy Doolan	69	69	73	69	280	15,699
Kelly Robbins	68	72	69	71	280	15,699
Jill McGill	66	72	71	71	280	15,699
Michele Redman	71	68	71	71	281	11,674
Kellee Booth	67	71	72	71	281	11,674
Fiona Pike	72	67	70	72	281	11,674
Michelle Ellis	68	69	75	70	282	9,862
Meg Mallon	71	71	69	71	282	9,862
Siew-Ai Lim	70	69	72	71	282	9,862
Marisa Baena	69	71	69	73	282	9,862
Carin Koch	72	70	70	71	283	7,753
Karrie Webb	68	73	71	71	283	7,753
Kelli Kuehne	72	70	69	72	283	7,753
Yu Ping Lin	72	69	70	72	283	7,753
Donna Andrews	68	71	72	72	283	7,753
Dawn Coe-Jones	70	73	67	73	283	7,753

	SCORES				TOTAL	MONEY
Mhairi McKay	66	70	71	76	283	7,753
Patricia Meunier-Lebouc	72	71	71	69	283	7,753
Gloria Park	70	71	73	70	284	5,729
Becky Iverson	68	69	76	71	284	5,729
Caroline McMillan	71	70	71	72	284	5,729
Cindy Flom	71	70	71	72	284	5,729
Caroline Blaylock	67	72	73	72	284	5,729
Cindy Figg-Currier	69	68	75	72	284	5,729
Lisa Hackney	70	72	68	74	284	5,729
Sherri Steinhauer	71	68	71	74	284	5,729
Hee-Won Han	70	73	70	71	284	5,729

Champions Classic

Country Club of the North, Beavercreek, Ohio
Par 36-36–72; 6,427 yards
(Shortened to 36 holes — rain.)

May 18-20
purse, $750,000

	SCORES		TOTAL	MONEY
Wendy Doolan	68	64	132	$112,500
Wendy Ward	64	68	132	69,819
(Doolan defeated Ward on fifth playoff hole.)				
Beth Daniel	68	65	133	45,288
Maria Hjorth	68	65	133	45,288
Janice Moodie	68	66	134	29,248
Dottie Pepper	67	67	134	29,248
Tina Barrett	71	64	135	19,876
Annika Sorenstam	69	66	135	19,876
Mhairi McKay	67	68	135	19,876
A.J. Eathorne	69	67	136	15,851
Becky Iverson	70	67	137	12,925
Jill McGill	68	69	137	12,925
Mi Hyun Kim	68	69	137	12,925
Kris Tschetter	68	69	137	12,925
Tracy Hanson	71	67	138	10,315
Karrie Webb	70	68	138	10,315
Heather Bowie	68	70	138	10,315
Kate Golden	73	66	139	8,175
Patricia Meunier-Lebouc	72	67	139	8,175
Nancy Scranton	71	68	139	8,175
Grace Park	69	70	139	8,175
Gloria Park	69	70	139	8,175
Michelle Estill	67	72	139	8,175
Smriti Mehra	67	72	139	8,175
Connie Wei	69	70	139	8,175
Eva Dahllof	73	67	140	5,987
Jamie Hullett	72	68	140	5,987
Akiko Fukushima	72	68	140	5,987
Becky Morgan	71	69	140	5,987
Luciana Bemvenuti	71	69	140	5,987
Annette DeLuca	70	70	140	5,987
Carri Wood	69	71	140	5,987
Marnie McGuire	68	72	140	5,987
Kristal Parker	68	72	140	5,987

Corning Classic

Corning Country Club, Corning, New York
Par 36-36–72; 6,062 yards

May 24-27
purse, $900,000

	SCORES				TOTAL	MONEY
Carin Koch	68	67	69	66	270	$135,000
Maria Hjorth	71	69	63	69	272	72,461
Mhairi McKay	69	65	68	70	272	72,461
Rosie Jones	68	72	67	66	273	43,023
Grace Park	70	66	70	67	273	43,023
Mi Hyun Kim	70	70	67	67	274	31,701
Dottie Pepper	69	71	66	69	275	26,720
Barb Mucha	70	69	69	69	277	22,417
Laura Diaz	70	67	69	71	277	22,417
Jane Crafter	66	74	69	69	278	16,803
Danielle Ammaccapane	68	72	68	70	278	16,803
Hiromi Kobayashi	68	72	68	70	278	16,803
Jenna Daniels	72	66	69	71	278	16,803
Janice Moodie	73	68	73	65	279	12,290
Tracy Hanson	71	71	71	66	279	12,290
Cindy Flom	68	70	74	67	279	12,290
Vickie Odegard	67	73	72	67	279	12,290
Michelle Estill	71	68	71	69	279	12,290
Becky Iverson	70	73	67	69	279	12,290
Sophie Gustafson	69	75	69	67	280	8,974
Moira Dunn	70	71	71	68	280	8,974
Catriona Matthew	69	72	71	68	280	8,974
Kathryn Marshall	69	71	71	69	280	8,974
Gloria Park	70	71	70	69	280	8,974
Helen Alfredsson	70	71	69	70	280	8,974
Alicia Dibos	71	68	70	71	280	8,974
Patricia Meunier-Lebouc	69	69	70	72	280	8,974
Vicki Goetze-Ackerman	73	66	69	72	280	8,974
Alison Nicholas	70	72	73	66	281	7,093
Eva Dahllof	67	72	72	70	281	7,093
Amy Fruhwirth	71	71	68	71	281	7,093
Kelli Kuehne	71	73	66	71	281	7,093

U.S. Women's Open

Pine Needles Lodge and Golf Club,
Southern Pines, North Carolina
Par 35-35–70; 6,256 yards

May 31-June 3
purse, $2,900,000

	SCORES				TOTAL	MONEY
Karrie Webb	70	65	69	69	273	$520,000
Se Ri Pak	69	70	70	72	281	310,000
Dottie Pepper	74	69	70	69	282	202,580
Cristie Kerr	69	73	71	70	283	118,697
Sherri Turner	72	70	71	70	283	118,697
Catriona Matthew	72	68	70	73	283	118,697
Lorie Kane	75	68	72	69	284	80,726
Kristi Albers	71	69	74	70	284	80,726
Kelli Kuehne	70	71	72	71	284	80,726
Wendy Doolan	71	70	70	73	284	80,726
Sophie Gustafson	74	66	74	71	285	66,581
Kelly Robbins	72	68	76	70	286	57,088

		SCORES			TOTAL	MONEY
A.J. Eathorne	67	71	75	73	286	57,088
Juli Inkster	68	72	71	75	286	57,088
Yuri Fudoh	73	68	70	75	286	57,088
Emilee Klein	72	69	75	71	287	46,885
Michele Redman	70	72	73	72	287	46,885
Annika Sorenstam	70	72	73	72	287	46,885
Maria Hjorth	70	71	77	70	288	37,327
Marisa Baena	71	72	75	70	288	37,327
Jill McGill	68	76	72	72	288	37,327
Wendy Ward	70	71	74	73	288	37,327
Dorothy Delasin	75	70	70	73	288	37,327
Beth Daniel	73	70	71	75	289	30,091
Audra Burks	70	72	72	75	289	30,091
Brandie Burton	73	70	77	70	290	24,649
Helen Alfredsson	71	73	74	72	290	24,649
Mi Hyun Kim	68	76	72	74	290	24,649
Janice Moodie	71	70	73	76	290	24,649
Kris Tschetter	72	74	77	68	291	20,472
Michelle Ellis	75	69	75	72	291	20,472
*Candy Hannemann	73	73	72	73	291	
Meg Mallon	72	70	76	73	291	20,472

Wegmans Rochester International

Locust Hill Country Club, Pittsford, New York
Par 35-37–72; 6,190 yards

June 7-10
purse, $1,000,000

		SCORES			TOTAL	MONEY
Laura Davies	68	68	69	74	279	$150,000
Wendy Ward	72	71	72	67	282	80,513
Maria Hjorth	70	71	69	72	282	80,513
Brandie Burton	68	69	73	73	283	52,836
Rosie Jones	74	73	69	68	284	31,500
Jenny Lidback	72	71	71	70	284	31,500
Mhairi McKay	70	73	70	71	284	31,500
Kelli Kuehne	73	69	70	72	284	31,500
Emilee Klein	68	74	69	73	284	31,500
Michelle Estill	70	76	69	71	286	21,135
Alicia Dibos	73	74	71	69	287	17,183
Heather Daly-Donofrio	72	73	73	69	287	17,183
Cindy Figg-Currier	73	71	74	69	287	17,183
Sherri Turner	71	73	75	69	288	13,921
Sherri Steinhauer	75	72	71	70	288	13,921
Jen Hanna	74	70	73	71	288	13,921
Danielle Ammaccapane	70	71	75	72	288	13,921
Tammie Green	70	72	71	75	288	13,921
Dorothy Delasin	71	74	74	70	289	11,113
Gloria Park	70	73	73	73	289	11,113
Nancy Scranton	68	75	73	73	289	11,113
Donna Andrews	70	73	72	74	289	11,113
Becky Iverson	70	75	68	76	289	11,113
Leta Lindley	67	78	76	69	290	9,493
Jill McGill	70	72	77	71	290	9,493
Barb Mucha	75	68	70	77	290	9,493
Deb Richard	74	73	72	72	291	8,436
Leslie Spalding	72	72	75	72	291	8,436
Liselotte Neumann	70	74	73	74	291	8,436
Laura Diaz	69	72	75	75	291	8,436

Evian Ladies Masters

See Ladies European Tour section.

McDonald's LPGA Championship

DuPont Country Club, Wilmington, Delaware
Par 35-36–71; 6,408 yards

June 21-24
purse, $1,500,000

	SCORES				TOTAL	MONEY
Karrie Webb	67	64	70	69	270	$225,000
Laura Diaz	67	71	66	68	272	139,639
Wendy Ward	65	69	71	69	274	90,577
Maria Hjorth	71	67	66	70	274	90,577
Annika Sorenstam	68	69	71	67	275	64,157
Becky Iverson	66	73	67	70	276	48,684
Laura Davies	67	68	70	71	276	48,684
Mi Hyun Kim	70	70	68	69	277	39,250
Helen Alfredsson	68	66	74	70	278	35,476
Maggie Will	68	74	67	70	279	30,245
Michele Redman	69	66	73	71	279	30,245
Rosie Jones	71	69	71	69	280	25,013
Lorie Kane	69	71	71	69	280	25,013
Liselotte Neumann	69	72	68	71	280	25,013
Wendy Doolan	70	71	72	68	281	21,239
Juli Inkster	71	71	69	70	281	21,239
Dottie Pepper	71	72	71	68	282	16,819
Kelly Robbins	69	74	71	68	282	16,819
Carin Koch	69	73	71	69	282	16,819
Meg Mallon	71	74	67	70	282	16,819
Leta Lindley	71	71	70	70	282	16,819
Pat Hurst	72	68	72	70	282	16,819
Terry-Jo Myers	70	71	69	72	282	16,819
Rachel Teske	68	72	70	72	282	16,819
Mhairi McKay	68	72	70	72	282	16,819
Heather Daly-Donofrio	75	68	71	69	283	13,162
Beth Daniel	71	71	70	71	283	13,162
Nancy Scranton	73	68	70	72	283	13,162
Akiko Fukushima	66	72	73	72	283	13,162
Catriona Matthew	71	72	72	69	284	11,603
Grace Park	71	72	71	70	284	11,603
Dawn Coe-Jones	72	69	71	72	284	11,603

ShopRite Classic

Marriott Seaview Resort, Bay Course,
Atlantic City, New Jersey
Par 36-35–71; 6,051 yards

June 29-July 1
purse, $1,200,000

	SCORES			TOTAL	MONEY
Betsy King	65	69	67	201	$180,000
Lorie Kane	65	68	70	203	111,711
Leslie Spalding	71	72	64	207	50,923
Donna Andrews	68	74	65	207	50,923
Tamie Durdin	68	72	67	207	50,923
Catriona Matthew	68	69	70	207	50,923
Rosie Jones	70	66	71	207	50,923

	SCORES			TOTAL	MONEY
Cristie Kerr	67	66	74	207	50,923
Karen Stupples	70	72	66	208	25,563
Terry-Jo Myers	66	75	67	208	25,563
Michelle Estill	67	69	72	208	25,563
Laura Davies	70	71	68	209	18,718
Danielle Ammaccapane	68	70	71	209	18,718
Janice Moodie	70	67	72	209	18,718
Marisa Baena	67	68	74	209	18,718
Pat Hurst	63	72	74	209	18,718
Sophie Gustafson	71	71	68	210	13,623
Nancy Scranton	69	73	68	210	13,623
Cindy Figg-Currier	71	70	69	210	13,623
Helen Alfredsson	70	70	70	210	13,623
Angela Stanford	66	74	70	210	13,623
Tammie Green	70	68	72	210	13,623
Juli Inkster	69	69	72	210	13,623
Carin Koch	66	70	74	210	13,623
Jenny Lidback	73	70	68	211	9,757
Becky Morgan	68	74	69	211	9,757
Hee-Won Han	68	73	70	211	9,757
Maggie Will	67	73	71	211	9,757
Vicki Goetze-Ackerman	67	73	71	211	9,757
Barb Mucha	69	70	72	211	9,757
Mi Hyun Kim	67	72	72	211	9,757
Shani Waugh	69	68	74	211	9,757
Marcy Newton	69	68	74	211	9,757
Moira Dunn	67	70	74	211	9,757

Jamie Farr Kroger Classic

Highland Meadows Golf Club, Sylvania, Ohio　　　　　　　July 5-8
Par 34-37–71; 6,365 yards　　　　　　　purse, $1,000,000

	SCORES				TOTAL	MONEY
Se Ri Pak	70	62	69	68	269	$150,000
Maria Hjorth	76	65	66	64	271	93,093
Marnie McGuire	70	69	69	65	273	60,384
Heather Bowie	68	66	71	68	273	60,384
Laura Diaz	70	67	70	67	274	33,463
Moira Dunn	68	68	70	68	274	33,463
Kris Tschetter	70	67	68	69	274	33,463
Meg Mallon	70	67	68	69	274	33,463
Mi Hyun Kim	72	68	74	62	276	19,625
Carin Koch	69	66	73	68	276	19,625
Mhairi McKay	75	67	65	69	276	19,625
Vicki Goetze-Ackerman	70	70	67	69	276	19,625
Kelly Robbins	68	71	68	69	276	19,625
Helen Alfredsson	71	71	71	64	277	15,599
Tracy Hanson	72	70	69	67	278	13,184
Jeong Jang	72	69	70	67	278	13,184
Tammie Green	70	68	73	67	278	13,184
Leta Lindley	72	67	71	68	278	13,184
Jenna Daniels	70	70	69	69	278	13,184
Sophie Gustafson	71	70	71	67	279	11,070
Rachel Teske	72	70	69	68	279	11,070
Heather Daly-Donofrio	70	71	68	70	279	11,070
Beth Daniel	72	72	70	66	280	9,623

	SCORES				TOTAL	MONEY
Michelle Estill	71	71	71	67	280	9,623
Amy Fruhwirth	72	71	69	68	280	9,623
Karrie Webb	70	68	69	73	280	9,623
Tamie Durdin	72	72	68	69	281	8,110
Brandie Burton	70	71	71	69	281	8,110
Smriti Mehra	68	70	74	69	281	8,110
Jennifer Hubbard	69	71	70	71	281	8,110
Alicia Dibos	67	71	69	74	281	8,110
Connie Masterson	73	67	73	68	281	8,110

Michelob Light Classic

Fox Run Golf Club, Eureka, Missouri   July 13-15
Par 36-36–72; 6,452 yards   purse, $800,000

	SCORES			TOTAL	MONEY
Emilee Klein	64	72	69	205	$120,000
Jill McGill	71	76	63	210	64,410
Annika Sorenstam	68	72	70	210	64,410
Shani Waugh	73	72	66	211	34,888
Mitzi Edge	71	73	67	211	34,888
Denise Killeen	68	71	72	211	34,888
Jeong Jang	72	73	67	212	18,316
Leta Lindley	69	75	68	212	18,316
Amy Fruhwirth	74	69	69	212	18,316
Diana D'Alessio	69	74	69	212	18,316
Kris Tschetter	68	73	71	212	18,316
Karrie Webb	70	69	73	212	18,316
Rosie Jones	74	70	69	213	11,213
Juli Inkster	72	71	70	213	11,213
Hee-Won Han	73	69	71	213	11,213
Rachel Teske	73	69	71	213	11,213
Lorie Kane	71	70	72	213	11,213
Nancy Scranton	69	72	72	213	11,213
Sherri Turner	68	70	75	213	11,213
Natascha Fink	70	72	72	214	8,856
Dina Ammaccapane	69	71	74	214	8,856
Nanci Bowen	71	68	75	214	8,856
Laurel Kean	73	72	70	215	7,575
Jamie Hullett	70	74	71	215	7,575
Cindy Schreyer	73	70	72	215	7,575
Jean Bartholomew	73	69	73	215	7,575
Yu Ping Lin	71	69	75	215	7,575
Audra Burks	76	72	68	216	6,722
Jennifer Hubbard	67	75	74	216	6,722
Akiko Fukushima	76	71	70	217	5,925
Tamie Durdin	73	73	71	217	5,925
Becky Morgan	71	73	73	217	5,925
Kristal Parker	70	74	73	217	5,925
Kelly Robbins	72	71	74	217	5,925

Sybase Big Apple Classic

Wykagyl Country Club, New Rochelle, New York
Par 35-36–71; 6,161 yards

July 19-22
purse, $950,000

	SCORES				TOTAL	MONEY
Rosie Jones	70	66	66	70	272	$142,500
Laura Diaz	68	71	68	66	273	88,438
Kris Tschetter	68	70	70	66	274	64,536
Michele Redman	66	70	70	69	275	50,195
Rachel Teske	70	72	70	64	276	34,099
Lorie Kane	69	71	68	68	276	34,099
Nancy Scranton	64	71	70	71	276	34,099
Annika Sorenstam	72	69	70	66	277	23,663
Mi Hyun Kim	68	68	70	71	277	23,663
Wendy Ward	68	69	72	69	278	20,078
Leta Lindley	73	69	68	70	280	17,448
Marnie McGuire	71	71	68	70	280	17,448
Meg Mallon	74	69	68	70	281	14,341
Mhairi McKay	70	68	72	71	281	14,341
Audra Burks	71	68	67	75	281	14,341
Betsy King	68	71	67	75	281	14,341
Beth Daniel	73	69	70	70	282	12,428
Dorothy Delasin	71	71	73	68	283	10,550
Cristie Kerr	69	68	76	70	283	10,550
Barb Mucha	76	71	65	71	283	10,550
Carri Wood	72	69	70	72	283	10,550
Emilee Klein	70	70	71	72	283	10,550
Silvia Cavalleri	70	72	68	73	283	10,550
Alicia Dibos	71	69	69	74	283	10,550
Yu Ping Lin	69	70	71	74	284	8,987
Siew-Ai Lim	73	69	69	74	285	8,700
Marilyn Lovander	73	70	76	67	286	7,445
Jackie Gallagher-Smith	73	71	74	68	286	7,445
Tina Barrett	72	74	68	72	286	7,445
Mitzi Edge	69	70	75	72	286	7,445
Vicki Goetze-Ackerman	74	68	71	73	286	7,445
Michelle McGann	70	70	73	73	286	7,445
Shani Waugh	69	71	73	73	286	7,445
Connie Wei	72	67	73	74	286	7,445

Giant Eagle Classic

Squaw Creek Country Club, Vienna, Ohio
Par 37-35–72; 6,361 yards

July 27-29
purse, $1,000,000

	SCORES			TOTAL	MONEY
Dorothy Delasin	69	69	65	203	$150,000
Tammie Green	69	67	68	204	93,093
Se Ri Pak	67	67	71	205	67,933
Janice Moodie	69	71	67	207	40,130
Dina Ammaccapane	69	70	68	207	40,130
Becky Iverson	68	70	69	207	40,130
Sherri Steinhauer	69	68	70	207	40,130
Mi Hyun Kim	69	72	67	208	26,167
Danielle Ammaccapane	73	69	67	209	20,396
Jen Hanna	70	70	69	209	20,396

	SCORES			TOTAL	MONEY
Donna Andrews	68	71	70	209	20,396
Marianne Morris	72	66	71	209	20,396
Vickie Odegard	69	70	71	210	16,135
Laurel Kean	68	70	72	210	16,135
Dawn Coe-Jones	75	70	66	211	12,685
Michele Redman	71	72	68	211	12,685
Deb Richard	71	71	69	211	12,685
Angela Stanford	70	72	69	211	12,685
Jenny Lidback	72	69	70	211	12,685
Laura Diaz	73	67	71	211	12,685
Dodie Mazzuca	70	69	72	211	12,685
Maggie Will	67	74	71	212	10,373
Heather Bowie	72	67	73	212	10,373
Betsy King	75	69	69	213	8,738
Amy Fruhwirth	73	71	69	213	8,738
Jenny Park-Choi	72	71	70	213	8,738
Patricia Baxter-Johnson	71	72	70	213	8,738
Audra Burks	69	71	73	213	8,738
Jane Geddes	69	70	74	213	8,738
Marnie McGuire	67	71	75	213	8,738
Suzy Green	69	74	70	213	8,738

Weetabix Women's British Open

See Ladies European Tour section.

Wendy's Championship for Children

New Albany Country Club, New Albany, Ohio
Par 36-36–72; 6,279 yards

August 10-12
purse, $1,000,000

	SCORES			TOTAL	MONEY
Wendy Ward	65	62	68	195	$150,000
Annika Sorenstam	67	65	66	198	80,513
Moira Dunn	67	64	67	198	80,513
Rosie Jones	66	69	66	201	52,836
Meg Mallon	70	65	67	202	42,772
Kelli Kuehne	68	70	65	203	30,360
Amy Fruhwirth	69	67	67	203	30,360
Karrie Webb	67	68	68	203	30,360
Kelly Robbins	69	70	65	204	21,313
Catriona Matthew	70	67	67	204	21,313
Mhairi McKay	72	63	69	204	21,313
Lorie Kane	72	66	67	205	15,632
Wendy Doolan	72	66	67	205	15,632
Vicki Goetze-Ackerman	68	70	67	205	15,632
Danielle Ammaccapane	67	69	69	205	15,632
Rachel Teske	66	69	70	205	15,632
Audra Burks	66	75	65	206	12,613
Nancy Scranton	70	69	67	206	12,613
Cindy Schreyer	69	69	68	206	12,613
Nanci Bowen	70	71	66	207	10,276
Suzy Green	69	70	68	207	10,276
Emilee Klein	66	73	68	207	10,276
Beth Daniel	69	69	69	207	10,276
Leta Lindley	64	72	71	207	10,276

	SCORES	TOTAL	MONEY
Tracy Hanson	66 69 72	207	10,276
Michelle Louviere	71 69 67	207	10,276
Hee-Won Han	69 72 67	208	8,436
Yu Ping Lin	66 75 67	208	8,436
Se Ri Pak	71 69 68	208	8,436
Dottie Pepper	67 72 69	208	8,436

Bank of Montreal Canadian Women's Open

Angus Glen Golf Club, South Course,　　　　　　　　　　　　August 16-19
Markham, Ontario, Canada　　　　　　　　　　　　　　　purse, $1,200,000
Par 36-36–72; 6,411 yards

	SCORES	TOTAL	MONEY
Annika Sorenstam	71 68 64 69	272	$180,000
Kelly Robbins	65 69 69 71	274	111,711
Se Ri Pak	65 72 71 68	276	72,461
Lorie Kane	69 69 68 70	276	72,461
Cristie Kerr	69 69 71 68	277	51,326
Mi Hyun Kim	71 72 69 67	279	36,431
Hiromi Kobayashi	69 75 67 68	279	36,431
Rosie Jones	65 69 71 74	279	36,431
Kelli Kuehne	75 70 69 66	280	23,550
Gloria Park	70 73 69 68	280	23,550
Emilee Klein	72 73 65 70	280	23,550
Wendy Doolan	71 69 70 70	280	23,550
Jill McGill	70 73 64 73	280	23,550
Maria Hjorth	68 69 70 74	281	18,718
Karrie Webb	71 75 67 69	282	16,907
Danielle Ammaccapane	70 71 70 71	282	16,907
Heather Daly-Donofrio	70 70 72 71	283	14,793
Jane Crafter	71 74 65 73	283	14,793
Meg Mallon	70 72 68 73	283	14,793
Tammie Green	69 73 64 77	283	14,793
Catriona Matthew	68 78 69 69	284	12,982
Hee-Won Han	68 72 72 72	284	12,982
Janice Moodie	73 70 70 72	285	11,363
Dawn Coe-Jones	68 74 71 72	285	11,363
Amy Fruhwirth	71 73 67 74	285	11,363
Kristal Parker	69 72 68 76	285	11,363
Barb Mucha	66 75 68 76	285	11,363
Joanne Morley	69 78 69 70	286	9,721
Vicki Goetze-Ackerman	73 71 70 72	286	9,721
A.J. Eathorne	69 74 69 74	286	9,721
Donna Andrews	67 73 71 75	286	9,721

First Union Betsy King Classic

Berkleigh Country Club, Kutztown, Pennsylvania　　　　　　August 23-26
Par 35-37–72; 6,197 yards　　　　　　　　　　　　　　　purse, $800,000

	SCORES	TOTAL	MONEY
Heather Daly-Donofrio	65 71 68 69	273	$120,000
Mhairi McKay	69 67 68 70	274	64,410
Moira Dunn	68 66 68 72	274	64,410

	SCORES				TOTAL	MONEY
Catriona Matthew	68	70	67	70	275	42,269
Mi Hyun Kim	72	67	72	65	276	34,217
Meg Mallon	71	67	67	72	277	28,179
Pat Hurst	68	71	70	69	278	23,751
Tina Barrett	71	72	69	67	279	18,028
Michelle Estill	71	72	67	69	279	18,028
A.J. Eathorne	73	69	67	70	279	18,028
Audra Burks	69	68	70	72	279	18,028
Alicia Dibos	72	67	72	69	280	13,742
Helen Alfredsson	69	70	69	72	280	13,742
Betsy King	71	74	69	67	281	11,166
Jane Crafter	71	69	70	71	281	11,166
Michele Redman	69	72	68	72	281	11,166
Rachel Teske	66	71	70	74	281	11,166
Wendy Doolan	67	68	70	76	281	11,166
Patricia Baxter-Johnson	70	71	72	69	282	9,113
Tina Fischer	71	71	70	70	282	9,113
Jean Bartholomew	76	67	67	72	282	9,113
Hee-Won Han	70	71	69	72	282	9,113
Lisa Kiggens	74	70	71	68	283	7,387
Beth Daniel	71	74	68	70	283	7,387
Kris Lindstrom	73	70	70	70	283	7,387
Vicki Goetze-Ackerman	71	73	68	71	283	7,387
Becky Morgan	71	67	72	73	283	7,387
Silvia Cavalleri	72	69	68	74	283	7,387
Kathryn Marshall	69	71	69	74	283	7,387
Karen Pearce	71	72	73	68	284	6,188
Jackie Gallagher-Smith	70	71	71	72	284	6,188
Kate Golden	73	70	66	75	284	6,188

State Farm Classic

Rail Golf Course, Springfield, Illinois
Par 36-36–72; 6,403 yards

August 30-September 2
purse, $1,000,000

	SCORES				TOTAL	MONEY
Kate Golden	69	65	70	63	267	$150,000
Annika Sorenstam	65	66	67	70	268	93,093
Moira Dunn	69	68	67	67	271	67,933
Emilee Klein	68	66	70	68	272	52,836
Laura Diaz	71	69	65	68	273	42,772
Wendy Ward	67	72	68	67	274	30,360
Tracy Hanson	66	73	68	67	274	30,360
Patricia Meunier-Lebouc	70	68	67	69	274	30,360
Jill McGill	68	69	72	66	275	21,308
Tina Fischer	65	70	70	70	275	21,308
Jean Bartholomew	71	65	68	71	275	21,308
Alicia Dibos	68	69	67	72	276	17,125
Cristie Kerr	73	67	63	73	276	17,125
Suzanne Strudwick	71	71	69	66	277	14,231
Karen Stupples	70	69	70	68	277	14,231
Chris Johnson	70	70	68	69	277	14,231
Helen Alfredsson	69	68	70	70	277	14,231
Rosie Jones	70	72	72	64	278	12,344
Charlotta Sorenstam	68	73	68	69	278	12,344
Danielle Ammaccapane	71	70	70	68	279	10,633
Barb Mucha	68	71	69	71	279	10,633

	SCORES				TOTAL	MONEY
Sherri Steinhauer	69	69	70	71	279	10,633
Marianne Morris	66	70	71	72	279	10,633
Gloria Park	70	66	69	74	279	10,633
Betsy King	72	70	72	66	280	9,023
Carri Wood	70	68	73	69	280	9,023
Shani Waugh	70	69	71	70	280	9,023
Jenny Park-Choi	68	69	72	71	280	9,023
Wendy Doolan	68	74	71	68	281	7,695
Donna Andrews	70	71	72	68	281	7,695
Pearl Sinn	67	71	74	69	281	7,695
Pat Hurst	70	69	70	72	281	7,695
Susie Redman	67	72	68	74	281	7,695

Williams Championship

Tulsa Country Club, Tulsa, Oklahoma
Par 35-35–70; 6,233 yards

September 7-9
purse, $1,000,000

	SCORES			TOTAL	MONEY
Gloria Park	68	69	64	201	$150,000
Donna Andrews	70	62	70	202	93,093
Rachel Teske	69	67	71	207	67,933
Nancy Scranton	71	67	70	208	52,836
Grace Park	72	68	69	209	31,500
Becky Iverson	73	66	70	209	31,500
Barb Mucha	72	67	70	209	31,500
Yu Ping Lin	72	66	71	209	31,500
Wendy Ward	70	66	73	209	31,500
Amy Fruhwirth	70	68	72	210	20,136
Rosie Jones	71	65	74	210	20,136
Dottie Pepper	75	68	68	211	15,196
Dorothy Delasin	74	69	68	211	15,196
Mhairi McKay	73	69	69	211	15,196
Cindy Schreyer	72	70	69	211	15,196
Kelly Robbins	68	71	72	211	15,196
Dawn Coe-Jones	72	66	73	211	15,196
Michelle McGann	72	70	70	212	11,589
Sherri Turner	73	68	71	212	11,589
Vicki Goetze-Ackerman	73	68	71	212	11,589
Karen Weiss	76	64	72	212	11,589
Becky Morgan	72	68	72	212	11,589
Danielle Ammaccapane	73	71	69	213	9,639
Annika Sorenstam	72	70	71	213	9,639
Tracy Hanson	70	72	71	213	9,639
Helen Alfredsson	70	67	76	213	9,639
Suzanne Strudwick	77	69	68	214	8,570
Shani Waugh	75	69	70	214	8,570
Jill McGill	74	67	73	214	8,570
Denise Killeen	74	72	69	215	7,423
Karrie Webb	74	70	71	215	7,423
Karen Stupples	78	65	72	215	7,423
Beth Bader	70	73	72	215	7,423
Michele Redman	74	68	73	215	7,423

	SCORES				TOTAL	MONEY
Maria Hjorth	73	73	69	69	284	15,596
Betsy King	73	71	70	70	284	15,596
Mi Hyun Kim	65	71	78	71	285	13,525
Nancy Scranton	73	69	71	72	285	13,525
Wendy Doolan	71	73	68	73	285	13,525
Juli Inkster	71	76	71	68	286	11,162
Catriona Matthew	72	70	75	69	286	11,162
Michele Redman	73	70	72	71	286	11,162
Kelly Robbins	69	72	73	72	286	11,162
Sherri Steinhauer	71	70	72	73	286	11,162
Wendy Ward	76	72	73	66	287	10,172
Gloria Park	77	71	72	68	288	9,647
Rosie Jones	73	72	69	74	288	9,647
Janice Moodie	73	70	73	73	289	9,082
Charlotta Sorenstam	69	78	71	72	290	8,593
Dorothy Delasin	72	74	71	73	290	8,593
Rachel Teske	70	74	70	76	290	8,593
Mardi Lunn	74	72	71	76	293	8,097
Kelli Kuehne	75	74	74	72	295	7,857
Beth Daniel	72	76	75	73	296	7,627
Jackie Gallagher-Smith	74	79	74	71	298	7,387

Samsung World Championship

Hiddenbrooke Golf Club, Vallejo, California   October 4-7
Par 36-36–72; 6,350 yards   purse, $750,000

	SCORES				TOTAL	MONEY
Dorothy Delasin	70	71	67	69	277	$157,000
Se Ri Pak	70	72	67	72	281	81,500
Karrie Webb	72	67	70	72	281	81,500
Kelly Robbins	71	75	72	66	284	52,000
Emilee Klein	71	75	65	75	286	42,000
Juli Inkster	74	70	68	75	287	34,000
Mi Hyun Kim	74	70	71	73	288	30,000
Laura Diaz	77	70	74	68	289	25,500
Lorie Kane	78	69	71	71	289	25,500
Sophie Gustafson	71	74	74	71	290	18,562
Wendy Ward	76	72	70	72	290	18,562
Janice Moodie	76	69	72	73	290	18,562
Annika Sorenstam	73	72	71	74	290	18,562
Rachel Teske	77	65	72	77	291	15,500
Michele Redman	76	72	70	74	292	15,000
Catriona Matthew	76	73	73	72	294	14,250
Maria Hjorth	78	70	71	75	294	14,250
Dottie Pepper	74	74	72	77	297	13,500
Rosie Jones	73	74	72	81	300	13,000
Ah Ram Suh	82	81	72	72	307	12,500

Asahi Ryokuken International Championship

Mount Vintage Plantation Golf Club,
North Augusta, South Carolina
Par 36-36–72; 6,321 yards
(Shortened to 54 holes — rain.)

September :
purse, $1,20

	SCORES			TOTAL	MONE
Tina Fischer	70	66	70	206	$180,00
Emilee Klein	69	68	70	207	96,61
Tracy Hanson	70	66	71	207	96,61
Annika Sorenstam	71	69	68	208	57,36
Lorie Kane	71	69	68	208	57,36
Sophie Gustafson	75	66	68	209	30,99
Charlotta Sorenstam	71	70	68	209	30,99
Meg Mallon	70	68	71	209	30,99
Nancy Scranton	68	68	73	209	30,99
Kris Tschetter	68	66	75	209	30,99
Jamie Hullett	70	70	69	209	30,99
Carin Koch	69	69	72	210	21,13
Kim Williams	73	73	65	211	18,718
Janice Moodie	74	70	67	211	18,718
Vickie Odegard	67	73	71	211	18,718
Jean Bartholomew	74	72	66	212	13,921
Donna Andrews	75	70	67	212	13,921
Alicia Dibos	73	71	68	212	13,921
Maria Hjorth	73	69	70	212	13,921
Kelli Kuehne	68	74	70	212	13,921
Mi Hyun Kim	73	68	71	212	13,921
Rosie Jones	71	68	73	212	13,921
Marianne Morris	67	72	73	212	13,921
Laura Diaz	67	69	76	212	13,921
Kristal Parker	72	73	68	213	10,091
Cindy Flom	74	70	69	213	10,091
Dawn Coe-Jones	70	74	69	213	10,091
Karen Pearce	73	70	70	213	10,091
Leslie Spalding	72	70	71	213	10,091
Jenny Rosales	70	71	72	213	10,091
Leta Lindley	73	67	73	213	10,091
Heather Bowie	69	68	76	213	10,091

AFLAC Champions

Robert Trent Jones Golf Trail at Magnolia Grove,
Mobile, Alabama
Par 36-36–72; 6,253 yards

September 27-3
purse, $750,00

	SCORES				TOTAL	MONEY
Se Ri Pak	70	67	64	71	272	$122,000
Lorie Kane	72	69	67	69	277	75,500
Grace Park	69	69	71	70	279	54,250
Emilee Klein	70	69	73	68	280	42,050
Carin Koch	70	73	71	67	281	30,550
Meg Mallon	71	69	72	69	281	30,550
Kate Golden	71	72	70	69	282	22,900
Karrie Webb	69	74	69	71	283	18,725
Dottie Pepper	67	73	69	74	283	18,725

Tyco/ADT Championship

Trump International Golf Club, West Palm Beach, Florida November 15-18
Par 36-36–72; 6,485 yards purse, $1,000,000

	SCORES				TOTAL	MONEY
Karrie Webb	67	71	73	68	279	$215,000
Annika Sorenstam	68	74	74	65	281	115,000
Janice Moodie	70	75	69	74	288	86,000
Rosie Jones	71	73	72	73	289	57,000
Meg Mallon	69	74	76	72	291	50,000
Betsy King	75	76	72	71	294	43,000
Sophie Gustafson	75	75	75	70	295	33,000
Grace Park	69	78	76	72	295	33,000
Laura Davies	73	71	80	72	296	21,650
Moira Dunn	71	73	75	77	296	21,650
Michele Redman	73	74	74	75	296	21,650
Maria Hjorth	77	73	69	77	296	21,650
Dottie Pepper	74	74	75	73	296	21,650
Juli Inkster	75	74	74	74	297	15,750
Wendy Doolan	69	73	83	72	297	15,750
Lorie Kane	73	74	78	75	300	13,875
Carin Koch	73	77	75	75	300	13,875
Kelly Robbins	74	79	77	71	301	12,000
Cristie Kerr	73	72	77	79	301	12,000
Wendy Ward	76	72	79	74	301	12,000
Marisa Baena	69	78	77	77	301	12,000
Emilee Klein	77	77	78	70	302	11,000
Dorothy Delasin	74	82	72	75	303	10,650
Catriona Matthew	78	79	77	72	306	10,150
Laura Diaz	77	77	81	71	306	10,150
Pat Hurst	81	76	77	73	307	9,500
Beth Daniel	77	77	80	73	307	9,500
Jill McGill	73	78	85	75	311	9,000
Mhairi McKay	75	83	78	80	316	8,850
Nancy Scranton	81	81	78	78	318	8,700

Hyundai Team Matches

Monarch Beach Golf Links, Dana Point, California December 8-9
Par 34-36–70; 6,094 yards purse, $1,200,000

FIRST-ROUND MATCHES

Grace Park and Wendy Ward defeated Juli Inkster and Dottie Pepper, 1 up.
Lorie Kane and Janice Moodie defeated Karrie Webb and Kelly Robbins, 2 and 1.

THIRD-PLACE MATCH

Webb and Robbins defeated Inkster and Pepper, 3 and 2.
(Webb and Robbins received $30,000 each; Inkster and Pepper received $20,000 each.)

CHAMPIONSHIP MATCH

Kane and Moodie defeated Park and Ward, 5 and 4.
(Kane and Moodie received $100,000 each; Park and Ward received $50,000 each.)

Evian Ladies European Tour

Australasian Ladies Masters

Royal Pines Resort, Ashmore, Gold Coast, Queensland
Par 35-37–72; 6,997 yards

March 1-4
purse, £200,000

	SCORES				TOTAL	MONEY
Karrie Webb	67	70	65	69	271	£30,391.51
Rachel Teske	71	68	71	69	279	20,260.94
Catriona Matthew	70	70	72	68	280	12,156.64
Kelly Robbins	68	67	75	71	281	10,130.56
Corinne Dibnah	68	70	74	71	283	7,901.71
Kathryn Marshall	67	73	68	75	283	7,901.71
Catrin Nilsmark	72	74	69	69	284	6,145.82
Maria Hjorth	70	75	68	71	284	6,145.82
Alison Munt	70	69	72	73	284	6,145.82
Patricia Meunier Lebouc	70	74	70	71	285	3,885.07
Fiona Pike	70	69	72	74	285	3,885.07
Tina Fischer	74	67	69	75	285	3,885.07
Lynette Brooky	66	65	76	78	285	3,885.07
So-Young Park	72	72	75	67	286	2,802.69
Karen Pearce	73	69	72	72	286	2,802.69
Diane Barnard	65	73	74	74	286	2,802.69
Alison Nicholas	71	72	74	70	287	2,384.08
Becky Morgan	74	72	71	70	287	2,384.08
Marine Monnet	71	73	71	72	287	2,384.08
Jane Leary	73	72	75	68	288	1,924.78
Gina Scott	73	74	73	68	288	1,924.78
Anne-Marie Knight	74	69	76	69	288	1,924.78
Joanne Morley	69	71	78	70	288	1,924.78
Carmen Hajjar	70	74	74	70	288	1,924.78
Shani Waugh	74	70	74	70	288	1,924.78
Il-Mi Chung	75	69	73	71	288	1,924.78
Esther Poburski	69	75	70	74	288	1,924.78
Helen Dobson	70	74	75	70	289	1,398
Soo-Yun Kang	73	74	72	70	289	1,398
Raquel Carriedo	71	71	75	72	289	1,398
Jan Stephenson	74	68	74	73	289	1,398
Laurette Maritz	69	73	74	73	289	1,398
Jane Crafter	71	75	70	73	289	1,398

AAMI Women's Australian Open

Yarra Yarra Golf Club, Melbourne, Victoria
Par 37-36–73; 6,054 yards

March 8-11
purse, £150,000

	SCORES				TOTAL	MONEY
Sophie Gustafson	70	69	66	71	276	£24,313.20
Karrie Webb	70	70	69	68	277	16,208.75
Jane Crafter	68	71	70	74	283	9,725.31
Corinne Dibnah	66	72	76	70	284	8,104.45

	SCORES				TOTAL	MONEY
Elisabeth Esterl	68	71	76	71	286	6,051.25
Alison Nicholas	68	74	73	71	286	6,051.25
Alison Munt	65	71	78	72	286	6,051.25
Patricia Meunier Lebouc	72	75	70	70	287	4,322.34
Marine Monnet	69	69	78	71	287	4,322.34
Becky Morgan	75	67	72	73	287	4,322.34
Paula Marti	72	74	74	69	289	2,684.17
Raquel Carriedo	72	74	74	69	289	2,684.17
Lynnette Brooky	77	67	74	71	289	2,684.17
Johanna Head	73	70	74	72	289	2,684.17
Soo-Yun Kang	70	74	71	74	289	2,684.17
Laura Davies	72	69	78	71	290	2,042.30
Karen Pearce	75	70	73	72	290	2,042.30
Virginie Auffret	72	70	75	73	290	2,042.30
Kelly Robbins	74	73	72	72	291	1,815.39
*Carlie Butler	74	71	72	74	291	
Sophie Sandolo	76	72	69	74	291	1,815.39
*Nikki Campbell	74	75	74	69	292	
Karine Icher	73	73	75	71	292	1,620.86
Samantha Head	75	72	74	71	292	1,620.86
*Helen Beatty	72	74	73	73	292	
Iben Tinning	71	73	72	76	292	1,620.86
Shani Waugh	76	72	67	77	292	1,620.86
Caroline Hall	75	74	67	77	293	1,458.79
Kate MacIntosh	75	71	74	74	294	1,394.02
*Rebecca Stevenson	76	72	70	76	294	

Taiwan Ladies Open

Ta Shee Golf & Country Club, Ta Shee, Taiwan
Par 36-36–72; 6,292 yards

March 15-17
purse, £100,000

	SCORES			TOTAL	MONEY
Raquel Carriedo	69	67	75	211	£15,000
Elisabeth Esterl	72	70	70	212	8,575
Anna Berg	74	66	72	212	8,575
Yu-Chen Huang	72	70	72	214	5,400
Nicola Moult	73	73	69	215	4,240
Hsui-Feng Tseng	72	75	69	216	3,000
Lisa Hed	71	73	72	216	3,000
Patricia Meunier Lebouc	74	67	75	216	3,000
Lora Fairclough	77	71	69	217	2,120
Irene Yeoh	73	70	74	217	2,120
Marlene Hedblom	72	76	70	218	1,780
Mia Lojdahl	71	76	71	218	1,780
Mei-Chi Cheng	72	75	73	220	1,610
Iben Tinning	78	71	72	221	1,425
Loraine Lambert	78	71	72	221	1,425
Johanna Head	76	73	72	221	1,425
Kirsty Taylor	72	75	74	221	1,425
Hsiao-Chuan Lu	77	70	74	221	1,425
Cherie Byrnes	76	71	74	221	1,425
Catherine Schmitt	74	76	72	222	1,200
Nienke Nijenhuis	76	74	72	222	1,200
Yu-Chuan Tai	76	73	73	222	1,200
Paula Marti	73	75	74	222	1,200
Judith Van Hagen	71	77	74	222	1,200

	SCORES			TOTAL	MONEY
Lynnette Brooky	72	76	74	222	1,200
Asa Gottmo	73	72	77	222	1,200
Ya-Huei Lu	75	76	72	223	1,020
Marina Arruti	79	72	72	223	1,020
Cecilie Lundgreen	77	70	76	223	1,020
*Kwan-Chih Lu	75	72	76	223	
Natascha Fink	75	71	77	223	1,020
Tatsuko Morimoto	74	70	79	223	1,020

Nedbank MasterCard South African Ladies Masters

See South African Women's Tour.

La Perla Ladies Italian Open

Poggio dei Medici Golf Club, Florence, Italy　　　　　　　　May 17-20
Par 37-36–73; 6,252 yards　　　　　　　　　　　　　　　purse, £120,000

	SCORES				TOTAL	MONEY
Paula Marti	70	73	72	68	283	£18,000
Raquel Carriedo	72	69	73	69	283	12,180
(Marti defeated Carriedo on first playoff hole.)						
Corinne Dibnah	65	73	72	74	284	8,400
Sophie Gustafson	68	73	76	70	287	6,480
Iben Tinning	73	71	73	72	289	4,644
Sophie Sandolo	72	72	70	75	289	4,644
Kirsty Taylor	72	74	73	71	290	3,300
Lora Fairclough	72	71	74	73	290	3,300
Natascha Fink	72	77	71	71	291	2,432
Giulia Sergas	69	71	78	73	291	2,432
Catherine Schmitt	70	73	74	74	291	2,432
Valerie Van Ryckeghem	72	75	73	72	292	2,064
Suzann Pettersen	74	73	74	72	293	1,856
Wendy Dicks	69	71	80	73	293	1,856
Laura Navarro	70	74	74	75	293	1,856
Alison Munt	74	73	74	73	294	1,704
Esther Poburski	71	72	74	77	294	1,704
*Federica Piovano	76	74	76	69	295	
Karine Mathiot	72	71	80	72	295	1,477.33
Laurette Maritz	71	76	76	72	295	1,477.33
Nicola Moult	75	73	74	73	295	1,477.33
Federica Dassu	71	72	77	75	295	1,477.33
Lara Tadiotto	73	74	73	75	295	1,477.33
Ludivine Kreutz	70	75	74	76	295	1,477.33
Susanna Berglund	73	73	72	77	295	1,477.33
Joanne Mills	71	72	73	79	295	1,477.33
Lynnette Brooky	74	74	67	80	295	1,477.33
Karen Lunn	72	74	77	73	296	1,278
Karine Icher	71	72	74	79	296	1,278
Erica Steen	74	76	75	72	297	1,170
Nicole Stillig	76	74	75	72	297	1,170
Trish Johnson	73	73	78	73	297	1,170
Elisabeth Esterl	74	73	75	75	297	1,170

Ladies French Open

Arras Golf Club, Anzin St. Aubin, France
Par 36-36–72; 5,800 yards

June 7-10
purse, £175,000

	SCORES				TOTAL	MONEY
Suzann Pettersen	71	70	70	69	280	£24,450
Becky Morgan	72	67	70	71	280	16,544.50
(Pettersen defeated Morgan on third playoff hole.)						
Giulia Sergas	69	72	68	72	281	10,106
Karine Icher	70	69	69	73	281	10,106
Raquel Carriedo	73	71	67	72	283	6,911.20
Judith Van Hagen	71	69	72	72	284	4,890
Laurette Maritz	70	72	70	72	284	4,890
Cecilie Lundgreen	71	71	70	72	284	4,890
Cherie Byrnes	72	70	70	73	285	3,651.20
Esther Poburski	73	72	69	72	286	3,020.93
Linda Ericsson	68	74	71	73	286	3,020.93
Valerie Van Ryckeghem	70	73	68	75	286	3,020.93
Jane Leary	74	72	70	71	287	2,567.25
Alison Munt	70	72	70	75	287	2,567.25
Paula Marti	73	71	73	71	288	2,352.63
Ana Belen Sanchez	73	72	69	74	288	2,352.63
Marine Monnet	73	67	72	76	288	2,352.63
Lara Tadiotto	74	71	74	70	289	2,157.03
Caroline Hall	75	71	70	73	289	2,157.03
Marlene Hedblom	74	72	66	77	289	2,157.03
Patricia Meunier Lebouc	76	73	70	71	290	1,931.55
Dale Reid	69	77	72	72	290	1,931.55
Patty Schremmer	71	74	71	74	290	1,931.55
Kirsty Taylor	80	66	70	74	290	1,931.55
Pernilla Sterner	73	74	68	75	290	1,931.55
Suzanne Dickens	71	72	71	76	290	1,931.55
Iben Tinning	74	74	75	68	291	1,638.15
Regine Lautens	75	71	75	70	291	1,638.15
Asa Gottmo	73	75	73	70	291	1,638.15
Eva-Lotta Stromlid	72	76	72	71	291	1,638.15
Catherine Knight	75	70	73	73	291	1,638.15
Corinne Dibnah	73	71	68	79	291	1,638.15

Evian Masters

Evian Masters Golf Club, Evians-les-Bains, France
Par 36-36–72; 6,085 yards

June 13-16
purse, £1,500,000

	SCORES				TOTAL	MONEY
Rachel Teske	71	68	66	68	273	£222,426
Maria Hjorth	69	65	71	69	274	148,372
Beth Daniel	67	68	70	72	277	108,994
Marine Monnet	73	69	70	66	278	84,754
Meg Mallon	70	75	67	67	279	68,595
Yu Ping Lin	68	72	72	68	280	43,548.20
Akiko Fukushima	72	66	72	70	280	43,548.20
Michele Redman	73	70	67	70	280	43,548.20
Dorothy Delasin	69	70	70	71	280	43,548.20
Jackie Gallagher-Smith	69	69	70	72	280	43,548.20
Laura Davies	76	70	71	64	281	27,591
Se Ri Pak	69	68	74	70	281	27,591

	SCORES				TOTAL	MONEY
Suzann Pettersen	70	69	72	70	281	27,591
Catriona Matthew	71	71	68	71	281	27,591
Mi Hyun Kim	71	67	73	71	282	22,561.50
Juli Inkster	73	70	67	72	282	22,561.50
Leta Lindley	72	69	72	70	283	19,754.25
Laura Diaz	73	67	72	71	283	19,754.25
Lorie Kane	71	70	71	71	283	19,754.25
Sophie Gustafson	69	66	73	75	283	19,754.25
Raquel Carriedo	69	73	72	70	284	16,622.50
Karen Weiss	71	71	71	71	284	16,622.50
Karrie Webb	71	73	67	73	284	16,622.50
Pat Hurst	69	70	71	74	284	16,622.50
Betsy King	74	72	72	67	285	13,693.85
Cristie Kerr	75	69	71	70	285	13,693.85
Karen Pearce	72	72	70	71	285	13,693.85
Wendy Ward	68	72	73	72	285	13,693.85
Kris Tschetter	74	68	69	74	285	13,693.85
Grace Park	73	69	69	74	285	13,693.85
Annika Sorenstam	69	69	72	75	285	13,693.85

Kellogg's All-Bran Ladies British Masters

Mottram Hall Golf Club, Cheshire, England
Par 36-37–73; 6,322 yards

July 6-8
purse, £100,000

	SCORES			TOTAL	MONEY
Paula Marti	71	70	68	209	£15,000
Raquel Carriedo	70	70	70	210	10,150
Dale Reid	70	69	72	211	7,000
Joanne Mills	68	72	72	212	4,820
Suzann Pettersen	69	69	74	212	4,820
Kirsty Taylor	72	67	74	213	3,500
Gina Scott	71	72	71	214	2,750
Lora Fairclough	65	75	74	214	2,750
Diane Barnard	74	73	68	215	2,026.66
Laura Davies	69	71	75	215	2,026.66
Trish Johnson	72	67	76	215	2,026.66
Anne-Marie Knight	73	73	70	216	1,443
Laurette Maritz	73	73	70	216	1,443
Linda Ericsson	72	74	70	216	1,443
Valerie Michaud	76	68	72	216	1,443
Ana Belen Sanchez	71	72	73	216	1,443
Corinne Dibnah	75	67	74	216	1,443
Marine Monnet	69	73	74	216	1,443
Esther Poburski	72	70	74	216	1,443
Malin Burstrom	74	67	75	216	1,443
Lynnette Brooky	69	72	75	216	1,443
Caroline Hall	77	70	70	217	1,185
Sara Eklund	73	71	73	217	1,185
Iben Tinning	70	73	74	217	1,185
Marie-Laure de Lorenzi	72	70	75	217	1,185
Vibeke Stensrud	75	73	70	218	1,035
Pernilla Sterner	73	75	70	218	1,035
Sophie Sandolo	73	72	73	218	1,035
Karine Icher	74	71	73	218	1,035
Marina Arruti	73	71	74	218	1,035
Johanna Head	73	70	75	218	1,035

WPGA Championship of Europe

Royal Porthcawl Golf Club, Bridgend, Wales
Par 36-37–73; 6,183 yards

July 26-29
purse, £400,000

	SCORES				TOTAL	MONEY
Helen Alfredsson	67	70	68	71	276	£60,000
Suzann Pettersen	70	68	68	74	280	40,600
Asa Gottmo	71	73	71	68	283	28,000
Lisa Hed	74	68	72	70	284	17,520
Becky Morgan	73	67	71	73	284	17,520
Karine Icher	70	69	70	75	284	17,520
Shani Waugh	74	70	68	73	285	12,000
Sophie Gustafson	71	74	73	68	286	8,986.66
Trish Johnson	73	74	68	71	286	8,986.66
Paula Marti	72	72	68	74	286	8,986.66
Joanne Morley	71	71	74	71	287	7,360
Johanna Head	71	75	72	71	289	6,660
Alison Munt	77	66	73	73	289	6,660
Carin Koch	74	72	76	68	290	6,060
Giulia Sergas	76	75	70	69	290	6,060
Kathryn Marshall	76	70	74	71	291	5,448
Alison Nicholas	72	75	72	72	291	5,448
Sara Eklund	75	74	69	73	291	5,448
Nicola Moult	71	75	71	74	291	5,448
Ana Belen Sanchez	72	71	73	75	291	5,448
Laura Davies	75	76	71	70	292	4,740
Suzanne Strudwick	74	77	70	71	292	4,740
Valerie Van Ryckeghem	71	73	75	73	292	4,740
Silvia Cavalleri	71	70	77	74	292	4,740
Elisabeth Esterl	71	72	75	74	292	4,740
Marina Arruti	73	72	70	77	292	4,740
Karen Pearce	73	76	74	70	293	4,080
Marine Monnet	77	71	73	72	293	4,080
Laurette Maritz	70	77	73	73	293	4,080
Riikka Hakkarainen	71	73	73	76	293	4,080
Raquel Carriedo	74	74	69	76	293	4,080

Weetabix Women's British Open

Sunningdale Golf Club, Old Course, Surrey, England
Par 36-36–72; 6,277 yards

August 2-5
purse, £1,000,000

	SCORES				TOTAL	MONEY
Se Ri Pak	71	70	70	66	277	£155,000
Mi Hyun Kim	72	65	71	71	279	100,000
Laura Diaz	74	70	69	67	280	51,812.50
Iben Tinning	71	69	72	68	280	51,812.50
Janice Moodie	67	70	71	72	280	51,812.50
Catriona Matthew	70	65	72	73	280	51,812.50
Kristal Parker	72	71	71	67	281	25,600
Marina Arruti	71	73	70	67	281	25,600
Kathryn Marshall	75	71	68	67	281	25,600
Kelli Kuehne	71	70	71	69	281	25,600
Kasumi Fujii	71	71	69	70	281	25,600
Raquel Carriedo	73	70	70	69	282	17,750
Tracy Hanson	72	69	70	71	282	17,750
Rosie Jones	70	69	71	72	282	17,750

	SCORES				TOTAL	MONEY
Brandie Burton	72	71	73	67	283	14,400
Pearl Sinn	74	70	72	67	283	14,400
Jill McGill	70	70	72	71	283	14,400
Karrie Webb	74	67	68	74	283	14,400
Becky Morgan	73	68	71	72	284	12,575
Trish Johnson	70	67	72	75	284	12,575
Johanna Head	68	70	75	72	285	11,125
Marlene Hedblom	70	74	69	72	285	11,125
Emilee Klein	71	70	71	73	285	11,125
Lora Fairclough	71	70	67	77	285	11,125
Danielle Ammaccapane	75	68	74	69	286	9,071.42
Dina Ammaccapane	72	71	74	69	286	9,071.42
Maria Hjorth	72	73	71	70	286	9,071.42
Silvia Cavalleri	71	73	72	70	286	9,071.42
Gloria Park	71	73	71	71	286	9,071.42
Ji Hee Lee	75	71	69	71	286	9,071.42
Laura Davies	68	73	69	76	286	9,071.42

Compaq Open

Osterakers Golf Club, Stockholm, Sweden
Par 37-36–73; 6,213 yards

August 9-12
purse, £325,000

	SCORES				TOTAL	MONEY
Raquel Carriedo	72	67	73	72	284	£48,750
Karine Icher	66	67	76	76	285	32,987.50
Sophie Gustafson	69	77	66	74	286	22,750
Elisabeth Esterl	72	75	73	70	290	15,665
Liselotte Neumann	73	75	68	74	290	15,665
Paula Marti	74	73	72	72	291	9,750
Carin Koch	75	72	71	73	291	9,750
Lynnette Brooky	72	73	72	74	291	9,750
Helen Alfredsson	76	74	70	72	292	6,890
Marine Monnet	74	75	66	77	292	6,890
Juli Inkster	75	75	75	68	293	5,451.87
Sara Eklund	74	72	75	72	293	5,451.87
Laura Davies	76	71	73	73	293	5,451.87
Maria Hjorth	76	74	70	73	293	5,451.87
Alison Munt	73	75	73	73	294	4,761.25
Iben Tinning	72	74	74	74	294	4,761.25
Joanne Morley	76	76	69	74	295	4,550
Esther Poburski	74	78	75	69	296	4,199
Dale Reid	73	73	76	74	296	4,199
Joanne Mills	78	71	72	75	296	4,199
Riikka Hakkarainen	77	73	71	75	296	4,199
Jessica Lindbergh	72	75	72	77	296	4,199
Lora Fairclough	76	72	79	70	297	3,900
Corinne Dibnah	71	76	78	73	298	3,705
Johanna Head	76	74	72	76	298	3,705
Anna Berg	73	74	72	79	298	3,705
Giulia Sergas	76	72	77	74	299	3,266.25
Gina Scott	75	76	74	74	299	3,266.25
Sophie Sandolo	76	78	71	74	299	3,266.25
Claire Duffy	74	74	76	75	299	3,266.25
Valerie Van Ryckeghem	77	72	75	75	299	3,266.25
Asa Gottmo	77	72	74	76	299	3,266.25

Palmerston Ladies German Open

Palmerston Golf Resort, Nick Faldo Course,
Berlin, Germany
Par 36-36–72; 6,213 yards

August 17-19
purse, £100,000

	SCORES			TOTAL	MONEY
Karine Icher	71	69	70	210	£22,500
Suzann Pettersen	72	67	72	211	15,225
Nicola Moult	74	69	69	212	10,500
Marina Arruti	76	72	66	214	6,052.50
*Martina Eberl	73	73	68	214	
Mette Hageman	74	70	70	214	6,052.50
Elisabeth Esterl	71	72	71	214	6,052.50
Gina Scott	75	68	71	214	6,052.50
Lisa Hed	75	74	66	215	3,555
Mandy Adamson	75	71	69	215	3,555
Ana Belen Sanchez	74	73	69	216	2,780
Lynnette Brooky	73	74	69	216	2,780
Marine Monnet	72	73	71	216	2,780
Federica Dassu	78	72	67	217	2,320
Veronica Zorzi	76	71	70	217	2,320
Laurette Maritz	74	69	74	217	2,320
Riikka Hakkarainen	73	75	70	218	2,100
Corinne Dibnah	71	75	72	218	2,100
Vibeke Stensrud	73	71	74	218	2,100
Samantha Head	79	71	69	219	1,845
Natascha Fink	70	79	70	219	1,845
Sara Eklund	76	73	70	219	1,845
Miriam Nagl	75	73	71	219	1,845
Joanne Mills	73	75	71	219	1,845
Julie Forbes	67	79	73	219	1,845
Valerie Van Ryckeghem	71	75	73	219	1,845
Erica Steen	73	79	68	220	1,597.50
Judith Van Hagen	77	73	70	220	1,597.50
Raquel Carriedo	75	73	72	220	1,597.50
Sophie Sandolo	74	74	72	220	1,597.50

Waterford Crystal Ladies Irish Open

Faithlegg Golf Club, Waterford, Ireland
Par 34-38–72; 6,001 yards

August 24-26
purse, £100,000

	SCORES			TOTAL	MONEY
Raquel Carriedo	68	66	66	200	£15,000
Sophie Gustafson	69	67	65	201	10,150
Laura Davies	70	67	65	202	6,200
Ana Belen Sanchez	66	68	68	202	6,200
Elisabeth Esterl	66	67	71	204	4,240
Marine Monnet	69	68	68	205	3,000
Karen Lunn	66	71	68	205	3,000
Trish Johnson	68	68	69	205	3,000
Diane Barnard	72	68	67	207	2,240
Corinne Dibnah	70	70	69	209	1,920
Kirsty Taylor	70	69	70	209	1,920
Judith Van Hagen	71	68	71	210	1,720
Sara Beautell	70	73	68	211	1,575
Filippa Helmersson	71	71	69	211	1,575

	SCORES			TOTAL	MONEY
Marlene Hedblom	73	71	69	213	1,422.50
Lynnette Brooky	72	71	70	213	1,422.50
Sophie Sandolo	71	71	71	213	1,422.50
Nicole Stillig	72	69	72	213	1,422.50
Marina Arruti	72	73	69	214	1,305
Cecilie Lundgreen	71	72	71	214	1,305
Gina Scott	75	73	67	215	1,155
Pernilla Sterner	73	73	69	215	1,155
Claire Duffy	72	73	70	215	1,155
Sara Forster	76	69	70	215	1,155
Mandy Adamson	72	71	72	215	1,155
Paula Marti	71	71	73	215	1,155
Joanne Mills	71	70	74	215	1,155
Laurette Maritz	67	72	76	215	1,155
Linda Ericsson	72	73	71	216	930
Riikka Hakkarainen	72	72	72	216	930
Alison Munt	71	72	73	216	930
Mia Lojdahl	69	74	73	216	930
Caryn Louw	72	70	74	216	930
Vibeke Stensrud	69	72	75	216	930
Lisa Hed	70	69	77	216	930

Mexx Sport Open

Kennemer Golf Club, Zandvoort, Netherlands
Par 36-36–72; 5,993 yards

August 31-September 2
purse, £100,000

	SCORES			TOTAL	MONEY
Karine Icher	70	70	72	212	£15,000
Suzann Pettersen	69	70	73	212	10,150
(Icher defeated Pettersen on third playoff hole.)					
Valerie Van Ryckeghem	71	71	71	213	6,200
Gina Scott	68	73	72	213	6,200
Dale Reid	74	74	66	214	3,310
Anna Berg	70	73	71	214	3,310
Catherine Knight	73	68	73	214	3,310
Iben Tinning	71	68	75	214	3,310
Marie Hedberg	71	75	69	215	2,026.66
Mandy Adamson	74	69	72	215	2,026.66
Judith Van Hagen	69	73	73	215	2,026.66
Ludivine Kreutz	72	76	68	216	1,623.33
Mette Hageman	73	70	73	216	1,623.33
Diane Barnard	69	71	76	216	1,623.33
Elaine Ratcliffe	69	80	69	218	1,402
Federica Dassu	73	75	70	218	1,402
Cecilie Lundgreen	75	71	72	218	1,402
Pernilla Sterner	70	76	72	218	1,402
Sophie Sandolo	74	71	73	218	1,402
Stephanie Arricau	73	74	72	219	1,200
Alison Munt	72	74	73	219	1,200
Julie Forbes	70	76	73	219	1,200
Riikka Hakkarainen	68	77	74	219	1,200
Marina Arruti	71	74	74	219	1,200
Natascha Fink	71	74	74	219	1,200
Sanet Marais	69	75	75	219	1,200
Eva-Lotta Stromlid	70	80	70	220	990
Filippa Helmersson	75	75	70	220	990

	SCORES			TOTAL	MONEY
Caryn Louw	74	73	73	220	990
Catrin Nilsmark	72	74	74	220	990
Giulia Sergas	72	73	75	220	990
Laurette Maritz	72	72	76	220	990
Sofia Gronberg Whitmore	70	74	76	220	990

WPGA International Match Play

Gleneagles Hotel, PGA Centenary Course,
Perth, Scotland
Par 36-36–72; 6,265 yards

September 6-9
purse, £400,000

FIRST ROUND

Dale Reid defeated Sandrine Mendiburu, 5 and 4.
Alison Munt defeated Anna Berg, 2 and 1.
Samantha Head defeated Cecilie Lundgreen, 21 holes.
Marina Arruti defeated Laurette Maritz, 4 and 3.
Gina Scott defeated Iben Tinning, 1 up.
Nicola Moult defeated Kirsty Taylor, 1 up.
Johanna Head defeated Giulia Sergas, 2 and 1.
Marie Laure de Lorenzi defeated Lara Tadiotto, 19 holes.

(Each losing player received £750.)

SECOND ROUND

Paula Marti defeated Reid, 1 up.
Suzann Pettersen defeated Munt, 21 holes.
Catrin Nilsmark defeated Samantha Head, 2 and 1.
Alison Nicholas defeated Arruti, 1 up.
Kathryn Marshall defeated Scott, 1 up.
Moult defeated Patricia Meunier-Lebouc, 1 up.
Elisabeth Esterl defeated Johanna Head, 3 and 2.
De Lorenzi defeated Karine Icher, 3 and 2.

(Each losing player received £1,500.)

THIRD ROUND

Sophie Gustafson defeated Marti (£7,000), 4 and 3.
Pettersen defeated Trish Johnson (£2,500), 2 and 1.
Laura Diaz defeated Nilsmark (£5,000), 1 up.
Laura Davies defeated Nicholas (£2,500), 3 and 2.
Maria Hjorth defeated Marshall (£3,500), 3 and 2.
Janice Moodie defeated Moult (£2,500), 2 up.
Carin Koch defeated Esterl (£9,000), 6 and 4.
De Lorenzi defeated Catriona Matthew (£2,500), 3 and 2.

QUARTER-FINALS

Gustafson defeated Pettersen (£16,000), 19 holes.
Davies defeated Diaz (£23,000), 19 holes.
Moodie defeated Hjorth (£30,000), 3 and 2.
Koch defeated de Lorenzi (£11,000), 1 up.

SEMI-FINALS

Davies defeated Gustafson, 19 holes.
Moodie defeated Koch, 2 and 1.

THIRD-PLACE MATCH

Gustafson defeated Koch, 4 and 3.

(Gustafson received £50,000; Koch received £38,000.)

FINAL

Davies defeated Moodie, 5 and 4.

(Davies received £110,000; Moodie received £70,000.)

Biarritz Ladies Classic

Biarritz Le Phare Golf Club, Biarritz, France
Par 35-35–70; 5,688 yards

September 27-29
purse, £100,000

	SCORES			TOTAL	MONEY
Rachel Kirkwood	70	65	67	202	£15,000
Marina Arruti	68	66	68	202	10,150
(Kirkwood defeated Arruti on first playoff hole.)					
*Sophie Giquel	63	73	67	203	
Marine Monnet	66	71	67	204	7,000
Nicola Moult	69	70	67	206	3,728
Elisabeth Esterl	68	71	67	206	3,728
Ana Larraneta	70	67	69	206	3,728
Loraine Lambert	64	72	70	206	3,728
Ana Belen Sanchez	66	69	71	206	3,728
Corinne Dibnah	71	70	66	207	1,882
Becky Morgan	70	70	67	207	1,882
Asa Gottmo	73	67	67	207	1,882
Kirsty Taylor	68	68	71	207	1,882
Jehanne Jail	63	71	73	207	1,882
Anna Berg	68	73	67	208	1,387.50
Lisa Hed	69	71	68	208	1,387.50
Samantha Head	71	69	68	208	1,387.50
Alexandra Armas	72	68	68	208	1,387.50
Veronica Zorzi	68	71	69	208	1,387.50
Suzann Pettersen	71	68	69	208	1,387.50
Regine Lautens	67	69	72	208	1,387.50
Raquel Carriedo	65	70	73	208	1,387.50
Riikka Hakkarainen	72	70	67	209	1,140
Cecilie Lundgreen	69	73	67	209	1,140
Filippa Helmersson	69	73	67	209	1,140
Erica Steen	71	71	67	209	1,140
Joanne Mills	70	71	68	209	1,140
Kathryn Marshall	72	68	69	209	1,140
Nina Karlsson	68	67	74	209	1,140
Nienke Nijenhuis	70	73	67	210	930
Patricia Meunier Lebouc	75	67	68	210	930
Caroline Grady	71	70	69	210	930
Karine Icher	68	72	70	210	930
Diane Barnard	70	69	71	210	930
Lara Tadiotto	69	70	71	210	930
Dale Reid	69	69	72	210	930

Princess Lalla Meriem Cup

Dar-es-Salam Golf Club, Red Course, Rabat, Morocco
Par 36-37–73; 6,400 yards

November 9-11
purse, US$50,000

	SCORES			TOTAL	MONEY
Marine Monnet	75	70	73	218	US$11,000
Joanna Head	74	76	73	223	6,000
Elisabeth Esterl	71	72	80	223	6,000
Patricia Meunier Lebouc	72	77	74	223	6,000
Lora Fairclough	75	75	76	226	4,000
Samantha Head	76	77	77	230	3,700
Regine Lautens	76	78	76	230	3,700
M. Amalou	77	78	81	236	3,400
Sofia Gronberg	80	78	84	242	3,200
Xonia Wunsch	85	78	83	246	3,000

Japan LPGA Tour

Daikin Orchid Ladies

Ryukyu Golf Club, Tamagusuku, Okinawa
Par 36-36–72; 6,270 yards

March 2-4
purse, ¥60,000,000

	SCORES			TOTAL	MONEY
Yuri Fudoh	73	71	69	213	¥10,800,000
Kasumi Fujii	75	69	72	216	4,360,000
Tomoko Ueda	70	72	74	216	4,360,000
Woo-Soon Ko	70	71	75	216	4,360,000
Nayoko Yoshikawa	69	74	74	217	2,160,000
Yu-Chen Huang	73	72	72	217	2,160,000
Mayumi Murai	74	70	73	217	2,160,000
Yuko Moriguchi	69	72	76	217	2,160,000
Riko Higashio	70	71	76	217	2,160,000
Yuri Kawanami	73	71	74	218	1,092,000
Toshimi Kimura	73	71	74	218	1,092,000
Aki Nakano	73	70	75	218	1,092,000
Ai-Yu Tu	71	70	77	218	1,092,000
Hisako Ohgane	74	71	74	219	712,000
Ikuyo Shiotani	74	70	75	219	712,000
Oh-Soon Lee	71	72	76	219	712,000
Takayo Bandoh	74	73	72	219	712,000
Yu-Chuan Tai	70	72	77	219	712,000
Aki Takamura	72	70	77	219	712,000
Nahoko Hirao	71	70	78	219	712,000
Chieko Nishida	71	70	78	219	712,000
Orie Fujino	68	70	81	219	712,000
Yukiyo Haga	75	70	75	220	522,000

	SCORES			TOTAL	MONEY
Mitsuko Kawasaki	72	71	77	220	522,000
Ae-Sook Kim	73	70	77	220	522,000
Midori Yoneyama	71	70	79	220	522,000
Hsiu-Feng Tseng	75	70	76	221	456,000
Mitsuko Hamada	73	72	76	221	456,000
Etsuko Kawakami	74	70	77	221	456,000
Chikayo Yamazaki	69	74	78	221	456,000
Yoko Tsuchiya	70	76	75	221	456,000
Mei-Chi Cheng	76	71	74	221	456,000
Mineko Nasu	79	68	74	221	456,000

Belluna Ladies Cup

Misatoroiyaru Golf Club, Misato, Saitama
Par 36-36–72; 6,361 yards

April 6-8
purse, ¥60,000,000

	SCORES			TOTAL	MONEY
Kasumi Fujii	75	67	67	209	¥10,800,000
Orie Fujino	74	72	69	215	4,740,000
Miyuki Shimabukuro	72	70	73	215	4,740,000
Emi Hyodoh	75	72	69	216	3,300,000
Rie Mitsuhashi	70	74	72	216	3,300,000
Yoko Inoue	71	75	71	217	2,400,000
Chieko Amanuma	74	74	70	218	1,545,600
Nahoko Hirao	74	73	71	218	1,545,600
Yu-Chen Huang	72	74	72	218	1,545,600
Woo-Soon Ko	75	71	72	218	1,545,600
Fuki Kido	74	71	73	218	1,545,600
Yuri Fudoh	78	71	70	219	978,000
Junko Omote	76	73	70	219	978,000
Kyoko Ono	72	74	73	219	978,000
Kasumi Adachi	71	74	74	219	978,000
Mayumi Inoue	76	72	72	220	768,000
Yoko Tsuchiya	71	75	74	220	768,000
Michie Ohba	72	74	74	220	768,000
Yuriko Ohtsuka	75	73	73	221	594,000
Ae-Sook Kim	75	75	71	221	594,000
Yuri Kawanami	74	75	72	221	594,000
Kaori Higo	72	74	75	221	594,000
Ikuyo Shiotani	78	71	73	222	534,000
Yuko Moriguchi	75	72	75	222	534,000
Yukiyo Haga	75	74	73	222	534,000
Toshimi Kimura	72	74	76	222	534,000
Ayako Okamoto	77	71	75	223	462,000
Yuko Motoyama	79	71	73	223	462,000
Michiko Hattori	76	74	73	223	462,000
Aki Takamura	72	76	75	223	462,000
Chihiro Nakajima	76	74	73	223	462,000
Namika Omata	76	72	75	223	462,000
Kayo Yamada	72	75	76	223	462,000
Ok-Hee Ku	73	76	74	223	462,000

Saishunkan Ladies Hinokuni Open

Kumamoto Kuukou Country Club, Kikuyo, Kumamoto
Par 36-36–72; 6,439 yards

April 13-15
purse, ¥60,000,000

	SCORES			TOTAL	MONEY
Kaori Higo	71	76	69	216	¥10,800,000
Ae-Sook Kim	73	73	73	219	5,280,000
Michiko Hattori	76	73	71	220	4,200,000
Aki Nakano	71	74	76	221	3,600,000
Hsiu-Feng Tseng	77	74	71	222	2,325,000
Yuri Fudoh	72	75	75	222	2,325,000
Riko Higashio	71	75	76	222	2,325,000
Rena Yamazaki	74	71	77	222	2,325,000
Ji-Hee Lee	73	78	72	223	1,230,000
Woo-Soon Ko	74	79	70	223	1,230,000
Kaori Harada	75	76	72	223	1,230,000
Chieko Nishida	74	75	74	223	1,230,000
Kyoko Ono	80	70	74	224	960,000
Chieko Amanuma	72	77	75	224	960,000
Shiho Ohyama	75	71	78	224	960,000
Ayumi Sobue	73	79	73	225	750,000
Junko Yasui	73	78	74	225	750,000
Yuko Moriguchi	78	72	75	225	750,000
Yuriko Ohtsuka	72	77	76	225	750,000
Nayoko Yoshikawa	75	78	73	226	588,000
Fuki Kido	75	77	74	226	588,000
Ok-Hee Ku	75	79	72	226	588,000
Ikuyo Shiotani	72	80	75	227	552,000
Mie Nakata	75	78	74	227	552,000
Hisako Ohgane	74	77	76	227	552,000
Rie Mitsuhashi	76	77	75	228	498,000
Kumiko Hiyoshi	74	78	76	228	498,000
Midori Yoneyama	74	78	76	228	498,000
Natsuko Noro	74	78	76	228	498,000
Oh-Soon Lee	79	74	75	228	498,000
Yu-Chuan Tai	75	78	75	228	498,000

Nasuogawa Ladies

Nasuogawa Golf Club, Ogawa, Tochigi
Par 36-36–72; 6,196 yards

April 20-22
purse, ¥50,000,000

	SCORES			TOTAL	MONEY
Michie Ohba	70	70	69	209	¥9,000,000
Miyuki Shimabukuro	69	71	72	212	4,400,000
Kasumi Adachi	71	72	70	213	3,500,000
Kumiko Hiyoshi	75	72	70	217	2,750,000
Ok-Hee Ku	71	73	73	217	2,750,000
Ji-Hee Lee	75	74	69	218	1,750,000
Woo-Soon Ko	70	73	75	218	1,750,000
Yu-Chen Huang	67	72	79	218	1,750,000
Toshimi Kimura	74	74	71	219	968,333
Chieko Amanuma	74	73	72	219	968,333
Orie Fujino	72	74	73	219	968,333
Kaori Suzuki	70	75	74	219	968,333
Kyoko Ono	71	72	76	219	968,333
Kaori Harada	73	69	77	219	968,333

	SCORES			TOTAL	MONEY
Shin Sora	76	74	70	220	650,000
Natsuko Noro	71	73	76	220	650,000
Kozue Azuma	72	72	76	220	650,000
Michiko Hattori	74	70	76	220	650,000
Rie Mitsuhashi	74	70	76	220	650,000
Hiroe Tani	75	73	73	221	475,000
Ikuyo Shiotani	74	75	72	221	475,000
Kyoko Kadokawa	70	76	75	221	475,000
Aki Takamura	74	75	72	221	475,000
Yu-Chuan Tai	73	73	75	221	475,000
Fuki Kido	78	72	71	221	475,000
Young-Me Lee	73	72	77	222	435,000
Keiko Arai	70	73	79	222	435,000
Ayako Okamoto	72	76	75	223	380,000
Mayumi Ishii	72	75	76	223	380,000
Nobuko Kizawa	76	73	74	223	380,000
Hisako Ohgane	73	74	76	223	380,000
Mitsuko Kawasaki	76	71	76	223	380,000
Junko Yasui	76	74	73	223	380,000
Chihiro Nakajima	77	73	73	223	380,000
Yuko Yamaguchi	74	71	78	223	380,000
Riyo Fukuroi	75	69	79	223	380,000

Katokichi Queens

Yashima Country Club, Mure, Kagawa
Par 36-36–72; 6,170 yards

April 27-29
purse, ¥50,000,000

	SCORES			TOTAL	MONEY
Chieko Amanuma	71	70	67	208	¥9,000,000
Junko Yasui	71	69	70	210	4,400,000
Hiroko Yamaguchi	72	65	74	211	3,500,000
Mineko Nasu	72	67	75	214	3,000,000
Yuri Fudoh	70	69	76	215	2,500,000
Ok-Hee Ku	73	72	71	216	1,500,000
Woo-Soon Ko	73	70	73	216	1,500,000
Yu-Chen Huang	73	70	73	216	1,500,000
Midori Yoneyama	73	70	73	216	1,500,000
Natsuko Noro	71	71	74	216	1,500,000
Etsuko Kawakami	72	72	73	217	910,000
Fuki Kido	76	67	74	217	910,000
Orie Fujino	71	76	71	218	735,000
Nobuko Kizawa	73	73	72	218	735,000
Mikino Kubo	73	71	74	218	735,000
Ji-Hee Lee	73	70	75	218	735,000
Kasumi Fujii	70	68	80	218	735,000
Ayako Okamoto	74	72	73	219	535,000
Fumiko Muraguchi	74	72	73	219	535,000
Michie Ohba	69	74	76	219	535,000
Hisako Ohgane	72	74	74	220	460,000
Toshimi Kimura	75	70	75	220	460,000
Mayumi Inoue	72	71	77	220	460,000
Kasumi Adachi	72	71	77	220	460,000
Yuriko Ohtsuka	74	75	72	221	410,000
Ayumi Sobue	76	71	74	221	410,000
Kayo Yamada	75	72	74	221	410,000
Chihiro Nakajima	75	72	74	221	410,000

	SCORES	TOTAL	MONEY
Ikuyo Shiotani	72 71 78	221	410,000
Harumi Kawano	72 70 79	221	410,000

Nichirei Cup World Ladies

Yomiuri Country Club, Tokyo   May 3-6
Par 36-36–72; 6,387 yards   purse, ¥60,000,000

	SCORES				TOTAL	MONEY
Karrie Webb	70	68	69	71	278	¥10,800,000
Kasumi Fujii	67	74	72	71	284	4,360,000
Chieko Amanuma	73	67	72	72	284	4,360,000
Carin Koch	70	70	67	77	284	4,360,000
Yuri Fudoh	73	74	72	67	286	2,160,000
Takayo Bandoh	72	68	78	68	286	2,160,000
Ji-Hee Lee	72	75	69	70	286	2,160,000
Junko Yasui	75	73	67	71	286	2,160,000
Harumi Sakagami	72	72	70	72	286	2,160,000
Aki Takamura	71	69	72	75	287	1,200,000
Yuriko Ohtsuka	72	70	72	74	288	1,098,000
Fumiko Muraguchi	71	76	68	74	289	1,008,000
Kumiko Hiyoshi	73	68	73	75	289	1,008,000
Kyoko Ono	75	74	70	71	290	768,000
Ayako Okamoto	71	73	74	72	290	768,000
Fuki Kido	77	71	70	72	290	768,000
Toshimi Kimura	69	72	75	74	290	768,000
Orie Fujino	70	78	68	74	290	768,000
Yu-Chen Huang	73	70	72	75	290	768,000
Kasumi Adachi	74	75	71	71	291	546,000
Chieko Nishida	75	71	73	72	291	546,000
Michiko Hattori	76	71	71	73	291	546,000
Yuko Moriguchi	75	70	74	73	292	522,000
Mayumi Murai	76	72	71	75	293	510,000
Eriko Moriyama	72	72	76	74	294	492,000
Becky Morgan	73	71	74	76	294	492,000
Mitsuko Kawasaki	74	72	75	74	295	438,000
Yuko Saitoh	77	70	73	76	295	438,000
Nobuko Kizawa	78	69	72	76	295	438,000
Emi Hyodoh	72	73	73	77	295	438,000
Yu-Chuan Tai	70	75	73	77	295	438,000
Kaori Harada	76	73	74	72	295	438,000
Yuko Motoyama	79	69	70	77	295	438,000

Vernal Ladies

Fukuoka Century Golf Club, Amagi, Fukuoka   May 11-13
Par 36-36–72; 6,516 yards   purse, ¥100,000,000

	SCORES		TOTAL	MONEY
Ikuyo Shiotani	73	73 70	216	¥18,000,000
Mineko Nasu	73	72 71	216	8,800,000
(Shiotani defeated Nasu on second playoff hole.)				
Ji-Hee Lee	76	74 68	218	6,000,000
Fuki Kido	74	73 71	218	6,000,000
Mei-Chi Cheng	76	70 72	218	6,000,000

	SCORES			TOTAL	MONEY
Kayo Segawa	74	75	71	220	3,250,000
Chieko Amanuma	78	71	71	220	3,250,000
Hiroko Yamaguchi	76	72	72	220	3,250,000
Kaori Harada	74	73	73	220	3,250,000
Kaori Higo	75	75	71	221	1,880,000
Yuri Fudoh	72	74	75	221	1,880,000
Kumiko Hiyoshi	74	72	75	221	1,880,000
Young-Me Lee	76	72	74	222	1,670,000
Ae-Sook Kim	78	71	74	223	1,520,000
Mari Nishi	76	70	77	223	1,520,000
Hisako Takeda	73	77	74	224	1,220,000
Rie Mitsuhashi	76	76	72	224	1,220,000
Shin Sora	76	73	75	224	1,220,000
Woo-Soon Ko	76	73	75	224	1,220,000
Kasumi Fujii	76	76	73	225	930,000
Hiroe Tani	75	74	76	225	930,000
Hisako Ohgane	75	77	73	225	930,000
Chihiro Nakajima	71	77	77	225	930,000
Toshimi Kimura	75	73	77	225	930,000
Fumiko Muraguchi	78	72	76	226	790,000
Kaori Suzuki	75	76	75	226	790,000
Michiko Hattori	72	77	77	226	790,000
Miyuki Shimabukuro	74	75	77	226	790,000
Orie Fujino	76	73	77	226	790,000
Michie Ohba	74	78	74	226	790,000
Yuko Saitoh	77	76	73	226	790,000
Aki Nakano	76	77	73	226	790,000
Chiharu Yamaguchi	76	77	73	226	790,000

Chukyo TV Bridgestone Ladies Open

Chukyo Golf Club, Toyota, Aichi
Par 36-36–72; 6,335 yards

May 18-20
purse, ¥50,000,000

	SCORES			TOTAL	MONEY
Michie Ohba	72	68	67	207	¥9,000,000
Ok-Hee Ku	73	70	67	210	4,400,000
Mineko Nasu	71	72	68	211	3,250,000
Yuri Fudoh	70	68	73	211	3,250,000
Fuki Kido	68	70	74	212	2,250,000
Junko Yasui	75	72	65	212	2,250,000
Aki Nakano	77	65	71	213	1,625,000
Kaori Higo	72	75	66	213	1,625,000
Kumiko Hiyoshi	73	69	72	214	1,012,500
Yuri Kawanami	72	74	68	214	1,012,500
Megumi Yamanaka	72	73	69	214	1,012,500
Kaori Harada	73	70	71	214	1,012,500
Shin Sora	70	73	72	215	750,000
Hsiu-Feng Tseng	73	74	68	215	750,000
Chieko Amanuma	70	72	73	215	750,000
Hiroko Yamaguchi	74	72	69	215	750,000
Aiko Hashimoto	74	70	72	216	520,000
Aki Takamura	68	73	75	216	520,000
Yoko Inoue	73	69	74	216	520,000
Mayumi Inoue	72	70	74	216	520,000
Mitsuko Kawasaki	75	68	73	216	520,000
Fumiko Kano	77	70	69	216	520,000

	SCORES			TOTAL	MONEY
Toshimi Kimura	73	71	73	217	425,000
Kayo Yamada	72	74	71	217	425,000
Etsuko Kawakami	70	73	74	217	425,000
Kinue Matsubara	68	73	76	217	425,000
Kuniko Maeda	75	69	73	217	425,000
Miyuki Shimabukuro	76	71	71	218	380,000
Shoko Asano	74	72	72	218	380,000
Hisako Ohgane	72	72	74	218	380,000
Mie Nakata	72	75	71	218	380,000

Kosaido Ladies Golf Cup

Chiba Kosaido Country Club, Ichihara, Chiba
Par 36-36–72; 6,260 yards

May 25-27
purse, ¥60,000,000

	SCORES			TOTAL	MONEY
Aki Takamura	72	70	70	212	¥10,800,000
Ae-Sook Kim	72	72	68	212	5,280,000
(Takamura defeated Kim on first playoff hole.)					
Hsiu-Feng Tseng	70	72	71	213	3,900,000
Chihiro Nakajima	71	69	73	213	3,900,000
Yu-Chen Huang	71	69	74	214	3,000,000
Toshimi Kimura	73	71	72	216	2,400,000
Ji-Hee Lee	72	73	72	217	1,950,000
Fumiko Muraguchi	72	73	72	217	1,950,000
Yoko Tsuchiya	73	75	70	218	1,126,000
Mayumi Murai	73	76	69	218	1,126,000
Rie Mitsuhashi	72	73	73	218	1,126,000
Fuki Kido	71	73	74	218	1,126,000
Kaori Harada	70	73	75	218	1,126,000
Nahoko Hirao	74	69	75	218	1,126,000
Masaki Maeda	72	76	71	219	690,857
Kaori Higo	73	74	72	219	690,857
Shiho Katano	74	75	70	219	690,857
Oh-Soon Lee	74	72	73	219	690,857
Yuko Motoyama	77	68	74	219	690,857
Orie Fujino	71	73	75	219	690,857
Michiko Hattori	72	71	76	219	690,857
Mayumi Ishii	74	74	72	220	498,000
Yoko Yamagishi	74	75	71	220	498,000
Shin Sora	73	74	73	220	498,000
Kasumi Fujii	73	74	73	220	498,000
Ikuyo Shiotani	72	74	74	220	498,000
Michie Ohba	70	75	75	220	498,000
Hiroko Yamaguchi	72	73	75	220	498,000
Hisako Ohgane	74	71	75	220	498,000
Akane Ohshiro	72	76	73	221	426,000
Kumiko Hiyoshi	69	77	75	221	426,000
Chieko Nishida	72	77	72	221	426,000
Kuniko Maeda	71	74	76	221	426,000

Resort Trust Ladies

Grandee Naruto Golf Club, Naruto, Tokushima
Par 36-36–72; 6,599 yards

June 1-3
purse, ¥50,000,000

	SCORES			TOTAL	MONEY
Aki Takamura	71	71	67	209	¥9,000,000
Chihiro Nakajima	69	71	72	212	4,400,000
Kaori Higo	71	72	71	214	3,500,000
Hisako Ohgane	71	72	72	215	2,500,000
Fuki Kido	67	74	74	215	2,500,000
Michie Ohba	71	69	75	215	2,500,000
Bie-Shyun Huang	70	74	72	216	1,375,000
Yuko Moriguchi	70	74	72	216	1,375,000
Nahoko Hirao	71	73	72	216	1,375,000
Chieko Amanuma	70	73	73	216	1,375,000
Hiroko Fujishima	76	70	71	217	850,000
Riko Higashio	73	72	72	217	850,000
Chiharu Yamaguchi	71	72	74	217	850,000
Namika Omata	73	70	74	217	850,000
Ok-Hee Ku	71	71	75	217	850,000
Mayumi Murai	69	78	71	218	625,000
Kayo Fukumoto	72	74	72	218	625,000
Kozue Azuma	75	71	72	218	625,000
Orie Fujino	73	71	74	218	625,000
Toshimi Kimura	72	75	72	219	490,000
Mitsuko Kawasaki	74	71	74	219	490,000
Shin Sora	72	72	75	219	490,000
Yuko Saitoh	78	71	71	220	450,000
Hsiu-Feng Tseng	71	77	72	220	450,000
Yoko Tsuchiya	73	74	73	220	450,000
Ji-Hee Lee	70	76	74	220	450,000
Woo-Soon Ko	73	73	74	220	450,000
Kayo Yamada	72	77	72	221	405,000
Ae-Sook Kim	70	77	74	221	405,000
Yuko Motoyama	72	74	75	221	405,000
Kumiko Fuchi	72	74	75	221	405,000

We Love Kobe Suntory Ladies Open

Japan Memorial Golf Club, Yokawa, Hyogo
Par 36-36–72; 6,419 yards

June 7-10
purse, ¥50,000,000

	SCORES				TOTAL	MONEY
Michiko Hattori	69	66	74	70	279	¥9,000,000
Kayo Yamada	69	71	70	71	281	4,400,000
Kaori Harada	73	74	69	69	285	3,500,000
Kyoko Kadokawa	71	74	73	68	286	2,312,500
Yoko Yamagishi	70	74	72	70	286	2,312,500
Namika Omata	65	75	74	72	286	2,312,500
Junko Omote	73	67	72	74	286	2,312,500
Ok-Hee Ku	71	73	74	69	287	1,375,000
Orie Fujino	72	74	68	73	287	1,375,000
Hsiu-Feng Tseng	71	74	75	68	288	895,000
Tomoko Ueda	70	71	75	72	288	895,000
Natsuko Noro	71	71	72	74	288	895,000
Aki Nakano	70	73	71	74	288	895,000
Rie Mitsuhashi	71	72	74	72	289	760,000

	SCORES				TOTAL	MONEY
Junko Yasui	73	72	76	69	290	610,000
Ikuyo Shiotani	73	73	73	71	290	610,000
Young-Me Lee	70	76	72	72	290	610,000
Akane Ohshiro	71	72	74	73	290	610,000
Mayumi Murai	72	69	74	75	290	610,000
Yoko Tsuchiya	73	73	75	70	291	440,000
Mie Nakata	71	75	73	72	291	440,000
Hiroko Yamaguchi	71	75	73	72	291	440,000
Shin Sora	71	75	73	72	291	440,000
Eika Ohtake	72	73	70	76	291	440,000
Yuri Kawanami	72	71	80	69	292	390,000
Yuko Moriguchi	74	71	76	71	292	390,000
Kozue Azuma	77	70	73	72	292	390,000
Yoko Inoue	70	77	73	72	292	390,000
Kaori Suzuki	73	71	73	75	292	390,000
Chihiro Nakajima	70	73	78	72	293	350,000
Fumiko Muraguchi	72	69	78	74	293	350,000
Riko Higashio	72	74	72	75	293	350,000

Apita Circle K Sankus Ladies

U Green Golf Club, Nakatsugawa, Gifu
Par 36-36–72; 6,355 yards

June 15-17
purse, ¥50,000,000

	SCORES			TOTAL	MONEY
Midori Yoneyama	70	67	68	205	¥9,000,000
Mayumi Murai	72	75	67	214	3,080,000
Yu-Chen Huang	72	72	70	214	3,080,000
Kyoko Ono	68	74	72	214	3,080,000
Aki Takamura	70	71	73	214	3,080,000
Kaori Harada	70	71	73	214	3,080,000
Kasumi Fujii	74	71	71	216	1,625,000
Natsuko Noro	72	72	72	216	1,625,000
Michie Ohba	70	75	72	217	1,025,000
Shoko Asano	73	72	72	217	1,025,000
Yuriko Ohtsuka	73	71	73	217	1,025,000
Ji-Hee Lee	74	69	74	217	1,025,000
Yuka Shiroto	73	76	69	218	675,000
Mikiyo Nishizuka	77	69	72	218	675,000
Aiko Hashimoto	73	72	73	218	675,000
Junko Yasui	74	71	73	218	675,000
Akane Ohshiro	69	75	74	218	675,000
Fuki Kido	71	73	74	218	675,000
Shin Sora	72	72	74	218	675,000
Atsuko Ueno	72	72	74	218	675,000
Hiroko Yamaguchi	71	77	71	219	455,000
Kaori Higo	72	76	71	219	455,000
Ayako Okamoto	74	74	71	219	455,000
Ok-Hee Ku	72	75	72	219	455,000
Kyoko Kadokawa	76	71	72	219	455,000
Toshimi Kimura	72	74	73	219	455,000
Yuri Fudoh	73	73	73	219	455,000
Harumi Kawano	75	71	73	219	455,000
Woo-Soon Ko	77	71	72	220	395,000
Kaori Suzuki	71	76	73	220	395,000
Chihiro Nakajima	74	73	73	220	395,000
Yuko Moriguchi	74	72	74	220	395,000

Friskies Osaka Ladies Open

Hanna Country Club, Daito, Osaka
Par 36-36–72; 6,345 yards

June 22-24
purse, ¥50,000,000

	SCORES			TOTAL	MONEY
Midori Yoneyama	69	71	71	211	¥9,000,000
Kayo Yamada	76	68	68	212	4,400,000
Chihiro Nakajima	73	72	68	213	3,250,000
Ayako Okamoto	74	70	69	213	3,250,000
Fuki Kido	71	72	71	214	2,250,000
Kaori Harada	70	71	73	214	2,250,000
Junko Yasui	72	74	69	215	1,223,333
Kaori Higo	74	71	70	215	1,223,333
Yuko Moriguchi	71	73	71	215	1,223,333
Yuri Fudoh	71	72	72	215	1,223,333
Mayumi Murai	67	75	73	215	1,223,333
Yu-Chen Huang	73	68	74	215	1,223,333
Kyoko Ono	71	73	72	216	820,000
Jae-Sook Won	73	71	72	216	820,000
Yu-Chuan Tai	72	74	71	217	645,000
Mayumi Inoue	72	73	72	217	645,000
Megumi Yamanaka	74	74	69	217	645,000
Kasumi Fujii	73	71	73	217	645,000
Junko Omote	71	71	75	217	645,000
Michiko Hattori	72	74	72	218	495,000
Yuriko Ohtsuka	72	74	73	219	470,000
Yuka Irie	72	73	74	219	470,000
Young-Me Lee	75	70	74	219	470,000
Yuko Motoyama	73	71	75	219	470,000
Ok-Hee Ku	76	72	72	220	430,000
Ayumi Sobue	72	75	73	220	430,000
Mikiyo Nishizuka	75	72	73	220	430,000
Shin Sora	73	71	76	220	430,000
*Yukiko Sakanoshita	72	74	75	221	
Fumiko Muraguchi	75	73	73	221	385,000
Toshimi Kimura	74	72	75	221	385,000
Etsuko Kawakami	76	71	74	221	385,000
Kasumi Adachi	70	76	75	221	385,000
Shoko Asano	74	70	77	221	385,000

Toyo Suisan Ladies Hokkaido

Sapporo Kitahiroshima Prince Golf Course, Hokkaido
Par 36-36–72; 6,541 yards

July 13-15
purse, ¥50,000,000

	SCORES			TOTAL	MONEY
Chieko Amanuma	72	68	71	211	¥9,000,000
Toshimi Kimura	73	71	71	215	4,400,000
Woo-Soon Ko	75	70	71	216	3,500,000
Aki Takamura	74	71	73	218	3,000,000
Ikuyo Shiotani	75	72	72	219	2,250,000
Kaori Harada	74	70	75	219	2,250,000
Kaori Higo	77	74	69	220	1,750,000
Yu-Chuan Tai	73	72	76	221	1,375,000
Akane Ohshiro	72	72	77	221	1,375,000
Kayo Yamada	77	72	73	222	933,333
Yoko Inoue	76	72	74	222	933,333

	SCORES			TOTAL	MONEY
Yoko Tsuchiya	73	74	75	222	933,333
Mie Nakata	74	77	72	223	775,000
Riko Higashio	80	69	74	223	775,000
Young-Me Lee	77	71	75	223	775,000
Yuko Motoyama	78	73	73	224	625,000
Natsuko Noro	78	71	75	224	625,000
Shin Sora	73	73	78	224	625,000
Aki Nakano	77	76	72	225	455,000
Ji-Hee Lee	80	73	72	225	455,000
Rie Fujiwara	80	71	74	225	455,000
Yu-Chen Huang	75	75	75	225	455,000
Nobuko Kizawa	76	74	75	225	455,000
Kozue Azuma	78	72	75	225	455,000
Kyoko Kadokawa	75	74	76	225	455,000
Ok-Hee Ku	73	74	78	225	455,000
Kyoko Ono	80	72	74	226	395,000
Keiko Arai	73	75	78	226	395,000
Michie Ohba	74	74	78	226	395,000
Yukiyo Haga	78	74	75	227	345,000
Kasumi Adachi	78	74	75	227	345,000
Jae-Sook Won	75	76	76	227	345,000
Kumiko Hiyoshi	78	73	76	227	345,000
Aiko Hashimoto	75	75	77	227	345,000
Mineko Nasu	78	72	77	227	345,000
Junko Omote	75	73	79	227	345,000

Taiheiyo Club Ladies Leben Cup

Taiheiyo Associates Sherwood Course, Oarai, Ibaraki
Par 36-36–72; 6,240 yards

July 20-22
purse, ¥50,000,000

	SCORES			TOTAL	MONEY
Kaori Higo	70	65	69	204	¥9,000,000
Michiko Hattori	66	75	64	205	3,950,000
Mikiyo Nishizuka	67	70	68	205	3,950,000
Ayako Okamoto	70	67	71	208	2,750,000
Ok-Hee Ku	64	69	75	208	2,750,000
Toshimi Kimura	71	69	69	209	2,000,000
Yu-Chen Huang	70	73	67	210	1,625,000
Hisako Ohgane	73	69	68	210	1,625,000
Kayo Yamada	69	73	69	211	1,250,000
Hiroko Yamaguchi	70	72	70	212	965,000
Michie Ohba	73	65	74	212	965,000
Shin Sora	68	72	73	213	855,000
Chiharu Yamaguchi	69	70	74	213	855,000
Takayo Bandoh	76	70	68	214	630,000
Junko Omote	74	72	68	214	630,000
Kaori Harada	74	71	69	214	630,000
Kumiko Hiyoshi	70	73	71	214	630,000
Ikuyo Shiotani	69	73	72	214	630,000
Michiko Okada	74	68	72	214	630,000
Harumi Kawano	70	71	73	214	630,000
Fumiko Kano	74	70	71	215	455,000
Miyuki Shimabukuro	71	72	72	215	455,000
Yuri Fudoh	72	71	72	215	455,000
Junko Yasui	68	72	75	215	455,000
Natsuko Noro	72	74	70	216	410,000

	SCORES			TOTAL	MONEY
Bie-Shyun Huang	75	71	70	216	410,000
Chieko Amanuma	71	74	71	216	410,000
Woo-Soon Ko	73	71	72	216	410,000
Aki Takamura	72	71	73	216	410,000
Mayumi Inoue	72	74	71	217	375,000
Aiko Hashimoto	72	72	73	217	375,000

Golf 5 Ladies

Mizunami Country Club, Mizunami, Gifu
Par 36-36–72; 6,471 yards

July 27-29
purse, ¥50,000,000

	SCORES			TOTAL	MONEY
Hsiao-Chuan Lu	73	69	73	215	¥9,000,000
Michie Ohba	73	70	72	215	4,400,000
(Lu defeated Ohba on second playoff hole.)					
Toshimi Kimura	72	73	71	216	3,000,000
Kumiko Hiyoshi	69	75	72	216	3,000,000
Midori Yoneyama	73	71	72	216	3,000,000
Chieko Nishida	73	74	70	217	1,750,000
Nobuko Kizawa	70	75	72	217	1,750,000
Woo-Soon Ko	73	71	73	217	1,750,000
Michiko Hattori	75	74	69	218	975,000
Mihoko Takahashi	73	72	73	218	975,000
Hisako Takeda	71	73	74	218	975,000
Fuki Kido	70	72	76	218	975,000
Ae-Sook Kim	67	72	79	218	975,000
Yu-Chen Huang	74	73	72	219	675,000
Chizuru Akiyama	75	73	71	219	675,000
Kaori Suzuki	74	71	74	219	675,000
Chiharu Yamaguchi	72	72	75	219	675,000
Eika Ohtake	70	73	76	219	675,000
Ok-Hee Ku	73	74	73	220	455,000
Hisako Ohgane	76	71	73	220	455,000
Kayo Yamada	73	73	74	220	455,000
Hsiu-Feng Tseng	74	74	72	220	455,000
Mayumi Ishii	74	75	71	220	455,000
Yuka Arita	68	76	76	220	455,000
Miyuki Shimabukuro	77	73	70	220	455,000
Mineko Nasu	72	71	77	220	455,000
Yuka Shiroto	74	73	74	221	385,000
Shoko Asano	75	73	73	221	385,000
Emi Hyodoh	73	72	76	221	385,000
Momoyo Kawakubo	72	72	77	221	385,000
Hikaru Kobayashi	73	71	77	221	385,000

Vernal Open

Privilege Golf Club, Narita, Chiba
Par 36-36–72; 6,271 yards

August 3-5
purse, ¥80,000,000

	SCORES			TOTAL	MONEY
Yuri Fudoh	68	66	73	207	¥14,400,000
Hisako Ohgane	69	70	71	210	7,040,000
Toshimi Kimura	70	72	70	212	5,200,000

	SCORES			TOTAL	MONEY
Ikuyo Shiotani	69	72	71	212	5,200,000
Mayumi Ishii	70	72	71	213	3,100,000
Yu-Chen Huang	71	70	72	213	3,100,000
Ae-Sook Kim	69	71	73	213	3,100,000
Natsuko Noro	67	71	75	213	3,100,000
Ayako Okamoto	71	72	71	214	1,800,000
Riko Higashio	68	72	74	214	1,800,000
Woo-Soon Ko	72	71	72	215	1,400,000
Nahoko Hirao	71	71	73	215	1,400,000
Masaki Maeda	70	71	74	215	1,400,000
Yuriko Ohtsuka	66	74	75	215	1,400,000
*Sakura Yokomine	71	72	73	216	
Bie-Shyun Huang	72	70	74	216	1,080,000
Akane Ohshiro	68	73	75	216	1,080,000
Eriko Moriyama	70	71	75	216	1,080,000
Mihoko Takahashi	71	70	75	216	1,080,000
Chieko Nishida	74	71	72	217	808,000
Mayumi Murai	71	73	73	217	808,000
Miyuki Shimabukuro	68	74	75	217	808,000
Momoyo Kawakubo	67	74	76	217	808,000
Midori Yoneyama	75	71	72	218	688,000
Aki Takamura	73	73	72	218	688,000
Mayumi Inoue	69	76	73	218	688,000
Shin Sora	71	74	73	218	688,000
Kasumi Adachi	74	71	73	218	688,000
Aki Nakano	71	72	75	218	688,000
Junko Yasui	69	73	76	218	688,000
Mie Nakata	70	72	76	218	688,000
Kiyo Kushida	71	71	76	218	688,000

NEC Karuizawa 72

Karuizawa 72 Golf Club, Nagano
Par 36-36–72; 6,485 yards

August 10-12
purse, ¥60,000,000

	SCORES			TOTAL	MONEY
Chieko Amanuma	69	71	67	207	¥10,800,000
Junko Yasui	73	69	66	208	5,280,000
Akane Ohshiro	70	72	67	209	3,600,000
Nobuko Kizawa	72	67	70	209	3,600,000
Mineko Nasu	69	69	71	209	3,600,000
Toshimi Kimura	71	68	71	210	2,250,000
Hsiao-Chuan Lu	68	69	73	210	2,250,000
Kasumi Fujii	72	73	66	211	1,344,000
Kaori Harada	72	70	69	211	1,344,000
Seiko Watanabe	72	70	69	211	1,344,000
Yuri Fudoh	67	72	72	211	1,344,000
Woo-Soon Ko	71	68	72	211	1,344,000
Yu-Chen Huang	69	73	70	212	870,000
Hsiu-Feng Tseng	73	68	71	212	870,000
Yuriko Ohtsuka	74	67	71	212	870,000
Ok-Hee Ku	69	71	72	212	870,000
Yu-Chuan Tai	69	71	72	212	870,000
Kayo Yamada	68	71	73	212	870,000
Man-Soo Kim	68	76	69	213	630,000
Ikuyo Shiotani	72	72	69	213	630,000
*Saori Ishikawa	72	71	70	213	

	SCORES			TOTAL	MONEY
Hiroko Fujishima	72	72	70	214	552,000
Shiho Ohyama	74	69	71	214	552,000
Eika Ohtake	73	69	72	214	552,000
Rie Mitsuhashi	69	72	73	214	552,000
Yuka Tonsho	71	70	73	214	552,000
Harumi Sakagami	71	70	73	214	552,000
Miyuki Shimabukuro	68	71	75	214	552,000
Kiyo Kushida	74	70	71	215	468,000
Yuka Shiroto	74	70	71	215	468,000
Chieko Nishida	73	71	71	215	468,000
Masaki Maeda	68	75	72	215	468,000
Akiko Fukushima	77	66	72	215	468,000
Yoko Inoue	70	72	73	215	468,000
Kaori Higo	71	65	79	215	468,000

Shin Caterpillar Mitsubishi Ladies

Daihakone Country Club, Hakone, Kanagawa
Par 36-37–73; 6,534 yards

August 17-19
purse, ¥60,000,000

	SCORES			TOTAL	MONEY
Chieko Amanuma	71	69	72	212	¥10,800,000
Masaki Maeda	71	69	73	213	5,280,000
Kaori Harada	72	74	69	215	3,900,000
Ai-Yu Tu	71	71	73	215	3,900,000
Hisako Ohgane	73	69	74	216	2,700,000
Ok-Hee Ku	67	73	76	216	2,700,000
Akiko Fukushima	74	73	70	217	1,950,000
Bie-Shyun Huang	73	73	71	217	1,950,000
Fumiko Muraguchi	72	75	71	218	1,350,000
Junko Yasui	68	74	76	218	1,350,000
Momoyo Kawakubo	77	73	69	219	1,032,000
Yuri Fudoh	76	70	73	219	1,032,000
Hsiu-Feng Tseng	70	73	76	219	1,032,000
Eika Ohtake	69	74	76	219	1,032,000
Kaori Higo	74	74	72	220	690,000
Ji-Hee Lee	72	74	74	220	690,000
Akane Ohshiro	75	71	74	220	690,000
Mayumi Murai	74	71	75	220	690,000
Aki Nakano	70	74	76	220	690,000
Chihiro Nakajima	71	73	76	220	690,000
Kasumi Fujii	75	69	76	220	690,000
Tomo Sakakibara	70	73	77	220	690,000
Jae-Sook Won	74	74	73	221	534,000
Kyoko Ono	72	74	75	221	534,000
Aki Takamura	77	69	75	221	534,000
Megumi Higuchi	75	75	72	222	480,000
Shin Sora	71	77	74	222	480,000
Woo-Soon Ko	71	76	75	222	480,000
Mizuho Ozawa	71	76	75	222	480,000
Fuki Kido	73	73	76	222	480,000
Chieko Nishida	75	71	76	222	480,000

Yonex Ladies Open

Yonex Country Club, Teradomari, Niigata
Par 36-36–72; 6,281 yards

August 24-26
purse, ¥60,000,000

	SCORES			TOTAL	MONEY
Yuri Fudoh	69	68	67	204	¥10,800,000
Hsiu-Feng Tseng	68	70	67	205	5,280,000
Kaori Harada	70	69	71	210	3,900,000
Miyuki Shimabukuro	71	65	74	210	3,900,000
Kasumi Fujii	70	70	71	211	2,500,000
Michiko Hattori	72	68	71	211	2,500,000
Mineko Nasu	69	70	72	211	2,500,000
Nobuko Kizawa	75	69	68	212	1,650,000
Mihoko Takahashi	72	70	70	212	1,650,000
Hiroko Yamaguchi	73	72	68	213	1,050,000
Midori Yoneyama	70	73	70	213	1,050,000
Keiko Arai	72	71	70	213	1,050,000
Yuka Arita	73	69	71	213	1,050,000
Kayo Segawa	69	71	73	213	1,050,000
Ae-Sook Kim	70	70	73	213	1,050,000
Yukiko Koyama	73	71	70	214	750,000
Mizuho Ozawa	75	68	71	214	750,000
Namika Omata	70	72	72	214	750,000
Kyoko Ono	72	70	72	214	750,000
Hsiao-Chuan Lu	73	72	70	215	558,000
Mika Tajiri	72	72	71	215	558,000
Kiyo Kushida	74	70	71	215	558,000
Toshimi Kimura	74	69	72	215	558,000
Kotomi Akiyama	71	71	73	215	558,000
Chie Yoshida	73	69	73	215	558,000
Chieko Nishida	64	77	74	215	558,000
Michie Ohba	70	70	75	215	558,000
Hiroko Fujishima	70	74	72	216	480,000
Kayo Yamada	72	72	72	216	480,000
Yuka Tonsho	74	69	73	216	480,000
Yu-Chen Huang	70	71	75	216	480,000
Yuko Motoyama	71	70	75	216	480,000

Fujisankei Ladies Classic

Fujizakura Country Club, Kawaguchiko, Yamanashi
Par 35-36–71; 6,297 yards

August 31-September 2
purse, ¥60,000,000

	SCORES			TOTAL	MONEY
Miyuki Shimabukuro	73	71	70	214	¥10,800,000
Ji-Hee Lee	72	69	74	215	4,740,000
Harumi Sakagami	68	72	75	215	4,740,000
Kaori Higo	70	76	70	216	3,600,000
Aiko Hashimoto	74	72	71	217	1,776,000
Kyoko Kadokawa	75	70	72	217	1,776,000
Dottie Pepper	74	71	72	217	1,776,000
Akane Ohshiro	71	73	73	217	1,776,000
Hiroko Fujishima	73	70	74	217	1,776,000
Hisako Takeda	72	70	75	217	1,776,000
Yoko Tsuchiya	69	71	77	217	1,776,000
Laura Davies	72	67	78	217	1,776,000
Midori Yoneyama	73	75	70	218	804,000

	SCORES			TOTAL	MONEY
Chieko Amanuma	73	74	71	218	804,000
Yu-Chen Huang	72	74	72	218	804,000
Ae-Sook Kim	73	73	72	218	804,000
Michie Ohba	73	72	73	218	804,000
Chieko Nishida	70	74	74	218	804,000
Mayumi Murai	71	71	76	218	804,000
Kayo Yamada	69	72	77	218	804,000
Yuri Kawanami	75	73	71	219	558,000
Michiko Hattori	72	74	73	219	558,000
Momoyo Kawakubo	75	71	73	219	558,000
Yoko Inoue	73	73	73	219	558,000
Kayo Segawa	71	72	76	219	558,000
Junko Yasui	73	75	72	220	492,000
Kayo Fukumoto	76	71	73	220	492,000
Mayumi Inoue	74	73	73	220	492,000
Junko Ishii	70	76	74	220	492,000
Woo-Soon Ko	71	73	76	220	492,000
Aki Nakano	72	72	76	220	492,000

Japan LPGA Championship Konica Cup

Rope Club, Shoiya, Tochigi
Par 36-36–72; 6,523 yards

September 6-9
purse, ¥70,000,000

	SCORES				TOTAL	MONEY
Kumiko Hiyoshi	70	67	72	73	282	¥12,600,000
Akiko Fukushima	72	69	69	73	283	5,530,000
Toshimi Kimura	73	68	69	73	283	5,530,000
Woo-Soon Ko	75	70	72	68	285	3,500,000
Kasumi Adachi	72	70	74	69	285	3,500,000
Kasumi Fujii	73	71	71	70	285	3,500,000
Kaori Higo	70	70	73	73	286	2,275,000
Yuri Fudoh	70	70	72	74	286	2,275,000
Michie Ohba	74	73	72	68	287	1,393,000
Chieko Amanuma	70	75	71	71	287	1,393,000
Mihoko Takahashi	69	72	72	74	287	1,393,000
Kaori Harada	69	73	71	74	287	1,393,000
Fumiko Muraguchi	70	72	74	72	288	1,071,000
Hsiao-Chuan Lu	73	72	71	72	288	1,071,000
Akane Ohshiro	73	72	72	72	289	896,000
Ae-Sook Kim	73	75	69	72	289	896,000
Yoko Inoue	67	69	75	78	289	896,000
Momoyo Kawakubo	74	73	74	69	290	665,000
Kotoko Uchida	72	74	73	71	290	665,000
Ji-Hee Lee	73	75	71	71	290	665,000
Mayumi Murai	74	74	71	71	290	665,000
Yuriko Ohtsuka	71	74	73	73	291	581,000
Harumi Sakagami	71	72	72	76	291	581,000
Hiroko Fujishima	71	73	74	74	292	546,000
Kayo Fukumoto	70	72	73	77	292	546,000
Shin Sora	73	71	71	77	292	546,000
Kayo Yamada	75	71	77	70	293	462,000
Rena Yamazaki	72	75	74	72	293	462,000
Masaki Maeda	70	77	74	72	293	462,000
Chieko Nishida	71	73	76	73	293	462,000
Aiko Hashimoto	72	75	73	73	293	462,000
Mayumi Inoue	71	76	73	73	293	462,000

	SCORES				TOTAL	MONEY
Hisako Ohgane	73	73	73	74	293	462,000
Hiromi Kobayashi	73	72	73	75	293	462,000
Ai-Yu Tu	71	75	71	76	293	462,000

Munsingwear Ladies Tokai Classic

Ryosen Golf Club, Inabe, Mie
Par 36-36–72; 6,388 yards

September 14-16
purse, ¥60,000,000

	SCORES			TOTAL	MONEY
Fuki Kido	69	65	71	205	¥10,800,000
Kasumi Fujii	71	69	67	207	4,360,000
Yuri Fudoh	68	70	69	207	4,360,000
Kaori Harada	69	69	69	207	4,360,000
Michie Ohba	66	71	72	209	3,000,000
Miyuki Shimabukuro	68	71	71	210	2,250,000
Mihoko Takahashi	68	70	72	210	2,250,000
Hsiu-Feng Tseng	72	71	68	211	1,500,000
Yun-Jye Wei	69	72	70	211	1,500,000
Aki Takamura	71	70	70	211	1,500,000
Shin Sora	72	69	71	212	1,032,000
Fumiko Muraguchi	69	71	72	212	1,032,000
Mineko Nasu	72	70	71	213	882,000
Kayo Yamada	73	68	72	213	882,000
Ji-Hee Lee	72	68	73	213	882,000
Hsiao-Chuan Lu	73	71	70	214	702,000
Orie Fujino	70	72	72	214	702,000
Eika Ohtake	70	71	73	214	702,000
Masaki Maeda	70	73	72	215	552,000
Kotoko Uchida	72	70	73	215	552,000
Chieko Amanuma	73	72	71	216	498,000
Yuka Shiroto	74	69	73	216	498,000
Harumi Sakagami	69	73	74	216	498,000
Yuriko Ohtsuka	70	76	71	217	432,000
Hiroko Yamaguchi	74	72	71	217	432,000
Keiko Arai	75	70	72	217	432,000
Junko Yasui	71	72	74	217	432,000
Woo-Soon Ko	72	71	74	217	432,000
Ae-Sook Kim	72	71	74	217	432,000
Bie-Shyun Huang	75	66	76	217	432,000
Yoko Inoue	70	70	77	217	432,000

Miyagi TV Cup Dunlop Ladies Open

Rainbow Hills Golf Club, Tomiya, Miyagi
Par 36-36–72; 6,483 yards

September 21-23
purse, ¥60,000,000

	SCORES			TOTAL	MONEY
Toshimi Kimura	69	73	71	213	¥10,800,000
Kayo Segawa	70	71	73	214	5,280,000
Ok-Hee Ku	72	75	68	215	3,600,000
Kaori Harada	72	72	71	215	3,600,000
Orie Fujino	72	72	71	215	3,600,000
Kasumi Fujii	74	74	68	216	2,100,000
Shin Sora	71	75	70	216	2,100,000

	SCORES			TOTAL	MONEY
Yun-Jye Wei	73	72	71	216	2,100,000
Mayumi Inoue	72	75	70	217	1,212,000
*Ai Miyazato	73	74	70	217	
Ai-Yu Tu	71	75	71	217	1,212,000
Kaori Higo	71	73	73	217	1,212,000
Ji-Hee Lee	73	71	73	217	1,212,000
Miyuki Shimabukuro	75	73	70	218	924,000
Mikino Kubo	72	75	71	218	924,000
Nahoko Hirao	72	74	72	218	924,000
Hisako Ohgane	73	72	74	219	804,000
Natsuko Noro	73	75	72	220	684,000
Yu-Chen Huang	74	72	74	220	684,000
Fumiko Muraguchi	71	73	76	220	684,000
Momoyo Kawakubo	75	73	73	221	534,000
Hsiao-Chuan Lu	73	74	74	221	534,000
Young-Me Lee	74	73	74	221	534,000
Riko Higashio	71	75	75	221	534,000
Mihoko Takahashi	73	73	75	221	534,000
Ikuyo Shiotani	73	72	76	221	534,000
Michiko Hattori	79	69	74	222	468,000
Aiko Takasu	71	76	75	222	468,000
Yumi Kokubo	73	76	73	222	468,000
Yuriko Ohtsuka	71	78	73	222	468,000
Misayo Fujisawa	73	73	76	222	468,000

Japan Women's Open

Muroran Golf Club, Muroran, Hokkaido
Par 36-36–72; 6,396 yards

September 27-30
purse, ¥70,000,000

	SCORES				TOTAL	MONEY
Miyuki Shimabukuro	71	75	77	79	302	¥14,000,000
Ayako Okamoto	75	76	75	80	306	7,700,000
Yu-Chen Huang	76	74	80	78	308	5,425,000
Woo-Soon Ko	76	77	78	78	309	3,570,000
Kasumi Fujii	72	82	82	74	310	2,464,666
Michiko Hattori	73	79	80	78	310	2,464,666
Ae-Sook Kim	76	82	76	76	310	2,464,666
*Ai Miyazato	74	79	77	80	310	
Yuri Fudoh	75	81	78	77	311	1,734,000
Tomoko Ueda	73	78	81	79	311	1,734,000
Junko Omote	80	80	80	72	312	1,290,666
Mayumi Inoue	72	82	83	75	312	1,290,666
Midori Yoneyama	77	80	76	79	312	1,290,666
Yoko Inoue	79	80	81	73	313	964,000
Fuki Kido	72	79	83	79	313	964,000
Aki Takamura	70	81	82	80	313	964,000
Young-Me Lee	75	82	82	75	314	819,000
Kumiko Hiyoshi	77	79	82	77	315	756,500
Yuri Kawanami	74	80	81	80	315	756,500
Aiko Hashimoto	77	81	81	77	316	649,200
Ji-Hee Lee	74	81	83	78	316	649,200
Chieko Amanuma	71	83	78	84	316	649,200
Miho Koga	76	81	75	84	316	649,200
Yumi Kokubo	76	80	75	85	316	649,200
Shin Sora	75	82	84	76	317	586,000
Kaori Harada	76	81	80	80	317	586,000

	SCORES			TOTAL	MONEY
Hiromi Kobayashi	76	81	83	78	318	563,000
Jae-Sook Won	79	79	74	86	318	563,000
Rie Mitsuhashi	74	79	83	83	319	541,000
Ai Kikuchi	76	83	83	78	320	519,000
Ikuyo Shiotani	73	81	86	80	320	519,000
Ai-Yu Tu	78	80	76	86	320	519,000

Sankyo Ladies Open

Akagi Country Club, Niisato, Gunma
Par 36-36–72; 6,390 yards

October 5-7
purse, ¥60,000,000

	SCORES			TOTAL	MONEY
Hiroko Yamaguchi	67	69	71	207	¥10,800,000
Toshimi Kimura	70	71	67	208	4,740,000
Aki Takamura	71	68	69	208	4,740,000
Kaori Higo	69	70	70	209	3,600,000
Kaori Harada	74	66	71	211	2,500,000
Kayo Yamada	69	70	72	211	2,500,000
Ai-Yu Tu	71	67	73	211	2,500,000
Oh-Soon Lee	72	72	68	212	1,500,000
Orie Fujino	68	73	71	212	1,500,000
Yuri Fudoh	65	74	73	212	1,500,000
Mayumi Inoue	72	71	70	213	960,000
Hiroko Fujishima	69	73	71	213	960,000
Hsiu-Feng Tseng	69	73	71	213	960,000
Harumi Sakagami	70	72	71	213	960,000
Yu-Chen Huang	72	70	71	213	960,000
Woo-Soon Ko	72	70	71	213	960,000
Fumiko Muraguchi	71	70	72	213	960,000
Junko Yasui	73	71	70	214	628,800
Akiko Fukushima	75	68	71	214	628,800
Ok-Hee Ku	67	75	72	214	628,800
Natsuko Noro	72	70	72	214	628,800
Fuki Kido	69	72	73	214	628,800
Kasumi Fujii	70	74	71	215	552,000
Hiroko Tanaka	73	69	73	215	552,000
Michie Ohba	74	67	74	215	552,000
Chie Yoshida	70	73	73	216	522,000
Shin Sora	75	68	73	216	522,000
Yukiyo Haga	72	72	73	217	486,000
Nahoko Hirao	72	71	74	217	486,000
Hisako Ohgane	74	69	74	217	486,000
Mayumi Ishii	71	71	75	217	486,000

Fujitsu Ladies

Tokyu Seven Hundred Club, Chiba
Par 36-36–72; 6,490 yards

October 12-14
purse, ¥60,000,000

	SCORES			TOTAL	MONEY
Yuri Fudoh	68	67	68	203	¥10,800,000
Michie Ohba	67	67	70	204	5,280,000
Mihoko Takahashi	68	70	67	205	3,600,000
Akiko Fukushima	65	70	70	205	3,600,000

	SCORES			TOTAL	MONEY
Orie Fujino	67	67	71	205	3,600,000
Aki Takamura	70	69	67	206	2,100,000
Kaori Higo	67	70	69	206	2,100,000
Toshimi Kimura	68	69	69	206	2,100,000
Hsiu-Feng Tseng	67	73	67	207	1,173,600
Chihiro Nakajima	67	70	70	207	1,173,600
Ikuyo Shiotani	70	67	70	207	1,173,600
Kayo Yamada	70	67	70	207	1,173,600
Misayo Fujisawa	67	68	72	207	1,173,600
Ayako Okamoto	71	71	66	208	906,000
Hsiao-Chuan Lu	70	67	71	208	906,000
Woo-Soon Ko	67	72	70	209	756,000
Yoko Inoue	68	71	70	209	756,000
Riko Higashio	68	69	72	209	756,000
Oh-Soon Lee	71	71	68	210	592,000
Kayo Segawa	70	71	69	210	592,000
Kasumi Fujii	72	65	73	210	592,000
Shin Sora	71	71	69	211	534,000
Junko Yasui	71	71	69	211	534,000
Eika Ohtake	71	70	70	211	534,000
Natsuko Noro	71	70	70	211	534,000
Masaki Maeda	71	71	70	212	492,000
Miyuki Shimabukuro	71	70	71	212	492,000
Kyoko Ono	69	71	72	212	492,000
Nahoko Hirao	72	70	71	213	426,000
Takayo Bandoh	70	71	72	213	426,000
Yun-Jye Wei	71	70	72	213	426,000
Kotoko Uchida	71	69	73	213	426,000
Tomoko Ueda	68	71	74	213	426,000
Kaori Suzuki	69	70	74	213	426,000
Chizuru Akiyama	69	70	74	213	426,000
Mayumi Ishii	67	71	75	213	426,000

Chako Higuchi Kibun Ladies Classic

Caledonian Golf Club, Yokoshima, Chiba
Par 36-37–73; 6,184 yards

October 19-21
purse, ¥60,000,000

	SCORES			TOTAL	MONEY
Chieko Amanuma	70	69	71	210	¥10,800,000
Kaori Harada	75	68	69	212	4,740,000
Miyuki Shimabukuro	70	70	72	212	4,740,000
Hisako Ohgane	73	68	72	213	3,600,000
Michie Ohba	71	71	72	214	3,000,000
Ikuyo Shiotani	75	71	69	215	1,594,285
Mieko Takano	71	74	70	215	1,594,285
Toshimi Kimura	73	72	70	215	1,594,285
Yun-Jye Wei	73	71	71	215	1,594,285
Yuri Kawanami	69	74	72	215	1,594,285
Oh-Soon Lee	70	71	74	215	1,594,285
Nahoko Hirao	71	69	75	215	1,594,285
Namika Omata	75	72	69	216	900,000
Kumiko Hiyoshi	73	71	72	216	900,000
Hiroko Yamaguchi	69	74	73	216	900,000
Jennifer Sevil	72	71	73	216	900,000
Junko Ishii	77	70	70	217	639,600
Hsiu-Feng Tseng	71	74	72	217	639,600

	SCORES			TOTAL	MONEY
Kyoko Ono	73	72	72	217	639,600
Yoko Tsuchiya	73	72	72	217	639,600
Aiko Hashimoto	74	67	76	217	639,600
Bie-Shyun Huang	73	74	71	218	522,000
Mikino Kubo	72	75	71	218	522,000
Akiko Fukushima	74	72	72	218	522,000
Woo-Soon Ko	73	72	73	218	522,000
Mihoko Takahashi	75	74	69	218	522,000
Yuriko Ohtsuka	72	75	72	219	474,000
Momoyo Yamazaki	73	69	77	219	474,000
Megumi Yamanaka	73	68	78	219	474,000
Kasumi Fujii	74	74	72	220	432,000
Michiko Hattori	74	72	74	220	432,000
Orie Fujino	71	74	75	220	432,000
Yuko Moriguchi	72	76	72	220	432,000

Cisco World Ladies Match Play

Sosei Country Club, Narita, Chiba
Par 36-36–72; 6,396 yards

October 25-28
purse, ¥100,800,000

FIRST ROUND

Annika Sorenstam defeated Mineko Nasu, 3 and 2.
Michele Redman defeated Kasumi Fujii, 2 and 1.
Mhairi McKay defeated Miyuki Shimabukuro, 2 and 1.
Catriona Matthew defeated Ko Woo-soon, 3 and 2.
Lorie Kane defeated Midori Yoneyama, 5 and 3.
Kaori Higo defeated Nancy Scranton, 1 up.
Laura Davies defeated Chieko Amanuma, 2 up.
Emilee Klein defeated Fuki Kido, 5 and 4.
Se Ri Pak defeated Michiko Hattori, 2 and 1.
Janice Moodie defeated Michie Ohba, 4 and 3.
Wendy Doolan defeated Toshimi Kimura, 1 up.
Rachel Teske defeated Ikuyo Shiotani, 19 holes.
Yu-Chen Huang defeated Maria Hjorth, 2 and 1.
Kaori Harada defeated Carin Koch, 20 holes.
Jill McGill defeated Yuri Fudoh, 19 holes.
Aki Takamura defeated Sophie Gustafson, 20 holes.

(Each losing player received ¥1,191,750.)

SECOND ROUND

Sorenstam defeated Redman, 5 and 3.
McKay defeated Matthew, 1 up.
Kane defeated Higo, 3 and 2.
Klein defeated Davies, 1 up.
Pak defeated Moodie, 2 and 1.
Teske defeated Doolan, 3 and 1.
Huang defeated Harada, 6 and 5.
Takamura defeated McGill, 1 up.

(Each losing player received ¥2,310,000.)

QUARTER-FINALS

Sorenstam defeated McKay, 3 and 1.
Kane defeated Klein, 4 and 3.
Pak defeated Teske, 3 and 2.
Huang defeated Takamura, 1 up.

(Each losing player received ¥4,620,000.)

SEMI-FINALS

Sorenstam defeated Kane, 4 and 2.
Pak defeated Huang, 6 and 4.

(Each losing player received ¥6,825,000.)

FINALS

Sorenstam defeated Pak, 1 up.

(Sorenstam received ¥15,120,000; Pak received ¥9,450,000

Mizuno Classic

Musashigaoka Golf Club, Hanno, Saitama
Par 36-36–72; 6,344 yards

November 2-4
purse, ¥118,800,000

	SCORES			TOTAL	MONEY
Annika Sorenstam	66	67	70	203	¥19,561,500
Laura Davies	70	65	71	206	12,140,205
Woo-Soon Ko	67	71	70	208	7,874,711
Marisa Baena	66	71	71	208	7,874,711
Aki Takamura	70	68	71	209	5,577,805
Ji -Hee Lee	72	71	68	211	4,593,451
Sophie Gustafson	73	71	68	212	3,281,140
Silvia Cavalleri	70	70	72	212	3,281,140
Yu Ping Lin	69	69	74	212	3,281,140
Kayo Yamada	67	71	74	212	3,281,140
Kasumi Fujii	70	73	70	213	2,110,710
Maria Hjorth	72	70	71	213	2,110,710
Lorie Kane	73	69	71	213	2,110,710
Akiko Fukushima	67	74	72	213	2,110,710
Karen Weiss	70	70	73	213	2,110,710
Yuri Fudoh	68	68	77	213	2,110,710
Nancy Scranton	74	68	72	214	1,640,510
Smriti Mehra	70	70	74	214	1,640,510
Hee-Won Han	70	69	75	214	1,640,510
Catriona Matthew	71	71	73	215	1,412,413
Kyoko Ono	71	70	74	215	1,412,413
Grace Park	70	70	75	215	1,412,413
Michie Ohba	72	67	76	215	1,412,413
Michiko Hattori	72	72	72	216	1,135,171
Toshimi Kimura	71	74	71	216	1,135,171
Kaori Higo	72	70	74	216	1,135,171
Leta Lindley	71	71	74	216	1,135,171
Michele Redman	73	73	70	216	1,135,171
Kris Tschetter	77	70	69	216	1,135,171
Jeong Jang	73	68	75	216	1,135,171
Ok-Hee Ku	72	68	76	216	1,135,171

Itoen Ladies

Great Island Club, Chonan, Chiba
Par 36-36–72; 6,365 yards

November 9-11
purse, ¥60,000,000

	SCORES			TOTAL	MONEY
Laura Davies	69	68	70	207	¥10,800,000
Junko Yasui	72	71	67	210	5,280,000
Kasumi Fujii	70	75	67	212	3,300,000
Ok-Hee Ku	72	70	70	212	3,300,000
Yun-Jye Wei	70	70	72	212	3,300,000
Woo-Soon Ko	70	69	73	212	3,300,000
Yuri Fudoh	75	69	69	213	1,800,000
Kaori Harada	70	73	70	213	1,800,000
Miyuki Shimabukuro	70	71	72	213	1,800,000
Akane Ohshiro	72	74	69	215	1,027,200
Momoyo Kawakubo	72	74	69	215	1,027,200
Chihiro Nakajima	72	73	70	215	1,027,200
Harumi Sakagami	71	73	71	215	1,027,200
Mayumi Nakajima	71	71	73	215	1,027,200
Shin Sora	76	73	67	216	642,000
Rie Mitsuhashi	72	76	68	216	642,000
Hiroko Yamaguchi	74	74	68	216	642,000
Michie Ohba	68	77	71	216	642,000
Hsiu-Feng Tseng	69	76	71	216	642,000
Mayumi Inoue	74	71	71	216	642,000
Midori Yoneyama	75	69	72	216	642,000
Oh-Soon Lee	71	71	74	216	642,000
Toshimi Kimura	75	75	67	217	480,000
Hiromi Kobayashi	76	73	68	217	480,000
Fumiko Muraguchi	73	75	69	217	480,000
Mihoko Takahashi	72	75	70	217	480,000
Kayo Segawa	74	73	71	218	444,000
Orie Fujino	76	70	72	218	444,000
Masaki Maeda	72	76	71	219	396,000
Chikako Matsuzawa	71	75	73	219	396,000
Yuri Kawanami	75	71	73	219	396,000
Ji-Hee Lee	71	74	74	219	396,000
Yoko Tsuchiya	73	72	74	219	396,000
Kaori Higo	75	68	76	219	396,000

Daioseishi Elleair Ladies Open

Elleair Golf Club, Matsuyama, Ehime
Par 36-36–72; 6,363 yards

November 16-18
purse, ¥100,000,000

	SCORES			TOTAL	MONEY
Ji-Hee Lee	71	69	68	208	¥18,000,000
Mineko Nasu	71	71	67	209	8,800,000
Shin Sora	69	70	71	210	7,000,000
Kaori Higo	73	68	70	211	6,000,000
Kasumi Fujii	75	69	68	212	3,600,000
Yuri Fudoh	71	72	69	212	3,600,000
Chihiro Nakajima	71	71	70	212	3,600,000
Akiko Fukushima	74	67	71	212	3,600,000
*Ai Miyazato	71	69	72	212	
Hiroko Yamaguchi	72	68	72	212	3,600,000
Yun-Jye Wei	69	72	72	213	1,905,000

	SCORES			TOTAL	MONEY
Keiko Arai	68	71	74	213	1,905,000
Mayumi Inoue	71	70	73	214	1,710,000
Fumiko Muraguchi	69	76	70	215	1,410,000
Hsiao-Chuan Lu	72	72	71	215	1,410,000
Orie Fujino	76	70	69	215	1,410,000
Mayumi Murai	75	68	72	215	1,410,000
Nahoko Hirao	76	72	67	215	1,410,000
Nayoko Yoshikawa	71	73	72	216	980,000
Oh-Soon Lee	69	74	73	216	980,000
Yuriko Ohtsuka	75	73	68	216	980,000
Harumi Sakagami	69	72	75	216	980,000
Ok-Hee Ku	73	71	73	217	820,000
Michie Ohba	74	70	73	217	820,000
Ae-Sook Kim	70	76	71	217	820,000
Hisako Ohgane	73	70	74	217	820,000
Fuki Kido	73	75	69	217	820,000
Toshimi Kimura	73	69	75	217	820,000
Kaori Harada	74	70	74	218	740,000
Yuka Arita	76	71	71	218	740,000

Japan LPGA Tour Championship

Hibiscus Golf Club, Sadowara, Miyazaki
Par 36-36–72; 6,495 yards

November 22-25
purse, ¥60,000,000

	SCORES				TOTAL	MONEY
Kaori Higo	67	71	66	71	275	¥15,000,000
Ikuyo Shiotani	70	69	69	70	278	8,700,000
Yuri Fudoh	71	71	72	65	279	6,000,000
Kasumi Fujii	74	65	69	72	280	4,800,000
Aki Takamura	69	70	74	68	281	4,170,000
Kumiko Hiyoshi	71	72	72	68	283	3,276,000
Michiko Hattori	67	71	72	73	283	3,276,000
Midori Yoneyama	69	76	70	71	286	1,780,000
Michie Ohba	70	76	68	72	286	1,780,000
Toshimi Kimura	70	73	69	74	286	1,780,000
Woo-Soon Ko	74	73	69	71	287	942,000
Yu-Chen Huang	70	73	72	72	287	942,000
Hiroko Yamaguchi	69	72	70	76	287	942,000
Miyuki Shimabukuro	73	72	71	73	289	642,000
Mineko Nasu	68	71	75	75	289	642,000
Junko Yasui	74	75	71	70	290	492,000
Hsiao-Chuan Lu	71	74	73	72	290	492,000
Fuki Kido	73	76	70	73	292	402,000
Chieko Amanuma	73	75	73	74	295	324,000
Kaori Harada	72	76	73	74	295	324,000
Ok-Hee Ku	73	75	73	76	297	294,000

South African Women's Tour

Nedbank MasterCard Classic

Glendower Golf Club, Johannesburg
Par 37-36–73; 5,849 yards

February 23-25
purse, R100,000

	SCORES			TOTAL	MONEY
Mandy Adamson	75	71	73	219	R17,250
Mara Larrauri	73	71	76	220	11,675
Annerie Wessels	72	76	73	221	8,050
Caryn Louw	77	72	74	223	5,545
Niina Laitinen	75	72	76	223	5,545
Andrea Hirschhorn	72	74	78	224	4,025
*Morgana Robbertze	79	74	73	226	
Joanne Norton	79	74	75	228	3,165
*Cas Bridge	78	73	77	228	
Letitia Moses	75	75	78	228	3,165
Vanessa Smith	75	76	79	230	2,330
Joanne Lefson	78	78	74	230	2,330
Zoe Grimbeek	78	79	73	230	2,330
Mariette Language	75	76	80	231	1,980
Cherry Moulder	77	78	77	232	1,810
Cecilia Sjoblom	80	78	74	232	1,810
*Leandri Pieterse	76	79	78	233	
Brenda Lunsford	79	78	76	233	1,715
Karen Pringle	82	77	75	234	1,650
*Esme Behrens	74	82	78	234	
Nicolle Flood	80	77	77	234	1,650
Alison Sheard	77	80	78	235	1,600
Michelle de Vries	73	84	79	236	1,560
*Sandra Winter	79	79	79	237	
Rae Hast	78	79	80	237	1,530
Barbara Plant	80	78	80	238	1,500
Elsabe Hefer	79	82	78	239	1,460
Shayne Wild	77	78	84	239	1,460
Tania Fourie	78	81	81	240	1,420
Donna Serino	82	82	76	240	1,420
Lesley Copeman	76	81	83	240	1,420

Telekom Ladies Classic

Woodhill Golf Club, Pretoria
Par 36-36–72; 5,969 yards

March 2-4
purse, R125,000

	SCORES			TOTAL	MONEY
Annerie Wessels	71	74	70	215	R22,500
Charlaine Coetzee-Hirst	75	69	71	215	14,600
(Wessels defeated Coetzee-Hirst on fourth playoff hole.)					
Caryn Louw	71	71	77	219	10,000
Niina Laitinen	78	71	73	222	7,700
Joanne Norton	77	74	72	223	5,950

	SCORES			TOTAL	MONEY
Cecilia Sjoblom	75	73	75	223	5,950
*Morgana Robbertze	76	70	77	223	
Vanessa Smith	74	78	72	224	5,800
Andrea Hirschhorn	74	77	74	225	4,500
Donna Serino	76	76	74	226	3,750
Shayne Wild	74	76	76	226	3,750
Barbara Plant	74	75	78	227	2,750
Brenda Lunsford	80	74	74	228	2,450
Mariette Language	79	77	72	228	2,450
Lesley Copeman	81	76	71	228	2,450
Elsabe Hefer	76	78	75	229	2,115
Karen Pringle	75	76	78	229	2,115
Zoe Grimbeek	78	73	78	229	2,115
Josefin Stalvant	76	78	77	231	1,975
Nicolle Flood	74	80	77	231	1,975
Cherry Moulder	78	77	77	232	1,900
*Esme Behrens	81	77	75	233	
Natou Soro	78	76	79	233	1,650
Jenny Germs	77	77	79	233	1,650
Letitia Moses	77	79	77	233	1,650
Mara Larrauri	77	78	79	234	1,550
Michelle de Vries	78	81	76	235	1,500
Rae Hast	79	80	77	236	1,400
Kajsa Gothman	80	81	76	237	1,350
Joanne Lefson	81	80	78	239	1,250
Sonia van Wyk	83	79	77	239	1,250
Sanet Marais	76	84	79	239	1,250

Vodacom Ladies Players Championship

Rondebosch Golf Club, Cape Town
Par 37-36–73; 5,592 yards

March 9-11
purse, R300,000

	SCORES			TOTAL	MONEY
Annerie Wessels	73	69	71	213	R52,000
Mandy Adamson	72	73	68	213	30,000
(Wessels defeated Adamson on second playoff hole.)					
Vanessa Smith	73	69	72	214	23,000
Nicolle Flood	72	71	72	215	16,250
Elsabe Hefer	70	72	73	215	16,250
Rae Hast	74	72	71	217	10,600
Josefin Stalvant	71	76	70	217	10,600
Charlaine Coetzee-Hirst	76	69	72	217	10,600
Caryn Louw	70	75	72	217	10,600
Federica Dassu	79	68	70	217	10,600
Andrea Hirschhorn	72	73	73	218	6,100
Joanne Lefson	74	73	73	220	5,600
Cherry Moulder	73	75	72	220	5,600
Mara Larrauri	73	74	73	220	5,600
Magali Ducres	76	72	73	221	5,100
Cecilia Sjoblom	75	72	74	221	5,100
Zoe Grimbeek	69	77	76	222	4,750
Tania Fourie	73	76	73	222	4,750
Joanne Norton	72	80	72	224	4,600
Natou Soro	78	75	72	225	4,200
Michelle de Vries	75	76	74	225	4,200
Mariette Language	79	72	76	227	3,650

	SCORES			TOTAL	MONEY
Karen Pringle	75	76	76	227	3,650
Shayne Wild	77	77	73	227	3,650
Lana Bassett	78	72	77	227	3,650
Letitia Moses	75	78	76	229	3,150
Donna Serino	81	73	75	229	3,150
Alison Sheard	76	79	75	230	3,000
Niina Laitinen	74	78	79	231	2,900
Debbie Gallop	75	78	81	234	2,750
Sonia van Wyk	82	77	75	234	2,750

Cape Times Women's South African Open

Devondale Golf Club, Stellenbosch
Par 36-36–72; 5,731 yards

March 16-18
purse, R100,000

	SCORES			TOTAL	MONEY
Vanessa Smith	70	70	71	211	R15,150
Charlaine Coetzee-Hirst	69	74	72	215	10,300
Mandy Adamson	69	72	75	216	6,350
Nicolle Flood	70	73	73	216	6,350
Julie Forbes	71	74	73	218	4,390
Federica Dassu	69	77	74	220	3,650
*Esme Behrens	72	72	77	221	
Mara Larrauri	78	72	71	221	3,150
Rae Hast	75	72	75	222	2,520
Caryn Louw	72	76	74	222	2,520
Shayne Wild	77	71	75	223	2,003
Zoe Grimbeek	72	75	76	223	2,003
Aideen Rogers	75	74	74	223	2,003
Lana Bassett	75	75	75	225	1,760
Andrea Hirschhorn	76	75	75	226	1,690
Annerie Wessels	78	77	72	227	1,615
Mariette Language	76	70	81	227	1,615
*Cas Bridge	71	78	78	227	
Lynn McCool	77	74	77	228	1,550
Josefin Stalvant	74	76	79	229	1,490
Michelle de Vries	71	77	81	229	1,490
Niina Laitinen	73	75	82	230	1,425
Cecilia Sjoblom	75	74	81	230	1,425
*Francis Botha	76	76	79	231	
*Morgana Robbertze	74	77	80	231	
Barbara Pestana	79	77	75	231	1,380
*Gilly Tebbutt	79	78	75	232	
Letitia Moses	77	77	78	232	1,350
Lesley Copeman	78	76	79	233	1,272
Cherry Moulder	79	76	78	233	1,272
Joanne Norton	77	75	81	233	1,272
Vibeke Stensrud	81	76	76	233	1,272

Nedbank MasterCard South African Ladies Masters

Gary Player Country Club, Sun City
Par 36-36–72; 6,330 yards

March 23-25
purse, R1,100,000

	SCORES			TOTAL	MONEY
Samantha Head	70	72	68	210	R165,000
Raquel Carriedo	74	70	67	211	82,683.26
Cecilie Lundgreen	71	72	68	211	82,683.26
Elisabeth Esterl	70	69	72	211	82,683.26
Paula Marti	70	72	72	214	46,640
Sophie Sandolo	76	70	70	216	35,750
Karine Icher	72	72	72	216	35,750
Lynnette Brooky	71	76	70	217	21,135.62
Federica Dassu	73	73	71	217	21,135.62
Nicola Moult	70	73	74	217	21,135.62
Joanna Head	74	75	68	217	21,135.62
Marie Hedberg	72	71	74	217	21,135.62
Anna Berg	74	72	71	217	21,135.62
Marina Arruti	71	74	72	217	21,135.62
Becky Morgan	73	72	73	218	16,390
Veronica Zorzi	76	73	70	219	15,400
Marlene Hedblom	72	76	71	219	15,400
Cherie Byrnes	74	73	72	219	15,400
Julie Forbes	73	72	75	220	14,190
Nicole Stillig	76	74	70	220	14,190
Nienke Nijenhuis	77	71	72	220	14,190
Laurette Maritz	74	73	74	221	12,540
Ana Larraneta	74	76	71	221	12,540
Kate MacIntosh	77	71	73	221	12,540
Suzanne Dickens	75	73	73	221	12,540
Jane Leary	77	71	73	221	12,540
Alison Munt	71	76	74	221	12,540
Kirsty Taylor	75	75	71	221	12,540
Christina Kuld	72	79	71	222	10,230
Mia Lojdahl	74	71	77	222	10,230
Alexandra Armas	74	73	75	222	10,230
Valerie Michaud	73	76	73	222	10,230
Lara Tadiotto	75	74	73	222	10,230
Sofia Gronberg Whitmore	77	70	75	222	10,230
Sara Forster	77	70	75	222	10,230

 **THE BEST-RUN E-BUSINESSES RUN SAP**